The Rebellion of Muḥammad al-Nafs al-Zakiyya in 145/762

Islamic History and Civilization

STUDIES AND TEXTS

VOLUME 118

The titles published in this series are listed at *brill.com/ihc*

The Rebellion of Muḥammad al-Nafs al-Zakiyya in 145/762

Ṭālibīs *and Early* ʿAbbāsīs *in Conflict*

By

Amikam Elad

TUTA SUB AEGIDE PALLAS · 1683 ·

BRILL

LEIDEN | BOSTON

Cover illustration: Reverse, field: "Muḥammad the Messenger of God." Obverse, field: "There is no God but God alone; He has no associate." Gold Dīnār. No mint, but probably struck at the seat of the caliphate in Iraq, 144 H / 761–762 AD. Copenhagen: The David Collection, Inv. no. C 26.

Library of Congress Cataloging-in-Publication Data

Elad, Amikam, author.
The rebellion of Muḥammad al-Nafs al-Zakiyya in 145/762 : Talibis and early 'Abbasids in conflict / by Amikam Elad.
pages cm
Includes bibliographical references and index.
ISBN 978-90-04-22989-1 (hardback : alk. paper) — ISBN 978-90-04-29622-0 (e-book : alk. paper)
1. Islamic Empire–History—750–1258. 2. Nafs al-Zakiyah, 711 or 712–762. 3. Manṣūr, Abū Ja'far, Caliph, approximately 712–775. I. Title.

DS38.6.E53 2016
909'.09767101—dc23

2015034770

This publication has been typeset in the multilingual "Brill" typeface. With over 5,100 characters covering Latin, IPA, Greek, and Cyrillic, this typeface is especially suitable for use in the humanities. For more information, please see www.brill.com/brill-typeface.

ISSN 0929-2403
ISBN 978-90-04-22989-1 (hardback)
ISBN 978-90-04-29622-0 (e-book)

This book is printed on acid-free paper.

To Einat

Contents

Acknowledgements XI

Introduction 1

PART 1
Muḥammad b. ʿAbdallāh in Historical Context

1 **Biographical Data of Muḥammad b. ʿAbdallāh al-Nafs al-Zakiyya** 17
- 1 Birth 17
- 2 Death 18
- 3 Mother 19
- 4 Siblings 21
- 5 The Residences of the Family 21
- 6 Wives and Children 25
- 7 Education 27
- 8 Physical Traits 27
- 9 The Image of Muḥammad b. ʿAbdallāh as Portrayed by the Sources 28

2 **Muḥammad b. ʿAbdallāh during the Umawī and ʿAbbāsī Periods** 49
- 1 The Umawī Period 49
- 2 Upon the Accession of the ʿAbbāsīs to Rule 82
- 3 The Caliphate of Abū l-ʿAbbās al-Saffāḥ (r. 132–136/749–754) 88
- 4 The Reign of al-Manṣūr (r. 136–158/754–775) 93
- 5 The Pre-Rebellion Phase: Propaganda and Espionage Activities 97

3 **On the Eve of the Rebellion** 103
- 1 Medina during the Early ʿAbbāsī Caliphate 103
- 2 The Imprisonment of the Ḥasanīs and Their Death 114
- 3 Propaganda and Followers of Muḥammad b. ʿAbdallāh in the Provinces 123

4 **Revolt** 145
- Introduction 145
- 1 Entering the City and Taking Control 148
- 2 Supporters and Warriors in the First Stage of the Revolt: General Observations 151

3 The First Actions: The Imprisonment of the ʿAbbāsī Family in Medina 155
4 The Financial Sources of the Rebellion 159
5 Organizing Medina 161
6 Appointing Governors in Arabia 165

5 **The ʿAbbāsī Reactions** 169
1 Al-Manṣūr's First Response 169
2 The Correspondence between al-Manṣūr and Muḥammad b. ʿAbdallāh 171
3 The ʿAbbāsī Army Headed by ʿĪsā b. Mūsā against Muḥammad al-Nafs al-Zakiyya 193

6 **The ʿAbbāsī Army's Campaigns Against Muḥammad b. ʿAbdallāh** 205
1 The First Stages 205
2 The Campaign Outside the City 209
3 The Last Battle and the Death of Muḥammad b. ʿAbdallāh 210
4 The Site Where Muḥammad b. ʿAbdallāh Was Killed 218
5 The ʿAbbāsīs' First Actions after the Suppression of the Revolt 225

PART 2
The Social, Ethnic, Political, and Religious Character of the Revolt

7 **Banū Quraysh** 233
1 The Ṭālibīs 234
2 Banū Umayya al-Akbar b. ʿAbd Shams b. ʿAbd Manāf b. Quṣayy b. Kilāb b. Murra b. Kaʿb b. Luʾayy b. Ghālib b. Fihr (Quraysh) (Chart V) 269
3 Banū Nawfal b. ʿAbd Manāf b. Quṣayy b. Kilāb b. Murra b. Kaʿb b. Luʾayy b. Ghālib b. Fihr (Quraysh) (Chart V) 275
4 Banū l-Muṭṭalib b. ʿAbd Manāf b. Quṣayy b. Kilāb … b. Ghālib b. Fihr (Quraysh) (Chart V) 275
5 Banū ʿAdī b. Kaʿb b. Luʾayy b. Ghālib b. Fihr (Quraysh) (Chart VI) 276
6 Banū Taym b. Murra b. Kaʿb b. Luʾayy b. Ghālib b. Fihr (Quraysh) (Chart VII) 284
7 Banū Makhzūm b. Yaqẓa b. Murra b. Kaʿb b. Luʾayy b. Ghālib b. Fihr (Quraysh) (Chart VIII) 287

8 Banū ʿĀmir b. Luʾayy b. Ghālib b. Fihr (Quraysh) (Chart IX) 294
9 Banū Jumaḥ b. ʿAmr b. Huṣayṣ b. Kaʿb b. Luʾayy b. Ghālib b. Fihr (Quraysh) (Chart X) 299
10 Banū Hāshim b. ʿAbd Manāf b. Quṣayy b. Kilāb b. Murra b. Kaʿb b. Luʾayy b. Ghālib b. Fihr (Quraysh) (Chart X) 301
11 Banū Zuhra b. Quṣayy b. Kilāb b. Murra b. Kaʿb b. Luʾayy b. Ghālib b. Fihr (Quraysh) (Chart XI) 302

8 Banū Asad b. ʿAbd al-ʿUzzā b. Quṣayy b. Kilāb b. Murra b. Kaʿb b. Luʾay b. Fihr (Quraysh) 310
1 The Family of al-Zubayr b. al-ʿAwwām 310
2 The Family of ʿAbdallāh b. Khālid b. Ḥizām b. Khuwaylid b. Asad b. ʿAbd al-ʿUzzā b. Quṣayy b. Kilāb 322
3 Some Notes on the Zubayrīs in Early Islam 323
4 ʿAbbāsīs and Zubayrīs 336
5 Transmissions of the Zubayrīs 341

9 The Tribal Support for/Opposition to Muḥammad b. ʿAbdallāh 343
1 The Anṣār 343
2 Banū Juhayna (... b. al-Ḥāfī b. Quḍāʿa) 346
3 Banū Muzayna (... b. al-Yās b. Muḍar) 348
4 Banū Sulaym (... b. Qays ʿAylān b. Muḍar) 349
5 Banū Ghifār b. Mulayl (... b. Kināna ... b. al-Yās b. Muḍar) 351
6 Banū Aslam (... b. Māzin b. al-Azd) 354
7 Banū Ashjaʿ (... b. Ghaṭafān b. Saʿd b. Qays ʿAylān b. Muḍar) 355
8 Banū Fazāra (... b. Ghaṭafān b. Saʿd b. Qays ʿAylān b. Muḍar) 355
9 Thaqīf (... b. Hawāzin ... b. Khṣafa b. Qays ʿAylān b. Muḍar) 356
10 Banū ʿĀmir b. Ṣaʿṣaʿa (... b. Hawāzin ... b. Khaṣafa b. Qays ʿAylān b. Muḍar) 356
11 Banū Bāhila (*mawālī*) 357
12 Banū Hawāzin (... b. Khaṣafa b. Qays ʿAylān b. Muḍar) (*mawlā*) 358
13 Banū Kinda 359
14 Banū Daws (al-Azd) (*mawlā*), or Banū Layth (Quḍāʿa) (*mawlā*) or Banū Ghifār (*mawlā*) 359
15 Unidentified 360
Conclusions 361

Appendix 1: The Attitude of the *ʿUlamāʾ* Towards the Rebellion 363
1 Mālik b. Anas 364
2 Hishām b. ʿUrwa b. al-Zubayr 367

3 Sufyān b. Saʿīd b. Masrūq (known as Sufyān al-Thawrī) 370
4 Abū Ḥanīfa al-Nuʿmān b. Thābit 371
5 Hārūn b. Saʿd al-ʿIjlī 372

Appendix 2: Transmitters and Transmission of the Historical Events of the Revolt 374
1 Transmitters from the Ṭālibī Families 374
2 The ʿAbbāsī Family 380
3 Transmission from Contemporaries of the Rebellion: Eyewitnesses, Supporters, and Opponents of the Revolt 381
4 ʿUmar b. Shabba: Direct Transmitters 394
5 Some Remarks on the Transmission of Abū l-Faraj al-Iṣfahānī in Maqātil al-ṭālibiyyīn Regarding the Events Surrounding the Rebellion of Muḥammad al-Nafs al-Zakiyya 422

Appendix 3: The Struggle for Legitimization Between the Ḥasanīs and the Ḥusaynīs as Reflected Mainly in Imāmī Literature 425
1 The Ḥusaynīs and Other Ṭālibī/Hāshimī Factions 425
2 The Ḥasanī and the Ḥusaynī Families: Animosity and Conflicts 429
3 The Symbols of Legitimacy of the Ḥusaynīs: The Inheritance of the ʿIlm of the Prophet; Holy Relics of Ādam, Moses, Joseph, and (mainly) of the Prophet Muḥammad 435
4 Ḥusaynīs and Ḥasanīs: The Struggle between Jaʿfar al-Ṣādiq and Muḥammad b. ʿAbdallāh b. al-Ḥasan 441
5 Jaʿfar al-Ṣādiq during the Rebellion and his Attitude Towards it According to Mainly Imāmī Traditions 446
6 Did Jaʿfar Regard Himself, or was he Regarded by his Adherents, as the Mahdī? 451
7 Jaʿfar al-Ṣādiq and the ʿAbbāsīs 452
8 The Treatise of Condolences from Jaʿfar al-Ṣādiq to the Ḥasanīs 463

Map of Medina 465
Genealogical Charts 466
Quraysh 466
Bibliography 478
Index 506

Acknowledgements

I am grateful to my wife, Einat, for her constant encouragement and support without which it would have been impossible to finish this book.

I owe many thanks to those who invested in the preparation of the manuscript for publication: Dr. Leigh Chipman, Dr. Yehudit Loebenstein, Dr. Keren Abbou-Hershkovitz, Mrs. Beverly Katz, and Ms. Valerie Joy Turner.

Introduction

1 The Purpose and Methodology of the Study

The original purpose of this book was to write a socio-political history of the revolt of Muḥammad b. ʿAbdallāh b. al-Ḥasan b. al-Ḥasan b. ʿAlī b. Abī Ṭālib, known as al-Nafs al-Zakiyya, in the year 145/762. Over the course of the book's long period of incubation, I wrote several additional chapters on various subjects, directly or indirectly connected to the revolt. These deal mainly with the relationship of the ʿAbbāsīs with the Ḥasanī and Ḥusaynī factions of the Shīʿa and with other Ṭālibī families, but also with the relationships between the ʿAlīd clans themselves, and largely concern the question of the struggle over legitimizing rule.[1]

2 The Importance of the Revolt for the ʿAbbāsīs

The revolt of Muḥammad al-Nafs al-Zakiyya was a serious threat to the legitimacy of the ʿAbbāsīs, a new dynasty that had come to power following a bloody military coup and that was immediately met by social, political, and religious opposition and resistance in various parts of the caliphate.[2] Some of the opposition movements that emerged were new, with largely socio-political coloring, but others were older. These older movements were composed mainly of factions of the Ṭālibī family, fueled by a religio-political ideology that had formed in opposition to Umawī rule. The rise of the ʿAbbāsīs hastened and sharpened the ideological aspects of the Ṭālibīs' protest, now turned against the ʿAbbāsīs and expressed in a series of revolts. Militarily, the ʿAbbāsīs had the upper hand; but from a religio-ideological point of view, the battle between the two parties was bitter in the extreme. Although from an Islamic perspective the ʿAbbāsīs belonged to the wider Hāshimī clan, i.e., they were members of the Prophet's family and eligible for the caliphate,[3] it was the Ṭālibīs, especially the Ḥasanīs and Ḥusaynīs, but also the Jaʿfarīs, rather than the ʿAbbāsīs, who for generations had cultivated the idea of their right to rule, using, among other things,

1 On some of the claims as they appear in Sunnī and Shīʿī *ḥādīth* literature, see Elad, "The *Ḥadīth* of al-Mahdī."

2 Omar, *ʿAbbāsid Caliphate*, esp. 153–210, 259–285, 311–315, 320–323; Cobb, *White Banners*, 23–26, 43–51, 75–82.

3 Madelung, "Hāshimiyyāt."

 | DOI 10.1163/9789004296220_002

the most important and widely-accepted tool of the day, the *ḥadīth* tradition. As Madelung put it, "It was the ʿAlid Shīʿa who more and more narrowed down the concept of the Prophet's *ahl al-bayt* to the Ṭālibids, the ʿAlids, the descendants of Fāṭima, and their specific lines of imams [...]."[4]

The ideological roots of the ʿAbbāsī revolution lie in the ʿAlīd Hāshimiyya movement and a sizeable part of its propagandists in Khurāsān belonged to the original Hāshimiyya movement.[5] It is widely believed, and correct, that the rise to power of the ʿAbbāsīs fragmented the Hāshimīs and pushed them into opposition to the government. From this stage onward, the ideological struggle between ʿAbbāsīs and ʿAlīds increased, finding expression in armed rebellion and suppression of rebellion.[6]

Emotional and ideological ties to the ʿAlīds did not end immediately with the ʿAbbāsī rise to power. Among some families, pro-ʿAlīd leanings continued long into the later ʿAbbāsī period, as shown by several fascinating pieces of evidence.[7] Even if the claim to legitimate rule by virtue of descent from al-ʿAbbās began to be formulated in the time of al-Manṣūr (r. 136–158/754–775),[8] it only received its final official stamp under al-Mahdī.[9] The revolt of Muḥammad b. ʿAbdallāh in 145/762, therefore, was a politico-religious challenge to the new ʿAbbāsī regime, according to which rule had to be handed over to the family of ʿAlī b. Abī Ṭālib. At the time, this view was acceptable to many groups of the Muslim community, and was not confined to Ṭālibī factions and their supporters. A detailed study of the supporters of Muḥammad b. ʿAbdallāh's revolt shows clearly that while a sizeable number were members of Ṭālibī families (Ḥasanīs, Ḥusaynīs, Jaʿfarīs, ʿAqīlīs, ʿUmarīs), many (perhaps even most) were members of a range of other clans of Quraysh, the Anṣār and other tribal groups, including non-Ṭālibī scholars of *ḥadīth* and *fiqh*. Obviously, all such

4 Madelung, "Hāshimiyyāt," 24.

5 Sharon, *Black Banners*, esp. 75–200; Omar, *ʿAbbāsid Caliphate*, 67–75, 80–95, 132–134; for additional bibliography, see Elad, "Transition," 89, n. 1, and idem, "The Ethnic Composition," 246, n. 1; for a different view, see Crone, "*al-Riḍā*," 100–106; idem, *Political Thought*, 91–93.

6 For example, see Omar, "Aspects," 171 (after Moscati, "Per una storia dell'antica šīʿa," *RSO*, 1955, 251); Zaman, *Religion and Politics*, 42; Cook, *Muslim Apocalyptic*, 229; Crone, *Political Thought*, 89–90.

7 E.g., the case of the families of Yaqṭīn b. Mūsā, see Elad, "Wāsiṭ," 83, n. 109; Madelung, "A Treatise," 19, n. 2; for the case of Jaʿfar b. Muḥammad b. al-Ashʿath, see appendix 3, 455f.; for Abū ʿAwn ʿAbd al-Malik b. Yazīd, see Crone, *Political Thought*, 90–91; Elad, "Abū ʿAwn"; and for the ʿAbbāsī *naqīb*, al-Qāsim b. Mujāshiʿ, see Crone, *Political Thought*, 90.

8 Zaman, *Religion and Politics*, 44–45; Elad, "The *Ḥadīth* of al-Mahdī," 57–67.

9 Sharon, *Black Banners*, 99 (according to *Akhbār al-ʿAbbās*, 165–166); Elad, "The *Ḥadīth* of al-Mahdī," 68ff.

groups supported the leader of the revolt, a Ḥasanī. Had his revolt succeeded, he would have become caliph.[10]

Serious though it was, this revolt's power in Medina and its environs lay in its questioning of ʿAbbāsī legitimacy rather than in its military might, which was small, despite the attempts of some accounts to give the impression of a near-total rallying of the Arab inhabitants of Medina and their *mawālī* and the Arab tribes of its hinterland.[11]

Already at a very early stage of research I realized that I could not discuss *all* of the subjects related to the revolt and its important political, religious, and social implications in appropriate depth. Such a discussion would require a long and winding journey through numerous and varying Arabic sources. Moreover, some of these subjects belong to disciplines that are not within my expertise. A clear example is the discussion in this book of the various Ṭālibī clans—Ḥasanīs, Ḥusaynīs, Jaʿfarīs, etc.—which requires expertise in the history of the early Shīʿa, which is not my field, hence the religious, doctrinal, and theological aspects of the revolt are not discussed here with the depth and breadth they deserve. These aspects are touched upon but not dealt with exhaustively in the discussion of the various personages and scholars who supported the revolt or played an active part in it, and those who opposed it. The sources mention dozens of scholars of various religious disciplines, belonging to different sects: Sunnīs, Muʿtazilīs, Zaydīs, and members of the Ṭālibī clans, among those who joined and/or supported the revolt. A partial list has already been given by Van Arendonk, and many others are mentioned or discussed by Van Ess.[12] The religio-theological character or doctrine of the revolt should be understood and defined among other things by examining the attitude of

10 It is hard to accept D. Cook's assertion (*Muslim Apocalyptic,* 192), that "[o]ne should be very cautious before saying that Muḥammad al-Nafs al-Zakīya was a Shīʿī figure. Virtually all of his followers were non-Shīʿīs. Messianic, yes; revolutionary, yes; but hardly Shīʿī." But it will be shown in this work that not all of Muḥammad b. ʿAbdallāh's supporters were "non-Shīʿīs" (see chapter 7). It seems that in the eyes of his contemporaries, Muḥammad b. ʿAbdallāh was certainly a Shīʿī figure, as was his distinguished Ḥasanī father. This is reflected very clearly in the traditions describing the conflicts, strife, and contentions between the Ḥusaynīs and the Ḥasanīs, mainly between Jaʿfar al-Ṣādiq and ʿAbdallāh b. al-Ḥasan, but also between Jaʿfar and Muḥammad b. ʿAbdallāh. It could be claimed, in many cases justifiably, that many of these traditions crystallized after the rebellion of al-Nafs al-Zakiyya; however, many circulated before it. (See appendix 3.)

11 See the discussion in chapter 7 (conclusion).

12 Van Arendonk, *L'Imamate Zaïdite,* esp. appendices 2:312–314 (the supporters of Muḥammad) and 3:314–317 (the supporters of Ibrāhīm); van Ess, *Theologie,* index: Nafs az-zakīya, s.v., esp. 1:187–188; 221–228; 2:249f., 286–288, 327–335, 672–687.

contemporaneous scholars from the numerous groups mentioned above towards the revolt and its instigator. The picture that emerges from some sources is that here, as in other aspects, the revolt is connected to that of Ibrāhīm, al-Nafs al-Zakiyya's brother, in al-Baṣra. Indeed, the traditions about support for al-Nafs al-Zakiyya among some of the extremist Shīʿī sects such as the Mughīriyya or the ʿIjliyya, or other groups such as the Zaydiyya and the Muʿtazila, should be treated with extreme caution.

3 The Case of the Zaydiyya

A number of questions connected to the politico-religious development of the early Zaydiyya immediately arise in this context. Some of these concern the doctrinal character of the early Zaydiyya in 145/762 and the extent to which they had developed and consolidated religious principles. I deal with this partially in my discussion of the "fourth letter" that Muḥammad b. ʿAbdallāh al-Nafs al-Zakiyya sent to al-Manṣūr and of other letters and speeches attributed to him quoted in Zaydī literature.[13] Another question which arises concerns whether al-Nafs al-Zakiyya was recognized as a Zaydī imām, and by whom? These and other matters pertaining to the Zaydiyya and other ʿAlīd groups are only partially discussed in this book, whose main focus is on the "Sunnīs."[14]

4 The Case of the Muʿtazila

There are conflicting reports about the Muʿtazila leaders' attitude towards Muḥammad al-Nafs al-Zakiyya and his revolt. Some reports highlight ʿAmr b. ʿUbayd's fierce objection to Muḥammad and his revolt and total rejection of his Mahdīship since he was to be killed,[15] while others describe ʿAmr b. ʿUbayd, Wāṣil b. ʿAṭāʾ, and other prominent leaders of the Muʿtazila as swearing allegiance to him in Medina.[16] It is obvious that at least these traditions were created after the revolt; but do they reflect the real attitude of these scholars towards al-Nafs al-Zakiyya and his revolt? The question is also relevant to their

13 See the discussion in chapter 5.

14 See also the discussion in chapter 1, 46f.

15 Al-Iṣfahānī, *Maqātil*, 246: أن عمرو بن عبيد كان ينكر أن يكون محمد بن عبد الله هو المهدي ويقول: كيف وهو يقتل.

16 Ibid., 293–294; Madelung, *al-Qāsim b. Ibrāhīm*, 72.

attitude towards Ibrāhīm and his revolt, but, as noted, this subject is beyond my expertise and therefore outside the frame of this book.[17]

Generally speaking, the positions of these factions regarding Muḥammad b. ʿAbdallāh were formulated after his death, and thus many, if not most, of the reports recording the relations between the leaders or members of the factions and Muḥammad b. ʿAbdallāh are later, post-rebellion products. Zaman evinces a sober view of this matter, albeit one based only on impressions.[18]

4.1 *Ibrāhīm b. ʿAbdallāh's Revolt*[19]

The history of this revolt is connected to and perhaps inseparable from the revolt of al-Nafs al-Zakiyya.[20] Although I do touch upon Ibrāhīm's revolt frequently in this work, this is not actually the main topic, and on the whole it requires—indeed deserves—a separate, in-depth research on al-ʿIrāq's political, social, economic, and religious, history during the late Umawī period and the first fifty years of ʿAbbāsī rule, especially in al-Baṣra.

5 The Correspondence between al-Manṣūr and Muḥammad b. ʿAbdallāh

This study dedicates a special chapter to this topic, which contains important and most probably authentic information on some of the doctrines of the Shīʿa during late Umawī and early ʿAbbāsī rule. Despite that, the study of the letters

17 Crone, *Political Thought*, 69, n. 10, mentioning that the Muʿtazilī *qāḍī* ʿAbd al-Jabbār (d. 415/1025) acknowledged al-Nafs al-Zakiyya and his brother Ibrāhīm as imāms.

18 Zaman, *Religion and Politics*, 74–75: "It is also difficult to be certain that all those who are said to have supported the revolt actually did so, or in what way. But to express these reservations is not to deny that the participation of the religious elite in this ʿAlid revolt was, in general, most impressive and that scholars from a wide range of backgrounds lent their support to it."

19 For general surveys of the rebellion, see Veccia Vagliery, "Ibrāhīm b. ʿAbdallāh"; Omar, *ʿAbbāsid Caliphate*, 240–247; Lassner, *Shaping*, esp. 81–87, 160–161, 266, n. 71; Kennedy, *ʿAbbāsid Caliphate*, 67–70, 202–204.

20 E.g., the support and participation of the Zubayrī families in the revolt in Medina and al-Baṣra; for al-Baṣra, see the entry on the family of ʿĀṣim b. al-Mundhir b. al-Zubayr b. al-ʿAwwām in al-Baṣra in chapter 7 (part 2); see also the active participation of some Arab dignitaries of al-Baṣra, the family of Banū Mismaʿ, in the rebellion in Medina (chapter 3, 140f.); Zaman, *Religion and Politics*, 73, n. 11: "Ibrāhīm's revolt in Basra, though politically more dangerous for the ʿAbbāsids than that of Muḥammad in Medina, was ideologically dependent upon, and a continuation of, the latter."

merits further comprehensive research. This should include an in-depth study of their contents as recorded in numerous sources, as well as an analytical, linguistic comparison of the texts.

6 The Historical Method of the Project

Special attention has been paid in this book to the following:

1) *Examining the people—scholars, military men, administrators, and others—who supported the revolt or opposed it*

Detailed studies of these people appears mainly in chapter 7, using the method of prosopographical research. This method allows access to much information about the social, cultural, religious, and even economic character of the revolt of Muḥammad al-Nafs al-Zakiyya; this information forms part of the greater picture of the social and tribal structure of Medina, and has not yet been studied in the requisite depth.[21] The prosopographical method is an initial attempt to provide an example for what can be done with the enormous potential of prosopographical data.[22]

An in-depth, detailed study of the social structure of Medina will add a significant amount of information to our understanding of the social background of the rebellion. At this point it is sufficient to mention that a large segment of Muḥammad's most distinguished adherents belonged to the "noble" and highly influential Zubayrī family.[23] This family was known, already in the Jāhiliyya, but also during the first two Islamic centuries, as a wealthy family that owned much property and many estates around Medina and elsewhere in Arabia. Many Zubayrīs joined al-Nafs al-Zakiyya's cause and played important roles in the rebellion. This support—despite the historical enmity between the Zubayrīs and the ʿAlīds—may be indicative of the frustration and resentment on the part of the Zubayrīs of ʿAbbāsī policies.[24]

21 T.H.R. Munt's forthcoming book, *The Holy City of Medina: Sacred Space in Early Islamic Arabia* (New York: Cambridge University Press, 2014) will undoubtedly shed a new and important light on Medina from the seventh to ninth centuries.

22 For example, studying members of Arab families often reveals individuals not mentioned in the standard *nasab* books, and thus we can reconstruct entire branches that were previously unknown. This is particularly true of the clans of Quraysh in Medina, and especially the Zubayrīs.

23 Already noted by Kennedy, *ʿAbbāsid Caliphate*, 201–202.

24 On the Zubayrīs and their attitude towards the rebellion, see chapter 8.

It should be remembered that, in the context of Medina, the information provided by the Arabic sources about ordinary people is limited. The sources focus mainly on the upper echelons of Arab society, largely members of Quraysh or the Anṣār, or on eminent and well-known scholars, and they do not aim to provide a cross-section of the city's society nor to give a detailed description of the complex internal relations between the families and clans of Medina.

2) *The socio-political, cultural, and geographical history of Medina*

The Arabic sources dealing with the revolt of Muḥammad al-Nafs al-Zakiyya are rich in detailed and accurate data about the physical and geographical aspects of Medina. Much of this information is taken from the writings of ʿUmar b. Shabba.[25] This helps reconstruct the city's topography from the end of the Umawī period to the end of the eighth century.[26] In this book I paid attention to the geographic details mentioned in the descriptions of the various stages of the revolt; but this subject, too, deserves a separate study.

3) *Examination of the transmitters and transmission of historical traditions*

It is well known that most of the traditions about the revolt of Muḥammad al-Nafs al-Zakiyya are preserved primarily in al-Ṭabarī's *Taʾrīkh al-rusul wa-l-mulūk*, and, to a lesser extent, in Abū l-Faraj al-Iṣfahānī's *Maqātil al-Ṭālibiyyīn*. Both are based largely on traditions discussing the background of the revolt, its course and its consequences, that appear in a work by ʿUmar b. Shabba Abū Zayd al-Numayrī (173–260/789–876),[27] *Kitāb akhbār Muḥammad wa-Ibrāhīm ibnay ʿAbdallāh b. al-Ḥasan.*[28] His traditions go back to transmitters who were

25 As is well-known. Ibn Shabba is also the author of a work on "The History of Medina" (*Akhbār [Taʾrīkh] al-Madīna*), of which only a part has been published. I have used this work extensively in this book.

26 In a similar fashion, it is possible to reconstruct the topography and geography of Baghdad in the early ninth century from the sources dealing with the civil war between al-Amīn and al-Maʾmūn, especially the detailed description of the siege of the city.

27 On him, see al-Mizzī, *Tahdhīb,* 21:386–390 and the comprehensive bibliography of the editor therein; Sezgin, 1:345–346: died in 264 or 263, but a more likely date is 262; Nagel, "Muḥammad b. ʿAbdallāh," esp. 230ff.; Günther, *Maqātil,* 220–225; Fleischhammer, *Kitāb al-Aghānī,* 104–106; Ibn Shabba, *Taʾrīkh al-Madīna,* 1: ح – ي; Leder, "ʿUmar b. Shabba," and the bibliography therein.

28 Ibn al-Nadīm, *al-Fihrist* (ed. Tajaddud), 125; Yāqūt, *Udabāʾ* (Beirut, 1993), 5:2093; al-Ṣafadī, *al-Wāfī,* 22:488; Sezgin, 1:345–346 and the bibliography, therein; Nagel, "Muḥammad b. ʿAbdallāh," 231.

active at the time of the revolt, the majority of whom are Medinese and provide contemporary evidence. While some supported the revolt and its leader, some opposed it, and yet others avoided political activism and remained neutral.

4) *Family traditions*

There are many examples of family members who relate traditions about themselves or other family members' activities in the revolt or the events connected with it, such as ʿAbdallāh b. ʿUmar b. al-Qāsim b. ʿAbdallāh b. ʿUbaydallāh b. ʿĀṣim b. ʿUmar b. al-Khaṭṭāb, who was a minor *muḥaddith*. He is mentioned twice by al-Ṭabarī as a close supporter of Muḥammad al-Nafs al-Zakiyya who took an active part in the fighting and related these events in the first person. Another example is ʿAbd al-Ḥamīd b. ʿAbd al-ʿAzīz b. ʿAbdallāh b. ʿAbdallāh b. ʿUmar b. al-Khaṭṭāb, who relates that his brother, ʿAbdallāh b. ʿAbd al-ʿAzīz, and his three sons revolted with Muḥammad b. ʿAbdallāh. A further example of the importance of these family traditions for the reconstruction of the events surrounding the revolt is the family traditions of ʿĪsā b. ʿAbdallāh b. Muḥammad b. ʿUmar b. ʿAlī b. Abī Ṭālib, related from his father and other family members, the descendants of ʿUmar b. ʿAlī b. Abī Ṭālib.[29]

Traditions transmitted from family members are early, but not necessarily factual or authentic. While occasionally they are simply tales with no hidden agenda, they are sometimes transmitted in order to highlight or glorify one's own deeds, or those of a family member, as I have shown elsewhere in the context of traditions about the Arab conquests.[30] One example among many is the case of Muḥammad al-Nafs al-Zakiyya's standard-bearer: both the Zubayrīs and the Ṭālibīs claimed him as their own.[31] A large part of this study is devoted to examining the earliest transmitters who reported on the revolt and whose traditions reached ʿUmar b. Shabba, apparently orally.

7 The Working Method: The Evaluation and Adaptation of Sources

Since the 1980s, great progress has been made in the study of early Islamic historiography and in the broader field of *ḥadīth* literature. More and more emphasis is being given to the study of the *isnād*, i.e., to the chain of transmitters.

29 Already noted by Nagel, "Muḥammad b. ʿAbdallāh," 242–245.

30 Elad, "Historical Writings," 114, 119–121; and see now the important study of Mazor, "al-Qudāmī": especially 19–21, 33, 36.

31 See the discussion in chapter 4, 161f.

Efforts are being made to develop a method and establish criteria that can contribute not only to determining the time of a *ḥadīth*'s formation and dissemination, but also to a more thorough understanding of the process by which the *ḥadīth* crystallized, the socio-religious environment in which this process took place, and a better understanding of the *ḥadīth*'s contents. The school pursuing these goals, whose main representatives today are Juynboll and especially Motzki and his disciples, like Görke, opposes the discrediting of all *isnād*s. In principle, they believe that *isnād*s are reliable, and, in Motzki's words, "the fact that some transmitters were indeed dishonest and forged *isnād*s cannot lead to the conclusion that the *isnād* system in general is unreliable and cannot be used for dating purposes."[32] I, too, came to this conclusion when I examined the *isnād*s in the literature on the praise of Jerusalem and found them valuable for dating traditions and understanding their social, political, religious, and geographical backgrounds.[33]

The study of transmitters and transmission in Arabic literature outside of *ḥadīth*, particularly in the areas of history and *adab*, is still in its infancy, but has raised considerable interest in the past few years; the names Conrad, Donner, Günther, Fleichhammer, al-Qāḍī, Landau-Tasseron, Mourad, and Mazor come to mind. I have discussed this subject elsewhere in the context of traditions about the Arab conquests and their raids (in the Syrian context) on Byzantium, which appear in the Arabic historical books. In this type of tradition there is even less room for the forging of *isnād*s and thus there is an opportunity to add important dimensions to our knowledge about the conquests. This kind of study can further our knowledge of the process of transmission and inform us how these traditions were transmitted by members of tribal groups who participated in the conquests, and by tribal groups who lived in a particular settlement or region.[34]

These early *isnād*s are to a large degree authentic and are not later inventions. Examining the transmission of historical traditions leads to a more

---

32 Elad, "Historical Writing," 118, quoting Motzki, "The Prophet and the Cat," 32, n. 44. The essence of the controversy among scholars, regarding the methodological approach towards *Ḥadīth*, from Goldziher through Schacht until the 1970s, is recorded by Crone, *Slaves*, 14–15, and 211 n.88. For a more recent bibliography about the controversy and the developments in the study of *ḥadīth*, see Elad, *Jerusalem*, 11, n. 33, and especially, Günther, "Source Criticism," 6ff.

33 Elad, *Jerusalem*, introduction, 15–22.

34 Elad, "Historical Writing," 119.

accurate understanding of their geographical origin, the transmitters' ethnic background, their education, occupations, and the duration of their activity.[35]

8 The *Isnād* in Shīʿī (Imāmī) *Ḥadīth*

In contrast to the study of the *isnād* (transmitters) and transmission that has developed among students of Sunnī *ḥadīth* literature and the various genres of early Islamic historiography, among scholars of Shīʿī literature this field is in its infancy. Few studies on the subject have been made, and Kohlberg and Moezzi have presented the severe methodological challenges well.[36] The Twelver/Imāmī doctrine of the character and characteristics of the Imām,[37] argues Kohlberg,

> had far-reaching effects not only on Shīʿī politico-religious theory but also on Shīʿī views on *ḥadīth.* The authority of the Imām in religious matters equals that of Muḥammad; any pronouncement of an Imām is automatically taken by the Shīʿīs to have been transmitted to him by the Prophet. It is not surprising, therefore, that virtually all Shīʿī *asānīd* have three basic forms:
> a. They either go back to an Imām; or

35 Ibid., 119–121; Mazor, "al-Qudāmī," esp. 30, n. 39 and 36; Elad, "Early Muslim Historiography," 289–290. I cannot accept the unequivocally negative view of D. Cook (*Muslim Apocalyptic,* 32), who said, criticizing Madelung's methodology: "In all of his work there is a tendency to spend a tremendous amount of time on the study of *isnād*s (the chain of transmitters, ostensibly leading back to the Prophet or one of his companions, but in practice of highly questionable value), and not nearly enough time with the traditions themselves." This presentation is not accurate, for Madelung seldom (if ever?) identifies the Prophet or a *ṣaḥābī* as the originators of a tradition. Also, ibid., 331: "… However, these conclusions must be seen as tentative for now, since absolute proof is lacking and the amount of serious research done in this field is very minimal concentrating far too much on the useless *isnāds* and too little on the traditions themselves." By using such phrases, Cook overlooks and disregards the serious and comprehensive studies on *isnāds* during the last decade, by Juynboll, and especially Motzki, Görke, and others, which cannot be dismissed in one or two unsubstantiated sentences.

36 Kohlberg, "Shīʿī *isnād,*" 142–143. On Imāmī *ḥadīth* of al-Bāqir but mainly of al-Ṣādiq, see Moezzi, *Divine Guide,* 24, 26–27, 102–103, 158, n. 143; see also Mitter, "Islamic Patronate," 70, n. 2.

37 For a summary of this doctrine, see Kohlberg, "Shīʿī *isnād,*" 142–143. Kohlberg in ibid., 142, in n. 2: refers the reader to the works of W. Madelung, "Hishām b. al-Ḥakam" [and] "Imāma," in *EI*[2] for a summary of the Shīʿī doctrine of the imamate.

b. They go back to an Imām who transmits from his forefathers (*ʿan abāʾihi*); or else
c. They go back to an Imām who transmits from Muḥammad, either directly or via the Imām's forefathers.

All three forms are regarded as possessing the same degree of authority. The Sunnīs, who do not adhere to the Shīʿī theory of the imāmate, regard most of these *asānīd* as being clearly unacceptable.[38]

Despite all the reservations and caution required when dealing with the Arabic sources, they preserve a wealth of data that few human civilizations have produced. The non-Muslim sources are scant, brief, and often of a strong, clearly tendentious character, no less—sometimes even more so—than the Muslim sources. However, some of the non-Muslim sources, especially the Syriac ones, are important for the study of the early history of Islam.[39] The Arabic sources remain, therefore, the best foundation for studying early Islamic history. Examining them and comparing their materials internally and externally can produce as objective a picture of an event or a historical process as possible. This method is indispensable because without it, the possibility of arriving at any grain of historical fact and exposing it is small.

Obviously all the available Arabic sources must be examined, and it is unfortunate that many studies of early Islamic history do not apply this method, utilizing, instead, the literary genre of sources that are strictly termed "historical" and neglecting other types.[40]

This method was made possible to a large extent thanks to the repository of Arabic literature recorded on several compact disks and hard drives, such as the CDs of *al-Turāth*, *Ahl al-Bayt*, and *al-Maktaba al-Shāmila*, containing many thousands of books from different genres of Arabic literature: *ḥadīth*,

38 Kohlberg, "Shīʿī *isnād*," 142–143.

39 This is clearly demonstrated in Robert Hoyland's new book, *Theophilus of Edessa's Chronicle*.

40 This method and approach to the Islamic primary sources has been accepted at the Hebrew University for decades. See Elad, *Jerusalem*, 9; ibid., n. 30: "Prof. A. Noth reached the same conclusion (independently), see Noth, "Charakter," 198; note also the (sober) reservation of Crone, *Slaves*, 11, n. 63." See also Donner's arguments in this vein (Donner, *Narratives*, 290): "Rather, it becomes necessary to compare an account with as many others on the same subject as possible, in an effort to gain a glimpse of the growth of the collective tradition on that subject over time. This is, of course, the time-tested approach of tradition and redaction criticism. Not by rejecting the whole Islamic tradition as 'opaque,' but rather by patiently unraveling the strands and layers of the complex of traditional material, will the Islamic origins story finally come, at least partially, to light."

adab, *fatāwā*, *fiqh*, *sīra*, *Qurʾān*, *tafsīr*, geography, biography, poetry, and more, that are at our disposal for the first time. Many of these books, including some of the best-known, lack an index, and therefore the phenomenon of the compact disks is revolutionary with respect to data and data mining. It has enabled me to collect, for the first time, the majority of the evidence for my specific research, but also for other studies as well.

My method regarding traditions consists of a) collecting every possible tradition on a specific topic, large or small, and then b) scrutinizing both the text and chain of transmitters (*isnād*). In many cases it is impossible to reveal the historical kernel of an event, and we are left with impressions or assumptions. Nevertheless, it is possible often to detect the socio-religious, and/or political bias of the tradition.

Historical traditions in general, and those relating to the rebellion of Muḥammad al-Nafs al-Zakiyya in particular, are intermingled with legendary literary motifs, miracles, and the like. These are numerous, but even they can be thoroughly checked and scrutinized, for instance, by checking the *isnād* and comparing all versions in search of common denominators, which enable one to find the historical axis around which these traditions revolve. The traditions about ʿAbdallāh al-Ashtar's journey to al-Sind serve as a typical example illustrating the methodological difficulties we face when trying to discern the kernels of historical events. Many pro-Ḥasanī traditions also serve as an example of the method mentioned. For example, the tradition about the political aspirations of Muḥammad b. ʿAbdallāh from his infancy should be categorized as pro-ʿAlīd, not only because of its content, but also due to its transmitters, the earliest of whom were scholars well-known for their Shīʿī leanings, and in many cases were eyewitnesses to or participants in the rebellion.[41]

41 See the full discussion in chapter 1; and for a discussion of the tradition according to which ʿAbdallāh b. al-Ḥasan propagandized for the Mahdīship of his son; this is an early tradition, narrated by al-Zuhrī's nephew [Muḥammad b. ʿAbdallāh b. Muslim, d. 152/769 or 770, or 157/773 or 774], transmitted by scholars who were either followers of the Ḥasanīs, and even took part in the rebellion of al-Nafs al-Zakiyya, or belonged to the Jaʿfarī branch of the ʿAlīd family. Many such examples are scattered throughout this book. Note that these traditions are different than matter-of-fact, descriptive traditions of the actual battles. Here we see the *Ayyām al-ʿArab* style of reporting, which makes the description more reliable.

9 Some Technical Details

The widespread use of the term "tradition" for the historical-literary accounts in this work is deliberate, and I normally prefer it to other words and terms such as anecdote, narration, discourse, or story, although at times I do use these terms, interchangeably.

This study was carried out in different libraries over a number of years, which resulted in the use of different editions of some of the bibliographical items.

PART 1

Muḥammad b. ʿAbdallāh in Historical Context

CHAPTER 1

Biographical Data of Muḥammad b. ʿAbdallāh al-Nafs al-Zakiyya

1 Birth

According to some sources Muḥammad b. ʿAbdallāh b. al-Ḥasan b. al-Ḥasan b. ʿAlī b. Abī Ṭālib was born in the year 100/718–719.[1] Shīʿī, mainly Imāmī, works add that there is no dispute regarding the year 100,[2] but experience has taught us that when such a phrase appears, its intent is to hide a dispute.[3] Some sources corroborate the date 100 H. by giving his age upon death as 45.[4] This year, however, is dubious due to its messianic connotations. As in the case of the first ʿAbbāsī caliph, Abū l-ʿAbbās al-Saffāḥ,[5] such traditions clearly demonstrate Muḥammad b. ʿAbdallāh's messianic character and are part of the corpus of traditions that build up his image as a Mahdī. Indeed, other sources, some quoting early *ahkbāriyyūn*, relate that he died at the age of 53,[6] and hence would have been born in the year 92/710–711.[7] According to several sources, his mother's pregnancy lasted four years and thus he may be defined as a *rāqid*

---

1 Al-Iṣfahānī, *Maqātil*, 237, where we find a garbled *isnād* from ʿUmar b. Shabba.

2 Al-Bukhārī, *Sirr al-silsila*, 7; Ibn ʿInaba, *ʿUmda*, 103. Abū Naṣr al-Bukhārī is Sahl b. ʿAbdallāh al-Nassāba (i.e., a genealogist who was alive in 341/952 or 953, and is the author of a Shīʿī genealogical book entitled *Sirr ansāb al-ʿAlawiyyīn* (see the bibliography).

3 For an example, see the statement of Ibn al-Murajjā in the early fourth/eleventh century that scholars agree that the *miʿrāj* of the Prophet took place from the Rock on the Ḥaram al-Sharīf in Jerusalem; see Elad, *Jerusalem*, 49.

4 Al-Masʿūdī, *Murūj*, 4:147; Ibn Abī Ḥātim, *al-Jarḥ* (Hyderabad edition), 3:295; Ibn Ḥajar, *Tahdhīb* (Hyderabad edition), 9:252: from Ibn Saʿd and others (إبن سعد وغير واحد); al-Bukhārī, *Sirr al-silsila*, 7: 45 and some months.

5 For the messianic meaning and importance of the year 100 H., see Landau-Tasseron, *al-Mujaddid*; see Sharon, *Black Banners*, 187–188 for the meaning of this year for the ʿAbbāsī *daʿwa*.

6 Ibn Saʿd, *al-Qism al-mutammim*, 378, from al-Wāqidī; Ibn Ḥajar, *Tahdhīb* (Hyderabad edition), 9:252, quoting al-Zubayr b. Bakkār and al-Wāqidī; al-Mizzī, *Tahdhīb*, 25:467, from al-Zubayr b. Bakkār; al-Ṣafadī, *al-Wāfī*, 3:297.

7 Al-Sayyid, "al-Nafs al-Zakiyya," 171, recording the two dates (92 H. [according to al-Ṣafadī] and 100 H.), commenting that "one of the dates must be incorrect," and concluding that al-Nafs al-Zakiyya was born ca. 92 H.

 | DOI 10.1163/9789004296220_003

(literally: "the sleeping child").[8] His special supernatural traits, as well as his titles, al-Mahdī and al-Nafs al-Zakiyya, are dealt with below.

2 Death

Most of the sources relate that he died on 14[9] or 15[10] Ramaḍān 145/6–7 December 762). Ibn ʿInaba, the Shīʿī author of *ʿUmdat al-ṭālib*, records another date: 25 Rajab 145/19 October 762).[11]

---

8 For the claim about the four-year pregnancy, see al-Bukhārī, *Sirr al-silsila*, 7 (copied by Ibn ʿInaba, *ʿUmda*, 104); al-ʿUmarī, *Ansāb*, 38; Ibn Kathīr, *al-Bidāya* (Cairo, 1351 H.), 10:101; Ibn Ḥajar, *Tahdhīb* (Beirut, 1984), 9:225; al-Sakhāwī, *al-Tuḥfa al-laṭīfa*, 2:492: حملت به أربع سنين. The editor of *Sirr al-silsila* (copied by the editor of the *ʿUmda*), remarks that this is accepted by the Shāfiʿīs but not by the Imāmiyya: هذا لا يوافق مذهب الإمامية؛ اللهم إلا الشافعية.

The term *rāqid* (plural *ruqqad* or *ruqūd*) denotes "a sleeping child," that is, a fetus that stays in its mother's womb for more than nine months. This idea is rooted in Islamic culture "and has been incorporated in the legal systems of the four leading *madhāhib*.... Jurists have disagreed about the possible duration of the prolonged pregnancy; some saw two years as a maximum, but according to others it could last much longer." See *EI*², "Rāḳid" (Odile Verberkmoes and Remke Kruk). Some famous cases of *ruqūd* are mentioned in the sources, the most famous of which is Mālik b. Anas (two or three years); Harim b. Ḥayyān (two years), Muḥammad b. ʿAjlān (more than three years), all mentioned by Ibn Qutayba, *al-Maʿārif* (Cairo edition), 594–595. A four year pregnancy is accepted by the Shāfiʿī, Ḥanbalī, and Mālikī schools. But there were opinions that accepted five, six, and even seven years of prolonged pregnancy. For a summary of the opinions of the different jurists and legal schools, see Ibn Qayyim al-Jawziyya, *Tuḥfat al-mawdūd*, 259–260; al-Malaṭī, *al-Muʿtaṣar min al-mukhtaṣar*, 1:317–318. The law, explain Verberkmoes and Kruk, created "a device to protect women as well as children against the sanctions attached to pregnancies and births out of wedlock: a *rāḳid* might be born legally long after his parents' marriage had come to an end by death or divorce. At the same time, the system offered barren wives an escape from the odium of infertility...." I do not know if the statement of the sources that the pregnancy of Hind, Muḥammad's mother, took four years, reflects any real event in her and her husband's life. This interesting matter merits further research, but is beyond the scope of this work.

9 Al-Ṭabarī, 3:249 (ll. 2–4); al-Balādhurī, *Ansāb* (ed. Madelung), 2:518.

10 Al-Ṭabarī, 3:265, from al-Wāqidī; al-Fasawī, *Maʿrifa*, 1:125–126; Ibn Saʿd, *al-Qism al-mutammim*, 378; al-Azdī, *Taʾrīkh al-Mawṣil*, 187; al-Mizzī, *Tahdhīb*, 25:467, from al-Zubayr b. Bakkār. See also al-Yaʿqūbī, *Taʾrīkh* (ed. Houtsma), 2:452–453; al-Masʿūdī, *Tanbīh*, 341; Ibn Saʿd, *al-Qism al-mutammim*, 259: all mentioning Ramaḍān, with no specific day.

11 Ibn ʿInaba, *ʿUmda*, 104, from [Abū Naṣr] al-Bukhārī.

3 Mother

His mother was Hind bt. Abī ʿUbayda[12] b. ʿAbdallāh b. Zamʿa (Zamaʿa[13]) b. al-Aswad b. al-Muṭṭalib b. Asad b. ʿAbd al-ʿUzzā b. Quṣayy. Her father, Abū ʿUbayda, who belonged to the most influential and prestigious clan of Banū Asad (which the Zubayrīs belonged to as well),[14] was one of the leaders of Quraysh.[15] He is described as a very generous person, who besides feeding many people from his family fed many guests as well.[16] Abū ʿUbayda lived in an estate in Wādī l-Farsh, near Medina, probably where Wādī Malal crosses al-Farsh, since the place he lived in is called Farsh Malal or al-Farsh min Malal. He seems to have lived near the Ḥasanī (and also the Jaʿfarī) families, who lived in Farsh Suwayqa.[17] Al-Zubayr b. Bakkār gives a more accurate name to his residence, calling it "Ṣafar that is in al-Farsh"[18] (see discussion below). Hind

---

12 Ibn al-Kalbī, *Jamhara* (ed. Ḥasan), 73, does not mention Abū ʿUbayda but mentions another son of ʿAbdallāh b. Zamʿa, named Kabīr. But Kabīr and Abū ʿUbayda are two different sons, see al-Zubayr b. Bakkār, *Jamhara*, [481], 506–507; al-Balādhurī, *Ansāb* (ed. ʿAbbās), 5:70; on her, see also Ahmed, *Religious Elite*, 159.

13 Ibn al-Kalbī, *Jamhara* (ed. Caskel), 2:605: Zamaʿa (ed. al-Ḥasan, 73: Zamʿa); Ibn Durayd, *al-Ishtiqāq*, 94: Zamaʿa (ed. Wüstenfeld), 58: Zamʿa.

14 His main, and longest, biography is recorded by al-Zubayr b. Bakkār, *Jamhara*, 482–505; the biography of Hind is on 496–505.

15 Ibn Ḥazm, *Jamhara*, 119–120: فكان من رؤساء قريش.

16 Al-Balādhurī, *Ansāb* (ed. ʿAbbās), 5:69: وكان أبو عبيدة سريا سخيا مطعاما للطعام يعده للأضياف ومن أتاه من إخوانه ; see also al-Zubayr b. Bakkār, *Jamhara*, 482; al-Iṣfahānī, *al-Aghānī* (Būlāq edition), 1:146, and 147; ibid., 18:208 (= Dār al-Kutub edition, 21:124).

17 Yāqūt, *Muʿjam* (ed. Wüstenfeld), 4:637: the residence of the Ḥasanīs and the Jaʿfarīs; ibid., 3:875: Abū ʿUbayda lives in al-Farsh min al-Malal; 400: Farsh Malal; al-Zubayr b. Bakkār, *Jamhara*, 482, 483, 486, 487 (in Ṣafar of Farsh); al-Iṣfahānī, *al-Aghānī* (Būlāq edition), 14:157 (= Dār al-Kutub edition, 16:121): al-Farsh min Malal; al-Bakrī, *Muʿjam*, 4:1258. We are unable to learn from the traditions whether Hind's father lived in this estate before or after she married ʿAbdallāh b. al-Ḥasan. It is noteworthy that the famous poet Kuthayyir used to live there at a certain period of his life; see al-Iṣfahānī, *al-Aghānī* (Būlāq edition), 8:36 (= Dār al-Kutub edition, 9:23).

18 Al-Zubayr b. Bakkār, *Jamhara*, 487: "Abū ʿUbayda b. ʿAbdallāh b. Zamʿa used to dwell in his abode, in Ṣafar that is in al-Farsh": كان أبو عبيدة بن زمعة نازلا في منزله بصفر من الفرش. Al-Ṣafar is described by al-Bakrī, *Muʿjam*, 4:1257–1258, as a fertile red mountain in al-Farsh, in which there was a hollow ground (ردهة) and a building (بناء) which belonged to Zayd b. Ḥasan. Further, al-Bakrī quotes the verses of ʿAmr b. ʿĀʾidh al-Hudhalī (not identified), who depicts two hills in the surroundings of al-Ṣafar, naming them "al-ʿAjūzayn" (the "two old ladies" [?]), while al-Samhūdī, *Wafāʾ*, 4:357, says: "this is a red mountain in Farsh Malal facing ʿAbūdā, and the road lies between them; there is a building belonging to al-Ḥasan

seemed to have loved her father very much; this we learn from an anecdote relating her deep mourning for him upon his death.[19] ʿAbdallāh b. al-Ḥasan was Hind's second husband. Before him she was married to ʿAbdallāh b. ʿAbd al-Malik b. Marwān,[20] from whom she inherited a large sum of money. ʿAbdallāh b. al-Ḥasan hence married a noble and rich woman. The importance of this combination, her pedigree and her wealth, is reflected in an anecdote recorded by al-Iṣfahānī.[21] This money enabled ʿAbdallāh b. al-Ḥasan to develop his estate, al-Bathna, which until his marriage was uncultivated and underdeveloped. Her husband rewarded her by giving her a large[?] part of this estate, including three rows of palm trees along the estate, which extended along Wādī l-Khayf. This property was given to her son Mūsā and was the cause of disputes between him and his half-brothers.[22]

It is noteworthy that Muḥammad al-Nafs al-Zakiyya's mother, Hind, and Rayṭa bt. ʿAbdallāh b. ʿAbd al-Madān had both been married to ʿAbdallāh b. ʿAbd al-Malik. Hind married ʿAbdallāh b. al-Ḥasan and bore him Muḥammad, who rebelled against the ʿAbbāsīs, while Rayṭa married Muḥammad b. ʿAlī b. ʿAbdallāh b. al-ʿAbbās and bore him Abū l-ʿAbbās al-Saffāḥ, the first ʿAbbāsī caliph.[23]

---

b. Zayd (rather than Zayd b. Ḥasan, as above), and behind it is a hollow ground that is called the hollow ground of the 'two old women': ردهة العجوزين. And the (meaning of) the 'two old women' [explains al-Samhūdī] is two hills, and Abū ʿUbayda b. ʿAbdallāh b. Zamʿa b. al-Aswad b. al-Muṭṭalib al-Zamʿī, the grandfather of the children of ʿAbdallāh b. Ḥasan b. Ḥasan … from their mother's side, used to dwell there." Cf. al-Bakrī, 3:878–879, where Ḍafir, is erroneously confused with Ṣafar.

19 Al-Iṣfahānī, *al-Aghānī* (Būlāq edition), 14:157 (= Dār al-Kutub edition, 16:122–123); (Būlāq edition), 18:208 (= Dār al-Kutub edition, 21:124–125), copied by Yāqūt, *Muʿjam* (ed. Wüstenfeld), 3:875–876. We also learn from these traditions, related from al-Zubayr b. Bakkār from Sulaymān b. ʿAyyāsh al-Saʿdī, about the close relations her father had with the Khārijī Muḥammad b. Bashīr, from Banū Khārija b. ʿUdwān. Sulaymān b. ʿAyyāsh al-Saʿdī was an important transmitter of al-Zubayr b. Bakkār, mainly of material relating to poets and their poetry. He related many traditions about the above-mentioned Khārijī, among them several which have some relation to Hind's father and the family of ʿAbdallāh b. al-Ḥasan and other ʿAlīds, Zayd b. al-Ḥasan b. ʿAlī b. Abī Ṭālib and his son, al-Ḥasan b. Zayd.

20 Al-Iṣfahānī, *Maqātil*, 235–236 (= idem, *al-Aghānī* (Būlāq edition), 18:208 (= Dār al-Kutub edition, 21:124–125). Another source mistakenly relates that it was the caliph himself, ʿAbd al-Malik b. Marwān, who was married to her, see al-Zubayrī, *Nasab Quraysh*, 227. For more about her, see Ibn Saʿd, *al-Qism al-mutammim*, 102, 372; al-Iṣfahānī, *Maqātil*, 233–236.

21 Al-Iṣfahānī, *al-Aghānī* (Būlāq edition), 18:208 (= Dār al-Kutub edition, 21:125): al-ʿAtakī < ʿUmar b. Shabba < Ibn Dāja < his father.

22 Al-Bakrī, *Muʿjam*, 1:227: فهو حق ابنه موسى منه الذي يقال له الشقة الذي خاصمه فيه إخوته من غيرها.

23 Al-Iṣfahānī, *al-Aghānī* (Būlāq edition), 18:208 (= Dār al-Kutub edition, 21:125).

4 Siblings

Muḥammad had eight brothers and five sisters. Muḥammad himself, Ibrāhīm, Mūsā, Idrīs (al-Akbar), Hārūn, Kulthūm, Umm Kulthūm, Fāṭima, Zaynab and Ruqayya were born to Hind bt. Abī ʿUbayda; ʿĪsā and Idrīs (al-Aṣghar) were born to ʿĀtika bt. ʿAbd al-Malik b. al-Ḥārith b. Khālid b. al-ʿĀṣ b. Hishām b. al-Mughīra b. ʿAbdallāh b. Makhzūm. Yaḥyā and Sulaymān were born to Hind's niece, Qarība bt. Rukayḥ b. Abī ʿUbayda b. ʿAbdallāh. b. Zamʿa.[24]

5 The Residences of the Family

It seems reasonable to assume that ʿAbdallāh b. al-Ḥasan's family had a house in Medina, but we do not have any evidence to corroborate this assertion.[25] They had an estate called Suwayqa or Farsh Suwayqa in Yanbuʿ district, near Medina.[26] Yāqūt says that Suwayqa was the dwelling place of ʿAlī b. Abī Ṭālib's family. The expression he uses (*yaskunu*) may denote that he was referring to his own period or was quoting a (much?) earlier source: سويقة موضع قرب المدينة يسكنه آل علي بن أبي طالب,[27] since al-Bakrī (d. 487/1094) also refers to Suwayqa as "the village which belongs to the family of Abū Ṭālib": سويقة القرية التي لآل أبي طالب.[28] Many testimonies bear witness to the fact that Suwayqa served as the main dwelling place of this family.[29] The descendants of al-Ḥasan

24 Ibn Saʿd *al-Qism al-mutammim*, 250–251, where Hārūn, Kulthūm, and Umm Kulthūm are only mentioned by him; Ibn ʿInaba, *ʿUmda*, 103; al-Zubayrī, *Nasab Quraysh*, 53–54; al-Iṣfahānī, *Maqātil*, 396, 431, 433, 487; al-Balādhurī, *Ansāb* (ed. Madelung), 2:495; cf. al-Iṣfahānī, *Maqātil*, 396, and al-Ṭabarī, 3:257 (l. 19), where the sons of ʿĀtika are ʿĪsā, Sulaymān, and Idrīs; on Zaynab and Ruqayya, see Ahmed, *Religious Elite*, 161 and n. 860; on ʿĀtika bt. ʿAbd al-Malik, see ibid. p. 159, n. 853; see also Bernheimer, *The ʿAlids*, 35, n. 9: on Zaynab, Ruqayya and Fāṭima, on ʿĀtika bt. ʿAbd al-Malik, see ibid., 39

25 The sentence in al-Ṭabarī, 3:192, does not refer to a dwelling place (*dār*) of the Ḥasanīs, as Williams mistakenly understood. The text: ودارَ محمد بالرحبة حتى جاء بيت عاتكة; Williams read: ودارُ محمد, instead of ودارَ محمد (see Williams' *Early ʿAbbāsī Empire*, 1:87).

26 For a short, general and superficial description of al-Suwayqa, see al-Jāsir, *Bilād Yanbuʿ*, 15–16, 189–194; see also Landau-Tasseron, "Arabia," 505.

27 Yāqūt, *Muʿjam* (ed. Wüstenfeld), 3:198 ("Suwayqa").

28 Al-Bakrī, *Muʿjam*, 4:1225 ("Masrūḥ"), locates it above (*fawq*) Suwayqa.

29 Al-Ṭabarī, 3:256 (l. 15): [ʿUmar b. Shabba] < Ismāʿīl b. Jaʿfar b. Ibrāhīm [b. Muḥammad b. ʿAlī b. ʿAbdallāh b. Jaʿfar b. Abī Ṭālib] from Muḥammad's brother, Mūsā b. ʿAbdallāh b. al-Ḥasan: "I came out from our residence (*manāzilinā*) in Suwayqa" (= al-Bakrī, *Muʿjam*, 3:768, with the following *isnād*: Yamūt b. al-Muzarriʿ < Ibn al-Mallāḥ < his father < Ismāʿīl b. Jaʿfar [b. Ibrāhīm] ***from*** Mūsā b. ʿAbdallāh b. al-Ḥasan. Ibn al-Mallāḥ may be Ḥabīb b.

b. ʿAbdallāh still lived there in much later periods: during the reigns of al-Hādī (r. 169–170/785–786), al-Rashīd (r. 170–193/786–809) and al-Mutawakkil (r. 232–247/847–861).[30] Suwayqa as described by al-Ḥarbī[?] was one mile from al-Sayāla and about twenty-three miles[31] from Medina. He describes the estate in his time, in the mid-ninth century,[32] as follows:

> At a distance of one mile from it [that is, al-Sayāla] there is a spring (*ʿayn*) that is known as Suwayqa which belongs to the descendants of ʿAbdallāh b. al-Ḥasan. Its waters are abundant and sweet, and it is situated towards the right side of the road: ناحية عن الطريق يُمْنَة. In it there are dwelling places (*manāzil*), sown fields (orchards? *mazāriʿ*) and a lot of palm groves.[33] Running water flows from this spring. When you leave the estate, to your left side is the "red mountain," which is called Wirqān.

---

al-Mallāḥ or one of his sons, ʿĀʾidh or al-Rabīʿ, who were called "Banū l- Mallāḥ." ʿĀiʾdh died in 190/805 or 806 and al-Rabīʿ between 150/767 and 160/777. Both brothers are considered faithful followers of the Shīʿī Imāms. Yamūt b. al-Muzarriʿ (d. 303 or 304/915, 916, or 917) was al-Jāḥiẓ's nephew and was the author (narrator?) of (*ṣāḥib*) أخبار وملح وآداب. On al-Suwayqa see also al-Ḥimyarī, *al-Rawḍ al-miʿṭār*, 1:328 (who copies al-Bakrī); al-Bakrī, *Muʿjam*, 1:56 ("Ashʿar"): وبأسفل الحورة عين عبدالله بن الحسن التي تدعى سويقة; al-Iṣfahānī, *Maqātil*, 250: "We were together with ʿAbdallāh b. al-Ḥasan in Suwayqa [...] Mūsā [b. ʿAbdallāh b. al-Ḥasan] stood on the rock (*al-ṣakhra*) in Suwayqa"; ibid., 293: a group of Muʿtazilīs comes to ʿAbdallāh b. al-Ḥasan in Suwayqa; al-Iṣfahānī, *al-Aghānī* (Būlāq edition), 4:91 (= Dār al-Kutub edition, 4:340); Ibn ʿAsākir, *Taʾrīkh*, 31:213, from al-Zubayr b. Bakkār from Sulaymān b. ʿAyyāsh al-Saʿdī (on him see above n. 19): The poet al-ʿAblī comes to the Ḥasanīs' estate in Suwayqa immediately after the ʿAbbāsī rise to power; al-Iṣfahānī, *al-Aghānī* (Būlāq edition), 11:83 (= Dār al-Kutub edition, 12:247): the poet Abū Wajza visits ʿAbdallāh b. al-Ḥasan in Suwayqa.

30 Al-Iṣfahānī, *Maqātil*, 445: the reign of al-Hādī (the year 169/776); 495: the reign of Hārūn al-Rashīd (d. 193/809); 600; al-Fīrūzābādī, *al-Maghānim al-muṭāba*, 191–192, during the reign of al-Mutawakkil (d. 247/861): the descendants of ʿAbdallāh b. al-Ḥasan still lived in Suwayqa.

31 According to Hinz, the length of the Arab *mīl* in the ʿAbbāsī period was approximately 2,000 m.; see Hinz, *Islamische Masse*, 63; but cf. van Berchem, *CIA*, 2:27, and Elad, "The Southern Golan," 48, who came to the conclusion that the ninth-century ʿAbbāsī mile ranges between 1500 and 2500 m.

32 Although al-Jāsir, the editor of *Kitāb al-Manāsik*, did his utmost to trace the author, and in the end came to the conclusion that it is highly plausible that he was Ibrāhīm b. Isḥāq al-Ḥarbī (198–285/814–898), the authorship is not unequivocally proven.

33 Mention of the palm groves of the Ḥasanīs is also recorded by al-Iṣfahānī, *Maqātil*, 298 (= al-Bakrī, *Muʿjam*, 3:268).

> In it there is (lives: *bihi*) a tribal branch of Juhayna. It is said that this mountain continues uninterrupted until Mecca: يقال انه متصل إلى مكة.[34]

We should bear in mind, however, that Suwayqa was completely demolished by the ʿAbbāsī troops after the rebellion of Muḥammad b. al-Ḥasan in 145/762.[35] A single tradition relates that al-Manṣūr gave back the estates (*amwālahum*) to the descendants of Muḥammad b. ʿAbdallāh, but no names of the estates are given.[36] It is highly plausible that these included Suwayqa, which was the large and main estate of the Ḥasanīs.

An interesting account is related by Abū l-Faraj al-Iṣfahānī regarding Suwayqa in 240/854–855, according to which the great-grandson of Mūsā b. ʿAbdallāh [al-Nafs al-Zakiyya's brother], Muḥammad b. Ṣāliḥ b. ʿAbdallāh b. Mūsā b. ʿAbdallāh, rebelled with other members of his family against the caliph al-Mutawakkil in 240/854–855. Their base was the family estate Suwayqa in al-Ḥijāz, so the caliph sent his well-known commander Abū l-Sāj against them. Muḥammad b. Ṣāliḥ and his family members were captured and put in chains. Some were killed, while Muḥammad b. Ṣāliḥ and others were brought to al-Sāmarrāʾ. Al-Zubayr b. Bakkār relates that Suwayqa was the base of the rebellion and that Abū l-Sāj laid waste to it: he uprooted many palm trees, and burnt the houses (of Banū l-Ḥasan).[37] According to this story, Suwayqa must

---

34 Al-Ḥarbī[?], *al-Manāsik*, 443; Suwayqa was situated at the lower end (*bi-asfal*) of Wādī l-Ḥawra, one of the *wādī*s of Mount al-Ashʿar. This mountain was one of the two mountains of the tribe of Juhayna; see al-Bakrī, *Muʿjam*, 1:156 ("Ashʿar").

35 Al-Ṭabarī, 3:256, from [ʿUmar b. Shabba] < ʿĪsā [b. ʿAbdallāh]: ʿĪsā b. Mūsā confiscates all the estates of Banū l-Ḥasan. In al-Bakrī, *Muʿjam*, 3:768 ("Suwayqa"), there are two anecdotes related by two eyewitnesses to the total destruction of the estate. The first narrates through (*wa-ḥaddatha*) Yamūt b. al-Muzarriʿ from Ibn al-Mallāḥ (that is, ʿĀʾidh b. Ḥabīb b. al-Mallāḥ al-ʿAbsī or al-Qurashī (d. 190/805 or 806), on him, see n. 29 above), from his father [Ḥabīb b. al-Mallāḥ?] from Ismāʿīl b. Jaʿfar b. Ibrāhīm [b. Muḥammad b. ʿAlī b. ʿAbdallāh b. Jaʿfar b. Abī Ṭālib] from Mūsā b. ʿAbdallāh b. al-Ḥasan, which ends with: "Muḥammad came out in rebellion afterwards and was killed and therefore our abodes were destroyed": فخرج محمد بعد هذا فقتل فخربت ديارنا. The second narrator is Saʿīd b. ʿUqba [b. Shaddād b. Umayya al-Dhuhlī l-Juhanī], whose daughter Fāṭima was married to ʿAbdallāh b. Mūsā b. ʿAbdallāh b. al-Ḥasan b. al-Ḥasan who describes the ruined Baṭḥāʾ Suwayqa. Large parts of the text were copied by al-Ḥimyarī, *al-Rawḍ al-Miʿṭār*, 328–329.

36 Al-Ṭabarī, 3:257–258 (l. 16 to l. 5).

37 Al-Iṣfahānī, *al-Aghānī* (Būlāq edition), 15:89 (= Dār al-Kutub edition, 16:360–361); idem, *Maqātil*, 600–601 (part of the tradition, related by ... Muḥammad b. Khalaf, Wakīʿ < Aḥmad b. Abī Khaythama). Yāqūt, *Muʿjam* (ed. Wüstenfeld), 3:198, seems to copy large parts of this tradition, without naming his source, though; see also al-Tanūkhī, *al-Faraj*, 4:354. Muḥammad b. Ṣāliḥ is worthy of further investigation; on him see, for example,

have been rebuilt sometime between 145/762 and 240/854–855.[38] Al-Ḥarbī's description of the flourishing estate in his times indicates that he saw it in this condition before 240/854–855, before it was demolished by al-Mutawakkil's general.

As noted, sometimes we find the mention of Farsh or the compound Farsh Suwayqa as denoting the estate of the Ḥasanīs.[39] Farsh was a (small) *wādī*, which was an offshoot of the bigger Wādī Malal.[40]

As already noted, ʿAbdallāh b. al-Ḥasan developed his estate, al-Bathna, with the help of his wife's money. Her money enabled him to invest in the development of the irrigation system.[41] The family of al-Ḥasan b. al-Ḥasan b. ʿAlī b. Abī

---

the beautiful story in al-Iṣfahānī, *al-Aghānī* (Dār al-Kutub edition), 16:364–367; idem, *Maqātil*, 605–608; al-Ḥimyarī, *al-Rawḍ al-miʿṭār*, 193–194. About the time he was a highway robber in al-Ḥijāz, a long anecdote is related by *him* through Ibrāhīm b. [Muḥammad b. ʿAbdallāh] b. al-Mudabbir (d. 279/892 or 893, on him, see *EI*², "Ibn al-Mudabbir" [H.L. Gottschalk]). From this story we learn that Muḥammad b. Ṣāliḥ married Ḥamdūna bt. ʿĪsā b. Mūsā b. Abī Khālid al-Ḥarbī [is he the nephew of al-Amīn's famous *Abnāwī* commander, Muḥammad b. Abī Khālid[?]; on him, see al-Ṭabarī, index; or he may be a descendant of the ʿAbbāsī commander ʿĪsā b. Mūsā l-Khurāsānī, who was active during al-Manṣūr's and al-Mahdī's reigns; see Ibn Khayyāṭ, *Taʾrīkh* (Beirut, 1993), 361; al-Yaʿqūbī, *Taʾrīkh* (ed. Houtsma), 2:464; Ibn al-Athīr, *al-Kāmil* (ed. Tornberg), 6:38]; but cf. the long, fascinating story, in the *al-faraj baʿda al-shidda* style, in Ibn ʿInaba, *ʿUmda*, 116–118. According to this story he married the daughter of Ibn al-Mudabbir; Ibn ʿInaba recorded the anectote from *Hidāyat al-ṭālib*, the work of Tāj al-Dīn, who is Tāj al-Dīn Muḥammad b. al-Qāsim b. al-Ḥusayn b. Maʿiyya al-Ḥasanī l-Ḥillī l-Dībājī (d. 776/1374); on him, see al-Ziriklī, *al-Aʿlām*, 7:5; Kaḥḥāla, *Muʿjam*, 11:138. In the two latter works *Hidāyat al-ṭālib* is not mentioned; it is mentioned by al-Ṭihrānī, *al-Dharīʿa* (Najaf and Tehran, 1398/1978), 25:180: هداية الطالب في نسب آل أبي طالب. For other biographies of Muḥammad b. Ṣāliḥ al-Ḥasanī, see al-Kutubī, *Fawāt*, 3:392; al-Ṣafadī, *al-Wāfī*, 3:154–155. The well-known historians such as al-Ṭabarī, al-Yaʿqūbī, and al-Masʿūdī do not mention his rebellion and his imprisonment.

38 It seems that it was flourishing again already in the year 169/785–786; see al-Iṣfahānī, *Maqātil*, 445. It was the dwelling place of the Ḥasanīs in the last quarter of the eighth century: the governor of Medina on behalf of Hārūn al-Rashīd, Bakkār b. ʿAbdallāh b. Muṣʿab b. Thābit b. ʿAbdallāh b. al-Zubayr, sent an envoy to arrest Muḥammad b. Yaḥyā b. ʿAbdallāh b. al-Ḥasan, who came to Suwayqa in Ramaḍān in order to fast there (see ibid., 495).

39 Al-Zubayrī, *Nasab Quraysh*, 227: "We were at (visited? *kunnā ʿinda*) ʿAbdallāh b. al-Ḥasan's in al-Farsh."

40 On Farsh and Farsh Suwayqa, see al-Bakrī, *Muʿjam*, 3:1019; Yāqūt, *Muʿjam* (ed. Wüstenfeld), 3:874–875. Wādī Malal was very fertile, and rich in water, see al-Bakrī, *Muʿjam*, 4:1256–1258; Yāqūt, *Muʿjam*, 4:637–638. It seems that Farsh was very close to Suwayqa, which was bigger and more centrally located. This is most probably the reason for the name Farsh Suwayqa.

41 Al-Bakrī, *Muʿjam*, 1:227.

Ṭālib had another estate just opposite Suwayqa called al-Ḥazra.[42] They also had other estates near Medina.[43]

6 Wives and Children

1) Umm Salama bt. Muḥammad b. al-Ḥasan b. al-Ḥasan b. ʿAlī b. Abī Ṭālib, his cousin. She bore him five children: three boys, ʿAbdallāh, who was called al-Ashtar, ʿAlī, and al-Ḥasan; and two girls, Fāṭima and Zaynab.
2) Fākhita bt. Fulayḥ b. Muḥammad b. al-Mundhir b. al-Zubayr b. al-ʿAwwām, who bore him one child, whose name was Ṭāhir.[44]
3) Ḥafṣa bt. ʿImrān b. Ibrāhīm b. Muḥammad b. Ṭalḥa b. ʿUbaydallāh. According to one source, Muḥammad was her third husband and after him she married another husband, but other sources do not mention Muḥammad as one of her husbands.[45]
4) A concubine, who bore him Ibrāhīm.[46]
5) Another[?] slave woman, who bore him al-Ḥasan.[47]

---

42 Ibid., 2:441.

43 Al-ʿAlī, *"Mulkiyyāt,"* 979–980.

44 Ibn Saʿd, *al-Qism al-mutammim*, 372–374; al-Zubayrī, *Nasab Quraysh*, 53–54 (al-Ḥusayn instead of al-Ḥasan); al-Bukhārī, *Sirr al-silsila*, 7–8 (= Ibn ʿInaba, *ʿUmda*, 105, n. 1 [editor's note], quoting *Sirr al-asrār* of Abū Naṣr al-Bukhārī): Salama, instead of Umm Salama; al-Ḥasan is described as the son of a slave woman. On Ṭāhir, and his mother, Fākhita, see al-Bukhārī, *Sirr al-silsila*, 7–8 (= Ibn ʿInaba, *ʿUmda*, 105–106); nothing more is known about him; al-Ḥasan b. Muḥammad died in the battle of Fakhkh in 169/786, see al-Bukhārī, *Sirr al-silsila*, 7–8; al-Iṣfahānī, *Maqātil*, 434, 443–446, 451–452.

45 Al-Madāʾinī, "Kitāb al-Murdifāt," 2:75–76; according to al-Madāʾinī, before Muḥammad she married al-Qāsim b. ʿAbdallāh b. ʿAmr b. ʿUthmān b. ʿAffān and Hishām b. ʿAbd al-Malik; according to Ibn Ḥabīb, *al-Muḥabbar*, 448, she married (in the following order) *six* husbands, al-Qāsim b. ʿAbdallāh b. ʿAmr b. ʿUthmān b. ʿAffān; Hishām b. ʿAbd al-Malik; then Muḥammad b. ʿAbdallāh b. ʿAmr b. ʿUthmān [al-Qāsim's brother!?]; ʿAwn b. Muḥammad b. ʿAlī b. Abī Ṭālib; ʿAbdallāh b. Ḥasan b. Ḥusayn, and ʿUthmān b. ʿUrwa b. al-Zubayr b. al-ʿAwwām. It is highly possible that Muḥammad b. ʿAbdallāh b. ʿAmr was mistakenly changed to Muḥammad b. ʿAbdallāh b. al-Ḥasan, see Ibn Ḥazm, *Jamhara*, 83: Ḥafṣa was married to Muḥammad b. ʿAbdallāh b. ʿAmr, to whom she bore Ruqayya al-Ṣughrā. Ibrāhīm b. ʿAbdallāh b. al-Ḥasan, Muḥammad's brother, was going to marry Ruqayya but he died before consummating the marriage and she married Muḥammad b. Ibrāhīm b. Muḥammad b. ʿAlī b. ʿAbdallāh b. al-ʿAbbās. See also Ahmed, *Religious Elite*, 90.

46 Al-Zubayrī, *Nasab Quraysh*, 54; for a brief history of Ibrāhīm b. Muḥammad, see Ibn ʿInaba, *ʿUmda*, 106.

47 Al-Bukhārī, *Sirr al-silsila*, 8 [= Ibn ʿInaba, *ʿUmda*, 105, n. 1, where the editor quotes Abū Naṣr al-Bukhārī's work].

6) Another[?] slave woman of his wife Fākhita by the name of Rukhayya, who bore him a son who died in an accident while Muḥammad b. ʿAbdallāh was in the mountains of Juhayna, fleeing from the governor of Medina.[48]
7) *Children*

Very little information about his children is found in the sources.

a) ʿAbdallāh, called al-Ashtar, was the most well-known. According to one tradition, he fled from al-Manṣūr during his father's rebellion, until he reached al-Sind, where he was killed.[49] Another version relates that his escape, hiding, and death occurred after the rebellion and his father's death.[50]
b) ʿAlī, who was sent to Egypt, most probably to incite it to mutiny, was arrested and sent to al-ʿIrāq, where he died in al-Manṣūr's prison.[51]
c) Zaynab was married to Muḥammad b. Abī l-ʿAbbās al-Saffāḥ, the son of the first ʿAbbāsī caliph. Muḥammad was one of the senior commanders of the ʿAbbāsī army sent to subdue the rebellion of Zaynab's father. Some sources relate that immediately upon the death of her father in battle, Muḥammad b. Abī l-ʿAbbās wanted to consummate the marriage. Along with traditions relating that indeed the marriage was consummated,[52] there are others that either make no mention of it or imply that it was never consummated. According to one source, after the death of Muḥammad b. Abī l-ʿAbbās al-Saffāḥ, she married ʿĪsā b. Mūsā l-ʿAbbāsī, who headed the ʿAbbāsī army against her father,[53] but according to other sources, she married ʿĪsā b. ʿAlī b. ʿAbdallāh b. al-ʿAbbās (not ʿĪsā b. Mūsā) and two or three husbands after him.[54]

48 Al-Ṭabarī, 3:167; al-Iṣfahānī, *Maqātil*, 230; according to al-Iṣfahānī, *al-Aghānī* (Būlāq edition), 7:96 (= Dār al-Kutub edition, 8:128–129), the name of his wife is Fulayḥa, who belonged to the Zubayrī family, but the text seems garbled and it should be: Fākhita bt. Fulayḥ (no. 2), who indeed belonged to the Zubayrī family.

49 Al-Ṭabarī, 3:359–364; al-Balādhurī, *Ansāb* (ed. Madelung), 2:534.

50 Ibn Saʿd, *al-Qism al-mutammim*, 372; al-Iṣfahānī, *Maqātil*, 310–314; Ibn ʿInaba, *ʿUmda*, 106.

51 Ibn Saʿd, *al-Qism al-mutammim*, 373; al-Bukhārī, *Sirr al-silsila*, 8; Ibn ʿInaba, *ʿUmda*, 105, n. 1 (the editor, quoting *Sirr al-silsila* of Abū Naṣr al-Bukhārī); al-Balādhurī, *Ansāb* (ed. Madelung), 2:540, mistakenly placed in the year 169/785, under the reign of al-Hādī; al-Masʿūdī, *Murūj*, 4:147: ʿAlī died in Egypt.

52 Ibn Saʿd, *al-Qism al-mutammim*, 373; Ibn Ḥabīb, *al-Muḥabbar*, 449.

53 Al-Balādhurī, *Ansāb* (ed. Madelung), 2:517.

54 Ibn Saʿd, *al-Qism al-mutammim*, 373: three husbands; Ibn Ḥabīb, *al-Muḥabbar*, 449–450: two husbands; see also the discussion of Ahmed, *Religious Elite*, 161 and n. 860; Bernheimer, *The ʿAlids*, 41–42.

7 Education

Little is known about Muḥammad's education. It seems that his father sought to give his sons Muḥammad and Ibrāhīm a formal knowledge of *ḥadīth* and *fiqh*, and for that purpose they were brought to ʿAbdallāh b. Ṭāʾūs (d. 132/749 or 750).[55] Among Sunnī scholars Muḥammad was not famous for any kind of scholarship.[56] He is mentioned in the books of *rijāl* (transmitters of *ḥadīth*) as a minor transmitter,[57] who is known to have transmitted only one *ḥadīth*. Among Zaydī scholars he was highly praised for being a *faqīh* with a firmly-established Zaydī doctrine (see the discussion below).

8 Physical Traits

Muḥammad is described as having a big body,[58] great strength,[59] and a very swarthy complexion.[60] On his face he had the remains of smallpox scars (*al-judarī*).[61] Between his shoulders he had a black mole, the size of an egg.[62] When he talked he stuttered.[63]

---

55 Al-Iṣfahānī, *Maqātil*, 238, 241; on Ibn Ṭāʾūs, see al-Mizzī, *Tahdhīb*, 15:130–132 and the comprehensive bibliography of the editor therein.

56 Cf. van Ess, *Theology*, 1:397, mentioning a work by Muḥammad b. ʿAbdallāh, *Kitāb al-Siyar*, according to Riḍwān al-Sayyid in *Majallat Kulliyyat al-Ādāb* (Sanaʿa, 1990), 9:105ff. I was unable to obtain this publication, and see the discussion in chapter 5, no. 4 (*Kitāb al-Siyar* of Muḥammad b. ʿAbdallāh).

57 Al-Wāqidī (if I understand him correctly) relates that Muḥammad transmitted a few traditions: وكان حديثه قليل; (perhaps unworthy traditions?), see al-Iṣfahānī, *Maqātil*, 241; Ibn Saʿd, *al-Qism al-mutammim*, 374: وكان قليل الحديث; the tradition is similar to that in al-Iṣfahānī's book, so it seems that he also quotes al-Wāqidī, without naming him. Ibn Ḥajar, *Tahdhīb* (Hyderabad edition), 9:252 (= al-Mizzī, *Tahdhīb*, 25:466) records that a number of *rijāl* critics regard him as a trustworthy transmitter, but some regard him as unworthy due to his rebellion, calling him and his brother Ibrāhīm *khawārij* (*khārijiyāni*).

58 Al-Ṭabarī, 3:203.

59 Al-Iṣfahānī, *Maqātil*, 250.

60 Al-Ṭabarī, 3:203: أدلم ,آدم شديد الأدمة ;أدلم is explained as a very dark complexioned man; idem, 254: أرقط ,آدم ;أرقط is a black man (but usually a sheep or a goat) speckled with white, or having patches of white and black, see Lane, *Lexicon*, s.v. *r.q.ṭ.*

61 Ibn Saʿd, *al-Qism al-mutammim*, 376: al-Wāqidī's testimony, serving as an eyewitness. Could this be the reason for the term *arqaṭ*, mentioned in the preceding note?

62 Al-Iṣfahānī, *Maqātil*, 238, 242, 243; Ibn ʿInaba, *ʿUmda*, 103, quoting Abū l-Ḥasan al-ʿUmarī (see also ibid., 106: قال شيخنا أبو الحسن العمري). Ibn ʿInaba died in 828/1425 in Kirmān.

63 Al-Ṭabarī, 3:230 (= al-Iṣfahānī, *Maqātil*, 242), where the expression used by an eyewitness is *tamtām*, adding that "he saw him (standing) on the *minbar*, while the words are stuck

Some of the physical traits attributed to Muḥammad b. ʿAbdallāh are similar to those of the Prophet Muḥammad. The resemblance to Moses (his stuttering) is also apparent (see also the discussion below: *Ṣāḥib al-khāl*).

9 The Image of Muḥammad b. ʿAbdallāh as Portrayed by the Sources

This part deals with some of the spiritual as well as physical traits of Muḥammad b. ʿAbdallāh, and with his charged epithets, which bear important religious significance in both Sunnī and Shīʿī Islam. In several instances it is possible to detect the way in which the biased sources constructed this spiritual and physical image.

9.1 *The Title al-Mahdī*

It seems plausible that ʿAbdallāh b. al-Ḥasan propagandized for the Mahdīship of his son. Whether this occurred already during the Umawī period, as some (mainly pro-Ḥasanī) traditions record,[64] or only in the early ʿAbbāsī period, is difficult to ascertain. The accepted view by scholars is that the title al-Mahdī was given to Muḥammad b. ʿAbdallāh towards the end of the Umawī period.[65]

---

and repeated [*yatalajlaju*] in his chest, and he hits his chest with his hands in order to get the words out"; the *isnād*: ʿUmar b. Shabba [al-Ṭabarī has *wa-ḥaddathanī*, omitting the name of ʿUmar b. Shabba] < ʿAbdallāh b. Nāfiʿ < Ibrāhīm b. ʿAlī l-Rāfiʿī, *min wuld Abī Rāfiʿ qāla:* كان محمد تمتاما فرأيته على المنبر يتلجلج الكلام في صدره فيضرب بيده عليه يستخرج الكلام; see also, al-ʿUmarī, *Ansāb*, 38 (copied by Ibn ʿInaba, *ʿUmda*, 103). The *tamtām* is explained by Lane, *Lexicon*, s.v. *t.m.m.* as "one who reiterates in uttering the letter *tāʾ* …, or one who jabbers, or hurries in his speech, so as not to make another understand"; *lajlaja*, or *talajlaja* is explained by Lane, *Lexicon*, s.v. *l.j.j.*: "He spoke with indistinct utterance: he spoke with a heavy tongue, and was defective in speech, not uttering one part of what he said immediately after another; he hesitated in speech, by reason of natural defect, or he reiterated, or stammered or stuttered (*taraddada*) in his speech."

64 E.g. al-Balādhurī, *Ansāb* (ed. Madelung), 2:496, who relates (no *isnād* is given) that ʿAbdallāh b. al-Ḥasan prepared his sons Ibrāhīm and Muḥammad to be caliphs before the first ʿAbbāsī caliph, Abū l-ʿAbbās, ascended the caliphate, "and he used to call his son Muḥammad al-Mahdī and al-Nafs al-Zakiyya." For the pro-Ḥasanī traditions, see below.

65 F. Buhl, "Muḥammad b. ʿAbdallāh," *EI*[1]; F. Buhl [and C.E. Bosworth], "Muḥammad b. ʿAbdallāh," *EI*[2]; Omar, *ʿAbbāsid Caliphate*, 215, argues, "that as early as in Hishām's reign … al-Mahd [read: al-Maḥḍ, that is ʿAbdallāh b. al-Ḥasan] started to spread the idea that his son Muḥammad was the Mahdī." Jafri, *Shīʿa*, 268, 275. Madelung, "al-Mughīriyya," argues that after the death of al-Bāqir (in ca. 117/735), al-Mughīra b. Saʿīd "backed the belief that the Ḥasanī Muḥammad b. ʿAbdallāh (al-Nafs al-Zakiyya) would come forth as the Mahdī." It is noteworthy that al-Mughīra was executed in 119/737! So he had two

An appropriate introduction to the topic is an early tradition, narrated by al-Zuhrī's nephew [Muḥammad b. ʿAbdallāh b. Muslim, d. 152/769–770 or 157/773–774],[66] transmitted by scholars who were either followers of the Ḥasanīs and even took part in the rebellion of al-Nafs al-Zakiyya, or belonged to a Ṭālibī (Jaʿfarī) family (see below). According to al-Zuhrī's nephew, he was sitting with ʿAbdallāh b. al-Ḥasan in Medina discussing the (issue of the) Mahdī, when ʿAbdallāh b. al-Ḥasan said that the Mahdī will be from the descendants of al-Ḥasan. The transmitter (Muḥammad b. ʿAbdallāh b. Muslim al-Zuhrī) says to him: "This is not accepted by the scholars belonging to your family": يأبى ذاك علماء أهل بيتك; to this ʿAbdallāh b. al-Ḥasan reaffirms that "the Mahdī will be from the descendants of al-Ḥasan b. ʿAlī and exclusively from among my descendants" (المهدي والله من ولد الحسن بن علي ثم من ولدي خاصة).[67] The direct transmitter from al-Zuhrī's nephew is ʿAbd al-ʿAzīz b. Muḥammad b. ʿUbayd al-Darāwardī (d. 182/798 or 799, or 186 or 187/802 or 803), one of the close supporters of Muḥammad b. ʿAbdallāh, who was appointed by the latter during the rebellion to be in charge of the arsenal (*al-silāḥ*), who transmitted to the Ṭālibī (Jaʿfarī) Medinan scholar, Dāwūd b. ʿAbdallāh (Abū l-Karrām) b. Muḥammad b. ʿAlī b. ʿAbdallāh b. Jaʿfar b. Abī Ṭālib. The latter often appears as a transmitter in Sunnī *ḥadīth* works, many times transmitting directly from ʿAbd al-ʿAzīz b. Muḥammad al-Darāwardī. It is impossible to establish any chronology from this tradition. If this event ever did take place, it could have happened during the Umawī as well as in the early ʿAbbāsī period.

---

years or less to spread this dogma; Madelung also believes that at that time [I understand this phrase to mean following the death of al-Bāqir], or in his words "it was evidently at this time that Muḥammad's father ʿAbdallāh b. al-Ḥasan b. al-Ḥasan began secretly to foster expectations that his son would be the expected Mahdī"; see also Cook, *Muslim Apocalyptic*, 215, who argues that "as the end of the Umayyad dynasty approached ... ʿAbd Allāh ibn al-Ḥasan ibn al-Ḥasan, apparently began to entertain messianic hopes for his son Muḥammad. ..." Cook provides no evidence for his claim. The pro-Ḥasanī traditions are well-known and serve as the basis for all scholars who hold this view; Ahmed, *Religious Elite*, 155, argues that two sources agree that ʿAbdallāh b. al-Ḥasan "had nominated his son Muḥammad to the caliphate, calling him al-Nafs al-Zakiyya and al-Mahdī, before al-Saffāḥ acceded the throne ... the movement that was to culminate in the revolution of his two sons had definitely begun during the caliphate of Hishām if not earlier. ..."; ibid., 166 (arguments in this vein).

66 On him, see al-Mizzī, *Tahdhīb*, 25:554–558; 24:638, reporting that in addition to being a transmitter of *ḥadīth*, he served the government as a secretary (*kātib*), and as head of the *shurṭa;* see also Elad, "Historical Writing," 123, n. 366.

67 Al-Mizzī, *Tahdhīb*, 25:467–468: Dāwūd b. ʿAbdallāh al-Jaʿfarī < al-Darāwardī [ʿAbd al-ʿAzīz b. Muḥammad b. ʿUbayd] < al-Zuhrī's nephew.

This is a very rare tradition. I was able to find it only in one source.[68] It is an eyewitness report by a non-Shīʿī scholar. The credibility of the tradition derives from its impartiality, that is, the mention that the scholars of the Hāshimī house do not approve of the ideas spread by ʿAbdallāh b. al-Ḥasan about his son being al-Mahdī. Some of the transmitters had a great interest in circulating the tradition.

It is different from other traditions that have clear pro-Ḥasanī tendencies, which were transmitted and circulated by scholars of the Ḥasanī family or their supporters. Such a typical tradition relates that Muḥammad b. ʿAbdallāh was called al-Mahdī from birth, due to the saying of the Prophet that the name of the Mahdī is Muḥammad b. ʿAbdallāh; this was the reason that "the family of Muḥammad" was so happy upon his birth, and "the Shīʿa" rejoiced with one another upon the annunciation of his appearance (وتباشرت به الشيعة).[69] Another typical pro-Ḥasanī tradition in this vein was related by ʿAbdallāh b. Mūsā b. ʿAbdallāh, al-Nafs al-Zakiyya's nephew,[70] or by ʿĪsā b. ʿAbdallāh b. Muḥammad b. ʿUmar b. ʿAlī.[71]

It is noteworthy that Balʿamī records that Muḥammad and Ibrāhīm started their propaganda before the ʿAbbāsīs ascended the caliphate. According to him, around the year 140/757–758, Muḥammad had told his adherents that he was the Mahdī of the family of Muḥammad and that his brother was *al-Hādī*, while al-Manṣūr, when nominating his son as the heir to the throne, said: my son is the Mahdī of the family of Muḥammad, and not the son of ʿAbdallāh b. al-Ḥasan.[72]

The Arabic version of al-Ṭabarī's *Taʾrīkh* is different in that it does not assert that al-Manṣūr nominated his son as heir to the throne in this year. Al-Ṭabarī

---

68 Al-Mizzī, *Tahdhīb*, 25:467–468.

69 Al-Iṣfahānī, *Maqātil*, 244–245; this tradition was not part of ʿUmar b. Shabba's work. Its *isnād* runs as follows: *ḥaddathanī* Aḥmad b. Saʿīd < Yaḥyā b. al-Ḥasan < ʿAbdallāh b. Muḥammad < Ḥumayd b. Saʿīd [unidentified]; the parallel tradition in al-Mizzī, *Tahdhīb*, 25:468 has: وقال يحيى بن الحسن بن جعفر العلوي النسابة. As to the transmitters: 1) Yaḥyā b. al-Ḥasan b. Jaʿfar (b. ʿUbaydallāh b. al-Ḥusayn b. ʿAlī b. al-Ḥusayn b. ʿAlī b. Abī Ṭālib, al-ʿUbaydalī l-ʿAqīqī [214–277/829–890]); ʿAbdallāh b. Muḥammad (b. Sulaymān b. ʿAbdallāh b. al-Ḥasan b. al-Ḥasan b. ʿAlī b. Abī Ṭālib), that is, the great-grandson of ʿAbdallāh b. al-Ḥasan, the father of Muḥammad al-Nafs al-Zakiyya.

70 Al-Iṣfahānī, *Maqātil*, 242–243: … Yaḥyā b. al-Ḥasan (al-ʿAqīqī) < Mūsā b. ʿAbdallāh b. Mūsā (b. ʿAbdallāh b. al-Ḥasan) < his father.

71 Al-Iṣfahānī, *Maqātil*, 244: … Yaḥyā b. al-Ḥasan (al-ʿAqīqī) < Ghassān b. Abī Ghassān < his father (Muḥammad b. Yaḥyā b. ʿAlī) < ʿĪsā b. ʿAbdallāh who reported "from infancy until he became mature, Muḥammad b. ʿAbdallāh used to hide and conceal himself (and all through this period) he was named al-Mahdī."

72 Balʿamī, 4:377–378.

relates (under the year 141/758–759) "in this year Abū Jaʿfar al-Manṣūr sent his son Muḥammad, who was at that time heir apparent (و لي عهد), to Khurāsān at the head of the armies ordering him to settle at al-Rayy."[73] It is commonly accepted that al-Mahdī was the second in line after ʿĪsā b. Mūsā who was at that time the heir to the throne. Al-Mahdī was officially nominated as heir only in 147/764–765.[74]

While the term و لي عهد (and not و لي العهد) in al-Ṭabarī's tradition may imply an heir apparent and not *the* heir apparent, Ibn Kathīr, who relies heavily on al-Ṭabarī for his *History*, records (under the year 141/758–759) "In this year al-Manṣūr appointed his son Muḥammad as the heir to the throne after him, named him al-Mahdī and appointed him over the land of Khurāsān" (و في هذه السنة و لى المنصور ابنه محمدا العهد من بعده ودعاه بالمهدي و ولاه بلاد خراسان).[75]

It seems that Muḥammad b. al-Manṣūr was entitled al-Mahdī on a copper coin from Bukhārā in 143/765 and on another copper coin from Samarqand in 144 H.[76] But from Balʿamī's (al-Ṭabarī) and Ibn Kathīr's texts we are informed that Muḥammad b. al-Manṣūr was given the title al-Mahdī by his father already in 140/757–758 or 141.[77]

The evidence for the scholars' assertions that the title al-Mahdī was given to Muḥammad b. ʿAbdallāh towards the end of the Umawī period is not unequivocal. It is highly plausible that he was entitled al-Mahdī during the reign of Abū l-ʿAbbās al-Saffāḥ (132–136/750–754) or that of al-Manṣūr, but before this title was officially given to al-Manṣūr's son, most probably in 143/760, which is the first time that this title is found on an official coin. From that time on, *the* ʿAbbāsī Mahdī was al-Manṣūr's son.[78]

---

73 Al-Ṭabarī, 3:133–134 (l. 20 to l. 1).

74 Al-Ṭabarī, 3:331ff.; H. Kennedy, "al-Mahdī, Abū ʿAbdallāh Muḥammad," *EI*².

75 Ibn Kathīr, *al-Bidāya* (ed. Shīrī), 10:82.

76 W. Spemann, *Katalog der Orientalischen Münzen/ Erster Band* (*Die Münzen der Östlichen Califen*) (Berlin, 1898), 326: Bukhārā, no. 2076 year 143: بسم الله ضرب بخارا في سنة ثلاث وأربعين ومائة.أمر به الأشعث [بن يحيى] في ولاية المهدي الأمير محمد بن أمير المؤمنين. My thanks are extended to Dr. Luke Treadwell for the source. See also the comprehensive discussion of Bates, "al-Mahdī," 292–295; 300 (table); 315, n. 36, quoting the Russian studies on the subject. Cf. al-Sayyid, "al-Nafs al-Zakiyya," 171, who believes that al-Manṣūr named his son al-Mahdī after the death of Muḥammad al-Nafs al-Zakiyya.

77 For further discussion, see Elad, "The *Ḥadīth* of al-Mahdī," 57–62.

78 *Akhbār al-ʿAbbās*, 238; in the tradition the young Abū l-ʿAbbās, ʿAbdallāh b. Muḥammad b. ʿAlī (the future first ʿAbbāsī caliph) is presented as the true redeemer of the Muslims against ʿAbdallāh b. al-Ḥasan b. al-Ḥasan's claim that his son, Muḥammad is the Mahdī. Accepting this tradition at face value leads to the unavoidable conclusion that the struggle between the ʿAbbāsīs and the Ḥasanīs over the legitimacy to rule began in the Umawī period. Nevertheless, it seems more plausible that the tradition was not invented before

Abū l-Faraj al-Iṣfahānī records six different small verses, some of which appear to bear witness to the fact that Muḥammad b. ʿAbdallāh was called al-Mahdī in the Umawī period. Two are from anonymous poets, one praises an unnamed newborn from the family of Muḥammad, who is called "*Imām hudā hādī*…" who is a descendant of ʿAlī and Muḥammad, who will put an end to the cruel tyrannical rule of the Abū l-ʿĀṣ family, and the Umawīs in general.[79]

A second group of verses was recited by ʿAbd al-ʿAzīz b. ʿImrān, Ibn Abī Thābit, a contemporary of the revolt, who did not know the identity of the poet "If what I thought about Muḥammad is true, then indeed what the non-Arabs relate about him in their books will come true."[80]

A third group of verses (two stanzas) by Ibrāhīm b. ʿAlī b. Harama (born 90/709, d. ca. 170/786) is quoted by al-Iṣfahānī.[81]

Three other groups of verses by Salama b. Aslum al-Juhanī were recorded by Abū l-Faraj. The first mentions "the son of ʿAbdallāh who has a seal that God has not given to any other besides him, who has marks of piety and true guidance."[82] In the second, the poet is named Salama b. Aslum, one of Banū Rabʿa of Juhayna who says "we wish that Muḥammad will be an Imām; the (Holy) Book that was sent down will be revived by him…and he will fill our

---

the ascendance of al-Saffāḥ to the caliphate, that is, not before the year 132/749–750. On the other hand, the tradition may imply that Muḥammad b. ʿAbdallāh was nicknamed al-Mahdī by his father during al-Saffāḥ's reign. The aim of the tradition was to pit the mahdīship of the ʿAbbāsī caliph, Abū l-ʿAbbās al-Saffāḥ, against that of Muḥammad b. ʿAbdallāh, the Ḥasanī; Elad, "al-Nafs al-Zakiyya, 157–159.

79 Al-Iṣfahānī, *Maqātil*, 245.

80 Al-Iṣfahānī, *Maqātil* 243, from ʿUmar b. Shabba < Muḥammad b. Ismāʿīl al-Jaʿfarī < "that Ibn Abī Thābit recited to him one stanza, and he does not know who composed it": إن يك ظني في محمد صادقا** يكن فيه ما تروي الأعاجم في الكتب

81 Al-Iṣfahānī, *Maqātil*, 243–244; idem, *al-Aghānī* (Dār al-Kutub edition), 4:376–377: four stanzas; for the historical background of these verses, see ibid. On Ibn Harama, see Ch. Pellat, "Ibn Harama," *EI*^{2}. In the Umawī period he seemed to have supported the ʿAlīd cause; although he praised ʿAbdallāh b. al-Ḥasan (al-Iṣfahānī, *al-Aghānī* [Dār al-Kutub edition], 4:372), at some point their relations deteriorated, their ways parted, and it seems that he preferred al-Ḥasan b. Zayd b. al-Ḥasan b. ʿAlī, the devout supporter of the ʿAbbāsīs (al-Iṣfahānī, *al-Aghānī* [Dār al-Kutub edition], 4:375–376) over ʿAbdallāh b. al-Ḥasan and his two sons, Muḥammad and Ibrāhīm (Ibn ʿAsākir, *Taʾrīkh*, 27:382; al-Mizzī, *Tahdhīb*, 6:154–155). When the ʿAbbāsīs came to power he did his best to get close to the ʿAbbāsī elite. He praised al-ʿAbbās b. ʿAbd al-Muṭṭalib (Ibn ʿAsākir, *Taʾrīkh*, 26:285), composed an elegy on Ibrāhīm b. Muḥammad al-Imām and a poem of praise for al-Saffāḥ (Ibn ʿAsākir, 7:211), al-Manṣūr (al-Iṣfahānī, *al-Aghānī* [Dār al-Kutub edition], 4:375, 397 in 140 H.!), and al-Sarī b. ʿAbdallāh the ʿAbbāsī, the governor of al-Yamāma (ibid., 4:382–386).

82 Al-Iṣfahānī, *Maqātil*, 243: له خاتم لم يعطه الله غيره***وفيه علامات من البر والهدى.

land with justice after it was filled with error and will bring us what I have been yearning for";[83] and the third piece "If there was among the people a Mahdī for us who will establish among us the way of life of the Prophet, he is Muḥammad, the godly, the pious."[84]

Who is this poet? I was not able to find any information on a poet by the name of Salama b. Aslum in the sources. Identifying him, however, with a certain Salama b. Aslum of Banū Rabʿa b. Rashdān b. Qays b. Juhayna, a minor Medinan transmitter of *ḥadīth*, is highly plausible. His son, ʿAbdallāh, was a *muḥaddith*[85] who flourished from the middle to the end of the second/eighth century; he seems to have had close relations with Mālik b. Anas (ca. 90/708 or 97/716 to 179/796), but also with ʿAbdallāh b. al-Ḥasan, whom he visited at his estate in Suwayqa.[86] Salama's son ʿAbdallāh is reported to have transmitted traditions from ʿUqba b. Shaddād al-Juhanī.[87] The authors of the *rijāl* books unanimously agree that Salama b. Aslum's main transmitter and teacher was Muʿāwiya b. Ḥudayj al-Juhanī, who was well known. He fought at the battle of Yarmūk, joined Muʿāwiya b. Abī Sufyān in his struggle against ʿAlī and served as the governor of Egypt on behalf of Muʿāwiya. He died in 52/672.[88]

Another direct transmitter of Salama b. Aslum was Busr b. Saʿīd, who died at the age of 87 or 97 in the year 100/718.[89]

If Salama b. Aslum al-Juhanī indeed heard directly from Muʿāwiya b. Ḥudayj who died in 52/672, he (Salama) was born ca. 40/660–661 and even if he lived for

83 Al-Iṣfahānī, *Maqātil*, 243 (= al-Mizzī, *Tahdhīb*, 25:468): إنا لنرجو أن يكون محمد*** إماما به يحيا الكتاب المنزل.. ويملأ عدلا أرضنا بعد ملئها*** ضلالا ويأتينا الذي كنت آمل

84 Al-Iṣfahānī, *Maqātil*, 243: إن كان في الناس لنا مهدي** يقيم فينا سيرة النبي** فإنه محمد التقي.

85 On him, see al-Dhahabī, *Mīzān* (Beirut, 1963), 2:431; Ibn Ḥajar, *Lisān*, 3:292; Ibn Nāṣir al-Dīn, *Tawḍīḥ*, 1:52.

86 Al-Khaṭīb al-Baghdādī, *al-Kifāya*, 433.

87 Ibn Ḥajar, *al-Iṣāba* (Beirut, 1415 H.), 3:257; al-ʿUqaylī, *al-Ḍuʿafāʾ*, 3:352; al-Albānī, *Silsila*, 1:479.

88 On him, see Ibn Ḥajar, *Tahdhīb* (Beirut, 1984), 10:183; al-Mizzī, *Tahdhīb*, 28:164–166; al-Dhahabī, *Siyar*, 3:37–40. The last three sources mention that he heard directly from Muʿāwiya b. Ḥudayj. See also Ibn al-Abbār, *al-Muʿjam*, 1:13, where Salama relates to his son that he heard Muʿāwiya b. Ḥudayj in Egypt; Ibn Mākūlā, *al-Ikmāl*, 1:74: سلمة بن أسلُم الجهني، تابعي سمع معاوية بن حديج; Ibn Nāṣir al-Dīn, *Tawḍīḥ*, 1:52, recording the detailed lineage, adding: حدث أيضا عن معاوية بن حديج. See also Ibn al-Abbār, *al-Muʿjam*, 1:13, quoting Salama's son, ʿAbdallāh, who relates that his father had told him that he heard Muʿāwiya b. Ḥudayj in Egypt; for the lineage of the family, see Ibn Ḥazm, *Jamhara*, 444; Salama b. Aslum is not mentioned by him, though.

89 Al-Dāraquṭnī, *Sunan*, 3:20. On Busr b. Saʿīd, see al-Dhahabī, *Siyar*, 4:594–595; al-Mizzī, *Tahdhīb*, 4:72–75: he died at the age of 87 or 97.

80 years, he did not die any later than 120/737–738. This leads to the conclusion that Salama b. Aslum could have composed the verses recorded by al-Iṣfahānī between 92/710–711 or 100/718 (when Muḥammad al-Nafs al-Zakiyya was born [see above]) and ca. 120/737–738. It indeed affirms the other pro-Ḥasanī traditions discussed thus far.

9.1.1 The Stuttering Mahdī

D. Cook has already shown that some of the descriptions of the Mahdī's traits in the Islamic tradition, especially his speech impediment (*thiqal*) "are consistent with what we know of Muḥammad al-Nafs al-Zakīya."[90]

"The messenger of God described the Mahdī, and described a speech impediment…, and [his] hitting his left thigh with his right hand when his speech comes slowly. His name is mine (Muḥammad) and his father's name is that of my father (ʿAbd Allāh)" (إن رسول الله وصف المهدي وذكر ثقلا في لسانه وضرب بفخذه اليسرى بيده اليمنى إذا أبطأ عليه الكلام إسمه إسمي وإسم أبيه إسم أبي).[91]

It seems that this tradition, recorded by Nuʿaym b. Ḥammād, was created for Muḥammad b. ʿAbdallāh, during his lifetime, to combine three of his characteristics: his speech impediment, his name and his father's name. The tradition is transmitted through Ibn Lahīʿa (97–174/715–790), its *isnād* ending with a *ṣaḥābī*, Abū l-Ṭufayl, ʿĀmir b. Wāthila who died in 107/725–726. This is most probably another example of the dubious ahistorical transmission of Ibn Lahīʿa in Nuʿaym's *Fitan*[92] as already noted by Madelung (see the discussion below).

It is noteworthy that al-Ḥasan b. ʿAlī b. Abī Ṭālib also had a speech impediment (*rutta*). The transmitter records the saying of Salmān al-Fārisī, that al-Ḥasan received it through "his uncle Mūsā b. ʿImrān, peace be upon him."[93]

Following are analyses of several traditions in al-Iṣfahānī's *Maqātil* regarding the speech impediment of Muḥammad al-Nafs al-Zakiyya.

---

90 Cook, *Muslim Apocalyptic*, 158.

91 Ibid. (quoting Nuʿaym b. Ḥammād, *Fitan*, 226).

92 Ibid.; with the *isnād*, al-Walīd (b. Muslim, d. 195/810) and Rishdīn (b. Saʿd, d. 188/804) < Ibn Lahīʿa (d. 174/790) < Isrāʾīl b. ʿAbbād (he is hardly mentioned in the biographical literature, for example see Ibn Mākūlā, *al-Ikmāl*, 3:20, where he is called *ṣāḥib akhbār al-malāḥim*; Ibn Abī Ḥātim, *al-Jarḥ* [Beirut edition], 2:331) < Maymūn al-Qaddāḥ (unidentified) < Abū l-Ṭufayl (ʿĀmir b. Wāthila, d. 107/725–726, on him, see al-Mizzī, *Tahdhīb*, 14:79–82).

93 Cook, *Muslim Apocalyptic*, 158, n. 107, according to al-Iṣfahānī, *Maqātil*, 50; the text is incomplete, some words are missing; the completion is according to Ibn Abī l-Ḥadīd, *Sharḥ* (Cairo, 1962), 16:29.

1) The first tradition is a short, clear-cut one, modeled after the well-known (above-mentioned) prophetic tradition about the Mahdī. It seems that it was created for Muḥammad al-Nafs al-Zakiyya most probably in his lifetime, “The name of al-Mahdī is Muḥammad b. ʿAbdallāh; he has a speech impediment.” The last links in the *isnād* are al-Qāsim b. al-Muṭṭalib al-ʿIjlī (unidentified) “al-Kalbī related to me 50 years ago” [!] that Abū Ṣāliḥ related to him 20 years earlier that he was told by Abū Hurayra. . . .[94]

Al-Kalbī is Muḥammad b. al-Sāʾib al-Kalbī (d. 146/763 or 764); Abū Ṣāliḥ is most probably Bādhām, Abū Ṣāliḥ, *mawlā* Umm Hāniʾ, the daughter of Abū Ṭālib who died ca. 120/737–738 (see the discussion on him above).

If, as I argue, the tradition was created for Muḥammad al-Nafs al-Zakiyya, then the *isnād* (or at least its last part) is fabricated. Both Abū Ṣāliḥ and Muḥammad b. al-Sāʾib al-Kalbī should have transmitted the tradition around the year 100/718 or even before that year. This seems impossible in light of the proposed dating and origin of the tradition.[95]

---

94 Al-Iṣfahānī, *Maqātil*, 242: إن المهدي اسمه محمد بن عبد الله، في لسانه رُتة. The *isnād* is of some interest: ʿUmar b. ʿAbdallāh < Abū Zayd [= ʿUmar b. Shabba] *ḥaddathanī* < Yaʿqūb b. al-Qāsim < *ḥaddathanī* ʿAlī b. Abī Ṭālib < *akhbaranī* al-Qāsim b. al-Muṭṭalib al-ʿIjlī < حدثني الكلبي منذ خمسين سنة ["al-Kalbī related to me 50 years ago" [!]] < أن أبا صالح حدثه قبل ذلك بعشرين سنة ["that Abū Ṣāliḥ related to him 20 years earlier"] < that he was told by Abū Hurayra. . . .

1) Yaʿqūb b. al-Qāsim b. Yaḥyā b. Muḥammad b. Yaḥyā b. Zakariyyāʾ b. Ṭalḥa b. ʿUbaydallāh (according to al-Iṣfahānī, *Maqātil*, 237; on him, see al-Khaṭīb al-Baghdādī, *Taʾrīkh* [Beirut edition], 14:274). 2) ʿAlī b. Abī Ṭālib b. Sarḥ (according to al-Iṣfahānī, *Maqātil*, 237). 3) Al-Qāsim b. al-Muṭṭalib al-ʿIjlī is not known. 4) Al-Kalbī, Muḥammad b. al-Sāʾib died in 146/763 or 764. 5) Following Goitein, I identified Abū Ṣāliḥ in another place as Dhakwān b. ʿAbdallāh al-Sammān (d. 101/718 or 719, see Elad, "The *Ḥadīth* of al-Mahdī," 189, n. 189); Madelung identified him as Abū Ṣāliḥ, Mīzān al-Baṣrī (in the index to al-Balādhurī, *Ansāb*, II); but it seems that he should be identified as Bādhām (or Bādhān), *mawlā* Umm Hāniʾ bt. Abī Ṭālib (d. ca 120/737 or 738). He is the only one of the two other Abū Ṣāliḥs mentioned above in this note who transmitted to al-Kalbī; in fact he is called in the sources "صاحب الكلبي", for example, see Ibn Ḥanbal, *al-ʿIlal*, 1:562. He was the author of a commentary of the Qurʾān; see Ibn Qutayba, *al-Maʿārif* (Cairo edition), 479; al-Bukhārī, *al-Kabīr* (Diyār Bakr edition), 2:144; al-ʿUqaylī, *Ḍuʿafāʾ*, 1:165–166; Ibn Ḥajar, *Tahdhīb* (Beirut, 1984), 10:344 (mentions the confusion between him and Mīzān al-Baṣrī); al-Mizzī, *Tahdhīb*, 4:4–7; according to al-Dhahabī, *Siyar*, 5:37–38, he survived 20 years after Abū Ṣāliḥ al-Sammān died; idem, *Taʾrīkh*, 7:325, mentions him among those who died between 111/729 or 730 and 120/737 or 738.

95 Abū Ṣāliḥ (died ca. 120/737 or 738) related to al-Kalbī "20 years ago"; al-Kalbī died in 146/762 or 763 and transmitted his link in the *isnād* "fifty years ago."

2) "… 'Umar b. Shabba < 'Abdallāh b. Nāfiʿ [b. Thābit b. 'Abdallāh b. al-Zubayr] < Ibrāhīm b. 'Alī l-Rāfiʿī, who belonged to the family of Abū Rāfiʿ, who said: 'Muḥammad was a stutterer. I saw him on the *minbar*, the words moving backwards and forwards in his chest. Then he would strike his chest with his hand to make the speech come forth.'"[96]

Nāfiʿ b. Thābit, the father of the second transmitter, was a Medinan who strongly refused to join the rebellion of al-Nafs al-Zakiyya.

The last link is an eyewitness and a pro-'Alīd scholar, Ibrāhīm b. 'Alī b. al-Ḥasan b. 'Alī b. Abī Rāfiʿ; I do not know if he took part in the rebellion. The thigh, which the Mahdī hit with his hand while stuttering in this tradition becomes the chest of Muḥammad b. 'Abdallāh. The transmitters shaped the anecdote according to the tradition of the stuttering Mahdī. The other possibility is that the *ḥadīth* was shaped to fit the traits of the real historic figure of Muḥammad b. 'Abdallāh.

9.2 *The Title al-Nafs al-Zakiyya*

Muḥammad b. 'Abdallāh was nicknamed al-Nafs al-Zakiyya ("the pure soul"). Al-Ṭabarī quotes verses from an elegiac poem on Muḥammad b. 'Abdallāh adding that people added at the end of this elegy a verse as follows: "May God kill 'Īsā [b. Mūsā] the killer of al-Nafs al-Zakiyya" (قتل الرحمان عيسى* قاتل النفس الزكية).[97] Abū l-Faraj al-Iṣfahānī relates that the scholars of the family of Abū Ṭālib used to say about Muḥammad b. 'Abdallāh that "he is the pure soul (النفس الزكية) and he is the one who was (or will be) killed in Aḥjār al-Zayt."[98]

Other traditions are related by Muḥammad b. 'Abdallāh himself, who knows that he will be killed in Aḥjār al-Zayt,[99] or by members of his family, e.g., in a tradition recorded by his nephew 'Abdallāh b. Mūsā b. 'Abdallāh b. al-Ḥasan, who relates that Muḥammad b. 'Abdallāh's cousin, 'Alī b. al-Ḥasan b.

96 Al-Ṭabarī, 3:203 (ll. 15–18); al-Iṣfahānī, *Maqātil*, 242: كان محمد تمتاما, فرأيته على المنبر يتلجلج الكلامُ في صدره فيضرب بيده عليه يستخرج الكلام. The translation is partly based on McAuliffe, *'Abbāsid Authority*, 160.

97 Al-Ṭabarī, 3:200 [= al-Iṣfahānī, *Maqātil*, 249]; this epithet is common, for example, see Ibn Khayyāṭ, *Ta'rīkh* (ed. al-'Umarī), 1:421; al-Dīnawarī, *al-Akhbār* (Leiden edition), 381; al-Dhahabī, *Mīzān* (Beirut, 1971), 7:363; Ibn Ḥajar, *Taqrīb* (1986 edition), 1:487; al-Sakhāwī, *al-Tuḥfa al-laṭīfa*, 1:43, 492.

98 Al-Iṣfahānī, *Maqātil*, 233: وكان علماء آل أبي طالب يروون فيه أنه النفس الزكية وأنه المقتول بأحجار الزيت; see also al-Masʿūdī, *Murūj*, 4:145, where he states that "he was named al-Nafs al-Zakiyya due to his piety and devotion"; al-Sayyid, "al-Nafs al-Zakiyya," 171–172, quoting al-Iṣfahānī and al-Masʿūdī.

99 Al-Ṭabarī, 3:248 (ll. 4–12); al-Samhūdī, *Wafā'*, 3:311.

al-Ḥasan b. al-Ḥasan, knew that "here in Aḥjār al-Zayt al-Nafs al-Zakiyya will be killed."[100] Imāmī scholars knew that the Prophet had predicted "that a pure soul (نفس زكية) of my family will be killed in Aḥjār al-Zayt."[101]

While the previous quoted traditions from members of the Ḥasanī family noting al-Nafs al-Zakiyya (the pure soul) who will be killed in Aḥjār al-Zayt certainly refer to Muḥammad b. ʿAbdallāh, these latter traditions mentioning a "pure soul" may refer to Muḥammad b. ʿAbdallāh, yet may possibly refer to another "pure soul" who was killed in Aḥjār al-Zayt.[102]

The Ḥasanīs distributed traditions that "al-Nafs al-Zakiyya is of the descendants of al-Ḥasan."[103] This was related through ʿUmar b. Mūsā from Muḥammad b. ʿAlī [(al-Bāqir) b. al-Ḥusayn b. ʿAlī?]. Another tradition was related by Yaḥyā b. al-Ḥusayn (d. 298/911), who was informed that Zayd b. ʿAlī [b. al-Ḥusayn?] related that "al-Nafs al-Zakiyya and al-Manṣūr [the Yamanī Messiah?] are of the descendants of al-Ḥasan. When al-Nafs al-Zakiyya (al-Ḥasanī) will be killed, the [Imāmī?] *Qāʾim* will arise."[104] But another tradition, this time related specifically by Muḥammad al-Bāqir, asserts that al-Nafs al-Zakiyya is of the descendants of al-Ḥusayn.[105]

D. Cook quotes two Imāmī traditions where al-Nafs al-Zakiyya is mentioned by name: Muḥammad b. al-Ḥasan (not b. ʿAbdallāh b. al-Ḥasan), a youth (*ghulām*) of the family of Muḥammad, who will be killed without committing a crime or sin. After he is killed God will send the *Qāʾim* of the family of Muḥammad.[106]

Cook argues that the Imāmī approach in these traditions is one of conciliation towards the Ḥasanīs by giving them a place in the messianic scenario.[107] "Afterwards, when the gap [between the two families] had become too wide to bridge, the figure of al-Nafs al-Zakīya was taken from the Ḥasanīds and reappropriated to the Ḥusaynids."[108]

---

100 Al-Iṣfahānī, *Maqātil*, 248.

101 Ibn ʿInaba, *ʿUmda*, 105 (عن رسول الله صلعم, تقتل بأحجار الزيت من ولدي نفس زكية); for a slightly different version, see al-Ṭabarsī l-Nūrī, *Nafas al-Raḥmān*, 302; ʿAlī Khān al-Madanī, *Riyāḍ al-sālikīn*, 567 (يقتل بأحجار الزيت رجل من ولدي نفس زكية). I was unable to find this tradition in other Imāmī or Sunnī *ḥadīth* works.

102 See the discussion below.

103 Al-Iṣfahānī, *Maqātil*, 248 (...حدثنا يحيى بن يعلى عن عمر بن موسى عن محمد بن علي عن آبائه قال النفس الزكية من ولد الحسن).

104 Al-Hādī ilā l-Ḥaqq, *al-Aḥkām*, 2:470.

105 Al-ʿAyyāshī, *Tafsīr*, 1:65 (copied by al-Majlisī, *Biḥār*, 52:223).

106 Cook, *Muslim Apocalyptic*, 159, 218.

107 Ibid., 219–220.

108 Ibid., 220.

This is indeed possible, but it seems that it is difficult to unequivocally assert that this person is from the Ḥasanī family. In theory he could have been from the Ḥusaynī family, e.g., Muḥammad b. al-Ḥasan b. al-Ḥusayn b. ʿAlī b. al-Ḥusayn b. ʿAlī b. Abī Ṭālib, a second cousin of Jaʿfar al-Ṣādiq or other members of the Ḥusaynī (or the Ḥasanī family) under this name.[109] It is also very difficult to unequivocally establish the chronology of these traditions. Another tradition in this vein is related by Muḥammad al-Bāqir (not his son, Jaʿfar al-Ṣādiq), who names the many (more than a dozen) portents of the coming of the Imāmī *Qāʾim*; the last ones are the emerging of the Sufyānī from Syria (al-Shām), al-Yamānī from Yemen (al-Yaman), the swallow-up (wasteland) in al-Baydāʾ, and the killing of a youth from the family of Muḥammad (Ṣ) between the Rukn and al-Maqām [in Mecca], "whose name is Muḥammad ibn al-Ḥasan, al-Nafs al-Zakīya, and a divine shout (*ṣayḥa*) will come from the heavens that the truth is with him and his party (*shīʿatihi*) (بأن الحق فيه و في شيعته), and then our *Qāʾim* will appear."[110] This is the most common and widely quoted version. It is a very interesting tradition, especially due to its ending, which explicitly acknowledges that the truth is with an obscure Muḥammad b. al-Ḥasan, al-Nafs al-Zakiyya and his supporters (party). A parallel tradition has another ending: "that the truth is with ʿAlī and his party" (بأن الحق مع علي وشيعته).[111] This ending is parallel to that in another well-known Imāmī tradition on the same subject, that is, the inevitable events (*al-maḥtūmāt*) preceding the coming of the *Qāʾim*. The "shout" (*ṣayḥa*) in the preceding tradition turns into a loud cry (*nidāʾ*) in the other *maḥtūmāt* traditions coming after the dissension among the ʿAbbāsīs (اختلاف بني العباس) and the killing of al-Nafs al-Zakiyya.[112] The aim of these

109 I was not able to find any information about Muḥammad b. al-Ḥasan b. al-Ḥusayn, Jaʿfar al-Ṣādiq's second cousin; he is often found in one of the genealogical links within a biography of his late descendants, e.g., Ibn Ḥamza al-Ṭūsī, *al-Wasīla*, 16; Ibn Bābawayh al-Qummī, *al-Amālī*, 18; al-Qāḍī l-Nuʿmān, *Sharḥ al-Akhbār*, 2:607; 3:577; al-Shaykh al-Mufīd, *al-Fuṣūl al-ʿashara*, 12. For a Ḥasanī under this name, for instance see Ibn Ḥazm, *Jamhara*, 44: Muḥammad b. al-Ḥasan b. Jaʿfar b. al-Ḥasan b. al-Ḥasan b. ʿAlī b. Abī Ṭālib, a second cousin of Muḥammad b. ʿAbdallāh al-Nafs al-Zakiyya.

110 Cook, *Muslim Apocalyptic*, 218, according to al-Majlisī, *Biḥār*, 62:191–192, and al-ʿĀmilī, *Ithbāt*, 7:392. See also Ibn Bābawayh, *Kamāl al-Dīn*, 331; al-Qummī, *al-Anwār al-bahiyya*, 374; al-Ṭabarsī, *Iʿlām*, 2:292; al-Irbilī, *Kashf al-ghumma*, 3:343 (الحق معه ومع شيعته) (instead of فيه), which does not change the meaning of the sentence; for "the swallow-up in al-Baydāʾ"(خسف البيداء), see Cook, *Muslim Apocalyptic*, 128ff.

111 Al-Kūrānī, *Muʿjam*, 3:493, and the sources quoted therein.

112 Al-Shaykh al-Mufīd, *al-Irshād*, 2:371; al-ʿĀmilī, *al-Ṣirāṭ al-mustaqīm*, 2:249; al-Qummī, *al-Anwār al-bahiyya*, 379; al-Irbilī, *Kashf al-ghumma*, 3:257; for a comprehensive bibliography, see al-Kūrānī, *Muʿjam*, 3:278.

Imāmī traditions is to unequivocally emphasize that al-Nafs al-Zakiyya was not the real Mahdī. The real *Mahdī l-Qāʾim* is from the Ḥusaynī family.

The nickname al-Nafs al-Zakiyya also appears in the Sunnī *ḥadīth*. These traditions are very early, and were already recorded by Nuʿaym b. Ḥammād in his *Kitāb al-Fitan*; some were noted and discussed by Madelung, but mainly by D. Cook.[113] One group of the traditions were connected with, or may have reflected, certain events of the caliphate of ʿAbdallāh b. al-Zubayr during Yazīd b. Muʿāwiya's reign, e.g., the tradition recording that the killing of al-Nafs al-Zakiyya will occur while Medina is ransacked.[114]

Madelung identifies the "pure soul" in Nuʿaym's traditions as the historical figure, Muḥammad b. ʿAbdallāh,[115] but in other traditions, as noted by D. Cook, the name al-Nafs al-Zakiyya appears as one of the *ʿalāmāt* (signs) of the Last Hour and the coming of the "real" *Mahdī*,

> it would appear, therefore, that the title [al-Nafs al-Zakiyya] is itself a messianic one, meaning a righteous person wrongfully killed by the government, who became one of the portents of the appearance of the real *Mahdī* afterwards[116].... Caution is indicated by the numerous traditions mentioning al-Nafs al-Zakīya or Nafs Zakīya by name (so it would seem).... The first figure [= al-Nafs al-Zakiyya], therefore, would be the idealized sacrificial messiah whose manner of death paves the way for the revelation of the true messiah, the Qāʾim.[117]

113 Madelung, "ʿAbdallāh b. al-Zubayr," 19, 34, originally proposed by Attema, *De Mohammedaansche opvattingen*, 74, 96–97 (Nuʿaym b. Ḥammād's *Fitan* and other major basic *fitan* literature were not printed yet); Attema's and Madelung's arguments are discussed by Cook, *Muslim Apocalyptic*, 159–160.

114 Nuʿaym b. Ḥammād, *Fitan*, 199; for the other traditions, see ibid., 110, 203, 204, 209; Madelung, "The Sufyānī," 34, n. 110; Cook, *Muslim Apocalyptic*, 160.

115 Madelung, "The Sufyānī," 19 and 34.

116 Cook, *Muslim Apocalyptic*, 160, and n. 113; ibid., n. 114, asserting that his name appears as one of the signs that will cause the downfall of the ʿAbbāsīs. Another tradition (ibid., quoting Nuʿaym b. Ḥammād, *Fitan*, 110 [see also al-Muttaqī l-Hindī, *Kanz*, 11:364]). It is noteworthy that in the quoted passage of Nuʿaym's *Fitan*, 110, the epithet appears as *al-Nafs al-Zākiya* not *al-Zakiyya*. On this, see also the discussion below.

117 Cook, Muslim Apocalyptic, 219. The author does not rule out the possibility that the real figure of al-Nafs al-Zakiyya, that is, Muḥammad b. ʿAbdallāh al-Ḥasanī, is meant in some of these traditions, but finds it more plausible to believe (219, last line to 220, first line) that in many of the traditions "there is no connection between the title and the historical figure."

Here it is worthwhile calling attention to another tradition, which appears in the early "Sunnī" *ḥadīth* collection, *al-Muṣannaf* of Ibn Abī Shayba (d. 235/849): ʿAbdallāh b. Numayr < Mūsā l-Juhanī < ʿUmar b. Qays al-Māṣir < Mujāhid [b. Jabr][118] < unnamed person of the companions of the Prophet (Ṣ):

> The Mahdī will not come out until al-Nafs al-Zakiyya is killed; when al-Nafs al-Zakiyya is killed, those in the sky and on earth will be angry with them; then the people will come to the Mahdī and will carry him in the same manner that a bride is carried to her husband on the night of her wedding. And he will fill the earth with justice and order. . . .[119]

Nuʿaym b. Ḥammād records a tradition that has some similarities to this *ḥadīth*, but with significant basic changes: "When al-Nafs al-Zakiyya will be killed, and his brother will be killed in Mecca while being abandoned and neglected (يقتل بمكة ضيعة), a herald will call from the sky: your Amīr is so and so and this is the Mahdī who will fill the Earth with justice."[120]

When discussing the universal signs for the return of the Mahdī in Imāmī traditions, Moezzi writes: "Five of these occur with such frequency that they were referred to as 'the five signs' (*al-ʿalāmāt al-khams*)." One of them (no. 4 in his list) is "'the assassination of the Pure Soul' (*qatl al-nafs al-zakiyya*); might this be, as some have believed, the assassination of the Ḥasanid Muḥammad b. ʿAbdallāh, who is called al-Nafs al-Zakiyya, killed in 145/762? Did the imams foresee the return as being imminent? I do not believe that this is probably,

118 On ʿUmar b. Qays al-Māṣir b. Abī Muslim al-Kūfī, *mawlā* Thaqīf, see Ibn Ḥajar, *Tahdhīb* (Beirut, 1984), 7:430; al-Mizzī, *Tahdhīb*, 21:484–486; on Mujāhid b. Jabr al-Makkī (d. between 100/720 and 104/722), see Ibn Saʿd, *Ṭabaqāt*, 5:466–467; al-Dhahabī, *al-Kāshif*, 240; Ibn Ḥajar, *Tahdhīb* (Beirut, 1984), 10:39–40; al-Mizzī, *Tahdhīb*, 27:228–235; Sezgin, 1:29; according to Sezgin, he died in 104/722.

119 Ibn Abī Shayba, *al-Muṣannaf*, 7:514, (حدثنا عبد الله بن نمير قال حدثنا موسى الجهني قال حدثني عمر بن قيس الماصر قال حدثني مجاهد قال حدثني فلان رجل من أصحاب النبي صلى الله عليه وسلم أن المهدي لا يخرج حتى تقتل النفس الزكية فإذا قتلت النفس الزكية غضب عليهم من في السماء ومن في الأرض فأتى الناس المهدي فزفوه كما تزف العروس إلى زوجها ليلة عرسها وهو يملأ الأرض قسطا وعدلا); for parallels in Sunnī writings, see al-Suyūṭī, *al-Durr al-manthūr* (Beirut edition), 6:58; idem, *al-ʿUrf al-Wardī* (Beirut, 1982), 2:65; al-Barazanjī, *al-Ishāʿa*, 113–114; al-Haythamī, *al-Mukhtaṣar*, 55 (all these sources quote Ibn Abī Shayba); and by the Imāmī author, Ibn Ṭāʾūs, *al-Tashrīf bi-l-minan*, 347; modern Imāmī scholars also mention the tradition of Ibn Abī Shayba, e.g., al-Bastawī, *al-Mahdī l-muntaẓar*, 214 (quoting also al-Barazanjī, *al-Ishāʿa*); and al-Kūrānī, *Muʿjam*, 1:478 (quoting all the above-mentioned parallels).

120 Nuʿaym b. Ḥammād, *Fitan*, 209.

since in some traditions al-Nafs al-Zakiyya is spoken of only al-Nafs" that is, وقتل النفس.[121]

But it seems that this is a single case (most probably a copyist's error) whereas all the other traditions that I came across record وقتل النفس الزكية.[122]

D. Cook has recently observed that according to a well-known Imāmī tradition, related through Jaʿfar al-Ṣādiq, only fifteen nights will pass between the emergence of the *Qāʾim* from the family of the Prophet and the killing of al-Nafs al-Zakiyya (ليس بين قيام قائم آل محمد وبين قتل النفس الزكية إلا خمسة عشر ليلة).[123]

In maintaining that Jaʿfar al-Ṣādiq is the source of the tradition, Cook hesitantly raises the possibility that this tradition may indicate that

> Jaʿfar al-Ṣādiq must have entertained messianic hopes for himself since he was the only Imām who could have benefited from this extremely limited period of time.... This is not in accordance with the usual traditions about him, but it is possible.... If this analysis is correct [adds Cook], then precisely at the time when Muḥammad al-Nafs al-Zakiyya revolted the Imāmī Shīʿīs were feeling a strong messianic pull, despite the quietist outlook of their Imām.[124]

Moezzi, as seen above, argued against this view.[125] Once again we face the unsolved problem of dating Imāmī traditions. Even if Jaʿfar al-Ṣādiq was the

121 Moezzi, *Divine Guide*, 118.

122 Ibid., n. 636, quoting one source: al-Nuʿmānī, *al-ghayba*, 266 that mentions وقتل النفس instead of وقتل النفس الزكية; in all **seven other traditions** that are recorded by al-Nuʿmānī, the phrase وقتل النفس الزكية appears (ibid. Bāb 15, 261, no. 9; 262, no. 11; 265, no. 15; 266, no. 16; 269, no. 21; 272, no. 26; Bāb 16, 301, no. 6. For other examples see, al-Shaykh al-Mufīd, *Irshād*, 2:371; al-Ṭūsī, *al-Ghayba*, 435, 437; Ibn Bābawayh al-Qummī (ʿAlī), *al-Imāma* (Qumm, 1404 H.), 128; Ibn Bābawayh al-Qummī, *al-Khiṣāl*, 303; al-Kulaynī, *al-Kāfī*, 8:310; al-Ḥillī, *al-Mustajād*, 258; al-Rāwandī, *al-Kharāʾij*, 3:1161, 1162; al-Majlisī, *Biḥār*, 52:203, 204, 206 (quoting *al-Ikmāl* of Ibn Bābawayh al-Qummī Muḥammad); 209, 289 (quoting, al-Ṭūsī's *Ghayba*); 119, 233, 235, 294 (quoting al-Nuʿmānī's *Ghayba*); 234 (quoting al-Nuʿmānī's *Ghayba*: النفس, instead of النفس الزكية); 304 (quoting al-Kulaynī's *al-Kāfī*).

123 Ibn Bābawayh, *Kamāl* (*Ikmāl*) *al-Dīn*, 649; al-Ṭūsī, *al-Ghayba*, 445; al-Majlisī, *Biḥār*, 52:203; al-Ṭabarsī, *Iʿlām*, 2:281.

124 Cook, *Muslim Apocalyptic*, 219.

125 Moezzi, *Divine Guide*, 118 and n. 636 on 224: "It was not the imams, and especially not Jaʿfar, who were responsible for the majority of the traditions about 'the assassination of the Pure Soul' that placed the coming of the *Qāʾim* just after the revolt of the Shīʿite insurgent. On the contrary, it was the insurgent who seems to have attempted to exploit

originator of the tradition—it could of course have been one of his close contemporaries, or it may have been of a slightly late provenance—the pure soul mentioned may have been an ahistoric figure, as in the other traditions of this kind mentioned above.

In Imāmī dogma "*qatl al-Nafs al-Zakiyya*" became one of the most important "Portents of the Hour" traditions (see Moezzi, above), and it seems that it was inserted into the many versions of the traditions dealing with this topic, sometimes clearly with no connection to the real figure of the rebel, Muḥammad b. ʿAbdallāh al-Nafs al-Zakiyya. Such widespread traditions mention, among the "Portents of the Hour," "the killing of al-Nafs al-Zakiyya, leading seventy [in some versions: seventy of the righteous] at the outskirts of al-Kūfa" (قتل النفس الزكية بظهر الكوفة في سبعين [or: سبعين من الصالحين]; in another version the name of the killed one, instead of al-Nafs al-Zakiyya, is Nafs Zakiyya, that means "a" pure soul.[126] This is an obvious parallelism to al-Ḥusayn b. ʿAlī.[127]

The tradition in this final[?] version was put into circulation after the ascendance of the ʿAbbāsīs since one of the "Portents of the Hour" is the appearance of the black flags from Khurāsān (وإقبال الرايات السود من خراسان).[128]

It should be noted that the phrase *nafs zakiyya* appears in the Qurʾān 18:74, when an unnamed figure (commonly identified by the commentators as al-Khiḍr) accompanies Moses and kills an innocent youth (*ghulām*). Moses reproaches him, saying: "Have you slain an innocent person who has slain no man? Verily you have done a horrid thing" (أقتلت نفسا زكية بغير نفس لقد جئت شيئا نكرا). Perhaps the motif of the innocent pure youth, al-Nafs al-Zakiyya, in the *ḥadīth* was remodeled according to the Qurʾānic verse. The expressions "*ghulām* who was killed without crime or sin" and "*nafs zakiyya*" could have been the origin of the epithet in the Sunnī as well as in the Imāmī tradition.[129] As far as I know, the first to note this possible connection was van Ess.[130] An

facts concerning the 'signs of Return' that had been circulating for a long time among the Muslims; he did so in the hope of passing himself off as the precursor of the Mahdi, if not the Mahdī himself...."

126 For the tradition of the killing on the outskirts of al-Kūfa, see al-Majlisī, *Biḥār*, 52:273; 53:82. It is related by ʿAlī b. Abī Ṭālib concerning future events, mainly in al-Kūfa, but also in Medina and other places; for the Nafs Zakiyya version, see ibid., 52:220.

127 Cook, *Muslim Apocalyptic*, 220.

128 For example, see al-Ḥillī, *Mukhtaṣar*, 199 (I did not find the tradition in al-Ṣaffār's *Baṣāʾir*); al-Shaykh al-Mufīd, *al-Irshād*, 2:368; al-Qummī, *al-Anwār al-bahiyya*, 377.

129 Interestingly, al-Masʿūdī, *Murūj*, 4:145, does not connect this epithet to the Qurʾānic verse. He relates that this epithet was given to Muḥammad b. ʿAbdallāh due to his piety and devotion (*li-zuhdihi wa-nuskihi*).

130 Van Ess, *Theologie*, 1:396; idem, "The Kāmiliyya," 151 [= 217], translating the term according to Qurʾān 18:74 as "unschuldige Blut" ("innocent blood") and adding in n. 53, "this is

examination of both Shīʿī and Sunnī exegetical literature regarding this verse would be extremely worthwhile, but that is beyond the scope of this study.

A version of the tradition about the appearance of *the* Mahdī following the killing of al-Nafs al-Zakiyya was most plausibly already in existence in the Umawī period.

Some of the traditions recorded by Nuʿaym b. Ḥammād are certainly of an Umawī provenance. It is noteworthy that in one of the traditions quoted in the *Ṣaḥīfa* of the Egyptian scholar Ibn Lahīʿa (97–174/715–790) the term "Nafs Zākiya" (instead of Nafs Zakiyya/al-Nafs al-Zakiyya), appears in connection with the events during ʿAlī b. Abī Ṭālib's reign, "Ibn Lahīʿa transmitted to us from Abū Qabīl who said: when ʿAlī killed the Ḥarūrā [that is, the Khawārij in Ḥarūrāʾ] […] Nafs Zākiya will be killed [… alḥ …] l killed him."[131]

Abū Qabīl is Ḥuyay b. Hāniʾ al-Maʿāfirī l-Miṣrī (d. 127 or 128/745). He was born in Yemen, and he himself reports that when ʿUthmān b. ʿAffān died (in 35/656) he was a young boy, still in Yemen.[132] He settled in Egypt and took part in the raid against Rhodes. He was the teacher and transmitter of some of the most distinguished scholars of Egypt, e.g., Ibn Lahīʿa, al-Layth b. Saʿd (d. 175/791) and Yazīd b. Abī Ḥabīb (d. 128/745).[133] The well-known *ḥadīth* scholar Yaʿqūb b. Shayba (182–262/798–875)[134] recorded that Ḥuyay had a (profound) knowledge in the *fitan* and *malāḥim* literature.[135]

If Abū Qabīl (who died in 128/745) indeed transmitted the tradition to Ibn Lahīʿa, then the Nafs Zākiya mentioned in it is not Muḥammad b. ʿAbdallāh, al-Nafs al-Zakiyya. Madelung argued that the transmission of Ibn Lahīʿa—in

---

the most likely translation of *al-nafs al-zakīya*." In this footnote he adds: "We can assume that the Shīʿa gave the name to Muḥammad Ibn ʿAbdallāh only after his death; during his lifetime he was called al-Mahdī"; see also Crone, *Political Thought*, 114, "For his name, cf. Q.18:74: "why have you killed an innocent soul (nafsan zakiyyatan)," with no further comment.

131 See Khouri, *Ibn Lahīʿa*, 245 (ll. 7–8): حدثنا ابن لهيعة عن ابن [=ابو] قبيل قال: لما قتل علي الحرورا […] نفس زاكية ستقتل […الح…] ل قتلوه; see also 257 (l. 81), from … Qays b. Saʿd < ʿAṭāʾ b. Abī Rabāḥ (d. 114/732 or 733, or 115/733 or 734, or 117/735 or 736) < Muḥammad b. ʿAlī b. Abī Ṭālib (Ibn al-Ḥanafiyya, d. between 73/692 or 693 and 93/711 or 712) "one of the four portents of the Last Day is the killing of *al-Nafs al-Zakiyya*" (not al-Zākiya); this tradition was most probably circulated after the ʿAbbāsīs' ascendance since it mentions the emergence of flags (not black flags) from the east; 289, (l. 303): Nafs Zākiya in the *isnād* of Ibn Lahīʿa < Abū Qabīl < Kaʿb al-Aḥbār.

132 Al-Bukhārī, *al-Ṣaghīr*, 2:11.

133 On him, see Ibn Ḥajar, *Tahdhīb* (Beirut, 1984), 3:64; al-Mizzī, *Tahdhīb*, 7:490–493; Madelung, "The Sufyānī," 31; Sezgin, 1:341.

134 On him, see Sezgin, 1:144; al-Ziriklī, *al-Aʿlām*, 8:199; Kaḥḥāla, *Muʿjam*, 13:249–250.

135 Al-Mizzī, *Tahdhīb*, 7:393; Madelung, "The Sufyānī," 31; Sezgin, 1:341.

Nuʿaym b. Ḥammād's *Fitan*—is highly dubious, even fabricated, including that of Abū Qabīl.[136]

In several specific cases Madelung is certainly correct (e.g., traditions from Abū Qabīl mentioning the *mulk* of Banū l-ʿAbbās; the black flags from Khurāsān, or the events of the year 204 H.). But these examples cannot serve as a total sweeping denial and disapproval of Abū Qabīl's transmission (which comprises different additional topics besides the *fitan* traditions) to many scholars, which are found by the dozens in the many variegated books of *ḥadīth* and history.

The term used in Ibn Lahīʿa's work is "*Nafs Zākiya*". The Qurʾānic term (in the Egyptian canonical version) is "*Nafs Zakiyya*," but it seems that most of the early *qirāʾāt* scholars read **Zākiya** instead of **Zakiyya.**[137] This rendering of the term is common in the early *ḥadīth* compilations and commentaries of the Qurʾān as well.[138]

9.3 *"Ṣāḥib al-khāl"*

The Ḥasanī family was responsible for spreading the tradition that Muḥammad was born with a black mole between his shoulders, as big as the size of an egg; he was called al-Mahdī and nicknamed "*Ṣarīḥ* [the purest lineage of] Quraysh."[139]

This tradition was related by Saʿīd b. ʿUqba al-Juhanī, a relation of the Ḥasanīs. Another very similar tradition was related by Mūsā b. ʿAbdallāh, Muḥammad's brother, where instead of "he was named al-Mahdī," it is rendered:

---

136 Madelung, "The Sufyānī," 31–34: "it is clear that the great majority of these chains of transmitters are unreal and fabricated. ..." (The quote is from 31, bottom).

137 See the summation of this topic by al-Ṭabarī, *Jāmiʿ al-bayān*, 15:354, who reports that most of the readers of the Qurʾān from al-Ḥijāz and al-Baṣra read "أقتلت نفسا زاكية", explaining the term as "the pure" [soul] without any sin, who has never sinned due to his very young age; while those readers from among the scholars of al-Kūfa read "نفسا زكية", meaning the penitent, whose sins are forgiven. See also ibid., 354f., the specific opinions of the readers of the Qurʾān on this topic; for other reports in this vein, see for example, al-Nawawī, *Sharḥ*, 15:140, who reports, "It was read in the seven [works on the reading of the Qurʾān] *zākiya* and *zakiyya*" (وفي السبع زاكية وزكية). See also the discussion in Ibn Khālawayh, *al-Ḥujja*, 1:227; Ibn Zanjala, *Ḥujja*, 1:427.

138 E.g., Muslim, *Ṣaḥīḥ*, 4:1849, 1851; Ibn Ḥibbān, *Ṣaḥīḥ*, 14:107; al-Ṭabarānī, *al-Aḥādīth al-ṭiwāl*, 1:289; see also Ibn Qutayba, *Gharīb al-ḥadīth*, 1:25; al-Shawkānī, *Fatḥ al-qadīr*, 3:302.

139 Al-Iṣfahānī, *Maqātil*, 237–238, citing ʿUmar b. Shabba < Muḥammad b. Ismāʿīl b. Jaʿfar al-Jaʿfarī < his mother, Ruqayya bt. Mūsā b. ʿAbdallāh b. al-Ḥasan b. al-Ḥasan < Saʿīd b. ʿUqba al-Juhanī – "ʿAbdallāh b. al-Ḥasan has taken him from her, since he [Saʿīd] was in his [probably Mūsā's, or perhaps ʿAbdallāh's] care and protection (وكان عبد الله بن الحسن أخذه منها فكان في حجره). He [that is, Saʿīd] said. ..."

"and he is the Mahdī."[140] Some of the traits and signs attributed to Muḥammad b. ʿAbdallāh are similar to those of the Prophet Muḥammad.[141] One of the most well-known signs is the black mole between his shoulders, similar to the Prophet's *khātam al-nubuwwa*, also between his shoulders.[142] The black mole is one of the physical traits of the Mahdī, mentioned in both the Sunnī and Imāmī literature. In the apocalyptic traditions, when the Prophet describes the war between the Muslims and the Byzantines, the Muslims are led by a forty-year-old man from the Prophet's family. One of the traits of this leader is the black mole (خال أسود) on his right cheek. In these traditions the leader is not termed al-Mahdī, but other Sunnī authors regarded him as the Mahdī.[143] In Imāmī sources he is unequivocally al-Mahdī.[144] Jaʿfar al-Ṣādiq is depicted as having a black mole on his cheek.[145] Other prominent persons and rebels also had black moles on their cheeks, or were called صاحب الخال or صاحب الشامة.[146]

Traditions depicting Muḥammad b. ʿAbdallāh's physical as well as spiritual-religious traits were disseminated, circulated, and transmitted by pro Shīʿī scholars, family members of the Ḥasanīs and other sections of the ʿAlīd family.

From these traditions it is clear that the inner, close circles of Muḥammad b. ʿAbdallāh were responsible for spreading traditions praising him. Of special interest are traditions, related from Saʿīd b. ʿUqba, describing the special,

140 Al-Iṣfahānī, *Maqātil*, 243

141 Al-Sayyid, "al-Nafs al-Zakiyya," 171, mentioning the moles of al-Nafs al-Zakiyya and that of the Prophet Muḥammad.

142 The common expression is خاتم النبوة, occasionally: سلعة (Ibn Saʿd, *Ṭabaqāt*, 1:426; al-Ṭabarānī, *al-Kabīr*, 22:279, 281; or علامة النبوة, see al-Ḥākim al-Naysābūrī, *al-Mustadrak* (Beirut, 1990), 2:657; or شامة النبوة, ibid., 631; Friedmann, *Prophecy Continuous*, 57, n. 29.

143 Sunnī sources, e.g., al-Ṭabarānī, *al-Kabīr*, 8:101; al-Haytamī, *Majmaʿ al-zawāʾid*, 7:319; Ibn Ḥajar, *Lisān*, 4:384; the leader is named *al-Mahdī* (based on this tradition), e.g., ʿAlī b. Burhān al-Dīn, *Sīra*, 1:314.

144 For example, see al-Majlisī, *Biḥār*, 51:80, 96; al-Irbilī, *Kashf al-Ghumma*, 3:269; al-Kūrānī, *Muʿjam*, 1:164–165, 338–340 and the exhaustive bibliography therein. For the physical description of the Mahdī in the *ḥadīth* literature, see Cook, *Muslim Apocalyptic*, 157–158.

145 Ibn Shahrāshūb, *Manāqib*, 3:401; al-Majlisī, *Biḥār*, 47:9, he had a black mole on his cheek and other red moles on his body.

146 E.g., al-Maʾmūn, who had black mole on his cheek, see al-Ṭabarī, 3:1141. According to Ibn ʿAsākir, *Taʾrīkh*, 33:338, he had a black mole on his right cheek, like the Mahdī in the apocalyptic tradition. According to Ibn Abī Uṣaybiʿa, *ʿUyūn al-anbāʾ* (Beirut, 1965), 81, Aristotle had a black mole on his lower chin; the well-known Qarmaṭī rebel, al-Ḥusayn b. Zikrawayh was called صاحب الشامة, see W. Madelung, "Ḳarmaṭī," *EI*², 4:660; al-Ziriklī, *al-Aʿlām*, 2:238; Ibn ʿAsākir, *Taʾrīkh*, 43:62–63: صاحب الخال.

sometimes extraordinary, physical as well as spiritual-religious traits of Muḥammad b. ʿAbdallāh. An example of one of these traditions follows:

> We were present in Suwayqa with ʿAbdallāh b. al-Ḥasan, in front of him there was a big rock. Muḥammad rose, prepared the rock for lifting (then lifted it) until it reached his knees, then his father forbade him to do it and he stopped. But when ʿAbdallāh [his father] went away, Muḥammad came back to the rock and lifted it up to his shoulders, and then he threw it. It was weighed and its weight was 1000 *raṭl*.[147]

9.4 *Zaydī Imām?*

It is well known that Muḥammad b. ʿAbdallāh was considered the sixth or seventh Imām of the Zaydiyya.[148] During his lifetime a group existed in al-Kūfa that is referred to in the sources as the Zaydiyya, whose nucleus was composed of supporters of Zayd b. ʿAlī b. al-Ḥusayn b. ʿAlī b. Abī Ṭālib. One of Muḥammad b. ʿAbdallāh's most loyal and active supporters was ʿĪsā b. Zayd b. ʿAlī b. al-Ḥusayn. The group of supporters united around him is often referred to as the Zaydiyya, but they are mainly mentioned in connection with al-Kūfa, at the time of Ibrāhīm b. ʿAbdallāh's revolt and the events connected with it. This group constituted the major nucleus of Ibrāhīm's army, and it is scarcely mentioned in connection with Muḥammad's rebellion and his campaign against the ʿAbbāsī army.[149]

---

147 Al-Iṣfahānī, *Maqātil*, 250, citing ʿUmar b. Shabba < Muḥammad b. Ismāʿīl [b. Jaʿfar] < his father < Saʿīd b. ʿUqba.

148 Strothmann, "Zaydiyya," 1197; Strothmann, *Zaiditen*, 107; Momen, *Shīʿī Islam*, 50; Madelung, *al-Qāsim ibn Ibrāhīm*, 189; Crone, *Political Thought*, 101; a (single) Imāmī source relates that Yaḥyā b. Zayd b. ʿAlī b. al-Ḥusayn b. ʿAlī b. Abī Ṭālib (d. 125/743) (on him, see van Arendonk, "Yaḥyā b. Zayd," *EI*[1]; Madelung, "Yaḥyā b. Zayd," *EI*[2]) appointed Muḥammad al-Nafs al-Zakiyya as his heir, but this is hardly plausible, see al-Shaykh al-Mufīd, *al-Masāʾil al-Jārūdiyya*, 3: وأوصى إلى محمد بن عبدالله بن الحسن بن الحسن بن علي عليه السلام الملقب بالنفس الزكية; Ibn Khaldūn, *al-ʿIbar* (Beirut, 1961), 1:354: وقال الزيدية بإمامة ابنه يحيى من بعده فمضى إلى خراسان وقتل بالجوزجان بعد أن أوصى إلى محمد بن عبد الله بن حسن بن الحسن السبط ويقال له النفس الزكية.

149 Al-Balādhurī, *Ansāb* (ed. Madelung), 2:530 (l. 21); 2:531 (l. 7); al-Ṭabarī, 3:254 (ll. 9–10); 3:302–303 (l. 17 to l. 1–2); al-Iṣfahānī, *Maqātil*, 331–332, 334, 335, 347, 357, 416, 418; 344 (ll. 9, 13); 348 [= al-Ṭabarī, 3:316 (l. 14)], Ibrāhīm is struck in the throat by a stray arrow, the Zaydiyya encircle him, to protect him (واطافت به الزيدية) (see McAuliffe, *ʿAbbāsid Authority*, 290: "until the Zaydīs [i.e., the former supporters of the ʿAlid claimant in al-Kūfa, Zayd b. ʿAlī b. al-Ḥusayn] encircled him."). Al-Iṣfahānī, *Maqātil*, 366, relates how Abū Ḥanīfa advises Ibrāhīm to come to al-Kūfa so that the Zaydiyya will help him

Nevertheless, Muḥammad's revolt is commonly defined by scholars as a Zaydī or Zaydī-Ḥasanī rebellion.[150]

Zaydī sources allegedly record public speeches and sermons of Muḥammad b. ʿAbdallāh, and these reveal a leader of a well-established movement with firm Zaydī doctrinal foundations. Some of these sermons were mentioned by al-Sayyid, including a detailed description of the alleged[?] *Kitāb al-Siyar of* Muḥammad b. ʿAbdallāh (see also the discussion in chapter 5, e.g., the speech in which he highly praises Zayd b. ʿAlī as the most distinguished Imām, who was most worthy of summoning the Muslims to God after al-Ḥusayn b. ʿAlī).[151]

As noted above, Sunnī sources do not attribute any special spiritual intellectual traits to Muḥammad b. ʿAbdallāh. They specifically assert that he was a minor *ḥadīth* transmitter who is known to have reported only one *ḥadīth*. However, some modern scholars regarded him as a great scholar, well versed in *ḥadīth* and *fiqh*. Their evidence, however, is far from conclusive. One set of evidence on which they base this conclusion is the long list of scholars that allegedly joined his cause, which in itself does not make al-Nafs al-Zakiyya a *faqīh* and/or *muḥaddith*.[152]

(كتب أبو حنيفة إلى إبراهيم يشير عليه أن يقدم الكوفة ليعينه الزيدية). The Zaydiyya appear only once in connection with Muḥammad b. ʿAbdallāh, at the beginning of his revolt, when he summons the dignitaries of the Zaydiyya and all the scholars that joined his cause to him: جمع إليه وجوه الزيدية وكل من حضر معه من أهل العلم, see ibid., 408. Several Zaydī dignitaries are mentioned at Muḥammad b. ʿAbdallāh's side during different stages of the revolt, see al-Iṣfahānī, *Maqātil*, 294, 413 (van Ess, *Theologie*, 1:262). The most famous of these was ʿĪsā b. Zayd b. ʿAlī, who is described as a commander of the right wings of both Muḥammad b. ʿAbdallāh's army and his brother's, see al-Iṣfahānī, 406, 413; on him, see n. 155 above.

150 Omar, *ʿAbbāsid Caliphate*, 246–248: a Ḥasanī-Zaydī revolt; Momen, *Shīʿī Islām*, 50; Watt, *Formative Period*, 162: Zaydite in inspiration; Newman, *Twelver Shīʿism*, 5: "The first of the great Zaydī rebellions was that of 145/762. ..."; Moezzi, *Divine Guide*, 27: "[A]s well as the revolts led by the Ḥasanid Zaydi Shīʿites Muḥammad b. ʿAbdAllāh (also called al-Nafs al-Zakiyya) and his brother Ibrāhīm"; ibid., n. 316: "The Zaydī revolt of the Ḥasanids Muḥammad b. ʿAbdAllāh, called al-Nafs al-Zakiyya, and his brother Ibrāhīm." In what follows, Moezzi describes the negative attitude of the Imāms in general and al-Bāqir and Jaʿfar al-Ṣādiq in particular, to the armed Zaydī [this is the term used by Moezzi] revolts; Madelung, "Zaydiyya," 478a: "Among the abortive revolts supported by Kūfan Zaydīs were those of Muḥammad al-Nafs al-Zakiyya and his brother Ibrāhīm."

151 Al-Sayyid, "al-Nafs al-Zakiyya," 176, n. 3, quoting *Kitāb al-Maṣābīḥ*, 218–220: وزيد إمام الأئمة وأولى من دعا إلى الله بعد الحسين بن علي.

152 For example, see Strothmann, "Die Literatur Zaiditen," 367; van Arendonk, *L'Imamat Zaïdite*, 50, among the sources that he quotes is Ibn Ḥajar, *Tahdhīb* (Hyderabad edition),

9.4.1 The Imāmiyya and the Zaydiyya

It is well known that most of Jaʿfar al-Ṣādiq's followers did not support Zayd b. ʿAlī's revolt in 120/740.[153] In Imāmī traditions, the Zaydīs are usually described as the followers of ʿAbdallāh b. al-Ḥasan (rarely of his son, Muḥammad), and as the adversaries of the Ḥusaynīs.[154] In these traditions the debate revolves largely around the figures of Jaʿfar al-Ṣādiq and ʿAbdallāh b. al-Ḥasan. However, we do occasionally find Muḥammad b. ʿAbdallāh al-Nafs al-Zakiyya within the framework of such traditions, e.g., where Jaʿfar al-Ṣadiq confronts the Zaydiyya. So far I have come across only two traditions of this kind that may be the "product" of a later phase in the struggle for legitimacy within the Banū Hāshim, mainly between the Ḥasanīs and the Ḥusaynīs. Of great interest in these traditions are the references to the "people of al-Zaydiyya" and in another, to the Zaydiyya and the Muʿtazila as the followers of Muḥammad b. ʿAbdallāh.[155]

9:252, but Ibn Ḥajar quotes Ibn Saʿd (probably from al-Wāqidī), who says that he transmitted (only) a few traditions (كان قليل الحديث); Sayyid, "al-Nafs al-Zakiyya," 178; among the sources he quotes is al-Iṣfahānī, *Maqātil*, 241 (from al-Wāqidī), where Ibrāhīm and Muḥammad are taken by their father to Ibn Ṭāʾūs, which does not necessarily turn each of them into a *faqīh* (see above); al-Wāqidī adds that Muḥammad heard two well-known *ḥadīth* transmitters, Nāfiʿ, *mawlā* Ibn ʿUmar and Abū l-Zinād ʿAbdallāh b. Dhakwān, and others (but) he transmitted a few traditions (وكان حديثه قليلا); these three scholars also rely on the evidence adduced by the Zaydī Imām al-Nāṭiq bi-l-Ḥaqq that Muḥammad b. ʿAbdallāh was the author of a book on the rules governing the conduct of war (كتاب السير); and see the discussion in chapter 5, no. 4 (*Kitāb al-Siyar* of Muḥammad b. ʿAbdallāh).

153 Madelung, "Zayd b. ʿAlī."

154 A group of traditions assess that the early Zaydīs were the followers of ʿAbdallāh b. al-Ḥasan: see al-Ṣaffār, *Baṣāʾir*, 194, nos. 1 and 2; 196, no. 4; 197, no. 6; 203, no. 31; 204, no. 37; al-Kulaynī, *al-Kāfī*, 7:376; Ibn Ḥamza al-Ṭūsī, *al-Thāqib fī l-manāqib*, 411; al-Khūʾī, *Rijāl*, 11:174; see also Cook, *Muslim Apocalyptic*, 216, 220–221.

155 Ibn Bābawayh al-Qummī, *al-Imāma*, 51, no. 36; al-Kulaynī, *al-Kāfī*, 1:242; al-Ṣaffār, *Baṣāʾir*, 176, no. 15, and the parallel traditions in al-Ṭabarsī, *Mustadrak*, 5:314–315, and al-Majlisī, *Biḥār*, 26:43; 47:271–272; cf. ibid., 26:40. See also the discussion in appendix 3, 546, no. 2.1.3; 557, no. 2.

CHAPTER 2

Muḥammad b. ʿAbdallāh during the Umawī and ʿAbbāsī Periods

1 The Umawī Period

There is little information on Muḥammad from the Umawī period. What there is deals for the most part with one subject, namely, the political aspirations ʿAbdallāh had for his son, Muḥammad (or for Muḥammad and his brother Ibrāhīm), namely fostering recognition among the Banū Hāshim that Muḥammad was the most deserving caliphal candidate. Many of the traditions regarding Muḥammad's political activity during the Umawī period were related by scholars and persons who supported the ʿAlīds and/or took an active part in Muḥammad's rebellion in 145/762. They contain chronological contradictions regarding his activities during this period. On the other hand, they share the same literary motifs, which cannot be considered historical. A large part of this information, therefore, does not reflect historical reality.

It is highly plausible that these traditions were created and disseminated following Muḥammad b. ʿAbdallāh's rebellion against the ʿAbbāsīs in 145/762, or possibly already a short time before the rebellion.[1] Following are a few of the relevant pieces of evidence.

1.1 *Traditions without Specific Dates and Names of Caliphs*

According to one group of traditions, Muḥammad b. ʿAbdallāh had been given the nickname "the Mahdī" from childhood. He was in constant hiding, writing people to join his cause and elect him as caliph.[2] These are early traditions that were spread already about twenty years or even less after his death.

1 But cf. Madelung, "al-Mughīriyya," *EI*², where he argues that "it was evidently at this time [that is after ca. 117/735 A.E.] that Muḥammad's father ʿAbdallāh b. al-Ḥasan b. al-Ḥasan secretly began to foster expectations that his son would be the expected Mahdī."

2 Al-Iṣfahānī, *Maqātil*, 239; the expression for a child is *ṣabiyy*; the *isnād*: we were told by [the transmitter is Abū l-Faraj al-Iṣfahānī] < Muḥammad b. Zakariyyā' al-Ṣaḥḥāf al-Baṣrī < Qaʿnab b. Muḥriz < al-Madā'inī < Ibn Da'b; ibid. 244: the expression for a child is *ghulām*; the *isnād*: … Ghassān b. Abī Ghassān < his father < ʿĪsā b. ʿAbdallāh; 244–245, the *isnād*: [al-Iṣfahānī] < Aḥmad b. Saʿīd < Yaḥyā b. al-Ḥasan < ʿAbdallāh b. Muḥammad < Ḥumayd b. Saʿīd [unidentified]; the last two versions lack the phrase calling for the cause.

© KONINKLIJKE BRILL NV, LEIDEN, 2016 | DOI 10.1163/9789004296220_004

It suffices here to deal with two traditions of this kind, to show their specific character. The first was related by the well-known ʿAlīd transmitter, ʿĪsā b. ʿAbdallāh b. Muḥammad b. ʿUmar b. ʿAlī b. Abī Ṭālib.[3] Another was related through al-Madāʾinī (d. ca. 225/840), from ʿĪsā b. Yazīd b. Daʾb b. Bakr, known as Ibn Daʾb (d. 171/787).[4] ʿĪsā b. Daʾb was a well-known scholar, versed in history and genealogy, a collector of ancient poetry (a *rāwī*) and also a poet in his own right. He had free access to the caliphs' courts, and is described as having close and even intimate relations with the Caliph al-Mahdī and especially with al-Hādī. He was accused by his contemporaries and later scholars of having forged all the different kinds of Arabic literature about which he was supposed to be knowledgeable. He seems to have been inclined towards the Shīʿa; therefore, if he himself did not invent the tradition (a supposition which in my view is doubtful),[5] he certainly was a worthy vessel for distributing it.[6] To sum up, this tradition about the political aspirations of Muḥammad b. ʿAbdallāh from his infancy should be categorized as pro-ʿAlīd, not only because of its content, but also because of its transmitters. In all cases I checked, the earliest transmitters were scholars well known for their Shīʿī tendencies, in many cases they

3 Al-Iṣfahānī, *Maqātil*, 244; on him and his family, see Nagel, "Muḥammad b. ʿAbdallāh," 242–243 (but especially, on ʿĪsā b. ʿAbdallāh).

4 Al-Iṣfahānī, *Maqātil*, 239: [Abū l-Faraj al-Iṣfahānī] < ʿĪsā b. al-Ḥusayn al-Warrāq < Aḥmad b. al-Ḥārith < al-Madāʾinī < Ibn Daʾb < ʿUmayr b. al-Faḍl al-Khathʿamī; mentioned by al-Sayyid, "al-Nafs al-Zakiyya," 171.

5 See the discussion on al-Yaʿqūbī, in Elad, "ʿAbd al-Malik."

6 On ʿĪsā b. Daʾb, see Ch. Pellat, "Ibn Daʾb," EI[2]; Ibn al-Nadīm, *al-Fihrist* (ed. Tajaddud), 103; Ibn Qutayba, *al-Maʿārif* (ed. Wüstenfeld), 267; he is greatly esteemed by al-Jāḥiẓ, *al-Bayān*, 1:42; see also ibid., 171; al-Khaṭīb al-Baghdādī, *Taʾrīkh* (Beirut, 1997), 11:150–153; Yāqūt, *Udabāʾ* (ed. Rifāʿī), 16:152–165 (ed. Margoliouth, 6:104–111); al-Suyūṭī, *al-Muzhir*, 2:354; Ibn Taghrī Birdī, *al-Nujūm*, 2:69; al-Qummī, *al-Kunā wa-l-alqāb*, 1:281–282; al-Ziriklī, *al-Aʿlām*, 5:111; on his Shīʿī persuasion, see Yāqūt, *Udabāʾ* (ed. Rifāʿī), 16:162 (ed. Margoliouth, 6:109; ed. ʿAbbās, 5:2149): وزعم العنزي (possibly he is al-Ḥasan b. ʿUlayl [d. 290/902], on him, see Sezgin, 1:374; or more plausibly, Muḥammad b. al-Muthannā b. ʿUbayd b. Qays b. Dīnār al-ʿAnazī l-Baṣrī [167–252/783–866], on him, see Kaḥḥāla, *Muʿjam*, 11:172; Rosenthal, *Historiography*, 392): أن ابن دأب كان يتشيع ويضع أخبار لبني هاشم; see also al-Shaykh al-Mufīd, *Kitāb al-ikhtiṣāṣ*, 144–160, who records the complete work of Ibn Daʾb entitled كتاب ابن دأب في فضل أمير المؤمنين عليه السلام (I thank Prof. Kohlberg for this reference); it is quoted from al-Shaykh al-Mufīd by al-Majlisī, *Biḥār*, 9:450–454; this work contained seventy traditions in praise of ʿAlī b. Abī Ṭālib and is quoted extensively both by medieval and modern Shīʿī authors. See, for example, al-Baḥrānī, *Ḥilya*, 2:434; al-Shāhrūdī, *Safīna*, 4:139; al-Kūfī, *Manāqib*, 2:363; al-Maḥmūdī, *Nahj al-saʿāda*, 1:213, 228; 8:320; al-Ṭabarī l-Nūrī, *Mustadrak al-wasāʾil*, 9:83; 11:93; 12:416.

were eyewitnesses to the events or even took part (they themselves or one of their family members) in the rebellion.[7]

Other traditions that can be connected to those mentioned above, almost without giving any indication of a specific date or name of a specific ruler, relate in general terms that already during the Umawī period, Muḥammad b. ʿAbdallāh used to hide and reappear intermittently, that people from his family and from Quraysh swore allegiance to him and that he was called al-Mahdī.[8]

Al-Wāqidī, on the other hand, "knows" that it was ʿAbdallāh b. al-Ḥasan who prepared his sons, Muḥammad and Ibrāhīm, as future caliphs worthy to rule already before the ascendance of Abū l-ʿAbbās to the throne, and that he was the one who nicknamed Muḥammad b. ʿAbdallāh "al-Nafs al-Zakiyya" and "al-Mahdī."[9]

1.2 *Traditions with Dates and Names of Caliphs*

1.2.1 Hishām b. ʿAbd al-Malik's Reign

Another group of traditions describes Muḥammad's activity (sometimes of his brother Ibrāhīm too) during Hishām b. ʿAbd al-Malik's reign (105–125/724–743). A key tradition of this group is directly related from ʿAbdallāh b. al-Ḥasan himself through the transmission of ʿAbd al-Raḥmān b. Abī l-Mawālī, the *mawlā* of the ʿAlīd family who took an active part in Muḥammad b. ʿAbdallāh's rebellion and related traditions about it. According to this tradition, Hishām asks ʿAbdallāh why his two sons, Muḥammad and Ibrāhīm, refrain from coming to the court along with the dignitaries that do appear there. ʿAbdallāh answers that his sons love to seclude themselves in the desert. The fact that they do not appear before the caliph does not indicate any concealed plot against him. These words left Hishām with no further comment (*fa-sakata*).[10]

Some literary motifs of this tradition appear in almost identical form and content in the traditions relating the history of Muḥammad and his brother Ibrāhīm during the caliphate of the first two ʿAbbāsī caliphs, Abū l-ʿAbbās al-Saffāḥ[11] and al-Manṣūr (see below).

---

7 But cf. Jafri, *Shīʿa*, 268; F. Buhl, "Ibrāhīm b. ʿAbdallāh," *EI*²; Omar, *ʿAbbāsid Caliphate*, 223: all accept these traditions at face value.

8 Al-Balādhurī, *Ansāb* (ed. Madelung), 2:498; al-Ṣafadī, *al-Wāfī*, 3:297.

9 Al-Balādhurī, *Ansāb* (ed. Madelung), 2:496 (= *Fragmenta*, 230: an identical parallel text [with small, mostly insignificant changes]. Al-Wāqidī is mentioned only in the *Fragmenta* and not in al-Balādhurī's *Ansāb*).

10 Ibn Saʿd, *al-Qism al-mutammim*, 374: al-Wāqidī from ʿAbd al-Raḥmān b. Abī l-Mawālī who heard ʿAbdallāh b. al-Ḥasan saying…; Ibn ʿAsākir, *Taʾrīkh*, 22:367 (a parallel tradition).

11 Ibn Saʿd, *al-Qism al-mutammim*, 252–253, citing the same phrases from al-Wāqidī, but about al-Saffāḥ and Muḥammad and Ibrāhīm. This has become a topos, a literary convention.

A most intriguing tradition belonging to this group was recorded in *Akhbār al-ʿAbbās* and was spread by people from Banū Musliya, who belonged to the inner circle of the ʿAbbāsī *daʿwa* in al-Kūfa. They heard Bukayr b. Māhān, the head of the Hāshimiyya movement, describing an episode that occurred in Muḥammad b. ʿAlī b. ʿAbdallāh b. al-ʿAbbās's house. Bukayr says that while staying in the house, Muḥammad's son, Abū l-ʿAbbās (the future first ʿAbbāsī caliph) entered and handed his father a letter. Muḥammad b. ʿAlī asks Bukayr: "Do you know who this letter is from? I [that is, Bukayr b. Māhān] said: No. He [Muḥammad] said: from the uncle on the mother's side of that [that is, Abū l-ʿAbbās], Ziyād b. ʿUbaydallāh al-Ḥārithī, the head of his tribe (*sayyid qawmihi*). Ho Abū Hāshim [i.e., the surname of relationship of Bukayr b. Māhān]—and he pointed to Abū l-ʿAbbās—this is the man who will appear (will be revealed) from among Banū Hāshim, the one who will undertake affairs, the Mahdī, contrary to what ʿAbdallāh b. al-Ḥasan says about his son" يا أبا هاشم وأشار إلى أبي العباس هذا المُجَلى عن بني هاشم القائم المهدي, لا ما يقول عبد الله بن الحسن في ابنه.[12]

The first aim of this tradition is to ascertain, from Muḥammad b. ʿAlī, the head of the ʿAbbāsī family, the legitimacy of the ʿAbbāsīs' rule in general, and that of of Abū l-ʿAbbās al-Saffāḥ in particular. It is one of several traditions that seek to legitimize the first ʿAbbāsī caliph, and is one of many traditions of an apocalyptic nature that depicts the first caliph as the Mahdī, which was his official title,[13] or as Ibn al-Ḥārithiyya, a name that pertains to his mother, who belonged to an important family of al-Ḥārith b. Kaʿb.[14]

In the tradition, the rivals of the ʿAbbāsīs in the struggle for legitimacy are the Ḥasanīs, namely, ʿAbdallāh b. al-Ḥasan b. al-Ḥasan and his son, Muḥammad. This would seem to reveal a struggle already in the Umawī period (Muḥammad b. ʿAlī died between 122/739 and 126/743).[15] Accepting this tradition at face value leads to the unavoidable conclusion that the struggle between the ʿAbbāsīs

12 *Akhbār al-ʿAbbās*, 238, from Asīd (Usayd) b. Dughaym al-Muslī from Bukayr b. Māhān, who stood at the head of the ʿAlīd Hāshimiyya movement, and later at the head of the ʿAbbāsī Hāshimiyya. For a parallel tradition, see *Nubdha*, fol. 256a (quoted by Omar, *ʿAbbāsid Caliphate*, 215); on Banū Musliya and their strong connections with the ʿAbbāsī *daʿwa*, see Sharon, *Black Banners*, 131, 141f.; on Bukayr b. Māhān, see Sharon, *Black Banners*, index, esp. 147–151, 155–157, 161–163. On Asīd (Usayd) b. Dughaym, see also *Akhbār al-ʿAbbās*, 249; *Nubdha*, fol. 256a; but cf. *Akhbār al-ʿAbbās*, 337: Ushaym b. Duʿaym al-Muslī; Agha, *Revolution*, 332, no. 47: Usayd.

13 Elad, "The First ʿAbbāsid *Mahdī*," 15–19; idem, "The *Ḥadīth* of al-Mahdī," 40–42.

14 Discussed by Sharon, *Black Banners*, 142f, 187; Elad, "al-Maʾmūn's Army," 311.

15 Ibn Saʿd, *al-Qism al-mutammim*, 244: year 125/743, during the reign of al-Walid b. Yazīd; *Akhbār al-ʿAbbās*, 239: between 122 and 125/739–740 and 743; al-Mizzī, *Tahdhīb*, 24:155: between 124 and 126/741–742 and 743–744.

and the Ḥasanīs over the legitimacy to rule had begun already in the Umawī period.[16] Nevertheless, it seems more plausible that the tradition was not conceived before the ascendance of al-Saffāḥ to the caliphate in 132/749–750.

One should keep in mind that in this period, and certainly after Muḥammad b. ʿAlī's death, it was his son Ibrāhīm who succeeded him, becoming the head of the ʿAbbāsī family. Only after his sudden and unexpected death at the hands of Marwān b. Muḥammad, when the armies of Qaḥṭaba b. Shabīb were on the verge of entering al-Kūfa, was Abū l-ʿAbbās probably chosen as the new leader of the ʿAbbāsī family, and eventually the new caliph.[17]

On the other hand, the tradition bears witness that during al-Saffāḥ's reign Muḥammad b. ʿAbdallāh was nicknamed al-Mahdī by his father. The aim of the tradition was to pit the mahdīship of the ʿAbbāsī caliph, Abū l-ʿAbbās al-Saffāḥ, against that of Muḥammad b. ʿAbdallāh, the Ḥasanī.

The tradition could have been created during al-Saffāḥ's reign, or at the beginning of al-Manṣūr's rule, when his son Muḥammad was not yet officially given the title al-Mahdī, that is, not after the year 143 H., the first time that this title is encountered on an official coin.[18] From that time on, "the" ʿAbbāsī Mahdī was al-Manṣūr's son.

The tradition also emphasizes the special connections between the ʿAbbāsīs and the tribe of al-Ḥārith b. Kaʿb. It aims at strengthening these connections, especially with the large family to which the first caliph's mother belonged. There is no evidence that connects Ziyād b. ʿUbaydallāh al-Ḥārithī to the ʿAbbāsīs before they ascended the caliphate. On the contrary, on the eve of the ʿAbbāsī takeover, we find him in Wāsiṭ, as one of the important commanders of Yazīd b. ʿUmar b. Hubayra, the Umawī governor of al-ʿIrāq. During the siege on the city by the ʿAbbāsīs, he defected to the ʿAbbāsīs.[19]

16 Omar, *ʿAbbāsid Caliphate*, 215, seems to accept the authenticity of the tradition, and argues (according to *Nubdha*, fol. 256a, which is the parallel text to the tradition in *Akhbār al-ʿAbbās*), "that as early as in Hishām's reign … al-Mahd [read: al-Maḥḍ, that is ʿAbdallāh b. al-Ḥasan] started to spread the idea that his son Muḥammad was the Mahdī."

17 On this complicated problem, see Sharon, *Revolt*, 225–242; Blankinship, "The Betrayal of the Imām Ibrāhīm," 591–592, 602–603.

18 *Katalog der Orientalischen Münzen*/Erster Band (*Die Münzen der Östlichen Califen*). Berlin, W. Spemann, 1898, 326: Bukhārā, no. 2076 year 143: بسم الله, ضرب بخاري في سنة ثلث [= ثلاث] ومئة. امر به الأشعث في ولية [= ولاية] المهدي الأمير محمد بن أمير المؤمنين.
My thanks to Dr. Luke Treadwell for the source. See also the comprehensive discussion of Bates, "al-Mahdī," 292–295; 300 (table); 315, n. 36 quoting the Russian studies on the subject.

19 On Ziyād b. ʿUbaydallāh al-Ḥārithī, see Crone, *Slaves*, 149; Elad, "Wāsiṭ," 59–60, 69 and n. 61; Elad, "Transition," 101; on the special connections and relations between al-Ḥārith b.

1.2.2 Al-Mughīra and Bayān

Several traditions dealing with the rebellion of al-Mughīra b. Saʿīd, and perhaps that of Bayān b. Samʿān, are evidence of the activity of Muḥammad b. ʿAbdallāh during Hishām's reign and of the propaganda generated during this period on his behalf as the Mahdī.

The two came out in open rebellion against Hishām and in 119/737 were defeated and executed by the governor of al-ʿIrāq, Khālid b. ʿAbdallāh al-Qasrī. The majority of the information is about al-Mughīra b. Saʿīd, who, it was said, was one of the supporters of Muḥammad (al-Bāqir) b. ʿAlī b. al-Ḥusayn b. ʿAlī b. Abī Ṭālib, and who, after the latter's death, began to disseminate propaganda for Muḥammad b. ʿAbdallāh al-Ḥasanī.

Scholars tend to accept this evidence as authentic. They rely mainly on heresiographic material, according to which after the death of Muḥammad b. ʿAbdallāh, a sect of the Mughīriyya continued to believe in him.[20] Watt, on the other hand, doubts the authenticity of the tradition relating the support of al-Mughīra for Muḥammad b. ʿAbdallāh at such an early stage, while he was still young, "but the latter [i.e., Muḥammad b. ʿAbdallāh], since he was only 19 in 737, may not have acknowledged al-Mughīra as his agent in any way."[21]

Watt's doubt was aroused most probably as a result of his belief that Muḥammad was born in 100 H., but as shown above, there are traditions that record his date of birth as 92 H., meaning that he would have been 27 during al-Mughīra's revolt.[22]

It is worth noting that early evidence recording al-Mughīra's propaganda supporting Muḥammad b. ʿAbdallāh's mahdīship is found in relatively early sources that are not heresiographic, e.g., *al-Muḥabbar* of Ibn Ḥabīb (d. 238/853),[23] and *Ansāb al-ashrāf* of al-Balādhurī, who records the evidence from al-Wāqidī (d. 207/823). In this tradition Bayān b. Samʿān is linked to al-Mughīra, both revolting against the Umawīs, propagandizing for Muḥammad b. ʿAbdallāh's

Kaʿb and the ʿAbbāsīs, see Sharon, *Black Banners*, 134, 141–143, 175; Elad, "Wāsiṭ," 69, n. 61; Elad, *The ʿAbbāsid Army*, 98–99.

20 Omar, *ʿAbbāsid Caliphate*, 215, 234 n. 93; Jafri, *Shīʿa*, 268; Tucker, "Mughīriyya," esp. 37–38; Madelung, "al-Mughīriyya"; on al-Mughīra and Bayān, see also the comprehensive bibliography of Pellat in al-Masʿūdī, *Murūj*, 7:695–696.

21 Watt, *Formative Period*, 51.

22 Yaḥyā b. Zayd b. ʿAlī b. al-Ḥusayn, who rebelled against the Umawīs in 125/742, was 18 or 28 when he died, see EI^1, "Yaḥyā b. Zayd" (C. van Arendonk); EI^2, "Yaḥyā b. Zayd" (W. Madelung): 28 years.

23 Ibn Ḥabīb, *al-Muḥabbar*, 483.

cause, while, at the same time accusing the followers of Muḥammad al-Bāqir, the Imām of the Ḥusaynī faction, of heresy.[24]

The tradition in al-Balādhurī, which describes Bayān's mutiny in the name of Muḥammad b. ʿAbdallāh (copied from al-Balādhurī [?] by the anonymous author of the *Fragmenta*, which was published by de Goeje), has been noted by several scholars, who greatly doubt it.[25]

These traditions that relate the support of al-Mughīra and his adherents for Muḥammad b. ʿAbdallāh during Hishām's caliphate are always accompanied by the explanation that this support occurred after Muḥammad al-Bāqir's death, when a rift occurred between the Mughīriyya and the Imāmiyya, that is, between al-Mughīra and his followers and Jaʿfar al-Ṣādiq and his followers.[26] The Shīʿa (that is the adherents) of Jaʿfar al-Ṣādiq, kept aloof, broke away from al-Mughīra,[27] and treated him as a liar.[28]

It is plausible that the provenance of these traditions seeking to tie the Mughīriyya movement to Muḥammad b. ʿAbdallāh during Hishām b. ʿAbd al-Malik's reign should be sought in a later period, i.e., they were formed in light of the historical connection and support of one part of the Mughīriyya for Muḥammad b. ʿAbdallāh and his rebellion against al-Manṣūr in 145/762.

---

24 Al-Balādhurī, *Ansāb* (ed. Madelung), 2:496–497 (= *Fragmenta*, 230–231): both Bayān and al-Mughīra circulated the idea that Muḥammad b. ʿAbdallāh was the Mahdī and al-Nafs al-Zakiyya; only Bayān is specifically mentioned as preaching this in his rebellion on Muḥammad's behalf. Although al-Wāqidī is not mentioned as the source of the tradition by al-Balādhurī, he is mentioned in the *Fragmenta* (which is a parallel identical text).

25 *EI*², "Bayān b. Samʿān" (M.G.S. Hodgson); Tucker, "Bayān b. Samʿān," 244 (and n. 14 quoting the *Fragmenta*, 230; he did not consult al-Balādhurī); Tucker argues that this information is inaccurate, and "resulted in all probability from confusing Bayān with Mughīra, who was an advocate of the Imāmate of al-Nafs al-Zakiyya" (ibid., n. 15 : quoting Saʿd b. ʿAbdallāh b. Abī Khalaf al-Ashʿarī l-Qummī, *Kitāb al-Maqālāt wa-l-firaq* [Tehran, 1964], 37). As to the Manṣūriyya sect, named after Abū Manṣūr al-ʿIjlī (d. between 120/738 and 126/744), according to some traditions they advocated for the Mahdīship of Muḥammad b. ʿAbdallāh, following the latter's death. Tucker, "Manṣūriyya," 69, is of the opinion that this group should be identified with the remains of the Mughīriyya, or alternatively, as a part of the Mughīriyya that joined Abū Manṣūr while he was still alive. In his view, there is no indication whatsoever that Abū Manṣūr himself supported Muḥammad b. ʿAbdallāh.

26 Al-Nawbakhtī, *Firaq* (ed. Ritter), 52; Tucker, "Mughīriyya," 37.

27 Al-Nawbakhtī, *Firaq*, 54.

28 Al-Balādhurī, *Ansāb* (ed. Madelung), 2:496–497 (= *Fragmenta*, 230): verses of the poet Abū Hurayra al-ʿIjlī about the lies spread by al-Mughīra against Jaʿfar al-Ṣādiq's *shīʿa* (the verses do not specifically relate to the propaganda of Muḥammad b. ʿAbdallāh); for the negative attitude of Jaʿfar al-Ṣādiq and his *shīʿa* against al-Mughīra b. Saʿīd, see for example, al-Shaykh al-Mufīd, *al-Ikhtiṣāṣ*, 204; al-Kashshī, *Rijāl*, 145–150.

This may be the historical kernel of the traditions. They could have been formulated a few years before the rebellion. It is highly possible that the *shīʿa* of Jaʿfar al-Ṣādiq were trying their best to defame the Mughīriyya in the eyes of the Muslims and the ʿAbbāsī rulers. This can be understood in light of the deep hatred between the two factions, whose roots crystallized following Muḥammad al-Bāqir's death, and intensified and gained momentum following Muḥammad b. ʿAbdallāh's rebellion, when Jaʿfar al-Ṣādiq did not join the man and his rebellion and did not take any active part in it.

This is therefore the nature of the connections between these traditions and others which we have already discussed, and those that are still to be discussed. They depict an active rebellious movement under the leadership and guidance of ʿAbdallāh b. al-Ḥasan and his son Muḥammad, with clear ideological-theological characteristics already in the Umawī period.

1.2.3 Discussion

It seems that the study of the Shīʿī movements towards the end of the Umawī period in general, as well as that of al-Mughīra and Bayān in particular, is far from exhausted. As already stated, the majority of the evidence comes from late heresiographic sources, and this poses difficult methodological problems, such as inconsistency. There would seem to be a clear desire to present an uninterrupted coherent narrative, thus creating anachronistic narratives that often present later events as if they happened earlier, and seeking to form consistent dogmatic developments in regard to the case discussed above, to relate it to al-Mughīra b. Saʿīd. My aim in this section is not the reconstruction of al-Mughīra's revolt, let alone the theological principles of his movement. This should be entrusted to scholars studying early Islamic religious movements. The methodological problems presented by the heresiographic sources are clearly demonstrated in the following examples.[29]

29 E.g., al-Ashʿarī, *Maqālāt*, 1:23; Ibn Taymiyya, *Minhāj al-sunna al-nabawiyya*, 3:479: "The Mughīriyya sect claims that the Imām after ʿAlī b. al-Ḥusayn is his son Muḥammad [al-Bāqir] Abū Jaʿfar.... and that Abū Jaʿfar passed on (*awṣā*) his *imāma* to al-Mughīra b. Saʿīd." This is in contrast to the common traditions about the split after the death of al-Bāqir, or even during his lifetime, for example. For a clear anachronism, see al-Shahrastānī, *al-Milal wa-l-niḥal*, 1:176: "al-Mughīriyya are the followers (*aṣḥāb*) of al-Mughīra b. Saʿīd al-ʿIjlī, who claimed falsely that after Muḥammad b. ʿAlī b. al-Ḥusayn (al-Bāqir) the *imāma* (passed on, literally belonged to) Muḥammad al-Nafs al-Zakiyya b. ʿAbdallāh b. al-Ḥasan b. al-Ḥasan, who rose in revolt in Medina and claimed (*zaʿama*) that he was still alive and had not died" (al-Nafs al-Zakiyya died in 145/762 while al-Mughīra died in 119/737). The translation is partly from Kazi and Flynn, *Muslim Sects*, 152. For another anachronistic description of the movement, see al-Isfarāʾīnī, *al-Tabṣīr fī l-dīn*, 1:35.

1) It is widely agreed that until al-Bāqir's death in ca. 117/735,[30] al-Mughīra was a close follower. But according to some traditions, the split had occurred already during al-Bāqir's life,[31] and then during Jaʿfar al-Ṣādiq's life.[32] According to Ibn Taymiyya, the last dogmatic principles which al-Mughīra stood for asserted that Muḥammad b. ʿAbdallāh b. al-Ḥasan was the Imām, and that the water of the Euphrates and any impure water (from a river, [canal?] spring, or well) is forbidden to drink. Upon hearing him profess such doctrines, those who asserted the dogma that the Imāma is vested in the descendants of al-Ḥusayn, left him.[33]
2) Al-Mughīra died in 119/737, a year or two after al-Bāqir's death. He must have developed these ideas and doctrines within a very short period.
3) Muḥammad al-Nafs al-Zakiyya was at that time between 19 and 27 years old, but it seems that in this case his age is of no relevance since:
4) It is well known that the head of the Ḥasanī house was ʿAbdallāh b. al-Ḥasan, who regarded himself as the true Imām of the family of the Prophet.
5) There was rivalry between the Ḥasanīs and the Ḥusaynīs over the leadership of the Hāshimī house (to be more precise, of the descendants of Fāṭima).
6) Until 117/735 the head of the Ḥusaynī house was Muḥammad al-Bāqir, after which his son, Jaʿfar al-Ṣādiq, held that position.
7) This struggle over the hegemony of the "Fāṭimīs" finds ample place in the sources, mainly in the Imāmī literature. The predominant figures in this struggle are ʿAbdallāh b. al-Ḥasan, the head, leader and Imām of the Ḥasanīs (and perhaps some other individuals and/or families from Banū Hāshim), while Jaʿfar al-Ṣādiq, the Imām of the Ḥusaynīs, is placed in opposition.
8) Muḥammad b. ʿAbdallāh al-Nafs al-Zakiyya <u>rarely</u> appears in these polemical traditions. From the Imāmī sources it is unequivocally clear that the main and only opponent of Jaʿfar al-Ṣādiq is ʿAbdallāh b. al-Ḥasan. (For further discussion on this topic, see appendix 3).

30 This is the most accepted date. Less accepted dates are 114/732, 116/737, 118/736. There are somehow much later, though improbable, dates, see Kohlberg, "Muḥammad b. ʿAlī. b. al-Ḥusayn."

31 Al-Haytamī, *al-Ṣawāʿiq al-muḥriqa* (Beirut, 1997), 1:159.

32 Al-Ḥiṣnī, *Dafʿ*, 1:26.

33 Ibn Taymiyya, *Minhāj al-sunna al-nabawiyya*, 2:350.

1.3 *The Period after al-Walīd b. Yazīd's Reign (126/743–744)*

Another group of traditions connects the political activity of Muḥammad and the propaganda generated in his favor to the period immediately after al-Walīd b. Yazīd's death (r. 126/743–744).[34] These traditions are connected to another group of traditions which report that Marwān b. Muḥammad (r. 126–132/744–750) did not see any reason to worry about the reports that Muḥammad b. ʿAbdallāh was conducting propaganda for himself (as the caliph) and was being called al-Mahdī. His view was that this was not the man or the family that should cause concern because they did not constitute any danger to the regime.[35]

In another tradition "Marwān explains" that he is not afraid of the Ḥasanīs since the rule is due to pass to the sons of their uncle, al-ʿAbbās. This is the reason he is bestowing honor and money on ʿAbdallāh b. al-Ḥasan and his son Muḥammad.[36] Another version of the tradition was related, most probably by a scholar who used to be on familiar terms with the caliph, since he opens the tradition, relating in the first person: "I said to Marwān b. Muhammad…." This scholar's name is Abū l-ʿAbbās al-Filasṭī[? read: al-Filasṭīnī?],[37] who transmitted directly to Ibn Abī Thābit [ʿAbd al-ʿAzīz b. ʿImrān b. ʿAbd al-ʿAzīz b. ʿUmar b. ʿAbd al-Raḥmān b. ʿAwf al-Zuhrī, d. 197/812–813] as follows: "I said to Marwān b. Muḥammad: Muḥammad b. ʿAbdallāh has become great (in the eyes of the people: *jadda*) and he is claiming this rule and naming himself al-Mahdī; Marwān said: I have nothing to do with him. He is not going to attain rule, nor does it belong to his father's family, for the rule is due to [pass to] the son of a slave woman. Marwān's anger was not roused against him until he was killed."[38]

This is an interesting tradition, since its aim is probably to name a specific (ʿAbbāsī?) ruler. The expression "son of a slave woman" makes the identification of this ruler difficult, and raises some unresolved questions. Assuming that the tradition was circulated sometime after Muḥammad b. ʿAbdallāh's revolt, we should then ask, to whom does it apply? It is not the first ʿAbbāsī caliph,

---

34 Al-Iṣfahānī, *Maqātil*, 257–258.

35 Al-Balādhurī, *Ansāb* (ed. Madelung), 2:498; al-Iṣfahānī, *Maqātil*, 247, 258–259, traditions in this vein.

36 Al-Iṣfahānī, *Maqātil*, 258.

37 Ibid., 247, 258 (this name also appears in the al-Najaf edition, 171 and 179). I was unable to trace this scholar.

38 Al-Iṣfahānī, *Maqātil*, 247; ibid., 258: a parallel tradition with an addition: instead of "not to his father": "not to his father's family." I prefer the second version, since the phrase *jadda* may also be rendered thus: he has become serious (in his affair), or he was or became fortunate, or possessed of good worldly fortune; see Lane, *Lexicon*, s.v. *j.d.d.*

Abū l-ʿAbbās al-Saffāḥ, whose mother was a noble Arab. It may imply Ibrāhīm (al-Imām) b. Muḥammad b. ʿAlī, whose mother was not an Arab.[39] In this case, this identification raises several chronological difficulties. Theoretically, the tradition could have been fabricated even before Muḥammad b. ʿAbdallāh's rebellion, during the late Umawī period, when Ibrāhīm was still alive and therefore relevant to parties that took part in the struggle to legitimize their rule. At the beginning of the ʿAbbāsī rule, the stage changes, at least from the ʿAbbāsī side, with new ʿAbbāsī caliphs becoming the subject of the debate for legitimacy. Ibrāhīm, as already stated, was no longer important in this struggle for legitimacy.

But since Muḥammad b. ʿAbdallāh and his family were the subject of the tradition, for it is Muḥammad b. ʿAbdallāh who was threatening Umawī rule, it is even more plausible to see al-Manṣūr as the "son of a slave woman" to whom Hishām allegedly refers.[40] The transmitter of this tradition, the contemporary of Marwān b. Muḥammad Abū l-ʿAbbās al-Filasṭīnī (if this identification is correct), lived and related traditions pertaining to the reign of the first ʿAbbāsī caliph.

However, the question posed above, i.e., the slave woman's identity, can be approached from a completely different direction, which may lead in turn to a completely different answer. Could the tradition be reflecting or echoing the Imāmī tradition that "the Mahdī/*Qāʾim* will be the son of a slave woman" (إبن الإماء/خيرة الإماء)? In this case, Marwān, the Umawī caliph, is being used by the Shīʿī/Imāmī fabricators of the tradition as a tool in their struggle for legitimacy, mainly against the Ḥasanīs.

Other traditions stress Caliph Marwān's specific order to his governor in Medina not to harm Muḥammad b. ʿAbdallāh. They give minute details of conversations between Marwān and ʿAbdallāh b. al-Ḥasan, the father of Muḥammad b. ʿAbdallāh, stressing time and again that Marwān is not afraid of the Ḥasanīs, because he knows that they pose no danger to his dynasty. More than that, he bestows upon them much money.[41]

The contents of these traditions, allegedly recording the relations between Marwān b. Muḥammad and the Ḥasanīs, cannot, under any circumstances, be

39 Al-Balādhurī, *Ansāb* (ed. al-Dūrī), 3:114; al-Zubayrī, *Nasab Quraysh*, 31; it cannot refer to al-Manṣūr's son, Muḥammad al-Mahdī (as argued by Zaman, "Muḥammad al-Nafs al-Zakiyya," 61), since al-Mahdī's mother was an Arab, see Ibn Khayyāṭ, *Taʾrīkh* (Beirut, 1993), 335, 354; al-Balādhurī, *Ansāb* (ed. al-Dūrī), 3:275; Ibn Ḥazm, *Jamhara*, 21.

40 Al-Manṣūr was indeed the son of a slave woman (*umm walad*), see al-Balādhurī, *Ansāb* (ed. al-Dūrī), 3:114; al-Zubayrī, *Nasab Quraysh*, 31.

41 Al-Iṣfahānī, *Maqātil*, 258–259.

accepted as genuine. This is not the kind of attitude expected from an experienced politician and distinguished military man such as Marwān. Reading the traditions, one can discern exact motifs and literary elements that can already be found in the traditions relating the Caliph Hishām b. ʿAbd al-Malik's attitude towards the Ḥasanīs, regarding Muḥammad and Ibrāhīm refraining from participating in missions of Arab dignitaries to him,[42] or their absence from a meeting in Medina with the representative of the caliph who was sent to fight the Khawārij.[43] This last motif of their absence is central in the traditions relating to the periods of the ʿAbbāsī caliphs, Abū l-ʿAbbās and al-Manṣūr (see discussion below).

Another literary motif appearing in other traditions about Muḥammad b. ʿAbdallāh and his family is that of the secret supernatural knowledge possessed by Marwān that enables him to be certain that Banū l-Ḥasan pose no danger to him or his rule. This is a recurrent motif in the traditions, and was also used in traditions recording the relations between the ʿAbbāsīs and the Ḥasanīs. One such example is the tradition in which the ʿAbbāsī general, ʿAbdallāh b. ʿAlī b. ʿAbdallāh b. al-ʿAbbās, the uncle of the two first ʿAbbāsī caliphs, prophesizes that he will be the one who will put an end to Umawī rule, and not members of the Ḥasanī family[44] (see below). The literary motif of esoteric supernatural knowledge finds its expression especially in the traditions dealing with the gathering of Banū Hāshim towards the end of the Umawī period, with the aim of choosing a suitable candidate for rule from among themselves.

1.3.1 The Meeting of Banū Hāshim in al-Abwāʾ: Introduction

Scholars have mentioned (for the most part briefly or incidentally) a well-known meeting of Banū Hāshim in al-Abwāʾ near Medina,[45] which several members of the ʿAbbāsī family attended. At the meeting, held after al-Walīd b. Yazīd's death (126/743), Banū Hāshim, including the ʿAbbāsīs, swore allegiance to Muḥammad b. ʿAbdallāh b. al-Ḥasan as caliph. The role of al-Manṣūr at this meeting is specifically emphasized.

---

42 Ibn Saʿd, *al-Qism al-mutammim*, 374.

43 Al-Iṣfahānī, *Maqātil*, 258.

44 Ibn Aʿtham al-Kūfī, *al-Futūḥ* (Hyderabad edition), 8:159–160.

45 A village in al-Ḥijāz, approximately midway between Mecca and Medina, see al-Ḥarbī[?], *al-Manāsik*, esp. 450–457; al-Bakrī, *Muʿjam*, 3:954 ("al-ʿAqīq"): 113 miles from Medina to al-Abwāʾ, but according to al-Ḥarbī[?], 96 miles; al-Ḥarbī, *al-Manāsik*, 468: the distance between Mecca and Medina is 200 miles. The miles are Arab miles, equivalent to approximately 1.9 km (see Elad, "The Golan," 46–48); Yāqūt, *Muʿjam* (Beirut edition), 1:79; al-Fīrūzābādī, *al-Maghānim al-muṭāba*, 5–6; al-Samhūdī, Wafāʾ, 3:443–444 ("Masjid al-Abwāʾ"); 4:108–109 ("al-Abwāʾ").

Scholars rely in this matter on the traditions recorded by Abū l-Faraj al-Iṣfahānī in *Maqātil al-Ṭālibiyyīn*.[46] They treat the many different traditions as one homogeneous tradition and usually accept their historicity.[47] Generally,

46 Al-Iṣfahānī, *Maqātil*, 205–208 (l. 10 to l. 11); 253–257 (l. 9 to l. 12).

47 See Veccia Vagliery, "Ibrāhīm b. ʿAbdallāh", *EI*², asserting that during the Umawī period the Hāshimī family gathered at al-Abwāʾ in order to swear an oath of allegiance to Muḥammad b. ʿAbdallāh. She adds that Jaʿfar al-Ṣādiq was not present at the meeting. It seems that Vagliery refers to the traditions recorded by al-Iṣfahānī, accepting them at face value and ignoring certain parts of them, as well as other parallel traditions. Other scholars have also taken these traditions literally, without critical approach, e.g., see Moscati, "Wāsiṭ," 183; ibid., n. 23 quoting 1) Nöldeke, "Manṣūr," 127 [English trans., 120–121]; 2) van Vloten, "Abbasidengeschichte," 213–218; 3) F. Buhl, "Muḥammad b. ʿAbdallāh", *EI*¹ and *EI*²; 4) Sourdel, "La Politique religieuse," 31; 5) van Arendonk, *L'Imamat Zaïdite*, 47–48; see also Jafri, *Shīʿa*, 269, who accepts these traditions at face value; Omar, *ʿAbbāsid Caliphate*, 216, argues that it is possible that a meeting really took place but it stands to reason that this is a Ḥasanī invention, created to besmirch al-Manṣūr's character. Elsewhere, Omar argues that this meeting indeed took place but no decisions were made; it does not stand to reason that the ʿAbbāsīs would swear to a Ḥasanī while a *daʿwa* was active on their behalf in Khurāsān. Another argument he raises is that this oath is not mentioned in Muḥammad's letter to al-Manṣūr, see Omar, "al-Rasāʾil," 19–20; but elsewhere Omar accepts these traditions about the meeting of Banū Hāshim in al-Abwāʾ at face value, and regards them as authentic, see Omar, "Aspects," 171 [p. 116 in his collected studies]; see also Madelung, "Hāshimiyyāt," 23, and El-Hibri, *Islamic Historiography*, 4. Nagel, "Muḥammad b. ʿAbdallāh," 258–262, gives a detailed description of the contents of the traditions of al-Abwāʾ meeting. He also categorically objects to the authenticity of the traditions in which Jaʿfar prophesizes that the two brothers, Muḥammad and Ibrāhīm, will die and that the ʿAbbāsīs will attain the caliphate, but at the same time he argues for the existence of an authentic kernel in these traditions; see Nagel, "Muḥammad b. ʿAbdallāh," 262, where he also maintains that the claims and arguments of Muḥammad b. ʿAbdallāh are based on an agreement that was made during the Umawī period; it is possible that the ʿAbbāsīs took part in the meeting and the agreement. Other scholars seem to accept Nagel's arguments and conclusions. Kennedy, *ʿAbbāsid Caliphate*, 67 (quoting al-Iṣfahānī, *Maqātil*, 207, 209) seems to have doubts regarding the authenticity of only part of this tradition: "Even before the revolution, Muḥammad's father had been putting him forward as the leader of the family and people swore allegiance to him as 'mahdi'. Pro-Alid sources even allege that Mansur himself had sworn allegiance to him in Umayyad times"; see also Kennedy, *ʿAbbāsid Caliphate*, 57 (quoting al-Iṣfahānī, *Maqātil*, 209): "In Shiʿite circles a story was later circulated to the effect that he had sworn allegiance to the Alid leader Muḥammad b. ʿAbd Allah." Crone, "*al-Riḍā*," 99–100, 105, also seems to accept at least the kernel of the tradition, that is, that the meeting between ʿAbbāsīs and ʿAlīds did take place (pp. 99 and 105), but concludes her discussion on this meeting by saying "Even so, however, the story may not be true" (p. 100); idem, *Islamic Thought*, 79, where she seems more certain of the authenticity of the tradition; Zaman, "al-Nafs al-Zakiyya," 60: "there are reports which emphasize that Muḥammad was, from early youth, generally

it can be said that there are two groups of traditions about the alleged meeting. At the beginning of each group the several links of transmission are mentioned, and then the composer of the story records a collective *matn*. This *matn*, or the main body of the text, consists of several truncated and fragmentary traditions of different transmitters, often recorded by Abū l-Faraj without mention of their names. Therefore, the traditions recorded by Abū l-Faraj al-Iṣfahānī on this topic are not homogeneous at all. These fragmented traditions were copied from al-Iṣfahānī's work mainly by Shīʿī Imāmī sources,[48] but traditions on the topic are also found in different kinds of non-Shīʿī Arabic literature.

There are fundamental differences and even contradictions between these different versions of this alleged meeting of Banū Hāshim. The assorted transmitters represent different interests and various political-ideological backgrounds. In many versions of the tradition, Banū Hāshim swear allegiance to Muḥammad b. ʿAbdallāh. In some of the traditions al-Manṣūr appears as having sworn allegiance to Muḥammad b. ʿAbdallāh, thus emphasizing his treachery.[49] But there are traditions in which the ʿAbbāsīs do not appear at

recognized as the Mahdī, and that even Abū Jaʿfar ʿAbdallāh, who was later to become the ʿAbbāsīd caliph as al-Manṣūr, was also one of those who so recognized and, therefore, greatly revered Muḥammad." Zaman relies on the tradition in al-Iṣfahānī, *Maqātil*, 239 (describing an alleged episode which occurred in Medina, not that in al-Abwāʾ). See also Arjomand, "The Crisis of the Imamate," 491 [in Kohlberg = 109]: "It is remarkable that Jaʿfar al-Sadiq avoided involvement in politics during the revolutionary era that began with the murder of Walid II in April 744. In that year, the Hashemite dignitaries met at the Abwa' near Mecca to elect a leader, and the Talibid ʿAbd Allah ibn Muʿawiya inaugurated the Hashemite revolution on behalf of 'the one agreed-upon' (*al-Riḍā*) from the house of Muhammad. Jaʿfar was the one dissident at the Hashemite meeting who refused to recognize his young cousin, Muhammad ibn ʿAbd Allah ibn al-Hasan, as the Mahdi of the House of the Prophet." See al-Sayyid, "al-Nafs al-Zakiyya," 172, 173, 175, accepting the traditions at face value; note also the (sober and perhaps morer optimistic) reservation of Ahmed, *Religious Elite*, 155, n. 831: "Though such accounts ought to be approached with caution, it is ineresting to note, for example, that the reports raise no doubts about the historicity of the Ḥasanid claim (advanced during the Umayyad period) and focus instead on the pre-ordained success of the ʿAbbāsids."

48 Al-Shaykh al-Mufīd, *al-Irshād*, 2:190–193; Ibn Sharāshūb, *Manāqib*, 4:228; al-Baḥrānī, *Madīnat al-maʿājiz*, 5:290; al-Kūrānī, *Muʿjam*, 433–435 (no. 989); al-Majlisī, *Biḥār*, 46:187–189; 47:276–278; al-Khūʾī, *Rijāl*, 11:173–174.

49 For example, see al-Ṭabarī, 3:143, 152, 262 (ll. 10–17), 3:263–264 (l. 17 to l. 2); al-Azdī, *Taʾrīkh al-Mawṣil*, 190 (an exact parallel); al-Iṣfahānī, *Maqātil*, 206, 287, 294–295 (l. 15 to l. 4); Ibn Kathīr, *al-Bidāya* (Cairo, 1351 H.), 10:80; al-Maqrīzī, *al-Nizāʿ wa-l-takhāṣum*, 56–57; Ibn ʿInaba, *ʿUmda*, 104.

all;[50] in other traditions, other dignitaries from the ʿAbbāsī family appear on the stage, including Abū l-ʿAbbās al-Saffāḥ, but when the latter is mentioned he is a passive character, and never delivers an enthusiastic speech in favor of Muḥammad b. ʿAbdallāh, as his brother al-Manṣūr does.[51] Al-Manṣūr is the only ʿAbbāsī who is accused of breaching the oath of allegiance to Muḥammad b. ʿAbdallāh. This may indicate that these traditions were crystallized following Muḥammad's rebellion against al-Manṣūr in 145/762. In some of the traditions, Jaʿfar al-Ṣādiq appears, refusing to take an oath of allegiance, foreseeing Muḥammad's death, and the failure of his revolt. The purpose of the traditions is evidently to stress his esoteric knowledge (*ʿilm*) and special traits and abilities (*muʿjizāt*) and to justify his doctrine of non-active political involvement (*quʿūd*).[52] These traditions in particular reflect the tensions and struggles between the Ḥasanīs and the Ḥusaynīs and the relations between the ʿAbbāsī and the ʿAlīd factions. Following is an analysis of these traditions.

1.3.1.1 *The Collective isnād of the First Group of the Traditions*

This group was related to Abū l-Faraj al-Iṣfahānī by three transmitters, **all** of whom heard ʿUmar b. Shabba and transmitted from him. Ibn Shabba heard three different transmitters, that is, we have three different chains of transmission.

Abū l-Faraj al-Iṣfahānī < Yaḥyā b. ʿAlī AND Aḥmad b. ʿAbd al-ʿAzīz AND ʿUmar b. ʿUbaydallāh al-ʿAtakī, [all] said we were related (*ḥaddathanā*) by ʿUMAR B. SHABBA who said:

1) *ḥaddathanī* Muḥammad b. Yaḥyā < ʿAbd al-ʿAzīz b. ʿImrān < ʿAbdallāh b. Jaʿfar b. ʿAbd al-Raḥmān b. al-Miswar b. Makhrama.

---

50 Al-Balādhurī, *Ansāb* (ed. Madelung), 2:498 [= *Fragmenta*, 231]; cf. al-Iṣfahānī, *Maqātil*, 207 (ll. 6–7).

51 Al-Iṣfahānī, *Maqātil*, 233–234 (l. 17 to l. 1), 255, (l. 4), 256, (l. 16), 287, (l. 4) (he is omitted in the parallel tradition in al-Ṭabarī's *Taʾrīkh*, 3:262).

52 For example, see al-Iṣfahānī, *Maqātil*, 254–255: Jaʿfar refuses to swear allegiance to Muḥammad b. ʿAbdallāh, indicating Abū l-ʿAbbās as the future caliph, telling ʿAbdallāh b. al-Ḥasan that his two sons will be killed; ibid., another version by another transmitter: Muḥammad b. ʿAbdallāh will be killed by al-Manṣūr; ibid., 255–256 (l. 15 to l. 8), another tradition from different transmitters: Jaʿfar tells ʿAbdallāh b. al-Ḥasan that the caliphate will pass not to him or his sons but first to al-Saffāḥ, then to al-Manṣūr, then to his descendants after him; ibid., 256 (ll. 5–6): Abū Jaʿfar al-Manṣūr will kill Muḥammad b. ʿAbdallāh in Aḥjār al-Zayt, then his brother will be killed by him; cf. ibid., 207–208 (a partially parallel tradition in this vein); it seems that Nagel was the first who regarded these traditions as mere fiction, see the short remark of Nagel, "Muḥammad b. ʿAbdallāh," 260.

2) *wa-ḥaddathanī* Jaʿfar b. Muḥammad b. Ismāʿīl b. al-Faḍl al-Hāshimī < a man from Banū Kināna.
3) *wa-ḥaddathanī* ʿAbd al-Raḥmān b. ʿAmr b. Ḥabīb < al-Ḥasan b. Ayyūb *mawlā Banī Numayr* < ʿAbd al-Aʿlā b. Aʿyan.

ʿUmar b. Shabba remarks at the end of his *isnād*: "all these transmitters have related this *ḥadīth* in different phrases and similar meaning, so I collected their transmissions [to one tradition] so the book will not be [too] long by repeating the chains of transmission [and mentioning it each and every time]."[53]

1.3.1.2 *The Collective isnād of the Second Group of the Traditions*

This time, Abū l-Faraj heard only one transmitter, who heard ʿUmar b. Shabba relating from FIVE different chains of transmitters:

1) *ḥaddathanā* al-Faḍl b. ʿAbd al-Raḥmān al-Hāshimī and Ibn Dāja.
2) *wa-ḥaddathanī* ʿAbd al-Raḥmān b. ʿAmr b. Jabala [= b. Ḥabīb?] < al-Ḥasan b. Ayyūb *mawlā Banī Numayr* < ʿAbd al-Aʿlā b. Aʿyan [= no. 3 in the first group].
3) *wa-ḥaddathanī* Ibrāhīm b. Muḥammad b. Abī l-Karrām al-Jaʿfarī < his father.
4) *wa-ḥaddathanī* Muḥammad b. Yaḥyā.
5) *wa-ḥaddathanī* ʿĪsā b. ʿAbdallāh b. Muḥammad b. ʿUmar b. ʿAlī < his father.

ʿUmar b. Shabba concludes by saying: "The *ḥadīth* of some of these transmitters is mixed with the *ḥadīth* of the others."[54]

In sum, ʿUmar b. Shabba heard this tradition, or better, these traditions, from **seven** different transmitters. In addition to these traditions, Abū l-Faraj records two additional traditions that were transmitted to him through al-Madāʾinī (one also by Ibn Dāja/Dāḥa), not by ʿUmar b. Shabba.[55]

1.3.1.3 *The Text of the First Group*

In spite of ʿUmar b. Shabba's declaration about mixing the *isnāds*, sometimes he mentions the transmitters of several paragraphs. This enables us to identify the transmitters and the texts in the second group of the *ḥadīth*, where the transmitters are seldom mentioned.

53 Al-Iṣfahānī, *Maqātil*, 253 (ll. 9–14); the complete text, ibid., 253–257 (l. 9 to l. 12).

54 Ibid., 205–206 (l. 10 to l. 3); the complete text, ibid., 205–208 (l. 10 to l. 11).

55 Ibid., 255–256 (l. 15 to l. 8); 256 (l. 13), 207 (l. 12); 255 (l. 17): Ibn Dāḥa; 205 (l. 11): Ibn Dāja.

a) The collective matn[56]

Banū Hāshim gathered (note that the location is not mentioned) after al-Walīd b. Yazīd's death (126/743). ʿAbdallāh b. al-Ḥasan addresses those present, describing the history of the Umawīs' harsh, cruel attitude towards their family, the advantages and superiority of *ahl al-bayt*, mentions the killing of al-Walīd b. Yazīd, and asks them to swear allegiance to his son, Muḥammad, "for you know that he is the Mahdī." Those who attend the meeting say that they do not see Jaʿfar b. Muḥammad (al-Ṣādiq) in this gathering. ʿAbdallāh sends for Jaʿfar but he refuses to come, so ʿAbdallāh goes to him in person. Jaʿfar is staying where the tent of al-Faḍl b. ʿAbd al-Raḥmān b. al-ʿAbbās b. Rabīʿa b. al-Ḥārith is pitched (*maḍrib*), whose daughter, ʿĀtika, was married to Jaʿfar al-Ṣādiq's cousin, ʿĪsā b. Zayd b. ʿAlī b. al-Ḥusayn. To ʿAbdallāh b. al-Ḥasan's request to swear allegiance to his son, Muḥammad, Jaʿfar answers, "You are an old and distinguished man but as to your son, I shall not swear [allegiance] to him and leave you."

Here the first version of the collective *matn* of the first group ends, and al-Iṣfahānī continues to quote part of the transmission of ʿAbd al-Aʿlā b. Aʿyan,[57] which can also be traced in the second group of the traditions.[58]

b) ʿAbd al-Aʿlā tells us that he attended the meeting, so his would appear to be an eyewitness report.[59] He says that ʿAbdallāh b. al-Ḥasan refused to send for Jaʿfar al-Ṣādiq, "for he will corrupt and ruin you," however, Jaʿfar was summoned and came to the meeting, but he categorically refused ʿAbdallāh's request to swear allegiance to his son, saying: "Do not do it, for the time is not yet ready for this matter." To the angry answer of ʿAbdallāh, that Jaʿfar is not candid, knowing the real truth and is jealous of his son, Jaʿfar answers that this is not the case; for this man, his brothers and their sons are going to take hold of the rule before you, and with his hand he patted Abū l-ʿAbbās [al-Saffāḥ]'s back and left the meeting. ʿAbd al-Ṣamad [b. ʿAlī b. ʿAbdallāh b. al-ʿAbbās] and Abū Jaʿfar [al-Manṣūr] follow him, reach him and ask him, "Oh Abū ʿAbdallāh, do you really believe this," and he says: "Yes, by God I swear, I believe this and I know it" (أتقول ذلك؟ قال نعم والله أقوله وأعلمه).[60] Without naming the transmitter, ʿAbd al-Aʿlā, this tradition, with some additions, is recorded by al-Iṣfahānī

56 Ibid., 253–254 (l. 16 to l. 15).
57 Ibid., 254–255 (l. 16 to l. 5).
58 Ibid., 207 (ll. 6–15).
59 Ibid., 254 (l. 17): فأتاهم [جعفر بن محمد] وأنا معهم
60 Ibid., 255 (l. 5).

in the second group of the traditions.[61] It is noteworthy that the second part of this tradition was combined in another tradition that deals with the Abū Salama affair, which happened several years after the alleged meeting.[62]

The main points of this fragmentary version can be summed up as follows:

1) No collective swearing of allegiance is mentioned.
2) Jaʿfar al-Ṣādiq's esoteric knowledge is emphasized: he knows that the ʿAbbāsīs will rule.
3) The members of the ʿAbbāsī family that attend the meeting are: a) Abū l-ʿAbbās al-Saffāḥ; b) his brother, Abū Jaʿfar al-Manṣūr; c) ʿAbd al-Ṣamad b. ʿAlī, the uncle of the former two.

It is noteworthy that in this version the ʿAbbāsīs did not swear allegiance to Muḥammad b. ʿAbdallāh.

c) The tradition of Muḥammad b. ʿAbdallāh (Abū l-Karrām) b. Muḥammad.[63]

He was a well-known Ṭālibī (Jaʿfarī) dignitary, who was one of the close associates of Caliph al-Manṣūr and one of the commanders of ʿĪsā b. Mūsā.[64] He provides two short sentences in which Jaʿfar al-Ṣādiq tells ʿAbdallāh b. al-Ḥasan: "I swear by God, the rule will not pass to you or your two sons but

61 Ibid., 207 (ll. 1, 6–17); 208 (ll. 4–6) [= 255 (ll. 4–5)]; the editor of *Maqātil* (ibid., 207 (ll. 8–10)), supplements the text with an addition from an exact parallel in al-Shaykh al-Mufīd, *Irshād* (Tehran, 1330 H., 253; al-Najaf, 1382/1962, 276–277), about Jaʿfar al-Ṣādiq's resentment of Muḥammad b. ʿAbdallāh, emphasizing that he is not the Mahdī, and this is not the time for his appearance; this addition is not found in the two places where the tradition is recorded by al-Iṣfahānī.

62 Ibn Sharāshūb, *Manāqib*, 2:355 (copied by al-Majlisī, *Biḥār*, 47:132), quoting (copying) from Ibn Kādish al-ʿUkbarī's book إبن كادش العكبري في مقاتل العصابة العلوية كتابة; the text is garbled: instead of أبو مسلم read أبو سلمة; instead of أبو جعفر محمد بن علي read أبو جعفر عبد الله بن محمد بن علي; Ibn Kādish is Abū l-ʿIzz Aḥmad b. ʿUbaydallāh b. Muḥammad b. Aḥmad ... b. Yazīd al-Sulamī l-Baghdādī, known as Ibn Kādish (431–526 or 527/1039 or 1040–1131 or 1133); on him, see Ibn al-Athīr, *al-Kāmil* (Beirut edition), 10:683: d. 526 H.; Ibn Kathīr, *al-Bidāya* (ed. Shīrī), 12:252: d. 527 H.; al-Dhahabī, *Taʾrīkh*, 36:141–143: d. 526 H.; Ibn Ḥajar, *Lisān*, 1:218: d. 556 H.[!]; Kaḥḥāla, *Muʿjam*, 1:308: d. 556/1161 (quoting only Ibn Ḥajar's *Lisān*).

63 Al-Iṣfahānī, *Maqātil*, 255 (ll. 6–9), from Ibrāhīm b. Muḥammad b. ʿAbdallāh b. [sic!] Abī Karrām from his father [the parallel tradition, with no name of the transmitter, ibid., 207 (ll. 15–17)].

64 Al-Ṭabarī, 3:231–232.

it will pass to those [the ʿAbbāsīs], and indeed your two sons shall be killed" (وإن ابنيك لمقتولون). Those attending the gathering dispersed and never reconvened after this meeting.

Also according to this version, those attending the meeting did not swear allegiance to Muḥammad. The ʿAbbāsīs are just mentioned, in passing, with no mention of specific names.

d) The tradition of ʿAbdallāh b. Jaʿfar b. ʿAbd al-Raḥmān b. al-Miswar b. Makhrama.

He was one of Muḥammad b. ʿAbdallāh's most loyal supporters. According to this fragmentary version, he escorted Jaʿfar al-Ṣādiq to this meeting, and described in the first person how Jaʿfar came out, "leaning on my hand, and he told me: do you see the one who is wearing the yellow mantle, that is Abū Jaʿfar, and I said yes; he said: by God I swear, indeed we find him as the one who will kill Muḥammad; I asked: will Muḥammad be killed? He said: yes. And I said to myself, I swear by the God of the Kaʿba, he is envious of him; but later, still being alive, I witnessed his killing by him."[65]

Al-Wāqidī reports that ʿAbdallāh b. Jaʿfar b. ʿAbd al-Raḥmān joined Muḥammad b. ʿAbdallāh's revolt, and when the latter died he went into hiding until he received safe conduct from the ʿAbbāsīs. He showed his regret in public for joining the revolt.[66] If this quoted version was really related by him, it may have been part of his public repentance and confession of his guilt.

It is worth noting that in this fragmentary version nothing is said about the swearing of allegiance to Muḥammad; al-Manṣūr appears on the stage, but his presence is required to emphasize the supernatural knowledge of Jaʿfar al-Ṣādiq.

Two additional traditions were not transmitted through ʿUmar b. Shabba.

e) The first is recorded through the following double *isnād*:

---

65 Al-Iṣfahānī, *Maqātil*, 255 (ll. 10–14) (= 207–208 (l. 17 to l. 3)), a parallel tradition with no *isnād*, but in the *matn*, instead of ʿAbdallāh b. Jaʿfar b. ʿAbd al-Raḥmān, Jaʿfar al-Ṣādiq leans on ʿAbd al-ʿAzīz b. ʿImrān [ibid. (l. 17)]; on 208 (l. 1) ʿAbd al-ʿAzīz b. ʿImrān asks Jaʿfar "will Muḥammad be killed?") It seems that in the first group of traditions (p. 255 (ll. 10–14)), the direct eyewitness transmitter is ʿAbdallāh b. Jaʿfar and in the second group (207–208 (l. 17 to l. 3)), the transmitter is ʿAbd al-ʿAzīz b. ʿImrān. It is noteworthy that in the chain of the transmitters (p. 253 (ll. 10–11)), ʿAbdallāh b. Jaʿfar is the last transmitter: *ḥaddathanī* [= ʿUmar b. Shabba] Muḥammad b. Yaḥyā < ʿAbd al-ʿAzīz b. ʿImrān < ʿAbdallāh b. Jaʿfar b. ʿAbd al-Raḥmān b. al-Miswar b. Makhrama.

66 Ibn Saʿd, *al-Qism al-mutammim*, 455.

1) Abū l-Faraj al-Iṣfahānī < ʿĪsā b. Ḥusayn al-Warrāq < al-Kharrāz (Aḥmad b. al-Ḥārith, d. 258/872)< al-Madāʾinī (d. ca. 225/840); and

2) Abū l-Faraj al-Iṣfahānī < al-Ḥasan b. ʿAlī < ʿAbdallāh b. Abī Saʿd (197–274/812 or 813–887)[67] < ʿAlī b. ʿAmr (unidentified) < Ibn Dāḥa.[68]

> Jaʿfar b. Muḥammad (al-Ṣādiq) said to ʿAbdallāh b. al-Ḥasan: "Indeed this rule, by God I swear, will not pass to you and not to your two sons, it will not pass but to that one—that one is al-Saffāḥ—then to that one—that is, al-Manṣūr, then to his descendants after him, and it will stay with them until they will put in charge young boys as *amīr*s and will consult the women." ʿAbdallāh said, "By God I swear oh Jaʿfar, God has not revealed to you His secrets, and you did not say this but out of sheer envy of my son." Jaʿfar answered: "No, by God I swear, I did not envy your son, but that (person), that is, Abū Jaʿfar will kill him in Aḥjār al-Zayt, then his brother will be killed after him in al-Ṭufūf, while the legs of his horse [are] in water." Then (Jaʿfar) rose, angry, dragging his cloak. Abū Jaʿfar (al-Manṣūr) followed him and said: "Do you know what you have said, Abū ʿAbdallāh?" Jaʿfar said: "By, God I know, and it is going to materialize." The transmitter (Ibn Dāḥa?) ends the tradition saying: When Abū Jaʿfar became caliph he named Jaʿfar "al-Ṣādiq"; and whenever he mentioned him he used to say: "I was told by al-Ṣādiq, Jaʿfar, so and so," thus this name became permanent.[69]

The last four traditions (b–e) record the words of Jaʿfar al-Ṣādiq to ʿAbdallāh b. al-Ḥasan. (Note that the meeting is not specifically described, certainly not its size, the number of its participants and their family-tribal affiliation.) Several notables of the ʿAbbāsī family are mentioned (in the last tradition, namely, al-Saffāḥ and al-Manṣūr), but it is not mentioned that they swore allegiance to Muḥammad b. ʿAbdallāh. The central issue and purpose in these traditions is to emphasize the esoteric supernatural knowledge of Jaʿfar al-Ṣādiq: the sons of ʿAbdallāh, that is, the Ḥasanīs, will not rule; the ʿAbbāsīs will rule; Jaʿfar even knows the sequence of caliphs, al-Saffāḥ and al-Manṣūr, and that the latter will kill Muḥammad in Aḥjār al-Zayt. It is noteworthy that the same literary motif, including the exact location of the killing (Aḥjār al-Zayt), is once again related

---

67 He is ʿAbdallāh b. ʿAmr b. ʿAbd al-Raḥmān Abū Muḥammad al-Warrāq; on him, see al-Khaṭīb al-Baghdādī, *Taʾrīkh* (Hyderabad edition), 10:25–26; ibid., 26: He is described as صاحب أخبار وآداب وملح; Fleischhammer, *Kitāb al-Aghānī*, 72–73.

68 Al-Iṣfahānī, *Maqātil*, 255 (ll. 15–17).

69 Ibid., 255–256 (l. 18 to l. 12).

by Jaʿfar al-Ṣādiq, but in another historical context, that is, several years later, in the Abū Salama affair[70] (see below).

e.1) This tradition was related to al-Iṣfahānī by ʿĪsā b. al-Ḥusayn < al-Kharrāz (Aḥmad b. al-Ḥārith) < al-Madāʾinī (d. ca. 225/840) < Suḥaym b. Ḥafṣ (Abū l-Yaqẓān, more commonly known as ʿĀmir b. Ḥafṣ, d. 190/806).[71]

The tradition has two distinct parts.[72] The second may not have been part of this original tradition and the transmission described above (e.1). It may have been part of the tradition of ʿĪsā b. ʿAbdallāh (see f below). According to the first part, a small number of men[73] of Banū Hāshim gathered at al-Abwāʾ, on the Meccan road. Among them were the ʿAbbāsīs Ibrāhīm al-Imām (b. Muḥammad b. ʿAlī b. ʿAbdallāh b. al-ʿAbbās), al-Saffāḥ,[74] al-Manṣūr, and Ṣāliḥ b. ʿAlī (b. ʿAbdallāh b. al-ʿAbbās). Among the Ḥasanīs, ʿAbdallāh b. al-Ḥasan and his two sons, Muḥammad and Ibrāhīm, and Muḥammad b. ʿAbdallāh b. ʿAmr b. ʿUthmān (ʿAbdallāh's brother from the same mother) are mentioned. Ṣāliḥ b. ʿAlī is the first speaker, speaking in general of the necessity to choose a worthy candidate for the caliphate from among them. Then ʿAbdallāh b. al-Ḥasan says: "You have already known that this son of mine is al-Mahdī, so come on, let us swear allegiance to him."[75] Then al-Manṣūr speaks about Muḥammad b. ʿAbdallāh and describes him as the most worthy candidate for the caliphate, and then they all swear allegiance to him. The only names specifically mentioned as those who took the oath for Muḥammad b. ʿAbdallāh are the ʿAbbāsīs: "Ibrāhīm al-Imām, al-Saffāḥ and al-Manṣūr, and the rest of those

70 Al-Yaʿqūbī, *Taʾrīkh* (ed. Houtsma), 2:418.

71 Al-Iṣfahānī, *Maqātil*, 256 (ll. 13–14); Suḥaym b. Ḥafṣ was a well-known scholar and the author of many compilations. The sources do not contain information regarding his sectarian inclination (on him, see Sezgin, 1:266 [he does not mention the *Fihrist* of Ibn al-Nadīm]; Rosenthal, *Historiography*, 381, n. 8: mentioning that Ibn Khallikān, *Wafayāt*, 6:354, quotes from *Kitāb al-Nasab* of Abū l-Yaqẓān; Ibn al-Nadīm, *al-Fihrist* (ed. Tajaddud), 107: كتاب أخبار تميم؛ كتاب حلف تميم بعضها بعضا؛ كتاب نسب خندف وأخبارها؛ كتاب النسب الكبير يحتوي على نسب إياد كنانة؛ أسد بن خزيمة (الهون بن خزيمة)؛ هذيل بن مدركة؛ قريش؛ بني طابخة؛ قيس عيلان؛ ربيعة بن نزار؛ تيم بن مرة وغير ذلك من النسب؛ كتاب النوادر; Yāqūt, *Udabāʾ* (ed. Margoliouth), 4:226; al-Baghdādī, *Hadiyyat al-ʿārifīn* (Istanbul, 1951), 1:435). Was he pro-Shīʿa? The tradition quoted above may tilt the balance in favor of this line of thought.

72 Al-Iṣfahānī, *Maqātil*, 256–257 (l. 13 to l. 8) (the first part); 257 (ll. 8–12) (the second part).

73 Ar. *nafar;* it denotes a group of not more than ten men.

74 In the partly parallel tradition, al-Iṣfahānī, *Maqātil*, 206 (l. 5), al-Saffāḥ is not mentioned.

75 The sentence of ʿAbdallāh b. al-Ḥasan is missing in this transmission, but it exists in the parallel tradition, ibid., 206 (ll. 10–11).

present": وسائر من حضر. The meeting occurred before the rule of Marwān II (127/744). In this period they gathered again and then a messenger came and told Ibrāhīm about the *bay'a* to him in Khurāsān and the gathering of armies in his name. When 'Abdallāh b. al-Ḥasan heard about it, he became angry with Ibrāhīm and feared him, and wrote to the caliph that he takes no responsibility, and has no part in Ibrāhīm's doings and in his affair.[76]

On the one hand, the 'Abbāsīs swear allegiance to Muḥammad b. 'Abdallāh, but on the other hand, 'Abdallāh b. al-Ḥasan reveals to Marwān II the secret of the 'Abbāsī *da'wa* and Ibrāhīm al-Imām's place within this movement (which may have been aimed at destroying the 'Abbāsī movement and eventually caused his death).

Analysis of the tradition

In this tradition, al-Abwā', the location where Banū Hāshim convened, appears for the first time, in fact the only time. This is the only tradition where al-Manṣūr speaks and demands that those present swear an oath to Muḥammad.

It is noteworthy that, in contrast to other traditions, Ja'far al-Ṣādiq is absent from the meeting. No one speaks ill of Muḥammad and/or prophesizes that he will be killed by al-Manṣūr, or that the rule will pass to the 'Abbāsīs.

There is room to doubt whether the second part, which deals with Ibrāhīm al-Imām and his movement in Khurāsān, was an integral part of this specific tradition related by Abū l-Yaqẓān. This part is woven within another tradition about this alleged meeting.

f) This tradition is recorded in *Akhbār al-'Abbās*, with the following *isnād*: 'Umar b. Shabba < I heard (*sami'tu*) 'Īsā b. 'Abdallāh (b. Muḥammad b. 'Umar b. 'Alī b. Abī Ṭālib) < his father,[77] describing the events in the first person. Small parts of this tradition have parallels in al-Iṣfahānī's *Maqātil*.[78]

According to this tradition, 'Īsā's father and grandfather reached Mecca during the *ḥajj*, when the *amīr* in charge of the *ḥajj* ceremonies was 'Abd al-Wāḥid b. Sulaymān b. 'Abd al-Malik. The tradition reads as follows:

> The messenger of 'Abdallāh b. al-Ḥasan came to my father with the following message: "Come to us, for we are gathering to decide upon

76 Al-Iṣfahānī, *Maqātil*, 256–257 (l. 13 to l. 12); partly parallel without the *isnād*, in ibid., 206 (ll. 4–9, 12–14) [= 256–257 (l. 15 to l. 5)]: the first part of this tradition. The second part, 257 (ll. 5–12), has no parallel.

77 *Akhbār al-'Abbās*, 385 (l. 11).

78 Al-Iṣfahānī, *Maqātil*, 206 (l. 16); 207 (ll. 2–6).

> a matter, and he also sent this message to Jaʿfar b. Muḥammad."[79] My father (says ʿĪsā) sent me to find out what they are convened for, and Jaʿfar al-Ṣādiq sent al-Arqaṭ, Muḥammad b. ʿAbdallāh b. ʿAlī [b. Abī Ṭālib] for the same purpose. I reached them [relates ʿĪsā's father] and found ʿAbdallāh b. al-Ḥasan, Ibrāhīm, and al-Manṣūr, the sons of Muḥammad b. ʿAlī b. ʿAbdallāh b. al-ʿAbbās, and a group of Banū Hāshim, and I found Muḥammad b. ʿAbdallāh b. al-Ḥasan standing, praying on a double-folded carpet of a saddle.[80] I [ʿĪsā's father] said: "My father has sent me to you to ask you for what purpose you have gathered." ʿAbdallāh b. al-Ḥasan answered: "We convened in order to swear allegiance to the Mahdī, Muḥammad b. ʿAbdallāh b. Ḥasan." He said: While we were discussing this, someone entered and whispered secretly in Ibrāhīm b. Muḥammad b. ʿAlī's ear; then Ibrāhīm came to them and said: "I do not see Abū Muḥammad, Jaʿfar b. Muḥammad b. ʿAlī present, nor the distinguished members of your house (وجوه شيعتكم), let us part this year and meet the next." Then he rose and we arose with him. The person who talked to him secretly said to him: "Are you going to swear allegiance to this young man, while your party (*shīʿatuka*) in Khurāsān conducts propaganda for you?" ʿAbd al-Wāḥid b. Sulaymān (the Umawī leader of the *ḥajj* caravan) sent a messenger to tell them: "If you want something, I'll give you what you want."

The tradition ends: "And when ʿAbdallāh b. al-Ḥasan despaired of Ibrāhīm, he wrote to Marwān [b. Muḥammad, the caliph] I am free of Ibrāhīm b. Muḥammad and am not responsible for the bad thing that he has done."[81]

1.3.1.4 *Discussion*

This tradition has several distinctive characteristics:

1) It is related by an eyewitness, one of the members of the ʿUmarī (ʿAlīd) family who attended the meeting.

---

79 The text here (*Akhbār al-ʿAbbās*, 385 (l. 13)), is garbled (some words are omitted): "A messenger from ʿAbdallāh b. al-Ḥasan came to Jaʿfar (al-Ṣādiq) b. Muḥammad (b. ʿAlī b. al-Ḥusayn)"; it is completed here according to al-Iṣfahānī, *Maqātil*, 206 (ll. 16–17): "ʿĪsā said…."

80 *Akhbār al-ʿAbbās*, 386 (l. 1): على طنفسة رحل مَثْنِيّة; in the MS: رجل; the editors corrected it to رحل; al-Iṣfahānī, *Maqātil*, 207 (l. 4): على طنفسة رجل مَثنيّة

81 *Akhbār al-ʿAbbās*, 385–386 (l. 11 to l. 10).

2) The meeting is in Mecca (not in al-Abwāʾ). Its date is Dhū l-Ḥijja 129/ August 747.[82]
3) Some important members of the Ṭālibī family, such as Jaʿfar al-Ṣādiq, or the ʿUmarī, ʿAbdallāh b. Muḥammad b. ʿUmar b. ʿAlī, did not attend the alleged meeting.
4) The representatives of the ʿAbbāsī family are Ibrāhīm al-Imām and Abū Jaʿfar al-Manṣūr (in other traditions, al-Saffāḥ and Ṣāliḥ b. ʿAlī are mentioned).
5) ʿAbdallāh b. al-Ḥasan was (at least partially) responsible for the death of Ibrāhīm al-Imām at the hands of Marwān.
6) Jaʿfar al-Ṣādiq does not take an active part in this meeting, and thus we "miss" his esoteric supernatural knowledge.
7) The actual swearing of allegiance did not materialize because of Ibrāhīm al-Imām.
8) Ibrāhīm al-Imām is the main protagonist in this tradition. In the other traditions related through ʿUmar b. Shabba, he does not appear. This is no accident. Although he was the head of the ʿAbbāsī family, the traditions that were circulated after the revolt wish to emphasize the roles of al-Manṣūr and al-Saffāḥ. More than this, in some of the traditions, al-Manṣūr wants, or even enthusiastically requests, to swear allegiance to Muḥammad b. ʿAbdallāh, and is "saved" by Jaʿfar al-Ṣādiq. Here, in the tradition last discussed, Ibrāhīm al-Imām is central, but unlike al-Manṣūr, he objects to Muḥammad b. ʿAbdallāh. The main contrast here is between Ibrāhīm and Muḥammad b. ʿAbdallāh b. al-Ḥasan, that is, the ʿAbbāsīs and the Ḥasanīs.

Jaʿfar al-Ṣādiq, and to a certain extent, Muḥammad b. ʿUmar b. ʿAlī, have passive secondary roles, and a completely different picture emerges from that of the other traditions, in which Jaʿfar is at the center of the conflict and the confrontational scenes with ʿAbdallāh b. al-Ḥasan. The same can be said about ʿAbdallāh b. al-Ḥasan. He, certainly not his young son Muḥammad, was the head of the Ḥasanī family. The meeting, according to this account occurred in Dhū l-Ḥijja 129/August–September 747. Abū Muslim came out in open armed revolt in Ramaḍān 129/May–June 747.[83] It is unreasonable to think that three months later, Ibrāhīm and his family members were unaware of Abū Muslim's armed insurrection in Khurāsān.

82 Al-Ṭabarī, 2:1983–1984; Ibn Khayyāṭ, *Taʾrīkh* (Beirut, 1993), 305; this is the only time when ʿAbd al-Wāḥid b. Sulaymān is mentioned as leading the *ḥajj* caravan.

83 Sharon, *Revolt*, 66f.

Moreover, the information about the armed revolt of *ahl Khurāsān*, "miraculously" arrived exactly when the ʿAbbāsīs (and the other Hāshimīs) were on the verge of swearing allegiance to Muḥammad b. ʿAbdallāh al-Ḥasanī.

As for ʿAbdallāh b. al-Ḥasan's letter to Marwān, most probably this accusation was circulated at a much later date, probably also after the revolt of Muḥammad al-Nafs al-Zakiyya. It seems that if this account was true, al-Manṣūr, or even al-Saffāḥ, would have killed him much earlier than 145/762.

This is a pro-ʿAbbāsī, anti-Ḥasanī, tradition. It is related through ʿĪsā b. ʿAbdallāh's al-ʿUmarī family, who had good relations with the ʿAbbāsīs. ʿĪsā's father and grandfather were contemporaries of the revolt. They transmitted many traditions on the rebellion of al-Nafs al-Zakiyya. It is possible that they were responsible for circulating the tradition.

g) The last tradition to be mentioned here tells that after al-Walīd b. Yazīd b. ʿAbd al-Malik was killed (126/744), ʿAbdallāh b. al-Ḥasan summoned a group from his family (*ahl baytihi*), to swear allegiance to his son Muḥammad. The only other ʿAlīd mentioned in this meeting is Jaʿfar al-Ṣādiq who refuses to respond to ʿAbdallāh's call, telling him "ʿThis rule is not within our family (*laysa fīnā*), it is only within the descendants of our uncle al-ʿAbbās. But if you refuse (to acknowledge this), call for yourself, for you are more distinguished than your son.' ʿAbdallāh held back and did not answer him."[84]

1.3.1.5 *The Role of al-Manṣūr in the Traditions about the Banū Hāshim Meeting*

It has been noted that **only one** of the seven traditions about the alleged meeting of Banū Hāshim in Abū l-Faraj al-Iṣfahānī's book presents al-Manṣūr as the central figure, where he speaks in favor of Muḥammad al-Nafs al-Zakiyya, and calls to swear allegiance to him. But there is other evidence about the activities of al-Manṣūr at this meeting. Many are mere repetitions and/or borrowings from the well-known (and above-mentioned) traditions. Some are clearly anti-ʿAbbāsī and/or pro-Imāmī.

1) One such tradition is recorded by al-Maqrīzī, whose anti-ʿAbbāsī attitude is known and well-attested to in his works, in which he emphasizes the cruel, unjust rule of the ʿAbbāsī caliphs. He mentions that al-Manṣūr was among

84 Al-Balādhurī, *Ansāb* (ed. Madelung), 2:498 (= *Fragmenta*, 231, a parallel tradition with minor insignificant changes); the ending is reminiscent of the text in al-Iṣfahānī, *Maqātil*, 207 (ll. 10–11).

those who swore allegiance to Muḥammad b. ʿAbdallāh when the Banū Hāshim conferred together concerning who they should elect as Imām.[85]

Another example is from an Imāmī (certainly anti-ʿAbbāsī) work, in which al-Manṣūr swears allegiance not only to Muḥammad, but also to his brother, Ibrāhīm.[86] These traditions do not mention the location of the meeting.

Some traditions mention that it was held in Mecca. Two mention that Muʿtazilīs were among those who were with al-Manṣūr when he swore allegiance to Muḥammad b. ʿAbdallāh.[87]

2) Traditions from "eyewitnesses" who accuse al-Manṣūr of denying the allegiance that he swore to Muḥammad b. ʿAbdallāh

This group of traditions is homogeneous and was related by transmitters from the Zubayrī family, who describe the death of a member of their family, ʿUthmān b. Muḥammad b. Khālid b. al-Zubayr, who was one of the most important supporters of Muḥammad b. ʿAbdallāh. When brought to al-Manṣūr, the caliph asked him "Have you sworn [allegiance] to him?" and ʿUthmān answered "Yes, (exactly) as you swore [allegiance] to him."[88]

In another tradition ʿUthmān accuses al-Manṣūr: "I and you have sworn [allegiance] to a man in Mecca; I kept my allegiance while you were perfidious. …"[89]

These traditions were related as firsthand evidence by members of the Zubayrī family. On the one hand, they seek to glorify one of their family mem-

---

85 Al-Maqrīzī, *al-Nizāʿ wa-l-takhāṣum*, 56–57 (Bosworth, *al-Maqrīzī*, 95).

86 E.g., Ibn ʿInaba, *ʿUmda*, 104; see also Ibn Kathīr, *al-Bidāya* (ed. Shīrī), 10:87: وكان في جملة من بايعه على ذلك ابو جعفر المنصور.

87 Al-Ṭabarī, 3:143, where al-Manṣūr swears allegiance to Muḥammad "together with all (or some) of the Muʿtazilīs that were there with them": مع سائر المعتزلة الذين كانوا معهم هناك; ibid., 152, where Abū Jaʿfar "swore [allegiance] to him in Mecca among (or perhaps while leading?) people from the Muʿtazila": كان عقد له بمكة في أناس من المعتزلة

88 Al-Ṭabarī, 3:262 (ll. 10–17), from Muḥammad b. ʿUrwa b. Hishām b. ʿUrwa (b. al-Zubayr), relating the tradition in the first person, witnessing the event in al-Manṣūr's court. See also al-Azdī, *Taʾrīkh al-Mawṣil*, 190, where we find an exact parallel; al-Iṣfahānī, *Maqātil*, 286–287, has a different *isnād*: al-Iṣfahānī < ʿĪsā b. al-Ḥusayn < Hārūn b. Mūsā, with slight changes and minor additions, but for an interesting addition, bearing evidence of the anti-ʿAbbāsī nature of the tradition, "He [al-Manṣūr] said: Have you sworn [allegiance] to him? He said: Yes, by God I swear, exactly as you swore to him, and your brothers and your family members, who are the perfidious."

89 Al-Ṭabarī, 3:263–264 (l. 17 to l. 2): (ʿUmar b. Shabba) < Saʿīd b. ʿAbd al-Ḥamīd b. Jaʿfar < Muḥammad b. ʿUthmān b. Khālid al-Zubayrī, reporting in the first person about his father's "heroic" stormy disputation with the caliph before he was executed; for a parallel tradition, see al-Iṣfahānī, *Maqātil*, 287.

bers, and thereby the extended Zubayrī family, but at the same time, they seek to undermine the caliph's credibility, and to besmirch him.[90]

2.1) Another tradition of this kind is recorded by al-Iṣfahānī in two different places by two different eyewitnesses[!]. Although the transmitters are different, and there are some verbal differences between them, it is clearly one tradition.

The first version is as follows:

> Abū Jaʿfar al-Manṣūr swore allegiance twice to Muḥammad b. ʿAbdallāh; one of them in Medina and the other, which I attended, in Mecca in the Great Mosque (al-Masjid al-Ḥarām). When he swore allegiance to him, he stayed with him until he [Muḥammad] came out of al-Masjid al-Ḥarām and rode, and Abū Jaʿfar held the stirrup of his riding beast for him, then he [Abū Jaʿfar] said to him: "Oh Abū ʿAbdallāh, but if (or when) **this** rule will pass **to you** you'll forget this event on this occasion, and will not acknowledge it (or requite this act) to me."[91]

The second version is a shorter, sometimes unclear, version of the first. The Arabic text is garbled and equivocal.[92]

---

90 See also ibid., 253, from Yaʿqūb b. ʿArabī; according to his testimony, ibid., 253 (ll. 7–8), he was one of the close associates of Muḥammad b. ʿAbdallāh, who was imprisoned after the revolt for many years.

91 Al-Iṣfahānī, *Maqātil*, 294–295 (l. 15 to l. 4): al-Iṣfahānī … Yaḥyā b. al-Ḥasan < ʿAbdallāh b. Ḥumayd al-Laythī (unidentified) < his father < ʿĪsā b. ʿAbdallāh (b. Muḥammad b. ʿUmar b. ʿAlī b. Abī Ṭālib; on him and his family, see esp. appendix 2) < his father: بايع أبو جعفر المنصور محمد بن عبد الله مرتين، إحداهما بالمدينة والأخرى أنا حاضرها بمكة في المسجد الحرام، فلما بايعه قام معه حتى خرج من المسجد الحرام فركب فأمسك له أبو جعفر بركاب دابته ثم قال له: يا أبا عبد الله أما إنه إن أفضى إليك هذا الأمر نسيت هذا الموقف و لم تعرفه لي.

92 Al-Iṣfahānī, *Maqātil*, 209 (ll. 6–10): al-Iṣfahānī … ʿAbdallāh b. Mūsā (b. ʿAbdallāh b. al-Ḥasan?) < ʿAbdallāh b. Saʿd al-Juhanī (unidentified) "Abū Jaʿfar (al-Manṣūr) swore allegiance to Muḥammad twice; I was attending one of them in Mecca in the great mosque. And when he (Muḥammad) came out he [al-Manṣūr] held the stirrup of his [Muḥammad's] horse's saddle. Then he said: 'But if (or when) the rule will pass to **the two of you** you'll not remember this event on this occasion for me'": بايع ابو جعفر محمدا مرتين، أنا حاضر إحداهما بمكة في المسجد الحرام، فلما خرج أمسك له بالركاب. ثم قال: أما إنه إن أفضى إليكما الأمر نسيت لي هذا الموقف. It is not clear why the dual form is used; it may be due to a printing (copyist) error. The only parallel text of the tradition appears in al-Amīn,

If the eyewitness (transmitter) in the first version is indeed the well-known scholar, ʿAbdallāh b. Muḥammad al-ʿUmarī, the father of ʿĪsā, one of the main transmitters of ʿUmar b. Shabba, it may strongly indicate pro-Ḥasanī, anti-ʿAbbāsī convictions. It is highly plausible that this link in the *isnād* was invented. If this is not the case, then it implies an anti-ʿAbbāsī attitude at least of ʿAbdallāh al-ʿUmarī. Were his and his son's name inserted in (or added to) the *isnād* on purpose, in order to give the tradition more credence? A well-known technique often used in the *ḥadīth* literature involves a person being highly praised by his enemy. ʿAbdallāh was the head of the Ṭālibī ʿUmarī family. He and his son are usually described as keen and loyal supporters of the ʿAbbāsīs. Moreover, they are described as followers of the Imāmiyya. These traditions are part of a larger corpus of traditions in this vein, i.e., traditions of "the rider and the stirrup" motif.[93] They depict, again by eyewitnesses, a scene that occurred in Medina, most probably still during the (end of) Umawī rule, when Abū Jaʿfar al-Manṣūr sees Muḥammad b. ʿAbdallāh coming out of his son's house,[94] or from the great mosque,[95] he leaps up, holding Muḥammad's cloak (*ridāʾ*), and then arranging it on the saddle[96] or, according to another tradition, standing beside Muḥammad's mule, laying his hand on its neck, while Muḥammad puts his hand on al-Manṣūr's shoulder.[97] And to the question of the somehow surprised eyewitness, "Who is this that you bestow upon him such a great honor?" he answers "Don't you know him?" The man answers "No," and al-Manṣūr answers: "This is Muḥammad b. ʿAbdallāh b. al-Ḥasan b. al-Ḥasan, our Mahdī, of the family of the Prophet."[98]

Mustadrakāt, 1:75, who copies al-Iṣfahānī's text, but the word إليكما, to you both, changes to إليك, to you.

93 Al-Iṣfahānī, *Maqātil*, 239 (ll. 1–8); 240 (ll. 9–16) [= 208 (ll. 12–16), a short parallel tradition].

94 Ibid., 239 (ll. 3–4).

95 Ibid., 240 (l. 11).

96 Ibid., 239 (l. 5).

97 Ibid., 240 (ll. 12–13).

98 Ibid., 239 (ll. 7–8): هذا محمد بن عبد الله بن الحسن بن الحسن, مهدينا أهل البيت; 240 (l. 16): إنك لجاهل به, هذا محمد بن عبدالله, مهدينا اهل البيت. The first tradition, ibid., 239 (ll. 1–8): … Aḥmad b. al-Ḥārith (al-Kharrāz) < al-Madāʾinī < Ibn Daʾb (d. 171/787) < ʿUmayr b. al-Faḍl al-Khathʿamī (unidentified), who was an eyewitness to the event. ʿĪsā b. Daʾb seems to have been inclined towards the Shīʿa, therefore, in case he himself did not invent the tradition (which in my view is doubtful), he was certainly a worthy tool in distributing it. The second tradition, ibid. 240 (ll. 9–16): Abū Zayd (ʿUmar b. Shabba) < Jaʿfar b. Muḥammad b. Ismāʿīl (b. al-Faḍl b. Yaʿqūb b. al-Faḍl b. ʿAbdallāh b. al-Ḥārith b. Nawfal b. ʿAbd al-Muṭṭalib) al-Hāshimī (on him, see below) < from his father < his grandfather; the parallel short tradition, ibid., 208 (ll. 12–16); on l. 14: change كنت أنا وجعفر to كنت أنا وابو

2.2) *Dāwūd b. ʿAlī l-ʿAbbāsī and the swearing of allegiance to Muḥammad b. ʿAbdallāh*

The last tradition in this group is connected to those discussed above, but approaches the issue from a different angle. Like other traditions in this vein, once more, it is an eyewitness's testimony, this time Abū l-Ḥasan ʿAbdallāh b. al-Ḥasan b. al-Furāt (unidentified, and see below). He relates that he went along with ʿAbdallāh b. al-Ḥasan b. al-Ḥasan (Muḥammad's father), and the two ʿAbbāsī dignitaries, ʿAbdallāh b. ʿAlī b. ʿAbdallāh b. al-ʿAbbās and his brother Dāwūd b. ʿAlī. Dāwūd addresses ʿAbdallāh b. al-Ḥasan, saying: "Oh Abū Muḥammad, if only you had told your sons, Muḥammad and Ibrāhīm, to publicly appear (in rebellion) and claim this rule, for the dynasty of Banū Umayya has already been shattered to pieces ... do you not hear the news about the bad unsound state of Naṣr b. Sayyār [the governor of Khurāsān]?" ʿAbdallāh b. al-Ḥasan answers that the time has not come yet for them to come out openly and then ʿAbdallāh b. ʿAlī l-ʿAbbāsī says: "Abū Muḥammad, you are not those who will overcome the Umawīs, on the contrary, we are, I swear by God, those that will overcome them. And it is I, by God I swear, who will kill them, destroy them and wreck their rule soon, if God wills ..." ʿAbdallāh b. al-Ḥasan kept quiet and did not speak.[99]

When analyzing some of the components of this tradition, one cannot but notice the coarse work that has gone into patching several literary components together. Ibn Aʿtham al-Kūfī transmitted it from al-Madāʾinī (d. ca. 225/840) from Abū l-Ḥasan Ibn al-Furāt, who gives an eyewitness report.

According to this tradition, this episode happened towards the end of Umawī rule. Dāwūd b. ʿAlī is given the role that is usually assigned in these traditions to al-Manṣūr, while ʿAbdallāh b. ʿAlī receives the role of Jaʿfar al-Ṣādiq. It is full of contradictions and improbabilities: a) The distinguished ʿAbbāsīs act and react as if there was no active propaganda dedicated to the ʿAbbāsī cause in Khurāsān; b) ʿAbdallāh b. ʿAlī's brother Dāwūd does not have secret

---

جعفر according to 240 (l. 11): كنت مع أبي جعفر ; Ibn ʿInaba, *ʿUmda*, 104 concluded (based on this text) that by Jaʿfar, Jaʿfar al-Ṣādiq is meant, but it seems that he was wrong.

99 Ibn Aʿtham al-Kūfī, *Futūḥ* (Hyderabad edition), 8:159–160 (Beirut edition, 8:318): Ibn Aʿtham < al-Madāʾinī < Abū l-Ḥasan b. al-Furāt; a parallel tradition (with some changes: 1) the name of ʿAbdallāh b. al-Ḥasan is garbled, instead of عبد الله بن الحسن بن الحسن بن علي بن أبي طالب in al-Kūfī's tradition, al-Iṣfahānī renders: عبد الله والحسن بن الحسن بن علي, that is, he adds ʿAbdallāh's brother, al-Ḥasan; 2) only Muḥammad is mentioned as the candidate to overthrow the Umawīs; 3) the ending [ʿAbdallāh's silence] is omitted), see al-Iṣfahānī, *Maqātil*, 347–348 (l. 12 to l. 3): ʿUmar b. Shabba < Muḥammad b. Yaḥyā < ʿAbdallāh b. Yaḥyā < ʿAbdallāh b. al-Ḥasan b. al-Furāt.

esoteric knowledge of his brother, i.e., he does not know that his brother will kill the Umawīs, etc. Therefore, he asks ʿAbdallāh b. al-Ḥasan the question about his sons.

But disregarding the bad craftsmanship of this tradition, it is clear that it could only have been invented after the ascendance of the ʿAbbāsīs, no earlier than the battle of the Zāb (132/750). Al-Madāʾinī died ca. 840. The transmitter, Abū l-Ḥasan Ibn al-Furāt, who relates to al-Madāʾinī in the first person, is unidentified, but he most probably belonged to the famous Banū l-Furāt family, several of whose members held the offices of secretaries and viziers under the ʿAbbāsīs (mainly from the end of the third/ninth century) and the Ikhshīdīs (in the fourth/tenth century). They were pro-Shīʿa. He may have been ʿUmar b. al-Furāt al-Kātib al-Baghdādī, who was one of the followers of the eighth Imām ʿAlī l-Riḍā, and was executed in Baghdad in 204/819.[100]

In conclusion, I would remind the reader that the esoteric knowledge, the knowledge of Muḥammad b. ʿAbdallāh's future, was not a unique trait of Jaʿfar al-Ṣādiq. ʿAbdallāh b. al-Ḥasan knows that his two sons will be killed;[101] Marwān b. Muḥammad, the last Umawī caliph, knows that he is not the real danger or threat to the Umawīs;[102] Abū l-ʿAbbās al-Saffāḥ, the first ʿAbbāsī caliph, foretells ʿAbdallāh b. al-Ḥasan that his sons will be killed, and that they do not pose any danger to him personally.[103] He has nothing to be afraid of, for ʿAbdallāh b. ʿAlī knows that he will overcome the Umawīs and that the rule will pass to the ʿAbbāsīs and not to the Ḥasanīs;[104] ʿAmr b. ʿUbayd, one of the Muʿtazila's leaders, knows that Muḥammad will be killed, therefore he cannot be *the* Mahdī.[105]

1.3.1.6 *Conclusion*

The last traditions mentioned above are clearly pro-Ḥasanī and anti-ʿAbbāsī. One group of traditions aims at emphasizing Abū Jaʿfar al-Manṣūr's role in the alleged meeting where Banū Hāshim swore allegiance to Muḥammad b. ʿAbdallāh. Another group is connected to the first one in emphasizing the great esteem that al-Manṣūr held for Muḥammad b. ʿAbdallāh, most probably

100 The well-known vizier, Abū l-Ḥasan, ʿAlī b. Muḥammad, died in 312/924; our transmitter may have been the ancient forefather of the Banū l-Furāt family. On Banū l-Furāt, see D. Sourdel, "Ibn al-Furāt," *EI*², 3:767a–768b, but esp. idem, *Le Vizirat* (index); on ʿUmar b. al-Furāt, see *Le Vizirat*, 514; al-Shākirī, *Mawsūʿat al-Muṣṭafā*, 13:415; al-Shāhrūdī l-Namāzī, *Rijāl*, 4:106; I do not know if he was called Abū l-Ḥasan; the sources I checked do not give his *kunya*.

101 Al-Iṣfahānī, *Maqātil*, 245–246 (l. 13 to l. 3).

102 Ibid., 247 (l. 10); al-Balādhurī, *Ansāb* (ed. Madelung), 2:498.

103 Ibid.

104 See 77, above.

105 Al-Iṣfahānī, *Maqātil*, 246 (ll. 9–10).

at the end of the Umawī period; both groups of traditions use similar literary motifs. It also has been noted that a whole group of traditions aims at emphasizing Jaʿfar al-Ṣādiq's view, especially his strong objection to the allegiance to Muḥammad al-Ḥasanī, and his supernatural knowledge of the future.

Placing al-Manṣūr in the center of these traditions is not the least bit surprising, because of the conviction that they crystallized after the revolts of Muḥammad and his brother Ibrāhīm in 145/762. In several traditions other members of the ʿAbbāsī family who swore allegiance to Muḥammad are mentioned, including Abū l-ʿAbbās al-Saffāḥ, the first ʿAbbāsī caliph. But he is always passive; it is never said that he spoke in favor of al-Nafs al-Zakiyya, or that he enthusiastically and unequivocally supported his claim to the caliphate, as his brother al-Manṣūr did.[106]

It should be remembered that at that time al-Manṣūr was not the head of the ʿAbbāsī family, rather his brother Ibrāhīm al-Imām was. It is even possible that within the hierarchy of the ʿAbbāsī family, the brother Abū l-ʿAbbās al-Saffāḥ was more distinguished than al-Manṣūr; after all it was al-Saffāḥ who became the successor of Ibrāhīm and not al-Manṣūr. If Abū l-ʿAbbās al-Saffāḥ indeed swore allegiance to Muḥammad b. ʿAbdallāh, why does no tradition, in all the many versions and sub-versions discussed so far about the Banū Hāshim meeting, accuse al-Saffāḥ of breaching his oath as his brother al-Manṣūr did? Indeed only one tradition puts al-Saffāḥ and al-Manṣūr together, relating that they made efforts to get hold of Muḥammad and Ibrāhīm "because of the allegiance they took for Muḥammad,"[107] but in the dozens of traditions that mention the relations between Abū l-ʿAbbās al-Saffāḥ and ʿAbdallāh b. al-Ḥasan, not even once does the latter accuse al-Saffāḥ of breaching his oath to his son.[108] The existence of such accusations against al-Manṣūr indicates that they were spread following the revolts of the two brothers.

1.3.1.7 *Transmitters of al-Abwāʾ Traditions*

1) **Ibn Dāḥa** is Ibrāhīm b. Sulaymān b. Dāḥa, Abū Isḥāq al-Muzanī (al-Madanī?). He was an Imāmī Shīʿī scholar, and a *mawlā* of the Ṭalḥa b. ʿUbaydallāh family who related traditions from Jaʿfar al-Ṣādiq. He was active in the mid-ninth century.[109]

---

106 Ibid., 233–234 (l. 17 to l. 1); 255 (l. 4); 256 (l. 16); 287 (l. 4) (he is omitted in the parallel tradition, al-Ṭabarī, 3:262).

107 Al-Iṣfahānī, *Maqātil*, 233–234 (l. 17 to l. 1).

108 See Elad, "Wāsiṭ" and below.

109 Al-Jāḥiẓ, *al-Bayān* (ed. Hārūn), 1:84 quotes him: I was related (*ḥaddathanī*) by Ibrāhīm b. Dāḥa from Muḥammad b. Abī ʿUmayr. They and Ṣāliḥ b. ʿAlī l-Afqam are described by

2) **Muḥammad b. Abī l-Karrām al-Jaʿfarī**: A pro-ʿAbbāsī.

3) **ʿĪsā b. ʿAbdallāh b. Muḥammad b. ʿUmar b. ʿAlī**. He and his father were pro ʿAbbāsīs; three members of this family were married to women of the Ḥusaynīs, including ʿĪsā's mother.

4) **ʿAbdallāh b. Jaʿfar b. ʿAbd al-Raḥmān b. Miswar b. Makhrama (al-Zuhrī).** One of the supporters of the revolt. The tradition cited in his name is anti-Ḥasanī, pro-Ḥusaynī, e.g., stressing the supernatural qualities of Jaʿfar al-Ṣādiq.

5) **Jaʿfar b. Muḥammad b. Ismāʿīl b. al-Faḍl b. ʿAbdallāh b. al-Ḥārith b. Nawfal b. al-Ḥārith b. ʿAbd al-Muṭṭalib**: I was unable to find any substantial information about him. His grandfather is mentioned in Imāmī *ḥadīth* literature as a trustworthy transmitter, a close associate of al-Bāqir and his son al-Ṣādiq.[110] His father Muḥammad is also mentioned as an Imāmī transmitter, and one of the close associates (*min aṣḥāb*) of Mūsā l-Kāẓim.[111] A cousin of his, al-Faḍl b. Ismāʿīl, married one of the daughters of Yaʿqūb b. al-Faḍl b. ʿAbd al-Raḥmān al-Hāshimī.[112]

6) **Al-Faḍl b. ʿAbd al-Raḥmān al-Hāshimī** is most probably al-Faḍl b. ʿAbd al-Raḥmān b. al-ʿAbbās b. Rabīʿa b. al-Ḥārith b. ʿAbd al-Muṭṭalib. He was a pro-ʿAlīd and supporter of the cause of both the Ḥusaynī and the Ḥasanī families. He was a poet, as was his father before him and his son, Isḥāq and the latter two sons, Muḥammad and ʿAbdallāh, after him.[113] Ibn Ḥazm records a very interesting report about him saying: "al-Faḍl b. ʿAbd al-Raḥmān b. al-ʿAbbās b. Rabīʿa b. al-Ḥārith b. ʿAbd al-Muṭṭalib, was brought up and prepared (*yurashshaḥ*) for the office of the caliphate [?!]; he maintained the opinion that the caliphate should pass to whoever is fit (for it) only from among Banū Hāshim": الفضل بن عبد الرحمان بن العباس بن الربيعة بن الحارث بن عبد المطلب, كان يُرَشَّح للخلافة... كان يرى أن

al-Jāḥiẓ as distinguished Shīʿīs. Ibn ʿUmayr adds that al-Jāḥiẓ was the most extreme Shīʿī among them (من مشايخ الشيعة وكان ابن عمير أغلاهم). Al-Jāḥiẓ died in 255/869 and Ibn ʿUmayr in 217/832 or 833. Ibrāhīm b. Dāḥa is sometimes called Ibn Abī Dāḥa, sometimes al-Madanī, or al-Muzanī, sometimes with both *nisbas*; on him, see al-Khaṭīb al-Baghdādī, *Taʾrīkh* (Beirut, 1997), 9:439 (= Ibn ʿAsākir, *Taʾrīkh*, 27:389); al-Ḥillī, *Rijāl*, 32; al-Tafrishī, *Naqd al-rijāl*, 1:63; al-Amīn, *Aʿyān al-Shīʿa*, 2:141; al-Tustarī, *Rijāl*, 11:606; he is quoted in al-Iṣfahānī, *Maqātil*, 205 (Ibn Dāja instead of Ibn Dāḥa) and 235, 255.

110 Al-Ḥillī, *Rijāl*, 51; al-Amīn, *Aʿyān al-Shīʿa*, 3:393.

111 Ibn Bābawayh al-Qummī, *Akhbār al-Riḍā* (Beirut, 1984), 2:31; al-Shāhrūdī, *Rijāl*, 6:465; al-Khūʾī, *Rijāl*, 16:114.

112 Al-Ṭabarī, 3:551.

113 Al-Jumaḥī, *Ṭabaqāt*, 1:76–77; al-Zubayrī, *Nasab Quraysh*, 89: al-Faḍl; al-Ṣafadī, *Wafayāt*, 8:273: his father, his son Isḥāq and the two sons; Madelung, "*al-Hāshimiyyāt*," 22–23, discussing the father (ʿAbd al-Raḥmān) and son (al-Faḍl); Ahmed, *Religious Elite*, 155, 179.

الخلافة فيمن صَلُحَ من بني هاشم دون غيرهم.[114] This was also the view of his son, Isḥāq[115] (on him, see below).

He and members of his family seem to have had long relations with the Ṭālibīs. He may have supported the revolt of Zayd b. ʿAlī, or at least he may have been sympathetic to his cause; his daughter, ʿĀtika, was married to Zayd's son, ʿĪsā and bore him Aḥmad al-Mukhtafī.[116] When Zayd b. ʿAlī died, al-Faḍl b. ʿAbd al-Raḥmān lamented him in a long *qaṣīda*. Three of Zayd's children were entrusted to his care.[117]

It is reported that during the *fitna* that broke out after al-Walīd b. Yazīd's death (126/744), he wrote a poem to ʿAbdallāh b. al-Ḥasan in which he incited him to an armed revolt.[118] Nothing is known of his fate after the revolt was crushed. His son ʿAbd al-Raḥmān related that some members of their family came out in rebellion with Ibrāhīm b. ʿAbdallāh. When Ibrāhīm was killed, the family went into hiding; al-Manṣūr arrested some of ʿAbd al-Raḥmān's brothers. When al-Mahdī became caliph, and gave a safe conduct (*amān*) to all the people and set the prisoners free, ʿAbd al-Raḥmān arrived in Baghdad with his brothers, seeking the caliph's *amān*; it was eventually given to them.[119] Among al-Faḍl's sons who took part in Ibrāhīm's revolt were Isḥāq and Yaʿqūb, who were imprisoned by al-Manṣūr with other brothers for eleven years.[120] During al-Mahdī's reign Yaʿqūb was accused of *zandaqa* and was imprisoned. He was executed by order of al-Hādī in 169/785.[121]

---

114 Ibn Ḥazm, *Jamhara*, 71.

115 Al-Ṭabarī, 3:507 (ll. 15–19): وكان إسحاق بن الفضل بن عبد الرحمن يرى أن الخلافة قد تجوز في صالحي بني هاشم جميعا.

116 Al-Zubayrī, *Nasab Quraysh*, 67; al-Iṣfahānī, *Maqātil*, 619; Ibn ʿInaba, *ʿUmda*, 289.

117 Al-Balādhurī, *Ansāb* (ed. Madelung), 2:634–635.

118 Ibid., 497–498 (= *Fragmenta*, 231); Ibn Aʿtham al-Kūfī, *al-Futūḥ* (ed. Shīrī), 8:318; Ibn Ḥazm, *Jamhara*, 71 (ʿAbdallāh b. al-Ḥasan is not mentioned); Madelung, "*al-Hāshimiyyāt*," 23 (quoting *Fragmenta*).

119 Al-Iṣfahānī, *al-Aghānī* (Dār al-Kutub edition), 3:179 (Būlāq edition, 3:39).

120 Al-Ṣafadī, *al-Wāfī*, 8:273: Isḥāq and his brothers are imprisoned for eleven years; but it seems that he stayed in prison at least until 158/775, when al-Mahdī became caliph, see al-Ṭabarī, 3:507, 509; al-Ṣafadī, *al-Wāfī*, 4:228, reports that Yaʿqūb took an active part in the revolt; his brother Muḥammad and other brothers were imprisoned by al-Manṣūr when Yaʿqūb joined the revolt.

121 Al-Zubayrī, *Nasab Quraysh*, 89; al-Ṭabarī, 3:549–551, relates that when he was killed his children were summoned to the caliph, and his daughter Fāṭima confessed that she was carrying her father's child; therefore she was frightened and died of fear; Ibn al-Athīr, *al-Kāmil* (ed. Tornberg), 6:60; al-Dhahabī, *Siyar*, 7:443; idem, *Taʾrīkh*, 10:33; Ibn Ḥajar, *Lisān*, 6:309–310.

When did al-Faḍl b.ʿAbd al-Raḥmān die? According to some sources he died in 128 or 129/745 or 747, that is, even before the ʿAbbāsīs came to power.[122] On the other hand, we have evidence attesting that he lived after the ʿAbbāsīs took power: 1) He composed poetry related to the killing of Marwān and the termination of Umawī rule (that is, not before the end of 132/750);[123] 2) He is mentioned as the direct transmitter of ʿUmar b. Shabba;[124] 3) From a tradition related by al-Ṣūlī from Abū ʿUbayda (d. 209/824 or 825), we learn that al-Faḍl b. ʿAbd al-Raḥmān was still alive during Hārūn al-Rashīd's reign. Al-Ziriklī therefore ascribes his death to ca. 173/790.[125]

7) **ʿAbd al-Aʿlā b. Aʿyan al-ʿIjlī, *mawlāhum,* al-Kūfī**. He is a pro-Ḥusaynī/Imāmī transmitter who was regarded by the Imāmīs as one of the jurisprudents who were close associates of Jaʿfar al-Ṣādiq: من فقهاء أصحاب الصادق.[126] The Sunnī critics of *rijāl* regard him as a completely unreliable, untrustworthy transmitter.[127]
8) **Muḥammad b. Yaḥyā b. ʿAlī b. ʿAbd al-Ḥamīd b. ʿUbayd b. Ghassān** al-Kinānī, Abū Ghassān al-Madanī.

2 Upon the Accession of the ʿAbbāsīs to Rule

2.1 *The Abū Salama Affair*

Several traditions report that after the news of the death of Ibrāhīm al-Imām reached al-Kūfa, Abū Salama, the chief *dāʿī* of the ʿAbbāsīs in that city, sent letters to three well-known ʿAlīds, offering each the caliphate. The three were: Jaʿfar (al-Ṣādiq) b. Muḥammad b. ʿAlī b. al-Ḥusayn; ʿAbdallāh b. al-Ḥasan b. al-Ḥasan; and ʿUmar b. ʿAlī b. al-Ḥusayn.[128]

---

122 Ibn Khayyāṭ, *Taʾrīkh* (ed. al-ʿUmarī), 1:215: year 128 H.; Ibn Ḥajar, *al-Iṣāba* (ed. al-Bijāwī), 5:399: year 129 H.

123 Ibn ʿAsākir, *Taʾrīkh*, 40:12.

124 Al-Iṣfahānī, *Maqātil*, 205 (l. 11): al-Faḍl b. ʿAbd al-Raḥmān al-Hāshimī.

125 Al-Ziriklī, *Aʿlām*, 5:150, quoting al-Marzubānī, *Muʿjam*, 310. See also al-Amīn, *Aʿyān al-Shīʿa*, 8:407 (also quoting al-Marzubānī's work); the quoted tradition is recorded by the editor of *Muʿjam al-shuʿarāʾ* in footnote 2 of the printed text; the tradition was written on the margin of the MS of the book: قال الصولي حدثنا محمد بن الحسن البلعي قال حدثنا أبو حاتم عن أبي عبيدة قال...; I was unable to find this tradition in the sources known to me.

126 Al-Ṭūsī, *Rijāl*, 242; al-Tafrishī, *Naqd al-rijāl*, 3:28; al-Khūʾī, *Rijāl*, 10:276–277.

127 Ibn Ḥibbān, *Majrūḥīn*, 3:156; al-Dhahabī, *Mīzān* (ed. al-Bijāwī), 2:529; Ibn Ḥajar, *Tahdhīb* (Beirut, 1984), 6:85; al-Mizzī, *Tahdhīb*, 16:347–348.

128 See for example, al-Jahshiyārī, *Wuzarāʾ*, 86; al-Yaʿqūbī, *Taʾrīkh* (ed. Houtsma), 2:418 (only Jaʿfar and ʿAbdallāh are mentioned); Ibn ʿInaba, *ʿUmda*, 101–102.

In all these traditions Jaʿfar al-Ṣādiq refuses bluntly to accept the offer and returns the letter. In some of them he warns ʿAbdallāh b. al-Ḥasan not to accept the offer, since *ahl Khurāsān* are not his *shīʿa* (that is, the supporters of his cause); more than that, he prophesies that Abū Salama will be killed.[129]

In another tradition, upon receiving the alleged letter of Abū Salama, ʿAbdallāh b. al-Ḥasan decides that his son should be sworn allegiance to, and he turns to a group of his brothers and half-brothers (lit., his father's sons) for this purpose. Jaʿfar al-Ṣādiq strongly opposes this move, and suggests that ʿAbdallāh b. al-Ḥasan not take any further steps in this matter, for he is afraid that ʿAbdallāh's son [the person mentioned in the tradition] will be killed in Aḥjār al-Zayt[130] (the place near Medina where Muḥammad b. ʿAbdallāh was killed thirteen years later). This prophecy and Jaʿfar al-Ṣādiq's ability to foresee the future is a recurrent motif found in other similar cases.

The concluding sentences of this tradition (the key point), could only have been related after the death of Muḥammad b. ʿAbdallāh. The main purpose here is to emphasize the quietism (*quʿūd*) of Jaʿfar al-Ṣādiq, which was cultivated by his father before him, and to justify this conviction. It aims to prove that this policy was right, using a very common literary device in medieval Islamic literature, that is, the esoteric knowledge, a person's inherent ability to foresee the future, in this case Jaʿfar al-Ṣādiq foreseeing the death and place of death of Muḥammad b. ʿAbdallāh. It also stresses the schism between the Ḥasanīs and the Ḥusaynīs. The tension and animosity between these two branches most probably existed long before the ascendance of the ʿAbbāsīs to power (see the discussion in appendix 3), but it certainly reached its peak during and after the rebellion of Muḥammad b. ʿAbdallāh. Some scholars tend to accept the authenticity of these traditions,[131] but

---

129 Al-Jahshiyārī, *Wuzarāʾ*, 86.

130 Al-Yaʿqūbī, *Taʾrīkh* (ed. Houtsma), 2:418.

131 See for instance, Wellhausen, *Arab Kingdom*, 546; Sourdel, *Le Vizirat*, 106; Shaban, *History*, 1:186–187; 2:1–2; Omar, *ʿAbbāsid Caliphate*, 139–144, 217, 246; idem, "Aspects," 172; Jafri, *Shīʿa*, 272–273; ibid., 273: "Jaʿfar aṣ-Ṣādiq, in all the sources which have recorded this story, is reported to have severely warned ʿAbd Allāh [b. al-Ḥasan] 'not to indulge and endanger his and his son's life in this game of power and treachery, as Abū Salama is not our Shīʿa and the Khurasānians are not our followers....' If this conversation is true it would throw light on Jaʿfar's extremely cautious policy of keeping entirely out of politics"; and see also Lassner, *Shaping*, 84; Kennedy, *Prophet*, 128; Crone, "*al-Riḍā*," 100–101; idem, *Islamic Thought*, 114; Halm, *Shiʿa Islam*, 22: "Kufan 'partisans' are said to have written to Imām Jaʿfar as-Sādiq, offering him the caliphate, but he supposedly declined. His reasons, assuming the truth of the reports, are not known." Arjomand, "The Crisis of the Imamate," 491–492 [in Kohlberg = 109–110] (after Jafri): "According to several traditions, Jaʿfar was invited by the Kufan revolutionary leader Abu Salama, presumably upon the death of the

following Sharon,[132] I would argue that they were put into circulation during the first two decades after the ascendance of the ʿAbbāsīs. Some of them were of an historical nature, combining history with religion, a common feature of writing in this period (and later periods, too) dealing with the history of the ascendance of the ʿAbbāsīs and the history of the first ʿAbbāsī caliphs. Many, like the last tradition mentioned above about the ascendance of the ʿAbbāsīs and the affair of Abū Salama, who allegedly wanted to pass the rule over to the ʿAlīds, were circulated by those close to the ʿAbbāsīs and/or their cause. Bearing in mind that Abū Salama was murdered by an envoy of Abū Muslim at the specific request of the Caliph Abū l-ʿAbbās, the tradition was most certainly put into circulation after Abū Salama's death (132/750) and most probably following Muḥammad b. ʿAbdallāh's rebellion. Its aim is twofold: the first is to malign Abū Salama, to justify his violent death by presenting him as a traitor to the ʿAbbāsī cause; and the second is to present the just cause of the ʿAbbāsīs through the attitude of Jaʿfar al-Ṣādiq, that is, his acknowledgment of the ʿAbbāsī rule, and his unequivocal attitude towards the Ḥasanī's rebellion. This is both a pro-ʿAbbāsī and pro-Ḥusaynī tradition. If it originated in the ʿAbbāsī court, or under its influence, it was put into circulation in an early period, perhaps immediately after the ʿAbbāsī revolution, when the relations between the Ḥusaynīs and the ʿAbbāsīs were still not very tense and full of hatred and animosity. But it does not necessarily belong to a "court tradition," that is, to a tradition that was circulated by scholars close to the ruling family or the caliph himself. These traditions could have been composed and circulated without this background, as they reflect a basic knowledge and historical facts, and combine them with literary motifs common in medieval Islamic literature. However, they are different from some of the traditions about the meeting in al-Abwāʾ that clearly reveal anti-ʿAbbāsī tendencies (see above).

2.2 *The Affair of Yazīd b. ʿUmar b. Hubayra*

Other traditions are linked to those discussed above, in that they accuse the last Umawī governor of al-ʿIrāq, Yazīd b. ʿUmar b. Hubayra, of communicating with the ʿAlīds, but mainly with Muḥammad b. ʿAbdallāh, during the siege of Wāsiṭ, the last stronghold of the Umawīs in al-ʿIrāq.[133] But other traditions tell of Ibn Hubayra's alleged communication not with Muḥammad b. ʿAbdallāh but with his father ʿAbdallāh b. al-Ḥasan,[134] or Muḥammad b. ʿAbdallāh and

---

ʿAbbasid Ibrahim al-Imam, to assume the leadership of the revolutionary movement, but he refused to get involved."

132 Sharon, *Revolt*, 246–256, esp. 249–251.

133 Al-Yaʿqūbī, *Taʾrīkh* (ed. Houtsma), 2:424; Ibn Ḥabīb, *al-Mughtālīn*, 190; al-Balādhurī, *Ansāb* (ed. al-Dūrī), 3:146: letters to Muḥammad b. ʿAbdallāh; Elad, "Wāsiṭ."

134 Al-Balādhurī, *Ansāb* (ed. al-Dūrī), 3:153.

other ʿAlīds, besides him.[135] Elsewhere I came to the conclusion that "the traditions regarding the correspondence between Ibn Hubayra and the ʿAlīds are ʿAbbāsī creations, written with the intent of justifying Ibn Hubayra's execution after he was given the *amān*."[136]

2.3 *ʿAbd al-Jabbār b. ʿAbd al-Raḥmān al-Azdī*

ʿAbd al-Jabbār b. ʿAbd al-Raḥmān al-Azdī was one of the seventy *duʿāt* of the ʿAbbāsīs in Khurāsān (from Abīward) and one of the chief commanders in the army of Qaḥṭaba b. Shabīb,[137] head of the *shurṭa* of Abū l-ʿAbbās al-Saffāḥ and al-Manṣūr, until 140/757–758, when he was appointed governor of Khurāsān by the caliph.[138] In 141/758–759 he rebelled against al-Manṣūr. Several sources state that ʿAbd al-Jabbār inclined towards the Shīʿīs[139] and that during his revolt he called Ibrāhīm b. ʿAbdallāh b. al-Ḥasan, who was in hiding, to come to him. Ibrāhīm did not comply with the request, therefore, ʿAbd al-Jabbār chose in his place a man by the name of Yazīd, *mawlā* of Bajīla, and proclaimed that he was Ibrāhīm b. ʿAbdallāh. This imposter used to deliver the Friday sermons

135 Ibid., 3:146.

136 Elad, "Wāsiṭ," 75–83 (the quote is from 82); some scholars regarded the traditions about Ibn Hubayra's correspondence with the ʿAlīds as authentic, see for example, Moscati, who finds it difficult to determine the truth regarding this correspondence. In one place he says that it is an ʿAbbāsī forgery, but adds that this story's background may be reasonable (Moscati, "Wāsiṭ," 178, 183). In the end Moscati presents a sort of compromise, according to which Ibn Hubayra did write a letter to the ʿAlīds, but it was an answer to Muḥammad b. ʿAbdallāh's letter and was written before his surrender to the ʿAbbāsīs and the drafting of the *amān* (ibid., 184–185). See also Omar, *ʿAbbāsid Caliphate*, 217, and Nagel, "Muḥammad b. ʿAbdallāh," 261, arguing for the authenticity of the correspondence of Ibn Hubayra with Muḥammad b. ʿAbdallāh.

137 *Akhbār al-ʿAbbās*, 218 (from Abīward), 221, 327.

138 On him and his family, see Crone, *Slaves*, 173–174; Omar, *ʿAbbāsid Caliphate*, 204–208; Kennedy, *ʿAbbāsid Caliphate*, 179–180; S. Moscati, "La rivolta di ʿAbd al-Ğabbār," 613–615; idem, "ʿAbd al-Djabbār b. ʿAbd al-Raḥmān," *EI*[2], using Balʿamī's translation of al-Ṭabarī, 4:378–380; Daniel, *Khurāsān*, 159–162 (and the exhaustive bibliography there); Agha, *Revolution*, 339–340, no. 105, using additional sources to those used by Omar, Crone, and Moscati, including *nasab* literature, and *Kitāb al-Muḥabbar* of Ibn Ḥabīb.

139 Al-Balādhurī, *Ansāb* (ed. al-Dūrī), 3:228 (ed. Zakkār, 4:304) from al-Madāʾinī; the expression is *yatashayyaʿ*, but the term may not have negative connotations, and may infer a positive attitude of the governor, who was a supporter of the ʿAbbāsī cause; this can be understood from the use and appearance of this phrase within the overall context of the sentence: وكان عبد الجبار يتشيع فسار سيرة حسنة ونظر في أمر الخراج وقوى الدعوة; but see ibid., 3:230 (ed. Zakkār, 4:307), also from al-Madāʾinī: وكان شيعي.

in the mosque pretending to be Ibrāhīm. He was killed by the ʿAbbāsī troops that came to Marw to subdue the revolt.[140]

But another tradition (again related by al-Madāʾinī) states that ʿAbd al-Jabbār wrote to Muḥammad b. ʿAbdallāh (not to his brother, Ibrāhīm), asking him to join him, or to send one of his children to him. Muḥammad b. ʿAbdallāh, with forty members of his family, had just left Medina to join ʿAbd al-Jabbār when the news reached him of the latter's defeat and they returned to Medina.[141]

Against these traditions, al-Ṭabarī relates (not mentioning the source) that upon his arrival in Khurāsān, ʿAbd al-Jabbār killed several of the most important commanders and notables, after accusing them of spreading pro-ʿAlīd propaganda. This may have happened following a strict direct order from the caliph. Balʿamī relates that this order came after ʿAbd al-Jabbār himself wrote to the caliph that there are a large number of people in Khurāsān who secretly recognize an imām from the family of ʿAlī.[142] Among the commanders mentioned are the governors of the provinces of Bukhārā and Qūhistān, who had had important roles in the ʿAbbāsī revolution. ʿAbd al-Jabbār also imprisoned some dignitaries who had played important roles in the ʿAbbāsī revolution, two (of whom only one is known to me) are mentioned by name. He also imprisoned several of the most distinguished commanders of *ahl Khurāsān*: عدة من وجوه قواد أهل خراسان.[143] Ibn Taghrī Birdī summarizes the affair by saying: "He seized a group of *ahl Khurāsān* and killed them."[144]

---

140 Al-Balādhurī, *Ansāb* (ed. al-Dūrī), 3:229 (ed. Zakkār, 4:305–306).

141 Al-Balādhurī, *Ansāb* (ed. al-Dūrī), 3:230 (ed. Zakkār, 4:307).

142 Balʿamī, 4:377, 378.

143 Al-Ṭabarī, 3:128: فأخذ بها ناس من القواد ذكر أنه إتخذهم بالدعاء إلى ولد علي بن أبي طالب; the two commanders are 1) Mūjāshiʿ b. Ḥurayth al-Anṣārī *ṣāḥib Bukhārā*. He was one of the early followers of al-Hāshimiyya movement. He was sent by Abū Salama to spread the ʿAbbāsī (Hāshimī) *daʿwa* to Transoxania, see *Akhbār al-ʿAbbās*, 248; Agha, *Revolution*, 363, no. 282; 2) Abū l-Mughīra Khālid b. Kathīr (b. Abī l-ʿAwrāʾ), who was one of the seventy *duʿāt* of the ʿAbbāsī revolution, see *Akhbār al-ʿAbbās*, 218; 220: originally he was one of the twelve *nuqabāʾ* called al-Tamīmī; al-Ṭabarī, 3:128: *mawlā Banī Tamīm*; Agha, *Revolution*, 356, no. 238. The commanders who were imprisoned are 1) al-Junayd b. Khālid b. Huraym al-Taghlibī (unidentified, Agha, *Revolution*, 355, no. 230, with no additional information); 2) Maʿbad b. al-Khalīl al-Maraʾī (that is, Imrūʾ al-Qays b. Zayd Manāt of Tamīm); al-Ṭabarī, 3:128, has al-Muzanī instead of al-Maraʾī; *Akhbār al-ʿAbbās*, 217: one of the seventy *duʿāt* (read al-Maraʾī instead al Murrī); ibid., 221 (al-Tamīmī); al-Yaʿqūbī, *Taʾrīkh* (ed. Houtsma), 2:449: al-Tamīmī, nominated as the governor of al-Sind by al-Manṣūr; Agha, *Revolution*, 358–359, no. 250: al-Tamīmī from Imruʾ al-Qays.

144 Ibn Taghrī Birdī, *al-Nujūm*, 1:340.

Al-Yaʿqūbī records that ʿAbd al-Jabbār killed many of those who belonged to *shīʿat Banī Hāshim*, which caused al-Manṣūr to write to him that he (that is, al-Manṣūr) had sworn to kill him.[145] It can be gathered, therefore, that the commanders and the senior commanders of *ahl Khurāsān* mentioned by al-Ṭabarī are *shīʿat Banī Hāshim*, who are mentioned by al-Yaʿqūbī. This supposition gains credence from the tradition related by al-Madāʾinī, whose last transmitter is Abū Ayyūb al-Khūzī, al-Manṣūr's chief secretary, that "when the news that ʿAbd al-Jabbār was killing the leaders of *ahl Khurāsān* reached al-Manṣūr, and a letter reached him from one (or some) of them … he said to Abū Ayyūb al-Khuzāʿī [sic! read al-Khūzī] indeed, ʿAbd al-Jabbār has already annihilated our devout partisans and followers of our cause: قد أفنى شيعتنا."[146] Ibn Kathīr, summarizing earlier chronicles, relates that ʿAbd al-Jabbār killed a group of the closest and most intimate adherents of the caliph: أنه قتل خلقا من شيعة الخليفة.[147]

It is well-known that the ʿAbbāsī *daʿwa* was initially an ʿAlīd movement. This phenomenon did not vanish with the ascendance of the ʿAbbāsīs. Many of the ʿAbbāsī senior veterans remained loyal to their old pro-ʿAlīd convictions. But it is hardly likely that al-Manṣūr would want to kill these veterans. Perhaps he meant those pro-ʿAlīd Imāmī or Ḥasanī followers in Khurāsān mentioned by Balʿamī. Indeed, Balʿamī states that Muḥammad b. ʿAbdallāh b. al-Ḥasan and his brother Ibrāhīm had spread propaganda secretly in al-Ḥijāz and Khurāsān. Balʿamī continues, telling of the letter of ʿAbd al-Jabbār to al-Manṣūr, from which it can be deduced that the adherents of a pro-ʿAlīd imām in Khurāsān are the followers of the two brothers and this is the reason for al-Manṣūr's order to kill [these?] ʿAlīds. But even if this was the course of events, it is doubtful that the old veterans of the ʿAbbāsī revolution were secret adherents of Muḥammad and Ibrāhīm, the sons of ʿAbdallāh b. al-Ḥasan. Some of them may still have followed the old Hāshimiyya line, that is, following Muḥammad b. al-Ḥanafiyya's line.

Scholars tend to believe that ʿAbd al-Jabbār was "a staunch ʿAlid supporter"[148] or, that "the key factor [in his revolt] seems to be that his affection for the *ghulāt* alienated the moderates."[149] But the material in the sources that deals with the revolt of ʿAbd al-Jabbār is not sufficient to support such unequivocal

145 Al-Yaʿqūbī, *Taʾrīkh* (ed. Houtsma), 2:445.

146 Al-Ṭabarī, 3:128; a parallel, abridged tradition in Ibn al-Athīr, *al-Kāmil* (Beirut edition), 5:131.

147 Ibn Kathīr, *al-Bidāya* (ed. Shīrī), 10:82; for the terms الشيعة/شيعة أمير المؤمنين/شيعة أهل خراسان/شيعة المنصور, see Elad, "Transition," 101.

148 Omar, *ʿAbbāsid Caliphate*, 206.

149 Daniel, *Khurāsān*, 162.

conclusions. Although the reports about this revolt have some common literary motifs similar to the other previous cases pertaining to the alleged communication of the Umawī caliphs, Abū Salama, Yazīd b. ʿUmar b. Hubayra, and especially the "al-Abwāʾ affair," this case is different, if only considering the element of the date. There is a gap of ten to fifteen years between the end of the Umawī period and the rebellion. In 140 or 141/757 or 758 we stand on firmer ground in regard to the history of the two brothers. In those years they were contemplating a rebellion and were considered to be a threat to the regime.

3 The Caliphate of Abū l-ʿAbbās al-Saffāḥ (r. 132–136/749–754)

3.1 *Abū l-ʿAbbās and the ʿAlīds (mainly ʿAbdallāh b. al-Ḥasan b. al-Ḥasan b. ʿAlī b. Abī Ṭālib)*

Very little is known of Muḥammad b. ʿAbdallāh from the time the ʿAbbāsī caliphate was established (132/749) until he came out in open rebellion in 145/762. Despite the most generous attitude of Caliph al-Saffāḥ towards ʿAbdallāh b. al-Ḥasan,[150] his brother, al-Ḥasan, on whom the caliph bestowed ʿUyūn Marwān in Dhū l-Khushub, and perhaps more significantly, gave into his custody al-Fadak,[151] other Ṭālibī families, e.g., the ʿUmarīs and the Ḥusaynīs[152]

150 For example, see Ibn ʿAbd Rabbihi, *al-ʿIqd* (Cairo edition), 5:74; al-Iṣfahānī, *Maqātil*, 173; *Fragmenta*, 214, where it is reported that the caliph gave him two million *dirhams* (Nagel, "Muḥammad b. ʿAbdallāh," 258 [quoting *Fragmenta*]); but see al-Balādhurī, *Ansāb* (ed. al-Dūrī), 3:166 (one million); (ed. Madelung), 2:498; Ibn ʿAsākir, *Taʾrīkh*, 27:387; al-Khaṭīb al-Baghdādī, *Taʾrīkh* (Beirut, 1997), 9:440 (one million); Sibṭ b. al-Jawzī, *Mirʾāt al-zamān*, fol. 283a (quoting al-Khaṭīb al-Baghdādī); al-Dhahabī, *Taʾrīkh* (ed. Tadmurī, *Ḥawādith wa-wafayāt 141–160*), 191 (one million *dirhams*); al-Balādhurī, *Ansāb* (ed. Madelung), 2:499 (ed. Zakkār, 3:309), reports that Abū l-ʿAbbās gave ʿAbdallāh b. al-Ḥasan estates which generated an annual income of 100,000 *dirhams*; Omar, *ʿAbbāsid Caliphate*, 218; see also Ahmed, *Religious Elite*, 154f.

151 ʿUyūn Marwān in Dhū l-Khushub: al-Iṣfahānī, *Maqātil*, 190: . . . ʿUmar b. Shabba < ʿAbd al-Jabbār b. Saʿīd al-Musāḥiqī < his father (Saʿīd b. Sulaymān b. Nawfal al-Qurashī [ʿĀmir b. Luʾayy]; al-Balādhurī, *Ansāb* (ed. Madelung), 2:499, without the *isnād*; for Fadak, see al-Samhūdī, *Wafāʾ*, 3:417.

152 1) The ʿUmarīs: e.g., the case of ʿAbdallāh b. Muḥammad b. ʿUmar b. ʿAlī b. Abī Ṭālib, who gained the favor of the first ʿAbbāsī caliph, Abū l-ʿAbbās al-Saffāḥ, who bestowed upon him two estates (in al-Ḥijāz?), al-ʿUshayra and ʿAyn Rustān, see al-ʿUmarī, *Ansāb*, 259. The Ḥusaynīs: e.g., the case of Muḥammad b. ʿAbdallāh b. ʿAlī b. al-Ḥusayn b. ʿAlī b. Abī Ṭālib to whom al-Saffāḥ gave ʿAyn Saʿīd b. Khālid, see Ibn ʿInaba, *ʿUmda*, 252; al-ʿUmarī, *Ansāb*, 144. His father, ʿAbdallāh b. ʿAlī, was in charge of the *ṣadaqāt* of both the Prophet and ʿAlī b. Abī Ṭālib, see ibid.; al-Khūʾī, *Rijāl*, 11:282 (from Ibn ʿInaba). Muḥammad's father,

and the ʿAlīds in general,[153] this attitude did not appease ʿAbdallāh b. al-Ḥasan, who is consistently described in the sources as ungrateful, never satisfied with the money and presents that he received from the caliph. One of the caliph's acts, which, on the one hand, expresses a desire to get close to and appease the Ḥasanīs, but, on the other hand, a desire to have control over and even neutralize the power of the Ḥasanī family, was the marriage of his son Muḥammad to Zaynab, the daughter of Muḥammad b. ʿAbdallāh b. al-Ḥasan. Muḥammad b. Abī l-ʿAbbās al-Saffāḥ wanted to consummate the marriage only after the annihilation of her father Muḥammad b. ʿAbdallāh.[154]

3.2 *Muḥammad b. ʿAbdallāh during the caliphate of Abū l-ʿAbbās al-Saffāḥ*

The sources are mostly unanimous in relating that from the ʿAbbāsīs' rise to power, the two brothers, Muḥammad and Ibrāhīm, were in hiding and did not swear allegiance to Caliph Abū l-ʿAbbās. They also add that Muḥammad b. ʿAbdallāh and his brother Ibrāhīm remained in hiding and did not appear before the caliph, despite his request to do so.[155]

A unique but ambiguous tradition relates that when Caliph Abū l-ʿAbbās' new governor came to Medina, "Muḥammad b. ʿAbdallāh b. al-Ḥasan b. al-Ḥasan came out towards him and swore allegiance [to the ʿAbbāsī caliph]—but [according to a different (less trustworthy?) version: *wa-qīla*] it was said that he did not swear [allegiance]—then he went into hiding."[156] This tradition is an echo of a longer tradition related by al-Balādhurī, according to

---

ʿAbdallāh b. ʿAlī (Zayn al-ʿĀbidīn) was the brother (from the same mother) of Muḥammad al-Bāqir. He was in charge of the revenues of the *ṣadaqāt* of both the Prophet and ʿAlī b. Abī Ṭālib. It is possible that the important role, the overseer of the *ṣadaqāt*, was the reason behind the conflict and strife between Jaʿfar al-Ṣādiq (b. Muḥammad b. ʿAlī) and his cousin, Muḥammad b. ʿAbdallāh b. ʿAlī; on this conflict, see al-Bukhārī, *Sirr al-silsila*, 50 (copied by Ibn ʿInaba, *ʿUmda*, 252).

153 Al-Balādhurī, *Ansāb* (ed. al-Dūrī), 3:165; al-Yaʿqūbī, *Taʾrīkh* (ed. Houtsma), 2:431–432; al-Muṭahhar b. Ṭāhir, *al-Badʾ*, 6:89–90; al-ʿIṣāmī, *Simṭ al-nujūm*, 3:240: quoting *Kitāb Qilādat al-naḥr* of Abū Makhrama [= *Qilādat al-naḥr fī wafayāt aʿyān al-dahr* of al-Ṭayyib b. ʿAbdallāh b. Aḥmad (A)bū Makhrama; on the author (d. 947/1540), see Brockelmann, *Supplementbände*, 2:239–240: his date of death 903/1497, but cf. Ibn al-ʿImād, *Shadharāt*, 10:382–383; al-Ziriklī, *al-Aʿlām*, 4:94; Kaḥḥāla, *Muʿjam*, 2:18–19: year 947/1540].

154 Al-Balādhurī, *Ansāb* (ed. Madelung), 2:517.

155 For instance, see Ibn Saʿd, *al-Qism al-mutammim*, 375; al-Yaʿqūbī, *Taʾrīkh* (ed. Houtsma), 2:431–432; al-Balādhurī, *Ansāb* (ed. Madelung), 2:498–500; al-Iṣfahānī, *Maqātil*, 173.

156 Al-Azdī, *Taʾrīkh al-Mawṣil*, 144.

which when the new 'Abbāsī governor, Ziyād b. 'Ubaydallāh al-Ḥārithī,[157] came to Medina in Rabī' al-Ākhar 133 (November–December 750), Muḥammad b. 'Abdallāh came from the desert and was among those who swore allegiance to the caliph in the presence of the governor. But when the governor wanted Muḥammad b. 'Abdallāh to swear to him personally, in front of all the other people, he went into hiding. "So the people spoke (about this incident), one person saying he [that is, Muḥammad b. 'Abdallāh] swore allegiance while another said: he did not swear."[158]

Abū l-Faraj al-Iṣfahānī relates, on one hand, that 'Abdallāh's two sons were afraid of the caliph and concealed themselves from him, but he does not explain the reason for this behavior.[159] However, elsewhere he (or, to be more accurate, his source) knows that the reason was the fact that both Abū l-'Abbās and his brother al-Manṣūr swore allegiance to Muḥammad b. 'Abdallāh in the Umawī period.[160] But besides this single tradition, all the others mention and sometimes even emphasize only the *bay'a* (the oath of allegiance) of al-Manṣūr. Abū l-'Abbās al-Saffāḥ is not mentioned among those dignitaries of Banū Hāshim, who were present in the al-Abwā' meeting. Moreover, as noted above, al-Manṣūr is the dominant figure in most of the traditions reporting this meeting. I would argue that these traditions mirror later events—they crystallized during and after the rebellion of Muḥammad b. 'Abdallāh. They reflect the struggle between the 'Abbāsīs and the Ḥasanīs during al-Manṣūr's reign. This is the reason why al-Saffāḥ's image is marginal in these traditions. Most of them do not even mention his presence in al-Abwā' (see the discussion above).

Several traditions relate that Muḥammad continuously advocated for himself as caliph (already) during the reign of Abū l-'Abbās al-Saffāḥ. One of these traditions tells about Muḥammad's propagandists in Medina,[161] while another such tradition is related by pro-'Alīd transmitters, concluding with 'Abdallāh b. al-Ḥasan himself, who relates (in the first person) that during his stay in al-Saffāḥ's court, while alone with the caliph, the latter showed him a letter from his son, Muḥammad b. 'Abdallāh, to one of the dignitaries in the 'Abbāsī court, Hishām b. 'Amr b. al-Bisṭām al-Taghlibī, calling him to join him and swear allegiance to him. 'Abdallāh assured the caliph that his two sons would

157 On him, see Crone, *Slaves*, 149.

158 Al-Balādhurī, *Ansāb* (ed. Zakkār), 3:310.

159 Al-Iṣfahānī, *Maqātil*, 173.

160 Ibid., 257: ['Umar b. Shabba?] < 'Īsā b. al-Ḥusayn < al-Khazzār (read: al-Kharrāz, Aḥmad b. al-Ḥārith, d. 258/872) < al-Madā'inī (d. ca. 225/840) < Suḥaym [or 'Āmir] b. Ḥafṣ (= Abū l-Yaqẓān d. 190/806); see the full discussion above.

161 Al-Balādhurī, *Ansāb* (ed. Madelung), 2:500.

never commit such an abominable deed.[162] On the face of it, this is firsthand evidence of Muḥammad b. ʿAbdallāh's activity during the reign of al-Saffāḥ. However, it is doubtful that this episode really happened. I tend to doubt the "letter motif," which is a very common literary motif in Islamic history, so much so that it can be considered a topos. It seems to belong to the "corpus of traditions" about the rebellion of al-Nafs al-Zakiyya that was spread after the death of the latter.

This is a pro-ʿAbbāsī tradition. On the one hand, its purpose is to vilify the Ḥasanī family and highlight their treacherous mendacious character, and on the other hand, it emphasizes the noble character of the ʿAbbāsī caliph. It was most probably circulated and spread from within the ʿAbbāsī court.

The letter is addressed to Hishām b. ʿAmr b. al-Bisṭām al-Taghlibī, a senior commander who also filled important administrative roles (as a governor) and was a close and intimate associate of Caliph al-Manṣūr. I found no traces that he had any pro-ʿAlīd (Ḥasanī) tendencies; on the contrary, as the governor of al-Sind he executed ʿAbdallāh al-Ashtar, the son of Muḥammad al-Nafs al-Zakiyya, who came to al-Sind after his father's death.[163]

But as noted above, the majority of the sources do not mention this specific point, but relate that both Muḥammad and Ibrāhīm stayed in hiding and refrained from appearing before the caliph, despite his specific order. In

---

162 Al-Iṣfahānī, *Maqātil*, 176–177 (idem, *al-Aghānī* (Būlāq edition), 18:206 (= Dār al-Kutub edition, 21:121); the *isnād*: … ʿUmar b. Shabba < ʿĪsā b. ʿAbdallāh b. Muḥammad b. ʿUmar b. ʿAlī b. Abī Ṭālib < al-Ḥasan (according to *al-Aghānī*; *Maqātil*: al-Ḥusayn [sic]) b. Zayd (b. al-Ḥasan b. ʿAlī b. Abī Ṭālib) < ʿAbdallāh b. al-Ḥasan (b. al-Ḥasan b. ʿAlī b. Abī Ṭālib); the text in *al-Aghānī* is garbled.

163 Hishām b. ʿAmr b. Bisṭām (b. Sufayḥ b. Marwān b. Yaʿlā b. Sufayḥ b. al-Saffāḥ, Salama b. Khālid b. Kaʿb b. Zuhayr b. Taym b. Usāma b. Mālik b. Hubayra b. ʿAmr b. Ghanm b. Taghlib b. Wāʾil). He is first mentioned in 132/749 as one of two dignitaries of al-Mawṣil, who changed their loyalty from the Umawīs to the ʿAbbāsīs (*qad sawwadā*) and turned over the besieged city to the ʿAbbāsī ʿAbdallāh b. ʿAlī. See al-Ṭabarī, 3:47; al-Azdī, *Taʾrīkh al-Mawṣil*, 133, 150 (called al-Zuhayrī, most probably after one of his ancestors; ibid., 136: al-Taghlibī). Next we find him as one of the commanders in the army of Abū Muslim fighting against ʿAbdallāh b. ʿAli in 136/754, see al-Balādhurī, *Ansāb* (ed. al-Dūrī), 3:107; al-Ṭabarī, 3:96; he was appointed by al-Manṣūr as the governor of al-Sind, where he executed ʿAbdallāh al-Ashtar, see al-Iṣfahānī, *Maqātil*, 312–314; idem, *al-Aghānī* (Būlāq edition), 12:86–87; al-Ṭabarī, 3:359; 362–364; 373, 379: on Kirmān and al-Sind; 380: discharged from office in the year 157/773 or 774; see also, Ibn Khayyāṭ, *Taʾrīkh* (Beirut, 1993), 351; al-Yaʿqūbī, *Taʾrīkh* (Beirut edition), 2:373. On his *nasab*, see Ibn al-Kalbī, *Jamhara* (ed. Ḥasan), 571 (ed. Caskel, 2:264; I, no. 165); Ibn Ḥazm, *Jamhara*, 306.

several instances their father, ʿAbdallāh b. al-Ḥasan, succeeded in appeasing the caliph's anger and suspicions.[164]

From two other traditions we learn that following his excuses to the caliph regarding his two sons, the caliph informed ʿAbdallāh b. al-Ḥasan that his sons will be killed. In one version he even describes the specific site of killing to ʿAbdallāh b. al-Ḥasan.[165]

It can be argued that if al-Saffāḥ had any concrete evidence of the rebellious intentions of one of the brothers, he would have acted more firmly, with a strong hand, to suppress the mutiny. On the other hand, he may not have wanted to light the fire of mutiny within the ʿAlīd family and subsequently throughout the whole Muslim community. The ʿAbbāsīs were related to the ʿAlīds with whom they had a strong and deep connection. The caliph did his utmost to reconcile them. The betrothal of his son Muḥammad to the daughter of Muḥammad b. ʿAbdallāh is intriguing. When was it arranged? During al-Saffāḥ's reign? If so, then it definitely served a political motive, i.e., the intention was to tie the Ḥasanī family to the ʿAbbāsī caliphate. It may indicate that the Ḥasanīs in general, led by ʿAbdallāh b. al-Ḥasan, were important (even dangerous) rivals of the ʿAbbāsīs.[166]

---

164 Ibn Saʿd, *al-Qism al-mutammim*, 375; al-Yaʿqūbī, *Taʾrīkh* (ed. Houtsma), 2:431–432.

165 Al-Balādhurī, *Ansāb* (ed. Madelung), 2:498: *qālū*; the specific sites: al-Iṣfahānī, *Maqātil*, 173: ʿUmar b. Shabba < Muḥammad b. Yaḥyā (most probably Yaḥyā b. ʿAbdallāh b. al-Ḥasan. For other parallel traditions of this text which is recorded in *Maqātil*, with changes, but by the same transmitter (the main difference is the omission of the identification of the sites where Muḥammad b. ʿAbdallāh and Ibrāhīm his brother will be killed), see al-Khaṭīb al-Baghdādī, *Taʾrīkh* (Hyderabad edition), 7:293; Ibn al-Jawzī, *al-Muntaẓam*, 8:90; al-Mizzī, *Tahdhīb*, 6:85; the *isnād*: … al-Ḥasan b. Muḥammad b. Yaḥyā l-ʿAlawī [Ibn al-Jawzī: al-Ḥasan b. Muḥammad al-ʿUkbarī] < his grandfather [Yaḥyā b. ʿAbdallāh b. al-Ḥasan] < Ghassān al-Laythī < his father. The identification of al-Ḥasan b. Muḥammad's father as Yaḥyā may be wrong; I was unable to find a son of Muḥammad b. Yaḥyā by the name of al-Ḥasan in the Shīʿī biographies.

166 For bibliography on the "marriage," see al-Balādhurī, *Ansāb* (ed. Madelung), 2:517, where we find contradictory narrations: Zaynab was brought to Muḥammad b. Abī l-ʿAbbās (another version: she was not brought to him, and ʿĪsā married her) and when he died ʿĪsā b. Mūsā married her; after him she married 1) Muḥammad b. Ibrāhīm al-Imām, then 2) Ibrāhīm b. Ibrāhīm b. al-Ḥasan b. Zayd b. al-Ḥasan b. ʿAlī, then 3) ʿAbdallāh b. al-Ḥasan b. Ibrāhīm b. ʿAbdallāh b. al-Ḥasan b. al-Ḥasan, and died while married to him. Note that al-Zubayrī, *Nasab Quraysh*, 55 says: Zaynab the daughter of Muḥammad was married to and stayed with (*kānat ʿinda*) Muḥammad b. Abī l-ʿAbbās Amīr al-Muʾminīn, then to ʿĪsā b. ʿAlī b. ʿAbdallāh b. al-ʿAbbās (! not to ʿĪsā b. Mūsā), then to Muḥammad b. Ibrāhīm (al-Imām) b. Muḥammad b. ʿAlī b. ʿAbdallāh b. al-ʿAbbās, then to two Ḥasanīs.

The literary motifs found in the traditions that depict Muḥammad's activities during Hishām b. ʿAbd al-Malik's and Marwān b. Muḥammad's reigns also exist in the traditions relating to al-Saffāḥ's reign. I refer here mainly to the repetitive motif describing the absence of Muḥammad and Ibrāhīm at the caliph's court and their hiding, but mainly to the intentional disregard of the reports about Muḥammad's claims to the caliphate. This is due to the secret knowledge of the Umawī and ʿAbbāsī caliphs that he does not constitute any danger to the caliphate (to this group Jaʿfar al-Ṣādiq should be added). They all know that he will not attain the caliphate.

4 The Reign of al-Manṣūr (r. 136–158/754–775)

Abū l-ʿAbbās al-Saffāḥ died in Dhū l-Ḥijja 136 (May 754), while his brother Abū Jaʿfar al-Manṣūr was in Mecca, leading the pilgrimage caravan. While visiting Mecca, the extended family members of Banū Hāshim came to pay him homage, except Muḥammad b. ʿAbdallāh and his brother Ibrāhīm.[167] The same incident occurred again in 138/756, when al-Manṣūr's cousin, al-Faḍl b. Ṣāliḥ b. ʿAlī, was the leader of the pilgrimage. All the dignitaries of Medina, among them all the Ḥasanī family, including their leading figure, ʿAbdallāh b. al-Ḥasan, paid him homage, except Muḥammad and Ibrāhīm.[168]

The two brothers were also absent in 139/757, when the governmental stipends (*al-ʿaṭāʾ*) were distributed among the Arab inhabitants of Medina (*ahl al-Madīna*).[169] Muḥammad and Ibrāhīm also refrained from appearing before the caliph during the *ḥajj* of the year 140/758.[170]

This and the aforementioned traditions explain the assertion of one of the sources, that from the first day of his rule al-Manṣūr's "sole concern was searching for Muḥammad [b. ʿAbdallāh], making inquiries about him and about his intentions."[171] He summoned every member of Banū Hāshim individually, asking each his opinion regarding Muḥammad. They all calmed the caliph's fear of Muḥammad, telling him that he does not wish to rebel against him. Only one member of Banū Hāshim, from the Ḥasanī family, al-Ḥasan b. Zayd (b. al-Ḥasan

167 Al-Ṭabarī, 3:143.

168 Ibid., 3:147.

169 Ibn ʿAbd Rabbihi, *al-ʿIqd*, 5:75.

170 Al-Yaʿqūbī, *Taʾrīkh* (ed. Houtsma), 2:444; al-Ṭabarī, 3:149–150.

171 al-Ṭabarī, 3:144 (trans. McAuliffe, *ʿAbbāsid Authority*, 87); see also al-Iṣfahānī, *al-Aghānī* (Būlāq edition), 18:206–207 (= Dār al-Kutub edition, 21:121); Ibn Saʿd, *al-Qism al-mutammim*, 253.

b. ʿAlī b. Abī Ṭālib) strongly warned him against Muḥammad's rebellious intentions.[172] We know that al-Ḥasan b. Zayd was a follower of the ʿAbbāsīs. Several years later we find him as the governor of Medina. His animosity towards the Ḥasanī rebellious section, that is, Muḥammad and his brother Ibrāhīm, is allegedly demonstrated in the tradition relating that he used to reveal the whereabouts of the two brothers and their places of hiding to al-Manṣūr.[173]

In 139/756–757, one of the caliph's trusted informers in Medina wrote to him that a messenger on behalf of ʿAbdallāh b. al-Ḥasan and his two sons, Muḥammad and Ibrāhīm, had left Medina with letters to some people (*rijāl*) in Khurāsān, in which they summon them to join their cause. The messenger was caught, brought to al-Manṣūr, who sent him with the unopened letters to ʿAbdallāh b. al-Ḥasan, telling him that he did not open the letters fearing that he would find in them something that he would not like and would change his heart towards him, asking him to send him his two sons. But the messenger was sent again by ʿAbdallāh b. al-Ḥasan and his two sons, was caught (again) by al-Manṣūr's agents in al-ʿIrāq, arrested, and the letters were delivered in Khurāsān by one of the caliph's trustworthy men, who was given supportive positive answers by the Ḥasanīs' followers in Khurāsān.[174]

Hishām b. ʿAmr, the intimate associate of Caliph al-Saffāḥ, did open the letter sent to him by Muḥammad b. ʿAbdallāh. Al-Manṣūr does not open the letter sent from the latter that falls into his hands. This would not make much sense, but should be regarded, once again, as a literary motif, perhaps a version of the famous story about *Ṣaḥīfat al-Mutalammis*.[175] While the literary motif is obvious, the endeavors to spread propaganda in Khurāsān, and the existence of supporters for the ʿAlīd-Ḥasanī cause there, is plausible. It finds corroboration in the traditions dealing with the governor of Khurāsān's rebel-

172 Al-Ṭabarī, 3:144; al-Iṣfahānī, *al-Aghānī* (Būlāq edition), 18:206–207.

173 Ibn Kathīr, *al-Bidāya* (ed. Shīrī), 10:87 (year 144 H.).

174 Ibn ʿAbd Rabbihi, *al-ʿIqd*, 5:75–76.

175 Al-Mutalammis and Ṭarafa b. ʿAbd, two Jāhilī poets, were sent by the king of al-Ḥīra, ʿAmr b. Hind (r. 554–569), with two sealed letters to the governor of al-Baḥrayn in which the governor was ordered to kill them. Al-Mutalammis opened his letter and was saved while Ṭarafa did not and was executed; see Ch. Pellat, "al-Mutalammis," *EI*². A similar case is that of the famous poet al-Farazdaq, who was sent by Marwān b. al-Ḥakam, the governor of Medina, with a letter to one of his governors, ordering the poet's immediate execution (or flogging and imprisonment), see Ibn Manẓūr, *Lisān al-ʿArab*, 6:41; Ibn Khallikān, *Wafayāt*, 6:91–94.

lion in 141/758–759, from which we learn of supporters of the Ḥasanī family in that province.[176]

Muḥammad b. ʿAbdallāh continued hiding from Caliph al-Manṣūr until he came out in open rebellion in 145/762. While staying in Medina in 140/758 al-Manṣūr ordered that ʿAbdallāh b. al-Ḥasan be put under house arrest, along with some of his family members. In 144/762 the Ḥasanī family was taken to al-ʿIrāq.[177]

Between 140/758 and 144/761–762, and especially between 143/760–761 and 145/762, the period of the governorship of Riyāḥ b. ʿUthmān, pursuit of the two brothers intensified. Already in 141/758–759, al-Manṣūr sent a special military expedition whose aim was to depose the governor (Ziyād b. ʿUbaydallāh) and find the two hiding brothers, Muḥammad and Ibrāhīm. Many traditions tell of Muḥammad's innumerable escapes from one place to another in Medina and its surroundings, and even outside the Arabian Peninsula. Some of the accounts contain material of a legendary-folkloristic nature, e.g., the long tradition about a magic mirror, which originally was given by God to Ādam and eventually passed into the hands of al-Manṣūr, by which he was able to see Muḥammad, follow him and watch his hiding places. One of the close courtiers of al-Manṣūr (أصحاب المنصور)[178] informed Muḥammad al-Nafs al-Zakiyya about the magic mirror and suggested that he not stay in one place more than the time it takes the government courier (*al-barīd*) to reach Medina from al-ʿIrāq.[179]

This tradition appears in many early and late sources. In most of them, this kind of story did not raise any amazement or questions. One of these sources was Ibn al-Jawzī.[180] Sibṭ b. al-Jawzī, the grandson of Ibn al-Jawzī, had a different attitude. Although he transmitted the tradition (from al-Ṭabarī), he conveyed his reservation in regard to one version of this story by saying:

176 See above, on the revolt of ʿAbd al-Jabbār.

177 See a detailed description in chapter 3.

178 On the "institute" of the *Ṣaḥāba* of Caliph al-Manṣūr, see Crone, *Slaves*, 67; Elad, "Transition," 93, n. 17.

179 Ibn Saʿd, *al-Qism al-mutammim*, 375; al-Ṭabarī, 3:155–156, 158, 167–168; the tradition about the magic mirror: ibid., 165–166, where we find the *isnād*: ʿUmar (b. Shabba) < ʿĪsā b. ʿAbdallāh < his uncle, ʿUbaydallāh b. Muḥammad b. ʿUmar b. ʿAlī (b. Abī Ṭālib); Sibṭ b. al-Jawzī, *Mirʾāt al-zamān*, fol. 280b (according to al-Ṭabarī).

180 Ibn al-Jawzī, *al-Muntaẓam*, 8:47.

> There is no need to be surprised regarding al-Ṭabarī, for his habit is to bring strange and miraculous stories, but the real wonder is my grandfather, for relating stories of this nature in *al-Muntaẓam*; for this is a matter that the well-reasoned and healthy brain will not accept. How is it possible that he [the caliph] sees Muḥammad and Ibrāhīm and does not recognize their location?[181]

In spite of the legendary-folkloristic components, some parts of the mirror tradition contain a grain of historical truth; its aim is to explain the failures of al-Manṣūr's well-oiled machine to find the two brothers for such a long time.

From another tradition we learn that after ʿAbdallāh b. al-Ḥasan was taken to al-ʿIrāq in 144/762, his two sons Muḥammad and Ibrāhīm fled first to ʿAdan [Aden], then to al-Sind and then to al-Kūfa, where the caliph, al-Manṣūr, stayed.[182] It is doubtful whether this information is trustworthy. Other traditions state that Muḥammad indeed intended to run away to Yemen, but al-Manṣūr made diverse plans, according to which he ordered his commanders to write to Muḥammad b. ʿAbdallāh, to express their loyalty and devotion to him, and by this convinced them not to leave Medina.[183] The function of al-Ḥasan b. Zayd as the one who revealed the whereabouts of the two brothers to al-Manṣūr is noteworthy.[184]

---

181 Sibṭ b. al-Jawzī, *Mirʾāt al-zamān*, fol. 280b: قال المصنف رحمه الله: و ليس العجب من الطبري فإن من عادته أن يأتي بالغرائب، وإنما العجب من جدي إذ حكى [تحكى؟] مثل هذا في المنتظم. وهذا شيء تأباه العقول السليمة والأدهان الصحيحة وكيف يرى محمد وإبراهيم ولا يعرف مكانهما؟

182 Al-Ṭabarī, 3:282; Sibṭ b. al-Jawzī, *Mirʾāt al-zamān*, fol. 280b (relying on al-Ṭabarī); al-Ṭabarī, 3:149: a shorter parallel tradition, where the part about the reason for their flight is missing, that is, the imprisonment of their father; also missing is the information about al-Manṣūr's stay at that time in al-Kūfa. According to this report the brothers continued from al-Kūfa to Medina; the *isnād* is as follows: Abū Zayd (= ʿUmar b. Shabba; he is omitted on 282) < ʿUbaydallāh b. Muḥammad b. Ḥafṣ < his father. See also Ibn Kathīr, *al-Bidāya* (Cairo, 1354 H.), 10:80–81 (= Beirut edition. 10:87), where we find a composite tradition, containing several events which were spread over a long period, but regarding this issue, Yemen and India are mentioned.

183 Al-Balādhurī, *Ansāb* (ed. Madelung), 2:514 (= *Fragmenta*, 242–243); al-Balādhurī, *Ansāb* (ed. al-Dūrī), 3:223–224: from ʿAbdallāh b. Ṣāliḥ < Abū Bakr b. ʿAyyāsh (al-Mantūf); see also al-Iṣfahānī, *Maqātil*, 268, where Muḥammad b. ʿAbdallāh is convinced that the commanders of al-Manṣūr will not attack him since they swore allegiance to him; the most prominent among them is Ḥumayd b. Qaḥṭaba.

184 Ibn Kathīr, *al-Bidāya* (ed. Shīrī), 10:87 (year 144 H.).

Towards the end of 144 (February–March 762) Muḥammad constituted a major danger to the ʿAbbāsī regime, which called for an immediate solution. The reverberations of Muḥammad's activities had spread through the entire caliphate and reached as far as Khurāsān, where they caused much tension among *ahl Khurāsān*'s army units. The governor of the province, Abū ʿAwn[185] wrote to the caliph that *ahl Khurāsān* believe that the affair of Muḥammad al-Nafs al-Zakiyya has been going on far too long and they would not submit to him (*taqāʿasū ʿannī*). To pacify this commotion Abū Jaʿfar al-Manṣūr ordered the execution of a prisoner in his jail in al-Hāshimiyya, Muḥammad b. ʿAbdallāh b. ʿAmr b. ʿUthmān, the maternal uncle of Muḥammad b. ʿAbdallāh, and his head was sent to Khurāsān and was presented there as Muḥammad b. ʿAbdallāh's head, with the solemn oath of al-Manṣūr attached, that "this is the head of Muḥammad b. ʿAbdallāh [b. al-Ḥasan] and that his mother is Fāṭima, the daughter of the Messenger of God."[186]

5 The Pre-Rebellion Phase: Propaganda and Espionage Activities

5.1 *The ʿAbbāsī Side*

1) Al-Manṣūr did his utmost to find Muḥammad and Ibrāhīm. In order to achieve this he established and developed a highly sophisticated network of spies and informers in Medina.[187] He bought some slaves from the Arab tribes (Bedouins?: من رقيق الأعراب) especially for this purpose and sent them to search for Muḥammad in the hinterlands of Medina and find information about him.[188] He also used merchants as a cover for intelligence and espionage purposes.[189] Al-Manṣūr used spies to penetrate ʿAbdallāh b. al-Ḥasan's inner circle in order to find information about his two sons, and their hiding places. These traditions are full of literary motifs, the most common being that of the anonymous man who spies on behalf of al-Manṣūr and succeeds in finding their hiding place but at the last moment Muḥammad b. ʿAbdallāh discovers him and the spy fails.[190]

185 On him, see Elad, "Abū ʿAwn."

186 Al-Ṭabarī, 3:183 (ll. 6–13).

187 Ibn ʿAbd Rabbihi, *al-ʿIqd*, 5:75–76.

188 Al-Ṭabarī, 3:145 (l. 10); McAuliffe, *ʿAbbāsid Authority*, 88: "some slaves held by the bedouins."

189 Al-Balādhurī, *Ansāb* (ed. Madelung), 2:502.

190 Ibid.: an anonymous merchant; al-Ṭabarī, 3:157–158: an anonymous spy.

One of these spies was ʿUqba b. Salm al-Hunāʾī (Azd),[191] who was sent to gain the confidence of ʿAbdallāh b. al-Ḥasan; he disguised himself as a messenger from the latter's faction (*shīʿa*) from one of the villages in Khurāsān, which used to send ʿAbdallāh b. al-Ḥasan voluntary alms from their property (صدقات أموالهم) as well as fine local products. ʿUqba reached ʿAbdallāh b. al-Ḥasan with a forged letter from this Ḥasanī faction in Khurāsān and eventually succeeded in gaining ʿAbdallāh b. al-Ḥasan's trust, the latter sent him back to his supporters in Khurāsān with the date on which his son will come out in open rebellion. ʿUqba revealed the information to al-Manṣūr. This event occurred in 144 H., a little while before the rebellion broke out. In Dhū l-Ḥijja 144 (March 762), while staying in al-Rabadha on his return from Mecca, al-Manṣūr ordered the Ḥasanīs to be brought to him. He planned a theatrical scene, in which ʿUqba was to appear in front of the perplexed and horrified ʿAbdallāh b. al-Ḥasan during the meal. It was there that ʿAbdallāh b. al-Ḥasan was imprisoned by the caliph.[192] According to another version ʿUqba b. Salm arrived in Medina disguised as a perfume merchant trying to find out Muḥammad's whereabouts.[193] In a similar version of this tradition, the name of the spy is Salm b. Qutayba [b. Muslim][194] and not ʿUqba b. Salm.[195] It is noteworthy that this tradition reverberated in Imāmī Shīʿī circles.[196]

2) Another technique developed by al-Manṣūr was to distribute letters from his senior commanders to Muḥammad b. ʿAbdallāh b. al-Ḥasan (as noted above), in which they express their alleged support and obedience[197] and urge

---

191 On him, see Elad, *ʿAbbāsid Army*, 101–103.

192 Al-Ṭabarī, 3:145–146, 151; al-Iṣfahānī, *Maqātil*, 211–212, 214 [= al-Iṣfahānī, *al-Aghānī* (Būlāq edition), 18:207 (= Dār al-Kutub edition, 21:122–123)]; al-Balādhurī, *Ansāb* (ed. Madelung), 2:503: the end of the tradition.

193 al-Balādhurī, *Ansāb* (ed. Madelung), 2:501–502; ibid., 2:503: the confrontation in al-Rabadha between him and ʿAbdallāh b. al-Ḥasan.

194 On him, see Crone, *Slaves*, 137.

195 Ibn ʿAbd Rabbihi, *al-ʿIqd*, 5:77–78.

196 For examples, see appendix 3.

197 Al-Balādhurī, *Ansāb* (ed. Madelung), 2:514 (= al-Iṣfahānī, *Maqātil*, 268, from al-Madāʾinī); al-Balādhurī, *Ansāb* (ed. al-Dūrī), 3:223–224, from Abū Bakr b. ʿAyyāsh al-Mantūf. Members of this family were well-known scholars, the most famous among them was ʿAbdallāh (d. 158/774 or 775), who was a historian (*akhbārī*), genealogist, transmitter of poetry, and one of the close associates of Caliph al-Manṣūr. Abū Bakr, his brother, was also a historian; on ʿAbdallāh, see McAuliffe, *ʿAbbāsid Authority*, 2, n. 8; also see al-Dhahabī, *Taʾrīkh*, 9:465; idem, *Mīzān* (Beirut, 1963), 2:470; al-Ṣafadī, *al-Wāfī*, 17:213. I did not find any biography of Abū Bakr b. ʿAyyāsh. He is mentioned in the vast Arabic literature as a *rāwī* of historical traditions, e.g., the indexes of Arabic historical and *adab* literature.

him to come out in open rebellion.[198] Muḥammad believed that the letters were authentic and that the caliphal army's senior commanders supported him and would defect to his camp upon their arrival in Medina.[199] When the armies met in battle, Muḥammad b. ʿAbdallāh allegedly said to Ḥumayd b. Qaḥṭaba: "Haven't you sworn allegiance to me? What is the meaning of this (behavior)?" and Ḥumayd answers: "This is the way we treat one who reveals his secret to the children": هكذا نفعل بمن يفشي سره إلى الصبيان.[200]

Traditions in this vein stress the success of the intelligence warfare developed by al-Manṣūr against Muḥammad b. ʿAbdallāh. Like many other traditions regarding the struggle, they are intermingled with legendary, literary motifs, miracles, etc. All the same, these legendary, literary motifs are woven around an historical nucleus, and reveal historical facts and details. Note that these traditions are different from the matter-of-fact, descriptive traditions of the actual battles. Here we are faced with the *Ayyām al-ʿArab* style of reporting, which makes the description more reliable. The traditions with the legendary, literary motifs are numerous, but even they can be thoroughly checked and discerned, for instance, by checking the *isnād*, comparing all the versions, and looking for common denominators; this leads to the historical axis around which these traditions were formulated. These traditions, that is, the use of spies by al-Manṣūr, were based on real cases. Even if the dialogues between the persons involved, e.g., al-Manṣūr and ʿUqba, al-Manṣūr and ʿAbdallāh b. al-Ḥasan, Muḥammad b. ʿAbdallāh and Ḥumayd b. Qaḥṭaba, were fabricated, in many cases the main facts are to be believed.

All of the traditions discussed above give us the clear impression that in intelligence warfare, al-Manṣūr had the upper hand. Muḥammad was certain that he had strong support in the provinces, in al-Shām, Khurāsān, and al-ʿIrāq. It is not clear whether this belief was part of the fabricated news spread by al-Manṣūr, or whether he may really have had supporters in these provinces (it seems that at least in Khurāsān he had some supporters). What is important is his preference to remain in al-Ḥijāz, living with grand illusions about his

198 Al-Ṭabarī, 3:198 (ll. 11–14).

199 Ibid.; al-Balādhurī, *Ansāb* (ed. al-Dūrī), 3:223–224; al-Iṣfahānī, *Maqātil*, 268.

200 That is, one who is simple-minded and acts like a child? Al-Iṣfahānī, *Maqātil*, 270, transmitting from al-Madāʾinī. For other traditions in this vein, see al-Balādhurī, *Ansāb* (ed. Madelung), 2:514 (ed. Zakkār, 3:327–328): "al-Manṣūr ordered his commanders to correspond with Muḥammad ... because he was on the verge of going to Yemen. When they did so he stayed and did not leave Medina. And it is said that Ḥumayd in person (or especially: *khāṣṣatan*) had sworn allegiance to him in Egypt, or assured him of his allegiance"; ibid. (ed. Madelung), 2:515 (ed. Zakkār, 3:328): Muḥammad b. ʿAbdallāh accuses Ḥumayd of breaking his oath to him.

power and supporters. According to such a tradition, when he told one of his close commanders(?), al-Ghāḍirī, about the supporters in al-Shām, Khurāsān, and al-ʿIrāq (*al-Miṣrayn*), the latter answered, "Oh son of my mother (يا ابن امي), you may claim the whole earth to yourself, while this ʿĪsā (b. Mūsā) is in Aʿwaṣ,[201] what good will you gain from it? By God I swear, there are no people who have become aware of their fate better than us."[202]

---

201 Al-Aʿwaṣ is located a few miles east of Medina, see al-Ḥarbī(?), *al-Manāsik*, 524–525; al-Bakrī, *Muʿjam*, 1:173: to the east of Medina, على بضعة عشر ميلا منها; Yāqūt, *Muʿjam* (ed. Wüstenfeld), 1:318; al-Samhūdī, *Wafāʾ*, 4:126.

202 Al-Balādhurī, *Ansāb* (ed. Zakkār), 3:331 (ed. Madelung, 2:517): وحدثني مصعب بن عبد الله الزبيري قال: قال محمد بن عبد الله للغاضري. As for al-Ghāḍirī, the man whom Muḥammad al-Nafs al-Zakiyya confided in, he is most probably mentioned by al-Ṭabarī, 3:231 (l. 3) (but see ibid., note c: Ms. B renders his name as al-ʿĀriḍī): in a tradition in the same vein as the one in al-Balādhurī, and with several identical phrases, transmitted from al-Ghāḍirī, a commander(?) in Muḥammad al-Nafs al-Zakiyya's camp, related in first-person form. McAuliffe, *ʿAbbāsid Authority*, 194, n. 943, identifies him with a gesture of certain fame, al-Ghāḍirī l-Muḍḥik (literarily: the funny [one]; one who makes people laugh), perhaps following the identification of Houtsma, the editor of this part of al-Ṭabarī in the *Introduction, Glossarium, Addenda et Emendanda to al-Ṭabarī's Taʾrīkh* (Leiden: E.J. Brill, 1901), dccxxxii, who cites as a reference on him al-Iṣfahānī, *al-Aghānī* (Būlāq edition), 17:101 (= Dār al-Kutub edition, 19:174). Both Houtsma and McAuliffe based the identification of al-Ghāḍirī (in al-Ṭabarī's work) on another tradition (al-Ṭabarī, 3:161 (l. 14) [McAuliffe, *ʿAbbāsid Authority*, 108]), where al-Ghāḍirī l-Muḍḥik is mentioned in an obscure passage in 141/758, long before the outbreak of the revolt. According to this tradition, it seems that al-Ghāḍirī is not a supporter of Muḥammad al-Nafs al-Zakiyya; on the contrary, he seems to contribute some of his property (cf. McAuliffe, *ʿAbbāsid Authority*, 108: camels) to the big search operation after al-Nafs al-Zakiyya. Houtsma, ibid., also mentions in this connection a parallel to this specific tradition (al-Ṭabarī, 3:161 (l. 14)) in Ibn ʿAsākir's *Taʾrīkh* (in the biography of Muḥammad b. Khālid al-Qasrī), but does not give the reference (he obviously read the MS); see now Ibn ʿAsākir, *Taʾrīkh*, 52:384 (idem, *al-Mukhtaṣar*, 22:131–132); here the sentence that mentions al-Ghāḍirī is missing, though. See the short biography on him in Ibn ʿAsākir, *Taʾrīkh*, 68:86, where we read that he was a storyteller of rare anecdotes (*nawādir*) and amusing stories of unknown origin; he came to Yazīd b. al-Walīd's court; ibid.: Sufyān al-Thawrī came to Medina and heard al-Ghāḍirī saying some amusing sentences that made the people laugh. As to the *nisba* al-Ghāḍirī, see Ibn al-Athīr, *al-Lubāb*, 2:372, who says that it can either relate to a sub-tribe of Khuzāʿa (see Ibn Durayd, *al-Ishtiqāq*, 473), or to Ghāḍira b. Mālik b. Thaʿlaba b. Dūdān b. Asad b. Khuzayma; but note that Ibn al-Kalbī, *Jamhara* (ed. Caskel), II, index, gives nine subtribes of this name; and see the comment in the tradition of al-Iṣfahānī, *al-Aghānī* (Būlāq edition), 17:101: "al-Ghāḍirī was a neglected foundling child whose father was not known (وكان الغاضري لقيطا منبوذا لا يعرف له أب). In my view, the person named al-Ghāḍirī in the tradition of al-Balādhurī, *Ansāb* (ed. Zakkār), 3:331 (ed. Madelung, 2:517) and al-Ṭabarī, 3:231, is not identical with the al-Ghāḍirī l-Muḍḥik mentioned in al-Ṭabarī, 3:161. Note

Al-Manṣūr also ordered that letters be composed in the name of Muḥammad b. ʿAbdallāh and sent to distinguished scholars; his intent was to learn of their loyalty to ʿAbbāsī rule.[203]

5.2 *Muḥammad b. ʿAbdallāh's Intelligence Operations*

Muḥammad also operated an intelligence system on his behalf in the caliph's court, although this was on a smaller scale.

According to one such tradition, Muḥammad or his brother Ibrāhīm sent a man from the tribe of Ḍabba to al-Musayyab b. al-Zuhayr al-Ḍabbī, the head of the *shurṭa* of al-Manṣūr,[204] in order to get information. The envoy sought to gain his confidence and to become close to al-Musayyab based on their common *nasab*, but the latter turned him in to the caliph, to whom he confessed his identity.

> Abū Jaʿfar al-Manṣūr asked, "What have you heard him [that is, Muḥammad or Ibrāhīm] say?" (The man) recited: "Fear banished him and disgraced him / Thus it is with one who hates the heat of battle."

that (al-Ṭabarī, 3:231) he calls Muḥammad al-Nafs al-Zakiyya "the son of my mother" (يا ابن أمي). This phrase is used to denote a real relationship, that is, the brother of the same mother (see Ibn Ḥajar, *al-Iṣāba* (ed. al-Bijāwī), 7:223: Umm Hāniʾ to her brother ʿAlī; al-Balādhurī, *Ansāb* (ed. al-Maḥmūdī, Beirut, 1394/1974), 2a:74: ʿAqīl to his brother ʿAlī; or real kinship, that is, relating to the same (large or small) family; for another example, see Wakīʿ, *Akhbār al-Quḍāt*, 1:188: Muḥammad b. ʿImrān (b. Ibrāhīm b. Muḥammad b. Ṭalḥa b. ʿUbaydallāh) al-Taymī calls al-Ḥakam b. al-Muṭṭalib (b. ʿAbdallāh b. al-Muṭṭalib b. Ḥanṭab b. al-Ḥārith b. ʿUbayd b. ʿUmar b. Makhzūm) al-Makhzūmī يا ابن أم; Both mothers of Muḥammad and his father ʿImrān belonged to the same family of the Makhzūm clan. Muḥammad b. ʿImrān's mother was Asmāʾ bt. Salama b. ʿUmar b. Abī Salama b. ʿAbd al-Asad al-Makhzūmī (al-Zubayrī, *Nasab Quraysh*, 285; Ibn Ḥazm, *Jamhara*, 139), and his father's mother was Zaynab bt. ʿUmar b. Abī Salama b. ʿAbd al-Asad (al-Zubayrī, *Nasab Quraysh*, 285); although al-Ḥakam's mother was not from the Makhzūm clan (she was from Banū Zuhra of Quraysh, ibid., 341), his father, al-Muṭṭalib was married to another woman from the Makhzūm clan, the daughter of the well-known *faqīh*, Saʿīd b. al-Musayyab (b. Ḥazn b.... ʿImrān b. Makhzūm) al-Makhzūmī (for a genealogical chart of the Makhzūm clan, see Ibn al-Kalbī, *Jamhara* [ed. Caskel], 1, table 22; on al-Ḥakam b. al-Muṭṭalib, see al-Balādhurī, *Ansāb* [ed. al-ʿAẓm], 8:341–344). See also the discussion about Muḥammad b. ʿImrān in chapter 7, 286.

203 Ibn Qutayba, *ʿUyūn*, 1:209: a letter to ʿAmr b. ʿUbayd, the distinguished leader of the Muʿtazila; al-Ṭabarī, 3:222–223 (l. 20 to l. 4): a letter to al-Aʿmash, Sulaymān b. Mihrān in al-Kūfa.

204 On him and his family, see Crone, *Slaves*, 186–187; McAuliffe, *ʿAbbāsīd Authority*, 150, n. 714; Agha, *Revolution*, 366, no. 300.

> Abū Jaʿfar said: Inform him therefore that we say: "O the shameful behavior we deem worse than death / Because of it we would bid death welcome." And he [the caliph] said: "Go away and tell him (that)."[205]

This tradition aims to emphasize the noble character of al-Manṣūr and his values: courage, endurance in the face of catastrophes, and generosity, all according to the ancient Arab spirit and ideals. It is difficult to ascertain whether this episode really occurred. The tradition could have been spread from within the inner circles of the ʿAbbāsī court, perhaps from the family of al-Musayyab b. Zuhayr, one of the most distinguished commanders of *ahl Khurāsān*, through a man from al-Anbār (but in this case it is tempting to accept another reading of the MSS of al-Ṭabarī: *al-Abnāʾ*).[206]

---

205 Al-Ṭabarī, 3:195; trans. McAuliffe, *ʿAbbāsid Authority*, 150.

206 Al-Ṭabarī, 3:195; the transmission is as follows: Ismāʿīl b. Ibrāhīm b. Hūd, a *mawlā* of Quraysh from a man from al-Anbār(?) whose patronym was Abū ʿUbayd; ibid., MS B renders another version of the name al-Anbār, e.g., al-*Abnāʾ*, that is, the man who related the tradition about al-Musayyab b. Zuhayr was a *Banawī*, that is, one of the descendants of *ahl Khurāsān*. Ayalon ("al-Muʿtaṣim," 33) remarked (a general observation with no citation) that "the sources frequently distort *Abnāʾ to* Anbār and *Abnāwī* to *Anbārī*."

CHAPTER 3

On the Eve of the Rebellion

1 Medina during the Early ʿAbbāsī Caliphate

1.1 *The Abbāsī Policy towards the City*

Throughout the Umawī caliphate and particularly from the reign of Hishām b. ʿAbd al-Malik, there was a slow decline in Medina's economic and geo-political status. With the ʿAbbāsīs' rise to power, this process was accelerated by the first two ʿAbbāsī caliphs' deliberate policy of giving preference to al-ʿIrāq and the eastern provinces, mainly Khurāsān, a lack of investment in Syria[1] and al-Ḥijāz, and massive confiscations of the properties and estates of the Umawīs and their supporters. The ʿAbbāsīs changed the custom of beginning the *iḥrām* (the sanctification ceremony of the pilgrims) from Medina. At the same time a gradual change occurred in the *ḥajj* route from the land to the sea. These processes and measures caused the deterioration of the socio-political and economic foundations of Medina.[2]

Looking in a more detailed manner into the confiscation of property and estates by the ʿAbbāsīs, we can see this as a general process encompassing the entire caliphal domains,[3] and as mentioned above, it also occurred in the Arabian Peninsula. The evidence is clear cut,[4] and bears witness to the confiscation of estates, but in some cases the chronological element is not entirely clear, that is, we do not know the specific dates of confiscations, and whether they took place immediately upon the accession of the ʿAbbāsīs. It is highly plausible, though, that when the expression "صارت في الصوافي" appears in the sources (that is, a certain estate was confiscated and became included in

1 For Syria under the early ʿAbbāsīs, see Cobb, *White Banners*, esp. 3–6, 17, 21f., 31, 44f., 67ff., 81f., 101–102.

2 This is a summary of Arazi's important discussion, "Mekke et Medine," 198–204; see also al-Ali, "*Mulkiyyāt*," 968, 971, 1004; Lassner, "Administration," 49; idem, *Shaping*, 69–79; Elad, "The Rebellion of Muhammad b. Abdallah, 185–186" (followed by Ahmed, *Religious Elite*, 159, n. 854); Munt's new book, *The Holy City of Medina*, undoubtedly sheds a new and important light on Medina during the seventh to ninth centuries.

3 For evidence (mainly for Syria), see Elad, "Two Inscriptions," 245–247.

4 Many of them were collected by Arazi, "Mekke et Medine," 202, note.

 | DOI 10.1163/9789004296220_005

the corpus of confiscated lands under a special *dīwān*),[5] it refers to the beginning of ʿAbbāsī rule.[6]

However, some evidence of the confiscation of estates by the first ʿAbbāsī caliph, Abū l-ʿAbbās al-Saffāḥ is clear-cut.[7] The confiscations were of Umawī property (with no mention of a specific family),[8] Marwānīs,[9] Sufyānīs,[10] and members of the Jaʿfarī family.[11]

5 For a discussion of the term *ṣawāfī* in the early ʿAbbāsī period, see Elad, "Two Inscriptions," 347 and the bibliography therein.

6 Al-Samhūdī, *Wafāʾ*, 3:22: Dār al-Qaḍāʾ in Medina: فصارت بعد في الصوافي; 49: Dār Marwān: فصارت في الصوافي; Ibn Shabba, *Taʾrīkh al-Madīna*, 1:233–234 (= al-Samhūdī [ed. al-Sāmarrāʾī], *Wafāʾ*, 3:22): فصارت في الصوافي... فهدمها أبو العباس أمير المؤمنين.

Al-Sāmarrāʾī, the editor of *Wafāʾ al-wafāʾ*, changed the name of the caliph to Abū Jaʿfar al-Manṣūr for historical-chronological reasons, see ibid., 22, n. 6. Indeed, according to Ibn Shabba, *Taʾrīkh al-Madīna*, 1:234 (= al-Samhūdī, *Wafāʾ*, 3:23), Dār al-Qaḍāʾ was demolished in 138/755 or 756 during al-Manṣūr's reign. This was most probably the case of al-Fayd, which was owned by a *mawlā* of the last Umawī governor of al-ʿIrāq, Yazīd b. ʿUmar b. Hubayra, and was confiscated by Banū l-ʿAbbās, see al-Bakrī, *Muʿjam*, 3:1033 ("Fayd"). On Yazīd b. ʿUmar b. Hubayra and his family, see Crone, *Slaves*, 107; Elad, "Wāsiṭ"; see also al-Samhūdī, *Wafāʾ*, 4:93: ʿAyn Ḍariyya and its running water upon the surface of the earth (عين ضرية وسيحها) was confiscated by the ʿAbbāsīs when they established their rule; the term أبيات الصوافي (in Medina), most probably denotes the houses confiscated by the ʿAbbāsīs, see al-Samhūdī, *Wafāʾ*, 3:14–15; Arazi, "Mekke et Medine," 202, note.

7 Abū l-ʿAbbās confiscated the estate called al-Bughaybigha from the family of ʿAbdallāh b. Jaʿfar b. Abī Ṭālib. He returned it to the ʿAlīds following a request from ʿAbdallāh b. al-Ḥasan but it was confiscated again by al-Manṣūr (most probably following Muḥammad b. ʿAbdallāh's rebellion), see Ibn Shabba, *Taʾrīkh al-Madīna*, 1:222 [= al-Samhūdī, *Wafāʾ*, 4:165 (quoted by al-Ali, "Mulkiyyāt," 973–974)]; al-Ḥāzimī, *al-Amākin*, 2:259; Yāqūt, *Muʿjam* (ed. Wüstenfeld), 1:696–698; for a different version of the history of this estate after the reign of al-al-Saffāḥ, see al-Samhūdī, *Wafāʾ*, 3:417 (= al-Fīrūzābādī, *al-Maghānim al-muṭāba*, 312–313): Abū l-ʿAbbās confiscated lands belonging to Marwān b. Muḥammad and gave them to al-Ḥasan b. al-Ḥasan b. ʿAlī b. Abī Ṭālib (quoted by al-Ali, "Mulkiyyāt," 993). This caliph also gave Ziyād b. ʿUbaydallāh, his maternal uncle and governor of Medina, a large residence, a palace (*dār*) which is defined as a *qaṭīʿa* (on this kind of estate, see, *EI*², "Iḳṭāʿ" and "Ḍayʿa" [Cl. Cahen]; al-Dūrī, "The Origins of Iqṭāʿ in Islam," *al-Abḥāth* [1969], 22:3–22). According to al-Balādhurī, *Ansāb* (ed. Madelung), 2:501, "this *dār* is located in al-Balāṭ, and is called Dār Muʿāwiya."

8 Al-Samhūdī, *Wafāʾ*, 4:35: no name of a family is given.

9 Ibid., 3:49.

10 Ibid., 4:93.

11 Ibn Shabba, *Taʾrīkh al-Madīna*, 1:232 (= al-Samhūdī, *Wafāʾ*, 2:295); Arazi, "Mekke et Medine," 202, note; al-Ali, "Mulkiyyāt."

This analysis of the politico-economic aspects of Medina during the beginning of the ʿAbbāsī rule is compatible with Lassner's analysis of the literary motifs revealed in the sources, which tell, on the one hand, of al-Manṣūr consulting with several of his confidential advisers when he first learned about the rebellion of Muḥammad and Ibrāhīm and, on the other hand, tell of Muḥammad b. ʿAbdallāh consulting with his confidential counselors. Both sides' advisers' recommendations and conclusions are paradoxically similar; they all bear witness to the low military-strategic importance of Medina in this period.[12]

The deterioration of the politico-economic situation of Medina was undoubtedly one of the main reasons for the outbreak of the rebellion in the city. An in-depth detailed study of Medina's social structure would add a significant layer to our understanding of the social background of the rebellion. Suffice it to mention at this point the fact that a large number of Muḥammad's most distinguished adherents belonged to the "noble" and highly-important Zubayrī family. This family was known already in the Jāhiliyya period and during the first two hundred years of Islamic rule as a rich family of great wealth that included many estates around Medina and elsewhere in Arabia. Many of them joined Muḥammad's cause, and played important roles in the rebellion. Their support for Muḥammad b. ʿAbdallāh—in spite of the historical animosity between the Zubayrīs and the ʿAlīds—may testify to the frustration and resentment of the Zubayrīs with the ʿAbbāsī policy.[13]

Despite the points raised above, Medina still held a certain importance for the ʿAbbāsīs, for the following reasons:

a) First and most important was the city's religious importance for the Muslim community—this in spite of the ʿAbbāsī endeavors to reduce its standing.[14]
b) The different families of the ʿAlīds, ʿAbbāsīs, of the Quraysh and al-Anṣār lived in Medina. They were the most important families of the Muslim community, comprising pre-Islamic "nobility" as well as new Islamic "nobility."

The fact that the rebellion was led by Muḥammad b. ʿAbdallāh b. al-Ḥasan was of great importance. His lineage and claim to the right to rule competed

12 Lassner, "Administration," 49.

13 On the Zubayrīs' estates, see chapter 8; Arazi, "Mekke et Medine," 189–190. This family and its attitude towards the rebellion are discussed in chapter 8.

14 Lassner, "Administration," 52; Landau-Tasseron, "Arabia," 403–404.

successfully with the arguments for the ʿAbbāsīs' legitimacy; at that time the latter were in a stage of transition, namely, from the legitimacy of the ʿAlīd-Hāshimiyya to that of al-ʿAbbās, the Prophet's uncle.

One of the main and crucial issues that engaged the ʿAbbāsīs from the day they rose to power was the question of their legitimacy to rule. It is no accident that Abū l-ʿAbbās al-Saffāḥ, the first ʿAbbāsī caliph, was nicknamed al-Mahdī, who is depicted in the traditions spread around the end of the Umawī period as the Messiah who will do away with oppression and injustice and bring salvation, peace, and security to the world.[15] At such an early stage after their ascent to the caliphate, the ʿAbbāsīs could not and would not bear any opposition that would undermine their legitimacy to rule.

This seems to be the main reason that compelled Abū l-ʿAbbās al-Saffāḥ to bestow presents and abundant sums of money upon ʿAbdallāh b. al-Ḥasan, as well as upon other ʿAlīds, and to marry his son Muḥammad to Zaynab, Muḥammad b. ʿAbdallāh's daughter. Al-Manṣūr also tried this policy of pacification at first. Al-Zubayr b. Bakkār reports that the large sums of money which al-Manṣūr bestowed were unprecedented. He gave large sums of money to the distinguished persons of Medina, especially to the ashrāf of Quraysh, to whom he gave 1000 *dīnār*s each. Not by accident, al-Zubayr b. Bakkār names only one of the ashrāf, Hishām b. ʿUrwa b. al-Zubayr, who was a relative.[16] Al-Manṣūr performed the *ḥajj* in 136/754 (before he became caliph), in 140/758, 144/762, and 152/769.[17] The accepted date of Hishām b. ʿUrwa's death is 146/763–764.[18] The event recorded by al-Zubayr b. Bakkār could have occurred either in 140 H. or in 144 H. It would seem that 140 is a better choice, as 144 may have been too late for al-Manṣūr. However, some traditions tell about an alleged discussion between al-Manṣūr and ʿĪsā b. Mūsā, before the latter was sent at the head of the ʿAbbāsī army against Muḥammad b. ʿAbdallāh. It is reported that the caliph ordered him to do his best to end the rebellion without bloodshed and unnecessary harm to Medinan dignitaries and to give the city's people safe conduct (*amān*),[19] and not to behave like Muslim b. ʿUqba or al-Ḥajjāj b. Yūsuf

---

15 Elad, "The *Ḥadīth* of al-Mahdī," esp. 39–43.

16 Al-Zubayr b. Bakkār, *Jamhara*, 303.

17 Al-Ṭabarī, 3:129, 172–173, 369 (respectively).

18 Other dates for his death are 145/762 or 763, or 147/764 or 765. He died in Baghdad. I was unable to ascertain the date he arrived in that city; on Hishām b. ʿUrwa, see Sezgin, 1:81–82; al-Mizzī, *Tahdhīb*, 30:232–241; Arazi, "Mekke et Medine"; and the discussion in chapter 7, 290f. chapter 8, 321f., and appendix 1, 367f.

19 Al-Ṭabarī, 3:225 (ll. 1–6); al-Balādhurī, *Ansāb* (ed. Madelung), 2:512–513.

(who were famous for their harsh measures, cruelty and tyranny).[20] The gist of this alleged conversation may have reflected al-Manṣūr's desire to cause as little tension as possible between the ʿAbbāsī regime and the ʿAlīds and other important families from among Quraysh and the Anṣār; but on the other hand, we have the context of an alleged[?] letter of al-Manṣūr to the Arab inhabitants of Medina and their *mawālī* (*ahl al-Madīna*) in which he threatens them, using harsh abusive terms. From the day he ascended the throne al-Manṣūr demonstrated a firm and uncompromising attitude towards the people of Medina when searching for the two brothers. Riyāḥ b. ʿUthmān was appointed governor of Medina entirely because of his blood relation to Muslim b. ʿUqba. Al-Manṣūr urged him to take harsh measures against the city's inhabitants, and indeed, he complied with the caliph's orders.[21]

The ʿAbbāsīs' economic interests in Medina served as another important factor; as noted above, the first ʿAbbāsī caliph confiscated buildings and estates from the Umawīs (and others) in Medina and its surroundings. Other members of the ʿAbbāsī family had some economic interests (estates and other kinds of properties) in Medina.[22]

1.2 *The ʿAbbāsīs and the Governors of Medina*

1.2.1 Introduction

It is plausible that Muḥammad b. ʿAbdallāh and his brother Ibrāhīm presented a real challenge to the ʿAbbāsīs' right to rule already during the reign of the first caliph, Abū l-ʿAbbās. The governors of Medina faced this challenge that quickly became a danger, and had to deal with it in their territory.

This problem decisively influenced al-Manṣūr's appointments of the governors of Medina. None of these governors belonged to the ʿAbbāsī family. Ziyād b. ʿUbaydallāh, al-Saffāḥ's maternal uncle, was dismissed from office in 141/758. His relationship to the ʿAbbāsīs and his being an important leader of the tribe of al-Ḥārith b. Kaʿb prevented al-Manṣūr from taking harsh steps towards him.

20 Ibn ʿAbd Rabbihi, *al-ʿIqd*, 5:86–87.

21 Al-Yaʿqūbī, *Taʾrīkh* (ed. Houtsma), 2:452.

22 ʿĪsā b. Mūsā had estates in Medina. His slave (*ghulām*) Saʿīd b. Dīnār was in charge of them (al-Ṭabarī, 3:205 (ll. 17–18)); al-Samhūdī, *Wafāʾ*, 3:49: Dār Yazīd b. ʿAbd al-Malik in Medina became the property of Zubayda bt. Jaʿfar b. al-Manṣūr, Hārūn al-Rashīd's wife; on her projects in Arabia along the *ḥajj* road, see Rāshid, *Darb Zubayda*, 31–35 (= the Arabic translation, 65–69). Al-Samhūdī, *Wafāʾ*, 3:56: mentioning buildings and properties belonging to the Barmakīs in Medina. It is highly plausible that they were purchased (probably confiscated, perhaps even immediately) upon the ascendance of the ʿAbbāsīs to rule; for other evidence about the ʿAbbāsī property in Medina, see the discussion of Muḥammad's entry to Medina in chapter 3.

According to an alleged conversation between al-Manṣūr and ʿĪsā b. Mūsā, the latter suggested sending a member of the ʿAbbāsī family to be governor of Medina. Al-Manṣūr objected to this suggestion, saying that blood relations would prevent such a person from taking hard measures against, and ill-treating, the family of Abū Ṭālib. In that case, suggested ʿĪsā, send someone from *ahl Khurāsān*, and al-Manṣūr answered "that the love for the family of Abū Ṭālib is merged in the hearts of *ahl Khurāsān* with the love towards us" (i.e., the ʿAbbāsī family). Al-Manṣūr continued, saying that he reached the conclusion that a governor must be chosen from among the *ahl al-Shām*, because of their hatred and constant struggle with the ʿAlīds. This was the reason he chose Riyāḥ b. ʿUthmān al-Murrī as the governor of Medina.[23]

Whether or not this conversation ever took place, it beautifully and convincingly represents al-Manṣūr's considerations in choosing his governor, Riyāḥ. This reasoning may also explain the choice of Muḥammad b. Khālid b. ʿAbdallāh al-Qasrī, the son of the well-known governor of al-ʿIrāq during Hishām b. ʿAbd al-Malik's reign, as governor after Ziyād b. ʿUbaydallāh. From the traditions we learn that he had substantial influence in Syria, as is evident from, e.g., the tradition according to which he sent his *mawlā* Rizām to Syria in order, allegedly, to conduct propaganda on behalf of Muḥammad b. ʿAbdallāh b. al-Ḥasan[24] (on Riyāḥ and Muḥammad b. Khālid, see the discussion below).

Although this tradition is filled with imaginary anecdotal material, it reflects an accepted opinion, or an opinion that could have been accepted as true and faithful to reality, about the close connection between the famous Umawī governor's son with the Arabs of Syria.

1.3 *The Governors of Medina (136–145/754–762)*

1.3.1 Ziyād b. ʿUbaydallāh b. ʿAbdallāh b. ʿAbd al-Madān al-Ḥārithī[25]

Abū l-ʿAbbās's policy, and to a lesser extent that of Abū Jaʿfar al-Manṣūr, was to appoint family members as governors of important towns and districts,[26] except for Khurāsān, to which persons from *ahl Khurāsān* and *al-Abnāʾ* were appointed.[27] As for Medina, the situation was different because of the special circumstances caused by the rebellion of Muḥammad b. ʿAbdallāh.

---

23 Al-Balādhurī, *Ansāb* (ed. Madelung), 2:520–521.

24 Ibid., 2:509; al-Ṭabarī, 3:215–216 (l. 15 to l. 10); Rizām is mentioned as the secretary (*kātib*) of Muḥammad b. Khālid al-Qasrī, see al-Balādhurī, *Ansāb* (ed. Madelung), 2:502 (l. 19).

25 On him, see Crone, *Slaves*, 149; see also Ibn ʿAsākir, *Taʾrīkh*, 19:156–162.

26 Lassner, *Shaping*, 77.

27 Crone, *Slaves*, 66; Kennedy, *ʿAbbāsid Caliphate*, 179; Elad, "Transition," 99, n. 43.

Ziyād b. ʿUbaydallāh b. ʿAbd al-Madān al-Ḥārithī, the governor of Medina who was chosen by the first caliph, Abū l-ʿAbbās, remained in office during al-Manṣūr's reign. As already mentioned, Ziyād was the maternal uncle of Abū l-ʿAbbās al-Saffāḥ from the family of ʿAbd al-Madān from al-Ḥārith b. Kaʿb. Families from this tribe had important roles in the ʿAbbāsī *daʿwa*.[28]

Ziyād was not completely devoted to searching for Muḥammad b. ʿAbdallāh.[29] At the end of 140/April 758, during his *ḥajj*, al-Manṣūr ordered him to place ʿAbdallāh b. al-Ḥasan under house arrest.[30] According to one tradition, Ziyād did not follow the caliph's command to kill ʿAbdallāh b. al-Ḥasan, rather he showed soft-heartedness toward him and arranged for comfortable conditions for him. As a result, he was discharged from office by al-Manṣūr in 141/758,[31] and a fine of 80,000 *dīnār*s was imposed on him.[32]

In that year the caliph sent some contingents to Medina headed by Abū l-Azhar,[33] in whose hands he entrusted letters of dismissal of Ziyād, and ordered the imprisonment of the governor and his relatives in Medina.[34] However, his status as a relative of the family, especially his relation to his brother, al-Saffāḥ,

28 On the importance of this tribe in connection with the ʿAbbāsī *daʿwa*, see Sharon, *Black Banners*, 141–145. On the relations of the ʿAbbāsī caliphs with this tribe, see Elad, *ʿAbbāsid Army*, 98–99; Elad, "Transition," 101, n. 57 and 125–126.

29 Al-Ṭabarī, 3:147–148, 158; Ibn Saʿd, *al-Qism al-mutammim*, 254; al-Balādhurī, *Ansāb* (ed. Madelung), 2:502.

30 Al-Balādhurī, *Ansāb* (ed. Madelung), 2:501; al-Ṭabarī, 3:152–153, reports his arrest in 140 AH. with no mention of Ziyād.

31 Al-Ṭabarī, 3:137, 159.

32 Ibn Ḥabīb, *al-Mughtālīn*, 207.

33 An ʿAbbāsī commander belonging to *ahl Khurāsān* army units. Like other dignitaries of *ahl Khurāsān* and *al-Abnāʾ* (e.g. Khālid b. Barmak and others), he was the *mawlā* of the caliph (al-Ṭabarī, 3:185 (ll. 1–2)). One source calls him[?] al-Tamīmī—see al-Khaṭīb al-Baghdādī, *Taʾrīkh* (Hyderabad edition), 1:77, where a commander named Abū l-Azhar al-Tamīmī, at the head of 1,000 soldiers, is in charge of the safekeeping of the al-Baṣra gate to Baghdad; but see al-Ṭabarī, 3:169 (l. 14), where he is named al-Mahrī, that is, from Banū Mahra of Quḍāʿa (on them, see Ibn Ḥazm, *Jamhara*, 485). He is first mentioned there in 141/758 or 759, when he was sent to arrest the governor Ziyād b. ʿUbaydallāh (see al-Ṭabarī, 3:159, where he is mentioned as "*rajul min ahl Khurāsān*"); he was sent by al-Manṣūr to Medina, imprisoned the Ḥasanīs, took them to al-Rabadha (al-Ṭabarī, 3:174; al-Iṣfahānī, *Maqātil*, 219, 223), and then to al-Hāshimiyya (al-Ṭabarī, 3:182), where he was entrusted with guarding them (ibid., 184; al-Balādhurī, *Ansāb* [ed. Madelung], 2:504; al-Iṣfahānī, *Maqātil*, 225), and there he (most probably) killed ʿAbdallāh b. al-Ḥasan (al-Ṭabarī, 3:185; al-Iṣfahānī, *Maqātil*, 226–227).

34 Al-Ṭabarī, 3:159–160.

prevented al-Manṣūr from executing him.[35] An example of this special status can be gleaned from the following story about Ziyād's secretary, Ḥafṣ b. ʿUmar from *ahl al-Kūfa*, who had Shīʿī sympathies (*yatashayyaʿ*) and used to obstruct Ziyād's search efforts. When al-Manṣūr became aware of this, he ordered the secretary to be brought to him. Trying to save his secretary, Ziyād sent letters on his behalf to ʿĪsā b. ʿAlī, the caliph's uncle, and to his nephew, ʿAbdallāh b. al-Rabīʿ b. ʿUbaydallāh, the governor of Yemen.[36] Their intercession on the secretary's behalf was successful and he was released and came back to Ziyād.[37]

1.3.2 ʿAbd al-ʿAzīz b. al-Muṭṭalib b. ʿAbdallāh

ʿAbd al-ʿAzīz b. al-Muṭṭalib b. ʿAbdallāh, the *qāḍī* of Medina,[38] was appointed (for a short term) as the governor replacing Ziyād b. ʿUbaydallāh. After his short term in office, he continued to serve as the *qāḍī* of Medina. According to most of the sources, he belonged to the family of Makhzūm (Quraysh),[39] but one source relates that he was of the family of Kathīr b. al-Ṣalt,[40] who belonged to one of the sub-tribes of Kinda.[41] Kathīr b. al-Ṣalt lived in Medina,[42] most probably with some of his brothers.[43] This exceptional, single tradition is of interest since Kathīr b. al-Ṣalt belonged to the family of the woman ʿAbdallāh b. al-ʿAbbās married.[44] Thus, if this lineage is correct, ʿAbd al-ʿAzīz b. al-Muṭṭalib

35 Ibid.

36 On him, see Crone, *Slaves*, 149.

37 Al-Ṭabarī, 3:147–148: ʿUmar b. Shabba < Muḥammad b. Yaḥyā < his father < his grandfather (ʿAlī); al-Balādhurī, *Ansāb* (ed. Madelung), 2:501 (= *Fragmenta*, 233): the secretary's name is Ḥafṣ; the caliph's nephew's name is ʿĪsā b. Mūsā (b. Muḥammad b. ʿAlī b. ʿAbdallāh b. al-ʿAbbās); the information about the secretary was revealed to al-Manṣūr by a "secret agent," a spy (*ʿayn*) of al-Manṣūr in Medina, ʿAbd al-ʿAzīz b. Saʿīd.

38 Al-Balādhurī, *Ansāb* (ed. Madelung), 2:502; al-Ṭabarī, 3:159–160.

39 Ibn al-Kalbī, *Jamhara* (ed. Ḥasan), 92; al-Zubayrī, *Nasab Quraysh*, 341; Ibn Saʿd, *al-Qism al-mutammim*, 460–461; Wakīʿ, *Quḍāt*, 1:202–210; Ibn Ḥajar, *Tahdhīb* (Hyderabad edition), 6:357–358; al-Mizzī, *Tahdhīb*, 18:206–208, and the comprehensive bibliography on him by the editor; Ahmed, *Religious Elite*, 88–89; Bernheimer, *The ʿAlids*, 40, n. 29 (according to al-Zubayrī).

40 Al-Balādhurī, *Ansāb* (ed. Madelung), 2:502.

41 I.e., to al-Ḥārith b. ʿAmr b. Muʿāwiya, see Ibn Ḥazm, *Jamhara*, 428; Ibn al-Kalbī, *Nasab maʿadd*, 1:176; idem, *Jamhara* (ed. Caskel), I, no. 239.

42 Ibn Ḥazm, *Jamhara*, 428.

43 Ibn al-Kalbī, *Nasab maʿadd*, 1:176: the text seems to be garbled.

44 He married Zurʿa (or Zuhra) bt. Mishraḥ b. Maʿdī Karib b. Walīʿa; see Ibn al-Kalbī, *Nasab maʿadd*, 1:176; al-Balādhurī, *Ansāb* (ed. al-Dūrī), 3:70: Zurʿa; Ibn Ḥazm, *Jamhara*, 19: Zuhra; al-Zubayrī, *Nasab Quraysh*, 28–29: Zurʿa. See also al-Azdī, *Taʾrīkh al-Mawṣil*, 234–235. For a

was related to the ʿAbbāsīs on his mother's side. But this lineage is mentioned in only one source.[45] When the new governor, Muḥammad b. Khālid, arrived in the city, ʿAbd al-ʿAzīz was reinstated as the *qāḍī*.[46]

1.3.3 Muḥammad b. Khālid b. ʿAbdallāh al-Qasrī[47]

Muḥammad reached Medina at the beginning of Rajab 141/November 758 with specific orders from the caliph to exert every effort to search for Muḥammad b. ʿAbdallāh.[48] Some traditions testify, as in the case of his predecessor, Ziyād, that Muḥammad b. Khālid did not try too hard to locate Muḥammad and Ibrāhīm.[49] Other traditions testify to the contrary, i.e., to the huge efforts and detailed planning by Muḥammad b. Khālid in searching for the two brothers.[50] On the other hand, they describe how, in the course of his futile search for Muḥammad b. ʿAbdallāh, he emptied the treasure house in Medina; these two elements, the failure to attain the target, and the large expenditures involved, led al-Manṣūr to discharge him and appoint Riyāḥ b. ʿUthmān in his place.

1.3.4 Riyāḥ b. ʿUthmān

Immediately upon entering Medina (on 23 Ramaḍān 144/5 January 761), the new governor arrested Muḥammad b. Khālid and his secretary, a *mawlā* named Rizām. The conditions of imprisonment were most uncomfortable, especially for the *mawlā* secretary, whom the new governor, Riyāḥ, used to summon every day for interrogation. During these interrogations, the governor sought incriminating details about Rizām's former master (يطالبه أن يسعى بصاحبه), and when he refused, he was flogged.[51] It is unclear what it was that the new governor wanted to uncover: a hidden treasure? A detailed report of all the

discussion on the importance of the lineage of the uncle from the mother's side, see Elad, "al-Maʾmūn's Army," 311–316, where the case of ʿAbdallāh b. al-ʿAbbās is discussed.

45 Perhaps at a certain stage, a connection was established between the clan of ʿAbd al-ʿAzīz (Makhzūm) and some families (or a family) from Kinda.

46 Wakīʿ, *Quḍāt*, 1:202. On him, see also chapter 3, no. 3.2 and chapter 7 (part 1), G, no. 3.2.

47 On this family, see Crone, *Slaves*, 102–103; on Muḥammad, see ibid., 102; al-Dīnawarī, *al-Akhbār al-ṭiwāl* (Cairo edition), 345, 349–350 (the Umawī period); 367–369 (his attitude towards the ʿAbbāsī army); Ibn ʿAsākir, *Taʾrīkh*, 52:384–386.

48 Al-Ṭabarī, 3:161.

49 Ibn Saʿd, *al-Qism al-mutammim*, 254; al-Balādhurī, *Ansāb* (ed. Madelung), 2:502 (= *Fragmenta*, 235).

50 Al-Ṭabarī, 3:161.

51 Al-Jahshiyārī, *al-Wuzarāʾ*, 124.

expenditures in regard to the searches and pursuit of Muḥammad and his brother?[52] Or a confession regarding support for Muḥammad b. ʿAbdallāh?

Muḥammad b. Khālid and his secretary stayed in prison until Muḥammad b. ʿAbdallāh came out in open rebellion and released them. After their release, Rizām led the force that broke into the governor's palace (*dār al-imāra*) and arrested the ʿAbbāsī governor, Riyāḥ b. ʿUthmān. Muḥammad b. Khālid's nephew, al-Nadhīr b. Yazīd, was ordered to ensure the safety of Riyāḥ and his close associates: بالاستيثاق من رياح وأصحابه.[53]

But later, relations between the ex-governor and Muḥammad b. ʿAbdallāh cooled down. The history of the relations between the two after Muḥammad b. Khālid was released from prison do not testify to any loyalty whatsoever to Muḥammad b. ʿAbdallāh and his rebellion, but rather to his loyalty to Caliph al-Manṣūr and the ʿAbbāsīs;[54] therefore he was re-arrested by Muḥammad b. ʿAbdallāh and imprisoned until the revolt ended.[55]

Riyāḥ's nomination was not merely by chance; it was decided upon following sound and balanced judgment and consultations.[56] Clearly his tribal lineage was inferior in comparison to that of the preceding Yemeni governors—indeed this could only have made it easier for the caliph, since his dependency upon the caliph would be much greater. However, it does not seem that this fact should be given much weight in the overall consideration of al-Manṣūr.[57]

---

52 See for example, al-Ṭabarī, 3:164, where he reports that Riyāḥ asks Muḥammad b. Khālid regarding the money (? in plural form: *al-amwāl*); Muḥammad does not answer and directs Riyāḥ to his secretary, Rizām. *Amwāl* can be rendered as money, wealth, estates and so forth; McAuliffe, *ʿAbbāsid Authority*, 111, translates it as "the [public] funds."

53 Al-Ṭabarī, 3:196 (ll. 4–12); in translating the word "*aṣḥābihi*" I followed the translation of McAuliffe, *ʿAbbāsid Authority*, 151; the names of al-Nadhīr and Rizām as well as this affair should be added to the biographies of this family in Crone, *Slaves*, 102–103.

54 Al-Balādhurī, *Ansāb* (ed. Madelung), 2:509 (= *Fragmenta*, 239–240); al-Ṭabarī, 3:215–216 (l. 15 to l. 10).

55 Al-Balādhurī, *Ansāb* (ed. Madelung), 2:510; al-Ṭabarī, 3:242 (ll. 6–12).

56 al-Ṭabarī, 3:162, 163, where it is stated that he was chosen due to the intercession of al-Rabīʿ, the *mawlā* of al-Manṣūr.

57 But cf. Omar, *ʿAbbāsid Caliphate*, 221: "He was a Syrian, a Qaysite and of humble origin," followed by Williams, *Early ʿAbbāsī Empire*, 1:63, n. 123: "Riyāḥ b. ʿUthmān b. Ḥayyān al-Murrī was a Syrian, a Qaysī and a nobody … and he was completely beholden to al-Manṣūr. …" Ibn ʿAsākir, *Taʾrīkh*, 18:365, records his lineage thus:

رياح بن عثمان بن حيان بن معبد بن شداد بن نعمان ابن رياح بن اسعد بن ربيعة بن عامر ابن يربوع بن غيظ بن مرة بن عوف بن سعد بن ذبيان ابن بغيض بن ريث بن غطفان بن سعد بن قيس عيلان أبو المغراء المري

It should be noted that Riyāḥ was most probably a courtier already during the Umawī period. Traditions mention him in the court of ʿUmar b. ʿAbd al-ʿAzīz (r. 99–101/717–720) at the side of the well-known scholar and statesman Rajāʾ b. Ḥaywa al-Kindī (d. 112/730), giving advice to the caliph.[58] Before his appointment as the governor of Medina during al-Manṣūr's caliphate, for a certain period, he was governor of Damascus on behalf of the general governor of Syria, the caliph's uncle, Ṣāliḥ b. ʿAlī b. ʿAbdallāh b. al-ʿAbbās, and also a governor of Egypt on behalf of the caliph.[59] Riyāḥ had other qualities which caused al-Manṣūr to send him to Medina, i.e., his connection with Medina was twofold. The first was through his father, ʿUthmān b. Ḥayyān, who served as the governor of the city during the reign of al-Walīd b. ʿAbd al-Malik (r. 86–96/705–715) for three years (93–96/712–715) and whose rule was distinguished as being tough and uncompromising.[60] The second connection is Riyāḥ's kinship with Muslim b. ʿUqba al-Murrī, Yazīd b. Muʿāwiya's general, who massacred the people of Medina in the battle of al-Ḥarra in 63/683.[61]

When ascending to the *minbar*, immediately upon his arrival in Medina (on Friday, 23 Ramaḍān 144/26 December 761),[62] Riyāḥ emphasized this relationship, telling his audience that he would follow and pursue the policy of

---

but in the biography of his father he asserts that he was a *mawlā* of Umm Dardāʾ or of ʿUtba b. Abī Sufyān b. Ḥarb[!]: مولى أم الدرداء ويقال مولى عتبة بن أبي سفيان بن حرب (Ibn ʿAsākir, *Taʾrīkh*, 38:338); this fact[?] does not appear in the *nasab* books, e.g., Ibn al-Kalbī, *Jamhara* (ed. Ḥasan), 422; al-Balādhurī, *Ansāb* (ed. Zakkār), 13:132; Ibn Ḥazm, *Jamhara*, 254. A certain Ḥayyān is mentioned in the sources (without naming his father and grandfather) as the *mawlā* of Umm al-Dardāʾ, see Ibn ʿAsākir, *Taʾrīkh*, 15:376–377; see also ibid., 22:357; 26:272, where he appears as a transmitter in an *isnād*; but see al-Mizzī, *Tahdhīb*, 35:356: عن عثمان بن حيان مولى أم الدرداء.

58 Ibn ʿAsākir, *Taʾrīkh*, 18:266 (his biography, ibid., 18:265–272); Sibṭ b. al-Jawzī, *Mirʾāt al-zamān*, fol. 283b (from al-Zubayr b. Bakkār); on Rajāʾ b. Ḥaywa, see Bosworth, "Rajāʾ"; Gil, *Palestine*, 121, no. 153; Elad, *Jerusalem*, 19, n. 65; Ibn ʿAsākir, *Taʾrīkh*, 18:96–116; al-Mizzī, *Tahdhīb*, 9:151–157, and the exhaustive bibliography therein.

59 Ibn ʿAsākir, *Taʾrīkh*, 18:265, 267; Sibṭ b. al-Jawzī, *Mirʾāt al-zamān*, fol. 283b; on Ṣāliḥ b. ʿAlī, see Ibn ʿAsākir, *Taʾrīkh*, 23:357–359; he was appointed the governor of Syria already in 137/754, ibid., 23:358; Cobb, *White Banners*, index.

60 On his rule, see al-Ṭabarī, 2:1254, 1255, 1258, 1266, 1281; his tough and uncompromising policy: ibid., 2:1259–1261; for his biographies, see for example, Ibn ʿAsākir, *Taʾrīkh*, 38:338–348; Ibn Ḥajar, *Tahdhīb* (Beirut, 1984), 7:104–105; al-Mizzī, *Tahdhīb*, 19:360–363.

61 On the genealogy of the families and the relations between them, see Ibn al-Kalbī, *Jamhara* (ed. Caskel), I, table 127; idem (ed. Ḥasan), 422; al-Balādhurī, *Ansāb* (ed. Zakkār), 13:132; Ibn Ḥazm, *Jamhara*, 254; on the battle, see Kister, "al-Ḥarra."

62 Al-Ṭabarī, 3:162.

his cousin, Muslim b. ʿUqba.[63] According to another tradition he said that he was the viper, the son of the viper, that is, ʿUthmān b. Ḥayyān, on the one hand, and the cousin of Muslim b. ʿUqba, on the other hand.[64]

The definition of Riyāḥ as رجل من أهل الشام, that is, an Arab from the Arabs of Syria, i.e., a man with an uncompromising hatred for the ʿAlīds, was supposedly said by al-Manṣūr in a conversation that, even if invented, was beautifully invented, and certainly reflects the real background of the selection of Riyāḥ as the governor of Medina.[65]

The background of the new governor, who took care to stress it during his first *khuṭba*, and his persistent search for Muḥammad and Ibrāhīm, caused permanent tension and hostility between him and the notables of Medina.[66] The most distinguished among these figures were men from Quraysh, on whom Riyāḥ based his military force, who on the crucial day, that is when the rebellion broke out, did not prove their loyalty.[67]

Riyāḥ was imprisoned when the revolt broke out. He was kept there till shortly before Muḥammad b. ʿAbdallāh was killed, after which he was killed together with his brother by Ibrāhīm b. Muṣʿab b. Muṣʿab b. al-Zubayr, known as Ibn Khuḍayr, one of Muḥammad's most loyal supporters.[68]

2 The Imprisonment of the Ḥasanīs and Their Death

2.1 *The Imprisonment of ʿAbdallāh b. al-Ḥasan and His Family in 140/758*

ʿAbdallāh b. al-Ḥasan was imprisoned for the first time at the end of the year 140/April–May 758 by order of Caliph al-Manṣūr,[69] most probably with other

63 Al-Balādhurī, *Ansāb* (ed. Madelung), 2:521; see also Sibṭ b. al-Jawzī, *Mirʾāt al-zamān*, fol. 283b.

64 Al-Yaʿqūbī, *Taʾrīkh* (ed. Houtsma), 2:452.

65 Al-Balādhurī, *Ansāb* (ed. Madelung), 2:520–521.

66 Al-Yaʿqūbī, *Taʾrīkh* (ed. Houtsma), 2:452.

67 Al-Ṭabarī, 3:192, 196; see also al-Mubarrad, *al-Kāmil*, 1:28: verses of the poet Ibn Mayyāda, who advises him not to put his confidence in the people of Quraysh; al-Iṣfahānī, *al-Aghānī* (Būlāq edition), 2:119, has a more detailed report, he advises the governor to establish a personal guard and army (*ḥaras wa-jund*) from Ghaṭafān and to leave the slaves (*al-ʿabīd*) to whom he gave his *dirhams*, and also to beware of Quraysh.

68 Al-Ṭabarī, 3:242 (ll. 1–12); see also 3:241 (ll. 15–16), where his brother is not mentioned; Sibṭ b. al-Jawzī, *Mirʾāt al-zamān*, fol. 283b; see also the discussion on Riyāḥ by Omar, *ʿAbbāsid Caliphate*, 220–222.

69 Al-Ṭabarī, 3:152–153 (= al-Iṣfahānī, *al-Aghānī* [Būlāq ed], 18:208).

members of his family.[70] At first they were kept in one of the rooms of Dār Marwān.[71]

Riyāḥ b. ʿUthmān, on the one hand, used harsh language and exercised harsh measures against ʿAbdallāh b. al-Ḥasan[72] but, on the other hand, allowed the Ḥasanīs to buy a residence (*dār*) large enough for them all, since their place of imprisonment was not large enough.[73] This *dār* was most probably located within the large complex of Dār Marwān, since al-Wāqidī relates that he saw with his own eyes the Ḥasanīs taken out of Dār Marwān in 144/762.[74] Other evidence reveals that people used to come and go from this prison, including ʿAbdallāh b. al-Ḥasan's wife,[75] and even his sons Muḥammad and Ibrāhīm (in disguise).[76] It was also possible to send letters to ʿAbdallāh b. al-Ḥasan in prison.[77] But this evidence is also full of literary motifs aimed at emphasizing the sublime character of Muḥammad and Ibrāhīm, who were willing to sacrifice themselves for those of their family who were imprisoned.

ʿAbdallāh b. al-Ḥasan's imprisonment in Medina lasted four years (Dhū l-Ḥijja 140/April–May 758 until Dhū l-Ḥijja 144/March 762).[78]

70 No specific name is given by the sources, though, see al-Iṣfahānī, *Maqātil*, 215, from Yaḥyā b. ʿAbdallāh b. al-Ḥasan: ("when my father ʿAbdallāh b. al-Ḥasan and his family"; 216: more than 10 people (بضعة عشر رجلا). According to Lane, *Lexicon, b.ḍ.ʿ*, it denotes between 13 to 19 people); Ibn ʿInaba, *ʿUmda*, 104: 8 people; al-Iṣfahānī, *Maqātil*, 218 (= al-Ṭabarī, 3:173); ibid., 3:172: from Mūsā b. ʿAbdallāh b. al-Ḥasan, who was in prison with his father. It can be understood that there was not enough room for them in prison.

71 Al-Iṣfahānī, *Maqātil*, 215, 217; al-Balādhurī, *Ansāb* (ed. Madelung), 2:501. See also al-Ṭabarī, 3:163 (ll. 17–18), where he writes: "while ʿAbdallāh [b. al-Ḥasan] is imprisoned inside the dome of the abode (*al-Dār*, i.e., Dār Marwān), which is on the road that leads to the *Maqṣūra*, he was imprisoned there by Ziyād b. ʿUbaydallāh": وعبد الله محبوس في قبة الدار التي على الطريق إلى المقصورة حبسه فيها زياد بن عبيد الله.

72 Al-Iṣfahānī, *Maqātil*, 216–217 (= al-Ṭabarī, 3:163–164 with minor additions).

73 Ibid., 172.

74 Ibn Saʿd, *al-Qism al-mutammim*, 255.

75 Al-Iṣfahānī, *Maqātil*, 215–216.

76 Ibn ʿInaba, *ʿUmda*, 104.

77 Al-Yaʿqūbī, *Taʾrīkh* (ed. Houtsma), 2:445.

78 Al-Ṭabarī, 3:173 (= al-Iṣfahānī, *Maqātil*, 218), has the following: …ʿUmar b. Shabba < Muḥammad b. Yaḥyā < al-Ḥārith b. Isḥāq, but there are traditions in which it is claimed that he stayed in prison three years, see ibid., 216; al-Ṭabarī, 3:153. It seems that four years is the correct number.

2.2 *The Imprisonment of the Ḥasanīs in 144/762*

Al-Manṣūr did not enter Medina on his way back from the *ḥajj* at Mecca. He encamped in al-Rabadha,[79] where he ordered ʿAbdallāh b. al-Ḥasan, his brothers, and sons to be brought to him. They were brought by Abū l-Azhar, one of the commanders of *ahl Khurāsān* units,[80] or by Riyāḥ, the governor,[81] their legs chained and their necks in iron collars.[82] The sources generally mention a total number of twelve or thirteen members of the Ḥasanī family,[83] and add at least four other dignitaries who were imprisoned with them (see below). But the number of Ḥasanī prisoners and those who accompanied them was much higher. The Ḥasanīs who were brought to al-ʿIrāq from al-Rabadha numbered ten sons of **al-Ḥasan b. al-Ḥasan b. ʿAlī b. Abī Ṭālib**, that is, the brothers of ʿAbdallāh b. al-Ḥasan, Muḥammad al-Nafs al-Zakiyya's father, and the sons of these brothers **1)** ʿAbdallāh b. al-Ḥasan b. al-Ḥasan,[84] and his son **2)** **[85] Mūsā b. ʿAbdallāh b. al-Ḥasan b. al-Ḥasan;[86] **3)** Ibrāhīm b. al-Ḥasan b. al-Ḥasan[87] and his five sons and one grandson: **4)** ** Isḥāq b. Ibrāhīm b. al-Ḥasan b. al-Ḥasan[88] and **5)** ** Ismāʿīl b. Ibrāhīm b. al-Ḥasan b. al-Ḥasan[89] and his son **6)** ** Ibrāhīm b. Ismāʿīl, known as Ṭabāṭibā;[90] **7)** ** ʿAlī b. Ibrāhīm b. al-Ḥasan b.

79 Al-Balādhurī, *Ansāb* (ed. Madelung), 2:503–504; al-Ṭabarī, 3:173.

80 al-Ṭabarī, 3:174 (ll. 15, 18) (on him, see above).

81 Ibid., 3:173–174.

82 Al-Ṭabarī, 3:171, 174 (ll. 5–13), 3:187; Ibn Saʿd, *al-Qism al-mutammim*, 255: a testimony of an eyewitness (al-Wāqidī).

83 This is the number specified by Jafri, *Shīʿa*, 275; Ahmed, *Religious Elite*, 156–157: 12 members of the Ḥasanī family.

84 Al-Ṭabarī, 3:182–183; al-ʿAqīqī, *Kitāb al-Muʿaqqibīn*, 123.

85 The double asterisk (**) denotes those prisoners of the Ḥasanī family who were pardoned and released.

86 Al-Ṭabarī, 3:170 (ll. 19–20); he was released from prison after the two brothers' revolts were crushed, see al-Iṣfahānī, *Maqātil*, 189 (ll. 1–2); al-Masʿūdī, *Murūj*, 4:151 (no. 2411).

87 On Ibrāhīm b. al-Ḥasan, see al-ʿAqīqī, *Kitāb al-Muʿaqqibīn*, 124: he was buried alive (دفن حيا); al-Ṭabarī, 3:180; al-Masʿūdī, *Murūj*, 4:150; al-Kulaynī, *al-Kāfī*, 1:361; but especially, al-Iṣfahānī, *Maqātil*, 187–189, where it is reported that he was the first of the Ḥasanīs to die in prison in al-Hāshimiyya, at the age of 67 on Rabīʿ I 145/May 762; he is mentioned in the *nasab* books, e.g., al-Balādhurī, *Ansāb* (ed. Madelung), 2:494; Ibn Ḥazm, *Jamhara*, 43; al-Bukhārī, *Sirr al-silsila*, 15.

88 Al-Iṣfahānī, *Maqātil*, 189; he is only mentioned by Ibn Ḥazm, *Jamhara*, 43 (who does not add that he was imprisoned by al-Manṣūr).

89 Al-ʿAqīqī, *Kitāb al-Muʿaqqibīn*, 131; for his biography, see al-Iṣfahānī, *Maqātil*, 199.

90 Al-Kulaynī, *al-Kāfī*, 1:361 (= al-Majlisī, *Biḥār*, 47:283), where we read that he was not killed in prison. He is not mentioned by other sources.

al-Ḥasan;[91] the latter four were released by al-Manṣūr;[92] the next (fourth) son died in prison: **8)** Muḥammad b. Ibrāhīm b. al-Ḥasan b. al-Ḥasan;[93] **9)** Yaʿqūb b. Ibrāhīm b. al-Ḥasan b. al-Ḥasan;[94] **10)** Abū Bakr b. al-Ḥasan b. al-Ḥasan;[95] **11)** Sulaymān b. al-Ḥasan b. al-Ḥasan;[96] **12)** Muḥammad b. al-Ḥasan b. al-Ḥasan; **13)** Yaʿqūb b. al-Ḥasan b. al-Ḥasan; **14)** Isḥāq b. al-Ḥasan b. al-Ḥasan;[97] **15)** ** Jaʿfar b. al-Ḥasan b. al-Ḥasan[98] and the latter's son, **16)** ** al-Ḥasan b. Jaʿfar;[99] **17)** ** Dāwūd b. al-Ḥasan b. al-Ḥasan, and his two sons, **18)** ** Sulaymān b.

---

91 Al-ʿAqīqī, *Kitāb al-Muʿaqqibīn*, 131, reports that he was released from prison to Medina; according to al-Kulaynī, *al-Kāfī*, 1:361–362 (= al-Majlisī, *Biḥār*, 47:283), he was not killed with his family members; al-Shāhrūdī, *Rijāl*, 273. On him see the short biography by al-Iṣfahānī, *Maqātil*, 403, where it is said that he was poisoned in Baghdad by order of Caliph al-Mahdī.

92 Al-Ṭabarī, 3:186 (ll. 8–9); al-Iṣfahānī, *Maqātil*, 189, mentions only Isḥāq and Ismāʿīl, but according to Muḥammad b. ʿAlī b. Ḥamza (on him see below), they were killed in prison; on Ibrāhīm b. al-Ḥasan b. al-Ḥasan, see also ibid., 199; Sibṭ b. al-Jawzī, *Mirʾāt al-zamān*, fol. 280a.

93 Al-Ṭabarī, 3:170; al-Iṣfahānī, *Maqātil*, 200, states that he was buried alive in a column (*usṭuwāna*); the column was dismantled, the Ḥasanī was put in it and then the column was rebuilt. His *nasab* is recorded by Ibn Ḥazm, *Jamhara*, 42, who adds: "it was said that he [the caliph] buried him alive."

94 He is only mentioned by al-ʿAqīqī, *Kitāb al-Muʿaqqibīn*, 124, recording that he died in prison.

95 Al-Masʿūdī, *Murūj*, 4:150; cf. al-Iṣfahānī's remark in *Maqātil*, 188: "Muḥammad b. ʿAlī b. Ḥamza al-ʿAlawī mentioned that Abū Bakr b. al-Ḥasan b. al-Ḥasan was killed with them, but I did not hear anyone mentioning this besides him, nor were we informed by anyone from among those who are knowledgeable in the science of genealogy that al-Ḥasan b. al-Ḥasan had a son called Abū Bakr." On Muḥammad b. ʿAlī b. Ḥamza b. al-Ḥasan b. ʿUbaydallāh b. al-ʿAbbās b. ʿAlī b. Abī Ṭālib (d. 287/900).

96 Al-Kulaynī, *al-Kāfī*, 1:361 (= al-Baḥrānī, *Madīnat al-maʿājiz*, 5:281; al-Majlisī, *Biḥār*, 47:282).

97 Al-Iṣfahānī, *Maqātil*, 228, from Muḥammad b. ʿAlī b. Ḥamza; Muḥammad b. al-Ḥasan b. al-Ḥasan's *nasab* is recorded by al-Balādhurī, *Ansāb* (ed. Madelung), 2:495, Ibn Ḥazm, *Jamhara*, 42 and al-Zubayrī, *Nasab Quraysh*, 51 and 53. I was unable to find Isḥāq and Yaʿqūb, the sons of al-Ḥasan b. al-Ḥasan, in the sources; Yaʿqūb may be identified with Yaʿqūb b. Ibrāhīm b. al-Ḥasan b. al-Ḥasan, who is mentioned by al-Zubayrī, *Nasab Quraysh*, 56.

98 Al-Ṭabarī, 3:186; al-Iṣfahānī, *Maqātil*, 189.

99 Al-Iṣfahānī, *Maqātil*, 189; al-Ṭabarī, 3:169–170; al-ʿAqīqī, *Kitāb al-Muʿaqqibīn*, 131; al-Masʿūdī, *Murūj*, 4:151; al-Kulaynī, *al-Kāfī*, 1:361–362 (= al-Majlisī, *Biḥār*, 47:283); according to al-Iṣfahānī and al-Kulaynī, he was not killed and was released after the death of the two brothers.

Dāwūd b. al-Ḥasan b. al-Ḥasan and **19)** ** ʿAbdallāh b. Dāwūd;[100] **20)** al-Ḥasan b. al-Ḥasan b. al-Ḥasan b. ʿAlī b. Abī Ṭālib,[101] and his two sons: **21)** ʿAlī l-Khayr b. al-Ḥasan b. al-Ḥasan b. al-Ḥasan;[102] **22)** al-ʿAbbās b. al-Ḥasan b. al-Ḥasan b. al-Ḥasan[103] and his son, **23)** ** ʿAlī b. al-ʿAbbās b. al-Ḥasan b. al-Ḥasan b. al-Ḥasan;[104] **24)** ʿAbdallāh b. al-Ḥasan b. al-Ḥasan b. al-Ḥasan.[105] Several prisoners of the Ḥasanī family were pardoned and released (nos. 2, 4, 5, 6, 7, 15, 16, 17, 18, 19, 23) by al-Manṣūr in al-Kūfa (that is, al-Hāshimiyya, see below).[106] The non-Ḥasanī

---

100 Al-ʿAqīqī, *Kitāb al-Muʿaqqibīn*, 131 (Sulaymān); al-Iṣfahānī, *Maqātil*, 189; al-Ṭabarī, 3:170 (Sulaymān and Dāwūd); al-Iṣfahānī, 189 (Dāwūd); Ibn Saʿd, *al-Qism al-mutammim*, 254; al-Masʿūdī, *Murūj*, 4:151 (Sulaymān and Dāwūd); al-Kulaynī, *al-Kāfī*, 1:361. Dāwūd and his two sons, according to al-Iṣfahānī and al-Kulaynī, were released from prison after the death of the two brothers.

101 Ibn Saʿd, *al-Qism al-mutammim*, 257. According to al-Iṣfahānī, *Maqātil*, 185–186, he died in prison at al-Hāshimiyya at the age of 68 in Dhū l-Qaʿda 145/January–February 763. According to al-ʿAqīqī, *Kitāb al-Muʿaqqibīn*, 124. he died in prison; al-Kulaynī, *al-Kāfī*, 361; al-Khaṭīb al-Baghdādī, *Taʾrīkh* (Cairo edition), 7:294; Sibṭ b. al-Jawzī, *Mirʾāt al-zamān*, fols. 283a–283b (copying Ibn Saʿd). In the two last sources the name is rendered incorrectly: al-Ḥasan b. al-Ḥasan b. ʿAlī instead of al-Ḥasan b. al-Ḥasan b. al-Ḥasan b. ʿAlī.

102 According to al-ʿAqīqī, *Kitāb al-Muʿaqqibīn*, 124, he died in prison; al-Ṭabarī, 3:180; Sibṭ b. al-Jawzī, *Mirʾāt al-zamān*, fol. 283a; and see his biography in al-Iṣfahānī, *Maqātil*, 190–195; he was the father of al-Ḥusayn, known as *Ṣāḥib al-Fakhkh*, who rebelled against al-Hādī in the year 169/786 and was married to Zaynab, the daughter of ʿAbdallāh b. al-Ḥasan b. al-Ḥasan, the father of Muḥammad al-Nafs al-Zakiyya. On him, see L. Veccia Vaglieri, "al-Ḥusayn b. ʿAlī, Ṣāḥib al-Fakhkh," EI^2; Haider, "Idrīs b. ʿAbdallāh," 459–460.

103 Al-ʿAqīqī, *Kitāb al-Muʿaqqibīn*, 124, relates that he died in prison; al-Ṭabarī, 3:170. On him, see al-Iṣfahānī, *Maqātil*, 197–198, where it is reported that he died in prison at the age of 53 on 23 Ramaḍān 145/15 December 762; al-Masʿūdī, *Murūj*, 4:151; Sibṭ b. al-Jawzī, *Mirʾāt al-zamān*, fol. 283a.

104 Al-ʿAqīqī, *Kitāb al-Muʿaqqibīn*, 131, relates that he was released from prison to Medina.

105 See al-Ṭabarī, 3:180; Sibṭ b. al-Jawzī, *Mirʾāt al-zamān*, fol. 283a; al-Masʿūdī, *Murūj*, 4:151 (no. 2411): ʿAbdallāh b. al-Ḥasan b. al-**Ḥusayn**, instead of **al-Ḥasan**. According to al-Iṣfahānī, *Maqātil*, 196, he died in al-Manṣūr's prison on 10 Muḥarram (يوم الأضحى) 145/10 April 762, aged 46; the mother of ʿAlī and ʿAbdallāh was Ḥubāba bt. ʿĀmir b. ʿAbdallāh b. ʿĀmir b. Bishr b. ʿĀmir Mulāʿib al-Asinna; al-ʿAbbās b. al-Ḥasan's mother was ʿĀʾisha bt. Ṭalḥa b. ʿUmar b. ʿUbaydallāh, see al-Ṭabarī, 3:180: [ʿUmar b. Shabba?] < Yaʿqūb b. al-Qāsim b. Muḥammad < ʿImrān b. Muḥriz from Banū l-Bakkāʾ.

106 Al-Masʿūdī, *Murūj*, 4:151 (no. 2411): nos. 2, 14, 15, 16, 17. The tradition mentions Muḥammad and Ibrāhīm, the sons of ʿAbdallāh b. al-Ḥasan, among the prisoners but this is most probably an error; see the note of the editor Ch. Pellat (note no. 3); al-Ṭabarī, 3:186, nos. 4, 5, 14, 17, and 18; al-Iṣfahānī, *Maqātil*, 189, nos. 2, 4, 5, 14, 15, 16, 17, 18 (but another version is recorded according to which nos. 4–5 were executed in prison); al-Kulaynī, *al-Kāfī*, 1:362: nos. 2, 6, 7, 15, 16, 17, 18.

dignitaries were 25–27) Muḥammad b. ʿAbdallāh b. ʿAmr b. ʿUthmān b. ʿAffān and his two sons.[107] He was the brother of ʿAbdallāh b. al-Ḥasan b. al-Ḥasan from the same mother (see below). And 28) ʿAbd al-Raḥmān b. Abī l-Mawālī, who was also imprisoned, sent to al-Rabadha, and related a personal report about the imprisonment of Muḥammad b. ʿAbdallāh b. ʿAmr b. ʿUthmān with other dignitaries from his family. According to his account, Ibn Abī l-Mawālī was taken separately to al-Manṣūr in al-Rabadha.[108]

From al-Rabadha (according to al-Masʿūdī) they were brought to al-Kūfa.[109] Al-Wāqidī, who was a young boy in Medina at that time, gives an eyewitness report, saying: "I saw ʿAbdallāh b. al-Ḥasan and his family members taken out [going out] from Marwān's abode after the evening prayer, in irons... carried on open/uncovered[?] litters (محامل أعراء), not having a carpet or seat under them. That day I was a young boy (*ghulām*) [but] I had already reached puberty, being capable of remembering what I see."[110] From al-Rabadha[111] the prisoners were brought to al-Hāshimiyya, near al-Kūfa, where they were put under the supervision of Abū l-Azhar.[112] Al-Haytham b. ʿAdī, the well-known

107 Al-Ṭabarī, 3:183 (al-ʿUthmānī and his two sons); for a long description of his imprisonment and torture at the hands of al-Manṣūr at al-Rabadha, and his execution in al-ʿIrāq, see al-Ṭabarī, 3:173–178. See also Ibn Saʿd, *al-Qism al-mutammim*, 260–262. Al-Balādhurī, *Ansāb* (ed. ʿAbbās), 4a:605–607; al-Iṣfahānī, *Maqātil*, 218, 220, 222; al-Zubayrī, *Nasab Quraysh*, 114; Ibn Ḥazm, *Jamhara*, p. 83; al-Masʿūdī, *Murūj*, 4:150; al-Khaṭīb al-Baghdādī, *Taʾrīkh* (Cairo edition), 5:385–388 [= al-Tanūkhī, *Nishwār*, 6:157–158]: his imprisonment and execution. See Ibn ʿAsākir, *Taʾrīkh*, 53:389–392, for traditions about his imprisonment, tortures, and execution (On him, see also Ahmed, *Religious Elite*, 89, 90, 120, 127, 154 and 121f. below).

108 Ibn Saʿd, *al-Qism al-mutammim*, 254–255; al-Ṭabarī, 3:187 (ll. 7–8); Ibn ʿAsākir, *Taʾrīkh*, 53:389–390.

109 Al-Masʿūdī, *Murūj*, 4:151 (no. 2411).

110 Ibn Saʿd, *al-Qism al-mutammim*, 255: ...فيحملون في محامل أعراء ليس تحتهم وطاء; محامل may also denote a basket. See al-Ṭabarī, 3:187, where the words *aʿrāʾ* and *ghulām* are missing. Ibn ʿAsākir, *Taʾrīkh*, 53:390, has a somewhat garbled parallel tradition, with a significant change: Muḥammad b. ʿAbdallāh b. ʿAmr b. ʿUthmān b. ʿAffān is mentioned instead of ʿAbdallāh b. al-Ḥasan and his household.

111 But note a different account according to which al-Manṣūr continued onwards from al-Rabadha to Mecca with the Ḥasanīs, and from there to al-ʿIrāq, see al-Balādhurī, *Ansāb* (ed. Madelung), 2:504. Al-Fasawī, *Maʿrifa*, 1:128, reports that he was on his way to the *ḥajj*; see also Ibn ʿAbd Rabbihi, *al-ʿIqd*, 5:78–79.

112 Al-Ṭabarī, 3:182 (ll. 9–11). Al-Hāshimiyya is usually mentioned as their place of imprisonment; see Ibn Saʿd, *al-Qism al-mutammim*, 257 (= Ibn ʿAsākir, *Taʾrīkh*, 53:384, 389–390), from ... al-Wāqidī < ʿAbd al-Raḥmān b. Abī l-Mawālī; ibid., 53:375, 383–385. See also al-Balādhurī, *Ansāb* (ed. Madelung), 2:504; al-Sakhāwī, *al-Tuḥfa al-laṭīfa*, 2:498. On

early historian (d. 207/822),[113] gives a detailed and accurate description of their prison and the horrible conditions of their imprisonment.

> They were locked by Abū Jaʿfar [al-Manṣūr] in a subterranean passage under the face of the earth, unable to distinguish between day and night. And the subterranean passage is located close to al-Kūfa Bridge, and it is a place that is visited (by pilgrims); they did not have a well for water nor a drinking tank. They used to urinate and relieve their bowels in the place, and if one of them died he was not buried and (his body) was consumed [...] while they were watching [...] the decay started at their feet and then went up their bodies until it reached their hearts and then they died.[114]

Already in al-Rabadha al-Manṣūr ordered the sale of ʿAbdallāh b. al-Ḥasan's property, including his slaves, and confiscated his estates. The money gained from this sale was put in the treasure-house (*bayt al-māl*) in Medina.[115]

---

al-Hāshimiyya, see J. Lassner, "al-Hāshimiyya," *EI*², but other locations are also mentioned by the sources, e.g., Qaṣr Ibn Hubayra in al-Ṭabarī, 3:183 (= al-Iṣfahānī, *Maqātil*, 225). Qaṣr Ibn Hubayra was situated near al-Kūfa, see J. Lassner, "Ḳaṣr Ibn Hubayra," *EI*²; al-Ḥīra: al-Yaʿqūbī, *Taʾrīkh* (ed. Houtsma), 2:445. On al-Kūfa itself, see for instance, al-Masʿūdī, *Murūj*, 4:151 (no. 2411), where it is clarified that their prison was situated "on the bank of the Euphrates, close to al-Kūfa's bridge" adding that "their place [of death? burial?] in al-Kūfa is visited until this time, which is the year 332/943 or 944; the place was destroyed over their very heads": "على شاطئ الفرات بالقرب من قنطرة الكوفة وموضعهم بالكوفة تزار إلى هذا الوقت وهو سنة اثنتين وثلاثين وثلاثمائة وكان قد هدم عليهم الموضع; see also Sibṭ b. al-Jawzī, *Mirʾāt al-zamān*, fol. 285a: *ʿinda Qanṭarat al-Kūfa*, but note that al-Masʿūdī himself says in another place [*Murūj*, 4:153ff. (no. 2413)] that when al-Manṣūr imprisoned the Ḥasanīs he ascended the *minbar* in al-Hāshimiyya addressing his loyal ʿAbbāsī troops (*ahl Khurāsān*) with a long speech; the contradiction (between al-Kūfa and al-Hāshimiyya) may not be so great since the two sites were very close.

113 On him, see Leder, *al-Haiṯam ibn ʿAdī*, esp. 286ff.

114 Sibṭ b. al-Jawzī, *Mirʾāt al-zamān*, fol. 285a:
وقال الهيثم: حبسهم أبو جعفر في سرداب تحت الأرض لا يعرفون ليلا ولا نهارا والسرداب عند قنطرة الكوفة وهو موضع يزار. ولم يكن عندهم بئر للماء ولا سقاية فكانوا يبولون ويتغوطون في مواضعهم. وإذا مات فيهم ميت لم يدفن بل تبلى وهم . . . ينظرون إليه . . . وكان الردم يبدو في أقدامهم ثم يترقى حتى يبلغ الفؤاد فيموتون . .
Cf. al-Masʿūdī, *Murūj*, 4:151 (no. 2411), for a partial shorter description with similar or even identical words and phrases; no transmitters are mentioned by al-Masʿūdī, though.

115 Al-Balādhurī, *Ansāb* (ed. Madelung), 2:503. See al-Ṭabarī, 3:153 (l. 11), where he has property and slaves: أمر ببيع متاعك ورقيقك; McAuliffe, *ʿAbbāsid Authority*, 99, has "your household goods and slaves."

A few words should be added about the two distinguished people who were imprisoned with the Ḥasanīs. The first was Muḥammad b. ʿAbdallāh b. ʿAmr b. ʿUthmān b. ʿAffān, called al-Dībāj, the brother of ʿAbdallāh b. al-Ḥasan on his mother's side.[116] Their mother (who was also the mother of al-Ḥasan and Ibrāhīm, the sons of al-Ḥasan b. al-Ḥasan b. ʿAlī b. Abī Ṭālib), was Fāṭima bt. al-Ḥusayn b. ʿAlī b. Abī Ṭālib.[117]

Muḥammad b. ʿAbdallāh b. ʿAmr was taken to Medina from his estate in Badr,[118] and from there, with two of his sons,[119] to al-Manṣūr in al-Rabadha, where he was severely flogged by order of the caliph, who was anxious to get him to reveal the whereabouts of Muḥammad and Ibrāhīm.[120] His daughter was married to Ibrāhīm b. ʿAbdallāh b. al-Ḥasan. Al-Manṣūr's informers revealed to him that she was pregnant, and since she lived with her father (her husband was constantly fleeing from al-Manṣūr's pursuers), he was accused of not notifying the authorities that Ibrāhīm used to frequent his wife in his abode.[121]

Versions of this tradition are recorded in several sources,[122] and comprise a detailed and verbatim report of the discussion between the caliph and Muḥammad al-Dībāj, but it seems that at least the main body of the story is a literary invention. The *nasab* books relate that Ruqayya al-Ṣughrā, Muḥammad al-Dībāj's daughter, was married to Ibrāhīm b. ʿAbdallāh b. al-Ḥasan, but they all add that Ibrāhīm was killed before consummating the

116 On him, see his entry in most of the biographical dictionaries, e.g., al-Bukhārī, *al-Kabīr* (Diyār Bakr edition), 1:138–139; Ibn Abī Ḥātim, *al-Jarḥ* (Beirut edition), 7:301; Ibn Ḥibbān, *al-Thiqāt*, 7:417; al-Khaṭīb al-Baghdādī, *Taʾrīkh* (Cairo edition), 5:385–388; Ibn ʿAsākir, *Taʾrīkh*, 53:379–392; al-Mizzī, *Tahdhīb*, 25:516–523, and the exhaustive bibliography of the editor therein. For the common explanation for his *laqab* "al-Dībāj" (initially meaning silk, silk brocade, and hence *dībāj al-wajh*, that is, the beauty of the skin), see for example, al-Samʿānī, *al-Ansāb*, 2:522: "he was called al-Dībāj due to his beautiful features"; al-Mizzī, *Tahdhīb*, 25:517.

117 Al-Balādhurī, *Ansāb* (ed. Madelung), 2:494; al-Zubayrī, *Nasab Quraysh*, 51–52; al-Ṭabarī, 3:173–174. Al-Iṣfahānī, *Maqātil*, 202–204; Fāṭima bore ʿAbdallāh b. ʿAmr b. ʿUthmān two other children, al-Qāsim and Ruqayya, al-Iṣfahānī, *Maqātil*, 180; Ibn ʿAsākir, *Taʾrīkh*, 70:16, 19; 53:382; 70:15: after ʿAbdallāh she married Ibn Abī ʿAtīq al-Bakrī and bore him Amīna, Umm Isḥāq b. Ṭalḥa.

118 Al-Iṣfahānī, *Maqātil*, 218 (= al-Ṭabarī, 3:174): فكان بماله في بدر.

119 Al-Ṭabarī, 3:183 (ll. 2–3).

120 Ibid., 3:176; Ibn Saʿd, *al-Qism al-mutammim*, 256–257; al-Balādhurī, *Ansāb* (ed. Madelung), 2:503–504; Ibn ʿAsākir, *Taʾrīkh*, 53:383, 390.

121 Al-Ṭabarī, 3:176.

122 E.g., al-Iṣfahānī, *Maqātil*, 221–222.

marriage.[123] Al-Balādhurī relates from Abū l-Yaqẓān[124] that "al-Dībāj gave his daughter in marriage to Muḥammad b. ʿAbdallāh OR to Ibrāhīm b. ʿAbdallāh b. Ḥasan b. Ḥasan b. ʿAlī, (therefore?) al-Manṣūr Amīr al-Muʾminīn summoned him to Medina, condemned him for his inclination towards the descendants of ʿAbdallāh b. al-Ḥasan b. Ḥasan, flogged him sixty times, and ordered his imprisonment. And when Muḥammad b. Ibrāhīm [sic! read ʿAbdallāh] mutinied, he ordered him brought [to al-ʿIrāq] and killed him while being tied up (or while being in prison: *ṣabr*an) in al-Hāshimiyya."[125]

The second person who was imprisoned with the Ḥasanīs, brought to al-Rabadha (and from there to al-Hāshimiyya and then to Baghdad) was ʿAbd al-Raḥmān b. Abī l-Mawālī (d. 173/789 or 790), a *mawlā* of ʿAlī b. Abī Ṭalib or Abū Rāfiʿ,[126] the *mawlā* of the Prophet.[127] He was whipped severely by order of the caliph.[128] Al-Wāqidī, who was a younger Medinan contemporary of his, knows that

> he intermingled and was intimate with Banū l-Ḥasan (مخالطا لبني الحسن), and knew the [hiding] place of Muḥammad and Ibrāhīm and used to come to them regularly; and it was said that he was one of their propagandists; this became known to Abū Jaʿfar (al-Manṣūr) who took him (as a prisoner) with them [the Ḥasanīs] [...][129]

Al-Khaṭīb al-Baghdādī quotes Aḥmad b. Ḥanbal, saying, "Ibn Abī l-Mawālī was imprisoned here with us in the Maṭbaq [i.e., the name of the prison, that is, in Baghdad].[130] Later he was released and came back to Medina": كان ابن أبي

123 Al-Zubayrī, *Nasab Quraysh*, 117; Ibn Ḥazm, *Jamhara*, 83; see also Ibn Saʿd, *al-Qism al-mutammim*, 256.

124 Suḥaym b. Ḥafṣ.

125 Al-Balādhurī, *Ansāb* (ed. ʿAbbās), 4a:606–607, from Abū l-Yaqẓān. Cf. ibid. (ed. Madelung), 2:503–504, where we find an abridged combined tradition (*qālū*): at first al-Dībāj gets 60 lashes and then an additional 150 lashes. Other sources tell of 100 lashes of the whip, for example, Ibn Saʿd, *al-Qism al-mutammim*, 256; Ibn ʿAsākir, *Taʾrīkh*, 53:383, 389, 391; al-Sakhāwī, *al-Tuḥfa al-laṭīfa*, 2:498.

126 On Abū Rāfiʿ's descendants who were close associates of ʿAlī b. Abī Ṭālib, see 390f. below.

127 On ʿAbd al-Raḥmān b. Zayd b. Abī l-Mawālī (who is commonly related to his grandfather), see Ibn Ḥibbān, *Mashāhīr*, 223; idem, *al-Thiqāt*, 7:91; al-Bājī, *al-Taʿdīl*, 2:982; al-Khaṭīb al-Baghdādī, *Taʾrīkh* (Beirut, 1997), 10:225–226; Ibn Ḥajar, *Muqaddimat fatḥ al-bārī*, 417; van Arendonk, *L'Imamat Zaïdite*, 312.

128 Al-Ṭabarī, 3:187, 188–189; al-Dhahabī, *Siyar*, 7:213; Ibn Saʿd, *al-Qism al-mutammim*, 256.

129 Al-Iṣfahānī, *Maqātil*, 287.

130 On this prison, see al-Munajjid, *al-Khulafāʾ wa-l-khulaʿāʾ*, 127–128.

المولي عندنا محبوسا في المطبق ثم خلي عنه ورجع إلى المدينة.[131] He is mentioned among the followers of Jaʿfar al-Ṣādiq.[132]

2.3 *Conclusion*

A careful reading of the sources reveals that twenty-four members of the Ḥasanī family were imprisoned by al-Manṣūr: ten sons of al-Ḥasan b. al-Ḥasan b. ʿAlī (that is, nine brothers of ʿAbdallāh, Muḥammad al-Nafs al-Zakiyya's father), their twelve sons, and two grandchildren. Two other, non-ʿAlīd persons and two sons of one of them were also imprisoned. Between eight and ten were released from prison.[133] The rest died (or were murdered) in prison.

3 Propaganda and Followers of Muḥammad b. ʿAbdallāh in the Provinces

There is more than a little evidence indicating that Muḥammad strove to give the rebellion as broad a character as possible and to extend it to other regions beyond the borders of the Arabian Peninsula. These traditions, like others depicting the rebellion, are loaded with repeated literary motifs that make it difficult to reconstruct the real course of events. Nevertheless, a careful scrutiny of these traditions enables us to reach partial conclusions regarding Muḥammad b. ʿAbdallāh's aims and ambitions in this matter.

These are traditions of a general nature, with no specific identifiable details, which relate that during the entire period in which Muḥammad b. ʿAbdallāh

---

131 Al-Khaṭīb al-Baghdādī, *Taʾrīkh* (Beirut, 1997), 10:226.

132 Al-Tafrishī, *Naqd al-rijāl*, 3:41; al-Shabastarī, *al-Imām al-Ṣādiq*, 223; al-Khūʾī, *Rijāl*, 10:325; and see also on him appendix 2, no. 9.

133 Al-Iṣfahānī, *Maqātil*, 189, 1) Jaʿfar b. al-Ḥasan b. al-Ḥasan b. ʿAlī b. Abī Ṭālib. On him, see also al-Ṭabarī, 3:186 (l. 9); 2) His son, al-Ḥasan (also according to al-ʿAqīqī, *Kitāb al-Muʿaqqibīn*, 131; on him, see also al-Masʿūdī, *Murūj*, 4:151); 3) Mūsā b. ʿAbdallāh b. al-Ḥasan b. al-Ḥasan (on him, see also al-Masʿūdī, *Murūj*, 4:151); 4) Dāwūd b. al-Ḥasan b. al-Ḥasan b. ʿAlī b. Abī Ṭālib; his two sons 5) Sulaymān b. Dāwūd (Dāwūd is also mentioned by al-ʿAqīqī, *Kitāb al-Muʿaqqibīn*, 131) and 6) ʿAbdallāh b. Dāwūd (on Sulaymān and ʿAbdallāh, see also al-Ṭabarī, 3:186 (l. 9); al-Masʿūdī, *Murūj*, 4:151); 7) Isḥāq b. Ibrāhīm b. al-Ḥasan b. al-Ḥasan b. ʿAlī (also according to al-Ṭabarī, 3:186 (l. 9)); 8) Ismāʿīl b. Ibrāhīm b. al-Ḥasan b. al-Ḥasan (also according to al-ʿAqīqī, *Kitāb al-Muʿaqqibīn*, 131 and al-Ṭabarī, 3:186 (l. 9)). According to a different tradition recorded from Muḥammad b. ʿAlī b. Ḥamza; the last two people (nos. 7 and 8) were killed in prison. Al-ʿAqīqī, *Kitāb al-Muʿaqqibīn*, 131, mentions two additional names of Ḥasanīs who were released from prison 9) ʿAlī b. Ibrāhīm b. al-Ḥasan b. al-Ḥasan and 10) ʿAlī b. al-ʿAbbās b. al-Ḥasan b. al-Ḥasan b. al-Ḥasan.

was hiding from the authorities, a network of propagandists was secretly active on his behalf in various parts of the caliphate.[134] Contact with his followers throughout the caliphate was maintained by correspondence[135] and entrusted to personal messengers, mainly from his family, but also not from his family.[136] According to such a tradition, "Muḥammad's sons and brothers have scattered in the lands propagating on his behalf as the Imām" (that is, the caliph). His son ʿAlī was sent to Egypt, where he was killed; ʿAbdallāh, to Khurāsān, from where he fled to al-Sind where he was killed; and al-Ḥasan was sent to Yemen, where he was imprisoned and died. As for his brothers, Mūsā was sent to al-Jazīra, Yaḥyā to al-Rayy and later on to Ṭabaristān, and Idrīs to al-Maghrib (where he was assassinated by order of al-Manṣūr).[137] This tradition combines a few well-known authentic facts about these persons in order to fabricate the main body of evidence, e.g., the idea of a wide comprehensive propaganda network spread throughout the Muslim world for the sake of Muḥammad b. ʿAbdallāh. His son ʿAlī indeed was in Egypt, but he was not killed there; he was brought to the caliph and died in al-ʿIrāq. As for ʿAbdallāh, he eventually arrived in al-Sind, but traditions differ as to whether he arrived there following the outbreak of the revolt or after it ended. In any case, this journey is described as a flight, certainly not for propaganda purposes. Idrīs eventually arrived in al-Maghrib, but as is known, a long time after the rebellion, and died in 175/791.[138] The sources do not tell of any propaganda activities on behalf of his son al-Ḥasan, nor of his brother Yaḥyā. Regarding Mūsā, his brother, it is related that he indeed tried to turn to Syria, to raise support there for his brother's cause, an attempt which ended in complete failure.[139]

This tradition, therefore, bases some of story on facts and adds the elements that are used as the basis of a fictitious story. This story is incorporated beautifully into other traditions that record some speeches of Muḥammad b. ʿAbdallāh in front of the people of Medina, e.g., "I did not come out in rebellion until *ahl al-Kūfa, ahl al-Baṣra*, Wāsiṭ, al-Jazīra, and al-Mawṣil swore allegiance to me, and promised to come out in rebellion on the night I came out."[140] Other

134 Al-Ṣafadī, *al-Wāfī*, 3:297.

135 Al-Yaʿqūbī, *Taʾrīkh* (ed. Houtsma), 2:450.

136 Al-Balādhurī, *Ansāb* (ed. Madelung), 2:523; Ibn ʿAbd Rabbihi, *al-ʿIqd*, 5:75–76.

137 Al-Masʿūdī, *Murūj*, 4:147 (copied by al-Shaykh al-Mufīd, *al-Masāʾil al-jārūdiyya*, 4).

138 Najam, "Idrīs b. ʿAbdallāh," 559–560. On him, see also 234f., below.

139 See below.

140 Al-Balādhurī, *Ansāb* (ed. Madelung), 2:519. Ibid., 2:508, where his first alleged speech in front of the people of Medina is described: "by God I swear, there is no big central city, in which Allāh is worshiped, that my propagandists did not take a swearing of allegiance to me from its inhabitants."

traditions present Muḥammad's deep conviction of the support he gained in the provinces and relate that even before the battle broke out, he still believed that his supporters in the provinces would come to his aid.[141]

It is impossible to know how much these speeches, allegedly delivered by Muḥammad b. ʿAbdallāh, reflect reality, or parts of it. Muḥammad is depicted in these traditions (at least) as naïve. We must take into consideration the policy of espionage and diversion implemented by the ʿAbbāsīs against Muḥammad, which, for instance, may have really caused him to believe that some of the most important commanders of the ʿAbbāsī army supported him, particularly the most important among them, Ḥumayd b. Qaḥṭaba; traditions record Muḥammad b. ʿAbdallāh's sheer astonishment and disappointment when Ḥumayd did not join his camp, contrary to his "solemn promise" to join his cause (see below).

3.1 *Egypt*

The propaganda in Egypt is connected to Muḥammad b. ʿAbdallāh's son, ʿAlī. According to several traditions he was sent by his father to promote his cause in Egypt, was discovered and caught by the governor, and sent to al-Manṣūr,[142] who ordered him imprisoned.[143] But according to another tradition, he left Egypt and was arrested only upon arriving in Medina.[144] Another detailed piece of evidence relates that ʿAlī was sent by his father to Egypt together with his brother, Mūsā and Maṭar Ṣāḥib al-Ḥammām (or al-Warrāq?), and Yazīd b. Khālid [b. ʿAbdallāh] al-Qasrī. All were sent to promote Muḥammad b. ʿAbdallāh's cause. ʿAlī was caught and brought to Abū Jaʿfar al-Manṣūr. Mūsā managed to escape.[145]

141 Al-Ṭabarī, 3:231. For a parallel shorter tradition, see al-Balādhurī, *Ansāb* (ed. Madelung), 2:517, where Muḥammad b. ʿAbdallāh reassures one of his followers (al-Ghāḍirī), that "a swearing of allegiance was already given in my name in al-Shām, Khurāsān and al-Miṣrayn" (that is, al-Baṣra and al-Kūfa).

142 Al-Ṭabarī, 3:171 (ll. 1–5).

143 Al-Balādhurī, *Ansāb* (ed. Madelung), 2:502, 540; Ibn Saʿd, *al-Qism al-mutammim*, 373; al-Ṭabarī, 3:172 (ll. 2–4); Ibn ʿInaba, *ʿUmda*, 105.

144 Al-Ṭabarī, 3:170 (ll. 17–20).

145 Al-Iṣfahānī, *Maqātil*, 201; ibid., from al-Madāʾinī, who explains that Maṭar was called Ṣāḥib al-Ḥammām (that is, the one who is in charge of the bath house) because he was in charge of al-Amīr's bath in al-Baṣra; ibid., 246, where he appears as an enthusiastic supporter of Muḥammad al-Nafs al-Zakiyya in a tradition that aims to disclose the negative attitude of the famous Muʿtazilī scholar ʿAmr b. ʿUbayd towards the revolt. I was unable to find more information about Maṭar and the Ḥammām.

As for Maṭar, al-Azdī records a detailed single tradition about the execution of two unknown and obscure people, Maṭar al-Warrāq and Bashīr al-Raḥḥāl, loyal and active supporters of Muḥammad al-Nafs al-Zakiyya in al-Manṣūr's court.[146] In the preceding tradition Maṭar was called Ṣāḥib al-Ḥammām, not al-Warrāq; this is obviously an error rooted in some confusion between him and the well-known *muḥaddith*, Maṭar b. Ṭahmān al-Warrāq, who died in 125/742–743 or 129/746–747.[147] As for Bashīr al-Raḥḥāl,[148] he is a somewhat obscure figure. Nothing is known of his family, e.g., the name of his father, his ethnic origin, or his place of birth.

He was a loyal supporter of the ʿAbbāsīs, and seemed to be a close associate of Caliph al-Manṣūr. After the death of ʿAbdallāh b. al-Ḥasan in al-Manṣūr's prison he transferred his loyalties to Muḥammad al-Nafs al-Zakiyya.[149] Nothing is heard of him during the latter's revolt, but he was one of Ibrāhīm's close advisers and supporters,[150] who, according to traditions died in Bashīr's lap.[151]

He is considered a Muʿtazilī by scholars[152] but in the Imāmī literature he is one of Muḥammad al-Bāqir's close associates (*aṣḥāb*).[153] Some sources have

146 Al-Azdī, *Taʾrīkh al-Mawṣil* (Cairo edition), 190: *Akhbaranī* [= Abū Zakariyyāʾ al-Azdī] < Ibn Mubārak < ʿUmar b. ʿAbīda < Ayyūb b. ʿUmar [b. Abī ʿAmr] < Muḥammad b. Khālid [b. Ismāʿīl b. Ayyūb b. Salama al-Makhzūmī?] < Muḥammad b. ʿUrwa b. Hishām b. ʿUrwa [b. al-Zubayr]. Al-Ṭabarī, 3:262, records a small part of the same tradition with a change in the *isnād*, e.g., *qāla wa-ḥaddathanī* [that is ʿUmar b. Shabba, see al-Ṭabarī, 3:260 (l. 18); McAuliffe, *ʿAbbāsid Authority*, 228], instead of ʿUmar b. ʿAbīda in al-Azdī's *Taʾrīkh*; the identification by McAuliffe, *ʿAbbāsid Authority*, 228 and index, Muḥammad b. Khālid as Muḥammad b. Khālid b. Ismāʿīl al-Makhzūmī on the basis of the *isnād* in al-Ṭabarī, 3:152, is reasonable.

147 Noticed by van Arendonk, *L'Imamat Zaïdite*, 316. Van Ess, *Theologie*, 2:62 and 83, reports that he died in 130/747. In the *rijāl* works that I consulted we find 125 H. or 129 H., for example, see Ibn Ḥibbān, *al-Thiqāt*, 5:435; al-Mizzī, *Tahdhīb*, 28:54.

148 On him, see van Arendonk, *L'Imamat Zaïdite*, 316; Madelung, *al-Qāsim b. Ibrāhīm*, 73. See esp. van Ess, *Theologie*, index, esp. 2:328–330; McAuliffe, *ʿAbbāsid Authority*, 137, n. 649, defining him (following Madelung) as a "Muʿtazilī ascetic." His *laqab* "al-raḥḥāl," was given due to his many *riḥlas* either to the *ḥajj* or to the borders to fight the enemies of Islām (وسمي الرحال لأنه رحل خمسين رحلة من حج إلى غزو); see al-Najāshī, *Rijāl*, 4:23; al-Nūrī l-Ṭabarsī, *Khātimat al-Mustadrak*, 4:23.

149 Al-Ṭabarī, 3:185–186.

150 Ibid., 3:311; al-Iṣfahānī, *Maqātil*, 339–341; Ibn ʿInaba, *ʿUmda*, 109; al-ʿUmarī, *Ansāb*, 350.

151 Al-Iṣfahānī, *Maqātil*, 347.

152 Van Arendonk, *L'Imamat Zaïdite*, 316; Madelung, *al-Qāsim b. Ibrāhīm*, 73; van Ess, *Theologie*, 2:328f.

153 See for example, al-Ṭūsī, *Rijāl*, 127.

him dying in battle along with Ibrāhīm,[154] but according to a single source, he was caught after the battle of Bākhamrā and brought to the caliph, who ordered him killed in a very cruel manner.[155]

Yazīd b. Khālid b. ʿAbdallāh al-Qasrī, who is mentioned in this tradition, had been dead for a long time; he died a short time before Marwān b. Muḥammad ascended the throne, in 744.[156] The inclusion of Mūsā b. ʿAbdallāh in this tradition in the Egyptian scene is unique, and I have not found a parallel report in the sources known to me. As opposed to this description, there is the accepted tradition according to which Mūsā was sent to conduct propaganda for his brother's cause in Syria.[157] This increases the suspicion of this version's veracity.

A single tradition mentions another[?] parallel rebellion in Egypt, but under the leadership of Ibrāhīm b. al-Ḥasan b. al-Ḥasan, the brother of ʿAbdallāh and uncle of Muḥammad b. ʿAbdallāh. Ibrāhīm was captured and sent to al-Manṣūr.[158] However, none of the evidence in which Ibrāhīm b. al-Ḥasan is mentioned connects him to any rebellion in Egypt. I have not found any evidence for this affair in the vast literature on the history of Egypt.[159] The accepted tradition is that he was imprisoned together with the Ḥasanīs in Medina, brought to al-Rabadha and then to al-ʿIrāq. According to one tradition, he was the first of the Ḥasanīs to die in prison at al-Hāshimiyya at the age of 67, in Rabīʿ I 145/ May–June 762.[160]

In spite of the contradictory, unreal and inaccurate elements discernible in the traditions dealing with the propaganda in Egypt, it is noteworthy that all traditions (except one, see below), mention ʿAlī b. Muḥammad b. ʿAbdallāh in connection with the pre-rebellion phase; that is, he conducted propaganda on behalf of his brother, was caught and arrested. These traditions do not supply additional socio-historical details. However, a unique long and detailed description recorded by al-Kindī (d. 350/961) adds some of the missing socio-historical elements of the rebellious movement in Egypt.

---

154 Ibn Khayyāṭ, *Taʾrīkh* (ed. al-ʿUmarī), 2:450. Al-Iṣfahānī, *Maqātil*, 347, reports that Ibrāhīm dies in Bashīr's lap and then Bashīr is killed; al-Dhahabī, *Siyar*, 6:224, called al-Amīr (the commander); van Ess, *Theologie*, 2:329.

155 Al-Azdī, *Taʾrīkh al-Mawṣil* (Cairo edition), 190; van Ess, *Theologie*, 2:330.

156 Crone, *Slaves*, 102.

157 See below; cf. the single tradition in al-Masʿūdī, *Murūj*, 4:174, telling that he was sent to al-Jazīra.

158 Al-Ṭabarī, 3:433–434.

159 Noted by de Goeje, ibid., 433, note g, where he remarks that it is ʿAlī b. Muḥammad b. ʿAbdallāh b. al-Ḥasan (and not Ibrāhīm), who is mentioned by the sources as connected to Egypt.

160 Al-Iṣfahānī, *Maqātil*, 188; see 116 above.

3.1.1 Al-Kindī's Description[161]

ʿAlī b. Muḥammad arrived in al-Fusṭāṭ during Ḥumayd b. Qaḥṭaba's governorship, between 5 Ramaḍān 143/18 December 760 and Dhū l-Qaʿda 144/February 762.[162] He came in order to summon the people to the cause of his father and his uncle (Ibrāhīm b. ʿAbdallāh). At first he stayed in ʿAssāma (ʿUsāma[?]) b. ʿAmr al-Maʿāfirī's house for a very short time.[163] Ḥumayd, the governor, was replaced by Yazīd b. Ḥātim al-Muhallabī, who arrived in Egypt on 15 Dhū l-Qaʿda 144/13 February 762.[164]

The following is part of al-Kindī's unique and detailed description:

> During his governorship the *daʿwa* of the Banū Ḥasan b. ʿAlī in Egypt appeared and people talked about it and many of them swore allegiance to ʿAlī b. Muḥammad b. ʿAbdallāh b. Ḥasan b. ʿAbdallāh [sic!] b. Ḥasan. He was the first ʿAlīd who came to Egypt. The person who undertook to implement his propaganda was Khālid b. Saʿīd b. Rabīʿa b. Ḥubaysh al-Ṣadafī, whose grandfather was one of the closest adherents (*khāṣṣat*) of ʿAlī b. Abī Ṭālib and his followers (*shīʿatihi*), and he was present in ʿUthmān's abode (وحضر الدار [= *Dār* ʿUthmān]) when he was killed.[165]

161 Al-Kindī, *Wulāt* (ed. Guest), 111–115.

162 Ibid., 110–111.

163 Ibid., 111; ʿAssāma [ʿUsāma ?] b. ʿAmr served as *ṣāḥib al-shurṭa* to some of the governors of Egypt in later years, see ibid., and Ibn Taghrī Birdī, *al-Nujūm*, vol. 2: index, s.v.; ʿAssāma is thus rendered by the editors of al-Kindī and Ibn Taghrī Birdī; but cf. Ibn Durayd, *al-Ishtiqāq*, 417: Banū ʿUsāma; al-Zabīdī, *Tāj al-ʿarūs*, 8:398, s.v. *ʿ.s.m*): "*wa-Banū ʿUsāma*, (the *ʿayn* is punctuated) with *ḍamma*, an Arab tribe"; but cf. Ibn Manẓūr, *Lisān al-ʿArab*, 12:402: "*wa-Banū ʿAssāma*: a tribe… *wa-ʿUsāma*: name (of a person)." The editor remarks, ibid., note, that some lexicographers write ʿUsāma, and others write ʿAssāma.

164 On him and his family, see Crone, *Slaves*, 134–135.

164 Al-Kindī, *Wulāt* (Beirut edition), 133.

165 Al-Kindī, *Wulāt* (ed. Guest), 111–112; text: وحضر الرأي instead of الدار; the editor of al-Kindī's *Wulāt* corrected the text according to the parallel text in al-Maqrīzī's *Khiṭaṭ* (Būlāq edition), 2:338: وحضر الدار في قتل عثمان (he was present in the residence [of ʿUthmān) at the time ʿUthmān was assassinated). Al-Maqrīzī copied al-Kindī's text. As for Khālid b. Saʿīd b. Rabīʿa, besides the very short but unique comment recorded by al-Kindī about him, little is added by the few other sources; he seems to be, as his father before him, a (minor) *ḥadīth* scholar: al-Mizzī, *Tahdhīb*, 22:532 (his father); al-Kindī, *Wulāt*, 104; Ibn Mākūlā, *al-Ikmāl*, 2:332 (Khālid); his grandfather, Rabīʿa b. Ḥubaysh b. ʿArfaṭa, was a jurisprudent (*faqīh*), who was nominated (against his will) over the judiciary in Egypt during the reign of Hishām b. ʿAbd al-Malik (r. 105–125/724–743), Ibn Mākūlā, *al-Ikmāl*, 2:332. As noted above, he is described by al-Kindī as belonging to ʿAlī's most intimate and distinguished associates and mentioned as one of those who were present in ʿUthmān's

Al-Kindī mentions the names of three other distinguished rebels. They are all descendants of Marwān b. al-Ḥakam, the Umawī caliph: 1) Diḥya b. Muṣʿab (Muʿaṣṣab?) b. al-Aṣbagh b. ʿAbd al-ʿAzīz b. Marwān b. al-Ḥakam; 2) Zayd b. al-Aṣbagh b. ʿAbd al-ʿAzīz; 3) Manṣūr al-Ashall b. al-Aṣbagh b. ʿAbd al-ʿAzīz.[166] In a consultation held by Khālid b. Saʿīd, the three mentioned Umawīs who were present, and some unidentified Arabs who were registered in the Dīwān

---

dār when he was killed. It is noteworthy that in another place he is accused of killing ʿUthmān, see Ibn ʿAsākir, *Taʾrīkh*, 62:433: he is besmirched by al-Mulāmis b. Khuzayma, who tells Muʿāwiya b. Abī Sufyān: "Indeed this is, meaning Rabīʿa b. Ḥubaysh al-Ṣadafī, the killer of ʿUthmān, the associate of the Devil and the father-in-law of Wirdān." Muʿāwiya asks Rabīʿa: "Did you marry your daughter to Wirdān? And he answers: Yes, oh Commander of the Faithful, I coupled a green sown field and a yellow dīnār.": أزوجت وردان ابنتك؟ قال نعم يا أمير المؤمنين، زوجت فدان أخضر ودينار أصفر. Wirdān was the *mawlā* of ʿAmr b. al-ʿĀṣ, the governor of Egypt. When the latter died, the caliph Muʿāwiya nominated Wirdān as the land-tax collector, see ibid., 62:430 and 431. The uncle of Khālid b. Saʿīd, ʿImrān b. Rabīʿa "was in charge of the *ʿirāfa* in Egypt for [the governor] ʿAbd al-ʿAzīz b. Marwān: كان يلي العرافة بمصر لعبد العزيز بن مروان, and he lived until the days of Abū Jaʿfar al-Manṣūr," al-Samʿānī, *al-Ansāb* (Hyderabad edition), 8:287. The office of the *ʿarīf* was connected to the military organization of the state and its major cities; the *ʿirāfa* is usually described as a military unit. "Each *ʿarīf* was assigned to an *ʿirāfa* and was responsible for the distribution of the stipend (*ʿaṭāʾ*) among its members, for this purpose he had to keep a register (*dīwān*) of the payees and their families. He was furthermore responsible for security inside his own *ʿirāfa*...." See Salih A. el-Ali and Cl. Cahen, "ʿArīf," *EI*²; it seems that ʿImrān b. Rabīʿa was the *ʿarīf* of his tribe (Ṣadif); on the *ʿarīf*, see also Elad, "The First ʿAbbāsid *Mahdī*," 36. On al-Ṣadif, see Ibn Ḥazm, *Jamhara*, 461; al-Samʿānī, *al-Ansāb* (Hyderabad edition), 8:286–287.

166 Al-Kindī, *Wulāt* (ed. Guest), 112; I was not able to find any further information about al-Manṣūr and Zayd. It seems that Diḥya's father's name was Muṣʿab, although in several sources it is rendered as Muʿaṣṣab, for example, see Ibn al-Kalbī, *Jamhara* (ed. Caskel), 2:232 (ed. Ḥasan, 40); R. Guest, the editor of al-Kindī's *Wulāt*, chose the form Muṣʿab, although in the ms. of the book it always appears as Muʿaṣṣab (the editor of the Beirut edition, 134, n. 2, remarks that he preferred the form Muʿaṣṣab throughout the book). Al-Samʿānī, *al-Ansāb* (Beirut edition), 1:331, has al-Mughaṣṣab; Ibn Taghrī Birdī, *al-Nujūm*, 2:49 (al-Muʿaṣṣab); on him see also ibid., 2:54, 58, 60, 61. But cf. Ibn Ḥazm, *Jamhara*, 104; al-Balādhurī, *Ansāb*, 4/2:101: Muṣʿab. See Ibn ʿAsākir, *Taʾrīkh*, 9:170, for a biography of al-Aṣbagh b. ʿAbd al-ʿAzīz where his son Muṣʿab and his grandson Diḥya b. al-Muṣʿab are mentioned; see also Ibn Mākūlā, *al-Ikmāl*, 3:314; Yāqūt, *Muʿjam* (Beirut edition), 1:284, 513; Ibn Qutayba, *al-Maʿārif* (Cairo edition), 362: *Diḥya bt.*[*!*] *Muṣʿab... kānat ʿālima*; Diḥya b. Muṣʿab rebelled in Egypt during al-Mahdī's and al-Hādī's caliphate and died in 169/785, see al-Kindī, *Wulāt*, (ed. Guest), 129–130; al-Yaʿqūbī, *Taʾrīkh* (Beirut edition), 2:405: Diḥya b. al-Aṣbagh (sic!); Yāqūt, *Muʿjam* (Beirut edition), 1:284, 513; al-Ziriklī, *al-Aʿlām*, 2:337 ("Diḥya b. Muṣʿab"); 5:149 ("al-Faḍl b. Ṣāliḥ").

(*ahl al-dīwān*), decide to gather on that night, 10 Shawwāl 145/1 January 763, in the great mosque and to come out from there in open rebellion.[167]

The rebels gathered at the great mosque at midnight. Their leader, Khālid b. Saʿīd wore a yellow mantle (قباء أصفر) and a yellow silk turban (عمامة خز صفراء).[168] He even put an *ʿimāma* on his horse. The plot was revealed to the authorities by one of the rebels. The city's important tribal leaders did not join the rebellion[169] and it seems that the number of those who did was small.[170] Some of them surrendered to the governor after he gathered troops around the great mosque. Khālid b. Saʿīd, the rebels' leader, was shot in the thigh with an arrow, but he managed to escape and hide in Yaḥyā b. Jābir Abā [sic!] Kināna al-Ḥaḍramī's house; he hid there for seventy nights until the search for him died down. Two of his sons, Ibrāhīm and Hudba, fled, too, and found shelter in the Banū Sahm residence (Dār Banī Sahm). Thirteen of the rebels were killed; al-Kindī stressed that only one of them was important: Kaltham (Kulthum/Kalthum) b. al-Mundhir al-Kalbī.[171] Perhaps another well-known person could be added to the list, ʿĪsā b. Lahīʿa b. ʿUqba b. Firʿān al-Ḥaḍramī l-Uʿdūlī, the brother of the famous scholar and *qāḍī* of Egypt, ʿAbdallāh b. Lahīʿa. "He died in Shawwāl 145/December 762–January 763; it is said that he was hit by an arrow on the night that Khālid b. Saʿīd b. Rabīʿa b. Ḥubaysh al-Ṣadafī came

---

167 Al-Kindī, *Wulāt* (ed. Guest), 112.

168 It is interesting that the color chosen by these rebels is neither white (the color of the pro-Umawī rebellions), nor green (the color chosen by al-Maʾmūn to distinguish his ʿAlīd preference).

169 Al-Kindī, *Wulāt*, 113.

170 Ibid., 112 (l. 14): if I understand the text correctly فانتهبوا بيت المال ثم تضاربوا عليه بسيوفهم فلم يصل منهم إليه إلا اليسير; see also the description on 113: the governor says: "if you saw the (light of the) lamps in the houses, it means that this is a comprehensive matter (*amr ʿāmm*) and then come to me, and if not come to the mosque"; eventually the army troops gather at the mosque, so it is most probably a sign that the houses in the streets remained dark.

171 Ibid., 114, has Kulthum (ed. Naṣṣār, 135: Kulthum); and see Ibn al-Kalbī, *Jamhara* (ed. Caskel), 2:369, where we read Kaltham; idem, *Nasab Maʿadd*, 2:611, remarking that Kalthum b. al-Mundhir b. ʿĀmir b. Abī ʿĀmir b. ʿAbdallāh b. Imruʾ al-Qays b. Ḥāritha b. ʿĀmir b. ʿAwf b. ʿĀmir [b. ʿAwf b. Bakr b. ʿAwf b. ʿUdhra b. Zayd Allāt b. Rafīda b. Thawr b. Kalb b. Wabara], "was the one who propagated in Egypt (al-Fusṭāṭ?) for the cause of Muḥammad b. ʿAbdallāh b. Ḥasan b. Ḥasan b. ʿAlī b. Abī Ṭālib and was killed in the night of the mosque campaign": وهو الذي دعا بمصر إلى محمد بن عبد الله بن حسن بن حسن بن علي بن أبي طالب وقتل ليلة المسجد. ; the reconstruction of the lineage is according to Ibn Ḥazm, *Jamhara*, 455–460; Ibn al-Kalbī, *Jamhara* (ed. Caskel), 2:603ff.]

out in the hideous attack (*nazwa*),[172] and he died from the arrow."[173] From this unique tradition we learn that notable members of the Marwānī Umawī family in Egypt, that of ʿAbd al-ʿAzīz b. Marwān b. al-Ḥakam took a leading part in the rebellion. Here is not the place to trace this family's history under the Umawīs and the early ʿAbbāsīs. Suffice it to say that many of its members were executed by the ʿAbbāsīs, with other members of the Marwānī house, either in Nahr Abī Fuṭrus (Antipatris), or in al-Qalansuwa (both in Jund Filasṭīn).[174]

The importance of al-Kindī's tradition lies in the detailed reliable information he records about the situation in Egypt on the eve of the revolt. It reveals that ʿAlī's propaganda in Egypt began about a year before his father came out in open rebellion; it also asserts that there was a positive response to the appeal by some of the Arab tribes in Egypt. It can be said that it involved some of the old and distinguished Arab families in Egypt from the Ṣadif and Ḥaḍramawt tribes, whose forefathers had taken part in the conquest of Egypt. The leadership of the revolt consisted of some pro-ʿAlīds, on the one side, and members of distinguished Umawī (Marwānī) families, on the other. However, it seems to have gained only limited support and was easily crushed by the professional ʿAbbāsī troops.

As for ʿAlī b. Muḥammad al-Nafs al-Zakiyya, the accepted opinion related in the sources is that he was caught and was brought to al-Manṣūr. One source specifically tells that he died in Baghdad.[175] Al-Kindī is aware of this tradition but says that there are different opinions about his fate. "One (some?) of the transmitters claimed that he was taken to Abū Jaʿfar (al-Manṣūr)"; but then he records a tradition whose *isnād* ends with Saʿīd b. Kathīr b. ʿUfayr (146–220/763 or 764–835, the well-known Egyptian scholar) that "ʿAlī b. Muḥammad

172 Dozy, *Supplément*, 664 (s.v. *n.z.w.*)

173 Al-Samʿānī, *al-Ansāb* (Hyderabad edition), 1:305; it is not stated in the tradition that he took part in the rebellion.

174 For the massacre in Nahr Abī Fuṭrus, see Moscati, "Le Massacre"; M. Sharon, "Nahr Abī Fuṭrus," *EI*²; Elad, "The Ethnic Composition," 286–289. For al-Qalansuwa, see al-Kindī, *Wulāt* (ed. Guest), 99–100. Regarding the conspirators: Zayd b. al-Aṣbagh, escaped to North Africa (Ifrīqiya) and came back due to an amnesty given to the family by al-Manṣūr (al-Kindī, *Wulāt*, 100). The son of his grandson, Wafāʾ b. Zayd b. al-Aṣbagh b. Zayd b. Abī[sic!] al-Aṣbagh b. ʿAbd al-ʿAzīz b. Marwān (d. Jumādā II 204/Nov.–Dec. 819), was a *ḥadīth* scholar, see Ibn Mākūlā, *al-Ikmāl*, 7:304. Al-Manṣūr b. al-Aṣbagh was also saved from the massacre (how is not known), see al-Kindī, *Wulāt*, 100. Diḥya b. Muṣʿab b. al-Aṣbagh is a better known figure, mainly due to his rebellion in Egypt (in 167/783 or 784) during al-Mahdī's reign, which was suppressed during Hādī's reign (in 169/785).

175 For example, see al-Balādhurī, *Ansāb* (ed. Madelung), 2:540, where it is reported that he died in Baghdad; al-Ṭabarī, 3:171; al-Iṣfahānī, *Maqātil*, 201, 295.

was given shelter and a hiding place by ʿAssāma b. ʿAmr [in whose house ʿAlī dwelled upon his arrival in Egypt]. ʿAssāma took him to one of his villages, named Ṭuwwa, where he became ill, died and was buried." As for ʿAssāma, he was brought to al-ʿIrāq and was imprisoned until al-Mahdī became caliph and set him free because of the intercession of his *wazīr*, Abū ʿUbaydallāh. Abū ʿUbaydallāh did this because of the close relations between Banū l-Maʿāfir (to which ʿAssāma belonged), and Banū Ashʿar (to which Abū ʿUbaydallāh belonged).[176] Al-Mahdī gave him *amān*, a pension of 200 (*dīnār*s) and sent him back to Egypt.[177]

Yāqūt adds some important geographic details about the village where ʿAlī b. Muḥammad died. He says:

> As for Ṭūkh al-Khayl, it is another village in the Saʿīd, west of the Nile. It is called Ṭūkh Bayt Yamūn, and it is also named Ṭuwwa. The grave of ʿAlī b. Muḥammad b. ʿAbdallāh b. al-Ḥasan b. al-Ḥasan b. ʿAlī b. Abī Ṭālib is located there. He had come out in rebellion in Egypt during al-Manṣūr's reign in the year 145. When Yazīd b. Ḥātim crushed his rebellion, ʿAssāma b. ʿUmar [read ʿAmr] al-Maʿāfirī hid him in this village and married him to his daughter (and he stayed there) until he died and was buried there.[178]

3.2 *Syria*

Muḥammad b. ʿAbdallāh made efforts to gain support and recruit supporters for his cause in Syria. These efforts, however, did not succeed in gathering large numbers of supporters from among the *ahl al-Shām* (the Arabs of Syria). According to one such tradition, Muḥammad b. ʿAbdallāh sent a messenger to *ahl al-Shām* calling them to swear allegiance to him as the caliph, but they refused.[179]

Other more detailed traditions describe how immediately upon the outbreak of the revolt, Muḥammad b. ʿAbdallāh sent a delegation to Syria to summon its people to his cause. But according to these traditions, this was Muḥammad b. Khālid b. ʿAbdallāh al-Qasrī's idea; although he was released by Muḥammad b. ʿAbdallāh from prison, he remained a follower of the ʿAbbāsīs and succeeded in persuading Muḥammad b. ʿAbdallāh to believe that

---

176 Abū ʿUbaydallāh, Muʿāwiya b. ʿUbaydallāh b. Yasār, al-Mahdī's *wazīr*, was a *mawlā* of Banū Ashʿar, on him, see Sourdel, *Le Vizirat*, 1:94ff.; Elad, "Transition," 113–114.

177 Al-Kindī, *Wulāt* (Beirut edition), 136.

178 Yāqūt, *Muʿjam* (Beirut edition), 4:46.

179 Ibn Kathīr, *al-Bidāya* (Cairo, 1351 H.), 10:86.

he would be able to conduct propaganda on his behalf in Syria. According to these traditions, this delegation included Rizām, the *mawlā* of Muḥammad b. Khālid, Mūsā b. ʿAbdallāh b. al-Ḥasan (Muḥammad b. ʿAbdallāh's brother)[180] or Rizām, Mūsā and ʿAbdallāh b. Jaʿfar b. ʿAbd al-Raḥmān b. Miswar b. Makhrama b. Nawfal al-Qurashī l-Zuhrī.[181]

According to another tradition, besides Mūsā b. ʿAbdallāh, this delegation included Rizām (the *mawlā* of Muḥammad b. Khālid) and the nephew of Muḥammad b. Khālid, Nadhīr b. Yazīd b. Khālid. Upon arriving in Syria, Rizām and Nadhīr abandoned Mūsā b. ʿAbdallāh (which was in fact their original plan) and fled to the caliph.[182] Mūsā returned to Medina after sending a letter to his brother in which he described the *ahl al-Shām*'s cold and negative reaction to his propaganda on his brother's behalf.[183] However, two other pieces of information may serve as evidence of certain support for Muḥammad b. ʿAbdallāh in Syria.

The first tells of a man from *ahl al-Shām* who joined Muḥammad b. ʿAbdallāh and fought with him.[184] While this tradition lacks any identifying details, and includes some literary motifs that undermine its credibility, the second testimony seems to be much more reliable, important, and interesting. It is related by the well-known early historian (*akhbārī*) al-Madāʾinī (d. ca. 225/840). According to him, Banū ʿAbs and all the inhabitants of (*min ahl*) Ḥiyār Banī l-Qaʿqāʿ who lived with them corresponded with Muḥammad b. ʿAbdallāh. One of the ʿAbsīs who wrote to him was Abū Dhufāfa, who was chosen in 154/771 by Caliph al-Manṣūr to be one of the close companions (*ṣaḥāba*) of al-Mahdī, his son. Abū Dhufāfa had a great influence on al-Mahdī, and this met with al-Manṣūr's approval (in contrast to the attitude of al-Rabīʿ b. Yūnus, the chief secretary of the caliph), who described Abū Dhufāfa as a "noble" man (*sharīf*), who educates his son according to the Arab values and customs.[185]

This tradition lacks apparent bias in regard to our topic of Muḥammad b. ʿAbdallāh's rebellion, for its aim was not to deal with the event itself, its

180 Al-Ṭabarī, 3:215–216 (l. 15 to l. 10).

181 Ibid., 3:216 (ll. 10–13).

182 Al-Balādhurī, *Ansāb* (ed. Madelung), 2:509–510.

183 Al-Ṭabarī, 3:216 (ll. 5–10); see also al-Balādhurī, *Ansāb* (ed. Madelung), 2:509–510; al-Iṣfahānī, *Maqātil*, 392: Mūsā was sent to Syria but Muḥammad b. ʿAbdallāh died before his arrival [in this province?]; according to another version, Mūsā returned to Medina before his brother's death.

184 Al-Ṭabarī, 3:222 (ll. 15–20).

185 Al-Balādhurī, *Ansāb* (ed. al-Dūrī), 3:261.

course or consequences. The mention of the correspondence of Banū ʿAbs in Ḥiyār Banī l-Qaʿqāʿ with Muḥammad b. ʿAbdallāh is related innocently, with no preconceived design, only as a background to the description of Abū Dhufāfa's distinctive position, and al-Manṣūr's wisdom and insight. This is not a tradition that uses literary motifs relating to unknown obscure persons, only relating that Banū ʿAbs, the inhabitants of Ḥiyār Banī l-Qaʿqāʿ in the Qinnasrīn district, and those who lived with them, supported Muḥammad b. ʿAbdallāh. This is further supported by other evidence, according to which Ibrāhīm b. ʿAbdallāh b. al-Ḥasan, in one of his constant wandering flights from al-Manṣūr, stayed in the dwellings of the family of al-Qaʿqāʿ b. Khulayd al-ʿAbsī in al-Ḥiyār.[186] These two pieces of information may testify to the connections of (and perhaps also support of) the Banū ʿAbs in al-Ḥiyār with the Ḥasanī family. This location and its inhabitants are well-known from the time of ʿAbd al-Malik b. Marwān (r. 65–86/685–705).

The aforementioned family members of Khulayd b. al-Qaʿqāʿ were relatives of ʿAbd al-Malik's family, and rose to great prominence during the Umawī period.[187] Members of this family were important leaders in their sub-tribal groups and even in larger tribal units. Zuhayr b. Jadhīma was the leader of Banū ʿAbs and Ghaṭafān.[188] Wallāda, the daughter of al-ʿAbbās b. Jazʾ b. al-Ḥārith b. Zuhayr al-ʿAbsī, married Caliph ʿAbd al-Malik and bore him al-Walīd and Sulaymān.[189] Al-Ḥuṣayn b. Khulayd b. Jazʾ was a tribal leader or notable dignitary in Syria (كان سيدا/شريفا بالشام).[190] He seems to have had close relations with Sulaymān b. ʿAbd al-Malik and is described as his maternal uncle.[191] His uncle, ʿAbdallāh b. Jazʾ was a notable dignitary in Syria (كان شريفا بالشام).[192] ʿAbd al-Malik granted estates to al-ʿAbbās and his nephew al-Qaʿqāʿ b. Khulayd; the most famous of these estates was the huge estate (which might

186 Al-Ṭabarī, 3:283; the rendering (al-Khiyār) in the Egyptian edition of Abū l-Faḍl Ibrāhīm, 7:623, is erroneous.

187 Elad, "The Southern Golan," 59–63; for the genealogical table of the family, see ibid., 60.

188 Ibn Ḥazm, *Jamhara*, 251.

189 Al-Zubayrī, *Nasab Quraysh*, 162; al-Balādhurī, *Ansāb* (ed. Zakkār), 7:2919, 2930; 13:5570; Ibn Ḥazm, *Jamhara*, 151; Ibn al-Kalbī, *Jamhara* (ed. Ḥasan), 442, erroneously identifies al-Qaʿqāʿ b. Khulayd b. Jazʾ as the grandfather of al-Walīd and Sulaymān, instead of al-ʿAbbās b. Jazʾ; this did not appear as clear-cut to other genealogists, see, for instance, Ibn al-ʿAdīm, *Bughya*, 1:125, 539.

190 Ibn al-Kalbī, *Jamhara* (ed. Ḥasan), 442 (*sharīf*); Ibn Ḥazm, *Jamhara*, 151; Ibn al-ʿAdīm, *Bughya*, 6:2818; Ibn ʿAsākir, *Taʾrīkh*, 14:373 (*sayyid*).

191 Al-Balādhurī, *Ansāb* (ed. Zakkār), 13:211.

192 Ibn al-Kalbī, *Jamhara* (ed. Ḥasan), 442.

have eventually become a town), Ḥiyār Banī l-Qaʿqāʿ.[193] Al-Qaʿqāʿ, who served as a scribe to al-Walīd b. ʿAbd al-Malik, was also granted estates in Damascus (*qaṭīʿa*)[194] and in the district of Manbij.[195] Al-Walīd b. al-Qaʿqāʿ was the governor of Qinnasrīn (or according to another source, of al-Balqāʾ) during the reign of Hishām b. ʿAbd al-Malik.[196] His brother, ʿAbd al-Malik b. al-Qaʿqāʿ, was the governor of Ḥimṣ during the reign of Hishām,[197] and in 119/737 he was appointed the commander-in-chief of the summer campaign.[198] A member of another branch of this tribe was Khālid b. Barz b. Kāmil b. Barz, who was the governor of Damascus on behalf of al-Walīd b. ʿAbd al-Malik.[199]

This maternal blood relationship paved the way for the ʿAbsīs access to the caliph's court, to prominent positions, and wealth.[200] Very little is known about this family's history during the early ʿAbbāsī caliphate. I do not know the background for their support of the Ḥasanīs. It may be connected to the general decline of Syria and its *ashrāf*, which resulted from the ascendance of the ʿAbbāsīs; it is possible that they specifically suffered at the hands of the

---

193 Elad, "Two Inscriptions," 313; see also Ibn al-ʿAdīm, *Bughya*, 1:125 (= Ibn Shaddād, *al-Aʿlāq al-khaṭīra*, 1 (pt 2): 38–39, 41), has "Ḥiyār Banī l-Qaʿqāʿ which is also known as Ḥiyār Banī ʿAbs." In Ibn al-ʿAdīm, *Bughya*, 1:125. and Ibn Shaddād, *al-Aʿlāq al-khaṭīra*, 1 (pt 2): 38–39, 41, quoting al-Yaʿqūbī, we read "and the district (*kūra*) of the second Qinnasrīn" (قنسرين الثانية); this passage is not found in the 1892 Leiden ed. of *Kitāb al-Buldān* of al-Yaʿqūbī, but in the appendix on 362 the editor quotes the passage from the ms. of *Taʾrīkh Ḥalab* of Ibn al-Shiḥna, who quotes al-Yaʿqūbī [= Muḥammad b. al-Shiḥna, *Taʾrīkh Ḥalab*, 231/164].

194 Ibn ʿAsākir *Taʾrīkh*, 49:347; Conrad, *Abū l-Ḥusayn al-Rāzī*, 57.

195 Ibn al-ʿAdīm, *Zubda*, 1:48; idem, *Bughya*, 1:540.

196 Ibn ʿAsākir, *Taʾrīkh*, 63:252: over Qinnasrīn; Ibn al-ʿAdīm, *Zubda*, 1:48: "governor of Qinnasrīn ... but it was said that he [i.e., Caliph Hishām] nominated ʿAbd al-Malik b. al-Qaʿqāʿ as governor of Qinnasrīn" (= Abū l-Fidāʾ[?], *al-Yawāqīt*, 41; Ibn Shaddād, *al-Aʿlāq al-khaṭīra*, 38); but cf. al-Ṭabarī, 2:1783 and Ibn ʿAsākir, *Taʾrīkh*, 63:253: "al-Walīd b. al-Qaʿqāʿ over Qinnasrīn and ʿAbd al-Malik b. al-Qaʿqāʿ over Ḥimṣ"[!]; al-Balādhurī, *Ansāb* (ed. al-Yaʿlāwī), 7/2:82 (ed. Zakkār, 13:211): governor of al-Balqāʾ[!].

197 Ibn ʿAsākir, *Taʾrīkh*, 63:253, adding that ʿAbd al-Malik and his brother al-Walīd were both tortured to death by Yazīd b.ʿUmar b. Hubayra, the governor of Qinnasrīn during the short reign of al-Walīd b. Yazīd (125–126/743–744).

198 Ibn ʿAsākir, *Taʾrīkh*, 37:90; al-Ṭabarī, 2:1593.

199 Ibn Ḥazm, *Jamhara*, 250; Ibn al-Kalbī, *Jamhara* (ed. Ḥasan), 441 (= ed. Caskel, 2:341); al-Balādhurī, *Ansāb* (ed. Zakkār), 13:211; Ibn ʿAsākir, *Taʾrīkh*, 16:5–6.

200 Al-Balādhurī, *Ansāb* (ed. Zakkār), 7:2919, 2930; this consanguinity served, on the other hand, as a motive in satires against the ʿAbsīs: "You were led in the Jāhiliyya by a slave, that is ʿAntara, and in (the time of) Islam by a woman, that is the mother of al-Walīd and Sulaymān," ibid., 13:211.

ʿAbbāsīs upon the ascendance of the latter. All this is speculative; I have not found any evidence to corroborate these assumptions. On the contrary, the aforementioned Abū Dhufāfa, who according to al-Madāʾinī's tradition corresponded with Muḥammad b. ʿAbdallāh, was not punished by al-Manṣūr; in 154/771 he was appointed to a high post by the caliph and was highly respected by him. One could argue that he supported Muḥammad b. ʿAbdallāh in 145/762 and it took him nine years to gain this senior position, if it were not for other evidence that Abū Dhufāfa al-ʿAbsī was one of the senior commanders in the army of Jaʿfar b. Sulaymān b. ʿAlī b. ʿAbdallāh b. al-ʿAbbās, the newly appointed governor of al-Baṣra, who led his army against Ibrāhīm b. ʿAbdallāh b. al-Ḥasan in Bākhamrā in the year145/762.[201] So far I have found only one source that mentions Abū Dhufāfa al-ʿAbsī: Ibn al-ʿAdīm mentions him briefly in one of the biographies of another member of the family (his descendant?), who lived more than two generations after Abū Dhufāfa. This other member is the poet ʿAbdallāh b. Muḥammad, known by his epithet (*laqab*) Abū l-Aḥwaṣ, or al-Muḥtariz al-Dhufāfī. The surname (*nisba*) al-Dhufāfī, adds Ibn al-ʿAdīm, is related to Dhufāfa b. ʿAbd al-ʿAzīz al-ʿAbsī, whose name before being mentioned offhandedly by Ibn al-ʿAdīm, had been unknown. The above-mentioned poet, al-Muḥtariz (al-Aḥwaṣ) al-Dhufāfī, was one of the close companions (*kāna yaṣḥab*) of the ʿAbbāsī Abū Ṭālib ʿAlī b. Ismāʿīl b. Ṣāliḥ b. ʿAlī [b. ʿAbdallāh b. al-ʿAbbās] al-Hāshimī in Ḥalab,[202] who lived most likely during al-Maʾmūn's reign (197–218/813–833).[203] Abū Dhufāfa, therefore, is ʿAbd al-ʿAzīz al-ʿAbsī.

201 Al-Balādhurī, *Ansāb* (ed. Madelung), 2:530; ibid.: Bākhumrā; cf. Yāqūt, *Muʿjam* (Beirut edition), 1 ("Bākhamrā"); al-Balādhurī, *Ansāb* (ed. Madelung), 2:530: Abū Dufāfa (instead of Dhufāfa), but it seems that the correct name should be Dhufāfa, see below.

202 Ibn al-ʿAdīm mentions the poet al-Muḥtariz al-Dhufāfī twice in the printed volumes of his monumental book: once under al-Aḥwaṣ al-Dhufāfī, see Ibn al-ʿAdīm, *Bughya*, 10:4717 (where ʿAlī b. Ismāʿīl b. Ṣāliḥ al-ʿAbbāsī is mentioned); the second time under al-Muḥtariz al-Dhufāfī, ibid., 10:4743. See also 10:4717, where he says that he is mentioned in the biographies of those who are named ʿAbdallāh (ذكرهم في العبادلة); these entries have not been published yet and the printed edition is incomplete. Ibn al-ʿAdīm adds that this poet married ʿAlwa al-Kurāʿa [Karrāʿa?], whom the poet al-Buḥturī described in his poetry (كان يشبب بها) (see al-Buḥturī, *Dīwān*, 4:2325, no. 875; and esp. 1:376, no. 146, noting that her mother's name was Zurayqa [see Ch. Pellat, "al-Buḥturī," *EI*², 1:1289b]); Yāqūt, *Muʿjam* (Beirut edition), 2:283, relates that ʿAlwa's abode (*dār*) in Ḥalab is situated in the middle of the city; this was the reason for the satirical poem of al-Buḥturī against her; see al-Buḥturī, *Dīwān*, 2:897, no. 354; 4:2325, no. 875; see also ibid., 3:1076–1077, where we find an elegy for the death of al-Dhufāfī's brother.

203 I found no information about ʿAlī b. Ismāʿīl. His father, Ismāʿīl b. Ṣāliḥ, was a close confidant of Hārūn al-Rashīd; on him, see Cobb, *White Banners*, 156, n. 31 and 158, n. 45. See also

I was unable to trace his exact lineage. Al-Ṣayrafī, the editor of the *Dīwān* of al-Buḥturī (206–284/821–897), does not identify the poet al-Aḥwaṣ al-Dhufāfī, but adds that he may belong to the family of Abū l-ʿAbbās Dhufāfa b. ʿAbd al-ʿAzīz al-ʿAbsī, "whom al-Rashīd ordered to kill a Byzantine prisoner who was brought to him."[204] According to this, Dhufāfa b. ʿAbd al-ʿAzīz was also probably a senior commander in the service of the ʿAbbāsī caliph. Another member of the family, Thumāma b. al-Walīd b. al-Qaʿqāʿ b. Khulayd, was appointed by Caliph al-Mahdī as the commander-in-chief of the summer expeditions in the years 160/777 and 161/778.[205]

3.3 *Al-ʿIrāq (al-Baṣra and al-Kūfa)*

It would have been reasonable to assume that Muḥammad b. ʿAbdallāh had substantial support in al-ʿIrāq, especially in al-Baṣra, where his brother Ibrāhīm came out in revolt. However, if this is correct, it was passive support, for no mission is known to have come from al-ʿIrāq to Medina to help Muḥammad b. ʿAbdallāh. On the other hand, if, as some of the sources record, Muḥammad and Ibrāhīm planned to revolt at the same time, then Ibrāhīm needed his Baṣrī supporters, as well as supporters from other places in al-ʿIrāq for his insurrection.

There is only general information about Muḥammad b. ʿAbdallāh's followers who swore allegiance to him in al-ʿIrāq.[206] On rare occasions a name is given, such as that of Yaʿqūb b. Dāwūd (who appears later as al-Mahdī's *wazīr*), of whom it is said that he used to roam the provinces, sometimes alone, sometimes with Ibrāhīm b. ʿAbdallāh, summoning the Muslims to swear allegiance to Muḥammad b. ʿAbdallāh.[207] A single interesting tradition related by al-Madāʾinī reveals that Muḥammad b. ʿAbdallāh

> reached al-Baṣra covertly with forty men. They went to ʿAbd al-Raḥmān b. ʿUthmān b. ʿAbd al-Raḥmān b. al-Ḥārith b. Hishām [b. Mughīra al-Makhzūmī], who said to him: "You have destroyed me and publicly exposed me. Stay with me but disperse your confederates." Muḥammad,

---

Ibn ʿAsākir, *Taʾrīkh*, 8:410–414. The history of the family of Ṣāliḥ b. ʿAlī l-ʿAbbāsī, especially of ʿAbd al-Malik b. Ṣāliḥ b. ʿAlī in Syria, was reconstructed by Bonner, *Aristocratic Violence*, index, esp. 88–94, and esp. Cobb, *White Banners*, 27–31.

204 Al-Buḥturī, *Dīwān*, 2:897, note by al-Ṣayrafī, the editor, who does not cite his source (= al-Iṣfahānī, *al-Aghānī* [Dār al-Kutub edition], 20:217).

205 Ibn Khayyāṭ, *Taʾrīkh* (ed. al-ʿUmarī), 2:459 and 468: years 160 H. and 161H.; al-Yaʿqūbī, *Taʾrīkh* (Beirut edition), 2:402; Ibn ʿAsākir, *Taʾrīkh*, 26:396: year 160 H.; al-Balādhurī, *Futūḥ*, 1:225; Ibn ʿAsākir, *Taʾrīkh*, 11:450: year 161 H.

206 Al-Balādhurī, *Ansāb* (ed. Madelung), 2:509.

207 Al-Ṭabarī, 3:507.

> however, refused, so ʿAbd al-Raḥmān said: "You may not stay with me; go stay with the Banū Rāsib." This Muḥammad did.[208]

This tradition has some grain of historical truth: some branches of the family of ʿAbd al-Raḥmān b. al-Ḥārith lived in al-Baṣra, including that of his son, ʿUthmān.[209] Ibrāhīm b. ʿAbdallāh lived among the Banū Rāsib (b. Maydaʿān [al-Azd])[210] in al-Baṣra, in the house of ʿAbd al-Raḥmān b. Ḥarb (unidentified).[211]

Other evidence is recorded by Sulaymān b. Muḥammad al-Sārī, who "heard Abū Habbār al-Muzanī saying: 'We stayed in al-Baṣra with Muḥammad b. ʿAbdallāh while he was summoning the people to his cause.'"[212] Abū Habbār was a confidant of Muḥammad b. ʿAbdallāh. It is worthwhile remembering that al-Manṣūr's first act upon hearing of the revolt was to leave Baghdad (still in its building stages) for al-Kūfa, which was the ʿAlīds' stronghold, in order to prevent its people from sending help and reinforcements to Muḥammad in Medina.[213] And indeed, nothing is heard of any active and meaningful help from the people of al-Kūfa. Most of Muḥammad b. ʿAbdallāh's supporters in al-Kūfa who corresponded with him were executed by order of al-Manṣūr.[214]

There is an exceptional case of two fairly well-known scholars, al-Ḥasan and ʿAlī, sons of Ṣāliḥ b. Ṣāliḥ b. Ḥayy (Ḥayyān) (al-Ḥasan was the most prominent scholar of the two),[215] who joined Muḥammad b. ʿAbdallāh in Medina

208 Al-Ṭabarī, 3:148 (ll. 2–7); trans. McAuliffe (*ʿAbbāsid Authority*, 92).

209 For general information on this family, see al-Zubayrī, *Nasab Quraysh*, 303–306; Ibn Ḥazm, *Jamhara*, 145; Ibn Saʿd, *Ṭabaqāt*, 5:5–7; Ibn Khayyāṭ, *Ṭabaqāt* (ed. Zakkār), 426f. As for ʿAbd al-Raḥmān b. ʿUthmān b. ʿAbd al-Raḥmān b. al-Ḥārith b. Hishām b. al-Mughīra al-Makhzūmī, I found him mentioned only once in al-Balādhurī, *Ansāb* (ed. ʿAbbās), 5:245, stating that the family lived in al-Baṣra; another family in al-Baṣra is that of ʿAbd al-Raḥmān b. Muḥammad b. Abī Bakr b. ʿAbdallāh (this should be corrected to ʿUbaydallāh according to Ibn Ḥazm, *Jamhara*, 145, and Wakīʿ, *Quḍāt*, 2:140; his biography, ibid., 140–142) b. ʿAbd al-Raḥmān b. al-Ḥārith b. Hishām; Ibn Ḥazm, *Jamhara*, 145, relates that he and his father lived in al-Baṣra; ibid., but esp. Wakīʿ, *Quḍāt*, 2:140: ʿAbd al-Raḥmān was the first Ḥanafī *qāḍī* in al-Baṣra during the governorship of Muḥammad b. Sulaymān [b. ʿAlī b. ʿAbdallāh b. al-ʿAbbās], during Hārūn al-Rashīd's reign; Muḥammad b. Sulaymān died in 173/789; on him, see al-Khaṭīb al-Baghdādī, *Taʾrīkh* (Beirut, 1997), 2:386–387; Ibn ʿAsākir, *Taʾrīkh*, 53:129–140.

210 Ibn Ḥazm, *Jamhara*, 474.

211 Al-Ṭabarī, 3:290; mentioned by Kennedy, *ʿAbbāsid Caliphate*, 202.

212 Al-Ṭabarī, 3:148 (ll. 7–9).

213 Al-Balādhurī, *Ansāb* (ed. Madelung), 2:521–522.

214 Ibid., 2:523.

215 On al-Ḥasan see van Ess, *Theologie*, 1:246–251; Crone, *Islamic Thought*, 103.

(most probably from al-Kūfa), ready to fight for him, and then were sent back immediately upon their arrival by Muḥammad.[216] The two scholars lived in al-Kūfa and belonged to the Hamdān (tribe).[217] The tradition which tells of their arrival in Medina does not appear in the long biographies of these two scholars.[218] They were pro-Zaydī and belonged (especially al-Ḥasan) to the inner circle of ʿĪsā b. Zayd b. ʿAlī b. al-Ḥusayn,[219] who was one of the close followers of Muḥammad b. ʿAbdallāh and took an active part in the rebellion. Al-Ḥasan (100–169/718 or 719–785 or 786) was especially known for holding the opinion that it is lawful to rise up in armed rebellion (against an unjust and wrongdoing sovereign): رجل كان يرى السيف على أمة محمد / كان الحسن بن حي يرى السيف.[220] Al-Dhahabī concludes his biography by saying that "al-Ḥasan considered that it is permissible to rebel against the rulers of his time because of their unjust and corrupt tyrannical rule, nevertheless he never fought (against the ruler). He objected to praying behind an unjust ruler."[221]

We find one other exceptional case, that of a minor transmitter, Yaʿqūb b. ʿArabī, originally from al-Kūfa. According to his (single) testimony, he was a close follower of Muḥammad b. ʿAbdallāh and was imprisoned for many years after the revolt.[222]

The same information regarding active support applies to al-Baṣra as well, except perhaps for two unequivocal cases:

---

216 Al-Iṣfahānī, *Maqātil*, 295; van Ess, *Theologie*, 1:247.

217 Ibn Ḥazm, *Jamhara*, 396; van Ess, *Theologie*, 1:246.

218 For example, see al-Mizzī, *Tahdhīb*, 6:177–191 (al-Ḥasan); 20:464–468 (ʿAlī); idem, *Siyar*, 7:361–371 (al-Ḥasan); 7:371–372 (ʿAlī), and the comprehensive bibliography of the editors therein.

219 They are mentioned several times in al-Iṣfahānī's *Maqātil*, see index; they (especially al-Ḥasan b. Ṣāliḥ) appear as the close companions of ʿĪsā b. Zayd , see al-Iṣfahānī's *Maqātil*, 415–416, 418.

220 Al-Mizzī, *Tahdhīb*, 6:181.

221 Al-Dhahabī, *Siyar*, 7:371.

222 Al-Iṣfahānī, *Maqātil*, 253 (ll. 7–8). As far as I know, he is mentioned only by Ibn Mākūlā, *al-Ikmāl*, 6:177, recording that he was a *muḥaddith* from al-Kūfa, who transmitted from ʿAdī b. Thābit (al-Anṣārī, d. 116/734, on him, see al-Ziriklī, *al-Aʿlām*, 4:219; al-Mizzī, *Tahdhīb*, 19:522–523: a Kūfan, "he was the *imām* of the Mosque of the Shīʿa and their *qāṣṣ*"; al-Shāhrūdī, al-Namāzī, *Rijāl*, 5:228) and from Abū Janāda, Ḥuṣayn b. Mukhāriq al-Salūlī (on him, see for example, al-Dhahabī, *Mīzān* [Beirut, 1963], 1:554; Ibn Ḥajar, *Lisān*, 2:319; Khūʾī, *Rijāl*, 7:134; Amīn, *Aʿyān al-Shīʿa*, 6:199: Khuḍayn b. Mukhāriq).

1) The first concerns members of the family of the well-known *ḥadīth* scholar Abū Bakr Azhar b. Saʿd b. Nāfiʿ al-Sammān, *mawlā* Bāhila, al-Baṣrī (d. 203/818 or 819).[223] Al-Ṭabarī transmitted through him thirteen traditions on the rebellion and related events. Two of his traditions clearly attest to his being in Medina during the rebellion,[224] but there is no statement by him that he himself took an active part in fighting, as did his two brothers, ʿUthmān and Muḥammad, who he says were with Muḥammad b. ʿAbdallāh.[225]

Although Azhar b. Saʿd's surname is al-Baṣrī, we do not know if he and his two brothers came from there with the specific intention of joining Muḥammad b. ʿAbdallāh. It is possible that in 145/762 they lived in Medina and moved to al-Baṣra at some later stage.

2) It is possible that some members of the Baṣrī family of ʿAbd al-Malik b. Mismaʿ b. Mālik b. Mismaʿ, who belonged to Banū Ḍubayʿa (Bakr b. Wāʾil), came to Medina in order to take part in the rebellion of Muḥammad b. ʿAbdallāh. Members of this family were the leaders of Bakr b. Wāʾil during large parts of the Umawī period, and held important roles during the early ʿAbbāsī period as well.[226]

When the rebellion broke out, al-Manṣūr attached Mismaʿ b. Muḥammad b. Shaybān b. Mālik b. Mismaʿ to ʿĪsā b. Mūsā's army, but the former withdrew from the ʿAbbāsī camp, and remained inactive until Muḥammad's death.[227] This may denote an inclination towards Muḥammad and his rebellion. Another member of this family, Zayd, the *mawlā* of Mismaʿ b. ʿAbd al-Malik, was in Medina during the rebellion. Al-Ṭabarī records through him three traditions concerning the rebellion;[228] in two he uses the first-person plural: "ʿĪsā b. Mūsā went forth [with his army] until he came upon us while we were in Medina": فسار حتى قدم علينا ونحن بالمدينة,[229] or "on the third day, he approached with [many] horses, men, and weapons, the like of which I've never seen.

223 On him, see Ibn Saʿd, *Ṭabaqāt*, 7:294; Ibn Ḥajar, *Tahdhīb* (Hyderabad edition), 1:202; al-Dhahabī, *Tadhkira* (Hyderabad, 1333 H.), 1:313; al-Dhahabī, *Siyar*, 9:441–442; al-Mizzī, *Tahdhīb*, 2:323–324.

224 Al-Ṭabarī, 3:195 (ll. 12–13): وقد شهد ذلك; 3:253 (l. 14): فرأيتهم صَفّيْن.

225 Ibid., 3:236 (ll. 6–13).

226 On this family, see Crone, *Slaves*, 116–118; Elad, "Transition," 110, n. 96.

227 Al-Ṭabarī, 3:224–225 (l. 11 to l. 1).

228 Ibid., 3:207 (ll. 13–20); 223 (ll. 18–21); 234 (ll. 6–17): all three have the same *isnād*: ʿUmar b. Shabba < ʿAbd al-Malik b. Shaybān [b. ʿAbd al-Malik b. Mismaʿ, according to McAuliffe, *ʿAbbāsid Authority*, 165, n. 801] < Mismaʿ b. ʿAbd al-Malik.

229 Al-Ṭabarī, 3:223 (ll. 18–20).

By God, we didn't have long to wait before he got the better of us": فلما كان اليوم الثالث أقبل بما لم أر مثله قط من الخيل والرجال والسلاح فوالله ما لبثنا ان ظهر علينا.[230] It is evident from his report that he was not a supporter of the ʿAbbāsīs. It is highly plausible that he was not the only one from this family in Medina. It is possible that Abū Sayyār, the *ḥājib* of Muḥammad b. ʿAbdallāh, was Mismaʿ b. ʿAbd al-Malik b. Mismaʿ b. Mālik, nicknamed Kurdīn/Kirdīn, who is mentioned in the Imāmī sources as the head of Bakr b. Wā'il in al-Baṣra and the head of his extended family: شيخ بكر بن وائل بالبصرة ووجهها وسيد المسامعة. He was regarded as a follower of Muḥammad al-Bāqir, but mainly of Jaʿfar al-Ṣādiq.[231] The Imāmī sources do not give any information about his participation in al-Nafs al-Zakiyya's rebellion, but it is noteworthy that he is mentioned by Ibn Ḥazm—who also relates, as the Imāmī sources do, that his *laqab* was "Kurdīn,"—as one of the supporters of Ibrāhīm b. ʿAbdallāh in al-Baṣra (see below).

Ibn Ḥazm reports on five members of this family who took an active part in the rebellion of Ibrāhīm b. ʿAbdallāh in al-Baṣra: 1) Shihāb b. ʿAbd al-Malik b. Mismaʿ; 2) his brother Mismaʿ b. ʿAbd al-Malik b. Mismaʿ, nicknamed "Kurdīn"; 3) ʿAwn b. Mālik b. Mismaʿ b. Mālik; 4) his brother Mismaʿ b. Mālik b. Mismaʿ b. Mālik; 5) ʿAbdallāh b. Shaybān b. ʿAbd al-Malik b. Mismaʿ.[232] In spite of the participation of members of this family in Ibrāhīm's rebellion, in the year 159/775–776, ʿAbd al-Malik b. Shihāb [b. Mismaʿ?] was the commander-in-chief of strong contingents which came from al-Baṣra to attack the Khawārij in the eastern Arabian Peninsula.[233]

The above-mentioned Yaʿqūb b. Dāwūd most probably did not reach as far as Medina and join Muḥammad b. ʿAbdallāh, but we are told that he took part in Ibrāhīm's rebellion in al-Baṣra with some of his brothers.[234] After the rebellion, he and his brother ʿAlī were arrested by order of al-Manṣūr and were released only after the caliph died.[235]

---

230 Ibid., 3:234 (ll. 15–16).

231 Al-Tafrishī, *Naqd al-rijāl*, 4:375; al-ʿĀmilī, *Wasā'il* (*Āl al-Bayt*), 30:492 (the quote is taken from the last two sources); on Abū Sayyār Mismaʿ b. ʿAbd al-Malik, see also al-Najāshī, *Rijāl*, 420; al-Ḥillī, *Rijāl*, 189; al-Khū'ī, *Rijāl*, 19:174–178.

232 Ibn Ḥazm, *Jamhara*, 320; these five should be added to the family's biographies in Crone's *Slaves*, 116–118.

233 Al-Ṭabarī, 3:460; Elad, "Transition," 109–110.

234 Al-Ṭabarī, 3:506–507.

235 On Yaʿqūb b. Dāwūd, see Sourdel, *Le Vizirat*, index, esp. 1:103–111; see ibid., 1:103–104, on his support of Muḥammad and Ibrāhīm.

3.4 *Al-Sind*

The traditions about ʿAbdallāh (al-Ashtar) b. Muḥammad b. ʿAbdallāh b. al-Ḥasan traveling to al-Sind are also typical examples that illustrate the methodological difficulties that can be faced when trying to uncover the reality of historical events.

According to one tradition, he went on this mission (to al-Sind) on his father's behalf, although it does not specifically state that his father asked him to summon people to his cause. In this tradition it is clear from the description of the governor of al-Sind, the Muhallabī ʿUmar b. Ḥafṣ [b. ʿUthmān b. Qabīṣa b. Abī Ṣufra, called Hazārmard], that he is one of al-Manṣūr's most loyal commanders although he is an adherent of the family of Abū Ṭālib. He gives the Ḥasanī delegation a warm reception, and even swears allegiance to Muḥammad b. ʿAbdallāh and summons to his court the notables and senior commanders, who all swear allegiance to Muḥammad b. ʿAbdallāh. According to this tradition ʿAbdallāh al-Ashtar found shelter in the court of one of the kings in al-Sind and later was killed by the governor's brother who replaced Ḥafṣ b. Umar. On the face of it, this tradition seems reliable. The long and detailed tradition (more than four pages) was transmitted to al-Ṭabarī by a member of the ʿAbbāsī family, ʿAlī b. Muḥammad b. Sulaymān b. ʿAlī b. ʿAbdallāh b. al-ʿAbbās,[236] who seemed to have been interested in the history of the early ʿAbbāsīs. He transmitted several traditions to al-Ṭabarī; these disclose inside information about the manners and customs of the early ʿAbbāsī caliphs and inside political information.[237] The affair of al-Ashtar is also recorded in *Maqātil al-ṭālibiyyīn* in several short traditions, most of them from an eyewitness, the tutor (*muʾaddib*) of the children of ʿAbdallāh b. al-Ḥasan, ʿAbdallāh b. Muḥammad b. Masʿada, who relates that he took ʿAbdallāh al-Ashtar with him after the death of his father Muḥammad, and accompanied him on his journey to al-Sind.[238] Another Shīʿī

236 Al-Ṭabarī, 3:359–364.

237 E.g., ibid., 3:414–415 (three traditions); 3:417–418; 3:549–551 (three traditions).

238 Al-Iṣfahānī, *Maqātil*, 310–314 (= al-Majlisī, *Biḥār*, 47:296). Scant information is found on ʿAbdallāh b. Muḥammad b. Masʿada, the tutor of ʿAbdallāh al-Ashtar in the Shīʿī/Imāmī literature, e.g., al-Shāhrūdī l-Namāzī, *Rijāl*, 103; on his father, a minor Imāmī transmitter, see ibid., 322; al-Khūʾī, *Rijāl*, 18:235. Another son, ʿAlī is mentioned frequently in the Imāmī literature, on him, see ibid., 13:172; 22:127. I was unable to find additional material about this tutor of al-Ashtar; he may be mentioned by al-Samʿānī, *al-Ansāb* (Hyderabad edition), 8:153 ("al-Shamīdīzakī"), and 9:236 ("al-ʿAthmī") as a transmitter of *ḥadīth;* in both texts he is called the Qurʾān reader (*al-muqriʾ*). In addition to ʿAlī and ʿAbdallāh, Muḥammad b. Masʿada's sons, the sources mention Masʿada b. Ṣadaqa, an Imāmī *muḥaddith*, and two

source supports this narrative, noting that al-Ashtar ran away to al-Sind after his father died. He was killed in Kābul on a mountain called ʿA.l.j. His head was brought to al-Manṣūr and was presented by al-Ḥasan b. Zayd b. al-Ḥasan b. ʿAlī from the top of the *minbar*.[239] There are still some reliable (stable) elements in these traditions in common, namely, the location (al-Sind), some ethnographical elements of the region's local population, the governors' names (ʿUmar b. Ḥafṣ and his substitute Hishām b. Bisṭām al-Taghlibī), and the arrival (at a certain stage) of ʿAbdallāh al-Ashtar b. Muḥammad al-Nafs al-Zakiyya in al-Sind. It is difficult to believe that ʿUmar b. Ḥafṣ supported the ʿAlīds in general and was a follower of Muḥammad b. ʿAbdallāh because it is recorded that he was a commander of ʿĪsā b. Mūsā and fought with him against Muḥammad al-Nafs al-Zakiyya.[240] It is also noteworthy that in 151 (which began 26 January 768 and ended 13 January 769), al-Manṣūr appointed him as governor of Ifrīqiya after his dismissal from al-Sind.[241] Furthermore, the tutor of ʿAbdallāh al-Ashtar does not ascribe any ʿAlīd tendency to ʿUmar b. Ḥafṣ, and definitely does not report that he swore allegiance to Muḥammad al-Nafs al-Zakiyya. This was related by the ʿAbbāsī *rāwī* of the family of Sulaymān b. ʿAlī [b. ʿAbdallāh b. al-ʿAbbās]. There was bitter animosity between the families of Sulaymān b. ʿAlī l-ʿAbbāsī and the Muhallabī family in al-Baṣra. Sufyān b. Muʿāwiya b. Yazīd b. al-Muhallab b. Abī Ṣufra replaced Sulaymān b. ʿAlī as governor of that city (after the latter was discharged from office by Caliph al-Manṣūr). Immediately upon his appointment, Sufyān was ordered by Caliph al-Manṣūr to bring ʿAbdallāh b. ʿAlī (Sulaymān's brother), who had been given shelter in al-Baṣra by Sulaymān b. ʿAlī after his unsuccessful rebellion, to him. He did this in spite of the strong resentment of Banū ʿAlī [b. ʿAbdallāh b. al-ʿAbbās], the Baṣrīs,

---

other scholars, Aḥmad and Jaʿfar, the sons of Muḥammad b. Masʿada, but I was unable to establish a connection between them and "our" ʿAbdallāh b. Muḥammad b. Masʿada.

239 Ibn ʿInaba, *ʿUmda*, 105; Ahmed, *Religious Elite*, 157, n. 850, where he briefly deals with ʿAbdallāh al-Ashtar's affair.

240 Al-Ṭabarī, 3:236: Hazārmard.

241 Ibid., 3:359; ʿUmar b. Ḥafṣ b. ʿUthmān b. Qabīṣa b. Abī Ṣufra belonged to the well-known family of al-Muhallab b. Abī Ṣufra al-Azdī. He was governor of al-Baṣra both for Abū l-ʿAbbās and al-Manṣūr; on him and his family, see P. Crone, "Muhallabids," *EI*², idem, *Slaves*, 133–135 (ʿUmar's biography is on 134); Crone, *Slaves*, 133–135, remarks that "according to one version he fought under ʿĪsā b. Mūsā against al-Nafs al-Zakiyya, but another has it that he stayed in Sind where, having ʿAlīd sympathies, he protected al-Nafs al-Zakiyya's son until he was dismissed in 151. **However that may be,** he was appointed to North Africa in 151..." [my emphasis].

ʿĪsā and Sulaymān. Sufyān b. Muʿāwiya, the new Muhallabī governor, also executed (again by order of the caliph) Ibn al-Muqaffaʿ, the *mawlā* and *kātib* of the family of Banū ʿAlī b. ʿAbdallāh b. al-ʿAbbās in al-Baṣra, who drafted the immutable *amān* for ʿAbdallāh b. ʿAlī, which was given to the caliph to sign.[242]

242 The Muhallabī family had a strong grip over al-Baṣra. ʿUmar b. Ḥafṣ governed the city on behalf of al-Saffāḥ and al-Manṣūr. On Sufyān b. Muʿāwiya b. Yazīd, see Crone, *Slaves*, 133–135; Robinson and Marsham, "ʿAbdallāh b. ʿAlī," 273–274. On ʿAbdallāh b. ʿAlī, see Elad, "The *Ḥadīth* of al-Mahdī," 39, n. 2; Robinson and Marsham, "ʿAbdallāh b. ʿAlī," esp. 247, n. 1 and 248–257; on the *amān* of ʿAbdallāh b. ʿAlī, see the excellent analysis of Robinson and Marsham, ibid. Ibn al-Muqaffaʿ was the secretary of Ṣāliḥ b. ʿAlī. On him, see F. Gabrieli, "Ibn al-Muqaffaʿ," *EI*²; J. Derek Lathham, "Ebn al-Moqaffaʿ," *EIr*, and the comprehensive bibliography therein (including D. Sourdel, "La biographie d'Ibn al-Muqaffaʿ d'après les sources anciennes").

CHAPTER 4

Revolt

Introduction

Riyāḥ b. ʿUthmān, the governor of Medina (from 23 Ramaḍān 144/25 December 761) went to great lengths in his intensive search for Muḥammad and Ibrāhīm, sons of ʿAbdallāh b. al-Ḥasan, who were continually fleeing the authorities. As noted, their father and, most probably, other members of their family were incarcerated in Medina. To intensify the pressure, the ʿAbbāsīs took twenty-four members of the Ḥasanī family to al-ʿIrāq as prisoners. The sources record that the immediate cause for Muḥammad's coming out in open rebellion was his father's imprisonment,[1] or his death,[2] or the death of his uncles in al-Manṣūr's prison.[3] These statements may be true, but it should be noted that Muḥammad waited for more than half a year after the imprisonment of his father and uncles, and several months after the first Ḥasanī was executed on al-Manṣūr's orders, before he came out in open rebellion.

The sources scarcely supply specific dates of death for the Ḥasanīs. Those mentioned date to after the revolt, after the end of Ramaḍān, or Dhū l-Qaʿda 145/January–February 763.[4] Most of the sources record that the first Ḥasanī to be killed in al-ʿIrāq was Ibrāhīm b. al-Ḥasan b. al-Ḥasan, Muḥammad's uncle. He was killed in Rabīʿ I 145/30 May–28 June 763.[5]

1 Al-Balādhurī, *Ansāb* (ed. Madelung), 2:505; al-Ṣafadī, *al-Wāfī,* 3:297.

2 Al-Balādhurī, *Ansāb* (ed. Madelung), 2:505.

3 Al-Kulaynī, *al-Kāfī,* 1:361–362.

4 E.g., the sons of al-Ḥasan b. al-Ḥasan b. al-Ḥasan b. ʿAlī b. Abī Ṭālib: 1) ʿAlī died on 23 Muḥarram 146/26 April 763 (al-Iṣfahānī, *Maqātil,* 195), or had already died, in 145 (Ibn Saʿd, *al-Qism al-mutammim,* 259, 385); 2) Al-ʿAbbās died on 23 Ramaḍān 145/15 December 762 (al-Iṣfahānī, *Maqātil,* 198); 3) ʿAbdallāh died on *yawm ʿīd al-aḍḥā* 145/1 March 763 (al-Iṣfahānī, *Maqātil,* 196).

5 For the date, see al-Iṣfahānī, *Maqātil,* 188:...ʿUmar b. Shabba < Abū Nuʿaym al-Faḍl b. Dukayn (130–219/748–834); on the latter, a well-known transmitter and scholar, see al-Mizzī, *Tahdhīb,* 23:197–220 and the comprehensive bibliography of the editor therein; Sezgin, 1:101; see also al-Ṭabarī, 3:183: *qāla* [= ʿUmar b. Shabba]< al-Faḍl b. Dukayn Abū Nuʿaym, a partial parallel tradition; the date is not mentioned.

 | DOI 10.1163/9789004296220_006

One single tradition records, however, that ʿAbdallāh b. al-Ḥasan, Muḥammad's and Ibrāhīm's father, was the first Ḥasanī to be killed in prison.[6] One tradition even states that he died several months before his son, or (according to another less common version) a little while before the latter's final defeat.[7] These traditions wish to give ʿAbdallāh b. al-Ḥasan the image of the first Ḥasanī martyr, but other traditions record that he lived after his son's death, e.g., the tradition that describes how his son's head was thrown towards him in prison while praying,[8] or the tradition that specifies that he died more than two months after his son's death.[9] But, as already noted, this contradicts the prevalent tradition that the first of the Ḥasanīs who died in prison was Ibrāhīm b. al-Ḥasan. It seems that the tradition that describes Abū l-Azhar, al-Manṣūr's commander, killing ʿAbdallāh b. al-Ḥasan by direct order of the caliph[10] should be preferred to the pro-ʿAbbāsī one that aims to clear the caliph from any responsibility for his death, stating that he died from a broken heart following the news of his son's death; according to this source he died at the end of Ramaḍān 145/December 763.[11]

Pro-Ḥasanī traditions claim that Muḥammad planned for him and his brother to rebel on the same day, but due to Ibrāhīm's illness the revolt of the latter was postponed.[12]

This pro-Ḥasanī tradition is contradicted by al-Wāqidī's version, describing what he saw with his own eyes in Medina when he was fifteen years old. Al-Wāqidī says that Ibrāhīm was sent from Medina to al-Baṣra by his brother Muḥammad only after the revolt broke out, when Muḥammad al-Nafs al-Zakiyya took control of Medina and Mecca.[13] Another version from the same historian states that Muḥammad sent Ibrāhīm to al-Baṣra only after he

6 Al-Ṭabarī, 3:188: al-Wāqidī < ʿAbd al-Raḥmān b. Abī l-Mawālī; al-Dhahabī, *Siyar,* 7:214.

7 Ibn ʿAsākir, *Taʾrīkh,* 27:370; Sibṭ b. al-Jawzī, *Mirʾāt al-zamān,* fol. 282b: he died before his son.

8 Al-Ṣafadī, *al-Wāfī,* 3:298.

9 Ibn ʿAsākir, *Taʾrīkh,* 27:390, from al-Ḥasan b. Muḥammad b. Yaḥyā l-ʿAlawī from his grandfather: he died in al-Kūfa on the day of the feast of *al-Aḍḥā* (that is, on 10 Dhū l-Ḥijja 145/29 February 763), aged 76; ibid., from al-Ḥasan b. Muḥammad b. Yaḥyā l-ʿAlawī from his grandfather from Mūsā b. ʿAbdallāh (possibly ʿAbdallāh b. al-Ḥasan's son): aged 75; ibid., 27:389, from al-Zubayr b. Bakkār: died in al-Hāshimiyya in 145, aged 72.

10 Al-Ṭabarī, 3:184–185 (l. 18 to l. 13) (= al-Iṣfahānī, *Maqātil,* 226–227).

11 Al-Ṭabarī, 3:186 (ll. 2–5).

12 Ibn ʿInaba, *ʿUmda,* 104; al-Ṭabarī, 3:189–190 (l. 20 to l. 3).

13 Ibn Saʿd, *al-Qism al-mutammim,* 376; al-Dhahabī, *Siyar,* 6:219, where he summarizes the tradition of Ibn Saʿd; Sibṭ b. al-Jawzī, *Mirʾāt al-zamān,* fol. 280a; al-Balādhurī, *Ansāb*

took control of Medina and Mecca and he was sworn in as caliph.[14] He arrived in al-Baṣra on the first day of Ramaḍān 145/23 November 762,[15] where he raised the banner of rebellion.[16]

Shortly before the revolt broke out, Muḥammad stayed in al-Madhād,[17] where he also hid two camel-loads of swords that were sent to him by his brother Ibrāhīm.[18] Al-Madhād was a cultivated and fertile valley (*mazraʿa*; *wādī*) on the western outskirts of Medina (in al-Sāfila). The *uṭum* (forts; "tower houses") of Banū Ḥarām b. Kaʿb b. Ghanm b. Salima, who belonged to the Khazraj, were situated there. Banū Salima lived in this area, and it was here that the Prophet dug the *khandaq*.[19]

And indeed, from another source, we learn that Muḥammad al-Nafs al-Zakiyya stayed among the Banū Salima of the Anṣār, where his followers and adherents (*aṣḥābuhu*) gathered around him.[20] Although al-Madhād is not specifically mentioned in the source, it is only natural to connect the two pieces of evidence. The Banū Salima were supporters of Muḥammad b. ʿAbdallāh, and that is why he hid his weapons in their territory, stayed there on the eve of the

(ed. Madelung), 2:505 and Ibn Ḥajar, *Tahdhīb* (Beirut, 1984), 4:465: Ibrāhīm was sent after the revolt broke out in Medina.

14 Al-Ṭabarī, 3:298.

15 Ibn Saʿd, *al-Qism al-mutammim*, 378–379; al-Ṭabarī, 3:298; Sibṭ b. al-Jawzī, *Mirʾāt al-zamān*, fol. 280a.

16 Al-Azdī, *Taʾrīkh al-Mawṣil*, 181; al-Iṣfahānī, *Maqātil*, 321, 349.

17 Al-Ṭabarī, 3:190, 193 (ll. 1–2), 194 (ll. 1–12), 195 (ll. 13–17): on the last night before the revolt broke out.

18 Ibid., 3:193 (ll. 16–17).

19 Al-Bakrī, *Muʿjam*, 2:498: Banū Salima lived in "Khazbā, a place facing the Qiblatayn Mosque, which extended until[?] al-Madhād, on the summit of al-Ḥarra; this is [al-Khazbā] the abode of Banū Salima of the Anṣār": خزبى موضع تلقاء مسجد القبلتين إلى المذاد في سند الحرة وهي دار بني سلمة من الأنصار; ibid., 4:1202: في سند الحيرة instead of الحرة; see also ibid., 3:823; 4:1399; al-Ḥāzimī, *al-Amkina*, 204, n. 1 (3): Khazbā or Khuzbā; al-Fīrūzābādī, *al-Maghānim al-muṭāba*, 373; Yāqūt, *Muʿjam* (Beirut edition), 5:88 (copying al-Fīrūzābādī): the *khandaq* of the Prophet. Banū Salima were among the earlier supporters of the Prophet in Medina, see McAuliffe, *ʿAbbāsid Authority*, 147, n. 697 (citing Watt, *Muḥammad at Medina*, 174–176); Guillaume, *The Life of Muḥammad*, 594; Ibn al-Kalbī, *Jamhara* (ed. Caskel), 1:190; 2:508 and Ibn Ḥazm, *Jamhara*, 358–359). For *uṭum as* "tower house," see Lecker, *Muslims, Jews and Pagans*, 12; ibid., 96: on the dwellings of Banū Salima; ibid., 72: on Banū Ḥarām. See also the map of Medina.

20 Al-Balādhurī, *Ansāb* (ed. Madelung), 2:507 (= *Fragmenta*, 138).

armed rebellion, and from there advanced with his followers to the center of the city.[21]

1 Entering the City and Taking Control

Muḥammad al-Nafs al-Zakiyya entered Medina, openly proclaiming rebellion, on 28 Jumādā II 145/ 23 September 762.[22] Al-Wāqidī (d. 207/823), who witnessed this event, described Muḥammad al-Nafs al-Zakiyya as riding a horse, dressed in a white, thick-lined robe (قباء أبيض محشو) and a white *ʿimāma,*[23] while other sources relate that he entered the city riding on a black Arab donkey: حمار عربي أسود.[24] Another eyewitness reports that he saw Muḥammad b. ʿAbdallāh on the night he came out wearing a quilted yellow headdress[25] (*qalansuwa muḍarraba*) and a yellow upper-gown with full long sleeves (*jubba*).[26]

---

21 Al-Ṭabarī, 3:192–193 (l. 20 to l. 2), where he reports that Muḥammad b. ʿAbdallāh chooses to advance with his supporters through the quarter [? abodes?] of Banū Salima: حتى إذا فقلنا له كيف نأخذ قال على :(ll. 1–2) 3:194 ;شرع على بني سلمة و بطحان قال أسلكوا بني سلمة... بني سلمة.

22 This is the most widely-accepted date, for instance, see Ibn Saʿd, *al-Qism al-mutammim*, 376, 378: from al-Wāqidī (= Ibn Ḥajar, *Tahdhīb* [Hyderabad edition], 9:252); al-Ṭabarī, 3:195 (ll. 18–20) (= al-Iṣfahānī, *Maqātil*, 262); al-Masʿūdī, *Tanbīh*, 341; al-Azdī, *Taʾrīkh al-Mawṣil*, 181. Al-Balādhurī, *Ansāb* (ed. Madelung), 2:509, records two dates: 1) the accepted date (28 Jumādā II); 2) 14 Ramaḍān (*wa-yuqālu*); it is noteworthy that this is the accepted date of his death. For other dates, see al-Ḥarbī[?], *al-Manāsik*, 372, where he records Jumādā II with no specific date. Al-Fasawī, *al-Maʿrifa*, 1:125, have two days earlier, that is 26 Jumādā II; al-Ṭabarī, 3:195 (ll. 14–15): 1 Rajab; Ibn Khayyāṭ, *Taʾrīkh* (Beirut, 1993), 340, 348: in Rajab, with no specific date; Omar, "al-Rasāʾil," 22: the beginning of Rajab with no source.

23 Ibn Saʿd, *al-Qism al-mutammim*, 376; see also al-Ṭabarī, 3:229 (ll. 8–13), where he describes Muḥammad b. ʿAbdallāh as wearing *qabāʾ abyaḍ* during the digging of his *khandaq*.

24 Ibid., 3:193–194 (l. 18 to l. 1); McAuliffe, *ʿAbbāsid Authority*, 148: "Muḥammad rode a bedouin donkey with a black coat."

25 According to McAuliffe, *ʿAbbāsid Authority*, 151, n. 719, who corrected the text following al-Ṭabarī, *Addenda et Emendanda*, dccxxvi, and *Glossarium*, s.v. *ḍaraba*; McAuliffe, *ʿAbbāsid Authority*, 151, n. 719: bibliography on the *qalansuwa* and the *jubba*.

26 Al-Ṭabarī, 3:195–196 (l. 20 to l. 1), l. 1: *qalansuwa miṣriyya*; but ibid., note a, according to MS B: *muḍarraba*; al-Ṭabarī (ed. Abū l-Faḍl Ibrāhīm), 7:557: *qalansuwa muḍariyya*.

The number of supporters that Muḥammad entered Medina with varies, according to the sources, and ranges from less than 100 to as many as 250[27] (see discussion below).

The route he chose is clearly depicted in the report of an eyewitness, ʿAbd al-ʿAzīz b. ʿImrān al-Zuhrī, a Medinan notable who at some stage joined the rebellion: from the Dār Banū Salima, Muḥammad continued through Ibn Ḥubayn Lane (*zuqāq*),[28] then he entered the market, passing through the date sellers' market and then to the basket sellers' market; from there he reached the prison, which (the transmitter adds) in those days was in the Dār Ibn Hishām, breached its gates, and released the prisoners.[29] He also broke down the doors of the treasury (*bayt al-māl*).[30] After releasing the prisoners (among whom were the former governor of Medina, Muḥammad b. Khālid al-Qasrī, his nephew, Nadhīr b. Yazīd and their *mawlā* Rizām),[31] Muḥammad b. ʿAbdallāh continued until he was between Dār Yazīd [b. ʿAbd al-Malik] and Dār Uways [b. Saʿd b. Abī Sarḥ al-ʿĀmirī], encircled the courtyard [of the mosque] until he reached the residence (*bayt*) of ʿĀtika bt. Yazīd [b. Muʿāwiya],[32] and sat on her doorstep, while small-scale skirmishes were taking place in the city. In one

---

27 Less than **100**: al-Ṭabarī, 3:193 (l. 18); **150**: al-Balādhurī, *Ansāb* (ed. Madelung), 2:507 (= *Fragmenta*, 238); **250**: al-Ṭabarī, 3:192–193 (l. 20 to l. 1); Ibn Kathīr, *al-Bidāya* (Cairo, 1351 H.), 10:83.

28 In the Jāhiliyya and during the earliest period of Islam Zuqāq b. Ḥubayn was the site of one of Medina's markets, called Muzāḥim, see Ibn Shabba, *Taʾrīkh al-Madīna*, 1:306 (= al-Samhūdī, *Wafāʾ*, 3:82; 4:470). At some point, it became the property of Ibn Ḥubayn, who was the *mawlā* of al-ʿAbbās b. ʿAbd al-Muṭṭalib, see Ibn Shabba, *Taʾrīkh al-Madīna*, 1:264; al-Samhūdī, *Wafāʾ*, 3:94; al-Samhūdī, ibid., relates that it is located to the west of the market of Medina. And see Lecker's map of the markets: east of Mount Salʿ and south of Thaniyyat al-Wadāʿ; I thank Prof. Lecker for drawing my attention to this site.

29 The long tradition of ʿAbd al-ʿAzīz b. ʿImrān al-Zuhrī, the eyewitness: al-Ṭabarī, 3:191–193 (l. 14 to l. 10); the description of the route of Muḥammad: ibid., 193 (ll. 1–5).

30 Al-Ṭabarī, 3:195 (l. 16).

31 Ibid., 3:196 (ll. 10–11): the report of another eyewitness, ʿUmar b. Rāshid; al-Iṣfahānī, *Maqātil*, 262–263: a partial parallel tradition.

32 On Dār Yazīd b. ʿAbd al-Malik, see Ibn Shabba, *Taʾrīkh al-Madīna*, 1:256–257; al-Samhūdī, *Wafāʾ*, 3:49–50; on Dār Uways b. Saʿd, see Ibn Shabba, *Taʾrīkh al-Madīna*, 1:50; al-Samhūdī, *Wafāʾ*, 3:257; the two *dārs* were facing each other; on Bayt ʿĀtika bt. Yazīd b. Muʿāwiya, see Ibn Shabba, *Taʾrīkh al-Madīna*, 1:257; Ibn ʿAsākir, *Taʾrīkh*, 32:201; al-Samhūdī, *Wafāʾ*, 1:377: Dār ʿĀtika; it seems that the *bayt* and the *dār* in this case denote the same buildings.

of these, Muḥammad's men killed a man of Sind, who was lighting lamps (candles?) in the mosque.[33]

Specific information is lacking regarding the identity of those against whom Muḥammad's men fought at this early stage of the revolt. Most probably they were contingents of the governor, Riyāḥ, although there is no evidence regarding armed posts in the city or the governor's military forces. On the night of the rebellion, Riyāḥ tried to mobilize men from Banū Zuhra of Quraysh, who scattered a short time before Muḥammad al-Nafs al-Zakiyya entered the city.[34] This information is given by ʿImrān b. ʿAbd al-ʿAzīz, a Zuhrī himself, who witnessed the events. His testimony is substantially supported by a different tradition, according to which the poet Ibn Mayyāda reproaches Riyāḥ, telling him to mobilize a guard (*ḥaras*) and soldiers from Ghaṭafān, that is, from his own tribe, and leave the slaves, to whom he gives the *dirhams*, and to beware the Quraysh.[35] When Riyāḥ was killed, Ibn Mayyāda composed a poem in which he criticized the governor, saying: "I prohibited you (to recruit) men from Quraysh"(نهيتك عن رجال من قريش).[36]

The city's governor, Riyāḥ, escaped to the governor's palace (*dār al-imāra*), which at that time was in Dār Marwān, and barricaded himself there.[37] Muḥammad's men entered Dār Marwān through one of the gates of the great mosque (Bāb al-Khawkha), from where there was a direct passage to the governor's palace. They burnt down the gate and captured Riyāḥ and his brother ʿAbbās b. ʿUthmān and imprisoned them.[38] According to another report,

33 Al-Ṭabarī, 3:193 (ll. 6–10); al-Iṣfahānī, *Maqātil*, 262: part of the tradition; the end of the tradition is garbled. See also al-Balādhurī, *Ansāb* (ed. Madelung), 2:507; lighting the lamps in the mosque: al-Ṭabarī, 3:193 (ll. 9–10): كان يستصبح في المسجد; McAuliffe, *ʿAbbāsid Authority*, 147 "began his morning observance in the mosque."

34 Al-Ṭabarī, 3:192: from ʿImrān b. ʿAbd al-ʿAzīz.

35 Al-Iṣfahānī, *al-Aghānī* (Būlāq edition), 2:119.

36 Al-Mubarrad, *al-Kāmil* (ed. Wright), 1:28 (l. 15).

37 Al-Balādhurī, *Ansāb* (ed. Madelung), 2:507; al-Ṭabarī, 3:196; the identification of Dār al-Imāra with Dār Marwān: Ibn Saʿd, *Ṭabaqāt*, 4:20: "the court (*raḥba*) of al-Faḍāʾ [sic! read al-Qaḍāʾ, see al-Samhūdī, *Wafāʾ*, 3:21ff; 25 (l. 2)] is opposite Dār al-Imāra, which today is called Dār Marwān…," but esp. al-Samhūdī, *Wafāʾ*, 3:24–25.

38 Al-Ṭabarī, 3:196. We also learn about the passageway between the mosque and Dār al-Imāra from the report that when the governor Riyāḥ was stoned by the people of Medina in the mosque, he hurried to the Maqṣūra, shut it and entered Dār Marwān, see al-Yaʿqūbī, *Taʾrīkh* (ed. Houtsma), 2:451; al-Samhūdī, *Wafāʾ*, 3:25, quoting Ibn Shabba's work: "Dār Marwān, which is situated on the southern side of the mosque; we have already written that the governors used to enter from one of its gates to the Maqṣūra." The *maqṣūra* in the mosque is the part which is partitioned off from the rest of the building and is reserved for

they also imprisoned a son of Muslim b. ʿUqba. According to an eyewitness report of Azhar b. Saʿīd (= Saʿd?), they were imprisoned in Dār Ibn Hishām;[39] "(and the prison) was in those days [adds the transmitter] in Dār Ibn Hishām" (وهو يومئذ في دار ابن هشام)[40] but according to another eyewitness report they were imprisoned in Dār Marwān.[41]

2 Supporters and Warriors in the First Stage of the Revolt: General Observations

As already noted, Muḥammad al-Nafs al-Zakiyya did not encounter any significant military opposition upon entering the city.[42] It most probably shows that the governor did not have any armed contingents; certainly he did not have any of the regular professional units of *ahl Khurāsān* at his disposal.

The questions of the scope of the support Muḥammad al-Nafs al-Zakiyya gained from among the Medinans, and the social/tribal and ethnic background of his supporters are addressed further on in this study. Some of the

---

the city's governor; it is well-known that in some of the major cities of the Muslim world there was a direct passageway between Dār al-Imāra and the great mosque, for example, see Elad, *Jerusalem*, 42, n. 89: Jerusalem, al-Kūfa, and Mosul.

39 Al-Ṭabarī, 3:195 (ll. 16–17).

40 Ibid., 3:193 (ll. 4–5): [ʿUmar b. Shabba] < Muḥammad b. Yaḥyā < ʿAbd al-ʿAzīz b. ʿImrān < his father (a shorter parallel tradition is recorded by al-Iṣfahānī, *Maqātil*, 262: the *isnād* is garbled, instead of ʿAbd al-ʿAzīz b. ʿAmmār, read ʿAbd al-ʿAzīz b. ʿImrān). Dār Ibn Hishām was in the great court of the city, al-Balāṭ, see al-Ṭabarī, 3:179 (l. 19) (= al-Iṣfahānī, *Maqātil*, 392); al-Ṭabarī, 3:216 (ll. 2–4): al-Ḥārith b. Isḥāq relates that Muḥammad al-Nafs al-Zakiyya imprisoned Muḥammad b. Khālid al-Qasrī (the second time) in "Dār Ibn Hishām, which is situated to the south of Muṣallā l-Janāʾiz, which is today the property of Faraj the eunuch" (on the latter, the *mawlā* of al-Rashīd, who served in important administrative/military posts under al-Rashīd, al-Amīn, and al-Maʾmūn, see Crone, *Slaves*, 190; Ayalon, *Eunuchs*, 109–113, 251, 253); al-Ṭabarī, 3:227: [ʿUmar b. Shabba] < Ayyūb b. ʿUmar b. Abī ʿAmr b. Nuʿaym b. Māhān < his father: several dignitaries of Quraysh and other tribes were imprisoned in Dār Ibn Hishām, which is in the Muṣallā; al-Samhūdī records the most detailed information about the houses that encircle the great court (*al-balāṭ al-aʿẓam*). According to him, Dār Ibn Hishām is the first *dār* on the left side of the *muṣallā*, see al-Samhūdī, *Wafāʾ*, 3:72; Ibn Hishām is Ibrāhīm b. Hishām b. Ismāʿīl al-Makhzūmī, the governor of Medina from 106/724 or 725 until 113/731 or 732, or 114/732 or 733, see al-Ṭabarī, vol. 2, index; his biography: Ibn ʿAsākir, *Taʾrīkh*, 7:259–266; his *dār* was adjacent to the northern border of al-Balāṭ, see al-Samhūdī, *Wafāʾ*, 3:68–69; 72.

41 Al-Ṭabarī, 3:196 (l. 9).

42 Ibid., 3:192–193.

sources assert that at least at the beginning of the rebellion, most of the Arab inhabitants of Medina supported him: "the offspring of ʿAlī, Jaʿfar, ʿAqīl, ʿUmar b. al-Khaṭṭāb, al-Zubayr b. al-ʿAwwām, and the rest of Quraysh and the offspring of the Anṣār."[43] This assertion, however, is misleading. This support was not uniform; there were those who opposed the rebellion, even among his close family, among the rest of the ʿAlīd families, and among the important Quraysh families.[44]

A contemporary of the events who lived in Medina during the uprising, Rashīd (Rushayd?) b. Ḥayyān b. Abī Sulaymān b. Samʿān, was one of the clan of Qurayṭ b. ʿAbdallāh b. Abī Bakr (Ubayd) b. Kilāb b. Rabīʿa b. ʿĀmir b. Ṣaʿṣaʿa. He related to his son, Abū Maslama (or Salama) Mawhūb, a minor poet and transmitter of poetry and literary anecdotes,[45] who transmitted to ʿUmar b. Shabba, that among Muḥammad al-Nafs al-Zakiyya's first actions upon entering Medina, was to collect and gather the inhabitants together, then to seize control of the entrances (أخذ عليهم المناقب) to the city. As a consequence of these actions, no one could enter or leave without encountering Muḥammad's men's close scrutiny. At first, he did not allow anyone to leave. When he heard of the approaching ʿAbbāsī army, he allowed those who wished to leave to do so, opening the roads and passageways of the city. "A world of people left, including me. When we were in al-ʿUrayḍ, which is about three *mīl*s[46] from Medina, ʿĪsā b. Mūsā's vanguard met up with us...."[47]

43 Al-Masʿūdī, *Murūj*, 4:146 (quoted by Ahmed, *Religious Elite*, 159, n. 854). For other traditions in this vein, see for example al-Yaʿqūbī, *Taʾrīkh* (ed. Houtsma), 2:452; al-Ṭabarī, 3:199 (ll. 6–11); 3:228; al-Azdī, *Taʾrīkh al-Mawṣil*, 187; Ibn Kathīr, *al-Bidāya* (Cairo, 1351 H.), 10:84.

44 See the detailed discussion in chapter 7.

45 He is rarely mentioned in the sources, see al-Ṭabarī, 3:203; 230: أحد بني قريط بن عبد الله بن أبي بكر بن كلاب; al-Iṣfahānī, *al-Aghānī* (Dār al-Kutub edition), 2:319 [= Būlāq edition, 2:111]; 2:272 [= 2:93]; 2:279 [= 2:96]: Abū Maslama; 2:283 [= 2:97]: Abū Maslama; 2:301 [= 2:105]; 2:319 [= 2:111]; 9:341 [= 8:195]: Abū Maslama; 17:93 [= 15:151]; 18:37–38 [= 16:124]; al-Marzubānī, *al-Muwashshaḥ*, 173 (Abū Maslama) and 245 (Abū Salama). Ibn ʿAsākir, *Taʾrīkh*, 18:376 (Abū Salama): in the last three sources he is the direct transmitter of al-Zubayr b. Bakkār; Yāqūt, *Muʿjam* (ed. Wüstenfeld), 1:159: al-Qurayṭī; 1:491; neither he nor his father are mentioned in the *nasab* books; on Banū Kilāb b. ʿĀmir b. Ṣaʿṣaʿa, see Ibn Ḥazm, *Jamhara*, 282–283: قريط بن عبد الله بن أبي بكر بن كلاب but cf. Ibn al-Kalbī, *Jamhara* (ed. Caskel), 2:471–472 (ed. al-Ḥasan, 322): قريط بن عبد بن أبي بكر بن كلاب.

46 On the length of the early ʿAbbāsī *mīl*, see chapter 1, n. 31.

47 Al-Ṭabarī, 3:230 (ll. 6–18); the translation of the last is after McAuliffe, *ʿAbbāsid Authority*, 193; ibid.: Rashīd and Qarīṭ, instead of Rushayd and Qurayṭ, but cf. Ibn Ḥazm, *Jamhara*, 282; Ibn Durayd, *al-Ishtiqāq*, 51; Ibn al-Kalbī, *Jamhara* (ed. Caskel), 2:471–472 (ed. al-Ḥasan, 322): Qurayṭ. Al-Marzubānī, *al-Muwashshaḥ*, 173 and 245; Yāqūt, *Muʿjam* (ed. Wüstenfeld),

Another tradition that conveys a similar description, that is, the desertion of the city by most of Muḥammad's supporters, is related by ʿUthmān b. Muḥammad b. Khālid b. al-Zubayr, one of al-Nafs al-Zakiyya's most loyal supporters, who estimates that at first 100,000 (!) men gathered with Muḥammad, but when ʿĪsā b. Mūsā and his army approached Medina, Muḥammad al-Nafs al-Zakiyya released his supporters from their oath to him and let those who wished to leave him. As a result, the people slipped away from the city, until Muḥammad was left with a small number of men: في شرذمة ليست بالكثيرة.[48] These traditions emphasize, first, the abandonment of Medina by its people, and, second, the fact that it was carried out with Muḥammad al-Nafs al-Zakiyya's full consent; he is revealed here as a forgiving and noble character. As opposed to these biased traditions, another tradition states that many men left Medina with their women and children. Muḥammad ordered Abū l-Qalammas to bring them back, but he managed to bring back only a small number of them.[49] Here Muḥammad is not depicted as a kind and noble person, rather he lacked both the moral and physical power to bring the fugitives back.

2.1 *The Size of the Army of Muḥammad b. ʿAbdallāh*

As noted above, the number of supporters that Muḥammad entered Medina with varies, according to the different sources, from fewer than 100 to 250. There is a noteworthy tradition recorded by one of the most loyal supporters of Muḥammad b. ʿAbdallāh, ʿAbd al-Ḥamīd b. Jaʿfar (on him, see below), that states that at the time of the major encounter between the two armies, Muḥammad b. ʿAbdallāh's army comprised a little more than 300 men, which is (adds the transmitter), the same number of the [Prophet's] men at Badr, when they fought the idolaters.[50]

The main battle between the ʿAbbāsī army and Muḥammad b. ʿAbdallāh's "army" is described as one between two armies built according to the classic Arab/Islamic warfare of wings: right and left wings that fight facing each other. But from the brief descriptions of the battle, we learn that it was short; that several senior commanders as well as many soldiers fled the battlefield, and that toward the end of the battle Muḥammad was left with a handful of

---

1:159 and 491: Rushayd (the editor's vocalization). However, cf. al-Iṣfahānī, *al-Aghānī* (Dār al-Kutub edition), 2:319: Rashīd, but see ibid., 17:93: Rushayd (also the editor's vocalization). The expression ألمناقب is equivalent to ألأنقاب, see chapter 5, nn. 172–173.

48 Al-Ṭabarī, 3:230 (ll. 1–6).

49 Ibid., 3:230–231 (l. 19 to l. 2).

50 Al-Ṭabarī, 3:237–238 (l. 17 to l. 2).

warriors from the tribes of Juhayna, who fought to the death (see the detailed description below).

Muḥammad's supporters and warriors were called al-Mubayyiḍa[51] while the act of rebellion and support for the revolt was called *bayyaḍa/tabyīḍ*. Muḥammad himself is depicted as wearing white garments: *qamīṣ abyaḍ* and *ʿimāma bayḍāʾ*,[52] or *qabāʾ abyaḍ*. White was the color of rebel movements against the early ʿAbbāsīs, mainly in Syria and al-Jazīra.[53]

2.2 *Muḥammad's Commanders*[54]

1) Khawwāt b. Bukayr b. Khawwāt b. Jubayr b. al-Nuʿmān [b. Umayya b. al-Burak b. Imruʾ al-Qays b. Thaʿlaba b. ʿAmr b. Mālik b. al-Aws] was in charge of the infantry corps when Muḥammad al-Nafs al-Zakiyya entered Medina,[55] and is termed "the leader (*sayyid*) of the Anṣār."[56]

2) ʿĪsā b. Zayd b. ʿAlī b. al-Ḥusayn b. ʿAlī b. Abī Ṭālib was in charge of the right wing (*maymana*) of Muḥammad's units.[57]

3–5) Yazīd, Ṣāliḥ, and al-Ḥasan, Muʿāwiya b. ʿAbdallāh b. Jaʿfar b. Abī Ṭālib's sons. Yazīd and Ṣāliḥ commanded the unit that faced the ʿAbbāsī unit of Kathīr b. al-Ḥuṣayn;[58] according to al-Kulaynī, it was Yazīd b. Muʿāwiya, who was in charge of the vanguard (*al-muqaddima*) of Muḥammad's army and was defeated by the *muqaddima* of ʿĪsā b. Mūsā.[59] Al-Ḥasan b. Muʿāwiya was appointed the governor of Mecca by Muḥammad b. ʿAbdallāh.

6) Ibrāhīm b. Khuḍayr [Muṣʿab] b. Muṣʿab b. al-Zubayr b. al-ʿAwwām.

7) ʿAlī b. Mālik b. Khuthaym b. ʿIrāk [b. Mālik] al-Ghifārī (unknown). His family lived in Medina. His grandfather Khuthaym was a *muḥaddith*, and served as the *qāḍī* of Medina.[60] His great-grandfather, ʿIrāk b. Mālik, was also

---

51 Al-Balādhurī, *Ansāb* (ed. al-Dūrī), 3:63 (cf. al-Zubayrī, *Nasab Quraysh*, 33).

52 Al-Ṭabarī, 3:223 (ll. 4–12).

53 See Cobb, *White Banners*, 5.

54 Nos. 2–7 and no. 9 are mentioned in al-Balādhurī, *Ansāb* (ed. Madelung), 2:514–515.

55 Al-Ṭabarī, 3:193 (ll. 12–13); Ibn al-Athīr, *al-Kāmil* (Beirut edition), 5:530.

56 Al-Ṭabarī, 3:201 (l. 19).

57 Al-Iṣfahānī, *Maqātil*, 407; al-Balādhurī, *Ansāb* (ed. Madelung), 2:514: as a commander.

58 al-Balādhurī, *Ansāb* (ed. Madelung), 2:514.

59 Al-Kulaynī, *al-Kāfī*, 1:364.

60 On him, see Ibn Abī Ḥātim, *al-Jarḥ* (Beirut edition), 3:388; Ibn Ḥajar, *Lisān*, 7:209; Ibn Ḥajar, *Tahdhīb* (Beirut, 1984), 3:118; al-Mizzī, *Tahdhīb*, 8:228–230. *Qāḍī* al-Madīna: Ibn Ḥajar, *Tahdhīb* (Beirut, 1984), 3:118, quoting from the *Book of Judicial Decisions* (*Kitāb al-Qaḍāʾ*) of Abū ʿAlī l-Ḥusayn b. ʿAlī l-Karābīsī (d. 245/859 or 248/862). On the author, see al-Ziriklī, *al-Aʿlām*, 2:244; Sezgin, 1:599–600.

a Medinan *muḥaddith* who died during the reign of Yazīd b. ʿAbd al-Malik (101–105/720–724).[61]

8) Abū l-Qalammas ʿUthmān b. ʿUbaydallāh b. ʿAbdallāh b. ʿUmar b. al-Khaṭṭāb.

9) ʿUthmān b. Muḥammad b. Khālid b. al-Zubayr.[62]

10) Saʿīd b. Abī Sufyān al-Ṣayrafī (unknown).

3 The First Actions: The Imprisonment of the ʿAbbāsī Family in Medina

As mentioned, immediately upon taking control of the city, Muḥammad and his supporters broke into the jail, imprisoned the ʿAbbāsī governor, Riyāḥ, and broke down the gates of *bayt al-māl*. One of his distinguished supporters (commanders?) from the Zubayrī family, a son of Muṣʿab (Khuḍayr) b. Muṣʿab b. al-Zubayr, named Ibn Khuḍayr, was sent to rescue Muḥammad's brother, Mūsā b. ʿAbdallāh, from the hands of Riyāḥ's people who were on their way to the caliph in al-ʿIrāq with the captive.[63]

In addition to Riyāḥ, he imprisoned all the ʿAbbāsīs' *mawālī* in Medina.[64] These *mawālī* were most probably in charge of the vast property of the ʿAbbāsīs in Medina and its surroundings. It can be safely assumed that Muḥammad confiscated this property and also the *mawālī*s' private property. This can be gleaned from the account about the theft of the merchandise/objects (*matāʿ*) of Ibn Abī Farwa, who was said to be the brother-in-law of Abū l-Khaṣīb,[65] who may be identified as Marzūq, the *mawlā* of Caliph al-Manṣūr.[66] Ibn Abī Farwa is most probably one of the descendants of ʿAbdallāh b. Abī Farwa, who was a

---

61 Al-Bukhārī, *al-Ṣaghīr*, 1:248; Ibn Abī Ḥātim, *al-Jarḥ* (Beirut edition), 7:38; Ibn Ḥibbān, *al-Thiqāt*, 5:281; Ibn Ḥajar, *Tahdhīb* (Beirut, 1984), 7:156; al-Mizzī, *Tahdhīb*, 19:545–548; al-Dhahabī, *Siyar*, 5:63–64: "died in the year 104 [722 or 723], or before that year."

62 One of the most loyal supporters of Muḥammad b. ʿAbdallāh, who was appointed governor of Medina by him (al-Ṭabarī, 3:168 (ll. 15–16)), fought with him (ibid., 3:234 (l. 19)), was caught and brought to al-Manṣūr, who executed him (ibid., 3:260–264); on him, see also chapter 7 (part 2), no. 3.3.

63 Al-Ṭabarī, 3:197–198 (l. 19 to l. 11) (= al-Iṣfahānī, *Maqātil*, 260: a partial epitomized tradition); on this family, see chapter 8.

64 Ibn Saʿd, *al-Qism al-mutammim*, 376.

65 Al-Ṭabarī, 3:201 (ll. 10–11) (= Ibn ʿAsākir, *Taʾrīkh*, 52:386: a parallel tradition).

66 On him, see Crone, *Slaves*, 190.

mawlā of al-Ḥārith b. al-Ḥifār, the *mawlā* of ʿUthmān b. ʿAffān.[67] ʿAbdallāh b. Abī Farwa was the secretary (*kātib*) of Muṣʿab b. al-Zubayr, and he was said to be the richest man in Medina: وكان أيسر أهل المدينة.[68]

Al-Rabīʿ b. Yūnus, the *mawlā* and the *ḥājib* of al-Manṣūr, was the (illegitimate) son of Yūnus b. Muḥammad b. Abī Farwa.[69] The above-mentioned Ibn Abī Farwa married the daughter of Abū l-Khaṣīb Marzūq, al-Manṣūr's *mawlā*.[70] This family's relationship to the ʿAbbāsīs is twofold—on the one hand through the family of al-Rabīʿ b. Yūnus, and on the other hand, through Marzūq, al-Manṣūr's *mawlā*. Plundering Ibn Abī Farwa was just one act of robbery carried out by Muḥammad b. ʿAbdallāh's supporters.[71]

3.1 *The ʿAbbāsī Families in Medina*

There is very little information on the ʿAbbāsīs who lived in Medina. At least two families lived in the city: 1) that of ʿAbdallāh b. ʿUbaydallāh b. al-ʿAbbās b. ʿAbd al-Muṭṭalib. ʿAbdallāh's son Ḥusayn lived in the city and also died there in 140/757–758 or 141/758–759. The city's governor, Muḥammad b. Khālid al-Qasrī, prayed over his dead body. He is mentioned in the Sunnī *rijāl* books of *ḥadīth,* mainly as an untrustworthy, very weak transmitter. This may be due to the nature of the ʿAbbāsī family traditions that he passed on, and/or also due to the fact that he was a poet and/or to his allegedly pro-Imāmī convictions (in the Imāmī literature he is described as the close associate of both Muḥammad al-Bāqir and Jaʿfar al-Ṣādiq). It is noteworthy that the well-known scholar Muḥammad b. Saʿd (d. 230/845) was Ḥusayn b. ʿAbdallāh [b. ʿUbaydallāh b. al-ʿAbbās] al-ʿAbbāsī's *mawlā.* In the Umawī period he married a distinguished woman from the Qurashī (Sahmī) family, ʿĀbida bt. Shuʿayb b. ʿAbdallāh b. ʿAmr b. al-ʿĀṣ (named ʿĀbida al-Ḥasnāʾ in the sources). When the ʿAbbāsīs came to power, they took hold of and confiscated the estates of (the family of) ʿAmr b. al-ʿĀṣ, as part of the general process of confiscating the property and estates of the Umawīs. At some (unknown) point, the estates were returned to (the

---

67 Al-Ṭabarī, 3:244 (ll. 2–15); perhaps he can be identified with Muḥammad. b. ʿAbd al-Wāḥid b. ʿAbdallāh b. Abī Farwa, a transmitter mentioned only once by al-Ṭabarī, who describes the entrance of the ʿAbbāsī army contingents into Medina vividly.

68 Al-Jahshiyārī, *Wuzarāʾ,* 44–45.

69 Ibid., 125.

70 Crone, *Slaves,* 190.

71 As may be gleaned from al-Ṭabarī, 3:201 (ll. 10–11): "We have never found such fine personal goods as those we found in the possession of Ibn Abī Farwa, the son in-law of Abū l-Khaṣīb." (McAuliffe's translation, 157): ما وجدنا من حر المتاع شيئا أجود من شيء وجدناه عند ابن أبي فروة ختن أبي الخصيب.

family of) ʿAmr b. al-ʿĀṣ. According to the sources, "because of her the estates of ʿAmr b. al-ʿĀṣ were given back after they were confiscated by Banū l-ʿAbbās": وبسببها ردت أموال عمرو بن العاصي، بعد أن قبضها بنو العباس,[72] that is, because of the marriage of ʿĀbida to al-Ḥusayn b. ʿAbdallāh al-ʿAbbāsī. An Imāmī source relates that he was [also] married to al-Ḥasan b. al-Ḥasan b. ʿAlī b. Abī Ṭālib's sister.[73]

Although al-Ḥusayn b. ʿAbdallāh al-ʿAbbāsī died in Medina in 140 or 141/758–759, that is, four years before the rebellion, some members of his family resided in the city. His son, ʿAbdallāh b. al-Ḥusayn, lived in the city, but very little is known about him. He was married to his cousin, Asmāʾ bt. al-Ḥasan

72 Ibn Ḥazm, *Jamhara,* 164; see also al-Zubayrī, *Nasab Quraysh,* 33: وبسبب عابدة رد على ولد عمرو بن العاص أموالهم; al-Iṣfahānī, *al-Aghānī* (Būlāq edition), 10:169 [= Dār al-Kutub edition, 12:67]: ... al-Zubayr b. Bakkār < Muḥammad b. Yaḥyā: وبسببها ردت على ولد عمرو بن العاص أموالهم في دولة بني العباس

Ibn ʿAsākir, *Taʾrīkh,* 10:367: "because of ʿĀbida's way of life [position?] the estates of ʿAmr b. al-ʿĀṣ were returned when Banū l-ʿAbbās ascended the caliphate, this after they were confiscated": ولسيرة عابدة ردت أموال عمرو بن العاص حين ولى بنو العباس بعدما قبضت.

On al-Ḥusayn b. ʿAbdallāh, see al-Balādhurī, *Ansāb* (ed. al-Dūrī), 3:62–65; 63, from al-Zubayr b. Bakkār: "al-Ḥusayn b. ʿAbdallāh b. ʿUbaydallāh b. al-ʿAbbās (used to) lived in Medina"; al-Iṣfahānī, *al-Aghānī* (Būlāq edition), 10:169–171 [= Dār al-Kutub edition, 12:66–71]. According to Ibn Ḥibbān, *al-Majrūḥīn,* 1:242, he was from Medina, and when he died in 141/758 or 759, the governor prayed over his body. Ibn Abī Ḥātim, *al-Jarḥ* (Beirut edition), 5:100, has Abū Zurʿa saying that he was a trustworthy Medinan transmitter of *ḥadīth*. This is not the accepted opinion of him, for example, see Ibn Ḥibbān, *al-Majrūḥīn,* 1:242; Ibn ʿAdī, *Ḍuʿafāʾ,* 2:349–351; al-ʿUqaylī, *Ḍuʿafāʾ,* 1:245; Ibn Ḥajar, *Taqrīb* (1986 edition), 1:167; al-Mizzī, *Tahdhīb*, 6:383–386. For his biography in the Shīʿī (mainly Imāmī) sources, see, for example, al-Ṭūsī, *Rijāl,* 130; al-Tafrishī, *Naqd al-rijāl,* 2:97 (من أصحاب الباقر والصادق); al-Amīn, *Aʿyān al-Shīʿa,* 6:81–82; al-Shāhrūdī, *Rijāl,* 148; al-Khūʾī, *Rijāl,* 7:18. Some of his verses are quoted by al-Zubayrī, *Nasab Quraysh,* 33; al-Balādhurī, *Ansāb* (ed. al-Dūrī), 3:62–65, but esp. al-Iṣfahānī, *al-Aghānī* (Būlāq edition), 10:169–171 [= Dār al-Kutub edition, 12:66–71]. The information about Ibn Saʿd, al-Ḥusayn's *mawlā*, is repeated in many sources, e.g., al-Khaṭīb al-Baghdādī, *Taʾrīkh* (Beirut, 1997), 2:370; Ibn ʿAsākir, *Taʾrīkh,* 53:65; al-Mizzī, *Tahdhīb*, 25:258; J.W. Fück, "Ibn Saʿd," *EI*[2].

73 If I understand the text correctly, see al-ʿUmarī, *Ansāb,* 36: وكان للحسن المثنى قسيمة خرجت إلى الحسين بن عبدالله بن عبيد الله بن العباس عم النبي (صلعم) (al-Ḥasan al-Muthannā [b. al-Ḥasan b. ʿAlī b. Abī Ṭālib] had a sister who went [to marry] al-Ḥusayn b. ʿAbdallāh b. ʿUbaydallāh b. al-ʿAbbās, the uncle of the Prophet [Ṣ]).

b. ʿAbdallāh b. ʿUbaydallāh b. al-ʿAbbās[74] and they both[?] lived in the city when the rebellion broke out.[75] Asmāʾ is mentioned in the sources as a courageous woman who publicly resisted Muḥammad b. ʿAbdallāh's revolt, and sent one of her *mawālī* to hang a black veil on a pole (black being the color and symbol of the ʿAbbāsīs) of the mosque's minaret. She also sent another one of her *mawālī*, called Mujīb al-ʿĀmirī, straight into Muḥammad al-Nafs al-Zakiyya's camp, where he cried out loud "Defeat, defeat, run for your lives (الهزيمة الهزيمة), the ʿAbbāsī army has already entered the city." When Muḥammad's supporters (*al-nās*) saw the black flag, they broke up and fled, but Muḥammad remained and continued to fight until he was killed.[76] When the mutiny was crushed, her house served as one of the sanctuaries for the Medinans.[77]

2) The second family is that of al-ʿAbbās b. ʿAbdallāh b. al-Ḥārith b. al-ʿAbbās b. ʿAbd al-Muṭṭalib. He was a distinguished Qurashī in Medina who was summoned to the governor for an emergency consultation, and then headed the patrol of the horsemen in Medina and its surroundings on the night the rebellion broke out.[78] At the end of the rebellion, his house (like that of Asmāʾ bt. al-Ḥasan b. ʿUbaydallāh) was one of those declared as sanctuaries for the Medinans.[79] His brother, al-Sarī, gained more fame in early ʿAbbāsī history. Ibn Ḥazm remarks that among the descendants of al-Ḥārith b. al-ʿAbbās, only al-Sarī gained fame. He was the deputy governor of Khurāsān in 141/758–759

74 Al-Ṭabarī, 3:244 (ll. 11–12).

75 Al-Balādhurī, *Ansāb* (ed. al-Dūrī), 3:63; only Asmāʾ is mentioned, but unless they were divorced, they most probably lived together in Medina.

76 Al-Yaʿqūbī, *Taʾrīkh* (ed. Houtsma), 2:453 (ll. 1–7) (her lineage is garbled); other sources record al-Asmāʾ''s actions; they all describe the hanging of the black veil on the minaret, but only al-Yaʿqūbī tells of the second *mawlā* who was sent to cause demoralization within Muḥammad b. ʿAbdallāh's army. All the sources relate that the black veil on the minaret shattered the morale of the army and caused its soldiers to flee, see al-Balādhurī, *Ansāb* (ed. al-Dūrī), 3:63 ("this act shattered the rebels": وكسر ذلك المبيضة); al-Zubayrī, *Nasab Quraysh*, 33; Ibn Ḥazm, *Jamhara*, 19: فكان ذلك سبب انهزام أهل المدينة; al-Ṭabarī, 3:244 (ll. 9–14): "when the supporters (أصحاب) of Muḥammad saw this [that is, the flag on the *manāra*] they shouted to each other: the ʿAbbāsī forces have entered the city [literally: "the city has been entered"] and they fled."

77 Al-Ṭabarī, 3:253 (ll. 3–4); her residence (*dār*) is also mentioned in Ibn Saʿd, *Ṭabaqāt*, 1:499–500; al-Ṭabarī, 3:199 (ll. 15–16).

78 Al-Ṭabarī, 3:191–192; he is not mentioned by Ibn Ḥazm or al-Balādhurī.

79 Al-Ṭabarī, 3:253.

and the governor of Mecca and al-Yamāma between 143/760–761 and 146/763–764, during al-Manṣūr's reign.[80]

4 The Financial Sources of the Rebellion

As noted, Muḥammad b. ʿAbdallāh broke down the treasury gates. It may be safely assumed that he took whatever was in it. In addition, a scholar and notable of Quraysh, Abū Bakr b. ʿAbdallāh b. Muḥammad b. Abī Sabra, who was in charge of collecting the *ṣadaqa* taxes from the tribes of Asad and Ṭayyiʾ, gave him money and this was an important source for financing the rebellion and establishing his short rule. According to the different sources, this sum amounted to something between 20,000 and 24,000 *dīnārs*.[81]

Two traditions tell of the efforts Muḥammad exerted to have magnificent and formal clothes made for his supporters. From the cloth coverings (*sutūr*) of the courtyard of the mosque of Medina, he made loose garments (tunics) with a slit in the front and wide sleeves (*darārīʿ*),[82] and from the heavy cloths that

---

80 Ibn Ḥazm, *Jamhara*, 18 (governor of Mecca and al-Yamāma for al-Manṣūr); al-Balādhurī, *Ansāb* (ed. al-Dūrī), 3:68–69 (governor of Mecca "and it is said (ويقال) that he was (also) nominated as the governor of Medina and al-Yamāma"); Ibn Khayyāṭ, *Taʾrīkh* (Beirut, 1993), 334 (al-Yamāma); al-Ṭabarī, 3:138 (year 141 H.: Khurāsān); 3:189 (year 143 H.: Mecca); 3:144–145, 328 (Mecca); 3:318 (year 145 H. at the head of the *ḥajj* (= Ibn Ḥabīb, *al-Muḥabbar*, 35; Sibṭ b. al-Jawzī, *Mirʾāt al-zamān*, fol. 280a); it is noteworthy that he is mentioned by the Imāmīs as the close associate of ʿAlī b. al-Ḥusayn b. ʿAlī b. Abī Ṭālib (known as Zayn al-ʿĀbidīn and al-Sajjād), for example, see al-Ṭūsī, *Rijāl*, 114, this is copied by many Imāmī sources, e.g., al-Tafrishī, *Naqd al-rijāl*, 2:302; al-Khūʾī, *Rijāl*, 9:44.

81 **20,000** *dīnārs*: Ibn Ḥajar, *Tahdhīb* (Hyderabad edition), 12:28: from Muṣʿab al-Zubayrī; **24,000** *dīnārs*: al-Zubayrī, *Nasab Quraysh*, 428–429; al-Tanūkhī, *al-Faraj*, 2:20–21; Ibn Ḥazm, *Jamhara*, 169; al-Khaṭīb al-Baghdādī, *Taʾrīkh* (Beirut, 1997), 14:371; Ibn ʿAsākir, *Taʾrīkh*, 66:24; al-Dhahabī, *Siyar*, 7:332; on him, see Ibn Saʿd, *al-Qism al-mutammim*, 458–460: his support of Muḥammad and the *ṣadaqa* tax affair is not mentioned in this biography; al-Khaṭīb al-Baghdādī, *Taʾrīkh* (Beirut, 1997), 14:370–374; Ibn ʿAsākir, *Taʾrīkh*, 66:22–29; al-Dhahabī, *Siyar*, 7:330–332; al-Mizzī, *Tahdhīb*, 33:102–108; on him, see also chapter 7 (part 1), no. 2.1.

82 Al-Ṭabarī, 3:236 (ll. 13–14): [ʿUmar b. Shabba] < Azhar [b. Saʿīd/Saʿd b. Nāfiʿ?]: وحدثني أزهر قال جعل محمد ستور المسجد دراريع لأصحابه; cf. McAuliffe, *ʿAbbāsid Authority*, 200: "Muḥammad made the mosque curtains into chain armor for his associates." As to the word *sutūr*, perhaps it should be rendered "cloth covering (above the courtyard of the mosque)," instead of curtains, thus translated by McAuliffe, see the discussion below in the next two footnotes). As to *darārīʿ*: McAuliffe rendered *darārīʿ* as from *dirāʿ/durūʿ/*

were stretched above the courtyard of the mosque and above the main routes in that courtyard to provide shade (*ẓilāl*), he made long wide garments with sleeves (*khafātīn,* plural of *khaftān*), which he distributed among his warriors.[83] It was recorded that the cloths that were hung in the courtyard of the mosque were installed by order of Caliph al-Manṣūr.[84]

---

adruʿ, plural form of *dirʿ*: breastplate, coat of mail; but it seems that *darārīʿ* is the plural form of *durrāʿa,* see Lane, *Lexicon,* s.v. *d.r.ʿ*; Dozy, *Vêtements,* 177–178. Al-Qaddūmī/Ibn al-Zubayrī, *Book of Gifts,* 325, n. 4; 420 (glossary); the Arabic text, *al-Dhakhāʾir wa-l-tuḥaf,* 133 (no. 161): *darārīʿ* made of brocade (*dībāj*); 146 (no. 167): white (*darārīʿ bīḍ*); al-Ṭabarī, 3:2243 (l. 4): the Qarmaṭī rebel Ṣāḥib al-Shāma was led in the streets of al-Raqqa on 26 Muḥarram 291/19 December 903 wearing a *durrāʿa* of silk (*ḥarīr*); ibid., (l. 18), the Qarmaṭī and his supporters were brought to Baghdad from al-Raqqa as captives, chained, wearing *darārīʿ* of silk (*ḥarīr*); Ibn ʿAsākir, *Taʾrīkh,* 61:116: *darārīʿ* from wool (*al-ṣūf*); and see also al-Rāwandī, *al-Kharāʾij,* 2:656: a black *durrāʿa* made of brocade (*durrāʿa dībāj sawdāʾ*). *Dārārīʿ* are mentioned immediately afterwards, and it is clear that this is the plural of the above mentioned *durrāʿa.*

83 Al-Ṭabarī, 3:236 (ll. 14–20): جعل محمد ظلال المسجد خَفاتِين لأصحابه; cf. McAuliffe, *ʿAbbāsid Authority,* 200: "Muḥammad made mosque covers into quilted armor for his associates." It seems that the term *ẓilāl* is the plural form of *ẓulla,* which denotes "a thing that covers, or protects [or shades] one overhead," see Lane, *Lexicon,* s.v. *ẓ.l.l.,* For the meaning of the term *ẓilāl* in the context of the mosque of Mecca and its courtyards, see al-Fākihī, *Akhbār Makka,* 2:185; see also ibid., 2:182–184. For another example of *ẓilāl* as the plural of *ẓulla* in the meaning of a shade cover of cloth, see also Ibn al-Jawzī, *al-Muntaẓam,* 9:104, reporting that one of the shade covers (of cloth; *ẓilāl*) of the mosque in Mecca was burnt by a bolt of lightning: ووقعت صاعقة في المسجد الحرام في رمضان هذه على بعض ظلال المسجد الحرام فأحرقت الظلة. For the meaning of the term *khaftān*, see Dozy, *Supplément,* s.v. *kh.f.t.*; idem., *Vêtements,* 162–168; al-Qaddūmī/al-Zubayrī, *Book of Gifts,* 207, no. 302 and n. 2 on 376; 333, n. 9, additional bibliography; they prefer the form *khuftān* instead *of khaftān,* but I chose the latter form following Dozy, *Vêtements,* 162–168; F. Steingass, *Arabic-English Dictionary* (London, 1884), 332; A. Biberstein Kazimirski, *Dictionnaire Arabe-Française* (Cairo, 1875), 1:763: *khaftān*; see also F. Steingass, *Persian-English Dictionary*[2] (London, 1930), 468; S. Haim, *The New Persian-English Dictionary* (Tehran, 2001), 354: *khaftān* (The meaning of the term in the dictionaries is not uniform and needs further research). For the Arabic text see Ibn al-Zubayr, *al-Dhakhāʾir,* 145 (no. 137), where we find it said that it was made of brocade (*khafātīn dībāj*). See also al-Ṭabarī, 3:556 (ll. 14–15, year 169/786, where he describes that when the Ṭālibī rebel, al-Ḥusayn b. ʿAlī b. al-Ḥasan b. al-Ḥasan b. al-Ḥasan (*Ṣāḥib al-Fakhkh*), took control of Medina, his supporters took the curtains of the mosque and prepared from them *khafātīn* for themselves: أخذ أصحاب الحسين ستور المسجد فجعلوها خفاتين لهم.

84 Al-Ḥarbī[?], *al-Manāsik,* 371–372; al-Ḥarbī quotes a contemporary (Muḥammad b. Ismāʿīl) who relates that in 140/758, when he was in Medina, al-Manṣūr ordered the installation

5 Organizing Medina

Muḥammad b. ʿAbdallāh nominated several people to military and administrative posts in the city. Some of the most important posts were given to notables of the Zubayrī family. As noted earlier, the deep involvement of the Zubayrī family in the rebellion is highly important and merits a separate study.[85]

5.1 *Governors of Medina*

Abū l-Faraj al-Iṣfahānī records a tradition transmitted to him from Yaḥyā b. Saʿīd b. Farrūkh al-Qaṭṭān (120–198/737 or 738–813 or 814) through the latter's son, Muḥammad b. Yaḥyā (d. 226/840 or 841), who heard his father (Yaḥyā) saying that "among those that came out in rebellion with Muḥammad b. ʿAbdallāh were ʿUbaydallāh b. ʿUmar, Hishām b. ʿUrwa, and Muḥammad b. ʿAjlān."[86] In another tradition, al-Iṣfahānī quotes al-Madāʾinī (d. ca. 225/840, through another chain of transmitters), that Hishām b. ʿUrwa b. al-Zubayr was nominated as governor of Medina after he swore allegiance to Muḥammad b. ʿAbdallāh.[87]

---

of a cloth covering above the courtyard of the mosque. It was installed on poles, and it had the shape of big tents. When Muḥammad b. ʿAbdallāh revolted he ordered that it be cut into *darārīʿ* for those who fought with him. The terms used for the cover is *sutūr*; it seems that here they should be understood as coverings and not curtains. Text: وأمر بستور يستر بها صحن المسجد على عمد لها رؤوس كهيئات الفساطيط . . . حتى خرج محمد بن عبد الله . . . فأمر بها فقطعت دراريع لمن كان يقاتل معه; and see al-Samhūdī, *Wafāʾ*, 2:467–468, a parallel tradition with small changes, quoting Ibn Zabāla Muḥammad b. al-Ḥasan (d. end of the eighth century.

85 On the Zubayrī family, see introduction but esp. chapter 7 (part 2).

86 Al-Iṣfahānī, *Maqātil*, 292–293: the *isnād*: *ḥaddathanī* [that is, al-Iṣfahānī:] < Aḥmad b. Muḥammad b. Saʿīd < ʿAbd al-Raḥmān b. Yūsuf [b. Kharrāsh (d. 238/852 or 853); a pro-Shīʿī transmitter (*wa-kāna rāfidiyyan*), see al-Dhahabī, *Mīzān* (Beirut, 1382 H.), 2:600–601] < ʿUbaydallāh b. Yūsuf al-Jubayrī [Abū Yūsuf al-Baṣrī, d. ca. 150/767 or 768; on him, see al-Khazrajī, *Khulāṣa*, 254; Ibn Ḥajar, *Tahdhīb* (Hyderabad edition), 7:57; al-Mizzī, *Tahdhīb*, 19:179–181 and the comprehensive bibliography therein] < Muḥammad b. Yaḥyā b. Saʿīd al-Qaṭṭān [on him, see Ibn Abī Ḥātim, *al-Jarḥ* (Beirut edition), 8:123; al-Mizzī, *Tahdhīb*, 26:610–612] < his father [Yaḥyā b. Saʿīd al-Qaṭṭān; on him, see al-Mizzī, *Tahdhīb*, 31:329–343, and the comprehensive bibliography therein]. ʿAbd al-Raḥmān b. Yūsuf, one of the links in the *isnād* adds: "I was informed that Musaddid [unidentified] related the same story (*ḥikāya*) about them taking part in his rebellion."

87 Al-Iṣfahānī, *Maqātil*, 296.

I was unable to find this report about his being a supporter of Muḥammad b. ʿAbdallāh and his appointment as the governor of Medina on the latter's behalf in the many biographies about him in the Sunnī *ʿilm al-rijāl*. Nor is it mentioned in the vast Shīʿī Imāmī literature of *ʿilm al-rijāl,* where he is mentioned as one of the followers (*aṣḥāb*) of the Imām Jaʿfar al-Ṣādiq.[88] Fortunately, this evidence is corroborated by al-Balādhurī, who relates that when the rebellion was over, the commander of the ʿAbbāsī army, ʿĪsā b. Mūsā, granted security and safety to the people of Medina (وآمن عيسى الناس) "... and Hishām b. ʿUrwa and Ayyūb b. Salama al-Makhzūmī had already sworn allegiance to Muḥammad b. ʿAbdallāh and they were granted security when they excused themselves and repented" (probably in public).[89]

However, another report relates that Muḥammad b. ʿAbdallāh nominated someone else from the Zubayrī family as the governor of Medina (استعمل عليها): ʿUthmān b. Muḥammad b. Khālid b. al-Zubayr b. al-ʿAwwām, who (also?) became the head of the *shurṭa* (see below).[90]

5.2 *The Ḥijāba*

According to one tradition, Muḥammad's *ḥājib* was Abū Sayyār.[91] It is possible that Abū Sayyār, the *ḥājib* of Muḥammad b. ʿAbdallāh, was Misma' b. ʿAbd al-Malik b. Misma' b. Mālik, who is mentioned in the Imāmī sources as the leader of Bakr b. Wā'il in al-Baṣra and the head of his extended family: شيخ بكر بن وائل بالبصرة و وجهها وسيد المسامعة. He was regarded as one of Muḥammad al-Bāqir's followers, but mainly of Jaʿfar al-Ṣādiq.[92] But according to another tradition, Muḥammad b. ʿAbdallāh's *ḥājib* was Ibn Abrūd (unidentified).[93]

---

88 Al-Ṭūsī, *Rijāl*, 318 (*bāb al-hā'* no. 15 (4747); idem, *al-Khilāf,* 6:484; al-Shabastarī, *al-Imām al-Ṣādiq,* 3:387, and the exhaustive bibliography therein; al-Tafrishī, *Naqd al-rijāl,* 5:51.

89 Al-Balādhurī, *Ansāb* (ed. Madelung), 2:518: وكان هشام بن عروة وايوب بن سلمة المخزومي قد بايعا محمد بن عبد الله فأومنا حين اعتذرا.

90 Al-Ṭabarī, 3:198 (l. 16) (= al-Iṣfahānī, *Maqātil,* 296): ʿUmar b. Shabba < Muḥammad b. Yaḥyā < al-Ḥārith b. Isḥāq.

91 Al-Ṭabarī, 3:222; ibid., according to MS B (in the *isnād*): Ibn Sayyār, but in the text: Abū Sayyār.

92 Al-Tafrishī, *Naqd al-rijāl,* 4:375; al-ʿĀmilī, *Wasā'il* (*Āl al-Bayt*), 30:492 (the quote is taken from the last two sources); on Abū Sayyār, Misma' b. ʿAbd al-Malik, see also al-Najāshī, *Rijāl,* 420; al-Ḥillī, *Rijāl,* 189; al-Khū'ī *Rijāl,* 19:174–178.

93 Al-Ṭabarī, 3:175 (l. 13).

5.3 *The Shurṭa*

Immediately upon entering Medina, Muḥammad b. ʿAbdallāh appointed ʿAbd al-Ḥamīd b. Jaʿfar b. ʿAbdallāh al-Anṣārī (al-Awsī), a *muḥaddith* (d. 153/770), as the head of his *shurṭa,* for a short time.

ʿAbd al-Ḥamīd b. Jaʿfar supported Muḥammad, took an active part in the uprising, and carried the *ḥarba* (a short spear) in front of him as part of the duties of the *ṣāḥib al-shurṭa.*[94] He related several traditions about aspects of the uprising that he experienced and witnessed, all of which became known through the work of ʿUmar b. Shabba, mainly in al-Ṭabarī's *Taʾrīkh,* but also in *Maqātil al-ṭālibiyyīn.* According to one testimony, at a certain stage he was replaced by the Zubayrī, ʿUthmān b. Muḥammad b. Khālid b. al-Zubayr b. al-ʿAwwām.[95] But according to many other testimonies this important post was filled by another member of the Zubayrī family, Ibrāhīm b. Muṣʿab (Khuḍayr) b. Muṣʿab b. al-Zubayr b. al-ʿAwwām, one of the senior commanders of Muḥammad b. ʿAbdallāh (if not the most senior of his commanders).[96]

Two others are mentioned by the sources as carrying out the duties of the *ṣāḥib al-shurṭa*: Imāmī sources mention the Ḥusaynī ʿĪsā b. Zayd b. ʿAlī b. al-Ḥusayn, who is described as one of Muḥammad's most loyal supporters and the head of his *shurṭa.*[97]

The second person was a descendant of ʿUmar b. al-Khaṭṭāb, ʿUthmān b. ʿUbaydallāh b. ʿAbdallāh b. ʿUmar b. al-Khaṭṭāb, nicknamed Abū l-Qalammas.[98]

5.4 *The Judiciary (al-Qaḍāʾ)*

According to one source, the man in charge of the judiciary was ʿAbd al-ʿAzīz b. al-Muṭṭalib b. ʿAbdallāh al-Makhzūmī (Quraysh),[99] but another source is less sure of this, saying: "Muḥammad b. ʿAbdallāh appointed as a judge ʿAbd al-ʿAzīz b. ʿAbd [sic!] al-Muṭṭalib, but it is said (*wa-yuqālu*) that he appointed as a judge, Abū Bakr b. ʿAbdallāh b. Abī Sabra."[100] Although the latter name is

---

94 Ibid., 3:193 (ll. 13–15): carrying the *ḥarba;* ibid., 3:199 (ll. 3–6): head of the *shurṭa;* on the connection between the *ḥarba* and the *shurṭa,* see, Crone, *Slaves,* 248, n. 474: read *ḥarba* instead of *ḥirba.*

95 Al-Ṭabarī, 3:199 (ll. 3–6); al-Iṣfahānī, *Maqātil,* 282.

96 Ibn al-Kalbī, *Jamhara* (ed. Caskel), 1:82 (ed. Ḥasan, 71); al-Balādhurī, *Ansāb* (ed. Madelung), 2:515; idem. (ed. ʿAbbās), 5:58; *Tāj al-ʿarūs,* s.v. *kh.ḍ.r.*

97 Al-Kulaynī, *al-Kāfī,* 1:362; al-Māzandarānī, *Sharḥ,* 6:315; al-Majlisī, *Biḥār,* 47:284–285; al-Baḥrānī, *Madīnat al-maʿājiz,* 5:285: وكان من ثقاته وكان على شرطه.

98 Al-Ṭabarī, 3:198; al-Iṣfahānī, *Maqātil,* 296.

99 Al-Ṭabarī, 3:198 (ll. 16–17) (= al-Iṣfahānī, *Maqātil,* 296).

100 Wakīʿ, *Quḍāt,* 1:223–224.

the less common version, it stands to reason that it is the correct one, since Abū Bakr b. Abī Sabra was one of the most zealous adherents of Muḥammad b. ʿAbdallāh.

5.5 *Dīwān al-ʿAṭāʾ*

Muḥammad al-Nafs al-Zakiyya appointed ʿAbdallāh b. Jaʿfar b. ʿAbd al-Raḥmān b. al-Miswar b. Makhrama al-Zuhrī [b. Nawfal b. Uhayb b. ʿAbd Manāf b. Zuhra b. Kilāb] in charge of *dīwān al-ʿaṭāʾ*.[101] His followers and soldiers were most probably listed in this *dīwān,* which was burned by Ibrāhīm b. Khuḍayr (Muṣʿab) al-Zubayrī, the chief[?] commander of al-Nafs al-Zakiyya during the last stage of the campaign, out of fear that the registers would fall into the ʿAbbāsīs' hands.[102]

5.6 *The Arsenal*

The man in charge of the arsenal (*ʿalā l-silāḥ*) was a well-known scholar, ʿAbd al-ʿAzīz b. Muḥammad b. ʿUbayd al-Darāwardī, *mawlā* Juhayna.[103]

5.7 *The Flag Bearer*

It has already been noted that ʿUthmān b. Muḥammad b. Khālid al Zubayrī was newly appointed by al-Nafs al-Zakiyya as governor of Medina. According to another testimony, he was the bearer of Muḥammad al-Nafs al-Zakiyya's flag; he entrusted the role to his son, Muḥammad. This tradition was spread by members of the Zubayrī family, its earliest transmitter being Muḥammad b. ʿUthmān himself.[104] But the Ṭālibīs spread a different tradition, according to which al-Ḥasan b. ʿAlī b. ʿAlī b. al-Ḥusayn b. ʿAlī b. Abī Ṭālib, nicknamed al-Afṭas, was the bearer of the white or yellow flag of al-Nafs al-Zakiyya. In this case, the source that transmitted this information took part in the revolt as well. The tradition was related to ʿUmar b. Shabba by ʿĪsā b. ʿAbdallāh b. Muḥammad b. ʿUmar b. ʿAlī b. Abī Ṭālib from his father. The complete tradition is recorded by al-Iṣfahānī (with some omissions by al-Ṭabarī):

---

101 Al-Ṭabarī, 3:198–199 (l. 18 to l. 1) (= al-Iṣfahānī, *Maqātil,* 296); al-Iṣfahānī, *Maqātil,* 282.

102 Al-Ṭabarī, 3:241 (ll. 14–15).

103 Ibid., 3:202 (ll. 9–10) (= al-Iṣfahānī, *Maqātil,* 283).

104 Al-Ṭabarī, 3:237 (ll. 11–14): [ʿUmar b. Shabba] < Ibrāhīm b. Muṣʿab b. ʿUmāra b. Ḥamza b. Muṣʿab b. al-Zubayr < Muḥammad b. ʿUthmān b. Muḥammad b. Khālid b. al-Zubayr. The tradition is not found in al-Iṣfahānī's *Maqātil.*

> al-Afṭas, who is al-Ḥasan b. ʿAlī b. ʿAlī b. al-Ḥusayn [b. ʿAlī b. Abī Ṭālib], had with him a yellow flag of Muḥammad with a picture of a serpent on it; each of his commanders (*aṣḥābihi*) from the family of ʿAlī b. Abī Ṭālib had a flag, and their battle cry was "(God is) One and one alone (*aḥad aḥad*)." The transmitter said [adding]: This was the same battle cry of the Prophet, may God pray for him and his family, in the battle of Ḥunayn [in the year 8/630].[105]

Other Imāmī sources mention the yellow flag,[106] but an early Imāmī author, Abū Naṣr al-Bukhārī, "knows" that the color of al-Ḥasan's flag was white.[107]

6 Appointing Governors in Arabia

Muḥammad sent governors to all parts of the Arabian Peninsula (to Mecca and al-Ṭā'if, al-Yamāma and Yemen), though not all of them reached their destination, and those who did (the governors of Mecca and al-Ṭā'if) spent a very short time there.

6.1 *Mecca*

To Mecca, the most important city in Arabia, Muḥammad al-Nafs al-Zakiyya sent a member of the Ṭālibī (Jaʿfarī) family, al-Ḥasan b. Muʿāwiya b. ʿAbdallāh b. Jaʿfar b. Abī Ṭālib.[108]

---

105 Al-Iṣfahānī, *Maqātil*, 284; al-Ṭabarī, 3:237 (ll. 11–14) (with some omissions: al-Iṣfahānī: علم لمحمد أصفر; al-Ṭabarī: omitting لمحمد; ibid., correct the name al-Ḥasan b. ʿAlī b. al-Ḥusayn, to al-Ḥasan b. ʿAlī **b. ʿAlī** b. al-Ḥusayn [b. Abī Ṭālib]). "أحد أحد" was also the battle cry of the Muslims in the battle of Badr, see Ibn Hishām, *al-Sīra*, 3:182. However, cf. al-Ḥalabī, *Insān al-ʿuyūn*, 2:426: in Badr, the battle cry (and password) of the Anṣār was أحد أحد and that of the Muhājirūn was يا بني عبد الرحمان. According to another version, the Prophet and the Muhājirūn's battle cry was يا منصور أمت or أحد أحد, that of the Khazraj was يا بني عبد الله, and that of the Aws: يا بني عبيد الله, but, adds the author, according to Ibn Saʿd, the battle cry of all the Muslims in Badr was: يا منصور أمت.

106 Al-ʿUmarī, *Ansāb*, 205 (= Ibn ʿInaba, *ʿUmda*, 339).

107 Al-Bukhārī, *Sirr al-silsila*, 77.

108 Al-Ṭabarī, 3:202 (ll. 3–6); al-Iṣfahānī, *Maqātil*, 301; his brother, Yazīd, was a senior commander in Muḥammad's army, see al-Kulaynī, *al-Kāfī*, 1:364 (= al-Majlisī, *Biḥār*, 47:286).

He left Medina accompanied by a small number of soldiers; according to one testimony, he was accompanied by seventy infantrymen and seven horse-riders.[109] The commander of his vanguard (*al-muqaddima*) was Abū ʿAdī ʿAbdallāh b. ʿAdī b. Ḥāritha b. Rabīʿa b. ʿAbd al-ʿUzzā b. ʿAbd al-Shams.[110] Another Qurashī who joined al-Ḥasan was from the family of Abū Lahab, al-ʿAbbās b. al-Qāsim.[111] Two others are mentioned with al-Ḥasan. The first is his cousin, al-Qāsim b. Isḥāq al-Jaʿfarī, who was appointed governor of Yemen (see further below); the second is Abū Jabra Muḥammad b. ʿAbdallāh b. ʿAnbasa [b. Saʿīd b. al-ʿĀṣ b. Umayya al-Akbar b. ʿAbd al-Shams (?)].[112]

It is difficult to ascertain the size and nature of the military forces that were at the disposal of the ʿAbbāsī governor of Mecca, al-Sarī b. ʿAbdallāh [b. al-Ḥārith b. al-ʿAbbās b. ʿAbd al-Muṭṭalib] al-ʿAbbāsī. According to one source, he had "thousands of soldiers" at his disposal;[113] another tradition states that al-Sarī did not have a military post in Mecca and had to recruit an army upon learning of the approaching (small) army of al-Ḥasan. According to this tradition, al-Sarī succeeded in recruiting more than two thousand seven hundred soldiers, under the command of his secretary Miskīn b. Hilāl and his *mawlā*, each at the head of one thousand men. Another commander from Mecca, Ibn Faras, led seven hundred men, who received 500 *dīnār*s from al-Sarī. Al-Ḥasan b. Muʿāwiya attacked Mecca with his force, killing seven of al-Sarī's men, causing the ʿAbbāsī Meccan troops and al-Sarī to flee[114] the city.[115] Al-Sarī's defeat might indicate that he had no intention of fighting al-Ḥasan b. Muʿāwiya. The number of his forces might not be exaggerated. The symbolic meaning of the number of al-Ḥasan's "army," (seventy), however, is clear.

Al-Ḥasan b. Muʿāwiya remained in Mecca for a short time. On hearing of the ʿAbbāsī army led by ʿĪsā b. Mūsā that was approaching Mecca, he left the city with new contingents from Mecca. On the way the news about Muḥammad al-Nafs al-Zakiyya's death reached them,[116] the army was dispersed and

109 Al-Ṭabarī, 3:202 (ll. 5–6); Ibn Kathīr, *al-Bidāya* (Cairo, 1351 H.), 10:86.

110 Al-Balādhurī, *Ansāb* (ed. Madelung), 2:508.

111 Al-Ṭabarī, 3:217 (l. 15); no additional information is given by the sources.

112 Ibid., 3:218 (ll. 11–12).

113 Ibn Kathīr, *al-Bidāya* (Cairo, 1351 H.), 10:86.

114 Al-Ṭabarī, 3:218–219; see also Ibn Kathīr, *al-Bidāya* (Cairo, 1351 H.), 10:86–87.

115 Al-Ṭabarī, 3:219–220; al-Balādhurī, *Ansāb* (ed. Madelung), 2:508.

116 According to a different tradition, he left Mecca when the news of Muḥammad's death reached him, see al-Balādhurī, *Ansāb* (ed. Madelung), 2:518.

al-Ḥasan fled by sea[117] to al-Baṣra, where he stayed until the death of Ibrāhīm b. ʿAbdallāh.[118]

6.2 *Yemen (al-Yaman)*

With al-Ḥasan b. Muʿāwiya, Muḥammad al-Nafs al-Zakiyya sent al-Qāsim b. Isḥāq [b. ʿAbdallāh b. Jaʿfar b. Abī Ṭālib], al-Jaʿfarī, who was appointed governor of Yemen.[119] But al-Qāsim never reached Yemen. He came with al-Ḥasan b. Muʿāwiya to Mecca, stayed there and then left the city with him. He found a hiding place in Medina, and remained hidden there until he and his brothers were granted a safe conduct (*amān*) by the caliph. This safe conduct was obtained through the mediation of their relative, the daughter of ʿAbdallāh b. Muḥammad b. ʿAlī b. ʿAbdallāh b. Jaʿfar b. Abī Ṭālib, who was married to ʿĪsā b. Mūsā l-ʿAbbāsī, the nephew of the two ʿAbbāsī caliphs.[120]

Ibn Ḥazm records a different version of the name of the person who was sent to govern Yemen:

> Al-Qāsim b. al-ʿAbbās b. Maʿmar [sic! read Muḥammad] b. Muʿattib **b. Abī Lahab**..., was a transmitter of *ḥadīth*. Muḥammad b. ʿAbdallāh b. al-Ḥasan b. al-Ḥasan b. ʿAlī b. Abī Ṭālib appointed him governor of Yemen, when he publicly appeared in Medina. (But) it was said (*wa-qīla*), that this is not correct, and that he was killed in the battle (*yawm*) of Qudayd [in 130/747]; the truth is [adds Ibn Ḥazm], that it was his son, al-ʿAbbās b. al-Qāsim who was killed in Qudayd.[121]

---

117 Al-Iṣfahānī, *al-Aghānī* (Dār al-Kutub edition), 11:301 (= Būlāq edition, 10:107).

118 Al-Ṭabarī, 3:221 (ll. 11–12); see also Ibn al-Athīr, *al-Kāmil* (ed. Tornberg), 5:413 (Beirut edition, 5:542), who mistakenly records that it was al-Ḥasan's son, Muḥammad, who was sent as the governor of Mecca and not his father. This tradition is also recorded by al-Fākihī, *al-Muntaqā*, 182, but al-Fākihī remarks that al-Zubayr b. Bakkār, in his *Kitāb al-Nasab*, specifies that the governor of Mecca on behalf of Muḥammad al-Nafs al-Zakiyya was al-Ḥasan b. Muʿāwiya, not his son.

119 Al-Ṭabarī, 3:202 (ll. 5–6); al-Iṣfahānī, *Maqātil*, 278, for his full lineage; 301: sent as the governor of Yemen; McAuliffe, *ʿAbbāsid Authority*, 158, n. 768; Kennedy, *ʿAbbāsid Caliphate*, 201, mentioning both al-Ḥasan b. Muʿāwiya and al-Qāsim b. Isḥāq.

120 Al-Ṭabarī, 3:221 (ll. 14–15); the sources I consulted do not give her name; in fact, her father, ʿAbdallāh, is not mentioned in the *nasab* books either.

121 Ibn Ḥazm, *Jamhara*, 72; on the battle of Qudayd, between Abū Ḥamza al-Khārijī and the Medinans, see al-Ṭabarī, 2:2006ff.

It seems that Ibn Ḥazm's assertion is not correct. Al-Qāsim b. al-ʿAbbās, and not his son, al-ʿAbbās, indeed died in 130/747, or 131.[122] Nothing is known about this son,[123] but he could be identified with "al-ʿAbbās b. al-Qāsim, a man from the family of Abū Lahab," who according to a tradition, left Medina with al-Ḥasan b. Muʿāwiya al-Jaʿfarī, the appointed governor of Mecca, on behalf of Muḥammad b. ʿAbdallāh.[124] There are no other specific details about this man. Was he the appointed governor of Yemen? The source does not say. According to another tradition, it was al-Qāsim b. Isḥāq al-Jaʿfarī who was appointed governor of Yemen by al-Nafs al-Zakiyya[125] (and see above).

6.3 *Al-Ṭāʾif*

Muḥammad al-Nafs al-Zakiyya appointed Abū ʿAdī ʿAbdallāh b. ʿUmar, al-ʿAblī l-Qurashī as the governor of al-Ṭāʾif. His force contained Bedouins (*aʿrāb*) from Muzayna, Juhayna, and Aslam, including several dignitaries: ʿAbd al-Malik b. Abī Zuhayr b. ʿAbd al-Raḥmān al-Thaqafī, a *ḥadīth* scholar, whose origin was most probably from al-Ṭāʾif, and eleven people from the Abū Bakr family. Another member of the family of ʿUmar b. al-Khaṭṭāb al-ʿUmarī, Muḥammad b. Abī Bakr [b. ʿUmar b. Ḥafṣ b. ʿĀṣim b. ʿUmar b. al-Khaṭṭāb], is mentioned in connection with the takeover of al-Ṭāʾif, but the Arabic text mentioning him is not clear to me. Abū ʿAdī took control of the city, but he left it after a stay of three days and fled to Yemen when he heard that the governor of Mecca appointed by Muḥammad al-Nafs al-Zakiyya left the city.[126]

6.4 *Al-Yamāma*

Another governor was sent to al-Yamāma, ʿUthmān b. Ibrāhīm al-Taymī, that is, from Abū Bakr's clan. The news about the death of al-Nafs al-Zakiyya reached him on his way to his destination, which he never reached.[127]

---

122 Ibn Saʿd, *al-Qism al-mutammim*, 268: year 130 H.: ومات ليالي الحرورية الذي قدموا المدينة في سنة ثلاثين ومائة; Ibn ʿAbd al-Barr, *al-Istīʿāb*, 3:1430: قتل يوم قديد; Ibn Ḥibbān, *Mashāhīr*, 221: year 131 H.; idem, *al-Thiqāt*, 7:355: year 131 or during the battles with the Ḥarūriyya in Medina (= year 130 H.); Ibn Ḥajar, *Taqrīb* (1986 edition), 1:450: "year 130 or after it"; on him, see also Ibn Abī Ḥātim, *al-Jarḥ* (Beirut edition), 7:114; al-Dhahabī, *Mīzān* (Beirut, 1995), 5:450–451; in all of the sources: al-Qāsim b. al-ʿAbbās b. **Muḥammad** instead of **Maʿmar** by Ibn Ḥazm; the same reading of the name is also rendered by al-Zubayrī, *Nasab Quraysh*, 273.

123 He is only mentioned once by Ibn Saʿd, *al-Qism al-mutammim*, 267.

124 Al-Ṭabarī, 3:217 (ll. 14–15).

125 Ibid., 3:202 (ll. 5–6).

126 Al-Iṣfahānī, *al-Aghānī* (Dār al-Kutub edition), 11:301 (Būlāq edition, 10:107).

127 Al-Balādhurī, *Ansāb* (ed. Madelung), 2:519.

CHAPTER 5

The ʿAbbāsī Reactions

1 Al-Manṣūr's First Response

The news about the outbreak of the revolt reached al-Manṣūr while he was in the area where he planned to build Baghdad. He left the site immediately and hurried to al-Kūfa.[1] (Most probably to al-Hāshimiyya in al-Kūfa's immediate surroundings). The tradition attributes to him the following saying: "I, Abū Jaʿfar, drew the fox out of his hole."[2] He ordered a tight curfew on al-Kūfa and surrounded it with armed posts. This was done following his uncle ʿAbdallāh b. ʿAlī's advice (who was at that time under house arrest).[3]

While still in Baghdad, he had a letter sent to Egypt, in which he ordered that the supply of food and grains (المادة والميرة) to Mecca and Medina be cut off.[4] He also ordered that the transfer of grain which passed through Wādī l-Qurā en route from Syria to Medina be blocked. According to al-Ṭabarī, this was done according to the advice of Jaʿfar b. Ḥanẓala al-Bahrānī, who was "the most knowledgeable among men in the (art) of war, and fought with Marwān [b. Muḥammad, the last Umawī caliph] in his wars."[5]

Other letters were sent to his brother al-ʿAbbās, who was the governor of al-Jazīra, and to the governors (*umarāʾ*)[6] of Syria (al-Shām), ordering them to send soldiers to him.[7]

1 Al-Ṭabarī, 3:206, 319; al-Balādhurī, *Ansāb* (ed. Madelung), 2:509, 521–522; al-Masʿūdī, *Tanbīh*, 360: al-Kūfa. However, cf. Agapius, *Taʾrīkh*, 126: al-Manṣūr leaves for al-ʿĀqūl. Al-ʿĀqūl is not mentioned by the Muslim geographers. An ʿĀqūl near al-Kūfa is mentioned by al-Kalāʿī, *al-Iktifāʾ*, 4:278; a Dayr al-ʿĀqūl, located south of Baghdad, between al-Madāʾin and al-Nuʿmāniyya, on the east bank of the Tigris is a well-known place; see Le Strange, *Eastern Caliphate*, 35–36; map II facing 25, but this is far from al-Kūfa.

2 Al-Ṭabarī, 3:206 (ll. 4–6).

3 Ibid.

4 Ibid., 3:280; al-Balādhurī, *Ansāb* (ed. al-Dūrī), 3:268: a similar tradition with some important changes; the word *al-mādda* is missing.

5 Al-Ṭabarī, 3:223–224 (l. 21 to l. 5).

6 Ibid., 3:180; McAuliffe, *ʿAbbāsid Authority*, 250, has commanders.

7 Al-Ṭabarī, 3:280–281 (al-Jazīra and Syria); al-Balādhurī, *Ansāb* (ed. al-Dūrī), 3:268 (Syria). In spite of the similarity between these two sources, there are some major differences between them: according to al-Ṭabarī, ibid., al-Manṣūr says (regarding recruiting soldiers from Syria: "It would be good if even one soldier reaches me every day, with them I'll increase the *ahl*

 | DOI 10.1163/9789004296220_007

Upon other advice from his uncle, ʿAbdallāh b. ʿAlī, al-Manṣūr summoned to al-ʿIrāq Salm b. Qutayba b. Muslim, the son of the well-known Umawī warrior and governor, who was in al-Rayy with al-Manṣūr's son, Muḥammad al-Mahdī. Upon his arrival, he was put at the head of some of the best contingents of *ahl al-Shām*.[8]

It is highly probable that al-Manṣūr did not need this specific advice, or the other advice supposedly given to him by various advisers. Although we have here a stereotypical literary narrative, built according to "the question and the answer motif," the advice of both ʿAbdallāh b. ʿAlī and of Jaʿfar b. Ḥanẓala was logical from a strategic point of view.

Most of the advice given was equally practical and it is certain that the caliph could have come up with it himself, such as the above-mentioned idea of blocking the transfer of grain from Syria to Medina. We have already seen that al-Manṣūr did not need anyone's advice in order to write to his governors in al-Jazīra and Syria and order them to send him troops.

Still, these traditions undoubtedly reflect the real situation on the eve of the outbreak of the revolt. They mirror real worry and anxiety on the caliph's part. They were put into circulation after the rebellion was crushed, together with others that, in retrospect, described the rebellion as if it had had no chance of succeeding at all and was doomed to failure.[9] In one such tradition the last Umawī caliph, Marwān b. Muḥammad, foretells that the rebellion will fail, as did all the other ʿAlīd rebellions in the past.[10] This esoteric knowledge, which the ʿAbbāsīs gain from Marwān, was also known to al-Manṣūr's astrologer,

Khurāsān units that are with me": ولو أن يرد علي في كل يوم رجل واحد أكثر به من معي من أهل خراسان, while al-Balādhurī's text (regarding recruitment from al-Jazīra) runs as follows: "even if he sent one man per day to him in order to break the *ahl Khurāsān* units with them, since their bad and corrupt behavior is not to be trusted, this in addition to their boldness (towards the caliph)": ولو أن يبعث إليه في كل يوم رجلا واحدا لينكسر بهم أهل خراسان فإنه لا يؤمن فسادهم مع دالتهم.

8 Al-Ṭabarī, 3:206–207.

9 E.g., ibid., 3:206.

10 Ibid., 3:204: ...ʿAbdallāh b. al-Rabīʿ b. ʿUbaydallāh b. ʿAbdallāh b. ʿAbd al-Madān < Saʿīd b. ʿAmr b. Jaʿda al-Makhzūmī, records a conversation between him and Marwān b. Muḥammad; ʿAbdallāh b. al-Rabīʿ b. ʿUbaydallāh b. ʿAbdallāh b. ʿAbd al-Madān, al-Manṣūr's relative (from the female side: the mother of Abū l-ʿAbbās al-Saffāḥ, al-Manṣūr's brother, was from their family; on him and his family, see Crone, *Slaves*, 149), relates his answer to al-Manṣūr, who confidentially disclosed to him the news of the revolt's outbreak.

who told the caliph that Muḥammad b. ʿAbdallāh would not live more than ninety days.[11]

In other traditions the advisers suggest that the caliph direct his efforts towards al-Baṣra, that is, to Ibrāhīm b. ʿAbdallāh's rebellion, which began only after al-Nafs al-Zakiyya's revolt was crushed, and thus echo the actual ending of the revolt in Medina.[12]

Immediately upon the outbreak of the revolt (and possibly even before), al-Manṣūr ordered the execution of Muḥammad b. ʿAbdallāh b. ʿAmr b. ʿUthmān b. ʿAffān, ʿAbdallāh b. al-Ḥasan's maternal half-brother, who was imprisoned with the Ḥasanīs in al-Hāshimiyya in al-ʿIrāq. His head was sent to Khurāsān and was presented there as that of Muḥammad b. ʿAbdallāh b. al-Ḥasan, the ʿAlīd rebel.[13]

2 The Correspondence between al-Manṣūr and Muḥammad b. ʿAbdallāh

When news of Muḥammad b. ʿAbdallāh's revolt reached al-Manṣūr, he sent him a letter in which he called him to surrender unconditionally, and offered him, his family, and his supporters an *amān* and a large sum of money. This opened an exchange of letters between the caliph and Muḥammad b. ʿAbdallāh.

The second letter is a long response by Muḥammad in which he claims that he is the only person who is entitled to the caliphate, and supports this claim with political-religious arguments for the unequivocal right of ʿAlī and

---

11 Al-Ṭabarī, 3:206; the name of the astrologer is Ḥārith *al-munajjim*. Another version in one of the MSS of al-Ṭabarī's *Taʾrīkh*, ibid., and Ibn al-Athīr, *al-Kāmil* (ed. Tornberg), 5:406 has al-Ḥārithī; this may be Ḥārith *al-munajjim*, who is mentioned by Ibn al-Nadīm, *Fihrist* (ed. al-Tajaddud), 337, according to whom he was very close (*munqaṭiʿ*) to al-Ḥasan b. Sahl. Abū Maʿshar (d. 272/885 or 886) transmitted from him. The editor of al-Ṭihrānī, *al-Dharīʿa* (Tehran, 1360 H.), 4:400, copies *al-Fihrist* and argues that the aforementioned al-Ḥasan b. Sahl is not the brother of the famous *wazīr* of al-Maʾmūn, al-Faḍl b. Sahl, but the Shīʿī al-Ḥasan b. Sahl b. Nawbakht *al-munajjim*.

12 Al-Ṭabarī, 3:292.

13 Al-Ṭabarī, 3:189, relates from Ibn Abī l-Mawālī that his head was sent to Khurāsān with a "group of the (ʿAbbāsī?) Shīʿa"; McAuliffe, *ʿAbbāsid Authority*, 141, has "group of the *shīʿa*"; other sources do not mention this term, e.g., al-Iṣfahānī, *Maqātil*, 226: ... ʿUmar b. Shabba < ʿĪsā < Miskīn b. ʿAmr; Ibn Saʿd, *al-Qism al-mutammim*, 257–258; Ibn al-Athīr, *al-Kāmil* (ed. Tornberg), 5:400; al-Balādhurī, *Ansāb* (ed. Madelung), 2:505, from Abū l-Yaqẓān relates that his head was sent to Khurāsān; but see al-Balādhurī, *Ansāb* (ed. ʿAbbās), 4/A:606, from al-Madāʾinī: his head was sent to Hind (= al-Sind?).

his descendants to rule: "ʿAlī was the *waṣiyy* (the inheritor) and the *imām* (the leader of the community), so how could you have inherited his *wilāya* (authority), when his own descendants are still alive?"[14] A major argument of Muḥammad's is his pure *nasab* and that of his predecessor, on both the male and female side (among them Fāṭima, the Prophet's daughter), implying that the lineage of al-Manṣūr, who was the son of a slave woman, was impure:

> You well know that no one who has lineage, nobility, and status equal to ours has laid claim to this office. By the nobility of our fathers, we are not the sons of the accursed [*al-luʿanāʾ*], the outcasts [*al-ṭuradāʾ*], and those who were freed from captivity [*al-ṭulaqāʾ*]. No one from the Banū Hāshim has the sort of bonds we can draw upon through kinship, precedence, and superiority. We are the descendants of the [fore]mother of God's messenger, Fāṭima bt. ʿAmr, in the Jāhiliyya and descendants of his daughter Fāṭima in Islam.[15]

---

14 Al-Ṭabarī, 3:209 (ll. 17–18) (trans. McAuliffe, *ʿAbbāsid Authority*, 167).

15 Al-Ṭabarī, 3:209–210 (l. 18 to l. 4) (trans. McAuliffe, *ʿAbbāsid Authority*, 167–168, with slight changes). *Al-ṭulaqāʾ* became a general term of defamation for those Meccans who became Muslims after the conquest of Mecca in 8/630; they were all captives and freed by the Prophet, who also gave them this epithet. See for example, Ibn Hishām, *al-Sīra*, 4:870; al-Ḥalabī, *Insān al-ʿuyūn*, 3:49, 65; Ibn Saʿd, *Ṭabaqāt*, 8:153; al-Yaʿqūbī, *Taʾrīkh* (Beirut edition), 2:60; Ibn Ḥibbān, *al-Thiqāt*, 2:56; al-Ṭabarī, 1:1642–1643. *Al-ṭuradāʾ*, pl. of *ṭarīd; al-luʿanāʾ*, pl. of *laʿīn*; as to *al-ṭuradāʾ*, al-Ḥakam b. Abī l-ʿĀṣ, the father of Marwān and grandfather of ʿAbd al-Malik, was expelled by the Prophet from Medina and was not allowed to return until the reign of ʿUthmān; the Prophet also cursed him upon his expulsion from Medina, thus he was called طريد رسول الله ولعينه. For example, see Ibn Qutayba, *al-Maʿārif* (Cairo edition), 353; al-Maqrīzī, *al-Nizāʿ wa-l-takhāṣum*, 14 [trans. Bosworth, *al-Maqrīzī*, 53–54, and 124, note]; al-Yaʿqūbī, *Taʾrīkh* (Beirut edition), 2:164 (*ṭarīd*). The three epithets, *al-ṭulaqāʾ, al-luʿanāʾ, and al-ṭuradāʾ*, became the common terms of defamation for the Sufyānīs and the Marwānīs or the Umawīs in general, mainly by the Shīʿīs: Muʿāwiya b. Abī Sufyān is often referred to as one of the *ṭulaqāʾ*, e.g., Ibn ʿAsākir, *Taʾrīkh*, 13:266; 25:180; 59:128; al-Mizzī, *Tahdhīb*, 17:343; and see Ibn Aʿtham al-Kūfī, *Futūḥ* (Beirut, 1411 H.), 4:323: the Umawīs who killed al-Ḥusayn are named *al-luʿanāʾ*; Ibn Saʿd, *Ṭabaqāt*, 5:109 (= al-Maqrīzī, *al-Nizāʿ wa-l-takhāṣum*, 14): Muḥammad b. al-Ḥanafiyya defames ʿAbd al-Malik and the Marwānīs: الطلقاء ولعناء رسول الله; Ibn Bābawayh al-Qummī, *Akhbār al-Riḍā*, 1:133: the Umawīs are الطرداء واللعناء; al-Majlisī, *Biḥār*, 99:166: الطلقاء واللعناء; al-Amīn, *Aʿyān al-Shīʿa*, 1:600: اللعناء وأولاد اللعناء; and see also Traini, "La corrispondenza," 778, n. 28; al-Ṭabarī, *Glossarium*, cccxlii; the three recipients of an *amān* are Yazīd b. ʿUmar b. Hubayra, ʿAbdallāh b. ʿAli, and Abū Muslim.

He mocks al-Manṣūr's consent to give him an *amān*, mentioning three famous *amān*s which al-Manṣūr did not honor—cases in which he had the recipients killed.

The third letter is a long and detailed answer by al-Manṣūr, in which he addresses each and every argument raised in Muḥammad's letter. A central argument is that God did not make women equal to uncles and fathers or paternal relations, therefore his relations cannot serve as an argument for the right to legitimate rule. "You are indeed the descendants of Fāṭima," writes the caliph, "which is a close kinship, but it does not legitimize inheritance, neither does it confer the *imāma* from her."[16] Regarding the claim that Muḥammad's lineage is pure on both sides, and that there is no non-Arab blood in his loins, al-Manṣūr answers:

> Truly you have gone beyond all bounds. You even hold yourself superior to one who was better than you in his essence (*nafs*) and his lineage, in the beginning and in the end, i.e., Ibrāhīm, the son of the Messenger of God [whose mother was Māriya the Copt] and [see yourself] superior, therefore, to the father who begot him[!] In particular, the best of your forefather's sons and the most excellent people among them are nothing but concubines' sons. After the death of God's Messenger, there was no one born among you who was more excellent than **ʿAlī b. Ḥusayn** [Zayn al-ʿĀbidīn], yet he was the son of a concubine. He was certainly better than your grandfather, Ḥasan b. Ḥasan. After ʿAlī there was no one among you to equal his son, **Muḥammad b. ʿAlī** [al-Bāqir], yet his grandmother was a concubine. He was certainly better than your father. Further, there is no one the equal of his son, **Jaʿfar** [al-Ṣādiq], yet his grandmother was a concubine.[17]

A large part of al-Manṣūr's answer is devoted to praising the ʿAbbāsīs who fought against the Umawīs and defeated them, and this after a series of unsuccessful pro-ʿAlīd revolts. With this victory the ʿAbbāsīs avenged the blood of the ʿAlīds, who were despised and cursed from the *minbar*s of the Umawīs' mosques. Here al-Manṣūr arrives at the central and most important point: After stating that "God gave uncles status equal to the father, giving them (legal) precedence in His book over the less significant mother,"[18] he asserts

16 Al-Ṭabarī, 3:213 (ll. 5–7) (trans. McAuliffe, *ʿAbbāsid Authority*, 173).

17 Al-Ṭabarī, 3:212–213 (l. 14 to l. 4) (trans. McAuliffe, *ʿAbbāsid Authority*, 171–172); the emphasis in bold in the square brackets are mine.

18 Al-Ṭabarī, 3:211 (ll. 9–10) (trans. McAuliffe, *ʿAbbāsid Authority*, 170).

that of the Prophet's three uncles (Ḥamza, Abū Ṭālib, al-ʿAbbās), the last was the most honored in the Jāhiliyya and Islam:

> You know very well that not one of ʿAbd al-Muṭṭalib's sons outlived the Prophet except al-ʿAbbās, who from among the Prophet's uncles, was his heir.... He carried out the duty of supplying the water for the pilgrims in Mecca [*al-siqāya*] during the Jāhiliyya and the Islamic period, as his inheritance from the Prophet, and the caliphate lies with his progeny. There is no eminence and excellence in the Jāhiliyya or in Islam, in this world or in the Hereafter, that al-ʿAbbās does not inherit and bequeath.[19]

Only three relatively small studies have been dedicated to the letters, those of Traini, Omar, and Nagel, who mainly give detailed contents of the letters, but also analyses of some of the political-religious-theological arguments revolving around the legitimization of each "party" (the ʿAbbāsīs and the ʿAlīds) to rule. However, they are far from exhaustive.[20] Other scholars, although well aware of the importance of the letters, only mention them briefly[21] or incidentally. Nevertheless, although scholars differ in regard to the letters' authenticity, or parts of them,[22] the accepted view is that they are early, and were composed not later than 200/815–816[23] (and see below).

The controversy surrounding the letters' authenticity is closely related to the discussion about the authenticity of the meeting of Banū Hāshim in al-Abwāʾ. A major issue that has puzzled scholars concerns the lack of any mention (in al-Nafs al-Zakiyya's letter to al-Manṣūr) of the traditions relating to the

19 Al-Ṭabarī, 3:215 (ll. 1–6) (trans. McAuliffe, *ʿAbbāsid Authority*, 175).

20 Traini, "La corrispondenza"; Omar, "al-Rasāʾil"; Nagel, "Muḥammad b. ʿAbdallāh."

21 E.g., Crone, *Islamic Thought*, 92.

22 E.g., 1) Van Vloten, "Zur Abbasidengeschichte," *ZDMG* 52 (1898), 213f., believed that the letters were not authentic (mentioned by Traini, "La corrispondenza," 775; Nagel, "Muḥammad b. ʿAbdallāh," 256, n. 21 [after Traini]); 2) cf. Margoliouth, *Lectures*, 90, who writes "The likelihood of letters being preserved becomes greater when the 'bureau of the seal' came into existence, and there is a probability that the correspondence between Manṣūr and the ʿAzid [sic!=Zaydī?] pretender Muḥammad b. ʿAbdallah is historical, though the copies produced by Tabari and Mubarrad differ in some important details"; 3) Van Arendonk, 90, stating that the letters are of doubtful authenticity: "Les lettres qu'al-Manṣūr et Muḥammad auraient échangées [in n. 2 he quotes al-Kāmil, 786 sqq.; Ṭab, III, 208 sqq.; *ʿIqd*, 3:36, 21 sqq.] sont vrai semblablement apocryphes [in n. 2b he says that this is contrary to Margoliouth: "cf. par contre D.S. Margoliouth ..."].

23 Nagel, "Muḥammad b. ʿAbdallāh," 247, 255–256; Zaman, *Religion and Politics*, 45, and n. 42 (quoting Nagel and accepting his analysis).

oath of allegiance (*bayʿa*) taken by dignitaries of Banū Hāshim, including some senior ʿAbbāsī family members, such as al-Manṣūr and al-Saffāḥ, towards the end of the Umawī period in al-Abwāʾ. This caused scholars such as van Vloten to argue that the letters were not authentic.[24] Traini, though arguing on the one hand for the authenticity of the letters, was also puzzled that the oath of allegiance in al-Abwāʾ was not mentioned in the letter sent to al-Manṣūr. To solve this problem, he argues that when al-ʿAbbās is mentioned in al-Manṣūr's letter, this also alludes to al-Abwāʾ, where according to some traditions al-ʿAbbās fed the Qurashīs during the Badr campaign.[25] However, his solution to the problem of the *bayʿa* in al-Abwāʾ is untenable and his arguments were rightly criticized and rejected by Nagel.[26] Omar is unequivocal in his view that the letters are authentic, in spite of minor changes to the texts of the letters by pro-ʿAlīd or pro-ʿAbbāsī transmitters. Regrettably, he does not adduce examples for such additions or changes.[27] He also adds that the two main important sources, al-Ṭabarī's *Taʾrīkh* and al-Mubarrad's *al-Kāmil*, differ considerably from each other, but again he does not give any examples for these textual differences.[28] Nagel categorically objects to the authenticity of the traditions in which Jaʿfar al-Ṣādiq prophecies that the two brothers, Muḥammad and Ibrāhīm, will die and that the ʿAbbāsīs will attain the caliphate,[29] but at the same time he argues for an authentic kernel in these traditions when saying that Muḥammad b. ʿAbdallāh's claims and arguments are based on an agreement reached during the Umawī period and that it is not impossible that this story (that is, the attendance of the ʿAbbāsīs in al-Abwāʾ and their oath of allegiance there) has a grain of truth to it.[30] It is not clear from Nagel's study what exactly the concrete nature of this grain of truth is, and why it is not referred to in al-Nafs al-Zakiyya's letter.

In Nagel's view, most of the arguments raised by Muḥammad and by al-Manṣūr are authentic. Some of those raised by Muḥammad were well-known during the Umawī period, in the middle of the second/eighth century.[31] However, Nagel adds, a small part of al-Manṣūr's letter, that which pertains to Muḥammad's pure lineage, especially through freeborn women, was not part

24 See n. 22 above.

25 Traini, "La corrispondenza," 797–798.

26 Nagel, "Muḥammad b. ʿAbdallāh," 229 and 256, n. 21.

27 Omar, "al-Rasāʾil," (*Buḥūth*), 104, 106.

28 Ibid., 105.

29 Nagel, "Muḥammad b. ʿAbdallāh," 260, 262.

30 Ibid., 262.

31 Ibid., 248–249, 255.

of the original letter. This is the part where al-Manṣūr mentions the heads of the Ḥusaynī family, ʿAlī b. al-Ḥusayn b. ʿAlī, whose mother was a slave woman; his son Muḥammad al-Bāqir, whose grandmother was a slave woman, and his grandson, Jaʿfar al-Ṣādiq, whose grandmother was a slave woman.[32] Nagel is referring to al-Manṣūr's statement: "the best of your forefather's sons and the most excellent people among them are nothing but concubines' sons."

Nagel argues that this view contradicts the total unequivocal defamation of the ʿAlīds in the other parts of the letter. The theological-religious concepts behind these sentences do not conform to the relations known to have existed between the ʿAlīds and the ʿAbbāsīs in that period. Therefore, he argues, this segment is a late redaction which can be explained in light of the historical relations that developed between the ʿAbbāsīs and the Ḥusaynīs before al-Maʾmūn's reign, a period when part of the Ḥusaynī family maintained good relations with the ʿAbbāsīs. This development reached its peak when al-Maʾmūn chose ʿAlī l-Riḍā as his heir. During al-Manṣūr's reign, continues Nagel, the Ḥusaynīs were divided among themselves; they were not united under a religious-political house or leadership. Nagel shows that some of the important members of the Ḥusaynī family, including two of Jaʿfar al-Ṣādiq's sons, supported the revolt.[33]

Nagel's view that the revolt was carried on the shoulders of various families of the Ṭālibīs, including the Ḥusaynīs, conforms to our conclusions on the subject. He may be correct in surmising that the doctrines of the Zaydīs or the Ḥusaynīs/Imāmīs were not fully developed in 145 H. But nevertheless, it seems that his view that the paragraph about the Ḥusaynīs is a product of a later redaction has some flaws. When was this paragraph added? Nagel mentions al-Maʾmūn and ʿAlī l-Riḍā; contrary to his description, the historical events, especially the history of the Imāmīs, do not reflect peaceful relations, or even co-existence, between the ʿAbbāsīs and the Ḥusaynīs. Mūsā b. Jaʿfar al-Kāẓim's history is well known: his relations with the ʿAbbāsīs were very tense; he was imprisoned by al-Mahdī and Hārūn al-Rashīd, and died in al-Rashīd's prison (possibly after being poisoned).[34] ʿAlī l-Riḍā was summoned to Marw and pro-

32 ʿAlī b. al-Ḥusayn's mother, Muḥammad al-Bāqir's grandmother, was indeed a slave woman; but Jaʿfar's mother was Umm Farwa bt. al-Qāsim b. Muḥammad b. Abī Bakr and her mother, that is his grandmother, was Asmāʾ bt. ʿAbd al-Raḥmān b. Abī Bakr (al-Kulaynī, *al-Kāfī* [1369 H.], 1:472; al-Majlisī, *Biḥār*, 47:5). I was not able to find out who the mother of Asmāʾ bt. ʿAbd al-Raḥmān was; however, the mother of Jaʿfar's grandmother (on his father's side) was a slave woman: Muḥammad b. ʿAlī's mother was Umm ʿAbdallāh bt. al-Ḥasan b. ʿAlī (al-Zubayrī, *Nasab Quraysh*, 59); her mother was a slave woman (ibid., 50).

33 Nagel, "Muḥammad b. ʿAbdallāh," 255–256.

34 Kohlberg, "Mūsā al-Kāẓim," 645–647.

claimed as the heir to the throne in 201/817 and died in 203/818, most possibly poisoned by order[?] of al-Maʾmūn.

If indeed, as Nagel argues, the letters were put into circulation at the end of the second *hijrī* century (ca. 815),[35] it is doubtful that they have any connection to al-Maʾmūn's religious policy, certainly not to that of al-Rashīd. It should be remembered that a long version of the letters was transmitted by Hishām b. Muḥammad al-Kalbī, who died in 204/819 or 206/821 (see below). It can be argued, therefore, that inserting the sentences which praise the Ḥusaynīs later than 145/762 is even less acceptable. This, however, does not resolve the problem. The obvious answer to the question of these sentences is that, on the one hand, al-Manṣūr mentioned the Ḥusaynīs in order to stress their descent from slave women, and to emphasize that they (the Ḥusaynīs) are still better than the "pure" Ḥasanīs, thus alluding to his (al-Manṣūr's) mother, who was a slave woman. On the other hand, this does not change the fact that the ʿAbbāsī family is nobler than both the Ḥasanīs and the Ḥusaynīs.

1.1 *The Text and its Transmission*

Nagel, as other scholars before him, studied the letters mainly according to al-Ṭabarī's text. The letters have been reproduced by many sources. Some record the letters in their entirety, others transmit either large sections or merely snippets, and some give only a summary of the letters. As noted in the introduction to this book, a comparative textual-contextual study of the letters is called for. Most of the sources were mentioned by Traini, some of which were (and still are) in manuscript form.[36] Two additional sources were mentioned by Omar.[37] Apparently not many parallel sources can be added to the list of sources provided by Traini and Omar.[38]

35 Nagel, "Muḥammad b. ʿAbdallāh," 255; 247: ca. 200 H.

36 Traini, "La corrispondenza," 785–786: al-Ṭabarī, *Taʾrīkh*; al-Mubarrad, *al-Kāmil*; Ibn ʿAbd Rabbihi, *al-ʿIqd*; Ibn Miskawayh, *Tajārib al-umam*, MS Cost.Aya Sofia 3118, f. 205r–210r (I did not consult this manuscript); *Ghurar al-siyar* (MS Bodl. 130, f. 182r–183r); *Fragmenta historicorum arabicorum*; Ibn al-Jawzī, *al-Muntaẓam*; Ibn al-Athīr, *al-Kāmil*; al-Dhahabī, *Taʾrīkh*; Ibn Kathīr, *al-Bidāya*; Ibn Khaldūn, *al-ʿIbar*; al-Nuwayrī, *Nihāya*; and al-Tibrīzī, MS Leiden Or. 2610 (the fourth letter).

37 Omar, "al-Rasāʾil," (*Buḥūth*), mentions the sources mentioned by Traini, adding two more (on 104): the MSS of al-Balādhurī, *Ansāb al-ashrāf*, and al-Azdī, *Taʾrīkh al-Mawṣil*; for the complete list of sources, see below.

38 Two sources, Balʿamī's Persian translation of al-Ṭabarī and Sibṭ b. al-Jawzī's *Tadhkirat al-khawwāṣ* can be added to the comprehensive list of sources of Traini: al-Ṭabarī, *Taʾrīkh*, 3:207–209 (l. 19 to l. 6) (the first letter); 3:209–211 (l. 6 to l. 5) (the second letter); 3:211–215 (l. 5 to l. 14) (the third letter); Balʿamī, 4:396–405 (see the discussion below); al-Balādhurī, *Ansāb* (ed. Madelung), 2:510–512: a large part of Muḥammad's letter (al-Ṭabarī, 3:209–210

Al-Ṭabarī and al-Azdī are the only sources who added a complete *isnād* before the text of the letters. Al-Ṭabarī's *isnād* is as follows: "[= 'Umar b. Shabba] < Muḥammad b. Yaḥyā [b. 'Alī, Abū Ghassān al-Kinānī] who said: I transcribed these letters from Muḥammad b. Bashīr (unidentified)[39] who testified to their authenticity. Abū 'Abd al-Raḥmān, a scribe from al-'Irāq (من كتّاب أهل العراق), AND al-Ḥakam b. Ṣadaqa b. Nizār (unidentified) related them to me. I also heard (*wa-sami'tu*) Ibn Abī Ḥarb declare them authentic." 'Umar b. Shabba gathered his information about the letters from four different transmitters. As for Abū 'Abd al-Raḥmān, McAuliffe identified him as Abū 'Abd al-Raḥmān al-Humānī, an unknown person (transmitter?), mentioned

(l. 14 to l. 5); 3:210 (ll. 14–16); 3:210–211 (l. 16 to l. 2); and a very large part of al-Manṣūr's answer, e.g., al-Ṭabarī, 3:211–212 (l. 13 to l. 1); 3:213 (ll. 8–10); 3:213–215 (l. 12 to l. 14); the name of Ja'far al-Ṣādiq is omitted by al-Balādhurī (*Ansāb* [Madelung ed.], 2:511); a Qur'ānic verse (2:133) is added by al-Balādhurī, where Ibrāhīm, Ismā'īl, and Isḥāq are mentioned; *Fragmenta*, 240–241: the first letter of al-Manṣūr, part of the second letter of Muḥammad; the third letter, the answer of al-Manṣūr, was omitted in its entirety by the author, who commented: "al-Manṣūr wrote an answer to this letter but this is not its place due to its length"; al-Mubarrad, *al-Kāmil* (Leipzig, 1864), 786–790 (Cairo 1953, 5:308–311; ed. Muḥammad Abū l-Faḍl Ibrāhīm [Cairo: Dār al-Fikr al-'Arabī, 1980], 113–120); Ibn 'Abd Rabbihi, *al-'Iqd*, 5:79–85; al-Mar'ashī, *Ghurar al-siyar*, 358–359; Abū 'Alī Aḥmad b. Muḥammad b. Ya'qūb (known as [Ibn] Miskawayh), *Tajārib al-umam*, MS Cost. Aya Sofia 3118, f. 205r–210r (I did not consult this manuscript); Ibn al-Jawzī, *al-Muntaẓam*, 8:64–66: large omissions and redactions of the text; Sibṭ b. al-Jawzī, *Tadhkira*, 221–224: minor and large omissions; change of word order (see below); the author sometimes inserts his own explanations and comments; Ibn Kathīr, *al-Bidāya* (ed. Shīrī), 10:91–92: a short version; many omissions; al-Dhahabī, *Ta'rīkh* (*ḥawādith wa-wafayāt 141 H.–160 H.*), 9:24–26: large omissions; Ibn Khaldūn, *'Ibar* (Beirut, 1971), 4:4–6: with omissions; al-Qalqashandī, *Ṣubḥ*, 1:277–282: a complete version; al-Nuwayrī, *Nihāyat al-arab*, 25:31–38.

39 Nagel, "Muḥammad b. 'Abdallāh," 247, suggests (but only as a possibility) identifying him with a Kūfan Shī'ī Imāmī scholar, who lived sometime between the end of the second/seventh century and the first quarter of the third/ninth century; on him, see al-Ṭūsī, *Ikhtiyār*, 2:774–778; al-Ṭūsī, *Fihrist*, 233; al-Najāshī, *Rijāl*, 344. Perhaps a better possibility may be Muḥammad b. Bashīr b. 'Aṭā' b. Marwān al-Kindī, al-Wā'iẓ; he was a *qāḍī* who died in Baghdad on 27 Jumādā II 236/5 January 851; on him, see Ibn Abī Ḥātim, *al-Jarḥ* (Beirut edition), 7:211; al-Khaṭīb al-Baghdādī, *Ta'rīkh* (Beirut, 1997), 2:97–98, where he is mentioned as the second transmitter in *isnāds* in *ḥadīth* works, e.g., al-Ṭabarānī, *al-Kabīr*, 3:128; 10:208; 11:210. However, there are other scholars with this name, e.g., Muḥammad b. Bashīr al-Qazzāz (Ibn 'Adī, *Ḍu'afā'*, 2:324) or Muḥammad b. Bashīr Abū Ja'far al-Zāhid (Ibn 'Adī, *Ḍu'afā'*, 2:327); it is noteworthy that other published texts of al-Ṭabarī have: ". . . I transcribed these letters from Muḥammad b. Bashīr, and **Bashīr** testified to their authenticity," while al-Azdī's version has Muḥammad b. **Bishr** (instead of **Bashīr**).

only once by al-Ṭabarī, who has him relating an anecdote about the building of a city near the site of Wāsiṭ by Solomon the son of David.[40] However, it makes more sense to identify him as the well-known *kātib* and *wazīr* of al-Maʾmūn, Muḥammad b. Yazdād b. Suwayd (d. 230/Dec. 844 in Sāmarrāʾ during al-Wāthiq's reign). He was also a poet. Ibn al-Nadīm mentions that Muḥammad b. Yazdād collected his poetry in a book and also composed a book of epistles (كتاب رسائل).[41] His son, ʿAbd al-Raḥmān, was also a poet;[42] he had another son, Abū Ṣāliḥ ʿAbdallāh (d. 261/875), a *kātib* who served as al-Mustaʿīn's *wazīr* in 249/863, who, like his father, also collected his letters in a book and wrote another book entitled *Kitāb al-Taʾrīkh*. His son, Ṣāliḥ, completed his father's history book up to the year 300/912–913.[43] Ibn Abī Ḥarb is Muḥammad b. Abī Ḥarb, a direct transmitter of ʿUmar b. Shabba. Al-Azdī received the texts of the letters not through ʿUmar b. Shabba[?] but through Muḥammad b. Yaḥyā and the transmission is identical (except for the omission of one transmitter) to that of al-Ṭabarī.[44]

It is noteworthy that the text of the three letters recorded by Sibṭ b. al-Jawzī's *Tadhkirat al-khawwāṣ* was related by Hishām b. Muḥammad al-Kalbī (d. 204/819).

1.2 *The Text of the Three Letters Recorded by Sibṭ b. al-Jawzī*

The three letters are reproduced by Sibṭ b. al-Jawzī in his book *Tadhkirat al-khawwāṣ*, which is a short history of ʿAlī's family and the twelve Imāms.[45] Sibṭ b. al-Jawzī recorded the text from Hishām b. Muḥammad al-Kalbī, relating: "Hishām b. Muḥammad said" (قال هشام بن محمد). This is not a single isolated mention of this famous *akhbārī*: he is quoted by Sibṭ b. al-Jawzī many times (see further below).

---

40 McAuliffe, *ʿAbbāsid Authority*, 165, n. 802.

41 On him, see Ibn ʿAsākir, *Taʾrīkh*, 56:237–238; al-Ṣafadī, *al-Wāfī*, 5:139–140; al-Ziriklī, *al-Aʿlām*, 7:143; Kaḥḥāla, *Muʿjam*, 12:114. For his works, see Ibn al-Nadīm, *Fihrist* (ed. Tajaddud), 138; al-Baghdādī, *Hadiyyat al-ʿārifīn*, 2:12.

42 On him, see al-Khaṭīb al-Baghdādī, *Taʾrīkh*, 10:281; Ibn ʿAsākir, *Taʾrīkh*, 56:238.

43 On ʿAbdallāh b. Muḥammad, see Ibn ʿAsākir, *Taʾrīkh*, 32:376–378; Ibn al-Nadīm, *al-Fihrist* (ed. Tajaddud), 138. On his son, Ṣāliḥ, see ibid; al-Baghdādī, *Hadiyyat al-ʿārifīn*, 1:422.

44 Al-Azdī, *Taʾrīkh al-Mawṣil*, 181 (ll. 15–18): فأخبرني محمد بن يزيد عن عمر بن عبيدة [= شبة؟] عن محمد بن يحيي قال: سمعت هذه الرسائل من محمد بن بشر [! = بشير؟] وكان يصححها وحدثنيها أبو عبد الرحمن من كتاب أهل العراق وسمعت ابن أبي حرب يصححها....

45 Sibṭ b. al-Jawzī, *Tadhkira*, 221–224.

In this work, Sibṭ b. al-Jawzī relied on diverse sources. Sometimes it is clear that he quotes a written book, e.g., when saying: such and such person wrote/said in such and such book. There are many examples of this kind in Sibṭ b. al-Jawzī's work.[46] Sometimes it is not clear that he used the actual book;[47] sometimes he combines several traditions from several different *akhbāriyyūn* and historians, sometimes he mentions their names, e.g., "al-Ṭabarī, al-Wāqidī, Hishām b. Muḥammad, and others besides them,"[48] and sometimes he does not.[49]

Hishām b. Muḥammad is mentioned two or three times as a link in a tradition recorded by a known author,[50] but he appears forty-six times as Sibṭ b. al-Jawzī's only source, e.g., *qāla* Hishām b. Muḥammad/*qāla* Ibn al-Kalbī/ *qāla* Hishām.[51] In these cases, Sibṭ b. al-Jawzī does not mention a specific work

---

46 E.g., 22: وقد أخرج أحمد [بن حنبل] في الفضائل; 24: قال أحمد في المسند; 27: وذكر أبو جعفر محمد بن جرير صاحب التأريخ فيه; 30: وذكر أبو إسحاق الثعلبي في تفسيره; 38: وذكره محمد بن إسحاق في المغازي أيضا; 55: وذكر أبو بكر الخطيب في تأريخ بغداد; 57: فذكر محمد بن سعد في الطبقات; 62: وذكر أبو حامد الغزالي في كتاب سر العالمين وكشف ما في الدارين; 68: وذكر المسعودي في مروج الذهب; 105: وقد ذكره أبو الفرج الإصفهاني في كتاب مرج البحرين; 112: وقال أبو نعيم في كتاب الحلية; 123: ذكر بعضها صاحب نهج البلاغة; 289: وذكر المدائني في كتاب الحرة; cf. Ibn al-Nadīm, *Fihrist* (ed. Tajaddud), 115: كتاب حرة راقم; Ms. ف: واقم, correct to: حرة واقم; 216 and 217: وذكر الصولي في كتاب الأوراق.

47 E.g., 58: وقال الزهري (a parallel tradition is found in al-Balādhurī, *Ansāb* [ed. al-Maḥmūdī, 1974], 219: a tradition with an *isnād* that is concluded with al-Zuhrī precedes the parallel tradition which has only: قال الزهري; another example is that of Sayf b. ʿUmar, who is mentioned several times: قال/وذكر سيف بن عمر, for instance, see 63, 65, 66, 73; but see on 67: وحكى ابن جرير عن سيف بن عمر.

48 Sibṭ b. al-Jawzī, *Tadhkira*, 56: قال علماء السير كالطبري والواقدي وهشام بن محمد وغيرهم; 175: قال أهل السير منهم محمد بن إسحاق وهشام بن محمد والسدي وغيرهم; see also 199, 214, 256, 275.

49 E.g., ibid., 79, 80, 81, 86, 87, 101, 172.

50 E.g., ibid., 68, 72: وحكى ابن سعد عن هشام بن محمد قال.

51 Ibid., 80 (l. 13); 81 (ll. 1, 3, and 8); 89 (l. 2 bottom); 91 (l. 7); 92 (l. 7); 94 (l. 5 bottom); 97 (ll. 10 and 20); 98 (l. 10); 99 (l. 1); 100 (l. 16); 107 (l. 16); 151 (l. 14); 175 (l. 9); 207 (l. 3 bottom); 219 (l. 4); 221 (l. 12); 231 (l. 9); 238 (l. 11); 239 (l. 11); 245 (l. 7); 249 (l. 4 bottom); 252 (l. 10); 254 (l. 14); 257 (l. 14); 258 (l. 8); 262 (l. 12); 263 (l. 1); 264 (l. 5 bottom); 270 (l. 1); 275 (l. 5); 278 (l. 14); 279 (l. 3 bottom); 281 (l. 18); 282 (l. 15); 294 (l. 5 bottom); 302 (l. 15); 304 (ll. 6, 9, and 2 bottom); 306 (l. 7); 328 (l. 8); 333 (l. 12) (the text is garbled); 335 (l. 15); 347 (l. 8).

by Hishām. He may have used one or several books or booklets of Hishām.[52] However, he quotes Hishām's book *Kitāb al-Mathālib* four times.[53]

A cursory comparison of the text of Sibṭ b. al-Jawzī/Hishām b. Muḥammad with that of al-Ṭabarī shows that the two texts are similar. However, both minor and major differences can be seen between the two texts, e.g., in the order of certain words, some words and sentences are omitted or added.[54]

1.3 *The Problem of Authenticity: The Question of the "Fourth Letter"*

Al-Manṣūr's third letter remained unanswered. Scholars stressed that the early sources do not record a fourth letter, nor do they give any hint of the existence of such a letter, although Traini had noticed that al-Marʿashī (d. 431/1030), the author of *Ghurar al-siyar*, alludes to a fourth letter.[55]

Al-Marʿashī records al-Manṣūr's first letter in full; the text is identical (with minor changes) to that of al-Ṭabarī;[56] Muḥammad b. ʿAbdallāh's answer is very short; it records the beginning and part of the end of the letter, and omits most of the second letter.[57] Al-Marʿashī does not record the contents of the third letter (that of al-Manṣūr), sufficing to say: "al-Manṣūr wrote him a long letter in which he contradicted and refuted Muḥammad's arguments and Muḥammad

52 The list of Hishām's works recorded by Ibn al-Nadīm, *Fihrist* (ed. Tajaddud), 108–111, is very long, dealing with variegated aspects of the cultural-social history of the Arabs in the Jāhiliyya and early Islam, and it is impossible within the framework of this study to examine the quoted texts more thoroughly.

53 Sibṭ b. al-Jawzī, *Tadhkira*, 202 (l. 19): قال الأصمعي وهشام بن محمد الكلبي في كتابه المسمى بالمثالب; 203 (l. 11): وذكر هشام بن محمد الكلبي أيضا في كتاب المثالب; 203 (l. 14) (*qāla*: a direct continuation of subject of the previous tradition); 205 (l. 3): قال ابن الكلبي (the same previous subject); 207 (l. 3 bottom): وذكر هشام بن محمد الكلبي عن محمد بن إسحاق (the same subject: defamation of al-Ḥakam b. Abī l-ʿĀṣ); *Kitāb al-Mathālib*, is mentioned among the list of Hishām's books, for example, see Ibn al-Nadīm, *Fihrist* (ed. Tajaddud), 108.

54 Muḥammad's letter: some sentences are omitted in Ibn al-Jawzī's work (al-Ṭabarī, 3:209 (l. 15); 3:210 (ll. 7–9)); the ending is rendered with small changes. In al-Manṣūr's second letter, the Qurʾānic verses (al-Ṭabarī, 3:211 (ll. 10–13)) are omitted; there are some minor changes in the wording as well as substantial additions in Sibṭ's text, regarding the paragraph about the excellence of the Ḥusaynīs (al-Ṭabarī, 3:212–213 (l. 17 to l. 4), e.g., *Tadhkira*, 223, adding Ismāʿīl the son of Abraham (al-Khalīl) to the list of the sons of the concubines; the grandmothers of Muḥammad b. ʿAlī l-Bāqir and Jaʿfar al-Ṣādiq his son (al-Ṭabarī, 3:213 (ll. 1–4)), become mothers by Sibṭ/Hishām.

55 Traini, "La corrispondenza," 773, n. 2 [= al-Marʿashī, *Ghurar al-siyar*, 359].

56 Al-Marʿashī, *Ghurar al-siyar*, 358.

57 Ibid., 359; the author omits the main body of al-Nafs al-Zakiyya's answer, saying that the letter was long (وأطال الكلام).

answered him with the same kind (of letter)."[58] It is possible that a fourth letter is alluded to here, as already noted by Traini.

1.3.1 The Fourth Letter

However, van Arendonk discovered "a fourth letter" of Muḥammad in unpublished Zaydī sources. According to van Arendonk, a short part of this letter is found in the MS of *al-Ḥadāʾiq al-wardiyya fī manāqib aʾimmat al-Zaydiyya* of Ḥumayd b. Aḥmad al-Muḥallī l-Hamdānī (d. 654/1254),[59] which copies from *Kitāb al-Maṣābīḥ* of Abū l-ʿAbbās Aḥmad b. Ibrāhīm b. al-Ḥasan b. Ibrāhīm b. Muḥammad b. Sulaymān b. Dāwūd b. al-Ḥasan b. al-Ḥasan b. ʿAlī l-Ḥasanī (flourished around the middle of the fourth/tenth century). This letter is entitled *"al-Dāmigha"* ("The Irrefutable," and see below). A complete letter is found in Leiden.[60] Van Arendonk also gave a very brief summary of some of the arguments raised in this letter.[61]

---

58 Ibid.: وكتب إليه المنصور كتابا طويلا في المعارضة والمناقضة, وأجابه محمد بمثله.

59 On the author and his work, see *Akhbār aʾimmat al-Zaydiyya*, ed. Madelung, 20–22 (editor's introduction), n. 2.
On the author and his work, see ibid.

60 Van Arendonk, *L'Imamat Zaïdite*, 53, n. 1: *al-Ḥadāʾiq al-wardiyya*: Munich cod.ar. 86; Brockelmann, *GAL*, 1:397 [325]; *Kitāb al-Maṣābīḥ*: MS Milan Ambrs. A 55, B 83 I, E 232 (Griffini, "Lista dei manoscr. arabi etc.," *RSO*, 3, 571, sq., no. 55, I; 4, 1033, no. 207, I); and see now *Akhbār aʾimmat al-Zaydiyya*, 16–17 (Madelung's introduction): an updated list of the manuscripts of *Kitāb al-Maṣābīḥ*, including two *MSS* in Ṣanʿāʾ; the Leiden MS: MS Leiden, or. 2610 (cat.2 II, 53:ar.1968), f. 60b–76a. According to al-Ziriklī, *al-Aʿlām*, 1:88, Aḥmad b. Ibrāhīm al-Ḥasanī, the author of *al-Maṣābīḥ* was a Yemenite *qāḍī* and grammarian. The title of the book is rendered by him as *Kitāb al-Maṣābīḥ*, but he mistakenly gives his death date as 1534. According to Brockelmann, *GAL*, *Supplementbände*, 1:556, the name of the book is *Kitāb al-Maṣābīḥ min akhbār al-Muṣṭafā wa-l-Murtaḍā wa-l-aʾimma min waladihimā l-ṭāhirīn*; he writes that he was alive in the beginning of the fifth century in Baghdad ("lebte zu Anfang des 5. Jahrh. in Baghdad"); al-Sayyid, "al-Nafs al-Zakiyya," 175, n. 3: gives the same title as Brockelmann, adding a date (352 H.) [= 963–964] after the name of the author; is it his death date? But see now *Akhbār aʾimmat al-Zaydiyya*, 16–17 (Madelung's introduction), who asserts that the author flourished around the middle of the fourth/tenth century; he died before finishing his *Kitāb al-Maṣābīḥ*. The author was the uncle (from his mother's side) of the two Caspian Zaydī Imāms (of the Qāsimiyya school), Aḥmad b. al-Ḥusayn b. Hārūn al-Muʾayyad (d. 411/1020) and his brother, al-Nāṭiq bi-l-Ḥaqq, Abū Ṭālib Yaḥyā b. al-Ḥusayn (d. 424/1033); see Madelung, *al-Qāsim b. Ibrāhīm*, index, esp. 172–175, 177f.; Madelung, "Zaydiyya," 479; idem, in *Akhbār aʾimmat al-Zaydiyya*, 17 (introduction). But cf. al-Shāhrūdī l-Namāzī, *Rijāl*, 1:300, where we read that he was born in 333/944 and died in 421/1130; a short comment on the author of *al-Maṣābīḥ* is transmitted by al-ʿUmarī, *Ansāb*, 341; Ibn ʿInaba, *ʿUmda*, 73.

61 Van Arendonk, *L'Imamat Zaïdite*, 54: "Il s'efforce de réfuter la démonstration d'al-Manṣūr sur le peu d'importance des femmes pour la descendance (Ṭab. III, 211, 5 seqq), en citant

His conclusion is that it is difficult to establish the authenticity of this letter, or, in his words: "Il est difficile d'établir si cette lettre faisait originellement partie de la correspondance transmise par la tradition, et si l'historiographie officielle ne laissait donc plus la parole au ʿAlide, ou bien si la tradition šīʿite avait comblé une lacune pour donner à Muḥammad le dernier mot."[62]

Traini also read this fourth letter in the same manuscript, adding that MS Leiden Or. 2610, entitled زهرة العيون وجلاء القلوب, is by an unknown Egyptian author and contains three parts. The third part (which contains the letter) is the work, تحفة الأولياء الأتقياء of Badr al-Dīn Badal b. Ismāʿīl al-Tibrīzī (d. 636/1238 or 1239). Traini seems determined to assert that this letter is not authentic.[63] Omar seems to accept Traini's evaluation and adds that al-Tibrīzī was biased towards the ʿAlīds.[64]

Al-Sayyid also mentions the fourth letter, citing the Zaydī sources, *Kitāb al-Maṣābīḥ* and *al-Ḥadāʾiq al-wardiyya*. This letter is entitled by these sources *al-dāmigha* ("the irrefutable").[65] He believes that this fourth letter, as well as all

des versets qui tendent à montrer la place honorable de la femme dans la révélation. A propos de la citation de Ṭab., III, 211, 10 seqq., il dit que le choix de Dieu n'est pas déterminé par la parenté, mais par la *sābiqa et la ṭāʿa*; il cite en autre des arguments contre le droit qu'on reconnaît à al-ʿAbbās sur la succession du Prophète. Pour terminer il déclare qu'il ne lui reste plus qu'à combattre son adversaire, dans l'espoir que Dieu lui donnera satisfaction dans le temps présent, ou s'il en décide autrement, en tout cas lorsque la dernière heure sera venu."

62 Van Arendonk, *L'Imamat Zaïdite*, 53–54.

63 Traini, "La corrispondenza," 773, n. 2. On Badr al-Dīn Badal b. Ismāʿīl al-Tibrīzī, see Brockelmann, *GAL*, 1:345; *Supplementbände*, 1:587; al-Dhahabī, *Taʾrīkh*, 46:5; idem, *Siyar*, 23:62. See also, Ḥājjī Khalīfa, *Kashf al-ẓunūn*, 1:363 and al-Baghdādī, *Hadiyyat al-ʿārifīn*, 1:231: تحفة الأولياء الأتقياء في ذكر حال سيد الأتقياء of Badr al-Dīn Badal b. Abī l-Maʿmar [Muʿammar?] Ismāʿīl. I was not able to find any details on *Zahrat al-ʿuyūn* and its author, but it was composed not later than the mid-tenth century since it is mentioned by al-Masʿūdī (d. 345/956), *Murūj*, 1:16: وكتاب زهرة العيون وجلاء القلوب تأليف المصري. It is also mentioned by al-ʿĀmilī, *Aʿyān al-Shīʿa*, 7:88: quoting *Majālis al-muʾminīn* (of al-ʿAllāma al-Qāḍī Nūr Allāh al-Shahīd al-Marʿashī l-Tustarī, d. 1019 H.), who quotes from "*Kitāb Zahrat al-ʿuyūn wa-jalāʾ al-qulūb* which was composed by one of the (religious) scholars of the Shāfiʿiyya": وفي مجالس المؤمنين عن كتاب زهرة العيون وجلاء القلوب تأليف بعض علماء الشافعية; Traini writes (in the footnote) that he intends to write a detailed study on the correspondance which includes editing and publishing the manuscript of the "fourth letter."

64 Omar, "al-Rasāʾil," 105, quoting a sentence from the manuscript; Omar quotes the text from a manuscript in the Bodleian Library, but with neither signature of the manuscript nor the folio of his citation.

65 This was also the name of the poem (*qaṣīda*) of Abū Dalfāʾ al-Ḥasan b. Zayd, which was composed in retaliation to the *qaṣīdas* of Diʿbil and Ibn Abī ʿUyayna; see Elad, "Transition," 123.

other letters and sermons of al-Nafs al-Zakiyya that are recorded by the Zaydī sources, are authentic.[66] Unfortunately, he does not give the detailed contents of the letter, but merely summarizes one of Muḥammad b. ʿAbdallāh's arguments that mothers are preferable to fathers, which refutes al-Manṣūr's argument that the uncle is preferable to the sons of the daughter; in the letter al-Nafs al-Zakiyya also adds that the legitimacy to rule in Islam is not determined according to the *nasab*, "God has not chosen from among his creatures and did not favor him (as the most worthy to rule) unless he had *al-sābiqa* (seniority in Islam) and *al-ṭāʿa* (obedience [to God]); this was the (particular) case of ʿAlī b. Abī Ṭālib."[67]

Al-Sayyid mentions other "letters of Muḥammad b. ʿAbdallāh" recorded in Zaydī sources that were sent to his supporters. One of these was the *Kitāb al-Daʿwa* ("epistle of the propaganda");[68] two others mentioned were one sent to the common people in the big cities (إلى العامة في الأمصار), and the second to his most trusted confidential adherents (إلى خواص أصحابه). The first epistle is of a general nature; it condemns the corrupt godless regime of al-Manṣūr, calls the people to act in accordance with the laws and commands of the Qurʾān, and summons them to return the right to legitimate rule to the Prophet's family, to disapprove of evil and abominable actions and to command right: وإلى إنكار المنكر والأمر بالمعروف.[69]

---

66 Al-Sayyid, "al-Nafs al-Zakiyya," 178.

67 Ibid., 176: ما اختار الله أحدا من خلقه ولا اختار له إلا على السابقة والطاعة, وكانت هذه حالة علي بن أبي طالب; al-Sayyid quotes a new printed offset copy of the manuscript of *al-Ḥadāʾiq al-wardiyya*, copied in Yemen with no date (ibid., 170–171, n. 2). Al-Sayyid confirms van Arendonk and Traini's assertions that the author of *al-Ḥadāʾiq al-wardiyya* copied the letters from *Kitāb al-Maṣābīḥ*, but he does not give the bibliographical reference for this manuscript. Ibid., 175, n. 3, he mentions a manuscript of Aḥmad al-Shāmī of Ṣanʿāʾ, *al-Radd fī l-maṣābīḥ* (no further bibliographical details are given; perhaps this is Aḥmad b. Ḥasan al-Shāmī, who according to Kaḥḥāla, *Muʿjam*, 1:193 was alive in 1041/1631). Elsewhere in his article al-Sayyid quotes *Kitāb al-Maṣābīḥ* many times, but since he does not give any bibliographical details for this work, one wonders whether he used the work of al-Shāmī as a reference.

68 Al-Sayyid, "al-Nafs al-Zakiyya," 176, n. 3, according to *al-Ḥadāʾiq al-wardiyya*, 1:157: وكتب كتاب الدعوة إلى الناس وأمر بإذاعته.

69 Al-Sayyid, "al-Nafs al-Zakiyya," 176–177 (quoting *Kitāb al-Maṣābīḥ* and *al-Ḥadāʾiq al-wardiyya*). For this theme in Zaydī doctrine, see Cook, *Commanding Right*, 237–251, esp. 231–233; 235: "Thus forbidding wrong appears repeatedly as an activity characteristic of (though far from confined to) imams and similar figures exercising religiously validated political power."

In the second epistle, which is addressed to the inner circle of his followers, al-Nafs al-Zakiyya highly praises ʿAlī b. Abī Ṭālib, his actions and deeds and the help and assistance he gave to the Prophet: all this make him the Prophet's most worthy successor. The letter also mentions ʿAlī's brother, uncle, and his two sons, al-Ḥasan and al-Ḥusayn, who are the leaders of the "young" (*shabāb*) people in Paradise, whose mother, Fāṭima, is the leader of the women of all worlds.[70]

The Zaydī Imām, Yaḥyā b. al-Ḥusayn b. Hārūn Abū Ṭālib al-Nāṭiq bi-l-Ḥaqq (340–424/951–1033), mentions another letter [letters?] of Muḥammad b. ʿAbdallāh.[71]

The Zaydī sources provide (besides the alleged letters) several sermons that were allegedly delivered by Muḥammad al-Nafs al-Zakiyya, such as that in which he highly praises Zayd b. ʿAlī as the most distinguished Imām, who had the most right to summon the Muslims to God after al-Ḥusayn b. ʿAlī.[72] The contents and themes of this sermon are essentially different from the first[?] sermon, delivered by al-Nafs al-Zakiyya in Medina, which is recorded by al-Ṭabarī. In al-Ṭabarī's version the ʿAbbāsīs are described as enemies of God who act against His laws; al-Manṣūr is depicted as a tyrant, the enemy of God, who is worse than Pharaoh, and is blamed for having constructed the Green Dome (al-Qubba al-Khaḍrā') in Baghdad and thus belittling the sacred Kaʿba; therefore, al-Nafs al-Zakiyya beseeches God to kill them all, without sparing a single one of them. Muḥammad b. ʿAbdallāh also praises the descendants

70 Al-Sayyid, "al-Nafs al-Zakiyya," 177 and nn. 1–3 (quoting *Kitāb al-Maṣābīḥ* and *al-Ḥadā'iq al-wardiyya*). Al-Ḥasan and al-Ḥusayn are described in a similar fashion in al-Nafs al-Zakiyya's letter responding to al-Manṣūr, see for instance al-Ṭabarī, 3:210 (ll. 8–9); (ll. 7–8), where Fāṭima is the most distinguished leader (*sayyida*) of the women of paradise: سيدة نساء أهل الجنة, while the Zaydī text describes her as "the universal leader of women": سيدة نساء العالمين.

71 Al-Sayyid, "al-Nafs al-Zakiyya," 177, n. 4, quoting the manuscript of *al-Ifāda fī ta'rīkh al-a'imma al-sāda*, Maktabat al-Awqāf bi-l-Jāmiʿ al-Kabīr in Ṣanʿā', fol. 17a; no further details of the manuscript are given. On al-Nāṭiq bi-l-Ḥaqq, see Brockelmann, *G*, 1:402; *Supplementbände*, 1:697–698; al-Ziriklī, *al-Aʿlām*, 8:141. On the work, *al-Ifāda fī ta'rīkh al-a'imma al-sāda*, see now *Akhbār a'immat al-Zaydiyya*, 17 (Madelung's introduction); ibid., 243–259, a long biography of al-Nāṭiq bi-l-Ḥaqq from *al-Ḥadā'iq al-wardiyya* of Ḥumayd b. Aḥmad al-Muḥallī. See also Madelung, "Zaydiyya," 478b; it is noteworthy that al-Nāṭiq bi-l-Ḥaqq studied with and related from his maternal uncle, Abū l-ʿAbbās Aḥmad b. Ibrāhīm, the author of *Kitāb al-Maṣābīḥ*, see Ibn ʿInaba, *ʿUmda*, 73; al-ʿUmarī, *Ansāb*, 341.

72 Al-Sayyid, "al-Nafs al-Zakiyya," 176, n. 3, quoting *Kitāb al-Maṣābīḥ*, 218–220: وزيد إمام الأئمة وأولى من دعا إلى الله بعد الحسين بن علي.

of the Anṣār and the Muhājirūn, who have the "strongest claim to uphold this religion"; he chose the people of Medina as his followers not due to their (military) strength and power but rather due to their loyalty to the Prophet and fidelity to Islam, and he reassured them that in every big city of the Islamic world the oath of allegiance was given to him.[73] It seems that some parts of this *khuṭba*, certainly the one mentioning al-Qubba al-Khaḍrāʾ in Baghdad, are anachronistic.[74]

1.4 *Kitāb al-Siyar of Muḥammad b. ʿAbdallāh*

Several scholars had noticed, while reading the manuscript of *al-Ifāda fī taʾrīkh al-aʾimma al-sāda* of the Zaydī Imām Abū Ṭālib al-Nāṭiq bi-l-Ḥaqq (d. 424/1033), that the latter mentions a book by Muḥammad al-Nafs al-Zakiyya titled *Kitāb al-Siyar* (the book on the law/conduct of war). They also noticed that al-Nāṭiq bi-l-Ḥaqq writes that he heard a group/many of the scholars/*fuqahāʾ* of Abū Ḥanīfa's school say that Muḥammad b. al-Ḥasan al-Shaybānī (132–189/750–805, the well-known and important Ḥanafī jurist)[75] took most of his responsa on the laws of war (*Masāʾil al-siyar*) from this book. They do not give further details about the book.[76]

Al-Sayyid also quotes the statement of al-Nāṭiq bi-l-Ḥaqq that was already noted by previous scholars.[77] Al-Sayyid adds that he mentioned this passage in 1989 to Wilferd Madelung, who told him that he has at his disposal several pages of this work of al-Nafs al-Zakiyya photocopied from the manuscript of *al-Jāmiʿ al-kāfī fī fiqh al-Zaydiyya* of Abū ʿAbdallāh Muḥammad b. ʿAlī l-Ḥasanī

73 Al-Ṭabarī, 3:197 (ll. 8–19): [ʿUmar b. Shabba] < Muḥammad b. Yaḥyā < Ismāʿīl b. Yaʿqūb al-Taymī; *Fragmenta*, 238: a partial parallel with some changes; Ibn al-Athīr, *al-Kāmil* (Beirut edition), 5:531.

74 Convincingly argued by McAuliffe: "As most sources date commencement of the construction of Baghdad to the year 145/762, reference to the dome in this sermon is probably an anachronism," see *ʿAbbāsid Authority*, 152, n. 730. For the green dome that rose above al-Manṣūr's palace, see the references, ibid.

75 On him, see Khadduri, *Islamic Law of Nations*, esp. 26–60; Chaumont, "al-Shaybānī," *EI*².

76 Strothmann, "Die Literatur der Zaiditen," 367; Griffini, "Arabischer Handschriften," 64 (both quote the Arabic text with slight differences); van Arendonk, 50 (quoting Strothmann and Griffini).

77 Al-Sayyid, "al-Nafs al-Zakiyya," 178, quoting *al-Ifāda*, fol. 17a: وله كتاب السير المشهور. وسمعت جماعة من فقهاء أصحاب أبي حنيفة وغيرهم يقولون إن محمد بن الحسن [الشيباني] نقل أكثر مسائل السير من هذا الكتاب؛ وفيه من غرائب الفقه ما يدل على مرتبته. No mention of this alleged[?] borrowing is related in the long discussion of Shaybānī's works on the *Siyar* by Khadduri (*Islamic Law of Nations*, 41–74).

(d. 445/1053).[78] According to al-Sayyid, part of *Kitāb al-Siyar* of Muḥammad b. ʿAbdallāh is found in the manuscript of *al-Jāmiʿ al-kāfī* in Ṣanʿāʾ. This part bears the title: *qitāl al-bughāt wa-masāʾiluhum*, i.e., dealing with those who are categorized as *bughāt* (rebels/dissenters).[79]

According to al-Sayyid, the text of *Kitāb al-Siyar* in *al-Jāmiʿ al-kāfī* is that of Muḥammad b. Manṣūr b. Yazīd al-Murādī (d. 290/903), and it concludes with the followers (*aṣḥāb*) of Muḥammad al-Nafs al-Zakiyya. The *isnād* recorded by al-Sayyid from *al-Sīra fī ahl al-baghy* of Muḥammad b. ʿAbdallāh b. al-Ḥasan is as follows:

> Muḥammad b. Manṣūr said in *Kitāb al-Sīra* < (*ḥaddathanī*) al-Ḥasan b. ʿAbdallāh al-Jazzār [unidentified] < (*ḥaddathanī*) Ḥasan b. Ḥusayn al-ʿUranī < (*ʿan*) Khālid b. Mukhtār < (*ʿan*) Rabīʿ b. Ḥabīb the brother of ʿĀʾidh b. Ḥabīb < (*ʿan*) Muḥammad b. ʿAbdallāh b. al-Ḥasan, peace be upon him, who said [...][80]

Muḥammad b. Manṣūr al-Murādī was a prominent Zaydī scholar, in whose name a legal school emerged in the third/ninth century.[81] In several places in the text his personal comments/additions are rendered.[82] I was unable to find any bibliography on al-Ḥasan b. ʿAbdallāh al-Jazzār.

The last three transmitters are known as Shīʿī Imāmī scholars. Al-Ḥasan b. Ḥusayn al-ʿUranī is said to have written a book about Imāmī scholars of *ḥadīth* from[?] Jaʿfar al-Ṣādiq: له كتاب عن الرجال عن جعفر بن محمد. He is described

78 Al-Sayyid, "al-Nafs al-Zakiyya," 178–179; al-Sayyid's article on *Kitāb al-Siyar* of al-Nafs al-Zakiyya in *Majallat Kulliyat al-Ādāb* 11 (1990), 105f., is mentioned by van Ess, *Theologie*, 1:397; 2:189; I was unable to obtain this article. On Muḥammad b. ʿAlī l-Ḥasanī l-ʿAlawī, see Brockelmann, *Supplementbände*, 1:698; Sezgin, 1:563; al-Sayyid, "al-Nafs al-Zakiyya," 178–179, n. 3. See also the introduction of Aḥmad al-Ḥusaynī and Maḥmūd al-Marʿashī, the editors of al-ʿAlawī, *Faḍl ziyārat al-Ḥusayn*, 1–24; ibid., 22–23: on *al-Jāmiʿ al-kāfī*.

79 Al-Sayyid, "al-Nafs al-Zakiyya," 179, n. 1: MS al-Jāmiʿ al-Kabīr, *fiqh* 160, no. 1117; five volumes; the relevant folios are in vol. 5, fols. 279b–288a. Al-Sarakhsī defines the *bughāt* (*ahl al-baghy*) as "rebels, who were not counted as unbelievers, though they were ignorant and their understanding [of Islam] was false"; see al-Sarakhsī, *al-Mabsūṭ*, 10:2; the translation is according to Khadduri, *Islamic Law of Nations*, 40; ibid., 230, n. 1, where we find an explanation of the term according to Ḥanafī law. Al-Sayyid, "al-Nafs al-Zakiyya," 179: quoting al-Sarakhsī; 180: "armed rebels who fight the lawful Imām."

80 Al-Sayyid, "al-Nafs al-Zakiyya," 181.

81 On him, see Madelung, *al-Qāsim b. Ibrāhīm*, index, esp. 80–84; Madelung, "Zaydiyya," 478a. See also al-Sayyid, "al-Nafs al-Zakiyya," 178–179, n. 3; Sezgin, 1:563.

82 E.g., al-Sayyid, "al-Nafs al-Zakiyya," 187, 188, 192.

by Sunnī authors as one of the most distinguished leaders of the Shīʿa: كان من رؤساء الشيعة.[83] Khālid b. al-Mukhtār flourished in the second half of the eighth century. He transmitted from Jaʿfar al-Ṣādiq and al-Aʿmash.[84] Al-Rabīʿ b. Ḥabīb (d. between 150/767 and 160/777) and his brother ʿA'idh (d. 190/805 or 806), the sons of al-Mallāḥ, are considered faithful adherents of the Shīʿī Imāms. As for al-Rabīʿ b. Ḥabīb, in the Shīʿī *rijāl* books he is mentioned, like his father, as one of the followers (*aṣḥāb*) of al-Bāqir and his son Jaʿfar al-Ṣādiq.[85] This did not escape the notice of the Sunnī authors of the *rijāl* books, who accuse him of being pro-Imāmī.[86] I did not find any evidence testifying to close relations between al-Rabīʿ b. Ḥabīb and Muḥammad b. ʿAbdallāh, nor to his being a student of the latter.

Al-Sayyid records the text of *Kitāb al-Bughāt* according to *al-Jāmiʿ al-kāfī*.[87] He believes that the text is authentic; he presents al-Nafs al-Zakiyya as a legitimate active Zaydī Imām, who most probably (*al-murajjaḥ*) composed this *siyar* work already in the Umayyad period as part of a complete theological-

83 On him, see Ibn Abī Ḥātim, *al-Jarḥ* (Beirut edition), 3:6: كان من رؤساء الشيعة; Ibn ʿAdī, *Ḍuʿafā'*, 2:332: روى أحاديث مناكير; al-Dhahabī, *Mīzān* (Beirut, 1963), 1:483–484; al-Najāshī, *Rijāl*, 51: له كتاب عن الرجال عن جعفر بن محمد; al-Khū'ī, *Rijāl*, 5:295; al-Amīn, *Aʿyān al-Shīʿa*, 5:54–55; al-Ṭihrānī, *al-Dharīʿa* (Tehran, 1365 H.), 6:321.

84 Al-Shaykh al-Mufīd, *al-Amālī*, 58; al-Majlisī, *Biḥār*, 32:186: from al-Aʿmash (d. 148/765); al-Shāhrūdī, *Rijāl*, 3:315: from Jaʿfar al-Ṣādiq; see also al-Ṭūsī, *al-Amālī*, 624; al-Majlisī, *Biḥār*, 38:30: transmits from al-Ḥārith b. Ḥuṣayn (al-Azdī).

85 Al-Māmaqānī, *Rijāl*, 1:424, no. 4003; al-Amīn, *Aʿyān al-Shīʿa*, 6:453; al-Khū'ī, *Rijāl*, 8:174; 10:224; al-Shabastarī, *al-Imām al-Ṣādiq*, 1:566.

86 Ibn Abī Ḥātim, *al-Jarḥ*, 3:458: كان شيعيا; Ibn ʿAdī, *Ḍuʿafā'*, 3:134–136; Ibn Ḥajar, *Tahdhīb* (Beirut, 1984), 3:208–209, who adds that al-Bukhārī mentioned him among those who died between 150/767 and 160/777; al-Mizzī, *Tahdhīb*, 9:67–69. On his brother, ʿĀ'idh, see Ibn Saʿd, *Ṭabaqāt*, 6:397; al-Bukhārī, *Kabīr* (ed. Diyār Bakr), 7:60–61 (his entry); Ibn Abī Ḥātim, *al-Jarḥ* (Beirut edition), 7:17; Ibn Ḥibbān, *al-Thiqāt*, 7:297: ʿĀ'idh and his brother al-Rabīʿ are called "Banū l-Mallāḥ"; Ibn ʿAdī, *Ḍuʿafā'*, 5:355; Ibn Maʿīn, *Ta'rīkh*, 1:309; Ibn Ḥajar, *Tahdhīb* (Beirut, 1984), 5:76–77; al-Mizzī, *Tahdhīb*, 14:95–98; Shīʿī (Imāmī) literature: al-Māmaqānī, 2:120, no. 6130. See also al-Khū'ī, *Rijāl*, 5:208: his father; 10:223–225: ʿĀ'idh (من أصحاب الصادق); ʿĀ'idh's son, Aḥmad was also one of al-Ṣādiq's followers, see al-Ṭūsī, *Rijāl*, 155: Aḥmad b. ʿĀ'idh b. Ḥabīb al-ʿAbsī l-Kūfī Abū ʿAlī, but cf. al-Najāshī, *Rijāl*, 98–99: Aḥmad b. ʿĀ'idh b. Ḥabīb al-Aḥmasī l-Bajalī [?!]. Al-Māmaqānī, *Rijāl*, 2:63, no. 364: the two different versions of the *nisba* with a discussion about the contradiction between the two *nisba*s.

87 Al-Sayyid, "al-Nafs al-Zakiyya," 181–198.

doctrinal program.[88] When published, his study[89] (and those of others) on this work should be able to establish its authenticity, as well as its relations to early Ḥanafī *siyar* literature and to other Zaydī *siyar* works.

In conclusion, al-Sayyid argues for the authenticity of all letters and sermons that are recorded by the Zaydī sources. The theological Zaydī character and content of these sermons and letters, and especially this part of *Kitāb al-Siyar*, present al-Nafs al-Zakiyya as a leader (*imām*) and a highly educated religious scholar with a defined and developed Zaydī doctrine.[90] It raises the possibility that they mirror a period certainly later than the Umawī period as argued by al-Sayyid,[91] but also later than 145/762. It seems that the doctrines of the Zaydiyya were not fully developed in 145/762,[92] but this topic is beyond the expertise of the present writer and deserves an in-depth study by scholars of the early Zaydiyya.

1.5 *The Letters according to Balʿamī (d. 974, or after 992?)*[93]

The fact that Balʿamī's Persian translation/adaptation of al-Ṭabarī's *Taʾrīkh* also records the three letters has escaped the scholars discussed above. But while the two letters of al-Manṣūr are relatively similar to those recorded in the Arabic text of al-Ṭabarī, the second letter recorded by Balʿamī, that of Muḥammad b. ʿAbdallāh, is completely different. In this version, the original Arabic text is hardly recognizable; on the one hand, the letter develops and expands on the Shīʿī-ʿAbbāsī polemics that exist in the Arabic version, but, on the other hand, it adds many new topics, all expressing bold, uncompromising contention and strife with the ʿAbbāsīs. A large part of this version refutes al-ʿAbbās's right to the *imāma*, and diminishes his image in the Jāhiliyya

88 Ibid., 180–181.

89 Ibid., 204, n. 3, writes that he intends to publish a book entitled: محمد النفس الزكية دعوته وثورته وكتابه في السيرة.

90 Muḥammad b. ʿAbdallāh was considered the sixth or seventh Imām of the Zaydiyya.

91 Al-Sayyid, "al-Nafs al-Zakiyya," 180–181.

92 Nagel, "al-Nafs al-Zakiyya," 255–256; Cook, *Commanding Right*, 228–237; on 231 he says (regarding the doctrine of forbidding wrong) that "it is not until Uṭrūsh [d. 304/917] that we encounter anything suggestive of an organized Zaydī doctrine of forbidding wrong." However, cf. Madelung, "Zaydiyya," 478a: "In religious law, the Zaydiyya relied at first on the teaching of various ʿAlid authorities, among them Muḥammad al-Bāḳir, D̲j̲aʿfar al-Ṣādiḳ, Zayd b. ʿAlī and Muḥammad al-Nafs al-Zakiyya"; Crone, *Islamic Thought*, 99–100: "For the first hundred years or so after Zayd's death, and to some extent even thereafter, the Zaydīs should be envisaged ... not as a party defined by a single set of shared beliefs ... they still did not have a unified stance."

93 Daniel, "Balʿamī's Account," 184, n. 4; for his biography, see Peacock, *Balʿamī*, 31–35.

and Islam. It is clear that these references are a direct answer to al-Manṣūr's arguments in his letter in favor of al-ʿAbbās. Other sections not found in the Arabic version deal with the praise of Abū Ṭālib, and praise of Muḥammad b. ʿAbdallāh's mother (of the Zubayrī family!), and the mother of al-Ḥasan b. al-Ḥasan, which ends with the unequivocal declaration: "Vous tous, grands et petits, vous êtes nés de femmes esclaves (la mère de Mançour était une esclave nommée Salāma)."[94] Towards the end of the letter, another name is added to those whose *amān* al-Manṣūr violated, that of Abū Salama al-Khallāl (who was not killed by al-Manṣūr but by his brother, al-Saffāḥ), who is mentioned here not by his name but by his epithet current during the ʿAbbāsī *daʿwa*, "the vizier of the family of Muḥammad," an early, charged Shīʿī epithet.[95] But perhaps the most interesting addition is the last paragraph of this version: after mentioning those persons whose *amāns* were breached by al-Manṣūr, Muḥammad says that it is al-Manṣūr who should ask for an *amān* from him because he is tied to Muḥammad by an oath which he gave him at Mecca, together with the other members of Banū Hāshim, during Marwān's reign. Therefore, if al-Manṣūr will repent of his disobedience, he'll be pardoned by Muḥammad.[96]

This is certainly "the fourth missing letter." This version merits an in-depth study of Balʿamī's History (*Taʾrīkhnāma*), which is beyond the scope of this study and beyond the expertise of this author. I will limit myself here with the following general observations, summarizing the scholars' conclusions with regard to Balʿamī.

Scholars accept that Balʿamī's *Taʾrīkhnāma* is not merely a copy or abbreviation of the Arabic text of al-Ṭabarī. Peacock's conclusions are that

> Balʿamī's version was never intended to be an exact, word-for-word translation of Ṭabarī, but rather an abridgement and adaptation. Accounts mentioned in Ṭabarī are missing in Balʿamī, while the translator often appears to have added material from elsewhere to supplement Ṭabarī's accounts. In other words, it is not so much a translation as a new,

94 Balʿamī, 4:399 (ll. 13–15); it seems that the explanation in brackets are those of Zotenberg, the translator.

95 This was the title of al-Mukhtār, see Goitein, "Vizierate," 171–172, 194–195; Sharon, *Black Banners*, 106; Zaman, "Wazīr," 185a.

96 Balʿamī, 4:399–400 (l. 29 to l. 3): "Mais c'est à toi de recevoir l'amān de moi; car tu es lié envers moi par le serment que tu as prêté, à la Mecque, avec les autres Beni-Hāschim, du temps de Merwān. Tu as violé ce serment."

> independent work which drew on the prestige of Ṭabarī's name to assert its own authoritative nature.[97]

Most surviving manuscripts of Balʿamī represent a later redaction.[98] Dunlop, following Spuler, remarks that "the translation of Ṭabarī into Persian under the Sāmānīs served no mere cultural purpose, but was intended to show the Persians that the destiny of their nation was linked with orthodox Islam."[99] Daniel also argues that the comments and personal criticism of Balʿamī "seem to indicate a pro-ʿAbbāsid stance on his part. He is generally regarded as a staunch Sunni and respected Shāfiʿī religious scholar."[100] But, he adds that "on the other hand, it should be noted that many passages favourable to ʿAlī may also be found in Balʿamī."[101]

In light of this, the question arises whether Balʿamī himself was responsible for the insertion of the "fourth letter" of Muḥammad b. ʿAbdallāh. Or is this perhaps a later insertion? Daniel touched indirectly upon this important point when he pointed out that there is evidence of sectarian tampering in Balʿamī's manuscripts. Three early manuscripts of Balʿamī

> are conspicuously pro-Shiʿite in their orientation. Naturally, one wonders what other changes in the manuscripts might have been introduced by copyists who were so conspicuously sectarian in outlook. This suspicion is only increased by the finding that topics with obvious sectarian implications, such as the date of conversion of prominent personalities such as Abū Bakr, ʿUmar or Zayd … and several Alid revolts are among the sections that vary widely among the manuscripts. The problem of how much, or which variety, of this material may be attributed to Balʿamī is not easy to resolve.[102]

---

97 Peacock, *Balʿamī*, 5; for further discussion, see ibid., 77, 105–140, 167, 171; see also Daniel, "Balʿamī's *Taʾrīkh*," 284; idem, "Balʿamī's Account," 170, 174, 180: for additional material inserted by Balʿamī (without any acknowledgment); Daniel, "Balʿamī's *Taʾrīkh*," 285; idem, "Balʿamī's Account," 172: comments and personal criticism of Balʿamī himself.

98 D. M. Dunlop, "Balʿamī," 984a–984b; Daniel, "Balʿamī's *Taʾrīkh*," 288: "there are more than 160 Balʿamī manuscripts in existence, dating from the twelfth down to the twentieth century."

99 Dunlop, "Balʿamī," 984b (quoting Bertold Spuler, "The Evolution of Persian Historiography," in B. Lewis and P. M. Holt (eds.), *Historians of the Middle East* [London, 1962], 126–132).

100 Daniel, "Balʿamī's Account," 173–174.

101 Ibid., 175.

102 Daniel, "Balʿamī's *Taʾrīkh*," 294.

Peacock clearly proved that with regard to the revolt of al-Ḥusayn b. ʿAlī, Balʿamī "exhibits a decided preference for information from Shīʿite authorities, despite the fact that they only represent a fraction of Ṭabarī's text."[103] Daniel adds that

> one's initial reaction [to pro-Shīʿī material] might well be to dismiss the obviously Shiʿite material as later additions by Persian Shiʿite copyists. However, some of the most conspicuously pro-Shiʿite manuscripts are also among the very oldest manuscripts; a Safavid manuscript could be expected to show signs of Shiʿite tampering, but the appearance of such material in manuscripts from the fourteenth century is not so easy to explain.[104]

The numerous surviving manuscripts of the *Taʾrīkhnāma* (more than 160)[105] present formidable textual problems that need to be resolved before the work can be studied adequately.[106] No manuscript from Balʿamī's own time exists; not a single manuscript has survived from the Sāmānī period, "with the earliest dating from several generations after Balʿamī's death."[107] Peacock argues that the earliest manuscript is an Arabic translation of the original Persian text of Balʿamī, copied in 442/1050.[108] In his view "it represents an unembellished translation of the Persian, following reasonably closely the text of the lost manuscript from which it was translated."[109] Most of the ten manuscripts used by Zotenberg for his French translation are of inferior quality and are outdated when compared to the much better manuscripts that are now available.[110] Today we have a much better scholarly edition of the Persian text by Raushan, which supersedes that of Zotenberg.[111]

103 Peacock, *Balʿamī*, 132.

104 Daniel, "Balʿamī's *Taʾrīkh*," 294, n. 42.

105 Peacock, *Balʿamī*, 52; ibid., 183–188: Addenda and corrigenda to Daniel's inventory of Balʿamī's manuscripts.

106 Ibid., x.

107 Peacock, *Balʿamī*, 6 and 51 (the quote is from 51).

108 Ibid., 66: this is MS Cambridge University Library Add. 836, from the fifteenth century, a copy of a manuscript dated 627/1230, which is a copy of one dated 442/1050; ibid., 66–73: discussing the manuscript.

109 Peacock, *Balʿamī*, 73; see also 182: arguments in this vein; 179–182: comparison of the Arabic translation and the Persian text.

110 Ibid., 175–176.

111 Muḥammad Raushan's edition was published in Tehran in 2001; see also Peacock, *Balʿamī*, 7, 53; Daniel, "Balʿamī's *Taʾrīkh*," 282, n. 1, and his criticism of the edition on 306–308.

An important and much-needed project would entail a comparison of Zotenberg's French translation, Raushan's edition, and other principle manuscripts of Balʿamī (especially the Arabic translation, MS Cambridge Add. 836) with the Arabic text of al-Ṭabarī.[112]

3 The ʿAbbāsī Army Headed by ʿĪsā b. Mūsā against Muḥammad al-Nafs al-Zakiyya

ʿĪsā b. Mūsā, the caliph's nephew, was appointed by al-Manṣūr as the commander-in-chief of the army against Muḥammad al-Nafs al-Zakiyya. He was chosen to lead this military, as well as political, campaign as the representative of the ʿAbbāsī family and the caliph.[113] Most of the sources agree that he was sent at the head of an army of 4,000 soldiers.[114] A single source tells of an army consisting of 4,000 horsemen and 2,000 infantrymen, followed by heavy reinforcements, headed by Ḥumayd b. Qaḥṭaba.[115] Eyewitnesses describe this army as a huge mass of locusts,[116] and an eyewitness from the rebel camp "knows" that the ʿAbbāsī army that surrounded them numbered 40,000 warriors.[117]

On 307–308, Daniel adds that since Raushan had not consulted manuscripts which preserve additional information not found in any of those that he used for his edition, researchers dealing with events pertaining to the early Islamic history "should not regard Raushan's edition as an absolute and infallible substitute for consulting other manuscripts that were not consulted by Raushan." (The quote is from 308).

112 But see the sober observation of Daniel, "Balʿamī's Account," 164, "Unfortunately, there are formidable problems involved in trying to answer such questions. It is not simply a matter of making side-by-side comparisons of two standard texts. Although there are now published editions of both works, it is not clear how closely they correspond to the author's original texts. There are so many manuscripts of Balʿamī's history, in several distinct if often jumbled recensions, that a truly definitive reconstruction of the source text is probably not possible"; Peacock, *Balʿamī*, 6, has reached the same conclusions: "Reconstructing the original text that Balʿamī wrote is fraught with difficulties, and we will probably never succeed in doing so entirely."

113 Omar, *ʿAbbāsid Caliphate*, 236; Lassner, *Shaping*, 74.

114 Al-Ṭabarī, 3:223 (ll. 14–15); al-Masʿūdī, *Tanbīh*, 341; al-Balādhurī, *Ansāb* (ed. Madelung), 2:513 [= *Fragmenta*, 241]; al-Azdī, *Taʾrīkh al-Mawṣil*, 187; al-Iṣfahānī, *Maqātil*, 267: from al-Madāʾinī.

115 Al-Masʿūdī, *Murūj*, 4:146 (cf. ibid., Paris edition, 6:192: only 4,000 cavalry, omitting the 2,000 infantry soldiers); the reinforcement of Ḥumayd (text: Muḥammad): في جيش كثيف.

116 Al-Ṭabarī, 3:230.

117 Ibid., 3:247–248 (l. 20 to l. 1).

Al-Manṣūr sent a man named Abū l-Aṣamm with them as a guide; his task was to arrange encampment sites for the army.[118] These army contingents were part of the regular ʿAbbāsī army, that is, the *ahl Khurāsān* contingents and their commanders[119] that comprised the decisive bulk of ʿĪsā b. Mūsā's army. Some military contingents from Syria (*ahl al-Shām*), headed by Salm b. Qutayba b. Muslim, the son of the famous Umayyad general, most probably joined ʿĪsā's army.[120]

Several dignitaries who belonged to the Ṭālibī family (see below) and other dignitaries of Arab families accompanied ʿĪsā, from al-Baṣra and al-Kūfa[?]. A noted Baṣrī dignitary was Mismaʿ b. Muḥammad b. Shaybān b. Mālik b. Mismaʿ, who belonged to a well-known and important family in al-Baṣra. Another dignitary from the family of the *ṣaḥābī* ʿAbdallāh b. Masʿūd, ʿAbd al-Raḥmān b. ʿAbdallāh b. ʿUtba b. ʿAbdallāh b. Masʿūd, a well-known *muḥaddith* from al-Kūfa, also accompanied ʿĪsā; but both dignitaries left the ʿAbbāsī camp and remained behind until Muḥammad al-Nafs al-Zakiyya was killed in Medina.[121]

118 Ibid., 3:231 (l. 11): وجه أبو جعفر مع عيسى بن موسى بابن الأصم ينزل له المنازل; McAuliffe, *ʿAbbāsid Authority*, 194: "Together with ʿĪsā b. Mūsā Abū Jaʿfar dispatched Ibn al-Aṣamm ["the deaf"], who attended to his staging posts for him"; Williams, *Early ʿAbbāsī Empire*, 1:114: "Abū Jaʿfar sent Ibn al-Aṣamm with ʿĪsā b. Mūsā as his quartermaster."

119 Al-Ṭabarī, 3:223 (ll. 14–16): أربعة آلاف من الجند; Ibn Saʿd, *al-Qism al-mutammim*, 376–377, the testimony of al-Wāqidī: "al-Manṣūr sends ... and Ḥumayd b. Qaḥṭaba al-Ṭāʾī and several commanders of *ahl Khurāsān* and their contingents."

120 According to the tradition in al-Ṭabarī, 3:206–207 (l. 16 to l. 2), al-Manṣūr, on his uncle, ʿAbdallāh b. ʿAlī's advice, summons Salm b. Qutayba from al-Rayy and sends him to lead *ahl al-Shām* units against Muḥammad al-Nafs al-Zakiyya. Lassner, *Shaping*, 75, argues that the Syrian armies entered at a later stage, after the rebellion was crushed in Medina. He bases his argument on the parallel text in al-Iṣfahānī, *Maqātil*, 265–266, but the end of the tradition is omitted in *Maqātil*, that is, the phrase that al-Manṣūr acted according to his uncle's advice. Lassner erroneously concluded that Salm came to al-ʿIrāq from Khurāsān with Khurāsānī contingents, and there the Syrian units were incorporated into his army. But all this is not mentioned in the text.

121 Al-Ṭabarī, 3:224–225 (l. 11 to l. 1); on the family of Mismaʿ b. Muḥammad, see Crone, *Slaves*, 116–118; on Mismaʿ b. Muḥammad, see ibid., 118; al-Ṭabarī, 3:224 (ll. 17–18): والمسعودي، عبد الرحمان بن عبد الله بن عبد الرحمان بن عبد الله بن مسعود. The name was corrected in the *Glossarium* of al-Ṭabarī, dccxxxviii, to عبد الرحمان بن عبد الله بن عتبة بن عبد الله بن مسعود, the well-known *muḥaddith* (d. 160/776 or 777), on him, see McAuliffe, *ʿAbbāsid Authority*, 187, n. 912; see also, al-Mizzī, *Tahdhīb*, 17:219–227; Ibn ʿAsākir, *Taʾrīkh*, 35:9–24.

The ʿAbbāsī army was well-equipped with riding horses and mules, weapons of all kinds, and food supplies.[122] The horsemen had armor that covered their faces and chests.[123] Among the cavalry there was a special unit (or units) of horses covered with armor.[124] It seems that the army also had a special unit of sappers (*faʿala*).[125]

The army was divided into the five classic divisions:[126] 1) the vanguard was headed by Ḥumayd b. Qaḥṭaba;[127] 2) the chief commander of the right wing was Muḥammad b. Abī l-ʿAbbās al-Saffāḥ; 3) the chief commander of the left wing was Dāwūd b. Karrāz al-Bāhilī;[128] 4) the rear guard (*al-sāqa/muʾakhkhara*) was headed by al-Haytham b. Shuʿba al-Nahshalī l-Tamīmī;[129] and 5) it seems plausible that ʿĪsā b. Mūsā was the head of the *qalb*. With the exception of Muḥammad b. Abī l-ʿAbbās, the other three commanders belonged to the top supreme command of *ahl Khurāsān*. Ḥumayd b. Qaḥṭaba was undoubtedly the most senior of the ʿAbbāsī commanders.[130]

No additional information is provided by the sources on the roles of Dāwūd b. Karrāz and al-Haytham b. Shuʿba in the battle. A little information is given on Muḥammad b. Abī l-ʿAbbās,[131] who filled important commanding roles

122 Ibn Saʿd, *al-Qism al-mutammim*, 376–377: the personal testimony of al-Wāqidī; al-Ṭabarī, 3:225 (l. 11): وجهزهم بالخيل والبغال والسلاح والميرة; ibid., 3:240: footsoldiers with arrows and shields: النشاب والتِّرَسة.

123 Ibid., 3:239 (ll. 11–17).

124 Ibid., 3:235 (ll. 8–9); horses clad with armor: *mujaffafa*.

125 Ibid., 3:240 (l. 6): ʿĪsā b. Mūsā sends *faʿala*, who demolish a high fence (*jidār*) that was erected in front of the *khandaq*; McAuliffe, *ʿAbbāsid Authority*, 204: "laborers"; Williams, *Early ʿAbbāsī Empire*, 1:120: "sappers."

126 Al-Ṭabarī, 3:238 (ll. 5–8).

127 On Ḥumayd b. Qaḥṭaba, see *Akhbār al-ʿAbbās*, 219 and 220: one of *nuẓarāʾ al-nuqabāʾ*; Crone, *Slaves*, 188; Agha, *Revolution*, 351, no. 198.

128 One of the seventy *duʿāt* of the ʿAbbāsī *daʿwa*, see *Akhbār al-ʿAbbās*, 218, 221; Agha, *Revolution*, 345–356, no. 153.

129 One of the senior commanders of *ahl Khurāsān* of the same sub-tribe as Khāzim b. Khuzayma al-Tamīmī l-Nahshalī, and one of the latter's commanders; on him, see Agha, *Revolution*, 350, no. 185.

130 On the central role of Ḥumayd in the battle, see al-Ṭabarī, 3:225 (ll. 10–11); 3:240 (ll. 1–6): commander of one hundred infantry men; 3:248 (ll. 18–19): commander of the horsemen; al-Balādhurī, *Ansāb* (ed. Madelung), 2:513–515; 2:516: administering al-Nafs al-Zakiyya the death blow, cutting off his head; al-Yaʿqūbī, *Taʾrīkh* (ed. Houtsma), 2:452.

131 Al-Ṭabarī, 3:225 (l. 9), 3:236 (ll. 11–12); al-Balādhurī, *Ansāb* (ed. Madelung), 2:513, 514, 517.

before and during the campaign.[132] He was married to Zaynab bt. Muḥammad al-Nafs al-Zakiyya. It is reported that after the latter's death he came to her demanding that they consummate the marriage, but the sources disagree as to whether they did. After Muḥammad, Zaynab married ʿĪsā b. Mūsā, and after his death she married three other husbands.[133] This raises the question of whether Muḥammad b. Abī l-ʿAbbās joined the military expedition because of his relation to Zaynab, Muḥammad al-Nafs al-Zakiyya's daughter?

In addition to the above-mentioned senior commanders, several other commanders are mentioned in the sources.

3.1 *Kathīr b. al-Ḥuṣayn al-ʿAbdī or al-ʿAbdarī*[134]

Kathīr is mentioned as a commander in the ʿAbbāsī army only in relation to the revolt. He was sent at the head of a vanguard towards Medina, then he encamped and fortified his contingents in al-Fayd until ʿĪsā b. Mūsā arrived with the main body of the army and together they turned towards Medina.[135] During the siege of the city he was stationed with his contingents near the *dār* of Ibn Aflaḥ which was in Baqīʿ al-Gharqad.[136] During the decisive battle he led a unit that fought against a unit headed by Ṣāliḥ and Yazīd, Muʿāwiya b. ʿAbdallāh b. Jaʿfar b. Abī Ṭālib's sons.[137] After Muḥammad's defeat and death, Kathīr was sent to Medina by ʿĪsā b. Mūsā, where he chased the supporters of the revolt and killed them. Al-Yaʿqūbī, who recorded this, added that afterwards Kathīr left Medina for al-ʿIrāq,[138] but according to other sources he was

132 Al-Ṭabarī, 3:236 (ll. 11–12): posted at Bāb Banī Salima; al-Balādhurī, *Ansāb* (ed. Madelung), 2:514: together with ʿUqba b. Salm facing the Juhayna troops of Muḥammad al-Nafs al-Zakiyya.

133 Al-Balādhurī, *Ansāb* (ed. Madelung), 2:517; after ʿĪsā b. Mūsā she married another ʿAbbāsī, Muḥammad b. Ibrāhīm al-Imām [b. Muḥammad b. ʿAlī b. ʿAbdallāh b. al-ʿAbbās], and two men of the Ḥasanī family.

134 Al-Ṭabarī, 3:224; al-Balādhurī, *Ansāb* (ed. Madelung), 2:514, 518, 525; al-Yaʿqūbī, *Taʾrīkh* (ed. Houtsma), 2:453: al-ʿAbdī, that is, belonging to ʿAbd Qays (Rabīʿa); but cf. Ibn Khayyāṭ, *Taʾrīkh* (ed. al-ʿUmarī), 2:449, 465: *aḥad Banī ʿAbd al-Dār* ("one of Banū ʿAbd al-Dār"), that is from the Qurashī family, but in this case the *nisba* is *al-ʿAbdarī*.

135 Al-Ṭabarī, 3:224 (ll. 6–11).

136 Ibid., 3:236 (ll. 10–11); Baqīʿ al-Gharqad was the cemetery of Medina within the city; see Ibn Shabba, *Taʾrīkh al-Madīna*, 1:89ff., 110–111; al-Bakrī, *Muʿjam*, 1:265; Yāqūt, *Muʿjam* (Beirut edition), 1:473; al-Samhūdī, *Wafāʾ*, index, esp. 4:170–171. On Dār Ibn Aflaḥ, see Ibn Shabba, *Taʾrīkh al-Madīna*, 1:125: the *dār* was a domed structure; al-Samhūdī, *Wafāʾ*, 3:299 (copies Ibn Shabba).

137 Al-Balādhurī, *Ansāb* (ed. Madelung), 2:514.

138 Al-Yaʿqūbī, *Taʾrīkh* (ed. Houtsma), 2:453; see also al-Ṭabarī, 3:252 (ll. 9–13).

appointed by ʿĪsā b. Mūsā as the governor of Medina, and he remained in this office for one month, until the caliph's new governor arrived.[139]

3.2 *Ḥamza b. Mālik b. al-Haytham al-Khuzāʿī*

Ḥamza was the son of one of the twelve *nuqabāʾ* of the ʿAbbāsī *daʿwa*. He himself was one of the most important *abnāʾ*; he carried out important military as well as administrative duties for the ʿAbbāsīs.[140] He is only mentioned once as a commander in ʿĪsā's army, when the latter tells Ḥumayd b. Qaḥṭaba to appoint Ḥamza in charge of the fighting against al-Nafs al-Zakiyya instead of him.[141]

3.3 *Muḥammad b. ʿUthmān, the brother of Asad b. al-Marzubān*

Muḥammad fought in the "Market of the Firewood Sellers" (سوق الحَطّابين)[142] against Abū l-Qalammas ʿUthmān b. ʿUbaydallāh b. ʿAbdallāh b. ʿUmar b. al-Khaṭṭāb, who killed him in this battle.[143] This is the only time he is mentioned in the sources. His brother, Asad b. al-Marzubān,[144] was one of the senior commanders in the army of Qaḥṭaba b. Shabīb[145] and is mentioned as a commander during al-Manṣūr's reign.[146] It is possible that he was also one of the commanders in this battle; later we hear that in al-Baṣra he crucified al-Mughīra b. al-Fazʿ, one of the senior commanders of Ibrāhīm b. ʿAbdallāh b. al-Ḥasan.[147] Asad b. al-Marzubān's mosque in Baghdad is mentioned in the year 197/813 and 224/839.[148]

---

139 Ibid., 265; Ibn Khayyāṭ, *Taʾrīkh* (ed. al-ʿUmarī), 2:449, 465.

140 Crone, *Slaves*, 181; on his father, Mālik b. al-Haytham, see ibid., but esp. Agha, *Revolution*, 359, no. 252.

141 Al-Ṭabarī, 3:248 (ll. 12–16); Ḥumayd bluntly objects to this request.

142 Ibn Shabba, *Taʾrīkh al-Madīna*, 1:268 [= al-Samhūdī, *Wafāʾ*, 3:103], locates the market in al-Jabbāna, which was in the north of Medina; ibid., editor's note, adding al-Fīrūzābādī, *al-Maghānim al-muṭāba*, 162 and al-Ḥarbī [?], *al-Manāsik*, 361–362.

143 Al-Ṭabarī, 3:238 (ll. 8–13).

144 Thus he is noted (al-Ṭabarī, 3:238 (ll. 8–13)): "the brother of Asad b. al-Marzubān"; but his name, rendered by al-Ṭabarī, is Muḥammad b. ʿUthmān [!].

145 *Akhbār al-ʿAbbās*, 354, 370; al-Ṭabarī, 3:16.

146 Al-Ṭabarī, 3:344: year 147/764 or 765; 368: year 151/768 or 769; McAuliffe, *ʿAbbāsid Authority*, 202, n. 975; Agha, *Revolution*, 343, no. 131.

147 On al-Mughīra b. al-Fazʿ, see al-Ṭabarī, index; al-Iṣfahānī, *Maqātil*, 318, 324, 327; his crucifixion: Ibn Ḥabīb, *al-Muḥabbar*, 487; Agha, *Revolution*, 343, no. 131.

148 Year 197/813: al-Ṭabarī, 3:920 (l. 16); year 224/838 or 839: Ibn Saʿd, *Ṭabaqāt*, 7:356: the biography of the *ḥadīth* scholar, ʿAbd al-Raḥmān b. Yūnus Abū Muslim, one of al-Manṣūr's *mawālī*, born in 164/780 or 781 "and died suddenly (*fujʾat*[an]) in the Mosque of Asad b. al-Marzubān on 10 Rajab 224/28 May 839."

3.4 *Hazārmard*

He is first mentioned upon the arrival of the ʿAbbāsī troops in Medina, when he was stationed near the bath house (*ḥammām*) of Ibn Abī l-Ṣaʿba.[149] He was killed in battle by the above-mentioned ʿUthmān b. ʿUbaydallāh b. ʿAbdallāh b. ʿUmar b. al-Khaṭṭāb, nicknamed Abū l-Qalammas.[150] The identity of this commander is not certain. He was not necessarily of non-Arab stock: ʿUmar b. Ḥafṣ al-Muhallabī, nicknamed Hazārmard, was one of the senior Arab Umayyad commanders who also served the ʿAbbāsīs during the reigns of al-Saffāḥ and al-Manṣūr, but at the time of the revolt he was the governor of al-Sind.[151]

3.5 *ʿUqba b. Salm b. Nāfiʿ al Hunāʾī, al-Azdī*

He was a close associate of al-Manṣūr and served in administrative as well as military roles, and in delicate diplomatic missions.[152] In the decisive battle against Muḥammad al-Nafs al-Zakiyya he was a wing commander, together with Muḥammad b. Abī l-ʿAbbās, facing the Juhayna troops of Muḥammad al-Nafs al-Zakiyya.[153] It is highly plausible that he had Syrian troops under his command.

3.6 A mawlā *of ʿAbdallāh b. Muʿāwiya [b. Jaʿfar b. Abī Ṭālib]*

He was in charge (perhaps commander) of the armored horsemen and horses: وكان على مجففته. He was ordered by ʿĪsā b. Mūsā to choose ten of his armored horsemen, and together with ten Ṭālibīs they set out for the city of Medina to negotiate the surrender of the city to the ʿAbbāsīs.[154] No further information is given about him.

---

149 Al-Ṭabarī, 3:236; I was unable to locate the site; perhaps it should be identified with Ḥammām Ṣaʿba which is mentioned by Ibn Shabba, *Taʾrīkh al-Madīna*, 1:268 [copied with one omission by al-Samhūdī, *Wafāʾ*, 3:103]. Several scholars are named Ibn Abī l-Ṣaʿba, see Ibn Mākūlā, *al-Ikmāl*, 5:188: ʿAbd al-Raḥmān b. Abī l-Ṣaʿba al-Madanī, *mawlā* Taym Quraysh; or his two brothers, Ḥumayd and ʿAbd al-ʿAzīz (but the latter is called al-Miṣrī, for example, see al-Mizzī, *Tahdhīb*, 18:146).

150 Al-Ṭabarī, 3:239 (ll. 3–7).

151 On him, see Crone, *Slaves*, 134; McAuliffe, *ʿAbbāsid Authority*, 78, n. 374 and the bibliography therein; see also the discussion in chapter 3 (§ al-Sind).

152 On him, see McAuliffe, *ʿAbbāsid Authority*, 89, nn. 422 and 423, but esp. Elad, "Transition," 108–109, n. 91. Add to the bibliography therein: al-Ṭabarī, volume 3 index, esp. 3:145–146, 151, 344, 352–353, 359, 367–368; Wakīʿ, *Quḍāt*, 2:58–60.

153 Al-Balādhurī, *Ansāb* (ed. Madelung), 2:514.

154 Ibid., 2:513; al-Ṭabarī, 3:235–236 (l. 6 to l. 5).

3.7 *Muḥammad b. ʿAbdallāh (Abū l-Karrām) b. Muḥammad b. ʿAlī b. ʿAbdallāh b. Jaʿfar b. Abī Ṭālib*

He was sent by ʿĪsā b. Mūsā at the head of 500 soldiers to block Muḥammad b. ʿAbdallāh's escape route.[155]

3.7.1 The Ṭālibīs in ʿĪsā b. Mūsā's Camp

Several important dignitaries from different Ṭālibī families accompanied ʿĪsā b. Mūsā to Medina. Some Ṭālibīs came from Medina to his camp. The purpose of their presence in the ʿAbbāsī army was to serve as mediators between ʿĪsā b. Mūsā and Muḥammad al-Nafs al-Zakiyya. They were sent several times from the ʿAbbāsī camp to Medina to persuade Muḥammad and his supporters to surrender; they guaranteed safety and security to the Medinans, but all their efforts were in vain.

One source mentions five (out of ten) Ṭālibīs by name in one of the delegations:

1) ʿAbdallāh b. Muḥammad b. ʿUmar b. ʿAlī [b. Abī Ṭālib].
2) ʿUmar b. Muḥammad b. ʿUmar b. ʿAlī [b. Abī Ṭālib].
3) Abū ʿAqīl, Muḥammad b. ʿAbdallāh b. Muḥammad b. ʿAqīl [b. Abī Ṭālib].
4) Al-Qāsim b. al-Ḥasan b. al-Ḥasan b. ʿAlī [b. Abī Ṭālib].
5) ʿAbdallāh b. Ismāʿīl b. ʿAbdallāh b. Jaʿfar [b. Abī Ṭālib].[156]

Other Ṭālibīs in the ʿAbbāsī camp were:

6) Muḥammad b. Zayd b. ʿAlī b. al-Ḥusayn [b. ʿAlī b. Abī Ṭālib].[157]

---

155 Al-Ṭabarī, 3:231–232.

156 Al-Ṭabarī, 3:235–236 (l. 6 to l. 5); ʿAbdallāh b. Muḥammad b. ʿUmar, his brother ʿUmar and Abū ʿAqīl Muḥammad b. ʿAbdallāh were among those who left Medina and joined the ʿAbbāsī camp, see ibid., 3:226–227 (l. 7 to l. 2). See also al-Iṣfahānī, *Maqātil*, 267, mentioning Muḥammad b. Zayd, al-Qāsim b. al-Ḥasan b. Zayd and Muḥammad b. ʿAbdallāh [Abū l- Karrām/Kirām] al-Jaʿfarī.

157 Al-Balādhurī, *Ansāb* (ed. Madelung), 2:513; al-Iṣfahānī, *Maqātil*, 267; Muḥammad b. Zayd appears in al-Ṭabarī four times but only as a *rāwī*, e.g., 3:234 (l. 4); 235, (l. 7); 240 (l. 2); 252 (l. 10); this is the reason that de Goeje defined him as a *rāwī*. McAuliffe, *ʿAbbāsid Authority*, 197–198, does not identify him; he is certainly a Ṭālibī, according to his own assertion, al-Ṭabarī, 3:235 (l. 11); his identification as one of the Ḥusaynīs, that is, Muḥammad b. Zayd b. ʿAlī b. al-Ḥusayn b. ʿAlī b. Abī Ṭālib, is mainly according to al-Iṣfahānī, *Maqātil*, 267; see also 387: وكان...مع أبي جعفر مسودا, and also according to al-Balādhurī, *Ansāb* (ed. Madelung), 2:513. On him and his family, see Ibn ʿInaba, *ʿUmda*, 69ff; it is noteworthy

7) Al-Qāsim b. al-Ḥasan b. Zayd [b. ʿAlī b. al-Ḥusayn b. ʿAlī b. Abī Ṭālib].[158]
8) Muḥammad b. ʿAbdallāh [Abū l-Karrām] b. Muḥammad b. ʿAlī b. ʿAbdallāh b. Jaʿfar b. Abī Ṭālib.[159]
9) A *mawlā* of ʿAbdallāh b. Muʿāwiya [b. Jaʿfar b. Abī Ṭālib], one of the commanders of the army (see the list of commanders above (f)).

These Ṭālibī dignitaries did not fill any military post, except the above-mentioned *mawlā* of ʿAbdallāh b. Muʿāwiya al-Jaʿfarī.

3.7.2 The Advancement of ʿĪsā's Army until Reaching Medina

As noted above, Abū Jaʿfar al-Manṣūr sent Ḥuṣayn b. Kathīr with his contingents as a vanguard. When Kathīr reached Fayd, an important strategic town on the *ḥajj* road mid-way between Mecca and al-Kūfa, he encamped there, built fortifications around his camp (وخندق عليه خندقا) and waited for the arrival of ʿĪsā b. Mūsā with the major forces of the army. With his arrival, the united army continued its way to Medina.[160]

While still in Fayd, ʿĪsā b. Mūsā sent letters to dignitaries of *ahl al-Madīna* (including ʿAbdallāh b. Muḥammad b. ʿAbd al-Raḥmān b. Ṣafwān al-Jumaḥī and ʿAbd al-ʿAzīz b. al-Muṭṭalib al-Makhzūmī, both Qurashīs). There are conflicting reports about the Medinans' reactions to these letters; al-Ḥārith b. Isḥāq relates that when the letters arrived in Medina, many followers of Muḥammad al-Nafs al-Zakiyya left him, including ʿAbd al-ʿAzīz b. al-Muṭṭalib.[161] Al-Madāʾinī, on the other hand, although adding two of the above-mentioned names of the ʿAbbāsī messengers from the Ṭālibī family, Muḥammad b. Zayd b. ʿAlī b. al-Ḥusayn b.

---

that his two brothers, al-Ḥusayn b. Zayd and ʿĪsā b. Zayd, supported the revolt and took an active part in it, see al-Iṣfahānī, *Maqātil*, 387, 389.

158 Al-Ṭabarī, 3:232 (ll. 9–10); 235 (l. 12); the unique information in the last tradition was narrated to ʿĪsā b. ʿAbdallāh (and from the latter to ʿUmar b. Shabba) by Muḥammad b. Zayd b. ʿAlī b. al-Ḥusayn b. ʿAlī b. Abī Ṭālib, who was one of the Ṭālibī dignitaries in ʿĪsā's camp. On him, see below; al-Balādhurī, *Ansāb* (ed. Madelung), 2:513: al-Qāsim b. al-Ḥusayn; correct to al-Ḥasan according to ibid. (ed. Madelung), 516; al-Ṭabarī, 3:232 (l. 10); al-Iṣfahānī, *Maqātil*, 267, 275: al-Qāsim b. al-Ḥasan.

159 Al-Ṭabarī, 3:232–233 (l. 20 to l. 7).

160 Fayd, says Yāqūt, *Muʿjam* (ed. Wüstenfeld), 3:927, was located on the only road that led to Syria; there is no alternative road, because the region is inaccessible, due to the sands; on al-Fayd, see also al-Ḥarbī[?], *al-Manāsik*, 306ff. and the note of the editor; al-Bakrī, *Muʿjam*, 3:1032–1034; the term *khandaq* in this case is not merely "a trench," see for example, al-Ṭabarī, 2:1956 (ll. 15–17), 2:1957 (ll. 1, 12–13), 2:1968 (ll. 4–5, 13, 15, 19), 2:1969 (ll. 1, 3, 13–17): Abū Muslim builds a fortified camp (a *khandaq*).

161 Al-Ṭabarī, 3:226 (ll. 1–5): [ʿUmar b. Shabba] < Muḥammad b. Yaḥyā < al-Ḥārith b. Isḥāq.

ʿAlī and al-Qāsim b. al-Ḥasan b. Zayd b. al-Ḥusayn b. ʿAlī, reports the unanimous bold and negative reaction of Medina's inhabitants towards the ʿAbbāsī delegation.[162]

ʿĪsā b. Mūsā advanced with the army on the main road to Medina. When he reached (Mount) Ṭaraf al-Qadūm, he sent Muḥammad b. Abī l-Karrām al-Jaʿfarī with 500 soldiers to al-Shajara (about 6 Arab miles from Medina) to block the main road from Medina to Mecca, anticipating that Muḥammad b. ʿAbdallāh might flee with his supporters to Mecca. According to the testimony of Muḥammad b. Abī l-Karrām himself, he stayed with his 500 men in al-Baṭḥāʾ until Muḥammad b. ʿAbdallāh's death.[163]

The ʿAbbāsī army's next stop was in al-Aʿwaṣ, east of Medina.[164] Al-Madāʾinī describes (based on unnamed sources) how ʿĪsā b. Mūsā continued until he reached a distance of one mile before the Mosque of the Prophet in Medina, but then, for tactical reasons, retreated to Siqāyat Sulaymān b. ʿAbd al-Malik

162 Al-Iṣfahānī, *Maqātil*, 267.

163 Al-Ṭabarī, 3:231–232; as for Ṭaraf al-Qadūm, all the sources refer to the mountain near Medina by the name of al-Qadūm. Ṭaraf al-Qadūm is mentioned in a *ḥadīth* of al-Furayʿa bt. Mālik, who told the Prophet that her husband was killed in Ṭaraf al-Qadūm: أن زوجها قتل في مكان من طريق المدينة يسمى طرف القدوم; it seems plausible that the meaning of the word Ṭaraf in this case is "the end," "fringes," but see Ibn Saʿd, *Ṭabaqāt*, 8:367 (copied by Ibn ʿAbd al-Barr, *al-Tamhīd*, 21:30), relating that Ṭaraf al-Qadūm is a name of a place on the road to Medina. On Mount Qadūm, see al-Ḥarbī[?], *Manāsik*, 408; al-Fīrūzābādī, *al-Maghānim al-muṭāba*, 276, 334; Yāqūt, *Muʿjam* (Beirut edition), 4:313; al-Samhūdī, *Wafāʾ*, 4:428–429; on 4:429, n. 1, the editor cites bibliography for the *ḥadīth* of al-Furayʿa. Ibn Abī l-Karrām relates that he advanced through al-Baṭḥāʾ, which is Baṭḥāʾ Ibn Azhar, located six miles from Medina. Al-Shajara and al-Baṭḥāʾ were located in Dhū l-Ḥulayfa; see al-Fīrūzābādī, *al-Maghānim al-muṭāba*, 199: al-Shajara is in Dhū l-Ḥulayfa, which is six miles from Medina; see also Yāqūt, *Muʿjam* (Beirut edition), 1:446 ("Baṭḥāʾ Dhī l-Ḥulayfa"): the Prophet sat under a tree in Baṭḥāʾ Abī Azhar, which is called Dhāt al-Sāq, and prayed there. A mosque was erected at this spot; ibid., 3:325 ("al-Shajara"): this is the tree, in Dhū l-Ḥulayfa, under which Asmāʾ bt. Muḥammad b. Abī Bakr had a child. It is six miles from Medina. Yāqūt copied the entries (with minor omissions) from al-Fīrūzābādī; al-Ḥarbī[?], *al-Manāsik*, 425, identifying al-Shajara with Dhū l-Ḥulayfa, quoting the *ḥadīth* stating that the Prophet encamped (? *anākha*) in al-Baṭḥāʾ which is in al-Ḥulayfa, and prayed there; ibid., 427: the distance between Medina to Dhū l-Ḥulayfa is five and a half miles.

164 Al-Bakrī, *Muʿjam*, 1:173: located more than ten miles [between thirteen to nineteen] from Medina (بضعة عشر ميلا من المدينة); see also al-Ḥarbī[?], *al-Manāsik*, 524: less than twenty miles; but see Ibn Saʿd, *al-Qism al-mutammim*, 358: the *muḥaddith* al-Ḥārith b. ʿAbd al-Raḥmān b. Saʿd b. Abī Dhubāb al-Dawsī "lived in al-Aʿwaṣ, which is situated eleven miles from Medina on the (main) road to al-ʿIrāq."

in al-Jurf, which is located four miles from Medina.[165] ʿĪsā reached Siqāyat Sulaymān, most probably also known as Qaṣr Sulaymān b. ʿAbd al-Malik, on Saturday morning, 12 Ramaḍān 145/4 December 762,[166] where he stayed until Monday morning.[167] On that morning, ʿĪsā moved towards Medina and took up position on Mount Salʿ,[168] an excellent observation point from where he could observe the city. He posted cavalry and foot soldiers at all the approaches to

---

165 Al-Ṭabarī, 3:231 (ll. 12–16): فرفعهم [عيسى بن موسى] إلى سقاية سليمان بن عبد الملك بالجرف وهي على أربعة أميال من المدينة; Professor Lecker wrote to me (personal communication, 20 Dec. 2009) that "al-Jurf is located at the end of Wādī l-ʿAqīq (see map of Medina), the Prophet encamped in al-Jurf before he went out to the Tabūk expedition; the prisoners of Caesarea were put there before they were distributed among the Muslims (al-Balādhurī, *Futūḥ*, 1:168); all this leads to a conclusion that it was a vast open area, convenient for the encampment of an army." Al-Jurf is described as being at a distance of three miles from Medina, see Ibn Saʿd, *Ṭabaqāt*, 3:163: the *ṣaḥābī* al-Miqdād b. ʿAmr died "in al-Jurf, at a distance of three miles from Medina" (مات المقداد بالجرف على ثلاثة أميال من المدينة); on al-Jurf, see al-Bakrī, *Muʿjam*, 2:376–378; Yāqūt, *Muʿjam* (ed. Wüstenfeld), 2:62–63; al-Samhūdī, *Wafāʾ*, 4:207–208 (quoting Ibn Saʿd); al-Fīrūzābādī, *al-Maghānim al-muṭāba*, 88–89; all the sources: three miles from Medina; al-Bakrī, *Muʿjam*, 2:377, gives also a different number (besides the three): "al-Zubayr said: al-Jurf is at a distance of one mile from Medina. And Ibn Isḥāq said: at a distance of one *farsakh*." In Islam, the *farsakh* was fixed to three Arab miles, see W. Hinz, "Farsakh," *EI*²; see also, al-ʿAlī, "Topography of Medina," 90.

166 12 Ramaḍān 145 indeed falls on Saturday.

167 Al-Ṭabarī, 3:233–234 (l. 17 to l. 1): سقاية سليمان; al-Balādhurī, *Ansāb* (ed. Madelung), 2:513–514, last line: ʿĪsā b. Mūsā advanced via بطن قناة until he reached al-Jurf and encamped in قصر سليمان بن عبد الملك; *Fragmenta*, 242, a verbatim parallel to al-Balādhurī, with minor changes: مضرب سليمان instead of فصر سليمان; ظهر فناة instead of بطن فناة. Al-Iṣfahānī, *Maqātil*, 268 (from al-Madāʾinī); al-Ṭabarī, al-Balādhurī and *Fragmenta*, do not name him as the source; on Siqāyat Sulaymān b. ʿAbd al-Malik, see al-Samhūdī, *Wafāʾ*, 4:321; al-Ḥāzimī, *al-Amākin*, 2:826; al-Fīrūzābādī, *al-Maghānim al-muṭāba*, 195 and 369: footnotes of the editor Ḥamad al-Jāsir. On Wādī l-Qanāt, one of the three main *wādī*s of the city, see Ibn Shabba, *Taʾrīkh al-Madīna*, 1:172; al-Bakrī, *Muʿjam*, 3:1096; Yāqūt, *Muʿjam* (ed. Wüstenfeld), 4:182; al-Fīrūzābādī, *al-Maghānim al-muṭāba*, 351–352, copies Yāqūt, adding (on 351) that it is located between Uḥud and Medina; further on, he quotes al-Madāʾinī that al-Qanāt is a *wādī* beginning in al-Ṭāʾif, and eventually reaches Ṭaraf al-Qadūm, at the bottom of the graves of the martyrs in Uḥud. See also al-Samhūdī, *Wafāʾ*, 4:58–59 (copying and using most of the quoted sources in this note).

168 Salʿ was a small mountain on the outskirts of Medina; al-Bakrī, *Muʿjam*, 3:747–748; al-Ḥāzimī, *al-Amākin*, 1:544. Late medieval sources describe it within the market of the city (al-Fīrūzābādī, *al-Maghānim al-muṭāba*, 183; Yāqūt, *Muʿjam* (Beirut edition), 3:236–237; al-Samhūdī, *Wafāʾ*, 4:324); see also al-ʿAlī, "Topography of Medina," 83; see map of Medina.

the city, except at the area of the Mosque of Abū l-Jarrāḥ[169] at Buṭḥān.[170] "This he left open as an exit for those wanting to flee."[171] Another source gives more detail and relates that:

* Hazārmard was stationed at (*ʿinda*) Ḥammām b. Abī l-Ṣaʿba.
* Kathīr b. Ḥuṣayn was stationed at (*ʿinda*) Dār Ibn Aflaḥ, which is in Baqīʿ al-Gharqad.
* Muḥammad b. Abī l-ʿAbbās was stationed to watch over (*ʿalā*) Bāb Banī Salima.

The rest of the commanders were stationed at the passageways and the entrances of Medina (أنقاب المدينة).[172] The strategic military importance of these roads or passageways to Medina is clearly recorded by the sources in other periods as well. During the *ridda* wars, Abū Bakr appointed ʿAbdallāh b. Masʿūd to guard over these roads (على حرس أنقاب المدينة), while ʿAlī, Ṭalḥa,

169 I was unable to locate it; Professor Lecker remarks that "it is clear that it is located to the west of mount Salʿ; this was the location of the 'mosques of the victory'" (of Islam), that is, commemorating the retreat of the besieging forces from Medina in the battle of the khandaq." (Personal communication, 20 Dec. 2009).

170 Wādī Buṭḥān is one of the three major *wādī*s of Medina (the other two are al-ʿAqīq and Qanāt), situated in the western part of Medina, see al-Bakrī, *Muʿjam* (Beirut edition), 1:237–238; al-Fīrūzābādī, *al-Maghānim al-muṭāba*, index, esp. 56–57 (and see map of Medina).

171 Al-Ṭabarī, 3:233–234 (l. 17 to l. 4).

172 Ibid., 3:236 (ll. 6–12); on Ḥammām b. Abī l-Ṣaʿba, see n. 149 above; Baqīʿ al-Gharqad was the cemetery of Medina, within the city; Dār Ibn Aflaḥ was located at the farthest end of al-Baqīʿ (see n. 136 above). The expression أنقاب المدينة (ibid., l. 12); appears in a well-known *ḥadīth* relating that the angels are watching over أنقاب المدينة and the plague and the Antichrist (al-Dajjāl) will not be able to enter Medina (for example, see al-Bukhārī, *Ṣaḥīḥ*, 2:664; al-Nasāʾī, *Sunan*, 2:485; al-Ṭabarānī, *al-Kabīr*, 7:36). For the explanation of the term, see for example, al-Zurqānī, *Sharḥ*, 4:289: "Ibn Wahb said: the meaning [of أنقاب المدينة] is its entrances, that is, its gates and the entrances (openings) of its roads, from which one enters": قال إبن وهب: يعني مداخلها وهي أبوابها وفوهات طرقها التي يدخل إليها منها; Ibn ʿAbd al-Barr, *al-Tamhīd*, 16:180: طرقها ومحاجها; al-Suyūṭī, *al-Dībāj*, 3:416: طرقها وفجاجها; Ibn Ḥajar, *Fatḥ al-Bārī*, 1:198: "the entrances of the city, its gates and the entrances (openings) of its roads": مداخل المدينة أبوابها وفوهات طرقها; but نقْب pl. أنقاب can also mean: "a road (or narrow road) in a mountain; a road between two mountains (Lane, *Lexicon*, s.v. *n.q.b.*); McAuliffe, *ʿAbbāsid Authority*, 200: "the passageways leading into Medina." An exactly similar word is مَنْقَب/مناقِب, see al-Ṭabarī, 3:230 (ll. 10, 12, 14): المناقب.

and al-Zubayr were each in charge of one *naqb* of these *anqāb* (بالقيام على نقب من أنقاب المدينة).[173]

Upon establishing his army in al-Salʿ, and having besieged the city, several attempts were made by ʿĪsā b. Mūsā to send messengers from his camp to Muḥammad b. ʿAbdallāh and the dignitaries of Medina, to call on them to surrender and receive *amān*. Muḥammad b. ʿAbdallāh rejected this demand, but several Medinan dignitaries who had supported Muḥammad deserted him and moved to ʿĪsā b. Mūsā's camp.[174] But it seems that the decisive majority of the people of Medina did not respond to several other attempts on ʿĪsā's part to persuade them to surrender and receive *amān*.[175] On the other hand, Muḥammad b. ʿAbdallāh sent ʿĪsā a letter in which he offered him *amān*, an offer which he turned down.[176] Another delegation (this time consisting of ʿAlīd dignitaries) was sent by ʿĪsā b. Mūsā to persuade Muḥammad and his supporters to surrender and receive *amān*, but it totally failed and they returned shamefacedly.[177]

173 Ibn Khayyāṭ, *Taʾrīkh* (Beirut, 1993), 64; see also al-Ṭabarī, 1:1874 (= Ibn ʿAsākir, *Taʾrīkh*, 25:159); ibid., 25:158 (I thank Professor Lecker for these sources).

174 Al-Ṭabarī, 3:226–227 (l. 7 to l. 2).

175 Ibid., 3:234 (ll. 6–7): ʿĪsā b. Mūsā himself calls the city's people to surrender, but this time he receives strong negative reactions; see also ibid. (ll. 4–5): ʿĪsā calls Muḥammad b. ʿAbdallāh to surrender on Friday, Saturday, and Sunday; for other examples, see ibid., 3:234–235 (l. 17 to l. 6); 3:236 (ll. 6–13).

176 Ibid., 3:232.

177 Ibid., 3:235–236 (l. 6 to l. 4).

CHAPTER 6

The ʿAbbāsī Army's Campaigns Against Muḥammad b. ʿAbdallāh

Many traditions that contain specific detailed evidence about the course of the campaigns are recorded in the different sources, but alas, not in any chronological order. In this work I undertake the task of arranging the chronological sequence of events. In some cases, therefore, the chronological order presented is the result of deduction and may possibly not reflect the "real" course of events.

1 The First Stages

The battle between ʿĪsā b. Mūsā's army and that of Muḥammad b. ʿAbdallāh was conducted in two stages. The first stage seems to have started with a softening of Muḥammad's forces by siege engines accompanied by a massive volley of arrows (نشاب ومقاليع).[1]

1.1 *Duel Combats*

It seems that in the first stages of the campaign, but also in later stages, several duels were held between the two sides' warriors. A number of testimonies relate the occurrence of several duels, some that took place outside the *khandaq* that surrounded parts of the city, others that were held within the city. All of these traditions were related by eyewitnesses, supporters of Muḥammad b. ʿAbdallāḥ or of the ʿAbbāsīs who took part in the battle. Some traditions belonged to the families or the tribes of the warriors, and were aimed at commemorating the bravery of their kinfolk. Many traditions are recorded in the ancient style of *ayyām al-ʿArab*, accompanied by stereotypical tribal praise of the warrior and slander of the enemy. In two of these duels, Abū l-Qalammas ʿUthmān b. ʿUbaydallāh b. ʿAbdallāh b. ʿUmar b. al-Khaṭṭāb (Muḥammad b. ʿAbdallāh's

1 Al-Ṭabarī, 3:236 (ll. 12–13); the phrase مقلاع is not found in al-Ṭabarī's *Glossarium* nor in Dozy's dictionary; see *Lisān al-ʿArab, q.l.ʿ.*: والمقلاع الذي يرمى به الحجر.

 | DOI 10.1163/9789004296220_008

commander) took part. In the first duel he killed Asad b. al-Marzubān's brother in Sūq al-Khaṭṭābīn;[2] in the second he killed Hazārmārd.[3]

The first of Muḥammad b. ʿAbdallāh's soldiers to be slain was Ibrāhīm b. Jaʿfar b. Muṣʿab b. al-Zubayr. The event was recorded by ʿUmar b. Shabba through a member of the Zubayrī family, Hishām b. Muḥammad b. ʿUrwa b. Hishām b. ʿUrwa b. al-Zubayr, from Māhān b. Bukht, the *mawlā* of Ḥumayd b. Qaḥṭaba, who describes how Ibrāhīm b. Jaʿfar b. Muṣʿab came out from the city alone "to look us over, riding around our army until he had spied out all of it." He aroused both fear and admiration in the ʿAbbāsī camp. Upon leaving after completing his mission, his horse stumbled and threw him to the ground and his armor (*tannūr*) broke his neck. "This armor was gilded," continues the narrator, "and it was said that it belonged to Muṣʿab b. al-Zubayr." Al-Ṭabarī's sources say that this event occurred in Medina: لما صرنا بالمدينة.[4] Al-Balādhurī's description of the event is concise and lacks the eyewitness's lively description. It is related by al-Madāʾinī (d. ca. 225/840), who adds topographical information, e.g., that the Zubayrī met the ʿAbbāsī army in Thaniyyat Wāqim, that is, in the mountain pass that leads to Wāqim, one of the *āṭām*s of Medina.[5] Ibrāhīm's father, Jaʿfar, was married to Mulayka bt. al-Ḥasan b. al-Ḥasan b. ʿAlī b. Abī Ṭālib, who was Muḥammad b. ʿAbdallāh's aunt, but Ibrāhīm b. Jaʿfar is not mentioned as her son in the *nasab* books. This marriage tie between the Zubayrīs and the Ḥasanīs may have contributed to Ibrāhīm's joining the rebellion.

2 Al-Ṭabarī, 3:238 (ll. 8–13).

3 Ibid., 3:238–239 (l. 13 to l. 2) and 3:239 (ll. 2–7); the description of a heavily armed ʿAbbāsī soldier challenging Muḥammad's soldiers, who had no armor at all, to a duel is noteworthy. He was killed by one of the latter's soldiers, who also killed another two ʿAbbāsī soldiers who set out to fight him (al-Ṭabarī, 3:239–240 (l. 7 to l. 1)). This is reminiscent of similar cases of duels during the siege of Baghdad by al-Maʾmūn's troops (in the year 197/812 or 813), when an *ʿayyār* with no armor or heavy weapons attacked a heavily-armored professional soldier of al-Maʾmūn's army, see al-Ṭabarī, 3:885–886.

4 Ibid., 3:233 (ll. 7–17); McAuliffe, *ʿAbbāsid Authority*, 196–197 (the quote is from 196); see also al-Iṣfahānī, *Maqātil*, 268: an epitomized tradition related by al-Madāʾinī; al-Dhahabī, *Taʾrīkh*, 9:27.

5 Al-Balādhurī, *Ansāb* (ed. Madelung), 2:513: al-Madāʾinī is not mentioned, but see the exact parallel tradition (with minor changes) in al-Iṣfahānī, *Maqātil*, 268, where al-Madāʾinī is mentioned as its source (ibid., بنية واقم instead of ثنية واقم). I was unable to find ثنية واقم in the sources; in Medina and/or its vicinity there were three sites named Wāqim, all *āṭām*s (fortified estates); see al-Fīrūzābādī, *al-Maghānim al-muṭāba*, 424–425; Yāqūt, *Muʿjam* (ed. Wüstenfeld), 4:893; al-Samhūdī, *Wafāʾ*, index, esp. 4:516.

1.2 *Assaulting and Bridging the Khandaq (Moat)*

As noted, after all efforts to negotiate failed, ʿĪsā b. Mūsā sent his chief commander, Ḥumayd b. Qaḥṭaba, at the head of 100 foot soldiers, to attack and penetrate the *khandaq*, which had been dug by Muḥammad b. ʿAbdallāh and his supporters on the original lines of the *khandaq* of the Prophet around some parts of Medina.[6] This contingent, armed with bows and arrows and iron shields, succeeded in defeating and dispersing Muḥammad's men who defended a (high) wall (*jidār*) that was put up in front of the *khandaq*. Ḥumayd informed ʿĪsā b. Mūsā that the wall should be razed and ʿĪsā sent him laborers ([?], *faʿala*), who razed it. In order to cross over the *khandaq*, ʿĪsā sent Ḥumayd doors or gates (*abwāb*) the size of the width of the *khandaq*, which his troops used to cross over to the other side, where they fought a very fierce battle from early morning until late afternoon.[7]

Another tradition gives a more detailed description: the *khandaq* itself was most probably deep enough to prevent it being crossed on foot or on horse. In order to fill it, ʿĪsā ordered that the saddlebags that were hung on the camels be thrown into it: حقائب الإبل. He also ordered two doors (gates?) be brought from Dār Saʿd b. Masʿūd in al-Thaniyya's quarters in order to put them over the *khandaq*; the ʿAbbāsī soldiers crossed over and fought in a place called Mafātiḥ Khashram (unidentified) until late afternoon.[8] It is most probable that these were not the ordinary doors of an ordinary room; they may have been the main gates of the *dār*, and thus may give us a certain impression of the *khandaq*'s width, which, according to this tradition, composed a real obstacle for the ʿAbbāsī army.

1.3 *Taking Control of the Outskirts of Medina and Entering the City*

Following the crossing of the *khandaq* (or perhaps at the same time, or even before this event, as the chronological sequence of events, as noted, cannot be established unequivocally), the ʿAbbāsī army took control of Mount Salʿ, which towers over the city, and which was under the control of the Arabs of Juhayna

6 On the digging of the *khandaq*, see al-Ṭabarī, 3:228–229; al-Iṣfahānī, *Maqātil*, 267; on the *khandaq* of the Prophet, see Ibn Saʿd, *Ṭabaqāt*, 2:65–67; al-Fīrūzābādī, *al-Maghānim al-muṭāba*, 133–134; and esp. al-Samhūdī, *Wafāʾ*, 4:265–270; Watt, *Muḥammad at Medina*, 35ff and the bibliography therein.

7 Al-Ṭabarī, 3:240 (ll. 1–9); ibid., 3:136 (l. 5): 100 (soldiers). The translation of *faʿala* as laborers is according to McAuliffe, *ʿAbbāsid Authority*, 204. Williams renders it as "sappers"; this is possible assuming that the ʿAbbāsī army had such a professional corps.

8 Al-Ṭabarī, 3:240 (ll. 15–18): [ʿUmar b. Shabba < Azhar]; late afternoon: حتى كان العصر, possibly afternoon prayer? On Khashram see below.

(أعاريب جهينة); they then "swooped down" (إنصبوا) the mountain towards Medina and entered it. An eyewitness vividly describes the "conquest" of the mountain: he saw an 'Abbāsī soldier "holding a spear on which he had stuck a man's head with the throat, liver, and entrails still attached...." When he reached the summit of Salʿ he called to his fellow soldiers in Persian (كوهبان) and they climbed up the mountain and planted a black flag...."[9]

At this very first stage, when the 'Abbāsīs had just begun to penetrate the city, Asmā' bt. al-Ḥasan b. 'Abdallāh b. 'Ubaydallāh b. al-'Abbās had a black scarf hung on the *manāra* of the Great Mosque. The pro-'Abbāsī transmitter relates that when the supporters (soldiers? *aṣḥāb*) of Muḥammad b. 'Abdallāh saw the "flag" they fled.[10]

Other contingents of the 'Abbāsī army entered the city from another direction, through the (quarter?) of Banū Ghifār. The members of Abū 'Amr's family of Banū Ghifār were the ones who opened a way before the 'Abbāsī troops through the Banū Ghifār quarter, enabling them to come upon Muḥammad b. 'Abdallāh's supporters (*aṣḥābihi*) from behind.[11] The way that Banū Abū 'Amr opened for the 'Abbāsīs was most probably through the *khandaq* of Banū Ghifār, which is described in another place and in a different context by Ismā'īl b. Abī 'Amr al-Ghifārī, who at the outbreak of the revolt was posted

9 Ibid., 3:244 (ll. 2–9): ['Umar b. Shabba]... < Muḥammad b. 'Abd al-Wāḥid b. 'Abdallāh b. Abī Farwa, whose family members were very close supporters of the 'Abbāsīs. This is the first (and last) time he is mentioned in the sources known to me. The rendering of إنصبوا is according to McAuliffe, *'Abbāsid Authority*, 208; ibid., n. 989: "The Persian phrase means 'mountain guards.'" As an alternative, the *Addenda et Emendanda*, dccxl, gives *kūhiyyān*, which could mean "mountain dwellers." Note that according to al-Ḥarbī[?], *al-Manāsik*, 412, Mount Salʿ was inhabited by the tribe of Ashjaʿ, but he may be referring to his time (mid-ninth century). Do Ashjaʿ and Juhayna belong to the same confederacy of tribes? Ashjaʿ b. Rayth b. Ghaṭafān b. Sa'd b. Qays 'Aylān b. Muḍar b. Nizār b. Ma'add b. 'Adnān (Ibn Ḥazm, *Jamhara*, 481; Ibn al-Kalbī, *Jamhara* [ed. Caskel], 1:201; II, tables 92 and 135); Juhayna b. Zayd b. Layth b. Sūd b. Aslam b. al-Ḥāfī b. Quḍā'a (Ibn Ḥazm, *Jamhara*, 444; Ibn al-Kalbī, *Jamhara* [ed. Caskel], 1:264; II, table 332).

10 Al-Ṭabarī, 3:244 (ll. 9–14): ['Umar b. Shabba]... Muḥammad b. 'Abd al-Wāḥid b. 'Abdallāh b. Abī Farwa; ibid., 3:246 (ll. 7–8); Ibn Ḥazm, describing this event adds: "and this was the reason for the defeat of the people of Medina": وكان ذلك سبب انهزام أهل المدينة; al-Balādhurī, *Ansāb* (ed. al-Dūrī), 3:63: "this broke down the rebels": وكسر ذلك المبيضة; al-Zubayrī, *Nasab Quraysh*, 33: "this was the breaking point for the rebels when 'Īsā b. Mūsā entered Medina": فكان ذلك كسرا للمبيضة حين دخل عيسى بن موسى المدينة; see also al-Ya'qūbī, *Ta'rīkh* (ed. Houtsma), 2:452–453.

11 Al-Ṭabarī, 3:244 (ll. 15–18); al-Kulaynī, *al-Kāfī*, 1:364.

(most probably as a commander) in the section of the moat (*khandaq*) that surrounded the territory of his tribe, Banū Ghifār.[12] Two of Ismāʿīl's brothers were imprisoned (perhaps held under house arrest) by Muḥammad al-Nafs al-Zakiyya.[13] Perhaps this was the reason that he[?] opened a way for the ʿAbbāsīs through his tribe's territory. When the last battle ended, and Muḥammad al-Nafs al-Zakiyya and his handful of supporters were all killed, Abū ʿAmr's house was one of the five places in which *amān* was given to whoever came there.[14]

ʿĪsā b. Mūsā himself encamped at Mount Dhubāb,[15] which according to al-Bakrī is located in the Jabbāna quarter of Medina, at the bottom of Thaniyyat (al-Wadāʿ).[16]

2 The Campaign Outside the City

A great many sources note that the main decisive battle between the two armies occurred on Monday, 15 Ramaḍān 145/7 December 762.[17] Several of these sources specifically state that it occurred outside the city;[18] from others this can be understood from their texts.[19]

The descriptions of the battles were related by men who took part in them, the supporters of the ʿAbbāsīs, on the one hand, and the supporters of Muḥammad b. ʿAbdallāh, on the other. Many of these testimonies are therefore contentious and biased. But in spite of these biased traditions, they enable us to reconstruct the main course of the battle, which was conducted according to the classic, traditional structure of five wings. The main battle lasted for

12 Al-Ṭabarī, 3:236–237 (l. 21 to l. 1), a family tradition, a first person narration from Ismāʿīl to his nephew: [ʿUmar b. Shabba] < Ayyūb b. ʿUmar [b. Abī ʿAmr] < Ismāʿīl b. Abī ʿAmr.

13 Ibid., 3:237 (ll. 10–11); see also ibid., 3:249 (ll. 5–13).

14 Al-Ṭabarī, 3:253 (ll. 6–7) (and see also below).

15 Al-Kulaynī, *al-Kāfī*, 1:364.

16 Al-Bakrī, *Muʿjam*, 2:609; al-Ḥarbī[?], *al-Manāsik*, 398; al-Ḥāzimī, *al-Amākin*, 1:259 (editor's note); 349: quoting al-Wāqidī (= al-Wāqidī, *al-Maghāzī*, 1:23); al-Samhūdī, *Wafāʾ*, 4:196, 280–282; according to him (d. 911/1505 or 1506) it is located north of Thaniyyat al-Wadāʿ, on which Masjid al-Rāya stood.

17 Al-Balādhurī, *Ansāb* (ed. Madelung), 2:514: no source is given by al-Balādhurī, but we can safely say that this is al-Madāʾinī, who is mentioned by name in the parallel tradition in al-Iṣfahānī, *Maqātil*, 268.

18 Al-Ṭabarī, 3:240 (ll. 9–14); al-Masʿūdī, *Tanbīh*, 341; Ibn ʿInaba, *ʿUmda*, 105; al-Kulaynī, *al-Kāfī*, 1:364.

19 Ibn Saʿd, *al-Qism al-mutammim*, 377–378: from al-Wāqidī; al-Azdī, *Taʾrīkh al-Mawṣil*, 187; al-Ṭabarī, 3:265: from al-Wāqidī.

a relatively short time, most certainly because of the decisive advantage the ʿAbbāsī army had in quality and quantity of manpower and equipment. The shortage of fighting men is evident when contingents from Muḥammad's army routed some ʿAbbāsī units, but were unable to take advantage of this victory, because they lacked men.[20]

Al-Balādhurī records a detailed tradition about the battle that reached him through al-Madāʾinī.[21] According to this tradition, at the beginning of the campaign, ʿĪsā b. Zayd was Muḥammad b. ʿAbdallāh's chief commander, while Muḥammad himself was in al-Muṣallā.[22] When the fighting intensified, he went down to command his forces and personally lead them in battle. He took command of a force that faced the forces led by Ḥumayd b. Qaḥṭaba. Yazīd and Ṣāliḥ, the sons of Muʿāwiya b. ʿAbdallāh b. Jaʿfar, heading their wing, faced the ʿAbbāsī wing headed by Kathīr b. Ḥuṣayn. Muḥammad b. Abī l-ʿAbbās (the son of the first caliph) and ʿUqba b. Salm [b. Nāfiʿ al-Hunāʾī (Azd)] faced the contingents of the Juhayna tribe (من ناحية جهينة). In the first stages of the battle, Ṣāliḥ and Yazīd, Muḥammad b. ʿAbdallāh's commanders, asked Kathīr b. Ḥuṣayn for an *amān*, which he granted them, but ʿĪsā b. Mūsā did not approve of the agreement. In spite of this refusal, Kathīr allowed them to go to wherever they wanted and they fled. The battle continued almost until the time of the noon prayer (قريب من الظهر). The arrows that were shot by *ahl Khurāsān* contingents injured many of al-Nafs al-Zakiyya's soldiers, so, the narrator continues flatly, "the people left Muḥammad."[23] Muḥammad b. ʿAbdallāh left al-Muṣallā and entered Dār Marwān where he prayed the noon prayer, washed and perfumed himself (تحنط) in preparation for death.[24]

3 The Last Battle and the Death of Muḥammad b. ʿAbdallāh

Returning to al-Balādhurī's (al-Madāʾinī's) long tradition: After the noon prayer, Muḥammad left Dār Marwān, and returned with those supporters who had not

20 Al-Ṭabarī, 3:243 (ll. 5–8); 3:250 (ll. 1–6).

21 For the complete tradition, see al-Balādhurī, *Ansāb* (ed. Madelung), 2:514–516 (= *Fragmenta*, 242–245).

22 This name, al-Muṣallā, was given to two places, one inside Medina also named *Muṣallā l-ʿĪd* (or *al-Aʿyād*), where the Prophet prayed, see al-Samhūdī, *Wafāʾ*, 3:106, 115, 118–119ff.; the other Muṣallā was Muṣallā (Wādī) al-ʿAqīq, ibid., 4:474, see al-Fīrūzābādī, *al-Maghānim al-muṭāba*, 384.

23 Al-Balādhurī, *Ansāb* (ed. Madelung), 2:514 (= *Fragmenta*, 242).

24 Al-Balādhurī, *Ansāb* (ed. Madelung), 2:514; Ibn ʿInaba, *ʿUmda*, 105.

left him to fight the ʿAbbāsī contingents in the last campaign which was held in Thaniyyat al-Wadāʿ and lasted until that evening. More supporters deserted his camp,[25] and at this stage Ibrāhīm b. Muṣʿab al-Zubayrī (Ibn Khuḍayr), Muḥammad b. ʿAbdallāh's *ṣāḥib al-shurṭa*, went to the prison and killed the ʿAbbāsī governor, Riyāḥ b. ʿUthmān and his son, who were imprisoned there. He wanted to kill the previous governor, Muḥammad b. Khālid al-Qasrī, who was also imprisoned there, but failed, went back to Muḥammad b. ʿAbdallāh, and was killed with him.[26] According to one testimony, Ibn Khuḍayr burned Muḥammad b. ʿAbdallāh's *dīwān*, in which all his supporters (soldiers) were registered;[27] but according to other traditions it was Muḥammad himself who entered his house and burned the "notebook" (*daftar*) in which there were lists of the names of his supporters and those who swore allegiance to him,[28] or it was his sister, whom he ordered to burn *al-kutub*,[29] which another source explains as "the letters of the swearings of allegiance to him that reached him from all the provinces."[30] The last battle occurred in the evening, before the evening prayer, when Muḥammad and his handful of supporters were killed.

It is difficult to follow the course of Muḥammad b. ʿAbdallāh's last battle and especially to crystallize the scores of details about his death into a coherent narrative. The reports in the different sources are not uniform and are full of contradictions. Generally, two main types of narratives regarding his death can be discerned. The first aims to describe a heroic traditional Arab type of death, e.g., Muḥammad b. ʿAbdallāh fought proudly and courageously until the last moment at the head of a handful of supporters (warriors) of Banū Shujāʿ of the Juhayna. According to this version, Muḥammad prayed in the Banū l-Du'il (Dayl?) Mosque,[31] in al-Thaniyya, then he went with the last remaining

25 Al-Balādhurī, *Ansāb* (ed. Madelung), 2:515; Thaniyyat al-Wadāʿ was the main northern[?] entrance to Medina; for the conflicting reports about the locations of this Thaniyya (whether on the way to Syria or to Mecca), see al-Fīrūzābādī, *al-Maghānim al-muṭāba*, 80–81; but especially al-Samhūdī, *Wafāʾ*, 4:195–201; al-Samhūdī's arguments for the northern direction seem highly plausible (cf. Yāqūt, *Muʿjam* [ed. Wüstenfeld], 1:937: unequivocally locates it on the road to Mecca).

26 Al-Balādhurī, *Ansāb* (ed. Madelung), 2:515; al-Ṭabarī, 3:241–242 (l. 16 to l. 3): from al-Wāqidī; Ibn Saʿd, *al-Qism al-mutammim*, 377–378; al-Iṣfahānī, *Maqātil*, 276: from al-Madāʾinī.

27 al-Iṣfahānī, *Maqātil*, 277.

28 Ibn ʿInaba, *ʿUmda*, 105; al-Ṣafadī, *al-Wāfī*, 3:297–298.

29 Al-Iṣfahānī, *Maqātil*, 272.

30 Ibn Abī l-Ḥadīd, *Sharḥ* (Cairo 1329 H.), 1:323: يعني كتب البيعة الواردة عليه من الآفاق.

31 Banū l-Du'il b. Bakr b. ʿAbd Manāt; on their places of dwelling in Medina, see Ibn Shabba, *Taʾrīkh al-Madīna*, 1:263; al-Samhūdī, *Wafāʾ*, 3:97–98: al-Dayl (probably the editor's vocalization) b. Bakr, quoting Ibn Shabba; this is a unique piece of evidence about the location and settlement of the tribe and their residence. McAuliffe, *ʿAbbāsid Authority*, 206, note:

warriors of Banū Shujāʿ to the bed of the watercourse of Mount Salʿ (بطن مسيل سلع), dismounted and hamstrung his mount and the Banū Shujāʿ hamstrung theirs. Each and every one broke his scabbard.[32] Al-Wāqidī also depicts the bravery and perseverance of a small group of Banū Shujāʿ of Juhayna who fought at Muḥammad's side until they were killed.[33]

Generally speaking, these traditions describe how Muḥammad b. ʿAbdallāh fought with his few loyal supporters, who were killed one after the other, until he himself was killed.[34] A typical tradition of this kind, which is related by an eyewitness, Abū l-Ḥajjāj al-Minqarī (unidentified), describes how Muḥammad fought bravely and skillfully, killing whoever came near him, until he closely resembled (so the narrator says) Ḥamza b. ʿAbd al-Muṭṭalib, the Prophet's uncle who was killed in the battle of Uḥud. Muḥammad, adds the eyewitness, was shot by an arrow and "I saw its colors, which were red and blue." Muḥammad leaned on a wall, while his men shielded him. When death came upon him he leaned against his sword and broke it.[35] The Ḥasanī family tradition relates that this was the Prophet's sword, Dhū l-Faqār.[36]

However, another group of traditions, completely different, describes Muḥammad b. ʿAbdallāh's death as less than honorable. This group can be divided into sub-divisions. In one such tradition, Muḥammad, on his knees, begged for his life, crying "woe to you, I am the son of your Prophet, wounded and wronged."[37] Another tradition describes in a laconic manner how Ḥumayd

---

Al-Dīl, also al-Duʾil, quoting Ibn al-Kalbī, *Jamhara* (ed. Caskel), 1:234; II, tables 36 and esp. 43; Ibn Ḥazm, *Jamhara*, 465.

32 Al-Ṭabarī, 3:242 (ll. 16–17); hamstringing a riding beast is an ancient Arab custom, by which "the warrior indicates that he was cutting off his only possible means of flight" (McAuliffe, *ʿAbbāsid Authority*, 206, n. 985, citing the example of Jaʿfar b. Abī Ṭālib in the battle of Muʾta).

33 Al-Ṭabarī, 3:240 (ll. 9–14); the heads of Banū Shujāʿ were sent to al-Manṣūr, ibid., 3:255 (l. 1).

34 Al-Balādhurī, *Ansāb* (ed. Madelung), 2:515–516; al-Ṭabarī, 3:245 (ll. 5–16); 246 (ll. 10–14) (= al-Iṣfahānī, *Maqātil*, 270).

35 Al-Ṭabarī, 3:246–247 (l. 19 to l. 5).

36 Ibid. 3:246–247 (ll. 6–7): [ʿUmar b. Shabba] < Muḥammad b. Ismāʿīl [b. Jaʿfar al-Jaʿfarī] < his grandfather [Mūsā b. ʿAbdallāh b. al-Ḥasan b. al-Ḥasan, Muḥammad b. ʿAbdallāh's brother]; according to another tradition, ibid., 3:247 (ll. 7–16), upon sensing his impending death Muḥammad gave his sword, Dhū l-Faqār, to a merchant to whom he owed 400 *dīnār*s. The sword was bought by the governor of Medina, was taken by Caliph al-Mahdī, who passed it on to his son al-Hādī, who tried it out on a dog and broke it into pieces.

37 Al-Ṭabarī, 3:246 (ll. 14–16): ويحكم أنا ابن نبيكم مجرَّح مظلوم; the version *mujarraḥ*, is also rendered by the parallel traditions in Ibn al-Athīr, *al-Kāmil* (ed. Tornberg), 5:419 and Ibn

b. Qaḥṭaba, the chief commander of the ʿAbbāsī army, came upon Muḥammad b. ʿAbdallāh through Ashjaʿ lane and killed him without his being aware, and took his head to ʿĪsā (b. Mūsā).[38] In the first group of traditions that describe a heroic death, Ḥumayd b. Qaḥṭaba is not mentioned. But in the decisive majority of the other traditions, he is the one who inflicts the death blow on Muḥammad and kills him.[39] It is clear that the aim of these traditions is to glorify Ḥumayd, to accord him the ultimate honor by ascribing the killing of Muḥammad al-Nafs al-Zakiyya to him. The question arises: did Ḥumayd indeed kill Muḥammad b. ʿAbdallāh? Recall that one group of traditions does not mention this. But it was important to Ḥumayd's family and to the ʿAbbāsīs to ascribe his death (at least the death blow) to Ḥumayd b. Qaḥṭaba, the son of the leader and the general who led the victorious *ahl Khurāsān* army towards al-ʿIrāq. More than anyone else, Ḥumayd personified the new ʿAbbāsī *dawla*. The importance of connecting him to the killing of Muḥammad b. ʿAbdallāh is clear from the following tradition, according to which Ḥumayd swears that when he sees Muḥammad he will deal him the death blow with his sword unless he is killed before (reaching) him. Ḥumayd passed over Muḥammad when he had already been killed and struck him a blow with his sword in order to fulfill his oath.[40]

The answer to the question raised above, therefore, is not unequivocal. But despite this uncertainty, it is highly plausible that Ḥumayd indeed killed Muḥammad b. ʿAbdallāh. This may be deduced from an interesting tradition that gives a highly accurate, detailed description of the circumstances surrounding the death of Muḥammad b. ʿAbdallāh, including unique topographic and geographic details of the last scene of the battle.

This very long and extremely interesting tradition is recorded (except for a short part with a few lines) by the Ḥasanī, Mūsā b. ʿAbdallāh b. al-Ḥasan, the brother of Muḥammad al-Nafs al-Zakiyya, who relates in the first person and in a very detailed manner the events that occurred in Medina after the outbreak of the revolt and the short period of Muḥammad's sovereignty

Kathīr, *al-Bidāya* (ed. Shīrī), 10:96; and see al-Iṣfahānī, *Maqātil*, 270–271: مجروح مظلوم; de Goeje, in al-Ṭabarī's *Addenda et Emendanda*, dccxl: suggests reading *muḥraj* (violated); the same word is rendered in the Egyptian edition of Abū l-Faḍl Ibrāhīm, 7:595; McAuliffe, *ʿAbbāsid Authority*, 210: *muḥraj* (after the *Addenda et Emendanda*) translating: "beset by difficulties."

38 Al-Ṭabarī, 3:246 (ll. 6–10) (= al-Iṣfahānī, *Maqātil*, 270: a parallel short tradition).

39 Al-Ṭabarī, 3:246 (ll. 10–14, 16–19); al-Balādhurī, *Ansāb* (ed. Madelung), 2:516.

40 Al-Ṭabarī, 3:248 (l. 16): [ʿUmar b. Shabba] < Jawwād b. Ghālib b. Mūsā *mawlā* Banī ʿIjl < Ḥumayd *mawlā* Muḥammad b. Abī l-ʿAbbās [al-Saffāḥ].

in Medina. A short part of the tradition is related by Khadīja bt. ʿUmar b. Muḥammad (al-Bāqir) b. ʿAlī b. al-Ḥusayn b. ʿAlī b. Abī Ṭālib. The long tradition was transmitted by Mūsā b. ʿAbdallāh al-Ḥasanī to ʿAbdallāh b. Ibrāhīm b. Muḥammad (b. ʿAlī b. ʿAbdallāh b. Jaʿfar b. Abī Ṭālib?). It records the key rift that occurred between the Ḥasanīs and the Ḥusaynīs following Muḥammad al-Nafs al-Zakiyya's rebellion.[41]

One part of this tradition describes several encounters between Jaʿfar al-Ṣādiq and ʿAbdallāh b. al-Ḥasan, in which Jaʿfar is requested to swear allegiance to Muḥammad b. ʿAbdallāh al-Nafs al-Zakiyya. Jaʿfar refuses and uses his esoteric knowledge (*ʿilm*) to foretell the misfortunes of the Ḥasanī family, and especially that of Muḥammad al-Nafs al-Zakiyya. Several times he gives accurate descriptions of certain events that will occur in the future. In a heated meeting between Muḥammad al-Nafs al-Zakiyya, accompanied by his loyal supporter ʿĪsā b. Zayd b. ʿAlī b. al-Ḥusayn, the two order Jaʿfar al-Ṣādiq to swear allegiance to al-Nafs al-Zakiyya. As the discussion turns into a bitter emotional confrontation, Jaʿfar al-Ṣādiq relates in minute details the circumstances of al-Nafs al-Zakiyya's killing: when, how, and where Muḥammad and his supporters will be killed by the ʿAbbāsī troops.[42]

The following is the translation of the text of the "apocalyptic prophecy" of Jaʿfar al-Ṣādiq:

> Indeed I see you going out from the gate of (Banū) Ashjaʿ into the interior of the Wādī, being attacked by a horseman distinguishing himself with the marks of men of courage (*fāris muʿlim*), in his hand he carries a short spear (*ṭarrādā*), half white and half black, riding on a horse aged five (كميت أقرح that is, a five-year-old horse with all his teeth in his mouth); he will spear you, but will not inflict upon you any damage. You will strike the edge of his horse and you will throw him down; and another (ʿAbbāsī soldier) will attack you, coming out from the lane of the family of Abū ʿAmmār al-Du'liyyūn; he has two plaited locks (غديرتان مضفورتان) that come out of his helmet, and a heavy mustache, by God I swear, he is your

41 Al-Kulaynī, *al-Kāfī*, 1:358–366; this tradition was copied from *al-Kāfī* by several Imāmī authors, e.g., al-Baḥrānī, *Madīnat al-maʿājiz*, 5:276–290; al-Māzandarānī, *Sharḥ*, 312–318, and the commentary of the editor, 318–326; al-Majlisī, *Biḥār*, 47:278–287.

42 ʿĪsā b. Zayd and Jaʿfar al-Ṣādiq: al-Kulaynī, *al-Kāfī*, 1:362–363; al-Majlisī, *Biḥār*, 47:283–285; see also al-Amīn, *Mustadrakāt*, 1:71.

> killer (literally: he is your master [فهو والله صاحبك]), may God have no pity on his decayed bones.[43]

In the actual description of the battle by Mūsā b. ʿAbdallāh following the "apocalyptic description" depicting the events after the defeat of Yazīd b. Muʿāwiya b. ʿAbdallāh b. Jaʿfar, who was in charge of Muḥammad b. ʿAbdallāh's vanguard, we read the following:

> ʿĪsā b. Mūsā reached Medina, and the battle (literally: the killing) started in Medina, and he encamped in Dhubāb. The ʿAbbāsī contingents came upon us from behind. Muḥammad came out with his supporters (*aṣḥābihi*), and proceeded until he reached the market where he left his supporters and went away. Then he followed them until he reached the Mosque of al-Khawwāmīn[?] and looked around at the empty courtyard (*al-faḍāʾ*), which had no ʿAbbāsī soldier and no rebel; he proceeded until he reached Shiʿb Fazāra, then he entered (the quarter of) Hudhayl, then he continued to Ashjaʿ (quarter), then the horseman, about whom Abū ʿAbdallāh (Jaʿfar al-Ṣādiq), peace be upon him, talked, came out behind him, from Sikkat Hudhayl, and speared him but did not do him any harm; Muḥammad attacked the horseman and struck the edge of his nose with his sword; the horseman speared him (Muḥammad) and pierced his armor, but Muḥammad bent over him, struck him and fatally wounded him. Then Ḥumayd b. Qaḥṭaba came out against him—while he [that is, Muḥammad] was preoccupied with striking the horseman—from al-ʿAmmārīn lane—and struck him once with his spear and the spear's teeth penetrated his armor, and the spear was broken; Muḥammad attacked Ḥumayd but Ḥumayd stabbed him with the pointed iron foot (*zujj*) of the spear and knocked him down, then (he dismounted and) went towards him, gave him the fatal stroke, killed him and took his head. The (ʿAbbāsī) army entered (the city) from every corner, Medina

---

43 Al-Kulaynī, *al-Kāfī*, 1:363; Ibn Ḥamza al-Ṭūsī, *al-Thāqib fī l-manāqib*, 409; al-Māzandarānī, *Sharḥ*, 6:316; al-Majlisī, *Biḥār*, 47:285; al-Baḥrānī, *Madīnat al-maʿājiz*, 5:285:
لكأني بك خارجا من سدة أشجع إلى بطن الوادي وقد حمل عليك فارس معلم في يده طرادة نصفها أبيض ونصفها أسود, على فرس كميت أقرح, فطعنك فلم يصنع فيك شيئا وضربت خيشوم فرسه فطرحته, وحمل عليك آخر خارج من زقاق آل أبي عمار الدئليين, عليه غديرتان مضفورتان وقد خرجتا من تحت بيضته, كثير شعر الشاربين فهو والله صاحبك, فلا رحم الله رمته.

> was taken by force and we fled out of fear and became dispersed in the countries.[44]

It is noteworthy that some place names that are mentioned in this long tradition also appear in the preceding traditions. It is also remarkable that Ḥumayd b. Qaḥṭaba is described as having a heavy bushy mustache and two plaits.

3.1 *Mūsā b. ʿAbdallāh*

The tradition was related by Mūsā b. ʿAbdallāh, Muḥammad b. ʿAbdallāh's brother. Mūsā was one of his brother's most loyal supporters.[45] At the end of the rebellion he fled with Muḥammad b. ʿAbdallāh's other supporters, was caught, brought to the caliph in Baghdad and whipped but not executed. There are, however, other different, contradicting testimonies on this matter. Al-Kulaynī remarks that Mūsā became very close and loyal to Mūsā b. Jaʿfar al-Ṣādiq's family and gained favor and benefited from his connections with them.[46]

---

44 Al-Kulaynī, *al-Kāfī*, 1:364–365; al-Majlisī, *Biḥār*, 47:286; al-Baḥrānī, *Madīnat al-maʿājiz*, 5:287–288; al-Māzandarānī, *Sharḥ*, 6:317:
وقدم عيسى بن موسى المدينة وصار القتال بالمدينة, فنزل بذباب ودخلت علينا المسودة من خلفنا وخرج محمد في أصحابه حتى بلغ السوق /365/ فأوصلهم ومضى ثم تبعهم حتى انتهى إلى مسجد الخوامين فنظر إلى ما هناك فضاء ليس فيه مسود ولا مبيض فاستقدم حتي انتهى إلي شعب فزارة ثم دخل هذيل ثم مضى إلى أشجع فخرج إليه الفارس الذي قال ابو عبد الله عليه السلام من خلفه من سكة هذيل فطعنه فلم يصنع فيه شيئا؛ وحمل على الفارس وضرب خيشوم فرسه بالسيف, فطعنه الفارس فأنفذه في الدرع, وانثنى عليه محمد فضربه فأثخنه. وخرج عليه حميد بن قحطبة -- وهو[= محمد بن عبد الله النفس الزكية] مدبر على الفارس يضربه -- من زقاق العمارين فطعنه طعنة أنفذ السنان فيه فكسر الرمح؛ وحمل على حميد فطعنه حميد بزج الرمح فصرعه, ثم نزل إليه فضربه حتى أثخنه وقتله وأخذ راسه. ودخل الجند من كل جانب وأخذت المدينة وأجلينا هربا في البلاد.

I was unable to find any information regarding the Mosque of al-Khawwāmīn; the word probably derives from *khām*, untanned skin, or unwashed coarse garments, or pieces of white cotton cloth, see, Lane, *Lexicon, kh.y.m*; al-Majlisī, *Biḥār*, 47:295; al-Ṭurayḥī, *Majmaʿ al-Baḥrayn*, 1:714: ومسجد الخوامين: مسجد بنواحي المدينة. والخام جلد لم يدبغ. I was unable to find any information regarding the lane of al-ʿAmmārīn.

45 Al-Kulaynī, *al-Kāfī*, 1:362: Mūsā declares that he was the third person who swore allegiance to his brother; al-Ṭabarī, 3:215–217: he was sent by his brother to conduct propaganda on his behalf in Syria; ibid. 3:202 (ll. 6–8): was sent as a governor of Syria on behalf of his brother.

46 Al-Kulaynī, *al-Kāfī*, 1:362.

Even if the chronological sequence of events regarding Mūsā's wanderings and history is confused (e.g., who gave him the *amān*, al-Manṣūr or al-Mahdī?),[47] more important for the issue at hand is Mūsā b. ʿAbdallāh's adherence to Mūsā b. Jaʿfar al-Ṣādiq's family. It seems that we can understand the tradition dealt with here, that is, Jaʿfar al-Ṣādiq's detailed prophecy regarding the precise manner by which Muḥammad b. ʿAbdallāh was killed. In fact, this is one of several traditions related directly by Mūsā b. ʿAbdallāh—describing the rebellion and the fierce arguments and clashes between Jaʿfar al-Ṣādiq and Muḥammad b. ʿAbdallāh—in which the Ḥusaynīs in general, and Jaʿfar specifically, are presented in a special, most favorable manner.[48] Mūsā concludes his long description by saying: "Mūsā b. Jaʿfar was very generous to me and has rewarded me lavishly. By God I swear, I am their slave (*mawlā*) after God: وجزا موسى بن جعفر عني خيرا وأنا والله مولاهم بعد الله."[49] The Imāmī *rijāl* scholars describe Mūsā as a close associate (*min aṣḥāb*) of Jaʿfar al-Ṣādiq.[50]

3.2 *Analysis of the Tradition*

This tradition was created after the rebellion and its aim was to emphasize the quietist (*quʿūd*) policy of Jaʿfar al-Ṣādiq, that is, his rejection of any sort of participation in the rebellion (see the exhaustive discussion in appendix 3). These descriptions are historically important, and seem to reflect the real course of events. In order to convince his reader that Jaʿfar al-Ṣādiq is the true Imām, the narrator describes the events and adds many small and large details, so that the reader who lived during the actual events and after they occurred and knew the real course of the events would believe in Jaʿfar's esoteric knowledge and recognize him as the true Imām. The unequivocal conclusion of the narrator (the Ḥasanī, Mūsā b. ʿAbdallāh) is to acknowledge Jaʿfar al-Ṣādiq's superiority and that of his family over all other families. He is the *true* Imām of the Muslim community. Even if we are faced here with a complete fabrication (a supposition which in my view is untenable), the geographical-topographical

---

47 Al-Khaṭīb al-Baghdādī, *Taʾrīkh* (Cairo edition), 13:25, supports the first option, that is, Mūsā was captured by Abū Jaʿfar al-Manṣūr after his two brothers were killed; the caliph pardoned him, and he (Mūsā) lived in Baghdad; ibid., 13:26: "as to Mūsā b. ʿAbdallāh, he hid in al-Baṣra and al-Manṣūr caught him and pardoned him."

48 Al-Kulaynī, *al-Kāfī*, 1:362–366.

49 Ibid., 1:366, and the parallel sources quoting him, e.g., al-Majlisī, *Biḥār*, 47:287.

50 E.g., al-Ṭūsī, *Fihrist*, 170; idem, *Rijāl*, 300; al-Māmaqānī, *Rijāl*, 257 no. 12,260; al-Khūʾī, *Rijāl*, 2:55–56.

details add a meaningful basis for a reconstruction of the physical features of Medina in this period.

This battle and the death of Muḥammad b. ʿAbdallāh occurred on Monday, 14 Ramaḍān 145,[51] or 15 Ramaḍān,[52] or on 25 Rajab.[53]

4 The Site Where Muḥammad b. ʿAbdallāh Was Killed

The sources give us names of several places in which Muḥammad was killed. They all may have been close to each other. The most common is:

4.1 *Aḥjār al-Zayt*

This is the most widely-accepted place.[54] The killing and place of death (أحجار الزيت) is often described in a "prophetic" tradition, which is often related on several occasions by Jaʿfar al-Ṣādiq in the framework of the Imāmī traditions that revolve around the struggle for the legitimization of rule between the Ḥasanīs and the Ḥusaynīs.[55] Other traditions are related by Muḥammad b. ʿAbdallāh himself, who knows that he will be killed in Aḥjār al-Zayt,[56] or by members of his family, e.g., his nephew, ʿAbdallāh b. Mūsā b. ʿAbdallāh b. al-Ḥasan, who relates that Muḥammad b. ʿAbdallāh's cousin, ʿAlī b. al-Ḥasan b. al-Ḥasan b. al-Ḥasan knew that "here in Aḥjār al-Zayt al-Nafs al-Zakiyya will be killed." [57]

---

51 Al-Balādhurī, *Ansāb* (ed. Madelung), 2:518; al-Ṭabarī, 3:249 (ll. 2–4): [ʿUmar b. Shabba] < Yaʿqūb b. al-Qāsim < ʿAlī b. Abī Ṭālib [b. Sarḥ, see al-Iṣfahānī, *Maqātil*, 237]: on Monday, after the evening prayer (= al-Iṣfahānī, *Maqātil*, 274–275: before the evening prayer); Ibn Kathīr, *al-Bidāya* (ed. Shīrī), 10:97; al-Dhahabī, *Siyar*, 6:218.

52 Ibn Saʿd, *al-Qism al-mutammim*, 378; al-Ṭabarī, 3:265 (ll. 2–4): from al-Wāqidī, middle of Ramaḍān; al-Fasawī, *Maʿrifa*, 1:125–126; al-Azdī, *Taʾrīkh al-Mawṣil*, 187: Monday, mid-Ramaḍān; Ibn ʿInaba, *ʿUmda*, 105: *wa-qīla*.

53 Ibn ʿInaba, *ʿUmda*, 105: *wa-qīla*; according to the Imāmī tradition, this is the date of the *mabʿath* of the Prophet, see Ibn Ṭāʾūs, *al-Iqbāl bi-l-aʿmāl*, 3:16; Mūsā b. Jaʿfar al-Ṣādiq died on that day, see al-Majlisī, *Biḥār*, 48:206.

54 Al-Ṭabarī, 3:248 (ll. 9, 12); al-Iṣfahānī, *Maqātil*, 272; al-Dhahabī, *Siyar*, 6:218; Ibn ʿInaba, *ʿUmda*, 103, 105.

55 E.g., the case of Abū Salama al-Khallāl, the chief *dāʿī* of the ʿAbbāsīs in al-Kūfa, for example, see al-Yaʿqūbī, *Taʾrīkh* (ed. Houtsma), 2:418; the case of the alleged meeting at al-Abwāʾ, for example, see al-Iṣfahānī, *Maqātil*, 256, 272 (and see chapter 2 (al-Abwāʾ Meeting) and appendix 3).

56 Al-Ṭabarī, 3:248 (ll. 4–12); al-Samhūdī, *Wafāʾ*, 3:311.

57 Al-Iṣfahānī, *Maqātil*, 248.

4.1.1 The Location of Aḥjār al-Zayt

Al-Samhūdī concludes the entry on Aḥjār al-Zayt by saying that two places by that name existed. The first was in Medina, in its old market; the second was in the dwelling area of Banū l-Ashhal in al-Ḥarra, where the battle of al-Ḥarra occurred in 63/683.[58] Both places are connected to bloody events.

4.1.1.1 *Aḥjār al-Zayt within the market of Medina*

This was a well-known place. In the Prophet's time and later on, perhaps even in the ninth century, Aḥjār al-Zayt was located within the market,[59] near al-Zawrāʾ (see below). The Prophet used to perform all kinds of prayers there. The most famous tradition is about the دعاء الإستسقاء (supplication for rain) performed by the Prophet "in Aḥjār al-Zayt near al-Zawrāʾ."[60]

Al-Zawrāʾ was built by ʿUthmān in 27/647–648.[61] Al-Samhūdī records that the forepart of the market of Medina, which began from the end of the courtyard of the Great Mosque and further beyond, was called al-Zawrāʾ.[62] Quoting Ibn Shabba, al-Samhūdī adds that ʿUmar b. al-Khaṭṭab gave al-ʿAbbās b. ʿAbd al-Muṭṭalib "his *dār* that is located in al-Zawrāʾ, [in] the market of Medina near Aḥjār al-Zayt."[63] Al-Samhūdī adds more specific details, saying that "Dār al-ʿAbbās was near the end of the above-mentioned courtyard (al-Balāṭ) [of the

58 Al-Samhūdī, *Wafāʾ*, 4:114–116.

59 Al-Ḥākim al-Naysābūrī, *al-Mustadrak* (Beirut, 1990), 3:571; al-Bayhaqī, *Shuʿab al-īmān*, 6:18 (= al-Suyūṭī, *al-Durr al-manthūr*, 6:221): Diḥya al-Kalbī arrived [in the lifetime of the Prophet] in Medina and "alighted with merchandise in Aḥjār al-Zayt which is [the transmitter explains] a place in the market of Medina": قد نزل بتجارة عند أحجار الزيت وهو مكان في سوق المدينة; Ibn Saʿd, *Ṭabaqāt*, 3:68: during the first *fitna*, "ʿAlī b. Abī Ṭālib goes out from the Great Mosque until he reaches Aḥjār al-Zayt, which is in the market of Medina."

60 The tradition is quoted in many *ḥadīth* compilations, for example, see Ibn Ḥanbal, *Musnad* (Būlāq edition), 5:223, 427; al-Samhūdī, *Wafāʾ*, 4:115: mentioning Abū Dāwūd, al-Tirmidhī, al-Ḥākim al-Naysābūrī, and Ibn Ḥibbān in his *Ṣaḥīḥ*, 3:163 (see the references for Abū Dāwūd's *Sunan* and al-*Mustadrak* of al-Ḥākim al-Naysābūrī in the footnotes of the editor of al-Samhūdī, ibid.); Yāqūt, *Muʿjam* (Beirut edition), 1:109.

61 Al-Yaʿqūbī, *Taʾrīkh* (Beirut edition), 2:166.

62 Al-Samhūdī, *Wafāʾ*, 3:89: أن مقدم سوق المدينة مما يلي خاتمة البلاط وما حول ذلك كان يسمى بالزوراء; see also al-Fīrūzābādī, *al-Maghānim al-muṭāba*, 173: "an elevated site near the market of Medina; and it was said that this is a name of the market of Medina."

63 Al-Samhūdī, *Wafāʾ*, 3:81 (I was unable to find this quote in the published edition of *Taʾrīkh al-Madīna* of Ibn Shabba); Ibn Shabba, *Taʾrīkh al-Madīna*, 1:16: الزوراء عند دار العباس بن عبد المطلب رضه بالسوق.

Great Mosque], and near "Mashhad Sayyidinā Mālik b. Sinān,[64] and to its east (of the Mashhad)... and there was Aḥjār al-Zayt."[65]

4.1.1.1.1 The Connection of Aḥjār al-Zayt in the Market of Medina to Bloody Events

Al-Shaybānī (d. 189/805), quoting traditions from *maghāzī* works (وفي المغازي ذكر), relates that Banū Qurayẓa were killed in the place where Dār Ibn Abī l-Jahm is located; their blood streamed until it reached Aḥjār al-Zayt.[66] Al-Samhūdī quotes a similar tradition from al-Bayhaqī through the transmission of Mūsā b. ʿUqba, the well-known author of the *Maghāzī*, "that the men of Banū Qurayẓa were killed near (*ʿinda*) Dār Abī l-Jahm that is in al-Balāṭ—and in those days al-Balāṭ did not exist—and it was claimed that their blood reached Aḥjār al-Zayt in the market."[67] Ḥuyay b. Akhṭab, the leader of Banū l-Naḍīr, was also executed by the Prophet on that day; "he was taken out to Ahjār al-Zayt which is located in the market, and his head was cut off."[68]

4.1.2 Aḥjār al-Zayt in Ḥarrat Wāqim

The other place named Aḥjār al-Zayt was located in the northeastern lava flow area, in the dwelling area of Banū ʿAbd al-Ashhal (Aws), where the well-known battle of al-Ḥarra took place (in 63/683).[69]

Where was Muḥammad b. ʿAbdallāh Killed?

Al-Samhūdī believes that the well-known tradition according to which the Prophet prophesies to Abū Dharr al-Ghifārī that much bloodshed will occur in Aḥjār al-Zayt, until Aḥjār al-Zayt "will be drowned with blood,"[70] alludes to the dwelling places of Banū ʿAbd al-Ashhal in al-Ḥarra, and to the bloodshed in the

64 A *ṣaḥābī* from the Khazraj, who died in the battle of Uḥud.

65 Al-Samhūdī, *Wafāʾ*, 3:81; my discussion of al-Zawrāʾ is based on the exhaustive discussion in Lecker, "Markets of Medina," 142–146.

66 Al-Shaybānī, *Siyar*, 2:592 (= al-Sarakhsī, *Sharḥ al-Siyar al-kabīr*, 2:173), quoted by Kister, "Banū Qurayẓa," 73, n. 31.

67 Al-Samhūdī, *Wafāʾ*, 3:79; I was not able to find the quotation in al-Bayhaqī's available works; al-Bayhaqī may have transmitted from Mūsā b. ʿUqba's *Maghāzī*; see al-Sarakhsī, *Sharḥ al-Siyar al-kabīr*, 2:591–592: "and it was mentioned in the *Maghāzī*": وفي المغازي ذكر, followed by a similar tradition; Kister, "Banū Qurayẓa," 73, n. 34.

68 Al-Ṭabarānī, *al-Kabīr*, 6:8.

69 Al-Samhūdī, *Wafāʾ*, 4:115–116.

70 Ibid., 4:115; for the *ḥadīth*, see ibid. (the editor's notes); Abū Dāwūd, *Sunan*, 2:305; al-Ḥākim al-Naysābūrī, *al-Mustadrak* (Beirut, 1990), 4:470; al-Bayhaqī, *al-Sunan al-kubrā*, 8:191;

battle of al-Ḥarra in 63/683.[71] Nevertheless, al-Samhūdī does not completely reject the possibility that the first location, that is, the market of Medina, is being referred to here and not al-Ḥarra (as other scholars believed), and that the *ḥadīth* may allude to the killing of Muḥammad al-Nafs al-Zakiyya in Aḥjār al-Zayt.[72]

Whether the tradition of Abū Dharr refers to those who were killed in the battle of al-Ḥarra or to Muḥammad al-Nafs al-Zakiyya and his supporters is not clear, but it seems that other traditions that were circulated may have alluded to Muḥammad al-Nafs al-Zakiyya's death. These traditions are found mainly in the *fitan* and *malāḥim* literature. One such tradition relates "that there will be a campaign in Medina in which Aḥjār al-Zayt will be drowned; compared to this battle (the battle of) al-Ḥarra is but one whip."[73]

4.2 *Mashhad al-Nafs al-Zakiyya in the Market of Medina*

Al-Samhūdī mentions Mashhad al-Nafs al-Zakiyya, which was located on the way to Thaniyyat al-Wadāʿ, near the water cistern (*birka*) of Medina.[74] It is unlikely that the Mashhad was built in honor of al-Nafs al-Zakiyya at the place that he was killed, that is, in Aḥjār al-Zayt in the market of Medina, because al-Samhūdī mentions this Mashhad as one of the three well-known Mashhads that were not in the main ancient cemetery of the city, Baqīʿ al-Gharqad.[75] When and by whom it was built is not known.

4.3 *Bayt Rūmī (A Byzantine House [?])*

According to a tradition recorded by al-Ṭabarī, Umm Ḥusayn bt. ʿAbdallāh b. Muḥammad b. ʿAlī b. al-Ḥusayn b. ʿAlī b. Abī Ṭālib (the mother of ʿĪsā b. ʿAbdallāh b. Muḥammad b. ʿUmar b. ʿAlī b. Abī Ṭālib) asked Jaʿfar al-Ṣādiq's opinion in regard to Muḥammad b. ʿAbdallāh, to which Jaʿfar answers that "this is a *fitna*; Muḥammad will be killed in it near a Byzantine house

al-ʿAẓīmābādī, *ʿAwn al-maʿbūd*, 11:228; al-Shawkānī, *Nayl al-awṭār*, 6:77; al-Mizzī, *Tahdhīb*, 28:10.

71 Al-Samhūdī, *Wafāʾ*, 4:115–116.

72 Ibid., 4:116.

73 Nuʿaym b. Ḥammād, *al-Fitan* 201; al-Barazanjī, *al-Ishāʿa*, 116; al-Sulamī, *ʿIqd al-durar*, 56–57; al-Suyūṭī, *al-ʿUrf al-wardī*, 2:71; al-Haytamī, *Mukhtaṣar*, 57.

74 Al-Samhūdī, *Wafāʾ*, 3:135; see also ibid., 3:91, 310; 400, quoting al-Maṭarī [Muḥammad b. Aḥmad, d. 741/1340], who mentions the grave (*qabr*) of al-Nafs al-Zakiyya outside the city.

75 Al-Samhūdī, *Wafāʾ*, 3:310.

(عند بيت رومي), and his brother from both his father's and his mother's side will be killed in al-ʿIrāq."[76]

4.4 *Ghanāʾim Khashram*

One of Muḥammad b. ʿAbdallāh's supporters reports in the first person "I was with Muḥammad b. ʿAbdallāh in Ghanāʾim Khashram when he told me: here al-Nafs al-Zakiyya will be killed. He said: and he was killed there."[77] This place[?] is mentioned with a different name (Mafātiḥ Khashram instead of Ghanāʾim Khashram) as a place where the two armies fought.[78]

Muḥammad's head was brought to ʿĪsā b. Mūsā,[79] who sent it to al-Manṣūr with Muḥammad b. Abī l-Karrām. ʿĪsā also sent al-Qāsim b. al-Ḥasan b. Zayd with him to inform the caliph about the victory.[80] The head reached al-Kūfa, where the caliph stayed, was put on a white tray and was displayed in the streets.[81] The next evening it was sent to the provinces with "a man (commander?) from the *ahl Khurāsān* (troops), from Banū Qarīʿ who belong to Banū Tamīm," who traveled with the head as far as Samarqand, and then went back to al-ʿIrāq with it. The same commander[?] did the same with Ibrāhīm's head. The two heads remained in al-Qarīʿī's possession, who buried them under the stairs (a stair?: *daraja*) in his house in Baghdad, which was in Abū Ḥanīfa's road

76 Al-Ṭabarī, 3:253–254 (l. 18 to l. 3) (= al-Iṣfahānī, *Maqātil*, 248): ʿUmar b. Shabba < ʿĪsā b. ʿAbdallāh < his mother Umm al-Ḥusayn; I am unable to identify this Bayt Rūmī.

77 Al-Iṣfahānī, *Maqātil*, 248–249.

78 Al-Ṭabarī, 3:240 (l. 18); I was unable to locate this site; several Arabs from al-Khazraj from Medina are named Khashram, see for example al-Dhahabī, *Taʾrīkh*, 15:354: Qudāma b. Muḥammad b. Qudāma b. Khashram al-Ashjaʿī l-Madanī; Ibn Ḥazm, *Jamhara*, 359: Khashram b. al-Ḥubāb b. al-Mundhir ... b. Kaʿb b. Salima; his father carried the flag in the battle of Badr, and his son Khashram fought at al-Ḥudaybiyya; and see also, al-Amīn, *Aʿyān al-Shīʿa*, 6:321 for other Madanīs from the Khazraj named Khashram. It seems that the meaning in the quoted texts is a toponym. The only source mentioning Khashram is Ibn Shabba, *Taʾrīkh al-Madīna*, 1:268: "Banū Mālik b. Ḥimār and Banū Zunaym and Banū Sukayn—who belong to Banū Fazāra b. Dhubyān b. Baghīḍ b. Ghayth b. Ghaṭafān—settled in the quarter named 'Banū Fazāra,' which is in front of (قبالة) Khashram, stretching further to Ḥammām al-Ṣaʿba, then to the woodsellers' market, which is in al-Jabbāna"; al-Samhūdī, *Wafāʾ*, 3:103, copies Ibn Shabba's text but omits the phrase "in front of Khashram."

79 Al-Ṭabarī, 3:265 (ll. 4–5).

80 Ibid., 3:252 (ll. 13–14); al-Iṣfahānī, *Maqātil*, 275.

81 Al-Ṭabarī, 3:254 (ll. 16–19); al-Iṣfahānī, *Maqātil*, 276: partial parallel tradition.

adjacent to Bāb al-Manṣūr. The transmitter of the tradition, ʿAlī b. Muḥammad (al-Madāʾinī?), remarks that "I had seen this/these stair/s."[82]

The heads of Banū Shujāʿ, the most loyal supporters of Muḥammad b. ʿAbdallāh, who did not desert him and fought with him until the end, were also sent to al-Manṣūr.[83]

4.5 *Muḥammad b. ʿAbdallāh's Burial Place*

Muḥammad's body remained where he was killed during a rainy night. During that night his body was plundered. The next morning, his sister, Zaynab and his daughter Fāṭima asked ʿĪsā's permission to bury him.[84] His neck was filled with cotton and he was buried in al-Baqīʿ (al-Gharqad) cemetery, "his grave [adds the transmitter] facing the alley of ʿAlī b. Abī Ṭālib situated on the main road or close to it."[85] Another tradition may give the Ḥasanī version of the location of his place of burial. According to this tradition, Muḥammad b. ʿAbdallāh tells his sister before the last campaign, to bury his headless body (for he knows for certain that his head will be cut off) at a distance of four or five cubits (*adhruʿ*) from the roofed enclosure (*ẓulla*) of Banū Nubayh.[86] They obeyed his wish and when they dug his grave they found a rock on which was engraved "this is the grave of al-Ḥasan b. ʿAlī b. Abī Ṭālib." Zaynab [his sister] said: May God have

---

82 Al-Azdī, *Taʾrīkh al-Mawṣil*, 194; al-Balādhurī, *Ansāb* (ed. Madelung), 2:536: a short summary of the long tradition in al-Azdī's work. It is highly plausible that this man from *ahl Khurāsān* was a commander.

83 Al-Ṭabarī, 3:254–255 (l. 20 to l. 3).

84 Al-Balādhurī, *Ansāb* (ed. Madelung), 2:516: only his daughter is mentioned; al-Ṭabarī, 3:252–253 (l. 15 to l. 3).

85 Al-Ṭabarī, 3:253 (ll. 1–3): ودفن في البقيع وكان قبره تجاه زقاق دار علي بن أبي طالب أو قريبا من ذلك; Baqīʿ al-Gharqad was the first central Muslim cemetery in Medina; it was located within the city. Al-Fīrūzābādī, *al-Maghānim al-muṭāba*, 61, remarks that in his days (he died in 823/1415), it was outside the walls of the city, while Yāqūt (d. 626/1229), *Muʿjam* (Beirut edition), 1:473, remarks that it was within the city; for a long and detailed description of those early Muslims who were buried in Baqīʿ al-Gharqad, see al-Samhūdī, *Wafāʾ*, 3:268ff.; see further, *EI*², s.v. "Baqīʿ al-Gharqad" (A. J. Wensink and A. S. Bazmee Ansari)

86 Nubayh b. Wahb b. ʿUthmān b. Abī Ṭalḥa [ʿAbdallāh] b. ʿAbd al-ʿUzzā b. ʿUthmān b. ʿAbd al-Dār al-ʿAbdarī l-Qurashī l-Madanī; on him, see al-Dhahabī, *Mīzān* (Beirut, 1995), 8:199; Ibn Ḥajar, *Lisān*, 7:345; idem, *Tahdhīb* (Beirut, 1984), 10:373; idem, *al-Iṣāba* (Beirut, 1415 H.), 6:333–334; for this lineage, see al-Zubayrī, *Nasab Quraysh*, 250ff. (Nubayh is not mentioned though); he is mentioned, ibid., 72; cf. Ibn Ḥibbān, *al-Thiqāt*, 7:545, and al-Ṭabarī, 1:1099, 1337: a different lineage: Nubayh b. Wahb b. ʿĀmir b. ʿIkrima al-ʿAbdarī (is he the same person?).

mercy on my brother, he was most knowledgeable when he conveyed his (last) wish to be buried in this place."[87]

This Ḥasanī version aims at praising Muḥammad b. ʿAbdallāh and showing his supernatural traits when he directs his sister to bury him near his great-grandfather, al-Ḥasan b. ʿAlī. On the face of it, this seems to be a sheer Ḥasanī invention. Otherwise, we have to believe that in 145/762 the location of al-Ḥasan's grave was not known even to members of his close family. Moreover, according to this story, there was no epitaph of al-Ḥasan's grave over the burial spot.

But it is highly probable that the tradition indicates the place where Muḥammad b. ʿAbdallāh's body was buried. According to the Muslim tradition, al-Ḥasan b. ʿAlī was buried in al-Baqīʿ, near Fāṭima, his mother. Abū l-Faraj al-Iṣfahānī records that al-Ḥasan was buried "at the side of Fāṭima's grave … in the Baqīʿ, in the Banū Nubayh's roofed (covered) enclosure": في جنب قبر فاطمة...في البقيع في ظلة بني نبيه.[88] Fāṭima was buried "in the corner (*zāwiya*) of Dār ʿAqīl which is adjacent to Dār al-Jaḥshiyyīn, in front of the passageway (*khawkha*) of Banū Nubayh, of the Banū ʿAbd al-Dār [of Quraysh], in al-Baqīʿ, and between her grave and the (main) road there is a distance of seven cubits."[89]

Ibn Shabba further describes that "al-Ḥasan was buried in the cemetery next to Fāṭima facing the passageway (*khawkha*) that extends from [or is within?] Nubayh b. Wahb's dwelling, and the (main) road of the people runs between

---

87 Al-Iṣfahānī, *Maqātil*, 272: instead of the grave of al-Ḥusayn b. ʿAlī read al-Ḥasan b. ʿAlī [in the Najaf 1965 edition, 183, and in the parallel tradition in Ibn Abī l-Ḥadīd, *Sharḥ* (Cairo, 1959–1964), 3:308: al-Ḥasan]. Al-Ḥasan was buried in the main cemetery of Medina, Baqīʿ al-Gharqad, see W. Madelung, "Ḥasan b. ʿAlī," *EIr*, 12:28 (see discussion below); Ḥusayn's body was buried in Karbalāʾ, see idem, "Ḥosayn b. ʿAlī," *EIr*, 12:497; *ẓulla* (see Lane, *Lexicon*, s.v. *ẓ.l.l.*) is anything that forms a covering over one; it is equivalent to *ṣuffa* or *saqīfa*, which is rendered (ibid, s.v. *ṣ.f.f.*): "a roof, or covering for shade and shelter, over the door of the house; or extending from a house to another house opposite the residence." Saqīfat Banī Sāʿida in Medina, where Abū Bakr was elected caliph, is also called Ẓullat Banī Sāʿida, for instance, see al-Ṭabarī, 1:1819 (l. 7) (trans. Poonawala), 9:188: "a roofed building of the Banū Sāʿidah"; this expression is much more common among the Imāmīs, e.g., al-Kulaynī, *al-Kāfī*, 4:8–9; al-Baḥrānī, *Madīnat al-maʿājiz*, 2:242; al-Majlisī, *Biḥār*, 28:262–263; 30:138.

88 Al-Iṣfahānī, *Maqātil*, 74.

89 Ibn Saʿd, *Ṭabaqāt*, 8:30:في زاوية دار عقيب [= عقيل] مما يلي دار الجحشيين مستقبل خرجة [= خوخة] بني نبيه من بني عبد الدار بالبقيع وبين قبرها وبين الطريق سبعة أذرع; al-Ṭabarī, 3:2436, a parallel tradition: the correction for *ʿAqīl* and *khawkha* is according to al-Ṭabarī's version and Ibn Shabba, *Taʾrīkh al-Madīna*, 1:106–107.

her grave and the passageway of Nubayh."[90] Some of the Prophet's wives were buried near the passageway of Nubayh (*khawkhat Nubayh*).[91]

5 The ʿAbbāsīs' First Actions after the Suppression of the Revolt

Immediately after the battle ended and Muḥammad b. ʿAbdallāh was killed, ʿĪsā b. Mūsā ordered most of his army contingents to leave the city, and, with the exception of Kathīr b. Ḥuṣayn and his units, not to stay the night there. ʿĪsā himself left for al-Jurf (where he had encamped a few days before), and stayed there until the next morning.[92]

The next morning, ʿĪsā arrived in Medina, gave permission to bury Muḥammad b. ʿAbdallāh, and ordered that his (dead) soldiers (*aṣḥābuhu*) be crucified in two rows from Thaniyyat al-Wadāʿ up to Dār ʿUmar b. ʿAbd al-ʿAzīz. A special guard was posted over the crucified body of Ibn Khuḍayr al-Zubayrī in order to prevent it being snatched, but this was in vain; his body was taken and hidden (and not found). The other soldiers remained crucified for three days. This caused the people of Medina great distress and suffering, so "ʿĪsā ordered the bodies thrown into the open area (*mafraj*) on Mount Salʿ, which is [adds the transmitter] the graveyard of the Jews. They were left there (for some time) and then they were thrown into a trench at the foot of Mount Dhubāb."[93] ʿĪsā b. Mūsā ordered that flags be posted on the gates of five of the houses of dignitaries of Medina: **1)** Asmāʾ bt. al-Ḥasan b. ʿAbdallāh [b. ʿUbaydallāh b. al-ʿAbbās b. ʿAbd al-Muṭṭalib]; **2)** al-ʿAbbās b. ʿAbdallāh b. al-Ḥārith [b. al-ʿAbbās b. ʿAbd al-Muṭṭalib]; **3)** Muḥammad b. ʿAbd al-ʿAzīz al-Zuhrī; **4)** ʿUbaydallāh

---

90 Ibid., 107: فدفن في المقبرة إلى جنب فاطمة مواجه الخوخة التي في دار نبيه بن وهب, طريق الناس بين قبرها و بين خوخة نبيه; ibid., 105 (= al-Samhūdī, *Wafāʾ*, 3:281): "the grave of Fāṭima faces the lane (*zuqāq*) of Nubayh; or "the grave of Fāṭima is in front of Dār ʿAqīl, near Dār Nubayh"; Ibn Shabba, *Taʾrīkh al-Madīna*, 1:106 (= al-Samhūdī, *Wafāʾ*, 3:281): "Fāṭima's grave (*rḍaʿ*) is at the exit of the lane that is between Dār ʿAqīl and Dār Abī Nubayh."

91 Al-Samhūdī, *Wafāʾ*, 3:295; 296 (*khawkhat āl Nubayh b. Wahb*); see also 3:212: "at the outset of al-Baqīʿ is a lane known as Nubayh's Lane and a passageway known as the passageway of the family of Nubayh": زقاقا يعرف بزقاق نبيه وخوخة تعرف بخوخة آل نبيه. Ibid., 3:211–212: a house (*bayt*) called Nubayh is mentioned, located at the site of the *uṭum* called Mishʿaṭ of Banū Ḥudayla (of Banū l-Najjār of the Khazraj). The *uṭum* was erected west of their mosque, called the Mosque of Ubayy b. Kaʿb; there are several readings of the *uṭum*, cf. al-Bakrī, *Muʿjam*, 4:1226: Musʿuṭ; al-Fīrūzābādī, *al-Maghānim al-muṭāba*, 382: Mashʿaṭ.

92 Al-Ṭabarī, 3:252 (ll. 11–13).

93 Ibid., 3:253 (ll. 11–18): [ʿUmar b. Shabba] < Azhar b. Saʿīd, an eyewitness report; text: *mafraḥ*, instead of *mafraj*, see McAuliffe, *ʿAbbāsid Authority*, 218, n. 1026.

b. Muḥammad b. Ṣafwān; and 5) Abū ʿAmr al-Ghifārī. His herald announced that whoever entered under the flags of one of these houses would be under the protection of the ʿAbbāsīs. This helped to pacify the city, and the next morning the markets were opened and business was conducted peacefully.[94] Al-Balādhurī (al-Madāʾinī?) explains that these acts (the amnesty) were done by ʿĪsā b. Mūsā upon al-Manṣūr's orders,[95] while another source relates that ʿĪsā gave a general amnesty to all the people.[96]

5.1 *Acts of Killing and Robbing by the Contingents of the ʿAbbāsī Army*

It seems that the picture drawn by these sources is far from reflecting the real course of events.

After the ʿAbbāsī victory, the ʿAbbāsī troops carried out acts of killing and robbery in Medina. One of those killed was Abū l-Shadāʾid Fāliḥ b. Maʿmar al-Fazārī, a blind satirical poet. When his head was brought to ʿĪsā, he sent a herald to the streets proclaiming that whoever comes in with a head will have his own head cut off.[97] This order most probably implies that such acts were not uncommon after the battle ended. The source telling about the killing of the poet presents it as a casual act by the ʿAbbāsī soldiers, certainly not one ordered by ʿĪsā b. Mūsā. We know almost nothing about this satirical poet. Was he a keen supporter of al-Nafs al-Zakiyya who composed satirical poems against the ʿAbbāsīs? One testimony describes him against a different historical background unrelated to the rebellion, satirizing the people of Medina and presenting ʿĪsā b. Mūsā in an unfavorable light.[98]

5.2 *The Persecution of Members of the Ḥasanī Family and other Supporters of the Rebellion*

Indeed, the sources record that the *amān* did not include all the active supporters of the rebellion. Al-Manṣūr's governors in Medina and other cities did not cease to persecute ʿAbdallāh b. al-Ḥasan's relatives,[99] and other notables

94 Al-Ṭabarī, 3:253 (ll. 3–11); see also al-Balādhurī, *Ansāb* (ed. Madelung), 2:516.

95 Ibid.

96 Al-Ṭabarī, 3:265 (l. 6): وآمن الناس كلهم; al-Balādhurī, *Ansāb* (ed. Madelung), 2:518: وآمن عيسى الناس.

97 Al-Ṭabarī, 3:251 (ll. 9–13).

98 Al-Iṣfahānī, *al-Aghānī* (Būlāq edition), 15:34–35 (Dār al-Kutub edition, 16:243); Ibn ʿAsākir, *Taʾrīkh*, 48:17–18 (a parallel tradition); see on him, also al-Iṣfahānī, *al-Aghānī*, 18:95 (Būlāq edition, 20:2); Sezgin, 2:647 (mentioning *al-Aghānī* and al-Ṭabarī); McAuliffe, *ʿAbbāsid Authority*, 160, n. 775.

99 Al-Ṭabarī, 3:438 (ll. 5–6).

who took an active part in the rebellion, such as members of the Zubayrī family,[100] or the descendants of ʿUmar b. al-Khaṭṭāb.[101] This policy was also applied to the supporters of Ibrāhīm's revolt in al-Baṣra.[102] It lasted and was in force during al-Manṣūr's entire reign. Al-Ṭabarī relates from al-Faḍl b. Sulaymān [b. ʿAlī l-ʿAbbāsī?] al-Hāshimī from his father, that in 157/773–774 (a year before al-Manṣūr's death), the *muḥtasib* of Baghdad gathered a group against al-Manṣūr; the reason for this was "that al-Manṣūr was pursuing those who had rebelled with Muḥammad and Ibrāhīm, sons of ʿAbdallāh b. al-Ḥasan." This *muḥtasib* had had some connections with them.[103] Some of these supporters stayed in hiding for a long time before they were caught, e.g., the family of Jaʿfar b. Abī Ṭālib, among them al-Ḥasan b. Muʿāwiya, the governor of Mecca appointed by Muḥammad b. ʿAbdallāh. Al-Ḥasan, and his other kinfolk came out from their hiding place in Medina during the governorship of Jaʿfar b. Sulaymān b. ʿAlī l-ʿAbbāsī. But even then, Jaʿfar ordered al-Ḥasan to be whipped, and sent him to jail where he stayed until Abū Jaʿfar al-Manṣūr's death (158/775). The governor also severely punished those who sheltered al-Ḥasan b. Muʿāwiya.[104]

Jaʿfar b. Sulaymān al-ʿAbbāsī undoubtedly acted on al-Manṣūr's orders and instructions. Muṣʿab b. ʿAbdallāh al-Zubayrī recorded the version of the instruction of al-Manṣūr to Jaʿfar b. Sulaymān upon his appointment as governor of Medina: "Look out for those who rebelled with Muḥammad b. ʿAbdallāh from among Quraysh and put them in prison; and whoever rebelled with him from among the ʿArabs, whip him; and whoever rebelled from among the *mawālī*, cut off his hand."[105]

The governor was prepared to carry out al-Manṣūr's instructions without reservation or hesitation. Thus, he ordered cutting off the hand of Muḥammad b. ʿAjlān Abū ʿAbdallāh *mawlā* Fāṭima bt. al-Walīd b. ʿUtba b. Rabīʿa (Quraysh),

---

100 Ibid., 3:262–264.

101 For example, see Ibn Saʿd, *al-Qism al-Mutammim*, 367–368; al-Ṭabarī, 3:264–265 (a member of ʿUbayd b. ʿUwayj b. ʿAdī b. Kaʿb).

102 Al-Ṭabarī, 3:327 (ll. 1–5): in 146/763 al-Manṣūr orders Salm b. Qutayba to demolish the houses of those who rebelled with Ibrāhīm and to uproot their palm groves.

103 Al-Ṭabarī, 3:324; the translation after Kennedy, *al-Manṣūr and al-Mahdī*, 9; I was unable to find any source upon which to establish my supposition that the transmitter, al-Faḍl b. Sulaymān al-Hāshimī, is a descendant of ʿAlī b. ʿAbdallāh b. al-ʿAbbās.

104 Al-Iṣfahānī, *Maqātil*, 301–302.

105 Al-Zubayr b. Bakkār, *al-Muwaffaqiyyāt*, 186: أنظر من خرج مع محمد بن عبد الله من قريش فاسجنه، ومن خرج معه من العرب فاجلده، ومن خرج من الموالي فاقطع يده; for the attitude of the first ʿAbbāsīs towards the *mawālī*, see Elad, "Transition," 118–127.

a well-known and important Medinan scholar (d. 148 or 149/765 or 766 or 767 in Egypt). It was only by the intervention of the most important *fuqahā*ʾ and notables of Medina that this sentence was not carried out.[106] Another example of the complete adherence to these instructions is the case of one of Muḥammad's supporters, the *ḥadīth* scholar, ʿAbdallāh b. ʿAṭāʾ b. Yaʿqūb *mawlā* Banū Sibāʿ, who remained in hiding and died in his hiding place. When his body was taken to the cemetery Jaʿfar b. Sulaymān ordered it to be removed from the bier and crucified; he permitted it to be buried only after three days.[107] This undoubtedly reflects his importance in the rebellion to both Muḥammad b. ʿAbdallāh's camp and the ʿAbbāsī's. He and his nine(!) children took part in the rebellion.

5.3 *Maritime Blockade*

Al-Manṣūr ordered a total economic maritime blockade of Medina that lasted until his death. As long as he lived, nothing was transported to the city by sea from al-Jār, the main port that served Medina. When al-Mahdī became caliph he put an end to this maritime blockade.[108] This interesting and most valuable tradition was related to al-Ṭabarī through ʿUmar b. Shabba from Hishām b. Ibrāhīm b. Hishām b. Rāshid al-Hamadhānī l-ʿAbbāsī, a scholar who was the tutor of al-ʿAbbās b. al-Maʾmūn.

5.4 *The Confiscation of Banū l-Ḥasan's and Jaʿfar al-Ṣādiq's Estates*

Another immediate action that was taken by ʿĪsā b. Mūsā after Muḥammad b. ʿAbdallāh's death was the confiscation of all the estates of Banū l-Ḥasan: أموال بني الحسن كلها; this was approved by the caliph.[109] As part of the punitive actions against the Ḥasanīs, the palm groves in their estate in Suwayqa were cut down.[110] Several years later, al-Manṣūr ordered that the Ḥasanīs be

106 Ibn Saʿd, *al-Qism al-mutammim*, 355–356 (from al-Wāqidī?); al-Iṣfahānī, *Maqātil*, 289 (= al-Suyūṭī, *Taʾrīkh*, 289); Abū l-ʿArab, *Kitāb al-miḥan*, 413.

107 Al-Iṣfahānī, *Maqātil*, 286, 297; see also al-Ṭabarī, 3:260 (ll. 3–6).

108 Al-Ṭabarī, 3:257 (ll. 13–16); الجار: ibid., footnote g) Codd. *al-x-iḥār*; ed. Abū l-Faḍl Ibrāhīm, 7:xx: *al-biḥār*; on al-Jār, see A. Dietrich, "al-Djār," *EI*[2]; besides the sources quoted by Dietrich, see also al-Fīrūzābādī, *al-Maghānim al-muṭāba*, 177–178, quoting the text of ʿArrām b. al-Aṣbagh al-Sulamī (d. ca. 275/888: *Asmāʾ jibāl Tihāma wa-sukkānihā*...; on him, see al-Ziriklī, *al-Aʿlām*, 4:223) through Abū l-Ashʿath ʿAbd al-Raḥmān b. Muḥammad b. ʿAbd al-Malik al-Kindī; see the comments of Ḥamad al-Jāsir to al-Ḥāzimī, *al-Amākin*, 1:177–179, n. 2; see also al-Samhūdī, *Wafāʾ*, 4:202.

109 Al-Ṭabarī, 3:257 (ll. 2–5); al-Azdī, *Taʾrīkh al-Mawṣil*, 193.

110 Al-Iṣfahānī, *Maqātil*, 298: from Ibrāhīm b. ʿAbdallāh b. al-Ḥasan relating that he met Mūsā b. ʿAbdallāh (his brother) who led him to Suwayqa to look at the palm trees that

given back their estates. According to one tradition, it was during the *ḥajj*, most probably of 152/769, that ʿĀtika bt. ʿAbd al-Malik al-Makhzūmiyya, ʿAbdallāh b. al-Ḥasan's wife, petitioned the caliph in Mecca and asked him to return their estates to them. On the order of the caliph, the governor of Medina, al-Ḥasan b. Zayd, returned their estates.[111] From this tradition and another with a different *isnād* (though both traditions were related by members of the Ṭālibī family),[112] we learn that ʿĪsā, Sulaymān, and Idrīs, the sons of ʿAbdallāh b. al-Ḥasan from his Makhzūmī wife, ʿĀtika bt. ʿAbd al-Malik, quarreled with the sons of their brother Muḥammad b. ʿAbdallāh about their father's inheritance, saying, "Your father Muḥammad was killed and ʿAbdallāh had made him his heir."[113] They took the dispute to al-Ḥasan b. Zayd [the governor], who, in turn, wrote to the Commander of the Faithful, Abū Jaʿfar, about the matter. The caliph replied as follows: "When this letter of mine reaches you, make them the heirs of their grandfather."[114] In another version of the tradition al-Manṣūr answered that the estates would be given back and divided according to ʿAbdallāh b. al-Ḥasan's

were cut down. The *isnād* is most probably garbled; Ibrāhīm b. ʿAbdallāh at that time was in al-Baṣra, preparing his revolt (see the remark of ʿUmar b. Shabba at the end of the long tradition, ibid., 299 (l. 9): "Abū Zayd said I transmitted or dictated this tradition to al-Madāʾinī but he criticised my narration [declared that my *isnād* is not sound] and found the two transmitters unreliable, saying: Mūsā has said" [that is, the only reliable transmitter is Mūsā b. ʿAbdallāh]: قال أبو زيد: حدثت المدائني هذا أو أمليت عليه فتركني وترك الرجلين وقال: قال موسى. It is possible to correct the *isnād* according to al-Bakrī, *Muʿjam*, 3:768:... Ismāʿīl b. Jaʿfar b. Ibrāhīm from Mūsā b. ʿAbdallāh b. al-Ḥasan; ibid., another tradition from an eyewitness, Saʿīd b. ʿUqba, a relation of the Ḥasanīs, who witnessed the destruction of Suwayqa.

111 Al- Iṣfahānī, *Maqātil*, 396–397; al-Iṣfahānī recorded the traditions through two chains of transmitters, the first through ʿUmar b. Shabba < ʿĪsā b. ʿAbdallāh, and the second:... Yaḥyā b. al-Ḥasan < Ismāʿīl b. Yaʿqūb; al-Manṣūr performed the *ḥajj* in 144/762, 147/765, and 152/769. Al-Ḥasan b. Zayd was appointed as the governor of Medina only in 150/767 or 768 (al-Ṭabarī, 3:359); according to Ibn Khayyāṭ, *Taʾrīkh* (Beirut, 1993), 353, in Ramaḍān 149/October–November 766.

112 Al-Ṭabarī, 3:257–258 (l. 16 to l. 5); the transmission is through the half-brother of Mūsā b. ʿAbdallāh b. al-Ḥasan, Muḥammad al-Nafs al-Zakiyya's brother: [ʿUmar b. Shabba] < Muḥammad b. Jaʿfar b. Ibrāhīm < his mother [Umm Salama bt. Muḥammad b. Ṭalḥa b. ʿAbdallāh b. ʿAbd al-Raḥmān b. Abī Bakr, the wife of Mūsā b. ʿAbdallāh].

113 Ibid., 3:258 (ll. 2–3); I relied on McAuliffe's translation, *ʿAbbāsid Authority*, 223; ibid., n. 1054, McAuliffe explains (quoting Schacht, *Islamic Law*, 170), that "Because there is no right of representation in Sunnī law, Muḥammad's sons would have had no de jure entitlement to their deceased father's inheritance from his father."

114 Al-Ṭabarī, 3:258 (ll. 3–4) (trans. McAuliffe).

decree.[115] The caliph was the supreme authority with regard to any judicial or religious decision.

5.5 *The Confiscation of Jaʿfar al-Ṣādiq's Estate*

Among the estates confiscated by ʿĪsā was one belonging to Jaʿfar al-Ṣādiq, ʿAyn Abī Ziyād.[116] It was only returned to him by Caliph al-Mahdī.[117]

Jaʿfar's estate[118] was confiscated after Muḥammad b. ʿAbdallāh's death.[119] Caliph al-Mahdī did not pursue his father's harsh policy against the Ṭālibīs. Upon becoming caliph, he performed the *ḥajj*, and on his way he visited Medina and distributed money lavishly among the Quraysh, the Anṣār and the rest of the people and gave them valuable presents. This he did after the troubles and the difficulties endured by the people during his father's reign, because they hastened (*li-tasarruʿihim*) to join Muḥammad b. ʿAbdallāh b. al-Ḥasan.[120] As already noted, al-Mahdī abolished the maritime blockade of Medina. He also initiated important construction projects in the Prophet's Mosque in Medina. Such enterprises had not been previously carried out in Medina by his father, al-Manṣūr.[121]

---

115 Al-Iṣfahānī, *Maqātil*, 396–397.

116 For the location of ʿAyn Abī Ziyād, see Ibn Shabba, *Taʾrīkh al-Madīna*, 1:172: further after the meeting of the *wādīs* of Medina; al-Bakrī, *Muʿjam*, 4:1333: in the *ʿāliya* of Medina; al-Samhūdī, *Wafāʾ*, 4:397: at the bottom of al-Ghāba, towards the meeting of the *wādīs* of Medina; this site was developed by Muʿāwiya b. Abī Sufyān, who dug the well of the spring, and also canals from the water source, see Ibn Qutayba, *Taʾwīl*, 142.

117 Al-Ṭabarī, 3:257 (ll. 12–13); and see also appendix 3.

118 The sources mention one estate, ʿAyn Abī Ziyād. Ibn al-Athīr, *al-Kāmil* (Beirut edition), 5:553, combines two different traditions, the one which tells of the confiscation of the Ḥasanīs' estates with that which tells of the confiscation of Jaʿfar al-Ṣādiq's estate. Instead of one estate he mentions estates.

119 Al-Iṣfahānī, *Maqātil*, 273.

120 Al-Iṣfahānī, *al-Aghānī* (Dār al-Kutub edition), 3:298 (Būlāq edition, 3:94): لتسرحهم instead of لتسرعهم.

121 For al-Mahdī's building enterprises in the Prophet's Mosque in Medina, see al-Samhūdī, *Wafāʾ*, 2:291–296; 3:5–6.

PART 2

The Social, Ethnic, Political, and Religious Character of the Revolt

CHAPTER 7

Banū Quraysh

> ʿĪsā [b. ʿAbdallāh b. Muḥammad b. ʿUmar b. ʿAlī b. Abī Ṭālib] related from his father, who said: Abū Jaʿfar [al-Manṣūr] asked ʿĪsā b. Mūsā: Who came to Muḥammad's assistance? The family of al-Zubayr, said ʿĪsā. When the caliph asked: Who else? ʿĪsā named ʿUmar [b. al-Khaṭṭāb's] family. At this the caliph exclaimed: By God, it certainly is for something other than his friendship for them or [their] love for him or his family. (ʿĪsā) said: Abū Jaʿfar used to say: Were I to find 1,000 from al-Zubayr's family, all of them good except one evildoer, I would kill the whole lot. But if I were to find 1,000 of ʿUmar's family, all of them evil except for one good man, I would forgive the whole lot.[1]

This chapter deals with those who supported the revolt, took passive and active parts in it, and those who opposed it.

Since we lack a comprehensive political-social and religious study of Medina in the late Umawī and early ʿAbbāsī periods, the data accumulated here will hopefully add substantial material for a future study of this topic. The list of persons in this chapter is, of course, selective and arbitrary, the result of the dependence on Arabic sources, which report mainly on the elite families of the "nobility," mainly from Quraysh. These people were more often also *ḥadīth* transmitters, in other words, they can also be considered scholars. These were emphasized in the discussion (every *muḥaddith* is marked by the ⓜ symbol; a *qāḍī* by the ⓠ symbol; a jurist (*faqīh*) by the ⓕ symbol. The discussion of the Muslim scholars and their attitude to the rebellion, however, is not exhausted in this work. It requires further deep, broad study by scholars of Islam. I hope that the material and the accompanying discussion on the learned persons will contribute to such research in the future.

It has been noted earlier that the assertion of some sources was that, at least at the beginning of the rebellion, most of the Arab inhabitants of Medina supported Muḥammad al-Nafs al-Zakiyya. However, statements such as "the offspring of ʿAlī, Jaʿfar, ʿAqīl, ʿUmar b. al-Khatṭṭāb, al-Zubayr b. al-ʿAwwām, and the

1 Al-Ṭabarī, 3:260 (ll. 12–18) (trans. McAuliffe, *ʿAbbāsid Authority*, 226); see also al-Azdī, *Taʾrīkh al-Mawṣil*, 193.

 | DOI 10.1163/9789004296220_009

rest of Quraysh and the offspring of the Anṣār,"[2] are misleading. This support was not uniform; there were those who opposed the rebellion, even among his close family, among the rest of the ʿAlīd families and among the important Qurashī families.

1 The Ṭālibīs

1.1 *Banū l-Ḥasan b. ʿAlī b. Abī Ṭālib* (Chart I)

Supporters of the Revolt

1.1.1 ʿAbdallāh b. al-Ḥasan b. al-Ḥasan b. ʿAlī b. Abī Ṭālib's sons

Most of the important male members of the family were imprisoned by order of the caliph and brought to al-Hāshimiyya in al-ʿIrāq and died in al-Manṣūr's prison (see chapter 3). The very few who escaped this fate were most probably several young boys, although one (single) source (al-Masʿūdī) relates this event differently, and includes some of those who took part in Muḥammad's revolt, e.g.:

1.1.1.1 *Yaḥyā b. ʿAbdallāh b. al-Ḥasan b. al-Ḥasan*

According to al-Masʿūdī, Yaḥyā was sent by Muḥammad al-Nafs al-Zakiyya to al-Rayy and later on to Ṭabaristān, promoting his brother's cause as the *imām* (that is, as caliph).[3] But the sources do not tell of any propaganda activities of his, and it is highly plausible (as Madelung asserts), that "he did not participate in that revolt."[4]

1.1.1.2 *Idrīs b. ʿAbdallāh b. al-Ḥasan b. al-Ḥasan*

Al-Masʿūdī also relates that Idrīs was sent by his brother, Muḥammad al-Nafs al-Zakiyya, to the Maghrib, where he was assassinated on the orders of al-Manṣūr,[5] but this is a total corruption of the real events. The first reliable information about Idrīs is recorded after 169/786, when he fought at the side of

2 Al-Masʿūdī, *Murūj*, 4:146; for other traditions in this vein, see, e.g., al-Yaʿqūbī, *Taʾrīkh* (ed. Houtsma), 2:452; al-Ṭabarī, 3:199 (ll. 6–11); 228; al-Azdī, *Taʾrīkh al-Mawṣil*, 187; Ibn Kathīr, *al-Bidāya* (Cairo, 1351 H.), 10:84; this was accepted by some scholars, e.g., Jafri, *Shīʿa*, 275, 278, 280 and esp. 281.

3 Al-Masʿūdī, *Murūj*, 4:147 (copied by al-Shaykh al-Mufīd, *al-Masāʾil al-jārūdiyya*, 4).

4 Madelung, "Yaḥyā b. ʿAbdallāh," 242a–243b

5 Al-Masʿūdī, *Murūj*, 4:147.

his nephew, al-Ḥusayn b. ʿAlī b. al-Ḥasan (*ṣāḥib* al-Fakhkh), managed to escape, remained in hiding a while, and only then managed to escape to the Maghrib, where he established an independent rule and died, poisoned most probably on the orders of Hārūn al-Rashīd (in 177/793).[6]

1.1.1.3 *Sulaymān b. ʿAbdallāh b. al-Ḥasan b. al-Ḥasan*

Being a small child, Sulaymān did not take part in Muḥammad's revolt,[7] but he joined his nephew's revolt in Fakhkh in 169/786, where he died.[8] But Abū l-Naṣr al-Bukhārī relates that he died at the age of 53,[9] which makes him 29 when his brother's revolt broke out. In this specific case, it is noteworthy that this age, 53, is a literary convention: King Sulaymān died at the age of 53, the same is related about many *ṣaḥābī*s and *tābiʿūn*, famous governors (Ziyād b. Abīhi and al-Ḥajjāj), and above all, this was the age of the Prophet Muḥammad when he made the *hijra* to Medina.

1.1.1.4 *Mūsā b. ʿAbdallāh b. al-Ḥasan b. al-Ḥasan*[10]

This is a different case. According to several Sunnī sources, Mūsā was among the members of the Ḥasanī family who were brought by orders of al-Manṣūr from al-Rabadha to al-ʿIrāq and among the very few who received an amnesty from the caliph after the revolts of the two brothers were crushed. But according to other traditions he was sent back to Medina and upon the outbreak of the revolt he was sent to Syria by his brother.

The Imāmī version of his biography is narrated by Mūsā b. ʿAbdallāh b. al-Ḥasan himself in a long, extremely interesting and important tradition recorded by al-Kulaynī and copied by other Imāmī sources. According to this complex tradition, when the revolt broke out he was the third from among Medina's inhabitants to swear allegiance to Muḥammad al-Nafs al-Zakiyya, and he described himself as a youth (young boy [?]: *ghulām*).[11] In this tradition, which serves as a song of praise to Jaʿfar al-Ṣādiq, Mūsā b. ʿAbdallāh alleges that

6 D. Eustache, "Idrīs I (al-Akbar)," *EI*²; R. Basset, "Idrīs I. b. ʿAbdallāh," *EI*¹; Najam, "Idrīs b. ʿAbdallāh"; al-Bukhārī, *Sirr al-silsila*, 12–13; al-Iṣfahānī, *Maqātil*, index, esp. 487–491; al-ʿUmarī, *Ansāb*, 62; al-Amīn, *Aʿyān al-Shīʿa*, 3:230–231.

7 This can be understood from the tradition in al-Iṣfahānī, *Maqātil*, 396, 433.

8 Ibid., 451.

9 Al-Bukhārī, *Sirr al-silsila*, 12; al-ʿUmarī, *Ansāb*, 60–62 (his biography, no mention of his age, though).

10 For his biography, see al-Iṣfahānī, *Maqātil*, 390–397; Ibn ʿAsākir, *Taʾrīkh*, 60:443–453; al-Khaṭīb al-Baghdādī, *Taʾrīkh* (Beirut, 1997), 13:27–29; Ibn ʿInaba, *ʿUmda*, 111ff; and see also the discussion of Nagel, "Muḥammad b. ʿAbdallāh," 243–244.

11 Al-Kulaynī, *al-Kāfī*, 1:362.

he witnessed a fierce and heated discussion between ʿAbdallāh b. al-Ḥasan, his son, Muḥammad al-Nafs al-Zakiyya, and Jaʿfar al-Ṣādiq regarding the legitimacy to rule. The purpose of the long tradition is to prove unequivocally that Jaʿfar al-Ṣādiq is the true Imām, and for that purpose it records "verbatim" Jaʿfar's "prophecies" about future events, mainly in regard to the fate of ʿAbdallāh b. al-Ḥasan and the revolts and the killing of his two sons. In the heated discussion Jaʿfar also referred to Mūsā b. ʿAbdallāh, foretelling his future, that he is going to join Muḥammad's rebellion and following Muḥammad's death, will join his brother Ibrāhīm, and after the latter is killed, will flee the authorities. Jaʿfar added, in Mūsā b. ʿAbdallāh's presence, that if he follows his advice, he had better seek a safeguard from the ʿAbbāsīs, and then God will bring him salvation.[12] This "prophecy," as well as all the others of Jaʿfar al-Ṣādiq, indeed materialized. The "prophecy" states that Mūsā says, indeed, immediately after the death of Muḥammad b. ʿAbdallāh I ran away and joined my brother Ibrāhīm. After he was killed, I joined Muḥammad's brother, ʿAbdallāh al-Ashtar, roamed the Islamic lands, reached al-Sind where my brother was killed, then returned and decided to give myself up to the mercy of Caliph al-Mahdī during one of his pilgrimages. Among the notables in Medina was Mūsā b. Jaʿfar al-Ṣādiq. Mūsā b. ʿAbdallāh al-Ḥasanī tells Caliph al-Mahdī that Jaʿfar, the father of Mūsā, was the one who foresaw his whole cycle of running and hiding and suggested that he give himself up to the mercy of the caliph. Upon hearing this, al-Mahdī is so moved that he gives Mūsā l-Ḥasanī a safe conduct (*amān*) and to Mūsā b. Jaʿfar al-Ḥusaynī, a large sum of money. Mūsā b. ʿAbdallāh ends his story by saying that this was what caused him to be an obedient servant (*mawlā*) of the family of Muḥammad b. ʿAlī b. al-Ḥusayn (Jaʿfar al-Ṣādiq's father).[13]

Other versions of Mūsā b. ʿAbdallāh's affairs during the revolt and after it are completely different from this Imāmī tradition. Some versions, although allegedly related by Mūsā himself, also give different and even contradictory information. According to one such tradition, related by Mūsā b. ʿAbdallāh in the first person, he was arrested with the other members of the Ḥasanī family in al-Rabadha, in the year 144/762; the caliph requested ʿAbdallāh b. al-Ḥasan, his father, to send him one member of his family. Mūsā, who according to his words was a very young boy (وأنا يومئذ حديث السن), is sent to the caliph and after being tortured at the caliph's court is sent to Medina as the caliph's informant, e.g., to provide information about his two brothers, but he does not

12 Al-Kulaynī, *al-Kāfī*, 1:360, and the parallel Imāmī sources, e.g., al-Baḥrānī, *Madīnat al-maʿājiz*, 5:280; al-Majlisī, *Biḥār*, 47:282.

13 Al-Kulaynī, *al-Kāfī*, 1:365–366; al-Baḥrānī, *Madīnat al-maʿājiz*, 5:288–289; al-Majlisī, *Biḥār*, 47:286–287.

carry out his task, and on the caliph's orders he is sent back by the governor of Medina to al-ʿIrāq, but is rescued on the way by Ibn Khuḍayr al-Zubayrī, the commander of Muḥammad al-Nafs al-Zakiyya, who brings Mūsā back to Medina.[14]

In another tradition Mūsā b. ʿAbdallāh is sent by his brother with Rizām, the *mawlā* of Muḥammad b. Khālid al-Qasrī, to Syria to summon its people to his cause. Upon their arrival in Syria, Mūsā was abandoned by Rizām who fled to the caliph and returned to Medina.[15] In another version, Mūsā went to Syria with Rizām and others, but when they arrived at Taymāʾ Rizām left them for al-ʿIrāq and the group returned to Medina.[16]

However, according to yet another tradition, related by ʿĪsā b. ʿAbdallāh al-ʿUmarī, Mūsā and another supporter of Muḥammad al-Nafs al-Zakiyya, ʿUthmān b. Muḥammad al-Zubayrī, reached Dūmat al-Jandal and from there went straight to al-Baṣra where they were recognized and captured.[17]

So far there are two different versions, both claiming that Mūsā b. ʿAbdallāh b. al-Ḥasan did not accomplish his mission in Syria, but according to one, he went back to Medina while according to the other, he fled to al-Baṣra and hid there, was discovered and brought to the caliph.[18]

The Zubayrī Version

The Zubayrī version has some parallels to ʿĪsā's short version, but also has some major differences. The tradition is related by Muḥammad b. ʿUthmān b. Muḥammad b. Khālid b. al-Zubayr b. al-ʿAwwām through Ibrāhīm b. Muṣʿab b. ʿUmāra b. Ḥamza b. Muṣʿab b. al-Zubayr, who transmitted the tradition to ʿUmar b. Shabba. According to this version, after the death of al-Nafs al-Zakiyya,

14 Al-Ṭabarī, 3:179–180, 198; a young boy: ibid., 3:179 (ll. 8–9); his rescue by Ibn Khuḍayr: ibid., 3:180; Ibn ʿAsākir, *Taʾrīkh*, 60:444; see also al-Iṣfahānī, *Maqātil*, 223–224, and a parallel tradition on 391–392, a combined tradition related by Mūsā b. ʿAbdallāh and Buthayna al-Shaybāniyya (who on 392 is defined as the one who suckled [*arḍaʿat*] Aḥmad b. ʿĪsā b. Zayd [b. ʿAlī b. al-Ḥusayn b. ʿAlī b. Abī Ṭālib] AND al-Faḍl b. Jaʿfar b. Sulaymān [b. ʿAlī b. ʿAbdallāh b. al-ʿAbbās?]); the part about Mūsā being sent to the caliph and his rescue by Muḥammad b. ʿAbdallāh's commander (al-Ṭabarī, 3:198) is missing in al-Iṣfahānī's version.

15 Al-Ṭabarī, 3:215–216 (l. 15 to l. 10): ʿUmar b. Shabba < Muḥammad b. Yaḥyā < al-Ḥārith b. Isḥāq.

16 Ibid., 3:216 (ll. 10–13): *qāla al-Ḥārith.*

17 Ibid., 3:216–217 (l. 13 to l. 3): [ʿUmar b. Shabba] < ʿĪsā < Mūsā b. ʿAbdallāh and Rizām together: وزرام معا in Baghdad; cf. McAuliffe, *ʿAbbāsid Authority*, 177: "Mūsā b. ʿAbdallāh informed me in Baghdad—Rizām being present as well"; perhaps the text should be rendered: معنا ; in that case McAuliffe's translation would make better sense.

18 Ibn ʿAsākir, *Taʾrīkh*, 60:443 (summarizing both traditions).

Mūsā b. ʿAbdallāh and some of the former supporters and commanders fled first to Mecca and then to al-Baṣra. One of them was the transmitter's father, ʿUthmān b. Muḥammad. There they were caught, brought to the governor who sent them to the caliph, who killed ʿUthmān, ordered Mūsā to be whipped fifty lashes and the same was done to the transmitter, whose father was killed before his eyes. The transmitter, Muḥammad b. ʿUthmān, does not tell us what happened to Mūsā after he was whipped. Rather, he is interested in relating his and his family's history and records that he himself was thrown into jail and was then released by the intercession of the caliph's vizier, Yaʿqūb b. Dāwūd, only after al-Mahdī became caliph.[19]

We shall return to this version, but suffice it here to remark that according to it, Mūsā escapes to al-Baṣra **after** his brother's death. What happened to Mūsā after he was whipped by order of al-Manṣūr is not told.

A similar tradition is related by al-Iṣfahānī through Buthayna al-Shaybāniyya.[20] According to her long account, Mūsā came from Syria to al-Baṣra (most probably) after his two brothers were killed, stayed in hiding, was caught, and brought to the governor, who sent him to the caliph. At the caliph's court he was whipped (500 lashes), which he bore admirably; the story emphasizes his bravery and formidable forbearance during the flogging. "After they finished flogging him they took him out"—then comes an alleged discussion with al-Manṣūr's *mawlā*, al-Rabīʿ, which ends with a line of poetry in which Mūsā praises his strength of will, his ability to endure suffering and hardships.[21] We do not know what happened to him according to this narration. Although it can be understood that he was not imprisoned, this is not stated specifically. After recording this version al-Iṣfahānī adds two other less reliable versions, using the phrases "it was said" (وقد قيل) that Mūsā remained in prison until [Caliph] al-Mahdī released him; and it also was said that he hid afterwards [that is, after he was flogged by order of al-Manṣūr and was released] until he died."[22]

The most common version narrating what happened to him after being whipped is recorded by Muṣʿab b. ʿAbdallāh al-Zubayrī: "As to Mūsā b. ʿAbdallāh, he hid himself in al-Baṣra and he [most probably the governor of

19 Al-Ṭabarī, 3:260–262.
20 On her see 237, n. 14 above.
21 Al-Iṣfahānī, *Maqātil*, 392–394; copied by al-Qāḍī l-Nuʿmān, *Sharḥ al-akhbār*, 3:326.
22 Al-Iṣfahānī, *Maqātil*, 394.

the city] seized him and sent him to al-Manṣūr, who pardoned him,"[23] and then he dwelled in Baghdad.[24]

Indirect evidence indeed testifies that Mūsā lived in Baghdad; it is related by the famous *ḥadīth* scholar, Yaḥyā b. Maʿīn (158–233/775–848), who relates "I came upon Mūsā here in Baghdad..." The aim of the description is to ascertain Mūsā's reliability as a transmitter of *ḥadīth*, and the mention of his residence in Baghdad is related in passing. This evidence rendered by Yaḥyā b. Maʿīn was received as genuine by critics of *ḥadīth*.[25] Yaḥyā b. Maʿīn could have met Mūsā during al-Rashīd's reign, certainly not in al-Manṣūr's, who died in 158/775, the year that Yaḥyā was born, and most probably not even during al-Mahdī's reign (158–168/775–785). And indeed, another testimony describes Mūsā b. ʿAbdallāh in al-Rashīd's court.[26]

Returning to the personal testimony of Mūsā b. ʿAbdallāh, as far as I know, part of this version is found only in one other Imāmī source, Ibn ʿInaba's *ʿUmda*, which combined the version that relates how Mūsā was sent from al-Rabadha (in this version to al-ʿIrāq) to Caliph al-Manṣūr, who tortured him (he was given 1,000 [!] lashes) and then sent him to Medina to spy for him and reveal his two brothers' hiding places. This version lacks the ending of the tradition in the *Maqātil*, and certainly is not that of al-Ṭabarī; instead of staying in Medina for several months and then being sent to the caliph and/or being rescued by Ibn

---

23 Al-Zubayrī, *Nasab Quraysh*, 53; the tradition is most probably garbled, perhaps it is part of a longer tradition cut and inserted by al-Zubayrī into his book; Ibn ʿAsākir, *Taʾrīkh*, 60:445, from al-Zubayr [b. Bakkār?]: "Mūsā b. ʿAbdallāh was hiding in al-Baṣra; he was taken to the caliph, who pardoned him after he gave him 70 lashes"; al-Khaṭīb al-Baghdādī, *Taʾrīkh* (Cairo edition), 13:25–26, another Imāmī tradition (Ḥusaynī transmitters):... al-Ḥasan b. Muḥammad b. Yaḥyā [b. al-Ḥasan b. Jaʿfar b. ʿUbaydallāh b. al-Ḥusayn b. ʿAlī b. al-Ḥusayn b. ʿAlī b. Abī Ṭālib] < his father < grandfather: "and Mūsā b. ʿAbdallāh was hiding in al-Baṣra and was seized by al-Manṣūr who forgave him his faults"; Ibn Ḥajar, *Lisān*, 6:123: "he was hiding for a certain period after his two brothers Muḥammad and Ibrāhīm were killed, then al-Manṣūr found him and caught him, had him whipped, then he pardoned him."

24 Al-Khaṭīb al-Baghdādī, *Taʾrīkh* (Cairo edition), 13:25 (copied by Ibn ʿAsākir, *Taʾrīkh*, 60:445); according to al-ʿUmarī, Umm Kulthūm, Mūsā b. ʿAbdallāh b. al-Ḥasan's daughter, was married to the nephew of al-Manṣūr. No name of the brother is given (al-ʿUmarī, *Ansāb*, 45). This may have been part of al-Manṣūr's considerations in pardoning Mūsā b. ʿAbdallāh.

25 Ibn ʿAsākir, *Taʾrīkh*, 60:447; al-Khaṭīb al-Baghdādī, *Taʾrīkh* (Cairo edition), 13:27; the comments of the critics of *ḥadīth*: e.g., Ibn Ḥajar, *Lisān*, 6:123: "Ibn Maʿīn saw him"; al-Dhahabī, *al-Mughnī*, 2:684: "Ibn Maʿīn saw him and considered him reliable in regard to a certain *ḥadīth*..."

26 This single anecdote is recorded by al-Iṣfahānī, *Maqātil*, 396, Ibn ʿAsākir, *Taʾrīkh*, 60:451, and al-Khaṭīb al-Baghdādī, *Taʾrīkh* (Cairo edition), 13:26–27.

Khuḍayr, according to al-Ṭabarī's version, in Ibn ʿInaba's version, immediately upon arriving in Medina, Mūsā b. ʿAbdallāh fled to Mecca. After his brother died in 145/762, al-Mahdī came to Mecca on a pilgrimage, Mūsā came out of his hiding place and asked al-Mahdī for absolution, which the latter gave him.[27] I intentionally refrain from calling al-Mahdī "caliph" in this tradition, since he became caliph only in 158/775, and according to the sources he did not stand at the head of the *ḥajj* pilgrims until the year 153/770.

Nevertheless, Ibn ʿInaba also relates the anecdote about Mūsā b. ʿAbdallāh at the court of Hārūn al-Rashīd, and states that he died on his estate in Suwayqa.[28]

Mūsā b. ʿAbdallāh was a minor transmitter of *ḥadīth*[29] and a poet.[30] He appears in the sources as a transmitter of the events relating to the revolt, e.g., the tradition in al-Ṭabarī which he transmitted to ʿĪsā b. ʿAbdallāh,[31] and other traditions, some strictly pro-Imāmī ones, which in this case may indeed verify the Imāmī sources that describe him as a close associate of Jaʿfar al-Ṣādiq: من أصحاب الصادق.[32]

1.1.2 Al-Ḥasan b. al-Ḥasan b. al-Ḥasan b. ʿAlī b. Abī Ṭālib

According to his nephew, Mūsā b. ʿAbdallāh, when al-Manṣūr's envoys came to the house where the Ḥasanīs were imprisoned and requested that Muḥammad and Ibrāhīm be delivered to them, al-Ḥasan b. al-Ḥasan b. al-Ḥasan cursed and condemned the two, saying

> This is all the doing of those two sons of an inauspicious mother. By God, this matter does not represent our view and is not the result of a consultation and consent on our part (ولا عن ملأ منا), and we do not have any capability to change this (situation) (ولا لنا فيه حيلة).[33]

27 Ibn ʿInaba, *ʿUmda*, 112.

28 Ibid.

29 For example, see Ibn Ḥajar, *Lisān*,6:123; al-Dhahabī, *al-Mughnī*, 2:684; al-ʿUqaylī, *Ḍuʿafāʾ*, 4:159; Ibn ʿAsākir, *Taʾrīkh*, 60:446–447; al-Khaṭīb al-Baghdādī, *Taʾrīkh* (Cairo edition), 13:27.

30 This is mentioned in his biographies, for example, see Ibn ʿInaba, *ʿUmda*, 112; Ibn ʿAsākir, *Taʾrīkh*, 60:446ff. and al-Khaṭīb al-Baghdādī, *Taʾrīkh* (Cairo edition), 13:26: quotations from his poetry.

31 Al-Ṭabarī, 3:216–217 (l. 14 to l. 1).

32 For example, see al-Ṭūsī, *Rijāl*, 300; al-Tafrishī, *Naqd al-rijāl*, 4:436; al-Khūʾī, *Rijāl*, 20:55.

33 Al-Ṭabarī, 3:173; the translation is after McAuliffe, *ʿAbbāsid Authority*, 122, with some changes.

It seems that this alleged view did not prevent the caliph from sending him with many members of his family to al-Hāshimiyya, where he died.

1.1.3 The Family of Zayd b. al-Ḥasan b. ʿAlī b. Abī Ṭālib

Opposition to the Revolt/ʿAbbāsī Supporters

Zayd b. al-Ḥasan b. ʿAlī b. Abī Ṭālib: Introductory Remarks

Zayd was in charge of the endowments (*ṣadaqāt*) of the Prophet.[34] Al-Khūʾī relates that he did not claim the Imāma for himself, nor did any of the Shīʿa or others besides them claim that he was entitled to it.[35] Abū Naṣr al-Bukhārī quotes Yaḥyā b. al-Ḥusayn al-ʿAqīqī (214–277/829–890 or 891), who relates that Zayd b. al-Ḥasan refrained from joining his uncle al-Ḥusayn in al-ʿIrāq, and after the latter's death, he swore allegiance to ʿAbdallāh b. al-Zubayr; this he did because his sister was married to Ibn al-Zubayr. He was with ʿAbdallāh b. al-Zubayr in his battles until the latter was killed, then "he took his sister's hand and returned to Medina. There is a story concerning him and al-Ḥajjāj in regard to this affair."[36] But this episode in his life did not seem to prevent close relations with the Marwānī family, that is, ʿAbd al-Malik and his son al-Walīd. His daughter Nafīsa was married to al-Walīd b. ʿAbd al-Malik (or, according to another version, to ʿAbd al-Malik himself) and bore him children. Ibn ʿInaba, who relates the two versions, asserts that the first was correct. He adds that ʿAbd al-Malik bestowed on Zayd much honor and gave him a large sum of 30,000 *dīnār*s as a present.[37] He may have served in a governmental post on their behalf.[38] He was dismissed from his high post by Caliph Sulaymān b.

---

34 Al-Shaykh al-Mufīd, *Irshād*, 2:21; Ibn ʿInaba, *ʿUmda*, 69; al-Majlisī, *Biḥār*, 44:163.

35 Al-Khūʾī, *Rijāl*, 8:351.

36 Al-Bukhārī, *Sirr al-silsila*, 21: quoting al-ʿAqīqī; Ibn ʿInaba, *ʿUmda*, 69 (quoting al-Bukhārī's *Sirr al-silsila*); regarding his abstaining from helping al-Ḥusayn, see, for example, the remark of a modern author, ʿAlī Najal Muḥammad Āl Sayf al-Khaṭī, *Wafāt al-imām al-Ḥasan b. ʿAlī …* in *Majmūʿa wafayāt al-aʾimma wa-yalīhi wafāt al-Sayyida Zaynab* [composed by several scholars: *marājiʿ min al-ʿulamāʾ al-aʿlām*] (Beirut: Dār al-Balāgha, 1412 H.), 132: Zayd was with his uncle in Karbalāʾ. Being a child who had not attained puberty he was taken prisoner. But according to the accepted tradition, he was 90 years when he died in 120/738. This means that he was about 32 when al-Ḥusayn died[!].

37 Ibn ʿInaba, *ʿUmda*, 70; on Nafīsa bt. Zayd, see also al-ʿUmarī, *Ansāb*, 231.

38 Al-Khūʾī, *Rijāl*, 8:351 (quoting al-Shaykh al-Mufīd's *Irshād*, 2:23): without the part about him serving in governmental posts: وكان مسلما لبني امية متقلدا من قبلهم الأعمال, though, he [?] continues, somewhat apologetically, he professed *taqiyya* against his enemies: وكان رأيه التقية لأعدائه.

ʿAbd al-Malik (r. 96–99/715–717), but was reinstated by ʿUmar II (d. 101/120).[39] Imāmī (but also Sunnī) sources tell at length about the conflict and animosity between him and the leading members of the ʿAlīd family, e.g., Abū Hāshim ʿAbdallāh b. Muḥammad b. al-Ḥanafiyya, ʿAlī b. al-Ḥusayn b. ʿAlī b. Abī Ṭālib[40] and Muḥammad (al-Bāqir), the latter's son.[41] He died in the year 120/738 aged somewhere between 90 and 100.[42]

1.1.3.1 *Al-Ḥasan b. Zayd b. al-Ḥasan b. ʿAlī b. Abī Ṭālib (d. 168/782 or 783)*[43]

Al-Ḥasan was ʿAbdallāh b. al-Ḥasan's cousin and an enthusiastic supporter of the ʿAbbāsīs in their contention against the Ḥasanīs. He was the first among the

39 Al-Mizzī, *Tahdhīb*, 10:53–54: quoting al-Zubayr b. Bakkār from Bakr b. ʿAbd al-Wahhāb al-Madanī < Abū Rāfiʿ Ruzayq b. Rāfiʿ < his father who saw the two letters that were kept by ʿAbd al-Wāḥid b. ʿAbdallāh al-Naṣrī, one ordering the dismissal by Sulaymān and the other the order of ʿUmar II to reinstate him, both sent to the governors of Medina; see also al-Shaykh al-Mufīd, *al-Irshād*, 2:21 and al-Majlisī, *Biḥār*, 44:163: quoting the letters without mentioning the tradition of al-Zubayr b. Bakkār and ʿAbd al-Wāḥid; ʿAbd al-Wāḥid served as the governor of Medina, Mecca, and al-Ṭāʾif from 104/723 until 106/724, on him, see Ibn ʿAsākir, *Taʾrīkh*, 37:244–253; al-Mizzī, *Tahdhīb*, 18:459–463 and the comprehensive bibliography therein.

40 See the note of the editor of *ʿUmdat al-Ṭālib*, 69, n. 1: Zayd was appointed in charge of the *ṣadaqāt* of the Prophet by al-Walīd b. ʿAbd al-Malik, due to Zayd's incitement against Abū Hāshim before the caliph, which caused the imprisonment of Abū Hāshim. ʿAlī b. al-Ḥusayn intervened on Abū Hāshim's behalf before the caliph; the complete tradition is quoted by Ibn ʿAsākir, *Taʾrīkh*, 19:375–377: ... al-Ḥusayn b. (it seems that the name of his father, Muḥammad, was omitted, see for example, al-Mizzī, *Tahdhīb*, 29:329 (l. 8)) [Muḥammad b.] Abī Maʿshar < his father < his grandfather Abū Maʿshar; according to this tradition al-Walīd was responsible for poisoning Abū Hāshim; most sources relate his death (poisoning) to Sulaymān b. ʿAbd al-Malik, see for example Ibn ʿAsākir, *Taʾrīkh*, 32:274–275; on Abū Maʿshar Najīḥ b. ʿAbd al-Raḥmān, *faqīh, muḥaddith*, and historian (d. 170/787), see *EI*², "Abū Maʿshar" (J. Horovitz-F. Rosenthal); al-Zirikli, *al-Aʿlām*, 8:328–329.

41 Al-Majlisī, *Biḥār*, 46:329–331 (quoted by al-Khūʾī, *Rijāl*, 8:351): Zayd's endeavors to cause Caliph ʿAbd al-Malik to kill Muḥammad al-Bāqir; al-Khūʾī regards this tradition forged and unreasonable due to historical considerations.

42 Ibid., quoting Abū Naṣr al-Bukhārī; al-Mizzī, *Tahdhīb*, 10:55: 90 years old; on Zayd, see also the discussion of Ahmed, *Religious Elite*, 147f.

43 On him, see Ibn Saʿd, *al-Qism al-Mutammim*, 386–387; al-Ṭabarī, 3:2518; al-Khaṭīb al-Baghdādī, *Taʾrīkh* (Beirut, 1997), 7:320–324; Ibn Ḥajar, *Tahdhīb* (Beirut, 1984), 2:243–244; al- Mizzī, *Tahdhīb*, 6:152–163 and the comprehensive bibliography therein; for the attitude of the Imāmīs towards him, see, for example, al-Shabastarī, *al-Imām al-Ṣādiq*, 1:366 and the comprehensive bibliography therein; al-Amīn, *Aʿyān al-Shīʿa*, 5:75–80; see also Landau-Tasseron, *Biographies*, 260–261 and n. 1157 on 260 and Ahmed, *Religious Authority*, 148f.

ʿAlīds to wear the black clothes (the color of the ʿAbbāsīs).[44] A single tradition (to which I found no parallels) relates that his daughter, Umm Kulthūm, was married to the first ʿAbbāsī caliph, Abū l-ʿAbbās al-Saffāḥ, and bore him two boys, who died at a young age.[45] His animosity towards the Ḥasanīs' rebellious faction, that is, Muḥammad and his brother Ibrāhīm, is allegedly demonstrated in the tradition relating that he used to reveal to al-Manṣūr the whereabouts of the two brothers and their places of hiding.[46] Mūsā b. ʿAbdallāh b. al-Ḥasan (al-Nafs al-Zakiyya's brother) is reported as saying: "Oh God, seek out Ḥasan b. Zayd for our bloodshed."[47] When the head of ʿAbdallāh b. Muḥammad al-Ashtar (Muḥammad al-Nafs al-Zakiyya's son) was brought to al-Manṣūr, it was presented by al-Ḥasan b. Zayd b. al-Ḥasan b. ʿAlī from the top of the *minbar*.[48] He served as the governor of Medina (from 149/766–767 or 150/767–768) and possibly filled other posts during al-Manṣūr's reign.[49] Although al-Ḥasan's daughter, Nafīsa, was married to Jaʿfar al-Ṣādiq's son, Isḥāq,[50] Imāmī sources emphasize the great animosity that existed between the two families, e.g., the tradition that records that al-Manṣūr ordered him to burn down Jaʿfar al-Ṣādiq's residence (*dār*). Then, the tradition describes Jaʿfar coming out of the burning house, walking unharmed through the flames saying: I am the son of أعراق الثرى and I am the son of Abraham, God's friend: انا ابن أعراق الثرى وانا ابن إبراهيم خليل الله عليه السلام. This tradition is found in chapters stressing Jaʿfar al-Ṣādiq's ability to perform miracles (*muʿjizāt*).[51] The expression *ʿirq/aʿrāq al-tharā* (literally: "the source of everything that is good upon earth"), is mainly applied to Ishmael (Ismāʿīl) or (rarely) to Abraham (Ibrāhīm),[52] that is, the root or source of all the Arabs.[53] Despite the miraculous elements woven in this

44 Al-Bukhārī, *Sirr al-silsila*, 21; copied by Ibn ʿInaba, *ʿUmda*, 70.

45 Al-Ṭabarī, 3:2518; I was unable to ascertain this information in the sources known to me; still I see no reason to doubt it.

46 Ibn Kathīr, *al-Bidāya* (ed. Shīrī), 10:87 (year 144 H.).

47 Al-Ṭabarī, 3:144 (ll. 11–12) (trans. McAuliffe, 87).

48 Ibn ʿInaba, *ʿUmda*, 105.

49 Al-Ṭabarī, 3:358 (year 150/767 or 768), 359, 368, 370–371, 373 (years 151–154/768–771); he was dismissed in 155/771 or 772, ibid., 3:377; Ibn Khayyāṭ, *Taʾrīkh* (Beirut, 1993), 353 (year 149/766 or 767); Ibn ʿInaba, *ʿUmda*, 70: Medina and other places in addition to it.

50 Ibn Ḥajar, *Tahdhīb* (Beirut, 1984), 1:200.

51 Al-Kulaynī, *al-Kāfī*, 1:473; al-Ṭabarī (al-Imāmī), *Manāqib*, 153; al-Baḥrānī, *Madīnat al-maʿājiz*, 5:295; al-Majlisī, *Biḥār*, 47:136.

52 See for example, Ibn Ḥajar, *al-Alqāb*, 1:82.

53 Lane's *Lexicon*, s.v. *ʿ.r.q.*; ibid., mentioning the verse of Imruʾ al-Qays, where he says that his origin is from *ʿirq al-tharā* (وانتسابـ[ي] إلى عرق الثرى), that is, "the root or source of all mankind"; the commentators of the poem explain that Adam or Ismāʿīl are meant by this

anecdote, it must have reflected a real historical background, that is, the animosity between al-Ḥasan b. Zayd and Jaʿfar al-Ṣādiq, and the harsh measures taken by al-Manṣūr against the latter. As already noted, some sources record the confiscation of Jaʿfar's estates by al-Manṣūr. The Imāmī sources emphasize mainly his harsh attitude towards both the Ḥasanī and Ḥusaynī families:

> He belonged to those *madhmūmūn* from among the *muḥaddithūn*, due to his vicious conduct and the weakness of his traditions. He treated harshly and opposed the two Imāms, al-Bāqir, may peace be on him, and al-Ṣādiq, may peace be on him, (while) assisting and supporting the ʿAbbāsīs against his cousin's sons, al-Ḥasan al-Muthannā.[54]

Some of the Sunnī critics of transmitters of *ḥadīth* considered him to be a trustworthy (transmitter) while others regarded him as a weak and unworthy transmitter.[55] Several of al-Ḥasan's sons were active supporters of the ʿAbbāsīs, but two sons, Zayd and ʿAlī, supported the rebellion (see below).

Al-Ḥasan b. Zayd's sons

Ten of his sons and one daughter are mentioned by the sources: Muḥammad, al-Ḥasan, al-Qāsim, ʿAlī, Zayd, Ibrāhīm, ʿĪsā, ʿAbdallāh, Isḥāq, Ismāʿīl, and Umm Kulthūm, who married Abū l-ʿAbbās al-Saffāḥ, the first ʿAbbāsī caliph.[56]

---

expression, see Imruʾ al-Qays, *Dīwān* (ed. De Slane, Paris, 1837), 33 (Ar. text); 103 (commentary); this name appears in a tradition in which the Prophet records the *nasab* of Maʿadd, e.g., Maʿadd b. ʿAdnān b. Udad b. Zanad b. Barā (Yarā; Barāʾ) b. *aʿrāq al-tharā*…; Umm Salama, the Prophet's wife, the (earliest) transmitter of the *ḥadīth* explains that what is meant by *aʿrāq al-tharā* is Ismāʿīl; see al-Ṭabarī, *Taʾrīkh*, 1:1113; al-Ḥākim al-Naysābūrī, *al-Mustadrak* (Beirut, 1411/1990), 2:437; al-Haythamī, *Majmaʿ al-zawāʾid*, 1:193; al-Majlisī, *Biḥār*, 35:141, all the latter sources identify Ismāʿīl as *ʿirq al-tharā*. As noted, Abraham is less mentioned in the sources as *ʿirq al-tharā*, for example, see al-Ṭabarī (al-Imāmī), *Manāqib*, 153; Ibn ʿAsākir, *Taʾrīkh*, 6:192: … al-Zubayr b. Bakkār < ʿAbd al-Raḥmān b. al-Mughīra al-Ḥizāmī: when the people saw that the fire did not harm Abraham and burn him they said: ما هو إلا عرق الثرى وما يذوقه إلا من لا تضره النار ولا تحرقه، فسمي عرق الثرى; the text is garbled, cf. al-Maqrīzī, *al-Muqaffā l-Kabīr*, 1:25: ما هو إلا عرق الندى [!] وما نعرفه، ألا ترى ما تضره النار ولا تحرقه فسمي عرق الندى.

54 Al-Shabastarī, *al-Imām al-Ṣādiq*, 1:366; Ibn ʿInaba, *ʿUmda*, 70: وكان مظاهرا لبني العباس على بني عمه الحسن المثنى وهو أول من لبس السواد من العلويين; al-Muthannā was the nickname of al-Ḥasan b. al-Ḥasan b. ʿAlī b. Abī Ṭālib.

55 For example, see al-Mizzī, *Tahdhīb*, 6:152–163 and the comprehensive bibliography therein.

56 Al-Ṭabarī, 3:2518, not mentioning al-Ḥasan, who is only mentioned by Ibn Ḥazm, *Jamhara*, 39–40, who does not mention Muḥammad, ʿĪsā, Isḥāq, and Umm Kulthūm, though; Ibn ʿInaba, *ʿUmda*, 70–71: omitting Muḥammad, ʿĪsā, al-Ḥasan, and Umm Kulthūm.

A single piece of evidence mentions that several of his sons served as commanding officers in ʿĪsā b. Mūsā's army. The Arabic text of this source is garbled and it is difficult to ascertain from it all the names of al-Ḥasan's sons who were in the ʿAbbāsī camp. If I understood it correctly they may have been: ʿAlī, Ibrāhīm, al-Qāsim, and perhaps also al-Ḥasan.[57]

1.1.3.2 *Ibrāhīm b. al-Ḥasan b. Zayd*

This is the only source mentioning his participation in the revolt.

1.1.3.3 *Al-Qāsim b. al-Ḥasan b. Zayd*

This evidence is corroborated by other sources, where al-Qāsim is mentioned as one of the most trusted commanders of ʿĪsā b. Mūsā.[58] He was sent by the latter to the caliph to announce the victory over Muḥammad b. ʿAbdallāh.[59]

1.1.3.4 *ʿAlī b. al-Ḥasan b. Zayd*

Another source mentions him among those who joined the revolt of Muḥammad b. ʿAbdallāh, so we have conflicting evidence about him.

1.1.3.5 *Isḥāq b. al-Ḥasan b. Zayd*

Isḥāq was a zealous adherent of the ʿAbbāsīs. He used to wear black clothes (the color of the ʿAbbāsīs) day and night. He was close to Hārūn al-Rashīd (r. 170–193/786–809) and was his adviser in regard to the ʿAlīds. He used to divulge information to the caliph about the members of the ʿAlīd families in Baghdad. As the result of such information and on the advise of Isḥāq, a group of ʿAlīds were executed by al-Rashīd.[60]

---

57 Al-Kulaynī, *al-Kāfī*, 1:364; al-Majlisī, *Biḥār*, 47:286; al-Māzandarānī, *Sharḥ*, 6:317: a long and detailed report of Mūsā b. ʿAbdallāh b. al-Ḥasan, who, upon mentioning the army of ʿĪsā b. Mūsā, says that "commanding ʿĪsā b. Mūsā's vanguard were the sons of al-Ḥasan b. Zayd b. al-Ḥasan b. al-Ḥasan [sic!, the second Ḥasan is an error] and [sic!] Qāsim and Muḥammad b. Zayd and ʿAlī and Ibrāhīm the sons of al-Ḥasan b. Zayd: وكان على مقدمة عيسى بن موسى ولد الحسن بن زيد بن الحسن بن الحسن [!] و[!؟] قاسم ومحمد ابن زيد وعلي وإبراهيم بنو الحسن بن زيد. As to Muḥammad b. Zayd, he may have been the brother of al-Ḥasan b. Zayd.

58 Al-Ṭabarī, 3:232 (l. 9f.); 3:235 (l. 12); 3:236 (ll. 7–8); al-Balādhurī, *Ansāb* (ed. Madelung), 2:513 (correct القاسم بن الحسين to القاسم بن الحسن); 2:516.

59 Al-Iṣfahānī, *Maqātil*, 275; al-Ṭabarī, 3:252; al-Qāsim is mentioned several times as one of the most trusted commanders of ʿĪsā b. Mūsā, see ibid., 3:233 (l. 9f.); 3:235 (l. 12); 3:236 (ll. 7–8); on him, see also Ahmed, *Religious Elite*, 151.

60 Al-Bukhārī, *Sirr al-silsila*, 25; Ibn ʿInaba, *ʿUmda*, 71: copies *Sirr al-silsila*.

Supporters of the Revolt

1.1.3.6 *ʿAlī b. al-Ḥasan b. Zayd b. al-Ḥasan b. ʿAlī b. Abī Ṭālib*

He is noted above as one of the commanders in ʿĪsā b. Mūsā's army, but he is also mentioned together with his brother, Zayd, as one of those who took part in the revolt.[61] In spite of this, he was not punished by al-Manṣūr (perhaps because of his father's position). According to Ibn ʿInaba, he died in al-Manṣūr's prison, but al-Iṣfahānī clarifies that he was imprisoned with his father when the latter was dismissed from his office as the governor of Medina, and died in prison.[62]

1.1.3.7 *Zayd b. al-Ḥasan b. Zayd b. al-Ḥasan b. ʿAlī b. Abī Ṭālib*

ʿAlī's brother, Zayd, is mentioned among those who took part in the revolt.[63]

1.2 ***Banū l-Ḥusayn b. ʿAlī b. Abī Ṭālib* (Chart 11)**

1.2.1 *The Family of ʿAlī b. al-Ḥusayn b. ʿAlī b. Abī Ṭālib*

Opposers of the Revolt/ʿAbbāsī supporters

Ⓜ1.2.1.1 *Al-Ḥusayn b. ʿAlī b. al-Ḥusayn b. ʿAlī b. Abī Ṭālib (d. 157/773 or 774)*[64]

Al-Ḥusayn, Jaʿfar al-Ṣādiq's uncle, was among the Ṭālibīs and other notables from among Quraysh who were summoned on the night of the revolt by the governor of Medina, Riyāḥ b. ʿUthmān. He is specifically quoted by an eyewitness as having assured the governor that they were obeying him unconditionally.[65]

61 Al-Ṭabarī, 3:258 (ll. 12–13); al-Iṣfahānī, *Maqātil*, 278 (l. 11); Nagel, "Muḥammad b. ʿAbdallāh," 257.

62 Ibn ʿInaba, *ʿUmda*, 70; al-Iṣfahānī, *Maqātil*, 398.

63 Al-Ṭabarī, 3:258 (ll. 12–13); al-Iṣfahānī, *Maqātil*, p . 398; Nagel, "Muḥammad b. ʿAbdallāh," 257.

64 On him, see al-Bukhārī, *Sirr al-silsila*, 69: died in 157/773 or 774; Ibn ʿInaba, *ʿUmda*, 318–319; al-ʿUmarī, *Ansāb*, 195; al-Shāhrūdī l-Namāzī, *Rijāl*, 5:181–182; al-Amīn, *Aʿyān al-Shīʿa*, 6:136. See also the short biographies in Sunnī *rijāl* works, e.g., Ibn Ḥajar, *Taqrīb* (Beirut, 1995), 1:216; al-Mizzī, *Tahdhīb*, 4:395–396; al-Ṣafadī, al-*Wāfī*, 12:266; on him and his family, see also Ahmed, *Religious Elite*, 172.

65 Al-Ṭabarī, 3:190–191 (l. 18 to l. 14); the quote is on 3:191 (ll. 9–10); a parallel tradition: al-Iṣfahānī, *Maqātil*, 261; the eyewitness (transmitter) is ʿAbdallāh b. ʿUmar b. ʿAlī b. Abī Ṭālib, the father of ʿĪsā who transmitted the tradition to ʿUmar b. Shabba.

(m)1.2.1.2 *His son, ʿUbaydallāh b. al-Ḥusayn b. ʿAlī b. al-Ḥusayn b. ʿAlī b. Abī Ṭālib (d. 157/773 or 774)*[66]

ʿUbaydallāh opposed Muḥammad's revolt, and when he was seized and brought before the latter, he closed his eyes and said "I am under oath to kill him if ever I see him (Muḥammad)."[67]

In Imāmī sources he is described as a close associate of Jaʿfar al-Ṣādiq: من أصحاب الصادق.[68] ʿUbaydallāh's mother was Khālida bt. Ḥamza b. Muṣʿab b. Thābit b. ʿAbdallāh b. al-Zubayr;[69] he married his cousin, Zaynab bt. Muḥammad (al-Bāqir) b. ʿAlī b. al-Ḥusayn b. ʿAlī b. Abī Ṭālib.[70] ʿUbaydallāh's daughter, Khadīja, was married to Jaʿfar al-Ṣādiq's son, Muḥammad.[71] Al-Iṣfahānī records a tradition of Muḥammad b. ʿAlī b. Ḥamza, according to which ʿUbaydallāh was poisoned by Abū Muslim in Khurāsān, but this is strongly refuted by al-Iṣfahānī, who adds that it is not mentioned by the Imāmī historian and genealogist Yaḥyā b. al-Ḥasan b. Jaʿfar, known as al-ʿAqīqī (d. 277/890 or 891), who belonged to ʿUbaydallāh's family.[72] Imāmī traditions do not mention this either. On the contrary, ʿUbaydallāh b. al-Ḥusayn b. ʿAlī had close relations

66 On him, see al-Bukhārī, *Sirr al-silsila*, 69–70; 69: died in 157 H.; al-Iṣfahānī, *Maqātil*, 170; Ibn ʿInaba, *ʿUmda*, 318–319; al-ʿUmarī, *Ansāb*, 195; al-Shāhrūdī, *Rijāl*, 5:181–182; al-Amīn, *Aʿyān al-Shīʿa*, 6:136; Ibn Ḥajar, *Taqrīb* (Beirut, 1995), 1:216; al-Ṣafadī, *al-Wāfī*, 12:266.

67 Al-Ṭabarī, 3:200–201 (l. 18 to l. 2); al-Iṣfahānī, *Maqātil*, 296: mistakenly عبد الله instead of عبيد الله; the tradition was copied by the Imāmī authors, e.g., al-Bukhārī, *Sirr al-silsila*, 70; Ibn ʿInaba, *ʿUmda*, 318–319; al-Shāhrūdī, *Rijāl*, 5:182.

68 E.g., al-Tafrishī, *Naqd al-rijāl*, 3:180.

69 Al-Bukhārī, *Sirr al-silsila*, 69.

70 Al-Ziryāṭī, *Muḥammad al-Bāqir*, 146.

71 Al-Iṣfahānī, *Maqātil*, 538.

72 Ibid., 170; on al-ʿAqīqī, see Günther, *Maqātil*, 226–228; al-Ziriklī, *al-Aʿlām*, 9:170 and the bibliography therein. Muḥammad b. ʿAlī b. Ḥamza [b. al-Ḥasan b. ʿUbaydallāh b. al-ʿAbbās b. ʿAlī b. Abī Ṭālib, d. 286/899] was the author of a book entitled *Maqātil al-ṭālibiyyīn* (al-Najāshī, *Rijāl*, 348), which was in the possession of his nephew, ʿAlī b. al-Ḥusayn b. ʿAlī b. Ḥamza (see Günther, *Maqātil*, 141). The latter gave it to Abū l-Faraj al-Iṣfahānī, who copied from the book, see al-Iṣfahānī, *Maqātil*, 13: وأخرج إلي كتاب عمه محمد بن علي بن حمزة فكتبته عنه; perhaps this book was the above-mentioned *Maqātil al-ṭālibiyyīn?* See ibid., 705: Abū l-Faraj most probably is quoting (from Muḥammad b. ʿAlī b. Ḥamza's book) a long list of Ṭālibīs who were killed: وذكر محمد بن علي بن حمزة مقاتل جماعة من الطالبيين; Abū l-Faraj used this book extensively, for example, see *Maqātil*, 94 (twice), 164, 165 (في كتابه), 189, 228; on Muḥammad b. ʿAlī b. Ḥamza, see Sezgin, 1:322; Günther, *Maqātil*, 190–191; see also al-Najāshī, *Rijāl*, 348; al-Bukhārī, *Sirr al-silsila*, 92 and the note of the editor therein; Ibn ʿInaba, *ʿUmda*, 358; al-Tustarī, *Rijāl*, 9:439; al-Khūʾī, *Rijāl*, 17:351: (copying al-Najāshī).

with Abū Muslim in Khurāsān before the ascendance of the ʿAbbāsīs.[73] Abū l-ʿAbbās al-Saffāḥ granted him an estate in al-Madāʾin called al-Bīdashīn (or Dhū Amarān/Dhū Amān), which gave him a large annual income.[74]

1.2.1.3 *Al-Ḥasan b. ʿAlī b. al-Ḥusayn b. ʿAlī b. al-Ḥusayn b. ʿAlī b. Abī Ṭālib*[75] *and*

(m)1.2.1.4 *ʿAlī b. ʿUmar b. ʿAlī b. al-Ḥusayn b. ʿAlī b. Abī Ṭālib*[76]

Both are mentioned in the presence of the governor Riyāḥ, on the eve of the outbreak of the revolt.[77] Nothing is known about their activity during the revolt.

1.2.2 The Family of Muḥammad (al-Bāqir) b. ʿAlī b. al-Ḥusayn b. ʿAlī b. Abī Ṭālib

Supporters of the Revolt

1.2.2.1 *Mūsā b. Jaʿfar (al-Ṣādiq) b. Muḥammad b. ʿAlī b. al-Ḥusayn b. ʿAlī b. Abī Ṭālib*

1.2.2.2 *ʿAbdallāh b. Jaʿfar (al-Ṣādiq)*[78]

ʿAbdallāh fought alongside Muḥammad and killed an ʿAbbāsī soldier in a duel.[79] On the face of it, this may raise a problem, due to the *quʿūd* policy of Jaʿfar,

73 Al-Bukhārī, *Sirr al-silsila*, 70 (= Ibn ʿInaba, *ʿUmda*, 319).

74 Al-Bukhārī, *Sirr al-silsila*, 69 (al-Bīdashīn); Ibn ʿInaba, *ʿUmda*, 319 (Dhū Amarān/Dhū Amān); Bernheimer, *The ʿAlids*, 19.

75 I was unable to identify him; this may be an error, and should be rendered as al-Ḥasan b. ʿAlī b. ʿAlī b. al-Ḥusayn b. ʿAlī b. Abī Ṭālib (al-Afṭas, see above). I was unable to find the name as rendered in al-Ṭabarī in the biographical dictionaries; note that in al-Ṭabarī, 3:191 (l. 2) he is al-Ḥasan, but cf. note b. according to MS A: Ḥusayn; also according to the parallel tradition in al-Iṣfahānī, *Maqātil*, 261 (l. 7); is he al-Ḥusayn b. ʿAlī b. al-Ḥusayn b. ʿAlī b. Abī Ṭālib? (see above).

76 On him, see ʿUmarī, *Ansāb*, 149; al-Shāhrūdī, *Rijāl*, 5:419; Ibn Abī Ḥātim, *al-Jarḥ*, 6:196; Ibn Ḥibbān, *al-Thiqāt*, 8:456; al-Ṣafadī, *al-Wāfī*, 21:348; these sources do not disclose any historical information about him.

77 Al-Ṭabarī, 3:191.

78 Al-Iṣfahānī, *Maqātil*, 277 (l. 8) (correct ولد الحسن to ولد الحسين according to the parallel tradition, ibid., 389 (l. 8)): from al-Ḥusayn b. Zayd [b. ʿAlī b. al-Ḥusayn b. ʿAlī b. Abī Ṭālib]; this error was noticed by Nagel, "Muḥammad b. ʿAbdallāh," 275, n. 24; Arjomand, "Crisis of the Imamate," 492 [in Kohlberg = 110]: according to al-Iṣfahānī; on Mūsā (al-Kāẓim) b. Jaʿfar, the seventh *Imām*, see Kohlberg, "Mūsā al-Kāẓim."

79 Al-Iṣfahānī, *Maqātil*, 278 (ll. 1–2): from an eyewitness, al-Ḥusayn b. Zayd b. ʿAlī, who was a supporter of the revolt; mentioned by Arjomand, "Crisis of the Imamate," 492 [in Kohlberg = 110]: according to al-Iṣfahānī; Crone, *Political Thought*, 114 (according to al-Iṣfahānī).

whom we know did not take an active part in the revolt. According to a pro-Ḥasanī tradition, Jaʿfar did not join Muḥammad, but permitted his two sons to join him and his cause.[80] (It is noteworthy that another son of Jaʿfar al-Ṣādiq, Ismāʿīl, was pro-ʿAbbāsī; see below.)

Opposers of the Revolt/ ʿAbbāsī Supporters

1.2.2.3 *Jaʿfar (al-Ṣādiq) b. Muḥammad (al-Bāqir)*[81]

The Sunnī and Shīʿī Imāmī sources supply extensive evidence regarding the tension, contention and strife between the Ḥasanīs and the Ḥusaynīs, mainly between Jaʿfar al-Ṣādiq and ʿAbdallāh b. al-Ḥasan and his son, Muḥammad.[82] It is accepted by scholars that Jaʿfar al-Ṣādiq "did not see it necessary for the Imām to rise in rebellion and try to become *de facto* ruler,"[83] and "at the time of the Shīʿī revolt of Muḥammad al-Nafs al-Zakiyya in al-Ḥijāz (145/762), he was again neutral, leading the Ḥusaynids in their passivity in that largely Ḥasanid affair, and was left in peace by al-Manṣūr."[84] This last statement, regarding the relations between al-Manṣūr and Jaʿfar al-Ṣādiq requires reconsideration.[85] In spite of this, and despite the well-known *quʿūd* doctrine of Jaʿfar (and his father before him) and the specific information about his refusal to take part in the revolt,[86] two of his sons took an active part in the revolt alongside Muḥammad

80 Al-Iṣfahānī, *Maqātil*, 252 (ll. 12–13): from Sulaymān b. Nahīk, a minor obscure Imāmī transmitter; the authors of Imāmī *rijāl* know almost nothing about him, for example, see al-Khūʾī, *Rijāl*, 9:295; al-Shāhrūdī, *Rijāl*, 4:153.

81 For a general bibliography on Jaʿfar al-Ṣādiq, see Jafri, *Shīʿa*, chapter 10, 259–288 and chapter 11, 289–316; for his central theological doctrines, see 281–283; 290–291: *naṣṣ* and *ʿilm*; 299–300: *taqiyya*; 249, 253, 260, 266, 267, 293, 299–300: his quiescent (*quʿūd*) policy; 300–304: the superhuman nature of the Imāms; Hodgson, "Djaʿfar al-Ṣādiḳ," 374a–375b; Hodgson, "Early Shīʿa," esp. 10–12; Gleave, "Jaʿfar al-Ṣādeq," 349–356 (life; teachings); Arjomand, "Crisis of the Imamate," 491–492 [in Kohlberg = 109–110]; Halm, *Shīʿa*, 21–24; Zaman, *Religion and Politics*, 35–56 and the bibliography in n. 11.

82 For an outstanding tradition in this vein, see al-Kulaynī, *al-Kāfī*, 1:362–364; this was partly dealt with in the discussion on "al-Abwāʾ Meeting" (chapter 2), and is further discussed in appendix 3.

83 Hodgson, "Early Shīʿa," 11.

84 Hodgson, "Djaʿfar al-Ṣādiḳ," 374; for similar views see, for example, Jafri, *Shīʿa*, 267, 293; Omar, "Aspects," 172; Arjomand, *Formation*, 492 [in Kohlberg = 110]; Gleave, "Jaʿfar al-Ṣādeq."

85 Arjomand, *Formation*, 492: "Jaʿfar even named the Caliph al-Manṣūr an executor of his will"; in n. 11, Arjomand quotes al-Ṭūsī, *Kitāb al-Ghayba* (Najaf, 1965), 119, 255, but the evidence is far from being unequivocal.

86 E.g., al-Ṭabarī, 3:252 (ll. 6–7); al-Iṣfahānī, *Maqātil*, 252 (ll. 9–13); see also al-Ṭabarī, 3:190–191 (l. 18 to l. 14).

b. ʿAbdallāh. It is noteworthy that al-Qāsim b. Isḥāq b. ʿAbdallāh b. Jaʿfar b. Abī Ṭālib, who was one of Muḥammad al-Nafs al-Zakiyya's loyal supporters and who was appointed by him as the governor of Yemen, was a cousin (on his mother's side) of Jaʿfar (al-Ṣādiq) and transmitted traditions from him.[87]

1.2.2.4 *Ismāʿīl (al-Aʿraj) b. Jaʿfar (al-Ṣādiq) b. Muḥammad (al-Bāqir) b. ʿAlī b. al-Ḥusayn b. ʿAlī b. Abī Ṭālib*

Ismāʿīl b. Jaʿfar warned al-Manṣūr at the end of 140/April–May 758 of a plot by Muḥammad b. ʿAbdallāh, who was cooperating with one of al-Manṣūr's commanders from *ahl Khurāsān* to assassinate him in Mecca during the *ḥajj* of the year 140 H. This is related by one of the most trusted adherents of Muḥammad b. ʿAbdallāh, Abū Habbār al-Muzanī.[88] Ismāʿīl is not mentioned by the sources during the revolt.

1.2.2.5 *The Family of ʿAbdallāh b. Muḥammad b. ʿAlī b. al-Ḥusayn b. ʿAlī b. Abī Ṭālib*

Supporters of the Revolt

1.2.2.5.1 Ḥamza b. ʿAbdallāh b. Muḥammad (al-Bāqir)

Ḥamza, Jaʿfar al-Ṣādiq's nephew, is described as one of the most courageous supporters of Muḥammad al-Nafs al-Zakiyya. This time, the well-known transmitters who belonged to the ʿUmarī (ʿAlīd) family know that in his case, unlike the case of his two sons, Jaʿfar al-Ṣādiq, his uncle, forbade him to join the revolt.[89] Perhaps this was also due to the fact that besides being his uncle, he was also his father-in-law, since Ḥamza was married to Jaʿfar's daughter, Asmāʾ, who bore him Umm Farwa and ʿAbdallāh.[90]

87 Al-Shabastarī, *al-Imām al-Ṣādiq*, 2:585; al-Shāhrūdī l-Namāzī, *Rijāl*, 6:234. On him, see also below.

88 Al-Ṭabarī, 3:153–154 (l. 16 to l. 9).

89 Al-Ṭabarī, 3:254 (ll. 5–6): ʿUmar b. Shabba < ʿĪsā b. ʿAbdallāh [b. Muḥammad b. ʿAlī b. ʿUmar b. ʿAlī b. Abī Ṭālib] < his father; ibid., 3:258 (ll. 11–12); Nagel, "Muḥammad b. ʿAbdallāh," 257: according to al-Ṭabarī, 3:258.

90 Al-Zubayrī, *Nasab Quraysh*, 63; see also al-Zirbāṭī, *Muḥammad al-Bāqir*, 112, 126, and his sources quoted therein. In the Imāmī literature he is described as one of the close supporters of Jaʿfar al-Ṣādiq (من أصحاب الصادق), for example, see al-Khūʾī, *Rijāl*, 7:285.

1.2.3 The Family of Zayd b. ʿAlī b. al-Ḥusayn b. ʿAlī b. Abī Ṭālib

Supporters of the Revolt

1.2.3.1 *Al-Ḥusayn b. Zayd b. ʿAlī b. al-Ḥusayn b. ʿAlī b. Abī Ṭālib*

He had special close relations with his cousin, Jaʿfar al-Ṣādiq, who raised him and took special care of him after his father's death.[91] The traditions in which he shows great sympathy towards Jaʿfar al-Ṣādiq may be due to their close relations.[92]

He supported both Muḥammad and Ibrāhīm and fought at their sides.[93] When the revolts ended, he stayed in hiding for a long time. After a certain period, when he understood that he was not wanted by the authorities, he came out of his hiding place gradually, appearing at first only to his family and his brothers, and then freely in Medina. This may have been possible because his brother Muḥammad b. Zayd b. ʿAlī, who was pro-ʿAbbāsī, stayed with (or supported) al-Manṣūr and did not join the revolts of Muḥammad and Ibrāhīm. It is related that al-Ḥusayn b. Zayd used to correspond with his brother, Muḥammad.[94]

1.2.3.2 *ʿĪsā b. Zayd b. ʿAlī b. al-Ḥusayn b. ʿAlī b. Abī Ṭālib (109–169/727–785 or 786)*[95]

He was one of the close supporters of Muḥammad. Together with his brother, al-Ḥusayn, he fought with Muḥammad and Ibrāhīm and subsequently went into hiding until his death during the rule of al-Hādī or al-Rashīd.[96] His loyalty to Muḥammad is emphasized by the sources.[97] In the battle against the ʿAbbāsī army he stood at the head of both the *maymana* of Muḥammad in Medina

91 Al-Iṣfahānī, *Maqātil*, 387.

92 E.g., al-Ṭabarī, 3:174–175 (l. 15 to l. 7); al-Iṣfahānī, *Maqātil*, 251–252; there is a noteworthy tradition in which he describes the arrival of Ibrāhīm al-Imām (al-ʿAbbāsī) to Medina; he distributes money to the ʿAlīds, and gives Jaʿfar al-Ṣādiq al-Ḥusaynī a sum double that of the Ḥasanīs.

93 Al-Iṣfahānī, *Maqātil*, 277, 389: at Muḥammad's side; 387, 406: both Muḥammad and Ibrāhīm; Ahmed, *Religious Elite*, 179, n. 954.

94 Ibid., 387: "stayed with (or supported) al-Manṣūr": وكان أخوه محمد بن زيد مع أبي جعفر المنصور.

95 Al-Bukhārī, *Sirr al-silsila*, 65.

96 On him, see al-Iṣfahānī, *Maqātil*, 405–428; al-Bukhārī, *Sirr al-ṣilsila*, 65–66; Ibn ʿInaba, *ʿUmda*, 285–289; 289–293 (his descendants); Ahmed, *Religious Elite*, 178f.

97 Al-Iṣfahānī, *Maqātil*, 296 (= al-Ṭabarī, 3:200–201 (l. 18 to l. 2): a parallel tradition lacking the beginning); al-Iṣfahānī, *Maqātil*, 283: an abbreviated tradition.

and that of Ibrāhīm at Bākhamrā in al-ʿIrāq.[98] According to an Imāmī tradition, he was appointed head of the *shurṭa* of Muḥammad al-Nafs al-Zakiyya.[99] Imāmī traditions add that he was designated by Ibrāhīm b. ʿAbdallāh as his heir and was the bearer of the latter's flag in battle.[100] These traditions record the fierce and violent arguments between Jaʿfar al-Ṣādiq and his cousin, ʿĪsā b. Zayd; ʿĪsā (together with Muḥammad al-Nafs al-Zakiyya) demanded that Jaʿfar join the revolt and swear allegiance to Muḥammad, while Jaʿfar strongly objected and warned his cousin that the rebellion was doomed, and gave them both a detailed picture of the circumstances of the death of Muḥammad al-Nafs al-Zakiyya. After the revolt ʿĪsā b. Zayd hid in ʿAlī b. Ṣāliḥ's house until he (ʿĪsā) died.[101]

Opposers of the Revolt/ʿAbbāsī Supporters

1.2.3.3 *Muḥammad b. Zayd b. ʿAlī b. al-Ḥusayn b. ʿAlī*[102]

Muḥammad was a pro-ʿAbbāsī zealot, one of the Ṭālibī notables in ʿĪsā b. Mūsā's army, who was sent by the latter to the people of Medina to call on them to accept safe conduct.[103] His two brothers, al-Ḥusayn and ʿĪsā, were active zealot supporters of Muḥammad b. ʿAbdallāh (see above).

---

98 Ibid., 406: … ʿAbbād b. Yaʿqūb < ʿĪsā b. ʿAbdallāh b. Muḥammad b. ʿUmar b. ʿAlī b. Abī Ṭālib.

99 Al-Kulaynī, *al-Kāfī*, 1:362; al-Baḥrānī, *Madīnat al-maʿājiz*, 5:283; al-Māzandarānī, *Sharḥ*, 6:315.

100 Ibn ʿInaba, *ʿUmda*, 285–286: وكان وصي إبراهيم . . . وحامل رايته.

101 Al-Iṣfahānī, *Maqātil*, 413, 420, 423–424; according to Ibn Saʿd, *Ṭabaqāt*, 6:375, al-Ḥasan b. Ṣāliḥ and ʿĪsā b. Zayd hid together in one place in al-Kūfa until the death of ʿĪsā in this hiding place.

102 On him, see al-Bukhārī, *Sirr al-silsila*, 67; al-Iṣfahānī, *Maqātil*, pp., 267, 387; al-Bukhārī, *Sirr al-silsila*, 67; al-Khaṭīb al-Baghdādī, *Taʾrīkh* (Beirut, 1997), 2:358; al-ʿUmarī, *Ansāb*, 183–186; 183: one of the Ṭālibī family who supported al-Manṣūr against the Ḥasanīs; al-Tafrishī, *Naqd al-rijāl*, 4:210; al-Tustarī, *Rijāl*, 9:275–276; al-Khūʾī, *Rijāl*, 17:103; Ahmed, *Religious Elite*, 179–180.

103 Al-Balādhurī, *Ansāb* (ed. Madelung), 2:513; al-Iṣfahānī, *Maqātil*, 267; ibid., 387: وكان مع أبي جعفر [المنصور] مسودا; al-ʿUmarī, *Ansāb*, 186.

1.2.4 The Family of ʿAlī b. ʿAlī b. al-Ḥusayn b. ʿAlī b. Abī Ṭālib

Supporters of the Revolt

1.2.4.1 *Al-Ḥasan (al-Afṭas) b. ʿAlī b. ʿAlī b. al-Ḥusayn b. ʿAlī b. Abī Ṭālib*[104]

Al-Ḥasan was a cousin of Jaʿfar al-Ṣādiq, one of the loyal supporters of Muḥammad al-Nafs al-Zakiyya. The Ṭālibīs spread a tradition, according to which it was al-Ḥasan b. ʿAlī b. ʿAlī b. al-Ḥusayn b. ʿAlī b. Abī Ṭālib, nicknamed al-Afṭas, who was the bearer of the white or yellow flag of al-Nafs al-Zakiyya. The source that transmitted this information took part in the revolt. The tradition was related to ʿUmar b. Shabba by ʿĪsā b. ʿAbdallāh b. Muḥammad b. ʿUmar b.ʿAlī b. Abī Ṭālib from his father. The complete tradition is recorded by al-Iṣfahānī (with some omissions by al-Ṭabarī):

> al-Afṭas, who is al-Ḥasan b.ʿAlī b. ʿAlī b. al-Ḥusayn [b. ʿAlī b. Abī Ṭālib], had a yellow flag of Muḥammad with a picture of a serpent on it with him; each of his commanders (*aṣḥābihi*) from the family of ʿAlī b. Abī Ṭālib had a flag, and their battle cry was "(God is) One and one alone" (*Aḥad Aḥad*).

The transmitter said [adding]: "This was the same battle cry of the Prophet, may God pray for him and his family, in the battle of Ḥunayn" [in the year 8/630].[105]

---

104 On him, see al-Bukhārī, *Sirr al-silsila*, 76–80; Ibn ʿInaba, *ʿUmda*, 339–340; al-ʿUmarī, *Ansāb*, 205ff.; al-Najāshī, *Rijāl*, 328–329; al-Tustarī, *Rijāl*, 12:92–93; al-Amīn, *Aʿyān al-Shīʿa*, 5:205–206.

105 Al-Iṣfahānī, *Maqātil*, 284 (mentioned by Nagel, "Muḥammad b. ʿAbdallāh," 257): ʿUmar b. Shabba < ʿĪsā b. ʿAbdallāh b. Muḥammad b. ʿUmar b. ʿAlī [b. Abī Ṭālib] < his father; al-Ṭabarī, 3:237 (ll. 14–15) (with some omissions); al-Iṣfahānī: علم لمحمد أصفر; al-Ṭabarī: omitting لمحمد; ibid., correct the name al-Ḥasan b. ʿAlī b. al-Ḥusayn, to al-Ḥasan b. ʿAlī b. ʿAlī b. al-Ḥusayn [b. Abī Ṭālib]). "*Aḥad Aḥad*," was also the battle cry of the Muslims in the battle of Badr, see Ibn Hishām, *al-Sīra*, 2:463; but cf. al-Ḥalabī, *Insān al-ʿuyūn*, 2:426: in Badr, the battle cry (and password) of the Anṣār was أحد أحد and that of the Muhājirūn was يا بني عبد الرحمان. According to another version, the Prophet and the Muhājirūn's battle cry was يا منصور أمت or أحد أحد, that of the Khazraj was يا بني عبد الله, and that of the Aws: يا بني عبيد الله, but, adds the author, according to Ibn Saʿd, the battle cry of all the Muslims in Badr was: يا منصور أمت; see also al-Maqrīzī, *Imtāʿ*, 1:106. Dr. Luke Treadwell informed me (personal correspondence, November 2009) of the coins that were issued in al-Baṣra by Ibrāhīm b. ʿAbdallāh, in 145 H., where the phrase "*aḥad aḥad*" appears; he wrote: "Q. xvii.81 is also on AR Basra 145 issued by Ibrahim b. ʿAbdallāh (Shamma, *Yarmouk Numismatics*, 4, 16) where it is combined with the phrase

Other Imāmī sources speak of the yellow flag,[106] but an early Imāmī author, Abū Naṣr al-Bukhārī, claimed that the color of al-Ḥasan's flag was white.[107]

Imāmī sources tell of the enmity and disdain between him and Jaʿfar al-Ṣādiq. The latter physically attacked and besmirched al-Ḥasan for his support of the revolt, while another tradition even tells of an alleged attempt by al-Ḥasan to kill Jaʿfar al-Ṣādiq. Despite this fierce dispute, on his deathbed Jaʿfar bequeathed al-Ḥasan 70 or 80 *dīnārs*.[108] After the revolt was crushed, al-Afṭas went into hiding. The Imāmī sources state that Jaʿfar al-Ṣādiq pleaded for him in the presence of Caliph al-Manṣūr, who pardoned him and gave him *amān*.[109]

A major aim of these traditions is to stress Jaʿfar al-Ṣādiq's sublime character. But even if these are literary motifs, they were woven around a grain of historical truth. Al-Ḥasan was an enthusiastic supporter of the revolt and Jaʿfar al-Ṣādiq clearly was not. There may have been other reasons for the hatred and enmity between the two; this topic merits a separate extended study.

1.3 *Banū Jaʿfar b. Abī Ṭālib* (Chart III)

Supporters of the Revolt

1.3.1 The Family of ʿAbdallāh b. Jaʿfar b. Abī Ṭālib

The Jaʿfarī version states that the sons of Muʿāwiya (b. ʿAbdallāh) hastened to join Muḥammad, except Muʿāwiya's brother Ismāʿīl (see below).[110] This is also vividly depicted by the Imāmī tradition, related by Mūsā b. ʿAbdallāh b.

---

aḥad aḥad (which Shamma proves, quoting from *Maqātil al-ṭālibiyyīn*, was a slogan of al-Nafs al-Zakiyya and his brother)."

106 Al-ʿUmarī, *Ansāb*, 205 (= Ibn ʿInaba, *ʿUmda*, 339).

107 Al-Bukhārī, *Sirr al-silsila*, 77; Ibn ʿInaba, *ʿUmda*, 339 (quoting Abū Naṣr al-Bukhārī).

108 Al-Bukhārī, *Sirr al-silsila*, 77. The source of the tradition is Yaḥyā b. al-Ḥasan al-Nassāba, known as al-ʿAqīqī (d. 277/890 or 891) and the parallel Imāmī sources that copy him, sometimes adding other versions, e.g., Ibn ʿInaba, *ʿUmda*, 339–340; al-ʿUmarī, *Ansāb*, 212; al-Majlisī, *Biḥār*, 46:182, 247; al-Tustarī, *Rijāl*, 12:93; al-Amīn, *Aʿyān al-Shīʿa*, 5:205.

109 Al-Bukhārī, *Sirr al-silsila*, 77 (= al-Tustarī, *Rijāl*, 12:93); Ibn ʿInaba, *ʿUmda*, 240. On him, see also al-Amīn, *Aʿyān al-Shīʿa*, 5:206; al-Zubayrī, *Nasab Quraysh*, 72–73; Ibn Ḥazm, *Jamhara*, 53, names al-Ḥusayn b. al-Ḥasan b. ʿAlī, who rebelled during al-Maʾmūn's period in Mecca, al-Afṭas; cf. al-Bukhārī, *Sirr al-silsila*, 46: Ibn al-Afṭas, al-Ḥusayn b. al-Ḥasan b. ʿAlī b. ʿAlī Zayn al-ʿĀbidīn.

110 Al-Ṭabarī, 3:200 (ll. 8–18): [ʿUmar b. Shabba] < Muḥammad b. Ismāʿīl.

al-Ḥasan.[111] Three sons and one daughter of Muʿāwiya are mentioned as the supporters of the revolt:[112]

1.3.1.1 *Yazīd b. Muʿāwiya b. ʿAbdallāh b. Jaʿfar b. Abī Ṭālib*

He is mentioned as one of Muḥammad b. ʿAbdallāh' supporters.[113] An Imāmī tradition states that he commanded the *muqaddima* of Muḥammad al-Nafs al-Zakiyya.[114]

1.3.1.2 *Ṣāliḥ b. Muʿāwiya b. ʿAbdallāh b. Jaʿfar b. Abī Ṭālib*[115]

From another tradition recorded by al-Balādhurī, we learn that in the decisive battle both Yazīd and Ṣāliḥ, the sons of Muʿāwiya b. ʿAbdallāh b. Jaʿfar, headed one of the wings of al-Nafs al-Zakiyya's army facing the ʿAbbāsī wing led by Kathīr b. al-Ḥuṣayn. The two brothers wanted to surrender and asked for (a letter of) protection and security (*amān*), which was given to them by Kathīr, the ʿAbbāsī commander. But ʿĪsā b. Mūsā did not approve the *amān*, so Kathīr let them escape from Medina. Al-Balādhurī adds that the mother of Yazīd and Ṣāliḥ was Fāṭima bt. al-Ḥasan b. al-Ḥasan b. ʿAlī b. Abī Ṭālib. This made Muḥammad al-Nafs al-Zakiyya their cousin on their mother's side.[116]

1.3.1.3 *Al-Ḥasan b. Muʿāwiya b. ʿAbdallāh b. Jaʿfar b. Abī Ṭālib*

He was appointed governor of Mecca by Muḥammad b. ʿAbdallāh. After Muḥammad's death he was caught and brought to al-Manṣūr in al-ʿIrāq, who imprisoned him for a long time.[117] He was released only after al-Mahdī became caliph (158/775).[118]

1.3.1.4 *Ḥammāda bt. Muʿāwiya b. ʿAbdallāh b. Jaʿfar b. Abī Ṭālib*

She is mentioned as an uncompromising supporter of Muḥammad b. ʿAbdallāh. She was married to her cousin, ʿAbdallāh b. Ismāʿīl b. ʿAbdallāh b. Jaʿfar.[119] When her father in-law confronted Muḥammad al-Nafs al-Zakiyya and refused to swear allegiance to him, she strongly denounced him, and according

111 Al-Kulaynī, *al-Kāfī*, 1:364; al-Majlisī, *Biḥār*, 47:285–286.

112 The three sons are mentioned by Nagel, "Muḥammad b. ʿAbdallāh," 257 (according to al-Ṭabarī and al-Iṣfahānī).

113 Al-Ṭabarī, 3:258 (ll. 5–7): [ʿUmar b. Shabba] < ʿĪsā [b. ʿAbdallāh al-Ṭālibī l-ʿUmarī].

114 Al-Kulaynī, *al-Kāfī*, 1:364; al-Majlisī, *Biḥār*, 47:286; al-Māzandarānī, *Sharḥ*, 6:317.

115 Al-Ṭabarī, 3:258 (ll. 5–7).

116 Al-Balādhurī, *Ansāb* (ed. Madelung), 2:514; ibid., 2:80: their mother.

117 Al-Balādhurī, *Ansāb* (ed. al-Maḥmūdī, 1974), 2a:67 (= ed. Zakkār and Ziriklī, 2:325 (827)).

118 Al-Iṣfahānī, *Maqātil*, 300, 305.

119 Ibid., 497.

to one tradition, she even killed him.[120] Another source relates the murder to "the sons of Muʿāwiya," without specifying a name.[121]

ⓜ1.3.1.5 *Al-Qāsim b. Isḥāq b. ʿAbdallāh b. Jaʿfar b. Abī Ṭālib*

As noted above, al-Qāsim was appointed governor of Yemen by Muḥammad al-Nafs al-Zakiyya[122] and was the cousin (on his mother's side) of Jaʿfar al-Ṣādiq, who transmitted traditions from him; he was (on his father's side) the cousin of al-Ḥasan, Yazīd, and Ṣāliḥ, the sons of Muʿāwiya. Traditions about the events concerning his appointment as governor were related to ʿUmar b. Shabba by his grandson, ʿAbdallāh b. Isḥāq b. al-Qāsim.[123] He was highly appreciated by the Imāmī scholars, who describe him as "one of the best *muḥaddithūn* of the Imāmiyya, and he was a governor of Yemen" (من حسان محدثي الإمامية وكان أميرا على اليمن). The Imāmī scholar does not bother to trouble us with the fact (likely well-known to every Imāmī scholar) that he was appointed to the the governorship by Muḥammad al-Nafs al-Zakiyya.[124]

Opposers of the Revolt/ʿAbbāsī Supporters

ⓜ1.3.1.6 *Ismāʿīl b. ʿAbdallāh b. Jaʿfar b. Abī Ṭālib*[125]

The Imāmī tradition is related by Mūsā b. ʿAbdallāh b. al-Ḥasan (Muḥammad al-Nafs al-Zakiyya's brother); it describes how Ismāʿīl b. ʿAbdallāh b. Jaʿfar was summoned to Muḥammad b. ʿAbdallāh al-Nafs al-Zakiyya, who demanded his *bayʿa*, but when Ismāʿīl refused, he was carried to his home and brutally killed (trampled upon) by the sons of his brother, Muʿāwiya b. ʿAbdallāh b. Jaʿfar: حتى دخل عليه بنو أخيه بنو معاوية بن عبد الله بن جعفر فتوطؤوه. He is described as a very old and weak man, who could not walk without assistance.[126] The

120 Al-Ṭabarī, 3:200 (ll. 8–18): the first part is transmitted by the Jaʿfarī family; the second part that tells about the murder of Ismāʿīl by Ḥammāda begins with: ويقال "and it is said," which implies a less trustworthy version.

121 Al-Kulaynī, *al-Kāfī*, 1:364.

122 Al-Ṭabarī, 3:202; he is mentioned by Nagel, "Muḥammad b. ʿAbdallāh," 257.

123 Al-Ṭabarī, 3:202 (ll. 3–4); 3:221 (ll. 5–7).

124 Al-Shabastarī, *al-Imām al-Ṣādiq*, 2:585.

125 On the family, see Ibn ʿInaba, *ʿUmda*, 38ff.; on Ismāʿīl, see 38–39 and the long note by the editor on 39.

126 Al-Kulaynī, *al-Kāfī*, 1:364; Ibn Ḥamza al-Ṭūsī, *al-Thāqib fī l-manāqib*, 381–382; al-Baḥrānī, *Madīnat al-maʿājiz*, 5:93–94, 286–287; al-Majlisī, *Biḥār*, 47:285–286 (all three sources copy al-Kulaynī). These facts are incorporated in a long tradition recorded (except for a few lines) by the Ḥasanī Mūsā b. ʿAbdallāh b. al-Ḥasan, the brother of Muḥammad al-Nafs al-Zakiyya, who relates in the first person and in a very detailed manner the events that

Jaʿfarī version states that he was killed by his niece, Ḥammāda, the daughter of Muʿāwiya, by order of Muḥammad b. ʿAbdallāh.[127]

Ismāʿīl b. ʿAbdallāh was very old (about 90), sick, and very weak, and still did not swear allegiance to al-Nafs al-Zakiyya. He most probably was not able to reach the ʿAbbāsī camp outside Medina, but his son ʿAbdallāh did.

1.3.1.7 *ʿAbdallāh b. Ismāʿīl b. ʿAbdallāh b. Jaʿfar b. Abī Ṭālib*

He came to the ʿAbbāsī camp from Medina upon the outbreak of the revolt with more than ten Ṭālibī dignitaries. They all stayed in ʿĪsā b. Mūsā's camp and later on he (with other Ṭālibīs) were sent by ʿĪsā b. Mūsā to persuade the inhabitants of Medina to surrender. They failed in this mission. This unique information was narrated to ʿĪsā b. ʿAbdallāh (and from the latter to ʿUmar b. Shabba) by the above-mentioned Muḥammad b. Zayd [b. ʿAlī b. al-Ḥusayn b. ʿAlī b. Abī Ṭālib], who was one of the Ṭālibī dignitaries in ʿĪsā's camp.[128]

The sources do not tell us whether he joined the ʿAbbāsī camp after his father was murdered, or before it happened. So much lies hidden behind the short sentences in al-Ṭabarī. Perhaps his mission in Medina served as an incentive for his father's murder, or perhaps he arrived in the city after his father's death.

1.3.1.8 *Muḥammad b. ʿAbdallāh (Abū l-Karrām [Kirām?]) b. Muḥammad b. ʿAlī b. ʿAbdallāh b. Jaʿfar b. Abī Ṭālib*[129]

He was a faithful supporter of the ʿAbbāsīs and their cause and was one of the closest confidential dignitaries of Caliph al-Manṣūr, that is, he belonged

---

occurred in Medina after the outbreak of the revolt and the short period of Muḥammad's sovereignty in Medina (see the full discussion in chapter 6, 279f., according to al-Kulaynī, *al-Kāfī*, 1:358–366). His short biographies in the Sunnī *rijāl* works do not mention the circumstances of his death, for example, see Ibn Ḥajar, *Taqrīb* (1986 edition), 1:108: died approximately 90 years old; al-Dhahabī, *al-Kāshif*, 1:246; al-Mizzī, *Tahdhīb*, 3:112.

127 Al-Ṭabarī, 3:200 (ll. 8–18): [ʿUmar b. Shabba] < Muḥammad b. Ismāʿīl [al-Jaʿfarī] < Ibn Abī Mulayka *mawlā* ʿAbdallāh b. Jaʿfar; ibid., Ismāʿīl's son ʿAbdallāh accuses Muḥammad b. ʿAbdallāh of ordering his father to be killed.

128 Al-Ṭabarī, 3:235–236 (l. 6 to l. 5); on him, see 252 above.

129 His lineage was rendered according to Ibn ʿInaba, *ʿUmda*, 51–52 (on the history of this family, see ibid., 38–55); al-ʿUmarī, *Ansāb*, 304–305; al-Zubayrī, *Nasab Quraysh*, 359; Ibn Mākūlā, *al-Ikmāl*, 7:128; correct al-Ṭabarī, 3:232–233 (l. 20 to l. 1): Muḥammad b. Abī l-Karrām b. ʿAbdallāh b. ʿAlī to Muḥammad b. Abī l-Karrām, ʿAbdallāh b. Muḥammad b. ʿAlī; Karrām is rendered by McAuliffe, *ʿAbbāsid Authority*, index; see Ibn Mākūlā, *al-Ikmāl*, 7:164: Kirām.

to the caliph's *ṣaḥāba*.[130] Al-Manṣūr sent him with ʿĪsā b. Mūsā to suppress the revolt of Muḥammad b. ʿAbdallāh. The latter's head was brought before him for identification,[131] and then he received the honor of carrying it, and most probably the heads of those who were killed with him, apparently mostly those of Banū Shujāʿ,[132] from Medina to the caliph.[133] He was also in the ʿAbbāsī army that was sent against Ibrāhīm b. ʿAbdallāh; he identified the head of the latter,[134] and then brought it to Egypt.[135] Muḥammad b. Abī l-Karrām, his son Ibrāhīm, and his brother Dāwūd transmitted traditions about the revolt of Muḥammad b. ʿAbdallāh.

1.3.1.9 *A* mawlā *of ʿAbdallāh b. Muʿāwiya* [*b. ʿAbdallāh b. Jaʿfar b. Abī Ṭālib*]
He was in charge [commander?] of the armored horsemen and horses: وكان على مجففته of ʿĪsā b. Mūsā's army. He was ordered by ʿĪsā b. Mūsā to choose ten of his armored horsemen, and together with ten Ṭālibīs they set out for the city of Medina to negotiate the surrender of the city to the ʿAbbāsīs.[136] No further information is given about him.

1.4 *Banū ʿUmar b. ʿAlī b. Abī Ṭālib*[137] (Chart IV)

1.4.1 The Family of Muḥammad b. ʿUmar b. ʿAlī b. Abī Ṭālib[138]

Opposers of the Revolt/ʿAbbāsī Supporters

So far, I have come across several descendants from this family who were active during the middle of the eighth century. Since they also lived during

130 Ibn Saʿd, *al-Qism al-mutammim*, 377; al-Ṭabarī, 3:225 (ll. 12–14).

131 Ibn Saʿd, *al-Qism al-mutammim*, 378.

132 Al-Ṭabarī, 3:254–255 (last line to line 1).

133 Ibid., 3:252 (ll. 12–14), 3:254 (ll. 8, 11); 3:302 (l. 20); al-Iṣfahānī, *Maqātil*, 275; Ibn ʿInaba, *ʿUmda*, 51.

134 Ibn Saʿd, *al-Qism al-mutammim*, 381 (= al-Ṭabarī, 3:316: part of the tradition).

135 Ibn ʿInaba, *ʿUmda*, 110.

136 Al-Ṭabarī, 3:235–236 (l. 6 to l. 5).

137 Re: the biographies of ʿUmar b. ʿAlī b. Abī Ṭālib and his descendants, see al-Zubayrī, *Nasab Quraysh*, 80; Ibn Ḥazm, *Jamhara*, 66–67; al-Bukhārī, *Sirr al-silsila*, 96ff.; Ibn ʿInaba, *ʿUmda*, 361ff.; 364: ʿUbaydallāh b. Muḥammad; 365: ʿAbdallāh b. Muḥammad; 367ff.: ʿĪsā b. ʿAbdallāh; al-ʿUmarī, *Ansāb*, 244ff.; 245ff.: Muḥammad b. ʿUmar; 260ff.: ʿAbdallāh b. Muḥammad; 292ff.: ʿĪsā b. ʿAbdallāh.

138 On him, see al-Zubayrī, *Nasab Quraysh*, 80; Ibn Saʿd, *Ṭabaqāt*, 5:329; al-Bukhārī, *Sirr al-silsila*, 97ff.; Ibn ʿInaba, *ʿUmda*, 362ff.; Ibn Ḥajar, *Tahdhīb* (Beirut, 1984), 9:321: lived until the beginning of the ʿAbbāsī caliphate; idem, *Taqrīb al-tahdhīb* (Damascus?, 1986), 1:498: died after the year [1]30/749; al-Mizzī, *Tahdhīb*, 26:172–173.

Muḥammad b. ʿAbdallāh's rebellion, they all would have had to react and respond to it. They all lived in Medina, and were among the most "noble" distinguished families of the city. As such, they played important, sometimes major, roles in the politics of the city. The "protaganists" during the revolt who are mentioned in the sources are all descendants of Muḥammad b. ʿUmar b. ʿAlī b. Abī Ṭālib (on him, see below). We learn about them mainly from the reports of ʿĪsā b. ʿAbdallāh b. Muḥammad b. ʿUmar that were directly transmitted to ʿUmar b. Shabba and were most probably incorporated into his lost work, parts of which were recorded mainly by al-Ṭabarī, but also to a lesser extent by al-Iṣfahānī.

ⓜ **Muḥammad b. ʿUmar b. ʿAlī b. Abī Ṭālib's** mother was Asmāʾ bt. ʿAqīl b. Abī Ṭālib. Of his five children, four were born to Khadīja bt. ʿAlī [Zayn al-ʿĀbidīn] b. al-Ḥusayn b. ʿAlī b. Abī Ṭālib, i.e., ʿUmar, ʿAbdallāh, ʿUbaydallāh, and Umm Kulthūm.[139] According to Abū Naṣr al-Bukhārī, another child, Jaʿfar, was born to a distinguished Makhzūmī woman, Umm Hāshim bt. Jaʿfar b. Jaʿda b. Hubayra b. Abī Wahb al-Makhzūmī,[140] but the same source cites another version which relates that his mother was an *umm walad*.[141]

The Descendants of Muḥammad b. ʿUmar b. ʿAlī b. Abī Ṭālib

Two of Muḥammad's children, ʿUmar and ʿAbdallāh, are mentioned as active participants in the events of the period (see below). Another son, ʿUbaydallāh, is only mentioned as a transmitter and we do not have any additional information in regard to his involvement in the historical events of the period. Nevertheless, a short biography is presented here in order to complete our picture of the family and to shed light on the political events in Medina on the eve of Muḥammad b. ʿAbdallāh's revolt.

ⓜ 1.4.1.1 *ʿUbaydallāh b. Muḥammad b. ʿUmar b. ʿAlī b. Abī Ṭālib*[142]

His mother was Khadīja bt. ʿAlī b. al-Ḥusayn b. ʿAlī b. Abī Ṭālib.[143] ʿUbaydallāh b. Muḥammad was married to Zaynab bt. Muḥammad (al-Bāqir) b. ʿAlī b. al-Ḥusayn b. ʿAlī b. Abī Ṭālib, who bore him al-ʿAbbās, Muḥammad, Khadīja,

139 Al-Zubayrī, *Nasab Quraysh*, 80; Ibn Saʿd, *Ṭabaqāt*, 5:329; see also the short account of the family by Ibn Ḥazm, *Jamhara*, 66–67; al-Mizzī, *Tahdhīb*, 16:94 (from al-Zubayr b. Bakkār).

140 Al-Bukhārī, *Sirr al-silsila*, 99; Ibn Saʿd, *Ṭabaqāt*, 5:329; al-Mizzī, *Tahdhīb*, 19:154.

141 Al-Bukhārī, *Sirr al-silsila*, 98 (= Ibn ʿInaba, *ʿUmda*, 362).

142 On him, see al-Zubayrī, *Nasab Quraysh*, 80; al-Bukhārī, *Sirr al-silsila*, 98–99; Ibn Ḥibbān, *al-Thiqāt*, 7:151; Ibn Abī Ḥātim, *al-Jarḥ*, 5:334; al-Mizzī, *Tahdhīb*, 19:153–155; al-ʿUmarī, *Ansāb*, 259.

143 Al-Bukhārī, *Sirr al-silsila*, 97 (she was also the mother of his brother ʿUmar, ibid.).

Fāṭima, and Umm Ḥasan.[144] Two other children, ʿAlī and Ilyās, were born to another Qurashī woman from the family of Nawfal b. al-Ḥārith b. ʿAbd al-Muṭṭalib.[145] His son ʿAlī was the author of a book, *Kitāb al-Aqḍiya*.[146] ʿUbaydallāh died at the age of 67.[147] This connection by marriage between the ʿUmarīs and the Ḥusaynīs is noteworthy; his nephew ʿĪsā b. ʿAbdallāh's mother was Umm al-Ḥusayn bt. ʿAbdallāh b. Muḥammad (al-Bāqir) b. ʿAlī (Zayn al-ʿĀbidīn) (see below). ʿUbaydallāh transmitted several traditions, all related to events of the revolt, to ʿĪsā b. ʿAbdallāh, his nephew.[148]

14.1.2 *ʿUmar b. Muḥammad b. ʿUmar b. ʿAlī b. Abī Ṭālib*[149]

He lived with his family in Medina.[150] He is mentioned among the Ṭālibīs who left Medina with his brother ʿAbdallāh at the request of ʿĪsā b. Mūsā and joined the ʿAbbāsī camp. Upon hearing this, Muḥammad al-Nafs al-Zakiyya seized ʿUmar's camels, but at the latter's request he gave them back.[151] A little later,

144 Al-Zubayrī, *Nasab Quraysh*, 80; al-ʿUmarī, *Ansāb*, 259; al-Mizzī, *Tahdhīb*, 19:154.

145 E.g., Ramla bt. Ḥasan b. al-Zubayr b. al-Walīd b. Saʿīd b. Nawfal b. al-Ḥārith b. ʿAbd al-Muṭṭalib, see al-Zubayrī, *Nasab Quraysh*, 80 (al-Mizzī, *Tahdhīb*, 19:154: ʿAlī and al-ʿAbbās instead of Ilyās). Ibn Ḥazm, *Jamhara*, 67, relates that ʿUbaydallāh was buried alive at the outskirts of Baghdad, and his grave is famous and known as "the grave of the vows" (قبر النذور); information in this vein is related by Ibn ʿInaba, *ʿUmda*, 364: وهو صاحب مقابر النذور ببغداد; and see also al-Tanūkhī, *Nishwār*, 5:36–38 (copied by al-Khaṭīb al-Baghdādī, *Taʾrīkh* [Beirut, 1997], 1:135–136 and Yāqūt, *Muʿjam* [Beirut edition], 4:305): the buried Ṭālibī is ʿUbaydallāh b. Muḥammad b. ʿUmar b. ʿAlī b. al-**Ḥusayn** b. ʿAlī b. Abī Ṭālib.

146 Al-Ṭūsī, *al-Fihrist*, 159; Ibn Shahrāshūb, *Maʿālim*, 101; al-Khūʾī, *Rijāl*, 13:96; al-Bukhārī, *Sirr al-silsila*, 98, records that his nickname was *al-ṭabīb*

147 Al-Bukhārī, *Sirr al-silsila*, 98.

148 E.g., see al-Ṭabarī, 3:165–166 (l. 10 to l. 17): ʿUmar [b. Shabba] < ʿĪsā b. ʿAbdallāh < his uncle: ʿUbaydallāh b. Muḥammad b. ʿUmar b. ʿAlī [b. Abī Ṭālib], recording the tradition about a magic mirror originally given by God to Ādam and eventually passed into the hands of al-Manṣūr, by which he was able to see Muḥammad, follow him and watch his hiding places; al-Ṭabarī, 3:167–168 (l. 13 to l. 3): [ʿUmar b. Shabba] < ʿĪsā b. ʿAbdallāh < my uncle, ʿUbaydallāh b. Muḥammad: quoting the narration of Muḥammad al-Nafs al-Zakiyya regarding his infant who died.

149 On him and his descendants, see al-Bukhārī, *Sirr al-silsila*, 98; Ibn ʿInaba, *ʿUmda*, 363; al-ʿUmarī, *Ansāb*, 263–264.

150 Al-Ṭabarī, 3:171 (ll. 11–12).

151 Ibid., 3:226–227 (l. 7 to l. 2).

both brothers were sent with other Ṭālibīs to persuade the people of Medina to receive an *amān* from the ʿAbbāsīs.[152]

ⓜ1.4.1.3 *ʿAbdallāh b. Muḥammad b. ʿUmar b. ʿAlī b. Abī Ṭālib*[153]

He was nicknamed Dāfin. He was married to Umm al-Ḥusayn, whose uncle was Jaʿfar (al-Ṣādiq). She bore him the above-mentioned ʿĪsā (nicknamed Mubārak), Muḥammad, Yaḥyā, and Umm ʿAbdallāh. According to al-Zubayrī, Muḥammad and another child by the name of Aḥmad were the children of an *umm walad*.[154] Aḥmad is reported to be an Imāmī transmitter, one of the transmitters (followers?) of Jaʿfar al-Ṣādiq (من أصحاب الصادق).[155]

ʿAbdallāh b. Muḥammad b. ʿUmar b. ʿAlī b. Abī Ṭālib was an Imāmī transmitter, but he is also mentioned as a transmitter in the Sunnī *rijāl* books, mainly about the ʿAlīds.[156] He is described as one of the followers of al-Sajjād and/or Jaʿfar al-Ṣādiq.[157]

ʿAbdallāh gained the favor of the first ʿAbbāsī caliph, Abū l-ʿAbbās al-Saffāḥ, who granted him two estates in al-Ḥijāz, al-ʿUshayra and ʿAyn Rustān.[158] This

---

152 Ibid., 3:235 (l. 11).

153 On him, see, for example, Ibn Ḥibbān, *al-Thiqāt*, 7:1–2; Ibn ʿAsākir, *Taʾrīkh*, 32:357–360; al-Dhahabī, *Mīzān* (Beirut, 1963), 2:484; al-Mizzī, *Tahdhīb*, 16:93–94; al-Ṣafadī, *al-Wāfī*, 17:229; al-Bukhārī, *Sirr al-silsila*, 97ff.; al-ʿUmarī, *Ansāb*, 259ff.

154 Al-Zubayrī, *Nasab Quraysh*, 80; Ibn ʿAsākir, *Taʾrīkh*, 32:357–358; al-Mizzī, *Tahdhīb*, 16:94; al-Bukhārī, *Sirr al-silsila*, 98: Aḥmad and Muḥammad from an *umm walad*; Ibn ʿInaba, *ʿUmda*, 365; al-ʿUmarī, *Ansāb*, 260–261; on 261: Mūsā is mentioned in the list of his children; he also mentions five daughters of ʿAbdallāh: Umm ʿAbdallāh, Fāṭima, Zaynab, Umm al-Ḥusayn, and Umm ʿĪsā. It is noteworthy that Umm ʿAbdallāh married Jaʿfar b. al-Manṣūr and after him al-Ḥasan b. Muḥammad b. Isḥāq al-Jaʿfarī; see al-ʿUmarī, *Ansāb*, 261.

155 Al-Ṭūsī, *Rijāl*, 155; al-Amīn, *Aʿyān al-Shīʿa*, 3:15.

156 E.g., see the traditions he related to al-Wāqidī in Ibn Saʿd, *Ṭabaqāt*, 4:38 (the battle of Muʾta); 8:22 (the marriage of ʿAlī and Fāṭima); 214 (about ʿAlī); on him, see Ibn ʿAsākir, *Taʾrīkh*, 32:357–360.

157 For example, see al-Ṭūsī, *Rijāl*, 117; al-Shabastarī, *al-Imām al-Ṣādiq*, 2:307 (and the bibliography therein); al-Khūʾī, *Rijāl*, 11:332; al-Māmaqānī, *Rijāl*, 2:214, no. 7060.

158 Al-ʿUmarī, *Ansāb*, 259; this is the only evidence. ʿAyn Rustān is not mentioned in the sources known to me; al-ʿUshayra (or Dhū l-ʿUshayra) is located by Yāqūt, *Muʿjam* (ed. Wüstenfeld), 3:679–680 ("al-ʿUshayra") in the area of Yanbuʿ between Mecca and Medina; see also, al-Ḥarbī[?], *al-Manāsik*, index, but esp. 302; al-Samhūdī, *Wafāʾ*, 4:388–389: it is also a small fortress between Yanbuʿ and Dhū l-Marwa, which is famous for its excellent dates.

may indicate that he was a wealthy man. It is also related that he used to give a lot in alms to the poor. According to a single tradition with no known parallels, he did not join Muḥammad b. ʿAbdallāh's revolt, and welcomed the ʿAbbāsīs' chief commander, ʿĪsā b. Mūsā, with other members of the ʿAlīd family. But when he witnessed the killing of Muḥammad's supporters by the ʿAbbāsīs, he showed signs of regret and was arrested and confined to his tent by the ʿAbbāsīs until the revolt was crushed.[159] This interesting unique information cannot be verified by any other source. It is possible that this is a pro-Shīʿī, biased tradition.

But the pro-ʿAbbāsī tendency of ʿAbdallāh may be corroborated by other testimonies. His son ʿĪsā describes in detail how his father led the pro-ʿAbbāsī Ṭālibīs who left Medina to ʿĪsā b. Mūsā's camp and then was sent by the latter at the head of a delegation to Medina that included ten Ṭālibīs who wanted to persuade its people to surrender to the ʿAbbāsīs and receive an *amān*. We learn from this description that ʿAbdallāh was the head of the Ṭālibī ʿUmarī family.[160]

According to one report he died during al-Manṣūr's reign (r. 136–158/754–775);[161] another gives a specific date, namely 152/769–770;[162] yet another source asserts that he died towards the end of al-Manṣūr's caliphate, adding that according to one piece of evidence he was buried in Damascus.[163] ʿAbdallāh b. Muḥammad is mentioned again thirteen years after the revolt, in 158/775, when he was arrested by the governor of Mecca, with other Sunnī scholars, on the order of Caliph al-Manṣūr. We are not told about the background and reasons for this imprisonment; it may have been connected to his behavior during and after the revolt of Muḥammad.[164] He most probably died in that year.

---

159 Al-ʿUmarī, *Ansāb*, 260, quoting the history[?] of Abū Bishr (وفي تأريخ أبي بشر). This is the only mention of this work in al-ʿUmarī's book. I was unable to find the work quoted in the sources known to me; is al-ʿUmarī quoting from a work of Abū Bishr Aḥmad b. Ibrāhīm b. Aḥmad al-ʿAmmī (d. 350/961), a Baṣrī Shīʿī jurisprudent and historian? Among his works are *al-Taʾrīkh al-kabīr, al-Taʾrīkh al-ṣaghīr, Akhbār ṣāḥib al-Zanj*, see al-Ziriklī, *al-Aʿlām*, 1:82.

160 Al-Ṭabarī, 3:226–227 (l. 7 to l. 2); 3:235–236 (l. 6 to l. 6).

161 Ibn Ḥibbān, *al-Thiqāt*, 7:2.

162 Al-Ṣafadī, *al-Wāfī*, 17:229.

163 Ibn ʿAsākir, *Taʾrīkh*, 32:357; ibid., 32:359: died towards the end of al-Manṣūr's caliphate; al-Mizzī, *Tahdhīb*, 16:94.

164 Al-ʿUmarī, *Ansāb*, 259: the governor is Muḥammad b. Ibrāhīm b. Muḥammad b. ʿAlī b. ʿAbdallāh b. al-ʿAbbās, the caliph's nephew; arrested with him were Sufyān al-Thawrī and ʿAbbād b. Kathīr; al-ʿUmarī states that he quotes al-Ṭabarī (*qāla ṣāḥib al-Taʾrīkh*), but in the parallel tradition in al-Ṭabarī, 3:386 (ʿUmar b. Shabba < Muḥammad b. ʿImrān the

A pro-Ḥasanī anti-ʿAbbāsī tradition is recorded by al-Iṣfahānī through ʿĪsā and his father, ʿAbdallāh.[165] ʿAbdallāh transmitted sixteen traditions to ʿĪsā, his son, all of which were related to the events of the revolt.

Two of ʿAbdallāh b. Muḥammad's sons, ʿAlī (who according to another text version may have been his nephew), but mainly ʿĪsā, are mentioned as active participants in the events of the period. A third son, Yaḥyā, is mentioned during Hārūn al-Rashīd's reign.

The Descendants of ʿAbdallāh b. Muḥammad b. ʿUmar b. ʿAlī b. Abī Ṭālib

1.4.1.4 *ʿAlī b. ʿAbdallāh b. [ʿUbaydallāh?] b. Muḥammad*
He is mentioned only once as a transmitter who gives an eyewitness testimony about the imprisonment of Banū l-Ḥasan by the governor of Medina, Riyāḥ.[166]

1.4.1.5 *Yaḥyā b. ʿAbdallāh b. Muḥammad b. ʿUmar b. ʿAlī b. Abī Ṭālib*
He was imprisoned on Hārūn al-Rashīd's order and was strangled in prison on the caliph's order.[167]

1.4.1.6 *ʿĪsā b. ʿAbdallāh b. Muḥammad b. ʿUmar b. ʿAlī b. Abī Ṭālib*[168]

His Biography
Very little is known about his life and career. He was called ʿĪsā l-Mubārak, a "noble" leader and a poet.[169] His mother was Umm al-Ḥusayn, the daughter of

mawlā of the governor), the name of the Ṭālibī, ʿAbdallāh b. Muḥammad b. ʿUmar, which appears in the Imāmī tradition (which should be a copy of al-Ṭabarī) is not mentioned; instead al-Ṭabarī (via his transmitters) defines him as "a man from the family of ʿAlī b. Abī Ṭālib who was in Mecca"; in al-Ṭabarī's version, a fourth scholar, Ibn Jurayj, is added to the list of prisoners.

165 Al-Iṣfahānī, *Maqātil*, 295; see chapter 2: the discussion on the al-Abwāʾ meeting.

166 Al-Ṭabarī, 3:171 (l. 9f.) (= al-Iṣfahānī, *Maqātil*, 218: b. ʿUbaydallāh, his nephew).

167 Al-ʿUmarī, *Ansāb*, 281–282; 291, 396: his descendants.

168 For some of his principal biographies, see Ibn Abī Ḥātim, *al-Jarḥ* (Beirut edition), 6:280; Ibn Ḥibbān, *al-Thiqāt*, 8:492; al-Ḥākim al-Naysābūrī, *al-Madkhal*, 1:170; Ibn ʿAdī, *al-Ḍuʿafāʾ* (Beirut, 1988), 5:242–244; al-Iṣfahānī, *al-Ḍuʿafāʾ*, 1:122; al-Dhahabī, *Mīzān* (Beirut, 1963), 3:315–316; Ibn Ḥajar, *Lisān*, 4:399; see also al-Zubayrī, *Nasab Quraysh*, 80. For Shīʿī Imāmī sources, see al-Bukhārī, *Sirr al-silsila*, 89 (quoting the lineage from ʿĪsā's book and from many other works the lineage of al-ʿAbbās b. ʿAlī b. Abī Ṭālib, who begot his son ʿUbaydallāh by his wife Lubāba bt. ʿUbaydallāh b. al-ʿAbbās b. ʿAbd al-Muṭṭalib; on her see Bernheimer, *The ʿAlids*, 41, n. 31); al-Bukhārī, *Sirr al-silsila*, 98: biographical details; 99: his son Aḥmad was an expert on genealogy (*nassāba*) and was also an author of a book; Ibn

ʿAbdallāh b. Muḥammad al-Bāqir b. ʿAlī b. al-Ḥusayn b. ʿAlī b. Abī Ṭālib.[170] He had a son, Aḥmad, who was a well-known scholar (on him see below). ʿĪsā lived with his family in Medina[171] and according to his testimony, in 145/762, when the rebellion of Muḥammad b. ʿAbdallāh broke out, he was a very young boy: فإني لصبي صغير.[172]

He was an important direct transmitter of ʿUmar b. Shabba (see appendix 2, 401f.). For the authors of the Shīʿī *rijāl* books he seems to be more important than his father. He transmitted from Jaʿfar al-Ṣādiq and according to the Imāmī *rijāl* books, was one of his close adherents. They also mention that he was the author of a book of traditions that were transmitted to him by his forefathers;[173] the book was defined by al-Ṭihrānī as كتاب الحديث.[174] The few Sunnī *rijāl* authors that mention him in their works almost unanimously describe him as an untrustworthy and unreliable transmitter, no doubt due to the boldly biased Shīʿī nature of the traditions he related from his family members (his father and grandfather).[175]

ʿInaba, *ʿUmda*, 367ff; al-ʿUmarī, *Ansāb*, 292–293; al-Najāshī, *Rijāl*, 295; al-Ṭūsī, *Rijāl*, 257; al-Ṭūsī, *Fihrist*, 188, 321; al-Māmaqānī, *Rijāl*, 2:362, no. 9316; al-Ḥillī, *Muntahā l-maṭlab*, 1:239; al-Ṭabarsī, *Mustadrak*, 5:64–71 (quoting many of the above-mentioned Shīʿī *rijāl* books); al-Khūʾī, *Rijāl*, 14:214–216; al-Shabastarī, *al-Imām al-Ṣādiq*, 2:535–536 (and the exhaustive list of sources of the editor therein); al-Amīn, *Aʿyān al-Shīʿa*, 8:383. See also the pioneering discussion of Nagel, "Muḥammad b. ʿAbdallāh," 242–243, but mainly the entry on him by Modarressi, *Tradition*, 194 (no. 109), with additional comprehensive bibliography.

169 Ibn ʿAsākir, *Taʾrīkh*, 32:358 [= al-Mizzī, *Tahdhīb*, 16:94]: from al-Zubayr b. Bakkār; al-ʿUmarī, *Ansāb*, 292: "a noble leader": وكان سيدا شريفا; Modarressi, *Tradition*, 194.

170 Al-ʿUmarī, *Ansāb*, 292.

171 The family abode (*dār*) in Medina is mentioned in al-Ṭabarī, 3:222 (l. 16).

172 Ibid., 3:226 (l. 9).

173 His book is mentioned by many of the Imāmī sources, e.g., al-Ṭūsī, *Fihrist*, 188, 321; al-Ḥillī, *Muntahā l-maṭlab*, 1:239; al-Shabastarī, *al-Imām al-Ṣādiq*, 2:535; as a transmitter of *ḥadīth* he is quoted abundantly in Shīʿī works and to a much lesser extent in Sunnī *ḥadīth* compilations. For some examples of his transmission in the Shīʿī sources, see al-Kulaynī, *al-Kāfī*, 6:380; al-Ṭūsī, *al-Amālī*, 55, 355; Ibn Ṭāʾūs, *al-Yaqīn*, 498, 510; al-Majlisī, *Biḥār*, 24:258; 27:297; 28:302; 40:25; 43:159; 97:227; al-ʿĀmilī, *Wasāʾil* (*ahl al-bayt*), 2:91; 23:198; 25:233. For traditions related through him by Sunnī authors, for example, see Ibn Shabba, *Taʾrīkh al-Madīna*, 2:645, 646, 755; al-Ṭabarānī, *al-Kabīr*, 3:41; al-Dāraquṭnī, *Sunan*, 1:302; al-Quḍāʿī, *Musnad*, 2:316; al-Muttaqī l-Hindī, *Kanz*, 14:184; Ibn ʿAsākir, *Taʾrīkh*, 13:227; 26:302; 27:283; 32:357; 42:245, 304, 308; 45:303, 344; 54:414; 65:323.

174 Al-Ṭihrānī, *al-Dharīʿa* (Tehran, 1365 H.), 6:356.

175 For example, see Ibn Ḥibbān, *al-Majrūḥīn* (Ḥalab edition), 2:121–123; 2:122: يروي عن أبائه أشياء موضوعة فمن ذلك . . .; in what follows, Ibn Ḥibbān records several examples, such

ʿĪsā b. ʿAbdallāh and the ʿAbbāsīs

ʿĪsā is described by al-ʿUmarī as a "noble" leader (سيد شريف) who transmitted *ḥadīth* and composed beautiful, pleasing poetry (وكان مليح الشعر). He adds that ʿĪsā composed a eulogy on

> *ṣāḥib al-Fakhkh* (al-Ḥusayn b. ʿAlī b. al-Ḥasan b. al-Ḥasan) and his family, but the governor of Medina, who belonged to the family of ʿUmar b. al-Khaṭṭāb [he was ʿUmar b. ʿAbd al-ʿAzīz b. ʿAbdallāh b. ʿAbdallāh b. ʿUmar b. al-Khaṭṭāb][176] forbade him to recite his poem in public. ʿĪsā wrote a letter on this matter to Muḥammad b. Sulaymān b. ʿAlī b. ʿAbdallāh b. al-ʿAbbās, who wrote to the governor to enable ʿĪsā to recite his poem.[177]

The question arises: Why would ʿĪsā communicate with the ʿAbbāsī "prince" Muḥammad b. Sulaymān b. ʿAlī b. ʿAbdallāh b. al-ʿAbbās, hoping to get his help, and why would this ʿAbbāsī "prince" treat him leniently? Muḥammad b. Sulaymān b. ʿAlī b. ʿAbdallāh b. al-ʿAbbās (d. 173/789, al-Saffāḥ's and al-Manṣūr's cousin)[178] was a very important ʿAbbāsī.[179] His mother was Umm al-Ḥasan, the daughter of Jaʿfar b. Ḥasan b. Ḥasan b. ʿAlī b. Abī Ṭālib,[180] the brother of ʿAbdallāh b. al-Ḥasan, the father of Muḥammad and ʿAbdallāh.

Muḥammad b. Sulaymān is described by the sources as the most distinguished and powerful member of the ʿAbbāsī family in general and of his own family (the descendants of ʿAlī b. ʿAbdallāh b. al-ʿAbbās) in particular.[181] He was

---

as the tradition related from his father from his grandfather from ʿAlī, praising ʿAlī b. Abī Ṭālib and his family; idem, *al-Thiqāt*, 8:498: في حديثه مناكير; al-Iṣfahānī, *al-Ḍuʿafāʾ*, 122: روى عن أبيه عن آبائه أحاديث مناكير لا يكتب حديثه لا شيء; al-Dhahabī, *Mīzān* (Beirut, 1963), 3:315–316: quoting Ibn Ḥibbān and others; Ibn Ḥajar, *Lisān*, 4:399; al-Munāwī, *Fayḍ al-qadīr*, 3:255; 6:360.

176 Al-Ṭabarī, 3:551ff.

177 Al-ʿUmarī, *Ansāb*, 292–293.

178 For the important roles played by the uncles of the two caliphs, al-Saffāḥ and al-Manṣūr, under these caliphs, see Lassner, *Shaping*, index (*ʿumūmah*), esp. 10–15, 35–38, 54–56; Kennedy, *ʿAbbāsid Caliphate*, 52–53.

179 On him, see Ibn Qutayba, *al-Maʿārif* (Cairo edition) 375 and 376; al-Balādhurī, *Ansāb* (ed. al-Dūrī), 3:94–96; Ibn ʿAsākir, *Taʾrīkh*, 53:128–140; al-Khaṭīb al-Baghdādī, *Taʾrīkh* (Beirut edition), 2:386–387; al-Dhahabī, *Siyar*, 240; al-Ṣafadī, *al-Wāfī*, 3:121–123; al-Ziriklī, *al-Aʿlām*, 6:148–149. On Sulaymān b. ʿAlī (Muḥammad's father), see al-Balādhurī, *Ansāb* (ed. al-Dūrī), 3:89–94; Lassner, *Shaping*, 12.

180 Ibn Qutayba, *al-Maʿārif* (Cairo edition), 375: the mother of Jaʿfar, Muḥammad, ʿĀʾisha, Zaynab, Asmāʾ, Fāṭima, Umm ʿAlī, and Umm al-Ḥasan; al-Balādhurī, *Ansāb* (ed. al-Dūrī), 3:94; ibid. (ed. Madelung), 2:543: only the males (Jaʿfar and Muḥammad) are mentioned.

181 Ibn ʿAsākir, *Taʾrīkh*, 53:130: كان عظيم أهله وجليل رهطه.

born in al-Ḥumayma in 122/739–740,[182] moved with his family to al-ʿIrāq, and inherited his father's post as the governor of al-Baṣra (in 142/759–760). Under al-Manṣūr he served as the governor of al-Kūfa and al-Baṣra; al-Balādhurī states that on al-Manṣūr's orders he destroyed the houses of the Kūfīs who participated in Ibrāhīm b. ʿAbdallāh's rebellion,[183] and al-Fasawī adds that upon his appointment as the governor of al-Kūfa in 146/763, he chased whoever was with Ibrāhīm, killed them, destroyed their houses, and uprooted their palm trees.[184] He was appointed twice as the governor of al-Baṣra under al-Mahdī, then under al-Hādī (160/776) and al-Rashīd (d. 194/809), and served until his death in Rajab 173/November–December 789.[185] His property was confiscated by order of al-Rashīd.[186]

In 169/786 he was among the ʿAbbāsī dignitaries that led the *ḥajj* pilgrimage from al-ʿIrāq to Mecca. While on their way to al-Ḥijāz, al-Ḥusayn b. ʿAlī b. al-Ḥasan b. al-Ḥasan b. al-Ḥasan b. ʿAlī's rebellion broke out in Medina. On 24 Dhū l-Qaʿda[187] al-Ḥusayn left the city with his supporters and headed towards Mecca, where they were defeated by an ʿAbbāsī army. It is noteworthy that according to one piece of evidence Muḥammad b. Sulaymān b. ʿAlī was appointed by al-Hādī as the head of this ʿAbbāsī army.[188]

Returning to the beginning of this discussion, al-ʿUmarī explains the lenient attitude of Muḥammad b. Sulaymān al-ʿAbbāsī to ʿĪsā b. ʿAbdallāh al-ʿUmarī l-Ṭālibī: he permitted him to recite his eulogy on the Ṭālibīs that were killed in al-Fakhkh, because his mother was an ʿAlīd:[189] وكانت أم محمد بن سليمان علوية (that is, Umm al-Ḥasan bt. Jaʿfar b. al-Ḥasan b. al-Ḥasan b. ʿAlī b. Abī Ṭālib, see above). It is noteworthy that Ḥusayn's (*ṣāḥib al-Fakhkh's*) mother was Zaynab bt. ʿAbdallāh b. al-Ḥasan b. al-Ḥasan. b. ʿAlī b. Abī Ṭālib.[190]

Also noteworthy is Jaʿfar b. al-Ḥasan b. al-Ḥasan b. ʿAlī's daughter, Umm al-Ḥasan, who married Jaʿfar b. Sulaymān b. ʿAlī b. ʿAbdallāh al-ʿAbbāsī, the brother of the above-mentioned Muḥammad b. Sulaymān b. ʿAlī.[191] An inter-

182 Ibn Khayyāṭ, *Taʾrīkh* (ed. al-ʿUmarī), 2:369.

183 Al-Balādhurī, *Ansāb* (ed. al-Dūrī), 3:94–95.

184 Al-Fasawī, *al-Maʿrifa*, 1:130–131; al-Fasawī is quoted by Ibn ʿAsākir, *Taʾrīkh*, 53:131 and Ibn Ḥajar, *Lisān*, 5:188; see also al-Balādhurī, *Ansāb* (ed. al-Dūrī), 3:94–95.

185 Ibn Khayyāṭ, *Taʾrīkh* (Beirut, 1993), 358, 364, 366, 378; Ibn ʿAsākir, *Taʾrīkh*, 53:129, 131, 136.

186 Ibn ʿAsākir, *Taʾrīkh*, 53:138–140.

187 Al-Ṭabarī, 3:556 (ll. 5–6).

188 Al-Ṭabarī, 3:556–557 (l. 20 to l. 7), but, see ibid., 3:558 (l. 15) and al-Iṣfahānī, *Maqātil*, 450: head of the *maymana*.

189 Al-ʿUmarī, *Ansāb*, 293.

190 Al-Bukhārī, *Sirr al-silsila*, 14; al-ʿUmarī, *Ansāb*, 66; al-Iṣfahānī, *Maqātil*, 431.

191 Ibn ʿInaba, *ʿUmda*, 184.

esting tradition enlightening this relationship is related through ʿUmar b. Shabba from Muḥammad b. Ismāʿīl b. Jaʿfar al-Jaʿfarī from his mother, Ruqayya bt. Mūsā b. ʿAbdallāh (al-Nafs al-Zakiyya's brother), from his father, ʿAbdallāh b. al-Ḥasan, who allegedly asked Sulaymān b. ʿAlī's [b. ʿAbdallāh b. al-ʿAbbās], opinion about the course of action that al-Manṣūr was liable to take regarding the revolt. He addressed Sulaymān with these words "Oh my brother, I am related to you by your wife, you are my relation ... so tell me what is your opinion (regarding the revolt)." Sulaymān answered that he thinks al-Manṣūr will act harshly with a tough hand towards the rebellion. The transmitter (Muḥammad b. Ismāʿīl) remarked that the family of ʿAbdallāh b. al-Ḥasan considered this frank and sincere attitude of Sulaymān b. ʿAlī the result of the kindness and affection that he had for his relations.[192]

1.4.1.7 *Aḥmad b. ʿĪsā b. ʿAbdallāh b. Muḥammad b. ʿUmar b. ʿAlī b. Abī Ṭālib (d. 266/879 or 880)*

His mother was an *umm walad* from Sind.[193] Aḥmad was most probably active during the last quarter of the eighth century (his father was a young boy in 145/762, see above). According to Ibn ʿInaba, he was a well-known scholar, versed in *fiqh* (jurisprudence), *nasab* (genealogy), and *ḥadīth*, the most knowledgeable and the most pious from among his (Ṭālibī) family: الفقيه النسابة المحدث كان شيخ أهله علما وزهدا.[194] His book on the genealogy of the Ṭālibīs was utilized by Abū Naṣr al-Bukhārī.[195] This *nasab* work may have preceded the *nasab* book of Yaḥyā b. al-Ḥasan b. Jaʿfar b. ʿUbaydallāh b. al-Ḥusayn b. ʿAlī b. al-Ḥusayn b. ʿAlī b. Abī Ṭālib al-ʿUbaydalī l-ʿAqīqī (214–277/829–890), which is commonly considered the earliest Ṭālibī *nasab* book.

---

192 Al-Ṭabarī, 3:145 (ll. 3–5): قال فكان آل عبد الله يرونها صلة من سليمان لهم; by *ṣila*, *ṣilat al-raḥim* is meant, see Lane, *Lexicon*, s.v. *w.ṣ.l.*

193 Al-Bukhārī, *Sirr al-silsila*, 98.

194 Ibn ʿInaba, *ʿUmda*, 367; al-Shāhrūdī l-Namāzī, *Rijāl*, 394.

195 See the comments of the editor of al-Bukhārī, *Sirr al-Silsila*, 9: وقد روى أبو نصر البخاري أيضا في كتابه عن جماعه ممن أخذ منهم العلم (منهم) الفقيه النسابة أبو طاهر أحمد بن عيسى بن عبد الله بن محمد بن عمر بن الإمام علي بن أبي طالب عليه السلام; ibid., p. 19: قال أحمد بن عيسى بن عبد الله بن محمد بن عمر بن علي بن أبي طالب عليه السلام في كتابه: إن عبيد الله بن عبد الله بن الحسن بن جعفر لم يعقب ... [Quoted by Ibn ʿInaba, ʿUmda, p. 186]; p. 99: قال أحمد بن عيسى بن عبد الله بن محمد بن عمر العمري النسابة في كتابه: أولاد جعفر بن محمد بن عمر ...; on Aḥmad b. ʿĪsā, see also al-ʿUmarī, Ansāb, p. 295.

1.5 *Banū ʿAqīl b. Abī Ṭālib* (Chart IV)

Opposers of the Revolt/ʿAbbāsī Supporters

1.5.1 The Family of Muḥammad b. ʿAqīl b. Abī Ṭālib

1.5.1.1 *Abū ʿAqīl Muḥammad b. ʿAbdallāh b. Muḥammad b. ʿAqīl b. Abī Ṭālib*
Very little is known about him and his career. He lived in Medina. Six of his sons are mentioned in the sources: ʿAlī, Ibrāhīm, al-Qāsim, Ṭāhir, Jaʿfar,[196] and ʿAqīl.[197] ʿAqīl and al-Qāsim were well-known transmitters of *ḥadīth*.[198]

Together with other Ṭālibī dignitaries, most probably led by ʿAbdallāh b. Muḥammad b. ʿUmar b. ʿAlī b. Abī Ṭālib (on him, see above), Muḥammad b. ʿAbdallāh b. Muḥammad b. ʿAqīl b. Abī Ṭālib left Medina and joined the ʿAbbāsī camp in al-Dhubāb.[199] He was sent with nine other Ṭālibī family members to Medina to persuade its inhabitants to surrender to the ʿAbbāsīs.[200] His father, ʿAbdallāh b. Muḥammad b. ʿAqīl, was a well-known *muḥaddith* and *faqīh*, who was a transmitter of Sufyān al-Thawrī. He is mentioned among the Jaʿfar al-Ṣādiq's supporters (*aṣḥāb al-Ṣādiq*),[201] but also in the Sunnī *rijāl* books. He died before the outbreak of Muḥammad b. ʿAbdallāh's revolt.[202]

Other Qurashī Clans

There are many testimonies mentioning the support and participation of various members of the Qurashī families in the revolt of Muḥammad al-Nafs al-Zakiyya.

196 Ibn Mākūlā, *al-Ikmāl*, 6:235.

197 Ibid., 6:230.

198 ʿAqīl: Ibn Mākūlā, *al-Ikmāl*, 6:230; Ibn ʿInaba, *ʿUmda*, 32; al-Qāsim: ibid.; Ibn Abī Ḥātim, *al-Jarḥ* (Beirut edition), 7:119; Ibn ʿAdī, *Ḍuʿafāʾ*, 6:35.

199 Al-Ṭabarī, 3:226.

200 Ibid., 3:235.

201 Al-Khūʾī, *Rijāl*, 11:330.

202 On him, see, for example, Ibn Saʿd, *al-Qism al-mutammim*, 264–267, from al-Wāqidī: he died before the revolt [= al-Mizzī, *Tahdhīb*, 16:84–85]; Ibn Ḥajar, *Tahdhīb* (Hyderabad edition), 6:13–16; 16: according to Ibn Qāniʿ [ʿAbd al-Bāqī b. Qāniʿ b. Marzūq, d. 351/926] he died in 142/759 or 760; al-Balādhurī, *Ansāb* (ed. Madelung), 2:83; al-Zubayrī, *Nasab Quraysh*, 85; Ibn Ḥazm, *Jamhara*, 69; Ibn ʿInaba, *ʿUmda*, 32: on him and his family.

2 Banū Umayya al-Akbar b. ʿAbd Shams b. ʿAbd Manāf b. Quṣayy b. Kilāb b. Murra b. Kaʿb b. Luʾayy b. Ghālib b. Fihr (Quraysh) (Chart v)

2.1 *The Family of al-ʿĀṣ b. Umayya al-Akbar b. ʿAbd Shams … b. Quṣayy … b. Fihr (Quraysh)*

Supporters of the Revolt

2.1.1 Muḥammad b. ʿAbdallāh b. ʿAmr b. Saʿīd b. al-ʿĀṣ [b. Saʿīd b. al-ʿĀṣ] b. Umayya [al-Akbar] b. ʿAbd Shams

He is mentioned thus by al-Ṭabarī as one of those who revolted with Muḥammad al-Nafs al-Zakiyya.[203]

2.1.2 Muḥammad b. ʿAbdallāh b. ʿAnbasa [b. Saʿīd b. al-ʿĀṣ b. Umayya al-Akbar b. ʿAbd Shams], named Abū Jabra

He was among those who were sent by Muḥammad b. ʿAbdallāh to Mecca with al-Ḥasan b. Muʿāwiya al-Jaʿfarī.[204] His father, ʿAbdallāh b. ʿAnbasa, was one of al-Yazīd b. al-Walīd's supporters and advisers.[205] He was killed by Dāwūd b. ʿAlī b. ʿAbdallāh b. al-ʿAbbās, the first ʿAbbāsī governor of Medina.[206] Dāwūd b. ʿAlī executed two other members of this family in Medina.[207]

---

203 Al-Ṭabarī, 3:259 (ll. 2–3). Some links in his lineage are missing; they were completed according to Ibn al-Kalbī, *Jamhara* (ed. Caskel), I, table 9, and Ibn Ḥazm, *Jamhara*, 81. I was not able to find more detail about him; cf. Ibn al-Athīr, *al-Kāmil* (ed. Tornberg), 5:421: correct Saʿīd b. al-ʿAbbās to Saʿīd b. al-ʿĀṣ.

204 Al-Ṭabarī, 3:218 (ll. 11–12). The affiliation with ʿAnbasa b. Saʿīd's family was made according to Ibn Ḥabīb, *al-Muḥabbar*, 440: فلان بن عبد العزيز بن عمر بن محمد بن عبد الله بن عنبسة بن سعيد بن العاص. The missing links in the lineage were completed with the help of the *nasab* books, Ibn al-Kalbī, *Jamhara* (ed. Caskel), I, table 9 and Ibn Ḥazm, *Jamhara*, 82.

205 Al-Ṭabarī, 2:1795–1796: year 126/743 or 744.

206 Ibn Ḥazm, *Jamhara*, 82; al-Zubayrī, *Nasab Quraysh*, 183; he is mentioned by Ibn al-Kalbī, *Jamhara* (ed. Ḥasan), 46. None of these sources mention a son of ʿAbdallāh b. ʿAnbasa named Muḥammad; I was able to find only one source mentioning Muḥammad.

207 1) Ismāʿīl b. Umayya b. ʿAmr b. Saʿīd b. al-ʿĀṣ b. Saʿīd b. al-ʿĀṣ b. Umayya b. ʿAbd Shams, a *faqīh* and *muḥaddith* (see Ibn Saʿd, *al-Qism al-mutammim*, 216; Ibn Ḥazm, *Jamhara*, 81–82; al-Zubayrī, *Nasab Quraysh*, 182; Ibn Ḥibbān, *al-Thiqāt*, 6:29; Ibn Ḥajar *Tahdhīb* [Beirut, 1984], 1:247–248; al-Mizzī, *Tahdhīb*, 3:46–47; Amīn, *Aʿyān al-Shīʿa*, 3:313). Only Ibn Ḥazm specifically relates that he was killed by Dāwūd b. ʿAlī; Ibn Saʿd, *al-Qism al-mutammim*, 216, records that he was imprisoned, but died in 144/760 or 761 (ibid., 217); the other sources quote Ibn Ḥibbān, who says that he died in Dāwūd b. ʿAlī's prison; for other dates

2.2 *Banū Abū l-ʿĀṣ b. Umayya al-Akbar*

Supporters of the Revolt

(m)2.2.1 Muḥammad (called al-Dībāj) b. ʿAbdallāh b. ʿAmr b. ʿUthmān b. ʿAffān [b. Abī l-ʿĀṣ b. Umayya (al-Akbar) b. ʿAbd Shams b. ʿAbd Manāf b. Quṣayy b. Kilāb b. Murra b. Kaʿb b. Luʾayy b. Ghālib b. Fihr][208]

Muḥammad al-Dībāj was a very distinguished Qurashī, a "noble" Arab on both his father's and his mother's side. Through the male lineage he was a descendant of Caliph ʿUthmān; his mother was Fāṭima bt. al-Ḥusayn b. ʿAlī b. Abī Ṭālib, who was also the mother of his brother, al-Qāsim.[209]

Al-Dībāj's lineage through his mother, Fāṭima, is repeatedly emphasized by the sources. This was one of the main themes in laudatory poetry dedicated

of his death, see the note of the editor of Ibn Saʿd, *al-Qism al-mutammim*, 217. 2) Ayyūb b. Mūsā b. ʿAmr b. Saʿīd b. al-ʿĀṣ b. Saʿīd b. al-ʿĀṣ b. Umayya, who died with Ismāʿīl in Dāwūd b. ʿAlī's prison, see Ibn Saʿd, *al-Qism al-mutammim*, 216: was arrested by Dāwūd; his biography, ibid., 217; Ibn Ḥibbān, *al-Thiqāt*, 6:53: "(Ayyūb b. Mūsā) died in Dāwūd b. ʿAlī's prison together with Ismāʿīl b. Umayya"; Ibn ʿAsākir, *Taʾrīkh*, 10:123–128; Ibn Ḥajar, *Tahdhīb* (Beirut, 1984), 1:360; al-Mizzī, *Tahdhīb*, 3:494–498; most of the sources agree that he died in 132/750; Ibn Khayyāṭ, *Taʾrīkh* (Beirut, 1993), 331: ʿImrān instead of Ayyūb: he was killed by Dāwūd b. ʿAlī; Ibn Khayyāṭ is quoted by Ibn ʿAsākir, *Taʾrīkh*, 10:127 and al-Mizzī, *Tahdhīb*, 3:497.

208 For his biographies, see, for example, al-Bukhārī, *al-Kabīr* (Diyār Bakr edition), 1:138–139; Ibn Saʿd, *al-Qism al-mutammim*, 260–262; al-Khaṭīb al-Baghdādī, *Taʾrīkh* (Beirut, 1997), 3:3–5; Ibn ʿAsākir, *Taʾrīkh*, 15:516–523; Ibn Ḥajar, *Tahdhīb* (ed. Hyderabad), 9:268–269; al-Dhahabī, *Taʾrīkh*, 9:273–275; al-Mizzī, *Tahdhīb*, 25:516–521.

209 Ibn ʿAsākir, *Taʾrīkh*, 53:382; it is noteworthy that al-Qāsim was married to Ḥafṣa bt. ʿImrān b. Ibrāhīm b. Muḥammad b. Ṭalḥa b. ʿUbaydallāh, see al-Madāʾinī, "Kitāb al-Murdifāt," 2:75–76. According to al-Madāʾinī, Ḥafṣa married other husbands after him: one was Muḥammad b. ʿAbdallāh b. al-Ḥasan; the other was Hishām b. ʿAbd al-Malik. According to Ibn Ḥabīb, *al-Muḥabbar*, 448, she married *six* husbands (in the following order): al-Qāsim b. ʿAbdallāh b. ʿAmr b. ʿUthmān b. ʿAffān; Hishām b. ʿAbd al-Malik; Muḥammad b. ʿAbdallāh b. ʿAmr b. ʿUthmān (al-Qāsim's brother [!?] not Muḥammad b. ʿAbdallāh b. al-Ḥasan); ʿAwn b. Muḥammad b. ʿAlī b. Abī Ṭālib; ʿAbdallāh b. Ḥasan b. Ḥusayn; ʿUthmān b. ʿUrwa b. al-Zubayr b. al-ʿAwwām. I am tempted to think that Muḥammad b. ʿAbdallāh b. ʿAmr was changed to Muḥammad b. ʿAbdallāh b. al-Ḥasan due to a copying error, see Ibn Ḥazm, *Jamhara*, 83: Ḥafṣa was married to Muḥammad b. ʿAbdallāh b. ʿAmr, to whom she bore Ruqayya al-Ṣughrā. Ibrāhīm b. ʿAbdallāh b. al-Ḥasan, Muḥammad's brother, married Ruqayya but he was killed before consummating the marriage and she married Muḥammad b. Ibrāhīm b. Muḥammad b. ʿAlī b. ʿAbdallāh b. al-ʿAbbās.

to him.[210] This highlights the importance of this noble pedigree through the mother in the eyes of the Arab-Muslim society in the first 200 years of Muslim rule. He was a transmitter of *ḥadīth*,[211] some of which he transmitted from his mother.[212] His mother's first husband was al-Ḥasan b. al-Ḥasan b. ʿAlī b. Abī Ṭālib. One of their children was ʿAbdallāh b. al-Ḥasan, Muḥammad al-Nafs al-Zakiyya's father. When al-Ḥasan b. al-Ḥasan died she married ʿAbdallāh b. ʿAmr and bore him Muḥammad (al-Dībāj) b. ʿAbdallāh.[213] Muḥammad (al-Dībāj) b. ʿAbdallāh b. ʿAmr b. ʿUthmān was, therefore, the brother of ʿAbdallāh b. al-Ḥasan b. al-Ḥasan from the mother's side.[214] The two brothers were very close to each other.[215]

Muḥammad b. ʿAbdallāh b. ʿAmr b. ʿUthmān was among the members of the Ḥasanī family who were sent to al-Manṣūr in al-Rabadha in 144/762. He was taken prisoner from his estate in Badr, where he was staying.[216] In al-Rabadha, al-Manṣūr personally interrogated the Ḥasanīs about the whereabouts of Muḥammad and Ibrāhīm, and their hiding places. He also interrogated Muḥammad al-Dībāj al-ʿUthmānī, and the sources reconstruct the alleged detailed, lengthy discussions held between the two. Before dealing with the detailed discussion, it is worth noting that it was Muḥammad al-ʿUthmānī who received the harshest treatment from al-Manṣūr. First, he was given numerous lashes by order of the caliph.[217] He was killed immediately upon the outbreak

210 E.g., the *madīḥ* (panegyric poem) of the poet Abū Wajza al-Saʿdī to Muḥammad b. ʿAbdallāh b. ʿAmr, transmitted (or rather, recited, to be precise) by Sulaymān b. ʿAyyāsh al-Saʿdī to al-Zubayr b. Bakkār. Sulaymān b. ʿAyyāsh was a Saʿdī so this is probably the reason for keeping and transmitting Abū Wajza's poetry, see al-Khaṭīb al-Baghdādī, *Taʾrīkh* (Beirut, 1997), 3:5; Ibn ʿAsākir, *Taʾrīkh*, 53:389; al-Mizzī, *Tahdhīb*, 25:521–522.

211 E.g., Ibn ʿAsākir, *Taʾrīkh*, 9:90; 16:69, 271; 27:377; 53:381: محدث أهل المدينة.

212 Al-Shāfiʿī, *al-Umm*, 2:103; Ibn Ḥanbal, *Musnad* (Beirut edition), 1:233; al-Dūlābī, *al-Dhurriyya al-ṭāhira*, 90–91; al-Ḥākim al-Naysābūrī, *al-Mustadrak* (Beirut, 1406 H.), 3:288; al-Ṭabarānī, *al-Kabīr*, 1:205; 3:131; 22:416; Ibn ʿAsākir, *Taʾrīkh*, 9:90; 53:379–380.

213 Al-Iṣfahānī, *Maqātil*, 202.

214 Ibn Ḥazm, *Jamhara*, 83; al-Zubayrī, *Nasab Quraysh*, 51–52; al-Balādhurī, *Ansāb* (ed. Madelung), 2:182; 547 (correct عبيد الله to عبد الله: the text is garbled); al-Iṣfahānī, *Maqātil*, 202–204; Ibn ʿAsākir, *Taʾrīkh*, 25:518.

215 Al-Zubayrī, *Nasab Quraysh*, 52.

216 Al-Ṭabarī, 3:173–174 (l. 14 to l. 2); al-Iṣfahānī, *Maqātil*, 218.

217 Al-Ṭabarī, 3:176: 150 lashes; 3:188: 100 lashes; Ibn Saʿd, *al-Qism al-mutammim*, 256; al-Balādhurī, *Ansāb* (ed. Madelung), 503–504: at first he was given 60 lashes and then another 150 lashes; al-Masʿūdī, *Murūj*, 4:150–151: 1,000 lashes.

of the revolt, his head was sent to Khurāsān and presented there as the head of Muḥammad b. ʿAbdallāh b. al-Ḥasan b. al-Ḥasan.[218]

What was the reason for al-Manṣūr's particularly severe attitude toward Muḥammad al-ʿUthmānī? In one place al-Manṣūr accuses him, saying:

> I bestowed upon you (estates?) and showed great generosity to you, and I did (this) and I did (that), and I did not condemn you and act against you due to the crimes of your family, and after all this, you prefer my enemy and hide his affair from me: أقطعتك ووصلتك وفعلت وفعلت ولم أؤاخذك بذنوب أهل بيتك ثم تستميل علي عدوي وتطوي أمره عني.[219]

The background to these accusations is not clear (if in fact they were true statements). They testify to earlier connections between the ʿAbbāsīs and Muḥammad al-Dībāj al-ʿUthmānī. "The crimes of your family" most probably alludes to his being an Umawī descendant. Many members of this family were executed by the ʿAbbāsīs in all parts of the caliphate. As noted above, Dāwūd b. ʿAlī, the governor of Medina, executed three distinguished members of Abū l-ʿĀṣ b. Umayya's family, the close relatives of Muḥammad b. ʿAbdallāh al-ʿUthmānī (see above). This Umawī lineage indeed could have been a real and considerable factor in al-Manṣūr's attitude towards Muḥammad al-Dībāj. This is echoed in a tradition according to which al-Manṣūr was afraid that Muḥammad al-Dībāj was able to cause *ahl al-Shām* (the Arab tribes of Syria) to support Muḥammad al-Nafs al-Zakiyya. According to a tradition it was Riyāḥ b. ʿUthmān, the governor of Medina, who called al-Manṣūr's attention to this, saying that *ahl al-Shām* do not incline towards the ʿAlīds, for ʿAlī b. Abī Ṭālib in their eyes is an infidel, but "their brother, Muḥammad b. ʿAbdallāh b. ʿAmr, if only he had called on *ahl al-Shām*, no one of them would have stayed behind (and not joined his call)."[220]

This point is not stressed by the sources; they generally only record the fierce discussion between al-Manṣūr and Muḥammad al-ʿUthmānī, when the caliph accuses him of knowing where Ibrāhīm b. ʿAbdallāh is hiding, since Muḥammad al-ʿUthmānī's daughter, Ruqayya, was married to Ibrāhīm. Moreover, al-Manṣūr knows that she is pregnant, and in that case, Muḥammad

---

218 Al-Balādhurī, *Ansāb* (ed. Madelung), 2:505; Ibn Saʿd, *al-Qism al-mutammim*, 257; al-Ṭabarī, 3:183 (ll. 6–13); 3:184 (ll. 5–9) (= al-Iṣfahānī, *Maqātil*, 226: a parallel tradition but lacking the beginning).

219 Al-Yaʿqūbī, *Taʾrīkh* (ed. Houtsma), 2:450.

220 Al-Ṭabarī, 3:178; al-Iṣfahānī, *Maqātil*, 221–222 (a partial parallel tradition): ʿUmar b. Shabba < Muḥammad b. Abī Ḥarb.

al-ʿUthmānī must have seen Ibrāhīm when he was visiting his wife (who was in her father's abode). Al-Manṣūr emphasizes again and again that Muḥammad al-ʿUthmānī swore to him that he would be faithful to him (this sentence may be related to the text quoted above). At the end of the fierce discussion, which is full of harsh expressions and blasphemy, al-ʿUthmānī claims that he does not know where Ibrāhīm is hiding, and al-Manṣūr orders him to be whipped.[221]

The accusation of al-Manṣūr that Ruqayya became pregnant by her husband Ibrāhīm may have had a basis in reality, since several sources testify that Ruqayya, Muḥammad al-ʿUthmānī's daughter, was indeed married to Ibrāhīm b. ʿAbdallāh al-Ḥasanī.[222] But a tradition (in the *nasab* books) relates that Ibrāhīm was killed before he consummated the marriage: فقتل قبل أن يدخل عليها, and after his death Ruqayya married a distinguished ʿAbbāsī, Muḥammad b. Ibrāhīm b. Muḥammad b. ʿAlī b. ʿAbdallāh b. al-ʿAbbās.[223] It is possible that this specific tradition is concerned with ʿAbbāsī interests, but it is also possible that the beautiful dialogue between al-Manṣūr and Muḥammad al-ʿUthmānī, and especially the accusations, are a literary invention.

2.3 *Banū ʿAbd al-ʿUzzā b. ʿAbd Shams b. ʿAbd Manāf*

2.3.1 Banū Rabīʿa b. ʿAbd al-ʿUzzā

Supporters of the Revolt

2.3.1.1 *Abū ʿAdī, nicknamed al-ʿAblī, ʿAbdallāh b. ʿUmar b. ʿAbdallāh b. ʿAlī b. ʿAdī b. Rabīʿa b. ʿAbd al- ʿUzzā b. ʿAbd Shams*[224]

He was a well-known poet, an enthusiastic supporter of Banū Hāshim, who during the Umawī period composed panegyric poems against these rulers. When the ʿAbbāsīs came to power, his family was arrested and his estates were confiscated by the governor of Medina, Dāwūd b. ʿAlī, al-Saffāḥ's uncle, but were later returned to him by the caliph. He became very close to ʿAbdallāh b. al-Ḥasan, and when the latter's son Muḥammad revolted, he joined his

221 Al-Ṭabarī, 3:175–177 (l. 17 to l. 3); see also 3:183–184 (l. 13 to l. 5) (with no curses and insults); Ibn Saʿd, *al-Qism al-mutammim*, 256.

222 Al-Balādhurī, *Ansāb* (ed. Madelung), 2:503; Ibn Saʿd, *al-Qism al-mutammim*, 256; al-Ṭabarī, 3:176; Ibn Kathīr, *al-Bidāya* (ed. Shīrī), 10:88.

223 Ibn Ḥazm, *Jamhara*, 83; al-Zubayrī, *Nasab Quraysh*, 117: ʿAlī b. ʿUbaydallāh instead of ʿAlī b. ʿAbdallāh; according to him, she died when giving birth.

224 His biography: al-Iṣfahānī, *al-Aghānī* (Dār al-Kutub edition), 11:293–309 (Būlāq edition. 10:103–110).

rebellion and was appointed as the governor of al-Ṭāʾif. When Muḥammad al-Nafs al-Zakiyya died he fled to Yemen.[225]

2.3.1.2 *Abū ʿAdī ʿAbdallāh b. ʿAdī b. Ḥāritha b. Rabīʿa b. ʿAbd al-ʿUzzā b. ʿAbd Shams*

He was in charge of the vanguard forces (المقدمة), of al-Ḥasan b. Muʿāwiya, the governor of Mecca designated by Muḥammad b. ʿAbdallāh.[226]

2.3.1.3 ⓜ ⓕ *Muḥammad b. ʿAjlān b. Hurmuz,* mawlā *Fāṭima bt.* [*al-Walīd* [?] *b.*] *ʿUtba b. Rabīʿa b. ʿAbd Shams b. ʿAbd Manāf* (*d. 148 or 149/765 or 766 or 767*)[227]

He was a well-known and important Medinan *muḥaddith* and *faqīh* who joined the rebellion of Muḥammad b. ʿAbdallāh. ʿUmar b. Shabba records from Qudāma b. Muḥammad "ʿAbdallāh b. Yazīd b. Hurmuz and Muḥammad b. ʿAjlān rebelled with Muḥammad. When the fighting came, each of the two girded a longbow. We assumed they wanted to show people that they were quite fit to do so."[228] After the revolt Muḥammad b. ʿAjlān was captured, and the new ʿAbbāsī governor, Jaʿfar b. Sulaymān, ordered that his hand be cut off.

225 Al-Iṣfahānī, *al-Aghānī* (Dār al-Kutub edition), 11:294–298, 300; 301: governor of al-Ṭāʾif; 4:340–341: visiting ʿAbdallāh b. al-Ḥasan and his brother al-Ḥasan at his estate, Suwayqa.

226 Al-Balādhurī, *Ansāb* (ed. Madelung), 2:508; he is not mentioned by Ibn al-Kalbī, *Jamhara* (ed. Caskel), I, table 14, and Ibn Ḥazm, *Jamhara*, 77–78.

227 On him, see van Arendonk, *L'Imamat Zaïdite*, 312–313, but especially the comprehensive discussion of van Ess, *Theologie*, 2:678–681; he (or his father) is usually described as the *mawlā* of Fāṭima bt. ʿUtba b. Rabīʿa, e.g., al-Bukhārī, *Ṣaghīr*, 2:70 (his father Hurmuz is mentioned); Ibn Abī Ḥātim, *al-Jarḥ* (Beirut edition), 7:18; 8:49–50; Ibn Ḥibbān, *al-Thiqāt*, 5:277; 7:386; al-Dhahabī, *Siyar*, 6:319: from Muṣʿab b. ʿAbdallāh al-Zubayrī (on her, see al-Maqrīzī, *al-Nizāʿ wa-l-takhāṣum*, 15–16 [ed. Ḥusayn Muʾnis, Cairo, Dār al-Maʿārif, 1988, 50–51])and in the biographical literature, e.g., Ibn Saʿd, *Ṭabaqāt*, 8:238–239; Ibn al-Athīr, *Usd al-ghāba*, 5:526; Ibn Ḥajar, *al-Iṣāba* (Beirut, 1415 H.), 8:275–276; Muḥammad b. ʿAjlān is not mentioned in her biographies. But cf. Ibn Qutayba, *al-Maʿārif* (Cairo edition), 595; Ibn Ḥajar, *Tahdhīb* (Beirut edition), 9:303; al-Mizzī, *Tahdhīb*, 26:101; al-Dhahabī, *Siyar*, 6:318: Fāṭima bt. **al-Walīd** b. ʿUtba b. Rabīʿa. The *nasab* books ascribe a daughter named Fāṭima both to ʿUtba (al-Balādhurī, *Ansāb* [ed. al-ʿAẓm], 7:696) and to al-Walīd b. ʿUtba, for example, see al-Zubayrī, *Nasab Quraysh*, 153; Ibn Ḥazm, *Jamhara*, 77.

228 Al-Ṭabarī, 3:251–252 (l. 18 to l. 1) (trans. McAuliffe, *ʿAbbāsid Authority*, 216, adding in footnote 1022: "Note *a* in the Leiden text offers the explanation that "they were, of course, educated men who were unaccustomed to carrying bows."); al-Iṣfahānī, *Maqātil*, 282, 292.

He was saved from this punishment by the intervention of the most important *fuqahā*ʾ and notables of Medina.[229] He died in Egypt in 148/765–766.[230]

3 Banū Nawfal b. ʿAbd Manāf b. Quṣayy b. Kilāb b. Murra b. Kaʿb b. Luʾayy b. Ghālib b. Fihr (Quraysh) (Chart v)

3.1 *The Family of ʿAdī b. Nawfal b. ʿAbd Manāf*

Supporters of the Revolt

3.1.1 Hishām b. ʿUmāra b. al-Walīd b. ʿAdī b. al-Khiyār [b. ʿAdī b. Nawfal b. ʿAbd Manāf b. Quṣayy b. Kilāb b. Murra b. Kaʿb b. Luʾayy b. Ghālib b. Fihr]

He fought, along with his *mawlā*, at Muḥammad b. ʿAbdallāh's side but fled after an arrow struck his shield, split it in two and stuck in his armor.[231]

4 Banū l-Muṭṭalib b. ʿAbd Manāf b. Quṣayy b. Kilāb … b. Ghālib b. Fihr (Quraysh) (Chart v)

Supporters of the Revolt

4.4.1 Jaʿfar b. ʿAbdallāh b. ʿAlī b. Yazīd b. Rukāna [b. ʿAbd Yazīd b. Hāshim b. al-Muṭṭalib b. ʿAbd Manāf, b. Quṣayy b. Kilāb b. Murra b. Kaʿb b. Luʾayy b. Ghālib b. Quraysh (Fihr) al-Qurashī l-Muṭṭalibī]

Nothing is known about him. He is only mentioned once by al-Ṭabarī, where he relates, in the first person, about the number of the supporters of Muḥammad al-Nafs al-Zakiyya. It is clear from the tradition that he took part in the revolt

229 Ibn Saʿd, *al-Qism al-mutammim*, 355–356 (from al-Wāqidī?); al-Ṭabarī, 3:259 (ll. 3–9); al-Azdī, *Taʾrīkh al-Mawṣil*, 193; al-Iṣfahānī, *Maqātil*, 281–282, 289 (= al-Suyūṭī, *Taʾrīkh*, 289); Abū l-ʿArab, *Kitāb al-Miḥan*, 413.

230 Al-Mizzī, *Tahdhīb*, 24:107. About ʿUtba b. Rabīʿa's family, see Ibn Ḥazm, *Jamhara*, 76–77; 77: al-Walīd b. ʿUtba died in 2/624 in the battle of Badr fighting against the Prophet Muḥammad, see al-Zubayrī, *Nasab Quraysh*, 153; Ibn Hishām, *al-Sīra*, 2:455–456; al-Maqrīzī, *al-Nizāʿ wa-l-takhāṣum*, 15–16 (ed. Muʾnis, 50–51).

231 Al-Ṭabarī, 3:243–244 (l. 13 to l. 2); on him and his family, see al-Zubayrī, *Nasab Quraysh*, 202–203; Ibn Ḥazm, *Jamhara*, 116: mentioning his brother, the poet al-Aswad, who was one of the *ṣaḥāba* of Caliph al-Mahdī, and his uncle, Hishām b. al-Walīd, the *muḥaddith*

at the latter's side.[232] His father was a transmitter of *ḥadīth*;[233] his grandfather ʿAlī is briefly mentioned in the *nasab* books,[234] as well as the ancestor of the family, Rukāna and his son Yazīd, who are mentioned for their activities during the period of the Prophet and the Rāshidūn.[235]

5 Banū ʿAdī b. Kaʿb b. Luʾayy b. Ghālib b. Fihr (Quraysh) (Chart VI)

Supporters of the Revolt

5.1 *The Family of ʿĀṣim b. ʿUmar b. al-Khaṭṭāb*

Ⓜ5.1.1 ʿAbdallāh b. ʿUmar b. al-Qāsim b. ʿAbdallāh b. ʿUbaydallāh b. ʿĀṣim b. ʿUmar b. al-Khaṭṭāb

He was a minor, almost unknown *muḥaddith*. His son, Muḥammad, gained slightly more fame in this field.[236]

Al-Ṭabarī mentions him twice, as a close supporter of Muḥammad and one who took an active part in the fighting, about which he relates in the first person; he describes the heroism of his fellow tribal members in battles.[237]

---

232 Al-Ṭabarī, 3:193 (l. 15) (Jaʿfar b. ʿAbdallāh b. Yazīd b. Rukāna should be corrected to Jaʿfar b. ʿAbdallāh b. **ʿAlī** b. Yazīd b. Rukāna).

233 Al-Dārimī, *Sunan* (Damascus, 1349 H.), 2:163; al-Dhahabī, *Mīzān* (Beirut, 1995), 4:149; al-Mizzī, *Tahdhīb*, 15:323.

234 E.g., Ibn Ḥazm, *Jamhara*, 73; al-Balādhurī, *Ansāb* (ed. ʿAbbās), 5:7–9: mentioning the ancestor, Rukāna, his son Yazīd, and the latter's son ʿAlī. Al-Balādhurī, *Ansāb* (ed. ʿAbbās), 5:8, relates that ʿAlī lived in the first half of the eighth century, and adds that the family have descendants that live in Medina (ولهم بقية في المدينة).

235 For example, see al-Ḥākim al-Naysābūrī, *al-Mustadrak* (Beirut, 1990), 3:511; al-Ṭabarānī, *al-Kabīr*, 5:70; Ibn Abī Ḥātim, *al-Jarḥ*, 3:519; Ibn Ḥibbān, *al-Thiqāt*, 3:130; Ibn Ḥajar, *Tahdhīb* (Beirut, 1984), 3:348; Ibn Ḥajar, *al-Iṣāba* (ed. al-Bijāwī), 2:497; al-Mizzī, *Tahdhīb*, 9:221; Ibn ʿAbd al-Barr, *al-Istīʿāb* (Beirut, 1412 H.), 4:1574; Ibn Qāniʿ, *Muʿjam al-ṣaḥāba*, 3:222–224.

236 The only brief biography of ʿAbdallāh b. ʿUmar b. al-Qāsim is recorded by Ibn Abī Ḥātim, *al-Jarḥ*, 5:110; for some of his transmissions, see Ibn ʿAsākir, *Taʾrīkh*, 31:392; 61:245; on his son, Muḥammad, as a *muḥaddith*, see al-ʿUqaylī, *Ḍuʿafāʾ*, 4:94 (instead of إبراهيم بن عاصم correct to عبيدالله بن عاصم).

237 Al-Ṭabarī, 3:238–239 (l. 13 to l. 2); 3:250 (ll. 11–17): [ʿUmar b. Shabba] < Muḥammad b. al-Ḥasan b. Zabāla < ʿAbdallāh b. ʿUmar b. al-Qāsim b. ʿAbdallāh al-ʿUmarī who said "we were with Muḥammad …".

ʿUmar b. Ḥafṣ b. ʿĀṣim b. ʿUmar b. al-Khaṭṭāb had three sons, ʿAbdallāh, Abū Bakr, and ʿUbaydallāh.[238] According to Ibn Saʿd, the first two participated in the rebellion.

ⓜ5.1.2 ʿAbdallāh b. ʿUmar b. Ḥafṣ b. ʿĀṣim b. ʿUmar b. al-Khaṭṭāb (d. 171, 172, or 173/787, 788, or 790)[239]

He was one of Muḥammad b. ʿAbdallāh's supporters who remained with him until his death. After the failure of the revolt he stayed in hiding, was caught, and brought to al-Manṣūr, who sent him to prison, where he stayed for many years. He was released by the caliph when he was informed that ʿAbdallāh had violent discussions and quarrels in prison with ʿAlīds that besmirched Abū Bakr, ʿUmar, and ʿUthmān.[240] Al-Manṣūr sent him to Medina, where he died.[241]

ⓠⓜ5.1.3 Abū Bakr b. ʿUmar b. Ḥafṣ b. ʿĀṣim b. ʿUmar b. al-Khaṭṭāb (the brother of the aforementioned)

Together with his brother he took an active part in the revolt and died shortly after it ended.[242] He served as the *qāḍī* of Medina under the governorship of Muḥammad b. Khālid b. ʿAbdallāh al-Qasrī (ca. 141–144/759–761).[243] His son, ʿAmr, was appointed as the *qaḍī* of (Jund) al-Urdunn,[244] and lived most probably in Tiberias, the capital of the district.

---

238 Al-Zubayrī, *Nasab Quraysh*, 362 (he does not mention their participation in the rebellion, though).

239 On him, see Ibn Ḥibbān, *al-Majrūḥīn*, 2:6–7; Ibn ʿAdī, *Ḍuʿafāʾ*, 4:141–143; al-Iṣfahānī, *Maqātil*, 289–290; al-ʿUqaylī, *Ḍuʿafāʾ*, 2:280–281; al-Khaṭīb al-Baghdādī, *Taʾrīkh* (Beirut, 1997), 10:20–22; al-Dhahabī, *Mīzān* (Beirut, 1963), 2:465–466; idem, *Siyar*, 5:339–341; Ibn Ḥajar, *Tahdhīb* (Beirut, 1984), 5:285–287 (some of the biographies only deal with him as a *muḥaddith* and do not mention his participation in the revolt); al-Mizzī, *Tahdhīb*, 15:327–332: his biography; 331: copying Ibn Saʿd's report about taking part in the rebellion; ibid.: *sanatayn* instead of *sinīn*).

240 Abū l-ʿArab, *Kitāb al-Miḥan*, 410–411; al-Balādhurī, *Ansāb* (ed. al-Dūrī), 3:260.

241 Ibn Saʿd, *al-Qism al-mutammim*, 367–368; al-Khaṭīb al-Baghdādī, *Taʾrīkh* (Beirut, 1997), 10:20–21 (quoting Ibn Saʿd).

242 Ibn Saʿd, *al-Qism al-mutammim*, 366; al-Iṣfahānī, *Maqātil*, 289: correct هو وأخوه وأبو بكر بن عمر to هو وأخوه أبو بكر بن عمر.

243 Wakīʿ, *Akhbār al-Quḍāt*, 1:210–211; al-Balādhurī, *Ansāb* (ed. ʿAbbās), 5:517; al-Zubayrī, *Nasab Quraysh*, 362; Ibn Ḥazm, *Jamhara*, 155.

244 Al-Balādhurī, *Ansāb* (ed. ʿAbbās), 5:517.

5.1.4 Muḥammad b. Abī Bakr b. ʿUmar b. Ḥafṣ b. ʿĀṣim b. ʿUmar b. al-Khaṭṭāb

A tradition in *al-Aghānī* mentions him in al-Ṭāʾif, swearing allegiance to Muḥammad b. ʿAbdallāh. The Arabic text is not clear to me, and I do not know what he was doing in al-Ṭāʾif, or if he was an ʿAbbāsī official (governor?) in the city.[245]

Opposers of the Rebellion/Supporters of the ʿAbbāsīs

ⓕⓜ5.1.5 ʿUbaydallāh b. ʿUmar b. Ḥafṣ b. ʿĀṣim b. ʿUmar b. al-Khaṭṭāb (the brother of ʿAbdallāh b. ʿUmar and Abū Bakr b. ʿUmar who supported the revolt; on them, see above)

He was a well-known *muḥaddith* and *faqīh*, and is described as one of the most distinguished notables of Quraysh, and a prominent leader in Medina. He died in 147/764–765.[246] In contrast to his two brothers, ʿAbdallāh and Abū Bakr, he did not join the rebellion. This is recorded in a detailed tradition by Ibn Saʿd, namely, that when the revolt broke out, ʿUbaydallāh retired (*iʿtazala*) to his estate and did not rebel with Muḥammad b. ʿAbdallāh, whereas his two brothers joined the rebellion. When Muḥammad asked ʿAbdallāh about their brother, he answered that the latter is at his estate, so Muḥammad allowed him to stay there and not join his revolt. This was his conduct, adds the transmitter, towards those who refused to join him; he did not force anyone to join him. When the revolt was terminated and Muḥammad was killed, ʿUbaydallāh returned to Medina and stayed there until he died in 147/764–765.[247] He is

245 Al-Iṣfahānī, *al-Aghānī* (Dār al-Kutub edition), 11:301 (Būlāq edition, 10:107): قال قدم أبو عدي العبلي الطائف واليا من قبل محمد بن عبد الله بن حسن أيام خروجه على أبي جعفر ومعه أعراب من مزينة وجهينة وأسلم فأخذ الطائف وأتى محمد بن أبي بكر العمري حتى بايع.

246 On him, see Ibn Ḥibbān, *al-Thiqāt*, 7:149; al-Bājī, *Taʿdīl* (ed. al-Bazzār), 2:990–991; al-Dhahabī, *Tadhkira* (Hyderabad edition), 1:151–152; idem, *Siyar*, 6:304–307; Ibn Ḥajar, *Tahdhīb* (Beirut, 1984), 7:35–36; al-Mizzī, *Tahdhīb*, 19:124–129; the year 147/764 or 765 as his death date is the most common; it is related through the transmission of al-Haytham b. ʿAdī (d. 207/822), e.g., al-Mizzī, *Tahdhīb*, 19:129; Ibn Ḥajar, *Tahdhīb* (Beirut, 1984), 7:36; but the years 144 and 145/761, 762, 763 are also mentioned as dates of his death, see ibid., quoting ʿUrwa [b. al-Zubayr (d. 93/712)]; Ibn Ḥibbān, *al-Thiqāt*, 7:149.

247 Ibn Saʿd, *al-Qism al-mutammim*, 365–366; Ibn Ḥajar, *Tahdhīb* (Beirut, 1984), 7:36 (quoting Ibn Saʿd); see also al-Dhahabī, *Tadhkira* (Beirut edition), 1:161: إعتزل فتنة إبن حسن.

sometimes confused with his brother, ʿAbdallāh, who took an active part in the revolt.[248]

5.2 *The Family of ʿAbdallāh b. ʿUmar b. al-Khaṭṭāb*

Supporters of the Revolt

5.2.1 Abū l-Qalammas ʿUthmān b. ʿUbaydallāh b. ʿAbdallāh b. ʿUmar b. al-Khaṭṭāb[249]

It is possible that his father, ʿUbaydallāh "had responded to Muḥammad's call to join his uprising but he died before he came out."[250] Abū l-Qalammas was one of the most loyal adherents and senior commanders of al-Nafs al-Zakiyya.[251] Immediately after the latter entered Medina, many men left the city with their women and children. Muḥammad ordered Abū l-Qalammas to bring them back, but he managed to bring back only a small number of them.[252] According to one tradition he was in charge of the *shurṭa* of Muḥammad b. ʿAbdallāh.[253] During battle he showed great courage and killed Hazārmard, one of the ʿAbbāsī commanders.[254] After the revolt he hid at his[?] estate in al-Furʿ, where he was killed by one of his slaves.[255]

5.2.2 His Son, Abū l-Qāsim Muḥammad b. ʿUthmān

He most probably took part in the revolt as well. This is not recorded in the sources, but it can be deduced by the matter-of-fact sentence of Ibn Ḥazm,

---

248 Al-Ṭabarī, 3:259 (l. 10): ʿUbaydallāh; in the parallel tradition in Ibn al-Athīr, *al-Kāmil* (ed. Tornberg), 5:421: it is ʿAbdallāh b. ʿUmar; but cf. al-Iṣfahānī, *Maqātil*, 292, who adds ʿUbaydallāh and Hishām b. ʿUrwa to the list of Muḥammad b. ʿAbdallāh's supporters; van Arendonk, *L'Imamat Zaïdite*, 313, cites the two conflicting pieces of evidence, but he does not analyze the ensuing contradiction.

249 For his lineage, see Ibn Ḥazm, *Jamhara*, 153; al-Zubayrī, *Nasab Quraysh*, 78.

250 Al-Ṭabarī, 3:259 (ll. 13–15); the tradition is related by Abū l-Qalammas' nephew, ʿAbd al-ʿAzīz b. Abī Salama b. ʿUbaydallāh (ʿUbaydallāh's grandson), who lists those who took part in the rebellion; he does not give his grandfather's full lineage, though, therefore it may have been another ʿUbaydallāh.

251 Al-Balādhurī, *Ansāb* (ed. Madelung), 2:515: one of his commanders.

252 Al-Ṭabarī, 3:230–231 (l. 19 to l. 2).

253 Ibid., 3:198 (ll. 17–18) (= al-Iṣfahānī, *Maqātil*, 295–296): ʿUmar b. Shabba < Muḥammad b. Yaḥyā < al-Ḥārith b. Isḥāq.

254 Al-Ṭabarī, 3:238 (ll. 8–13); 3:239 (ll. 3–7): killing Hazārmard; 3:250–251 (l. 17 to l. 3): his personal military skills and courage.

255 Ibid., 3:250–251 (l. 17 to l. 3).

saying, "as for Abū l-Qāsim Muḥammad b. ʿUthmān b. ʿUbaydallāh b. ʿAbdallāh b. ʿUmar, al-Manṣūr killed him while he was bound in captivity": قتله المنصور صبرا.[256] Nothing is known about his son, al-Qalammas.[257]

It is noteworthy that Abū Salama, ʿUthmān's (Abū l-Qalammas') brother, was among those who did not join the rebellion[258] (on him, see below).

(m) 5.2.3 ʿAbd al-ʿAzīz b. ʿAbdallāh b. ʿAbdallāh b. ʿUmar b. al-Khaṭṭāb[259]

He was a *ḥadīth* scholar, and one of the most distinguished notables of Quraysh.[260] He fought at Muḥammad's side. When Muḥammad's army was defeated and dispersed, he fled but was caught and brought back to the city,[261] and brought from there in chains to al-Manṣūr in al-ʿIrāq, who accused him of fighting, together with his three sons (see further below). At ʿAbd al-ʿAzīz's pleading, al-Manṣūr pardoned him and set him free.[262] Some of ʿAbd al-ʿAzīz's sons and grandsons served in high official roles in the caliphate, which indeed may serve as proof that his past behavior was forgiven.[263]

256 Ibn Ḥazm, *Jamhara*, 153 (last line).

257 Al-Qalammas' son Abū Bakr was married to Umm Kulthūm bt. Ibrāhīm b. Muḥammad b. ʿAlī b. Abī Ṭālib, see al-Zubayrī, *Nasab Quraysh*, 78 (ll. 8–9).

258 Al-Ṭabarī, 3:199 (ll. 10–11): [ʿUmar b. Shabba] < Azhar b. Saʿīd b. Nāfiʿ.

259 For some of his principal biographies, see Ibn Saʿd, *al-Qism al-mutammim*, 220–222; Ibn ʿAsākir, *Taʾrīkh*, 36:298–303; al-Khaṭīb al-Baghdādī, *Taʾrīkh* (Beirut, 1997), 10:433–434; Ibn Ḥajar, *Tahdhīb* (Beirut, 1984), 6:307; al-Mizzī, *Tahdhīb*, 18:158–159.

260 Al-Zubayrī, *Nasab Quraysh*, 357.

261 Al-Ṭabarī, 3:243 (ll. 9–12).

262 Al-Tanūkhī, *Nishwār*, 6:155–156: ... Aḥmad b. Sulaymān al-Ṭūsī < al-Zubayr b. Bakkār < Muṣʿab b. ʿUthmān [al-Zubayrī?] < AND Muḥammad b. al-Ḍaḥḥāk al-Ḥizāmī < AND Muḥammad b. al-Ḥasan al-Makhzūmī < AND others beside them; the tradition was copied by several sources, e.g., al-Khaṭīb al-Baghdādī, *Taʾrīkh* (Beirut, 1997), 10:433–434; Ibn ʿAsākir, *Taʾrīkh*, 36:302; al-Mizzī, *Tahdhīb*, 18:159.

263 His son ʿUmar (al-Aṣghar) b. ʿAbd al-ʿAzīz was appointed governor of Medina, Kirmān, and al-Yamāma, see al-Zubayrī, *Nasab Quraysh*, 358: governor of Medina and Kirmān on behalf of Hārūn al-Rashīd and of al-Yamāma on behalf of ʿĪsā b. Jaʿfar b. al-Manṣūr; al-Balādhurī, *Ansāb* (ed. ʿAbbās), 5:512, and Ibn Qutayba, *al-Maʿārif* (Cairo edition), 186: governed Kirmān on behalf of al-Mahdī, and Medina on behalf of al-Hādī; Ibn Ḥazm, *Jamhara*, 153: Kirmān and Medina for al-Hādī. Another son, Isḥāq, was in charge of the *ṣadaqa* of ʿUmar b. al-Khaṭṭāb; both he and another brother of his, Muḥammad, are mentioned as notables of Quraysh: من وجوه قريش, see al-Zubayrī, *Nasab Quraysh*, 358. His grandson, Ibrāhīm b. Muḥammad b. ʿAbd al-ʿAzīz, was appointed by al-Muʿtaṣim over the judiciary of al-Raqqa, see ibid., 358–359; Ibn Ḥazm, *Jamhara*, 153.

5.2.4–7 ⓜ *His Son, ʿAbdallāh b. ʿAbd al-ʿAzīz b. ʿAbdallāh b. ʿAbdallāh b. ʿUmar b. al-Khaṭṭāb, and his three sons: Isḥāq, Muḥammad, and ʿAbdallāh*

ʿAbdallāh b. ʿAbd al-ʿAzīz (d. 184/800 or 801)[264] is described as a great scholar, extremely pious, the most prominent ascetic of his period, called *al-zāhid al-ʿābid* by the sources that emphasize his great moral power in caliphal circles; he preached to caliphs against unworthy conduct (النهي عن المنكر), and so forth. Nowhere is it mentioned that he took part in the revolt of Muḥammad b. ʿAbdallāh. His extreme piety, and his renunciation of the earthly world is well demonstrated in the tradition that relates that when his brother ʿUmar became the governor of Medina, he left and did not speak with him until the day he died[265] or according to an alternative version, he left his brother, went away from Medina to his residence (estate? *manzilihi*), where he worshiped God and secluded himself, not mixing with people, until he died.[266]

A single rare tradition discloses that ʿAbdallāh and his three sons, Isḥāq, Muḥammad, and ʿAbdallāh, took an active role in the revolt. This is related by ʿAbd al-Ḥamīd, ʿAbd al-ʿAzīz's son (the brother of ʿAbdallāh).[267]

Opposers of the Revolt/ʿAbbāsī Supporters

5.2.8 Abū Salama b. ʿUbaydallāh b. ʿAbdallāh b. ʿUmar b. al-Khaṭṭāb

Abū Salama was among those from his family who did not join the revolt, unlike his brother, Abū l-Qalammas (and probably the latter's son, Muḥammad), who took an active part in the revolt. This is mentioned in only one tradition,[268] but this is most probably the reason that his son, ʿAbd al-Raḥmān, was appointed as head of the *shurṭa* of Medina and another son, ʿUbaydallāh, was appointed

264 On him, see Ibn Saʿd, *Ṭabaqāt*, 5:435; Ibn Ḥibbān, *al-Thiqāt*, 7:19–20; idem, *Mashāhīr*, 207; Ibn Ḥajar, *Tahdhīb* (Beirut, 1984), 5:264–265; al-Mizzī, *Tahdhīb*, 15:241–242, and the exhaustive bibliography therein; al-Mubārakfūrī, *Tuḥfat al-aḥwadhī*, 7:373–374; al-Ṣafadī, *al-Wāfī*, 17:157; Ibn Ḥazm, *Jamhara*, 153, and al-Zubayrī, *Nasab Quraysh*, 358–359, dedicate a relatively long biography to him and his family, but do not mention the revolt. Several of his sons are mentioned but not the three who are mentioned by Wakīʿ as the supporters of the revolt.

265 Ibn Ḥibbān, *al-Thiqāt*, 7:20.

266 Ibn Ḥibbān, *Mashāhīr*, 207–208.

267 Wakīʿ, *Akhbār al-quḍāt*, 1:196–197: *akhbaranī* ʿAbdallāh b. Shuʿayb < Zubayr [b. Bakkār?] < ʿAbd al-Ḥamīd b. ʿAbd al-ʿAzīz b. ʿAbdallāh b. ʿAbdallāh b. ʿUmar.

268 Al-Ṭabarī, 3:199 (ll. 10–11): (ʿUmar b. Shabba) < Azhar b. Saʿīd b. Nāfiʿ.

as the *qāḍī* of the city during the governorship of ʿAbd al-Ṣamad b. ʿAlī l-ʿAbbāsī (between 157 and 158/773–774 and 774–775).[269]

5.3 *The Family of ʿAbd al-Raḥmān b. ʿUmar b. al-Khaṭṭāb*

ⓜ 5.3.1 Abū l-Yaḥāmīm Muḥammad b. ʿAbd al-Raḥmān b. ʿAbd al-Raḥmān (al-Mujabbar) b. ʿAbd al-Raḥmān b. ʿUmar b. al-Khaṭṭāb

His father was a minor transmitter of *ḥadīth*. His son, Muḥammad, was also a minor (sometimes strongly criticized) *muḥaddith*, who according to some sources lived in al-Baṣra.[270] Ibn Ḥazm relates that he joined the revolt of Muḥammad b. ʿAbdallāh.[271]

5.4 *The Family of ʿUbayd b. ʿUwayj b. ʿAdī b. Kaʿb b. Luʾayy b. Ghālib b. Fihr (Quraysh)*

Supporters of the Revolt

---

269 Al-Zubayrī, *Nasab Quraysh*, 360; Ibn Ḥazm, *Jamhara*, 153; al-Balādhurī, *Ansāb* (ed. Zakkār), 10:461: mentioning only ʿAbd al-Raḥmān: correct بن سلمة to بن أبي سلمة as the editor of the other edition, Iḥsān ʿAbbās does. See also al-Balādhurī, *Ansāb* (ed. ʿAbbās), 5:517, who adds the missing word أبي in brackets; Ibn al-Kalbī, *Jamhara* (ed. Ḥasan), 106–107: the name of ʿAbd al-Raḥmān and his position is missing and the editor completed the name (according to al-Zubayrī, *Nasab Quraysh*, 362) to عبد الرحمن بن عبد الله بن عمر بن حفص بن عاصم بن عمر but he was wrong; he should have consulted 360, where the correct lineage and the position (*al-shurṭa*) is given; ʿAbd al-Ṣamad b. ʿAlī (b. ʿAbdallāh b. al-ʿAbbās) was the governor of Medina between 157/773–774 and 158/774–775 (al-Ṭabarī, 3:370, 458); he was dismissed in 159/775 or 776 (ibid., 3:460); in 147/764 or 765, 148/765 or 766, and 150/767–768, he served as the governor of Mecca and al-Ṭāʾif, not of Medina (ibid., 3:328, 353, 359).

270 Muḥammad is mentioned (briefly) in some of the biographical dictionaries of *ḥadīth*, and in the corpora as a transmitter, for example see al-Nasāʾī, *Man lam yarwi ʿanhu ghayr wāḥid*, 274; Ibn Ḥibbān, *al-Majrūḥīn*, 2:263; Ibn Ḥamza al-Ḥusaynī l-Shāfiʿī, *Man lahu riwāya*, 379; Ibn Mākūlā, *al-Ikmāl*, 7:208; al-Dhahabī, *Mīzān* (ed. Bijāwī), 3:621; Ibn Ḥajar, *Lisān*, 5:245–246; as a transmitter in *isnād*s: al-Bayhaqī, *Sunan*, 2:9; 6:212; al-Khaṭīb al-Baghdadī, *Taʾrīkh* (Beirut, 1997), 11:294; Ibn ʿAsākir, *Taʾrīkh*, 62:286; Ibn al-Jawzī, *Mawḍūʿāt*, 2:160; al-Dhahabī, *Taʾrīkh*, 10:447; al-Dāraquṭnī, *Sunan*, 1:278; al-Mizzī, *Tahdhīb*, 10:484; 29:146; on his father, see Ibn Ḥamza al-Ḥusaynī l-Shāfiʿī, *Man lahu riwāya*, 367; as an *isnād* transmitter: Ibn Mākūlā, *al-Ikmāl*, 7:208; Ibn Ḥibbān, *al-Thiqāt*, 7:76.

271 Ibn Ḥazm, *Jamhara*, 156 (the only source which mentions his *kunya*: Abū l-Yaḥāmīm, with variants in different MSS: al-Ḥayāmīm; al-Maḥāmīm).

5.4.1 ʿAbd al-ʿAzīz b. Ibrāhīm b. ʿAbdallāh b. Muṭīʿ [b. al-Aswad b. Ḥāritha b. Naḍala b. ʿAwf b. ʿUbayd b. ʿUwayj b. ʿAdī b. Kaʿb][272]

He took part in the rebellion. After it was crushed he was brought to al-Manṣūr, together with ʿAlī b. al-Muṭṭalib b. ʿAbdallāh b. al-Muṭṭalib b. Ḥanṭab from Makhzūm, was given 500 lashes, and was pardoned afterwards by the caliph.[273]

5.4.2 His brother, ʿAbd al-Raḥmān b. Ibrāhīm b. ʿAbdallāh b. Muṭīʿ

He is mentioned with his brother as someone who rebelled with Muḥammad b. ʿAbdallāh.[274]

5.5 *Banū l-Khaṭṭāb b. Nufayl b. ʿAbd al-ʿUzzā b. Riyāḥ b. ʿAbdallāh b. Qurṭ b. Rizāḥ b. ʿAdī b. Kaʿb*

Opposers of the Rebellion/Supporters of the ʿAbbāsīs

5.5.1 The Family of Zayd b. al-Khaṭṭāb (mawlā of ?).

(m) 5.51.1 *Abū Yaḥyā Fulayḥ b. Sulaymān b. Abī l-Mughīra b. Ḥunayn, commonly known as* mawlā *Zayd b. al-Khaṭṭāb, but also as* mawlā *al-ʿAbbās, or* mawlā *Khuzāʿa or* mawlā *Aslam*[275]

He was a well-known scholar who lived in Medina, where he died in 168/782–783. The first time he is mentioned by the sources is in 141/758, when he advises

272 The reconstruction of his complete lineage is according to Ibn Ḥazm, *Jamhara*, 156–159.

273 Al-Ṭabarī, 3:264–265 (l. 8 to l. 2); al-Azdī, *Taʾrīkh al-Mawṣil*, 192–193; Ibn Ḥazm, *Jamhara*, 158–159.

274 Ibn Ḥazm, *Jamhara*, 159.

275 His biographies: Ibn Saʿd, *Ṭabaqāt*, 5:515: مولى زيد بن الخطاب بن نفيل العدوي; al-Bukhārī, *al-Ṣaghīr*, 2:162: الخزاعي الأسلمي مولاهم; Ibn Ḥibbān, *Mashāhīr*, 225: الخزاعي الأسلمي; Ibn Ḥibbān, *al-Thiqāt*, 7:324: الخزاعي الأسلمي, but cf. ibid., 5:133: it was said of his father's uncle, ʿUbayd b. Ḥunayn, that he was 1) مولى زيد بن الخطاب and it is said 2) ويقال مولى آل العباس; but it was said 3) مولى بني زريق; it was said of his uncle, ʿUbayd b. Ḥunayn, says Ibn Saʿd, *Ṭabaqāt*, 5:285, that he was one of the captives of ʿAyn al-Tamr (in al-ʿIrāq), who was sent by Khālid b. al-Walīd to Abū Bakr in Medina; and see al-Bājī, *al-Taʿdīl* (ed. al-Bazzār), 3:1189–1190: 1) مولى زيد بن الخطاب 2) يقال مولى العباس 3) ويقال وقال البخاري في التأريخ الصغير الخزاعي ويقال الأسلمي 4–5) مولى علي بن أبي طالب مولاهم; there is a noteworthy mention of Fulayḥ by Ibn Shabba, *Taʾrīkh al-Madīna*, 1:311: حدثنا فليح بن سليمان الأسلمي; Ibn Abī Ḥātim, *al-Jarḥ*, 7:84; al-Mizzī, *Tahdhīb*, 23:317–318; al-Dhahabī, *Taʾrīkh*, 10:397–399; al-Dhahabī, *Siyar*, 7:351–355: ...الخزاعي ويقال الأسلمي, المدني الحافظ... من موالي آل زيد بن الخطاب; al-Ṣafadī, *al-Wāfī*, 24:62–63.

ʿAbd al-ʿAzīz b. Saʿīd [b. Saʿd b. ʿUbāda al-Khazrajī?], the confidential agent (spy: *ʿayn*) of the caliph and the person in charge of the *ṣadaqāt* in Medina, to write to the caliph and urge him to imprison the Ḥasanīs. When ʿAbd al-ʿAzīz died, the caliph appointed Fulayḥ to his (ʿAbd al-ʿAzīz's) position, that is, *ṣāḥib al-ṣadaqāt*.[276] Whether he was also the confidential agent of the caliph in Medina is not known. He was certainly highly esteemed by the caliph. During al-Ḥasan b. Zayd's governorship of Medina, Fulayḥ was appointed as a superintendent over the governor: وكان فليح ضاغطا على حسن بن زيد بن حسن بن علي حين ولي المدينة لأبي جعفر. This caused great tension and conflict between the two.[277] The next time we meet Fulayḥ b. Sulaymān is in 155/771–772. In that year al-Manṣūr dismissed the governor of Medina, al-Ḥasan b. Zayd, and in his place appointed ʿAbd al-Ṣamad b. ʿAlī l-ʿAbbāsī. He also assigned Fulayḥ b. Sulaymān to supervise him: وجعل معه فليح بن سليمان مشرفا عليه.[278] Al-Dhahabī renders معينا له, that is, as a helper and assistant (not a supervisor).[279] Fulayḥ is also mentioned in the Imāmī *rijāl* literature as one of the close associates of Jaʿfar al-Ṣādiq.[280] His son Sulaymān is mentioned in 145/762 during the revolt of the blacks (*al-sūdān*) in Medina. He left Medina to inform the caliph of the grave situation in the city.[281] He was a minor *ḥadīth* scholar.[282]

6 Banū Taym b. Murra b. Kaʿb b. Luʾayy b. Ghālib b. Fihr (Quraysh) (Chart VII)

Supporters of the Revolt

6.1.1–1.11 *The Family of Abū Bakr b. Abī Quḥāfa b. ʿĀmir b. ʿAmr b. Kaʿb b. Saʿd b. Taym b. Murra*

Among the dignitaries from Quraysh who joined the force of Abū ʿAdī, al-ʿAblī, the governor of al-Ṭāʾif appointed by Muḥammad b. ʿAbdallāh, were eleven members of Abū Bakr's family.[283]

---

276 Al-Ṭabarī, 3:169 (ll. 5–12).

277 Ibn Saʿd, *Ṭabaqāt*, 5:415.

278 Ibid., 5:377 (ll. 7–9).

279 Al-Dhahabī, *Taʾrīkh*, 9:360; see also Ibn ʿAsākir, *Taʾrīkh*, 32:342–343: a personal report about his "casual" talk with al-Manṣūr who in 158/775 asks him his age, which was then 63, the same as that of al-Manṣūr, who died in that year.

280 Al-Khūʾī, *Rijāl*, 14:366.

281 Al-Ṭabarī, 3:267 (ll. 15–19); Ibn al-Athīr, *al-Kāmil* (ed. Tornberg), 5:244 (last line): Sulaymān b. Mulayḥ (but cf. n. 2: MS A: Fulayḥ).

282 See for example Ibn Abī Ḥātim, *al-Jarḥ* (Beirut edition), 4:135; Ibn Ḥajar, *Lisān*, 3:101.

283 Al-Iṣfahānī, *al-Aghānī* (Dār al-Kutub edition), 11:301; this is the only source that mentions them.

6.2 *The Family of ʿUbaydallāh b. Maʿmar b. ʿUthmān b. ʿAmr b. Kaʿb. . . . b. Taym b. Murra*

6.2.1 ʿUthmān b. Ibrāhīm [b. Muḥammad b. Muʿādh b. ʿUbaydallāh b. Maʿmar b. ʿUthmān b. ʿAmr b. Kaʿb b. Saʿd b. Taym b. Murra] al-Taymī[284]

He was sent by Muḥammad b. ʿAbdallāh to seize al-Yamāma, but Muḥammad died before he arrived at his destination.[285]

Opposers of the Revolt/ʿAbbāsī Supporters

6.2.2 Ibrāhīm b. Ṭalḥa b. ʿUmar b. ʿUbaydallāh b. Maʿmar [b. ʿUthmān b. ʿAmr b. Kaʿb b. Saʿd b. Taym b. Murra][286]

He was one of the notables and leaders of his family and Quraysh.[287] He may have supported the rebellion in its initial stages, but he was one of the notables of Quraysh to whom ʿĪsā b. Mūsā, while on the outskirts of Medina, sent a letter. Because of that he was imprisoned (with others) by Muḥammad b. ʿAbdallāh and was released by ʿĪsā when he took over the city.[288] His brother Jaʿfar owned a very large and rich estate, Umm ʿIyāl, which yielded an income of 4,000 *dīnār*s annually from its fruit crop (dates) alone; the spring on the estate supplied water to more than 20,000 palm trees.[289]

6.2.3 Ibrāhīm b. Muḥammad b. Ibrāhīm b. Ṭalḥa b. ʿUmar b. ʿUbaydallāh b. Maʿmar [b. ʿUthmān b. ʿAmr b. Kaʿb b. Saʿd b. Taym b. Murra]

The grandson of Ibrāhīm b. Ṭalḥa. Al-Balādhurī relates that Muḥammad b. ʿAbdallāh ordered the grandson to swear allegiance to him, but he refused,

284 The reconstruction of the complete lineage is according to Ibn Ḥazm, *Jamhara*, 140: ʿUthmān b. Ibrāhīm b. Muḥammad b. Muʿādh b. ʿUbaydallāh b. Maʿmar; several people of this family served as judges for al-Manṣūr in Baghdad and al-Baṣra.

285 Al-Balādhurī, *Ansāb* (ed. Madelung), 2:519.

286 The reconstruction of the lineage is according to Ibn Ḥazm, *Jamhara*, 140.

287 Ibid.

288 Al-Ṭabarī, 3:227 (ll. 2–16).

289 Ibn Ḥazm, *Jamhara*, 140; on Umm ʿIyāl, see al-Bakrī, *Muʿjam*, 1:196: locates it in al-Furʿ (one of the oases at the foot of Mount Āra); it is the property of Jaʿfar b. Ṭalḥa. See also ibid., 3:1050–1052 ("al-Quds" [mountain]); Yāqūt, *Muʿjam* (ed. Wüstenfeld), 1:363: a village between Mecca and Medina at the foot of Mount Āra, which is in al-Tihāma; further, Yāqūt quotes ʿArrām b. al-Aṣbagh al-Sulamī (d. ca. 275/888): Umm al-ʿIyāl is a village, the endowment (*ṣadaqa*) of Fāṭima, the daughter of the Prophet; al-Fīrūzābādī, *al-Maghānim al-muṭāba*, 4 ([Mount] "Āra"): the mountain is near Medina, parallel to (the mountain chain of) Quds; al-Samhūdī, *Wafāʾ*, 4:128–129 (quoting Yāqūt and Ibn Ḥazm); 106: quoting ʿArrām: Umm al-ʿIyāl is both a name of a spring and a village; one of the springs at the foot of Mount Āra.

saying, "I have already sworn allegiance to Abū Jaʿfar al-Manṣūr, *amīr al-muʾminīn*."[290]

6.3 *The Family of ʿUbaydallāh b. ʿUthmān b. ʿAmr b. Kaʿb b. Saʿd b. Taym*

ⓠ 6.3.1 Muḥammad b. ʿImrān b. Ibrāhīm b. Muḥammad b. Ṭalḥa b. ʿUbaydallāh b. ʿUthmān b. ʿAmr b. Kaʿb b. Saʿd b. Taym b. Murra (d. 154/770 or 771)[291]

He served as a *qāḍī* of Medina under the last Umawī caliph, and also under al-Manṣūr al-ʿAbbāsī.[292]

He was considered loyal and trustworthy by Caliph al-Manṣūr. This is reflected in the following tradition: Upon his arrival to al-Rabadha near Medina in 144/762, and before the imprisonment of the Ḥasanīs, al-Manṣūr sent two envoys on his behalf to ʿAbdallāh b. al-Ḥasan, to convince him to turn in his sons. The first envoy was Muḥammad b. ʿImrān b. Ibrāhīm b. Muḥammad b. Ṭalḥa [from Taym Quraysh] and the second emissary was Mālik b. Anas[!].[293]

Muḥammad b. ʿImrān did not join the rebellion of Muḥammad al-Nafs al-Zakiyya; this is known from a tradition related by Wakīʿ from ʿAbdallāh b. Shabīb < Zubayr < ʿAbd al-Ḥamīd b. ʿAbd al-ʿAzīz b. ʿAbdallāh b. ʿAbdallāh b. ʿUmar [b. al-Khaṭṭab].[294] This may have been the reason for his selection as the *qāḍī* of Medina during al-Manṣūr's reign. His son, ʿAbdallāh, was appointed to be *qaḍāʾ* of Medina by al-Mahdī (or al-Rashīd), then of Mecca, then he moved to al-ʿIrāq, when he became a close associate of al-Rashīd, joined the latter in his journey to Khurāsān and died the same year as al-Rashīd died in al-Ṭūs[295] (or according to another tradition in al-Rayy).[296]

---

290 Al-Balādhurī, *Ansāb* (ed. Madelung), 2:509; the family's genealogy is recorded by Ibn Ḥazm, *Jamhara*, 140, who mentions Ibrāhīm b. Ṭalḥa (no. 1) and his son Muḥammad. The grandson Ibrāhīm is not mentioned, though, and we can add this person to the family tree.

291 On him, see al-Zubayrī, *Nasab Quraysh*, 284–285; Ibn al-Kalbī, *Jamhara* (ed. Caskel), I, table 21; Ibn Saʿd, *al-Qism al-mutammim*, 393 (no. 319); Ibn Ḥazm, *Jamhara*, 139; al-Iṣfahānī, *al-Aghānī* (index: many anecdotes); Ibn Abī Ḥātim, *al-Jarḥ* (Beirut edition), 8:41; Ibn Ḥibbān, *al-Thiqāt*, 7:367–368; a comprehensive biography is found in Wakīʿ, *Akhbār al-quḍāt*, 1:181–199.

292 Ibn Saʿd, *al-Qism al-mutammim*, 393.

293 Al-Ṭabarī, 3:172–173; the family of Mālik was the *ḥulafāʾ* of Banū Taym, see Ibn Ḥazm, *Jamhara*, 436.

294 Wakīʿ, *Akhbār al-quḍāt*, 1:196–197.

295 Ibn Ḥazm, *Jamhara*, 139; ibid.: Two other family members were appointed in charge of the *shurṭa* of ʿĪsā b. Mūsā in al-Kūfa.

296 Ibn Saʿd, *Ṭabaqāt*, 5:435.

7 Banū Makhzūm b. Yaqẓa b. Murra b. Kaʿb b. Luʾayy b. Ghālib b. Fihr (Quraysh) (Chart VIII)

Supporters of the Revolt

7.1 *The Family of al-Mughīra b. ʿAbdallāh b. ʿUmar b. Makhzūm*

The family of al-Mughīra b. ʿAbdallāh was the most important family of Banū Makhzūm.[297]

7.1.1 ʿAbdallāh b. ʿAbd al-Raḥmān b. al-Ḥārith b. ʿAbdallāh b. ʿAyyāsh b. Abī Rabīʿa (ʿAmr) b. al-Mughīra b. ʿAbdallāh b. ʿUmar b. Makhzūm b. Yaqẓa b. Murra

ʿAbdallāh took (most probably an active) part in the revolt of Muḥammad b. ʿAbdallāh. After the revolt he was imprisoned and executed by order of al-Manṣūr, while being bound (فقتله المنصور صبرا).[298] Nothing further is known about him.

A Short History of the Family

ʿAyyāsh b. Abī Rabīʿa was a well-known *ṣaḥābī* who died (according to most versio4ns) in Syria during the Arab conquest.[299] His son ʿAbdallāh b. ʿAyyāsh joined him and also took part in the campaigns in Syria. Al-Wāqidī reports that he had a *dār* in Medina.[300] He died in Mecca in 64/683 aged 62, on the same day that Caliph Yazīd b. Muʿāwiya died. ʿAbdallāh b. al-Zubayr prayed over his body.[301] According to another version, he died in 78/697–698 in

297 Ibn Ḥazm, *Jamhara*, 144: وفيه بيت بني مخزوم وعددهم; of his son, Hishām, it was said that Quraysh used his death date as their calendar, see al-Zubayrī, *Nasab Quraysh*, 301: وزعموا أن قريشا كانت تؤرخ بموته تقول: عام مات هشام. ʿAbd al-Raḥmān b. al-Ḥārith was one of the collectors and editors of the Qurʾān, for example, see al-Balādhurī, *Ansāb* (ed. al-ʿAbbās), 5:240ff.

298 Ibn Ḥazm, *Jamhara*, 147; al-Zubayrī, *Nasab Quraysh*, 319: قتله المنصور أسيرا; al-Balādhurī, *Ansāb* (ed. ʿAbbās), 5:262: فأخذ أسيرا فقتله; the full reconstruction of his lineage is according to Ibn Ḥazm, *Jamhara*, 144–147; Ibn al-Kalbī, *Jamhara* (ed. Caskel), I, tables 22 and 23 (the last two names: ʿAbdallāh and ʿAbd al-Raḥmān are missing); al-Balādhurī, *Ansāb* (ed. ʿAbbās), 5:262–263 (partial); Bernheimer, *The ʿAlids*, 40, n. 29.

299 On him, see Ibn Saʿd, *Ṭabaqāt*, 5:443; Ibn ʿAsākir, *Taʾrīkh*, 47:234–247; died in Syria during the conquests: 237–238, 240, 247 (the battle of Yarmūk); but cf. 238: died in the battle of al-Yamāma; Ibn Ḥajar, *Tahdhīb* (Beirut 1984), 8:176.

300 Ibn ʿAsākir, *Taʾrīkh*, 31:388; see also ibid., 47:237–238.

301 Ibn Ḥibbān, *al-Thiqāt*, 3:218.

Sijistān.[302] Al-Ḥārith b. ʿAbdallāh b. ʿAyyāsh, the grandfather of ʿAbdallāh b. ʿAbd al-Raḥmān, was one of the adherents of ʿAbdallāh b. al-Zubayr and was appointed by the latter as the governor of al-Baṣra and by Muṣʿab b. al-Zubayr as the governor of al-Kūfa.[303] Despite his role in the camp of the rival caliph, ʿAbd al-Malik regarded him highly, and he used to come to the caliph after the campaign was over.[304]

His son, ʿAbd al-Raḥmān b. al-Ḥārith (80–143/699–700 to 760–761, aged 63),[305] the father of ʿAbdallāh, was appointed as the governor of Tabāla (in al-Tihāma, on the road to Yemen)[306] by the ʿAbbāsī governor of Mecca and Medina, Ziyād b. ʿUbaydallāh b. ʿAbd al-Madān al-Ḥārithī. This appointment was most probably made before 141/758–759, when Ziyād, the governor, was dismissed from office. This post made ʿAbd al-Raḥmān rich. With the money he gained from his post he came to Medina and built a residence (*dār*) there, which he called Tabāla. Mūsā b. Jaʿfar b. Muḥammad [b. ʿAlī b. al-Ḥusayn b. ʿAlī b. Abī Ṭālib?] bought this residence from ʿAbd al-Raḥmān's heirs,[307] perhaps after the execution of ʿAbd al-Raḥmān's son ʿAbdallāh by al-Manṣūr (see above). ʿAbd al-Raḥmān's son al-Mughīra (124 or 125–186/741 or 742 or 743–802) was a well-known *faqīh* in Medina, and is described as a devout student and close associate (*ṣāḥib*) of Mālik b. Anas.[308]

---

302 Ibn Khayyāṭ, *Ṭabaqāt* (ed. al-ʿUmarī), 1:234: died in 78/697 or 698 in Sijistān[!?]; Ibn Ḥajar, *Taʿjīl al-manfaʿa*, 1:231: died in 64/683 or 684 (according to Ibn Ḥibbān), or 78 (according to Ibn Khayyāṭ); on him, see also al-Mizzī, *Tahdhīb*, 15:410–411 (also quoting Ibn Ḥibbān but gives the date of his death erroneously as 70 instead of 64); Ibn ʿAsākir, *Taʾrīkh*, 31:385–392.

303 Al-Balādhurī, *Ansāb* (ed. ʿAbbās), 5:251–252.

304 Ibid., 5:252: When the news of his death in Mecca reached Damascus, al-Walīd b. ʿAbd al-Malik said: "the head and leader of Banū Makhzūm has perished" and his father corrected him saying: "say: the head and leader of Quraysh has died": هلك سيد بني مخزوم فقال [عبد الملك] أهكذا تقول؟ قل: مات سيد قريش. About al-Ḥārith b. ʿAbdallāh, see also Ibn ʿAsākir, *Taʾrīkh*, 11:436–447; al-Mizzī, *Tahdhīb*, 5:239–244.

305 Ibid., 17:38.

306 On Tabāla, see Yāqūt, *Muʿjam* (ed. Wüstenfeld), 1:816–817; *EI*², "Tabāla."

307 Ibn Saʿd, *al-Qism al-mutammim*, 269–270; al-Balādhurī, *Ansāb* (ed. ʿAbbās), 5:262; for his biographies, see, for example, Ibn Ḥibbān, *al-Thiqāt*, 7:73; Ibn Ḥajar, *Taqrīb* (ed. ʿAwāma), 1:338; al-Mizzī, *Tahdhīb*, 17:37–38.

308 Ibn Ḥazm, *Jamhara*, 147: صاحب مالك بن أنس; Ibn Ḥajar, *Tahdhīb* (Beirut, 1984), 10:236 and al-Mizzī, *Tahdhīb*, 28:381–383: كان فقيه أهل المدينة بعد مالك.

Opposers of the Revolt/ʿAbbāsī Supporters

7.1.2 Ayyūb b. Salama b. ʿAbdallāh b. al-Walīd b. al-Walīd b. al-Mughīra b. ʿAbdallāh b. ʿUmar b. Makhzūm [b. Yaqẓa b. Murra b. Kaʿb b. Luʾayy b. Ghālib b. Fihr] al-Madanī

Ayyūb belonged to a very distinguished and wealthy family of Makhzūm.[309] He inherited from the family of Khālid b. al-Walīd because the latter lacked a direct descendant. This inheritance included several "houses" (*dūr*) in Medina.[310] The family residence was still in the hands of the descendants of Ayyūb b. Salama in the time of ʿUmar b. Shabba (d. 262/876).[311] Ayyūb was related to the family of Hishām b. ʿAbd al-Malik through the latter's mother.[312] He was related both to the Umawīs and the ʿAbbāsīs through the marriage of the daughter of his brother, Umm Salama bt. Yaʿqūb b. Salama, to Maslama b. Hishām b. ʿAbd al-Malik and later to Abū l-ʿAbbās al-Saffāḥ, the first ʿAbbāsī caliph.[313]

Ayyūb married the sister of ʿAbdallāh b. al-Ḥasan, Fāṭima. A severe quarrel occurred between Ayyūb and ʿAbdallāh b. al-Ḥasan regarding this marriage, and this led to the direct interference of Caliph Hishām: Ayyūb asked for her hand from her son, Ṣāliḥ b. Muʿāwiya b. ʿAbdallāh b. Jaʿfar, and ʿAbdallāh b. al-Ḥasan claimed that only he, as her *walīyy*, was legally allowed to give her hand in marriage. This led to the imprisonment of Ayyūb and the intercession of his son on the matter before Caliph Hishām b. ʿAbd al-Malik.[314]

---

309 On him, see Ibn al-Kalbī, *Jamhara* (ed. Ḥasan), 89; Ibn Ḥazm, *Jamhara*, 148; al-Zubayrī, *Nasab Quraysh*, 228, 230; al-Balādhurī, *Ansāb* (ed. ʿAbbās), 5:269; Ibn ʿAsākir, *Taʾrīkh*, 10:98–101.

310 Al-Zubayrī, *Nasab Quraysh*, 228; Ibn Ḥazm, *Jamhara*, 148; al-Fākihī, *Akhbār Makka*, 3:345; Ibn ʿAsākir, *Taʾrīkh*, 10:101; 16:214; Ibn al-Athīr, *Usd al-ghāba*, 2:96; Ibn Ḥajar, *Tahdhīb* (Beirut 1984), 3:104; al-ʿAynī, *ʿUmdat al-qārī*, 16:245; al-Sakhāwī, *al-Tuḥfa al-laṭīfa*, 1:209.

311 Ibn Shabba, *Taʾrīkh al-Madīna*, 1:231, 244.

312 Al-Ṭabarī, 2:1669: Umm Hishām bt. Hishām b. Ismāʿīl b. Hishām b. al-Walīd b. al-Mughīra; on him and his family, see Ibn Ḥazm, *Jamhara*, 148; al-Zubayrī, *Nasab Quraysh*, 330.

313 For example, see Ibn ʿAsākir, *Taʾrīkh*, 70:242; her biography: 70:242–247; Ibn Ḥabīb, *al-Muḥabbar*, 445: she was married 1) to ʿAbdallāh (or Maslama) b. ʿAbd al-Malik; 2) Abū l-ʿAbbās al-Saffāḥ; 3) Ismāʿīl b. ʿAlī b. ʿAbdallāh b. al-ʿAbbās.

314 See Ibn ʿAsākir, *Taʾrīkh*, 8:375–377; 8:377: إن هذا تجوز هذه المرأة إلى غير ولي هي امرأة من آل حسن والمزوج من آل جعفر. For a detailed description of the marriage affair, see Wakīʿ, *Akhbār al-quḍāt*, 1:172–174; al-Balādhurī, *Ansāb* (ed. ʿAbbās), 5:269.

According to al-Balādhurī, he and Hishām b. ʿUrwa participated in the rebellion. They both received *amān* from al-Manṣūr after conveying excuses for their participation.[315]

The evidence of Ayyūb b. Salama swearing allegiance to Muḥammad b. ʿAbdallāh appears only in al-Balādhurī's work. It seems, however, that this evidence is not reliable. Ayyūb is mentioned together with Hishām b. ʿUrwa among those who supported the revolt, which is very doubtful. Ayyūb and his sons were present in the year 144/762 in the camp of al-Manṣūr in al-Rabadha, to which Banū l-Ḥasan were brought. When the sound of the flogging of Muḥammad b. ʿAbdallāh al-ʿUthmānī was heard, Ayyūb said to his sons "watch out for yourselves, and don't let a word escape you."[316] It is not stated in the source that some of the prisoners were Ayyūb's family, and it seems plausible that they were there as part of a delegation of dignitaries from Medina to the caliph. The next mention of Ayyūb b. Salama is on the eve of the rebellion, in the palace of the governor of Medina, Riyāḥ, where Ayyūb advised him how to put down the fire of mutiny among the inhabitants of the city: "Cut off their hands and whip them."[317] Ayyūb b. Salama is described as a counselor to the ʿAbbāsī governor and not as a supporter of Muḥammad b. ʿAbdallāh. Bearing in mind that Ayyūb's marriage to Fāṭima bt. al-Ḥasan was annulled by Hishām b. ʿAbd al-Malik, on the demand of ʿAbdallāh b. al-Ḥasan, Muḥammad al-Nafs al-Zakiyya's father, the feelings of Ayyūb towards ʿAbdallāh were naturally charged with hate and enmity. On the other hand, Ayyūb was related to the ʿAbbāsīs and was considered a maternal uncle (*khāl*) of the ruling family.[318] He was a rich man and had a great deal to lose.[319] All this tilts the balance against the evidence of his swearing allegiance to Muḥammad al-Nafs al-Zakiyya.

315 Al-Balādhurī, *Ansāb* (ed. Madelung), 2:518; *Fragmenta*, 246, with a slight change: وكان هشام بن عروة وأيوب بن سلمة المخزومي قد بايعا محمد بن عبد الله فأومنا حين اعتذرا.

316 Al-Ṭabarī, 3:177 (l. 10): لا تسقطوا بشيء; the translation is according to McAuliffe, *ʿAbbāsid Authority*, 127 (based on al-Ṭabarī's *Glossarium*, s.v. *s.q.ṭ.*); cf. Lane, *Lexicon*, s.v. *s.q.ṭ.*: أسقطوا له بالكلام: "they reviled him with evil speech"; how many sons were with him is not noted; according to Ibn Ḥazm, *Jamhara*, 148, Ayyūb had 14[!] sons.

317 Al-Yaʿqūbī, *Taʾrīkh* (ed. Houtsma), 2:451–452.

318 On this important term (and institution) among the Arabs during the Jāhiliyya and the Islamic period, see Elad, "al-Maʾmūn's Army," 306–316.

319 He was the sole heir of the last descendant of Khālid b. al-Walīd.

7.1.2.1–2 *Two of Ayyūb's sons are mentioned in connection with the revolt:* **Ismāʿīl b. Ayyūb b. Salama** was appointed by Abū l-ʿAbbās al-Saffāḥ as the governor of Mecca.[320] He and his brother, **Khālid,** were among the notables of Quraysh who were summoned for consultation by Riyāḥ, the governor of Medina, on the eve of the outbreak of the revolt. It can be assumed that at that crucial moment, they were loyal to the ʿAbbāsīs. One of the participants of this meeting declared that they were loyal and obedient to the ʿAbbāsīs.[321]

Another son, **Hishām b. Ayyūb**, was in charge of the *shurṭa* of Medina. It is not stated when he held this post.[322]

7.1.3 Al-Ḥārith b. ʿĀmir [= al-ʿAyyāsh] b. ʿAbd al-Raḥmān b. al-Ḥārith b. Hishām b. al-Mughīra b. ʿAbdallāh b. ʿUmar b. Makhzūm

When Banū l-Ḥasan were brought to al-Manṣūr in al-Rabadha, they met al-Ḥārith b. ʿĀmir [read ʿAyyāsh?] b. ʿAbd al-Raḥmān b. al-Ḥārith b. Hishām [b. al-Mughīra … b. Makhzūm] there, who cursed them, saying, "Praised be God who expelled you from our land (country?: بلادنا)."[323]

It is plausible that another important family of Banū Makhzūm resided in Medina, i.e.:

7.1.4 The Family of Abū Umayya (Ḥudhayfa, called Zād al-Rakb) b. al-Mughīra b. ʿAbdallāh b. ʿUmar b. Makhzūm

Al-Ṭabarī records that **Rubayḥa bt. Abī Shākir al-Qurashiyya,** after the evening prayer, before the decisive battle, gave Muḥammad b. ʿAbdallāh [water to] drink, then urged him to run away.[324] It is possible to identify this woman as Rubayḥa bt. Muḥammad b. ʿAbdallāh b. ʿAbdallāh b. Ḥudhayfa (Abū Umayya, called Zād al-Rakb) b. al-Mughīra b. ʿAbdallāh, the wife of Ibrāhīm b. al-Ḥasan

320 Al-Balādhurī, *Ansāb* (ed. ʿAbbās), 5:269 (bottom line).

321 Al-Ṭabarī, 3:190–191 (l. 18 to l. 14); al-Iṣfahānī, *Maqātil*, 261 (with minor omissions and additions): ʿUmar b. Shabba < ʿĪsā b. ʿAbdallāh < his father, an eyewitness testimony.

322 Ibn al-Kalbī, *Jamhara* (ed. Ḥasan), 89.

323 Al-Ṭabarī, 3:175 (ll. 9–11); ibid.: al-Ḥārith b. ʿĀmir; but in footnote d: MS A has: عباس (which is most probably a copying error of عياش), instead of ʿĀmir; the *nasab* books do not mention a son of ʿAbd al-Raḥmān b. al-Ḥārith named ʿĀmir or al-ʿAbbās, but do mention a son named ʿAyyāsh, see al-Zubayrī, *Nasab Quraysh*, 305; Ibn Ḥazm, *Jamhara*, 145; al-Balādhurī, *Ansāb* (ed. ʿAbbās), 5:241; but a son named al-Ḥārith b. ʿAyyāsh is not mentioned in these *nasab* books; only Abū Bakr b. ʿAbd al-Raḥmān had a son named al-Ḥārith.

324 Al-Ṭabarī, 3:242 (ll. 14–16).

b. al-Ḥasan, ʿAbdallāh's brother, the first Ḥasanī who died in al-Manṣūr's prison in al-ʿIrāq.[325]

7.2 *The Family of Asad (Abū Junda[u?]b) [al-Mughīra b. ʿAbdallāh's brother] b. ʿAbdallāh b. ʿUmar b. Makhzūm*

Supporters of the Revolt

7.2.1 Al-Arqam b. Abī l-Arqam (ʿAbd Manāf) [b. Asad b. ʿAbdallāh b. ʿUmar b. Makhzūm]

He had a residence in Medina, which was endowed as a family *waqf:* وكانت داره صدقة على ولده. One (or some: *baʿḍ*) of his descendants joined the revolt of Muḥammad b. ʿAbdallāh; therefore this family residence was bought [confiscated? فصارت لأبي جعفر ابتياعا] by al-Manṣūr and then was given to al-Khayzurān, al-Mahdī's female slave (Hārūn al-Rashīd's mother).[326]

7.3 *The Family of ʿUbayd b. ʿUmar b. Makhzūm*

Supporters of the Revolt

7.3.1 ʿAlī b. al-Muṭṭalib b. ʿAbdallāh b. al-Muṭṭalib b. Ḥanṭab b. al-Ḥārith b. ʿUbayd b. ʿUmar b. Makhzūm

He was one of those who rebelled with Muḥammad b. ʿAbdallāh,[327] and was one of his most loyal supporters.[328] After the revolt he was caught, brought to the caliph and whipped 500 lashes.[329] (It is noteworthy that his brother, ʿAbd al-ʿAzīz, joined the ʿAbbāsīs, see below).

---

325 Al-Iṣfahānī, *Maqātil*, 199, calls her: Rubayḥa bt. Muḥammad b. ʿAbdallāh b. ʿAbdallāh b. Abī Umayya, called Zād al-Rakb, copied by al-Amīn, *Aʿyān al-Shīʿa*, 3:310. See also al-Bukhārī, *Sirr al-silsila*, 15: Rubayḥa bt. [Muḥammad b. ʿAbdallāh?] b. ʿAbdallāh b. Umayya [read Abī Umayya?] al-Makhzūmī; she is not mentioned in the *nasab* books that I have consulted. On the important Makhzūmī family of Abū Umayya, called Zād al-Rakb, see al-Zubayrī, *Nasab Quraysh*, 315; Ibn Ḥazm, *Jamhara*, 146–147; al-Balādhurī, *Ansāb* (ed. ʿAbbās), 5:263–266; Abū Umayya was the father of Umm Salama (Hind), the Prophet's wife, for example, see Ibn Saʿd, *Ṭabaqāt*, 8:87; Ibn Ḥazm, *Jamhara*, 146; al-Mizzī, *Tahdhīb*, 35:317.

326 Al-Balādhurī, *Ansāb* (ed. ʿAbbās), 5:278; on him and his family, see Ibn Ḥazm, *Jamhara*, 143 (nothing is related about the rebellion).

327 Ibn Ḥazm, *Jamhara*, 142.

328 Al-Ṭabarī, 3:226 (ll. 5–6).

329 Ibid., 3:264 (ll. 10–11); al-Azdī, *Taʾrīkh al-Mawṣil*, 192.

Opposers of the Revolt/ʿAbbāsī Supporters

(q) 7.3.2 ʿAbd al-ʿAzīz b. al-Muṭṭalib b. ʿAbdallāh b. al-Muṭṭalib b. Ḥanṭab b. al-Ḥārith b. ʿUbayd b. ʿUmar b. Makhzūm[330]

ʿAbd al-ʿAzīz b. al-Muṭṭalib is described as one of the most distinguished notables of Quraysh; he served as the *qāḍī* of Medina during the governorship of Ziyād b. ʿUbaydallāh. When the latter was dismissed (in 141/758), ʿAbd al-ʿAzīz was appointed as the new governor,[331] until the arrival of Muḥammad b. Khālid al-Qasrī, when he was reinstated as the *qāḍī*.[332]

When Muḥammad b. ʿAbdallāh took control of Medina and appointed dignitaries to official posts, according to one source, the person in charge of the judiciary was ʿAbd al-ʿAzīz b. al-Muṭṭalib b. ʿAbdallāh al-Makhzūmī,[333] but another source is less certain, saying, "Muḥammad b. ʿAbdallāh appointed as a judge ʿAbd al-ʿAzīz b. ʿAbd [sic!] al-Muṭṭalib, but it is said (*wa-yuqālu*) that he appointed as a judge, Abū Bakr b. ʿAbdallāh b. Abī Sabra."[334] Although the second name is the less accepted version (in the author's view), it stands to reason that it is the correct one, since Abū Bakr b. Abī Sabra was one of the most zealous supporters of Muḥammad b. ʿAbdallāh. If he served as the *qāḍī* of Medina under Muḥammad b. ʿAbdallāh, it may indeed imply that he supported him and his cause, but only for a very short period, even before the initial skirmishes between the ʿAbbāsīs and Muḥammad's supporters. ʿAbd al-ʿAzīz left Muḥammad's camp upon receiving a letter from ʿĪsā b. Mūsā, but was seized and brought back. He stayed for a short while and then left again, but was seized once again. His brother ʿAlī b. al-Muṭṭalib, who was among Muḥammad's most loyal supporters, persuaded Muḥammad al-Nafs al-Zakiyya to leave his brother ʿAbd al-ʿAzīz alone.[335]

330 The brother of ʿAlī (see above); this is a good example for the split within families, where we find two brothers on opposite sides; on him, see al-Balādhurī, *Ansāb* (ed. ʿAbbās), 5:191; Wakīʿ, *Akhbār al-quḍāt*, 1:202–210; Ibn Ḥibbān, *al-Thiqāt*, 7:113; Ibn Abī Ḥātim, *al-Jarḥ* (Beirut edition), 5:393; Ibn Ḥajar, *Tahdhīb* (Beirut, 1984), 6:318; al-Mizzī, *Tahdhīb*, 6:206–208.

331 Al-Ṭabarī, 3:159 (ll. 2–19).

332 Wakīʿ, *Akhbār al-quḍāt*, 1:202.

333 Al-Ṭabarī, 3:198 (= al-Iṣfahānī, *Maqātil*, 296).

334 Wakīʿ, *Akhbār al-quḍāt*, 1:223–224.

335 Al-Ṭabarī, 3:226 (ll. 2–7).

8 Banū ʿĀmir b. Luʾayy b. Ghālib b. Fihr (Quraysh) (Chart IX)

8.1 *The family of ʿAbdallāh b. Abī Qays b. ʿAbd Wudd b. Naṣr b. Mālik b. Ḥisl b. ʿĀmir b. Luʾayy b. Ghālib b. Fihr (Quraysh)*

Supporters of the Revolt

Ⓜ8. 1.1 ʿUbaydallāh b. ʿAmr b. Abī Dhiʾb (Hishām) [b. Shuʿba b. ʿAbdallāh b. Abī Qays b. ʿAbd Wudd b. Naṣr b. Mālik b. Ḥisl b. ʿĀmir b. Luʾayy[?]]

Al-Faḍl b. Dukayn (d. 219/834) relates that he [al-Faḍl] was informed that "ʿUbaydallāh b. ʿAmr b. Abī Dhuʾayb [read Dhiʾb] and ʿAbd al-Ḥamīd b. Jaʿfar came to Muḥammad before the uprising and said to him, 'Why are you waiting to come out in open revolt? By God, in this community we find no one more ill-fated for it than you. What keeps you from revolting on your own?'"[336]

If the version of ʿUbaydallāh b. ʿAmr b. Abī Dhiʾb is to be trusted, then he may have been the grandson of Abū Dhiʾb Hishām b. Shuʿba of ʿĀmir b. Luʾayy (Quraysh), although the *nasab* books that I consulted do not mention a son of Abū Dhiʾb named ʿAmr.[337] An unidentified *muḥaddith* by the name of ʿUbaydallāh b. ʿAmr b. Abī Dhiʾb is mentioned only once by Ibn Ḥibbān.[338]

Opposers of the Revolt/ʿAbbāsī Supporters

ⓂⒻ8.1.2 Muḥammad b. ʿAbd al-Raḥmān b. al-Mughīra b. al-Ḥārith b. Hishām (Abū Dhiʾb) b. Shuʿba [b. ʿAbdallāh b. Abī Qays b. ʿAbd Wudd b. Naṣr b. Mālik b. Ḥisl b. ʿĀmir b. Luʾayy], who is commonly named Ibn Abī Dhiʾb (d. 159/776)[339]

Ibn Abī Dhiʾb was a well-known Medinan scholar. It seems that he is not to be identified with ʿUbaydallāh b. ʿAmr b. Abī Dhiʾb discussed above.[340]

---

336 Al-Ṭabarī, 3:190 (ll. 14–18) (trans. McAuliffe, *ʿAbbāsid Authority*, 143–144); al-Ṭabarī, 3:190: أبي ذؤيب; ibid. note g: MS A renders أبي ذيب; Ibn al-Athīr, *al-Kāmil* (Beirut edition), 5:529 (ed. Tornberg, 5:402–403): بن أبي ذئب; al-Iṣfahānī, *Maqātil*, 261: إبن ذئب; al-Dhahabī, *Siyar*, 6:214 and idem, *Taʾrīkh* (*Ḥawādith wa-wafayāt*, 141–160), 9:21: ابن أبي ذئب, relating the same tradition of al-Faḍl b. Dukayn, but the two supporters of Muḥammad become three: 1) ʿUbaydallāh b. ʿUmar[!] 2) Ibn Abī Dhiʾb and 3) ʿAbd al-Ḥamīd b. Jaʿfar. As for ʿUbaydallāh b. ʿUmar he is discussed above (Banū ʿAdī).

337 E.g., Ibn al-Kalbī, *Jamhara* (ed. Ḥasan), 110; al-Zubayrī, *Nasab Quraysh*, 423; Ibn Ḥazm, *Jamhara*, 168.

338 Ibn Ḥibbān, *al-Thiqāt*, 6:214; Ibn Ḥajar, *Taʿjīl al-manfaʿa*, 102 (quoting Ibn Ḥibbān).

339 On him, see van Ess, *Theologie*, 2:681–687; Cook, *Commanding Right*, 56.

340 But cf. van Arendonk, *L'Imamat Zaïdite*, 313: according to al-Iṣfahānī and al-Dhahabī.

Al-Wāqidī states that Muḥammad b. ʿAbd al-Raḥmān did not support and certainly did not join the rebellion. When Muḥammad b. ʿAbdallāh came out in open revolt Ibn Abī Dhiʾb stayed in his house and did not leave it until Muḥammad was killed. Moreover, the governors of Medina honored him and gave him special treatment. Jaʿfar b. Sulaymān gave him 100 *dīnār*s as a present while al-Ḥasan b. Zayd gave him a monthly pension of five *dīnār*s, which was later raised to ten. When he arrived in Baghdad he received 1,000 *dīnār*s.[341]

8.2 *The Family of ʿAbd al-ʿUzzā b. Abī Qays b. ʿAbd Wudd b. Naṣr b. Mālik b. Ḥisl b. ʿĀmir b. Luʾayy*

Supporters of the Revolt

ⓠ8.2.1 Abū Bakr b. ʿAbdallāh b. Muḥammad b. Abī Sabra b. Abī Ruhm b. ʿAbd al-ʿUzzā b. Abī Qays b. . . . b. Ghālib b. Fihr (Quraysh)[342]

He belonged to a distinguished family of Qurashī scholars. He served as the *qāḍī* of Mecca under the governorship of Ziyād b. ʿUbaydallāh al-Ḥārithī, while his brother, Muḥammad, served as a *qāḍī* in Medina under the same governor.[343] According to one report he was appointed the *qāḍī* of Medina by the first ʿAbbāsī governor of al-Ḥijāz, Dāwūd b. ʿAlī, the uncle of the caliphs al-Saffāḥ and al-Manṣūr.[344] He is commonly described as a *muftī* in Medina: وكان يفتي بالمدينة.[345] Upon the outbreak of the revolt he was among the dignitaries of Quraysh who received letters from ʿĪsā b. Mūsā l-ʿAbbāsī summoning them to

---

341 Ibn Saʿd, *al-Qism al-mutammim*, 416, 417, 419–420; al-Dhahabī copied Ibn Saʿd's/al-Wāqidī's tradition, see *Siyar*, 7:141–142; idem, *Taʾrīkh*, 9:601; idem, *Tadhkira* (Hyderabad edition), 1:192; see also van Arendonk, *L'Imamat Zaïdite*, 44, 313 (quoting al-Dhahabī's *Tadhkira* and Zaydī sources).

342 On him, see al-Zubayrī, *Nasab Quraysh*, 428–429; Ibn Ḥazm, *Jamhara*, 169; Ibn Saʿd, *al-Qism al-mutammim*, 458–460: his support of Muḥammad and the affair of the *ṣadaqa* taxes is not mentioned in this biography; Ibn Qutayba, *al-Maʿārif* (Cairo edition), 489. See Wakīʿ, *Akhbār al-quḍāt*, 1:200–202, where we find a comprehensive biography; Ibn Ḥibbān, *al-Majrūḥīn* (ed. al-Bāz), 3:147–148; al-Khaṭīb al-Baghdādī, *Taʾrīkh* (Hyderabad edition), 14:367–371 [Beirut, 1997 edition, 14:370–374]; Ibn ʿAsākir, *Taʾrīkh*, 66:22–29; al-Dhahabī, *Siyar*, 7:330–332; al-Mizzī, *Tahdhīb*, 33:102–108; McAuliffe, *ʿAbbāsid Authority*, 189, n. 923; van Arendonk, *L'Imamat Zaïdite*, 312.

343 Al-Mizzī, *Tahdhīb*, 33:103: his brother; Ibn Saʿd, *al-Qism al-mutammim*, 458; Ibn ʿAsākir, *Taʾrīkh*, 66:23 (copying Ibn Saʿd): as the *qāḍī* of Mecca.

344 Al-Balādhurī, *Ansāb* (ed. ʿAbbās), 5:550: correct أبو بكر بن عبد الله بن محمد بن عبد الله بن أبي سبرة to أبو بكر بن عبد الله بن محمد بن أبي سبرة.

345 Ibn ʿAdī, *Ḍuʿafāʾ*, 7:295; al-Khaṭīb al-Baghdādī, *Taʾrīkh* (Beirut, 1997), 14:372; Ibn ʿAsākir, *Taʾrīkh*, 66:23.

join him and leave Muḥammad b. ʿAbdallāh, who imprisoned them all except two, one of whom was Abū Bakr b. ʿAbdallāh b. Abī Sabra.[346] At the time of the outbreak of the revolt of al-Nafs al-Zakiyya, he was in charge of the *ṣadaqāt* of Ṭayy' and Asad. The sum that was collected by him according to the different sources was between 20,000 and 24,000 *dīnār*s and was given to Muḥammad b. ʿAbdallāh, and this contributed to the latter's power.[347]

He was captured after the rebellion, whipped 70 lashes, and imprisoned by the temporary ʿAbbāsī governor (Kathīr b. Ḥuṣayn) of Medina,[348] but was released by the new governor of Medina, Jaʿfar b. Sulaymān b. ʿAlī l-ʿAbbāsī, by order of al-Manṣūr, because of his conduct during the mutiny of the *sūdān* (black slaves) in Medina in 145/762. He was released from prison by these rebels, but refused to speak against the authorities and incite Medina's inhabitants to join the rebellion against the ʿAbbāsīs.[349] Later, he resided in Baghdad, serving as a *qāḍī* on behalf of Caliph al-Manṣūr,[350] and still later he served as the *qāḍī* for the heir apparent Mūsā b. al-Mahdī and escorted him to Jurjān.[351] He died in Baghdad in 162/778–779 at the age of 60.[352]

Opposers of the Revolt/ʿAbbāsī Supporters

8.2.2 Sulaymān b. ʿAbdallāh b. [Muḥammad b.?] Abī Sabra [b. Abī Ruhm b. ʿAbd al-ʿUzzā b. Abī Qays b. ... b. Ghālib b. Fihr (Quraysh)]

He disclosed to Riyāḥ b. ʿUthmān, the governor of Medina, the movements of Muḥammad b. ʿAbdallāh, and that the latter intended to go to al-Madhād.[353]

---

346 Al-Ṭabarī, 3:227 (ll. 7–8).

347 20,000 *dīnārs*: Ibn Ḥajar, *Tahdhīb* (Beirut, 1984), 12:26: from Muṣʿab al-Zubayrī; 24,000 *dīnārs*: al-Zubayrī, *Nasab Quraysh*, 428–429; al-Tanūkhī, *al-Faraj*, 2:20–21; Ibn Ḥazm, *Jamhara*, 169; al-Khaṭīb al-Baghdādī, *Taʾrīkh* (Beirut, 1997), 14:367; Ibn ʿAsākir, *Taʾrīkh*, 66:24; al-Dhahabī, *Siyar*, 7:332.

348 Al-Ṭabarī, 3:266 (l. 1).

349 For example, see ibid., 3:265–271: ʿUmar b. Shabba < Muḥammad b. Yaḥyā < al-Ḥārith b. Isḥāq; al-Balādhurī, *Ansāb* (ed. Madelung), 2:524–526: al-Ḥasan b. ʿAlī l-Ḥirmāzī [on him, see Ibn al-Nadīm, *al-Fihrist* (ed. Tajaddud), 54; al-Ṣafadī, *al-Wāfī*, 12:88]; AND Abū l-ʿAbbās al-Faḍl b. al-ʿAbbās [b. Mūsā b. ʿĪsā?] al-Hāshimī < al-Zubayr b. Bakkār < his uncle Muṣʿab b. ʿAbdallāh and others besides them (both); al-Tanūkhī, *al-Faraj*, 2:20–24; Ibn ʿAsākir, *Taʾrīkh*, 66:25–26.

350 Ibn ʿAsākir, *Taʾrīkh*, 66:25; Ibn Ḥibbān, *al-Majrūḥīn* (ed. al-Bāz), 3:147.

351 Ibn Saʿd, *al-Qism al-mutammim*, 459; Ibn ʿAsākir, *Taʾrīkh*, 66:23: escorting Mūsā b. al-Mahdī to Jurjān.

352 For example, see Ibn Saʿd, *al-Qism al-mutammim*, 459; Ibn ʿAsākir, *Taʾrīkh*, 66:29.

353 Al-Ṭabarī, 3:190 (ll. 13–14); Ibn al-Athīr, *al-Kāmil* (ed. Tornberg), 5:402; Sulaymān is not mentioned in the *nasab* books that I consulted, nor this special lineage: سليمان بن عبد

If this identification is correct, Sulaymān may have been the brother of Abū Bakr b. ʿAbdallāh, one of the most devout supporters of Muḥammad al-Nafs al-Zakiyya (on him, see above), or if the lineage recorded by al-Ṭabarī is accepted, his father may have been the brother of Abū Bakr's grandfather.

ⓠⓜ8.2.3 Saʿīd b. Sulaymān b. Nawfal b. Musāḥiq b. ʿAbdallāh b. Makhrama b. ʿAbd al-ʿUzzā b. Abī Qays b. ʿAbd Wudd b. Naṣr b. Mālik b. Ḥisl b. ʿĀmir b. Luʾayy b. Ghālib b. Fihr, and his son, ʿAbd al-Jabbār

There is no information on Saʿīd during the rebellion, but it stands to reason that during the revolt in 145/762 he was already in the service of the ʿAbbāsīs or was at least a supporter. The first information about this family is from al-Mahdī's period.

It seems that contrary to the distinguished member of their clan, Abū Bakr b. ʿAbdallāh b. Muḥammad b. Abī Sabra, who was one of the great supporters of Muḥammad al-Nafs al-Zakiyya, Saʿīd b. Sulaymān and his son, ʿAbd al-Jabbār, were close adherents of the ʿAbbāsīs.

Saʿīd b. Sulaymān b. Nawfal's mother was Amat al-Wahhāb bt. ʿAmr b. Musāḥiq b. ʿAbdallāh b. Makhrama (that is, the daughter of his grandfather's brother).[354] He served as a *qāḍī* in al-Mahdī's reign and came in a delegation to Hārūn al-Rashīd and was an intimate associate (كان ينقطع) of the ʿAbbāsī, al-ʿAbbās b. Muḥammad b. ʿAlī b. ʿAbdallāh b. al-ʿAbbās (al-Manṣūr's brother). He had an estate called al-Jafr, near al-Ḍariyya in al-Ḥijāz, situated at a distance approximately 18 miles from Medina. He is described as one of the most learned and distinguished men of Quraysh in his time.[355]

الله بن أبي سبرة; the only sons of ʿAbdallāh b. Muḥammad b. Abī Sabra mentioned in the *nasab* books are Muḥammad and Abū Bakr (see Ibn Ḥazm, *Jamhara*, 169). It seems that we should correct his lineage according to al-Ṭabarī, 3:269 (l. 15), when he mentions سليمان بن عبد الله بن محمد بن أبي سبرة in a tradition that records the revolt of the blacks (*sūdān*) in Medina in 145/762, immediately after Muḥammad b. ʿAbdallāh's revolt was crushed.

354 Al-Zubayrī, *Nasab Quraysh*, 428.

355 Ibid., 427; for further details about the estate, see al-Bakrī, *Muʿjam*, 3:863 ("Ḍariyya"); Yāqūt, *Muʿjam* (ed. Wüstenfeld), 2:91–92. On him, see Ibn Ḥazm, *Jamhara*, 169; al-Khaṭīb al-Baghdādī, *Taʾrīkh* (Cairo edition), 9:65–67; al-Zubayrī, *Nasab Quraysh*, 427. Several late sources mention the tradition about Saʿīd's close relations with al-ʿAbbās b. Muḥammad al-ʿAbbāsī; it was transmitted by Muṣʿab b. ʿAbdallāh al-Zubayrī to his uncle al-Zubayr b. Bakkār, e.g., al-Khaṭīb al-Baghdādī, *Taʾrīkh* (Cairo edition), 9:66; Ibn ʿAsākir, *Taʾrīkh*, 26:397. See also al-Sakhāwī, *al-Tuḥfa al-laṭīfa*, 1:399: *qāḍī al-Madīna*; Ibn al-Jawzī, *al-Muntaẓam*, 9:167.

ⓠ ⓜ 8.2.4 ʿAbd al-Jabbār b. Saʿīd b. Sulaymān b. Nawfal

He was a minor transmitter of *ḥadīth*, some of which he transmitted from his father.[356] He was also a poet. Ibn al-Nadīm saw his *dīwān*.[357] During al-Maʾmūn's reign he served as a *qāḍī* of Medina, where he died in 229/843–844.

The grandfather of Saʿīd b. Sulaymān, Nawfal b. Musāḥiq,[358] was one of the *ashrāf* of Quraysh. He was appointed as the *qāḍī* of Medina during ʿAbd al-Malik's reign,[359] and was later an intimate associate of al-Walīd b. ʿAbd al-Malik.[360] Nawfal was a minor transmitter of *ḥadīth*.[361] He married Umm ʿAbdallāh bt. Abī Sabra b. Abī Ruhm [b. ʿAbd al-ʿUzzā b. Abī Qays], who bore Saʿd.[362] He and his son Saʿd after him officiated in exacting the alms for the poor (الصدقات).[363] Some sources relate that he died during ʿAbd al-Malik's reign,[364] but this information does not conform to the traditions (related from al-Zubayr b. Bakkār and Muṣʿab b. ʿAbdallāh al-Zubayrī) that he lived under the caliphate of al-Walīd b. ʿAbd al-Malik.

356 Ibn Saʿd, *Ṭabaqāt*, 5:440; transmitting from his father, e.g., the interesting tradition which relates that Abū l-ʿAbbās al-Saffāḥ bestowed ʿUyūn Marwān in Dhū l-Khushub upon al-Ḥasan b. al-Ḥasan b. al-Ḥasan b. ʿAlī b. Abī Ṭālib, see al-Iṣfahānī, *Maqātil*, 190: ... ʿUmar b. Shabba < ʿAbd al-Jabbār b. Saʿīd al-Musāḥiqī < his father [Saʿīd b. Sulaymān b. Nawfal]; see also al-Balādhurī, *Ansāb* (ed. Madelung), 2:499 (ed. Zakkār, 3:309: ʿAyn Marwān; no *isnād* is given). For more evidence where he appears as a link in a chain of transmitters of *ḥadīth*, see al-Dāraquṭnī, *Sunan* (Beirut, 1966), 2:242, 4:103, 219; al-Ṭabarānī, *al-Awsaṭ*, 4:180; al-Ṭabarānī, *al-Kabīr*, 1:63; 5:136; 22:441–442; 23:173; 24:216; al-Bayhaqī, *al-Sunan al-kubrā*, 5:244; al-Majlisī, *Biḥār*, 39:313; 66:140.

357 Ibn al-Nadīm, *al-Fihrist* (ed. Tajaddud), 187.

358 On him, see al-Zubayrī, *Nasab Quraysh*, 427; Wakīʿ, *Akhbār al-quḍāt*, 1:232–233; al-Khaṭīb al-Baghdādī, *Taʾrīkh* (Beirut, 1997), 9:67–68; Ibn ʿAsākir, *Taʾrīkh*, 62:293–302; al-Mizzī, *Tahdhīb*, 30:67–70.

359 Ibn Saʿd, *Ṭabaqāt*, 5:152.

360 Al-Zubayrī, *Nasab Quraysh*, 427; al-Mizzī, *Tahdhīb*, 30:68–69.

361 Ibn Saʿd, *Ṭabaqāt*, 5:242.

362 Ibid.: Saʿd; al-Zubayrī, *Nasab Quraysh*, 427: Saʿīd instead of Saʿd; Ibn ʿAsākir, *Taʾrīkh*, 62:299, 301: Saʿīd or Saʿd.

363 Ibn ʿAsākir, *Taʾrīkh*, 62:301 and al-Mizzī, *Tahdhīb*, 30:69: وكان يسعي على الصدقات.

364 Al-Mizzī, *Tahdhīb*, 30:69: year 74/693 or 694, quoting Ibn Ḥibbān (= *al-Thiqāt*, 5:478); see also Ibn Abī Ḥātim, *al-Jarḥ* (Hyderabad edition), 4/1:488: at the beginning of his reign.

8.3 *The Family of Jadhīma b. Mālik b. Ḥisl b. ʿĀmir b. Luʾayy*

Opposers of the Revolt/ʿAbbāsī Supporters

8.3.1 Al-Ḥusayn b. Ṣakhr of the family (*min āl*) Uways b. [Saʿd? b.] Abī Sarḥ [b. al-Ḥārith b. Ḥubayyib b. Jadhīma b. Mālik b. Ḥisl b. ʿĀmir b. Luʾayy b. Ghālib b. Fihr]

When the revolt broke out he left Medina for al-ʿIrāq, and after nine days arrived at the caliph's court, announcing the outbreak of the revolt.[365]

9 Banū Jumaḥ b. ʿAmr b. Huṣayṣ b. Kaʿb b. Luʾayy b. Ghālib b. Fihr (Quraysh) (Chart X). See also Banū Kinda

Opposers to the Revolt/Supporters of the ʿAbbāsīs

9.1 *The Family of Khalaf b. Wahb b. Ḥudhāfa b. Jumaḥ*

ⓠ 9.1.1 ʿUbaydallāh b. Muḥammad b. Ṣafwān [b. ʿUbaydallāh b. Ubayy b. Khalaf b. Wahb b. Ḥudhāfa b. Jumaḥ b. ʿAmr b. Huṣayṣ b. Kaʿb b. Luʾayy b. Ghālib b. Fihr (Quraysh)]

His father, Muḥammad b. Ṣafwān, served as the *qāḍī* of Medina during Hishām b. ʿAbd al-Malik's reign.[366] ʿUbaydallāh is mentioned among the notables of Quraysh to whom ʿĪsā b. Mūsā sent letters calling them to join the ʿAbbāsī camp. It is not specifically mentioned that he deserted al-Nafs al-Zakiyya,[367] though this may be deduced from the fact that at the end of the revolt his house was one of the five in which the people of Medina could seek shelter and receive an *amān*.[368] After the revolt he lived in Mecca, from whence he was summoned by Caliph al-Manṣūr to Baghdad, and there he was appointed to be in charge of the judiciary. Al-Mahdī appointed him governor, and put him in charge of the judiciary (القضاء والصلاة والحرب) of Medina. He was dismissed by al-Mahdī in

---

365 Al-Ṭabarī, 3:205 (ll. 5–8), 217 (ll. 18–19); Ibn al-Athīr, *al-Kāmil* (ed. Tornberg), 5:405–406 (bottom line to line 1); Ibn Khaldūn, *ʿIbar* (Beirut, 1971), 3:191; he and his father are not mentioned among the distinguished members of this family in the *nasab* books, e.g., Ibn al-Kalbī, *Jamhara* (ed. Caskel), I, table 27; al-Zubayrī, *Nasab Quraysh*, 433; Ibn Ḥazm, *Jamhara*, 170; in all the genealogical sources: Uways b. Saʿd b. Abī Sarḥ.

366 Ibn Ḥazm, *Jamhara*, 161; Wakīʿ, *Akhbār al-quḍāt*, 1:168.

367 Al-Ṭabarī, 3:226 (l. 3).

368 Ibid., 3:253 (ll. 6–7).

159/775–776, and died shortly after in Medina in the year 160/785–786.[369] His son, ʿAbd al-Aʿlā, was appointed to his father's position.[370]

9.2 *The Family of Ḥabīb b. Wahb b. Ḥudhāfa b. Jumaḥ*

Opposers of the Revolt?

ⓜ9.2.1 Qudāma b. Mūsā [b. ʿUmar b. Qudāma b. Maẓʿūn b. Ḥabīb b. Wahb b. Ḥudhāfa b. Jumaḥ b. ʿAmr b. Huṣayṣ b. Kaʿb b. Luʾayy b. Ghālib b. Fihr (Quraysh)]

Qudāma b. Mūsā is mentioned twice by al-Ṭabarī, in both cases as a very distinguished Qurashī. He is first mentioned as the close associate of the governor of Medina, Riyāḥ b. ʿUthmān[371] (r. 23 Ramaḍān 144–28 Jumādā II 145/26 December 761–23 September 762). The second time was after the revolt was suppressed, again he is described as a very distinguished Qurashī who advised the ʿAbbāsī governor of the city.[372] These are the only testimonies regarding this Qudāma b. Mūsā. He may possibly be identified as the well-known *muḥaddith* who was also the *imām* of the mosque of Medina, Qudāma b. Mūsā b. ʿUmar al-Jumaḥī (d. 153/770). His short biographies in the *rijāl* books do not yield any details besides the obvious customary details that are provided by this kind of literature, that is, his teachers, students, one or two traditions that he transmitted (the reason for his inclusion in that genre of literature) and sometimes the year of his death.[373]

369 Al-Khaṭīb al-Baghdādī, *Taʾrīkh* (Beirut, 1997), 7:357: summoned from Mecca; 10:305: appointed by al-Manṣūr and later by al-Mahdī; Ibn Ḥazm, *Jamhara*, 160; al-Zubayrī, *Nasab Quraysh*, 392; Ibn al-Kalbī, *Jamhara* (ed. Ḥasan), 96: appointed by al-Manṣūr to be in charge of the judiciary of al-ʿIrāq and by al-Mahdī of the judiciary of Medina; see also Wakīʿ, *Akhbār al-quḍāt*, 1:228: a governor of Medina during al-Mahdī's reign; al-Ṭabarī, 3:458 (ll. 4–5): *qāḍī* in Baghdad until al-Manṣūr's death; 3:460 (ll. 4–5): the governor of Medina in 159/775–776 (his name is rendered: عبيد الله بن محمد بن عبد الرحمن [!] بن صفوان الجمحي and on 3:469 (ll. 14–15) and 3:482 (ll. 5–6): عبيد الله بن صفوان الجمحي, instead of عبيد الله بن محمد بن صفوان; this is the correct lineage of this notable Qurashī rendered by the quoted sources); ibid.: died in 160/776 or 777; see also al-Dhahabī, *Taʾrīkh*, 9:518; Ibn Ḥajar, *Tahdhīb* (Beirut, 1984), 9:205; al-Mizzī, *Tahdhīb*, 21:319; al-Ṣafadī, *al-Wāfī*, 19:270.

370 Al-Khaṭīb al-Baghdādī, *Taʾrīkh* (Beirut, 1997), 10:305.

371 Al-Ṭabarī, 3:171 (l. 16) (= al-Iṣfahānī, *Maqātil*, 191): ʿUmar b. Shabba < ʿĪsā b. ʿAbdallāh [from the family of ʿUmar b. ʿAlī b. Abī Ṭālib] < his father, who relates in the first person about the meeting with the governor, which he also attended.

372 Al-Ṭabarī, 3:270 (ll. 18–21).

373 On him, see Ibn Saʿd, *al-Qism al-mutammim*, 389; Ibn Ḥibbān, *al-Thiqāt*, 7:340; Ibn Abī Ḥātim, *al-Jarḥ*, 7:128; al-Dhahabī, *Taʾrīkh*, 9:575; al-Khazrajī, *Khulāṣa*, 315; Ibn Ḥajar, *Fatḥ*

10 Banū Hāshim b. ʿAbd Manāf b. Quṣayy b. Kilāb b. Murra b. Kaʿb b. Luʾayy b. Ghālib b. Fihr (Quraysh) (Chart x)

10.1 *The Family of Abū Lahab (ʿAbd al-ʿUzzā) b. ʿAbd al-Muṭṭalib b. Hāshim b. ʿAbd Manāf, Supporters of the Revolt*

10.1.1 Al-ʿAbbās b. al-Qāsim "a man from the family of Abū Lahab" (رجل من آل أبي لهب)

He was in the company of the new governor of Mecca, appointed by Muḥammad b. ʿAbdallāh.[374] Nothing else is known about him. He may be identified as the son of al-Qāsim b. al-ʿAbbās b. Muḥammad b. Muʿattib b. Abī Lahab.[375]

10.1.2 Sudayf b. Maymūn,[376] *mawlā* Āl Abī Lahab[377]
Sudayf b. Maymūn was a *mukhaḍram* poet and an enthusiastic supporter of Banū Hāshim during the Umawī period.[378] When the ʿAbbāsīs seized power he joined their cause and we find him in the courts of the first two ʿAbbāsī caliphs, Abū l-ʿAbbās al-Saffāḥ and al-Manṣūr, but at a certain time he became an enthusiastic supporter of Muḥammad al-Nafs al-Zakiyya, joined his

---

al-bārī, 10:263; Ibn Ḥajar, *Tahdhīb* (Beirut, 1984), 8:327; al-Mizzī, *Tahdhīb*, 23:553–555; al-Ziriklī, *al-Aʿlām*, 5:191. About this Jumaḥī's lineage, see al-Zubayrī, *Nasab Quraysh*, 394; Ibn Ḥazm, *Jamhara*, 161; Ibn al-Kalbī, *Jamhara* (ed. Ḥasan), 97 (ed. Caskel, I, table 24): Qudāma, his father and grandfather are not mentioned.

374 Al-Ṭabarī, 3:217 (ll. 14–15).

375 On him, see chapter 4, 168f.

376 For his biographies, see al-Iṣfahānī, *al-Aghānī* (Dār al-Kutub edition), 4:344–351; 16:135–136; al-Fākihī, *Akhbār Makka*, 3:145–147; al-ʿUqaylī, *Ḍuʿafāʾ*, 2:180–181; Ibn ʿAsākir, *Taʾrīkh*, 20:148–152; al-Ṣafadī, *al-Wāfī*, 15:125–127 (no. 179); Sibṭ b. al-Jawzī, *Mirʾāt al-zamān*, fols. 284a–284b; see also al-Balādhurī, *Ansāb* (ed. al-ʿAẓm), 3:254 (ed. al-Dūrī, 224); (ed. Madelung), 2:536–537; al-ʿĀmilī, *Aʿyān al-Shīʿa*, 7:188–192; Taieb El Acheche, "Sudayf b. Maymūn," *EI*[2].

377 In all the sources he is mentioned as the *mawlā* of Abū Lahab (the Prophet's uncle), but see the interesting remark by al-Iṣfahānī, *al-Aghānī* (Dār al-Kutub edition), 16:135: "He is Sudayf b. Maymūn *mawlā* Khuzāʿa. The reason that he fabricated a lineage (إدّعاء) from the *mawālī* of Banū Hāshim was that he married a freed slave girl of the family of Abū Lahab and so he claimed to be their *mawlā* and in the course of the years he became known as one of their *mawālī*; but it was said that it was his father who was married to the slave girl of the family of Abū Lahab and she bore him Sudayf." For the custom of *iddiʿāʾ* at the beginning of the ʿAbbāsī caliphate, see Elad, "Transition," 125–127.

378 Al-Iṣfahānī, *al-Aghānī* (Dār al-Kutub edition), 16:135; al-Ṣafadī, *al-Wāfī*, 15:126–127 (copying *al-Aghānī*); al-Fākihī, *Akhbār Makka*, 3:145, 147: he was imprisoned by the governor of Mecca and whipped because of his strong and blunt anti-Umawī attitude.

rebellion (giving him money that the caliph gave him), and according to one tradition, he became one of his close associates (*khāṣṣatihi*), calumniating and besmirching the caliph, on the one hand, and praising Banū ʿAlī, on the other hand. When the rebellion was crushed, he joined Muḥammad's brother Ibrāhīm in al-Baṣra. After the latter was killed he was persecuted by order of the caliph and captured by the governor of Medina (where he was hiding), who executed him in a very cruel manner.[379]

11 Banū Zuhra b. Quṣayy b. Kilāb b. Murra b. Kaʿb b. Luʾayy b. Ghālib b. Fihr (Quraysh) (Chart XI)

11.1 *The Family of Uhayb b. ʿAbd Manāf b. Zuhra*

Supporters of the Revolt

Ⓜ︎Ⓕ︎11.1.1 ʿAbdallāh b. Jaʿfar b. ʿAbd al-Raḥmān b. al-Miswar b. Makhrama [b. Nawfal b. Uhayb b. ʿAbd Manāf b. Zuhra][380]

He was one of the well-known scholars of Medina who joined al-Nafs al-Zakiyya's revolt; in fact, he supported the cause[381] long before the outbreak

379 All the colorful details are found in the biographies that are quoted in n. 388; close associate of Muḥammad al-Nafs al-Zakiyya: al-ʿUqaylī, *Ḍuʿafāʾ*, 2:181 (an identical parallel tradition is given by Ibn ʿAsākir, *Taʾrīkh*, 20:151 with the same *isnād* (although he received the tradition orally and did not copy it from al-ʿUqaylī's book); see also Sibṭ b. al-Jawzī, *Mirʾāt al-zamān*, fol. 284a. The *isnād* of al-ʿUqaylī: حدثني أبو محمد الخزاعي يعني نافع بن محمد قال حدثني عمي قال أخبرني عبد الرحمن بن محمد الكندي قال أخبرني محمد بن داود العباسي وكان أمير مكة قال; this ʿAbbāsī is most probably Muḥammad b. Dāwūd b. ʿĪsā b. Mūsā b. Muḥammad b. ʿAlī b. ʿAbdallāh b. al-ʿAbbās. His father (Dāwūd) was the governor of Mecca and Medina during al-Amīn's reign (al-Balādhurī, *Ansāb* (ed. al-Dūrī), 3:280; al-Ṭabarī, 3:775, 832, 860ff.); his son, Muḥammad, was a well-known ʿAbbāsī dignitary (al-Ṭabarī, index; ibid., 3:1194: year 221/835 or 836: governor of Mecca; he was the leader of the *ḥajj* caravan from 221/836 to 232/846 or 847 during al-Muʿtaṣim's reign, see Ibn Kahayyāṭ, *Taʾrīkh* (ed. Zakkār, Damascus 1968), 2:885–898).

380 On him, see Ibn Saʿd, *al-Qism al-mutammim*, 454–456; Ibn ʿAsākir, *Taʾrīkh*, 27:299–307; Ibn Ḥajar, *Tahdhīb* (Beirut, 1984), 5:150–151; al-Dhahabī, *Taʾrīkh*, 10:291–292; al-Mizzī, *Tahdhīb*, 14:372–376 and the comprehensive bibliography of the editor on 372–373, n. 5; for his lineage, see Ibn Ḥazm, *Jamhara*, 128–129; van Arendonk, *L'Imamat Zaïdite*, 312.

381 Al-Ṭabarī, 3:260 (ll. 1–2); al-Balādhurī, *Ansāb* (ed. Madelung), 2:514 (ll. 19–20): in both editions: instead of عبدالله بن جعفر بن عبد الله correct to عبد الله بن جعفر بن عبد الرحمن;

of the revolt. Al-Wāqidī describes him as one of the notables of Medina, a scholar versed in the Prophet's raids and conquest literature and in handing down legal decisions: من رجال المدينة وكان عالما بالمغازي والفتوى; al-Wāqidī adds that he was one of the confidants and trustworthy supporters (من ثقات) of Muḥammad b. ʿAbdallāh. Whenever the latter came to Medina under cover he used to stay in ʿAbdallāh b. Jaʿfar's abode. The latter was close to the ruling elites, and had free access to the governors; he was thus able to hear their plots and plans against Muḥammad b. ʿAbdallāh and reveal them to him. When the latter came out in rebellion, he joined him, and when Muḥammad b. ʿAbdallāh died, he went into hiding until he was granted an assurance of safety and security (*amān*).[382]

According to one of the sources, he was sent by Muḥammad b. ʿAbdallāh with his (Muḥammad's) brother Mūsā to Syria, for the purpose of propagating for their cause.[383] He was appointed by Muḥammad b. ʿAbdallāh to be in charge of *dīwān al-ʿaṭāʾ* (that is, in charge of payments to supporters/soldiers).[384] Al-Wāqidī related from ʿAbd al-Raḥmān b. Abī l-Zinād (100–174/718 to 790–791)[385] that each time a *qāḍī* in Medina died or was dismissed, the best and most suitable person for the position was ʿAbdallāh b. Jaʿfar, but he was never appointed to the post, most probably due to his participation in the revolt of Muḥammad b. ʿAbdallāh.[386]

Ⓜ11.1.2 ʿAbd al-Wāḥid b. Abī ʿAwn al-Dawsī (al-Azdī, *mawlā* of) (or al-Uwaysī); or *ḥalīf Banū Zuhra* (*mawlā* of al-Miswar b. Makhrama b. Nawfal b. Uhayb b. ʿAbd Manāf b. Zuhra)[387]

Ibn Saʿd relates that he was a *muḥaddith* who was very close (كان منقطعا) to ʿAbdallāh b. al-Ḥasan. He was persecuted by al-Manṣūr, who accused him

---

it is noteworthy that the index to Madelung's edition has: عبد الرحمن. See *Fragmenta*, 243, for the same mistake, but the editor (de Goeje) corrects it in the footnote.

382 Ibn Saʿd, *al-Qism al-mutammim*, 454–455 (quoted by al-Mizzī, *Tahdhīb*, 14:375 and Ibn ʿAsākir, *Taʾrīkh*, 27:306); mention of the *amān*: Ibn Saʿd, *al-Qism al-mutammim*, 455; Ibn ʿAsākir, *Taʾrīkh*, 27:307.

383 Al-Ṭabarī, 3:216 (ll. 10–13).

384 Ibid., 3:168–169 (l. 19 to l. 1); al-Iṣfahānī, *Maqātil*, 296.

385 On him, see Ibn Saʿd, *Ṭabaqāt*, 5:415; Ibn Ḥajar, *Tahdhīb* (Beirut, 1984), 6:155–156; al-Mizzī, *Tahdhīb*, 17:95–101.

386 Ibn Saʿd, *al-Qism al-mutammim*, 455; Ibn ʿAsākir, *Taʾrīkh*, 27:306; al-Mizzī, *Tahdhīb*, 14:375.

387 On him, see Ibn Saʿd, *al-Qism al-mutammim*, 349–350; Ibn Ḥibbān, *al-Thiqāt*, 7:123; Ibn Abī Ḥātim, *al-Jarḥ* (Beirut edition), 6:226; Ibn Ḥajar, *Tahdhīb* (Beirut, 1984), 6:388 (relying on Ibn Saʿd and other sources); al-Mizzī, *Tahdhīb*, 18:363–366; van Arendonk, *L'Imamat Zaïdite*, 313.

of knowing Muḥammad b. ʿAbdallāh's hiding place. ʿAbd al-Wāḥid escaped to Ṭaraf al-Qadūm, a mountain north of Medina behind Mount Uḥud,[388] where he was given shelter by Muḥammad b. Yaʿqūb b. ʿUtba al-Thaqafī.[389] He died there suddenly in the year 144/761–762,[390] that is, before the revolt broke out, although in another testimony he is named among those who took part in the revolt.[391] He is described as the *mawlā* of Daws (Azd), or al-Uwaysī, that is, the descendant of Uways [most probably: b. Saʿd b. Abī Sarḥ al-ʿĀmirī l-Qurashī],[392] but one source relates that he was from Daws but was an ally of Quraysh: وكان له حلف في قريش.[393] Another source makes his descent clearer, stating that his father, Abū ʿAwn, was a *mawlā* of al-Miswar b. Makhrama [al-Zuhrī, al-Qurashī].[394] It is noteworthy that ʿAbdallāh b. Jaʿfar b. ʿAbd al-Raḥmān b. al-Miswar b. Makhrama al-Zuhrī, who was one of the well-known scholars of Medina, joined the revolt of al-Nafs al-Zakiyya and supported its cause.[395] ʿAbd al-Wāḥid b. Abī ʿAwn (his *mawlā/ḥalīf*) also joined the cause of Muḥammad b. ʿAbdallāh. ʿAbd al-Wāḥid b. Abī ʿAwn was a *muḥaddith* but also a historian who recorded many historical traditions. Some of them he transmitted to ʿAbdallāh b. Jaʿfar b. ʿAbd al-Raḥmān b. al-Miswar b. Makhrama al-Zuhrī.[396]

---

388 Yāqūt, *Muʿjam* (Beirut edition), 4:312; al-Fīrūzābādī, *al-Maghānim al-muṭāba*, 334; al-Samhūdī, *Wafāʾ*, 4:429.

389 His father, Yaʿqūb b. ʿUtba al-Thaqafī, held official governmental posts under the Umawīs. He died in 120/738 in Medina, see al-Mizzī, *Tahdhib*, 32:350–353; much less is known of his son, who was a minor transmitter of *ḥadīth*, see al-Bukhārī, *Kabīr* (Dār al-Fikr edition), 1:267; Ibn Abī Ḥātim, *al-Jarḥ* (Beirut edition), 8:121.

390 Ibn Saʿd, *al-Qism al-mutammim*, 349–350; al-Iṣfahānī, *Maqātil*, 288: from Hārūn b. Mūsā l-Farwī, relating an exact parallel of Ibn Saʿd's tradition; note that Ibn ʿUyayna should be corrected to read Ibn ʿUtba.

391 Al-Ṭabarī, 3:259–260 (l. 18 to l. 1) and al-Iṣfahānī, *Maqātil*, 285: *mawlā* al-Azd.

392 On Uways b. Saʿd b. Abī Sarḥ, see Ibn al-Kalbī, *Jamhara* (ed. Caskel), 1:580; II, table 27; Ibn Ḥazm, *Jamhara*, 170; al-Samʿānī, *al-Ansāb* (Beirut, 1988), 1:230.

393 Ibn Saʿd, *Ṭabaqāt*, 4:227 [= Ibn ʿAsākir, *Taʾrīkh*, 25:11; al-Maqrīzī, *Imtāʿ*, 4:357; Ibn Sayyid al-Nās, *ʿUyūn al-athar*, 1:184].

394 Al-Mizzī, *Tahdhīb*, 14:373: وأبي عون والد عبد الواحد بن أبي عون مولى المسور بن مخرمة.

395 On him, see above.

396 E.g., Ibn Saʿd, *Ṭabaqāt*, 4:227 [= Ibn ʿAsākir, *Taʾrīkh*, 25:11]; Ibn Ḥanbal, *Musnad* (Būlāq edition), 6:11; al-Bayhaqī, *al-Sunan al-kubrā* (Hyderabad edition), 9:213.

Opposers of the Revolt/ʿAbbāsī Supporters

11.1.3 Ibrāhīm b. Yaʿqūb b. ʿUmar b. Saʿd b. Abī Waqqāṣ b. Uhayb b. ʿAbd Manāf b. Zuhra

He is mentioned only once, on the eve of the outbreak of the revolt, when he came with other warriors of Banū Zuhra to the aid of Riyāḥ b. ʿUthmān, the governor of Medina. He is described as one of the finest archers who came with his bow slung over his shoulder.[397]

11.2 *The Family of al-Ḥārith b. Zuhra b. Kilāb*

11.2.1 The Family of ʿAbd al-ʿAzīz b. ʿUmar b. ʿAbd al-Raḥmān b. ʿAwf b. ʿAbd ʿAwf b. ʿAbd b. al-Ḥārith b. Zuhra

This is a very important family whose members constituted the elite of the people of Medina, a family of great scholars and politicians with wealth and influence in Medina and other centers of the Islamic world.[398] Here I only deal with those directly connected to the events of the revolt of al-Nafs al-Zakiyya.

It is very interesting to learn that this family was split; two brothers supported the revolt, and one opposed it and served the ʿAbbāsīs.

Supporters of the Revolt

A long tradition is recorded by al-Ṭabarī, related by two dignitaries from Banū Zuhra, who describe the attitude of their family towards the ʿAbbāsīs and the rebellion, and the role they played on the eve of the revolt. Two leaders of the family are mentioned. They were summoned by the governor to his palace, and they were ordered to summon their kinfolk. So at least at the beginning, on the eve of the revolt, they seemed to support (or at least were loyal to) the ʿAbbāsīs. The two are:

397 Al-Ṭabarī, 3:162 (ll. 9–10).

398 Useful initial sources for the family are the *nasab* books, e.g., al-Zubayrī, *Nasab Quraysh*, 271–272; Ibn Ḥazm, *Jamhara*, 134; and see also the useful information of Ahmed, *Religious Elite*, 58–59.

(m)11.2.2 ʿImrān b. ʿAbd al-ʿAzīz b. ʿUmar b. ʿAbd al-Raḥmān b. ʿAwf... b. al-Ḥārith b. Zuhra al-Zuhrī and the second is his brother:

(q)11.2.3 Muḥammad b. ʿAbd al-ʿAzīz b. ʿUmar, who also served as a *qāḍī*[399] (on them, see below).

But at a later stage, ʿImrān b. ʿAbd al-ʿAzīz seems to have joined the revolt, with another brother:

11.2.4 Mūsā [b. ʿAbd al-ʿAzīz b. ʿUmar b. ʿAbd al-Raḥmān b. ʿAwf... b. al-Ḥārith b. Zuhra]

Nothing is known about him. He is mentioned by Ibn Ḥazm only once, together with his brother ʿImrān.[400]

In a family tradition, ʿAbd al-ʿAzīz b. ʿImrān relates from his father about the last day of ʿAbbāsī rule in Medina. ʿImrān b. ʿAbd al-ʿAzīz is sitting with his brother Muḥammad, who is defined by the governor as "the judge of the Commander of the Faithful." He complies with the governor's request, and goes out and recruits soldiers from among his family, which is described as the biggest in the city: وأنت أكثر من ههنا عشيرةً.[401]

Ibn Ḥazm described ʿImrān as a supporter of the revolt, while according to the family tradition he was one of the close associates of the ʿAbbāsī governor (before Muḥammad b. ʿAbdallāh took control of the city). ʿImrān was a minor *muḥaddith*; he was severely criticized by the authors of *rijāl* books of *ḥadīth*, who defined his transmission as totally unreliable.[402] His brother, Muḥammad b. ʿAbd al-ʿAzīz, was a zealous supporter of the Abbāsīs (see below).

Opposers of the Revolt/ʿAbbāsī Supporters

(m)(q)11.2.3 Muḥammad b. ʿAbd al-ʿAzīz b. ʿUmar b. ʿAbd al-Raḥmān b. ʿAwf... b. al-Ḥārith b. Zuhra[403]

He was the most important representative of the family in Medina. He served as the *qāḍī* of the city already during the governorship of Muḥammad b.

399 Al-Ṭabarī, 3:191 (l. 18); 3:192 (l. 5): *qāḍī*

400 Ibn Ḥazm, *Jamhara*, 134, flatly records that ʿImrān b. ʿAbd al-ʿAzīz and his brother Mūsā were among those who revolted with Muḥammad b. ʿAbdallāh b. al-Ḥasan.

401 Al-Ṭabarī, 3:191–192 (l. 14 to l. 19); "judge of the Commander of the Faithful": 3:192 (l. 5).

402 E.g., Ibn Ḥibbān, *al-Majrūḥīn*, 2:125; al-ʿUqaylī, *Ḍuʿafāʾ* (Beirut, 1984), 3:300; Ibn al-Jawzī, *al-Ḍuʿafāʾ*, 2:221: the two sources rely on Ibn Ḥibbān.

403 On him, see Wakīʿ, *Akhbār al-quḍāt*, 1:213–222; al-Khaṭīb al-Baghdādī, *Taʾrīkh* (Beirut, 1997), 3:152–153; all the authors of the *rijāl* books categorically regard him as an untrustworthy, unreliable transmitter, e.g., al-Nasāʾī, *Ḍuʿafāʾ*, 232; Ibn Abī Ḥātim, *al-Jarḥ*, 8:7;

Khālid al-Qasrī, then during the governorship of Riyāḥ b. ʿUthmān, until the revolt broke out.[404] On the eve of the revolt he was with the governor, and both he and Riyāḥ hid from Muḥammad b. ʿAbdallāh.[405] Despite Muḥammad b. ʿAbdallāh's expectations that he would help him and stand together with him, Muḥammad b. ʿAbd al-ʿAzīz made excuses, promised that he would join him, but secretly slipped away from the city and moved to Mecca.[406] We do not know if or when he came back from Mecca, but when the rebellion was suppressed, his house was one of the houses in which an ʿAbbāsī flag was posted, and whoever came there received an *amān*.[407] A few months after the revolt we find him in Medina, taking an active part in the political-social activities of the city.[408]

Muḥammad b. ʿAbd al-ʿAzīz had three sons; none of them are mentioned in connection with the revolt.[409] One of the most distinguished notables of the family was ʿAbd al-ʿAzīz b. ʿImrān b. ʿAbd al-ʿAzīz. It is noteworthy that Muḥammad b. ʿAbd al-ʿAzīz's two brothers, ʿImrān and Mūsā, supported the revolt of al-Nafs al-Zakiyya (see above).

11.3 *Allies of Banū Zuhra*

Supporters of the Revolt

ⓜ11.3.1–10 ʿAbdallāh b. ʿAṭāʾ b. Yaʿqūb, "*mawlā* of Banū Sibāʿ; and Ibn Sibāʿ [adds the transmitter] is from Khuzāʿa, an ally (حليف) of Banū Zuhra" He joined the revolt with his nine[!] sons: **1) Ibrāhīm; 2) Isḥāq; 3) Rabīʿa; 4) Jaʿfar; 5) ʿAbdallāh; 6) ʿAṭāʾ; 7) Yaʿqūb; 8) ʿUthmān; 9) ʿAbd al-ʿAzīz**.[410]

Ibn ʿAdī, *Ḍuʿafāʾ*, 6:239; al-ʿUqaylī, *Ḍuʿafāʾ* (Beirut, 1418 H.), 4:104; al-Dhahabī, *Mīzān* (ed. al-Bijāwī), 3:628.

404 Wakīʿ, *Akhbār al-quḍāt*, 1:213; al-Ṭabarī, 3:192: *qāḍī* under Riyāḥ; al-Zubayrī, *Nasab Quraysh*, 271; Ibn Ḥazm, *Jamhara*, 134; the family had estates near Medina, for example, see, Wakīʿ, *Akhbār al-quḍāt*, 1:213: Muḥammad b. ʿAbd al-ʿAzīz had an estate (أرض) in al-Jurf; Ibn Ḥazm, *Jamhara*, 134 (ll. 8, 21): the family estate in al-ʿĪṣ, which belonged administratively to Medina (ضيعة بالعيص من أعمال المدينة).

405 Al-Ṭabarī, 3:191 (ll. 10–11).

406 Ibid., 3:199 (ll. 1–3).

407 Ibid., 3:253.

408 Ibid., 3:269.

409 On Aḥmad, Ibrāhīm, and ʿAbd al-ʿAzīz, see Ibn Ḥazm, *Jamhara*, 134; al-Zubayrī, *Nasab Quraysh*, 271–272.

410 Al-Ṭabarī, 3:260 (ll. 3–6) (= al-Iṣfahānī, *Maqātil*, 286): ʿUmar b. Shabba < ʿAbd al-ʿAzīz b. Abī Salama b. ʿUbaydallāh b. ʿAbdallāh b. ʿUmar [b. al-Khaṭṭāb]; Ibn al-Athīr, *al-Kāmil* (ed. Tornberg), 5:422 (a parallel to al-Ṭabarī); van Arendonk, *L'Imamat Zaïdite*, 313.

ʿUmar b. Shabba records a tradition related to him by Mutawakkil b. Abī l-ʿAjwa (al-Faḥwa?), that Abū Jaʿfar al-Manṣūr used to say: "ʿAbdallāh b. ʿAṭāʾ causes us great wonder, for yesterday he was on my carpet and afterwards he hit me with ten swords."[411] Abū l-Faraj al-Iṣfahānī relates from Hārūn b. Mūsā l-Farwī's [work?],[412] that ʿAbdallāh b. ʿAṭāʾ "was one of the close associates (*khāṣṣa*) of Muḥammad b. ʿAlī (al-Bāqir); he transmitted [information] about ʿAbdallāh b. al-Ḥasan b. al-Ḥasan and had a special interest in them": وكان ذا خصوص بهم.[413] Another relative of Hārūn b. Mūsā l-Farwī, Ḥumayd b. ʿAbdallāh b. Abī Farwa (unknown), lived through the rebellion and related that when the battle ended, ʿAbdallāh b. ʿAṭāʾ went into hiding and died in Medina during the governorship of Jaʿfar b. Sulaymān al-ʿAbbāsī. When ʿAbdallāh b. ʿAṭāʾ was carried to the cemetery, Jaʿfar b. Sulaymān ordered that he be removed from his bier and crucified. He stayed in this condition for three days until Jaʿfar b. Sulaymān permitted his burial.[414] Ḥumayd b. ʿAbdallāh al-Farwī also relates the following tradition:

> When the people erected gates at the openings of the roads in the days of Muḥammad b. ʿAbdallāh, **we wanted** to close our road, but ʿAbdallāh b. ʿAṭāʾ forbade us, saying: (If our road will be closed) from where shall we cross to *amīr al-muʾminīn* Muḥammad?

The same transmitter, Ḥumayd b. ʿAbdallāh b. Abī Farwa, adds that ʿAbdallāh b. ʿAṭāʾ was a trustworthy transmitter of *ḥadīth*, and that he transmitted from Abū Jaʿfar Muḥammad b. ʿAlī (al-Bāqir) and ʿAbdallāh b. Burayda and others besides them from the *tābiʿūn;* trustworthy transmitters related from him, such as Mālik b. Anas and others like him (of his standing).[415] I was not able to find any additional information about him. This means that he was not a known *ḥadīth* scholar[416] like his father ʿAṭāʾ and his brother Rabīʿa.

---

411 Al-Iṣfahānī, *Maqātil*, 297; van Arendonk, *L'Imamat Zaïdite*, 313; al-Iṣfahānī, *Maqātil*, 297: Mutawakkil b. Abī l-ʿAjwa; al-Ṭabarī, 3:244: a different tradition related by ʿUmar b. Shabba from Mutawakkil b. Abī l-Faḥwa.

412 Al-Iṣfahānī, *Maqātil*, 286: قال هارون الفروي في خبره خاصة may imply a written source?

413 Ibid.

414 Al-Iṣfahānī, *Maqātil*, 286, 297; McAuliffe, *ʿAbbāsid Authority*, 225, n. 1064, quoting van Arendonk, *L'Imamat Zaïdite*, 313 = *Opkomst*, 286: "ʿAbdallāh b. ʿAṭāʾ, a *muḥaddith* and *faqīh*, went into hiding after Muḥammad's uprising but was eventually put to death during Jaʿfar b. Sulaymān's tenure as governor of Medina."

415 Al-Iṣfahānī, *Maqātil*, 297.

416 Several *muḥaddithūn* by this name flourished in that period, but it seems that none of them matches "our" ʿAbdallāh b. ʿAṭāʾ; the editor of *Maqātil*, 297, n. 2, refers us to the

His father ʿAṭāʾ was a *ḥadīth* scholar, mentioned in the sources as مولى بني سباع, sometimes with the *nisba* al-Kaykhārānī (or al-Kanjārānī, or al-Kūkhārānī), said to derive from a place in Yemen.[417] His brother Rabīʿa was also a well-known *ḥadīth* scholar, commonly known as the "*mawlā* of Banū Sibāʿ," but one source also calls him the *mawlā* of Banū Zuhra al-Madanī.[418] Since the members of this family were the allies of Banū Zuhra, it is possible that they lived in their quarter in Medina, and were considered part of the Banū Zuhra tribe.[419]

---

biography of a different person by that name in al-Dhahabī's *Mīzān;* even transmitting from Ibn Burayda cannot serve as unequivocal evidence, cf. for example, al-Dhahabī, *Taʾrīkh*, 3:633, with Ibn Ḥajar, *Tahdhīb* (Beirut, 1984), 5:281–282: "ʿAbdallāh b. ʿAṭāʾ al-Ṭāʾifī l-Makkī ... *ṣāḥib* Ibn Burayda."

417 On him, see ʿAbd al-Razzāq, *al-Muṣannaf*, 10:33: his brother Muḥammad is also mentioned (the period of Marwān b. al-Ḥakam (r. 64/683–684)); al-Bukhārī, *al-Kabīr* (ed. al-Nadwī), 4:467: al-Kaykhārānī; Ibn Ḥibbān, *al-Thiqāt*, 7:252; Ibn Abī Ḥātim, *al-Jarḥ* (Beirut edition), 6:338; al-Nawawī, *Sharḥ*, 9:33: al-Kūkhārānī.

418 Ibn Ḥajar, *Tahdhīb* (Beirut, 1984), 3:225; on him, see Ibn Saʿd, *al-Ṭabaqāt*, 5:346; al-Bukhārī, *al-Kabīr* (ed. al-Nadwī), 3:289; Ibn Ḥibbān, *al-Thiqāt*, 6:300.

419 On Banū Sibāʿ of Khuzāʿa, see Ibn Ḥazm, *Jamhara*, 242: Sibāʿ b. ʿAbd ʿAmr; but see Ibn al-Kalbī, *Nasab Maʿadd*, 2:460: Sibāʿ b. ʿAbd al-ʿUzzā, and see ibid., n. 4, the editor's comment; their alliance with Banū Zuhra is not mentioned, though; ibid., and Ibn Ḥazm, *Jamhara*, 242, another member of the close family of Sibāʿ is mentioned as the ally (حليف) of Banū Zuhra.

CHAPTER 8

Banū Asad b. ʿAbd al-ʿUzzā b. Quṣayy b. Kilāb b. Murra b. Kaʿb b. Luʾay b. Fihr (Quraysh)

(Chart XII)

1 The Family of al-Zubayr b. al-ʿAwwām

1.1 *The Family of Muṣʿab b. al-Zubayr b. al-ʿAwwām b. Khuwaylid b. Asad Supporters of the Revolt*

The Sons of Muṣʿab (known as Khuḍayr) b. Muṣʿab b. al-Zubayr

Immediately upon taking control of the city, Muḥammad and his supporters broke into the jail, imprisoned the ʿAbbāsī governor, Riyāḥ, and broke open the gates of *bayt al-māl*. One of his supporters, called Ibn Khuḍayr, was sent to rescue Muḥammad's brother, Mūsā b. ʿAbdallāh, from the hands of Riyāḥ's people, who were on their way with him to the caliph in al-ʿIrāq.[1]

De Goeje [Houtsma?] identified him as a descendant of Muṣʿab b. al-Zubayr,[2] and McAuliffe followed suit.[3] De Goeje most probably concluded this Zubayrī origin from the tradition which relates that the daughter of Khuḍayr (Amīna) was married to a Zubayrī, al-Zubayr b. Khubayb b. Thābit b. ʿAbdallāh b. al-Zubayr[4] (on him, see below). De Goeje also probably assumed that since she was married to a Zubayrī, she was also of the same family, and indeed he was right. Khuḍayr was the nickname of Muṣʿab b. Muṣʿab b. al-Zubayr b. al-ʿAwwām.[5] Two of his sons, ʿĪsā and Ibrāhīm (and perhaps a third son,

1 Al-Ṭabarī, 3:197–198 (l. 19 to l. 11) (Ibn Khuḍayr is mentioned in line 11) (= al-Iṣfahānī, *Maqātil*, 260 [a partial epitomized tradition], and Ibn ʿAsākir, *Taʾrīkh*, 60:444: a parallel tradition).

2 In al-Ṭabarī, *indices*, 169.

3 McAuliffe, *ʿAbbāsid Authority*, 153, n. 738: "Ṭabarī, *Indices*, identifies him as a descendant of Muṣʿab b. al-Zubayr."

4 Al-Ṭabarī, 3:260; Ibn Ḥazm, *Jamhara*, 122; al-Zubayr b. Bakkār, *Jamhara*, 337 (correct Amīna bt. Muḥammad to Amīna bt. Muṣʿab).

5 Ibn Saʿd, *Ṭabaqāt*, 5:183; al-Zubayr b. Bakkār, *Jamhara*, 337; al-Zubayrī, *Nasab Quraysh*, 250; Ibn Ḥazm, *Jamhara*, 124; al-Balādhurī, *Ansāb* (ed. Madelung), 2:515; but cf. idem, *Ansāb* (ed. ʿAbbās), 5:58: Khuḍayr is Ibrāhīm b. Muṣʿab, who was in charge of the *shurṭa* of

 | DOI 10.1163/9789004296220_010

Khālid), were dedicated supporters of Muḥammad b. ʿAbdallāh, fought with him, and died at his side.[6]

In the case of the tradition in al-Ṭabarī quoted above (3:260), Ibn Khuḍayr could be either Ibrāhīm or ʿĪsā, the sons of Khuḍayr (Muṣʿab b. Muṣʿab b. al-Zubayr).

1.1.1 Ibrāhīm b. Muṣʿab (Khuḍayr) b. Muṣʿab b. al-Zubayr, nicknamed Ibn Khuḍayr

He was the most distinguished supporter of Muḥammad al-Nafs al-Zakiyya from among the Zubayrīs. His military skills and his exceptional bravery in battle at Muḥammad b. ʿAbdallāh's side until his death are described by transmitters from the Zubayrī family.[7] He is usually called Ibn Khuḍayr in the sources. He served as the head of Muḥammad al-Nafs al-Zakiyya's *shurṭa*, and fought with him to the end. Shortly before the final defeat, he entered the prison and killed the former ʿAbbāsī governor Riyāḥ b. ʿUthmān and his brother, ʿAbbās, but was not able to break into Dār Ibn Hishām, where Muḥammad b. Khālid al-Qasrī was imprisoned.[8] He then burned the *dīwān* of Muḥammad b. ʿAbdallāh, which contained the names of his supporters.[9] He was among the close supporters of al-Nafs al-Zakiyya who were crucified in two rows in Medina. His body was snatched at night, in spite of the special guard that was posted to watch it.[10]

Muḥammad al-Nafs al-Zakiyya "… but it is said (*wa-yuqālu*) that the name of Khuḍayr is Muṣʿab b. Muṣʿab"; the identification of Ibrāhīm with Khuḍayr is mistaken, it should be rendered: Ibn Khuḍayr (see below). In the following sources he is identified as Ibn Khuḍayr, e.g., Sibṭ b. al-Jawzī, *Mirʾāt al-zamān*, fol. 283b: from al-Zubayr b. Bakkār (al-Zubayrī): فلما قصد عيسى بن موسى المدينة واقتتلا دخل إبراهيم بن خضير, وخضير اسمه مصعب [بن مصعب] بن الزبير ... وذبحه كما تذبح الشاة; ibid., fol. 284a: ورجع إبراهيم بن خضير فقاتل مع محمد حتى قتل.; Ibn al-Kalbī, *Jamhara* (ed. Ḥasan), 71 (= Ibn Mākūlā, *al-Ikmāl*, 2:482: quoting Ibn al-Kalbī); al-Zubayr b. Bakkār, *Jamhara*, 338: ومن ولد مصعب بن المصعب بن الزبير إبراهيم بن مصعب المعروف بابن خضير قتل مع محمد بن عبد الله وكانت له شجاعة موصوفة. (= Ibn ʿAsākir, *Taʾrīkh*, 18:281).

6 Ibn Ḥazm, *Jamhara*, 125.

7 E.g., al-Ṭabarī, 3:242–243 (l. 12 to l. 5); 3:245 (ll. 5–16).

8 Ibid., 3:241–242 (l. 16 to l. 2), (ll. 6–12); al-Balādhurī, *Ansāb* (ed. Madelung), 2:515.

9 Al-Ṭabarī, 3:241 (ll. 10–16); 3:242–243 (l. 12 to l. 5).

10 Ibid., 3:253 (ll. 13–15); on him, see also, Ibn Saʿd, *al-Qism al-mutammim*, 377–378; Ibn al-Kalbī, *Jamhara* (ed. Caskel), I, table 19.

1.1.2 ʿĪsā b. Muṣʿab (Khuḍayr) b. Muṣʿab b. al-Zubayr

It was said that **ʿĪsā b. Muṣʿab (Khuḍayr)'s** role among Muḥammad b. ʿAbdallāh's supporters was like that of a *wazīr*. He was killed in battle, fighting with Muḥammad b. ʿAbdallāh.[11]

1.1.3 Khālid b. Muṣʿab (Khuḍayr) b. Muṣʿab b. al-Zubayr

It seems highly plausible that like his two brothers, Ibrāhīm and ʿĪsā, Khālid b. Muṣʿab (Khuḍayr) was also a loyal adherent of Muḥammad b. ʿAbdallāh, and died with him on the battlefield.[12]

1.2 *The Family of Jaʿfar b. Muṣʿab b. al-Zubayr*[13]

Supporters of the Revolt

1.2.1 Ibrāhīm b. Jaʿfar b. Muṣʿab b. al-Zubayr

A certain Ibrāhīm b. Jaʿfar was sent by Muḥammad b. ʿAbdallāh with a letter to ʿĪsā b. Mūsā, summoning him to yield and join his cause.[14] He may be identified as Ibrāhīm b. Jaʿfar b. Muṣʿab b. al-Zubayr, the first of Muḥammad b. ʿAbdallāh's soldiers slain.

Jaʿfar b. Muṣʿab, Ibrāhīm's father, lived on his estate in Wādī Fāḍija with his children until he died.[15] He was married to Mulayka bt. al-Ḥasan b. al-Ḥasan b. ʿAlī b. Abī Ṭālib, who was Muḥammad b. ʿAbdallāh's aunt. Mulayka bore Jaʿfar a girl named Fāṭima and maybe several other daughters.[16] Although Ibrāhīm

---

11 Ibn Ḥazm, *Jamhara*, 125 (ll. 4–6). *Wazīr* can be understood here as an intimate adviser and supporter.

12 I was unable to find additional information about him other than the short sentence by Ibn Ḥazm, *Jamhara*, 125: وقتل [= عيسى بن خضير] معه [= مع محمد النفس الزكية] وأخواه إبراهيم وخالد. Ibrāhīm and Khālid are mentioned here together; since we know that Ibrāhīm also died at the side of al-Nafs al-Zakiyya, it is plausible to translate the sentence thus: ʿĪsā was killed with him and also his two brothers Ibrāhīm and Khālid (were killed with him), understanding the و before the أخواه as واو المعية. Khālid is briefly mentioned by al-Zubayr b. Bakkār, *Jamhara*, 341: خالد بن مصعب بن مصعب وكانت له مروؤة وحال جميله (there is no mention of his support of the rebellion of Muḥammad b. ʿAbdallāh).

13 This branch is missing in Ibn al-Kalbī's work (ed. Caskel).

14 Al-Ṭabarī, 3:232 (ll. 18–20).

15 Al-Samhūdī, *Wafāʾ*, 4:91; this is the only historical piece of evidence that I found about him. The *nasab* books only mention his name and lineage, e.g., al-Zubayrī, *Nasab Quraysh*, 250; al-Zubayr b. Bakkār, *Jamhara*, 334; al-Balādhurī, *Ansāb* (ed. al-ʿAẓm), 8:73; Ibn Ḥazm, *Jamhara*, 125 (l. 1), is the only source that mentions Ibrāhīm b. Jaʿfar b. Muṣʿab.

16 Al-Zubayrī, *Nasab Quraysh*, 53: the name of her daughter was Fāṭima; Ibn Qutayba, *al-Maʿārif* (Cairo edition), 224 (ed. Wüstenfeld, 116): bore him daughters; Ibn Ḥazm,

b. Jaʿfar is not mentioned as her son by the sources, this marriage tie between the Zubayrīs and the Ḥasanīs may have contributed to Ibrāhīm's joining the rebellion.

1.2.2 Muḥammad b. Jaʿfar b. Muṣʿab b. al-Zubayr

He joined the rebellion of Muḥammad b. ʿAbdallāh. When the latter died, he fled to al-Baṣra and then returned to his estate in Wādī Fāḍija.[17]

1.3 *The Family of Khālid b. al-Zubayr b. al-ʿAwwām*[18]

Supporters of the Revolt

1.3.1 Khālid b. ʿUthmān b. Khālid b. al-Zubayr b. al-ʿAwwām

He took part in Muḥammad b. ʿAbdallāh's revolt in Medina. He was captured on orders of Caliph al-Manṣūr, killed, and then crucified.[19]

1.3.2 ʿUthmān b. Muḥammad b. Khālid b. al-Zubayr and His Son

1.3.3 Muḥammad b. ʿUthmān b. Muḥammad b. Khālid b. al-Zubayr

ʿUthmān b. Muḥammad b. Khālid b. al-Zubayr is described as one of the closest and important supporters of Muḥammad b. ʿAbdallāh al-Nafs al-Zakiyya. After the revolt, he and his son fled from the ʿAbbāsīs, were captured in al-Baṣra and were brought to the caliph, who ordered ʿUthmān b. Muḥammad to be executed. His son, Muḥammad, was flogged, but his life was spared.[20]

Jamhara, 42 (bore him a daughter); but cf. al-Balādhurī, *Ansāb* (ed. Zakkār), 9:448: Jaʿfar b. Muṣʿab married Mulayka bt. al-Ḥusayn b. ʿAlī (but cf. idem, ed. al-ʿAẓm, 8:73: Mulayla (instead of Mulayka) bt. al-Ḥasan b. ʿAlī. To my knowledge, no source mentions a daughter of al-Ḥusayn b. ʿAlī named Mulayka; however, ʿAlī b. al-Ḥusayn b. ʿAlī had a daughter named Mulayka, see al-Balādhurī, *Ansāb* (ed. Madelung), 2:458.

17 Al-Samhūdī, *Wafāʾ*, 4:91; he is not mentioned in the *nasab* books.

18 This family is not mentioned by Ibn al-Kalbī's *Jamhara.*

19 Ibn Ḥabīb, *al-Muḥabbar,* 486–487; al-Balādhurī, *Ansāb* (ed. ʿAbbās), 5:50–51 (ed. al-ʿAẓm, 8:64).

20 Al-Ṭabarī, 3:260–262 (l. 18 to l. 10): a long tradition narrated by Muḥammad b. ʿUthmān himself; the *isnād:* ʿUmar [b. Shabba] < Ibrāhīm b. Muṣʿab b. ʿUmāra b. Ḥamza b. Muṣʿab < Muḥammad b. ʿUthmān b. Khālid b. al-Zubayr; 3:262 (ll. 10–17): a tradition from Muḥammad b. ʿUrwa b. Hishām b. ʿUrwa b. al-Zubayr (= al-Iṣfahānī, *Maqātil,* 287; al-Azdī, *Taʾrīkh al-Mawṣil,* 190); al-Ṭabarī, 3:262–264 (l. 17 to l. 2): another long tradition by Muḥammad b. ʿUthmān b. Muḥammad; see also ibid., 3:264 (ll. 2–5): ʿUmar < ʿĪsā < his father, about the execution of ʿUthmān; ibid. (ll. 5–6); al-Iṣfahānī, *Maqātil,* 286.

ʿUthmān b. Muḥammad b. Khālid was appointed as the governor of Medina by Muḥammad al-Nafs al-Zakiyya,[21] and (then?) served as the head of his *shurṭa*.[22] He (allegedly?) related several traditions that contain firsthand information about several stages of the revolt, mainly information about Muḥammad al-Nafs al-Zakiyya's camp, e.g., the number of his supporters, his bravery in battle, the final campaign, and so forth.[23]

His son, Muḥammad related the long, detailed tradition describing the flight, capture, and the execution of his father before his eyes. When the caliph ordered him executed as well, al-Manṣūr's uncle, ʿĪsā b. ʿAlī [b. ʿAbdallāh b. al-ʿAbbās], said to the caliph that he thought that at the time of the revolt, Muḥammad b. ʿUthmān was a youth who had not attained puberty: والله ما أحسبه بلغ. Muḥammad b. ʿUthmān said: "Oh *amīr al-muʾminīn*, I was (then) a young boy inexperienced and ignorant of affairs (*ghirran*), my father commanded me and I obeyed him." This long, detailed tradition was transmitted to ʿUmar b. Shabba by members of the Zubayrī family from Muḥammad b. ʿUthmān.[24] Muḥammad b. ʿUthmān may have indeed been a young boy, who according to Islamic law had not attained puberty, and he may have "only" obeyed his father, e.g., the tradition in which he relates that the flag of Muḥammad al-Nafs al-Zakiyya was handed to his father, "and I used to carry it for him."[25]

1.4 *The Family of ʿAbdallāh b. al-Zubayr*

Supporters of the Revolt

1.4.1 Muṣʿab b. Thābit b. ʿAbdallāh b. al-Zubayr b. al-ʿAwwām and His Son

1.4.2 ʿAbdallāh b. Muṣʿab b. Thābit

Al-Iṣfahānī mentions that Muṣʿab b. Thābit b. ʿAbdallāh b. al-Zubayr and his son, ʿAbdallāh, revolted with Muḥammad al-Nafs al-Zakiyya.[26] This matter

21 Al-Ṭabarī, 3:198 (l. 16) (= al-Iṣfahānī, *Maqātil*, 295–296): ʿUmar b. Shabba < Muḥammad b. Yaḥyā < al-Ḥārith b. Isḥāq.

22 Al-Ṭabarī, 3:199 (l. 6): al-Zubayrī, no name is mentioned but see al-Iṣfahānī, *Maqātil*, 282, a parallel tradition with the full name.

23 E.g., al-Ṭabarī, 3:229–230 (l. 18 to l. 6), 3:234–235 (l. 17 to l. 6), 3:237 (ll. 12–14) (from ʿUthmān b. Muḥammad); 260–263 (from his son, Muḥammad b. ʿUthmān); al-Iṣfahānī, *Maqātil*, 286–287 (= al-Ṭabarī, 3:262); on him, see also Ibn Ḥazm, *Jamhara*, 125; he is not mentioned by Ibn al-Kalbī, al-Zubayrī, or al-Zubayr b. Bakkār.

24 The whole story: al-Ṭabarī, 3:260–262; his words to the caliph, ibid., 3:262 (ll. 5–6).

25 Ibid., 3:237 (ll. 12–14): ʿUmar b. Shabba < Ibrāhīm b. Muṣʿab b. ʿUmāra b. Ḥamza b. Muṣʿab b. al-Zubayr < *ḥaddathanī* Muḥammad b. ʿUthmān b. Muḥammad b. Khālid b. al-Zubayr.

26 Al-Iṣfahānī, *Maqātil*, 285: [Abū l-Faraj al-Iṣfahānī] < ʿĪsā b. al-Ḥusayn [al-Warrāq] < Hārūn b. Mūsā [al-Farwī].

is not mentioned in the long biographies of Muṣʿab b. Thābit and his son ʿAbdallāh in al-Zubayr b. Bakkār's work. Al-Iṣfahānī relates that ʿAbdallāh b. Muṣʿab b. Thābit b. ʿAbdallāh b. al-Zubayr was a poet who used to compose poetry about Muḥammad which instigated the people to revolt.[27] He, says al-Iṣfahānī, joined the rebellion of Muḥammad b. ʿAbdallāh and was among the rebels from al-Zubayr's family. When Muḥammad was killed he stayed in hiding until al-Manṣūr came to Mecca during the *ḥajj* "and granted an amnesty to all the people."[28] He composed lamentation poems on Muḥammad b. ʿAbdallāh, his brother Ibrāhīm, and two members of the Zubayrī family.[29] He most probably gained the favor of al-Manṣūr, but especially of those who ruled after him. This we learn from the long and detailed biography of him by his son Muṣʿab in his *Nasab Quraysh*, and by his grandson, al-Zubayr b. Bakkār [b. ʿAbdallāh b. Muṣʿab b. Thābit b. ʿAbdallāh b. al-Zubayr b. al-ʿAwwām].[30] He was one of the *ṣaḥāba* of Caliph al-Mahdī, who appointed him governor of al-Yamāma. Hārūn al-Rashīd nominated him as governor of Medina, then of Yemen (which included governance over the territory of the ʿAkk tribe, which was usually included within the governorship of Mecca).[31] He died in al-Raqqa, on 27 Rabīʿ I 184/26 April 800.[32] (On his son, Bakkār, see below).

The active participation of ʿAbdallāh b. Muṣʿab b. Thābit in the revolt is mentioned in a long tradition, according to which at a gathering at Hārūn al-Rashīd's court, Yaḥyā b. ʿAbdallāh b. al-Ḥasan (Mūsā b. ʿAbdallāh in al-Masʿūdī's *Murūj*) accuses him of having taken an active part in the rebellion of al-Nafs al-Zakiyya, encouraging the warriors by reciting some poetry in support of Banū l-Ḥasan.[33] In the longer parallel tradition in al-Ṭabarī's

27 Ibid.

28 Al-Iṣfahānī, *al-Aghānī* (Būlāq edition), 20:180 (= Dār al-Kutub edition 24:237); general amnesty to all the people: وآمن الناس جميعا this phrase should be treated with great reservation.

29 Al-Ṭabarī, 3:255; al-Iṣfahānī, *Maqātil*, 307; al-Azdī, *Taʾrīkh al-Mawṣil*, 191.

30 Al-Zubayrī, *Nasab Quraysh*, 242; al-Zubayr b. Bakkār, *Jamhara*, 125: he had gained a special position, and was highly esteemed by al-Mahdī, al-Hādī, and Hārūn al-Rashīd (no mention of al-Manṣūr); his long biography, ibid., 124–156; see also 209–211.

31 Al-Zubayrī, *Nasab Quraysh*, 242 (al-Yamāma, Medina, and Yemen); al-Zubayr b. Bakkār, *Jamhara*, 129 (Medina); 130 (al-Yaman and ʿAkk); ibid., 209–211: governor of Yemen; al-Ṭabarī, 3:739 (Medina); Ibn Khayyāṭ, *Taʾrīkh* (ed. al-ʿUmarī), 2:497; al-Yaʿqūbī, *Taʾrīkh* (ed. Houtsma), 2:498, and Ibn Ḥazm, *Jamhara*, 123 (Yemen).

32 Al-Zubayr b. Bakkār, *Jamhara*, 146.

33 Al-Iṣfahānī, *Maqātil*, 476; al-Masʿūdī, *Murūj*, 4:200; cf. al-Ṭabarī, 3:617: Bakkār b. ʿAbdallāh b. Muṣʿab instead of ʿAbdallāh b. Muṣʿab.

Ta'rīkh, instead of ʿAbdallāh b. Muṣʿab b. Thābit [b. ʿAbdallāh b. al-Zubayr], the latter's son, Bakkār b. ʿAbdallāh b. Muṣʿab b. Thābit, is mentioned[34] (see below).

ʿAbdallāh b. Muṣʿab, his son and his grandson, all gained the favor of the ʿAbbāsī caliphs, and served the "blessed dynasty" with great vigor. It is natural that they did their best to conceal their family past, that is, their support of the revolt of al-Nafs al-Zakiyya. Abū l-Faraj al-Iṣfahānī (284–356/897–967) is the only source that records the participation of Muṣʿab b. Thābit and his son ʿAbdallāh in the revolt. He received this information from ʿĪsā b. al-Ḥusayn al-Marwazī l-Warrāq through Hārūn b. Mūsā b. ʿAbdallāh (Abū ʿAlqama) b. Muḥammad b. ʿAbdallāh b. Abī Farwa al-Qurashī l-Madanī, *mawlā* ʿUthmān b. ʿAffān (b. ca. 152/770, d. 232 or 233/847–848). Hārūn b. Mūsā was a *muḥaddith*, as well as a *rāwī* of historical traditions (on him, see appendix 2). The positive attitude of many members of the Zubayrī family towards the revolt is rarely echoed in the sources. The fierce confrontation in the above-noted anecdote between Yaḥyā b. ʿAbdallāh (or alternatively, his brother Mūsā b. ʿAbdallāh) and ʿAbdallāh b. Muṣʿab (or, alternatively, his son Bakkār) is indeed a rare example. According to this narrative, Bakkār b. ʿAbdallāh died immediately after the fierce confrontation and contention with the ʿAlīd Yaḥyā b. ʿAbdallāh, because he lied to the caliph.[35] The version in which ʿAbdallāh b. Muṣʿab is the one who dies immediately after leaving the caliph's palace was related by a member of the ʿAbbāsī family, the grandson of al-Manṣūr, ʿĪsā b. Jaʿfar b. Abī Jaʿfar al-Manṣūr.[36] It is noteworthy that neither the report about his participation in the revolt of al-Nafs al-Zakiyya nor the alleged confrontation with the Ḥasanī Yaḥyā b. ʿAbdallāh b. al-Ḥasan in the presence of Hārūn al-Rashīd is mentioned by al-Zubayr b. Bakkār, the grandchild of ʿAbdallāh b. Muṣʿab.

We can rule out the participation of Bakkār b. ʿAbdallāh in this alleged dispute (if it took place at all). Al-Ṭabarī chose to chronicle this episode under

34 Al-Ṭabarī, 3:616–618; the name of Bakkār: 3:616 (ll. 9–10); *Fragmenta*, 293–294; but see the same long tradition in al-Masʿūdī, *Murūj*, 4:200–202: the name of the ʿAlīd at al-Rashīd's court is Mūsā b. ʿAbdallāh, Yaḥyā's brother; the name of the Zubayrī is ʿAbdallāh b. Muṣʿab; but see the remark of al-Masʿūdī, *Murūj*, 4:202: "it is said that the hero of this story is Yaḥyā b. ʿAbdallāh, the brother of Mūsā," noted by the editor, Pellat, on 200, n. 8; al-Khaṭīb al-Baghdādī, *Ta'rīkh* (Cairo edition), 14:111: ʿAbdallāh b. Muṣʿab against Yaḥyā b. ʿAbdallāh in al-Rashīd's court; it is noteworthy that al-Ṭabarī records another long tradition dealing with the same topic, where the main figures are ʿAbdallāh b. Muṣʿab al-Zubayrī and not Bakkār, his son, and Yaḥyā b. ʿAbdallāh; and cf. Madelung, "Yaḥyā b. ʿAbdallāh," 11:243.

35 Al-Ṭabarī, 3:618 (l. 15).

36 Ibid., 3:620 (ll. 7–9) (the *isnād*); 3:623 (ll. 5–20) (his death).

the year 176/792–793;[37] it occurred most plausibly in Baghdad, where Yaḥyā was imprisoned, and ʿAbdallāh (or Bakkār), therefore, must have died in that year.

However, Bakkār served as the governor of Medina and died in this city in 195/811 (see below). It is hardly plausible for ʿAbdallāh b. Muṣʿab to be the hero of this anecdote as well. He died in al-Raqqa in 184/801. Al-Zubayr b. Bakkār related from his relative, ʿAbdallāh b. Nāfiʿ b. Thābit [b. ʿAbdallāh b. al-Zubayr] that on the same day that ʿAbdallāh b. Muṣʿab died, Hārūn al-Rashīd conquered al-ʿIrq; therefore he sent his son al-Maʾmūn to pray over ʿAbdallāh b. Muṣʿab's body and later he accompanied him to the grave.[38]

1.4.3 Bakkār b. ʿAbdallāh b. Muṣʿab b. Thābit b. ʿAbdallāh b. al-Zubayr [the Father of al-Zubayr b. Bakkār]

Abū Bakr Bakkār b. ʿAbdallāh b. Muṣʿab was appointed by Hārūn al-Rashīd as the governor of Medina, where he governed for more than twelve years.[39] His son, the well-known scholar al-Zubayr b. Bakkār, reported that his father's yearly salary was 1,000 *dīnār*s.[40]

According to a single tradition of legendary character, Bakkār b. ʿAbdallāh al-Zubayrī took part in a long anti-ʿAlīd confrontation at al-Rashīd's court with Yaḥyā b. ʿAbdallāh b. al-Ḥasan b. al-Ḥasan b. ʿAlī b. Abī Ṭālib, the brother of Muḥammad al-Nafs al-Zakiyya, who led an ʿAlīd rebellion in Daylam in 176/792. In this confrontation, Yaḥyā cursed Bakkār and accused him of supporting the revolt of his brother, Muḥammad b. ʿAbdallāh. According to this version, Bakkār insisted that Yaḥyā was lying, swore a solemn oath to the caliph, but due to Yaḥyā's curses died almost instantly. To the transmitter of the tradition it is clear that his death was due to his false oath and Yaḥyā's curse.[41] It is worth noting that al-Ṭabarī himself, after recording the long tradition about the curse on Bakkār by Yaḥyā b. ʿAbdallāh and the former's subsequent death, says that the Zubayrī family's version of the death of Bakkār is entirely different, i.e.,

---

37 Ibid., 3:616–618; 620–624; Madelung, "Yaḥyā b. ʿAbdallāh," relying on al-Ṭabarī, believes that the episode occurred in 184/800.

38 Al-Zubayr b. Bakkār, *Jamhara*, 146; the editor of the book, Maḥmūd Muḥammad Shākir, was unable to locate this site (al-ʿIrq); I was not able to locate it either; it is most probably somewhere along the borders with Byzantium.

39 Al-Zubayr b. Bakkār, *Jamhara*, 163: 12 years, three months, and 11 days; al-Zubayrī, *Nasab Quraysh*, 242: 13 years; Ibn Ḥazm, *Jamhara*, 123 (l. 2): 12 years and several months; al-Ṭabarī, 3:739 (ll. 15–16); al-Iṣfahānī, *Maqātil*, 495; Ibn Taghrī Birdī, *al-Nujūm*, 2:148: 12 years.

40 Al-Zubayr b. Bakkār, *Jamhara*, 296.

41 Al-Ṭabarī, 3:618 (Bakkār); 3:623 (ʿAbdallāh).

that he was killed by his wife and two of his slaves who suffocated him with a pillow in his sleep.[42]

Other sources record the same tradition but his name (Bakkār) is replaced by that of his father, ʿAbdallāh.[43] Be it as it may, Yaḥyā b. ʿAbdallāh was killed by orders of al-Rashīd in Baghdad.[44] Bakkār b. ʿAbdallāh al-Zubayrī, records al-Ṭabarī,

> had a violent hatred for the house of ʿAlī b. Abī Ṭālib and used to send reports to Hārūn [al-Rashīd] about them and put the worst construction on information about their doings. Also al-Rashīd had appointed him as governor of Medīna and ordered him to press hard on the ʿAlids.[45]

Bakkār indeed followed al-Rashīd's policy against the Ṭālibīs. While governor of Medina, he imprisoned Yaḥyā b. ʿAbdallāh's son, Muḥammad, who died in prison.[46] Bakkār died in 195/811, long after Yaḥyā b. ʿAbdallāh died in al-Rashīd's prison.[47]

1.4.4 ʿAbd al-Wahhāb b. Yaḥyā b. ʿAbbād b. ʿAbdallāh b. al-Zubayr

ʿAbd al-Wahhāb supported Muḥammad b. ʿAbdallāh's revolt. This we learn from a very interesting tradition, related by his wife [Umm?]Kulthu[=ū?]m bt. Wahb to her grandson, Yaʿqūb b. al-Qāsim b. Muḥammad b. Yaḥyā b. Zakariyyāʾ b. Ṭalḥa b. ʿUbaydallāh (al-Taymī l-Qurashī), that her husband joined the revolt

42 Ibid., 3:618–619: Isḥāq b. Muḥammad [b. Aḥmad b. Abbān, d. 286/899 or 900] al-Nakhaʿī < al-Zubayr b. Hishām < his father; on Isḥāq b. Muḥammad al-Nakhaʿī, an extreme Shīʿī scholar, see al-Khūʾī, *Rijāl*, 3:229–232; al-Amīn, *Aʿyān al-Shīʿa*, 3:277–278; al-Khaṭīb al-Baghdādī, *Taʾrīkh* (Beirut, 1997), 4:57 (= Ibn ʿAsākir, *Taʾrīkh*, 42:290); Ibn al-Jawzī, *Mawḍūʿāt*, 2:75. I was not able to identify al-Zubayr b. Hishām and his father. It is highly plausible that they are from the Zubayrī family.

43 See the discussion above.

44 For the different versions of the ways he was killed, see al-Iṣfahānī, *Maqātil*, 479–483; Madelung, "Yaḥyā b. ʿAbdallāh."

45 Al-Ṭabarī, 3:616 (ll. 9–11) (trans. Bosworth, *ʿAbbāsid Caliphate in Equilibrium*, 121).

46 Al-Iṣfahānī, *Maqātil*, 495–496; not mentioned by Madelung, "Yaḥyā b. ʿAbdallāh."

47 Al-Zubayr b. Bakkār, *Jamhara*, 187: 20 Rabīʿ II 195/20 January 811; al-Dhahabī, *Taʾrīkh* (*Ḥawādith wa-wafayāt 191–200 H.*), 13:131: year 195; Yaḥyā died most probably in 187/803, see Madelung, "Yaḥyā b. ʿAbdallāh."

and she hid in the house of Asmāʾ bt. Ḥusayn b. ʿAbdallāh b. ʿUbaydallāh b. ʿAbbās.[48]

Opposers of the Revolt/ʿAbbāsī Supporters

1.4.5 Khubayb b. Thābit b. ʿAbdallāh b. al-Zubayr[49]

Khubayb b. Thābit is specifically mentioned among the few distinguished people of Medina who did not join the rebellion.[50] As to his son,

1.4.6 Al-Zubayr b. Khubayb b. Thābit b. ʿAbdallāh b. al-Zubayr[51]

He was a *ḥadīth* scholar who was married to Amīna bt. Khuḍayr, Muṣʿab b. Muṣʿab b. al-Zubayr. He is described as a pious ascetic(?) (*nāsik*). When the rebellion broke out he withdrew (*iʿtazala*) to [his estate?] in Wādī Murr in Baṭn Iḍam with his family (his wife? مع أهله).[52] Al-Zubayr b. Khubayb related to his relative, Ibrāhīm b. Muṣʿab b. ʿUmāra b. Ḥamza b. Muṣʿab b. al-Zubayr, that he and his wife met a man in Baṭn Iḍam, who informed them about the failure of the rebellion and the death of Muḥammad al-Nafs al-Zakiyya and his wife's brother, [Ibrāhīm] b. Khuḍayr.[53] At a certain stage of his life he lived in Baghdad and, together with his brother, al-Mughīra b. Khubayb, was among

48 Al-Ṭabarī, 3:199–200 (l. 13 to l. 2); the name of the transmitter is Kulthum (Kalthum/Kaltham); cf. al-Iṣfahānī, *Maqātil*, 239: a different tradition: Yaʿqūb b. al-Qāsim < his mother Fāṭima bt. ʿUmar < Umm Kulthūm bt. Wahb; Yaʿqūb b. al-Qāsim transmitted this unique tradition to ʿUmar b. Shabba.

49 On him, see al-Zubayr b. Bakkār, *Jamhara*, 97–98; 99–115: his descendants.

50 Al-Ṭabarī, 3:199 (l. 11).

51 On him, see al-Zubayr b. Bakkār, *Jamhara*, 99–109; Ibn Ḥibbān, *al-Thiqāt*, 4:211; Ibn Abī Ḥātim, *al-Jarḥ* (Beirut edition), 3:584; Ibn al-Jawzī, *al-Muntaẓam*, 9:166; al-Khaṭīb al-Baghdādī, *Taʾrīkh* (Beirut, 1997), 8:467–468.

52 Ibn Ḥazm, *Jamhara*, 122 إعتزل بِأمر من بطن إضم (= al-Samhūdī, *Wafāʾ*, 4:132: بالأمر; the text is corrupted and should be rendered بالمر instead of بالأمر); al-Amar or Dhū l-Amar is a well-known place in Najd, mentioned among the Prophet's *ghazawāt* (for example, see Ibn Hishām, *al-Sīra*, 2:560: غزوة ذي أمر; al-Samhūdī, *Wafāʾ*, 4:132; al-Ḥāzimī, *al-Amākin*, 2:83–84); Ibn Ḥazm and al-Samhūdī (who copied the latter) confused Murr with Amar; on "Murr, one of the *wādī*s of Baṭn Iḍam, but it is said that it is Baṭn Iḍam," see al-Ḥāzimī, *al-Amākin*, 2:836 (= Yāqūt, *Muʿjam* [ed. Wüstenfeld], 4:494: from al-Ḥāzimī); the confusion in Ibn Ḥazm and al-Samhūdī was already noticed by Ḥamad al-Jāsir, see al-Fīrūzābādī, *al-Maghānim al-muṭāba*, 24, and also in al-Jāsir, *Bilād Yanbuʿ*, 210–211.

53 Al-Ṭabarī, 3:260 (ll. 6–12); al-Azdī, *Taʾrīkh al-Mawṣil*, 192 (Beirut edition, 1:398); al-Ṭabarī, 3:260 (l. 8) and al-Azdī, *Taʾrīkh al-Mawṣil*, 192 (ll. 7–8): "We were in (*wādī*) Murr in Baṭn

those who had access to caliphs al-Mahdī and Hārūn al-Rashīd. They both received money from these caliphs.[54] Towards the end of his life he withdrew to his estate in al-Muraysīʿ, and lived in its mosque (not leaving it except for ablutions) until his death at the age of 74.[55]

1.4.7 Nāfiʿ b. Thābit b. ʿAbdallāh b. al-Zubayr (d. 155/771 or 772)[56]

He was a *ḥadīth* scholar, the brother of the above-mentioned Khubayb, who also strongly refused to join the rebellion of al-Nafs al-Zakiyya. This is recorded by his two sons, ʿAbdallāh *al-Aṣghar* and ʿAbdallāh *al-Akbar*.[57] Al-Zubayr b. Bakkār relates that he strongly objected to any disobedience to the government.[58]

1.5 *The Family of al-Mundhir b. al-Zubayr b. al-ʿAwwām*

Supporters of the Revolt

1.5.1 Al-Mundhir b. Muḥammad b. al-Mundhir b. al-Zubayr b. al-ʿAwwām

A single tradition in *Maqātil al-ṭālibiyyīn* mentions him among those who joined the rebellion of Muḥammad b. ʿAbdallāh. He is described as an honest and righteous man, versed in Muslim jurisprudence, who was accepted as

---

Iḍam" إنا لبالمرمن بطن إضم ; the text of al-Azdī is corrupted: al-Ḥuṣayn instead of al-Khuḍayr; Ḥabīb instead of Khubayb.

54 Al-Zubayr b. Bakkār, *Jamhara*, [107] (al-Zubayr b. Khubayb); al-Zubayrī, *Nasab Quraysh*, 243; on al-Mughīra b. Khubayb, see al-Zubayr b. Bakkār, *Jamhara*, 109–114; 113: al-Mahdī gave him (as an *iqṭāʿ*) two springs in Iḍam; al-Zubayrī, *Nasab Quraysh*, 242: he belonged to the *ṣaḥāba* of Caliph al-Mahdī; Ibn Ḥazm, *Jamhara*, 122; al-Khaṭīb al-Baghdādī, *Taʾrīkh* (Beirut, 1997), 13:196.

55 Al-Zubayr b. Bakkār, *Jamhara*, 99 (his withdrawal to his estate); 99–109 (his biography) (= al-Khaṭīb al-Baghdādī, *Taʾrīkh* (Beirut, 1997), 13:467, mainly from al-Zubayr b. Bakkār); al-Bakrī, *Muʿjam*, 4:1220; al-Maqrīzī, *Imtāʿ*, 8:369; on al-Muraysīʿ, located by the sources in Wādī l-Qurā, see al-Bakrī, *Muʿjam*, 4:1220; Yāqūt, *Muʿjam* (ed. Wüstenfeld), 4:515; al-Fīrūzābādī, *al-Maghānim al-muṭāba*, 380; al-Maqrīzī, *Imtāʿ*, 8:369; al-Samhūdī, *al-Wafāʾ*, 4:470; on his brother, al-Mughīra, see al-Khaṭīb al-Baghdādī, *Taʾrīkh*, 8:467–468; 13:196 (his biography); al-Bakrī, *Muʿjam*, 1:166 (al-Mahdī gives him an estate in Iḍam).

56 On him, see al-Zubayr b. Bakkār, *Jamhara*, 92–94; Ibn Ḥazm, *Jamhara*, 123; Ibn Khayyāṭ, *Taʾrīkh* (ed. al-ʿUmarī), 2:456; al-Bukhārī, *Kabīr* (Beirut, 2001), 7:391.

57 Al-Ṭabarī, 3:217 (ll. 3–12); his sons related traditions about the revolt, for example, see al-Iṣfahānī, *Maqātil*, 242, 353; al-Ṭabarī, 3:203 (ll. 15–18); 3:217 (ll. 3–12).

58 Al-Zubayr b. Bakkār, *Jamhara*, 92: أنه كان يعظم المعاصي إعظاما شديدا ويفزع منها إذا ذكرت.

a *ḥadīth* transmitter by the family of Muḥammad [i.e., the [Imāmī] ʿAlīds?].[59] ʿĪsā b. ʿAbdallāh (b. Muḥammad b. ʿUmar b. ʿAlī b. Abī Ṭālib) describes how he saw al-Mundhir b. Muḥammad passing by al-Ḥasan b. Zayd b. al-Ḥasan b. ʿAlī b. Abī Ṭālib. The latter embraced him, crying bitterly, and said, "among those who supported Muḥammad b. ʿAbdallāh there was no braver and fiercer horse rider than that [man, i.e., al-Mundhir b. Muḥammad]."[60]

1.5.2–3 ʿUmar and al-Zubayr, the sons of ʿĀṣim b. al-Mundhir b. al-Zubayr b. al-ʿAwwām

According to Ibn Ḥazm, they both took part in Ibrāhīm b. ʿAbdallāh's revolt in al-Baṣra.[61] ʿĀṣim b. al-Mundhir b. al-Zubayr and his children lived in al-Baṣra.[62]

1.6 *The Family of ʿUrwa b. al-Zubayr*

Supporters[?] of the Revolt

1.6.1 Hishām b. ʿUrwa b. al-Zubayr

Several traditions mention Hishām b. ʿUrwa among those who took part in Muḥammad b. ʿAbdallāh's revolt, but it is highly probable that Hishām b. ʿUrwa

59 Al-Iṣfahānī, *Maqātil*, 284 (ll. 10–13): حدثنا عيسى بن الحسين قال: حدثنا هارون بن موسى الفروي عن داود ابن القاسم وغيره من أهل المدينة قال: خرج المنذر بن محمد بن المنذر بن الزبير مع محمد بن عبدالله وكان رجلا صالحا, فقيها, قد حمل عنه أهل البيت الحديث; on the transmitters, see appendix 2.

60 Al-Iṣfahānī, *Maqātil*, 284–285 (l. 14 to l. 1); for an identical parallel tradition, see ibid., 279 (ll. 3–5): the names of the transmitters are omitted, only ʿĪsā is mentioned; the lineage of al-Mundhir seems to be garbled: المنذر بن محمد بن الزبير instead of المنذر بن محمد بن المنذر بن الزبير. Muḥammad b. al-Mundhir b. al-Zubayr is a well-known person (al-Zubayr b. Bakkār, *Jamhara*, 236–246; no son under the name of al-Mundhir is mentioned, though); although the date of Muḥammad b. al-Mundhir's death is not given in the sources, it is hardly plausible that he took part in the rebellion of Muḥammad b. ʿAbdallāh (in 145/762), since he was active ca. the first quarter of the eighth century, see ibid., 242–243: with ʿAbd al-Malik (d. 86/705) and Sulayman (d. 99/717); no other caliph is mentioned; and see also the anecdote in al-Balādhurī, *Ansāb* (ed. ʿAbbās), 5:57, when Muḥammad b. al-Mundhir ridicules ʿAbdallāh b. ʿAmr b. ʿUthmān [b. ʿAffān], who died in 96/714 or 715.

61 Ibn Ḥazm, *Jamhara*, 123; they are not mentioned by al-Zubayr b. Bakkār in his *Jamhara*.

62 Al-Balādhurī, *Ansāb* (ed. ʿAbbās), 5:57: ʿĀṣim; al-Zubayr b. Bakkār, *Jamhara*, 256: ʿAbdallāh b. ʿĀṣim (who lived with his children in al-Baṣra) and had several estates in the city. Ibn Ḥazm, *Jamhara*, 123: mentions a Shāfiʿī *faqīh* and *muḥaddith*, a descendant of Sulaymān b. ʿĀṣim and adds that the rest of the descendants of ʿĀṣim b. al-Mundhir live in al-Baṣra: وبقية ولد عاصم بن المنذر بالبصرة.

did not take part at all and that he lived in al-ʿIrāq during the revolt and even before it broke out.

2 The Family of ʿAbdallāh b. Khālid b. Ḥizām b. Khuwaylid b. Asad b. ʿAbd al-ʿUzzā b. Quṣayy b. Kilāb

Opponents of the Revolt

2.1 *Al-Ḍaḥḥāk b. ʿUthmān b. ʿAbdallāh b. Khālid b. Ḥizām b. Khuwaylid (d. 153/770), and His Second Cousin*

2.2 *ʿAbdallāh b. al-Mundhir b. al-Mughīra b. ʿAbdallāh b. Khālid b. Ḥizām b. Khuwaylid*

A single tradition relates that al-Ḍaḥḥāk b. ʿUthmān and ʿAbdallāh b. al-Mundhir were among the few Medinan notables who did not join Muḥammad b. ʿAbdallāh's rebellion.[63]

Banū Asad: *Mawālī* of the Zubayrī family

Supporters of the Revolt

2.3 *ʿAbdallāh b. al-Zubayr b. ʿUmar b. Dirham al-Zubayrī* [mawlāhum], *al-Kūfī,* mawlā *Banī Asad*

Al-Iṣfahānī records an eyewitness testimony of ʿAbdallāh b. al-Zubayr b. ʿUmar that describes Muḥammad b. ʿAbdallāh's ornamented sword on the day that he rebelled openly. According to al-Iṣfahānī's sources, ʿAbdallāh b. al-Zubayr b. ʿUmar was one of Muḥammad b. ʿAbdallāh's close associates.[64] He was a

---

63 Al-Ṭabarī, 3:199 (ll. 8–10); only al-Ḍaḥḥāk and his descendants are mentioned in the *nasab* and *rijāl* books, for example, see al-Zubayr b. Bakkār, *Jamhara,* 401–404; al-Zubayrī, *Nasab Quraysh,* 234; as a *ḥadīth* transmitter: Ibn Ḥibbān, *al-Thiqāt,* 6:482; al-Mizzī, *Tahdhīb,* 13:272–274. ʿAbdallāh b. al-Mundhir (d. 236/850 or 851) is not mentioned or discussed in the sources; his son, al-Mundhir, and grandson, Ibrāhīm, were distinguished notables and scholars of *ḥadīth* in Medina, for example, see al-Zubayr b. Bakkār, *Jamhara,* 395; Ibn Ḥazm, *Jamhara,* 121; Ibn Ḥajar, *Tahdhīb* (Hyderabad edition), 10:301: al-Mundhir b. ʿAbdallāh; Ibn Ḥajar, *Tahdhīb* (ed. Hyderabad), 1:166–167; al-Mizzī, *Tahdhīb,* 2:207–211: Ibrāhīm b. al-Mundhir.

64 Al-Iṣfahānī, *Maqātil,* 290.

minor transmitter of *ḥadīth*, highly criticized by Sunnī scholars.[65] His father was a well-known Kūfan *muḥaddith* (d. 203/818 or 819).[66]

3 Some Notes on the Zubayrīs in Early Islam

The Zubayrī family played an important and sometimes crucial role in the early history of Islam: during the Prophet's lifetime, the Battle of the Camel, the caliphate of ʿUthmān, the caliphate of ʿAbdallāh b. al-Zubayr, the Battle of al-Ḥarra (63/683), the Battle of Qudayd (130/747)[67] and, of course, the revolt

---

65 I was able to find very few biographies of him, e.g., Ibn Abī Ḥātim, *al-Jarḥ* (Beirut edition), 5:56; al-Dhahabī, *Mīzān* (Beirut, 1995), 4:99.

66 On him, see for example al-Dhahabī, *Siyar*, 9:529–532; al-Mizzī, *Tahdhīb*, 25:476–481, and the comprehensive bibliography therein; al-Khaṭīb al-Baghdādī, *Taʾrīkh* (Beirut, 1997), 3:19–21.

67 The scale and significance of the Zubayrīs and other families closely related to the Zubayrīs in the opposition movements should be assessed through a comprehensive in-depth study. Suffice it to mention here several families, branching from Zamʿa b. al-Aswad b. Muṭṭalib b. Asad. Al-Muṭṭalib and Khuwaylid al-Zubayr b. al-ʿAwwām's grandfather were brothers. It is noteworthy that Hind and Qarība, the wives of ʿAbdallāh b. al-Ḥasan, belonged to the family of Zamʿa b. al-Aswad, which had a long history of taking part in the opposition to the Umawīs. Members of this extended family were killed in the battle of al-Ḥarra, e.g.:
1) **Yazīd b. ʿAbdallāh b. Zamʿa** was among the prisoners who were killed by Muslim b. ʿUqba in the battle of al-Ḥarra, see al-Zubayrī, *Nasab Quraysh*, 222; al-Zubayr b. Bakkār, *Jamhara*, 473; Ibn Ḥazm, *Jamhara*, 119: قتل يوم الحرة صبرا إذ أبى أن يبايع ليزيد أنه عبد قن; see also al-Balādhurī, *Ansāb* (ed. ʿAbbās), 5:69; but cf. Ibn al-Kalbī, *Jamhara* (ed. Ḥasan), 73: the one who was killed is ʿAbdallāh b. Wahb b. Zamʿa [b. al-Aswad b. ʿAbd al-Muṭṭalib b. Asad b. ʿAbd al-ʿUzzā b. Quṣayy]. Other members of the extended family were among those of *ahl al-Madīna* killed in the battle of Qudayd against Abū Ḥamza al-Khārijī, e.g.:
2–3) **Wahb and al-Miqdād, the sons of ʿAbdallāh (al-Aṣghar) b. Wahb b. Zamʿa,** see Ibn Ḥazm, *Jamhara*, 119.
4–8) **ʿUbaydallāh and ʿAbdallāh the sons of Abū ʿUbayda b. ʿAbdallāh b. Zamʿa, and three sons of ʿAbdallāh b. Abī ʿUbayda, Hishām, Muḥammad, and ʿAbd al-Raḥmān,** see ibid., 119–120.
It is related about another member of this family, al-Mundhir b. al-Zubayr [b. ʿAbd al-Raḥmān b. Habbār b. al-Aswad b. al-Muṭṭalib b. Asad b. ʿAbd al-ʿUzzā b. Quṣayy], the descendant of Habbār b. al-Aswad, who was the brother of Zamʿa, that he revolted during al-Saffāḥ's reign (r. 132–136/750–754) in Qirqīsiyā in al-Jazīra, was captured and crucified, see Ibn Ḥazm, *Jamhara*, 119: المنذر بن الزبير قد قام بقرقيسيا أيام السفاح فأسر وصلب; this is the only source that mentions him in general, and/or in connection with the

of Muḥammad b. ʿAbdallāh. Though a detailed, extensive study of this family's history is much needed, this cannot be addressed in the framework of this study. An important pioneering study of one of the influential families of the Zubayrīs in the Umawī and early ʿAbbāsī period has been carried out by A. Arazi, who examined the historical background for the emergence of the literature in praise of Medina (*Faḍāʾil al-Madīna*) that developed in light of the political-economic and social crises that developed in the city during the Umawī period, especially towards the end of the period and the beginning of ʿAbbāsī rule. Arazi concluded that the Zubayrīs, and especially ʿUrwa b. al-Zubayr and his son Hishām, played a central role in consolidating and spreading the traditions in praise of Medina. In light of this phenomenon, Arazi examines the history of the Zubayrī family in Medina,[68] especially their economic standing and interest in Medina and its environment.[69]

The following sections mainly deal with the role of the Zubayrī family in Muḥammad al-Nafs al-Zakiyya's revolt. It was clearly shown that a large segment of Muḥammad's most distinguished adherents belonged to the "noble" and highly important Zubayrī family. Many of them played important roles in the rebellion. There are, therefore, two aspects which should be discussed: 1) The political-social, and the economic position of the Zubayrīs, and 2) the relations between the Zubayrīs and the Ṭālibīs.

3.1 *The Political-Social and Especially the Economic Position of the Zubayrīs*

This family was known already in the Jāhiliyya and during the first two hundred years of Islamic rule, as a prosperous family whose wealth included many estates around Medina and in other locations in Arabia. Hasson concludes this matter by saying:

> After the *hijra*, al-Zubayr had become one of the wealthiest companions. He owned a large number of properties, including some large estates,

---

revolt, in particular; this evidence is faithfully copied by Ibn Khaldūn, *ʿIbar* (Beirut, 1961), 2:277–278, except for his name, al-Mundhir b. al-Rabīʿ which should be corrected to al-Mundhir b. al-Zubayr. For his complete genealogy, see Ibn Ḥazm, *Jamhara*, 118; al-Zubayrī, *Nasab Quraysh*, 220; is this revolt one of the revolts in al-Jazīra following the accession of the ʿAbbāsīs? Qirqīsiyā is mentioned briefly by the sources in 132/750 (the name of al-Mundhir b. al-Zubayr and his fate are not mentioned, though); on the insurrection in al-Jazīra during al-Saffāḥ's rule, see Cobb, *White Banners*, 46–51.

68 Arazi, "Mekke et Medine," 186–206.

69 Ibid., esp. 186, 189–191, 195; see also the discussion on the Zubayrīs by Landau-Tasseron, "Arabia," 406–407.

> such as al-Ghāba in the vicinity of Medina, al-Salīla in al-Rabadha; Dār al-Zubayr and Masjid al-Zubayr in Sūq Wardān of al-Fusṭāṭ; and estates in Alexandria and Kūfa. Some were grants of land in Arabia from the Prophet, others were granted by ʿUthmān b. ʿAffān, especially in ʿIrāq. His estate (*dār*) in the quarter of Banū Sulaym in al-Baṣra was vast and included markets and stores .... To give an example of his fortune, it was reported that he sold one of his *dūr* for 600,000 dirhams.[70]

Against the pro-Zubayrī tradition that seeks to portray al-Zubayr as a pious, almost penniless warrior who did not leave any money and had "only" two estates (one of them al-Ghāba) and eleven residences (*dār*/*dūr*) in Medina, one in Egypt, one in al-Kūfa and two in al-Baṣra,[71] other evidence bears witness to many other estates al-Zubayr had received during his lifetime, e.g., the Prophet granted (أقطع) al-Zubayr a plot of land with palm groves that belonged to Banū l-Naḍīr: أرضا من أرض بني النضير ذات نخل.[72] Abū Bakr granted him (أقطع) al-Jurf, and ʿUmar granted him the entire area of al-ʿAqīq (العقيق أجمع).[73]

3.1.1 The Houses (dūr) of Banū l-Zubayr in Medina, mainly in Baqīʿ al-Zubayr

The land was owned by Kaʿb b. al-Ashraf, one of the leaders of the Jewish tribes in Medina.[74] After the assassination of Kaʿb b. al-Ashraf by order of the Prophet, the Prophet confiscated the land and granted it to al-Zubayr b. al-ʿAwwām. From that day on the place was known as Baqīʿ al-Zubayr.[75]

ʿUmar b. Shabba (d. 262/876) gives an important list of the dwellings of the Banū l-Zubayr in Medina:

> Al-Zubayr asked the Prophet (Ṣ) to grant him al-Baqīʿ as an *iqṭāʿ*, and the Prophet gave it to him, and this is Baqīʿ al-Zubayr. The following large-size dwellings (*dūr*) that al-Zubayr possessed were:

---

70 Hasson, "al-Zubayr b. al-ʿAwwām," 550.

71 Al-Balādhurī, *Ansāb* (ed. ʿAbbās), 5:36–37; ibid., 5:39, another tradition in this vein.

72 Ibid., 5:38; al-Balādhurī, *Futūḥ*, 1:21 (transmitted by Hishām b. ʿUrwa b. al-Zubayr from his father).

73 Al-Balādhurī, *Ansāb* (ed. ʿAbbās), 5:38; ibid.: al-Jurf until Qanāt; al-Balādhurī, *Futūḥ*, 1:22.

74 On him, see M. Watt, "Kaʿb b. al-Ashraf," *EI*²; Lecker, "Wāqidī's Account."

75 Kister, "The Market of the Prophet," 273; Lecker, "Markets of Medina," 139–140.

1) **Dār ʿUrwa b. al-Zubayr,** the *dār* in which the slaughter house exists; then, behind it, to its east;
2) **Dār al-Mundhir b. al-Zubayr,** extending to ʿUrwa's alley (*zuqāq*). Banū Muḥammad b. Fulayḥ b. al-Mundhir reside there. In it (that is, Baqīʿ al-Zubayr);
3) **Dār Muṣʿab b. al-Zubayr,** the *dār* on the left when heading towards Banū Māzin, to the side next to **Dār al-Ḥijāra;** it (Dār Muṣʿab) is in the hands of Banū Muṣʿab today;[76] in it (Baqīʿ al-Zubayr);
4) **The *dār* of the family of ʿUkāsha b. Muṣʿab b. al-Zubayr.** This is the *dār* above [on?: *ʿalā*] the gate of the alley in which there is the *kuttāb* [i.e., elementary school] that **leads you** towards the houses (*dūr*) of **Nafīs** b. Muḥammad, that is, the *mawlā* of Banū l-Muʿallā, which is located within the (quarter) of Banū Zurayq of the Anṣār. In it (Baqīʿ al-Zubayr);
5) **The *dār* of the family of ʿAbdallāh b. al-Zubayr,** in which Ṣiddīq b. Mūsā l-Zubayrī dwelled. Its houses (*adyāruhā*) belong to Banū l-Mundhir, among them the house (*bayt*) of Abū ʿA.w.d al-Zubayrī and his son; then (you reach) Dār ʿAbdallāh, that extends until Dār Asmāʾ bt. Abī Bakr al-Ṣiddīq, may God be pleased with both of them. In it (Baqīʿ al-Zubayr);
6) **The house (*bayt*) of Nāfiʿ b. Thābit b. ʿAbdallāh b. al-Zubayr.** From its upper edge the road diverges into two.[77] All this is a charitable endowment of al-Zubayr to his children.

Al-Zubayr, may God be pleased with him, (also) built Dār ʿUrwa [b. al-Zubayr] and Dār ʿAmr, which are close to each other, located in al-Qawārīr's Lane (*khawkha*). He granted these dwellings to ʿUrwa and ʿAmr and their descendants as separate charitable endowments, which are in their hands, according to the original conditions of the endowment, until today.[78]

---

76 See also al-Zubayr b. Bakkār, *Jamhara*, 38: the *dār* of ʿUmar b. Muṣʿab b. al-Zubayr in Baqīʿ al-Zubayr is mentioned.

77 Al-Samhūdī, *Wafāʾ*, 4:170: "the house (*bayt*) of Nāfiʿ al-Zubayrī, located in the place where the road branches off" (بمفترق الطريق).

78 Ibn Shabba, *Taʾrīkh al-Madīna*, 1:229–230:

ذكر الدور والمساكن

استقطع الزبير النبيَّ صلى الله عليه وسلم البقيعَ فقطعه، فهو بقيع الزبير، ففيه من الدور للزبير: دار عُرْوَة بن الزبير، وهي التي فيها المجزرة، ثم خلفها في شرقيها دار المنذر بن الزبير إلى زقاق عروة،

ʿUrwa and Jaʿfar, the sons of al-Zubayr, inherited the *dār* of ʿUmāra b. Ḥamza b. al-Zubayr in Baqīʿ al-Zubayr, known as Dār ʿUrwa. ʿUrwa exchanged his legal rights in the stores of the market of Medina for his brother's (Jaʿfar) rights in the aforementioned *dār*, in order to have the full rights to the *dār*.[79]

In the entry "al-Furʿ," which belonged to the region of Medina, al-Bakrī records a detailed report about the estates of the Zubayrī family. He quotes al-Zubayr b. Bakkār from his informants: عن رجاله,[80] that ʿAbdallāh b. al-Zubayr developed and cultivated (*iʿtamala*) al-Furʿ and took estates there for himself. Among the estates he developed and cultivated was ʿAyn al-Fāriʿa and al-Sanām.[81] It is reported that he sold his estate in al-Ghāba,[82] which was named al-Siqāya, to Muʿāwiya b. Abī Sufyān for 100,000 *dīnār*s. With part of the money from the sale he bought an estate in al-Mujāḥ, near Mecca, for his brother ʿUrwa b. al-Zubayr.[83] This was not the only estate of the Zubayrīs in al-Ghāba (see below). ʿAbdallāh b. al-Zubayr also purchased (developed—*ittakhadha*) al-Jathjātha, which is described as one of the uncultivated areas of

---

فيها يسكن بنو محمد بن فُلَيح بن المنذر، وفيه دار مصعب بن الزبير، وهي الدار التي على يسارك إذا أَردتَ بني مازن، إلى جنب دار الحجارة، وهي بأَيدي بني مُصْعَب اليوم، وفيه دار آل عكاشة بن مصعب بن الزبير، وهي الدار التي على باب الزقاق الذي فيه الكتّاب الذي يخرجك إلى دُورِ نفيس بن محمد يعني مولى بني المعلى في بنِي زريق من الأنصار، وفيه دار آل عبد الله بن الزبير التي كان فيها صدّيق بن موسى، الزبيري، وأُديارها لبني المنذر، فيها بيت أَبي عود الزبيري وابنه، ثم دار عبد الله، ممدودة إلى دار أَسماء بنت أَبي بكر الصديق رضي الله عنهما. وفيه بيت نافع بن ثابت بن عبد الله بن الزبير الذي يفترق علوه الطريقان. كل هذا صدقة من الزبير بن العوام وتجويز منه لولده. واتخذ الزبير رضي الله عنه أَيضًا دارَ عروةَ ودارَ عمرو، وهما متلازمتان عند خوخة القوارير، فتصدق بهما متفرقتين على عروة وعمرو وأَعقابهما، فهما بأَيديهم على ذلك إلى اليوم.
Al-Samhūdī, *Wafāʾ*, 4:169–170, copied most of Ibn Shabba's text.

79 Al-Zubayr b. Bakkār, *Jamhara*, 350.

80 Al-Bakrī, *Muʿjam*, 3:1020; al-Bakrī copied al-Zubayr b. Bakkār's work, see below.

81 Al-Zubayr b. Bakkār, *Jamhara*, 54 (= al-Bakrī, *Muʿjam*, 3:1020).

82 Near Medina, at a distance of eight miles to the north of Medina, see al-Fīrūzābādī, *al-Maghānim al-muṭāba*, 299; al-Samhūdī, *al-Wafāʾ*, 4:404–406: locating al-Ghāba towards the edge of Sāfilat Medina; see also ibid., n. 7 of the editor.

83 Ibn ʿAsākir, *Taʾrīkh*, 54:212; al-Dhahabī, *Siyar*, 4:429; see also al-Samhūdī, *Wafāʾ*, 4:405: al-Zubayr bought al-Ghāba for 170,000 (*dirhams*?) and it was sold as part of his legacy [تركته that is, his inheritance] for 1,600,000 (*dirhams*?); for the location of al-Mujāḥ, see Yāqūt, *Muʿjam* (ed. Wüstenfeld), 4:415–416.

Medina (بادية من بوادي المدينة). The families of Ḥamza, ʿAbbād and Thābit, the sons of ʿAbdallāh b. al-Zubayr, had dwelling places there.[84] Muḥammad b. ʿAbbād b. ʿAbdallāh b. al-Zubayr owned an estate in Namira [?]: صدقته بنمرة.[85]

3.1.2 The Estates of ʿUrwa b. al-Zubayr

Al-Bakrī, quoting al-Zubayr b. Bakkār al-Zubayrī, reports that Mujāḥ is a well-known oasis (*māʾ*) of the Banū ʿAbdallāh b. al-Zubayr. ʿUrwa b. al-Zubayr gave it to his brother.[86] ʿUrwa developed and cultivated ʿAyn al-Muhd (Nahd?) and ʿAyn ʿAskar.[87] He owned other estates in Arabia, e.g., in Wādī l-ʿAqīq, where his well-known *qaṣr* [large house of stone?; a "palace"], Qaṣr al-ʿAqīq, with its famous well (in addition to other wells) were located.[88] It is reported that

84 Al-Zubayr b. Bakkār, *Jamhara*, 68; al-Bakrī, *Muʿjam*, 2:367; al-Jathjātha is sixteen or seventeen miles from Medina. Al-Zubayr b. Bakkār defines this mile as the "small mile": الميل الصغير; I do not know the meaning of this term.

85 Al-Zubayr b. Bakkār, *Jamhara*, 73; Namira is described near (at) ʿArafa near Mecca, al-Bakrī, *Muʿjam*, 4:1334 ("Namira"); ibid., 1:134 ("al-Arāk"); al-Samhūdī, *Wafāʾ*, 4:505 (in al-Qudayd). Al-Qudayd is in al-Furʿ region; see the note of the editor of al-Zubayr b. Bakkār's work, ibid., 73–74, who concludes that the Namira mentioned in the tradition is in al-Furʿ region (based on Ibn Khurdādhbeh, *Masālik*, 129, where it is mentioned together with al-Furʿ in the district belonging to the jurisdiction [*aʿrād*] of Medina; for the term *aʿrād al-Madīna*, see Lecker, *Banū Sulaym*, 105, n. 30, and 225, n. 27).

86 Al-Bakrī, *Muʿjam*, 4:1160–1161 ("Laqf"); al-Zubayrī, *Nasab Quraysh*, 246: mentions ʿAbdallāh b. ʿUrwa's estates in al-Furʿ; they may be the above-mentioned estates of ʿUrwa or different ones.

87 Al-Zubayr b. Bakkār, *Jamhara*, 54 ("ʿAyn al-Muhd"); al-Bakrī, *Muʿjam*, 3:1020–1021: ʿAyn al-Nahd ("al-Furʿ"); ibid., 4:1336.

88 Al-Zubayr b. Bakkār, *Jamhara*, 132, 283; 301: "مجلس بئر عروة" is mentioned; al-Iṣfahānī, *Ḥilya*, 2:180 (Cairo edition, 2:204); Yāqūt, *Muʿjam* (Beirut edition), 4:360–361; 360: ʿUrwa's well; al-Dhahabī, *Siyar*, 4:427–428. See also the important detailed report about the history of ʿUrwa's estate in al-ʿAqīq in al-Samhūdī, *Wafāʾ*, 4:16–22; 18: the *qaṣr* and the wells were built by his grandson, ʿUmar b. ʿAbdallāh b. ʿUrwa; ʿUmar b. ʿAbd al-ʿAzīz orders that the well be destroyed; 19: ʿUrwa endowed (*taṣaddaqa*) the *qaṣr* to his children and the well to the Muslims. His two sons, Yaḥyā and ʿAbdallāh, were nominated as the overseers in charge of the *qaṣr*, then 40 years after ʿUrwa's death it was given to Hishām b. ʿUrwa, then to his son, ʿUbaydallāh; 20: the *qaṣr* and the well were destroyed by the governor of Medina during Hishām b. ʿAbd al-Malik's reign, but were rebuilt and reinstated by orders of the caliph. It is noteworthy is that some other famous *ṣaḥāba* had estates in al-ʿAqīq, for example, Saʿd b. Abī Waqqāṣ had a *qaṣr* in al-ʿAqīq, see Ibn Saʿd, *Ṭabaqāt*, 3:147–148; al-Balādhurī, *Ansāb* (ed. ʿAbbās), 5:83, 279; Abū Hurayra had an estate (*arḍ*), in al-ʿAqīq, see al-Dhahabī, *Siyar*, 2:610.

al-Zubayr b. Hishām b. ʿUrwa b. al-Zubayr died in al-ʿAqīq, most probably in one of the family estates there. His father, Hishām b. ʿUrwa, prayed over his body.[89] Another estate owned by ʿUrwa was al-Muqtariba, located in Jīzat (Wādī) Buṭḥān. Hishām b. ʿUrwa and his wife Fāṭima bt. al-Mundhir loved the place and used to live there. When ʿUrwa died Hishām gave his share in the estate to his brother, Yaḥyā b. ʿUrwa, for the latter's rights in their father's inheritance.[90] Hishām b. ʿUrwa also had an estate in al-Sarāt.[91] According to al-Wāqidī, ʿUrwa died in al-Furʿ.[92]

3.1.3 The Family of Ḥamza b. ʿAbdallāh b. al-Zubayr

Ḥamza developed and cultivated ʿAyn al-Rubuḍ (Rubḍ?) and [ʿAyn] al-Najafa (both in al-Furʿ).[93] The canals of the two estates supplied water to more than 20,000 palm trees.[94] Al-Rubuḍ was owned by the Zubayrīs, and was still passed as inheritance in the Zubayrī family during Hārūn al-Rashīd's rule.[95] Al-Athaba in al-Baqīʿ region (في أرض البقيع) was owned by ʿAbbād b. Ḥamza b. ʿAbdallāh b. al-Zubayr, as a (family?) *waqf*.[96] He also had a *qaṣr* on the outskirts (*fī ẓāhir*) of Qubāʾ.[97]

3.1.4 The Family of Muṣʿab b. al-Zubayr

Members of the Muṣʿab b. al-Zubayr family, al-Mundhir b. Muṣʿab b. Muṣʿab and his brother, Khālid b. Muṣʿab, owned ʿAyn al-Nahd (al-Mundhir) and al-Jawwāniyya (Khālid) (also in al-Furʿ).[98] Al-Zubayr b. Bakkār relates from Ayyūb b. Ḥasan al-Rāfiʿī, "how they used to go out every Friday, together with the other young boys of the primary school (*kuttāb*) of Medina, sit at Naqb

---

89 Al-Zubayr b. Bakkār, *Jamhara*, 295.

90 Ibid., 299–300; Wādī Buṭḥān (Baṭiḥān, Baṭḥān), was one of the three principle *wādīs* in Medina, see the map of Medina; for the reading of the name, see the comment of Maḥmūd Muḥammad Shākir the editor of al-Zubayr b. Bakkār, *Jamhara*, 299, n. 4.

91 Ibid., 300; I do not know the location of this estate. The Sarāt range is very long, stretching from the Gulf of Aqaba to the Gulf of Aden.

92 Al-Balādhurī, *Ansāb* (ed. ʿAbbās), 5:54: ʿUrwa b. al-Zubayr died in an estate (*māl*) *bi-nāḥiyat al-Furʿ*; for the location of al-Furʿ on the map, see Lecker, *Banū Sulaym*, xiii.

93 Al-Zubayr b. Bakkār, *Jamhara*, 54: al-Rubuḍ; al-Bakrī, *Muʿjam*, 3:1020: al-Rubḍ.

94 Ibid., 1021; al-Zubayr b. Bakkār, *Jamhara*, 52.

95 Ibid., 62.

96 Al-Bakrī, *Muʿjam*, 1:107 ("al-ʿAthaba"); 4:1028 ("al-Naqīʿ").

97 Al-Zubayr b. Bakkār, *Jamhara*, 55.

98 Ibid., 340–341; al-Bakrī, *Muʿjam*, 3:1021.

Wāqim and watch the sons of Muṣʿab b. al-Zubayr entering from al-Jawwāniyya leaping on Arab horses."[99] The family (of Muṣʿab b. al-Zubayr) also owned estates in Ḥaṣīr, in Wādī l-Naqīʿ.[100]

3.1.5 The Family of Thābit b. ʿAbdallāh b. al-Zubayr

Another Zubayrī family, the descendants of Thābit b. ʿAbdallāh b. al-Zubayr, e.g., al-Zubayr b. Bakkār b. ʿAbdallāh b. Muṣʿab b. Thābit b. ʿAbdallāh b. al-Zubayr, owned an estate at Thaniyyat al-Sharīd, which had sown lands, wells, different kinds of trees (عضاه: species of acacia trees) and آجام and some kinds of herbage (الكلأ).[101] Muṣʿab b. Thābit b. ʿAbdallāh b. al-Zubayr had a *qaṣr* and *qarāra* in his estate in al-ʿAqīq.[102]

Al-Zubayr b. Khubayb b. Thābit b. ʿAbdallāh b. al-Zubayr owned an estate (*ḍayʿa*) in al-Muraysīʿ, which belonged to al-Qudayd region.[103] He died in (another?) estate in Wādī l-Qurā.[104]

99 Al-Zubayr b. Bakkār, *Jamhara*, 340; al-Jawwāniyya was near Uḥud, to the north of Medina; al-Samhūdī relates that it was the abode of the Jews of Medina, see al-Samhūdī, *Wafāʾ*, 4:216–217; Wāqim is in Ḥarrat Wāqim, one of the strongholds (*uṭum*) of Medina, see al-Bakrī, *Muʿjam*, 4:1365; al-Fīrūzābādī, *al-Maghānim al-muṭāba*, 424; al-Samhūdī, *Wafāʾ*, 4:516; Lecker, *Muslims, Jews and Pagans*, 8.

100 Al-Bakrī, *Muʿjam*, 4:1327.

101 Ibid., 1331; according to Lane, *Lexicon*, s.v. *a.j.m.*, the meaning of آجام (plural of أجمة) is a thicket, wood or forest; abundant collection of dense trees or shrubs; or of reeds and canes. To understand the word in the sentence as the plural form of *ujum*, which means forts or strongholds seems out of context.

102 Al-Zubayr b. Bakkār, *Jamhara*, 121; *qārāra* is rendered by Lane, *Lexicon*, s.v. *q.r.r.*, as a depressed piece of ground; any depressed piece of ground into which water pours and where it remains.

103 Al-Zubayr b. Bakkār, *Jamhara*, 99: he stayed in a mosque in his estate in al-Muraysīʿ for years, not leaving it but for ablutions (= al-Khaṭīb al-Baghdādī, *Taʾrīkh* [Beirut, 1997], 8:467). Al-Muraysīʿ is described as belonging to al-Qudayd region in the direction of the seashore (من ناحية قديد إلى الساحل), see al-Ṭabarī, 1:1500, 1511; Yāqūt, *Muʿjam* (Beirut edition), 5:118; al-Samhūdī, *Wafāʾ*, 4:470 (recording the contradictory data regarding its distance from al-Furʿ, one hour or one day). In terms of administration, al-Qudayd belonged to al-Furʿ, see al-Bakrī, *Muʿjam*, 3:1021; it is described as located between Mecca and Medina, or near Mecca, see al-Fīrūzābādī, *al-Maghānim al-muṭāba*, 334; for a general description, see al-Ḥarbrī[?], *al-Manāsik*, 459–461; and see the location of al-Qudayd in Lecker's map, *Banū Sulaym*, xiii.

104 Al-Zubayr b. Bakkār, *Jamhara*, 109 (= al-Khaṭīb al-Baghdādī, *Taʾrīkh* [Beirut, 1997], 8:466); al-Bakrī, *Muʿjam*, 4:88, mistakenly locates al-Muraysīʿ in Wādī l-Qurā (*qarya min Wādī l-Qurā*), adding the tradition about the seclusion of al-Zubayr b. Khubayb in his estate in

3.1.6 The Confiscation of ʿAbdallāh b. al-Zubayr's Estates (and Those of Other Zubayrīs) by ʿAbd al-Malik

After the submission of al-Ḥijāz, ʿAbd al-Malik confiscated the property of ʿAbdallāh b. al-Zubayr and other members of al-Zubayr's family.[105] This was part of a general policy of ʿAbd al-Malik, who also stopped the payment of the annual governmental stipends to all the Arabs in al-Ḥijāz, including notables from Quraysh. One of those Qurashī notables was the father of the famous scholar Ibn Shihāb al-Zuhrī, Muḥammad b. Muslim b. ʿUbaydallāh (d. 124/742).[106]

I do not know whether all (or most) of the estates of the Zubayrīs were given back to their owners by the Umawī caliphs. Several specific testimonies, however, bear witness to the return of the estates of the Zubayrīs confiscated by Caliph ʿAbd al-Malik and other Umawī caliphs. Al-Zubayr b. Bakkār relates that Thābit b. ʿAbdallāh b. al-Zubayr came to Caliph ʿAbd al-Malik asking for the return of the family estates. The caliph ordered that the sons of ʿAbdallāh b. al-Zubayr be given some (or one: *baʿḍ*) of their estates.[107]

One of the Zubayrīs whose estate was confiscated was Muḥammad b. al-Mundhir b. al-Zubayr b. al-ʿAwwām,[108] who was one of the senior supporters and commanders of ʿAbdallāh b. al-Zubayr.[109] His story was recorded by the

al-Muraysīʿ. It seems that al-Bakrī combined this tradition (that does not mention Wādī l-Qurā) with the second, which states that al-Zubayr died in his estate in Wādī l-Qurā, thus mistakenly concluding that al-Muraysīʿ was located in that *wādī*.

105 Al-Zubayr b. Bakkār, *Jamhara*, 242; 82: the estates of ʿAbdallāh b. al-Zubayr; al-Zubayrī, *Nasab Quraysh*, 247.

106 Since al-Zuhrī's father fought at the side of ʿAbdallāh b. al-Zubayr against ʿAbd al-Malik (Lecker, "al-Zuhrī," 47; Abū Zurʿa, *Taʾrīkh*, 1:408; Ibn ʿAsākir, *Taʾrīkh*, 55:297 [= idem, *al-Mukhtaṣar*, 23:227]; al-Dhahabī, *Siyar*, 229, 230; Ibn al-Jawzī, *al-Muntaẓam*, 7:232); this caliph ordered the removal of the names of the members of this family from the *dīwān* (Ibn ʿAsākir, *Taʾrīkh*, 55:300 (= Ibn ʿAsākir, *Mukhtaṣar*, 23:229); Ibn al-Jawzī, *al-Muntaẓam*, 7:233; al-Fasawī, *al-Maʿrifa*, 1:628) and other Arab tribes in his city [? or the entire Ḥijāz?] (Ibn ʿAsākir, *Taʾrīkh*, 55:300 [= idem, *al-Mukhtaṣar*, 23:229]: إن بلدك لبلد ما فرضنا فيها لأحد منذ كان هذا الأمر; al-Fasawī, *al-Maʿrifa*, 1:628); ʿAbd al-Malik renewed and even increased to al-Zuhrī's annual pension, appointing him as one of the *ṣaḥāba* of the caliph, with the salary of that class (Ibn ʿAsākir, *Taʾrīkh*, 55:324; Ibn al-Jawzī, *al-Muntaẓam*, 7:234; al-Dhahabī, *Siyar*, 331).

107 Al-Zubayr b. Bakkār, *Jamhara*, 82 (= Ibn ʿAsākir, *Taʾrīkh*, 11:128).

108 On him, see al-Zubayr b. Bakkār, *Jamhara*, 236–244; Ibn ʿAsākir, *Taʾrīkh*, 56:25–31.

109 Al-Zubayr b. Bakkār, *Jamhara*, 239.

Zubayrī historians, e.g., al-Zubayr b. Bakkār from his uncle, Muṣʿab b. ʿAbdallāh [b. Muṣʿab b. Thābit b. ʿAbdallāh b. al-Zubayr]. It attests to the confiscation of the estates of ʿAbdallāh b. al-Zubayr and other Zubayrīs who supported Ibn al-Zubayr:

> Muḥammad b. al-Mundhir [b. al-Zubayr b. al-ʿAwwām] came to ʿAbd al-Malik b. Marwān, (and this was) after the execution of ʿAbdallāh b. al-Zubayr, asking for his estate, which was confiscated with estates of Ibn al-Zubayr. ʿAbd al-Malik ordered in a letter the return of Muḥammad b. al-Mundhir's estate, mentioning Ibn al-Zubayr in his letter saying: "from what was confiscated from the liar"; [reading this] Muḥammad [b. al-Mundhir] said: "A man like me does not carry the curse of his uncle," so ʿAbd al-Malik ordered that this be erased from the letter.[110]

Another similar case is the story of Yaḥyā b. ʿUrwa b. al-Zubayr, who according to ʿAbdallāh b. Muṣʿab al-Zubayrī, came to ʿAbd al-Malik asking for the return of the confiscated estates of the family of al-Zubayr. The caliph gave him back his confiscated estate/s (it is noteworthy that here the text refers to his estates, not to the estates of all the Zubayrīs).[111]

ʿAbd al-Malik did not give the Zubayrīs all their estates back. Al-Zubayr b. Bakkār relates that Sulaymān b. ʿAbd al-Malik had great respect for the Zubayrī family, for Thābit b. ʿAbdallāh b. al-Zubayr in particular. Therefore he restored estates [property?: *ashyāʾ*] to the sons of ʿAbdallāh b. al-Zubayr that ʿAbd al-Malik did not return.[112]

The above noted traditions do not give names or locations of the estates that were returned to the Zubayrīs. It is known that the Zubayrīs had had large estates in al-Furʿ, and it is highly plausible that the estates that are mentioned (with no actual location), or some of them, were in al-Furʿ. This we learn from another tradition recording the case of another member of ʿUrwa's family, ʿAbdallāh b. ʿUrwa b. al-Zubayr, during the governorship of Khālid b. ʿAbd al-Malik b. al-Ḥārith b. al-Ḥakam b. Abī l-ʿĀṣ of Medina (between 114/732–733

---

110 Ibid., 242 (a parallel tradition: Ibn ʿAsākir, *Taʾrīkh*, 25:25).

111 Al-Zubayrī, *Nasab Quraysh*, 247: فسأله يرد [= برد؟] ماقبض من أموال آل الزبير ... ورد عليه ماقبض له.

112 Al-Zubayr b. Bakkār, *Jamhara*, 89 (= Ibn ʿAsākir, *Taʾrīkh*, 11:132): ورد عليهم أشياء لم يكن ردها عبد الملك.

and 118 or 119/736–738), during the caliphate of Hishām b. ʿAbd al-Malik.[113] The estates were in al-Furʿ. In these years there was an extreme drought and Abdallāh b. ʿUrwa permitted the people to enter his palm groves in al-Furʿ and eat freely. [114]

3.2 *The Relations between the Zubayrīs and the Ṭālibīs*

It is reported that Khālid b. ʿUthmān b. Khālid b. al-Zubayr b. al-ʿAwwām took part in Muḥammad b. ʿAbdallāh's revolt in Medina. When al-Manṣūr heard about this he said: "What has the family of al-Zubayr to do with the family of ʿAlī? (Then) he was captured by the caliph who killed him and (then) crucified him."[115] Other traditions in this vein aim at stressing the hatred between the Zubayrīs and the Ṭālibīs.[116]

Al-Manṣūr's alleged statement about the animosity between the two families most probably reflects the general view of the Muslims in the early Islamic period. It was reported (as already noted above) that another dignitary of another Zubayrī family, Bakkār b. ʿAbdallāh [b. Muṣʿab b. Thābit b. ʿAbdallāh b. al-Zubayr], the father of the famous scholar al-Zubayr b. Bakkār, "had a violent hatred for the house of ʿAlī b. Abī Ṭālib and used to send reports to Hārūn [al-Rashīd] about them and put the worst construction on information about their doings."[117] This attested animosity between the two families is accepted by scholars. Bosworth, commenting on the above-quoted text, writes of Bakkār b. ʿAbdallāh b. Muṣʿab: "His hatred for the ʿAlids would be explicable in the light of the ancient hostility between the two Meccan leading companions ʿAlī and al-Zubayr, dating back at least to the time of the Battle of the Camel in which ʿAlī's forces killed al-Zubayr, and their descendants";[118] while Madelung, when analyzing the reports about the revolt of Yaḥyā b. ʿAbdallāh

113 The duration of Khālid b. ʿAbd al-Malik's rule: al-Ṭabarī, 2:1561, 1592: from 114/732 or 733 to 118/736 or 737; Ibn Khayyāṭ, *Taʾrīkh* (ed. al-ʿUmarī), 2:373, 378–379: from 114 until 119.

114 Al-Zubayrī, *Nasab Quraysh*, 246.

115 Al-Balādhurī, *Ansāb* (ed. ʿAbbās), 5:50–51 (ed. Zakkār, 9:440; ed. al-ʿAẓm, 8:64): خالد بن عثمان بن خالد بن الزبير، وكان خرج مع محمد بن عبد الله بن حسن بن حسن بن علي بالمدينة. فقال أبو جعفر أمير المؤمنين المنصور: ما آل الزبير وآل علي؟ وأخذه أبو جعفر فقتله وصلبه.; Ibn Ḥabīb, *al-Muḥabbar*, 486–487.

116 Al-Ṭabarī, 3:161–162.

117 Ibid., 3:616 (trans. Bosworth, *ʿAbbāsid Caliphate in Equilibrium*, 121).

118 Ibid., al-Ṭabarī (trans. Bosworth, *ʿAbbāsid Caliphate in Equilibrium*, 121 n. 461).

b. al-Ḥasan in Daylam (in 176/792), says: "But the caliph ... appointed two members of the fiercely anti-ʿAlid family of al-Zubayr as governors of Medina, first ʿAbdallāh b. Muṣʿab b. Ṭhābit (180/796–7) and then his son Bakkār (181–193/797–809)." It was Bakkār who informed the caliph that Yaḥyā was engaged in treason "and advised the caliph to recall him in order to forestall a major rebellion."[119]

3.2.1 Zubayrīs and ʿAlīds: Intermarriage

3.2.1.1 *Ḥasanī Men with Zubayrī (Asadī) Women*

1) ʿAbdallāh b. al-Ḥasan, Muḥammad al-Nafs al-Zakiyya's father, married Hind bt. Abī ʿUbayda b. ʿAbdallāh (al-Akbar) b. Zamʿa [b. al-Aswad b. Muṭṭalib b. Asad; al-Muṭṭalib being the brother of Khuwaylid, al-Zubayr b. al-ʿAwwām]. Hind's father was one of the leaders of Quraysh, highly esteemed, and also wealthy. The two families (the Ḥasanīs and the Muṭṭalibīs) lived near each other on their estates, Farsh Malal and Farsh Suwayqa (see discussion in chapter 1). The close relations between the two families are clearly demonstrated by the following evidence: Kulthum bt. Wahb [b. ʿAbd al-Raḥmān b. Wahb b. ʿAbdallāh al-Akbar b. Zamʿa b. al-Aswad b. Muṭṭalib b. Asad b. ʿAbd al-ʿUzzā b. Quṣayy] married ʿAbd al-Wahhāb b. Yaḥyā b. ʿAbbād b. ʿAbdallāh b. al-Zubayr. ʿAbd al-Wahhāb joined Muḥammad al-Nafs al-Zakiyya's revolt.[120] His wife, Kulthum, belonged to the family of Hind bt. Abī ʿUbayda b. ʿAbdallāh al-Akbar, who was, as noted, the wife of ʿAbdallāh b. al-Ḥasan and the mother of Muḥammad al-Nafs al-Zakiyya.[121]

2) ʿAbdallāh b. al-Ḥasan married another Asadī woman, who bore him Yaḥyā. She was Hind's niece, Qarība bt. Rukayḥ (ʿAbdallāh?) b. Abī ʿUbayda b. ʿAbdallāh. b. Zamʿa.[122]

3) It is noteworthy that Muḥammad al-Nafs al-Zakiyya married Fākhita bt. Fulayḥ b. Muḥammad b. al-Mundhir b. al-Zubayr b. al-ʿAwwām, who bore him one child whose name was Ṭāhir.[123]

---

119 Madelung, "Yaḥyā b. ʿAbdallāh," 11:242a–243b.

120 Al-Ṭabarī, 3:199 (ll. 12–20); 3:200 (l. 1).

121 The reconstruction of her full lineage is according to al-Zubayrī, *Nasab Quraysh*, 65.

122 Al-Balādhurī, *Ansāb* (ed. Madelung), 2:495; al-Zubayrī, *Nasab Quraysh*, 54; al-Zubayr b. Bakkār, *Jamhara*, 505–506; al-Iṣfahānī, *Maqātil*, 463: bt. ʿAbdallāh.

123 Ibn Saʿd, *al-Qism al-mutammim*, 374; al-Zubayrī, *Nasab Quraysh*, 54; al-Bukhārī, *Sirr al-silsila*, 8 (= Ibn ʿInaba, *ʿUmda*, 105–106, n. 1 [editor's note, quoting *Sirr al-asrār* of Abū Naṣr al-Bukhārī]).

4) ʿAbdallāh b. al-Zubayr married Tumāḍir bt. Manẓūr b. Sayyār b. ʿAmr al-Fazārī,[124] who bore him Khubayb, Ḥamza, ʿAbbād, and Thābit.[125] Al-Ḥasan b. ʿAlī b. Abī Ṭālib married Khawla bt. Manẓūr, the sister of Tumāḍir, who bore him al-Ḥasan [b. al-Ḥasan, ʿAbdallāh's father].[126]

Al-Ḥasan b. al-Ḥasan b. ʿAlī b. Abī Ṭālib was the cousin (on the mother's side) of Thābit, Khubayb, Ḥamza, and ʿAbbād, the sons of ʿAbdallāh b. al-Zubayr. These Zubayrīs were the second cousins of ʿAbdallāh b. al-Ḥasan, Muḥammad al-Nafs al-Zakiyya's father.

3.2.1.2 *Marriage between Zubayrī Men and Ḥasanī Women*

1) ʿAbdallāh b. al-Zubayr married Umm al-Ḥasan Nafīsa bt. al-Ḥasan b. ʿAlī b. Abī Ṭālib. This was the reason, explains the Imāmī source, Zayd b. al-Ḥasan swore allegiance to ʿAbdallāh b. al-Zubayr after al-Ḥusayn was killed: وبايع بعد قتل عمه الحسين عبد الله بن الزبير لأن أخته لامه وأبيه كانت تحت عبد الله بن الزبير.[127] Al-Balādhurī (most probably) erroneously, renders her name as Umm al-Ḥasan bt. ʿAlī b. Abī Ṭālib.[128]

2) ʿAmr b. al-Mundhir b. al-Zubayr married Umm Salama Ruqayya bt. al-Ḥasan b. ʿAlī.[129]

---

124 Al-Zubayrī, *Nasab Quraysh*, 48, 239–240; al-Balādhurī, *Ansāb* (ed. Madelung), 2:463; for the full lineage of her father, see Ibn Ḥazm, *Jamhara*, 258.

125 Al-Zubayrī, *Nasab Quraysh*, 240.

126 Al-Zubayr b. Bakkār, *Jamhara*, 83 (ibid., 35: Zujla instead of Khawla); al-Zubayrī, *Nasab Quraysh*, 46; 48: قدم [ثابت بن عبد الله بن الزبير] وهو ابن خالة الحسن بن الحسن: أمه تماضر بنت منظور, أخت خولة بنت منظور لأبيها وأمها; Ibn Ḥazm, *Jamhara*, 258; see also Ibn al-Kalbī, *Jamhara* (ed. Caskel), 1, table 130; 2:398 (Manẓūr); 345 (Khawla, the daughter). Tumāḍir is not mentioned by Ibn al-Kalbī.

127 Al-Bukhārī, *Sirr al-silsila*, 21 (= Ibn ʿInaba, *ʿUmda*, 69; al-ʿUmarī, *Ansāb*, 20); al-Zubayrī, *Nasab Quraysh*, 50; see also ibid., 112: her name was Umm al-Ḥusayn, she was married to ʿAbdallāh b. al-Zubayr and bore him Bakr and Ruqayya, but according to other sources, Bakr was born to ʿĀʾisha bt. ʿUthmān b. ʿAffān, see al-Zubayr b. Bakkār, *Jamhara*, 33; Ibn Ḥazm, *Jamhara*, 122; Nafīsa: Ibn Ḥazm, *Jamhara*, 122; Ibn ʿAsākir, *Taʾrīkh*, 11:128: Muḥammad b. al-Ḥanafiyya visits his niece, Nafīsa, who is married to ʿAbdallāh b. al-Zubayr; and cf. al-Zubayr b. Bakkār, *Jamhara*, 33–34, her name is: Umm Ḥasan Nafīsa bt. al-Ḥasan b. ʿAlī. (On Zayd b. al-Ḥasan b. ʿAlī.

128 Al-Balādhurī, *Ansāb* (ed. Madelung), 2:177.

129 Al-Zubayrī, *Nasab Quraysh*, 50; Ibn Ḥazm, *Jamhara*, 123: ʿAmr b. al-Mundhir. It is noteworthy that al-Zubayr b. Bakkār, *Jamhara*, 252–253, mentions a son of al-Mundhir named ʿUmar, who was the son of a slave woman (*umm walad*), but see the correction of the

3) Jaʿfar b. Muṣʿab b. al-Zubayr married Mulayka bt. al-Ḥasan b. al-Ḥasan b. ʿAlī b. Abī Ṭālib. She bore him one daughter and one son.[130]

3.2.3 Zubayrīs and Jaʿfarīs: Intermarriage

1) Ḥamza b. ʿAbdallāh b. al-Zubayr married Fāṭima bt. al-Qāsim b. Muḥammad b. Jaʿfar b. Abī Ṭālib. She bore him Abū Bakr and Yaḥyā.[131]

4 ʿAbbāsīs and Zubayrīs

In chapter 2, it was argued that throughout the Umawī caliphate and particularly from the reign of Hishām b. ʿAbd al-Malik (105–125/724–743), there was a slow decline in the economic and geo-political status of Medina. With the ʿAbbāsīs' rise to power, this process was accelerated by the deliberate policy of the first two ʿAbbāsī caliphs. The processes and measures taken by these two caliphs caused the deterioration of the socio-political and economic foundations of Medina. The ensuing adversity was undoubtedly one of the main reasons for the rebellion that broke out in the city. The loyal support of members of the Zubayrī family in the rebellion of Muḥammad b. ʿAbdallāh—in spite of the historical animosity between the Zubayrīs and the ʿAlīds—may testify to the frustration and resentment of the Zubayrīs against the ʿAbbāsī policy.

The sources mention eighteen members of the Zubayrī family who supported and took an active part in Muḥammad al-Nafs al-Zakiyya's revolt. Some served as his most senior commanders and held important positions in his very short caliphate. Five members of the family opposed the revolt; two other supporters were from Khālid b. Ḥizām's family. It has been shown that after the revolt, al-Manṣūr punished the inhabitants of the city severely.

---

editor, ibid., 252, n. 4; cf. Ibn Saʿd, *Ṭabaqāt*, 5:182: ʿUmar and ʿAmr are mentioned among the sons of al-Mundhir; both are the children of slave women; Umm Salama was also married to ʿUmar b. ʿAlī b. al-Ḥusayn b. ʿAlī b. Abī Ṭālib, see Ibn ʿInaba, *ʿUmda*, 68, the editor quotes al-ʿUmarī's *Ansāb*.

130 Al-Zubayrī, *Nasab Quraysh*, 53 and al-Zubayr b. Bakkār, *Jamhara*, 117: the name of the daughter is Fāṭima; al-Balādhurī, *Ansāb* (ed. ʿAbbās), 5:58: the name of the male is Ḥamza who died with his son, ʿUmāra, in the battle of Qudayd; ibid., correct Mulayla to Mulayka; Ibn Ḥazm, *Jamhara*, 42: an unnamed daughter is mentioned.

131 Al-Zubayr b. Bakkār, *Jamhara*, 60; al-Zubayrī, *Nasab Quraysh*, 82; Ibn Ḥazm, *Jamhara*, 123; al-Balādhurī, *Ansāb* (ed. al-ʿAẓm), 8:75; Ḥamza lived in al-Baṣra (ibid., 8:74) ʿĀṣim b. al-Mundhir, also lived in al-Baṣra (ibid., 8:71).

His reign is characterized by the lack of any building or development in the city.

The situation changed when al-Mahdī became caliph (r. 158–169/775–785). The change can be seen in several aspects: government investments in the city that included huge amounts of money were granted to the distinguished (mainly Qurashī) families, mostly for construction projects, the most important of which was the huge project of the renovation (extension) of the Prophet's mosque, and the removal of the economic siege on the city. We can gain much information on the subject from the work of al-Zubayr b. Bakkār, who informs us of the special favorable attitude of Caliph al-Mahdī towards the notables of Medina. This author also provides important information pertaining to the reigns of al-Hādī (r. 169–170/785–786) and Hārūn al-Rashīd (r. 170–193/786–809), who bestowed great sums of money on the people of Medina, especially on Banū Quraysh. The (only published) volume of al-Zubayr b. Bakkār deals with the Zubayrī family. The picture that emerges from this work is of a large family, whose members were very wealthy, many of whom were well-known scholars (*muḥaddithūn, fuqahāʾ*, and *qāḍīs*) who were also deeply involved in ʿAbbāsī affairs in Medina and elsewhere. This information sheds significant light on the superior position of the Quraysh and its important families during the early history of Islam.

4.1 *The Position and Roles of Members of the Zubayrī Family in the Early ʿAbbāsī State*

Evidence provided by al-Zubayr b. Bakkār [b. ʿAbdallāh b. Muṣʿab], but also by the latter's uncle, Muṣʿab b. ʿAbdallāh b. Muṣʿab, shows that several members of the Zubayrī family gained highly esteemed positions in the ʿAbbāsī court, mostly from al-Mahdī's reign on. But we should also remember that several distinguished members of the family of ʿUrwa b. al-Zubayr had already gained high positions in al-Manṣūr's court. It was noted above that Hishām b. ʿUrwa (d. 145 or 146/762 or 763) was among the *ṣaḥāba* of al-Manṣūr.[132] His grandson, Muḥammad b. ʿUrwa b. Hishām b. ʿUrwa b. al-Zubayr, also gained the favor of al-Manṣūr. He is mentioned once by al-Ṭabarī as a transmitter who described the execution of another Zubayrī, ʿUthmān b. Muḥammad b. Khālid b. al-Zubayr in al-Manṣūr's court.[133] He carried out some administrative posts for al-Ḥasan b. Zayd b. al-Ḥasan b. ʿAlī b. Abī Ṭālib, the governor of Medina, on

132 See for example, al-Zubayrī, *Nasab Quraysh*, 248.

133 Al-Ṭabarī, 3:262 (ll. 10–17).

behalf of Caliph al-Manṣūr from 149/767 until 155/772,[134] and later was one of the close associates of al-Mahdī. Hārūn al-Rashīd appointed him as the overseer of the *zanādiqa*.[135]

As for al-Mahdī's period, the family of ʿAbdallāh b. al-Zubayr gained a particularly favored position, as did other Zubayrī families, e.g., the family of ʿUrwa b. al-Zubayr.

4.1.1 Members of the Family of ʿAbdallāh b. al-Zubayr

1) ʿAbdallāh b. Muṣʿab b. Thābit b. ʿAbdallāh b. al-Zubayr: ʿAbdallāh b. Muṣʿab, like his father, supported the revolt but was pardoned by al-Manṣūr. He gained a high position in the caliphate of al-Mahdī and al-Rashīd (see above).

2) His son, Bakkār, served as the governor of Medina for more than twelve years during al-Rashīd's reign (see the discussion above).

Special relations between other families of ʿAbdallāh b. al-Zubayr and the ʿAbbāsī caliph are further noted by al-Zubayr b. Bakkār, who reports that while visiting Medina, Caliph al-Mahdī honored

3) Yaḥyā b. al-Zubayr b. ʿAbbād b. Ḥamza b. ʿAbdallāh b. al-Zubayr, who was called the elder [the most distinguished?: شيخ] and the person who was in charge of the collection of the Zubayrī family's *ṣadaqa*.[136]

4) Another distinguished Zubayrī was ʿAbd al-Malik b. Yaḥyā b. ʿAbbād b. ʿAbdallāh b. al-Zubayr. When Caliph al-Mahdī wrote to the people of Medina and requested that they send him a notable person from among them to represent them at court and take care of their interests, they chose ʿAbd al-Malik b. Yaḥyā, who stayed in Baghdad in the caliph's court. He is described as a very rich man, who was in charge of collecting the *ṣadaqa* of (the family of) al-Zubayr and that of ʿAbbād (his grandfather).[137] He sold al-Mahdī's *wazīr*, Abū

---

134 Al-Zubayr b. Bakkār, *Jamhara*, 297 [= al-Khaṭīb al-Baghdādī, *Taʾrīkh* (Beirut 1997), 3:354]; administrative posts: وكان قد ولي قبل مصيره مع أمير المؤمنين المهدي للحسن بن زيد غير مرة; the governorship of al-Ḥasan b. Zayd: Ibn Khayyāṭ, *Taʾrīkh* (ed. al-ʿUmarī), 2:466: year 149 H.; al-Ṭabarī, 3:358, 377: years 150–155 H.; al-Azdī, *Taʾrīkh al-Mawṣil* (Cairo edition), 211: year 150 H.; on al-Ḥasan b. Zayd, see McAuliffe, *ʿAbbāsid Authority*, 87, n. 410.

135 Al-Zubayr b. Bakkār, *Jamhara*, 296–297 (= al-Khaṭīb al-Baghdādī, *Taʾrīkh* [Beirut 1997], 3:354); overseer of the *zanādiqa*: فاستعمله على الزنادقة.

136 Al-Zubayr b. Bakkār, *Jamhara*, 69: شيخ آل الزبير و والي صدقتهم.

137 Ibid., 76; part of the tradition of al-Zubayr b. Bakkār was copied by al-Khaṭīb al-Baghdādī, *Taʾrīkh* (Beirut, 1997), 10:407–408.

ʿUbaydallāh, an estate with water installations [?: *ʿayn*] called Malaḥ in (*wādī*) Sāya for 10,000 *dīnārs*.[138] He owned another spring/estate (*ʿayn*) called ʿAyn al-Riḍā.[139]

---

138 Al-Zubayr b. Bakkār, *Jamhara*, 76–77; 76: *bi-Sāya*; al-Khaṭīb al-Baghdādī, *Taʾrīkh* (Beirut, 1997) 10:407: Sibāba; Sāya belonged to the region of Medina, see al-Bakrī, *Muʿjam*, 3:1021 ("al-Furʿ"): its taxes were collected by the ruler of al-Furʿ (that is, in respect to its administration, it belonged to al-Furʿ); ibid., 811 ("Shamanṣīr"): quoting Ibn al-Aʿrābī [Muḥammad b. Ziyād Abū ʿUbaydallāh, 150–231/767 or 768–845 or 846; on him, see al-Ziriklī, *al-Aʿlām*, 6:131]: "Sāya is a vast *wādī* in which there are more than 70 springs that flow in canals: أكثر من سبعين عينا نهرا تجري, the Muzayna and Sulaym dwell there"; the somehow unequivocal text becomes clear in light of another paragraph in al-Bakrī's work, this time quoting Abū ʿUbaydallāh, ʿAmr b. Bishr al-Sakūnī [who was active in the mid second/eighth century], 3:787 ("Sharāʾ"): "[Sāya] is a *wādī* situated among two great and wide masses of stones, which are two black lava areas in which there are many villages; its inhabitants are a mixture of people of unknown origin; its water are springs that flow under the earth; they are all *fuqur*. *Al-fuqur* is a subterranean canal; the single form is *faqīr*. The ruler of Sāya is under the jurisdiction of the governor of Medina. In it there are palm groves and planted fields, banana plantations and vineyards. It is the source of wealth for [or it is the principle place of abode of: أصلها] the descendants of ʿAlī b. Abī Ṭālib": وهو واد بين حاميتين هما حرّتان سوداوان به قرى كثيرة, سكانها من أفناء الناس, ومياهها عيون تجري تحت الأرض, فقر كلها. والفقر: القُنِيّ تحت الأرض واحدها فقير. و والي ساية من قبل صاحب المدينة. وفيها نخل ومزارع وموز وعنب, أصلها لولد علي بن أبي طالب. In the introduction to his work, al-Bakrī states that "most of the material of this book [of mine] is taken from al-Sakūnī, that is the book of Abū ʿUbaydallāh, ʿAmr b. Bishr al-Sakūnī, in his book *Jibāl Tihāma wa-maḥālluhā*; (al-Sakūnī himself) took all of this material from Abū l-Ashʿath ʿAbd al-Raḥmān b. Muḥammad b. ʿAbd al-Malik al-Kindī, who (took it) from ʿArrām b. al-Aṣbagh al-Sulamī l-Aʿrābī" (d. ca. 150/767 or 768); al-Fīrūzābādī, *al-Maghānim al-muṭāba*, 175–176 (copied by al-Samhūdī, *Wafāʾ*, 4:315), indeed tells us that he took his material from Ibn ʿArrām, adding pomegranate groves to the list of the agricultural crops, and also that the inhabitants of unknown origin were merchants from every area (وتجار من كل بلد). It is noteworthy that ʿArrām's published text is different from al-Bakrī's. Al-Bakrī leads us to believe that all along the *wādī* of Sāya there were subterranean canals, while ʿArrām relates that "in the upper part of Sāya there is a village named al-Fāriʿ which has many palm groves and its inhabitants are all of unknown origin, and its waters are *ʿuyūn*, that flow under the ground, all are *fuqur*. And the *fuqur* and the canal are the same: والفقر والقنا واحد, and the single form of *al-fuqur* is *faqīr*" (Ibn al-Aṣbagh, *Jibāl Tihāma*, 413).

139 Al-Zubayr b. Bakkār, *Jamhara*, 77–78.

4.1.2 The Family of ʿUrwa b. al-Zubayr

1) Muṣʿab b. ʿUthmān b. Muṣʿab b. ʿUrwa b. al-Zubayr was a *muḥaddith*[140] in charge of the collection of the *ṣadaqa/zakāt* taxes for Abū Bakr [Bakkār] b. ʿAbdallāh [b. Muṣʿab b. Thābit b. ʿAbdallāh b. al-Zubayr].[141]

2) ʿUthmān b. al-Mundhir b. Muṣʿab b. ʿUrwa b. al-Zubayr was in charge of the *shuraṭ* of Medina on behalf of Dāwūd b. ʿĪsā b. Mūsā [b. Muḥammad b. ʿAlī b. ʿAbdallāh b. al-ʿAbbās]; he was also in charge of the collection of the *ṣadaqa/zakāt* taxes for Abū Bakr (Bakkār) b. ʿAbdallāh [b. Muṣʿab b. Thābit b. ʿAbdallāh b. al-Zubayr][142] (on Bakkār, see above).

4.2 *Marriage and Relations between the Zubayrīs and the ʿAbbāsīs*

The noble status of the Zubayrīs made their daughters highly desirable brides among the noble families of Quraysh; the most distinguished among these families were the Banū Hāshim: the Ṭālibīs and the ʿAbbāsīs. The old principle of *kufʾ* (plural: *akfāʾ*) was still important in this period.[143]

1) Muḥammad b. Abī l-ʿAbbās al-Saffāḥ was married to Zaynab bt. Muḥammad al-Nafs al-Zakiyya. The marriage was initiated by the caliph,[144] that is, not later than 132/754 (the year of the caliph's death), at least eight years before the outbreak of the revolt. This may have been an important political marriage, part of the policy of reconciliation on the part of the caliph towards the Ḥasanīs, whose leader was ʿAbdallāh b. al-Ḥasan, Muḥammad's father.

2) Al-Zubayr b. Bakkār records a personal communication related to him from the ʿAbbāsī Muḥammad b. Dāwūd b. ʿĪsā [b. Mūsā b. Muḥammad b. ʿAlī b. ʿAbdallāh b. al-ʿAbbās] about the latter's father, Dāwūd b. ʿĪsā, who was married to the Zubayrī woman, Asmāʾ bt. Abī Bakr b. ʿAbdallāh b. Ṣāliḥ b. ʿAbdallāh b. al-Zubayr. After she died, he married another woman from the same family, this time Umm Ḥasan bt. ʿAbd al-Malik b. Yaḥyā [b. ʿAbbād b. ʿAbdallāh b. al-Zubayr]. The ceremony was held in Medina and was conducted by Caliph al-Mahdī himself.[145]

---

140 Ibn Ḥazm, *Jamhara*, 124.

141 Al-Zubayr b. Bakkār, *Jamhara*, 298.

142 Al-Zubayr b. Bakkār, *Jamhara*, 298.

143 Ibid., 78–79; the term *kufʾ* is not mentioned in the text, though; on this term, see Goldziher, *Muslim Studies*, 1:123–124; Elad, "Transition," 103, n. 59, but especially the important discussion by Bernheimer, *The ʿAlids*, 32–33, 44–47.

144 Al-Balādhurī, *Ansāb* (ed. Madelung), 2:517.

145 Al-Zubayr b. Bakkār, *Jamhara*, 78–79; Dāwūd b. ʿĪsā b. Mūsā appears as a distinguished ʿAbbāsī, during the reigns of Hārūn al-Rashīd, al-Amīn, and al-Maʾmūn; for example, see al-Ṭabarī, 3:709: a commander in al-Rashīd's campaign against Byzantium; in 193/808 or

3) When Banū Sulaymān b. ʿAlī b. ʿAbdallāh b. al-ʿAbbās heard that Muṣʿab b. Thābit b. ʿAbdallāh b. al-Zubayr arrived in al-Baṣra, they came to him and asked for his daughters Khadīja and Asmāʾ as brides for members of their ʿAbbāsī family.[146] Khadīja's and Asmāʾ's mother was Fāṭima bt. Jaʿfar b. Muṣʿab b. al-Zubayr; her mother was Mulayka bt. al-Ḥasan b. al-Ḥasan b. ʿAlī b. Abī Ṭālib, that is, the sister of ʿAbdallāh b. al-Ḥasan, Muḥammad al-Nafs al-Zakiyya's father.[147]

5 Transmissions of the Zubayrīs

Some of the traditions about the family members taking part in the battles were transmitted by members of the Zubayrī family to ʿUmar b. Shabba.[148] Some of these transmitters were supported by evidence from other Zubayrī family members who lived during the revolt. The old Arab tradition of relating the heroic stories of members of one's tribe continued in this period as well. One example is Ibrāhīm b. Muṣʿab b. ʿUmāra b. Ḥamza b. Muṣʿab b. al-Zubayr.

He appears several times in al-Ṭabarī and in al-Iṣfahānī's *Maqātil*. In several of the traditions his direct transmitters were members of the Zubayrī family relating the events of the revolt of al-Nafs al-Zakiyya.[149]

Other well-known scholars of the Zubayrī family, such as al-Zubayr b. Bakkār, recorded many traditions that deal with the events of the revolt. As

---

809 he was the governor of Mecca (al-Ṭabarī, 3:937) and stood at the head of the *ḥajj* pilgrimage of that year (al-Ṭabarī, 3:775; Ibn Khayyāṭ, *Taʾrīkh* [ed. al-ʿUmarī], 2:502); in 195/810 or 811 he was appointed the governor of Medina by al-Amīn (al-Ṭabarī, 3:832); his appointment was confirmed by Ṭāhir b. al-Ḥusayn on behalf of al-Maʾmūn in 196 H. (ibid. 3:857; and see also about him, ibid., 3:860–864); Ibn Ḥabīb, *al-Muḥabbar*, 39; al-Yaʿqūbī, *Taʾrīkh* (Beirut edition), 2:442; Ibn ʿAsākir, *Taʾrīkh*, 17:174.

146 Al-Zubayr b. Bakkār, *Jamhara*, 117; Ahmed, *Religious Elite*, 153.

147 Ibid.

148 E.g., al-Ṭabarī, 3:233 (ll. 7–11) (= al-Iṣfahānī, *Maqātil*, 268: from al-Madāʾinī, a short summary of the long, colorful tradition in al-Ṭabarī) about the single attack of Ibrāhīm b. Jaʿfar b. Muṣʿab al-Zubayrī on ʿĪsā's troops. For other examples, see al-Ṭabarī, 3:245 (ll. 5–16).

149 E.g., al-Ṭabarī, 3:237 (ll. 11–12): [ʿUmar b. Shabba] < Ibrāhīm b. Muṣʿab b. ʿUmāra b. Ḥamza b. Muṣʿab b. al-Zubayr < Muḥammad b. ʿUthmān b. Muḥammad b. Khālid b. al-Zubayr; 255 (l. 3f.): one of several transmitters of ʿUmar b. Shabba who recited to the latter an elegy for Muḥammad b. ʿAbdallāh by the Zubayrī ʿAbdallāh b. Muṣʿab b. Thābit b. ʿAbdallāh b. al-Zubayr; 260 (ll. 6–12): from al-Zubayr b. Khubayb b. Thābit b. ʿAbdallāh b. al-Zubayr; on Ibrāhīm b. Muṣʿab b. ʿUmāra.

for al-Zubayr b. Bakkār, his contribution to the transmission of early Arabic poetry and genealogy is tremendous. A special part of his contribution came in the form of traditions about Hind's father and the Ḥasanī family through Sulaymān b. ʿAyyāsh al-Saʿdī. He also recorded traditions relating to the revolt from his uncle, Muṣʿab b. ʿAbdallāh al-Zubayrī.[150]

150 E.g., al-Balādhurī, *Ansāb* (ed. Madelung), 2:460, 524.

CHAPTER 9

The Tribal Support for/Opposition to Muḥammad b. ʿAbdallāh

ʿUmar b. Shabba < Muḥammad b. Ismāʿīl b. Jaʿfar < someone close whom he trusted related: At the time of the uprising, the people of Medina and its environs as well as certain Arab tribes: أهل المدينة وأعراضها وقبائل من العرب, among them Juhayna, Muzayna, Sulaym, Banū Bakr, Aslam, and Ghifār, responded to Muḥammad, but he gave precedence to Juhayna, which angered the Qaysī tribes.[1]

According to another tradition, those who joined Muḥammad were a (tribal) group from Juhayna and others beside them, of unknown origin: من أفناء العرب, and many people of *ahl al-Madīna* from Quraysh and others besides them, and bedouins from the districts belonging to the jurisdiction of Medina and those who joined them: ومن الأعراض من الأعراب ومن ضوى إليهم.[2] However, there is no evidence that the above-mentioned tribes fought alongside Muḥammad as coherent units. The only evidence is of the Banū Shujāʿ from Juhayna, who fought with him till the end.[3]

1 The Anṣār

We lack specific evidence about the participation of large units (families) of the Anṣār in the rebellion. The Anṣār are not mentioned during the campaign with ʿĪsā b. Mūsā. According to an interesting tradition, when the Ḥasanīs were carried in chains to al-Rabadha, Jaʿfar al-Ṣādiq cursed the Anṣār who do not help the sons of the Prophet and protect them as they committed to do at the ʿAqaba meeting in the Prophet's presence.[4] The aim of the tradition is to present Jaʿfar al-Ṣādiq in a positive light, but it probably reflects the real situation

1 Al-Ṭabarī, 3:228 (ll. 7–11) (trans. McAuliffe, *ʿAbbāsid Authority*, 191).

2 Ibn Saʿd, *al-Qism al-mutammim*, 375; for *aʿrāḍ* Medina, see Lecker, *Banū Sulaym*, 105, n. 30 and 225, n. 27.

3 Ibn Saʿd, *al-Qism al-mutammim*, 377: from al-Wāqidī [= al-Ṭabarī, 3:240 (ll. 9–14)].

4 Al-Iṣfahānī, *Maqātil*, 220.

 | DOI 10.1163/9789004296220_011

in which the Anṣār, as a collective entity (if it existed at all), did not actively support Muḥammad b. ʿAbdallāh.

Supporters of the Revolt

1.1 *Banū Aws*

1) Khawwāt b. Bukayr b. Khawwāt b. Jubayr b. al-Nuʿmān [b. Umayya b. al-Burak b. Imruʾ al-Qays b. Thaʿlaba b. ʿAmr b. Mālik b. al-Aws]

He was in charge of the infantry corps of Muḥammad al-Nafs al-Zakiyya when the latter entered Medina,[5] and is termed "the leader" (*sayyid*) of the Anṣār.[6] He belonged to a well-known family of the Anṣār (from Banū Aws). His grandfather was a poet, and a *sayyid* in the Jāhiliyya, and one of the dignified *ṣaḥāba* of the Prophet.[7] The brother of his grandfather, ʿAbdallāh b. Jubayr, was listed among those who attended the famous ʿAqaba meeting with the Prophet and later he was in charge of Muḥammad's archers in the battle of Uḥud.[8] Khawwāt b. Jubayr fought in the battle of Ṣiffīn at ʿAlī's side.[9] Perhaps this explains the pro-Ṭālibī bias of Khawwāt b. Bukayr.

Allies of the Aws

2) ʿAbd al-Ḥamīd b. Jaʿfar b. ʿAbdallāh b. [Abī] al-Ḥakam b. Rāfiʿ b. Sinān al-Awsī l-Anṣārī Abū l-Faḍl or Abū Ḥafṣ

He was a *muḥaddith* who died in 153/770. According to one version in the *nasab* books, his forefathers originally belonged to al-Ḥārith b. ʿAmr b. Muzayqāʾ of the Azd, who are described in these sources as "the leading family (within their extended family) in Medina (living) together with the Anṣār."[10] Ibn Saʿd adds

---

5 Al-Ṭabarī, 3:193 (ll. 12–13).

6 Al-Ṭabarī, 3:201 (l. 19).

7 His lineage: Ibn Ḥazm, *Jamhara*, 336; 337: one of the loyal supporters of (*min aṣḥāb*) Muḥammad; Ibn al-Kalbī, *Jamhara* (ed. Caskel), 2:346; 1, table 177 (ed. al-Ḥasan, 631); idem, *Nasab Maʿadd*, 2:373: biography of Khawwāt the grandfather; his grandson is not mentioned; on Khawwāt b. Jubayr, see Ibn Ḥibbān, *al-Thiqāt*, 3:109; Ibn Ḥajar, *Tahdhīb* (Beirut, 1984), 3:147; al-Dhahabī, *Siyar*, 2:329–330; al-Mizzī, *Tahdhīb*, 8:347–350, and the comprehensive bibliography of the editor therein.

8 Al-Dhahabī, *Siyar*, 2:330.

9 Ibn Ḥajar, *Tahdhīb* (Beirut, 1984), 3:147; al-Mizzī, *Tahdhīb*, 8:348.

10 Ibn a-Kalbī, *Jamhara* (ed. Ḥasan), 619; idem, *Nasab Maʿadd*, 1:438; Ibn Ḥazm, *Jamhara*, 373: وهم أهل بيت بالمدينة مع الأنصار; Ibn al-Kalbī, *Jamhara* (ed. Caskel), 1:195; see also table 196: their relations to the Aws and the Khazraj; 2:124 (mentioned by McAuliffe, *ʿAbbāsid Authority*, 144, n. 674); Ibn al-Kalbī, *Nasab Maʿadd*, 1:436–438 (ʿAbd al-Ḥamīd is not

that "it is said that he is of the descendants of al-Fiṭyawn, who are the allies (*ḥulafāʾ*) of the Aws."[11] But he is mostly described (in the biographical dictionaries) as belonging to the Aws.[12]

He supported Muḥammad b. ʿAbdallāh's revolt, took an active part in the uprising, and was appointed by the latter for a short time as the head of the *shurṭa and* carried the *ḥarba* (a short spear) in front of the latter as part of the duties of the *ṣāḥib al-shurṭa*.[13]

3) **His son, Saʿd b. ʿAbd al-Ḥamīd** (d. 219/834 or 835) was a direct transmitter of ʿUmar b. Shabba (on him, see appendix 2).

1.2 *Banū l-Khazraj*

1) Banū Salima [b. Saʿd b. ʿAlī b. Asad b. Sārida b. Tazīd b. Jusham b. al-Khazraj].[14]

Supporters of the Revolt

Banū Salima were the supporters of Muḥammad b. ʿAbdallāh. Before the armed rebellion he hid his weapons in their territory. On the eve of the armed rebellion he stayed among Banū Salima of the Anṣār, where his followers and adherents (*aṣḥābuhu*) gathered around him, and from there he chose to advance with his followers [to the center of the city].

---

mentioned); al-Ṭabarī, 3:200 (ll. 3–4): his son is called "the brother of the Anṣār"; al-Ḥārith b. ʿAmr b. ʿĀmir, says Ibn al-Kalbī, *Nasab Maʿadd*, 1:436, begot ʿAdī, ʿAmr, Sawāda, and Rifāʿa.

11 Ibn Saʿd, *al-Qism al-mutammim*, 400; Fiṭyawn was the ancient Arab-Jewish king in Yathrib, who applied the *ius primae noctis* over the Aws and the Khazraj women, see W. M. Watt, "al-Madīna," *EI*²; Lecker, *Muḥammad and the Jews*, 42ff.

12 On him, see McAuliffe, *ʿAbbāsid Authority*, 144, n. 674; Ibn Abī Ḥātim, *al-Jarḥ* (Hyderabad edition), 3/1:10; al-Dhahabī, *Mīzān*, 2:539; al-Dhahabī, *Siyar*, 7:20–22; Ibn Ḥajar, *Tahdhīb* (Hyderabad edition), 6:111; Ibn Ḥajar, *al-Iṣāba* (Beirut, 1415 H.), 2:365; al-Ṣafadī, *al-Wāfī*, 18:70; al-Mizzī, *Tahdhīb*, 16:416–420 and the comprehensive bibliography therein (including Ibn Saʿd, *al-Qism al-mutammim*, 400); van Ess, *Theologie*, 2:678; a certain ʿAbd al-Ḥamīd who was one of the eunuchs of Abū l-ʿAbbās (al-Saffāḥ the Caliph?: حدثني عبد الحميد وكان من خدم أبي العباس) is mentioned by al-Ṭabarī, 3:292, but this is most probably not the same person; cf. McAuliffe, *ʿAbbāsid Authority*, 144, n. 674: "Ṭabarī later identifies him as a servant to Abū l-ʿAbbās."

13 Al-Ṭabarī, 3:193 (ll. 13–15): carrying the *ḥarba*; ibid., 3:199 (ll. 3–6): head of the *shurṭa*; on the connection between the *ḥarba* and the *shurṭa*, see Crone, *Slaves*, 248, n. 474.

14 For this *nasab*, see Ibn Ḥazm, *Jamhara*, 358; Ibn al-Kalbī (ed. Caskel), 1, table 190.

Opposition to the Revolt/ʿAbbāsī Supporters

2) ʿAbd al-ʿAzīz b. Saʿīd [b. Saʿd b. ʿUbāda b. Dulaym b. Ḥāritha b. Abī Khuzayma b. Thaʿlaba b. Ṭarīf b. al-Khazraj ?]

He is described by al-Ṭabarī through the transmission of ʿĪsā b. ʿAbdallāh from ʿAbdallāh b. ʿImrān b. Abī Farwa as a spy (*ʿayn*) of al-Manṣūr in Medina who was in charge of the collection of the voluntary alms (*ṣadaqāt*). He induced al-Manṣūr to imprison the Ḥasanī family. Then the caliph summoned him and asked him who suggested this idea to him; ʿAbd al-ʿAzīz answered that it was Fulayḥ b. Sulaymān.[15]

ʿAbd al-ʿAzīz b. Saʿīd may be identified as the grandson of Saʿd b. ʿUbāda, the well-known leader of the Khazraj at the time of the Prophet.[16] ʿAbd al-ʿAzīz was a minor transmitter of *ḥadīth*, and his biographies in the *rijāl* books do not add any historical information about him beyond what is given by al-Ṭabarī.[17] It is highly plausible that he was already mentioned in 141/758–759 during the governorship of Ziyād b. ʿUbaydallāh over Medina, fulfilling his task as "a secret agent" (*ʿayn*) of the caliph in Medina, informing al-Manṣūr (in writing) about the Shīʿī sympathies of the governor's secretary.[18]

2 Banū Juhayna (… b. al-Ḥāfī b. Quḍāʿa)[19]

Supporters of the Revolt

Banū Juhayna dwelled in Yanbuʿ and its close surroundings during ʿAlī b. Abī Ṭālib's reign.[20] ʿArrām b. al-Aṣbagh al-Sulamī (d. ca. 275/888) relates that Banū

15 Al-Ṭabarī, 3:169 (ll. 5–12).

16 On him, see, for example, Ibn Ḥajar, *Tahdhīb* (Beirut, 1984), 3:412; al-Mizzī, *Tahdhīb*, 10:277–281; M. Watt, "Saʿd b. ʿUbāda," *EI*².

17 There are very few biographies of him, for example, see Ibn Ḥibbān, *al-Thiqāt*, 5:125; Ibn Ḥajar, *al-Iṣāba* (ed. al-Bijāwī), 5:248; as a link in the *isnād*: Ibn ʿAdī, *Ḍuʿafāʾ*, 5:329; al-Ṭūsī, *al-Amālī*, 475 [= al-Majlisī, *Biḥār*, 22:243]; Ibn ʿAsākir, *Taʾrīkh*, 49:427 and 428; Ibn al-Jawzī, *Ṣafwa*, 1:505; Ibn Ḥajar, *Lisān*, 4:43.

18 Al-Ṭabarī, 3:147–148 (l. 18 to l. 2); the name of the spy is ʿAbd al-ʿAzīz b. Saʿd, corrected by de Goeje, in al-Ṭabarī's *Addenda et Emendanda*, dccxxxi, to ʿAbdallāh [this is a typographical error, read ʿAbd al-ʿAzīz] b. Saʿīd; and indeed the name should be rendered ʿAbd al-ʿAzīz b. Saʿīd, basing the reading on the two times this name appears on 169 (ll. 5, 10–11), and in Ibn al-Athīr, *al-Kāmil* (ed. Tornberg), 5:398; McAuliffe, *ʿAbbāsid Authority*, 91, n. 432: ʿAbdallāh b. Saʿīd.

19 On Juhayna (b. Zayd b. Layth b. Sūd b. Aslum b. al-Ḥāfī b. Quḍāʿa), see Kister, "Ḳuḍāʿa," 5:315a–317a; Ibn al-Kalbī (ed. Caskel), 1, no. 332; 2:264.

20 Al-Samhūdī, *Wafāʾ*, 4:526 (entry Yanbuʿ).

l-Ḥasan b. ʿAlī own Yanbuʿ; al-Anṣār, Juhayna, and (Banū) Layth used to dwell there.[21] Jabal Juhayna belonged to Yanbuʿ district (عمل ينبع).[22]

Several traditions record that Muḥammad b. ʿAbdallāh hid from al-Manṣūr and the governors of Medina in Jabal Juhayna.[23] Some Arabs of Juhayna are mentioned together with Muḥammad b. ʿAbdallāh, hiding in Jabal Juhayna.[24]

The fact that Banū Juhayna supported Muḥammad did not escape al-Manṣūr. In 144 H., together with the Ḥasanīs who were brought to him as prisoners to al-Rabadha, there were also 400[!?] prisoners from Juhayna, Muzayna, and other tribes as well. This is related by ʿAbd al-Raḥmān b. Abī l-Mawālī, who was taken prisoner together with the Ḥasanīs.[25]

The Qaysī tribes were angered by Muḥammad b. ʿAbdallāh's preference of Juhayna, as mentioned above.[26] The sources tell of Juhanīs in the presence of Muḥammad b. ʿAbdallāh; it was a Juhanī who advised him to dig the *khandaq*, against the advice of a Sulamī,[27] and it is related that the governor of al-Ṭāʾif appointed on behalf of Muḥammad b. ʿAbdallāh, Abū ʿAdī l-ʿAblī, took control of the city with the help of Arabs from Juhayna, Muzayna, and Aslam.[28]

But more important is the fact that the most loyal group of supporters who stood at his side and fought with him until they all died were from Juhayna. They fought in the wing that confronted the ʿAbbāsī forces under the command of Muḥammad b. Abī l-ʿAbbās and ʿUqba b. Salm.[29] It is possible that more Arabs of the Juhayna tribe joined him at the first stages of the campaign, but left him at some later stage.[30] The last stages of the campaign are depicted by the sources in a very precise manner: in this last stage a group of Banū Juhayna called Banū Shujāʿ stayed with Muḥammad, who fought until all

21 Yāqūt, *Muʿjam* (Beirut edition), 5:450: quoting ʿArrām b. al-Aṣbagh; al-Samhūdī, *Wafāʾ*, 4:525 and al-Fīrūzābādī, *al-Maghānim al-muṭāba*, 440: quoting ʿArrām (or Yāqūt) without acknowledging it.

22 Al-Ṭabarī, 3:167 (l. 2).

23 Ibid., 3:156–158, 167; al-Balādhurī, *Ansāb* (ed. Madelung), 2:502.

24 Al-Ṭabarī, 3:157.

25 Ibn Saʿd, *al-Qism al-mutammim*, 255.

26 Al-Ṭabarī, 3:228; Juhayna belongs to the Quḍāʿa confederation of Qaysī origin, whose *nasab* was changed by order of Muʿāwiya b. Abī Sufyān (d. 680), see Kister, "Ḳuḍāʿa," 5:315a.

27 Al-Ṭabarī, 3:228.

28 Al-Iṣfahānī, *al-Aghānī* (Būlāq edition), 10:107.

29 Al-Balādhurī, *Ansāb* (ed. Madelung), 2:514.

30 Al-Ṭabarī, 3:244 (ll. 3–7).

of them were killed.[31] At the last moment they hamstrung their riding beasts and broke the scabbards of their swords.[32] After the battle their heads were carried to the caliph.[33]

Two *Mawālī* of Juhayna are mentioned as the supporters of Muḥammad b. ʿAbdallāh.

The first is the well-known scholar, **ʿAbd al-ʿAzīz b. Muḥammad b. ʿUbayd al-Darāwardī *mawlā* Juhayna/Quḍāʿa**, one of the most important supporters of Muḥammad b. ʿAbdallāh, who was in charge of the arsenal (*ʿalā l-silāḥ*).

The second was **Isḥāq b. Ibrāhīm b. Dīnār.**[34]

3 Banū Muzayna (… b. al-Yās b. Muḍar)[35]

Muzayna is mentioned among the tribes that supported Muḥammad b. ʿAbdallāh.[36]

The support of the members of this tribe for Muḥammad and his cause was substantial. Four hundred men from Juhayna, Muzayna, and other tribes (not mentioned by name), were carried with the chained Ḥasanīs to al-Rabadha, where al-Manṣur encamped in the year 144 H.[37] After the revolt broke out, during the very short caliphate of Muḥammad, the latter sent a governor to al-Ṭāʾif with tribal men [soldiers ?] from Muzayna, Juhayna, and Aslam.[38]

Contrary to Juhayna, on which we have more information, especially details of their participation in the revolt and in the last battle, the sources mention only some individuals of Muzayna who supported Muḥammad b. ʿAbdallāh before the revolt, e.g., messengers sent to his hiding place,[39] a confidential

31 Ibid., 3:240 (ll. 9–14); Ibn Saʿd, *al-Qism al-mutammim*, 377: a parallel tradition from al-Wāqidī.

32 Al-Ṭabarī, 3:242 (ll. 16–17); al-Dhahabī, *Siyar*, 7:218.

33 Al-Ṭabarī, 3:254–255 (l. 20 to l. 3).

34 Al-Iṣfahānī, *Maqātil*, 286; nothing is known about him.

35 On Muzayna (b. Udd b. Ṭābikha b. al-Yās b. Muḍar b. Nizār b. Maʿadd b. ʿAdnān), see Donner, "Muzayna," 7:824a–825a.

36 Al-Ṭabarī, 3:228; al-Balādhurī, *Ansāb* (ed. Madelung), 2:509; for the location of their dwellings in Medina, see al-Samhūdī, *Wafāʾ*, 3:99–101.

37 Al-Ṭabarī, 3:187 (ll. 17–19): an eyewitness testimony of ʿAbd al-Raḥmān b. Abī l-Mawālī, who was among those who were taken to al-Rabadha.

38 Al-Iṣfahānī, *al-Aghānī* (Būlāq edition), 10:107.

39 Al-Balādhurī, *Ansāb* (ed. Madelung), 2:502; except for the messenger, 100 additional men of Muzayna are mentioned, but it is not stated explicitly that they were supporters of Muḥammad.

adviser,[40] or an escort to al-Baṣra, where Muḥammad called the people to his cause.[41]

1) Abū Habbār al-Muzanī

The person who accompanied Muḥammad b. ʿAbdallāh to al-Baṣra was Abū Habbār al-Muzanī, a close associate of his who undertook some very confidential and dangerous missions for him. According to one piece of evidence, when the revolt was crushed he fled with Mūsā b. ʿAbdallāh, al-Nafs al-Zakiyya's brother, and ʿUthmān b. Muḥammad b. Khālid b. al-Zubayr to al-Baṣra. These last two were caught and brought to the caliph. The transmitter, the latter's son, does not tell us what happened to Abū Habbār. If he was caught he was most probably executed.[42]

As noted above, we do not have any testimonial evidence that Muzayna fought as a homogeneous tribal unit at Muḥammad's side, and there is no testimony as to their fate after the revolt and Muḥammad's death, except for one piece of evidence pertaining to the above-mentioned Abū Habbār (see above).

4 Banū Sulaym (... b. Qays ʿAylān b. Muḍar)[43]

Regrettably we lack even an initial history of those clans of Banū Sulaym who remained in Arabia after the conquest. It seems that the tribal leaders of Banū Sulaym supported Muḥammad b. ʿAbdallāh, at least at the beginning of his revolt, before the ʿAbbāsī army entered Medina. We learn this from an

40 Al-Ṭabarī, 3:157–158.

41 Ibid., 3:148.

42 Al-Ṭabarī, 3:260–262 (l. 18 to l. 10); on him see, ibid., 3:148 (ll. 7–9) (MS A: al-Murrī): relating in the first person about his stay in al-Baṣra with Muḥammad b. ʿAbdallāh; ibid., 3:153–154 (l. 18 to l. 14): relating in the first person a long tradition that, in 140 H., ʿAbdallāh b. al-Ḥasan (Muḥammad's father) sent a pro-Shīʿī conspiring commander of al-Manṣūr with his slave to Khurāsān. And see ibid., 3:156–158 (l. 15 to l. 5): the *isnād* is as follows: ʿUmar b. Shabba < Muḥammad b. Yaḥyā < al-Ḥārith b. Isḥāq, but from 3:157–158 (l. 6 to l. 19) (for partial parallels, see Ibn al-Athīr, *al-Kāmil* [ed. Tornberg], 5:391–392; Ibn Khaldūn, *ʿIbar* [Beirut, 1971], 3:188; al-Nuwayrī, *Nihāya*, 25:4): a first person testimony from Abū Habbār on how he was sent to warn Muḥammad b. ʿAbdallāh about a spy sent over by the caliph. He escaped punishment because the spy, who managed to escape to al-Manṣūr, confused the name of Abū Habbār, and gave another name instead (Wabar al-Muzanī according to al-Ṭabarī, 3:158 (ll. 3–4); Ibn al-Athīr, *al-Kāmil* [ed. Tornberg], 5:392 (l. 16): Wabār al-Murrī).

43 On Sulaym b. Manṣūr b. ʿIkrima b. Khaṣafa b. Qays ʿAylān in the Jāhiliyya and the beginning of the Islamic period (outside Arabia), see Lecker, *Banū Sulaym*; idem, "Sulaym."

important tradition related by ʿAbdallāh b. Maʿrūf, a Sulamī, a descendant of the clan of Riyāḥ b. Mālik b. ʿUṣayya b. Khufāf [b. Imruʾ al-Qays b. Buhtha b. Sulaym],[44] who was an eyewitness to the event:

> The Banū Sulaym came to Muḥammad under the leadership of their headmen. Their spokesman, Jābir b. Anas al-Riyāḥī, said, "Commander of the Faithful, we are your maternal uncles and your neighbors, and we have weapons and mounts in our possessions. By God, Islam came at a time when the Banū Sulaym owned more horses than there were in the Ḥijāz. Indeed, if a bedouin had what we have remains with us now, the entire desert would be at his disposal. Do not dig a trench (*khandaq*). The Messenger of God dug his trench for reasons God knows best. If you dig a trench, the footsoldiers will not be able to fight effectively and the horses will not be able to be moved on our behalf between the lines. Those in front of whom a trench is dug are those who must fight in it, while it prevents them from getting at those against whom it is dug." At this one of the Banū Shujāʿ intervened, saying, "The Messenger of God dug a trench, so follow his way of thinking, or do you intend to set aside the Messenger of God's way for your own?" "O Ibn Shujāʿ," Jābir responded, "nothing weighs more heavily on you and your associates than actually meeting them [in battle], and nothing is more to my liking and that of my associates than fighting them directly." "With the *khandaq*," Muḥammad added, "we have simply followed the Messenger of God's footsteps. No one can turn us from him nor will I forsake him."[45]

From another piece of evidence we learn of a man from Sulaym, Jubayr b. ʿAbdallāh al-Sulamī, who hid in al-Madhād before the break out of the revolt together with two other supporters of Muḥammad b. ʿAbdallāh.[46]

However, nothing is known about the Sulamīs conduct during the battles; it is not known whether they fought at his side. There is only one testimony mentioning one man:

Supporters of the Revolt

---

44 The reconstruction of this *nasab* is according to Ibn al-Kalbī, *Jamhara* (ed. Caskel), 1:122; 2:488 (quoted by McAuliffe, *ʿAbbāsid Authority*, 191, n. 934: Riyāḥ b. Mālik were a clan of the Banū Sulaym); on the lineage of Banū ʿUṣayya b. Yaqẓa, see Ibn al-Kalbī, *Jamhara* (ed. Ḥasan), 398; ʿAbdallāh b. Maʿrūf and Jābir b. Anas are not mentioned by him, nor does he appear in the long entry on Sulaym in Ibn Ḥazm, *Jamhara*, 261–264.

45 Al-Ṭabarī, 3:228–229 (l. 11 to l. 5); trans. McAuliffe, *ʿAbbāsid Authority*, 191–192.

46 Al-Ṭabarī, 3:190 (ll. 7–12).

1) Jahm b. ʿUthmān, *mawlā* Banū Bahz of Sulaym

Jahm b. ʿUthmān was born in 105/723–724. He was a supporter of Muḥammad b. ʿAbdallāh and fought at his side. He is described as one of the close associates (*wa-ṣaḥiba*) of Jaʿfar al-Ṣādiq. He was persecuted by al-Manṣūr, fled to Yemen and died there.[47]

5 Banū Ghifār b. Mulayl (... b. Kināna ... b. al-Yās b. Muḍar)

Supporters of the Revolt

Some branches of Ghifār families took part in the revolt at the side of al-Nafs al-Zakiyya. One part of the moat (*khandaq*) that was dug by orders of the latter was in the territory of Banū Ghifār, and a commander from this tribe was most probably in charge of this section.[48]

47 Traditions emphasizing his personal active participation in the revolt: al-Ṭabarī, 3:193 (ll. 10–15), 3:237–238 (l. 17 to l. 2) (= al-Iṣfahānī, *Maqātil*, 283–284); al-Ṭabarī, 3:200: [ʿUmar b. Shabba = *wa-ḥaddathanī*] < Saʿīd [read Saʿd] b. ʿAbd al-Ḥamīd b. Jaʿfar b. ʿAbdallāh b. al-Ḥakam b. Sinān al-Ḥakamī, the brother of al-Anṣār < others (غير واحد)...; the parallel tradition in al-Iṣfahānī, *Maqātil*, 283: *qāla Abū Zayd* [= ʿUmar b. Shabba] < Saʿīd [read Saʿd] b. ʿAbd al-Ḥamīd < Jahm b. Jaʿfar al-Ḥakamī < غير واحد أن مالك بن أنس...; the *isnād* is garbled and perhaps should be rendered according to al-Ṭabarī, 3:237 (ll. 18–19) thus: ʿUmar b. Shabba < Saʿīd [Saʿd] b. ʿAbd al-Ḥamīd b. Jaʿfar b. ʿAbdallāh b. al-Ḥakam b. Sinān al-Ḥakamī < Jahm b. ʿUthmān, the *mawlā* of Banū Sulaym of the family of Banū Bahz; on Bahz b. Imruʾ al-Qays b. Buhtha b. Sulaym, see Lecker, *Sulaym*, index, esp. 75–80, 124–125 and 246 (the genealogical chart of Sulaym); he is mentioned as an adherent of Jaʿfar al-Ṣādiq by the Sunnī and the Shīʿī books of *rijāl*, e.g., al-Ṭūsī, *Rijāl*, 176; al-Shabastarī, *al-Imām al-Ṣādiq*, 1:319 (and the bibliography therein); al-Tafrishī, *Naqd al-rijāl*, 1:378; Ibn Abī l-Ḥātim, *al-Jarḥ*, 2:522. The historical information about him is given by the Sunnī author Ibn Ḥajar, *Lisān*, 2:142–143 who records his birth date, that he was closely associated (وصحب) with Jaʿfar al-Ṣādiq and that al-Manṣūr looked for him, so he fled to Yemen and died there; this information was copied by al-Amīn, *Aʿyān al-Shīʿa*, 4:253. Traditions emphasizing his personal active participation in the revolt: al-Ṭabarī, 3:193.

48 Al-Ṭabarī, 3:236–237 (l. 21 to l. 11); ibid., 3:227: Ismāʿīl b. Abī ʿAmr; see the discussion on him and his family below; for a general brief survey of the tribe (Banū Ghifār b. Mulayl b. Ḍamra b. Bakr b. ʿAbd Manāt b. Kināna b. Khuzayma b. Mudrika b. al-Yās b. Muḍar), see J. W. Fück, *EI*², "Ghifār"; Ibn Ḥazm, *Jamhara*, 186; for a very important detailed description of their territory in Medina during the time of the Prophet, see Ibn Shabba, *Taʾrīkh al-Madīna*, 1:260–261: ...نزول بني غفار بن مليل...القطيعة التي قطع لها النبي صلعم

5.1 *The Family of Abū ʿAmr b. Nuʿaym b. Mukarram [Māhān?] b. Thaʿlaba b. Jarīr b. ʿAmr b. ʿAbdallāh b. Ghifār b. Mulayl b. Ḍamra b. Bakr b. ʿAbd Manāt b. Kināna*

This branch of the descendants of ʿAbdallāh b. Ghifār are not specifically mentioned in the *nasab* books; only one branch of this family is specifically mentioned, namely, Mālik b. ʿAbdallāh.[49] The family of Abū ʿAmr b. Nuʿaym is reconstructed here according to other sources.[50] Three dignitaries belonged to this family:

1) ʿUmar b. Abī ʿAmr b. Nuʿaym b. Māhān and his two brothers, Yūsuf and Ismāʿīl

The family was split in their attitude towards the revolt: ʿUmar and Yūsuf did not join the revolt, while Ismāʿīl was among its supporters, probably one of the commanders of Muḥammad al-Nafs al-Zakiyya.

Supporters of Muḥammad

2) Ismāʿīl b. Abī ʿAmr

He seems to have been one of the commanders of Muḥammad al-Nafs al-Zakiyya, but deserted him, opened a way in his tribe's territory for the ʿAbbāsī forces, and this was most probably the reason that when the last battle ended, his house was one of the five places where *amān* was given to whoever took refuge there.

Opposers of the Revolt/Supporters of the ʿAbbāsīs

---

49 Ibn al-Kalbī, *Jamhara* (ed. Caskel), II, table 42; Ibn Ḥazm, *Jamhara*, 186: not even one branch; al-Balādhurī, *Ansāb* (ed. Zakkār), 11:123f., 129: Mālik b. ʿAbdallāh.

50 Al-Ṭabarī, 3:227: Ayyūb b. ʿUmar b. Abī ʿAmr b. Nuʿaym b. Māhān; Ibn Ḥajar, *Lisān*, 4:286: the biography of ʿUmar b. Ayyūb b. ʿUmar b. Abī ʿAmr b. Nuʿaym, who is defined as al-Ghifārī. Only two sources mention the complete lineage of the family: Ibn ʿAsākir, *Taʾrīkh*, 26:340 (in a random *isnād*, not in a special biography): … ʿUmar b. Ayyūb [b. ʿUmar] b. Abī ʿAmr b. Mukarram b. Thaʿlaba b. Jarīr b. ʿAmr b. ʿAbdallāh [b. Ghifār]; and see Ibn Shabba, *Taʾrīkh al-Madīna*, 1:261, in a very important tradition about the settlement of Banū Ghifār in Medina, and the allotment of the lands in the city by the Prophet; the family of Abū ʿAmr appears among the families of the tribe that are specifically mentioned by ʿUmar b. Shabba: "Banū Abī ʿAmr b. Nuʿaym b. Māhān, and they are from Banū ʿAbdallāh b. Ghifār, settled to the north and west of Banū Mubashshir b. Ghifār…". (ونزل بنو أبي عمرو بن نعيم بن ماهان وهم من بني عبد الله بن غفار شامي وغربي بني مبشر بن غفار....)

3–4) ʿUmar and Yūsuf, the sons of Abū ʿAmr b. Nuʿaym

ʿUmar seems to be the senior member of his family. When the army of ʿĪsā b. Mūsā approached Medina, ʿUmar was one of the dignitaries of Medina to whom al-Manṣūr sent a messenger with private letters. The messenger and the letters were seized by Muḥammad's guards, and ʿUmar and his brother Yūsuf were imprisoned by Muḥammad al-Nafs al-Zakiyya, who accused ʿUmar of wanting to kill him. He ordered ʿUmar and his brother to be flogged and imprisoned them under very harsh conditions. They were released from prison only when the ʿAbbāsī armies entered Medina. This specific firsthand evidence was passed to ʿUmar b. Shabba by the same members of the Ghifārī family, e.g., ʿUmar b. Abī ʿAmr, who related the history of the family's history during the revolt to his son, Ayyūb, who transmitted it directly to ʿUmar b. Shabba.[51]

When ʿĪsā b. Mūsā entered Medina, continues ʿUmar b. Abī ʿAmr in another place, they were released and were asked to identify Muḥammad al-Nafs al-Zakiyya's head, which they reluctantly did, and then ʿUmar was nominated as governor of the territory between Mecca and Medina. "And I stayed in my office until Jaʿfar b. Sulaymān had me brought down to him [to Medina] and ordered me to join and cleave to him constantly."[52]

5.2 *ʿAlī b. Mālik b. Khaytham (Khuthaym?) b. ʿIrāk al-Ghifārī*

Supporters of the Revolt

He was killed with Ibn Khuḍayr in battle. Nothing else is known about him.[53]

---

51 Al-Ṭabarī, 3:227; the name of the other brother, Yūsuf: ibid., 3:249 (l. 7).

52 Al-Ṭabarī, 3:249: ثم ولاني ما بين مكة والمدينة فلم أزل واليا عليه حتى قدم جعفر بن سليمان فحدرني إليه وألزمني نفسه; McAuliffe, *ʿAbbāsid Authority*, 213: "At this time Jaʿfar had me brought down to him and placed me under his own jurisdiction." A certain Ibn Abī ʿAmr is mentioned in an anecdote in 152/769 or 770, when al-Manṣūr stood at the head of the pilgrimage to Mecca. It relates that he is complaining to the caliph that al-Ḥasan b. Zayd, the governor of Medina, flogged him. The transmitter intervenes in the middle of the narration and adds that he was punished by al-Ḥasan because he hit Muḥammad al-Nafs al-Zakiyya's corpse with his sword, see al-Azdī, *Taʾrīkh al-Mawṣil*, 176; the name of the complainer is Ibn Abī ʿAmr. It is plausible that this is ʿUmar b. Abī ʿAmr, but his name is not specifically mentioned; the transmitter is Muṣʿab b. al-Zubayr, but see the note of the editor, who suggests that the name may have been corrupted, and perhaps it should be read: Muṣʿab b. ʿAbdallāh b. Muṣʿab b. Thābit b. ʿAbdallāh b. al-Zubayr, the famous scholar, the author of *Nasab Quraysh*.

53 Al-Balādhurī, *Ansāb* (ed. Madelung), 2:515: Khaytham; ed. al-Maḥmūdī, 108: Khuthaym; *Fragmenta* (an exact parallel), 244: Khaytham.

6 Banū Aslam (... b. Māzin b. al-Azd)[54]

They are mentioned together with other tribes (Juhayna, Muzayna, Sulaym, Banū Bakr, and Ghifār) as tribes who responded to Muḥammad b. ʿAbdallāh's call.[55] But, as in the case of most of the tribes mentioned, there is no evidence of the participation of large groups, or even of many individuals, from this tribe in the battles.

Supporters of the Revolt

1) The only evidence concerning this tribe is that related about **Abū ʿAdī l-ʿAblī**, who was nominated by Muḥammad as the governor of al-Ṭāʾif. He left Medina with Arabs from Muzayna, Juhayna, and Aslam (most probably also as armed units),[56] but nothing is said about the size of this force.

2) ʿAbdallāh b. ʿĀmir
The only Aslamī mentioned in the sources who supported Muḥammad b. ʿAbdallāh is ʿAbdallāh b. ʿĀmir, a *muḥaddith* and Qurʾān reader (d. 150 or 152/767 or 769), who according to one source is noted as "from Banū Mālik b. Afṣā, the brothers of Aslam."[57] He is described as one of the loyal supporters of Muḥammad b. ʿAbdallāh, who hid with the latter before the outbreak of the revolt,[58] and later fought with him against the ʿAbbāsī army.[59]

---

54 This Yamanī (southern) *nasab* is partially given by ʿUmar b. Shabba, *Taʾrīkh al-Madīna*, 1:364, describing the settlement and dwellings of the different families of Banū Aslam in Medina (copied with additional important information by al-Samhūdī, *Wafāʾ*, 3:98–99); for the full *nasab* (Banū Aslam b. Afṣa b. Ḥāritha b. ʿAmr (Muzayqiyāʾ) b. ʿĀmir b. Ḥāritha b. Imruʾ al-Qays b. Thaʿlaba b. Māzin b. al-Azd), see Ibn Ḥazm, *Jamhara*, 330–331, 367; Ibn al-Kalbī, *Nasab Maʿadd*, 2:456–457; but cf. Ibn Ḥazm, *Jamhara*, 240–241: a different Qaysī/Muḍarī (northern) *nasab* of Aslam (b. Afṣā b. ʿĀmir b. Qamaʿa b. al-Yās b. Muḍar).

55 Al-Ṭabarī, 3:228 (ll. 9–10).

56 Al-Iṣfahānī, *al-Aghānī* (Būlāq edition), 10:107.

57 Ibn Saʿd, *al-Qism al-mutammim*, 410: "from Banū Mālik b. Afṣā, the brothers of Aslam"; on him, see also Ibn Abī Ḥātim, *al-Jarḥ* (Beirut edition), 5:122; Ibn ʿAdī, *Ḍuʿafāʾ*, 4:154–155; Ibn Ḥajar, *Tahdhīb* (Beirut, 1984), 5:241; al-Mizzī, *Tahdhib*, 15:150–152.

58 Al-Ṭabarī, 3:157 (l. 8); 3:190 (ll. 8–9).

59 Ibid., 3:248 (ll. 4–12).

7 Banū Ashjaʿ (… b. Ghaṭafān b. Saʿd b. Qays ʿAylān b. Muḍar)[60]

Families of this tribe supported Muḥammad b. ʿAbdallāh, who before the revolt hid in al-Bayḍāʾ, which belonged to Ashjaʿ and was located at a distance of approximately 20 miles from Medina.[61] When Abū l-ʿAbbās al-Saffāḥ became caliph, Muḥammad b. ʿAbdallāh hid in the territory of Ghaṭafān, sheltered by the family of the famous poet, Arṭāt b. Suhayya.[62] Several families of Banū Ashjaʿ dwelled in Medina.[63] According to one tradition, Ḥumayd b. Qaḥṭaba entered through Ashjaʿ lane: زقاق أشجع, attacked Muḥammad b. ʿAbdallāh, and killed him.[64]

8) Banū Fazāra (… b. Ghaṭafān b. Saʿd b. Qays ʿAylān b. Muḍar)[65]

Supporters of the Revolt

There is no evidence of the participation of members of this tribe in the revolt. The blind Medinan poet, **Abū l-Shadāʾid Fāliḥ b. Maʿmar**, was killed by ʿAbbāsī soldiers in his house, which was in Banū Fazāra's gorge (*shiʿb*). The tradition is related by the poet's grandson, most probably from his father, who gives the impression that his father was an innocent victim.[66] However, this poet may have been a (passive) supporter of Muḥammad b. ʿAbdallāh.[67]

---

60 On Ashjaʿ b. Ghayth b. Ghaṭafān b. Saʿd b. Qays ʿAylān, see Ibn Ḥazm, *Jamhara*, 249–250; Ibn al-Kalbī, *Jamhara* (ed. Ḥasan), 453–455 (= ed. Caskel, 1, no. 135).

61 Al-Ṭabarī, 3:166 (ll. 14–15).

62 Al-Balādhurī, *Ansāb* (ed. Madelung), 2:498 (= *Fragmenta*, 231); this poet belonged to the Dhubyān (b. Bughayḍ b. Rayth b. Ghaṭafān), but also to a smaller sub-clan of ʿUqfān ([Ghaṭafān?] b. Abī Ḥāritha b. Murra … b. Dhubyān … b. Ghaṭafān), see Ibn Ḥazm, *Jamhara*, p, 252: Ghaṭafān; Ibn al-Kalbī, *Jamhara* (ed. Ḥasan), 446: ʿUqfān; al-Iṣfahānī, *al-Aghānī* (Dār al-Kutub edition), 13:29: ʿUqfān.

63 ʿUmar b. Shabba, *Taʾrīkh al-Madīna*, 1:267; copied with additions by al-Samhūdī, *Wafāʾ*, 3:101–103.

64 Al-Ṭabarī, 3:246 (ll. 6–10).

65 On the tribe (Fazāra b. Dhubyān b. Burayḍ b. Rayth b. Ghaṭafān b. Saʿd b. Qays ʿAylān) in the Jāhiliyya and Muḥammad's period, see W. M. Watt, "Fazāra," *EI*^{2}, 2:873; Ibn al-Kalbī, *Jamhara* (ed. Caskel), 2:246; 1, no. 92; Ibn Ḥazm, *Jamhara*, 255–259.

66 Cf. al-Ṭabarī, 3:251 (ll. 3–15).

67 Ibid., 3:203 (ll. 4–6): sending some poetry verses to Muḥammad when ʿĪsā b. Mūsā approached Medina; see also the interesting tradition that records the satirical verses that Abū l-Shadāʾid composed against ʿĪsā b. Mūsā (no indication for the date of this poem is given, it must have occurred sometime before 145/762), al-Iṣfahānī, *al-Aghānī* (Dār al-

9 Thaqīf (… b. Hawāzin … b. Khṣafa b. Qays ʿAylān b. Muḍar)[68]

1) ʿAbd al-Malik b. Abī Zuhayr b. ʿAbd al-Raḥmān al-Thaqafī

He was in the forces sent by Muḥammad al-Nafs al-Zakiyya to conquer al-Ṭāʾif. When the nominated governor, Abū ʿAdī l-ʿAblī, left the city after a short stay, ʿAbd al-Malik was nominated by Abū ʿAdī as governor of the city on his behalf.[69] His *nisba*, al-Thaqafī, may imply that he was not chosen at random; his origin was most probably al-Ṭāʾif. He was a minor *ḥadīth* scholar who transmitted from and to scholars of the same origin, with the *nisba* al-Thaqafī.[70]

10 Banū ʿĀmir b. Ṣaʿṣaʿa (… b. Hawāzin … b. Khaṣafa b. Qays ʿAylān b. Muḍar)[71]

10.1 *Banū Numayr b. ʿĀmir b. Ṣaʿṣaʿa* (mawālī)[72]

An unnamed *mawlā* of this tribe supported the rebellion and may have been killed in battle. This is known from the brother of a supporter whose name was al-Faḍl b. Sulaymān.[73]

Kutub edition), 16:243–244 (this source is mentioned by Sezgin, 2:647). Did ʿĪsā b. Mūsā remember this and order the killing of this blind poet?

68 On this important tribe (Thaqīf b. Munabbih b. Bakr b. Hawāzin b. Manṣūr b. ʿIkrima b. Khaṣafa b. Qays ʿAylān), see M. Lecker, "Thaḳīf," *EI*², 10:432; Ibn al-Kalbī, *Jamhara* (ed. Caskel), 1, nos. 92 and 118.

69 Al-Iṣfahānī, *al-Aghānī* (Dār al-Kutub edition), 11:301 (Būlāq edition, 10:107).

70 He is mentioned in the *rijāl* books of *ḥadīth*, e.g., al-Bukhārī, *al-Kabīr* (Diyār Bakr edition), 5:414–415; al-Dhahabī, *Mīzān* (Beirut, 1995), 4:398; Ibn Abī Ḥātim, *al-Jarḥ* (Beirut edition), 5:351; Ibn Ḥajar, *Lisān*, 4:1986; I could not find any additional information about him.

71 On this large confederation of tribes (ʿĀmir b. Ṣaʿṣaʿa b. Muʿāwiya b. Bakr b. Hawāzin b. Manṣūr b. ʿIkrima b. Khaṣafa b. Qays b. ʿAylān b. Muḍar), see W. Caskel, "ʿĀmir b. Ṣaʿṣaʿa," *EI*², 1:441a–442b; Ibn al-Kalbī, *Jamhara* (ed. Caskel), 1, no. 92.

72 On Banū Numayr, see Ibn Ḥazm, *Jamhara*, 279–280; G. Levi Della Vida, "Numayr," *EI*², 7:120.

73 Al-Ṭabarī, 3:245–246 (l. 17 to l. 2): "I heard al-Faḍl b. Sulaymān the *mawlā* of Banū Numayr relate from his brother—and a brother of his had been killed with Muḥammad—who said …"; what follows is an eyewitness report of the battle; the underlined sentence was omitted in MS A in de Goeje's edition; it is also omitted in the parallel tradition in al-Iṣfahānī, *Maqātil*, 269: the name of the *mawlā* is Fuḍayl (noted by McAuliffe, *ʿAbbāsid Authority*, 209, n. 994). A second tradition about the battle from al-Faḍl related through his brother is recorded by al-Ṭabarī, 3:247–248 (l. 20 to l. 4); it is not stated that the brother had died, though.

10.2 *The Family of Qurayṭ . . . b. Rabīʿa b. ʿĀmir b. Ṣaʿṣaʿa*

1) Rashīd (Rushayd?) b. Ḥayyān b. Abī Sulaymān b. Samʿān *aḥad* Banī Qurayṭ
He was a contemporary of the events; he lived in Medina during the uprising. He related to his son, Abū Maslama (or Salama) Mawhūb, a minor poet and transmitter of poetry and literary anecdotes, who transmitted to ʿUmar b. Shabba about Muḥammad al-Nafs al-Zakiyya's first actions after entering Medina. Rashīd may have supported Muḥammad b. ʿAbdallāh's cause at the initial stages of the revolt but deserted him along with many people of Medina when they heard that the ʿAbbāsī army was approaching the city.[74]

11 Banū Bāhila (*mawālī*)[75]

11.1 *The Family of Azhar b. Saʿd b. Nāfiʿ* (mawlā *Bāhila*)

Supporters of the Revolt

1–3) Azhar b. Saʿd b. Nāfiʿ, Abū Bakr al-Sammān al-Baṣrī (d. 203/818 or 819, or 207/822 or 823) and his two brothers, ʿUthmān b. Saʿd b. Nāfiʿ and Muḥammad b. Saʿd b. Nāfiʿ
Azhar b. Saʿd b. Nāfiʿ was in Medina during the rebellion, but it seems that he himself did not take an active part in the fighting, though his two brothers, ʿUthmān and Muḥammad, fought with Muḥammad al-Nafs al-Zakiyya. Many traditions are related from him in first person. They all deal with and pertain to the rebellion and to events related to it.

---

74 Al-Ṭabarī, 3:230 (ll. 6–18); on the family of Qurayṭ (b. ʿAbdallāh (ʿAbd) b. Abī Bakr ʿUbayd b. Kilāb b. Rabīʿa b. ʿĀmir b. Ṣaʿṣaʿa), see Ibn al-Kalbī (ed. Caskel), I, no. 95 (ed. al-Ḥasan, 222, 224): Qurayṭ b. ʿAbd; but see Ibn Ḥazm, *Jamhara*, 282; al-Ṭabarī, 3:230 (l. 8), and al-Nuwayrī, *Nihāya*, 2:339: Qurayṭ b. ʿAbdallāh.

75 On Bāhila, see W. Caskel, "Bāhila," *EI*², 1:920b–921a; 920b: "the genealogy of the tribe is somewhat complicated, Bāhila is the mother of one son of Mālik b. Aʿṣur [b. Saʿd b. Qays Aʿylān] and through *nikāḥ al-maqṭ* with the other son, Maʿn by name, the mother of two of the latter's sons and the foster-mother of ten other sons"; on Bāhila, see Ibn al-Kalbī, *Jamhara* (ed. Ḥasan), 458–463; Ibn Ḥazm, *Jamhara*, 245–247.

12 Banū Hawāzin (… b. Khaṣafa b. Qays ʿAylān b. Muḍar) (*mawlā*)

The Family of ʿUrwa b. Muḥammad b. ʿAṭiyya b. ʿUrwa b. al-Qayn b. ʿĀmir b. ʿAmīra b. Millān b. Nāṣira b. Fuṣayya b. Naṣr b. Saʿd b. Bakr b. Hawāzin b. Manṣūr b. ʿIkrima b. Khaṣafa b. Qays ʿAylān[76]

Supporters of the Revolt

1) ʿAbdallāh b. Jaʿfar b. Najīḥ al-Madīnī/Madanī l-Saʿdī (*mawlā* Saʿd b. Bakr/ *mawlā* ʿUrwa [b. Muḥammad?] b. ʿAṭiyya al-Saʿdī, d. 178/794–795)[77]
Abū l-Faraj al-Iṣfahānī remarks that ʿAbdallāh b. Jaʿfar b. Najīḥ was the father of ʿAlī l-Madanī *al-muḥaddith*.[78] He (ʿAbdallāh) was a Qurʾān reciter and one of the great *muḥaddithūn* who joined Muḥammad b. ʿAbdallāh's revolt and remained with him until Muḥammad was killed; he then hid from al-Manṣūr, who ordered him caught. "And I [adds al-Iṣfahānī] have mentioned (previously) his affair when I dealt with the killing of Ibrāhīm."[79] The "previous mention" in al-Iṣfahānī's work indeed mentions ʿAbdallāh b. Jaʿfar al-Madāʾinī [read al-Madīnī] in two traditions, but both traditions mention him as a supporter of Ibrāhīm b. ʿAbdallāh, accompanying him in his camp.[80] Al-Ṭabarī also records a similar tradition, with similar content.[81] It seems therefore reasonable that in the first tradition al-Iṣfahānī confuses Muḥammad and his brother Ibrāhīm. ʿAbdallāh b. Jaʿfar was a Medinan scholar, but at a certain unknown date moved to al-Baṣra. His son ʿAlī was born in al-Baṣra in 161/777–778.[82] ʿAbdallāh b. Jaʿfar was a *ḥadīth* transmitter who was unanimously considered unreliable by Sunnī critics of *ḥadīth* transmitters. He is mentioned by Imāmī sources as one of the close associates of Jaʿfar al-Ṣādiq: من أصحاب الصادق.[83]

76 The reconstruction of this family lineage is according to Ibn Ḥazm, *Jamhara*, 266; Ibn al-Kalbī, *Jamhara* (ed. Caskel), 2:574.

77 On him, see al-Mizzī, *Tahdhīb*, 14:379–384 and the comprehensive bibliography of the editor therein; Ibn ʿAbd al-Barr, *al-Istīʿāb*, 3:1072: the identification of his *walāʾ* to Saʿd b. Bakr b. Hawāzin; al-Mizzī, *Tahdhīb*, 21:5 (biography of his son, ʿAlī): *mawlā* ʿUrwa [b. Muḥammad?] b. ʿAṭiyya al-Saʿdī.

78 On him, see al-Dhahabī, *Siyar*, 11:41–60; al-Mizzī, *Tahdhīb*, 21:5–34 and the comprehensive bibliography of the editor therein.

79 Al-Iṣfahānī, *Maqātil*, 414.

80 Ibid., 357.

81 Al-Ṭabarī, 3:309 (ll. 11 to l. 15).

82 Al-Khaṭīb al-Baghdādī, *Taʾrīkh* (Beirut, 1997), 11:456; al-Dhahabī, *Siyar*, 11:43.

83 E.g., al-Ṭūsī, *Rijāl*, 234; al-Tafrishī, *Naqd al-rijāl*, 3:94.

13 Banū Kinda

Supporters of the Revolt

An unnamed man from the family of Kathīr b. al-Ṣalt (Muʿāwiya b. Kinda):[84] He supported Muḥammad b. ʿAbdallāh, joined the rebellion and after the latter's death hid from the authorities, together with ʿUthmān b. Muḥammad b. Khālid b. al-Zubayr b. al-ʿAwwām. Together they left Medina for al-Baṣra, were caught and brought to the caliph's court, where the man from Kathīr's family was released and set free and the Zubayrī was executed. The long tradition was narrated by Muḥammad b. ʿUthmān who was then a little child and was spared by the caliph.[85]

Three sons of Kathīr b. al-Ṣalt emigrated to Medina, settled there, and became allies (*ḥulafāʾ*) of Banū Jumaḥ (Quraysh) [b. ʿAmr b. Huṣayṣ b. Kaʿb b. Luʾayy b. Ghālib b. Quraysh]. Their tribal status was changed by Caliph al-Mahdī, who ordered that they no longer be the allies of Banū Jumaḥ and instead should become allies of al-ʿAbbās b. ʿAbd al-Muṭṭalib.[86] It seems that their father, Kathīr, came with them to Medina,[87] where he had a large mansion.[88]

14 Banū Daws (al-Azd) (*mawlā*), or Banū Layth (Quḍāʿa) (*mawlā*) or Banū Ghifār (*mawlā*)

Supporters of the Revolt

1) ʿAbdallāh b. Yazīd[?] b. Hurmuz (d. 148/765 or 766), *mawlā* Banū Daws, or Layth or Ghifār[89]

---

84 Kathīr b. al-Ṣalt b. Maʿdī Karib b. Walīʿa b. Shuraḥbīl b. Muʿāwiya b. Ḥujr al-Qarid b. al-Ḥārith al-Wallāda b. ʿAmr b. Muʿāwiya b. al-Ḥārith al-Akbar b. Muʿāwiya b. Thawr b. Murattiʿ b. Muʿāwiya b. Kinda; the reconstruction of his lineage is according to Ibn al-Kalbī, *Jamhara* (ed. Caskel), 1, nos. 233 and 239; Ibn Ḥazm, *Jamhara*, 427–428 (he is mentioned on 428).

85 Al-Ṭabarī, 3:262–264 (l. 17 to l. 2).

86 Ibn Saʿd, *Ṭabaqāt*, 5:13; see also Ibn Khayyāṭ, *Ṭabaqāt* (ed. Zakkār), 415; Ibn ʿAsākir, *Taʾrīkh*, 50:36 (quoting Muṣʿab [b. ʿAbdallāh] al-Zubayrī; I did not find this quote in al-Zubayrī's *Nasab Quraysh*); al-Ṣafadī, *al-Wāfī*, 15:59; al-Mizzī, *Tahdhīb*, 24:128.

87 Ibn Ḥazm, *Jamhara*, 428: سكن المدينة.

88 Ibn Saʿd, *Ṭabaqāt*, 5:14: وله دار بالمدينة كبيرة.

89 On him, see Ibn Saʿd, *Ṭabaqāt*, 5:284; idem, *al-Qism al-mutammim*, 327–328; al-Samʿānī, *Ansāb* (Beirut, 1988), 5:151: *mawlā* of the family of Banū Dhubāb of Daws; Ibn Qutayba,

He was a Medinan *faqīh* and a minor *muḥaddith*. He (together with Muḥammad b. ʿAjlān) took an active part in the rebellion.[90] After the battle he was brought to ʿĪsā b. Mūsā who set him free.[91] His father Yazīd was one of *abnāʾ al-Furs* who were in Medina,[92] and is described as the *mawlā* of the family of Dhubāb from Daws, who stood at the head of the *mawālī* in the battle of al-Ḥarra.[93]

2) ʿAbd al-Wāḥid b. Abī ʿAwn al-Dawsī (al-Azdī, *mawlā* of) (see under Banū Zuhra, *mawālī* of) Al-ʿIrāq: al-Kūfa and al-Baṣra
For a brief discussion, see chapter 3.

15 Unidentified

Supporters of the Revolt

Abū Ḥunayn

He was an active supporter of Muḥammad b. ʿAbdallāh; we learn this from two pieces of evidence. In the first he related to al-Ḥārith b. Isḥāq that he entered the house where ʿAbdallāh b. al-Ḥasan was confined in Medina.[94] The second testimony states that ʿAlī b. Muḥammad al-Nafs al-Zakiyya, who came to Egypt as a propagandist for his father, was caught by the governor, and sent to the caliph's court where he informed on his father's supporters. Among those he named were ʿAbd al-Raḥmān b. Abī l-Mawālī and Abū Ḥunayn. Al-Manṣūr

al-Maʿārif (Cairo edition), 584: *mawlā al-Dawsiyyīn*; on Daws b.ʿUdthān b. ʿAbdallāh b. Zahrān b. Kaʿb b. al-Ḥārith b. Kaʿb b. ʿAbdallāh b. Mālik b. Naṣr b. al-Azd, see Ibn al-Kalbī, *Jamhara* (ed. Caskel), I, no. 210; 2:232; Ibn al-Kalbī, *Nasab Maʿadd*, 2:487; Ibn Ḥazm, *Jamhara*, 473. I was unable to find Banū Dhubāb of the Daws; al-Bukhārī, *Ṣaghīr*, 2:84; Ibn Abī Ḥātim, *al-Jarḥ* (Beirut edition), 9:294–295; Ibn Ḥibbān *al-Thiqāt*, 7:12: *mawlā* Banī Layth, that is, Layth b. Sūd b. Aslum b. al-Ḥāfī b. Quḍāʿa, see Ibn al-Kalbī, *Jamhara* (ed. Caskel), I, no. 330; 2:376; Ibn Ḥazm, *Jamhara*, 443–444; al-Mizzī, *Tahdhīb*, 32:270–273: *mawlā* of the family of Dhubāb of Banū Daws, or Ghifār or Layth; van Arendonk, *L'Imamat Zaïdite*, 313; van Ess, *Theologie*, 665.

90 Al-Ṭabarī, 3:251 (ll. 18–19); al-Iṣfahānī, *Maqātil*, 279 (Ibn Hurmuz), 281; 285 (Yazīd b. Hurmuz instead of ʿAbdallāh b. Yazīd ...); al-Azdī, *Taʾrīkh al-Mawṣil*, 188: Ibn Hurmuz.

91 Al-Ṭabarī, 3:252 (ll. 1–4); al-Azdī, *Taʾrīkh al-Mawṣil*, 187.

92 Ibn Saʿd, *Ṭabaqāt*, 5:284; al-Mizzī, *Tahdhīb*, 32:270, 272.

93 Ibn Saʿd, *Ṭabaqāt*, 5:284; idem, *al-Qism al-mutammim*, 327; al-Mizzī, *Tahdhīb*, 32:270.

94 Al-Ṭabarī, 3:153; on al-Ḥārith b. Isḥāq.

ordered both men to be imprisoned. Abū Ḥunayn was flogged one hundred times.[95] I was not able to find out more about this person.

Conclusions

Elsewhere in this work I noted the assertion of the sources that, at least at the beginning of the rebellion, most of the Arab inhabitants of Medina supported Muḥammad al-Nafs al-Zakiyya. This assertion, however, is misleading. The material assembled in this book clearly shows that this support was not uniform; there were those who opposed the rebellion, even among the immediate offspring of the Anṣār family, among the rest of the ʿAlīd families, and among the important families of Quraysh. It is noteworthy that Jaʿfar al-Ṣādiq did not support Muḥammad and his rebellion, though despite this, six people belonging to Jaʿfar's immediate family are known to have taken an active part in the uprising. First and foremost, his sons, Mūsā and ʿAbdallāh, and his brother's son, Ḥamza b. ʿAbdallāh (who is described as one of the closest and most courageous adherents) should be mentioned, but there were also other Ḥusaynīs, all uncles and cousins of Jaʿfar al-Ṣādiq, who participated in the rebellion. Nonetheless, a greater number of family members (between seven and nine) opposed it. It is not clear how developed Jaʿfar al-Ṣādiq's *quʿūd* doctrine was at the beginning of the ʿAbbāsī period and to what extent the ʿAbbāsīs were aware of it and its implications, for after their rise to power, tense relations and hostility prevailed between the ʿAbbāsīs and Jaʿfar al-Ṣādiq. ʿAbbāsī fears, no doubt, greatly increased, seeing that the Ḥusaynī family was neither united in their attitude towards the rebellion nor, evidently, in backing Jaʿfar al-Ṣādiq's leadership. They were displeased with Jaʿfar's "quietism" in the rebellion. He refrained from appearing openly before ʿĪsā b. Mūsā as a sign of loyalty to the ʿAbbāsīs and this led to the confiscation of his estate, ʿAyn Abī Ziyād, with the approval of al-Manṣūr, who also may have ordered his house in Medina burned down.

Families from Quraysh, e.g., Makhzūm, Zuhra, Taym b. Murra, Jadhīma b. Mālik, Jumaḥ, and ʿAdī b. Kaʿb, were split between the supporters of Muḥammad b. ʿAbdallāh and those opposing him, the latter outnumbering the former. Among the Zubayrī (Banū Asad b. ʿAbd al-ʿUzzā) and the ʿUmarī (that is, the descendants of ʿUmar b. al-Khaṭṭāb: Banū ʿAdī) families, however, most supported Muḥammad and only a few opposed him. The Zubayrīs constituted the main military and administrative backbone of the rebellion; the ʿUmarīs

95 Al-Ṭabarī, 3:170–171; on ʿAbd al-Raḥmān b. Abī l-Mawālī.

were second to them in importance.[96] Also noted among Muḥammad's supporters are families or individuals from Arab tribes: the Juhayna, Muzayna, Sulaym, Bakr, Aslam, Ghifār, Numayr (*mawālī*), and Bāhila (*mawālī*). With the help of the Arabs from Juhayna, Muzayna, and Aslam, the governor sent by Muḥammad to al-Ṭā'if gained the upper hand there. However, there is no evidence that the above-mentioned tribes fought alongside Muḥammad as coherent units. The only evidence is of the Banū Ashjaʿ from Juhayna, who fought with him till the end.[97]

Several distinguished persons from the Anṣār supported the rebellion, but it seems that as a homogeneous unit they did not make any special effort to defend Muḥammad's family when they were arrested by the ʿAbbāsīs,[98] nor is there evidence that they participated in the battle against ʿĪsā b. Mūsā.[99]

96 This was already noted by Kennedy, *Abbāsid Caliphate*, 201–202.

97 Ibn Saʿd, *al-Qism al-mutammim*, 377: from al-Wāqidī [= al-Ṭabarī, 3:240 (ll. 9–14)].

98 Al-Iṣfahānī, *Maqātil*, 220.

99 For evidence of the support of several Anṣārīs in the rebellion, see above, e.g., al-Ṭabarī, 3:199 (ll. 3–6) [= al-Iṣfahānī, *Maqātil*, 280 (read ʿAbd al-Ḥamīd instead of ʿAbd al-Majīd)]; al-Ṭabarī, 3:193 (ll. 12–13); 3:194 (ll. 1–2) (equivocal evidence).

Appendix 1: The Attitude of the *'Ulamā'* Towards the Rebellion

It is commonly accepted by scholars that several of the important *'ulamā'* of this period from Medina, as well as from other cities, supported and joined the rebellion. Some of them had Shī'ī tendencies, though a large number were not pro-Shī'ī. Notable among them, to mention a few, are Mālik b. Anas, Sufyān al-Thawrī, Abū Ḥanīfa, and Hishām b. 'Urwa b. al-Zubayr.[1] Nevertheless, when this list of scholars is thoroughly examined, it becomes clear that at least for some of them, their leanings towards the rebellion and their support of Muḥammad was not unequivocal.

Zaman argues in the same vein when saying that these claims "are extremely dubious, however: several scholars of Medina and Basra are, in fact, known to have abstained from backing the revolt, and even many 'Alīds opposed it."[2] And,

> In general, there is little doubt that opinion in religious circles, both in Medina and Basra, was no less divided than it would have been among people in general. Apart from other possible reasons—such as pro-'Abbāsid attitudes of some religious figures, or the fear of 'Abbāsid reprisals, etc.—quietist scruples probably led many to disapprove of the revolt.[3]

The support for the rebellion of the distinguished Mu'tazilīs, particularly that of Wāṣil b. 'Aṭā' (who died in 131 H., fourteen years before Muḥammad's revolt), as well as that of

1 See a list of 14 scholars in van Arendonk's appendix, 312–314; many more can be added to this list; Omar, *'Abbāsid Caliphate*, 223: Mālik b. Anas supported Muḥammad b. 'Abdallāh; other scholars like Abū Ḥanīfa, Muḥammad b. Hurmuz, Muḥammad b. 'Ajlān, and Abū Bakr b. Abī Sabra sympathized with the rebellion; "the body of traditionists ... [adds Omar] was moderately pro-'Alid in its leanings in this early Islamic period"; see also El-Hibri, *Islamic Historiography*, 5, 48 (Mālik b. Anas) and Abū Ḥanīfa (p. 5); but esp. Zaman, *Religion and Politics*, 73–76; ibid., 73: "This revolt is unique ... for the large number of scholars who are said to have supported it. The more prominent among those mentioned include: Mālik b. Anas and Abū Ḥanīfa ... Mis'ar b. Kidām ... Muḥammad b. 'Ajlān and Ibn Abī Dhi'b ... Abū Bakr b. Abī Sabra, Shu'ba b. Ḥajjāj, Ḥusayn b. Bashīr, 'Abbād b. al-'Awwām and Yazīd b. Hārūn"; ibid., 148f.: discussing Mālik b. Anas; van Ess, *Theologie*, 1:187–188: Abū Ḥanīfa; 237: Sulaymān b. Mihrān (al-A'mash); 2:677–687: the supporters of Muḥammad b. 'Abdallāh from among the Qadariyya scholars.

2 Zaman, *Religion and Politics*, 74.

3 Ibid., 75, n. 22.

 | DOI 10.1163/9789004296220_012

ʿAmr b. ʿUbayd is doubtful.[4] Arguments in favor of Muḥammad b. ʿAbdallāh's support of the Muʿtazilī doctrine lack solid evidence.[5]

Following is an initial study of Mālik b. Anas's case and some remarks on Abū Ḥanīfa, Sufyān al-Thawrī, Hishām b. ʿUrwa b. al-Zubayr, and Hārūn b. Saʿd al-ʿIjlī.

The discussion of these scholars is of course partial and deals only with their attitude towards al-Nafs al-Zakiyya's revolt. But despite this, the emerging picture differs from the accepted view about these scholars' attitude to the ʿAbbāsīs in general and to the revolt in particular. All the *ʿulamāʾ* who are mentioned in connection with the revolt deserve a thorough detailed study. Only then will the complete picture be revealed.

1 Mālik b. Anas

1) A pro-Shīʿī tradition reports that Mālik b. Anas swore allegiance to Muḥammad b. ʿAbdallāh. This was the cause of al-Manṣūr's change of attitude towards Mālik b. Anas.[6]

2) A more common tradition, often quoted by scholars, which is related through one of the leading supporters of Muḥammad who belonged to the Anṣār, records that

> Mālik b. Anas was asked to give a *fatwā* as to whether it was lawful to rebel with Muḥammad; it was said to him, truly, we are bound by our oath of allegiance to Abū Jaʿfar, so he said: you only gave your oath under duress, and no oath is binding when given under compulsion. At this, people rushed off to join Muḥammad, but Mālik stayed in his house.[7]

This and other traditions contradict other pieces of evidence, according to which a short time before the rebellion broke out (and also after its suppression) the relationship between al-Manṣūr and Mālik was good, as attested to by the following evidence:

---

4 See van Ess, *Theologie*, 2:249f.: Wāṣil b. ʿAṭāʾ; 286–288: ʿAmr b. ʿUbayd; 327–335: Muʿtazilī participation in Ibrāhīm's revolt; for Muḥammad and Ibrāhīm and the Muʿtazila, see also Madelung, *al-Qāsim b. Ibrāhīm*, 36, 41, 72–74.

5 See Zaman, *Religion and Politics*, 74, n. 19, quoting van Ess' article "Une lecture," 64ff.

6 Ibn ʿInaba, *ʿUmda*, 105.

7 Al-Ṭabarī, 3:200 (ll. 3–7); the *isnād* reads as follows: ʿUmar b. Shabba < Saʿīd b. ʿAbd al-Ḥamīd b. Jaʿfar b. ʿAbdallāh b. al-Ḥakam b. Sinān al-Ḥakamī, *akhū l-Anṣār* < from more than one person: إن مالك بن أنس استفتي في الخروج مع محمد وقيل له إن في أعناقنا بيعة لأبي جعفر؛ فقال إنما بايعتم مكرهين وليس على كل مكره يمين. فأسرع الناس إلى محمد ولزم مالك بيته; al-Iṣfahānī, *Maqātil*, 283 and al-Suyūṭī, *Taʾrīkh* (Cairo, 1305 H.), 102: a parallel tradition without the ending: *wa-lazima Mālik baytahu.*

3) Upon his arrival at al-Rabadha near Medina in 144/762, and before the imprisonment of the Ḥasanīs, al-Manṣūr sent two envoys on his behalf to ʿAbdallāh b. al-Ḥasan, to convince him to turn his sons in. The first was Muḥammad b. ʿImrān b. Ibrāhīm b. Muḥammad b. Ṭalḥa (from Taym Quraysh), and the second emissary was Mālik b. Anas.[8]

4) After the failure of this mission al-Manṣūr imprisoned ʿAbdallāh b. al-Ḥasan and his extended family, confiscated his property, which was sold and brought to the *bayt al-māl* in Medina. The originator of the tradition goes on, saying "Mālik b. Anas the *faqīh* took his pension [salary? *rizq*] from this same money, out of free choice": فأخذ مالك بن أنس الفقيه رزقه من ذلك المال بعينه اختيارا منه.[9]

5) Upon the suppression of the revolt, al-Wāqidī relates that "When Muḥammad b. ʿAbdallāh came out in open rebellion in Medina, Mālik remained in his house and did not leave it until Muḥammad was killed."[10]

In this tradition, and in others in this vein,[11] the same expression as in paragraph 1, appears: *wa-lazima Mālik baytahu* (and Mālik remained in his house), but in these traditions it is mentioned with no connection whatsoever to the breaching of the oath to al-Manṣūr. Here, Mālik prefers not to be involved in any way with the rebellion and abstains from any active participation in the political events. This position was taken by some other well-known scholars in Medina.

6) Mālik's negative attitude towards the rebellion is depicted in the following tradition, according to which Abū Zayd b. Abī l-Ghamr asks ʿAbd al-Raḥmān b. al-Qāsim

> Did Mālik come out (in open rebellion) on the day that Muḥammad came out (in rebellion) [?] he said, I said: He did not come out. He said: I do not think that he saw something that pleased him. I said: Did he [Mālik] use to say we shall be

8 Al-Ṭabarī, 3:172–173; the family of Mālik were the *ḥulafāʾ* of Banū Taym (Ibn Ḥazm, *Jamhara*, 436).

9 Al-Balādhurī, *Ansāb* (ed. Madelung), 2:503; *Fragmenta*, 236: without the ending of the tradition: بعينه اختيارا منه; al-Maḥmūdī, the Shīʿī editor of this volume (ibid., n. 2) adds a note regarding this tradition, saying: "by this act and other similar acts the man became one of the *fuqahāʾ* of the Muslim nation (*al-umma*), and the ʿAbbāsīs exerted themselves to publish his books and *fatāwā* in all the countries of the Islamic world."

10 Ibn Saʿd, *al-Qism al-Mutammim*, 440; Abū l-ʿArab, *Kitāb al-Miḥan*, 232: a parallel tradition, correct Muḥammad b. ʿAmr to Muḥammad b. ʿUmar.

11 Al-Dhahabī, *Siyar*, 6:215: ثم إن محمدا استعمل عمال على المدينة ولزم مالك بيته; Ibn Kathīr, *al-Bidāya* (ed. Shīrī), 10:187 (year 179 H.): ومن وقت خروج محمد بن عبد الله بن حسن لزم مالك بيته فلم يكن يأتي أحدا الا لعزاء ولا لهناء ولا يخرج لجمعة ولا لجماعة.

rewarded by praying behind them [that is the *imāms* of the ʿAbbāsīs] during the Friday prayers [?] he said yes (he did).[12]

1.1 *Mālik b. Anas after al-Nafs al-Zakiyya's Rebellion*

The major incident that is connected to Mālik b. Anas occurred in 147/764, about two years after Muḥammad's revolt. Mālik was flogged by order of the governor of Medina, Jaʿfar b. Sulaymān b. ʿAlī l-ʿAbbāsī, and publicly humiliated by the latter. The sources differ as to the reason for this severe punishment. According to one version, in 147 Mālik b. Anas was flogged 70 times because he gave a *fatwā* that did not meet with the sovereign's approval (*gharaḍ al-sulṭān*).[13] Another tradition explains that he was punished because he spread a *ḥadīth* against divorce by coercion, which he considered to be illegal: ليس على مستكره طلاق. Abū Jaʿfar al-Manṣūr forbade him to circulate this *ḥadīth*, and when Mālik did not comply and circulated it in public, al-Manṣūr ordered him to be flogged.[14] He was flogged by the governor of Medina, his beard was shaved, and he was put on a donkey which carried him through the city,[15] and his books (notes? *kutub*) were hung round his neck.[16] A different version combining two accusations was recorded by al-Wāqidī, who explains that Mālik b. Anas' good relations with the ʿAbbāsī government, the acceptance of his opinions and his legal sayings [? by the caliph?] (لما دعي مالك بن أنس وشوور وسمع منه وقبل قوله) caused much jealousy among the people. When Jaʿfar b. Sulaymān was nominated as the governor of Medina, Mālik was accused of considering the oath of allegiance to the ʿAbbāsīs worthless and considering divorce by coercion unlawful (طلاق المكره أنه لا يجوز).[17]

The author of *al-Dībāj al-Mudhhab* also records this tradition, which combines the two accusations against Mālik. He adds that this is commonly agreed upon by most of

12 Abū l-ʿArab, *Kitāb al-Miḥan*, 413: قلت لعبد الرحمان بن القاسم: أخرج مالك يوم خرج[؟] قال قلت: لم يخرج. قال: لا أراه رأى ما يعجبه. قلت: أفكان يقول تجزينا الصلاة خلفهم والجمعة[؟] قال: نعم.

13 Ibn Khallikān, *Wafayāt*, 4:136, quoting Ibn al-Jawzī's *Shudhūr al-ʿuqūd*: في سنة سبع وأربعين ومائة وفيها ضرب مالك بن أنس سبعين سوطا لأجل فتوى لم توافق غرض السلطان.

14 Al-Dhahabī, *Siyar*, 8:80.

15 Al-Iṣfahānī, *Ḥilya* (Cairo edition), 6:316: two parts with two *isnāds* 1) … Aḥmad b. Isḥāq < Abū Bakr b. Muḥammad b. Aḥmad b. Rāshid < Abū Dāwūd; 2) "I was told by one of the followers (*aṣḥāb*) of Ibn Wahb from Ibn Wahb."

16 Al-Dhahabī, *Siyar*, 11:295.

17 Ibn Saʿd, *al-Qism al-mutammim*, 441; al-Dhahabī, *Siyar*, 8:80; Ibn Khallikān, *Wafayāt*, 4:136: from al-Wāqidī, a composite tradition, mentioning only the first accusation, that is, that the oath of allegiance to the ʿAbbāsīs is worthless; with no mention of the *ḥadīth* against divorce by coercion.

the transmitters (على هذا أكثر الرواة), except for Ibn Bukayr, who said that Mālik was flogged because he considered ʿUthmān more important than ʿAlī. This was the reason, continues Ibn Bukayr, that the ʿAlīds slandered Mālik, until he was flogged. It was said to Ibn Bukayr: you have disagreed with your fellow companions (*khālafta aṣḥābaka*), so he said, I know better than my associates.[18]

The *qāḍī* of Medina, Muḥammad b. ʿAbd al-ʿAzīz b. ʿUmar b. ʿAbd al-Raḥmān b. ʿAwf al-Zuhrī l-Qurashī, issued the *fatwā* allowing Mālik b. Anas to be flogged.[19]

2 Hishām b. ʿUrwa b. al-Zubayr

Abū l-Faraj al-Iṣfahānī records two traditions that mention Hishām b. ʿUrwa among those who took part in Muḥammad b. ʿAbdallāh's revolt. The first tradition was transmitted to him from Yaḥyā b. Saʿīd b. Farrūkh al-Qaṭṭān (120–198/737 or 738–813 or 814) through the latter's son, Muḥammad b. Yaḥyā (d. 226/840 or 841), who heard his father saying that "among those who rebelled with Muḥammad b. ʿAbdallāh were ʿUbaydallāh b. ʿUmar, Hishām b. ʿUrwa, and Muḥammad b. ʿAjlān." One chain in the *isnād*, ʿAbd al-Raḥmān b. Yūsuf, added, "I was informed by Musaddid that he related a similar account regarding their having rebelled with Muḥammad."[20] The second tradition was copied from the book (*kitāb*) of the historian and poet Aḥmad b. al-Ḥārith b. al-Mubārak al-Kharrāz (d. 258/872), who heard it from al-Madāʾinī. According to

---

18 Ibn Farḥūn, *al-Dībāj al-mudhhab*, 1:28: عدا ذلك كله ابن بكير وقال: ما ضرب إلا في تقديمه عثمان على علي رضي الله عنهما. فسعا به الطالبيون حتى ضرب. فقيل لأبي بكر: خالفت أصحابك فقال: أنا أعلم من أصحابي.

19 Ibn Ḥazm, *al-Iḥkām*, 5:91: محمد بن عبد العزيز بن عمر بن عبد الرحمان بن عوف ولي قضاء المدينة وبفتياه ضرب جعفر بن سليمان بن على بن عبد الله بن العباس مالك بن أنس; see also al-Dhahabī, *Siyar*, 11:295.

20 Al-Iṣfahānī, *Maqātil*, 292–293, with the following *isnād: ḥaddathanī* [that is, al-Iṣfahānī:] < Aḥmad b. Muḥammad b. Saʿīd < ʿAbd al-Raḥmān b. Yūsuf [b. Kharrāsh (d. 238/852 or 853), a pro-Shīʿī transmitter (وكان رافضيا), see al-Dhahabī, *Mīzān* (Beirut, 1382 H.), 2:600–601] < ʿUbaydallāh b. Yūsuf al-Jubayrī [Abū Yūsuf al-Baṣrī, d. ca. 150/767 or 768; on him, see al-Khazrajī, *Khulāṣa*, 254; Ibn Ḥajar, *Tahdhīb* (Hyderabad edition), 7:57; al-Mizzī, *Tahdhīb*, 19:179–181 and the comprehensive bibliography therein] < Muḥammad b. Yaḥyā b. Saʿīd al-Qaṭṭān [d. 226/840 or 841, on him, see Ibn Abī Ḥātim, *al-Jarḥ* (Beirut edition), 8:123–124; al-Mizzī, *Tahdhīb*, 26:610–612] < his father [Yaḥyā b. Saʿīd al-Qaṭṭān (120–198/737 or 738–813 or 814), on him, see al-Mizzī, *Tahdhīb*, 31:329–343, and the comprehensive bibliography therein].

this tradition Hishām b. ʿUrwa swore allegiance to Muḥammad b. ʿAbdallāh and was appointed governor of the city.[21]

I was unable to find this report about him being a supporter of Muḥammad b. ʿAbdallāh or of his appointment as governor of Medina by the latter in his numerous biographies in the Sunnī *ʿilm al-rijāl*. Nor is it mentioned in the vast Shīʿī literature of *ʿilm al-rijāl*, where he is mentioned as one of the adherents (*aṣḥāb*) of the Imām Jaʿfar al-Ṣādiq.[22] This evidence is, however, corroborated by al-Balādhurī, who relates that when the rebellion was over, the chief commander of the ʿAbbāsī army, ʿĪsā b. Mūsā, granted security and safety to the people of Medina: وآمن عيسى الناس "... and Hishām b. ʿUrwa and Ayyūb b. Salama al-Makhzūmī, had already sworn allegiance to Muḥammad b. ʿAbdallāh and they were granted security and safety when they gave excuses for themselves and repented" (probably in public).[23]

Hishām was a well-known scholar, a *faqīh* (one of the seven *fuqahāʾ* of Medina), and a *muḥaddith*. He was greatly esteemed by the authors of the Sunnī *ʿilm al-rijāl* books (e.g., the knowledge and evaluation of transmitters of *ḥadīth*). Many sources state that he was close to Caliph al-Manṣūr, and was one of the intimate group of scholars and notables that belonged to the confidential institution called "the *ṣaḥāba* of the Caliph," in this case صحابة المنصور.[24] When he died al-Manṣūr himself prayed over his body.[25] His grandson, Muḥammad b. ʿUrwa b. Hishām, gained al-Manṣūr's favor and later was one of the close associates of al-Mahdī and Hārūn al-Rashīd. In light of the information on the close and intimate relations of Hishām b. ʿUrwa with the ʿAbbāsī caliph, it is surprising to read that he supported Muḥammad b. ʿAbdallāh's revolt. According to some sources Hishām died in 145/762–763 (the year of the revolt), but most of the sources give his year of death as 146/763–764 (one source gives the year 147/764–765).[26]

---

21 Al-Iṣfahānī, *Maqātil*, 296: دفع إلي عيسى بن الحسين الوراق كتابا ذكر أنه كتاب أحمد بن الحارث فقرأت فيه: حدثنا المدائني أن هشام بن عروة بن الزبير بايع محمد بن عبدالله وجعل له ولاية المدينة; on Aḥmad b. al-Ḥārith, see Appendix 2, 388 n., 423f.

22 Al-Ṭūsī, *Rijāl*, 318 (*bāb al-hāʾ* no. 15 (4747); al-Shabastarī, *al-Imām al-Ṣādiq*, 3:387, and the exhaustive bibliography therein; al-Tafrishī, *Naqd al-rijāl*, 5:51.

23 Al-Balādhurī, *Ansāb* (ed. Madelung), 2:518; *Fragmenta*, 246: a similar parallel tradition: وكان هشام بن عروة وأيوب بن سلمة المخزومي قد بايعا محمد بن عبدالله فأومنا حين اعتذرا.

24 Al-Zubayr b. Bakkār, *Jamhara*, 304 (= al-Khaṭīb al-Baghdādī, *Taʾrīkh* (Beirut, 1997), 14:40); al-Zubayrī, *Nasab Quraysh*, 248; for this term, see Elad, "Transition," 93, n. 17.

25 Al-Zubayr b. Bakkār, *Jamhara*, 304; al-Khaṭīb al-Baghdādī, *Taʾrīkh* (Beirut, 1997), 14:41.

26 On Hishām b. ʿUrwa, see, for example, al-Zubayr b. Bakkār, *Jamhara*, 291–293, 299–304; 303–304: he died in Baghdad in 146/763 or 764; al-Zubayrī, *Nasab Quraysh*, 248: died in 145 H. or 146 H.; al-Balādhurī, *Ansāb* (ed. Iḥsān ʿAbbās), index, but esp. 5:55–56 (died in Baghdad in 146 H.); Ibn Abī Ḥātim, *al-Jarḥ* (Beirut edition), 9:63–64; 64: he died after the

One source emphasizes that he died after Ibrāhīm b. ʿAbdallāh's defeat[27] (the accepted date is 25 Dhū l-Qaʿda 145/14 February 763).[28]

From what has been said thus far, it is highly plausible that Hishām b. ʿUrwa died in 146, several months after the end of the rebellion of Ibrāhīm in al-Baṣra. Is it possible that the 86-year-old man (he died at the age of 87) supported Muḥammad b. ʿAbdallāh in Medina, arrived in Baghdad in late 145 H., requested and received *amān* from the caliph, who not only gave him a full pardon, but appointed him as one of his intimates in the *ṣaḥāba*, and when he died, bestowed on him the ultimate honor of praying over his dead body?

It is highly probable that Hishām b. ʿUrwa did not take any part in the revolt and that he lived in al-ʿIrāq during the revolt and even before it broke out. Ibn Saʿd records that Hishām "came to Abū Jaʿfar al-Manṣūr in al-Kūfa, and (then) joined him in Baghdad, where he died in 146 (H.)": وفد على أبي جعفر المنصور بالكوفة ولحق به ببغداد فمات بها في سنة ست وأربعين ومائة.[29]

While Baghdad was being built al-Manṣūr resided in al-Hāshimiyya, near al-Kūfa. It seems that Hishām b. ʿUrwa came first to al-Hāshimiyya, and then moved to Baghdad, while it was being built. However, from this text it is not possible to conclude unequivocally that Hishām went with the caliph from al-Kūfa [= al-Hāshimiyya] to Baghdad. When Hishām b. ʿUrwa left Medina for al-ʿIrāq is not known. Al-Zubayr b. Bakkār records that in one of his pilgrimages to Mecca, al-Manṣūr arrived in Medina and gave each of the *ashrāf* of that city 1,000 *dīnār*s. Al-Zubayr b. Bakkār mentions only one name, that of Hishām b. ʿUrwa.[30]

Al-Manṣūr's pilgrimage may have been in 136/754, while he was the heir apparent, in 140/758, or in 144/763. But since in 144 he did not enter Medina (he encamped in al-Rabadha, whence the Ḥasanīs were brought), it is possible that the pilgrimage occurred in 140/758. Hishām b. ʿUrwa could have left Medina after that year.

---

defeat of Ibrāhīm in 145 H.; al-Bukhārī, *al-Kabīr* (ed. al-Nadwī), 8:193–194; 194: "died after the defeat which occurred in 145"; al-Khaṭīb al-Baghdādī, *Taʾrīkh* (Beirut, 1997), 14:37–42; 41, from al-Zubayr b. Bakkār: he died in Baghdad in 146 H.; 42, from Abū Nuʿaym: died in 145 H., but according to ʿAbdallāh b. Dāwūd, ʿAbda b. Sulaymān al-Kilābī and al-Haytham b. ʿAdī: in 146 H.; ibid., according to ʿAmr b. ʿAlī: year 147 H.; Ibn Ḥajar, *Tahdhīb* (Beirut, 1984), 11:44–46; 46 and al-Mizzī, *Tahdhīb*, 30:232–242, and al-Ṣafadī, *al-Wāfī*, 27:358–359: all the dates are mentioned; Sezgin, 1:88–89: died in 146/763.

27 Al-Fasawī, *Maʿrifa*, 1:129.

28 Vaglieri, "Ibrāhīm b. ʿAbdallāh," 984b.

29 Ibn Saʿd, *Ṭabaqāt*, 7:321.

30 Al-Zubayr b. Bakkār, *Jamhara*, 303.

3 Sufyān b. Saʿīd b. Masrūq (known as Sufyān al-Thawrī, 97–161/715 or 716–778)[31]

Certain facts are well-known: His politico-religious pro-Umawī, "conservative" attitude; his antagonism towards the ʿAbbāsīs, his persecution already by al-Manṣūr and especially by al-Mahdī; and his having concealed himself from the ʿAbbāsī authorities until his death.[32]

Very little is known about his career and relations with the ʿAbbāsī authorities before ca. 150 H. It is well-known that he rejected the post of *qāḍī* in al-Kūfa in 153/769 and escaped to Ṣanʿāʾ.[33]

Al-Iṣfahānī records a tradition from Muḥammad b. Ismāʿīl b. Rajāʾ al-Zubaydī l-Kūfī (d. 167/783 or 784), who is considered in the Sunnī *rijāl* books as one of those who were defined as Shīʿa supporters.[34] Imāmī *rijāl* books describe him as one of the close supporters (*min aṣḥāb*) of Jaʿfar al-Ṣādiq.[35] This scholar relates in the first person that [already] in 140/757–758 Sufyān al-Thawrī praised Muḥammad b. ʿAbdallāh as one who is worthy of the Muslim community being unanimous in his regard, adding that the best people are the Shīʿīs.[36] Another tradition recorded by al-Iṣfahānī may testify to Sufyān's favorable view of Muḥammad b. ʿAbdallāh's revolt. It is recorded from ʿUmar b. Shabba through al-Walīd b. Hishām b. Qaḥdham [b. Sulaymān b. Dhakwān; d. 222/836 or 837], a *muḥaddith* and historian, and also according to the Imāmīs a close supporter of Jaʿfar al-Ṣādiq,[37] from Sahl b. Bishr (not identified), who heard Sufyān [al-Thawrī?] saying: "I wish that this Mahdī had come out, that is (relating to) Muḥammad b. ʿAbdallāh b. al-Ḥasan."[38] But in another parallel tradition Sahl heard a young girl (*fatāt*) instead of Sufyān.[39]

On the face of it, these traditions may be regarded as authentic, in light of what is known about the tense and hostile relations between Sufyān al-Thawrī and the ʿAbbāsīs. But according to different traditions we learn that Sufyān attacked the

31 On him, see Raddatz, "Sufyān al-Thawrī"; van Ess, *Theologie*, index, esp. 1:221–228; Zaman, *Religion and Politics*, index, esp. 79–80; Sezgin, 1:518–519.

32 Raddatz, "Sufyān al-Thawrī," 771b; Zaman, *Religion and Politics*, 79; for the tense/hostile relations, for example, see al-Dhahabī, *Siyar*, 7:244, 246, 251, 257–259, 262–266.

33 Raddatz, "Sufyān al-Thawrī," 771a.

34 Ibn ʿAdī, *Ḍuʿafāʾ*, 247; al-Mizzī, *Tahdhīb*, 24:473–474.

35 E.g., al-Ṭūsī, *Rijāl*, 276; Khūʾī, *Rijāl*, 16:113–114.

36 Al-Iṣfahānī, *Maqātil*, 292.

37 On him, see Ibn Khayyāṭ, *Ṭabaqāt* (ed. Zakkār), 399; Ibn Ḥibbān, *al-Thiqāt*, 7:555; al-Samʿānī, *al-Ansāb* (Beirut, 1988), 4:455; Ibn Abī Ḥātim, *al-Jarḥ* (Beirut edition), 9:20; Ibn Ḥajar, *Lisān*, 6:228. Imāmī literature: al-Ṭūsī, *Rijāl*, 317; al-Shabastarī, *al-Imām al-Ṣādiq*, 3:407–408; see also Ibn ʿAsākir, *Taʾrīkh*, 70:165: a family of secretaries.

38 Al-Iṣfahānī, *Maqātil*, 205.

39 Ibid., 244.

muḥaddith ʿAbd al-Ḥamīd b. Jaʿfar al-Anṣārī al-Awsī, and declared him a weak (unreliable: *ḍaʿīf*) transmitter. One criticism of *ḥadīth* transmitters explains that it was due to his Qadarī (free will) doctrine,[40] but another explains that it was due to his participation in Muḥammad b. ʿAbdallāh's revolt.[41] The well-known scholar Abū Dāwūd al-Sijistānī (d. 275/888) is quoted as saying:

> Sufyān al-Thawrī used to speak ill against ʿAbd al-Ḥamīd b. Jaʿfar because he rebelled with Muḥammad, adding the following: if the Mahdī passes by you while you are at home, do not come out to him until the people gather together against him.[42]

Abū Dāwūd adds that Sufyān did not speak with another scholar, Abū Khālid al-Aḥmar Sulaymān b. Ḥayyān, who joined the rebellion of Ibrāhīm b. ʿAbdallāh until his (Sufyān's) death.[43] Sufyān is said to have had a very negative opinion of the scholar al-Ḥasan b. Ṣāliḥ b. Ṣāliḥ, who believed that it is permissible to rise up in arms against the ruler.[44]

These traditions bear witness to Sufyān's total and general rejection of armed rebellion against the ruler, on the one hand, and to his negative attitude towards Muḥammad b. ʿAbdallāh's revolt in particular, on the other hand.

4 Abū Ḥanīfa al-Nuʿmān b. Thābit (d. 150/767)

> There are numerous references in Abū Ḥanīfa's biographical reports to his unequivocal support of the Ḥusaynīd anti-Umayyad rebellion of Zayd b. ʿAlī (in 120/738)... and the Ḥasanid anti-ʿAbbasid rebellion of Muḥammad al-Nafs al-Zakiyya and his younger brother Ibrāhīm... he was so vociferous in his support for Ibrāhīm....[45]

Schacht's view is less unequivocal, "the truth is probably that he compromised himself by unguarded remarks at the time of the rising of the ʿAlids al-Nafs al-Zakiyya and his brother Ibrāhīm, in 145, was transferred to Baghdad and imprisoned there."[46]

---

40 Ibn Ḥajar, *Tahdhīb* (Beirut edition), 6:101; al-Mizzī, *Tahdhīb*, 16:418–419.

41 Ibn Abī Ḥātim, *al-Jarḥ* (Beirut edition), 6:10; al-Mizzī, *Tahdhīb*, 16:419.

42 Al-Dhahabī, *Taʾrīkh*, 9:23; idem, *Siyar*, 6:215; al-Khaṭīb al-Baghdādī, *Taʾrīkh* (Beirut, 1997), 23 (correct Sulaymān to Sufyān).

43 Al-Khaṭīb al-Baghdādī, *Taʾrīkh* (Beirut, 1997), 23.

44 Al-Dhahabī, *Siyar*, 7:363; Ibn Ḥajar, *Tahdhīb* (Beirut, 1984), 2:249; al-Mizzī, *Tahdhīb*, 6:181.

45 ʿAbdallāh, "Abū Ḥanīfa," 299.

46 Schacht, "Abū Ḥanīfa," 123a; van Ess, *Theologie*, 1:187–188.

It is noteworthy that the sources I checked speak of his favorable view and support of Ibrāhīm's revolt and not that of his brother, Muḥammad.[47] It seems that this was also van Arendonk's conclusion; he based his findings mainly on Zaydī sources and mentioned Abū Ḥanīfa as the supporter of Zayd b. ʿAlī b. al-Ḥusayn and of Ibrāhīm b. ʿAbdallāh, and not of Muḥammad.[48]

5 Hārūn b. Saʿd al-ʿIjlī[49]

There are conflicting reports about the well-known Kūfan scholar, Hārūn b. Saʿd al-ʿIjlī, and his support of the rebellions of the two brothers. Abū l-Faraj al-Iṣfahānī relates that Hārūn b. Saʿd al-ʿIjlī was appointed by Ibrāhīm to govern Wāsiṭ, and the latter sent a large army of the Zaydiyya: جيشا كثيفا من الزيدية with him.[50] Other traditions state that Hārūn reached Wāsiṭ and was besieged by the ʿAbbāsī commander ʿĀmir b. Ismāʿīl.[51] Ibn Ḥibbān accuses him of being an extreme *rāfiḍī*, the "head of the *Zaydiyya*; he used to pray near the piece of the wood on which Zayd [b. ʿAlī] was crucified and propagated for Zayd's doctrines (respecting religion). It is forbidden to transmit from him or to cite his opinions under any circumstance."[52] Ibn Abī Ḥātim specifically says that he took part in the rebellion of Ibrāhīm b. ʿAbdallāh b. al-Ḥasan. When the latter was defeated he fled to Wāsiṭ, so the people of Wāsiṭ wrote down (*ḥadīth*) from him.[53]

---

47 Cf. Schacht, "Abū Ḥanīfa," 123a, quoting al-Khaṭīb al-Baghdādī, *Taʾrīkh* (Cairo edition), 10:329; but ibid., Abū Ḥanīfa speaks in favor of Ibrāhīm; all the many traditions recorded by al-Iṣfahānī, *Maqātil*, 361, 364–368, 378, 379, speak of the favorable attitude of Abū Ḥanīfa to Ibrāhīm, for example, see ibid., 366: Abū Ḥanīfa writes to Ibrāhīm to come to al-Kūfa in order to receive assistance from the Zaydiyya: كتب أبو حنيفة إلى إبراهيم يشير عليه أن يقدم الكوفة ليعينه الزيدية.

48 Van Arendonk, *L'Imamat Zaïdite*, 30–31, 307: Zayd b. ʿAlī; 58, 315–316: Ibrāhīm b. ʿAbdallāh; and see Zaman, *Religion and Politics*, 74, n. 13 (quoting al-Iṣfahānī and Van Arendonk).

49 On him, see Van Arendonk, *L'Imamat Zaïdite*, 309, 314; Sezgin, 1:560; McAuliffe, *ʿAbbāsid Authority*, 219, n. 1032, with additional bibliography; Van Ess, *Theologie*, index, esp. 1:252–253, and the exhaustive bibliography therein.

50 Al-Iṣfahānī, *Maqātil*, 359; see also al-Ṭabarī, 3:302 (l. 10): appointed by Ibrāhīm over Wāsiṭ; but no mention of his army or al-Zaydiyya.

51 Al-Ṭabarī, 3:254 (ll. 9–10), 3:302 (ll. 17–19); on ʿĀmir b. Ismāʿīl, see Agha, *Revolution*, 342, no. 125; McAuliffe, *ʿAbbāsid Authority*, 218–219, n. 1031.

52 Ibn Ḥibbān, *al-Majrūḥīn* (Ḥalab edition), 3:94: كان غاليا بالرفض وهو رأس الزيدية كان ممن يعتكف عند خشبة زيد بن علي وكان داعيا إلى مذهبه ولا يحل الرواية عنه ولا الإحتجاج به بالحال.

53 Ibn Abī Ḥātim, *al-Jarḥ* (Beirut edition), 9:91 [copied by al-Mizzī, *Tahdhīb*, 30:87].

In contrast to this assertion, al-Balādhurī tells us that "Hārūn b. Saʿd al-ʿIjlī was a Shīʿī, and (therefore?) he maligned Ibrāhīm's rebellion": وكان هارون بن سعد العجلي شيعيا فعاب خروج إبراهيم. Hārūn, adds al-Balādhurī, recited three poetry verses before Ibrāhīm b. ʿAbdallāh, and stated that in spite of the fact that Ibrāhīm is his leader and they follow his example in religion, he is forced to turn away from him in regard to his innovation (*mubtadiʿ*).[54]

But according to al-Zubayr b. Bakkār, Hārūn's negative attitude was towards the rebellion of Muḥammad and not Ibrāhīm; the verses were recited in front of Muḥammad.[55] Ibn Ḥajar also quotes scholars who describe Hārūn as a devout, extreme Shīʿī, but adds that "Abū l-ʿArab al-Ṣiqillī [Muṣʿab b. Muḥammad, d. 506/1112][56] related from Ibn Qutayba that Hārūn recited some verses to him that prove that he pulled away from the Shīʿī [Zaydī?] persuasion": أنشد له شعرا يدل على نزوعه عن الرفض.[57]

It is possible that the verses referred to by Ibn Ḥajar are those that are quoted by al-Balādhurī and al-Dhahabī, who in another place, when commenting on Ibn Abī Ḥātim's criticism of Hārūn b. Saʿd, says that "he was not an extreme *rāfiḍī* because al-Rāfiḍa separated themselves from Zayd b. ʿAlī and abandoned him": لم يكن غاليا في رفضه فإن الرافضة رفضت زيد بن علي وفارقه.[58]

---

54 Al-Balādhurī, *Ansāb* (ed. Madelung), 2:532 [ed. al-ʿAẓm, 2:442–443].

55 Al-Dhahabī, *Taʾrīkh*, 9:272; al-Mizzī, *Tahdhīb*, 25:467; both quoting al-Zubayr b. Bakkār: وقال هارون بن سعد العجلي يعيب خروجه وكان هارون بن سعد العجلي شيعيا.

56 On him, see al-Ziriklī, *al-Aʿlām*, 7:249.

57 Ibn Ḥajar, *Tahdhīb* (Hyderabad edition), 11:11.

58 Al-Dhahabī, *Taʾrīkh*, 9:316.

Appendix 2: Transmitters and Transmission of the Historical Events of the Revolt

This appendix provides information regarding the transmission and transmitters of traditions pertaining to events and circumstances related to the rebellion of Muḥammad b. ʿAbdallāh. Part of the appendix deals with scholars and members of the Ṭālibī family who transmitted intimate firsthand traditions related to members of their family and the rebellion. The central part deals with the direct transmitters of ʿUmar b. Shabba and their transmitters, most of whom were contemporaries of the rebellion, some eyewitnesses, some active participants. Eyewitness transmitters are designated EW.

1 Transmitters from the Ṭālibī Families

1.1 *The Descendants of ʿUmar b. ʿAlī b. Abī Ṭālib*

1) The Descendants of Muḥammad b. ʿUmar b. ʿAlī b. Abī Ṭālib

For ʿAbdallāh b. Muḥammad b. ʿUmar, his son ʿĪsā in particular, and his brother ʿUbaydallāh, see below: Ibn Shabba's direct transmitters and also chapter 7 (part 1).

1.2 *The Descendants of al-Ḥasan b. ʿAlī b. Abī Ṭālib*

1) Abdallāh b. Muḥammad b. Sulaymān b. ʿAbdallāh b. al-Ḥasan b. al-Ḥasan b. ʿAlī b. Abī Ṭālib

The great-grandson of ʿAbdallāh b. al-Ḥasan, the father of Muḥammad al-Nafs al-Zakiyya.[1] He transmitted from his Ḥasanī relatives pro-ʿAlīd traditions in general, and pro-Ḥasanī ones in particular, but he is also quoted in non-Shīʿī works.[2]

---

1 He was identified with the help of several traditions in al-Iṣfahānī's *Maqātil*, 236 (ll. 3–4), 706 (l. 2), 720 (l. 3); on him, see also Ibn ʿInaba, *ʿUmda*, 157, quoting "al-Mūḍiḥ [Muwaḍḍiḥ?] al-Nassāba" (quoted several times by Ibn ʿInaba), who is Abū ʿAlī, ʿUmar b. ʿAlī b. al-Ḥusayn (flourished in the first half of the fifth/eleventh century); he was the teacher of al-ʿUmarī, ʿAlī b. Abī l-Ghanāʾim Muḥammad, who flourished also in the first half of the fifth/eleventh century (he was alive in 443/1051), and of his father as well; see the introduction of Shihāb al-Dīn al-Marʿashī to al-ʿUmarī's book, *al-Majdī fī ansāb al-ṭālibiyyīn*, 9; ibid., al-Marʿashī suggests that he died in 459 H.; for a comprehensive bibliography on al-ʿUmarī, see Kohlberg, *Ibn Ṭāʾūs*, 239–240; al-Muwaḍḍiḥ is mentioned by al-ʿUmarī several times, see *Ansāb*, 10, 11, 13, 20, 61, 130–131.

2 Pro-Ḥasanī tradition: al-Iṣfahānī, *Maqātil*, 159, relating from the grandson of ʿAbdallāh b. al-Ḥasan: "Aḥmad b. Saʿīd < Yaḥyā b. al-Ḥasan [b. Jaʿfar b. ʿUbaydallāh b. al-Ḥusayn b. ʿAlī b. al-Ḥusayn b. ʿAlī b. Abī Ṭālib, al-ʿUbaydalī l-ʿAqīqī, the genealogist and historian, on him, see below] < ʿAbdallāh b. Muḥammad b. Sulaymān b. ʿAbdallāh b. al-Ḥasan, who said: I heard ʿAbdallāh b. Mūsā [b. ʿAbdallāh b. al-Ḥasan] saying: My grandmother, Hind, was pregnant

 | DOI 10.1163/9789004296220_013

He transmitted a typical tradition, relating that Muḥammad b. ʿAbdallāh was called al-Mahdī from birth, this was attributed to the saying of the Prophet that the name of the Mahdī is Muḥammad b. ʿAbdallāh; this was the reason that "the family of Muḥammad was so happy upon his birth, and the Shīʿa rejoiced with one another by the annunciation of his appearance (وتباشرت به الشيعة)." It is related in *Maqātil al-ṭālibiyyīn*, and was most probably not taken from ʿUmar b. Shabba's work. Its *isnād* runs as follows: *ḥaddathanī* Aḥmad b. Saʿīd < Yaḥyā b. al-Ḥasan [b. Jaʿfar b. ʿUbaydallāh al-ʿUbaydalī] < ʿAbdallāh b. Muḥammad < Ḥumayd b. Saʿīd.[3]

2) EW/Mūsā b. ʿAbdallāh b. al-Ḥasan b. al-Ḥasan b. ʿAlī b. Abī Ṭālib, Muḥammad al-Nafs al-Zakiyya's brother

Nine of Mūsā b. ʿAbdallāh's traditions were recorded by al-Ṭabarī, all of them firsthand, eyewitness testimonies about the events. Three traditions were related from him to Muḥammad b. Ismāʿīl [b. Jaʿfar b. Ibrāhīm b. Muḥammad b. ʿAlī b. ʿAbdallāh b. Jaʿfar b. Abī Ṭālib; on him, see below: Ibn Shabba's direct transmitters], who transmitted them to ʿUmar b. Shabba; four were transmitted to his son ʿAbdallāh who transmitted them to his son Mūsā, who was a direct transmitter of ʿUmar b. Shabba [on Mūsā b. ʿAbdallāh, see below: Ibn Shabba's direct transmitters], one tradition to ʿĪsā b. ʿAbdallāh who transmitted to ʿUmar b. Shabba and one to Ismāʿīl b. Jaʿfar b. Ibrāhīm, the father of Muḥammad, mentioned above (on him, see below: Ibn Shabba's direct transmitters).[4] Interestingly, in *Maqātil al-ṭālibiyyīn*, only five traditions were recorded from him, of which only two are parallel to traditions recorded in al-Ṭabarī's *Taʾrīkh*.[5] Most of the traditions deal with the imprisonment of the Ḥasanīs.

---

with my uncle Muḥammad b. ʿAbdallāh four years; al-Ṭabarī (al-Imāmī), *Manāqib*, 74: also relating from Mūsā b. ʿAbdallāh b. al-Ḥasan < his father < his grandfather: God has chosen ʿAlī b. Abī Ṭālib as the heir of the Prophet; for non-Shīʿī works, for example, see al-Ṣāliḥī l-Shāmī, *Subul al-hudā*, 11:29.

3 Al-Iṣfahānī, *Maqātil*, 244–245 [= al-Mizzī, *Tahdhīb*, 25:468: adding the title *al-nassāba* (the geneaology expert) to Yaḥyā's name: وقال يحيى بن الحسن بن جعفر النسابة حدثني....].

4 **1)** Al-Ṭabarī, 3:144 (ll. 10–13): ʿUmar b. Shabba < Muḥammad b. Ismāʿīl < my grandfather Mūsā b. ʿAbdallāh; **2)** 3:172 (ll. 4–15): ʿUmar b. Shabba < Mūsā b. ʿAbdallāh b. Mūsā b. ʿAbdallāh b. Ḥasan < my father < his father, Mūsā b. ʿAbdallāh; **3)** 3:172–173 (l. 20 to l. 9): ʿUmar b. Shabba < Mūsā b. ʿAbdallāh < my father < his father; **4)** 3:173 (ll. 11–14): ʿUmar b. Shabba < Mūsā b. ʿAbdallāh < his father < his grandfather; **5)** 3:179–180 (l. 4 to l. 2): ʿUmar b. Shabba < Mūsā b. ʿAbdallāh b. Mūsā < my father < his father; **6)** 3:180 (ll. 2–11): ʿUmar b. Shabba < Muḥammad b. Ismāʿīl < Mūsā; **7)** 3:185 (ll. 13–15): ʿUmar b. Shabba < Muḥammad b. Ismāʿīl < I heard my grandfather Mūsā b. ʿAbdallāh; **8)** 3:216–217 (l. 13 to l. 3): ʿUmar b. Shabba < ʿĪsā [b. ʿAbdallāh] < Mūsā b. ʿAbdallāh in Baghdad; **9)** 3:256–257 (l. 15 to l. 2): ʿUmar b. Shabba < Ismāʿīl b. Jaʿfar b. Ibrāhīm < Mūsā b. ʿAbdallāh b. Ḥasan.

5 Al-Iṣfahānī, *Maqātil*, 192 [= al-Ṭabarī, 3:185 (ll. 13–15)]: two strands of transmission; 192:... Aḥmad b. Saʿīd < Yaḥyā b. al-Ḥasan [al-ʿAqīqī] < Mūsā b. ʿAbdallāh b. Mūsā; 223–224:

3) Al-Ḥasan b. Zayd b. al-Ḥasan b. ʿAlī b. Abī Ṭālib

1.3 *The Descendants of al-Ḥusayn b. ʿAlī b. Abī Ṭālib*

1) EW/al-Ḥusayn b. Zayd b. ʿAlī b. al-Ḥusayn b. ʿAlī b. Abī Ṭālib

He was a supporter of Muḥammad al-Nafs al-Zakiyya, took an active part in the revolt and transmitted firsthand reports about the revolt.[6]

2) EW/Muḥammad b. Zayd b. ʿAlī b. al-Ḥusayn b. ʿAlī b. Abī Ṭālib

He was the brother of the aforementioned. He was a supporter of the ʿAbbāsīs, who came to Medina with the ʿAbbāsī army headed by ʿĪsā b. Mūsā; it is noteworthy that his brothers, al-Ḥusayn and ʿĪsā, the sons of Zayd b. ʿAlī b. al-Ḥusayn b. ʿAlī b. Abī Ṭālib, were two of the loyal supporters of Muḥammad al-Nafs al-Zakiyya.[7] Muḥammad b. Zayd was a direct transmitter of ʿĪsā b. ʿAbdallāh, who related to the latter reports in the first person about the revolt.[8]

3) Yaḥyā b. al-Ḥasan b. Jaʿfar b. ʿUbaydallāh b. al-Ḥusayn b. ʿAlī b. al-Ḥusayn b. ʿAlī b. Abī Ṭālib al-ʿUbaydalī l-ʿAqīqī (214–277/829–890)

He was a historian and genealogist. He compiled a work on the genealogy of the Ṭālibīs: أنساب/نسب آل أبي طالب, which is commonly considered as the earliest Ṭālibī *nasab* book,[9] but see the discussion on Aḥmad b. ʿĪsā b. ʿAbdallāh b. Muḥammad b. ʿUmar b. ʿAlī b. Abī Ṭālib (d. 266/879 or 880), who also compiled a book on the genealogy of the Ṭālibīs. This *nasab* work may have preceded the *nasab* book of al-ʿAqīqī.

ʿUmar b. Shabba < Mūsā b. ʿAbdallāh < his father < his grandfather [= al-Ṭabarī, 3:179–180 (l. 4 to l. 2)]; 238: ʿUmar b. Shabba < Muḥammad b. Ismāʿīl < Mūsā b. ʿAbdallāh; 437: ... al-Ḥasan b. al-Ḥusayn b. Jāmiʿ < Mūsā b. ʿAbdallāh b. al-Ḥasan.

6 Al-Ṭabarī, 3:174–175 (l. 15 to l. 7); al-Iṣfahānī, *Maqātil*, 251–252, 277. See also the interesting tradition in *Akhbār al-ʿAbbās*, 383–384, related from al-Ḥusayn b. Zayd in the first person: Ibrāhīm b. Muḥammad b. ʿAlī *al-Imām* arrives in Medina and distributes money among the Ḥasanīs and the Ḥusaynīs; to the Ḥasanīs ʿAbdallāh b. al-Ḥasan and his brother Ibrāhīm he gives 500 (*dīnārs* ?) and to Jaʿfar al-Ṣādiq 1,000(!).

7 On Muḥammad b. Zayd and his family, see Ibn ʿInaba, *ʿUmda*, 69ff.; he is not "just" a *rāwī*, as defined by de Goeje in the *Index to al-Ṭabarī*; he is not identified by McAuliffe, *ʿAbbāsid Authority*, 197.

8 Al-Ṭabarī, 3:234 (ll. 4–5); 3:235–236 (l. 6 to l. 5); 3:240 (ll. 1–9); 3:252 (ll. 10–14); the transmission is recorded below.

9 Al-Ṭihrānī, *al-Dharīʿa* (al-Najaf, 1355 H.), 2:285 and 378: quoting Ibn ʿInaba's *ʿUmda*: هو أول من صنف في نسب الطالبين (I was unable to find the quote in Ibn ʿInaba's book); al-Amīn, *Aʿyān al-Shīʿa*, 5:283; al-Baghdādī, *Hadiyyat al-ʿārifīn*, 1:674; al-Ziriklī, *al-Aʿlām*, 8:141; Kaḥḥāla, *Muʿjam*, 13:190; Abū Zayd, *Ṭabaqāt*, 66–67; on him, see Sezgin, 1:273; Bernheimer, *The ʿAlids*, 18.

Apart from *nasab* material about the Ṭālibīs, Yaḥyā b. al-Ḥasan al-ʿAqīqī appears as a link in many traditions relating to the Ḥasanī family during and after the rebellion.[10]

1.4 *The Family of Jaʿfar b. Abī Ṭālib*

1) EW/Muḥammad b. ʿAbdallāh (Abū l-Karrām [Kirām?]) b. Muḥammad b. ʿAlī b. ʿAbdallāh b. Jaʿfar b. Abī Ṭālib

He was a faithful supporter of the ʿAbbāsīs and their cause and was one of the closest confidents and dignitaries of Caliph al-Manṣūr. Muḥammad b. Abī l-Karrām transmitted a few eyewitness traditions on the revolt to ʿĪsā b. ʿAbdallāh b. Muḥammad b. ʿUmar b. ʿAlī.[11]

2) His son, Ibrāhīm, was a direct transmitter of ʿUmar b. Shabba (on him, see below: Ibn Shabba's direct transmitters), in several cases he relied on his father.[12] One such tradition records one of the versions of the al-Abwāʾ affair, that is, the alleged meeting of the Hāshimīs in al-Abwāʾ towards the end of Umawī rule, where they swore allegiance to Muḥammad b. ʿAbdallāh as the future caliph. This specific version is very interesting, introducing onto the stage Jaʿfar al-Ṣādiq, who clearly and bluntly tells ʿAbdallāh b. al-Ḥasan that the caliphate will not pass to his sons but to the ʿAbbāsīs, and that his two sons will be killed.[13]

Perhaps it is not merely a coincidence that this version is related by Muḥammad b. Abī l-Karrām and his son, that is, due to their extreme loyalty to the ʿAbbāsīs and their being an integral component of the political-social and religious regime. This tradition was most probably circulated immediately after the death of Muḥammad and Ibrāhīm. It reflects a bias towards both the ʿAbbāsīs and Jaʿfar al-Ṣādiq, the Ḥusaynī. It may be interesting to look for special relations between Muḥammad b. Abī l-Karrām and Jaʿfar al-Ṣādiq, a task beyond the scope of this work.[14]

3) His brother, Dāwūd b. ʿAbdallāh (Abū l-Karrām), b. Muḥammad b. ʿAlī b. ʿAbdallāh b. Jaʿfar b. Abī Ṭālib, Abū Sulaymān

---

10 He appears as a link in the *isnād* of dozens of traditions in Abū l-Faraj al-Iṣfahānī's *Maqātil*. More than 30 traditions deal with the Ḥasanī family and the events of the rebellion: see ibid., 175, 176, 180–187, 192, 199, 203, 209, 216, 236, 242, 244–245 [the parallel tradition in al-Mizzī, *Tahdhīb*, 25:468: وقال يحيى بن الحسن بن جعفر العلوي النسابة...], 248, 252, 253, 279, 280, 293, 294, 316, 352–353, 396, 408, 432.

11 E.g., al-Ṭabarī, 3:231–232 (l. 7 to l. 8); 3:254 (ll. 7–16).

12 Al-Ṭabarī, 3:232–233 (l. 20 to l. 1), 3:316 (l. 15).

13 Al-Iṣfahānī, *Maqātil*, 206, 255; and see the discussion of al-Abwāʾ in chapter 2.

14 Some Imāmī sources mention him as one of Jaʿfar al-Ṣādiq's close associates: من أصحاب الصادق, see al-Khūʾī, *Rijāl*, 15:310; al-Shāhrūdī l-Namāzī, *Rijāl*, 394; quoting al-Barqī's *Rijāl* (not available to me).

He was a Medinese scholar. He often appears as a transmitter in Sunnī *ḥadīth* works, many times transmitting directly from ʿAbd al-ʿAzīz b. Muḥammad al-Darāwardī.[15] He appears as a link in the tradition according to which ʿAbdallāh b. al-Ḥasan propagandized for the Mahdīship of his son. This we learn from an early tradition, narrated by al-Zuhrī's nephew [Muḥammad b. ʿAbdallāh b. Muslim, d. 152 or 157/769–770 or 773–774], transmitted through scholars who were either followers of the Ḥasanīs and even took part in the rebellion of al-Nafs al-Zakiyya's rebellion, or belonged to the ʿAlīd (Jaʿfarī) family.[16]

4) Muḥammad b. Jaʿfar b. Ibrāhīm b. Muḥammad b. ʿAlī b. ʿAbdallāh b. Jaʿfar b. Abī Ṭālib

5) Ismāʿīl b. Jaʿfar b. Ibrāhīm b. Muḥammad b. ʿAlī b. ʿAbdallāh b. Jaʿfar b. Abī Ṭālib, and

6) Muḥammad b. Ismāʿīl b. Jaʿfar b. Ibrāhīm b. Muḥammad b. ʿAlī b. ʿAbdallāh b. Jaʿfar b. Abī Ṭālib (the aforementioned son)[17]

Non-Ḥasanī families related to the Ḥasanīs by marriage:

1) EW/Saʿīd b. ʿUqba b. Shaddād b. Umayya al-Juhanī
His origin is not known. So far I have found only one reference on his grandfather, Shaddād b. Umayya, who was a *ṣaḥābī*.[18] It is possible that the family belonged to Banū

15 On him, see Ibn Ḥibbān, *al-Thiqāt*, 8:235; Ibn Abī Ḥātim, *al-Jarḥ* (Beirut edition), 3:416: he had in his possession, through the transmission of [?*ʿan*] Ḥātim b. Ismāʿīl, 30 volumes of the (*ḥadīth*) works of Sharīk [b. ʿAbdallāh b. Abī Sharīk, 95–177/713 or 714–793 or 794]: كان عنده عن حاتم بن إسماعيل مصنفات شريك نحو ثلاثين جزءا; Ibn Ḥajar, *Taqrīb* (Beirut, 1995), 1:607; al-Dhahabī, *Taʾrīkh*, 15:147; Ibn Ḥajar, *Tahdhīb* (Beirut, 1984), 3:165; al-Mizzī, *Tahdhīb*, 8:409–410; the last three sources quote Ibn Abī Ḥātim on the works of Sharīk; transmitting traditions: e.g., al-Ṭabarānī, *al-Awsaṭ*, 7:302; idem, *al-Kabīr* (Cairo edition), 19:98; 24:323; Ibn ʿAsākir, *Taʾrīkh*, 18:8; 41:355; 52:5.

16 Al-Mizzī, *Tahdhīb*, 25:467–468: Dāwūd b. ʿAbdallāh al-Jaʿfarī < al-Darāwardī [ʿAbd al-ʿAzīz b. Muḥammad b. ʿUbayd] < al-Zuhrī's nephew.

17 On him, see al-Bukhārī, *al-Kabīr* (ed. al-Nadwī), 1:37 (his entry); Ibn Abī Ḥātim, *al-Jarḥ* (Beirut edition), 7:189; al-Samʿānī, *Ansāb* (Beirut, 1988), 2:68 ("al-Jaʿfarī"); Nagel, "Muḥammad b. ʿAbdallāh," 244–245 (and see also below under Ibn Shabba's direct transmitters).

18 Al-Bakrī, *Muʿjam*, 1:155 ("al-Ashʿar"): Shaddād b. Umayya al-Dhuhlī came to the Prophet with a gift of honey; his *nisba*: Dhuhlī, from Juhayna, see al-Bakrī, *Muʿjam*, 1:155: وبني عوف بن ذهل الجهنيين.

Rabʿa b. Rashdān b. Qays b. Juhayna; we learn this from the report on a certain Salama b. Aslum, a minor Medinan transmitter of *ḥadīth* (and possibly also a poet) from Banū Rabʿa b. Rashdān, whose father may have been ʿUqba b. Shaddād b. Umayya al-Juhanī. Salama b. Aslum's son ʿAbdallāh is reported to have transmitted traditions from ʿUqba b. Shaddād, who was a minor *ḥadīth* transmitter.[19]

Saʿīd stayed with (in the house of) the daughter of Ruqayya bt. Mūsā b. ʿAbdallāh, and ʿAbdallāh b. al-Ḥasan took him from her, and the transmitter adds that he was under the care and protection of ʿAbdallāh b. al-Ḥasan (كان في حجره).[20] Fāṭima, Saʿīd b. ʿUqba's daughter, was married to Mūsā's son ʿAbdallāh.[21]

Because of this relationship with ʿAbdallāh b. al-Ḥasan's family, Saʿīd was able to record several traditions on this family.

Two anecdotes are related by two people who witnessed the total destruction of the estate of the Ḥasanīs. The second anecdote of these two is the eyewitness testimony of Saʿīd b. ʿUqba [b. Shaddād b. Umayya al-Juhanī], who describes the ruined Baṭḥāʾ Suwayqa.[22] It is plausible to assume that this testimony was passed on to Ismāʿīl b. Jaʿfar b. Ibrāhīm b. Muḥammad b. ʿAlī b. ʿAbdallāh b. Jaʿfar b. Abī Ṭālib, although he is not specifically mentioned in the text. We remember that the two families, that of Saʿīd and that of Ismāʿīl, were related by marriage ties: Ismāʿīl was a relative of Mūsā b. ʿAbdallāh and apparently close to him; he married Ruqayya, the daughter of Mūsā b. ʿAbdallāh; and Saʿīd's daughter married Mūsā's son, ʿAbdallāh. The preceding two traditions in al-Bakrī's book are related from Ismāʿīl b. Jaʿfar. Other traditions related by Saʿīd were passed on to Ismāʿīl. They all reveal the close family relations between Saʿīd and ʿAbdallāh b. al-Ḥasan's family, telling of intimate events of this family.

---

19 On ʿUqba b. Shaddād, see al-ʿUqaylī, *Ḍuʿafāʾ* (ed. Qalʿajī), 3:352; al-Dhahabī, *Mīzān* (ed. al-Bijāwī), 3:85; al-Bakrī, *Muʿjam*, 1:155 ("al-Ashʿar"); see also Ibn ʿAsākir, *Taʾrīkh*, 50:97; al-Mizzī, *Tahdhīb*, 26:150: . . . al-Zubayr [b. Bakkār] < Muḥammad b. Ismāʿīl b. Jaʿfar < Saʿīd b. ʿUqba < his father: ʿUqba reciting a poem of Kuthayyir that he himself heard from the poet, in praise of Muḥammad b. ʿAlī [Ibn al-Ḥanafiyya].

20 Al-Iṣfahānī, *Maqātil*, 238.

21 Al-Khaṭīb al-Baghdādī, *Taʾrīkh* (Beirut, 1997), 13:41: موسى بن عبد الله بن موسى بن عبد الله بن الحسن بن الحسن بن علي بن أبي طالب، مديني الأصل سكن بغداد وحدث بها عن أبيه وعن أمه فاطمة بنت سعيد بن عقبة الجهني; ibid., a tradition, related through him < [his mother] Fāṭima bt. Saʿīd b. ʿUqba b. Shaddād b. Umayya < her father [Saʿīd b. ʿUqba] < Zayd b. ʿAlī [b. al-Ḥusayn b. ʿAlī b. Abī Ṭālib] < his father < his grandfather [al-Ḥusayn b. ʿAlī] < ʿAlī b. Abī Ṭālib (it is not stated in this case that Fāṭima is his mother, that is, *ḥaddathatnī ummī* . . .). The tradition tells of the first object created by God, the pen and then the inkstand; Ibn al-Jawzī, *al-Muntaẓam*, 1:120 and al-Suyūṭī, *al-Laʾālīʾ al-maṣnūʿa*, 1:121–122 (a parallel tradition).

22 Al-Bakrī, *Muʿjam*, 3:768 ("Suwayqaʾ"); large parts of the text were copied by al-Ḥimyarī, *al-Rawḍ al-miʿṭār*, 328–329.

Of special interest are traditions related from Saʿīd describing the special, sometimes extraordinary physical as well as spiritual-religious traits of Muḥammad b. ʿAbdallāh. From these traditions it is clear that the inner circles of those close to Muḥammad b. ʿAbdallāh were responsible for the spreading of traditions praising him. Two of these traditions that describe Muḥammad b. ʿAbdallāh's physical traits have been dealt with elsewhere in this study.[23]

Other traditions of Saʿīd b. ʿUqba were related through his son-in-law, ʿAbdallāh b. Mūsa, e.g., the two traditions: Mūsā b. ʿAbdallāh b. Mūsā b. ʿAbdallāh b. al-Ḥasan [b. al-Ḥasan b. ʿAlī b. Abī Ṭālib] < his father < Saʿīd b. ʿUqba: describing the generosity of ʿAbdallāh's family towards the poet Abū ʿAdī.[24]

2 The ʿAbbāsī Family

In a long tradition (more than four pages long) ʿAlī b. Muḥammad b. Sulaymān b. ʿAlī b. ʿAbdallāh b. al-ʿAbbās describes how ʿAbdallāh al-Ashtar, Muḥammad b. ʿAbdallāh's son, traveled to al-Sind, found shelter in the court of one of the kings there and later was killed by the brother of the governor who replaced ʿUmar b. Ḥafṣ.[25] ʿAlī b. Muḥammad b. Sulaymān b. ʿAlī b. ʿAbdallāh b. al-ʿAbbās seems to have had an interest in the history of the early ʿAbbāsīs; he related to al-Ṭabarī several traditions that disclose inside information about the manners and customs of the early ʿAbbāsī caliphs, as well as inside political information.[26]

2.1 *ʿAbbāsī Dignitaries*

EW/Jaʿfar b. Muḥammad b. al-Ashʿath al-Khuzāʿī l-Abnāʾī

He relates that his father was ordered to choose a secret envoy to Medina who would pretend to be a Shīʿī follower; the aim of the tradition is to emphasize the supernatural knowledge of Jaʿfar al-Ṣādiq; this event caused Jaʿfar b. Muḥammad to follow the Imāmī dogma.

---

23 See chapter 1, 27f., 45f.

24 The first anecdote: al-Iṣfahānī, *al-Aghānī* (Būlāq edition), 18:205–206 [= Dār al-Kutub edition, 21:119]; the second anecdote: ibid. (Būlāq edition), 10:105 [= idem, *Maqātil*, 183–184].

25 Al-Ṭabarī, 3:359–364.

26 He appears in al-Ṭabarī several times; in all instances we read *wa-dhakara*, or *wa-dhukira*; does it denote a quotation from a work? See al-Ṭabarī, 3:414–415 (three traditions); 3:417, 549–551 (three traditions); see *Akhbār al-ʿAbbās*, 228 for traditions relating inner customs of the court, inner stories of the ʿAbbāsī caliphs and family, ʿAbbāsī politics and so forth. Mostly he transmits from his father, Muḥammad b. Sulaymān. Note that he is not to be confused with ʿAlī b. Muḥammad b. Sulaymān al-Nawfalī, the well-known *rāwī*.

3 Transmission from Contemporaries of the Rebellion: Eyewitnesses, Supporters, and Opponents of the Revolt

1) EW/**ʿAbdallāh b. ʿImrān b. Abī Farwa**

He lived in Medina and related eyewitness information about the events slightly preceding the rebellion, mainly about the imprisonment of the Ḥasanīs; he gained this information directly from Abū l-Azhar, the commander who was appointed by al-Manṣūr to be in charge of the imprisonment. ʿAbdallāh b. ʿImrān seems to have had friendly relations with this commander. All the traditions of ʿAbdallāh were transmitted to ʿĪsā b. ʿAbdallāh[27] (and see also below). ʿImrān, ʿAbdallāh's father, was a poet.[28] ʿAbdallāh b. ʿImrān was well versed in poetry,[29] and had an interest in history. Several traditions about historical events in the Umawī period were transmitted by him.[30] He was a minor *ḥadīth* transmitter.[31]

2) EW/? **ʿAbdallāh (al-Akbar) b. Nāfiʿ b. Thābit b. al-Zubayr b. al-ʿAwwām and his brother, ʿAbdallāh al-Aṣghar** (see below under Ibn Shabba's Direct Transmitters).

3) EW/**ʿAbdallāh b. al-Rabīʿ b. ʿUbaydallāh b. ʿAbd al-Madān b. ʿUbaydallāh al-Ḥārithī**

He was the uncle on his mother's side of the first ʿAbbāsī caliph; he served as a governor of Yemen and Medina for al-Manṣūr. He transmitted one tradition about the reaction of al-Manṣūr to the news of the revolt's outbreak.[32]

4) EW/**ʿAbdallāh b. ʿUmar b. al-Qāsim b. ʿAbdallāh b. ʿUbaydallāh b. ʿĀṣim b. ʿUmar b. al-Khaṭṭāb**

He was a minor, almost unknown *muḥaddith*. His son Muḥammad gained slightly more fame in this field.[33]

---

27 Al-Ṭabarī, 3:160 [= al-Iṣfahānī, *Maqātil*, 226–227]: he is strolling along with Abū l-Azhar, relating what had occurred during that stroll; 169, 174 [= al-Iṣfahānī, *Maqātil*, 218], 182; al-Iṣfahānī, *Maqātil*, 198.

28 Ibn ʿAsākir, *Taʾrīkh*, 10:294–295.

29 Ibid., 48:87: strolling with al-Ghamr b. Yazīd b. ʿAbd al-Malik [killed in 132/750 in Abū Fuṭrus by ʿAbdallāh b. ʿAlī l-ʿAbbāsī, see Ibn Ḥazm, *Jamhara*, 91], reciting poetry by ʿUmar b. ʿAbdallāh b. Abī Rabīʿa.

30 E.g. Ibn ʿAsākir, *Taʾrīkh*, 20:64; 33:218; 48:87; 59:331.

31 Ibn Abī Ḥātim, *al-Jarḥ* (Beirut edition), 5:130; Ibn ʿAsākir, *Taʾrīkh*, 2:64; Ibn al-ʿImād, *Bughya*, 9:413; Ibn Ḥajar, *Taʿjīl al-manfaʿa*, 1:233; I was not able to detect his full lineage in the sources. He was most probably a descendant of Abū Farwa, who was a *mawlā* of al-Ḥārith b. al-Ḥifār, the *mawlā* of ʿUthmān b. ʿAffān.

32 Al-Ṭabarī, 3:204–205 (l. 3 to l. 5).

33 The only brief biography of ʿAbdallāh b. ʿUmar b. al-Qāsim b. ʿAbdallāh b. ʿUbaydallāh b. ʿĀṣim b. ʿUmar is recorded by Ibn Abī Ḥātim, *al-Jarḥ*, 5:110, with only his partial

ʿAbdallāh b. ʿUmar is mentioned twice in al-Ṭabarī as a close follower of Muḥammad and one who took an active part in the fighting, about which he relates in the first person. In the first tradition he vividly describes a frightening soldier of the ʿAbbāsī camp, the sight of whom caused one of Muḥammad b. ʿAbdallāh's warriors to flee, but (and this is the crux of the story) then the courageous, fearless Abū l-Qalammas came out and fought a duel with this ʿAbbāsī, and killed him.[34]

In the second tradition, ʿAbdallāh b. ʿUmar b. al-Qāsim once again relates in the first person an episode that occurred after their defeat. He was in a group that included Abū l-Qalammas, who is, once again, the dominant and central figure of the story.[35]

5) EW/ʿAbdallāh b. al-Zubayr b. ʿUmar b. Dirham al-Zubayrī [*mawlāhum*] al-Kūfī, *mawlā* Banī Asad

He relates an eyewitness testimony that describes Muḥammad b. ʿAbdallāh's ornamented sword on the day that he rebelled openly.[36]

6) ʿAbd al-ʿAzīz b. ʿImrān b. ʿAbd al-ʿAzīz b. ʿUmar b. ʿAbd al-Raḥmān b. ʿAwf al-Zuhrī, known as Ibn Abī Thābit (d. 197/812 or 813)[37]

---

lineage; his full lineage was reconstructed with the help of the following sources where he is mentioned as a transmitter in an *isnād*, for example, see al-Bayhaqī, *al-Sunan al-kubrā*, 5:43 (his full lineage); Ibn ʿAsākir, *Taʾrīkh*, 20:64; 31:392; 61:245 (partial lineage); al-Dhahabī, *Mīzān* (ed. al-Bijāwī), 3:597 (full, complete lineage). On his son Muḥammad as a *muḥaddith*, see al-ʿUqaylī, *Ḍuʿafāʾ* (Beirut 1418 H.), 4:94 (instead of إبراهيم بن عاصم read عبيد الله بن عاصم); al-Dhahabī, *Mīzān* (ed. al-Bijāwī), 3:610; Ibn Ḥajar, *Lisān*, 5:227 (all give the complete lineage).

34 Al-Ṭabarī, 3:238–239 (l. 13 to l. 2): (ʿUmar b. Shabba) < Muḥammad b. al-Ḥasan b. Zabāla < ʿAbdallāh b. ʿUmar b. al-Qāsim b. ʿAbdallāh al-ʿUmarī "who said we were with Muḥammad. …"

35 Al-Ṭabarī, 3:250 (ll. 11–17): The same *isnād* as in the preceding note.

36 Al-Iṣfahānī, *Maqātil*, 290.

37 On his father, ʿImrān b. ʿAbd al-ʿAzīz, who at a certain (later?) stage, seems to have joined the revolt, with another brother, Mūsā see chapter 7, 306f. and 391 below; on ʿAbd al-ʿAzīz b. ʿImrān, see al-Zubayrī, *Nasab Quraysh*, 271; Ibn Khayyāṭ, *Ṭabaqāt* (ed. Zakkār), 483; Ibn Saʿd, *Ṭabaqāt*, 5:436; Ibn Ḥibbān, *al-Majrūḥīn*, 2:139–140; Ibn Abī Ḥātim, *al-Jarḥ* (Beirut edition), 5:390–391; Ibn ʿAdī, *Ḍuʿafāʾ*, 5:285–286; al-Khaṭīb al-Baghdādī, *Taʾrīkh* (Beirut, 1997), 439–440; al-Dhahabī, *Mīzān* (Cairo edition), 2:138; Ibn Ḥajar, *Tahdhīb* (Hyderabad edition), 6:350–351; al-Mizzī, *Tahdhīb*, 18:178–181; al-Ṣafadī, *al-Wāfī* (Beirut, 2009), 18:537; al-Sakhāwī, *al-Tuḥfa al-laṭīfa*, 2:184–185; the date of his death according to most sources is 197 H., see for instance, Ibn Khayyāṭ, *Ṭabaqāt* (ed. Zakkār), 483; al-Khaṭīb al-Baghdādī, *Taʾrīkh* (Beirut, 1997), 440; al-Mizzī, *Tahdhīb*, 18:181, according to Khalīfa b. Khayyāṭ, Muḥammad b. Saʿd and Muḥammad b. ʿAbdallāh al-Ḥaḍramī, Maṭīn (d. 297/910, on him, see al-Zirikli, *al-Aʿlām* [Beirut 1980], 6:223); cf. al-Ṣafadī, *al-Wāfī* (Beirut, 2009), 18:537: d. in

On the eve of the revolt he was most probably a young boy, while his father, ʿImrān b. ʿAbd al-ʿAzīz, is mentioned as one of the supporters of the governor of Medina, Riyāḥ. This we learn from the father's personal testimony. The chain of transmission in al-Ṭabarī is as follows: [ʿUmar b. Shabba] < Muḥammad b. Yaḥyā < ʿAbd al-ʿAzīz b. ʿImrān < my father related to me:

> While Riyāḥ was in Dār Marwān, news reached him that Muḥammad was about to rebel openly that very night. He sent for my brother, Muḥammad b. ʿImrān [sic!? Read: b. ʿAbd al-ʿAzīz?], and for al-ʿAbbās b. ʿAbdallāh b. al-Ḥārith b. al-ʿAbbās, and for several others. He said: "My brother came out leading the forces for the governor and I came out with him until we entered his presence after the final evening prayer. …" We sat down and my brother said: "May God give you prosperity, I will be your surety for him [that is, Muḥammad al-Nafs al-Zakiyya]". … To this Riyāḥ responded: "You have the largest number of kinfolk of anyone here, and you are the *qāḍī* of the Commander of the Faithful. Go summon your kinfolk." My brother jumped up ready to go, but Riyāḥ said: "sit down, Thābit, you go." So I rose quickly and sent word to the Banū Zuhra, who live in Ḥashsh Ṭalḥa, Dār Saʿd and Dār Banū Azhar: "Come with your weapons. …"[38]

The identification of the figures here raises several problems. If indeed ʿImrān b. ʿAbd al-ʿAzīz is the narrator, then his brother's name cannot be Muḥammad b. ʿImrān, but Muḥammad **b.** ʿAbd al-ʿAzīz. Indeed, ʿImrān b. ʿAbd al-ʿAzīz had a brother by the name of Muḥammad, who served as a *qāḍī* in Medina during al-Manṣūr's reign.[39] Ibn al-Athīr summarized and redacted the tradition, as he very often did with al-Ṭabarī's texts, omitting the *isnād*, some of the names, and difficult words and phrases, inserting in their place some ordinary, simple idioms and phrases: "The news came to Riyāḥ that Muḥammad is going to come out in open revolt at night, so he summoned Muḥammad b. ʿImrān b. Ibrāhīm b. Muḥammad, the *qāḍī* of Medina. …"[40] The name of the *qāḍī* in the tradition turns out to be a different person, someone from another clan of Quraysh, Taym b. Murra, not Banū Zuhra. This is Muḥammad b. ʿImrān b. Ibrāhīm b. Muḥammad. b. Ṭalḥa b. ʿUbaydallāh b. ʿUthmān b. ʿAmr b. Kaʿb b. Saʿd b. Taym (d. 154/770 or 771), who was indeed a *qāḍī* of Medina during al-Manṣūr's reign.

---

the 160s or 170s. However, see the remark of al-Sakhāwī, *al-Tuḥfa al-laṭīfa*, 2:185: "whoever said 70 … [instead of 90] made a mistake." This error, the changing of تسعين to سبعين, is common in the Arabic sources.

38 Al-Ṭabarī, 3:191–192 (l. 14 to l. 8); trans. McAuliffe, *ʿAbbāsīd Authority*, 145–146 (with slight changes).

39 Al-Zubayrī, *Nasab Quraysh*, 271; Ibn Ḥazm, *Jamhara*, 134.

40 Ibn al-Athīr, *al-Kāmil* (Beirut edition), 5:530.

ʿAbd al-ʿAzīz was born, lived, and died in Medina. He visited Baghdad and was close to Yaḥyā b. Khālid al-Barmakī, who used to bestow large sums of money upon him.[41] He is described as a scholar who was well versed in poetry (*shiʿr*) and genealogy (*nasab*), but all the *rijāl* critics describe him as a very weak, unreliable, and untrustworthy transmitter of *ḥadīth*. Some stress the fact that his fame was due to his knowledge of poetry and genealogy, not his knowledge of *ḥadīth*.[42] It seems that this allegation is in itself sufficient to form a negative opinion against a transmitter of *ḥadīth*. The fact that he was closely associated with Jaʿfar al-Ṣādiq could have added to suspicion of him and his unreliability in the eyes of the Sunnī critics of *ḥadīth*.[43]

ʿAbd al-ʿAzīz was a transmitter (*rāwī*) of historical traditions.[44] Some of these traditions (ten in number), are recorded by al-Ṭabarī, all dealing with or connected to the rebellion of Muḥammad b. ʿAbdallāh al-Nafs al-Zakiyya. Seven were transmitted by ʿAbd al-ʿAzīz to Muḥammad b. Yaḥyā (see below), who related them to ʿUmar b. Shabba. All ten traditions seem to have been included in the latter's work. All the intimate descriptions of Muḥammad b. ʿAbdallāh's camp, the battle, and the way the latter died were related to ʿAbd al-ʿAzīz b. ʿImrān by eyewitnesses, or those who took part in the rebellion.[45]

---

41 Al-Khaṭīb al-Baghdādī, *Taʾrīkh* (Beirut, 1997), 10:440–441.

42 See for instance Ibn Ḥibbān, *al-Majrūḥīn*, 2:139: فكان الغالب عليه الشعر والأدب دون العلم; Ibn ʿAdī *Ḍuʿafāʾ* (Beirut, 1984), 5:285: إنما كان صاحب شعر.

43 For his Imāmī inclinations and association with Jaʿfar al-Ṣādiq, see al-Iṣfahānī, *Maqātil*, 207–208; ibid., 243, reciting a verse in praise of Muḥammad b. ʿAbdallāh, to Muḥammad b. Ismāʿīl al-Jaʿfarī (the grandchild of Mūsā b. ʿAbdallāh b. al-Ḥasan from his mother's side; his father, Ismāʿīl b. Ibrāhīm, was married to Ruqayya, Mūsā b. ʿAbdallāh's daughter [see above]); he was regarded by the Imāmīs (with slight reservations) as a trustworthy (Imāmī) transmitter, for example, see al-Ḥillī, *Khulāṣat al-aqwāl*, 376; al-Tafrishī, *Naqd al-rijāl*, 3:64; al-Khūʾī, *Rijāl*, 11:32; al-Ṭūsī, *Rijāl*, 239. It is noteworthy, in this context, that ʿAbd al-ʿAzīz's father ʿImrān and his uncle Mūsā joined the rebellion of Muḥammad b. ʿAbdallāh, see Ibn Ḥazm, *Jamhara*, 134.

44 E.g., Ibn Ḥabīb, *al-Munammaq*, 221 (about حلف الأحابيش in the Jāhiliyya), 261: the well-known traditions about the validity and importance of *ḥilf* in the Jāhiliyya and Islam; al-Ṭabarī, 1:967 and 968: the birth and age of the Prophet; 1:2722, 2788, 2795: the death of ʿUmar.

45 For example, note al-Ṭabarī, 3:144 (from ʿAbdallāh b. Abī ʿAbīda b. Muḥammad b. ʿAmmār b. Yāsir); 3:191–192 (from his father ʿImrān b. ʿAbd al-ʿAzīz); 3:196 (from his maternal uncle, Rāshid b. Ḥafṣ); 3:204 (from Muḥammad b. ʿAbd al-ʿAzīz from ʿAbdallāh b. al-Rabīʿ b. ʿUbaydallāh b. ʿAbd al-Madān b. ʿUbaydallāh): al-Manṣūr's reaction to the rebellion; 3:222 (from Abū Sayyār, the *ḥājib* of Muḥammad b. ʿAbdallāh): information about Muḥammad b. ʿAbdallāh's camp; 3:227–228 (from ʿAbd al-Ḥamīd b. Jaʿfar b. ʿAbdallāh b. Abī l-Ḥakam [one of the supporters of Muḥammad b. ʿAbdallāh]): "while staying with Muḥammad one night…"; 3:240–241 (from ʿAbdallāh b. Jaʿfar, another supporter of Muḥammad [perhaps

7) ʿAbd al-ʿAzīz b. Muḥammad b. ʿUbayd b. Abī ʿUbayd al-Darāwardī, *mawlā* Juhayna (Quḍāʿa) [d. 182 or 186 or 187/798–799 or 802 or 803][46]
He was one of the close supporters of Muḥammad b. ʿAbdallāh, who was appointed by him during the rebellion in charge of the arsenal (*al-silāḥ*).[47] He appears as a link in the tradition according to which ʿAbdallāh b. al-Ḥasan propagandized for the Mahdīship of his son. It was transmitted to al-Darāwardī by al-Zuhrī's nephew [Muḥammad b. ʿAbdallāh b. Muslim, d. 152 or 157/769–770 or 773–774]. Al-Darāwardī related the tradition to the Medinan ʿAlīd (Jaʿfarī) scholar, Dāwūd b. ʿAbdallāh [Abū l-Karrām] b. Muḥammad b. ʿAlī b. ʿAbdallāh b. Jaʿfar b. Abī Ṭālib, Abū Sulaymān.[48]

8) EW/ʿAbd al-Ḥamīd b. Jaʿfar b. ʿAbdallāh b. [Abī] l-Ḥakam b. Rāfiʿ b. Sinān al-Awsī l-Anṣārī Abū l-Faḍl or Abū Ḥafṣ (d. 153/770)
He supported Muḥammad, took an active part in the uprising and was appointed, for a short time, by the latter as the head of the *shurṭa* and carried the *ḥarba* (a short spear) in front of the *shurṭa* as part of the duties of صاحب الشرطة.[49] Several traditions about aspects of the uprising that he experienced and witnessed were transmitted by him, all which reach us through the work of ʿUmar b. Shabba, mainly in al-Ṭabarī's work, but also in *Maqātil al-ṭālibiyyīn*.[50]

---

this is ʿAbdallāh b. Jaʿfar b. ʿAbd al-Raḥmān b. al-Miswar b. Makhrama al-Zuhrī?]); 3:244 (he is the first transmitter, i.e., the *isnād* ends with him); 3:246 (from ʿAbdallāh b. Jaʿfar *qāla*): a description of the killing of Muḥammad al-Nafs al-Zakiyya from an eyewitness; see also al-Iṣfahānī, *Maqātil*, 167: from ʿAbdallāh b. Muḥammad b. Ismāʿīl al-Jaʿfarī from his father (Muḥammad) from ʿAbd al-ʿAzīz b. ʿImrān from Muḥammad b. Jaʿfar b. al-Walīd *mawlā* Abū Hurayra and Muḥriz b. Jaʿfar (on the rebellion of ʿAbdallāh b. Muʿāwiya); al-Iṣfahānī, *al-Aghānī* (Būlāq edition), 11:75 (ʿUmar b. Shabba from Muḥammad b. Yaḥyā from ʿAbd al-ʿAzīz b. ʿImrān from ʿAbdallāh b. al-Rabīʿ from Saʿīd b. ʿAmr b. Jaʿda b. Hubayra [= al-Iṣfahānī, *Maqātil*, 169: a parallel tradition with a garbled *isnād*]): a tradition about the battle of the Zāb connecting Marwān, ʿAbdallāh b. ʿAlī, and ʿAbdallāh b. Muʿāwiya.

46 On him, see Ibn Saʿd, *Ṭabaqāt*, 5:424 and Ibn Khayyāṭ, *Ṭabaqāt* (ed. Zakkār), 482: *mawlā* al-Birak b. Wabara of Quḍāʿa; al-Bukhārī, *al-Ṣaghīr* (Beirut, 1406 H.), 2:218, idem, *al-Kabīr*, 6:25; Ibn Ḥibbān, *Mashāhīr*, 225 and idem, *Thiqāt*, 7:116: *mawlā* Juhayna; al-Iṣfahānī, *Maqātil*, 286: *mawlā* Baliyy [= Quḍāʿa]; al-Dhahabī, *Tadhkira* (Beirut edition), 1:269–270; al-Samʿānī, *al-Ansāb* (Hyderabad edition), 5:330; Ibn Ḥajar, *Tahdhīb* (Beirut 1984), 6:315–316; idem, *Lisān*, 7:507: *al-Juhanī aw al-Quḍāʿī*; al-Mizzī, *Tahdhīb*, 18:187–195 and the comprehensive bibliography of the editor therein.

47 Al-Ṭabarī, 3:202 (ll. 9–10); al-Iṣfahānī, *Maqātil*, 283; van Arendonk, *L'Imamat Zaïdite*, 312.

48 Al-Mizzī, *Tahdhīb*, 25:467–468: Dāwūd b. ʿAbdallāh al-Jaʿfarī < al-Darāwardī [ʿAbd al-ʿAzīz b. Muḥammad b. ʿUbayd] < al-Zuhrī's nephew.

49 Al-Ṭabarī, 3:193: carrying the *ḥarba*; ibid., 3:199: head of the *shurṭa*

50 The following bibliography relates to his historical transmission and his reliability as a transmitter; 1) as a transmitter on the events of the revolt: al-Ṭabarī, 3:190, 193, 199 (direct

His son, Saʿd b. ʿAbd al-Ḥamīd (d. 219/834 or 835) was a direct transmitter of ʿUmar b. Shabba.[51]

9) EW/ ʿAbd al-Raḥmān b. Abī l-Mawālī (d. 173/789 or 790)
He was imprisoned with the Ḥasanīs and was sent to al-ʿIrāq. He recorded several traditions relating to the early phases of the rebellion, especially about the imprisonment of the Ḥasanīs and himself. One such tradition records the names of several of the Ḥasanīs that were taken to al-Rabadha. Some of his personal accounts were told to al-Wāqidī, e.g., when the latter relates from ʿAbd al-Raḥmān b. Abī l-Mawālī that about four hundred tribesmen from Juhayna, Muzayna, and other tribes were brought to al-Rabadha with the Ḥasanīs. "I [remarks Ibn Abī l-Mawālī] saw them, their hands tied up behind their backs in the sun."[52]

10) EW/Abū l-ʿAbbās al-Filasṭī[nī?]
He transmitted one tradition about Marwān b. Muḥammad, the last Umayyad caliph, and his attitude to Muḥammad b. ʿAbdallāh. I was unable to identify this scholar. The *nisba* al-Filasṭī does not exist in the sources known to me. It is probably a misprint of al-Filasṭīnī, although this tradition with the same garbled[?] name is recorded twice by Abū l-Faraj al-Iṣfahānī.[53] A scholar by the name of Abū l-ʿAbbās al-Filasṭīnī is mentioned as a transmitter of the famous scholar, al-Madāʾinī. So far I was able to find him quoted only once, in a tradition in which he related an anecdote regarding *ahl al-Shām*, immediately upon the ascendance of the ʿAbbāsīs to the caliphate.[54]

---

transmitter), 3:201 (direct transmitter), 3:227 and 237 (direct transmitter); al-Iṣfahānī, *Maqātil*, 283–284; 2) as a transmitter of *ḥadīth*, see, for example, Ibn Ḥibbān, *al-Thiqāt*, 7:122; al-Ājurrī, *Suʾālāt*, 1:94: Sufyān al-Thawrī severely criticizes the integrity of ʿAbd al-Ḥamīd as a transmitter due to his participation in the revolt of Muḥammad; Ibn Abī Ḥātim, *al-Jarḥ* (Beirut edition), 6:10; al-Ṣafadī, *al-Wāfī*, 18:42–43: al-Wāqidī criticized him because of his participation in the revolt: وكان الواقدي ينكر عليه خروجه مع محمد بن عبد الله; see also van Ess, *Theologie*, 2:678.

51 In both al-Ṭabarī's and al-Iṣfahānī's printed works he is rendered as Saʿīd. Corrected in al-Ṭabarī's *Addenda et Emendana*, dccxxxvi; see McAuliffe, *ʿAbbāsid Authority*, 145, n. 701; on him, see al-Khaṭīb al-Baghdādī, *Taʾrīkh* (Beirut, 1997), 9:126–128; al-Mizzī, *Tahdhīb*, 10:285–287, and the comprehensive bibliography therein.

52 Al-Ṭabarī, 3:187; Ibn Saʿd, *al-Qism al-mutammim*, 255; Ibn ʿAsākir, *Taʾrīkh*, 53:389–392: the complete[?] tradition is much longer than that recorded in the two preceding sources.

53 Al-Iṣfahānī, *Maqātil*, 247, 258.

54 See Ibn Aʿtham al-Kūfī, *al-Futūḥ* (Hyderabad edition), 8:195: قال أبو الحسن المدائني أخبرني أبو العباس الفلسطيني وكان من غلبة أهل العلم في عصره (Abū l-Ḥasan al-Madāʾinī said:

11) EW/Abū Habbār al-Muzanī

He was one of the most confidential and close supporters of Muḥammad b. ʿAbdallāh, who hid with him and accompanied him to al-Baṣra before the revolt, most probably fought with him, and fled after the revolt was crushed. He relates three traditions, describing some events in the first person.

12) EW/Abū Ḥunayn

Abū Ḥunayn was one of the active supporters of the rebellion in Medina. He described to al-Ḥārith b. Isḥāq (on him, see below) how he entered the house where ʿAbdallāh b. al-Ḥasan was confined in Medina.[55]

13) EW/Abū Sayyār

He was the *ḥājib* of Muḥammad b. ʿAbdallāh. This we learn from a tradition related by him in the first person about how he came to Muḥammad b. ʿAbdallāh at night announcing that Ibrāhīm had seized al-Baṣra.[56] Nothing more is known about this person. He might be Mismaʿ b. ʿAbd al-Malik b. Mismaʿ b. Mālik.

14) EW/ʿAlī b. ʿAbd al-Ḥamīd

ʿAlī b. ʿAbd al-Ḥamīd was, most plausibly, the grandfather of the important scholar Muḥammad b. Yaḥyā [b. ʿAlī b. ʿAbd al-Ḥamīd b. ʿUbayd al-Kinānī] (on him, see below). Three traditions of his disclose interesting, as well as important, historical information regarding Medina during the governorship of Ziyād b. ʿUbaydallāh al-Ḥārithī; the most interesting of them is about al-Manṣūr's stay in Medina in 140/758. From these traditions we learn that ʿAlī b. ʿAbd al-Ḥamīd was a close associate of the governor. Two traditions were related to Muḥammad b. Yaḥyā by his father through his grandfather. Another was transmitted by al-Ḥārith b. Isḥāq, who was ʿAlī b. ʿAbd al-Ḥamīd's nephew (see below).[57]

15) EW/Azhar b. Saʿd b. Nāfiʿ Abū Bakr al-Sammān and his two brothers

16) EW/ʿUthmān b. Saʿd b. Nāfiʿ and

I was informed by Abū l-ʿAbbās al-Filasṭīnī, who was one of the preeminent scholars of his period).

55 Al-Ṭabarī, 3:153: دخلت على عبد الله بن الحسن وهو محبوس.

56 Al-Ṭabarī, 3:222 (ll. 5–14).

57 Al-Ṭabarī, 2:1885 (from his father); traditions about Ziyād b. ʿUbaydallāh: 3:147–148 (l. 18 to l. 2); 3:154 (l. 15f.) (from his father from his grandfather: al-Manṣūr in Medina); 3:160 (l. 4f.) (described as "al-Ḥārith's uncle from his mother's side").

17) EW/ **Muḥammad b. Saʿd b. Nāfiʿ**: On this family, see below.

18) Hārūn b. Mūsā b. ʿAbdallāh b. Muḥammad b. ʿAbdallāh b. Abī Farwa
He is not a direct transmitter of Ibn Shabba, nor an eyewitness; however, he is still important and interesting, among other things, with respect to the history of Medina. Hārūn b. Mūsā b. ʿAbdallāh [= Ibn Abī ʿAlqama] b. Muḥammad b. ʿAbdallāh b. Abī Farwa (174–252 or 253/790 or 791–867 or 868) was a *ḥadīth* transmitter. The family were the *mawālī* of ʿUthmān b. ʿAffān.[58] He appears in al-Iṣfahānī's *Maqātil* eleven times as the third transmitter after al-Iṣfahānī himself, in most of them transmitting to ʿĪsā b. al-Ḥusayn al-Warrāq, one of al-Iṣfahānī's main direct transmitters.[59] Ten traditions deal with events that are connected to the revolt, and one to the revolt of Zayd b. ʿAlī. In all of the traditions (but one), he is not the last transmitter.[60] One tradition was related to him by his mother (about the battle cries of Muḥammad's army أحد أحد محمد بن عبد الله).[61] Three traditions about the revolt were transmitted to Hārūn b. Mūsā by Dāwūd b. al-Qāsim.[62] Did Hārūn b. Mūsā have written notes or a book

58 On Hārūn b. Mūsā, see al-Ṭabarī, index, esp. 2:2006–2015 (reporting on the revolt of Abū Ḥamza al-Khārijī in 130/747 or 748); Ibn Abī Ḥātim, *al-Jarḥ* (Beirut edition), 9:95; al-Dhahabī, *Mīzān* (ed. al-Bijāwī), 4:287; Ibn Ḥajar, *Tahdhīb* (Beirut 1984), 13–14; idem, *Taqrīb* (1986 edition), 1:569; al-Mizzī, *Tahdhīb*, 30:113–115 (29:122: his father; 16:63–65: his grandfather); Ibn ʿAsākir, *Taʾrīkh*, 43:548, records a tradition which is found in his book *The mosque of Medina in history*, see the discussion below; Günther, *Maqātil*, 167–168.

59 ʿĪsā b. al-Ḥusayn al-Warrāq al-Marwazī appears in *al-Aghānī* 108 times as the direct transmitter of Abū l-Faraj al-Iṣfahānī, see Günther, *Maqātil*, 167–168; Fleischhammer, *Kitāb al-Aghānī*, 52–53; he is mentioned in *Maqātil* 19 times as the direct transmitter of al-Iṣfahānī, many of his traditions record events of the rebellion. Some of them were found in a book by Aḥmad b. al-Ḥārith al-Kharrāz (d. 258/872), that was in the possession of ʿĪsā b. al-Ḥusayn, who gave it to Abū l-Faraj al-Iṣfahānī, who quotes directly from the MS of the book (Günther, *Maqātil*, 118–121); Aḥmad b. al-Ḥārith al-Kharrāz was a devout pupil of al-Madāʾinī, who copied the latter's works and transmitted his works either by oral transmission or directly from the written works (Sezgin, 1:319; Fleischhammer, *Kitāb al-Aghānī*, 76–77). Günther, *Maqātil*, 121, showed that most of the traditions of al-Kharrāz that deal with Muḥammad al-Nafs al-Zakiyya's revolt and other Ṭālibī revolts and/or events that are connected to the Ṭālibīs were taken from al-Madāʾinī, and he argued convincingly that al-Kharrāz transmitted from al-Madāʾinī's book *Kitāb man qutila min al-Ṭālibiyyīn* (Günther, *Maqātil*, 119).

60 Al-Iṣfahānī, *Maqātil*, 128 (l. 13) (about Zayd b. ʿAlī's revolt); 183 (l. 1); 276 (l. 10), 282 (l. 5), 283 (l. 11), 284 (l. 10), 285 (l. 2), 285 (l. 5), 285 (l. 8), 286 (l. 7), 286 (l. 15), 288 (l. 13) (about al-Nafs al-Zakiyya's revolt).

61 Ibid., 276 (ll. 10–12).

62 Ibid., pp. 282 (l. 5), 283 (l. 11), 284 (l. 10).

about al-Nafs al-Zakiyya's revolt at his disposal?[63] Al-Samhūdī records about 200 traditions from the book *Akhbār al-Madīna* of Yaḥyā b. al-Ḥasan b. Jaʿfar al-Ḥusaynī l-ʿAqīqī (d. 277/890).[64] Al-Samhūdī records Yaḥyā's traditions from Hārūn b. Mūsā l-Farwī five times. It is possible that Yaḥyā b. al-Ḥasan al-ʿAqīqī relied on a written work of Hārūn b. Mūsā, based on the following testament of Ibn ʿAsākir: "… *ḥaddathanā* Hārūn b. Mūsā l-Farwī in the book *The mosque of Medina in history*: نا هارون بن موسى الفروي في كتاب مسجد المدينة في الأخبار."[65]

Al-Ṭabarī recorded sixteen traditions related through Hārūn b. Mūsā l-Farwī, all of which, except one, deal extensively with the events of the revolt of Abū Ḥamza al-Khārijī, mainly in Medina, in 129–130/746–748. Hārūn b. Mūsā is the second transmitter after al-Ṭabarī himself, and in most of the traditions he transmitted to al-ʿAbbās b. ʿĪsā l-ʿUqaylī. It is noteworthy that al-Ṭabarī's traditions of Hārūn b. Mūsā consist of about 13 pages, and it is highly plausible that he had a written work on the subject. A large part of these traditions is recorded in Abū l-Faraj al-Iṣfahānī's *Kitāb al-aghānī*.[66] I cannot tell whether the events of Muḥammad b. ʿAbdallāh's revolt and the events of the revolt of Abū Ḥamza al-Khārijī were included in one composition or in the book *The mosque of Medina in history*. He was a prolific writer who was also interested in poetry. The traditions that were recorded through him by al-Iṣfahānī in his *al-Aghānī* bear evidence to this.[67]

19) EW/Ḥumayd b. ʿAbdallāh b. Abī Farwa/al-Farwī

Another member of Hārūn b. Mūsā l-Farwī's family, Ḥumayd b. ʿAbdallāh b. Abī Farwa/al-Farwī (not identified) was a contemporary of the rebellion of al-Nafs al-Zakiyya and recorded two traditions about the revolt, one in the first person; both traditions were related by him to Muḥammad b. al-Ḥasan b. Zabāla and from the latter to ʿUmar b.

---

63 It is possible that al-Iṣfahānī's remark, *Maqātil*, 286: قال هارون الفروي في خبره خاصة refers to a written source.

64 For example, see al-Samhūdī, *Wafāʾ*, 1:155, 424; 2:310; 5:61.

65 Ibn ʿAsākir, *Taʾrīkh*, 43:548.

66 Al-Ṭabarī, 2:1942, 1981–1983 (l. 11 to l. 16), 2006–2015 (l. 14 to l. 3): Mūsā b. Hārūn is mentioned several times in these pages; 3:594 (l. 21): recording some poetry that was recited to Caliph al-Mahdī; al-Iṣfahānī, *al-Aghānī* (Dār al-Kutub edition), 23:227, 23:236–244 (l. 13 to l. 18): more than eight pages dealing with the revolt of Abū Ḥamza al-Khārijī in Medina, partly from the *riwāya* of al-Ṭabarī through al-ʿAbbās b. ʿĪsā l-ʿUqaylī; Mūsā b. Hārūn is mentioned as the transmitter several times in these pages.

67 Al-Iṣfahānī, *al-Aghānī* (Dār al-Kutub edition), 2:10 (l. 9); 3:328 (l. 15); 9:216 (l. 11); 11:302 (l. 3); 13:264 (l. 3); 24:164.

Shabba.[68] The *nisba* al-Farwī refers to the relation to Abū Farwa, most probably one of the descendants of ʿAbdallāh b. Abī Farwa, who was a *mawlā* of al-Ḥārith b. al-Ḥifār, the *mawlā* of ʿUthmān b. ʿAffān.

20) EW/Ibrāhīm b. ʿAlī b. al-Ḥasan b. ʿAlī b. Abī Rāfiʿ

He records an eyewitness testimony about the speech impediment of Muḥammad al-Nafs al-Zakiyya.[69]

Abū Rāfiʿ, the forefather of this family, was a slave of al-ʿAbbās b. ʿAbd al-Muṭṭalib and became the *mawlā* of the Prophet. Two of his sons, ʿAlī and ʿUbaydallāh b. Abī Rāfiʿ (d. ca. 80/700), served as the secretaries of ʿAlī b. Abī Ṭālib. In the Shīʿī, as well as in the Sunnī, biographical literature, ʿUbaydallāh is mentioned as the author of several works. Of special interest is "The Book that contains the names of the Companions of the Prophet who witnessed [that is, took the side of and fought] with the Commander of the Faithful [that is ʿAlī b. Abī Ṭālib] at the battles of al-Jamal, Ṣiffīn and al-Nahrawān."[70]

The transmitter in this case, Ibrāhīm b. ʿAlī b. al-Ḥasan b. ʿAlī b. Abī Rāfiʿ al-Madanī, moved to Baghdad at an old age and died there. It is not known whether he supported the Ḥasanī cause or took an active part in the rebellion. He is mentioned as one of the followers of Jaʿfar al-Ṣādiq.[71] Most of the Sunnī critics of transmitters of *ḥadīth* question his credibility; he transmitted traditions from Jaʿfar al-Ṣādiq about al-Ḥusayn's death, and a well-known tradition about Fāṭima bringing her two sons al-Ḥasan and al-Ḥusayn to the Prophet, who blesses them.[72]

---

68 Al-Iṣfahānī, *Maqātil*, 286: Abū Zayd [= ʿUmar b. Shabba] < Muḥammad b. al-Ḥasan [b. Zabāla] < Ḥumayd b. ʿAbdallāh al-Farwī; 297: ʿUmar b. Shabba < Muḥammad b. al-Ḥasan b. Zabāla < Ḥumayd b. ʿAbdallāh b. Abī Farwa.

69 Al-Ṭabarī, 3:203 (ll. 15–18); al-Iṣfahānī, *Maqātil*, 242.

70 On Abū Rāfiʿ and his two sons, especially ʿUbaydallāh, see Elad, "Early Muslim Historiography," 272–273; Elad, "Historical Writing," 124–125.

71 Al-Ṭūsī, *Rijāl*, 158; al-Shāhrūdī, *Rijāl*, 177; al-Tustarī, *Rijāl*, 12:372.

72 On him, see al-Khaṭīb al-Baghdādī, *Taʾrīkh* (Beirut, 1997), 6:129; al-Mizzī, *Tahdhīb*, 2:155–156. See also the bibliography of the editor on 156, nn. 1–6: the opinions of the Sunnī critics of transmitters of *ḥadīth*; transmission from Jaʿfar al-Ṣādiq: al-ʿĀmilī, *Wasāʾil* (*Āl al-bayt*), 25:201; al-Majlisī, *Biḥār*, 59:145; 63:232; Ibn ʿAsākir, *Taʾrīkh*, 70:24: Jaʿfar al-Ṣādiq who relates from his father < his grandfather the tradition about al-Ḥusayn's death; al-Shaykh al-Mufīd, *al-Irshād*, 2:6 [= Ibn ʿAsākir, *Taʾrīkh*, 13:229; al-Majlisī, *Biḥār*, 43:263]: his father < his grandmother, Zaynab, the daughter of Abū Rāfiʿ, the tradition about Fāṭima.

21) EW/Ibrāhīm b. Ziyād b. ʿAnbasa [b. Saʿīd b. al-ʿĀṣ b. Umayya b. ʿAbd Shams?]
He is mentioned only once by al-Ṭabarī, where he describes Muḥammad b. ʿAbdallāh ascending the *minbar* in the mosque of Medina.[73] We cannot know from this short descriptive tradition if he took part in the rebellion or opposed it.

22) EW/ʿImrān b. ʿAbd al-ʿAzīz b. ʿUmar b. ʿAbd al-Raḥmān b. ʿAwf al-Zuhrī
He was one of the Qurashīs (from Banū Zuhra) of Medina. On the eve of the revolt, he seemed to have supported (or at least was loyal to) the ʿAbbāsīs. But at a later stage, ʿImrān b. ʿAbd al-ʿAzīz seems to have joined the revolt with another brother, Mūsā. On him, but mainly on his son, ʿAbd al-ʿAzīz, who transmitted many traditions concerning the events of the revolt, see above. He transmitted to his son ʿAbd al-ʿAzīz a long eyewitness tradition.[74]

23) EW/[?] Ismāʿīl b. Yaʿqūb al-Taymī
He appears only once as a transmitter in al-Ṭabarī's *Taʾrīkh*, where he relates to Muḥammad b. Yaḥyā, Abū Ghassān al-Kinānī (on him, see below) the version of the (first?) *khuṭba* of Muḥammad b. ʿAbdallāh in Medina.[75] He was a transmitter of *ḥadīth* as well as a transmitter of historical anecdotes. Among those he heard *ḥadīth* from was Hishām b. ʿUrwa (61–146/680–763). He was a direct transmitter of Muṣʿab b. ʿAbdallāh al-Zubayrī (156–236/773–848) and al-Zubayr b. Bakkār (172–256/788 or 789–870).[76]

---

73 Al-Ṭabarī, 3:203 (ll. 9–11): ʿUmar b. Shabba < ʿĪsā [b. ʿAbdallāh] < al-Ḥasan b. Zayd b. al-Ḥasan b. ʿAlī; Ibrāhīm b. Ziyād b. ʿAnbasa is not mentioned in any other historical source known to me but it is plausible to identify him with Ibrāhīm b. Ziyād b. ʿAnbasa b. Saʿīd b. al-ʿĀṣ b. Umayya b. ʿAbd Shams, who is only mentioned by Ibn Ḥazm, *Jamhara*, 82; Ibrāhīm b. Ziyād b. ʿAnbasa b. Saʿīd b. al-ʿĀṣ is mentioned (thus) in al-Iṣfahānī, *al-Aghānī* (Dār al-Kutub edition), 1:249 [= Būlāq edition, 1:97] recording the physical traits of the Umawī singer Ibn Surayj.

74 For an example of such eyewitness evidence of ʿImrān b. ʿAbd al-ʿAzīz, see al-Ṭabarī, 3:191 (l. 14–15), 3:193 (l. 10): a long detailed tradition: *wa-ḥaddathanī* [= ʿUmar b. Shabba] < Muḥammad b. Yaḥyā < ʿAbd al-ʿAzīz b. ʿImrān < his father. Part of the long text [an exact parallel] is recorded by al-Iṣfahānī, *Maqātil*, 262: correct (in the *isnād*) b. ʿAmmār to b. ʿImrān.

75 Al-Ṭabarī, 3:197 (ll. 8–19).

76 As a *muḥaddith*: al-Bukhārī, *al-Kabīr* (Diyār Bakr edition), 1:377; Ibn Abī Ḥātim, *al-Jarḥ* (Beirut edition), 2:204: from Hishām b. ʿUrwa; Ibn Ḥibbān, *al-Thiqāt*, 8:93; al-Dhahabī, *Mīzān* (Beirut, 1963), 1:254; transmitting to Muṣʿab b. ʿAbdallāh: Ibn ʿAsākir, *Taʾrīkh*, 56:50; al-Dhahabī, *Siyar*, 5:358; idem, *Taʾrīkh*, 8:256; transmitting to al-Zubayr b. Bakkār: Ibn Abī l-Dunyā, *al-Iʿtibār*, 67; Ibn ʿAsākir, *Taʾrīkh*, 28:172–173; Ibn Abī l-Ḥadīd, *Sharḥ*, 20:113; see also Ibn Abī l-Barr, *al-Tamhīd*, 9:10–11.

24) EW/ Jaʿfar b. ʿAbdallāh b. ʿAlī b. Yazīd b. Rukāna [b. ʿAbd Yazīd b. Hāshim b. al-Muṭṭalib b. ʿAbd Manāf b. Quṣayy b. Kilāb b. Murra b. Kaʿb b. Luʾayy b. Ghālib b. Quraysh (Fihr) al-Qurashī l-Muṭṭalibī]
He is only mentioned once by al-Ṭabarī, where he relates in the first person information regarding the number of the supporters of Muḥammad al-Nafs al-Zakiyya. It is clear from the tradition that he took part in the revolt at the latter's side.[77]

25) EW/Jahm b. ʿUthmān *mawlā* Banī Sulaym *thumma aḥad Banī Bahz* (born in 105/723–724)
He was a supporter of Muḥammad, fought at his side and transmitted specific detailed information about the revolt (see the entry on Saʿd b. ʿAbd al-Ḥamīd b. Jaʿfar below). He was a pro-Shīʿī transmitter and one of the close followers (*aṣḥāb*) of Jaʿfar al-Ṣādiq. He was persecuted by al-Manṣūr, fled to Yemen and died there.

26) EW/Maʿmar b. Fāliḥ (Abū l-Shadāʾid)
He relates how his father, the blind poet, was killed in his house by the ʿAbbāsī soldiers, while his sister cried for help, and her alleged[?] conversation with one of the ʿAbbāsī soldiers.[78]

27) EW/Rashīd b. Ḥayyān b. Abī Sulaymān b. Samʿān *aḥad Banī Qurayṭ* [ʿĀmir b. Ṣaʿṣaʿa]
He related to his son Mawhūb, one, or perhaps two traditions about the revolt. Mawhūb was a direct transmitter of ʿUmar b. Shabba.[79]

28) Sulaymān b. ʿAyyāsh al-Saʿdī (flourished in the second half of the second/eighth century and the first quarter of the third/ninth century).[80]
He was an important transmitter of al-Zubayr b. Bakkār (172–256/788–870), mainly on material relating to poets and their poetry. He transmitted many traditions about Muḥammad b. Bashīr the Khārijī from Khārija b. ʿUdwān, among them several that have some relation to Hind's father and the family of ʿAbdallāh b. al-Ḥasan and other

77 Al-Ṭabarī, 3:193 (l. 15) (correct Jaʿfar b. ʿAbdallāh b. Yazīd b. Rukāna to Jaʿfar b. ʿAbdallāh b. ʿAlī b. Yazīd b. Rukāna).

78 Al-Ṭabarī, 3:251 (ll. 3–13).

79 Al-Ṭabarī, 3:203 (ll. 3–4); 3:230 (l. 7): أحد بني قريط بن عبد الله بن أبي بكر بن كلاب [بن ربيعة بن عامر بن صعصعة]; On this lineage, see Ibn Ḥazm, *Jamhara*, 282. On his father, Mawhūb, see below.

80 This is determined according to those from whom he heard *ḥadīth*, e.g., Mūsā b. ʿUqba, d. 141/758, and those who heard him, e.g., Muḥammad b. Salām al-Jumaḥī, 150–232/767–848 and al-Zubayr b. Bakkār, 172–256/788–870.

ʿAlīds, e.g., Zayd b. al-Ḥasan b. ʿAlī b. Abī Ṭālib and his son, al-Ḥasan b. Zayd.[81] More than thirty-five traditions of Sulaymān b. ʿAyyāsh appear in *Kitāb al-Aghānī*, all of them transmitted by him to al-Zubayr b. Bakkār. These are not merely traditions dealing with the Zubayrī family but, on the contrary, as noted above, they deal mainly with different poets and the transmission of their poetry, e.g., al-ʿIblī, Kuthayyir, Maʿn b. Aws al-Muzanī, Muḥammad b. Bashīr al-Khārijī, and others. As a by-product, some very important evidence regarding the Ḥasanī family is revealed, e.g., information about Suwayqa, the Ḥasanīs, and the poet al-ʿIblī.[82] Many traditions were recorded by al-Zubayr b. Bakkār from Sulaymān on the history of the Khārijī, Muḥammad b. Bashīr, and his close relations with ʿAbdallāh b. al-Ḥasan's family.[83] He is mentioned twice in al-Bakrī's geographical work, explaining to al-Zubayr b. Bakkār the etymology of two geographical toponyms.[84]

29) EW/ʿUmar b. Abī ʿAmr b. Nuʿaym b. Māhān al-Ghifārī
He opposed the rebellion together with one of his brothers, and they were imprisoned by Muḥammad b. ʿAbdallāh. He transmitted to his son Ayyūb two pieces of personal evidence relating to the history of the family during the revolt.

30) EW/ʿUmar b. Rāshid
He was a direct transmitter of ʿUmar b. Shabba but also an eyewitness to the rebellion (on him, see below).

31) EW/ʿUthmān b. Saʿd b. Nāfiʿ and Muḥammad b. Saʿd b. Nāfiʿ: On them, see below.

32) Yamūt b. al-Muzarriʿ
Yamūt b. al-Muzarriʿ (d. 303 or 304/915, 916, or 917) was al-Jāḥiẓ's nephew and was the author of (*ṣāḥib*) *Akhbār wa-mulaḥ wa-ādāb*. In one case he was a link in a tradition

81 See al-Iṣfahānī, *al-Aghānī* (Būlāq edition), 14:157 (Yazīd b. al-Ḥusayn and al-Ḥasan b. Yazīd; the correction is according to Dār al-Kutub edition, 16:121, and the Beirut edition Dār al-Thaqāfa [1959], 16:77); see also ibid. (Būlāq edition), 14:161 [= 16:131–132]: lamentation for Zayd b. Ḥasan.

82 Al-Iṣfahānī, *al-Aghānī* (Būlāq edition), 4:91 (= Dār al-Kutub edition, 4:340); Ibn ʿAsākir, *Taʾrīkh*, 31:213; and see Ibn ʿAsākir, *Taʾrīkh*, 53:389; al-Khaṭīb al-Baghdādī, *Taʾrīkh* (Beirut, 1997), 3:5; al-Mizzī, *Tahdhīb*, 25:521: *madīḥ* poetry about Muḥammad b. ʿAbdallāh b. ʿAmr b. ʿUthmān b. ʿAffān (the maternal brother of ʿAbdallāh b. al-Ḥasan b. al-Ḥasan).

83 See, for example, an anecdote that tells of Hind's deep mourning for her father upon his death, al-Iṣfahānī, *al-Aghānī* (Būlāq edition), 14:157 [= Dār al-Kutub edition, 16:122–123]; ibid. (Būlāq edition), 18:208 [= Dār al-Kutub edition, 21:124–125 and idem, *Maqātil*, 234–235], copied by Yāqūt, *Muʿjam* (Beirut edition), 4:250–251.

84 Al-Bakrī, *Muʿjam*, 3:805 ("al-Shuqra"); 1020 ("al-Furuʿ").

about the Ḥasanī's estate, Suwayqa. The sources do not mention that he had any special Shīʿī inclinations.[85]

33) EW/Zayd, the *mawlā* of Mismaʿ b. ʿAbd al-Malik [b. Mismaʿ b. Mālik b. Mismaʿ... b. Ḍubayʿa ... b. Bakr b. Wāʾil?]
He was in Medina during the rebellion. Al-Ṭabarī records through him three traditions concerning the rebellion; in two he uses the first person plural describing the huge, well-equipped ʿAbbāsī army.[86] It is evident from his report that he was not an ʿAbbāsī supporter.

4 ʿUmar b. Shabba: Direct Transmitters

General comment: Al-Ṭabarī and al-Iṣfahānī's use of ʿUmar b. Shabba's book
It is well-known that ʿUmar b. Shabba's work on the rebellion of Muḥammad and Ibrāhīm was the principal source for al-Ṭabarī's *Taʾrīkh* and al-Iṣfahānī's *Maqātil*. This was already noticed and commented upon by Günther, and it was Nagel who emphasized this phenomenon in regard to the rebellion of al-Nafs al-Zakiyya. The work that was used extensively was most probably كتاب محمد وإبراهيم ابني عبد الله بن الحسن بن الحسن, although some parts of the traditions quoted by al-Ṭabarī and al-Iṣfahānī could have belonged to other works of Ibn Shabba, such as: كتاب/أخبار المدينة؛ كتاب أمراء كتاب أمراء المدينة; كتاب أخبار المنصور, or even كتاب التأريخ.[87]

85 Al-Bakrī, *Muʿjam*, 3:768, with the following *isnād*: Yamūt b. al-Muzarriʿ < Ibn al-Mallāḥ < his father < Ismāʿīl b. Jaʿfar [b. Ibrāhīm] ***from*** Mūsā b. ʿAbdallāh b. al-Ḥasan; the tradition is found in Ibn al-Muzarriʿ's work, *al-Āmālī*, 1:13, quoted from the digital sites al-Maktaba al-Shāmila (http://www.islamport.com) and al-Warrāq (http://www.alwaraq.net) (I was unable to read the published book); on Yamūt, see Ibn ʿAsākir, *al-Mukhtaṣar*, 28:64–66; al-Khaṭīb al-Baghdādī, *Taʾrīkh* (Beirut, 1997), 14:360–361; al-Dhahabī, *Taʾrīkh*, 23:150–151; idem, *Siyar*, 14:247–248; al-Rabaʿī, *Mawlid al-ʿulamāʾ*, 2:634; and esp. Ibn Khallikān, *Wafāyāt*, 7:53–59: a long biography of him and his son, the poet Muhalhil; al-Ziriklī, *al-Aʿlām*, 8:209.

86 Al-Ṭabarī, 3:207 (ll. 13–20); 3:223 (ll. 18–21); 3:234 (ll. 6–17) (the use of the first person is in the last two); all three have the same *isnād*: ʿUmar b. Shabba < ʿAbd al-Malik b. Shaybān [b. ʿAbd al-Malik b. Mismaʿ, according to McAuliffe, *ʿAbbāsid Authority*, 165, n. 801; see also Ibn Ḥazm, *Jamhara*, 320] < Mismaʿ b. ʿAbd al-Malik.

87 Nagel, "Muḥammad b. ʿAbdallāh," 231; Günther, *Maqātil*, esp. 220–225; Sezgin, 1:345–346; Leder, "ʿUmar b. Shabba," 827r; McAuliffe, *ʿAbbāsid Authority*, xxi–xxii (mentioning both Nagel and Günther); the titles of these works are mentioned by Ibn al-Nadīm, *Fihrist* (ed. Tajaddud), 125; Yāqūt, *Udabāʾ* (ed. Rifāʿī), 16:61; al-Baghdādī, *Hadiyyat al-ʿārifīn*, 1:780; Ḥājjī

Al-Ṭabarī very often does not mention ʿUmar b. Shabba by name, rendering "*wa-qāla*" or "*ḥaddathanī*." In most of the parallel traditions in al-Iṣfahānī's *Maqātil*, the name of ʿUmar b. Shabba appears either in full, or just the first name or his *kunya* (Abū Zayd).[88] This is most probably the reason that McAuliffe translated each and every case "according to ʿUmar," instead of "*wa-ḥaddathanī*" or "*wa-qāla*"—and rightly so.

1) **ʿAbdallāh (al-Aṣghar) b. Nāfiʿ b. Thābit b. ʿAbdallāh b. al-Zubayr:** ʿAbdallāh (al-Aṣghar)'s father Nāfiʿ was a *ḥadīth* scholar, who, like his brother Khubayb, also strongly refused to join the rebellion of al-Nafs al-Zakiyya. This is recorded by ʿUmar b. Shabba through Nāfiʿ's son, ʿAbdallāh al-Aṣghar, who received the information about the negative attitude of their father against the revolt and of the harsh discussion between his father and Muḥammad al-Nafs al-Zakiyya from his brother, ʿAbdallāh (al-Akbar).[89]

ʿAbdallāh b. Nāfiʿ al-Aṣghar was a well-known *muḥaddith* (he is called صاحب مالك بن أنس), but also a scholar who transmitted historical traditions, a large number of them on the history of the Zubayrī family in general, and his family in particular. He was a major source of al-Zubayr b. Bakkār (d. 256/870), who related that Nāfiʿ died in Muḥarram 216/February–March 831 at the age of 70; this means that he would have been born in 146/763–764, about a year after the revolt of Muḥammad al-Nafs al-Zakiyya, but there are other dates for his death, as well.[90]

Khalīfa, *Kashf al-ẓunūn*, 1:29 (أخبار المدينة); several other works of ʿUmar b. Shabba were extensively used by al-Iṣfahānī in his *Kitāb al-Aghānī*, see Leder, "ʿUmar b. Shabba," 827r, but esp. Fleischhammer, *Kitāb al-Aghānī*, index, esp. 104–106.

88 E.g., al-Ṭabarī, 3:191 (l. 14): *wa-ḥaddathanī* [= ʿUmar b. Shabba] < Muḥammad b. Yaḥyā.... Part of the long text (an exact parallel) is recorded by al-Iṣfahānī, *Maqātil*, 262: *qāla* Abū Zayd [= ʿUmar b. Shabba] *wa-ḥaddathanī Muḥammad b. Yaḥyā*...; al-Iṣfahānī, *Maqātil*, 283–284 (once Abū Zayd; twice ʿUmar b. Shabba [= al-Ṭabarī, 3:220 and 237: *wa-ḥaddathanī*]); 287: ʿUmar b. Shabba [= al-Ṭabarī, 3:262: *wa-ḥaddathanī*]; al-Ṭabarī, 3:195 (l. 19): *qāla* [= ʿUmar b. Shabba] *ḥaddathanī* Yaʿqūb b. al-Qāsim... [= al-Iṣfahānī, *Maqātil*, 262: Yaḥyā b. ʿAlī < ʿUmar b. Shabba < *ḥaddathanī* Yaʿqūb b. al-Qāsim...]; al-Ṭabarī, 3:253: *ḥaddathanī* ʿĪsā b. ʿAbdallāh... [= al-Iṣfahānī, *Maqātil*, 248: *akhbaranā* ʿUmar b. ʿAbdallāh < ʿUmar b. Shabba < *ḥaddathanī* ʿĪsā b. ʿAbdallāh].

89 Al-Ṭabarī, 3:217 (ll. 3–12); he is almost unknown in the Sunnī *rijāl* literature, except for three or four instances where he is recorded as the transmitter of his brother's material; the only source that provides some detail about him is al-Zubayr b. Bakkār, *Jamhara*, 94–95.

90 On him, see al-Zubayr b. Bakkār, *Jamhara*, 95–96; ibid., 96: d. in Muḥarram 216; Ibn Saʿd, *Ṭabaqāt*, 5:439; Ibn ʿAsākir, *Taʾrīkh*, 22:70; 27:381; 30:315; 32:244; 35:35; 58:248; 59:253 (most of the traditions are related to al-Zubayr b. Bakkār); al-Khaṭīb al-Baghdādī, *Taʾrīkh* (Beirut, 1997), 10:172; Ibn Ḥajar, *Tahdhīb* (Beirut, 1984), 6:46: transmitted from his brother, عبد الله

ʿAbdallāh b. Nāfiʿ was a direct transmitter of ʿUmar b. Shabba. Of the three traditions recorded by him about the revolt, two were transmitted to ʿUmar b. Shabba.[91]

2) ʿAbdallāh b. Isḥāq b. al-Qāsim b. Isḥāq b. ʿAbdallāh b. Jaʿfar b. Abī Ṭālib
His grandfather, al-Qāsim b. Isḥāq b. ʿAbdallāh b. Jaʿfar b. Abī Ṭālib, was one of the senior supporters of Muḥammad al-Nafs al-Zakiyya, and was appointed as the governor of Yemen. His grandson transmitted to ʿUmar b. Shabba family traditions about events connected to his grandfather's nomination as the governor on behalf of Muḥammad, but also about other topics connected to the revolt.[92]

3) ʿAbd al-ʿAzīz b. Abī Salama b. ʿUbaydallāh b. ʿAbdallāh b. ʿUmar b. al-Khaṭṭāb
He was a *muḥaddith* of Medinan origin, who lived in Baghdad and died there in 166/782–783.[93] He transmitted to ʿUmar b. Shabba a list of names of those who joined the revolt of Muḥammad b. ʿAbdallāh, including ʿUbaydallāh [his grandfather?], who intended to join the revolt but died before it broke out.[94]

بن نافع الأكبر: d. in Muḥarram 216 aged 75[!], but according to other versions, in 210/825 or 826; 215/830 or 831; 225/839 or 840; al-Dhahabī, *Taʾrīkh*, 15:223–224: transmitted from his brother, عبد الله بن نافع الأكبر: d. in Muḥarram 216 aged 70 (from al-Zubayr b. Bakkār); al-Ṣafadī, *al-Wāfī*, 17:347; al-Maqqarī, *Nafḥ al-ṭīb*, 2:42, 630: صاحب مالك بن أنس.

91 For example, see al-Iṣfahānī, *Maqātil*, 242; al-Ṭabarī, 3:203 (ll. 15–18) (= al-Iṣfahānī, *Maqātil*, 242); al-Ṭabarī, 3:217 (ll. 3–12); see also al-Iṣfahānī, *Maqātil*, 353: transmitting to Hārūn b. Mūsā about Ibrāhīm b. ʿAbdallāh's head that was put in front of al-Manṣūr.

92 E.g., al-Ṭabarī, 3:202; see also 3:221 (سمعت من لا أحصى من أصحابنا: I heard countless of our close associates [i.e., our family?; McAuliffe, *ʿAbbāsid Authority*, 183: "countless of our associates"]); al-Ṭabarī, 3:236: relating from ʿUmar, an Anṣārī *shaykh*; his complete lineage is rendered in al-Ṭabarī, 3:153–154 (l. 16 to l. 9): ʿUmar [b. Shabba] < ʿAbdallāh b. Isḥāq b. al-Qāsim b. Isḥāq b. ʿAbdallāh b. Jaʿfar b. Abī Ṭālib < Abū Ḥarmala Muḥammad b. ʿUthmān, *mawlā* of the family of ʿAmr b. ʿUthmān < Abū Habbār al-Muzanī: year 140/757 or 758: about a plot of the Ḥasanīs to assassinate al-Manṣūr.

93 Ibn Abī Ḥātim, *al-Jarḥ* (Beirut edition), 5:384; Ibn Ḥibbān, *al-Thiqāt*, 7:110 (the date of his death); al-Khaṭīb al-Baghdādī, *Taʾrīkh* (Beirut, 1997), 10:447–448; Ibn Ḥajar, *Tahdhīb* (Hyderabad edition), 6:339–340; al-Mizzī, *Tahdhīb*, 18:141–142.

94 Al-Ṭabarī, 3:259–260 (l. 13 to l. 6); see also al-Iṣfahānī, *Maqātil*, 285 (the ʿUmarī, ʿUbaydallāh b. Muʿāwiya, is not mentioned in this *riwāya*); 316–317: an anecdote about Muḥammad b. ʿAbdallāh, his brother Ibrāhīm and their father: ʿUmar b. Shabba < ʿAbd al-ʿAzīz b. Abī Salama al-ʿUmarī and Saʿīd b. Harīm. On his family, see chapter 7, 297f.

4) Ayyūb b. ʿUmar b. Abī ʿAmr b. Nuʿaym b. Mukarram [Māhān?] b. Thaʿlaba b. Jarīr b. ʿAmr b. ʿAbdallāh b. Ghifār b. Mulayl b. Ḍamra b. Bakr b. ʿAbd Manāt b. Kināna b. Khuzayma

He appears several times in the sources, mainly in al-Ṭabarī's *Taʾrīkh* (11 times). In all of them he is the direct transmitter of ʿUmar b. Shabba. Nine out of the eleven traditions deal with events that are connected to the revolt, related to Ayyūb from people who lived in Medina during the time of the revolt, and/or took an active part (like his father) in it. Some specific evidence about the history of the family in the revolt was passed to Ayyūb by his father, ʿUmar b. Abī ʿAmr,[95] who with his brother opposed the rebellion and was imprisoned by Muḥammad b. ʿAbdallāh. Ayyūb b. ʿUmar appears in other sources also as the direct transmitter of ʿUmar b. Shabba, relating to the him events in Medina that are not related to the time or events of the revolt.[96]

5) Azhar b. Saʿd b. Nāfiʿ, Abū Bakr al-Sammān and his two brothers, ʿUthmān b. Saʿd b. Nāfiʿ and Muḥammad b. Saʿd b. Nāfiʿ

Al-Ṭabarī recorded thirteen traditions that were directly transmitted to ʿUmar b. Shabba by Azhar b. Saʿīd [read Saʿd] b. Nāfiʿ.[97] Al-Iṣfahānī records four such traditions.[98] It is noteworthy that all the traditions (except three) end with him, that is, there is no earlier transmitter before him in the *isnād*. Three traditions he related directly from his brothers who fought at the side of Muḥammad al-Nafs al-Zakiyya. Many other traditions are related from him in the first person. They all deal with and pertain to the

95 Al-Ṭabarī, 1:3468: Ayyūb transmits from Jaʿfar al-Ṣādiq; 2:1675: from Muḥammad b. ʿAbd al-ʿAzīz al-Zuhrī: the two traditions deal with the ʿAlīds but not with the revolt; 3:147 (l. 1); 152 (l. 12); 163 (l. 12); 201 (l. 3); 218 (l. 2); 227 (ll. 2–16): from his father; 236–237: from his uncle Ismāʿīl; 249 (l. 5): his father; 257 (l. 5): concludes with him; see also al-Iṣfahānī, *Maqātil*, 175; 202 [? cf. the parallel tradition in al-Iṣfahānī, *al-Aghānī* (Būlāq edition), 18:204 [Dār al-Kutub edition, 21:116]: instead of Ayyūb b. ʿUmar, read: Ayyūb < ʿUmar b. Abī l-Mawālī.

96 Ibn Abī l-Dunyā, *Makārim al-akhlāq*, 108: Abū Zayd al-Numayrī [= ʿUmar b. Shabba] < Ayyūb b. ʿUmar b. Abī ʿAmr < ʿAbdallāh b. Muḥammad al-Farwī: ʿAbdallāh b. ʿĀmir b. Kurayz b. Khālid b. ʿUqba b. Abī Muʿayṭ buys his *dār* in the market of Medina; Wakīʿ, *Quḍāt*, 1:172: al-Numayrī [= ʿUmar b. Shabba] < Ayyūb b. ʿUmar b. Abī ʿAmr < Mūsā b. ʿAbd al-ʿAzīz: the tradition about the marriage of Fāṭima bt. al-Ḥusayn b. ʿAlī to Ayyūb b. Salama al-Makhzūmī; Ibn ʿAsākir, *Taʾrīkh*, 40:264: ʿUmar b. Shabba < Ayyūb b. ʿUmar b. Abī ʿAmr < Muslim b. ʿAbdallāh b. ʿUrwa [b. al-Zubayr] < his father: about the amputation of ʿUrwa b. al-Zubayr's leg.

97 Al-Ṭabarī, 3:195 (l. 13f.); 3:199 (l. 6f.); 3:202 (l. 9f.); 3:217 (l. 13f.); 3:236 (l. 6f.); 3:236 (l. 13f) (from his two brothers); 3:239 (l. 2f.); 3:240 (l. 15f.); 3:242 (l. 4f.) (from his brother); 3:243 (l. 5f.) (from his two brothers); 3:246 (l. 6f.); 3:253 (l. 11f.).

98 Al-Iṣfahānī, *Maqātil*, 263, 270, 283: all pertaining to Muḥammad's revolt; all have Azhar b. Saʿd. On 361–362, Azhar b. Saʿd relates in the first person that he saw Hushaym [b. Bashīr] fighting for Ibrāhīm b. ʿAbdallāh in Wāsiṭ.

rebellion and to related events. It is clear from his traditions that he was in Medina during the rebellion; two traditions clearly attest to this,[99] but he does not state that he himself took an active part in the fighting as did his two brothers, ʿUthmān and Muḥammad, whom he says were with Muḥammad b. ʿAbdallāh.[100] His brothers narrated to him episodes from the battle that in turn were related by him to others.[101]

I was unable to find any information about Azhar b. Saʿīd b. Nāfiʿ. I was able to find him thus mentioned (Azhar b. Saʿīd b. Nāfiʿ) only in one other source besides al-Ṭabarī, e.g., in al-Fākihī's *Akhbār Makka*, where he is one of a group of informants of al-Fākihī about the history of the Khawārij during the time of Marwān b. Muḥammad, mainly about Abū Ḥamza al-Khārijī's speech in Mecca.[102]

Three traditions of his are recorded by Abū l-Faraj al-Iṣfahānī in *Maqātil al-ṭālibiyyīn* through ʿUmar b. Shabba. Two have exact parallels in al-Ṭabarī's book. It is noteworthy that our transmitter's name in *Maqātil* is Azhar b. Saʿd (instead of Saʿīd). In one place he is called Azhar b. Saʿd al-Sammān.[103] It seems highly plausible, therefore, to identify Azhar b. Saʿīd b. Nāfiʿ with the *ḥadīth* scholar Azhar b. Saʿd Abū Bakr al-Sammān, *mawlā* Bāhila, al-Baṣrī (d. 203/818 or 819, or 207/822 or 823).[104]

According to some sources, Azhar b. Saʿd had close and friendly relations with Caliph al-Manṣūr.[105] If the proposed identification is correct, and he is the Azhar b. Saʿīd who is mentioned by al-Ṭabarī, the question which arises is what was he doing in

99 Al-Ṭabarī, 3:195 (ll. 12–13): ʿUmar b. Shabba remarks in one of the cases: "It was related by Azhar b. Saʿīd b. Nāfiʿ who had witnessed the event ..." وقد شهد ذلك; see also 253 (l. 14), a first person report: رايتهم صفين.

100 Al-Ṭabarī, 3:236 (ll. 6–13).

101 Ibid., 3:243 (ll. 5–8): the two brothers relating in the first person plural about the battle: هزمنا يومئذ أصحاب عيسى; ibid., 3:242 (ll. 4–5): from one of his brothers about the killing of Riyāḥ b. ʿUthmān by Ibn Khuḍayr.

102 Al-Fākihī, *Akhbār Makka*, 3:140: Azhar b. Saʿīd b. Nāfiʿ < Yazīd b. Khālid al-Ḍamrī (not identified).

103 The first tradition: al-Iṣfahānī, *Maqātil*, 283: Abū Zayd [= ʿUmar b. Shabba] < Azhar b. Saʿd al-Sammān; the parallel tradition in al-Ṭabarī, 3:202 (ll. 9–10): *wa-ḥaddathanī* Azhar b. Saʿīd [ibid., n. c: according to MS A: Saʿd]; the second tradition, al-Iṣfahānī, *Maqātil*, 263: Abū Zayd < Azhar b. Saʿd; the third tradition, al-Iṣfahānī, *Maqātil*, 270: Abū Zayd < Azhar b. Saʿd; the parallel more complete tradition in al-Ṭabarī, 3:246 (ll. 6–10): *wa-ḥaddathanī* Azhar b. Saʿīd.

104 On him, see Ibn Saʿd, *Ṭabaqāt*, 7:294; Ibn Qutayba, *al-Maʿārif* (Cairo edition), 513; Ibn Ḥajar, *Tahdhīb* (Hyderabad edition), 1:202; al-Dhahabī, *Tadhkira* (Hyderabad, 1333 H.), 1:313; al-Mizzī, *Tahdhīb*, 2:323–325; al-Bājī, *al-Taʿdīl*, 1:379; see also al-Masʿūdī, *Murūj* (index), 6:141–142 (the comments of the editor, Ch. Pellat).

105 Al-Masʿūdī, *Murūj*, 4:331 nos. 2761–2762; al-Dhahabī, *Siyar*, 9:441–442; al-Ṣafadī, *al-Wāfī*, 8:240; Ibn al-ʿImād, *Shadharāt*, 3:12; in spite of the clear anecdotal elements in the

Medina at the time of the rebellion; his two brothers, according to his report, participated in the mutiny; did he change sides and join the rebellion? He never stated that he did so.

It is possible that Azhar and his brothers lived in Medina in in 145/762 and moved to al-Baṣra at some later stage, perhaps following the death of Muḥammad b. ʿAbdallāh. It is noteworthy that al-Iṣfahānī records a tradition from Azhar b. Saʿd relating in the first person that he saw Hushaym b. Bashīr in Wāsiṭ, fighting alongside Ibrāhīm b. ʿAbdallāh, shooting arrows from behind the wall at the ʿAbbāsī army.[106]

6) Hishām b. Ibrāhīm b. Hishām b. Rāshid from Hamadhān, known as al-ʿAbbāsī

This *nisba* appears in a tradition in which he relates to ʿUmar b. Shabba (following the latter's direct question) the circumstances of the death of ʿAbdallāh b. al-Ḥasan, Muḥammad al-Nafs al-Zakiyya's father, in prison.[107]

He also gave ʿUmar b. Shabba two additional pieces of valuable information, one about the confiscation of the estate of Jaʿfar al-Ṣādiq by orders of al-Manṣūr, and the second about the maritime economic blockade of Medina during al-Manṣūr's reign.[108]

Very little is known about Hishām and his family. His father is mentioned once as a transmitter in *Akhbār al-ʿAbbās* who relates from ʿĪsā b. Idrīs b. Maʿqal the ethnic origin of Abū Muslim al-Khurāsānī.[109] Valuable information is gained about him in the Imāmī sources. Some copy in full and verbatim the text in al-Kashshī's *Rijāl*.[110] Through this biography we learn that at some (first?) stages of his life he was pro-Imāmī, and traditions bear evidence of his somewhat ambiguous relations with Mūsā b. Jaʿfar al-Ṣādiq (in Baghdad, during al-Rashīd's reign) and his son ʿAlī l-Riḍā in Khurāsān (ca. 201/816–817). But all in all, ʿAlī l-Riḍā cursed him because Hishām and his disciple Yūnus affirmed a false doctrine in regard to al-Ḥasan and al-Ḥusayn: يقولان بالحسن والحسين; he calls Hishām and his father *zindīqs*. As to his *nisba*, al-ʿAbbāsī, the Imāmī sources explain that at the beginning he was one of the Shīʿa (كان من الشيعة) and was persecuted by the authorities; for that reason he changed his ways and wrote books about the Zaydiyya and a book affirming and verifying al-ʿAbbās's imamate: إثبات إمامة العباس. The authorities (ruler) became aware of his books and said that "this is

---

tradition, it seems that the main protaganists, that is, al-Manṣūr and Azhar b. Saʿd al-Sammān, are not just inventions.

106 Al-Iṣfahānī, *Maqātil*, 361–362: "I saw Hushaym carrying a sword hung upon his neck in a shoulder belt made of rope of (twisted) palm tree, shooting arrows behind the wall at the ʿAbbāsīs": رأيت هشيما عليه سيف حمائله شريط يرامي المسودة من وراء السور.

107 Al-Ṭabarī, 3:186 (ll. 2–5).

108 Ibid., 3:257 (ll. 11–13): Jaʿfar's estate; ibid. (ll. 13–16): the maritime blockade.

109 *Akhbār al-ʿAbbās*, 264.

110 Al-Kashshī, *Rijāl*, 311–312; al-Ṭūsī, *Ikhtiyār*, 2:790–791); al-Tustarī, *Rijāl*, 513–517 (with some additions); al-Tafrishī, *Naqd al-rijāl*, 5:41–42 (partially parallel).

an ʿAbbāsī": هذا عباسي.[111] Another explanation for this *nisba* is that al-Maʾmūn's son, al-ʿAbbās, was under his (Hishām b. Ibrāhīm's) protection and care: لجعل المأمون ابنه في حجره.[112] Another source states that al-Maʾmūn entrusted his son to the care of Hishām for his education.[113] The same source knows that Hishām was one of ʿAlī l-Riḍā's closest and most loyal supporters before turning his back on him, and when al-Riḍā arrived in Marw, al-Maʾmūn appointed Hishām b. Ibrāhīm as the *ḥājib* of ʿAlī l-Riḍā.[114] On some unknown date al-Maʾmūn sent Hishām b. Ibrāhīm from Khurāsān to al-ʿIrāq.[115]

7) Ibrāhīm b. Muḥammad b. ʿAbdallāh (Abū l-Karrām) b. Muḥammad b. ʿAlī b. ʿAbdallāh b. Jaʿfar b. Abī Ṭālib

He was a direct transmitter of ʿUmar b. Shabba. In several cases he based his *riwāya* on his father.[116] One such tradition records one of the versions of the al-Abwāʾ affair, that is, the alleged meeting of the Hāshimīs in al-Abwāʾ towards the end of Umawī rule, where they swore allegiance to Muḥammad b. ʿAbdallāh as the future caliph. This specific version is very interesting, as it introduces on the stage Jaʿfar al-Ṣādiq, who clearly and bluntly tells ʿAbdallāh b. al-Ḥasan that the caliphate will not pass to his sons but to the ʿAbbāsīs, and that his two sons will be killed[117] (on his father, see above).

8) Ibrāhīm b. Muṣʿab b. ʿUmāra b. Ḥamza b. Muṣʿab b. al-Zubayr

He appears several times in al-Ṭabarī's *Taʾrīkh* and al-Iṣfahānī's *Maqātil*. In several of the traditions his direct transmitters were scholars/members of the Zubayrī family relating the events of the revolt of al-Nafs al-Zakiyya.[118]

---

111 Al-Kashshī, *Rijāl*, 312; al-Ṭūsī, *Ikhtiyār*, 2:766; al-Tustarī, *Rijāl*, 514; ibid., 516–517, the author argues that the correct text should be كتب الراوندية في إثبات إمامة العباس; van Ess, *Theologie*, 3:98 n. 46: mentioning the work according to al-Kashshī.

112 Al-Tustarī, *Rijāl*, 10:515.

113 Ibn Bābawayh al-Qummī, *Akhbār al-Riḍā* (Beirut, 1984), 1:165; al-Khūʾī, *Rijāl*, 20:290 (copies Ibn Bābawayh al-Qummī).

114 Ibn Bābawayh al-Qummī, *Akhbār al-Riḍā* (Beirut, 1984), 1:164–165; al-Khūʾī, *Rijāl*, 20:290–291 (copies Ibn Bābawayh al-Qummī).

115 Al-Tustarī, *Rijāl*, 516.

116 Al-Ṭabarī, 3:232–233 (l. 20 to l. 1), 3:316 (l. 15).

117 Al-Iṣfahānī, *Maqātil*, 206, 255; and see the discussion on al-Abwāʾ in chapter 2.

118 E.g., al-Ṭabarī, 3:237 (ll. 11–12): [ʿUmar b. Shabba] < Ibrāhīm b. Muṣʿab b. ʿUmāra b. Ḥamza b. Muṣʿab b. al-Zubayr < Muḥammad b. ʿUthmān b. Muḥammad b. Khālid b. al-Zubayr; 3:255 (l. 3f.): one of several transmitters of ʿUmar b. Shabba who recited to the latter an elegy for Muḥammad b. ʿAbdallāh by the Zubayrī, ʿAbdallāh b. Muṣʿab b. Thābit b. ʿAbdallāh b. al-Zubayr; 3:260 (ll. 6–12): from al-Zubayr b. Khubayb b. Thābit b. ʿAbdallāh b. al-Zubayr.

Ibn Zabāla, see Muḥammad b. al-Ḥasan b. Zabāla

9) ʿĪsā b. ʿAbdallāh b. Muḥammad b. ʿUmar b. ʿAlī b. Abī Ṭālib[119]

9.1) The importance of ʿĪsā b. ʿAbdallāh's transmission

The highly important value of ʿĪsā b. ʿAbdallāh b. Muḥammad's traditions is clearly demonstrated in the following example: ʿĪsā b. ʿAbdallāh relates that upon approaching Medina, ʿĪsā b. Mūsā, who headed the ʿAbbāsī army that was sent to subdue the revolt, wrote to his father, ʿAbdallāh [b. Muḥammad b. ʿUmar], asking him to gather with him any dignitaries from among his Ṭālibī kinfolk who did not support the revolt in Medina (فادع من أتاك من قومك) and leave the city and join the ʿAbbāsī camp. This unique information was passed on by ʿAbdallāh b. Muḥammad's son, ʿĪsā, who gives the exact contents of the letter, explicitly stating that he saw the letter with his own eyes, adding that at that time he was a very young boy (فإني لصبي صغير). He mentions the names of three Ṭālibīs, two from his (ʿUmarī) family, i.e., his father ʿAbdallāh and his uncle ʿUmar b. Muḥammad and one from the ʿAqīl family, Abū ʿAqīl, Muḥammad b. ʿAbdallāh b. Muḥammad b. ʿAqīl b. Abī Ṭālib.[120] The number of the Ṭālibīs that stayed in ʿĪsā b. Mūsā's camp was considerably high, for further on we hear of ten Ṭālibī dignitaries from different families, among them the two aforementioned ʿUmarīs, ʿAbdallāh and ʿUmar, the above-mentioned Abū ʿAqīl Muḥammad b. ʿAbdallāh (of the ʿAqīl b. Abī Ṭālib family), al-Qāsim b. al-Ḥasan b. Zayd b. al-Ḥasan b. ʿAlī, ʿAbdallāh b. Ismāʿīl b. ʿAbdallāh b. Jaʿfar b. Abī Ṭālib, and Muḥammad b. Zayd b. ʿAlī b. al-Ḥusayn b. ʿAlī b. Abī Ṭālib, who were sent by ʿĪsā b. Mūsā to persuade the people of Medina to surrender. They failed in this mission. This unique information was narrated to ʿĪsā b. ʿAbdallāh (and from him to ʿUmar b. Shabba) by the abovementioned Muḥammad b. Zayd, who was one of the Ṭālibī dignitaries in ʿĪsā's camp.

The above-mentioned members of the ʿUmarī family, especially ʿAbdallāh b. Muḥammad b. ʿUmar related numerous traditions about the revolt, most of which were directly transmitted to ʿĪsā b. ʿAbdallāh [b. Muḥammad b. ʿUmar], who was one of the main direct sources of ʿUmar b. Shabba. Since they sided with the ʿAbbāsīs, and actually stayed in their camp, they were able to transmit the stories they heard in the ʿAbbāsī camp from ʿAbbāsī commanders and dignitaries during the events, and also later after the revolt was crushed. But ʿĪsā b. ʿAbdallāh also supplies most valuable (sometimes unique) information about several aspects of Muḥammad's camp, firsthand inside information that he received from Ṭālibīs and non-Ṭālibīs; some were mere supporters of Muḥammad b. ʿAbdallāh, others took an active part in the revolt, some carried out important roles in the latter's short caliphate.

---

119 See also the important pioneering discussion of Nagel, "Muḥammad b. ʿAbdallāh," 242ff.

120 Al-Ṭabarī, 3:226–227 (l. 7 to l. 2); being a small boy: 3:226 (l. 9).

From the information that accumulated about ʿĪsā b. ʿAbdallāh, it seems highly plausible that he himself had at his disposal either a written work (book?) on the rebellion of Muḥammad (and his brother Ibrāhīm?), or at least extensive written notes on the subject, which were transmitted orally to ʿUmar b. Shabba.

As already noted, ʿĪsā b. ʿAbdallāh was a direct transmitter of Ibn Shabba. Al-Ṭabarī recorded fifty traditions that were transmitted from ʿĪsā to ʿUmar b. Shabba, and al-Iṣfahānī recorded sixteen (fifteen through Ibn Shabba), all pertaining to different aspects of the revolt, related to ʿĪsā from contemporaries of the revolt, often people who were directly involved, either on the rebel side or the ʿAbbāsī side. Many were from different branches of the Ṭālibīs, some from ʿĪsā's family, e.g., his father, his mother, his brother, and his uncle.

9.2) The transmission and transmitters of ʿĪsā b. ʿAbdallāh

A) In *Maqātil al-ṭālibiyyīn*

‖ = a parallel tradition in al-Ṭabarī.

† = A tradition from his father.

‡ = A tradition from his father concluding with the latter.

○ = A tradition from his mother.

⁝ = A tradition from his uncle/cousin.

∴ = A tradition from his father from his grandfather.

⊗ = ʿĪsā is the last (earliest) transmitter; the *isnād* is concluded with him.

The pre-rebellion period

1) p. 176: ʿUmar b. Shabba < ʿĪsā b. ʿAbdallāh < al-Ḥasan b. Zayd < ʿAbdallāh b. al-Ḥasan (about al-Saffāḥ and ʿAbdallāh b. al-Ḥasan).

‡ 2) p. 206: ʿUmar b. Shabba < ʿĪsā < his father (al-Abwāʾ affair; it is closely connected to the biography of Muḥammad b. ʿAbdallāh and to his rebellion).

The period of the rebellion

⊗ 3) p. 189: ʿUmar b. Shabba < ʿĪsā.

‡ 4) p. 191: ʿUmar b. Shabba < ʿĪsā < his father.

5) p. 198: ʿUmar b. Shabba < ʿĪsā < ʿAbdallāh b. ʿImrān b. Abī Farwa.

6) p. 211: ʿUmar b. Shabba < ʿĪsā < Muḥammad b. ʿImrān < ʿUqba b. Salm.

⁝ ‖ 7) p. 218: ʿUmar b. Shabba < ʿĪsā < [his cousin] ʿAlī b. ʿUbaydallāh b. Muḥammad b. ʿUmar b. ʿAlī b. Abī Ṭālib [= al-Ṭabarī, 3:171 (ll. 9f.): ʿAlī b. ʿAbdallāh, that is, his brother!].

‖ 8) p. 218: ʿUmar b. Shabba < ʿĪsā < ʿAbdallāh b. ʿImrān b. Abī Farwa [= al-Ṭabarī, 3:174].

⁝ ‖ 9) p. 230: ʿUmar b. Shabba < ʿĪsā < [his uncle] ʿUbaydallāh b. Muḥammad b. ʿUmar b. ʿAlī b. Abī Ṭālib [= al-Ṭabarī, 3:168–169].

10) p. 240: ʿUmar b. Shabba < ʿĪsā < Abū Salama al-Ma[i?]ṣbaḥī [al-Muṣabbiḥī?]< a *mawlā* of Abū Jaʿfar al-Manṣūr.

⊗ 11) p. 244: [ʿUmar b. Shabba?] < ʿĪsā.
○ ‖ 11) p. 248: ʿUmar b. Shabba < ʿĪsā < his mother Umm al-Ḥusayn [= al-Ṭabarī, 3:253].
⊗ 12) p. 278: ʿUmar b. Shabba < ʿĪsā.
⊗ 13) p. 278: ʿUmar b. Shabba < ʿĪsā.
⊗ 14) p. 279: ʿUmar b. Shabba < ʿĪsā.
⊗ 15) p. 279: ʿUmar b. Shabba < ʿĪsā.
‖ 16) p. 281: ʿUmar b. Shabba < ʿĪsā < al-Ḥusayn b. Ziyād [= al-Ṭabarī, 3:252 (ll. 1–4): al-Ḥusayn b. Yazīd instead Ziyād].
† 17) p. 296: ʿUmar b. Shabba < ʿĪsā < his father [= p. 407: a short parallel; the tradition ends with ʿĪsā, his father is omitted].
⊗ 18) p. 406: Instead of ʿUmar b. Shabba: ʿAbbād b. Yaʿqūb < ʿĪsā: (ʿĪsā b. Zayd [b. ʿAlī b. al-Ḥusayn] commanding the *maymana* of both Muḥammad al-Nafs al-Zakiyya and his brother Ibrāhīm).

Summary

Seventeen traditions were transmitted by ʿĪsā to ʿUmar b. Shabba; fifteen or seventeen traditions dealing with different aspects of the rebellion were related through the transmission of ʿĪsā b. ʿAbdallāh; seven traditions conclude with ʿĪsā, that is, he is the last transmitter. He may have heard some from his father, but he may have had notes or a group of traditions about the revolt. Three traditions were transmitted to ʿĪsā by his father. Two traditions do not deal specifically with the rebellion; one was transmitted to ʿUmar b. Shabba; five traditions have parallels in al-Ṭabarī.

B) In al-Ṭabarī's Taʾrīkh, III

In the vast majority of the traditions ʿUmar b. Shabba's name is omitted in the *isnād.* Al-Ṭabarī mentions him occasionally, but afterwards, in the preceding traditions, sometimes very frequently, he uses the phrase *wa-qāla /qāla* instead. In parallel traditions in *Maqātil,* the name of ʿUmar b. Shabba appears in the *isnād* (for some examples, see below).

Pre-rebellion period

1) p. 25 (ll. 7–19): Abū Zayd, ʿUmar b. Shabba < ʿĪsā b. ʿAbdallāh b. Muḥammad b. ʿUmar b. ʿAlī b. Abī Ṭālib < ʿUthmān b. ʿUrwa b. Muḥammad b. ʿAmmār b. Yāsir (relating in the first person about the search of the messengers of the Umawī caliph for Ibrāhīm b. Muḥammad al-ʿAbbāsī in al-Ḥumayma; concludes with him).

The period of the rebellion

⊗ 2) p. 148 (ll. 9–11): *qāla* [= ʿUmar b. Shabba] < ʿĪsā b. ʿAbdallāh < *qāla: qāla Abū Jaʿfar* [al-Manṣūr].
3) p. 158 (ll. 15–18): ʿUmar < ʿĪsā b. ʿAbdallāh < حدثني من أصدق (concludes with him).

4) pp. 160–161 (l. 15 to l. 2): *qāla* [= ʿUmar b. Shabba] < ʿĪsā b. ʿAbdallāh < ʿAbdallāh b. ʿImrān b. Abī Farwa < *qāla:* كنت أنا والشعباني قائدكان لأبي جعفر (first person report; concludes with him).

5) pp. 161–162 (l. 19 to l. 8): *qāla* [= ʿUmar b. Shabba] < ʿĪsā b. ʿAbdallāh < Ḥusayn b. Yazīd < Ibn Ḍabba.

⁝ 6) pp. 165–166 (l. 10 to l. 17): *qāla* [= ʿUmar b. Shabba] < ʿĪsā b. ʿAbdallāh < my uncle, ʿUbaydallāh b. Muḥammad b. ʿUmar b. ʿAlī (concludes with him).[121]

⁝ 7) pp. 167–168 (l. 13 to l. 3): *qāla* [= ʿUmar b. Shabba] < ʿĪsā b. ʿAbdallāh < my uncle, ʿUbaydallāh b. Muḥammad (concludes with him).

8) p. 169 (ll. 5–12): [ʿUmar b. Shabba?] "in what has been mentioned from ʿĪsā b. ʿAbdallāh" < ʿAbdallāh b. ʿImrān b. Abī Farwa (concludes with him).

9) p. 169 (ll. 13–17): *qāla* ʿĪsā < ʿAbdallāh b. ʿImrān b. Abī Farwa (concludes with him).

⁝ 10) p. 171 (ll. 9–15): *qāla* [= ʿUmar b. Shabba] < ʿĪsā < [his cousin] ʿAlī b. ʿAbdallāh [sic! read ʿUbaydallāh, see al-Iṣfahānī, *Maqātil*, pp. 14, 218] b. Muḥammad b. ʿUmar b. ʿAlī قال حضرنا باب رياح (concludes with him).

‡ 11) pp. 171–172 (l. 15 to l. 4): *qāla* [= ʿUmar b. Shabba] < ʿĪsā < my father (first person report on the events; concludes with him).

12) p. 174 (ll. 13–15): *qāla* [= ʿUmar b. Shabba] < ʿĪsā < ʿAbdallāh b. ʿImrān [b. Abī Farwa, according to the parallel tradition in al-Iṣfahānī, *Maqātil*, pp. 218–219] (first person report on the events; concludes with him).

13) p. 175 (ll. 12–17): *qāla* [= ʿUmar b. Shabba] < ʿĪsā < Ibn Abrūd حاجب محمد بن عبد الله قال (first person report on the events; concludes with him).

14) pp. 178–179 (l. 17 to l. 4): *qāla* [= ʿUmar b. Shabba] < ʿĪsā b. ʿAbdallāh b. Muḥammad < Sulaymān b. Dāwūd b. Ḥasan < *qāla mā raʾaytu*... (first person report on the events; concludes with him).

15) p. 182 (ll. 9–11): *qāla* [= ʿUmar b. Shabba] < ʿĪsā < ʿAbdallāh b. ʿImrān b. Abī Farwa (first person report on the events; concludes with him).

16) pp. 182–183 (l. 17 to l. 1): *qāla* ʿUmar < ʿĪsā < ʿAbdallāh b. ʿImrān [b. Abī Farwa] < Abū l-Azhar (first person report on the events; concludes with him).

17) p. 184 (ll. 5–9): *qāla* [= ʿUmar b. Shabba] < ʿĪsā b. ʿAbdallāh < Miskīn b. ʿAmr (concludes with him).

18) pp. 184–185 (l. 18 to l. 13): *qāla* [= ʿUmar b. Shabba] < ʿĪsā b. ʿAbdallāh < ʿAbdallāh b. ʿImrān b. Abī Farwa (first person report on the events; concludes with him).

---

121 A tradition of legendary-folkloristic nature, e.g., the long tradition about a magic mirror which originally was given by God to Ādam and eventually passed into the hands of al-Manṣūr. This mirror enabled him to see Muḥammad, follow him and see his hiding places; see also chapter 2, 95f.; Nagel, "Muḥammad b. ʿAbdallāh," 243.

19) p. 186 (ll. 6–10): *qāla* [= ʿUmar b. Shabba] < ʿĪsā b. ʿAbdallāh < *qāla man baqiyā minhum*... (first person report on the events).

⨂ 20) p. 186 (ll. 10–12): *qāla ʿĪsā*.

‡ 21) pp. 190–191 (l. 18 to l. 14): *qāla* [= ʿUmar b. Shabba] < ʿĪsā < my father (first person report on the events; concludes with him).

22) pp. 193–194 (l. 15 to l. 3): *qāla* [= ʿUmar b. Shabba] < ʿĪsā < Jaʿfar b. ʿAbdallāh b. [ʿAlī b.] Yazīd b. Rukāna [b. ʿAbd Yazīd b. Hāshim b. al-Muṭṭalib b. ʿAbd Manāf] (first person report on the events; concludes with him).[122]

‡ 23) p. 196 (ll. 12–14): *qāla* [= ʿUmar b. Shabba] < ʿĪsā < my father (concludes with him).

‡ 24) pp. 200–201 (l. 18 to l. 2): *qāla* [= ʿUmar b. Shabba] < ʿĪsā < my father (concludes with him).

⨂ 25) p. 203 (ll. 7–9): *qāla* [= ʿUmar b. Shabba] < ʿĪsā *qāla*.

26) p. 203 (ll. 9–11): *qāla* [= ʿUmar b. Shabba] < ʿĪsā < Ibrāhīm b. Ziyād b. ʿAnbasa (first person report on the events; concludes with him).

‡ 27) pp. 203–204 (l. 18 to l. 3): *qāla* [= ʿUmar b. Shabba] < ʿĪsā < my father (concludes with him).

28) pp. 216–217 (l. 13 to l. 3): *qāla* [= ʿUmar b. Shabba] < ʿĪsā < Mūsā b. ʿAbdallāh [b. al-Ḥasan b. al-Ḥasan] in Baghdad and also by Rizām[?][123] (a report in the first person on the events; concludes with him).

⨂ 29) p. 217 (ll. 1–3): *qāla ʿĪsā* (personal communication of ʿĪsā to ʿUmar b. Shabba, from notes/book?).

⨂ 30) p. 222 (ll. 15–19): *qāla* [= ʿUmar b. Shabba] < ʿĪsā *qāla* (a report in the first person on the events from Medina).

‡ 31) p. 225 (ll. 1–6): *wa-ḥaddathanī* [= ʿUmar b. Shabba] < ʿĪsā b. ʿAbdallāh b. Muḥammad b. ʿUmar b. ʿAlī b. Abī Ṭālib < my father (concludes with him).

‡ 32) p. 225 (ll. 15–20): *qāla* ʿUmar [b. Shabba] < ʿĪsā < his father (concludes with him).

⨂ 33) pp. 226–227 (l. 7 to l. 2): *qāla* [= ʿUmar b. Shabba] < ʿĪsā *qāla* (a report in the first person on the events from Medina).

34) p. 231 (ll. 3–10): *qāla* [= ʿUmar b. Shabba] < ʿĪsā < al-Ghāḍirī (concludes with him; first person report on the events from Medina).

---

122 This is the only source which mentions him. I was unable to find any additional information about him. His family and ancestors are relatively well known.

123 Al-Ṭabarī, 3:216 (ll. 14–15): حدثني موسى بن عبد الله ببغداد و رزام معا قال: بعثني; perhaps the text should be read معنا (that is, "with us") instead of معا; McAuliffe, *ʿAbbāsid Authority*, 177: "Mūsā b. ʿAbdallāh informed me in Baghdad—Rizām being present as well—as follows ..."; this is also the rendering of the version of Abū l-Faḍl Ibrāhīm's text (7:572).

∵ 35) p. 231 (ll. 10–16): *qāla* [= ʿUmar b. Shabba] < ʿĪsā < his father < his grandfather[124] (concludes with him; first person report on the events).

36) pp. 231–232 (l. 17 to l. 8): *qāla* [= ʿUmar b. Shabba] < ʿĪsā < Muḥammad b. Abī Karrām [Kirām?] (concludes with him; first person report on the events).

37) p. 234 (ll. 4–5): *qāla* [= ʿUmar b. Shabba] < ʿĪsā < Muḥammad b. Zayd [b. ʿAlī b. al-Ḥusayn] (concludes with him; first person report on the events).[125]

38) pp. 235–236 (l. 6 to l. 5): *qāla* [= ʿUmar b. Shabba] < ʿĪsā < Muḥammad b. Zayd [b. ʿAlī b. al-Ḥusayn] (concludes with him; first person report on the events).

‡ 39) p. 237 (ll. 14–17): *qāla* [= ʿUmar b. Shabba] < ʿĪsā < his father [= al-Iṣfahānī, *Maqātil*, 284: Abū Zayd < ʿĪsā b. ʿAbdallāh b. ʿUmar b. ʿAlī < my father].

40) p. 240 (ll. 1–9): *wa-ḥaddathanī* [= ʿUmar b. Shabba] < ʿĪsā < Muḥammad b. Zayd [b. ʿAlī b. al-Ḥusayn] (concludes with him; first person report on the events).

⊗ 41) p. 243 (ll. 9–13): *wa-ḥaddathanī* [= ʿUmar b. Shabba] < ʿĪsā *qāla* (report on the events from Medina).

42) pp. 243–244 (l. 13 to l. 2): *wa-ḥaddathanī* [= ʿUmar b. Shabba] < ʿĪsā < *mawlā* of Hishām b. ʿUmāra b. al-Walīd b. ʿAdī b. al-Khiyār (concludes with him; first person report on the events of the battle).

‡ 43) pp. 250–251 (l. 17 to l. 3): *fa-ḥaddathanī* [= ʿUmar b. Shabba] < ʿĪsā < his father (reports on the aftermath of the battle).

44) p. 252 (ll. 1–4): *ḥaddathanī* [= ʿUmar b. Shabba] < ʿĪsā < Ḥusayn b. Yazīd (concludes with him; reports on the aftermath of the battle).[126]

45) p. 252 (ll. 10–14): *wa-ḥaddathanī* [= ʿUmar b. Shabba] < ʿĪsā < Muḥammad b. Zayd [b. ʿAlī b. al-Ḥusayn] (concludes with him; first person report on the events).

○ 46) p. 253–254 (l. 18 to l. 3): *ḥaddathanī* [= ʿUmar b. Shabba] < ʿĪsā b. ʿAbdallāh < my mother Umm Ḥusayn bt. ʿAbdallāh b. Muḥammad b. ʿAlī b. Ḥusayn (concludes with her; first person report on the events of the revolt).

‡ 47) p. 254 (ll. 3–7): *qāla* [= ʿUmar b. Shabba] < ʿĪsā < his father (reports on the aftermath of the revolt).

48) p. 254 (ll. 7–16): *ḥaddathanī* [= ʿUmar b. Shabba] < ʿĪsā < Muḥammad b. Abī l-Karrām [Kirām?] (concludes with him; first person report on the events).

⊗ 49) p. 257 (ll. 2–4): *wa-ḥaddathanī* [= ʿUmar b. Shabba] < ʿĪsā *qāla* (reporting on the aftermath of the revolt).

---

124 According to MS A: instead of *from* his grandfather: *and* his grandfather.

125 The full name is reconstructed according to al-Iṣfahānī, *Maqātil*, 267; on him see above; on him and his brothers, see also chapter 5, n. 157 and chapter 7, 252.

126 Unidentified; this might be al-Ḥusayn b. Zayd b. ʿAlī b. al-Ḥusayn b. ʿAlī b. Abī Ṭālib, the brother of Muḥammad mentioned above.

⊗ 50) pp. 258 (ll. 5–8) [11–14; 17–19][127]and 259 (ll. 2–3): [*wa-ḥaddathanī* = ʿUmar b. Shabba] < ʿĪsā *qāla* (a list of the supporters of Muḥammad al-Nafs al-Zakiyya from among the Ṭālibīs).

⊗ 51) pp. 258 (ll. 8–11): *wa-ḥaddathanī* [= ʿUmar b. Shabba] < ʿĪsā *qāla* (about the Ṭālibīs who took part in the revolt).

⊗ 52) p. 258 (ll. 13–17): *qāla* ʿĪsā (this is a continuous transmission of ʿĪsā's tradition about the Ṭālibīs who took part in the revolt).

⊗ 53) pp. 258–259 (l. 19 to l. 1): *qāla ʿĪsā* (this is a continuous transmission of ʿĪsā's tradition about the Ṭālibīs who took part in the revolt).

‡ 54) p. 260 (ll. 12–15): *qāla* [= ʿUmar b. Shabba] < ʿĪsā < my father (reports on the aftermath of the revolt).

⊗ 55) p. 260 (ll. 15–18): *qāla* [ʿĪsā] (reporting on the aftermath of the revolt).

‡ 56) p. 264 (ll. 2–8): *wa-ḥaddathanī* [= ʿUmar b. Shabba] < ʿĪsā < my father (reports on the aftermath of the revolt: the prisoners who are brought to al-Manṣūr, some executed, some pardoned).

57) pp. 264–265 (l. 8 to l. 2): *wa-ḥaddathanī* [= ʿUmar b. Shabba] < ʿĪsā < *samiʿtu* Ḥasan b. Zayd *yaqūlu* (concludes with him; first person report from the caliph's court on the aftermath of the revolt: prisoners brought to al-Manṣūr and flogged).

The revolt of the blacks (sūdān) in Medina

⊗ 58) p. 267 (ll. 10–12): *wa-ḥaddathanī* [= ʿUmar b. Shabba] < ʿĪsā *qāla* (the names of the leaders of the *sūdān;* they defeat the governor of Medina who leaves the city and encamps in Baṭn Nakhl).

Different subjects: Tradition about al-ʿAbbās b. ʿAbd al-Muṭṭalib and the Prophet

∵ 59) Ibn ʿAsākir, *Taʾrīkh*, 26:302; Ibn ʿAdī, *Ḍuʿafāʾ*, 5:245: ʿUmar b. Shabba < ʿĪsā b. ʿAbdallāh b. Muḥammad b. ʿUmar b. ʿAlī [b. Abī Ṭālib] < my father < his father < his grandfather < ʿAlī.

Summary

In total there are seventy-three traditions in al-Ṭabarī's *Taʾrīkh* and in al-Iṣfahānī's *Maqātil* that were transmitted to ʿUmar b. Shabba by ʿĪsā b. ʿAbdallāh. Fifty-six traditions in al-Ṭabarī's *Taʾrīkh* deal with the revolt. Fifteen (out of seventeen) traditions in al-Iṣfahānī's *Maqātil* deal directly with the revolt, while two others are connected in a way that they are part of the historical background to the revolt, e.g. a tradition about al-Saffāḥ and ʿAbdallāh b. al-Ḥasan, and another one reporting about the al-Abwāʾ

127 This is a long tradition of ʿĪsā, a list of the Ṭālibī supporters of al-Nafs al-Zakiyya; it is interrupted three times by ʿUmar b. Shabba, by anecdotes about the persons, also related to him by ʿĪsā b. ʿAbdallāh.

affair. Two traditions in al-Ṭabarī deal with different historical events: 1) The description of the search for Ibrāhīm b. Muḥammad *al-Imām al-ʿAbbāsī* in al-Ḥumayma by the messengers of the Umawī caliph Marwān b. Muḥammad (no. 1); and 2) A tradition recording information regarding the *sūdāns*' (blacks') revolt in Medina immediately following the crushing of the revolt of Muḥammad al-Nafs al-Zakiyya (no. 55).

The transmitters of ʿĪsā b. ʿAbdallāh

The *isnād* of seventeen traditions end with ʿĪsā b. ʿAbdallāh. Twenty-two traditions were related to ʿĪsā by his relatives. Sixteen traditions were transmitted to ʿĪsā by his father (thirteen in al-Ṭabarī's *Taʾrīkh*, nos. 11, 21, 23, 24, 27, 31, 32, 39, 43, 47, 54, 56; three in al-Iṣfahānī's *Maqātil*, nos. 2, 4, and 17). Two traditions were transmitted to ʿĪsā by his father from his grandfather (both in al-Ṭabarī's *Taʾrīkh*). Two traditions were transmitted to ʿĪsā by his uncle, ʿUbaydallāh (in al-Ṭabarī's *Taʾrīkh*, nos. 6 and 7; *Maqātil*, no. 9). One tradition was transmitted to ʿĪsā by his cousin ʿAlī (al-Ṭabarī, *Taʾrīkh*, no. 10; *Maqātil*, no. 7). One tradition was transmitted to ʿĪsā by his mother (al-Ṭabarī's *Taʾrīkh*).

Other transmitters

Eight traditions were transmitted to ʿĪsā by ʿAbdallāh b. ʿImrān b. Abī Farwa (on him, see above), seven in al-Ṭabarī's *Taʾrīkh*; one in al-Iṣfahānī's *Maqātil*. Four traditions were transmitted to ʿĪsā by Muḥammad b. Zayd b. ʿAlī b. al-Ḥusayn b. ʿAlī b. Abī Ṭālib (on him, see above) in al-Ṭabarī's *Taʾrīkh*. Two traditions were transmitted to ʿĪsā by al-Ḥusayn b. Yazīd [Ziyād?] [= al-Ḥasan b. Zayd?].

Two traditions were transmitted to ʿĪsā by Muḥammad b. Abī l-Karrām (al-Ṭabarī's *Taʾrīkh*). One tradition was transmitted to ʿĪsā by Muḥammad b. ʿImrān [b. Abī Farwa?] (al-Iṣfahānī's *Maqātil*).[128] One tradition was transmitted to ʿĪsā by Sulaymān b. Dāwūd b. al-Ḥasan (al-Ṭabarī's *Taʾrīkh*). One tradition was transmitted to ʿĪsā by Mūsā b. ʿAbdallāh b. al-Ḥasan b. al-Ḥasan b. ʿAlī (al-Ṭabarī's *Taʾrīkh*). One tradition was transmitted to ʿĪsā by Ibn Abrūd (the *ḥājib* of Muḥammad al-Nafs al-Zakiyya (al-Ṭabarī's *Taʾrīkh*). One tradition was transmitted to ʿĪsā by al-Ghāḍirī (al-Ṭabarī's *Taʾrīkh*). One tradition was transmitted to ʿĪsā by Ibrāhīm b. Ziyād b. ʿAnbasa (al-Ṭabarī's *Taʾrīkh*). One tradition was transmitted to ʿĪsā by Miskīn b. ʿUmar (al-Ṭabarī's *Taʾrīkh*). One tradition was transmitted to ʿĪsā by al-Ḥasan b. Zayd b. al-Ḥasan b. ʿAlī b. Abī Ṭālib (al-Ṭabarī's *Taʾrīkh*). One tradition was transmitted to ʿĪsā by Jaʿfar b. ʿAbdallāh b. ʿAlī b. Yazīd b. Rukāna (al-Ṭabarī's *Taʾrīkh*). One tradition was transmitted to ʿĪsā by *mawlā* Hishām b. ʿUmāra b. al-Walīd b. ʿAdī b. al-Khiyār (al-Ṭabarī's *Taʾrīkh*). One tradition was transmitted to ʿĪsā by Abū Salama al-Muṣabbiḥī (al-Maṣbaḥī?), in al-Iṣfahānī's *Maqātil*.

128 Is he Muḥammad b. ʿImrān al-Taymī?

One tradition was transmitted to ʿĪsā by an anonymous person: "حدثني من أصدق" (al-Ṭabarī's *Taʾrīkh*).

An analysis of the contents of the traditions of ʿĪsā b. ʿAbdallāh strongly indicates that he had at his disposal a large number of traditions about Muḥammad al-Nafs al-Zakiyya's rebellion (but also about the revolt of Ibrāhīm, see above no. 18), which he received (collected) from different sources—his father, his uncle and cousin, his mother, and other informants, most of whom witnessed the events or actively participated in the events evolving around the revolt. Both al-Ṭabarī and al-Iṣfahānī record many traditions (some of them are long) in which ʿUmar b. Shabba transmits directly from ʿĪsā, using the term "*qāla ʿĪsā*" with no further transmitter after the latter. No less than seventeen traditions of Ibn Shabba (eleven in al-Ṭabarī and six in al-Iṣfahānī) were transmitted by ʿĪsā, with no further *isnād* link (noteworthy is the long transmission relating to one subject, e.g., al-Ṭabarī, 3:257 (ll. 2–14); 3:258 (ll. 5–8, 13–19); 3:259 (ll. 1–3)). This would seem to support the hypothesis about the notes or work that ʿĪsā had at his disposal. It is thus possible that Ibn Shabba copied from a written work of ʿĪsā. But some further conclusions can be drawn about ʿĪsā's activity as a historian. It seems that he transmitted historical traditions dealing with the end of the Umayyad period and the beginning of the ʿAbbāsī period, as well as other traditions relating to the history of Medina after the revolt of al-Nafs al-Zakiyya, e.g., the tradition about the *sūdān*'s revolt in Medina, which may have been part of Ibn Shabba's book on the history of Medina.

10) Ismāʿīl b. Jaʿfar b. Ibrāhīm b. Muḥammad b. ʿAlī b. ʿAbdallāh b. Jaʿfar b. Abī Ṭālib
The sources do not disclose his mother's name, but he may have been a son of Umm Salama bt. Muḥammad b. Ṭalḥa b. ʿAbdallāh b. ʿAbd al-Raḥmān b. Abī Bakr, who was also the wife of Mūsā b. ʿAbdallāh b. al-Ḥasan, and the mother of his brother, Muḥammad (see below). He married Ruqayya, the daughter of Mūsā b. ʿAbdallāh,[129] which means, as in the case of his brother, Muḥammad, that his marriage to Ruqayya was consummated before his mother married Mūsā b. ʿAbdallāh (Ruqayya was most probably not her daughter).[130] Apparently he was close to Mūsā b. ʿAbdallāh (see below). The sources state that Ismāʿīl and Ruqayya had two sons, Ibrāhīm and Muḥammad,[131] the latter being a known transmitter of *ḥadīth* as well as of historical traditions. He was

129 Al-Iṣfahānī, *Maqātil*, 237; Ibn ʿInaba, *ʿUmda*, 47–48; al-ʿUmarī, *Ansāb*, 45.

130 Ibid.: Mūsā's children from Umm Salama are ʿAbdallāh, Ibrāhīm, Muḥammad, Umm al-Ḥasan, Khadīja, and Ṣafiyya. Ruqayya is not mentioned among them, and she was most probably not his half (step) sister.

131 Al-ʿUmarī, *Ansāb*, 45: Muḥammad; al-Shāhrūdī, *Mustadrakāt*, 1:125: Muḥammad and Ibrāhīm.

one of the direct transmitters of ʿUmar b. Shabba and related some inside information from and about the Ḥasanī family and events during the revolt.[132]

Ismāʿīl b. Jaʿfar was a minor scholar of *ḥadīth*.[133] He is mentioned a few times in the sources as the direct transmitter of ʿUmar b. Shabba. So far I have managed to detect only five such traditions, all relating to the Ḥasanī family and/or the events of the revolt.[134] On his brother, and his son, both named Muḥammad, see below.

11) Maḥmūd b. Maʿmar b. Fāliḥ (Abū l-Shadāʾid) al-Fazārī

He related two traditions to ʿUmar b. Shabba about his grandfather, the blind poet: 1) how the latter sent some verses to Muḥammad b. ʿAbdallāh before the ʿAbbāsī army entered Medina; and 2) describing how he was killed in his house by the ʿAbbāsī soldiers.

12) Muḥammad b. Abī Ḥarb

He was a direct transmitter of ʿUmar b. Shabba on the events of the revolt. All the traditions are found in al-Ṭabarī's *Taʾrīkh* and al-Iṣfahānī's *Maqātil*, and they all (except one) conclude with him (*qāla*), with no further transmitters. This may denote that he had written notes about the revolt. He was one of the transmitters who related to ʿUmar

132 The son of Ruqayya and Ismāʿīl: al-ʿUmarī, *Ansāb*, 45; al-Iṣfahānī, *Maqātil*, 237; he is mentioned by Nagel, "Muḥammad b. ʿAbdallāh," 244, and see the discussion further below.

133 For example, see al-Bukhārī, *al-Kabīr* (ed. al-Nadwī), 1:350; Ibn Abī Ḥātim, *al-Jarḥ* (Beirut edition), 2:163–164; Ibn Ḥibbān, *al-Thiqāt*, 8:92; Ibn Ḥajar, *Lisān*, 1:397.

134 1) Al-Ṭabarī, 3:256 (l. 15) [= al-Bakrī, *Muʿjam*, 3:768]: [ʿUmar b. Shabba] < Ismāʿīl b. Jaʿfar b. Ibrāhīm [b. Muḥammad b. ʿAlī b. ʿAbdallāh b. Jaʿfar b. Abī Ṭālib], from Mūsā b. ʿAbdallāh b. al-Ḥasan, where we find a testimony concerning Suwayqa being a [the main?] residence for the Ḥasanī family, "I came out of our dwellings (*manāzilinā*) in Suwayqa"; 2) Al-Ṭabarī, 3:170 (ll. 6–7): ʿUmar b. Shabba < Ismāʿīl b. Jaʿfar b. Ibrāhīm; 3) Al-Iṣfahānī, *Maqātil*, 183: ʿUmar b. Shabba < Ismāʿīl b. Jaʿfar al-Jaʿfarī < Saʿīd b. ʿUqba al-Juhanī (on him, see below); 4) Al-Bakrī, *Muʿjam*, 3:768: (*wa-ḥaddatha*) Yamūt b. al-Muzarriʿ from Ibn al-Mallāḥ [that is, ʿĀʾidh b. Ḥabīb b. al-Mallāḥ al-ʿAbsī or al-Qurashī (d. 190/805 or 806), on him, see below] from his father [Ḥabīb b. al-Mallāḥ] from Ismāʿīl b. Jaʿfar b. Ibrāhīm [b. Muḥammad b. ʿAlī b. ʿAbdallāh b. Jaʿfar b. Abī Ṭālib] from Mūsā b. ʿAbdallāh b. al-Ḥasan; another testimony regarding Suwayqa, related in the first person by Mūsā b. ʿAbdallāh; 5) Ibid., the same *isnād* as before, describing in the first person how he met Mūsā b. ʿAbdallāh, who leads the former through the devastated estate of Suwayqa; the text was copied, almost verbatim, by al-Ḥimyarī, *al-Rawḍ al-miʿṭār*, 328–329; a parallel tradition, al-Iṣfahānī, *Maqātil*, 298 with a changed (garbled?) *isnād* and simpler text; the poetry, though, is longer and more complete.

b. Shabba about the letters between Muḥammad b. ʿAbdallāh and al-Manṣūr. I was unable to find any further information about him.[135]

13) Mawhūb b. Rashīd b. Ḥayyān *aḥad* Banī Qurayṭ [ʿĀmir b. Ṣaʿṣaʿa]

He transmitted two traditions to ʿUmar b. Shabba: 1) from his father who witnessed the entrance of Muḥammad b. ʿAbdallāh to Medina and described some of the first actions of al-Nafs al-Zakiyya in Medina and the reactions of the people of that city;[136] 2) in which he records some verses of the poet Abū l-Shadāʾid, relating to Muḥammad b. ʿAbdallāh's rebellion and the sending of the ʿAbbāsī army of ʿĪsā b. Mūsā against him.[137]

14) Muḥammad b. al-Ḥasan b. Zabāla

Muḥammad b. al-Ḥasan b. Zabāla was one of ʿUmar b. Shabba's direct transmitters. He was a scholar well-known to his contemporaries and medieval Muslim scholars, but less known in modern research.[138] He was a Medinan scholar, who was a *muḥaddith* as well as a historian. He was active during the middle of the second/eighth century and died, according to Ibn Ḥajar, a little before the end of the second *hijrī* century/815–816, although al-Dhahabī included him in the volume of the biographies of those who died between 211/826 and 220/835.[139] He is severely criticized by critics of transmitters of *ḥadīth* as a totally unreliable, untrustworthy forger, and a thief (of *ḥadīth*). It is very rare to find a scholar of *ḥadīth* who is unanimously viewed by *rijāl al-ḥadīth* scholars as unequivocally negative as a *muḥaddith*.[140] However, Ibn Zabāla was also (mainly?) a historian, about whom al-Dhahabī commented (after quoting faithfully all the

135 Al-Ṭabarī, 3:178, 183, 184; 206 and 208: Ibn Abī Ḥarb; al-Iṣfahānī, *Maqātil*, 193; the *isnād* does not end with him; 221, 265; 326 (Ibrāhīm's revolt).

136 Al-Ṭabarī, 3:230 (ll. 6–18).

137 Al-Ṭabarī, 3:203 (ll. 3–6).

138 On him, see Rosenthal, *Historiography*, 475; Brockelmann, GAL, 1:137–138; Sezgin, 1:343–344; Kaḥḥāla, *Muʿjam*, 9:191; but esp. the comprehensive study of Munt, "Ibn Zabāla"; ibid., 11, n. 45: additional modern bibliography on Ibn Zabāla, including Ṣalāḥ ʿAbd al-ʿAzīz Salāma, *Akhbār al-Madīna li-Muḥammad b. al-Ḥasan b. Zabāla* (Medina: Markaz Buḥūth wa-Dirāsāt, 1424/2003); not available to me.

139 Ibn Ḥajar, *Taqrīb* (Beirut 1995), 2:66: مات قبل المائتين; quoted by Sezgin, 1:343–344, and Munt, "Ibn Zabāla," 2; but cf. Rosenthal, *Historiography*, 475, n. 6, quoting Brockelmann: "wrote 199/814" [!?]; al-Dhahabī, *Taʾrīkh* (ed. al-Tadmurī: *Ḥawādith wa-wafayāt 211–220*), 364–365.

140 For example, see Ibn Abī Ḥātim, *al-Jarḥ* (Beirut edition), 7:227–228; Ibn Ḥibbān, *al-Majrūḥīn*, 2:272; Ibn ʿAdī, *Ḍuʿafāʾ*, 6:171–172; Ibn Ḥajar, *Tahdhīb* (Beirut edition), 9:101–102; al-Dhahabī, *Taʾrīkh* (ed. al-Tadmurī: *Ḥawādith wa-wafayāt 211–220*), 364–365, and the exhaustive bibliography of the editor; idem, *Siyar*, 12:163; and see the exhaustive list of his critics recorded by al-Maqrīzī, *Imtāʿ*, 10:362–364; Nagel, "Muḥammad b. ʿAbdallāh," 235.

defamations vilifying him) "I have not seen anyone more versed than him in the (subjects of) the raids of the Prophet and the early campaigns (*al-maghāzī*) and the (Arab) genealogy (*al-ansāb*)..."[141] and then he says "I say, he was a historian (and) a very learned man, from whom al-Zubayr [b. Bakkār, d. 256/870] took a great deal."[142] This remark connects us to an important topic which is one of Ibn Zabāla's historical works (the most well-known, and probably the most important), that is, *Kitāb al-Madīna wa-akhbāriha*.[143] This work has not survived, but as already noted by Sezgin, some quotations from it appear in later sources (under *Ta'rīkh al-Madīna* or the more common title: *Akhbār al-Madīna*), e.g., Ibn Ḥajar and al-Samhūdī.[144] Al-Zubayr b. Bakkār wrote a history of Medina, which was also lost, but is quoted by Arabic sources much more widely than Ibn Zabāla's work.[145] Several scholars pointed out the connection between al-Zubayr b. Bakkār and Ibn Zabāla.[146] And indeed, a simple check with the help of the digital databases that contain thousands of early Arabic sources show that in his work on Medina, al-Zubayr b. Bakkār quotes Ibn Zabāla many times.

---

141 Al-Dhahabī, *Ta'rīkh* (ed. al-Tadmurī: *Ḥawādith wa-wafayāt, 211–220*), 364: وما رأيت أحدا أعلم بالمغازي والأنساب منه.

142 Ibid., 365: قلت كان أخباريا علامة أكثر عنه الزبير.

143 For an extensive discussion of this work, see now Munt, "Ibn Zabāla," 14ff; Ibn al-Nadīm, *Fihrist* (ed. Tajaddud), 121, mentions three works: *Kitāb al-Madīna wa-akhbāriha*; *Kitāb al-Shuʿarāʾ*; and *Kitāb al-Alqāb*; a single source, Ibn Ḥajar, *Tahdhīb* (Hyderabad edition), 9:117 (quoting Zakariyyāʾ b. Yaḥyā l-Sājī, d. 307/919 or 920), mentions *Kitāb mathālib al-ansāb*; see Munt, "Ibn Zabāla," 14, n. 62); other sources mention only his work on Medina, e.g., Ḥājjī Khalīfa, *Kashf al-ẓunūn* (Beirut 1992), 1:29; al-Baghdādī, *Hadiyyat al-ʿārifīn*, 2:9 (تأريخ المدينة).

144 Sezgin, 1:343–344, where he also directs our attention to the connection between al-Zubayr b. Bakkār and Ibn Zabāla. The work is noted in all the studies mentioned in note 161 above; for discussion about the citations of Ibn Zabāla by al-Samhūdī and the reliability of this transmission, see Munt, "Ibn Zabāla," 5–6, 8, 13. Ibn Zabāla is quoted by al-Samhūdī more than 600 times; Munt, "Ibn Zabāla," 16–17, 19; 23–27, where he mentions the citation of this work by early, but mainly (and extensively) by later medieval sources.

145 On al-Zubayr b. Bakkār, see Sezgin, 1:317–318; about his work, ibid., 318, bringing a few citations from his *Akhbār al-Madīna* quoted by Ibn Ḥajar in his *al-Iṣāba*. Hundreds of additional examples are found in the vast Arabic literature, and they can be easily processed with the help of the digital databases of the early Arabic sources at our disposal.

146 Ibid., 343; but especially Munt, "Ibn Zabāla," 14–15; 26: emphasizing the citations in al-Zubayr b. Bakkār's *al-Muwaffaqiyyāt* and *Jamharat al-nasab*.

A similar study shows that ʿUmar b. Shabba [d. 264/877] relied heavily[?][147] on Ibn Zabāla in his work. Suffice it here to remark that many traditions that deal with the rebellion of Muḥammad al-Nafs al-Zakiyya that are recorded by al-Ṭabarī and al-Iṣfahānī through the transmission (work?) of Ibn Shabba were directly transmitted to him by Ibn Zabāla, and it is highly plausible that they contained parts of the latter's lost book. Muḥammad b. al-Ḥasan b. Zabāla is mentioned nineteen times (by al-Ṭabarī and al-Iṣfahānī) as the direct transmitter of ʿUmar b. Shabba; seventeen relate to Muḥammad b. ʿAbdallāh and his revolt.[148]

15) Muḥammad b. Ismāʿīl b. Jaʿfar b. Ibrāhīm b. Muḥammad b. ʿAlī b. ʿAbdallāh b. Jaʿfar b. Abī Ṭālib (the aforementioned son, no. 10)[149]

He was a direct transmitter to ʿUmar b. Shabba, relating to him reports about the events of the revolt from firsthand sources, most of whom witnessed and/or took an active part in the events revolving around the revolt; some are recorded in the first person from his mother, Ruqayya, the daughter of Mūsā b. ʿAbdallāh b. al-Ḥasan, and many from the latter, who was his grandfather. Al-Ṭabarī and al-Iṣfahānī record twenty-one traditions that were transmitted through 1) ʿUmar b. Shabba from 2) Muḥammad b. Ismāʿīl; the ⓡ symbol designates a direct quote or first person/firsthand report; the ⓝ symbol may designate personal independent notes (work?).

a) Traditions about the revolt and the events that are connected to it in al-Ṭabarī's *Taʾrīkh* [TT] and al-Iṣfahānī's *Maqātil* [IM].

1) TT, 3:144 (l. 2): 1 < 2 < ʿAbd al-ʿAzīz b. ʿImrān < ʿAbdallāh b. Abī ʿUbayda b. Muḥammad b. ʿAmmār b. Yāsir [= *Maqātil*, 209–210]

ⓡ 2) TT, 3:144 (l. 11): *wa-qāla* Muḥammad [b. Ismāʿīl] < I heard my grandfather Mūsā b. ʿAbdallāh say.

---

147 But cf. Nagel, "Muḥammad b. ʿAbdallāh," 235, and Munt, "Ibn Zabāla," 124: "He very rarely appears as a source in the Iraqi Ibn Šabba's *Taʾrīḫ al-Madīna l-munawwara*, even though he is often listed as someone with whom Ibn Šabba studied."

148 Al-Ṭabarī, 3:168, 173, 174, 175, 182 (x2), 202, 229, 238, 241, 250 (x2), 252, 255, 269; in only two places is ʿUmar b. Shabba mentioned by name, otherwise the tradition starts by *wa-qāla* or *wa-ḥaddathanī*; McAuliffe is right in rendering these words by ʿUmar b. Shabba; two of the fifteen traditions in al-Ṭabarī do not deal with the rebellion; al-Iṣfahānī, *Maqātil*, 200 (x2), 219, 248, 279, 286, 297 (seven traditions), in all of them ʿUmar b. Shabba is specifically mentioned by name in the *isnād*. Three traditions in the two works are parallel, e.g., al-Ṭabarī, 3:174, 182, and 252 [= al-Iṣfahānī, *Maqātil*, 219, 200, and 279, respectively].

149 On him, see al-Bukhārī, *al-Kabīr* (ed. al-Nadwī), 1:37; Ibn Abī Ḥātim, *al-Jarḥ* (Beirut edition), 7:189; al-Samʿānī, *Ansāb* (Beirut, 1988), 2:68 ("al-Jaʿfarī"); Nagel, "Muḥammad b. ʿAbdallāh," 244–245.

ⓡ 3) TT, 3:144 (l. 14): 1 < 2 < I heard al-Qāsim b. Muḥammad b. ʿAbdallāh b. ʿAmr b. ʿUthmān b. ʿAffān < Muḥammad b. Wahb al-Sulamī < his father [= *Maqātil*, 210].
ⓝ 4) TT, 3:145 (l. 1): *qāla* Muḥammad.
ⓡ 5) TT, 3:145 (l. 3): *qāla* Muḥammad < My mother related to me [Ruqayya: وحدثتني أمي] < her father [Mūsā b. ʿAbdallāh] [= *Maqātil*, 210 (l. 11)].
ⓡ 6) TT, 3:180 (ll. 2–3): 1 < 2 < from Mūsā b. ʿAbdallāh [= *Maqātil*, 224 (l. 4)].
ⓡ 7) TT, 3:185, ll. 13–14: I heard (*samiʿtu*) from my grandfather, Mūsā b. ʿAbdallāh [= al-Iṣfahānī, *Maqātil*, 192].
8) TT, 3:200, ll. 8–9: 1 < 2 < Ibn Abī Mulayka *mawlā* ʿAbdallāh b. Jaʿfar. This shows that he relied on both sides of his family, the Jaʿfarīs and the Ḥasanīs.
9) TT, 3:228, ll. 7–8: 1 < 2 < from his trustworthy informants (عن الثقة عنده).
ⓝⓡ 10) TT, 3:228, ll. 11–12: *qāla* Muḥammad < ʿAbdallāh b. Maʿrūf, one of the Banū Riyāḥ b. Mālik b. ʿUṣayya b. Khufāf, and he had witnessed this already (وقد شهد ذلك).
11) TT, 3:232, ll. 8–9: 1 < 2 < from his trustworthy informants (عن الثقة عنده).
12) TT, 3:244, l. 16: 1 < 2 < from his trustworthy informants (عن الثقة عنده).
ⓡ 13) TT, 3:246–247 (l. 19 to l. 1): 1 < 2 < Abū l-Ḥajjāj al-Minqarī *qāla raʾaytu*.
ⓡ 14) TT, 3:247 (l. 6): *qāla* < I heard my grandfather say (فسمعت جدي يقول) [= al-Iṣfahānī, *Maqātil*, 271].
15) IM, 210–211 (l. 16 to l. 6): 1 < 2 < al-Ḥasan b. ʿAlī b. al-Ḥasan b. al-Ḥasan b. al-Ḥasan.
16) IM, 212: 1 < 2 < I heard from my grandfather Mūsā b. ʿAbdallāh and a group from those that revered ʿAbdallāh b. al-Ḥasan.
ⓡ 17) IM, 237–238 (l. 16 to l. 3): 1 < 2 < from his mother Ruqayya bt. Mūsā b. ʿAbdallāh b. al-Ḥasan b. al-Ḥasan < Saʿīd b. ʿUqba al-Juhanī.[150]
ⓡ 18) IM, 238 (ll. 8–11): 1 < 2 < Mūsā b. ʿAbdallāh.
ⓡ 19) IM, 243 (ll. 5–7): 1 < 2 < Ibn Abī Thābit [ʿAbd al-ʿAzīz b. ʿImrān al-Zuhrī].
ⓡ 20) IM, 249 (ll. 8–11): 1 < 2 < ʿAbd al-ʿAzīz b. ʿImrān al-Zuhrī < his father.
ⓡ 21) IM, 275–276 (l. 14 to l. 6): 1 < 2 < I heard my grandmother, Umm Salama bt. Muḥammad b. Ṭalḥa < I heard Zaynab bt. ʿAbdallāh [b. al-Ḥasan b. al-Ḥasan] saying.

b) Traditions on other subjects related through Muḥammad b. Ismāʿīl (not through ʿUmar b. Shabba)
1) Al-Iṣfahānī, *Maqātil*, 167 (ll. 5–6): . . . ʿAbdallāh b. Muḥammad b. Ismāʿīl al-Jaʿfarī < his father, about the revolt of ʿAbdallāh b. Muʿāwiya in the Umawī period.

---

150 Al-Iṣfahānī, *Maqātil*, 237–238: "Saʿīd b. ʿUqba al-Juhanī—and ʿAbdallāh b. al-Ḥasan had already taken him from her, and he was under his care and protection" [that is, he educated him?]: وكان عبد الله بن الحسن أخذه منها فكان في حجره. Was he a slave? A young child who could be in her residence? The two families were related.

ⓡ 2) Al-Iṣfahānī, *Maqātil*, 394 (l. 16): ... al-Zubayr [b. Bakkār] < Muḥammad b. Ismāʿīl al-Jaʿfarī, quoting a poem of Mūsā b. ʿAbdallāh.

ⓡ 3) Al-Mizzī, *Tahdhīb*, 26:150: ... al-Zubayr [b. Bakkār] < Muḥammad b. Ismāʿīl b. Jaʿfar < Saʿīd b. ʿUqba al-Juhanī < his father: reciting a poem he heard recited by the poet Kuthayyir in front of ʿAlī b. ʿAbdallāh b. Jaʿfar [b. Abī Ṭālib], in which he praised Muḥammad b. ʿAlī [Ibn al-Ḥanafiyya].

16) Muḥammad b. Jaʿfar b. Ibrāhīm b. Muḥammad b. ʿAlī b. ʿAbdallāh b. Jaʿfar b. Abī Ṭālib (the brother of Ismāʿīl [no. 10] and the uncle of Muḥammad [no. 15])

He was the son of Umm Salama bt. Muḥammad b. Ṭalḥa b. ʿAbdallāh b. ʿAbd al-Raḥmān b. Abī Bakr, who was married to Jaʿfar b. Ibrāhīm al-Jaʿfarī. She married Mūsā b. ʿAbdallāh b. al-Ḥasan, the brother of Muḥammad al-Nafs al-Zakiyya, at an unknown date and under unknown circumstances.[151] Muḥammad b. Jaʿfar was married to Zaynab, the daughter of Mūsā b. ʿAbdallāh al-Ḥasanī.[152] It is highly plausible that the marriage was consummated before his mother married Mūsā b. ʿAbdallāh. Al-Ṭabarī records only two traditions of his that are related directly to ʿUmar b. Shabba. The first was related by his grandfather, Mūsā b. ʿAbdallāh, and the second by his mother, Umm Salama.[153] This is in contrast to his brother, and mainly to his nephew, from whom much more written material was left on the revolt.

17) Muḥammad b. Yaḥyā b. ʿAlī b. ʿAbd al-Ḥamīd b. ʿUbayd [b. Ghassān?] b. Yasār, Abū Ghassān al-Madanī l-Kinānī

He was one of the main direct informants of ʿUmar b. Shabba on the revolt of Muḥammad b. ʿAbdallāh (but on other topics as well).[154] In al-Ṭabarī's *Taʾrīkh* he appears fifty-three times, always as the direct transmitter of ʿUmar b. Shabba. Forty-seven traditions deal with events pertaining to the revolt, six to the uprising of the blacks (*sūdān*) in Medina immediately after the termination of Muḥammad b. ʿAbdallāh's revolt; thirty-one were transmitted to him by al-Ḥārith b. Isḥāq (on him see below) and eight by ʿAbd al-ʿAzīz

151 For this assertion (identification), see al-Ṭabarī, 3:257 (ll. 16–18): her full lineage is given; for Mūsā's marriage to Umm Salama, see al-ʿUmarī, *Ansāb*, 45, his wife (although her full lineage is not given, she is named [ibid., 46] al-Ṭalḥiyya, and al-Ṭalḥiyya al-Taymiyya, that is, of Taym Quraysh, Abū Bakr's family); see also Ibn ʿAsākir, *Taʾrīkh*, 60:448: Mūsā married Umm Salama bt. Muḥammad b. Ṭalḥa; al-Zubayrī, *Nasab Quraysh*, 55: Mūsā b. ʿAbdallāh marries "Umm Salama bt. Muḥammad b. Ṭalḥa b. ʿAbdallāh b. ʿAbd al-Raḥmān b. Abī Bakr al-Ṣiddīq."

152 Al-ʿUmarī, *Ansāb*, 45: Zaynab bore Muḥammad b. Jaʿfar, Ibrāhīm, ʿĪsā, Dāwūd, and Mūsā; but cf. Ibn ʿAsākir, *Taʾrīkh*, 60:448, who mistakenly records that she married his brother, Ismāʿīl, who married Ruqayya, another daughter of Mūsā.

153 Al-Ṭabarī, 3:185 (ll. 13–15) (from his grandfather); 3:257–258 (l. 16 to l. 5) (his mother).

154 Nagel, "Muḥammad b. ʿAbdallāh," 236–238.

b. ʿImrān, Ibn Abī Thābit (on him, see above); six are historical traditions pertaining to the Umawī period.[155] In al-Iṣfahānī's *Maqātil* he is recorded eight times, in all of them he is the direct transmitter of ʿUmar b. Shabba; three traditions have parallels in al-Ṭabarī. Those that have no parallel in al-Ṭabarī are of great importance, especially those that record the affair of the meeting in al-Abwāʾ[156] (see chapter 2).

He was an early *akhbārī* who recorded historical traditions from the early Umawī period (from the time of Muʿāwiya's reign) to the end of the eighth century. He was well versed in the history of Arabic poetry and poets (see below). ʿUmar b. Shabba relates that he belonged to a family of secretaries (*kuttāb*): He was a *kātib*, as was his father, his two grandfathers (from his father and his mother's sides), and his uncle, Ghassān b. ʿAlī b. ʿAbd al-Ḥamīd. Muḥammad himself was the *kātib* of Sulaymān b. ʿAlī b. ʿAbdallāh b. al-ʿAbbās.[157]

His father was also a scholar of *ḥadīth*, who for a certain time was in charge of the *shurṭa* in Medina.[158] One of the scholars he heard *ḥadīth* from was Ibn Isḥāq (d. 150/767 or 768). His son Muḥammad was among those that heard *ḥadīth* from him.[159]

---

155 For the early period, see al-Ṭabarī, 2:199, 428, 818, 863, 868, 1885; for the events of the revolt (al-Ḥārith b. Isḥāq = *; ʿAbd al-ʿAzīz b. ʿImrān = **), see ibid., 3:147, 149*, 153*, 154, 156*, 158*, 159*, 160*, 161*, 162, 163, 164*, 166*, 170*, 173*, 175*, 189*, 190*, 191**, 196**, 197 (from Ismāʿīl b. Yaʿqūb al-Taymī, recording the version of Muḥammad b. ʿAbdallāh's *khuṭba*), 198*, 202, 204**, 205*, 207, 215*, 222**, 223*, 225*, 227**, 229*, 230*, 233*, 240**, 242*, 244**, 246**, 246*, 252*, 255; the uprising of the blacks (*sūdān*) in Medina: 265*, 266*, 267*, 268*, 269*, 271*.

156 Al-Iṣfahānī, *Maqātil*, 173, 196 [= al-Ṭabarī, 3:173], 202, 215, 218 [= al-Ṭabarī, 3:173]; 247, 253 (traditions on the meeting in al-Abwāʾ), 270; Nagel, "Muḥammad b. ʿAbdallāh," 237.

157 Al-Mizzī, *Tahdhīb*, 26:638; see also Ibn Ḥajar, *Tahdhīb* (Hyderabad edition), 9:518 (part of the tradition of Ibn Shabba); Nagel, "Muḥammad b. ʿAbdallāh," 236 (according to Ibn Ḥajar).

158 Al-Mizzī, *Tahdhīb*, 26:638.

159 Al-Bukhārī, *al-Kabīr* (ed. al-Nadwī), 8:297; on Muḥammad b. Yaḥyā, see Ibn Abī l-Dunyā, *Makārim al-akhlāq*, 134; al-Ḥākim al-Naysābūrī, *al-Mustadrak* (Beirut, 1406 H.), 4:350; al-Dāraquṭnī, *Sunan*, 1:29: relating from ʿAbd al-ʿAzīz b. Abī Thābit b. ʿAbd al-ʿAzīz b. ʿUmar b. ʿAbd al-Raḥmān b. ʿAwf; al-Khazrajī, *Khulāṣa*, 364; Ibn Abī Ḥātim, *al-Jarḥ* (Beirut edition), 8:123; Ibn Ḥibbān, *al-Thiqāt*, 9:74; al-Samʿānī, *Ansāb* (Beirut, 1988), 2:134; Ibn Ḥajar, *Tahdhīb* (Hyderabad edition), 9:517–518; al-Mizzī, *Tahdhīb*, 26:636–638; the usual lineage is Muḥammad b. Yaḥyā b. ʿAlī b. ʿAbd al-Ḥamīd b. ʿUbayd b. Yasār al-Kinānī Abū Ghassān al-Madanī; sometimes Ghassān is added after ʿUbayd; his *nisba* al-Kinānī is sometimes rendered by mistake as al-Kattānī, see for instance Ibn ʿAsākir, *Taʾrīkh*, 12:312; 36:359; 37:157; see also McAuliffe, *ʿAbbāsid Authority*, 91, n. 431: "Muḥ. b. Yaḥyā b. ʿAlī l-Kinānī (Abū Ghassān) was a member of the family of Medinese *kātibs* and a respected *muḥaddith*. Ibn Ḥajar, *Tahdhīb*, 9:436–457; Ṣafadī, *al-Wāfī*, 5:187; Nagel, 'Bricht,' 236–238"; in the index of McAuliffe, *ʿAbbāsid Authority*, his name is mistakenly rendered Muḥammad b. Yaḥyā

As mentioned above, Muḥammad b. Yaḥyā was well versed in Arabic poetry. He is mentioned more than fifty times in al-Iṣfahānī's *Kitāb al-Aghānī*, as the transmitter of poetry verses, anecdotal material about poets and their poetry, genealogical material about poets, and so forth. About forty traditions were directly transmitted by him to ʿUmar b. Shabba. Thirteen were transmitted to al-Zubayr b. Bakkār.[160]

Muḥammad b. Yaḥyā merits separate research, which is beyond the scope of this study. Here I will mention only three of his direct earlier transmitters who passed him information about the rebellion of al-Nafs al-Zakiyya: a) al-Ḥārith b. Isḥāq; b) ʿAbd al-ʿAzīz b. ʿImrān (Ibn Abī Thābit); and c) his father (Yaḥyā), but more worthy of attention than his father is his grandfather, ʿAlī b. ʿAbd al-Ḥamīd, who transmitted important and interesting firsthand evidence to his son.

a) Al-Ḥārith b. Isḥāq

Of the forty-seven traditions in al-Ṭabarī's *Taʾrīkh*, thirty were directly transmitted to Muḥammad b. Yaḥyā by al-Ḥārith b. Isḥāq. I was unable to find any substantial biographical data about him;[161] in fact, besides al-Ṭabarī I found only three additional traditions with the same *isnād*, that is, al-Ḥārith b. Isḥāq > Muḥammad b. Yaḥyā > ʿUmar b. Shabba. Two traditions deal with various aspects of the rebellion and the third is a historical tradition about a governor of Medina; with regard to the third, it is not clear whether it is part of the work on the rebellion by ʿUmar b. Shabba.[162] Of the thirty-one traditions in al-Ṭabarī, twenty-five deal unequivocally with the rebellion of Muḥammad b. ʿAbdallāh and six deal with the rebellion of the blacks (*sūdān*) in Medina immediately after the termination of the rebellion. In all the traditions, except two, al-Ḥārith b. Isḥāq is the last (earliest) transmitter. The two transmitters of al-Ḥārith b. Isḥāq were two contemporaries of the rebellion: Abū Ḥunayn, one of the active supporters of the rebellion in Medina; and the second, ʿAlī b. ʿAbd al-Ḥamīd, his uncle from his mother's side, who related a firsthand, eyewitness tradition about

---

b. Muḥammad instead of Muḥammad b. Yaḥyā b. ʿAlī. In all the cases that he appears in al-Ṭabarī's *Taʾrīkh* he is Muḥammad b. Yaḥyā; once (3:154 (l. 14)): Muḥammad b. Yaḥyā b. Muḥammad, which is most probably a mistake.

160 Al-Iṣfahānī, *al-Aghānī* (index): in most of the traditions his *kunya* Abū Ghassān is mentioned before or after his name.

161 He is not identified by Nagel, "Muḥammad b. ʿAbdallāh," 237; McAuliffe does not identify him when he is first mentioned in her translation on 94.

162 Two traditions: al-Iṣfahānī, *Maqātil*, 186 and 259; the third piece of evidence: Ibn Abī l-Dunyā, *Makārim al-akhlāq*, 149: Abū Zayd al-Numayrī [= ʿUmar b. Shabba] < Abū Ghassān Muḥammad b. Yaḥyā l-Kinānī < al-Ḥārith b. Isḥāq; other sources record traditions that are found in al-Ṭabarī's *Taʾrīkh*, e.g., Ibn ʿAsākir, *Taʾrīkh*, 18:270 [= al-Ṭabarī, *Taʾrīkh*, 3:242]; Ibn ʿAsākir, *Taʾrīkh*, 52:385 [= al-Ṭabarī, *Taʾrīkh*, 3:161].

an event concerning the rebellion.[163] The above-mentioned ʿAlī b. ʿAbd al-Ḥamīd was also, most plausibly, the grandfather of Muḥammad b. Yaḥyā, the transmitter discussed above. The fact that al-Ḥārith b. Isḥāq had at his disposal thirty-one traditions about a specific historical subject may testify to the existence of written notes or even a written work about the history of Medina, or the history of Muḥammad b. ʿAbdallāh's revolt, which was transmitted to ʿUmar b. Shabba. These traditions may have contained parts of Ibn Shabba's book on the rebellion of the two brothers (perhaps another work, *Taʾrīkh al-Madīna*). They are clear evidence of the nature of the firsthand material that ʿUmar b. Shabba collected about the revolt and Medina.

b) ʿAbd al-ʿAzīz b. ʿImrān b. ʿAbd al-ʿAzīz b. ʿUmar b. ʿAbd al-Raḥmān b. ʿAwf al-Zuhrī, Ibn Abī Thābit

ʿAbd al-ʿAzīz b. ʿImrān was a transmitter (*rāwī*) of historical traditions. Al-Ṭabarī records ten traditions, all dealing with or connected to the rebellion of Muḥammad b. ʿAbdallāh. Eight were transmitted by Ibn Abī Thābit to Muḥammad b. Yaḥyā (see above), who related them to ʿUmar b. Shabba. All ten traditions seem to have been included in the latter's work. All the intimate descriptions from Muḥammad b. ʿAbdallāh's camp, the battle, and the way the latter died were related to Ibn Abī Thābit by eyewitnesses, or those who took part in the rebellion.

c) Traditions related to Muḥammad b. Yaḥyā by his father (Yaḥyā) and his grandfather (ʿAlī b. ʿAbd al-Ḥamīd)

Two traditions were related to Muḥammad b. Yaḥyā by his father through his grandfather. Another was transmitted by al-Ḥārith b. Isḥāq, who was ʿAlī's nephew (see above).

18) Mūsā b. ʿAbdallāh b. Mūsā b. ʿAbdallāh b. al-Ḥasan b. al-Ḥasan b. ʿAlī b. Abī Ṭālib (d. 256/870)

He was the grandson of Mūsā b. ʿAbdallāh, al-Nafs al-Zakiyya's brother.[164] He was a direct transmitter of ʿUmar b. Shabba and he related family traditions mainly through his father from his grandfather, Mūsā b. ʿAbdallāh. The traditions are all in the first

163 The two traditions: al-Ṭabarī, *Taʾrīkh*, 3:153: from Abū Ḥunayn, one of the active supporters of the rebellion in Medina; the second, al-Ṭabarī, *Taʾrīkh*, 3:160 (l. 5): from his uncle on his mother's side, ʿAlī b. ʿAbd al-Ḥamīd, on him, see al-Khaṭīb al-Baghdādī, *Taʾrīkh* (Beirut, 1997), 13:41–42; al-ʿUmarī, *Ansāb*, 53–54; Ibn ʿInaba, *ʿUmda*, 126.

164 He was arrested by orders of Caliph al-Muhtadī, and was poisoned in 259/872 in Zabāla on the way to al-ʿIrāq, see al-Iṣfahānī, *Maqātil*, 679; on him, see al-Khaṭīb al-Baghdādī, *Taʾrīkh* (Beirut, 1997), 13:41–42; al-ʿUmarī, *Ansāb*, 53–54; Ibn ʿInaba, *ʿUmda*, 126.

person and concern the Ḥasanī family before, during and after the revolt;[165] he also transmitted material to other scholars about the Ḥasanī family.[166] As a minor transmitter of *ḥadīth*, he related from his mother, Fāṭima bt. Saʿīd b. ʿUqba, and transmitted to scholars in Baghdad, where he settled.[167] He is also quoted in Imāmī *ḥadīth* literature.[168]

19) Saʿd b. ʿAbd al-Ḥamīd b. Jaʿfar (d. 219/834 or 835)[169]

He was a direct transmitter of ʿUmar b. Shabba. He transmitted to ʿUmar b. Shabba traditions containing detailed specific information about the revolt from people who took part in the rebellion, fought with Muḥammad, and played important roles in his short-lived caliphate.[170] It is noteworthy that, although his father was one of Muḥammad b. ʿAbdallāh's important supporters, he did not record the traditions directly from his father, although he relates to him several times, but from other different supporters of Muḥammad b. ʿAbdallāh, e.g., Jahm b. ʿUthmān *mawlā* Banī Sulaym, who was a pro-Shīʿī transmitter and one of the followers (*aṣḥāb*) of Jaʿfar al-Ṣādiq (see above) and Muḥammad b. ʿUthmān [b. Muḥammad] b. Khālid b. al-Zubayr.[171] Saʿd b. ʿAbd al-Ḥamīd is not mentioned as one of the transmitters of his father in his or in his father's biographies. Perhaps he was too young when his father died. In one place he relates from his sister who related directly from their father.[172]

---

165 E.g. al-Ṭabarī, 3:172 (ll. 4–15); 3:172–173 (l. 20 to l. 9); 3:173 (ll. 11–14); 3:179–180 (l. 4 to l. 2) [= al-Iṣfahānī, *Maqātil*, 223–224; 391–392].

166 E.g., Al-Iṣfahānī, *Maqātil*, 192, 242–243, 432: relating to Yaḥyā b. al-Ḥasan al-ʿAqīqī (d. 277/890), the historian and the genealogist who, as scholars commonly agree, was the first to compose a book about the genealogy of the Ṭālibīs (on him, see below); al-ʿAqīqī transmitted the traditions to Aḥmad b. Muḥammad b. Saʿīd, the direct transmitter of al-Iṣfahānī (on him, see Fleischhammer, *Kitāb al-Aghānī*, index).

167 Al-Khaṭīb al-Baghdādī, *Taʾrīkh* (Beirut, 1997), 13:41.

168 E.g., al-Majlisī, *Biḥār*, 8:188; 71:192; 89:260; 91:219; 92:90; most of the traditions were transmitted to him by members of the Ḥasanī, Zaydī, and Ḥusaynī families.

169 In both al-Ṭabarī's and al-Iṣfahānī's printed works he is rendered as Saʿīd. Corrected in al-Ṭabarī's *Addenda et Emendana*, dccxxxvi; see McAuliffe, *ʿAbbāsid Authority*, 145, n. 701; on him, see al-Khaṭīb al-Baghdādī, *Taʾrīkh*, 9:124–126; al-Mizzī, *Tahdhīb*, 10:285–287, and the comprehensive bibliography therein.

170 Al-Ṭabarī, 3:193, 200 (= al-Iṣfahānī, *Maqātil*, 283), 3:201, 229, 237 (= al-Iṣfahānī, *Maqātil*, 283–284), 259, 262; al-Iṣfahānī, *Maqātil*, 287 (no parallel in al-Ṭabarī); part of the text is probably garbled; perhaps instead of وقال لأبي it should be read: وقال له أبي.

171 For Muḥammad b. ʿUthmān b. Khālid b. al-Zubayr, see al-Ṭabarī, 3:262.

172 Al-Ṭabarī, 3:201–202 (l. 14 to l. 3): [ʿUmar b. Shabba] وحدثني سعيد بن عبد الحميد بن جعفر قال: حدثتني أختي بريكة بنت عبد الحميد عن أبيها قال: إني لعند محمد يوما; note the phrase

20) Sahl b. ʿAqīl b. Ismāʿīl

He was a direct transmitter of ʿUmar b. Shabba, relating nine traditions to him mainly about Ibrāhīm b. ʿAbdallāh's revolt in al-Baṣra. One tradition relates to the two revolts. He transmitted from his father and from Salm b. Farqad, who was the *ḥājib* of Sulaymān b. Mujālid, one of the close associates of al-Manṣūr.[173] I was not able to find any more information about him.[174] He may possibly be identified as a minor *ḥadīth* transmitter from Wāsiṭ, who was the *muʾadhdhin* of his cousin's mosque, the scholar ʿAmr b. ʿAwn, who died in 225/839–840.[175]

21) Sulaymān b. Muḥammad al-Sārī

He is mentioned only once as a direct transmitter of Ibn Shabba, relating a tradition that he heard from Abū Habbār al-Muzanī, one of al-Nafs al-Zakiyya's closest and most loyal supporters.[176]

"from Burayka's father" (*ʿan abīhā*) not "from my father" (*abī*), for ʿAbd al-Ḥamīd was the father of both.

173 He was the foster brother (أخ من الرضاعة) of al-Manṣūr (that is, both were nursed by the same woman); he served in important military and administrative roles, see Ibn Khayyāṭ, *Taʾrīkh* (Beirut, 1993), 354; al-Ṭabarī, 3:294–295; al-Jahshiyārī, *al-Wuzarāʾ*, 100; Ibn ʿAsākir, *Taʾrīkh*, 22:365–367; al-Khaṭīb al-Baghdādī, *Taʾrīkh* (Beirut, 1997), 1:97, 103; al-Ṣafadī, *al-Wāfī*, 15:257.

174 Transmitting to ʿUmar b. Shabba: al-Ṭabarī, 3:206 (ll. 4–6): from his father on the revolts of Muḥammad and Ibrāhīm (text: Suhayl, corrected in the *Addenda et Emendanda*, dccxxxvii, noticed by McAuliffe, *ʿAbbāsid Authority*, 163, note); 291 (ll. 4–14): from his father; 292 (ll. 13–18): from Salm b. Farqad; 294–295 (l. 14 to l. 3): from Salm b. Farqad *ḥājib Sulaymān b. Mujālid*; ibid., 298–299 (l. 17 to l. 2): فذكر سهل بن عقيل عن أبيه; 317–318 (l. 2 to l. 1): فذكر سلم بن فرقد حاجب سليمان بن مجالد, but part of the tradition is recorded by al-Iṣfahānī, *Maqātil*, 346, from which we learn that it was transmitted to al-Iṣfahānī's sources through ʿUmar b. Shabba: [Abū l-Faraj al-Iṣfahānī: حدثنا] < ʿUmar AND Yaḥyā < ʿUmar b. Shabba < Sahl b. ʿAqīl < Salm b. Farqad; he [ʿUmar] said I was related by another person (وحدثني غيره).

175 On Sahl b. ʿAqīl, see Ibn Abī Ḥātim, *al-Jarḥ* (Beirut edition), 4:202: قرابة عمرو بن عون ومؤذن مسجده; 5:69: the *muʾadhdhin* of ʿAmr b. ʿAwn's mosque; Ibn Abī Ḥātim, *ʿIlal*, 1:273: إبن عم عمرو ابن عون; Baḥshal al-Wāsiṭī, *Taʾrīkh Wāsiṭ*, 1:191; for ʿAmr b. ʿAwn, for example, see al-Bājī, *al-Taʿdīl*, 3:1106; al-Mizzī, *Tahdhīb*, 22:177–180; and see also Nagel, "Muḥammad b. ʿAbdallāh," 240.

176 Al-Ṭabarī, 3:148 (l. 7).

22) ʿUbaydallāh b. Muḥammad b. Ḥafṣ b. ʿUmar b. Mūsā b. ʿUbaydallāh b. Maʿmar b. ʿUthmān b. ʿAmr b. Kaʿb b. Saʿd b. Taym (Quraysh), Abū ʿAbd al-Raḥmān, known as Ibn ʿĀʾisha (d. 228/843)

He was a famous Baṣrī scholar, historian (*akhbārī*), and *muḥaddith* who related directly to ʿUmar b. Shabba three traditions regarding events that were connected to the revolt of Muḥammad but also to that of his brother Ibrāhīm. Two traditions were related to him by his father, Muḥammad, who was not as famous as his son.[177] He transmitted other historical traditions on various topics and periods to ʿUmar b. Shabba.[178]

23) ʿUmar b. Rāshid

He was a direct transmitter of ʿUmar b. Shabba but also an eyewitness to the rebellion. Al-Ṭabarī records seven traditions that he related to ʿUmar b. Shabba. One of them deals with the rebellion and gives a very detailed and accurate description of the initial stages of the revolt.[179] Two others describe in great detail the events in Mecca during the rebellion, e.g., the clash and struggle between the newly nominated governor of the city by Muḥammad b. ʿAbdallāh and the ʿAbbāsī governor. ʿUmar b. Rāshid says that he was at that time in Mecca. In these two traditions ʿUmar b. Rāshid is called *mawlā* ʿAnaj/ʿAnj [*or ghanj*?].[180] However, in the first tradition this relationship (*mawlā* ʿAnaj/ʿAnj [or *ghanj*?]) is not mentioned. He relates in the first person that he was in Medina the night Muḥammad b. ʿAbdallāh appeared, and describes his appearance vividly.[181] Are we dealing here with the same transmitter? We do not know how much time elapsed between Muḥammad's arrival in Medina and the sending of the new governor to Mecca. No specific date is given by the sources. It is merely stated that Muḥammad b. ʿAbdallāh sent his new governor to Mecca when he rebelled openly.[182] The transmitter, ʿUmar b. Rāshid, could have left Medina immediately after the out-

---

177 Al-Ṭabarī, 3:149 (ll. 11–14) [a similar, longer tradition on 3:282 (ll. 12–16)]; 3:287 (ll. 2–3): all from his father; 3:285–286 (l. 15 to l. 2); on him and his lineage, his family see Ibn Ḥazm, *Jamhara*, 140; Ibn Saʿd, *Ṭabaqāt*, 7:301; Ibn Abī Ḥātim, *al-Jarḥ* (Beirut edition), 5:335; Ibn Ḥibbān, *al-Thiqāt*, 8:405; al-Khaṭīb al-Baghdādī, *Taʾrīkh* (Beirut, 1997), 10:313–318; Ibn Ḥajar, *Tahdhīb* (Beirut, 1984), 7:41; al-Mizzī, *Tahdhīb*, 19:147–152; al-Ziriklī, *al-Aʿlām*, 4:196; Rosenthal, *Historiography*, 505, n. 3; McAuliffe, *ʿAbbāsid Authority*, 94, n. 446.

178 E.g., al-Ṭabarī, 2:1136: ... ʿUmar b. Shabba < ʿUbaydallāh b. Muḥammad b. Ḥafṣ < Saʿīd b. ʿUbaydallāh: a historical anecdote about ʿAbd al-Malik and Ibn al-Ashʿath.

179 Al-Ṭabarī, 3:195–196 (l. 19 to l. 12).

180 Ibid., 3:218 (ll. 11–12) (staying in Mecca); 221; I was not able to find this tribe/person in the sources known to me.

181 Ibid., 3:195–196 (l. 19 to l. 12) (= al-Iṣfahānī, *Maqātil*, 262–263): A detailed eyewitness testimony about the entrance of Muḥammad b. ʿAbdallāh to Medina: description of his clothes, his route in the city, and his initial activities.

182 Al-Ṭabarī, 3:217 (l. 13).

break of the rebellion. Still, it raises the possibility that we are dealing with two different people.

The next four traditions from ʿUmar b. Shabba through ʿUmar b. Rāshid deal with the insurrection of the blacks (*sūdān*) in Medina in 145/762.[183] These traditions may have been part of ʿUmar b. Shabba's book on the rebellion of the two brothers, or of his *Akhbār al-Madīna*.

24) Yaʿqūb b. al-Qāsim b. Muḥammad b. Yaḥyā b. Zakariyyāʾ b. Ṭalḥa b. ʿUbaydallāh al-Taymī l-Qurashī:[184] He appears nine times in al-Ṭabarī's *Taʾrīkh* and five times in al-Iṣfahānī's *Maqātil* as the direct transmitter of ʿUmar b. Shabba. Yaʿqūb transmitted many of his traditions from the scholar ʿAlī b. Abī Ṭālib b. Sarḥ.[185] All the traditions deal with events related to the revolt,[186] some of them unique, e.g., the tradition he relates from his grandmother, Kulthum bt. Wahb, who was married to the Zubayrī ʿAbd al-Wahhāb b. Yaḥyā b. ʿAbbād b. ʿAbdallāh b. al-Zubayr. She relates to her grandson Yaʿqūb that her husband[187] joined the revolt and she hid in the house of Asmāʾ bt. Ḥusayn b. ʿAbdallāh b. ʿUbaydallāh b. ʿAbbās.[188]

5 Some Remarks on the Transmission of Abū l-Faraj al-Iṣfahānī in Maqātil al-ṭālibiyyīn Regarding the Events Surrounding the Rebellion of Muḥammad al-Nafs al-Zakiyya

Nagel, in his pioneering research, pointed out that ʿUmar b. Shabba (d. 264/877) was the main source of al-Ṭabarī and al-Iṣfahānī for the history of the revolt of Muḥammad b. ʿAbdallāh. Although ʿUmar b. Shabba was al-Iṣfahānī's main source, the latter used many other sources. Sometimes, in the same tradition he relies on Ibn Shabba, on the one hand, and on the other hand, on other chains of transmitters, among them important *akhbāriyyūn* such as Abū l-Ḥasan ʿAlī b. Muḥammad al-Madāʾinī (d. ca. 225/840),[189]

183 Ibid., 3:266–267, 269, 271.

184 For his biography, see al-Khaṭīb al-Baghdādī, *Taʾrīkh* (Beirut, 1997), 14:274; Nagel, "Muḥammad b. ʿAbdallāh, 245.

185 According to al-Iṣfahānī, *Maqātil*, 237: ʿAlī b. Abī Ṭālib b. Sarḥ; al-Ṭabarī, 3:224 (ll. 11–12): Yaʿqūb b. al-Qāsim < ʿAlī b. Abī Ṭālib "whom I met in Ṣanʿāʾ": و لقيته بصنعاء.

186 Al-Ṭabarī, 3:180 (l. 12) (Yaʿqūb b. al-Qāsim b. Muḥammad), 172, 195, 199, 219, 224, 249 (Yaʿqūb b. al-Qāsim); al-Iṣfahānī, *Maqātil*, 237 (Yaʿqūb b. al-Qāsim b. Muḥammad b. Yaḥyā b. Zakariyyāʾ b. Ṭalḥa b. ʿUbaydallāh), 238, 262, 274, 365 (Yaʿqūb b. al-Qāsim).

187 ʿAbd al-Wahhāb b. Yaḥyā l-Zubayrī; this means that he was not the grandfather of our transmitter, Yaʿqūb b. al-Qāsim b. Muḥammad.

188 Al-Ṭabarī, 3:199–200 (l. 13 to l. 2).

189 On him, see Sezgin, 1:314–315, and the bibliography therein.

who was a direct transmitter of another important *akhbārī* and littérateur, Aḥmad b. al-Ḥārith al-Kharrāz (d. 258/872).

Aḥmad b. al-Ḥārith al-Kharrāz[190]

As shown by Günther,[191] al-Iṣfahānī used Aḥmad b. al-Ḥārith's book extensively. One important testimony regarding Hishām b. ʿUrwa's participation in the rebellion was discussed elsewhere.[192] Al-Iṣfahānī used the copy of this book that was at his disposal several times in his *Maqātil*,[193] but even more so in *al-Aghānī*. Most of the traditions that are cited by al-Iṣfahānī from Aḥmad b. al-Ḥārith were transmitted to Aḥmad b. al-Ḥārith from the important and well-known *akhbārī*, al-Madāʾinī (d. ca. 225/840).[194] Aḥmad b. al-Ḥārith was a Baghdadi scholar, the *mawlā* of Caliph al-Manṣūr. He is

---

190 On him, see Ibn al-Nadīm, *al-Fihrist* (ed. al-Tajaddud), 117 (ed. Flügel, 104–105; Dodge, 1:229); al-Khaṭīb al-Baghdādī, *Taʾrīkh* (Beirut, 1997), 4:345; Yāqūt, *Udabāʾ* (ed. Margoliouth), 1:407–409; Sezgin, 1:318–319. These sources are mentioned by Günther, *Maqātil*, 121; ibid., 118–121: a detailed discussion of his transmission in al-Iṣfahānī's *Maqātil*; see also al-Masʿūdī, *Murūj* (annotated index by Pellat, the editor), 6:122; Pellat, ibid., renders one of Aḥmad b. al-Ḥārith's books: *Kitāb akhbār Banī l-ʿAbbās* instead of *Kitāb akhbār Abī l-ʿAbbās* [?] (in most of the printed texts that I checked: *akhbār Abī l-ʿAbbās*); al-Ṣafadī, *al-Wāfī*, 6:184 (*akhbār Banī l-ʿAbbās*); ibid., 184–185: his biography.

191 Günther, *Maqātil*, 118–121.

192 Al-Iṣfahānī, *Maqātil*, 296: دفع إلي عيسى بن الحسين الوراق كتابا ذكر أنه كتاب أحمد بن الحارث فقرأت فيه (ʿĪsā b. al-Ḥusayn al-Warrāq gave me a book and mentioned that it is the book of Aḥmad b. al-Ḥārith, and this is what I read in it).

193 E.g., al-Iṣfahānī, *Maqātil*, 390–391; the important evidence was already noted by Günther, *Maqātil*, 119: "... from ʿUmar b. Shabba from his authorities; and I copied this (information) from the book of Aḥmad b. al-Ḥārith al-Kharrāz, I did not hear its transmission, what happened was that ʿĪsā b. al-Ḥusayn gave me the book from which I copied this and said to me: this is the book of Aḥmad b. al-Ḥārith": ...عمر بن شبة عن رجاله ونسخت من كتاب أحمد بن الحارث الخراز ذلك ولم أسمعه، إلا أن عيسى بن الحسين دفع الكتاب الذي نسخت هذا منه إلي وقال لي هذا كتاب أحمد بن الحارث.

194 Al-Iṣfahānī, *Maqātil*, records 20 traditions from him, most of them through al-Madāʾinī (pp. 79, 86, 90, 95, 123, 160, 162, 163, 166, 259, 267, 276, 296, 384, 390, 392, 443, 451, 588 (= Günther, *Maqātil*, 121; most of the pages are missing in the index to the printed edition); attestation by al-Iṣfahānī for copying from the book of Aḥmad b. al-Ḥārith that was at his disposal, ibid., 296, 384, 390, and 443 (= Günther, *Maqātil*, 119–120; see also Günther, "Medieval Arabic Author," 144 and 148). In *Kitāb al-Aghānī* he is quoted 138 times (the vast majority from al-Madāʾinī), see Fleischhammer, *Kitāb al-Aghānī*, index, esp. 76–77 (no. 13); 113 (no. 12).

described as al-Madāʾinī's closest pupil (صاحب المدائني),[195] to whom, according to one testimony, his teacher (al-Madāʾinī) read (dictated) all his books.[196] It is impossible to know which book of Aḥmad is quoted by al-Iṣfahānī. The list of his books that are given by Ibn al-Nadīm and Yāqūt, who copies him, is much shorter than that of al-Madāʾinī. Sixteen of his books are mentioned by Ibn al-Nadīm, and al-Ṣafadī.[197] Likewise, it is impossible to know which of al-Madāʾinī's many dozens of works Aḥmad b. al-Ḥārith quotes.[198]

Sometimes al-Iṣfahānī used combined reports, that is, he mentioned several chains of transmission, gave a summary or combined several transmissions into one.[199]

---

195 Ibn al-Nadīm, *Fihrist* (ed. Tajaddud), 113; al-Khaṭīb al-Baghdādī, *Taʾrīkh* (Beirut, 1997), 4:345.

196 Yāqūt, *Udabāʾ* (ed. Margoliouth), 1:408: أسمع المدائني كتبه كلها; see also al-Khaṭīb al-Baghdādī, *Taʾrīkh* (Beirut, 1997), 4:345: روى عن المدائني تصانيفه.

197 Ibn al-Nadīm, *Fihrist* (ed. Tajaddud), 117 (= al-Ṣafadī, *al-Wāfī*, 6:184): وله من الكتب المصنفة 1) كتاب المسالك والممالك 2) كتاب أسماء الخلفاء وكتّابهم والصحابة (الصفدي: وكتّابهم والصحبة) 3) كتاب مغازي البحر في دولة بني هاشم وذكر أبي حفص صاحب اقريطش 4) كتاب القبائل 5) كتاب الأشراف 6) كتاب ما نهى النبي صلى الله عليه وسلم عنه 7) كتاب أبناء السراري 8) كتاب نوادر الشعر (الصفدي: الشعراء) 9) كتاب مختصر كتاب البطون 10) كتاب مغازي النبي صلى الله عليه وسلم وسراياه وذكر أزواجه 11) كتاب جمهرة ولد (الصفدي: نسب) الحارث بن كعب وأخبارهم في الجاهلية 12) كتاب أخبار أبي العباس 13) كتاب الأخبار والنوادر 14) كتاب شحنة (الصفدي: سجيّة) البريد 15) كتاب النسيب (الصفدي: النسب) 16) كتاب الحلائب والرهان.

198 Possibly from one (or more) of the following books: كتاب أسماء من قتل من الطالبيين؛ كتاب تأريخ الخلفاء؛ كتاب الخلفاء الكبير؛ كتاب مكة؛ كتاب المدينة, Ibn al-Nadīm, *al-Fihrist* (ed. Tajaddud), 114–115; Günther argues that some of the traditions of Aḥmad b. al-Ḥārith about the revolt were transmitted to him by al-Madāʾinī (d. ca. 225/840), most probably from the lost book of the latter كتاب أسماء من قتل من الطالبيين; Günther, *Maqātil*, 119. This work is mentioned by Ibn al-Nadīm, *Fihrist* (ed. Tajaddud), 114; al-Ṣafadī, *al-Wāfī*, 22:30; al-Ṭihrānī, *al-Dharīʿa* (al-Najaf/Tehran, 1393/1974), 22:230.

199 E.g., al-Iṣfahānī, *Maqātil*, 391: وقد دخل بعض الحديث في بعض; 206: وقد دخل حديث كل هولاء قد روى هذا الحديث بألفاظ مختلفة ومعان; 256: بعضهم في حديث الآخرين قريبة فجمعت روايتهم لئلا يطول الكتاب بتكرير الأسانيد.

Appendix 3: The Struggle for Legitimization Between the Ḥasanīs and the Ḥusaynīs as Reflected Mainly in Imāmī Literature

This appendix deals with the attitude of some of the Ṭālibī families, mainly the Ḥasanīs and the Ḥusaynīs, towards Muḥammad b. ʿAbdallāh's rebellion insofar as it manifested itself in the struggle for legitimization between the Ḥasanīs and the Ḥusaynīs in the Shīʿī-Imāmī literature. This survey should be treated only as an introduction to the topic, certainly not as a (highly needed) comprehensive study of the inter-relations of the ʿAlīd families during the time of the Rāshidūn and the Umawīs. It mainly concentrates on two persons, ʿAbdallāh b. al-Ḥasan b. al-Ḥasan b. ʿAlī b. Abī Ṭālib, the head of the Ḥasanīs,[1] and Jaʿfar b. Muḥammad b. ʿAlī b. al-Ḥusayn b. ʿAlī b. Abī Ṭālib, known as Jaʿfar al-Ṣādiq, the head of the Ḥusaynīs.

In many cases the struggle between these two families occurs within a specific well-defined context, e.g.,: the al-Abwāʾ meeting; Abū Salama's affair; and other cases with specific geographical settings, often an event that was documented and can be dated. In these cases it can be argued that they reflect a tension, a struggle or even animosity between the two branches of the ʿAlīd family, the roots of which were most probably planted earlier, but it is far beyond the aim of the present work to reconstruct this struggle historically. In the cases of al-Abwāʾ and Abū Salama, the traditions were not formulated before the rebellion of al-Nafs al-Zakiyya. But there are traditions that lack a specific date or geographical setting but that bear evidence of the complete, unequivocal reservations of Jaʿfar al-Ṣādiq on the aspirations of ʿAbdallāh b. al-Ḥasan and his or the Ḥasanīs' claims to rule.

1 The Ḥusaynīs and Other Ṭālibī/Hāshimī Factions

It is well known that Jaʿfar al-Ṣādiq did not join Muḥammad b. ʿAbdallāh's rebellion in 145/762. In many ways this marks the culmination of a long struggle between the

---

* For a general introduction about the relations between the two houses, see the brief but very perceptive observations of D. Cook, *Muslim Apocalyptic*, 214ff.; 215: The messianic hopes ʿAbdallāh b. al-Ḥasan entertained for his son at the end of the Umawī dynasty; the merits of al-Ḥasan in Imāmī literature; 215–220: The reconstruction of al-Ḥasan's image by the Ḥasanīs, and the efforts to establish the legitimization to rule; 216–217: some further short observations about the polemics and arguments between the two families.

1 K. V. Zetterstéen, "ʿAbdallāh b. al-Ḥasan," *EI*[2]; Jafrī, *Shīʿa*, 247, 266, 268–269, 273, 275.

 | DOI 10.1163/9789004296220_014

two families, with roots stemming from personal, ideological, and economic reasons. Jaʿfar al-Ṣādiq (as his father before him) was the head of the Ḥusaynī family, but he had higher aspirations for himself as the head and leader, i.e., the Imām, certainly of the descendants of Fāṭima, possibly of all Banū Hāshim.[2] This caused deep antagonism between the Ḥusaynīs and other factions of the Ṭālibī families, e.g., the Jaʿfarīs,[3] but mainly the Ḥasanīs, especially al-Ḥasan b. al-Ḥasan b. ʿAlī b. Abī Ṭālib, and mainly his son ʿAbdallāh b. al-Ḥasan, who nurtured the same aspirations regarding the leadership of Banū Hāshim.[4]

The basic principle inherent in the Imāmī Shīʿa is that the *imāma* was transferred by explicit designation, *naṣṣ*, from ʿAlī b. Abī Ṭālib to his sons, al-Ḥasan, then to al-Ḥusayn, then to al-Ḥusayn's descendants: his son, ʿAlī (Zayn al-ʿĀbidīn), then to ʿAlī's son Muḥammad (al-Bāqir) and then to Jaʿfar b. Muḥammad (al-Ṣādiq).[5] The inheritance of the *imāma* in the Ḥusaynī family is paternal rather than maternal (Muḥammad

2 See the discussion below in this appendix; but cf. Crone, *Political Thought*, 114–115: Jaʿfar al-Ṣādiq regarded himself as a scholar rather than an *imām* in the sense of a savior; he did not claim to be the *imām* in the sense of ruler; in fact, "at the time he was no imam at all."

3 Members of the Jaʿfarī family circulated traditions from the Prophet, in which he recognizes their legitimate right to rule, for example, see Abū l-Shaykh al-Anṣārī, *Ṭabaqāt al-muḥaddithīn*, 1:433–434; Ibn ʿAsākir, *Taʾrīkh*, 33:210; al-Maqdisī, *al-Aḥādīth al-mukhtāra*, 9:199–200: … Muḥammad b. Ismāʿīl b. Jaʿfar b. Ibrāhīm b. Muḥammad b. [ʿAlī b. (after al-Maqdisī)] ʿAbdallāh b. Jaʿfar < Ṣāliḥ b. Muʿāwiya < his brother ʿAbdallāh b. Muʿāwiya < his father Muʿāwiya b. ʿAbdallāh b. Jaʿfar < ʿAbdallāh b. Jaʿfar who said: The messenger of God said: ʿAlī is my roots and Jaʿfar is my branch, or Jaʿfar is my root and ʿAlī is my branch: علي أصلي وجعفر فرعي أو جعفر أصلي وعلي فرعي. See also al-Haythamī, *Majmaʿ al-zawāʾid*, 9:273; al-Majlisī, *Biḥār*, 40:76 (without an *isnād*); the Jaʿfarīs' aspiration to rule culminated with the rebellion of ʿAbdallāh b. Muʿāwiya in 127/744, see Zettersteen, "ʿAbdallāh b. Muʿāwiya," *EI*[2].

4 This is the opinion of modern Imāmī scholars, e.g., al-Khūʾī, *Rijāl*, 11:173: "I say, this tradition [that is the tradition about Ibn al-Najāshī, see below] proves that ʿAbdallāh b. al-Ḥasan assigned himself to the *imāma* and used to give decisions in matters of law not in accordance with the Qurʾān: أقول هذه الرواية تدل على أن عبد الله بن الحسن كان قد نصب نفسه للإمامة وكان يفتي بغير ما أنزله الله" see also the comment of al-Maḥallātī, the editor of *Tafsīr al-ʿAyyāshī*, 1:368, n. 2; it corresponds to Madelung's assertion in "Zayd b. ʿAlī b. al-Ḥusayn": "ʿAbdallāh b. al-Ḥasan who harboured ambitions at first for himself and later for his son al-Nafs al-Zakiyya."

5 Hodgson, "Early Shīʿa," 9–11; Gleave, "Jaʿfar al-Ṣādeq," 350: the principle of the *naṣṣ;* Crone, *Political Thought*, 110; Jafri, *Shīʿa*, 281–283, 290–291: a comprehensive discussion of Jaʿfar's principles.

al-Bāqir's mother was the daughter of al-Ḥasan b. ʿAlī b. Abī Ṭālib),[6] but only **through sons**; brothers or uncles (*ʿumūma*) have no right to the *imāma*.[7]

Zayd b. ʿAlī b. al-Ḥusayn (d. 122/740), Muḥammad al-Bāqir's half-brother, was a rival of the latter, claiming the inheritance of the Prophet. "When an opportunity presented itself, he [al-Bāqir] did not hesitate to contest Zayd's rights quite sharply," denying his right to the *imāma*.[8]

This principle excludes the right of any other Hāshimī family to the *imāma*, that is, to rule. This is clearly demonstrated in the Imāmī literature,[9] in which sometimes the specific names of the Hāshimī families are mentioned, e.g., the Jaʿfarīs, the Ḥasanīs, and the ʿAbbāsīs[!].[10] Muḥammad b. ʿAlī Ibn al-Ḥanafiyya in particular was discussed separately (see below).

The exclusion of all the brothers of Muḥammad al-Bāqir is demonstrated in the following tradition:

> From Muḥammad (al-Bāqir): his father ʿAlī b. al-Ḥusayn gave him the chest (*safaṭ/ṣundūq*) that contained the weapons and the books of the Prophet. When ʿAlī died, his sons came to their brother, Muḥammad (al-Bāqir) claiming their share in the contents of the *ṣundūq* and he said: "I swear by God, you are not entitled to any share of it, if you were entitled to a share in it, he would not have given it to me.[11]

1.1 *Jaʿfar al-Ṣādiq and Muḥammad Ibn al-Ḥanafiyya*

Muḥammad b. al-Ḥanafiyya gained some importance in the Imāmī *ḥadīth*, most probably because of his group of adherents, al-Kaysāniyya/al-Hāshimiyya.[12] In the Imāmī

6 Al-Bukhārī, *Sirr al-silsila*, 69: Umm ʿAbdallāh bt. al-Ḥasan b. ʿAlī, married ʿAlī b. al-Ḥusayn and bore him ʿAbdallāh and Muḥammad (al-Bāqir); she was Jaʿfar al-Ṣādiq's grandmother.

7 Al-Ṣaffār, *Baṣāʾir*, 209, no. 57.

8 Jafri, *Shīʿa*, 251; on Zayd b. ʿAlī, see Madelung, "Zayd b. ʿAlī b. al-Ḥusayn."

9 See for example, Ibn Bābawayh al-Qummī, *al-Imāma*, 48–49, nos. 31 and 32; 50, no. 33; 54, no. 38; 56, no. 40ff.

10 Ibn Bābawayh al-Qummī, *ʿIlal*, 1:207; al-Kulaynī, *al-Kāfī*, 1:288; Ibn Bābawayh al-Qummī, *al-Imāma*, 48, no. 30 (and the parallels of the editor in n. 9): from Muḥammad b. ʿAlī l-Bāqir, who except for the Ḥusaynīs, negates the right of the descendants of the Hāshimī families of Jaʿfar, al-ʿAbbās and al-Ḥasan to the *imāma*. In sum, he says: "No Muslim has a share in the *imāma* except us: ما لمحمدي فيها نصيب غيرنا." Can the mention of the ʿAbbāsīs in the tradition date the tradition to at least after 132/750?

11 Al-Ṣaffār, *Baṣāʾir*, 200, no. 18; 201, no. 24.

12 Jafri, *Shīʿa*, 298–299; We must bear in mind the possible implications of these traditions regarding the attitude of the Imāmīs towards the ʿAbbāsīs, who continued, at least until al-Mahdī's reign, to base their legitimacy to rule on that of the old Hāshimiyya.

literature special chapters were dedicated to refuting Ibn al- Ḥanafiyya's claim to the *imāma*. There one finds a tradition in which Muḥammad al-Bāqir is asked if Ibn al-Ḥanafiyya was an *imām* and he answers, no, but he was a *mahdī*: ولكنه كان مهديا.[13] Traditions were circulated in the name of Muḥammad al-Bāqir, in which Muḥammad b. al-Ḥanafiyya acknowledged ʿAlī b. al-Ḥusayn's priority over him regarding legitimacy to the *imāma*. A prevailing tradition records that Ibn al-Ḥanafiyya came to ʿAlī b. al-Ḥusayn, claiming the *imāma* for himself because: 1) al-Ḥusayn b. ʿAlī died without nominating an heir; 2) Ibn al-Ḥanafiyya is the uncle and equals his father: وأنا عمك وصنو أبيك [this recalls the argument of the ʿAbbāsīs in their struggle for legitimacy [!]]; 3) he is the son of ʿAlī, being older than ʿAlī b. al-Ḥusayn, therefore more entitled to the *imāma*. To this ʿAlī answers: 1) his father bequeathed him the *imāma* before he left for al-ʿIrāq; 2) in order to remove any doubt about this they go to the Kaʿba, where the black stone verifies the words of ʿAlī b. al-Ḥusayn, saying: Indeed the *waṣiyya* and *al-imāma* after al-Ḥusayn b. ʿAlī was transferred to ʿAlī b. al-Ḥusayn … **b. Fāṭima**. This last argument was therefore part of the competition between the Ḥusaynīs and the followers of Ibn al-Ḥanafiyya.[14]

In other traditions, this time transmitted from Jaʿfar al-Ṣādiq, the latter strongly refuted the claims of the adherents of Muḥammad b. al-Ḥanafiyya to the *imāma* [rule]. In one of the traditions they are called al-Kaysāniyya. The most decisive argument against their claims is that the *silāḥ* of the Prophet is not in their possession, but in that of the Ḥusaynīs. When Muḥammad b. ʿAlī (Ibn al-Ḥanafiyya) was in need of some part of the testament (*al-waṣiyya*) of the Prophet, he used to ask for it from ʿAlī b. al-Ḥusayn, who had it in his possession.[15]

1.2 *Ḥusaynīs and Jaʿfarīs/Jaʿfar al-Ṣādiq and the Jaʿfarīs*

The attitude of Jaʿfar al-Ṣādiq to the rebellion of ʿAbdallāh b. Muʿāwiya [b. ʿAbdallāh b. Jaʿfar b. ʿAlī b. Abī Ṭālib] may be reflected in the tradition in which Ḥammād b. ʿUthmān (d. 190/805 or 806)[16] heard Jaʿfar al-Ṣādiq saying: "The heretics (*al-zanādiqa*)

---

13 Ibn Bābawayh al-Qummī, *al-Imāma*, 60, no. 47: باب إمامة علي بن الحسين عليه السلام وإبطال إمامة محمد بن الحنفية.

14 Al-Ṣaffār, *Baṣāʾir*, 522, and the parallels in Ibn Bābawayh al-Qummī, *al-Imāma*, 60–61, no. 49; al-Ḥillī, *Mukhtaṣar*, 14; al-Ṭabarī l-Imāmī, *Dalāʾil*, 206–208.

15 Al-Ṣaffār, *Baṣāʾir*, 198, no. 11: Ḥamrān < Jaʿfar al-Ṣādiq; 198, no. 14; 204, no. 38: adding at the end: but I do not blame a cousin of mine; al-Majlisī, *Biḥār*, 108:368; for other traditions in this vein, see al-Ṣaffār, *Baṣāʾir*, 180, no. 29: Abū Ḥamza al-Thamālī < ʿAlī b. al-Ḥusayn: al-Ḥusayn b. ʿAlī discloses some *ʿilm* from ʿAlī's *ṣaḥīfa* to Ibn al-Ḥanafiyya.

16 On him, see Modarressi, *Tradition*, index, esp. 239.

will appear in the year 128; this (knowledge came to me) as the result of looking through the scroll (*muṣḥaf*) of Fāṭima, peace be upon her."[17]

2 The Ḥasanī and the Ḥusaynī Families: Animosity and Conflicts

2.1 *Economic Reasons: Some Preliminary Remarks*

A major aspect of this strife is the economic aspect, mainly the dispute and struggle over the endowments (*ṣadaqāt*) of the Ṭālibī family. This aspect was already emphasized by Madelung[18] and is dealt with here briefly. This topic warrants a broader and deeper discussion.

ʿAbdallāh b. al-Ḥasan b. al-Ḥasan b. ʿAlī b. Abī Ṭālib, Muḥammad al-Nafs al-Zakiyya's father, was in charge of the *ṣadaqāt* (i.e., the endowment lands, estates etc., from which alms are given, or the poor rate [*ṣadaqa*]) of ʿAlī b. Abī Ṭālib after his father (al-Ḥasan b. al-Ḥasan) died[19] (see below). Zayd b. ʿAlī b. al-Ḥusayn b. ʿAlī b. Abī Ṭālib disputed him in respect to this.[20] The strife between the ʿAlīd families over the control of ʿAlī's *ṣadaqāt* had earlier roots. Al-Ḥasan b. al-Ḥasan, as noted, was in control of

17 Al-Ṣaffār, *Baṣāʾir*, 177, no. 18; in the tradition al-Ṣādiq explains that *muṣḥaf Fāṭima* is a compendium of tales and secret knowledge that was transferred to Fāṭima by an angel who came to comfort her after the Prophet's death. ʿAlī b. Abī Ṭālib listened to it in secret and wrote the esoteric knowledge that was transmitted to Fāṭima; for parallel traditions, see al-Baḥrānī, *Madīnat al-maʿājiz*, 5:330; al-Majlisī, *Biḥār*, 26:44; 47:65 (quoting al-Ṣaffār); Moezzi, *Divine Guide*, 74; ʿAbdallāh b. Muʿāwiya's revolt broke out in 127/744 and lasted until 129/747, see Zettersteen, "ʿAbdallāh b. Muʿāwiya," *EI*²; or 130/747 or 748, as argued by Bernheimer, "ʿAbdallāh b. Muʿāwiya," 390; Tucker, "ʿAbdallāh b. Muʿāwiya," 44:129 H. or 130 H. For a bibliography on the revolt, see Bernheimer, "ʿAbdallāh b. Muʿāwiya," 381, n. 2; it is noteworthy that this year (128) is also mentioned in connection with rebellion and rebels in Khurāsān, in the epistle of Yaḥyā b.ʿAbd al-Ḥamīd al-Kātib, most probably relating to al-Ḥārith b. Surayj's revolt, see al-Qāḍī, "Nābiṭa," 32–37; Elad, "The Ethnic Composition," 289–292; see also Cook, *Muslim Apocalyptic*, 220, who quotes another Imāmī tradition regarding the revolt of ʿAbdallāh b. Muʿāwiya: "Other branches of the family are dismissed more cursorily. The Jaʿfarīds ... are said to have a rebellion in their future that will not amount to anything, probably the rebellion of ʿAbdallāh b. Muʿāwiya." (Ibid., n. 126, quoting al-Majlisī, 52:246; for additional parallels, see al-Majlisī, *Biḥār*,52:270; al-Nuʿmānī, *Ghayba*, 291). But it seems that this is not an Imāmī tradition; it is related by Ibn al-Ḥanafiyya. The flag of the Jaʿfarīs is indeed mentioned, though.

18 Madelung, "Zayd b. ʿAlī b. al-Ḥusayn"; and see also Landau-Tasseron, "Arabia," 405, n. 23, but especially, Ahmed, *Religious Elite*, 152f.

19 Al-Zubayrī, *Nasab Quraysh*, 46; al-Ardabīlī, *Jāmiʿ al-ruwāt*, 2:332.

20 Ibn ʿInaba, *ʿUmda*, 103: وكان يتولى صدقات أمير المؤمنين علي (ع) بعد أبيه الحسن و نازعه في ذلك زيد بن علي بن الحسين (ع) ولهما في ذلك حكايات لا تليق بهذا المختصر; Madelung, "Zayd b. ʿAlī b. al-Ḥusayn."

his grandfather's *ṣadaqāt*. At a certain point ʿAlī b. al-Ḥusayn b. ʿAlī b. Abī Ṭālib (Zayn al-ʿĀbidīn) contested this, but later accepted it.[21] From al-Zubayr b. Bakkār we learn that at a certain stage, his uncle, ʿUmar b. ʿAlī b. Abī Ṭālib, wished to be nominated as co-partner of al-Ḥasan b. al-Ḥasan to this important post, but the latter refused. The dispute was brought before al-Ḥajjāj b. Yūsuf, governor of Medina at the time (between 73/692 and 75/694),[22] who ruled in ʿUmar's favor. Al-Ḥasan went to the caliph's court, and the latter wrote a letter to al-Ḥajjāj ordering that al-Ḥasan's control of ʿAlī's *ṣadaqāt* should not be shared by anyone else.[23]

This dispute was brought again before the governor of Medina, Ibrāhīm b. Hishām (106–114/723–732). This time Zayd b. ʿAlī b. al-Ḥusayn was entrusted by his brother Muḥammad al-Bāqir to litigate on their behalf.[24] The Ḥasanīs were at first represented by Jaʿfar b. al-Ḥasan b. al-Ḥasan[25] and then by his brother ʿAbdallāh b. al-Ḥasan, who was in fact in control of the endowments after the death of his father.

> The case evidently involved the leadership of the descendants of Muḥammad through Fāṭima and thence their potential claim on the caliphate. ʿAbdallāh b. al-Ḥasan, who harboured ambitions at first for himself and later for his son al-Nafs al-Zakiyya, is reported to have accused Zayd before the governor of aspiring to the caliphate.[26]

2.2 *The Exclusive Right of the Ḥusaynīs to the Imāma: The Struggle between Jaʿfar al-Ṣādiq and ʿAbdallāh b. al-Ḥasan*

The most important rivals among the Banū Hāshim families were the Ḥasanīs; according to Imāmī traditions (usually related from Jaʿfar al-Ṣādiq), the descendants of al-Ḥasan are not mentioned in the *Kitāb Fāṭima* [Book of Fāṭima], where every ruler is mentioned by name.[27]

---

21 Al-Balādhurī, *Ansāb* (ed. Madelung), 2:613: during Hishām's rule; Ibn ʿInaba, *ʿUmda*, 99.

22 A. Dietrich, "al-Ḥadjdjādj b. Yūsuf," *EI*², 3:40.

23 Al-Shaykh al-Mufīd, *al-Irshād*, 2:23–25: quoting al-Zubayr b. Bakkār; al-Zubayrī, *Nasab Quraysh*, 46–47: not mentioning al-Zubayr b. Bakkār; Ibn ʿInaba, *ʿUmda*, 99: with minor changes, not mentioning al-Zubayr b. Bakkār, though; al-Irbilī, *Kashf al-ghumma*, 2:201 (an abridged tradition); Ahmed, *Religious Elite*, 159.

24 Al-Balādhurī, *Ansāb* (ed. Madelung), 2:613.

25 Madelung, "Zayd b. ʿAlī b. al-Ḥusayn"; see al-Balādhurī, *Ansāb* (ed. Madelung), 2:543: A general description of the dispute between the Ḥasanīs and the Ḥusaynīs (no mention of the city or the governor): Jaʿfar on behalf of the Ḥasanīs and Zayd on behalf of the Ḥusaynīs; ibid., 2:614: Jaʿfar b. al-Ḥasan and after him ʿAbdallāh b. al-Ḥasan.

26 Madelung, "Zayd b. ʿAlī b. al-Ḥusayn"; on ʿAbdallāh b. al-Ḥasan, see the exhaustive discussion in Ahmed, *Religious Elite*, 154ff.

27 Al-Ṣaffār, *Baṣāʾir*, 189, no. 3 [= al-Majlisī, *Biḥār*, 26:155]; al-Ṣaffār, *Baṣāʾir*, 189, no. 6 [= al-Majlisī, *Biḥār*, 26:156]: Fāṭima's scroll (*ṣaḥīfat Fāṭima*) is mentioned; for other

2.2.1 Abdallāh b. al-Ḥasan versus Jaʿfar al-Ṣādiq

This struggle for exclusive legitimacy is clearly demonstrated in the Shīʿī Imāmī traditions that stress personal conflict, antagonism, competition, and contention between the aforementioned leaders of the two main branches of the ʿAlīd family. Shīʿī *ḥadīth* are known to record the personal stories of scholars, some of whom were followers of ʿAbdallāh b. al-Ḥasan and considered him to be the Imām, but because of their disappointment in his personality and poor juridical knowledge, chose to follow Jaʿfar al-Ṣādiq as their Imām. The supernatural nature and the esoteric knowledge of Jaʿfar al-Ṣādiq is strongly emphasized in these traditions.[28] Although it is difficult to accurately ascertain the date of these traditions, it seems that many of them reflect a pre-ʿAbbāsī period, that is, they pertain to conditions prevailing in the Umawī period. The pre-rebellion phase and the rebellion itself in the ʿAbbāsī period led to the creation of many other traditions of this kind and added some specific characteristics of this period. Two examples are given below, the first, that of the well-known scholar [Ibn] al-Kalbī, and the second, that of ʿAbdallāh b. al-Najāshī.

2.2.1.1 *The Case of [Ibn?] al-Kalbī l-Nassāba*

A long detailed tradition related through an *isnād* concludes with Samāʿa b. Mihrān,[29] who heard the following story from al-Kalbī l-Nassāba:

I entered Medina, "knowing nothing of these Imāmī-Ḥusaynī doctrines": ولست أعرف شيئا من هذا الأمر. In the great mosque he met a group of Banū Quraysh and asked them, who was the most knowledgeable from among the people of this house [of the Prophet] (من عالم أهل هذا البيت). They sent him to ʿAbdallāh b. al-Ḥasan whom he asked four juridical questions. In all four answers ʿAbdallāh b. al-Ḥasan deviated from the laws of the Qurʾān, saying to al-Kalbī, the Qurʾān states so and so, or the people do so and so according to the Qurʾān, but we, the family of the [noble] house (ونحن أهل البيت) do not perform this and this. The answers he received startled al-Kalbī,

---

traditions in this vein, see Ibn Bābawayh al-Qummī, *al-Imāma*, 47, no 29: باب أن الإمامة لا تصلح إلا في ولد الحسين من دون ولد الحسن, and the parallels of the editor, therein; ibid., 50, no. 34; 51–52, no. 37.

28 For a discussion on the sources of knowledge of the Imāms, see Moezzi, *Divine Guide*, 73–74 (written sources); 91ff. (sacred power of the Imāms, the "miraculous powers of the Imāms are presented as the result of their initiatory knowledge"; they work miracles; 92: "Their power devolves from their knowledge. Most of these powers are associated with the knowledge of magic"); 93–96: the supernatural, prodigious powers of the Imāms.

29 He lived in al-Kūfa, where he was a silk merchant and died in Medina. He was one of the followers of Jaʿfar al-Ṣādiq and appears hundreds of times in the Shīʿī literature as a direct transmitter of al-Ṣādiq. On him, see Modarressi, *Tradition*, 369–370; and see the note of the editors of al-Ṭūsī, *al-Khilāf*, 1:56, n. 7.

who left him saying: this family lies regarding this family [of the Prophet]: هذه العصابة تكذب على أهل هذا البيت. Al-Kalbī returned to the mosque, asked the Qurashīs again, who is the most knowledgeable among the people of *ahl al-bayt*, and they reluctantly direct him to Jaʿfar b. Muḥammad (al-Ṣādiq). Already at the entrance to al-Ṣādiq's residence (*dār*), al-Kalbī is perplexed by the uncanny knowledge of the slave (*ghulām*) of al-Ṣādiq, who knows his tribal affinity. Al-Kalbī asked al-Ṣādiq the same questions, admired his answers so much that he clapped his hands out of pleasure, saying: "If there exists a true doctrine—this is it" (إن كان شيء فهذا). The transmitter of al-Kalbī adds: "[From that day] al-Kalbī continued to worship God by the love of the family of this house until he died." (فلم يزل الكلبي يدين الله بحب آل البيت حتى مات).[30]

The tradition is woven around the famous scholar Ibn al-Kalbī (see below), who acknowledges Jaʿfar al-Ṣādiq as the true Imām and reveals the false and unworthy true personality of ʿAbdallāh b. al-Ḥasan. At least one small part in the tradition is of a legendary nature (the esoteric knowledge of al-Ṣādiq's slave). Even if the whole story is fabricated, it was woven around some grains of historical truth, e.g., it reflects the rivalry between the Ḥasanīs and the Ḥusaynīs over the leadership of Banū Hāshim, and over the identity of the true *imām*.

2.2.1.2 *Who is al-Kalbī l-Nassāba?*

The transmitter is one of two well-known and extremely important scholars, Muḥammad b. al-Sāʾib al-Kalbī (d. 146/763), or his son Hishām b. Muḥammad (d. 204/819). Both father and son were pro-Imāmī Shīʿīs. Muḥammad was one of the adherents of Muḥammad b. ʿAlī l-Bāqir and his son, Jaʿfar al-Ṣādiq. Hishām was close to Jaʿfar and he appears many times as a direct transmitter from Jaʿfar al-Ṣādiq in the Imāmī Shīʿī books of *ḥadīth*. Both were experts on the genealogy of the Arabs,[31] but regarding the identity of the transmitter in the tradition discussed, the Shīʿī scholars of *ḥadīth* identify him as the son, Hishām b. Muḥammad.[32] In the tradition from al-Kalbī, which is discussed at length, four matters of law are mentioned. Some of the topics appear in Shīʿī law and *ḥadīth* books separately, all transmitted directly by al-Kalbī from Jaʿfar al-Ṣādiq.[33]

30 Al-Kulaynī, *al-Kāfī* (1963 H.), 1:349–351 (the quote is on 351); al-Baḥrānī, *Madīnat al-maʿājiz*, 5:460.

31 W. Atallah, "al-Kalbī," *EI*²; Elad, "The Dome of the Rock," 42.

32 See the note of the editor of al-Thaqafī l-Kūfī, *Kitāb al-ghārāt*, 2:746 [quoting al-Qummī's *al-Kunā wa-l-alqāb*]: "al-Kalbī, the genealogy expert, is also called Ibn al-Kalbī, Abū l-Mundhir Hishām b. b. Abī l-Naḍr Muḥammad ..."; al-Anṣārī, *al-Mawṣūʿa*, 1:132, quoting al-ʿAllāma al-Ṭihrānī in his *al-Dharīʿa*: "He [that is, Muḥammad b. al-Sāʾib] is the father of Hishām al-Kalbī, the famous expert on genealogy and the author of the Great Tafsīr."

33 See for instance, al-Kulaynī, *al-Kāfī*, 6:416; al-Ṭūsī, *al-Istibṣār*, 1:16; al-Ṭūsī, *al-Khilāf*, 1:56. For other traditions related by al-Kalbī from Jaʿfar al-Ṣādiq, see for example al-Baḥrānī,

2.2.1.3 *The Repentance of ʿAbdallāh b. al-Najāshī: The Motif of the 'Good, Rightly-Guided' Companion and the 'Bad, Misguided One'*

The tradition (I am tempted to say, the story) has at least three versions with common motifs. The first group lacks some developed motifs found in other versions of this tradition, e.g., the supernatural characteristics of Jaʿfar al-Ṣādiq and the repentance of ʿAbdallāh b. al-Najāshī. It is transmitted by Abū ʿĀṣim al-Sijistānī, who together with ʿAbdallāh b. al-Najāshī, came to Medina. ʿAbdallāh was a follower of the Zaydiyya and upon arriving in Medina went to ʿAbdallāh b. al-Ḥasan, while Abū ʿĀṣim, an Imāmī by inclination, went to Jaʿfar al-Ṣādiq. In the morning when they met, ʿAbdallāh asks Abū ʿĀṣim to introduce him to Jaʿfar al-Ṣādiq, which he does. ʿAbdallāh b. al-Najāshī tells al-Ṣādiq that he had killed seven people who cursed ʿAlī b. Abī Ṭālib and ʿAbdallāh b. al-Ḥasan tells him that he will not be cleansed of this murder, neither in this world, nor in the next. Jaʿfar al-Ṣādiq asks him about the specific background of each killing, then tells him that if he had received permission from the Imām, he would have been innocent of any sin, both in this world and in the next, but in order to repent of his acts he tells him to sacrifice seven rams (*kabsh*) in al-Minā. Here the tradition ends.[34] However, in a sub-version of this tradition that lacks the opening of the preceding tradition, without any indication of his sectarian affiliation, ʿAbdallāh b. al-Najāshī, tells Jaʿfar al-Ṣādiq that he had killed **thirteen** of the Khawārij [the **seven Muslims** are from then on described as **Khawārij**). The rest of the tradition is almost identical to the preceding one.[35]

The second version lacks any anecdotal background, i.e., no geographical settings (Sijistān, Medina), no former sectarian affiliation (e.g., no mention of the Zaydiyya, of ʿAbdallāh b. al-Ḥasan or the consultation with him beforehand). ʿAbdallāh b. al-Najāshī comes to Jaʿfar al-Ṣādiq, tells him that he had killed thirteen [!] men of the Khawārij, who cursed ʿAlī. Jaʿfar tells him that he should have consulted the Imām and received his consent for the killing, but since he came quickly to the Imām (*li-sabqika al-imām*) he should sacrifice thirteen sheep, give the meat to charity, and is not obliged to do anything else.[36]

The third version is almost completely different, with some elements of the preceding traditions. According to this tradition, narrated by ʿAmmār al-Sijistānī, ʿAbdallāh b. al-Najāshī, who was a close adherent of ʿAbdallāh b. al-Ḥasan and supported the doctrine of the Zaydiyya: وكان منقطعا إلى عبد الله بن الحسن ويقول بالزيدية, asks Jaʿfar

---

al-Ḥadāʾiq, 5:224; al-Najafī, *Jawāhir*, 1:169; al-Majlisī, *Biḥār*, 21:153; 24:5, 159, 274; 27:74; al-Khūʾī, *al-Ṭahāra*, 4:197: *al-Kalbī l-Nassāba*.

34 Al-Kulaynī, *al-Kāfī*, 7:376; al-Ṭūsī, *Tahdhīb*, 10:213–214.

35 See al-ʿĀmilī, *Wasāʾil* (*al-Islāmiyya*), 19:170.

36 Al-Iṣfahānī, *Kashf al-lithām*, 2:416; al-Najafī, *Jawāhir*, 41:438; al-Ṭabāṭabāʾī, *Riyāḍ al-masāʾil*, 13:537; al-ʿĀmilī, *Wasāʾil* (*Āl al-Bayt*), 29:230–231.

al-Ṣādiq's follower to arrange a meeting for him with the latter. Jaʿfar al-Ṣādiq astonishes him by disclosing to him some hidden episode from his past. Here the tradition ends.[37]

It is noteworthy that some of the background details regarding ʿAbdallāh b. al-Najāshī are lacking, e.g., the geographical background, the nature of his problem, that is, the killing of seven or thirteen men, his consultation with ʿAbdallāh b. al-Ḥasan, the latter's answer, and in particular, there is no mention of his problem and his deed to Jaʿfar al-Ṣādiq, and the latter's juridical answer to the problem to his deed. It is noteworthy that in some sources ʿAbdallāh b. al-Ḥasan is rendered as al-Ḥasan b. al-Ḥasan, that is, the father of the former. This is most probably a copyist's mistake.

The combined version is a combination of most parts of versions 1 and 2 (thirteen of the Khawārij instead of seven are killed) and version 3, that is the full story of ʿAbdallāh b. al-Najāshī from beginning to end, his place of origin, his Zaydī-Ḥasanī affiliation, his consultation with ʿAbdallāh b. al-Ḥasan, the latter's legal decision, his coming to Jaʿfar al-Ṣādiq, the detailed questioning, the legal decision of al-Ṣādiq, and then, at the end the disclosure of the secret past. Both the judgment and the supernatural character of Jaʿfar cause ʿAbdallāh b. al-Najāshī to say "Oh ʿAmmār, I hereby testify that this is the most knowledgeable of the family of Muḥammad, and that everything that I believed in until now is canceled and that this is the sovereign [*imām*] who is entitled to rule": وأن الذي كنت عليه باطل وأن هذا صاحب الأمر.[38]

This rivalry between ʿAbdallāh b. al-Ḥasan and Jaʿfar al-Ṣādiq over the identity of the "true" Imām, that is, over the leadership of the Banū Hāshim in particular and the whole Muslim community in general, is manifested in other traditions as well. They utilize several motifs of the preceding traditions. According to one of these traditions, a man who regards ʿAbdallāh b. al-Ḥasan as an *imām* comes to him with a specific question in law (about the *ḥajj*) and ʿAbdallāh b. al-Ḥasan sends him to Jaʿfar al-Ṣādiq because he is the expert on this topic [literally: he exerted himself for the study of this subject?: قد نصب نفسه لهذا].[39]

37 Al-Ṣaffār, *Baṣāʾir*, 265; Ibn Ḥamza al-Ṭūsī, *al-Thāqib fī l-manāqib*, 411: al-Ḥasan b. al-Ḥasan instead of ʿAbdallāh b. al-Ḥasan b. al-Ḥasan; al-Rāwandī, *al-Kharāʾij wa-l-jarāʾiḥ*, 2:722–723: al-Ḥasan instead of ʿAbdallāh b. al-Ḥasan; al-Baḥrānī, *Madīnat al-maʿājiz*, 5:317–318; al-Majlisī, *Biḥār*, 47:73.

38 Al-Ṭūsī, *Ikhtiyār*, 2:633–634; al-ʿĀmilī, *Wasāʾil* (*al-Islāmiyya*), 20:245–246 and the parallel sources therein; al-Khūʾī, *Rijāl*, 11:383 and the parallel sources therein.

39 Al-ʿAyyāshī, *Tafsīr*, 1:368, no. 55 and the parallels of the editors on 1:269, n. 1.

3 The Symbols of Legitimacy of the Ḥusaynīs: The Inheritance of the ʿIlm of the Prophet; Holy Relics of Ādam (Adam), Mūsā (Moses), Yūsuf (Joseph), and (mainly) of the Prophet Muḥammad

ʿAlī b. al-Ḥusayn, his son Muḥammad, and his grandson Jaʿfar inherited, along with the *imāma*, some holy relics (mainly of the Prophet) that distinguished them from every other family of Banū Hāshim, including the ʿAbbāsīs. These symbols of legitimacy gave them the right to rule as the Imāms of the Muslims. Special chapters in the Imāmī *ḥadīth* literature deal with this topic. The figures that play central roles in these traditions are ʿAlī b. Abī Ṭālib, ʿAlī b. al-Ḥusayn and his son Muḥammad al-Bāqir, but it seems that Jaʿfar al-Ṣādiq is the main and dominant figure in most of them.

The inheritance of these holy objects serves, in the Imāmī sources, as the core argument for the right of this specific Ḥusaynī house to rule. The majority of these relics were given by ʿAlī b. Abī Ṭālib to al-Ḥasan, then to al-Ḥusayn, and from him they were passed on only among his descendants and only to sons: ʿAlī b. al-Ḥusayn (Zayn al-ʿĀbidīn), then to Muḥammad b. ʿAlī (al-Bāqir) and then to Jaʿfar al-Ṣādiq.[40]

3.1 *The Prophet's Weapons*

Besides the Prophet's *ʿilm* (esoteric religious knowledge),[41] another major theme appears in these traditions, i.e., the weapons (*silāḥ*) of the Prophet, which serve as a central basis of legitimization. They appear in the Shīʿī-Imāmī sources in several ways:

1) In a general manner, with no polemic emphasis and with no relation to any specific family of the ʿAlīds.

This group of traditions establishes the equation between the Covenant of the Children of Israel (*Banū Isrāʾīl*) and the weapons of the Prophet, for as kingship prevailed among the family in which the Ark of the Covenant remained, so kingship prevailed within the family that had the weapons of the Prophet (literally: circulated among them: *dāra*).[42] An interesting addition appears in one of the parallel versions:

---

40 Al-Ṣaffār, *Baṣāʾir*, 197, no. 8: ʿAlī inherited from the Prophet his weapons and esoteric religious knowledge (*silāḥ* and *ʿilm*) then they were passed on to al-Ḥasan > al-Ḥusayn > ʿAlī [Zayn al-ʿĀbidīn]; idem, no. 10: with the addition ... ʿAlī [Zayn al-ʿĀbidīn] > Muḥammad [al-Bāqir].

41 For a discussion of this principle, see Jafri, *Shīʿa*, 291–293.

42 Al-Ṣaffār, *Baṣāʾir*, 197, no. 7; al-Kulaynī, *al-Kāfī*, 1:238; al-Ṣaffār, *Baṣāʾir*, 196–197, no. 5, 200, no. 20: instead of *mulk*: *ʿilm*; 200, no. 19; al-Kulaynī, *al-Kāfī*, 1:238: *al-imāma* instead of *mulk* or *ʿilm*. See also al-Ṣaffār, *Baṣāʾir*, nos. 33, 34, 35 on 203.

the transmitter, the adherent of al-Bāqir, asks him: "Are the weapons separated from the knowledge?" He says no: قلت فيكون السلاح مزايلا للعلم؟ قال لا.[43]

This seems to be a refutation of the Ḥasanī claim that they have in their possession the sword of the Prophet (see below). The Ḥusaynī house inherited both *ʿilm* and *silāḥ*.

These traditions usually serve as the core argument against:

1.2) the Ḥasanī family in general, who claim that the sword of the Prophet was in their possession[44] or categorically deny the possession and existence of *al-Jafr* by the Ḥusaynī family (see below) or belittle its importance.[45] The Ḥasanī family (Banū l-Ḥasan) knows, claims Jaʿfar al-Ṣādiq, that the *Jafr* and Fāṭima's scroll (*muṣḥaf* Fāṭima) are in the possession of the Ḥusaynī family, but they are motivated by jealousy and the desire for this earthly world instead of seeking the true way (*al-ḥaqq*) [of the Ḥusaynīs].[46] The Ḥasanī side in this strife between the families hardly appears on its own; we learn about it mainly from the debate in the Imāmī sources.

1.3) ʿAbdallāh b. al-Ḥasan in particular. Following are a few examples of these traditions:

a) "... from Sulaymān b. Hārūn who said: I said to Abū ʿAbdallāh [that is, Jaʿfar al-Ṣādiq]: the ʿIjliyya (see below) claim (إن العجلية يزعمون) that ʿAbdallāh b. al-Ḥasan claims falsely (*yaddaʿī*) that the Prophet's sword is in his possession." Jaʿfar al-Ṣādiq accuses him of lying, saying that ʿAbdallāh b. al-Ḥasan saw the sword in the possession of ʿAlī b. al-Ḥusayn [Zayn al-ʿĀbidīn]. Then he continues, saying that the rule will not pass to them [the Ḥasanīs], they are not worthy of it, they are not those who were chosen by God to rule.[47]

b) ... from ʿAlī b. Saʿīd, who relates in the first person, that while in the presence of Abū ʿAbdallāh [that is, Jaʿfar al-Ṣādiq], with him was Muḥammad b. ʿAbdallāh b. ʿAlī [b. al-Ḥusayn b. ʿAlī b. Abī Ṭālib], when al-Ṣādiq was asked by one of our (the Imāmī) group (رجل من أصحابنا): ʿAbdallāh b. al-Ḥasan says that they have rights in this rule that others beside them do not have; Jaʿfar al-Ṣādiq answers that ʿAbdallāh b. al-Ḥasan

---

43 al-Ṣaffār, *Baṣāʾir*, 203, no. 33; al-Kulaynī, *al-Kāfī*, 1:238, no. 3.

44 Al-Ṣaffār, *Baṣāʾir*, 199, no. 16; 204, no. 37.

45 Ibid., 174, no. 10; 175, no. 11.

46 Ibid., 171, no. 1; see also, 179, no. 26.

47 Ibid., 194, no. 1; 197, no. 6; 203, no. 31: it is possible that ʿAbdallāh b. al-Ḥasan's father al-Ḥasan saw it when he was a little boy under the care of (صبي في حِجْر) ʿAlī b. al-Ḥusayn; al-Khūʾī, *Rijāl*, 11:171, quoting *Baṣāʾir al-darajāt* and al-Majlisī, *Biḥār*, 7:324, chapter: ما عند الأئمة عليهم السلام من سلاح رسول الله صلعم.

claims (wrongly) that his father ʿAlī was not an Imām and also says "that we do not have esoteric religious knowledge (*ʿilm*) and the truth (*ṣidq*). I swear by God, indeed he has no esoteric religious knowledge."[48]

c) …from ʿAlī b. Saʿīd, who relates that Muḥammad b. ʿAbdallāh b. ʿAlī in the presence of Jaʿfar al-Ṣādiq says that ʿAbdallāh b. al-Ḥasan mocks (you), saying this is (found) in your *Jafr*,[49] to which you call [? Or: which is the source of your prayers?]: أنه يهزأ ويقول في جفركم الذي تدعون; this makes Jaʿfar al-Ṣādiq angry and he says: "Indeed when Abdallāh b. al-Ḥasan says that there is no *imām* among us, he speaks the truth, he is not an *imām*, nor was his father an *imām*, for he claims falsely that ʿAlī b. Abī Ṭālib was not an *imam*."[50]

d) In another tradition Jaʿfar al-Ṣādiq says:

> Indeed ʿAbdallāh b. al-Ḥasan claims that he does not have knowledge that other common people do not have and he said: I swear by God, he speaks the truth, ʿAbdallāh b. al-Ḥasan does not have any different knowledge than that which exists among the common people. But (contrary to this) in our possession is the

---

48 Al-Ṣaffār, *Baṣāʾir*, 173; al-Khūʾī, *Rijāl*, 11:171, quoting al-Ṣaffār: يزعم أن أباه علي لم يكن إماما ويقول إن ليس لنا علم وصدق والله ما عنده علم; see also al-Ṣaffār, *Baṣāʾir*, 176, no. 15: a partial parallel.

49 About the *Jafr*, see Moezzi, *Divine Guide*, 74; it is a tanned skin, containing different, various kinds of knowledge kept by the Imāms. It is made of bull skin (al-Ṣaffār, *Baṣāʾir*, 176, no. 15), or of goat and sheep skins (ibid., 177, no. 19; 179, no. 26), or a camel skin (ibid., 173, no. 5); ibid., 181, no. 34: "a bull's tanned skin, in the shape of a leather travelling bag, containing books and knowledge that people need until the Last Day"; p, 180, no. 31: a skin, known as "skin of ʿUkāẓ" (*adīm ukāẓī*), that is, a skin sold in the ʿUkāẓ market (near Mecca), see *Lisān al-ʿArab*, s.v., *ʿ.k.ẓ.*; al-Ṣaffār, *Baṣāʾir*, 170, no. 1: two kinds of *Jafr*; 1) the white *Jafr* (*al-Jafr al-Abyaḍ*), containing the *Zabūr* of David, the Torah of Moses, the *Injīl* of Jesus, and the scrolls of Abraham, and all the laws regarding what is lawful and forbidden, and the Scroll of Fāṭima (but see ibid., 177, no. 19: it is the *Jāmiʿa* [see below] that contains these laws). 2) "The Red *Jafr*… containing the weapons (*silāḥ* [of the Prophet], the meaning of the name is that it is opened for the shedding of blood, the owner of the sword opens it for the killing."

50 Al-Ṣaffār, *Baṣāʾir*, 176, no. 15; 180, no. 30; al-Khūʾī, *Rijāl*, 11:172, quoting *Baṣāʾir*; see also al-Ṣaffār, *Baṣāʾir*, 173, no. 5.

> *Jāmiʿa*,[51] which contains the laws of what is lawful and forbidden, and we have the *Jafr* … and in our possession is Fāṭima's Scroll.[52]

The weapons (*silāḥ*), the sword (*sayf*) of the Prophet that the Ḥusaynī Imāms inherited are only part of a long list of holy objects that were passed on in their family. A nearly full list is found in the following tradition:

3.2 *Holy Relics of Adam, Moses, Joseph, and (mainly) of the Prophet Muḥammad*

2.1) … ʿAbdallāh b. Muskān [d. 183/790–800] < Sulaymān b. Khālid [al-Aqṭaʿ, d. ca. 148/765–766],[53] who were with a group of followers in Jaʿfar al-Ṣādiq's presence, when some men from al-Kūfa arrived (in another similar tradition they are two people from the Zaydiyya),[54] who say that people say that "within your family, the family of the Prophet, there is an *imām muftaraḍ al-ṭāʿa*." Al-Ṣādiq answers that he does not know of this phenomenon among the family of his house. They claim that it is you [who is the Imām], but Jaʿfar said: I did not tell them so. When the people see that they made him angry they go away. Sulaymān is asked who these people are and he answers that they are from the ʿIjliyya (see below), the curse of God on them (in the parallel tradition: "they belong to our lowest people, from the Zaydiyya" (هما من أهل سوقنا من الزيدية),[55] they claim that the sword of the Prophet is in the possession of ʿAbdallāh b. al-Ḥasan. To this al-Ṣādiq responds: No, neither he nor his father have ever seen it; he may have seen it in the possession of ʿAlī b. al-Ḥusayn (the grandfather of Jaʿfar al-Ṣādiq).

51 This is a large scroll, described as "seventy cubits in length and its width is the width of the thigh of a two-humped camel, and in it everything a man needs is found": فيها كلما يحتاج الناس إليه, al-Ṣaffār, *Baṣāʾir*, 173–174, no. 6; ibid., 180, no. 31: "its length is seventy cubits; it contains everything, even the fine (or mulct) for a wounded (scratched) skin (see Lane, *Lexicon*, s.v. *a.r.sh.* and *kh.d.sh*), it is a dictation of the messenger of God and written by ʿAlī [b. Abī Ṭālib]": وهي سبعون ذراعا فيهاكل شيء حتى أرش الخدش إملاء رسول الله وخط علي عليه السلام; 177, no. 19; 181, no. 33: contains what is lawful and forbidden (فيها الحلال والحرام; see also ibid., 172–173, no. 3; 173, no. 6.

52 Al-Ṣaffār, *Baṣāʾir*, 177, no. 19; 181, no. 33: a parallel tradition.

53 On ʿAbdallāh b. Muskān, see Modarressi, *Tradition*, 150–153; on Sulaymān b. Khālid, see ibid., 374–375.

54 Al-Ṣaffār, *Baṣāʾir*, 194, no. 2.

55 Ibid., 195, no. 2; al-Kulaynī, *al-Kāfī*, 1:234–235.

> By God I swear [continues al-Ṣādiq], we have in our possession (*ʿindanā*) (in the parallel tradition: I have in my possession: *ʿindī*)[56] 1) the Prophet's sword, 2) his armor (*dirʿ*), 3) his weapons (*silāḥ*), 4) his breastplate (*laʾma*), 5) his seal,[57] 6) the (magic) name (of God: *al-ism*) used by the Prophet in the battle between the idolaters and the Muslims,[58] 7) the Covenant that was brought by the angels, 8) the basin (*ṭast*) on which Moses offered up sacrifices, 9) Moses's Tablets, 10) Moses's staff.[59]

As to the coat of mail of the Prophet, al-Ṣādiq says that his father wore it but it was too long on him and dragged on the ground, I put it on and it was also too big,[60] "but our Messiah will be whoever wears the coat of armor of the Messenger of God and it will fit him [completely]": وإن قائمنا من لبس درع رسول الله فملأها.[61]

2.2) Other traditions add the following holy objects that were in the possession of Jaʿfar al-Ṣādiq: 1) the helmet [?] (*maghfar*) of the Prophet;[62] 2) his flag called

56 Ibid., 194, no. 2; 198, no. 12: "indeed in my possession are the seal of the Prophet, his coat of arms and his flag."

57 Ibid., 198, no. 12.

58 Most plausibly the name of God (الإسم الأعظم/الأكبر), which was composed of 73 letters; the Prophet received 72 (one was left with God), which he passed on to the Imāms, see Moezzi, *Divine Guide*, 92.

59 Al-Ṣaffār, *Baṣāʾir*, 194–195, no. 2; Moses's staff was bequeathed by Adam to Shuʿayb then to Moses and finally it reached ʿAlī b. Abī Ṭālib, al-Ṣaffār, *Baṣāʾir*, 204, no. 36.

60 Al-Kulaynī, *al-Kāfī*, 1:234: لبس أبي درع رسول الله... فخطت و لبستها أنا ففضلت.

61 Al-Ṣaffār, *Baṣāʾir*, 196, no. 4; 197, no. 9, from al-Ṣādiq: his father put on the coat of mail of the Prophet (يجرها على الأرض). For parallel or very similar traditions, see al-Kulaynī, *al-Kāfī*, 1:232–234; al-Shaykh al-Mufīd, *al-Irshād*, 2:187–188; al-Irbilī, *Kashf al-ghumma*, 2:384–385; al-Majlisī, *Biḥār*, 26:207. On al-Qāʾim, see W. Madelung, "Ḳāʾim Āl al-Bayt," *EI*²; Cook, *Muslim Apocalyptic*, 195; Madelung renders the term as "the riser," that is the one who will "rise against the illegitimate regime and restore justice on earth, evidently in contrast to the *ḳāʾid*, or 'sitting,' members of the family, who refused to be drawn into ventures of armed revolt. The term thus was often qualified as *al-ḳāʾim bi 'l-sayf*." In its specific sense among the Imāmiyya, "the term meant the eschatological Mahdī, since their Imāms, especially from Djaʿfar al-Ṣādiq on, made it a principle to refuse involvement in revolutionary activities." Cf. D. Cook, *Muslim Apocalyptic*, 195 for a different interpretation of the term, e.g., the name "would appear to emphasize the sudden appearance (*qiyām*) of the messianic figure"; ibid., p, 196: the verbs *qāma* and *kharaja* "convey the idea of sudden appearance."

62 A *maghfar* is a helmet, or head covering worn under the helmet (Lane, *Lexicon*, s.v. *l.ʾ.m.*).

al-mughalliba (the conqueror); 3) Solomon's seal;[63] 4) Fāṭima's scroll (*muṣḥaf Fāṭima*);[64] 5) the *Jāmiʿa* (scroll); 6) the two sandals (*naʿlān*) of the Prophet;[65] 7 [?]) the long shirt (*qamīṣ*) of Joseph, which came into the possession of the Prophet and his family.[66]

2.3) In a rare tradition three of the most important leaders of the Ḥasanī family are mentioned—al-Ḥasan b. al-Ḥasan [b. ʿAlī b. Abī Ṭālib], his son, ʿAbdallāh, and Muḥammad b. ʿAbdallāh b. al-Ḥasan—as the main rivals of the Ḥusaynī family within the ʿAlīd family.[67] The aim of the tradition is to emphasize the total enmity and rivalry between the Ḥasanīs and the Ḥusaynīs from an early date. The mention of al-Ḥasan b. al-Ḥasan and Muḥammad b. ʿAbdallāh in this kind of tradition is rare. Can this give us any clue as to its date?

3.3 *Historical Note on al-ʿIjliyya*

The editor of *Baṣāʾir* (p. 196, n. 2) remarks that according to *Firaq al-Shīʿa*, al-ʿIjliyya are the weak/defective members of al-Zaydiyya (ضعفاء الزيدية), and they were named thus because they were the followers of Hārūn b. Saʿīd [read Saʿd], al-ʿIjlī. But according to al-Shahrastānī, they maintained that after Abū l-Khaṭṭāb the *imām* was ʿUmayr b. Bayān al-ʿIjlī. Their beliefs are the same as those of the first group though they admit that they do die. They set up a tent at Kunāsat al-Kūfa where they all gathered to worship al-Ṣadiq. A report about them was sent to Yazīd b. ʿUmar b. Hubayra, who took ʿUmayr prisoner and crucified him in Kunāsat al-Kūfa. This group is called the ʿIjliyya, or also the ʿUmayriyya.[68]

If the mention of Yazīd b. ʿUmar is historically reliable, then the episodes described in the preceding traditions in which the ʿIjliyya are mentioned occurred between 128/745 (the year in which Yazīd became governor of al-ʿIrāq) and 132/750, when he was executed by the ʿAbbāsīs.[69]

---

63 Al-Ṣaffār, *Baṣāʾir*, 195, no. 2.

64 Ibid., 173, no. 5; 173–174, no. 6; 206, no. 47: from al-Bāqir; al-Kulaynī, *al-Kāfī*, 1:240: from al-Ṣādiq.

65 Al-Ṣaffār, *Baṣāʾir*, 202, no. 29.

66 Al-Majlisī, *Biḥār*, 26:215, no. 28; it does not specifically mention that it is in Jaʿfar al-Ṣādiq's possession; besides the sword and coat of mail, ʿAlī also inherited from the Prophet his (camel) saddle, and his mule called al-Shahbāʾ, al-Ṣaffār, *Baṣāʾir*, 206, no. 44.

67 Al-Ṣaffār, *Baṣāʾir*, 176, no. 15: al-Ḥasan b. al-Ḥasan is mentioned by al-Muʿallā b. Khunays (Jaʿfar al-Ṣādiq's *mawlā*), who speaks ill of al-Ḥasan b. al-Ḥasan without making specific accusations against his conduct: جعلت فداك ما لقيت من الحسن بن الحسن [it could also be read: *laqītu*, in this case the subject would be the *mawlā*, but the first reading (*laqīta*) seems the correct one].

68 The translation is mainly according to Kazi and Flynn, *Muslim Sects*, 155.

69 See Elad, "Wāsiṭ."

4 Ḥusaynīs and Ḥasanīs: The Struggle between Jaʿfar al-Ṣādiq and Muḥammad b. ʿAbdallāh b. al-Ḥasan

4.1 *Historical Traditions: The al-Abwāʾ Meeting, Abū Salama's Affair, and Other Events*

In some of the traditions relating the al-Abwāʾ meeting, Jaʿfar al-Ṣādiq appears, refusing to take an oath of allegiance to Muḥammad al-Nafs al-Zakiyya and foreseeing the death of Muḥammad, evidently to stress his *ʿilm* and to justify his *quʿūd* doctrine.[70] These traditions in particular reflect the tensions and struggles between the Ḥasanīs and the Ḥusaynīs and the relations between the ʿAbbāsīs and the ʿAlīd factions. This may also hold true for other traditions concerning the correspondence of Abū Salama, the head of the ʿAbbāsī *daʿwa* in al-Kūfa, with a few ʿAlīds, among them Jaʿfar al-Ṣādiq and ʿAbdallāh b. al-Ḥasan, who wanted to nominate his son, Muḥammad as the *imām* of the Muslim community. These traditions aimed to malign Abū Salama, but mainly also to justify the *quʿūd* (quiescent) policy of Jaʿfar al-Ṣādiq,[71] who refused the call of Abū Salama.[72] The supernatural nature of Jaʿfar al-Ṣādiq is also demonstrated in other traditions that are connected to ʿAbdallāh b. al-Ḥasan and his son, but have no connection to the meeting of Banū Hāshim and the oath of allegiance to Muḥammad b.

70 For example, see al-Iṣfahānī, *Maqātil*, 254–255: Jaʿfar refuses to swear allegiance to Muḥammad b. ʿAbdallāh, indicating Abū l-ʿAbbās as the future caliph, telling ʿAbdallāh b. al-Ḥasan that his two sons will be killed; ibid.; another version by another transmitter: Muḥammad b. ʿAbdallāh will be killed by al-Manṣūr; ibid., 255–256 (l. 1 to l. 8); another tradition from different transmitters: Jaʿfar tells ʿAbdallāh b. al-Ḥasan that the caliphate will pass not to him or his sons but first to al-Saffāḥ, then to al-Manṣūr then to his descendants after him; ibid., 256 (ll. 5–6): Abū Jaʿfar al-Manṣūr will kill Muḥammad b. ʿAbdallāh in Aḥjār al-Zayt, and after this he will kill his brother. Cf. ibid., 207–208 (a partially parallel tradition in this vein); it seems that Nagel was the first to regard these traditions as mere fiction, see the short remark of Nagel, "Muḥammad b. ʿAbdallāh," 260; for a detailed discussion of the al-Abwāʾ meeting, see chapter 2).

71 About the quiescent doctrine of Jaʿfar al-Ṣādiq, see for instance Hodgson, " Early Shīʿa," 11–12; idem, "Djaʿfar al-Ṣādiḳ," 374; Jafri, *Shīʿa*, 249, 253, 260, 266, 267, 293, 299–300; according to Jafri, this doctrine was already cultivated by his grandfather, ʿAlī b. al-Ḥusayn (ibid., 237–239, 242) and especially his father, Muḥammad (ibid., 249, 251, 253, 267); Gleave, "Jaʿfar al-Ṣādeq," 350; Ahmed, *Religious Elite*, 181.

72 For example, see al-Yaʿqūbī, *Taʾrīkh* (Leiden edition), 2:418: Jaʿfar prophesies to ʿAbdallāh b. al-Ḥasan that his son will be killed in Aḥjār al-Zayt; Ibn Shahrāshūb, *Manāqib*, 3:355–356: a tradition similar in its expressions and phrases to the "al-Abwāʾ meeting" tradition (also al-Iṣfahānī, *Maqātil*, 256): Jaʿfar prophesies to Abū Salama that the rule will pass to Abū l-ʿAbbās, then to his brother; the garbled text of Ibn Shahrāshūb was most probably copied by al-Majlisī, *Biḥār*, 47:132. For a detailed discussion of the Abū Salama affair, see chapter 2.

ʿAbdallāh. In these traditions Jaʿfar al-Ṣādiq prophesies in the ʿAbbāsī period[!] that Muḥammad b. ʿAbdallāh will be killed.[73]

4.2 *The Struggle According to Imāmī Traditions*

It has already been mentioned above that the conflict between the Ḥasanīs and the Ḥusaynīs in the Imāmī *ḥadīth* is mainly between Jaʿfar al-Ṣādiq and ʿAbdallāh b. al-Ḥasan, both leaders and heads of their extended families. But there are several cases in which Jaʿfar expressed an unequivocally negative opinion on Muḥammad's revolt, e.g., his revolt is *fitna*;[74] whenever Jaʿfar al-Ṣādiq saw Muḥammad b. ʿAbdallāh his eyes filled with tears, and when asked for the reason for this he answered, "The people say about him that he is the Mahdī, but he is going to be killed (وإنه لمقتول); he is not mentioned in the book of his father ʿAlī as one of the caliphs of this community."[75]

In the Imāmī traditions, Muḥammad b. ʿAbdallāh rarely appears as al-Ṣādiq's opponent. So far I have come across very few such traditions; all are from the early work of al-Ṣaffār in the section on the books that are in the possession of the Imāms, in which the names of the kings who will rule (are listed): باب في الأئمة عندهم الكتب التي فيها أسماء الملوك الذي يملكون.

In these traditions Jaʿfar al-Ṣādiq tells his *mawlā* Khunays, or, alternatively, an adherent of his, or a group of his followers, that he looked in the book (*kitāb*) of ʿAlī/ or Fāṭima or Fāṭima's scroll (*ṣaḥīfa*), where the names of all the prophets and kings are mentioned and the name of Muḥammad b. ʿAbdallāh b. al-Ḥasan is not one of them.[76] *Kitāb* ʿAlī/Fāṭima or the *ṣaḥīfa* of Fāṭima were some of the written sources of the Imāms' knowledge.[77]

---

73 Al-Ṭabarī, 3:253–254 (l. 1 to l. 3); 254 (ll. 3–7); al-Iṣfahānī, *Maqātil*, 208 (a parallel tradition: al-Shaykh al-Mufīd, *al-Irshād*, 2:193, quoted by the editor of *Maqātil*, ibid., note); al-Kulaynī, *al-Kāfī*, 8:395. For other traditions in this vein, see al-Kulaynī, *al-Kāfī*, 1:358–360.

74 Al-Ṭabarī, 3:253–254 (l. 18 to l. 3).

75 Al-Iṣfahānī, *Maqātil*, 208 (ll. 7–11)]= al-Shaykh al-Mufīd, *al-Irshād*, 2:193]; al-Kulaynī, *al-Kāfī*, 8:395; al-Majlisī, *Biḥār*, 46:189.

76 1) Al-Ṣaffār, *Baṣāʾir*, 188–189, no. 1 [= al-Majlisī, *Biḥār*, 26:155]: Al-Muʿallā b. Khunays: Muḥammad b. ʿAbdallāh is not mentioned in *Kitāb ʿAlī* among the caliphs and kings of this nation; 2) al-Ṣaffār, *Baṣāʾir*, 189, no. 2 [= al-Majlisī, *Biḥār*, 26:155; 47:272]: from a group [of his followers]; 3) al-Ṣaffār, *Baṣāʾir*, 189, no. 4 [= al-Majlisī, *Biḥār*, 26:156]: al-Muʿallā b. Khunays: a book in his possession in which every prophet, designated heir (*waṣiyy*), and ruler (*malik*) is mentioned by name [= Ibn Bābawayh al-Qummī, *al-Imāma*, 51, no. 35); 4) al-Ṣaffār, *Baṣāʾir*, 189, no. 6 [= al-Majlisī, *Biḥār*, 26:156]; see also Moezzi, *Divine Guide*, 187 (n. 316).

77 Moezzi, *Divine Guide*, 73–74.

Another tradition, which combines some possibly authentic historical elements, was circulated:

> ʿAbd al-Malik b. Aʿyan said to Abū ʿAbdallāh [Jaʿfar al-Ṣādiq], peace be upon him: The Zaydiyya and the Muʿtazila already had approached Muḥammad b. ʿAbdallāh b. al-Ḥasan and came to him. Will he rule? And he said: By God I swear, I have in my possession two books in which are the names of every prophet and every king that will rule; no, by God I swear, Muḥammad b. ʿAbdallāh does not appear in either of these books.[78]

The last two traditions seem to have originated in the ʿAbbāsī period, mainly during al-Manṣūr's reign, when Muḥammad b. ʿAbdallāh was on the verge of mutiny, was termed al-Mahdī by his father and his followers, and became a threat not only to the ʿAbbāsīs, but also to the Imāmīs. Another tradition in the same vein is as follows:

4.2.1 The case of Yazīd b. Abī Ḥāzim and a man from al-Mughīriyya: The qā'im is the son of a captive/slave woman (ibn sabiyya)

This is a rare tradition which uses the well-known motif of the famous *ḥadīth* "the name of *al-mahdī* is like my name and that of his father is like my father,"[79] as a tool within the framework of the competition for rule between the Ḥasanīs and the Ḥusaynīs. The two factions are represented in this tradition by ʿAbdallāh b. al-Ḥasan and Jaʿfar al-Ṣādiq:

Akhbaranā Aḥmad b. Saʿīd < ʿAlī b. al-Ḥasan al-Taymalī [?] < Muḥammad wa Aḥmad ibnay al-Ḥasan < their father < Thaʿlaba b. Maymūn < Yazīd b. Abī Ḥāzim, who said:

He went [the story is told in first person] from al-Kūfa to Medina, went to Jaʿfar al-Ṣadiq who asked him if he was escorted by someone in his journey, he said yes, by a man from the Mughīriyya (رجل من المغيرية), who claimed (كان يزعم) that Muḥammad b. ʿAbdallāh b. al-Ḥasan is the *Qā'im*. The proof (*al-dalīl*) for this is that this is the name of the Prophet and his father's name is like the name of the father of the Prophet. I answered him that if you are dealing with names (إن كنت تأخذ بالأسماء), then he is from the descendants of al-Ḥusayn, that is, Muḥammad b. ʿAbdallāh b. ʿAlī [b. al-Ḥusayn b. ʿAlī b. Abī Ṭālib], but he [that is the man of the Mughīriyya] answered: this is the son of a slave woman (*ibn ama*), that is, Muḥammad b. ʿAbdallāh b. ʿAlī, and that one is *ibn mahīra*[80] that is, Muḥammad b. ʿAbdallāh b. al-Ḥasan b. al-Ḥasan.

---

78 Ibn Bābawayh al-Qummī, *al-Imāma*, 51, no. 36; al-Kulaynī, *al-Kāfī*, 1:242; al-Majlisī, *Biḥār*, 26:156.

79 On the tradition, see D. Cook, *Muslim Apocalyptic*, 140–141, but esp. Elad, "The *Ḥadīth* of *al-Mahdī*," 53–57.

80 That is, *ghāliyat al-mahr*: a free woman having a rich dowry (*Lisān al-ʿArab*, s.v. *m.h.r.*).

"Then Abū ʿAbdallāh (Jaʿfar al-Ṣādiq) said to me: and how did you respond to him and I said: I did not have any answer to refute him, so he said to me: Didn't you (plural form) know that he is the son of a captive woman, that is the *qāʾim*, peace be on Him": أو لم تعلم أنه إبن سبية يعني القائم.[81]

"*Al-Qāʾim* in Shīʿī terminology commonly denotes al-Mahdī."[82] This is not a common and widespread tradition. The term *ibn sabiyya* is not very common either. The scene depicted in the tradition occurred no later than 145/762, the year Muḥammad b. ʿAbdallāh died. The main points of the tradition are as follows:

1) Jaʿfar al-Ṣādiq (or whoever used his name) asserts that the mother of the *Qāʾim* [= al-Mahdī] is a female slave.
2) The *ḥadīth* "The name of al-Mahdī is like my name and his father's name is like my father" exists and serves as a tool of contention and strife between the Ḥasanīs and the Ḥusaynīs.
3) The followers of Muḥammad b. ʿAbdallāh (in this case a man from the Mughīriyya sect) regard this *ḥadīth* as confirming the Mahdīship of Muḥammad b. ʿAbdallāh.
4) A proposal (that may have existed) in favor of a Ḥusaynī Mahdī, that is Muḥammad b. ʿAbdallāh b. ʿAlī b. al-Ḥusayn, is rejected by Jaʿfar al-Ṣādiq,
5) Who gives the ultimate Ḥusaynī/Imāmī answer: "He is the son of a captive woman."

Does Jaʿfar al-Ṣādiq refer to a specific person? And if so does he refer to someone in his lifetime? The past? Or the future? His unequivocal answer takes the Ḥasanīs out of the race for the Mahdīship and of course the rule of the Muslim community. This seems to be the main objective of the tradition. But this raises the question of the substitute for the Ḥasanīs. If the past is our object, then it is well-known that the mother of Muḥammad b. ʿAlī b. Abī Ṭālib (Ibn al-Ḥanafiyya) was brought as a prisoner to Medina after the battle of ʿAqrabāʾ and came into ʿAlī's possession.[83]

It seems that the captive woman, the mother of the Mahdī, is identical to another mother who is mentioned in another tradition, allegedly related from ʿAlī b. Abī Ṭālib, who swore that the Mahdī is "the son of the chosen from among the slave women" (بأبي إبن خيرة الإماء).[84] When Muḥammad al-Bāqir (d. 117/735) was asked whether

81 Al-Nuʿmānī, *al-Ghayba*, 228–229; al-Majlisī, *Biḥār*, 51:42; al-Kawrānī, *Muʿjam*, 3:435.
82 W. Madelung, "Ḳāʾim Āl al-Bayt," *EI*²: Cook, *Muslim Apocalyptic*, 195.
83 F. Buhl, "Muḥammad Ibn al-Ḥanafiyya," *EI*²
84 Al-Ṭūsī, *al-Ghayba*, 470; al-Shaykh al-Mufīd, *Irshād*, 2:382; al-Nuʿmānī, *al-Ghayba*, 233; al-Majlisī, *Biḥār*, 51:36.

Fāṭima is meant by this phrase, he said no, she is the chosen from among the freeborn women (خيرة الحرائر).[85]

Another potential candidate for the Mahdīship whose mother was a captive woman was Zayd b. ʿAlī b. al-Ḥusayn, who rebelled against the Umawīs in 122/740. In all likelihood Zayd was called al-Mahdī by his followers,[86] but he was not regarded as the Mahdī by Jaʿfar al-Ṣādiq.[87] It is related that one of his (al-Ṣādiq's) followers came rejoicing, telling him that al-Ṣādiq's uncle, Zayd b. ʿAlī had rebelled. He informs al-Ṣādiq that Zayd claims: 1) that he is the son of a captive woman and therefore he is the *Qāʾim* of

85 Al-Nuʿmānī, *al-Ghayba*, 234, no. 9 [= al-Majlisī, *Biḥār*, 51:42].

86 Sharon, *Black Banners*, 179, n. 78; Duri, "*Fikra*," 125, but mainly Crone and Hinds, *God's Caliph*, 103 and the bibliography therein (Ibn ʿAbd Rabbihi, *al-ʿIqd al-farīd*, 4:483; al-Masʿūdī, *Murūj*, 4:43, no. 2222; al-Maqrīzī, *al-Nizāʿ wa-l-takhāṣum*, 5; al-Mubarrad, *al-Kāmil*, 710; Ibn ʿAsākir, *Tahdhīb* [*Taʾrīkh Madīnat Dimashq*], 4:426 [= Beirut edition, 15:134]); Duri quotes only al-Masʿūdī's *Murūj*, and Sharon quotes only al-Maqrīzī and the *Anonyme* (MS Leiden, fol. 3b); all the sources quoted by the authors, record **one** evidence, the verses of an Umawī poet, Ḥakīm b. ʿAyyāsh, known as al-Aʿwar al-Kalbī, boasting in front of the adherents of Zayd b. ʿAlī in al-Kūfa:

صلبنا لكم زيدًا على جذع نخلة ** ولم نرى مهديا على الجذع يُصلب
وقِسْتم بعثمان عليًا سفاهةً ** وعثمانُ خير من علي وأطيب

(We crucified Zayd for you on the trunk of a palm tree / and we have never seen a Messiah crucified on the trunk / You compared ʿAlī with ʿUthmān out of ignorance / while ʿUthmān is better than ʿAlī and worthier); the tradition in Ibn ʿAsākir's work is copied by Yāqūt, *al-Udabāʾ* (ed. Margoliouth), 10:248–249, in both sources the verses are recited by a man from al-Kūfa to ʿAbdallāh b. Jaʿfar al-Ṣādiq, but it seems that the correct name should be Jaʿfar al-Ṣādiq (Abū ʿAbdallāh) and not his son ʿAbdallāh, see Ibn Shahrāshūb, *Manāqib*, 3:360; al-Irbilī, *Kashf al-ghumma*, 2:421 [= al-Majlisī, *Biḥār*, 46:192; 47:136; 62:72]; Ibn Ḥajar, *al-Iṣāba* (Beirut, 1415 H.), 2:182; the last four sources: Abū ʿAbdallāh, or Jaʿfar al-Ṣādiq (most of the sources quote only the first verse). Cf. Madelung, "Mahdī," 1232, who argues that the supporters of Zayd b. ʿAlī in al-Kūfa "did not try to identify him with the Mahdī but with the Manṣūr," that is, argues Madelung, the Messiah of the southern tribes. Madelung relies on the tradition in al-Ṭabarī, 2:1676, related from Hishām b. Muḥammad al-Kalbī from Abū Mikhnaf "that the Shīʿa in al-Kūfa began to come repeatedly time after time to Zayd b. ʿAlī, telling him to come out in a rebellion saying: we hope that you would be al-Manṣūr (the victorious?) and that this will be the time in which Banū Umayya will perish." I follow Sharon, *Black Banners*, 179, n. 78, who translated the term *al-Manṣūr* in al-Ṭabarī as "the victorious," saying: "It is questionable whether the term *manṣūr* here has a messianic meaning"; and Hillenbrand, *al-Ṭabarī*, 13, n. 57: "the one to whom victory is given." It seems that the verses mentioned in this note strongly support the opinion of Sharon, Duri, Crone and Hinds, that Zayd b. ʿAlī was titled al-Mahdī by his supporters.

87 Muḥammad al-Bāqir strongly opposed Zayd's revolt, see Jafri, *Shīʿa*, 249, 251–253; and his son Jaʿfar followed suit, see ibid., 266–267; Gleave, "Jaʿfar al-Ṣādeq," 350.

this nation; and 2) he is the son of "the chosen from among the slave women": يزعم أنه ابن سبية وهو قائم هذه الأمة وإنه ابن خيرة الإماء. To this al-Ṣādiq comments briefly and dryly: "He is not what he says; if he will come out (rebels) he will be killed": ليس هو كما قال إن خرج قتل.[88]

The phrase "a captive slave woman," denoting the mother of the Imāmī *Qā'im*/*Mahdī* within the framework of the Imāmī-Zaydī struggle for legitimacy, may perhaps bear evidence of its early provenance, at least not much later than 122/740, when Zayd was executed and crucified.

In other traditions the captive female slave becomes a black female slave (*ama sawdā'*),[89] but mainly the phrase "the chosen from among the slave women": ابن خيرة الإماء becomes "the pure/the most excellent Nubian [that is, black] chosen from among the slave women": ابن خيرة الإماء النوبية الطيبة. The Imāmī scholars identified this Nubian slave woman as the mother of the ninth Imām, Muḥammad b. ʿAlī [al-Riḍā b. Mūsā b. Jaʿfar] al-Jawād (d. 220/835), whose mother was a Nubian slave woman.[90] It is noteworthy, in connection with this, that the mother of the seventh Imām, Mūsā b. Jaʿfar al-Ṣādiq, was called "the one who is purified from any sin or stain" (*al-miṣfāt*),[91] which, according to Imāmī sources was the epithet for Eve: "purified from any stain" (المصفاة من الدنس).[92] The mother of the eighth Imām, ʿAlī b. Mūsā l-Riḍā was a slave woman who was given the epithet "the pure" (*al-ṭāhira*) by her husband, Mūsā b. Jaʿfar.[93]

It seems that it is not a mere coincidence that the mothers of the seventh, eighth, and ninth Imāms are either identified with or connected to the tradition of the chosen slave woman mother of the Mahdī, but this topic merits a separate discussion.

5 Jaʿfar al-Ṣādiq during the Rebellion and his Attitude Towards it According to Mainly Imāmī Traditions

There are conflicting reports about Jaʿfar al-Ṣādiq on the eve of the outbreak of the revolt.

---

88 Al-Nuʿmānī, *al-Ghayba*, 229, no. 10 [= al-Khū'ī, *Rijāl*, 8:363].

89 Al-Nuʿmānī, *al-Ghayba*, 228, no. 8.

90 Al-Qummī, *al-Anwār al-bahiyya*, 249; al-Shaykh al-Mufīd, *al-Irshād*, 2:276; al-Ṭabarsī, *Iʿlām*, 2:92.

91 Kohlberg, "Mūsā al-Kāẓim," 645a; for example, see Ibn Shahrāshūb, *Manāqib*, 3:437; al-Baḥrānī, *Madīnat al-maʿājiz*, 7:7, 9; al-Majlisī, *Biḥār*, 48:1, 6.

92 Ibn Ṭā'ūs, *al-Iqbāl bi-l-aʿmāl*, 3:244; al-Majlisī, *Biḥār*, 95:401.

93 Al-Baḥrānī, *Madīnat al-maʿājiz*, 7:7, 9; al-Majlisī, *Biḥār*, 49:5.

1) According to some reports transmitted by and through Imāmī transmitters, on the night of the outbreak of the rebellion Jaʿfar left Medina and withdrew to his estate al-Ṭayyiba. One chain of transmitters is worthy of mention: ʿĪsā b. ʿAbdallāh b. Muḥammad b. ʿUmar b. ʿAlī b. Abī Ṭālib < his mother Umm Ḥusayn bt. ʿAbdallāh b. Muḥammad [al-Bāqir] b. ʿAlī b. al-Ḥusayn b. ʿAlī b. Abī Ṭālib who relates an alleged eyewitness report from her uncle, Jaʿfar al-Ṣādiq:

On that night Jaʿfar orders [someone] to bring him his chest ["basket": *safaṭ*], where the flag of the Prophet (*al-ʿuqāb*) was deposited, [he] takes out 200 *dīnār*s which were put there by his grandfather, ʿAlī b. al-Ḥusayn, received from [the selling? revenues of] ʿAmūdān. Jaʿfar adds that he was keeping this sum of money for "this event that happened tonight in Medina, so he took it and went away, and the money served for his maintenance in [his estate] Ṭayyiba."[94]

The *safaṭ* was in the exclusive possession of the Ḥusaynīs. As already noted, the Ḥasanī side in this strife between the families hardly appears on its own, we learn about it mainly from the debate in the Imāmī sources. One such rare tradition claims that Muḥammad b. ʿAbdallāh received the *safaṭ* (the basket) from Fāṭima bt. ʿAlī b. Abī Ṭālib, who received it from her brother al-Ḥusayn, without knowing what was inside it.[95] This is a rare tradition that managed to survive despite the dominant Imāmī

94 Al-Ṣaffār, *Baṣāʾir*, 195, no. 3 (and the parallels in al-Majlisī, *Biḥār*, 26:204 and al-Rāwandī, *al-Kharāʾij*, 2:770): وكانت نفقته بطيبة; the *isnād*: Aḥmad b. al-Ḥusayn < his father < Ẓarīf b. Nāfiʿ; according to this tradition, ʿAlī b. al-Ḥusayn gained this sum from the selling[?] of ʿAmūdān: عزلها علي بن الحسين عليهما السلام عن ثمن عمودان (in other variants: رفعها/ دفعها); a short version of the tradition, al-Ṣaffār, *Baṣāʾir*, 201, no. 26: from … al-Ḥasan b. Ẓarīf < his father < al-Ḥasan b. Zayd: Jaʿfar takes out 100 (instead of 200) *dīnār*s. The text is simpler than the first one: he takes out the money in order to spend it in al-ʿAmūdān (لينفقها لعمودان) [a parallel text: al-Majlisī, *Biḥār*, 26:216: لينفقها بعمودان]; see also another parallel tradition, al-Ṣaffār, *Baṣāʾir*, 207, no. 50: from ʿĪsā b. ʿAbdallāh [b. Muḥammad b. ʿUmar b. ʿAlī b. Abī Ṭālib] < his mother [whose uncle was Jaʿfar al-Ṣādiq] [= al-Majlisī, *Biḥār*, 26:215–216]: Jaʿfar takes out the money that his father[!] not his grandfather, ʿAlī b. al-Ḥusayn received from selling ʿAmūdān. I was unable to locate ʿAmūdān. Al-Majlisī, ibid., 26:204, assumed that this is the name of his estate but does not give its location; al-Ṭayyiba was an estate of Jaʿfar al-Ṣādiq (most probably of his family), see al-Ṣaffār, *Baṣāʾir*, 254 (no. 3): from Muʿattab, the *mawlā* of Jaʿfar al-Ṣādiq: "I went with Abū ʿAbdallāh [that is, Jaʿfar al-Ṣādiq], peace be upon him, to an estate of his called Ṭayyiba"; see also the comment of al-Majlisī, *Biḥār*, 26:204–205.

95 Al-Iṣfahānī, *Maqātil*, 241; Cook, *Muslim Apocalyptic*, 216 [quoting al-Iṣfahānī and al-Majlisī, 45:82: an irrelevant/erroneous quote]: "a *safaṭ* (a "basket") of knowledge (or "a basket of books") supposedly left for him [that is, for Muḥammad b. ʿAbdallāh] from the latter" [that is al-Ḥusayn b. ʿAlī]; but we do not learn all this from the text of the tradition, 1) al-Ḥusayn did not leave the *safaṭ* to Muḥammad b. ʿAbdallāh, it was given to him by al-Ḥusayn's daughter; 2) the contents of the *safaṭ* is not mentioned in this tradition.

view according to which it was in the possession of Jaʿfar al-Ṣādiq. According to these traditions he was well aware of the contents of this *safaṭ*.

2) The above mentioned Umm Ḥusayn relates to her son, ʿĪsā b. ʿAbdallāh, that when she asked her uncle Jaʿfar al-Ṣādiq for his opinion about the rebellion of Muḥammad b. ʿAbdallāh, he said to her:

> this is a *fitna* (that is, an abominable war between brothers of the faith);[96] Muḥammad will be killed near a Byzantine house (*bayt rūmī*) and his brother from both his mother and father will be killed in al-ʿIrāq while the hooves of his horse were in the water.[97]

3) A very long, extremely interesting tradition[98] is recorded (except for a short part with a few lines) by Mūsā b. ʿAbdallāh b. al-Ḥasan, the brother of Muḥammad al-Nafs al-Zakiyya, who relates in the first person and in a very detailed manner the events that occurred in Medina after the outbreak of the revolt and the short period of Muḥammad's sovereignty in Medina. A short part of the tradition is related by Khadīja bt. ʿUmar b. Muḥammad (al-Bāqir) b. ʿAlī b. al-Ḥusayn b. ʿAlī b. Abī Ṭālib. The long tradition was transmitted by Mūsā b. ʿAbdallāh al-Ḥasanī to ʿAbdallāh b. Ibrāhīm b. Muḥammad [b. ʿAlī b. ʿAbdallāh b. Jaʿfar b. Abī Ṭālib?]. The tradition records the rift that occurred between the Ḥasanīs and the Ḥusaynīs following the rebellion of Muḥammad al-Nafs al-Zakiyya. Like other traditions in this vein, the two main representatives of the families are ʿAbdallāh b. al-Ḥasan and Jaʿfar al-Ṣādiq, but the central figure in the long tradition is Jaʿfar al-Ṣādiq (and to some extent also his father), and the events, plot, and scenes depicted in the tradition are woven around him in order to emphasize his supernatural character, mainly his and his father's ability to foresee the future, to distinguish truth from falsehood, due to their preeminent knowledge (*ʿilm*). This trait, which distinguishes Jaʿfar, and marks him as the true Imām, is the main

96 *Fitna* is often used to refer to civil war, disagreement, and division in Islam and specifically alludes to a time involving trials of faith.

97 Al-Iṣfahānī, *Maqātil*, 248: Umar b. Shabba < ʿĪsā b. ʿAbdallāh, his mother Umm Ḥusayn: قالت قلت لعمي جعفر بن محمد; al-Ṭabarī, 3:253–254: instead of ʿUmar b. Shabba: *ḥaddathanī*; ibid., his *fitna* (*fitnatuhu*) instead of *fitna;* cf. the edition of Abū l-Faḍl Ibrāhīm, 7:600, n. 6: in MS ت: *fitna;* Ibn al-Athīr, *al-Kāmil* (Beirut edition), 5:553: *fitna;* I was unable to locate the "Byzantine house"; McAuliffe, *ʿAbbāsid Authority*, 218, n. 1028 and Nagel, "Muḥammad b. ʿAbdallāh," 261: mentioning the tradition with no identification; for the horses' hooves, see McAuliffe, *ʿAbbāsid Authority*, 218, n. 1029, my translation of this text is slightly different from hers.

98 Al-Kulaynī, *al-Kāfī*, 1:358–366; this tradition was copied from *al-Kāfī* by several Imāmī authors, e.g., al-Baḥrānī, *Madīnat al-maʿājiz*, 5:276–290; al-Māzandrānī, *Sharḥ*, 312–318, and the commentary of the editor, 318–326; al-Majlisī, *Biḥār*, 47:278–287.

motif of the tradition. It was created after the rebellion and its aim was to emphasize the *quʿūd* policy of Jaʿfar al-Ṣādiq, that is, his rejection of any sort of participation in the rebellion.

It begins when the narrator records an alleged discussion between ʿAbdallāh b. al-Ḥasan and Jaʿfar al-Ṣādiq, when the latter categorically refuses to swear allegiance to ʿAbdallāh's son, Muḥammad al-Nafs al-Zakiyya. The discussion becomes fierce and turns to the question of legitimacy: who is better, that is, worthy to rule, the Ḥasanīs or the Ḥusaynīs. Then Jaʿfar al-Ṣādiq categorically denies the right of Banū l-Ḥasan through the ages (from al-Ḥasan b. ʿAlī to ʿAbdallāh b. al-Ḥasan) to the *imāma* and tells the latter that he and his family (the Ḥasanīs) as well as his son, Muḥammad b. ʿAbdallāh, will be killed.[99] The main recurrent motif, the secret knowledge of Jaʿfar (and his father before him) is exploited in the tradition to totally denounce the revolt of al-Nafs al-Zakiyya. Jaʿfar repeatedly stresses Muḥammad al-Nafs al-Zakiyya's death.

This tradition has some outstanding features in regard to Jaʿfar al-Ṣādiq's attitude: his resistance is indeed passive, but here, in this tradition, another element is added, that is, a public verbal objection; his attitude towards Muḥammad b. ʿAbdallāh and his rebellion is unequivocally contemptuous: "He is the squint-eyed one with the curled locks at his forehead, the black man, who will be killed on the threshold of (the quarter of Banū) Ashjaʿ between its residential courts."[100] Jaʿfar is described as standing at the gate of the mosque preaching to the people of Medina: "May God curse you (repeating this three times). This is not what you have obligated yourselves to the Messenger of God—may God bless him and his family—for nor did you swear allegiance to him on these terms." Then he withdrew to his residence for twenty days.[101]

In a heated meeting between Muḥammad al-Nafs al-Zakiyya accompanied by his loyal supporter ʿĪsā b. Zayd b. ʿAlī b. al-Ḥusayn, the two order Jaʿfar al-Ṣādiq to swear allegiance to al-Nafs al-Zakiyya. As the discussion turns into a bitter emotional confrontation, Jaʿfar al-Ṣādiq relates in minute detail the circumstances of the killing of al-Nafs al-Zakiyya: when, how, and where Muḥammad and his supporters will be killed by the ʿAbbāsī troops.[102]

This confrontation ends with the imprisonment of Jaʿfar al-Ṣādiq, and the confiscation of his estates (property?) and the property (estates) that belonged to those family

99 The fierce discussion: al-Kulaynī, *al-Kāfī*, 1:359–361; al-Māzandrānī, *Sharḥ*, 313–314; al-Majlisī, *Biḥār*, 47:281–282.

100 Al-Kulaynī, *al-Kāfī*, 1:360; al-Baḥrānī, *Madīnat al-maʿājiz*, 5:279; al-Majlisī, *Biḥār*, 47:281: فإنه الأحول الأكشف والأخضر المقتول بسدة أشجع بين دورها عند بطن مسيلها; these terms are defined by the commentators as contemptuous towards the Arabs.

101 Cursing the Medinese and withdrawing to his house: Al-Kulaynī, *al-Kāfī*, 1:361, and the parallel traditions in the sources quoted in the preceding note.

102 ʿĪsā b. Zayd and Jaʿfar al-Ṣādiq: Al-Kulaynī, *al-Kāfī*, 1:362–363; al-Majlisī, *Biḥār*, 47:283–285.

members of Jaʿfar who did not join the rebellion. When Muḥammad b. ʿAbdallāh orders Jaʿfar's imprisonment, he is reminded that the city prison is ruined and does not have locks, so he is put under house arrest in "Dār al-Makhba'" which is, adds the narrator, Dār Rayṭa today.[103]

These descriptions are historically important and seem to reflect the real course of events, e.g., the specific details of the location of the battle, its course, the names of commanders, the location of the place where Muḥammad al-Nafs al-Zakiyya was killed, the description of the commander that killed him, the location of the house arrest of Jaʿfar al-Ṣādiq—all these seem to have a strong basis of authenticity and reality since they are cited in order to emphasize the esoteric knowledge and the supernatural traits of Jaʿfar al-Ṣādiq and his father before him. This is the purpose of the sub-story in this long narration about Ismāʿīl b. ʿAbdallāh b. Jaʿfar b. Abī Ṭālib, in which the exact details and circumstances of his death was foretold already in the Umawī period by Jaʿfar's father Muḥammad al-Bāqir,

> when you will be summoned to the false matter [that is, the rebellion against the ʿAbbāsīs] and refused (to join) it, and when you looked at the squint-eyed (*al-aḥwal*) the inauspicious (*al-mash'ūm*) whose origin is traced back (*yantamī*) to al-Ḥasan's family on the *minbar* of the Prophet—may Allāh pray for him and his family and grant them peace—summoning (the people) to swear allegiance to him, who was called by a name that is not his name [that is, al-Mahdī], renew your will, for you will be killed on that day or the next.

Ismāʿīl refused al-Nafs al-Zakiyya's demand to join his cause and swear allegiance to him. Because of this strong resistance to the revolt he was brutally murdered (trampled) by his nephews [members of his brother's family?: حتى دخل عليه بنو أخيه بنو معاوية بن عبد الله بن جعفر فتوطؤوه.[104] After his murder Jaʿfar al-Ṣādiq was released from his house arrest.[105]

In order to convince his reader that Jaʿfar al-Ṣādiq is the true Imām, the transmitter describes the real events, adds many large and small details so that the reader, who lived during the actual events and after they had occurred and knows the real course of

103 Jaʿfar's imprisonment and the confiscation of his estates/property: Al-Kulaynī, *al-Kāfī*, 1:362– 363; al-Baḥrānī, *Madīnat al-maʿājiz*, 5:285–286; al-Māzandrānī, *Sharḥ*, 6:316; al-Majlisī, *Biḥār*, 47:284–285; al-Majlisī, *Biḥār*, 47:292, suggests that Rayṭa is the daughter of ʿAbdallāh b. Muḥammad b. al-Ḥanafiyya.

104 Al-Kulaynī, *al-Kāfī*, 1:364; Ibn Ḥamza al-Ṭūsī, *al-Thāqib*, 381–382; al-Baḥrānī, *Madīnat al-maʿājiz*, 5:93–94, 286–287; al-Majlisī, *Biḥār*, 47:285–286 (all three sources copy al-Kulaynī).

105 Al-Kulaynī, *al-Kāfī*, 1:364, and the verbatim parallels in the preceding note.

the events, would believe in the esoteric knowledge of Jaʿfar and would recognize him as the true Imām. This method is similar to that used in the apocalyptic traditions. The unequivocal conclusion of the narrator (the Ḥasanī Mūsā b. ʿAbdallāh) is to acknowledge Jaʿfar al-Ṣādiq's (and his family's) superiority over all other families. He is the true Imām of the Muslim community.

The main topic of the tradition reminds us of many other traditions that emphasize the better judgment of Jaʿfar al-Ṣādiq, due to his esoteric knowledge. It certainly brings to mind some versions of the al-Abwāʾ tradition. But this tradition is much longer and more detailed than the known traditions about the meeting in al-Abwāʾ recorded mainly by al-Iṣfahānī in *Maqātil al-ṭālibiyyīn*.

6 Did Jaʿfar Regard Himself, or was he Regarded by his Adherents, as the Mahdī?

When discussing the universal signs for the Mahdī's return, Moezzi says:

> One of them is [no. 4 in his list] [...] the assassination of the Pure Soul (قتل النفس الزكية); might this be, as some have believed, the assassination of the Ḥasanid Muḥammad b. ʿAbd Allāh, who is called al-Nafs al-Zakiyya, killed in 145/762.... Did the imams foresee the return as being imminent? This is not probable, especially since in some traditions al-Nafs al-Zakiyya is not spoken of, but merely al-Nafs [that is, وقتل النفس A.E].[106]

But it seems that this is a single case (most probably a copyist's error) whereas all the other traditions that I came across have: وقتل النفس الزكية.[107]

106 Moezzi, *Divine Guide*, 118.

107 Ibid., n. 636, quoting one source: al-Nuʿmānī, *Kitāb al-ghayba*, 266 that mentions وقتل النفس instead of وقتل النفس الزكية ; in all **seven other traditions** that are recorded by al-Nuʿmānī, the phrase وقتل النفس الزكية appears (ibid., *Bāb* 15: 261, no. 9; 262, no. 11; 265, no. 15; 266, no. 16; 269, no. 21; 272, no. 26; *Bāb* 16: 301, no. 6; for other examples, see al-Shaykh al-Mufīd, *Irshād*, 2:371; al-Ṭūsī, *al-Ghayba*, 435, 437; Ibn Bābawayh al-Qummī, *al-Imāma*, 128; Ibn Bābawayh al-Qummī, *al-Khiṣāl*, 303; al-Kulaynī, *al-Kāfī*, 8:310; al-Ḥillī, *al-Mustajād*, 258; al-Rāwandī, *al-Kharāʾij*, 3:1161, 1162; al-Majlisī, *Biḥār*, 52:203, 204, 206 (quoting *al-Ikmāl* of Ibn Bābawayh Muḥammad al-Qummī); 209, 289 (quoting al-Ṭūsī's *Ghayba*); 119, 233, 235, 294 (quoting al-Nuʿmānī's *Ghayba*); 234 (quoting al-Nuʿmānī's *Ghayba*: النفس, instead of النفس الزكية); 304 (quoting al-Kulaynī's *al-Kāfī*). Note that on

D. Cook has recently observed that according to a well-known Imāmī tradition, related through Jaʿfar al-Ṣādiq, only fifteen nights will pass between the rising of the *qā'im* from the family of the Prophet and the killing of al-Nafs al-Zakiyya: ليس بين قيام قائم آل محمد و بين قتل النفس الزكية إلا خمسة عشر ليلة.[108] Cook maintains that this tradition may indicate that

> Jaʿfar al-Ṣādiq must have entertained messianic hopes for himself, since he was the only Imām who could have benefited from this extremely limited period of time.... If this analysis is correct [adds Cook], then precisely at the time when Muḥammad al-Nafs al-Zakiyya revolted the *Imāmī* Shīʿīs were feeling a strong messianic pull, despite the quietist outlook of their imām.[109]

Cook may be correct in assuming that Jaʿfar al-Ṣādiq is the source of the tradition,[110] but it could also have been one of his close contemporary followers.

Moezzi, as seen above, argued against this view.[111] It seems, however, that it is an Imāmī tradition that may reflect the view at the time of Jaʿfar al-Ṣādiq and/or his close followers.

7 Jaʿfar al-Ṣādiq and the ʿAbbāsīs

The accepted view among scholars is that Jaʿfar al-Ṣādiq "appears to have maintained the politically quietist stance of his father, Imam Moḥammed al-Bāqer,"[112] and that

273 [= al-Majlisī, *Biḥār*, 52:273 and 53:82]: وقتل النفس الزكية بظهر الكوفة في سبعين, but it seems that this is a different matter, not connected to al-Ṣādiq's previous traditions. It is related from ʿAlī b. Abī Ṭālib concerning future events mainly in al-Kūfa, but also in Medina and other places.

108 Ibn Bābawayh, *Kamāl (Ikmāl) al-Dīn*, 649; al-Ṭūsī, *al-Ghayba*, 445; al-Majlisī, *Biḥār*, 52:203; al-Ṭabarsī, *Iʿlām*, 2:281.

109 Cook, *Muslim Apocalyptic*, 219.

110 Ibid.

111 Moezzi, *Divine Guide*, 118 and n. 636 on 224: "It was not the imams, and especially not Jaʿfar, who were responsible for the majority of the traditions about 'the assassination of the Pure Soul' that placed the coming of the *Qā'im* just after the revolt of the Shīʿite insurgent. On the contrary, it was the insurgent who seems to have attempted to exploit facts concerning the 'signs of Return' that had been circulating for a long time among the Muslims; he did so in the hope of passing himself off as the precursor of the Mahdī, if not the Mahdī himself...."

112 Gleave, "Jaʿfar al-Ṣādeq," 350; see also Jafri, *Shīʿa*, 249, 251, 253 (al-Bāqir's quiescent policy); Hodgson, "Djaʿfar al-Ṣādiḳ," 374; idem, "The Early Shīʿa," 10–11: according to Hodgson,

> Just as he had refused to be involved in the uprisings of Zayd or the ʿAbbāsids against Umayyad rule, Jaʿfar al-Ṣādeq offered no support to the uprising of his own cousin Muḥammad b. ʿAbd-Allāh b. Ḥasan, called al-Nafs al-Zakiyya (the Pure Soul) and referred to as al-Mahdī ... in 145/762.[113]

Some scholars even argue that Caliph al-Manṣūr maintained good relations with Jaʿfar al-Ṣādiq:

> Once the ʿAbbasids emerged as the victors in the Hashemite revolution, Jaʿfar showed no signs of opposition to the new regime and visited the second ʿAbbasid caliph, Abu Jaʿfar ʿAbd Allah ibn Muhammad al-Mansur (754–75) in Iraq. Mansur ... was ruthless in his violent treatment of the ʿAlids in general. Yet his relations with Jaʿfar al-Sadiq were good. He solicited Jaʿfar's legal advice and reportedly restored the tomb of ʿAli in Najaf at his request. Furthermore, Mansur retained some of Jaʿfar's important followers in his service thus creating a permanent niche for an Imami office-holding aristocracy within the ʿAbbasid state.[114]

"Jaʿfar even named the Caliph al-Manṣūr an executor of his will." These assertions are far from being unequivocal.[115]

---

this doctrine was introduced by Muḥammad al-Bāqir and was well developed in Jaʿfar al-Ṣādiq's life; Omar, *ʿAbbāsid Caliphate*, 182, n. 169, and esp. 246–248, discussing the passive policy of Jaʿfar al-Ṣādiq as part of his analysis of what he calls "the Ḥasanī Zaydī" revolt of Muḥammad and Ibrāhīm; Madelung, "A Treatise," 18: "The Imams from the fourth, ʿAlī Zayn al-ʿĀbidīn, had ceased activity to seek the rule through the overthrow of the usurpatory caliphate. The sixth Imam, Jaʿfar al-Ṣādiq, rejected in particular any offer or help to restore him to his rightful position by force and strictly forbade his followers to engage in revolutionary activity on behalf of the Imams until the rise of the Qāʾim Imam who would claim his right to rule with the sword"; and see also, Kennedy, *Prophet*, 133; van Ess, *Theologie*, 1:274ff.

113 Gleave, "Jaʿfar al-Ṣādeq," 350; Jafri, *Shīʿa*, 267, 275–283; see also Omar, "Aspects," 172; Arjomand, "The Crisis of the Imamate," 492; Moezzi, *Divine Guide*, 65: "He had the same negative, passive attitude toward the Zaydī Shīʿite insurgents led by [h]is paternal uncle Zayd b. ʿAlī in 122/740 and by his cousin Yaḥyā b. Zayd in 125/743, and finally in 145/762 by the Ḥasanid Shīʿite al-Nafs al-Zakiyya and his brother Ibrāhīm."

114 Arjomand, "The Crisis of the Imamate," 492 [in Kohlberg = 110], and n. 4 on page 509 [in Kohlberg = 127]; and see also Omar, "Aspects," arguing in this vein.

115 Arjomand, "The Crisis of the Imamate," 492 [in Kohlberg = 110], and n. 11 on 510 [in Kohlberg = 128], quoting a tradition related by Abū Jaʿfar Muḥammad b. al-Ḥasan al-Ṭūsī, *Kitāb al-ghayba* (Najaf, 1965), 119, 255. This tradition was (originally?) recorded by al-Kulaynī, *al-Kāfī*, 1:310 (no. 13), who quotes Abū Ayyūb al-Naḥawī [read al-Khūzī, according to al-Ṭūṣī's *Ghayba*; this is the well-known *kātib* of al-Manṣūr, Abū Ayyūb

While Hodgson claims in this vein that "At the time of the Shīʿī revolt of Muḥammad al-Nafs al-Zakiyya in the Hijāz (145/762), he was again neutral, leading the Ḥusaynids in their passivity in that largely Ḥasanid affair, and was left in peace by al-Manṣūr. . . ."[116] Omar argues that "it was this peaceful disposition of al-Ṣādiq and his lack of interest in the politics of the time that enabled him to live on comparatively good terms with the Caliph al-Manṣūr. . . . It was al-Manṣūr who gave Ǧaʿfar the title of al-Ṣādiq."[117] "Al-Manṣūr was pleased to have him in Madīna as a deterrent to militant ʿAlids and

al-Mūriyānī, also nicknamed al-Khūzī (after Khūzistān)]; Abū Ayyūb relates in the first person that one night he was summoned to the caliph, who was crying, with a letter in his hand. al-Manṣūr told Abū Ayyūb that the letter is from Muḥammad b. Sulaymān [his cousin], the governor of Medina, reporting the death of Jaʿfar al-Ṣādiq. After praising Jaʿfar, the caliph orders Abū Ayyūb to write a letter to the governor that if in his will Jaʿfar had appointed a specific heir whom he preferred, then he (the governor) should kill him. The governor's answer was that Jaʿfar appointed five people in his will, al-Manṣūr himself, Muḥammad b. Sulaymān (the ʿAbbāsī governor), ʿAbdallāh and Mūsā, Jaʿfar's sons, and Ḥumayda, Jaʿfar's wife. The response of al-Manṣūr was: there is no possible way to kill those (people mentioned): وروى أبو أيوب النحوي[= الخوزي] قال: بعث إلي ابو جعفر المنصور في جوف الليل فدخلت عليه...وفي يده كتاب...وهو يبكي وقال هذا كتاب محمد بن سليمان يخبرنا أن جعفر ابن محمد قد مات فإنا لله وإنا إليه لراجعون ثلاثا وأين مثل جعفر؟ ثم قال لي أكتب... إن كان قد أوصى إلى رجل بعينه فقدمه واضرب عنقه. قال فرجع الجواب إليه أنه قد أوصى إلى خمسة, أحدهم أبو جعفر المنصور ومحمد بن سليمان وعبد الله وموسى ابني جعفر وحميدة. فقال المنصور: ليس إلى قتل هؤلاء سبيل; for a parallel tradition, see ibid., no. 14: instead of Ḥumayda: an unnamed *mawlā* of Jaʿfar al-Ṣādiq is mentioned; see also al-Amīn, *Aʿyān al-Shīʿa*, 1:677: Abū Ayyūb الجوزي instead of الخوزي; several late Imāmī authors, relying on al-Kulaynī's version (النحوي), tried in vain to discover any information about "Abū Ayyūb al-Naḥawī," for example, see al-Tustarī, *Rijāl*, 11:218; al-Jawāhirī, *Rijāl*, 685; al-Khūʾī, *Rijāl*, 22:44.

116 Hodgson, "Djaʿfar al-Ṣādiḳ," 374.

117 Omar, "Aspects," 172–173. As evidence Omar relies on the letter from al-Manṣūr to Muḥammad b. ʿAbdallāh where the latter is praised by the caliph; the epithet "al-Ṣādiq": according to al-Iṣfahānī, *Maqātil*, 256: "When Abū Jaʿfar became caliph he named Jaʿfar "al-Ṣādiq" [that is "one who speaks the truth"]; this tradition comes immediately after one version of the traditions on the al-Abwāʾ meeting (Ibn Dāja's), where Jaʿfar al-Ṣādiq boldly claims that the rule will not pass to the hands of the Ḥasanīs but to the ʿAbbāsīs: al-Saffāḥ, al-Manṣūr, and then to al-Manṣūr's son. It is not possible to accept this tradition at its face value; cf. Nagel, "Muḥammad b. ʿAbdallāh," 261: Jaʿfar al-Ṣādiq was an intimate associate of al-Manṣūr who named him "al-Ṣādiq." For other explanations of the epithet (*laqab*) al-Ṣādiq in Imāmī sources, for example, see Ibn Sharāshūb, *Manāqib*, 3:393–394; al-Majlisī, *Biḥār*, 47:33.

consequently to weaken the ʿAlid revolutionary front. The Caliph even used to consult al-Ṣādiq on legal questions as well as the political condition in the Ḥiǧāz."[118]

The Imāmī traditions expand and elaborate on this theme and bring it to perfection when describing the great esteem and admiration of al-Manṣūr towards Jaʿfar al-Ṣādiq. These traditions, however, without any doubt are not authentic. Two examples will suffice:

1) One such tradition is of special interest since it is related by one of the most important dignitaries in Hārūn al-Rashīd's court, Jaʿfar b. Muḥammad b. al-Ashʿath al-Khuzāʿī. His father (d. 149/766 or 777) was one of the deputy *naqīb*s of the ʿAbbāsī revolution and was appointed to important military and administrative posts by the first two ʿAbbāsī caliphs. His son Jaʿfar, as a member of the elite social stratum, *al-Abnā*ʾ (that is, *Abnā*ʾ *Ahl Khurāsān*) was head of the caliph's *shurṭa*, the head of *dīwān al-khātam*, and later (in 173 [?]/789 or 790)[119] was appointed as the governor of Khurāsān. However, Jaʿfar b. Muḥammad al-Khuzāʿī was at the same time one of the followers of Jaʿfar al-Ṣādiq. The possibility that one of the most important dignitaries in the ʿAbbāsī court who belonged to the innermost circle of the *Abnā*ʾ whose fathers established the ʿAbbāsī caliphate ["one of the Mayflower"], was an Imāmī Shīʿī has an important bearing on the religious-social infrastructure of the early ʿAbbāsī caliphate. We have a few examples of other important dignitaries of the *Abnā*ʾ who were followers of the Imāmī Shīʿa,[120] but this topic deserves a special, separate study. Returning to the Imāmī tradition, Jaʿfar b. Muḥammad b. al-Ashʿath asks Ṣafwān b. Yaḥyā l-Bajalī (d. 210/825 or 826)[121] "Do you know what caused us to enter into this matter (that is, to accept the Imāmī dogma) and to acknowledge it?" Abū l-Dawānīq (Caliph al-Manṣūr)[122] called his father and asked him to choose a reliable man for an espionage mission. His father chose his

118 Omar, "Aspects," 173 (no evidence is provided for these assertions).

119 Al-Ṭabarī, 3:609: year 173 H., Jaʿfar b. Muḥammad is dismissed from his governorship; in 171/787 or 788 he is still in Baghdad, in charge of the *dīwān al-khātam*, ibid., 3:605–606.

120 E.g., ʿAlī b. Yaqṭīn and his family, on him, see Elad, "Wāsiṭ"; and the case of Abū ʿAwn ʿAbd al-Malik b. Yazīd al-Azdī (al-Ṭabarī, 3:537 [= Ibn ʿAsākir, *Taʾrīkh*, 37:180–181]). The text is quoted and discussed by Zaman, *Religion and Politics*, 47–48; Crone, *Political Thought*, 90–91; and see Elad, "Abū ʿAwn." Abū ʿAwn was one of the twelve (or twenty) deputy *naqīb*s (نظراء النقباء), see *Akhbār al-ʿAbbās*, 219–220; and for the ʿAbbāsī *naqīb*, al-Qāsim b. Mujāshiʿ, see Crone, *Islamic Thought*, 90.

121 A well-known Imāmī scholar, on him, see al-Ḥillī, *Rijāl*, 111; Ibn al-Nadīm, *Fihrist* (ed. Tajaddud), 278; al-Baghdādī, *Hadiyyat al-ʿārifīn*, 1:427; Kaḥḥāla, *Muʿjam*, 5:20; Kohlberg, *Ibn Ṭāwūs*, 228; Modarressi, *Tradition*, index.

122 An epithet of scorn which means the father of the (small) coins, alluding to the stinginess of Caliph al-Manṣūr; the more common name of al-Manṣūr in the Imāmī literature was al-Dawānīqī.

uncle from his mother's side for the mission. He was sent to Medina, pretending to be a messenger from Khurāsān who came to distribute money that was collected for the Medinese by their Shīʿa faction in Khurāsān. The Medinese were asked to acknowledge the receipt of the money by signing, so all signed except Jaʿfar al-Ṣadiq, who perceived the true identity of the messenger, and even disclosed to him the exact wording of the conversation between the messenger and Caliph al-Manṣūr. Upon hearing this from his messenger, the caliph said: "Know, that there is no prophethood among the people of the family of the Prophet, except that among them is a *muḥaddath*, and indeed Jaʿfar b. Muḥammad is a *muḥaddath* today" (*al-yawm*, that is, this time?). This (event) (says Jaʿfar b. Muḥammad b. al-Ashʿath, the transmitter of the tradition) was the right indication [to become a follower of Jaʿfar al-Ṣādiq].[123]

The tradition combines some elements that we have already encountered in previous traditions of this kind. Its ultimate aim though is to demonstrate Jaʿfar al-Ṣādiq's supernatural knowledge and to give him semi-official recognition by al-Manṣūr as a *muḥaddath*, that is, "those to whom an angel speaks," a term that establishes the "special position of the Imām as receiving knowledge in a manner denied to ordinary mortals."[124] A common method used in the Sunnī as well as the Imāmī *ḥadīth* literature involves one being praised by his enemy. Al-Manṣūr acknowledges that Jaʿfar al-Ṣādiq is a *muḥaddath*.

2) On another occasion, al-Manṣūr acknowledges that the Mahdī will be from the descendants of Fāṭima. To the "astonishment" of the listener and transmitter (an Imāmī scholar, Sayf b. ʿUmayra), al-Manṣūr says that if he had not heard it from Abū Jaʿfar Muḥammad b. ʿAlī [al-Bāqir] personally, and it had not been related to him by

---

123 Al-Ṣaffār, *Baṣāʾir*, 265–266; al-Kulaynī, *al-Kāfī*, 1:476; al-Rāwandī, *al-Kharāʾij wa-l-jarāʾiḥ*, 2:720–721, no. 25; Ibn Shahrāshūb, *Manāqib*, 3:348; Ibn Ḥamza al-Ṭūsī, *al-Thāqib fī l-manāqib*, 406; al-Majlisī, *Biḥār*, 48:207. See also al-Shaykh al-Mufīd, *al-Irshād*, 2:237; al-Ṭūsī, *al-Ghayba*, 27; Ibn Ṭāʾūs, *al-ʿAmal al-mashrūʿ*, 288, records that Jaʿfar al-Ṣādiq gave Muḥammad b. al-Ashʿath [sic! read Jaʿfar b. Muḥammad b. al-Ashʿath, see two parallel traditions in al-Majlisī, *Biḥār*, 87:89 and 91:43] an epistle (*kitāb*) containing supplications and prayers (دعاء والصلاة) for the Prophet; see also al-Kūrānī, *Muʿjam*, 4:115 for another parallel; al-Shabastarī, *al-Imām al-Ṣādiq*, 304, with bibliography of Shīʿī works. For additional details about him, see Ibn Bābawayh al-Qummī, *Akhbār al-Riḍā*, 2:70–72; al-Amīn, *Aʿyān al-Shīʿa*, 4:153. For the "Sunnī" literature about Muḥammad b. al-Ashʿath and his family, see Crone, *Slaves*, 184–185; he was one of the senior commanders of *al-Abnāʾ* who carried out very important administrative as well as military roles in the ʿAbbāsī caliphate, mainly under the reign of Hārūn al-Rashīd (d. 193/809). Crone does not mention the Imāmī affiliation of Jaʿfar b. Muḥammad, nor the Imāmī sources mentioned here.

124 Kohlberg, "*Muḥaddath*"; the quotations are from 40 and 46, respectively. On *al-muḥaddath*, see also Moezzi, *Divine Gide*, 70ff.

everyone, he would not have accepted it (its authenticity): لولا أني سمعته من أبي جعفر محمد بن علي وحدثني به أهل الأرض كلهم، ما قبلته.[125]

It seems that the descriptions of the two Imāmī traditions and the views held by scholars arguing for the close and intimate relations between al-Manṣūr and Jaʿfar al-Ṣādiq are far from being a reflection of the real course of events. Relations between the caliph and Jaʿfar al-Ṣādiq were very tense and even hostile.[126] It should be remembered that the accepted view of the Imāmī sources (and the scholars as well) is that Jaʿfar al-Ṣādiq was poisoned by al-Manṣūr.[127] (See the discussion below.)

So far, the lack of socio-historical research on the life of Jaʿfar al-Ṣādiq during the ʿAbbāsī rule means that the following comments can only serve as a preliminary introduction to this topic.

7.1 *The Period of Abū l-ʿAbbās al-Saffāḥ (r. 132–136/750–754)*

One of the major questions that should be raised is whether Jaʿfar al-Ṣādiq acted according to the principle of the *quʿūd* which dictates that the true Imām must keep aloof from political activism and should not attempt to seize power unless the time is ripe, and should be content to teach. There are several testimonies that indeed corroborate such principles of Jaʿfar al-Ṣādiq.

125 Al-Kulaynī, *al-Kāfī*, 8:210; al-Shaykh al-Mufīd, *al-Irshād*, 2:370–371; al-Majlisī, *Biḥār*, 52:288, 300; al-Sulamī, *ʿIqd al-durar*, 110. Sayf b. ʿUmayra al-Nakhaʿī l-Kūfī is a well-known Imāmī scholar, considered by the Imāmīs as a close associate (من أصحاب) of Jaʿfar al-Ṣādiq and his son, Mūsā l-Kāẓim, see al-Ṭūsī, *al-Fihrist*, 140; al-Māmaqānī, *Tanqīḥ al-rijāl*, part II, 79, no. 5460; al-Amīn, *Aʿyān al-Shīʿa*, 7:326; al-Khūʾī, *Rijāl*, 9:379–387. In Sunnī *rijāl* works: Ibn Ḥajar, *Tahdhīb* (Hyderabad edition), 4:296; al-Mizzī, *Tahdhīb*, 12:327–328; Ibn al-Nadīm, *Fihrist* (ed. Tajaddud), 275: mentioned as one of the Imāmī scholars who composed a work of a legal nature.

126 The evidence of Arjomand (n. 120 above) is far from conclusive and unequivocal, e.g., Arjomand, "The Crisis of the Imamate," 492 [in Kohlberg = 110], and n. 4 on 509 [in Kohlberg = 127], quoting al-Shaykh al-Mufīd, *al-Irshād* (Qumm: Basirati, n.d.), 12–13, trans. Howard, 6: evidence for the restoration of the tomb of ʿAlī in Najaf by orders of al-Manṣūr at Jaʿfar's request; but according to *al-Irshād*, 1:10, Jaʿfar visits ʿAlī's grave on his journey to the caliph, who was at that time in al-Ḥīra; another assertion, that al-Manṣūr "solicited Jaʿfar's legal advice" (quoting Ibn Shahrāshūb, *Manāqib*, 3:378–379, 389), is far from accurate.

127 Hodgson, "Djaʿfar al-Ṣādiḳ," 374a–375b: "Djaʿfar died in 148/765 (poisoned according to the unlikely Twelver tradition, on the orders of al-Manṣūr"); 375 (l. 2): "He left a cohesive following with an active intellectual life, well on the way to becoming a sect"; Gleave, "Jaʿfar al-Ṣādeq," 351, "According to most sources, Jaʿfar al-Ṣādiq died in 148/765…, supposedly poisoned by the ʿAbbāsid caliph al-Manṣūr, though to what political end is unclear."

7.1.1 The Revolt of Bassām b. Ibrāhīm

According to one testimony, Bassām b. Ibrāhīm, one of the senior commanders in the army of Qaḥṭaba b. Shabīb, rebelled against the first ʿAbbāsī caliph in 132/750. He wrote to Jaʿfar al-Ṣādiq, offering him his allegiance. Jaʿfar, afraid of a caliphal intention to test his loyalty, hurried with the letter to the caliph, who asked him to send his son Ismāʿīl to al-Ḥīra to meet Bassām, where the latter was caught, brought to the court of the caliph; his limbs were amputated, and then he was crucified.[128]

7.1.2 The Abū Salama Affair

Several traditions report that Abū Salama, the chief *dāʿī* of the ʿAbbāsīs in al-Kūfa, sent letters to three well-known ʿAlīds, offering each one the caliphate. One of them was Jaʿfar al-Ṣādiq. In all these traditions Jaʿfar al-Ṣādiq bluntly refuses to accept the offer and demonstratively burns the letter. He knows that Abū Salama and Muḥammad b. ʿAbdallāh b. al-Ḥasan will be killed.

Elsewhere in this book I argued that these traditions could only have been related after the death of Muḥammad b. ʿAbdallāh. The main purpose of the traditions was to emphasize the quietism (*quʿūd*) of Jaʿfar al-Ṣādiq, which was cultivated already by his father before him, and to justify this conviction.

7.1.3 Imāmī Sources

Nevertheless, some reports testify to the tension and enmity between Jaʿfar al-Ṣādiq and the ʿAbbāsīs already during Abū l-ʿAbbās' reign.

a) Imāmī sources record that Dāwūd b. ʿAlī [b. ʿAbdallāh b. al-ʿAbbās], Abū l-ʿAbbās' uncle, who served as governor of Medina, executed al-Muʿallā b. Khunays, the *mawlā* of Jaʿfar al-Ṣādiq, and confiscated his money. After the murder of his *mawlā*, Jaʿfar al-Ṣādiq came to Dāwūd b. ʿAlī and threatened him. That same night Jaʿfar prayed for God's help and Dāwūd b. ʿAlī died the following morning.[129] Disregarding the legendary and miraculous, supernatural elements of this Imāmī tradition, it is highly plausible that the execution of al-Muʿallā b. Khunays is not an invention. It certainly attests to the strained relations between the governor of al-Ḥijāz, Dāwūd b. ʿAlī, and Jaʿfar al-Ṣādiq. Other Imāmī traditions may testify to this as well.[130] It is quite possible that

---

128 Al-Balādhurī, *Ansāb* (ed. al-Dūrī), 3:171 [= al-Maqrīzī, *al-Muqaffā l-kabīr*, 4:171]; on Bassām, see Agha, *Revolution*, 344–345, and the comprehensive bibliography therein.

129 This tradition is not recorded in "Sunnī" sources. For the Imāmī sources, see the sources quoted by Modarressi, *Tradition*, 326 (among them: al-Ṣaffār, *Baṣāʾir* [Tehran, 1365 H.], 238; al-Kulaynī, *al-Kāfī* [1363 H.], 2:513, 557); see also al-Shaykh al-Mufīd, *Irshād*, 2:184–185; al-Kashshī, *Rijāl* (Najaf edition), 323–324.

130 E.g. al-Kulaynī, *al-Kāfī*, 8:210–212 [= al-Majlisī, *Biḥār*, 47:342–343].

the caliph knew about these strained relations between his uncle Dāwūd b. ʿAlī and Jaʿfar al-Ṣādiq.

b) The caliph was most probably aware of the fact that Jaʿfar al-Ṣādiq maintained an active and organized *shīʿa* with its own financial establishment. Yaqṭīn b. Mūsā, one of the most distinguished ʿAbbāsī *duʿāt* in al-Kūfa, who, together with his sons, served several ʿAbbāsī caliphs, belonged to the Ḥusaynī/Imāmī faction headed by Jaʿfar al-Ṣādiq. It is reported that he used to carry money and presents: وكان يحمل الأموال والألطاف for Jaʿfar.[131]

c) This may have been the reason for a unique (single) report by al-Māmaqānī, who quotes Ibn Bābawayh al-Qummī's work من لا يحضره الفقيه, that during Abū l-ʿAbbās' caliphate, "al-Imām al-Ṣādiq" was brought from Medina to al-Kūfa, was imprisoned in al-Ḥīra for a lengthy period, and kept in isolation. Later, the conditions of imprisonment were eased and Jaʿfar al-Ṣādiq was placed under house arrest in al-Ḥīra on condition that he would not contact anyone (literally: sit with anyone). Subsequently he was returned under guard to Medina, where he lived until Abū l-ʿAbbās' death in 136/754.[132]

---

131 Ibn al-Nadīm, *Fihrist* (ed. Tajaddud), 279; al-Ṭūsī, *Fihrist*, 155: وكان يحمل الأموال; al-Khūʾī, *Rijāl*, 13:243; Ibn al-Najjār, *Dhayl Taʾrīkh Baghdād*, 4 [19], 202 (all three latter sources seem to rely on Ibn al-Nadīm); on Yaqṭīn and his family, see Elad, "Wāsiṭ," 83; Madelung, "A Treatise," 19; Arjomand, "The Crisis of the Imamate," 492 [in Kohlberg = 110].

132 Al-Māmaqānī, *Rijāl*, no. 7047: the biography of the first ʿAbbāsī caliph, ʿAbdallāh b. Muḥammad Abū l-ʿAbbās al-Saffāḥ: عبد الله بن محمد أبو العباس السفاح وقع في طريق الصدوق ره في باب ما يصلى فيه وما لا يصلى فيه من الفقيه...ومن جرائمه العظام بعد غصب الخلافة حمله الإمام الصادق ع من المدينة إلى الكوفة وحبسه إياه في الحيرة زمنا طويلا لا يقربه أحد ولا يقرب من أحد ثم أطلقه من الحبس واعتقله في الحيرة على أن لا يقعد لأحد أبدا ثم رده إلى المدينة مرصودا حتى هلك السفاح وولي الخلافة أخوه أبو جعفر الدوانيقي لعنة الله عليهما; Elad, "Wāsiṭ," 84. My thanks are extended to Prof. Etan Kohlberg, who drew my attention to the fact that al-Māmaqānī is quoting Ibn Bābawayh's book; he also added that the text should have been found in *Man lā yaḥḍuruhu al-Faqīh* (Tehran, 1390 H.), 1:160–174: باب ما يصلى فيه وما لا يصلى فيه من الثياب وجميع الأنواع—but the text quoted by al-Māmaqānī is not found in that chapter. There are two possible explanations for this: 1) al-Māmaqānī made a mistake and the quote is taken from another source; 2) al-Māmaqānī used a different version from that of the printed edition. Kohlberg is inclined towards the second explanation mainly for two reasons: 1) Generally al-Māmaqānī is accurate when citing his sources; 2) Ibn Bābawayh relates several traditions in the above-mentioned chapter which condemn wearing black clothes, the color of the ʿAbbāsīs (ibid., 1:163). Kohlberg assumes that the quoted text by al-Māmaqānī (about al-Saffāḥ and Jaʿfar al-Ṣādiq) appeared in the MS of *Man lā yaḥḍuruhu al-faqīh* in the chapter mentioned. It is

7.2 *The Caliphate of Abū Jaʿfar al-Manṣūr*

7.2.1 Confiscation of His Estates by the ʿAbbāsīs

ʿĪsā b. Mūsā confiscated all the Ḥasānī family's estates; this gained the caliph's approval.[133] By orders of the caliph he also confiscated the estates of those ʿAlīds who did not (refused to?) meet him. ʿUmar b. Shabba relates from ʿĪsā b. ʿAbdallāh from his father that ʿĪsā b. Mūsā therefore seized Jaʿfar al-Ṣādiq's estate, ʿAyn Abī Ziyād "because Jaʿfar b. Muḥammad absented himself from him (تغيب عنه). When Abū Jaʿfar [al-Manṣūr] came [to Medina] Jaʿfar spoke with him about his seized estate. The caliph answered: 'Your Mahdī has already seized it.'"[134] According to this tradition al-Manṣūr mocks Jaʿfar al-Ṣādiq and accuses him of at least believing that Muḥammad b. ʿAbdallāh was the Mahdī. Another tradition states that Jaʿfar al-Ṣādiq met al-Manṣūr and asked him to give back his estate, ʿAyn Abī Ziyād, "so that I may eat from its palm boughs." Al-Manṣūr became angry over this request, saying "How dare you speak in such a manner; by God, I shall really give you a bad time." As in other traditions, Jaʿfar managed to calm down the caliph, who forgave him.[135] It seems that in this case no distinction was made by the ʿAbbāsīs between the Ḥasanīs and the Ḥusaynīs. Ibn al-Athīr sums up this matter, saying that ʿĪsā b. Mūsā seized all the estates of the Ḥasanīs and the estates of Jaʿfar.[136]

The estate was not returned to Jaʿfar al-Ṣādiq during al-Manṣūr's reign but al-Mahdī gave it back to his descendants.[137]

2.2) Imāmī sources record that al-Manṣūr ordered his governor of Mecca and Medina, al-Ḥasan b. Zayd b. al-Ḥasan b. ʿAlī b. Abī Ṭālib (one of the close associates of al-Manṣūr and a supporter of the ʿAbbāsīs and their cause), to burn down Jaʿfar al-Ṣādiq's residence (*dār*); and he carried this out in full. Then, the tradition describes Jaʿfar coming out of the burning house, walking through the flames, walking in the fire with no harm at all done to him, saying: "I am the son of أعراق الثرى and I am the son of Abraham, God's friend." This tradition is found in chapters stressing the supernatural traits and powers of Jaʿfar al-Ṣādiq (*muʿjizāt*).[138] Several details in this tradition do not

---

difficult to ascertain whether the text was omitted from Ibn Bābawayh's work/MSS due to considerations of *taqiyya*, or due to other unknown reasons.

133 Al-Ṭabarī, 3:257 (ll. 2–5); al-Azdī, *Taʾrīkh al-Mawṣil*, 193.

134 Al-Ṭabarī, 3:225 (ll. 15–20); al-Iṣfahānī, *Maqātil*, 273 [= al-Majlisī, *Biḥār*, 47:210]: without the ending; Nagel, "Muḥammad b. ʿAbdallāh," 257–258.

135 Al-Ṭabarī, 3:257 (ll. 5–11); McAuliffe, *ʿAbbāsid Authority*, 222; Nagel, "Muḥammad b. ʿAbdallāh," 257–258.

136 Ibn al-Athīr, *al-Kāmil* (Beirut edition), 5:553: قبض عيسى أموال بني الحسن كلها وأموال جعفر.

137 Al-Ṭabarī, 3:257 (ll. 11–13).

138 Al-Kulaynī, *al-Kāfī*, I, 473; al-Ṭabarī (al-Imāmī), *Manāqib*, 153; al-Baḥrānī, *Madīnat al-maʿājiz*, 5:295; Ibn Shahrāshūb, *Manāqib*, 3:362; al-Majlisī, *Biḥār*, 47:136. On the

correspond to what is known from historical sources: 1) Al-Ḥasan b. Zayd is mentioned as the governor of Medina only, not of Mecca; 2) According to al-Ṭabarī, al-Ḥasan b. Zayd was appointed as the governor of Medina in 149/766–767[139] or 150/767,[140] whereas Jaʿfar al-Ṣādiq died in 148!

It certainly joins other traditions that depict the supernatural nature of Jaʿfar al-Ṣādiq, his ability to perform miracles, and to foresee the future. Several traditions in this vein are scattered in the chapters of this book. Here the great personality of Jaʿfar manifests itself and the caliph understands that he is a special man; this time he is not acknowledged because of his supernatural traits as the Imām, but al-Manṣūr certainly understands that he is faced with a charismatic leader of the family of al-Ḥusayn. Despite the miraculous elements woven into this anecdote, it must have reflected some real historical background, that is, the animosity between al-Ḥasan b. Zayd and Jaʿfar al-Ṣādiq and the harsh measures taken by al-Manṣūr against the latter. We remember that other "Sunnī" sources relate the confiscation of Jaʿfar's estates by al-Manṣūr. The burning down of Jaʿfar's *dār* may have really occurred.

3) It seems that, as in al-Saffāḥ's reign, Jaʿfar's *shīʿa* continued to collect money and send it to their leader during al-Manṣūr's reign as well. The accusations of al-Manṣūr that Jaʿfar's *shīʿa* collected taxes for him may have been based on reality. Al-Iṣfahānī records a long tradition related in the first person by Jaʿfar al-Ṣādiq to Yūnus b. Abī Yaʿqūb. It was copied by several Imāmī and non-Imāmī authors.[141] Jaʿfar relates that after Ibrāhīm b. ʿAbdallāh was killed in Bakhamrā, the caliph ordered all the adult men who attained puberty be collected[142] from their families [that is, the Ḥusaynī family], and brought to al-Kūfa. A month later Jaʿfar al-Ṣādiq, accompanied by al-Ḥasan b. Zayd (b. al-Ḥasan b. ʿAlī b. Abī Ṭālib, who played a role in the previous tradition), were summoned to the caliph, who addressed Jaʿfar al-Ṣādiq, asking: "You are the one that knows the hidden unknown things?" أنت الذي تعلم الغيب؟ and Jaʿfar answers: "Only God knows the hidden things." The second question was "You are the one for whom this 'land tax' (خراج) is collected?" And Jaʿfar reconstructs his answer: "I said it is for you—oh Amīr al-Muʾminīn—that the land tax is collected." The initial intention of the caliph was to destroy the houses of the Ḥusaynīs in Medina, to uproot their palm

expression *ʿirq/aʿrāq al-tharā* (literally: "the source/the origin of everything that is good upon earth"), see chapter 7, 243f.

139 Ibn Khayyāṭ, *Taʾrīkh* (ed. al-ʿUmarī), 2:466.

140 Al-Ṭabarī, 3:358.

141 Al-Iṣfahānī, *Maqātil*, 350–352; al-Tanūkhī, *al-Faraj*, 1:313–315; Sibṭ b. al- Jawzī, *Mirʾāt al-zamān*, fol. 283a; al-Majlisī, *Biḥār*, 47:211; al-Amīn, *Aʿyān al-Shīʿa*, 2:180.

142 Al-Iṣfahānī, *Maqātil*, 350: حسرنا عن المدينة but in all the other versions: وحشرنا/حشرنا من المدينة; Sibṭ b. al-Jawzī, *Mirʾāt al-zamān*, fol. 283a: حشرنا أبو جعفر من المدينة.

groves, and to exile them to al-Sarāt, but Jaʿfar al-Ṣādiq managed to completely change the caliph's intentions by relating traditions from the Prophet about the advantages and benefits given to those who favor their family, help them, and do good for them (صلة الرحم). The caliph especially favored the *ḥadīth* about one of the kings on earth that had only three years to live, but after he did good deeds and helped his family, God turned these three years into thirty. So their fate reversed and the caliph sent Jaʿfar with the Ḥusaynīs back to Medina.

The tradition aims at praising Jaʿfar and describing his superior traits; the caliph's accusation regarding the collection of taxes by Jaʿfar's *shīʿa*, may have reflected a real situation.

4) Jaʿfar al-Ṣādiq had a "cohesive following with an active intellectual life, well on the way to becoming a sect."[143] Several Imāmī traditions attest to this. Some, like the above tradition, tell of the serious conflict and enmity between the Ḥusaynīs and the ʿAbbāsīs. Many times their aim is to emphasize the supernatural traits of Jaʿfar al-Ṣādiq, but it seems that the traditions were invented and woven around a real core of historical facts, that is, the basic situation of suspicion and enmity that existed between the two families.

One such tradition is related in the first person by Hishām b. Sālim al-Jawālīqī, a well-known Shīʿī theologian (*mutakallim*) of his time, a transmitter of Jaʿfar al-Ṣādiq and his son Mūsā l-Kāẓim[144] He describes the situation in Medina immediately after Jaʿfar al-Ṣādiq's death, when the ʿAbbāsīs' spies were looking for Jaʿfar's followers and executing them. The aim of the tradition is to praise Mūsā l-Kāẓim and to emphasize that he, and not his brother ʿAbdallāh, is his father's heir.[145]

We remember that money was collected for Jaʿfar al-Ṣādiq already during al-Saffāḥ's reign. These accusations raised by al-Manṣūr appear again and again in Imāmī sources, and it is highly probable that they mirror the real circumstances. Al-Tanūkhī records a tradition related from ʿAbdallāh b. al-Faḍl b. al-Rabīʿ from his father (al-Faḍl, the famous *wazīr* of al-Amīn), that al-Manṣūr, on his way to the *ḥajj* (in 147/December 764–January 765), arrives in Medina, summons Jaʿfar al-Ṣādiq, and accuses him: "You deviate from my rule, acting in a corrupt way to destroy it."[146] A parallel tradition recorded by the Imāmī author al-Irbilī (d. 692/1292 or 1293) adds to the accusations

143 Hodgson, "Djaʿfar al-Ṣādiḳ," 375.

144 On him, see van Ess, *Theologie*, 1:342–348; Modarressi, *Tradition*, 269–271.

145 Al-Kulaynī, *al-Kāfī*, 1:351–352: وذلك أنه كان له بالمدينة جواسيس ينظرون إلى من إتفقت عليه شيعة جعفر عليه السلام عليه فيضربون عنقه. For parallel sources, see al-Ṭūsī, *Ikhtiyār*, 2:566; al-Baḥrānī, *Madīnat al-maʿājiz*, 6:209; al-Māzandarānī, *Sharḥ*, 6:296.

146 Al-Tanūkhī, *al-Faraj*, 1:318.

the following: "the people of al-ʿIrāq took you as *imām*, giving you the *zakāt* of their property/money (*amwāluhum*); and you deviate from my rule, acting in a corrupt way to destroy it."[147]

As mentioned above, the accepted view among scholars is that Jaʿfar al-Ṣādiq refused to be involved in any uprisings against the Umawīs or the ʿAbbāsīs. He offered no support to the uprising of Muḥammad b. ʿAbdallāh al-Nafs al-Zakiyya. This view is expressed in the tradition that relates that Jaʿfar played no active part in the revolt, and withdrew (تنحى) (in order not to be involved in the rebellion).[148] The Imāmī tradition is more explicit in relating that when the revolt broke out Jaʿfar al-Ṣādiq ran away to his estate in al-Furʿ. Only after Muḥammad was killed and the people received *amān* from the authorities did he come back to Medina, where he died in 148 H.[149]

It is noteworthy that Ismāʿīl, Jaʿfar al-Ṣādiq's son, supported the ʿAbbāsīs (before the rebellion broke out), but two other sons, Mūsā and ʿAbdallāh, supported al-Nafs al-Zakiyya. What was Jaʿfar's attitude to this support? On the face of it he should have categorically objected, but such an attitude is not disclosed by the sources. A single pro-Ḥasanī tradition relates that Jaʿfar asked Muḥammad b. ʿAbdallāh to free him from the obligation to join his revolt, which the latter did. Moreover, Muḥammad told Jaʿfar's sons to return to their home, to their father, but Jaʿfar allowed them to go back to join Muḥammad, so they did and took part in his revolt.[150] As noted, this is a single, pro-Ḥasanī tradition which aims to stress his noble character and Muḥammad b. ʿAbdallāh's kindness towards Jaʿfar and his sons. It is to be remembered that it stands in strict contradiction to other traditions, that may be termed pro-Ḥusaynī (pro-Jaʿfarī), that describe the bold uncompromising attitude towards Jaʿfar al-Ṣādiq by Muḥammad and his supporters, and his short-term imprisonment by the latter.[151]

The participation of Jaʿfar's sons in the rebellion must have affected al-Manṣūr's attitude towards Jaʿfar al-Ṣādiq and the Ḥusaynīs.

8 The Treatise of Condolences from Jaʿfar al-Ṣādiq to the Ḥasanīs

Raḍī l-Dīn ʿAlī b. Mūsā b. Jaʿfar b. Ṭāʾūs (d. 664/1266), records a letter of condolences sent from Jaʿfar al-Ṣādiq to ʿAbdallāh b. al-Ḥasan when he was taken with his family

147 Al-Irbilī, *Kashf al-ghumma*, 371: إتخذك أهل العراق إماما يجبون إليك زكاة أموالهم وتلحد في سلطاني وتبغيه الغوائل; copied by Imāmī authors, e.g., al-Majlisī, *Biḥār*, 47:182; 92:223; al-Amīn, *Aʿyān al-Shīʿa*, 1:666.

148 Al-Ṭabarī, 3:254 (l. 7).

149 Al-Majlisī, *Biḥār*, 47:5; al-Irbilī, *Kashf al-ghumma*, 2:374.

150 Al-Iṣfahānī, *Maqātil*, 252; I did not find any parallel source for this tradition.

151 E.g., al-Kulaynī, *al-Kāfī*, 8:358ff.; and see above.

to prison.[152] Ibn Ṭā'ūs quotes the letter from his grandfather, al-Shaykh al-Ṭūsī, through two chains of transmitters, which conclude with Isḥāq b. ʿAmmār b. Ḥayyāsh (d. ca. 181/797 or 798), a transmitter from Jaʿfar al-Ṣādiq and his son Mūsā l-Kāẓim.[153] The letter was copied from Ibn Ṭā'ūs' work by later authors, all endeavoring to explain and compromise between the affectionate and encouraging words in this letter and the harsh and abominable expressions found in traditions besmirching ʿAbdallāh b. al-Ḥasan by Jaʿfar al-Ṣādiq,[154] some which were dealt with in this appendix.

In spite of what has been said about the sometimes fierce and almost merciless struggle and animosity, the Ḥasanīs and the Ḥusaynīs were of the same stock, the descendants of ʿAlī and of Fāṭima, and the two families intermarried.[155] Several traditions transmitted through Jaʿfar's cousins, ʿAlī b. ʿUmar b. ʿAlī b. al-Ḥusayn, and Ḥusayn b. Zayd b. ʿAlī, relate that Jaʿfar wept when he saw the Ḥasanīs led in chains to al-Rabadha, he blessed Muḥammad and Ibrāhīm, spoke boldly against al-Manṣūr and the ʿAbbāsīs,[156] or the Anṣār, who, as they broke their promise to the Prophet during the ʿAqaba meeting, continued in this abominable behavior by not helping the Prophet's family.[157] Another source states that Jaʿfar regretted not joining Muḥammad and Ibrāhīm's rebellion.[158]

152 Ibn Ṭā'ūs, *al-Iqbāl bi-l-aʿmāl*, 3:82–85.

153 On him, see Modarressi, *Tradition*, 299.

154 E.g., al-Majlisī, *Biḥār*, 48:299–301; al-Shāhrūdī-Namāzī, *Rijāl*, 6:153–154

155 1) Umm ʿAbdallāh, the daughter of al-Ḥasan b. ʿAlī married ʿAlī b. al-Ḥusayn b. ʿAlī b. Abī Ṭālib; 2) Umm Salama bt. al-Ḥasan b. ʿAlī married ʿUmar b. ʿAlī b. al-Ḥusayn b. ʿAlī b. Abī Ṭālib, see Ibn ʿInaba, *ʿUmda*, 68 (quoting al-ʿUmarī's *Ansāb*; I was unable to locate this information in al-ʿUmarī's book); 3) Nafīsa, bt. al-Ḥasan b. Zayd b. al-Ḥasan b. ʿAlī b. Abī Ṭālib was married to Isḥāq b. Jaʿfar (al-Ṣādiq) [b. Muḥammad b. ʿAlī b. al-Ḥusayn b. ʿAlī b. Abī Ṭālib], see Ibn Ḥajar, *Tahdhīb* (Beirut 1404 H.), 1:200; Ibn Kathīr, *al-Bidāya* (ed. Shīrī), 10:286–287; Ibn ʿInaba, *ʿUmda*, 70; al-Abṭaḥī, *Tahdhīb al-maqāl*, 4:267; al-Ziriklī, *al-Aʿlām*, 8:44; Ahmed, *Religious Elite*, 154 n. 825; 168f. (for earlier marriage ties between the two families); 173; Bernheimer, *The ʿAlids*, 34–35.

156 Al-Iṣfahānī, *Maqātil*, 251–252; al-Ṭabarī, 3:174–175 (l. 15 to l. 7).

157 Al-Iṣfahānī, *Maqātil*, 219–220 [= al-Ṭabarī, 3:174–175 (l. 15 to l. 7), omitting the mention of the Anṣār].

158 Al-Iṣfahānī, *Maqātil*, 252.

Map of Medina

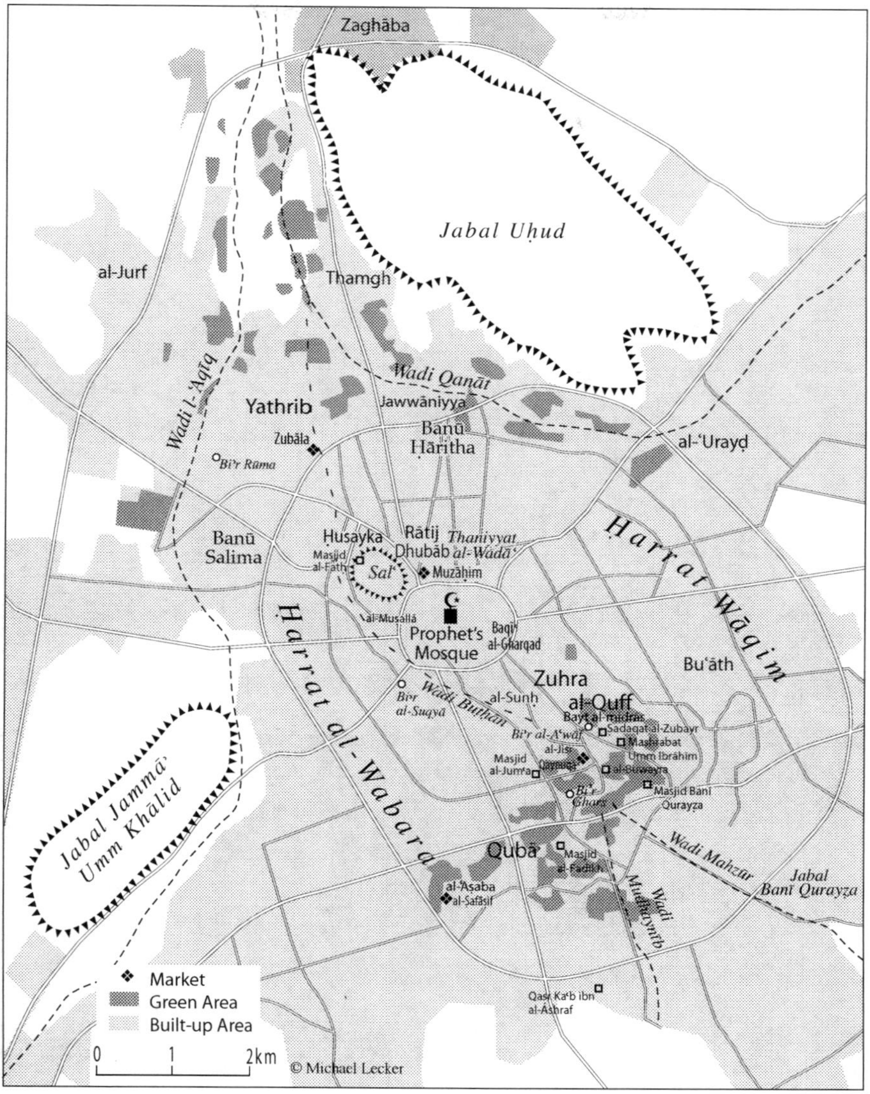

Al-Madīna on the Eve of Islām
(After M. Lecker, *Muslims, Jews and Pagans*)

Genealogical Charts

Quraysh

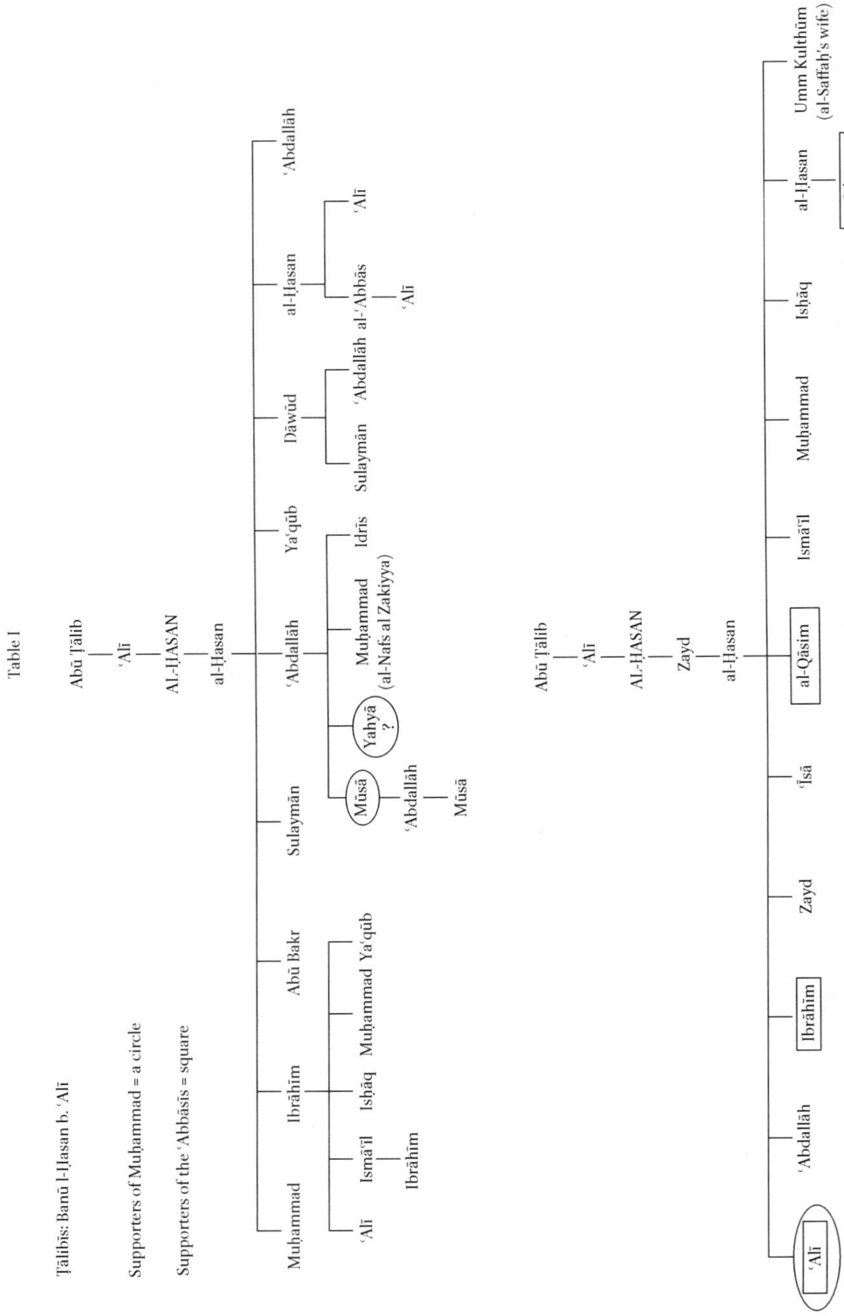

Chart II

Quraysh: The Ṭālibīs

Banū ʿAlī b. al-Ḥusayn b. ʿAlī b. Abī Ṭālib

Supporters of Muḥammad = circle
Supporters of the ʿAbbāsīs = square

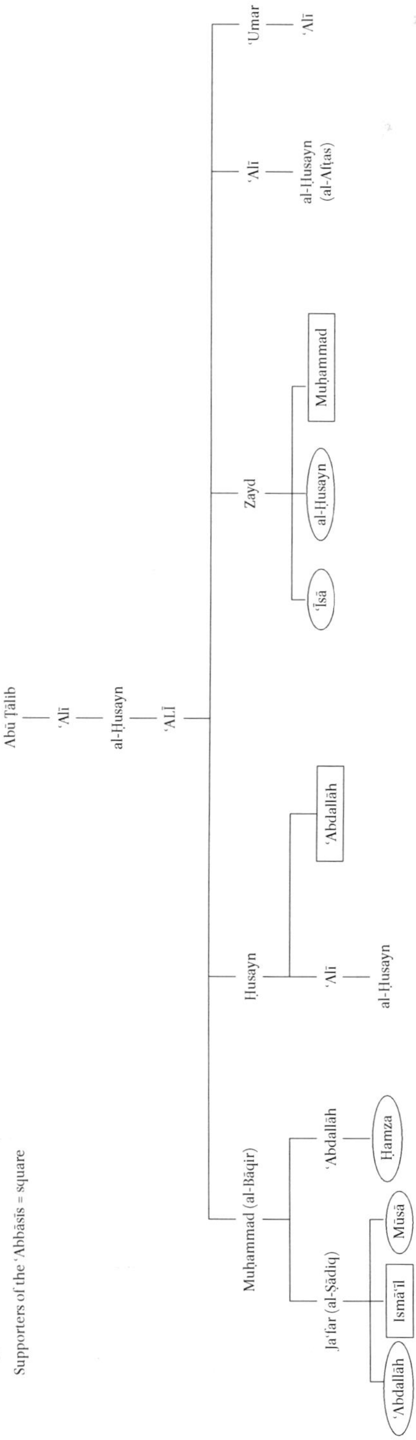

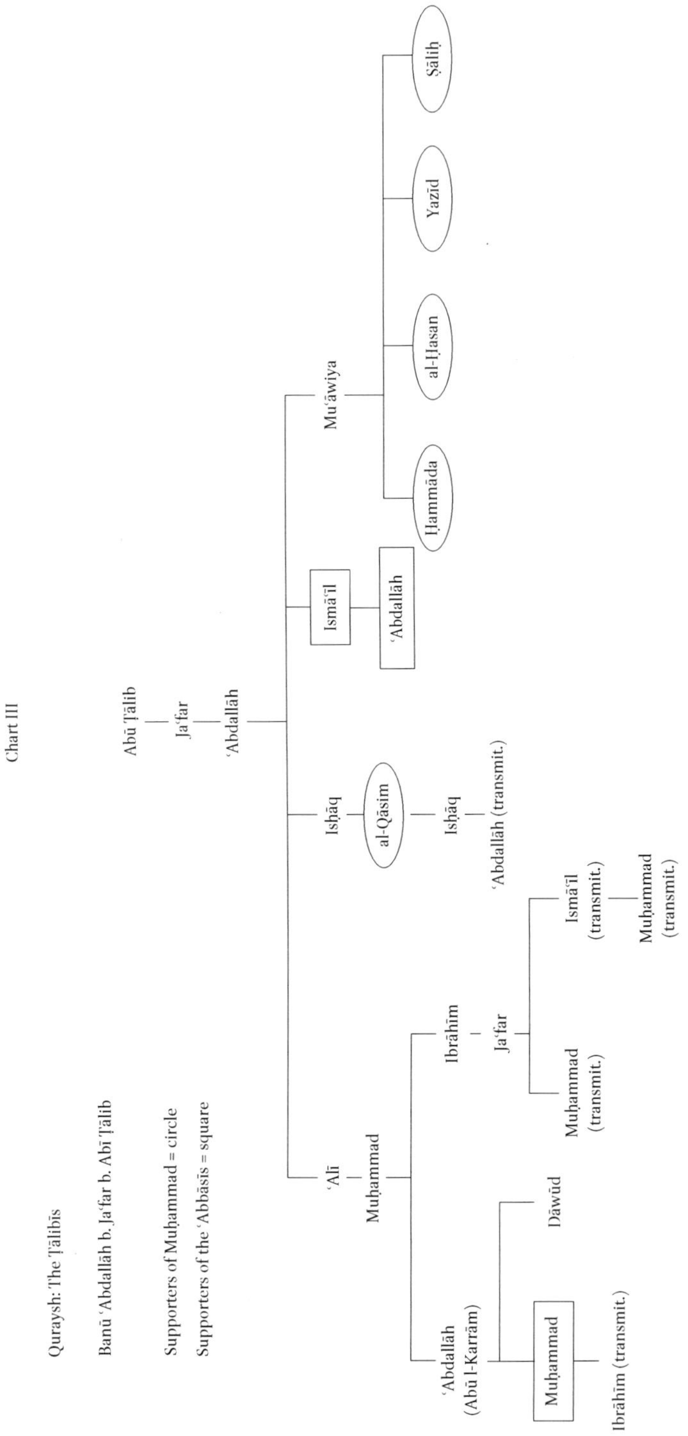
Chart III
Quraysh: The Ṭālibīs
Banū ʿAbdallāh b. Jaʿfar b. Abī Ṭālib
Supporters of Muḥammad = circle
Supporters of the ʿAbbāsīs = square
Abū Ṭālib
Jaʿfar
ʿAbdallāh
Muʿāwiya
Ḥammāda
al-Ḥasan
Yazīd
Ṣāliḥ
Ismāʿīl
ʿAbdallāh
Isḥāq
al-Qāsim
Isḥāq
ʿAbdallāh (transmit.)
ʿAlī
Muḥammad
Ibrāhīm
Jaʿfar
Ismāʿīl (transmit.)
Muḥammad (transmit.)
Muḥammad (transmit.)
ʿAbdallāh (Abū l-Karrām)
Dāwūd
Muḥammad
Ibrāhīm (transmit.)

Chart IV

Quraysh: The Ṭālibīs

Banū ʿUmar b. ʿAlī b. Abī Ṭālib
Banū Muḥammad b. ʿAqīl b. Abī Ṭālib

Supporters of Muḥammad = circle
Supporters of the ʿAbbāsīs = square

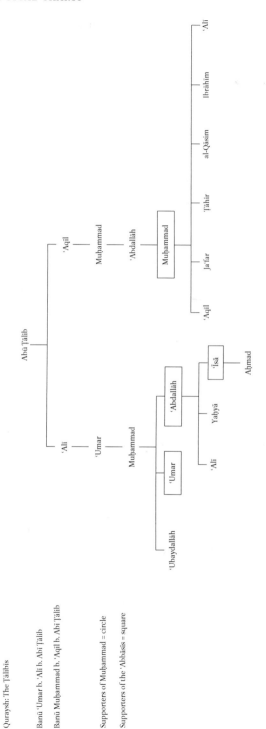

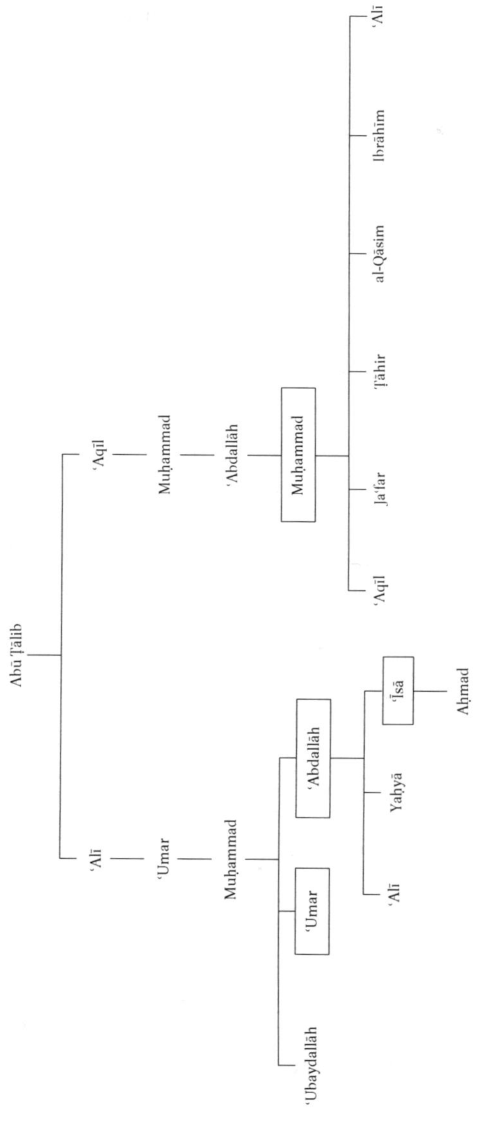

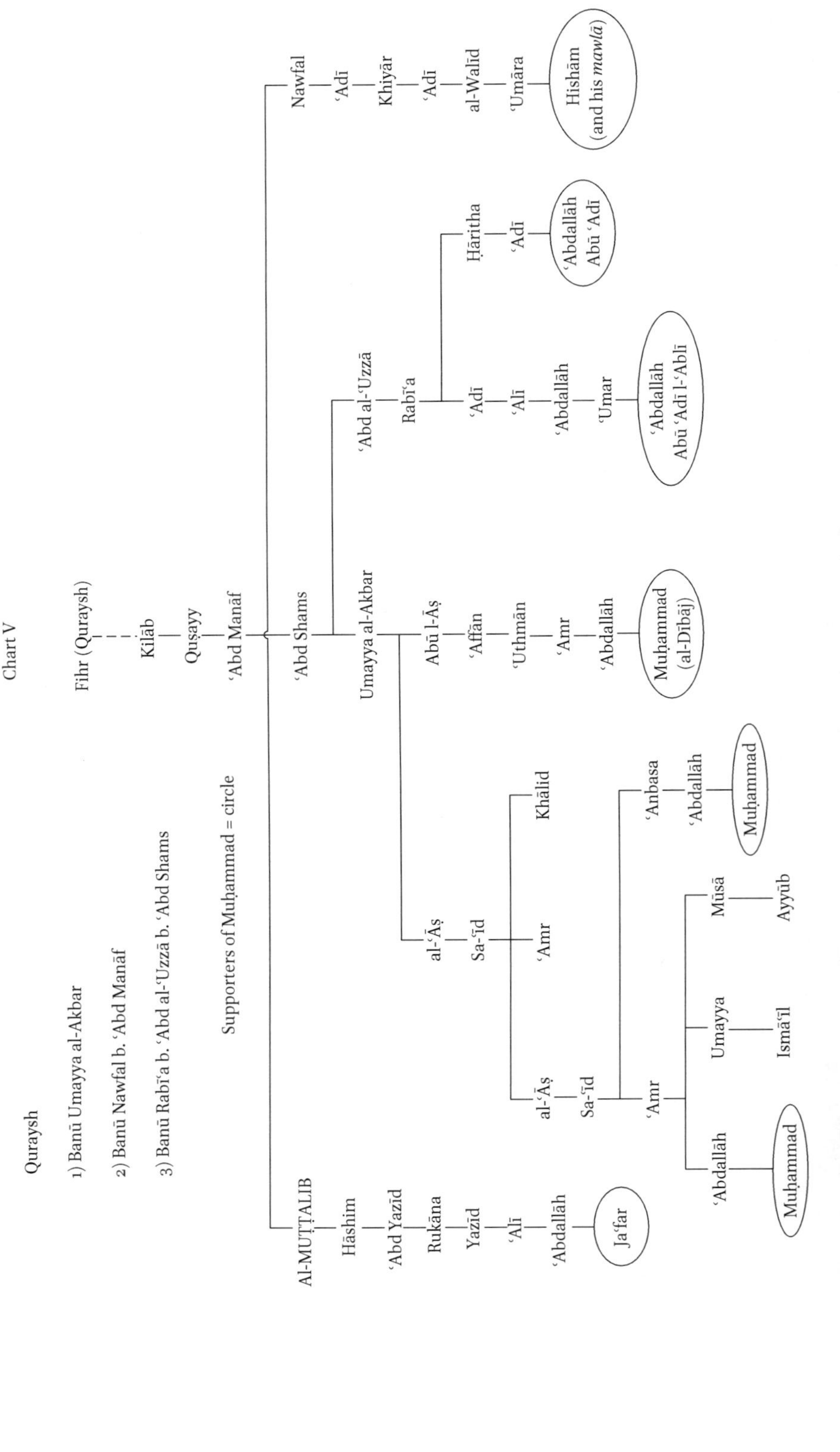
Chart V
Quraysh
1) Banū Umayya al-Akbar
2) Banū Nawfal b. ʿAbd Manāf
3) Banū Rabīʿa b. ʿAbd al-ʿUzzā b. ʿAbd Shams
Supporters of Muḥammad = circle
Fihr (Quraysh)
Kilāb
Quṣayy
ʿAbd Manāf
Nawfal
ʿAdī
Khiyār
ʿAdī
al-Walīd
ʿUmāra
Hishām (and his *mawlā*)
ʿAbd Shams
ʿAbd al-ʿUzzā
Rabīʿa
Ḥāritha
ʿAdī
ʿAbdallāh Abū ʿAdī
ʿAdī
ʿAlī
ʿAbdallāh
ʿUmar
ʿAbdallāh Abū ʿAdī l-ʿAblī
Umayya al-Akbar
Abū l-ʿĀṣ
ʿAffān
ʿUthmān
ʿAmr
ʿAbdallāh
Muḥammad (al-Dībāj)
al-ʿĀṣ
Saʿīd
Khālid
ʿAmr
al-ʿĀṣ
Saʿīd
ʿAnbasa
ʿAbdallāh
Muḥammad
ʿAmr
Mūsā
Ayyūb
Umayya
Ismāʿīl
ʿAbdallāh
Muḥammad
Al-MUṬṬALIB
Hāshim
ʿAbd Yazīd
Rukāna
Yazīd
ʿAlī
ʿAbdallāh
Jaʿfar

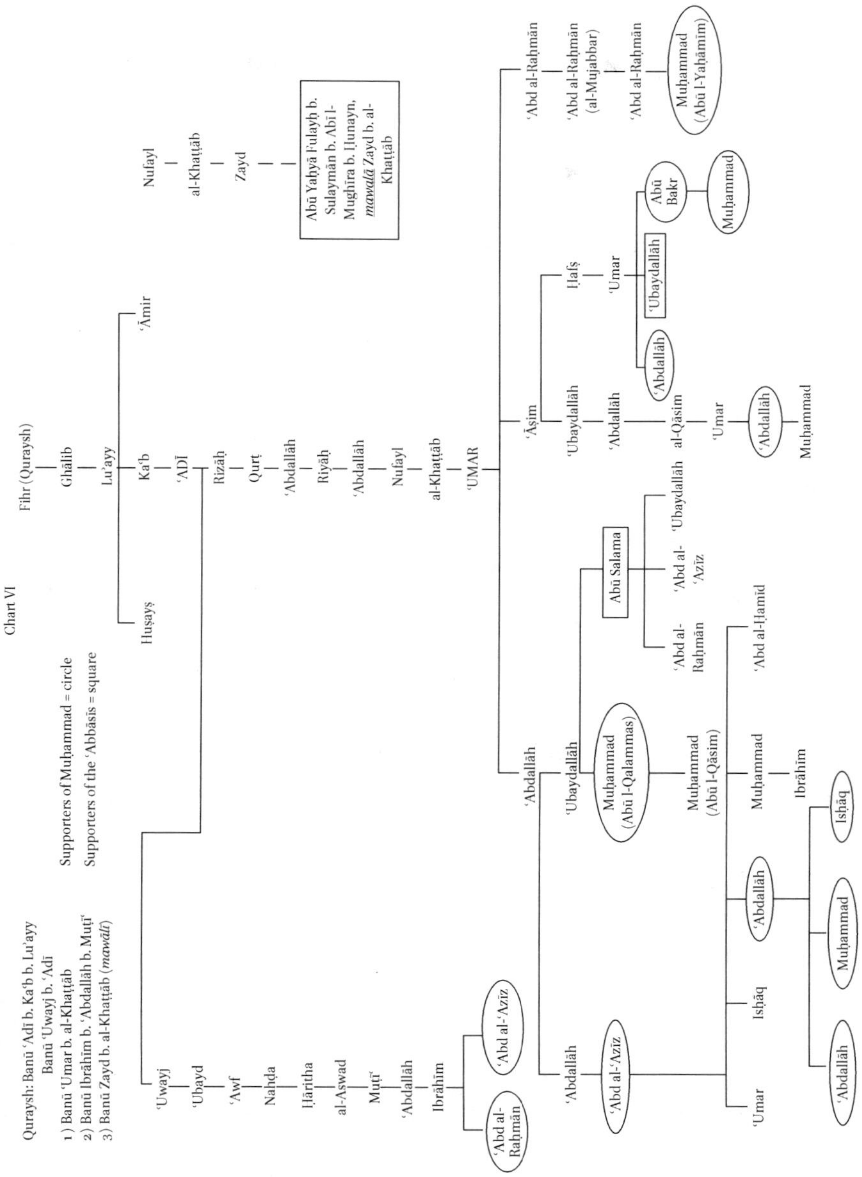
Chart VI
Quraysh: Banū ʿAdī b. Kaʿb b. Luʾayy
Banū ʿUwayj b. ʿAdī
1) Banū ʿUmar b. al-Khaṭṭāb
2) Banū Ibrāhīm b. ʿAbdallāh b. Muṭīʿ
3) Banū Zayd b. al-Khaṭṭāb (*mawālī*)
Supporters of Muḥammad = circle
Supporters of the ʿAbbāsīs = square
Fihr (Quraysh)
Ghālib
Luʾayy
Ḥuṣayṣ
Kaʿb
ʿĀmir
ʿADĪ
Nufayl
al-Khaṭṭāb
Zayd
Abū Yaḥyā Fulayḥ b. Sulaymān b. Abī l-Mughīra b. Ḥunayn, *mawlā* Zayd b. al-Khaṭṭāb
ʿUwayj
ʿUbayd
ʿAwf
Naḍla
Ḥāritha
al-Aswad
Muṭīʿ
ʿAbdallāh
Ibrāhīm
ʿAbd al-Raḥmān
ʿAbd al-ʿAzīz
Rizāḥ
Qurṭ
ʿAbdallāh
Riyāḥ
ʿAbdallāh
Nufayl
al-Khaṭṭāb
ʿUMAR
ʿAbdallāh
ʿĀṣim
ʿAbd al-Raḥmān
ʿAbdallāh
ʿUbaydallāh
Abū Salama
ʿAbd al-Raḥmān
ʿAbd al-ʿAzīz
ʿUbaydallāh
Muḥammad (Abū l-Qalammas)
Muḥammad (Abū l-Qāsim)
ʿAbd al-ʿAzīz
ʿUmar
Isḥāq
ʿAbdallāh
Muḥammad
ʿAbd al-Ḥamīd
Ibrāhīm
ʿAbdallāh
Muḥammad
Isḥāq
ʿUbaydallāh
ʿAbdallāh
al-Qāsim
ʿUmar
ʿAbdallāh
Muḥammad
Ḥafṣ
ʿUmar
ʿAbdallāh
ʿUbaydallāh
Abū Bakr
Muḥammad
ʿAbd al-Raḥmān
ʿAbd al-Raḥmān (al-Mujabbar)
ʿAbd al-Raḥmān
Muḥammad (Abū l-Yaḥāmīm)

Chart VII

Quraysh; Banū Taym b. Murra

Supporters of Muḥammad = circle

Supporters of the ʿAbbāsīs = square

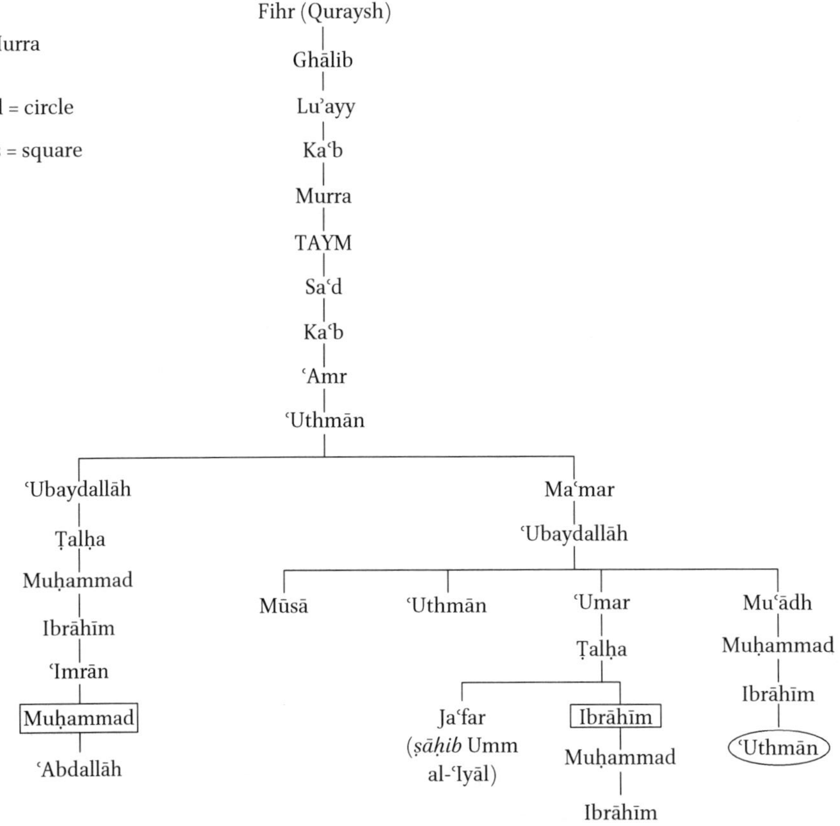

Chart VIII

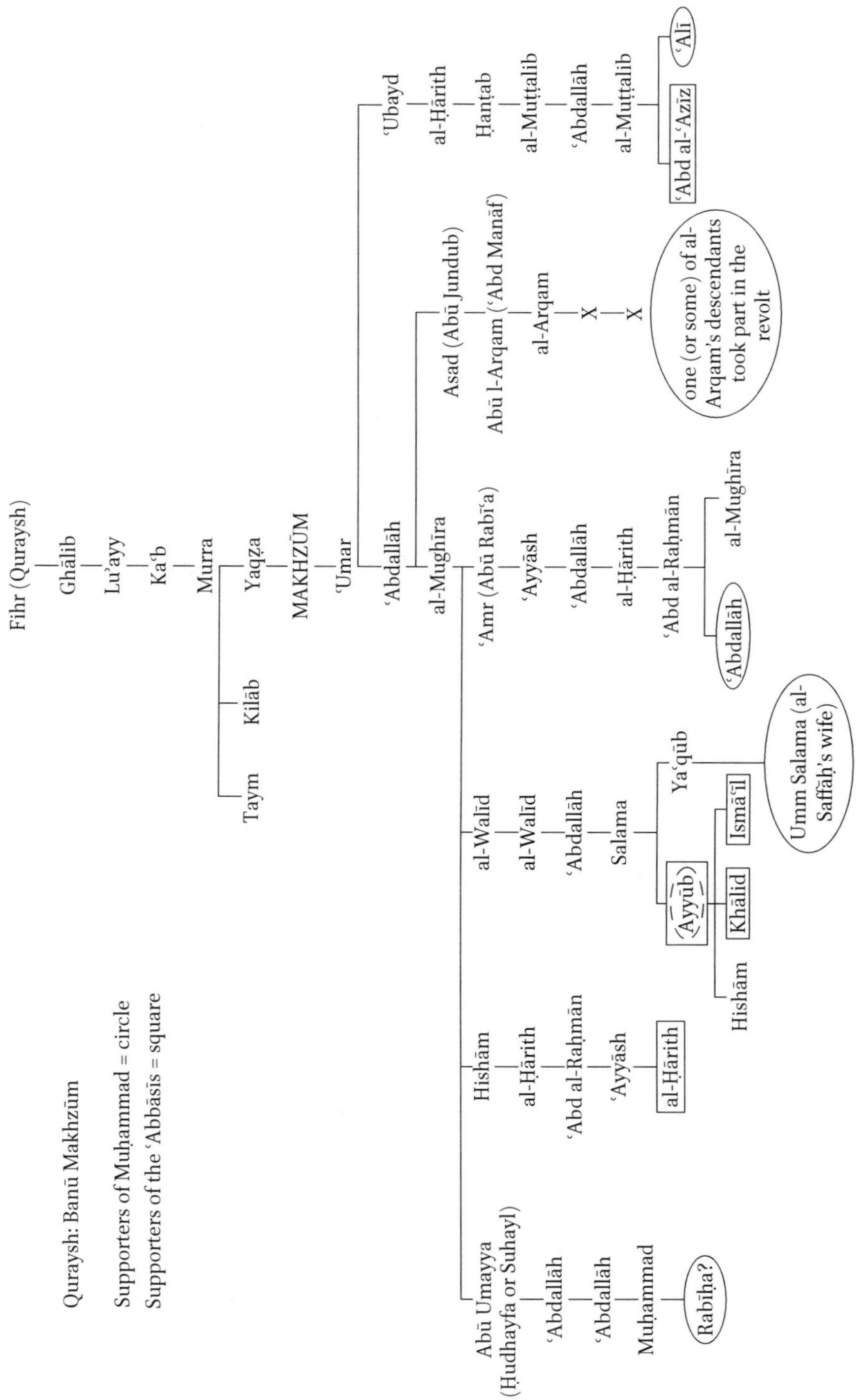
Quraysh: Banū Makhzūm
Supporters of Muḥammad = circle
Supporters of the ʿAbbāsīs = square
Fihr (Quraysh)
Ghālib
Luʾayy
Kaʿb
Murra
Taym
Kilāb
Yaqẓa
MAKHZŪM
ʿUmar
ʿAbdallāh
ʿUbayd
al-Ḥārith
Ḥanṭab
al-Muṭṭalib
ʿAbdallāh
al-Muṭṭalib
ʿAbd al-ʿAzīz
ʿAlī
al-Mughīra
Asad (Abū Jundub)
Abū l-Arqam (ʿAbd Manāf)
al-Arqam
X
X
one (or some) of al-Arqam's descendants took part in the revolt
ʿAmr (Abū Rabīʿa)
ʿAyyāsh
ʿAbdallāh
al-Ḥārith
ʿAbd al-Raḥmān
ʿAbdallāh
al-Mughīra
al-Walīd
al-Walīd
ʿAbdallāh
Salama
Yaʿqūb
Umm Salama (al-Saffāḥ's wife)
Ayyūb
Hishām
Khālid
Ismāʿīl
Hishām
al-Ḥārith
ʿAbd al-Raḥmān
ʿAyyāsh
al-Ḥārith
Abū Umayya (Ḥudhayfa or Suhayl)
ʿAbdallāh
ʿAbdallāh
Muḥammad
Rabīḥa?

Chart IX

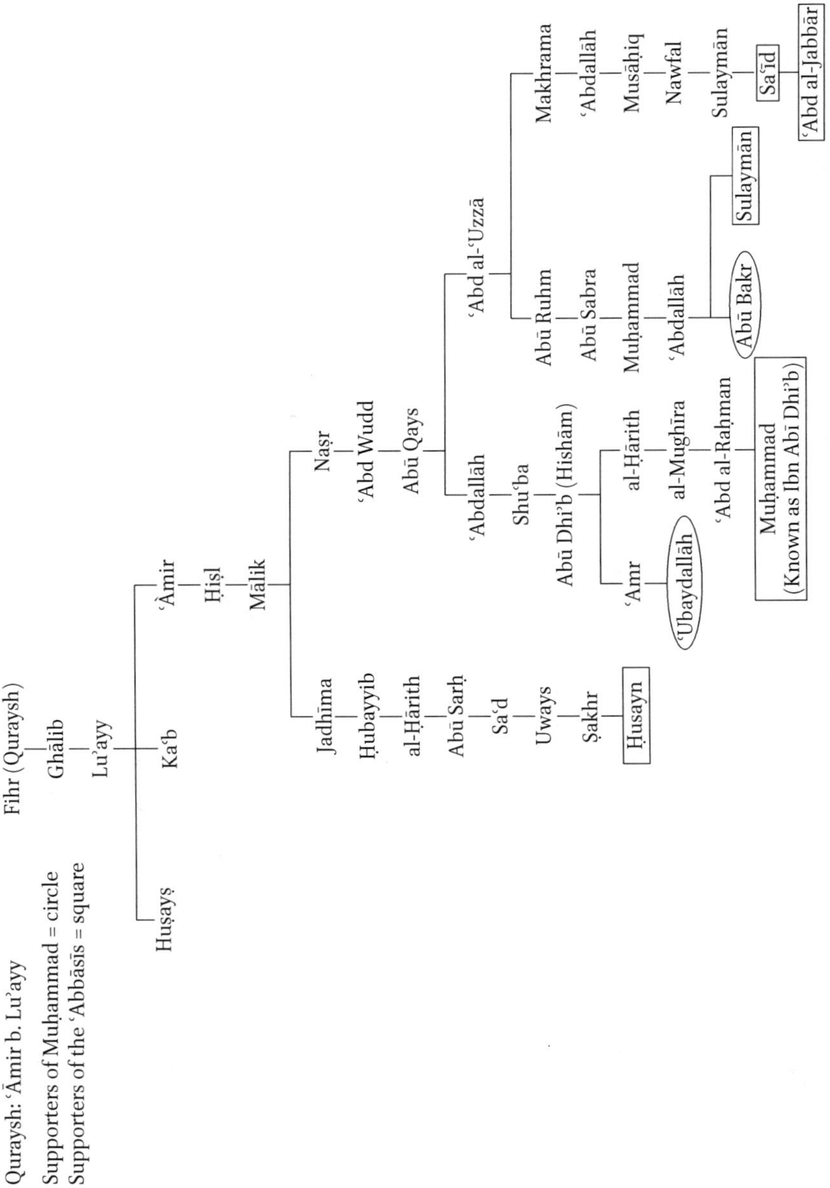
Quraysh: ʿĀmir b. Luʾayy
Supporters of Muḥammad = circle
Supporters of the ʿAbbāsīs = square
Fihr (Quraysh)
Ghālib
Luʾayy
Huṣayṣ
Kaʿb
ʿĀmir
Ḥiṣl
Mālik
Jadhīma
Ḥubayyib
al-Ḥārith
Abū Sarḥ
Saʿd
Uways
Ṣakhr
Ḥusayn
Naṣr
ʿAbd Wudd
Abū Qays
ʿAbdallāh
Shuʿba
Abū Dhiʾb (Hishām)
ʿAmr
ʿUbaydallāh
al-Ḥārith
al-Mughīra
ʿAbd al-Raḥman
Muḥammad (Known as Ibn Abī Dhiʾb)
ʿAbd al-ʿUzzā
Abū Ruhm
Abū Sabra
Muḥammad
ʿAbdallāh
Abū Bakr
Sulaymān
Makhrama
ʿAbdallāh
Musāḥiq
Nawfal
Sulaymān
Saʿīd
ʿAbd al-Jabbār

Chart X

Quraysh: Banū Jumaḥ

Abū Lahab's clan

Supporters of Muḥammad = circle
Supporters of the ʿAbbāsīs = square

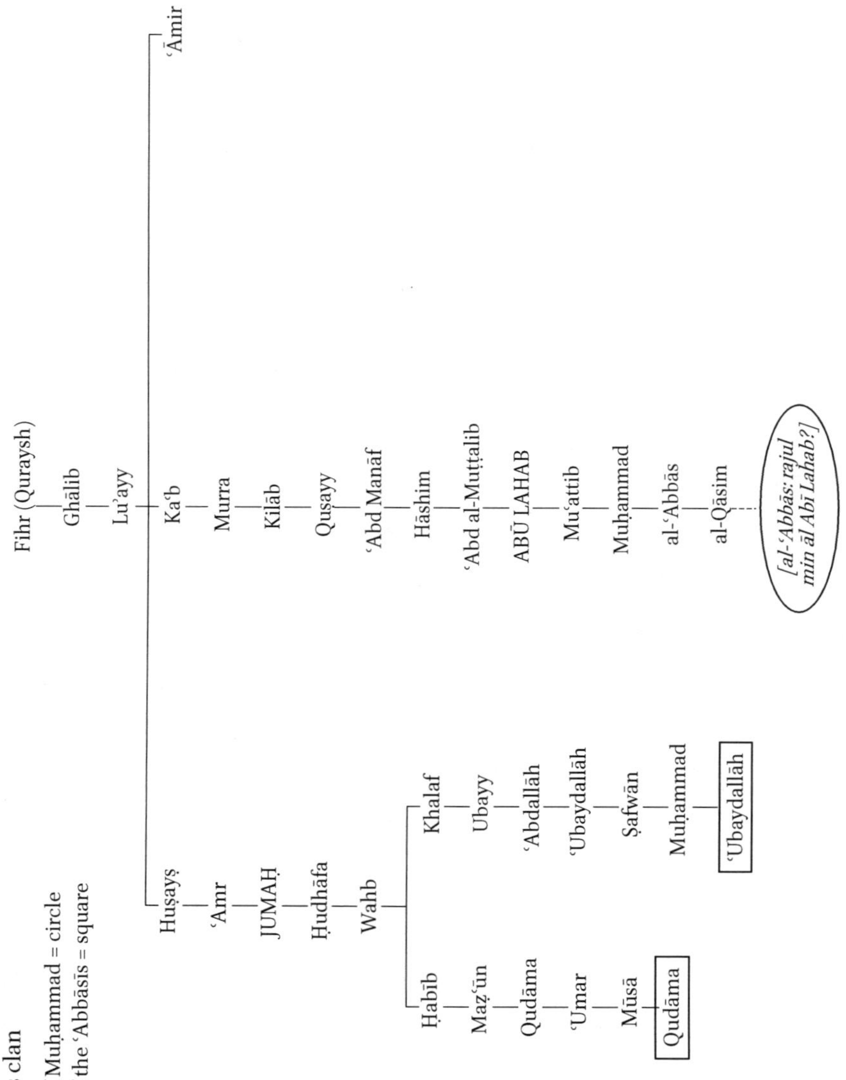

Chart XI

Quraysh: Banū Zuhra and their allies

Supporters of Muḥammad = circle
Supporters of the ʿAbbāsīs = square

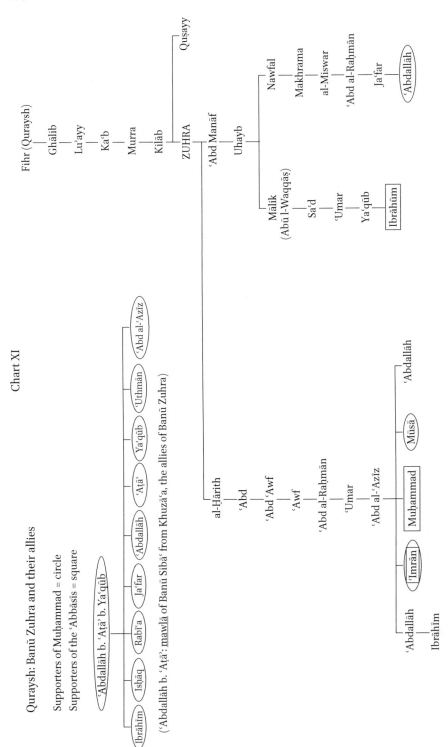

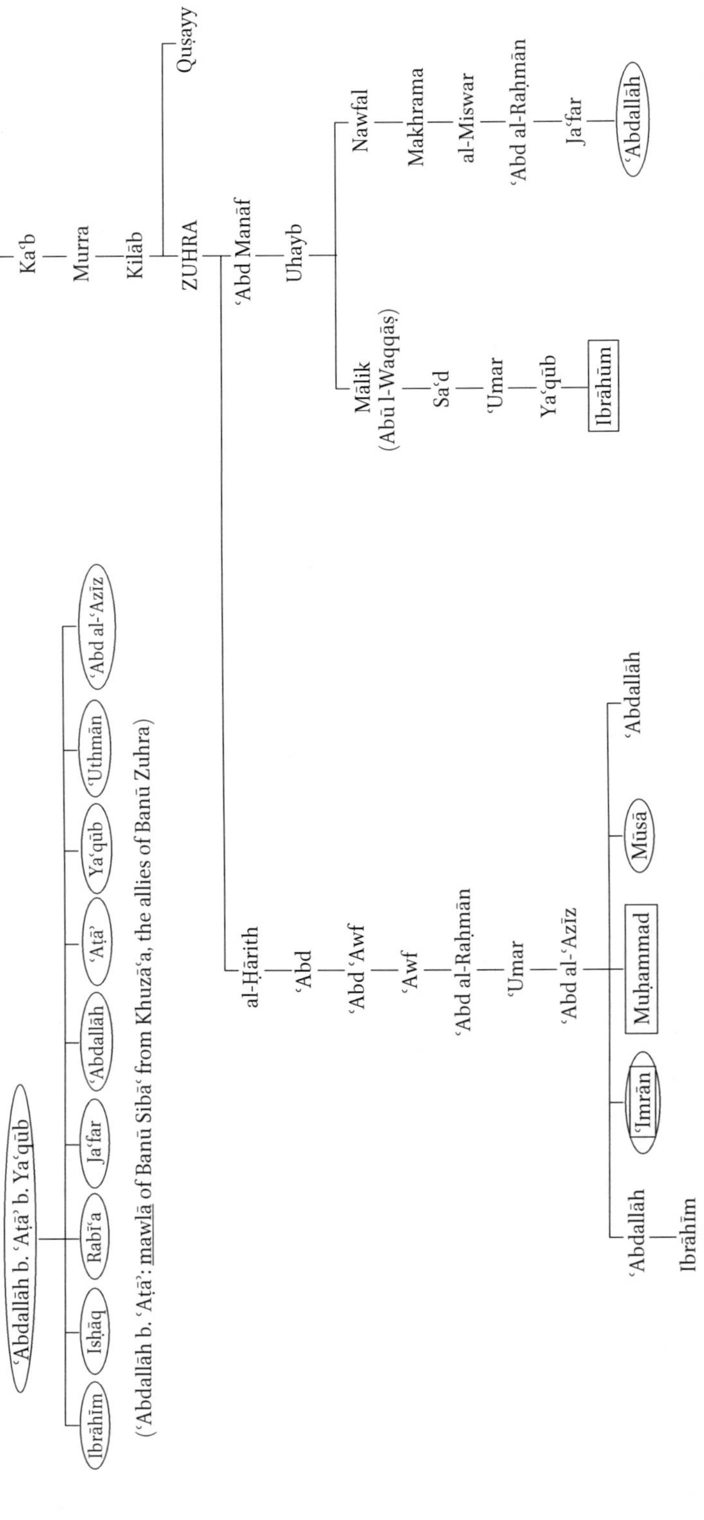

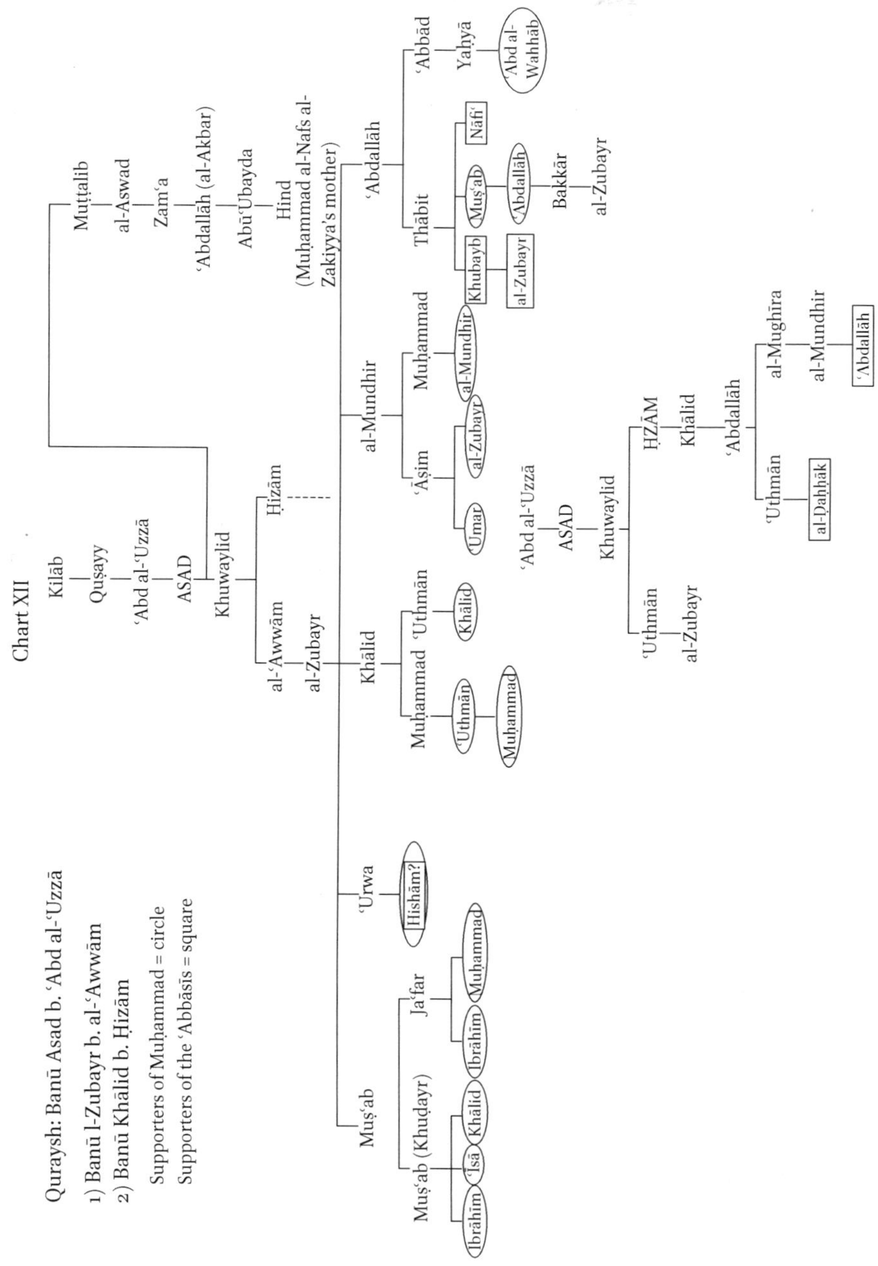
Chart XII
Quraysh: Banū Asad b. ʿAbd al-ʿUzzā
1) Banū l-Zubayr b. al-ʿAwwām
2) Banū Khālid b. Ḥizām
Supporters of Muḥammad = circle
Supporters of the ʿAbbāsīs = square
Kilāb
Quṣayy
ʿAbd al-ʿUzzā
ASAD
Muṭṭalib
al-Aswad
Zamʿa
ʿAbdallāh (al-Akbar)
Abū ʿUbayda
Hind
(Muḥammad al-Nafs al-Zakiyya's mother)
Khuwaylid
al-ʿAwwām
Ḥizām
al-Zubayr
Muṣʿab
ʿUrwa
Khālid
al-Mundhir
ʿAbdallāh
Muṣʿab (Khuḍayr)
Jaʿfar
Ibrāhīm
ʿĪsā
Khālid
Ibrāhīm
Muḥammad
Hishām?
Muḥammad
ʿUthmān
ʿUthmān
Muḥammad
Khālid
ʿĀṣim
Muḥammad
ʿUmar
al-Zubayr
al-Mundhir
Thābit
ʿAbbād
Khubayb
Muṣʿab
Nāfiʿ
al-Zubayr
ʿAbdallāh
Bakkār
al-Zubayr
Yaḥyā
ʿAbd al-Wahhāb
ʿAbd al-ʿUzzā
ASAD
Khuwaylid
ʿUthmān
al-Zubayr
ḤIZĀM
Khālid
ʿAbdallāh
ʿUthmān
al-Ḍaḥḥāk
al-Mughīra
al-Mundhir
ʿAbdallāh

Bibliography

ʿAbd al-Bāqī b. Qāniʿ, see Ibn Qāniʿ.

ʿAbdallāh, U.F. "Abū Ḥanīfa." *EIr*, 1:295b–301b.

ʿAbd al-Razzāq b. Hammām al-Ṣanʿānī. *Al-Muṣannaf.* Ed. Ḥabīb al-Raḥmān al-Aʿẓamī. Beirut²: n.p., 1403 H.

Al-Abṭaḥī, Muḥammad ʿAlī l-Muwaḥḥid. *Tahdhīb al-maqāl fī tanqīḥ kitāb al-rijāl.* Qumm: n.p., 1412 H.

Abū l-ʿArab, Muḥammad b. Aḥmad b. Tamīm. *Kitāb al-Miḥan*. Ed. Yaḥyā Wuhayb al-Jabbūrī. Beirut: Dār al-Gharb al-Islāmī, 1983.

Abū Dāwūd, Sulaymān b. al-Ashʿath al-Sijistānī. *Sunan*. Ed. Saʿīd Muḥammad al-Laḥām. Beirut: Dār al-Fikr li-l-Ṭibāʿa wa-l-Nashr wa-l-Tawzīʿ, 1410/1990.

Abū l-Fidāʾ, Ismāʿīl b. ʿAlī. *Al-Yawāqīt wa-l-ḍarab fī taʾrīkh Ḥalab*. Ed. Muḥammad Kamāl and Fāliḥ al-Bukūr. Aleppo: Dār al-Qalam al-ʿArabī bi-Ḥalab, 1410/1989.

Abū l-Shaykh al-Anṣārī, ʿAbdallāh b. Muḥammad b. Jaʿfar b. Ḥayyān. *Ṭabaqāt al-muḥaddithīn bi-Iṣfahān wa-l-wāridīna ʿalayhā*. Beirut²: Muʾassasat al-Risāla, 1412/1992.

Abū Zayd, Bakr b. ʿAbdallāh. *Ṭabaqāt al-nassābīn*. Riyadh: Dār al-Rushd li-l-Nashr wa-l-Tawzīʿ, 1407/1987.

Abū Zurʿa al-Dimashqī, ʿAbd al-Raḥmān b. ʿAmr. *Taʾrīkh Abī Zurʿa al-Dimashqī.* Ed. Niʿmat Allāh al-Qūjānī. Damascus: Maṭbaʿat Majmaʿ al-Lugha al-ʿArabiyya bi-Dimashq, 1980.

Agapius b. Qusṭanṭīn al-Manbijī. *Taʾrīkh = Al-Muntakhab min taʾrīkh al-Manbijī.* Ed. ʿUmar ʿAbd al-Salām Tadmurī. Tripoli: Dār al-Manṣūr, 1406/1986.

Agha, Saleh Said. *The Revolution which Toppled the Umayyads: Neither Arab nor ʿAbbāsid.* Leiden: E.J. Brill, 2003.

Ahmed, Q. Asad. *The Religious Elite of the Early Islamic Ḥijāz: Five Prosopographical Case Studies.* Oxford: Prosopographica Research, Linacre College, University of Oxford, 2011.

Al-Ājurrī, Muḥammad b. ʿAlī Abū ʿUbayd. *Suʾālāt Abī ʿUbayd al-Ājurrī Abā Dāwūd Sulaymān b. al-Ashʿath al-Sijistānī fī maʿrifat al-rijāl wa-jarḥihim wa-taʿdīlihim.* Ed. Muḥammad ʿAlī Qāsim al-ʿUmarī. Medina: al-Jāmiʿa al-Islāmiyya, 1399/1979.

Akhbār al-ʿAbbās = Anonymous. *Akhbār al-dawla al-ʿabbāsiyya wa-fīhi akhbār al-ʿAbbās wa-wuldihi*. Ed. ʿAbd al-ʿAzīz al-Dūrī and ʿAbd al-Jabbār al-Muṭṭalibī. Beirut: Dār Ṣādir, 1971.

Akhbār aʾimmat al-Zaydiyya = Akhbār aʾimmat al-Zaydiyya fī Ṭabaristān, Daylamān, wa-Jīlān. Nuṣūṣ Taʾrīkhiyya. Jamaʿahā wa-ḥaqqaqahā Fīlfrd Mādīlūngh. English title: *Arabic Texts Concerning the History of the Zaydī Imāms of Ṭabaristān, Daylamān and Gilān.* Collected and edited by Wilferd Madelung. Beirut and Wiesbaden: Franz Steiner, 1987 [Beiruter Texte und Studien, 28].

Al-ʿAlawī l-Shajarī, Muḥammad b. ʿAlī. *Faḍl ziyārat al-Ḥusayn*. Ed. Aḥmad al-Ḥusaynī and Maḥmūd al-Marʿashī. Qumm: Maktabat Āyatullāh al-Marʿashī, 1403 H.

Al-Albānī, Muḥammad Nāṣir al-Dīn b. al-Ḥājj Nūḥ. *Silsilat al-aḥādīth al-ḍaʿīfa wa-l-mawḍūʿa wa-atharuhā l-sayyiʾ fī l-umma*. Riyadh: Dār al-Maʿārif, 1412/1992.

Al-ʿAlī, Ṣ.A. "Mulkiyyāt al-arāḍī fī l-Ḥijāz fī l-qarn al-awwal al-hijrī." *Majallat al-ʿArab* 3, no. 11 (1969), 961–1005.

———. "Studies in the Topography of Medina (during the 1st Century A.H.)." IC 35 (1961), 65–92.

ʿAlī Khān al-Madanī = ʿAlī Khān b. Aḥmad b. Muḥammad al-Shīrāzī Ṣadr al-Dīn al-Madanī. *Riyāḍ al-sālikīn fī sharḥ ṣaḥīfat Sayyid al-Sājidīn*. Ed. Muḥsin al-Ḥusaynī l-Amīnī. [Qumm?]: Muʾassasat al-Nashr al-Islāmī, 1415 H.

Al-ʿĀmilī, ʿAlī b. Yūnus Abū Muḥammad. *Al-Ṣirāṭ al-mustaqīm ilā mustaḥiqqī l-taqdīm*. Ed. Muḥammad al-Bāqir al-Bahbūdī. N.p.: Maṭbaʿat al-Ḥaydarī. Al-Maktaba al-Murtaḍawiyya li-Iḥyāʾ al-Āthār al-Jaʿfariyya, 1384 H.

Al-ʿĀmilī, Muḥammad b. al-Ḥasan b. ʿAlī l-Ḥurr. *Tafṣīl wasāʾil al-Shīʿa ilā taḥṣīl masāʾil al-sharīʿa*. Qumm[2]: Muʾassasat Āl al-Bayt li-Iḥyāʾ al-Turāth, 1414 H.

———. *Wasāʾil (al-Islāmiyya) = Wasāʾil al-Shīʿa al-Islāmiyya*. Ed. Muḥammad al-Rāzī. Beirut: Dār Iḥyāʾ al-Turāth al-ʿArabī, n.d.

———. *Wasāʾil (Āl al-Bayt) = Wasāʾil al-Shīʿa Āl al-Bayt*. Ed. Muḥammad Riḍā l-Jalālī. Qumm[2]: Muʾassasat Āl al-Bayt li-Iḥyāʾ al-Turāth, 1414 H.

Al-Amīn, Muḥsin b. ʿAbd al-Karīm. *Aʿyān al-Shīʿa*. Beirut: Dār al-Taʿāruf li-l-Maṭbūʿāt, 1406–1413/1985–1993.

———. *Mustadrakāt aʿyān al-shīʿa*. Beirut: Dār al-Taʿāruf, n.d.

Anonyme Leiden = *Dhikr Banī l-ʿAbbās wa-sabab ẓuhūrihim*. MS Leiden. Cod.or. 14.023 (see P.S. van Koningsveld in *Bibliotheca Orientalis*, 5–6 (Sept.–Nov. 1973), 370–385).

Al-Anṣārī, Muḥammad ʿAlī. *Al-Mawsūʿa al-fiqhiyya al-muyassara*. Qumm: Majmaʿ al-Fiqh al-Islāmī, 1415 H.

Al-ʿAqīqī, Yaḥyā b. al-Ḥasan b. Jaʿfar b. ʿUbaydallāh. *Kitāb al-Muʿaqqibīn min wuld al-Imām Amīr al-Muʾminīn*. Ed. Muḥammad al-Kāẓim. Qumm: Maktabat Āyatullah al-ʿUẓmā l-Marʿashī l-Najafī, 2001.

Arazi, A. "Mekke et Medine" = "Materiaux pour l'étude du conflit de préséance entre la Mekke et Medine." *JSAI* 5 (1984), 177–235.

Al-Ardabīlī, Muḥammad b. ʿAlī. *Jāmiʿ al-ruwāt*. [Najaf ?]: Maktabat Āyatullāh al-Marʿashī l-Najafī, 1403 H.

Arjomand, Said Amir. "The Crisis of the Imamate and the Institution of Occultation in Twelver Shiʿism: A Sociohistorical Perspective." IJMES 28 (1996), 491–515. [Republished in E. Kohlberg (ed.), *Shīʿism* (*The Formation of the Classical Islamic World* 33), pp. 109–133. Burlington, VT: Ashgate Variorum, 2003].

Al-Ashʿarī, ʿAlī b. Ismāʿīl Abū l-Ḥasan. *Maqālāt al-Islāmiyyīn wa-ikhtilāf al-muṣallīn*. Ed. Hellmut Ritter. Beirut[3]: Dār Iḥyāʾ al-Turāth al-ʿArabī, n.d. [Reprint of 1929 Istanbul edition.]

Attema, D.S. *De Mohammedaanse opvattingen omtrent het tijdstip van den jongsten dag en zijn voorteekenen.* Amsterdam: Nord-Hollandsche Uitgeverns Maatschappij, 1942.

Ayalon, D. *Eunuchs, Caliphs and Sultans: A Study in Power Relationships.* Jerusalem: Magnes Press of the Hebrew University of Jerusalem, 1999.

Al-ʿAynī, Maḥmūd b. Aḥmad b. Mūsā Badr al-Dīn al-Ḥanafī. *ʿUmdat al-qārī fī sharḥ al-Bukhārī.* Beirut: Dār Iḥyāʾ al-Turāth al-ʿArabī, [198–?].

Al-ʿAyyāshī, al-Naḍr b. Muḥammad b. Masʿūd b. ʿAyyāsh al-Sulamī l-Samarqandī. *Tafsīr.* Ed. Hāshim al-Rasūlī l-Maḥallātī. Tehran: Al-Maktaba al-ʿIlmiyya al-Islāmiyya, n.d.

Al-Azdī, Yazīd b. Muḥammad b. Iyyās Abū Zakariyyāʾ. *Taʾrīkh al-Mawṣil.* Ed. ʿAlī Ḥabība. Cairo: N.p., 1387/1967.

Al-ʿAẓīm Ābādī, Muḥammad Shams al-Ḥaqq Abū l-Ṭayyib. *ʿAwn al-Maʿbūd: Sharḥ Sunan Abī Dāwūd maʿa Sharḥ al-ḥāfiẓ Ibn Qayyim al-Jawziyya.* Beirut[2]: Dār al-Kutub al-ʿIlmiyya, 1415 H.

Al-Baghdādī, Ismāʿīl Bāshā b. Muḥammad. *Hadiyyat al-ʿārifīn: Asmāʾ al-muʾallifīn wa-āthār al-muṣannifīn.* Istanbul: Maṭbaʿat Wikālat al-Maʿārif, 1951. [Reprinted: Beirut: Dār Iḥyāʾ al-Turāth al-ʿArabī, n.d.]

Al-Baḥrānī, al-Sayyid Hāshim b. Sulaymān. *Al-Ḥadāʾiq al-nāḍira.* Ed. Muḥammad Taqī l-Īrānī. Qumm: Jamāʿat al-Mudarrisīn, n.d.

———. *Ḥilyat al-abrār fī aḥwāl Muḥammad wa-ālihi al-aṭhār.* Ed. Ghulām Raḍiyy mawlānā l-Baḥrānī. N.p: Muʾassasat al-Maʿārif al-Islāmiyya, 1411 H.

———. *Madīnat maʿājiz al-aʾimma al-ithnay ʿashar wa-dalāʾil al-ḥujaj ʿalā l-bashar.* Ed. ʿIzzatullāh al-Mawlāʾī l-Hamadānī. Qumm: Muʾassasat al-Maʿārif al-Islāmiyya, 1413 H.

Baḥshal al-Wāsiṭī, Aslam b. Sahl b. Aslam. *Taʾrīkh Wāsiṭ.* Ed. Kūrkīs ʿAwwād. Beirut: ʿĀlam al-Kutub, 1406 H.

Al-Bājī, Sulaymān b. Khalaf b. Saʿd b. Ayyūb. *Al-Taʿdīl wa-l-takhrīj.* Ed. Aḥmad al-Bazzār. Marrakech: Wizārat al-Awqāf wa-l-Shuʾūn al-Islāmiyya, n.d.

Al-Bakjarī l-Ḥikrī, Mughulṭāy b. Qilīj b. ʿAbdallāh ʿAlāʾ al-Dīn. *Ikmāl tahdhīb al-kamāl.* Ed. Abū ʿAbd al-Raḥmān ʿĀdil b. Muḥammad and Abū Muḥammad Usāma b. Ibrāhīm. Cairo: al-Fārūq al-Ḥadītha li-l-Ṭibāʿa wa-l-Nashr, 1422/2001.

Al-Bakrī, ʿAbdallāh b. ʿAbd al-ʿAzīz Abū ʿUbayd. *Muʿjam mā istaʿjam min asmāʾ al-bilād wa-l-mawāḍiʿ.* Ed. Muṣṭafā l-Saqqā. Cairo: Maṭbaʿat Lajnat al-Taʾlīf wa-l-Tarjama wa-l-Nashr, 1364–1371/1945–1951.

Al-Balādhurī, Aḥmad b. Yaḥyā. *Ansāb al-Ashrāf.* 1) Ed. Suhayl Zakkār and Riyāḍ Ziriklī. Beirut: Dār al-Fikr li-l-Ṭibāʿa wa-l-Nashr wa-l-Tawzīʿ, 1417/1996. 2) Ed. Mahmoud al-Fardous al-Azem [Maḥmūd Firdaws al-ʿAẓm]. Damascus: Dār al-Yaqẓa al-ʿArabiyya, 1997–2002. 3) Vol. 2 [a] (the biographies of the Jaʿfarīs and part of the ʿAlīds). Ed. Muḥammad Bāqir al-Maḥmūdī. Beirut: Muʾassasat al-Aʿlamī li-l-Maṭbūʿāt, 1394/1974. 4) Vol. 2. Ed. W. Madelung. Beirut/Berlin: Klaus Schwarz, 1424/2003. 5) Vol. 3, Ed. ʿAbd al-ʿAzīz al-Dūrī. Beirut/Wiesbaden: Franz Steiner, 1978. 6) Vol. 4/a. Ed. Iḥsān ʿAbbās. Beirut. N.p., 1979. 7) Vol. 4/2. Ed. ʿAbd al-ʿAzīz al-Dūrī and ʿIṣām ʿUqla. Beirut/Berlin: N.p., 2001. 8) Vol. 5. Ed. Iḥsān ʿAbbās. Beirut/Stuttgart: Al-Sharika al-Muttaḥida li-l-Tawzīʿ/Franz Steiner, 1996. 9) Vol. 7/2. Ed. Muḥammad al-Yaʿlāwī. Beirut/Berlin: Klaus Schwarz, 1423/2002.

———. *Kitāb Futūḥ al-buldān*. Ed. Ṣalāḥ al-Dīn al-Munajjid. Cairo: Maktabat al-Nahḍa al-Miṣriyya, 1956.

Balʿamī, see al-Ṭabarī.

Al-Barazanjī, Muḥammad b. ʿAbd Rasūl al-Ḥusaynī. *al-Ishāʿa li-ashrāṭ al-sāʿa*. Cairo: Maktabat wa-Maṭbaʿat al-Mashhad al-Ḥusaynī, 1393 H. [Photocopy: Beirut: Dār al-Kutub al-ʿIlmiyya, n.d.].

Al-Barqī, Aḥmad b. Abī ʿAbdallāh Abū Jaʿfar. *Kitāb al-rijāl*. Tehran: N.p., 1342 H.

Al-Bastawī, ʿAbd al-ʿAlīm ʿAbd al-ʿAẓīm. *Al-Mahdī l-muntaẓar (ʿA) fī ḍawʾ al-aḥādīth wa-l-āthār al-ṣaḥīḥa*. Mecca: al-Maktaba al-Makkiyya, 1420/1999.

Bates, M.L. "al-Mahdī" = "Khurāsānī Revolutionaries and al-Mahdī's Title." In Farhad Daftary and Josef W. Meri (eds.), *Culture and Memory in Medieval Islam: Essays in Honour of Wilferd Madelung*, pp. 279–317. London and New York: I.B. Tauris, 2003.

Al-Bayhaqī, Aḥmad b. al-Ḥusayn b. ʿAlī b. Mūsā Abū Bakr. *Al-Qirāʾa khalf al-Imām*. Ed. Muḥammad al-Saʿīd Basyūnī Zaghlūl. Beirut: Dār al-Kutub al-ʿIlmiyya, 1405 H.

———. *Shuʿab al-īmān*. Ed. Muḥammad al-Saʿīd Basyūnī Zaghlūl. Beirut: Dār al-Kutub al-ʿIlmiyya, 1410 H.

———. *Al-Sunan al-kubrā = Sunan al-Bayhaqī l-kubrā*. Ed. Muḥammad ʿAbd al-Qādir ʿAṭā. Mecca: Maktabat Dār al-Bāz li-l-Nashr wa-l-Tawzīʿ, 1414/1994.

Bernheimer, T. *The ʿAlids. The First Family of Islam, 750–1200*. Edinburgh: Edinburgh University Press, 2013.

———. "The Revolt of ʿAbdallāh b. Muʿāwiya, AH 127–130: A Reconsideration through the Coinage." *BSOAS* 69 (2006), 381–393.

Blankinship, K.Y. "The Tribal Faction in the ʿAbbāsid Revolution: The Betrayal of the Imām Ibrāhīm b. Muḥammad." *JAOS* 108 (1988), 589–603.

Bonner, M. *Aristocratic Violence and Holy War: Studies in Jihād and the Arab-Byzantine Frontier*. New Haven, CT: American Oriental Society, 1996.

Bosworth, C.E. *The ʿAbbāsid Caliphate in Equilibrium = The History of al-Ṭabarī*. Vol. 30: *The ʿAbbāsid Caliphate in Equilibrium*. Albany: State University of New York Press, 1989.

——— (trans.). *Al-Maqrīzī's "Book of Contention and Strife Concerning the Relations Between the Banū Umayya and the Banū Hāshim."* Manchester: University of Manchester (*Journal of Semitic Studies Monographs No. 3*), 1980[?].

———. "Rajāʾ b. Ḥaywa al-Kindī and the Umayyad Caliphs." *IQ* 14 (1972), 36–80.

Brockelmann, C. *Geschichte der Arabischen Litteratur*. Vol. 1, Weimar, 1898; vol. 2, Berlin, 1902 (second edition: Leiden: E.J. Brill, 1945–1949); *Supplementbände*, vols. 1–3, Leiden: E.J. Brill, 1937–1942.

Al-Buḥturī, al-Walīd b. ʿUbayd (Allāh) Abū ʿUbāda. *Dīwān al-Buḥturī*[2]. Ed. Ḥasan Kāmil al-Ṣayrafī. Cairo: Dār al-Maʿārif, 1972–1977.

Al-Bukhārī, Muḥammad b. Ismāʿīl. *Kitāb al-Ḍuʿafāʾ al-ṣaghīr.* Ed. Maḥmūd Ibrāhīm Zāyid. Beirut: Dār al-Maʿrifa li-l-Ṭibāʿa wa-l-Nashr wa-l-Tawzīʿ, 1406/1986.

———. *Al-Kabīr = Al-Taʾrīkh al-kabīr.* 1) Ed. Hāshim al-Nadwī. [Damascus?]. Dār al-Fikr, [198–?]. 2) Diyār Bakr. Al-Maktaba al-Islāmiyya, n.d.

———. *Al-Ṣaghīr = Al-Taʾrīkh al-ṣaghīr.* Ed. Muḥmūd Ibrāhīm Zāyid. Beirut: Dār al-Maʿrifa, 1406 H.

———. *Ṣaḥīḥ.* Ed. Muṣṭafā Dīb al-Bughā. Beirut[2]: Dār Ibn Kathīr, 1407/1987.

Al-Bukhārī, Sahl b. ʿAbdallāh b. Dāwūd b. Sulaymān Abū Naṣr. *Sirr al-silsila al-ʿAlawiyya.* Najaf: Al-Maktaba wa-l-Maṭbaʿa al-Ḥaydariyya, 1381/1962.

Caskel, *Ǧamhara* see Ibn al-Kalbī, *Jamhara.*

Cobb, M.P. *White Banners: Contention in ʿAbbasid Syria, 750–880.* Albany: State University of New York Press, 2001.

Conrad, G. *Abū l-Ḥusayn al-Rāzī (–347/958) und seine Schriften: Untersuchungen zur frühen Damaszener Geschichtsschreibung.* Stuttgart: Franz Steiner, 1991.

Cook, D. *Studies in Muslim Apocalyptic.* Princeton, NJ: Darwin Press, 2002.

Cook, M. *Commanding Right and Forbidding Wrong in Islamic Thought.* Cambridge: Cambridge University Press, 2000.

Crone, P. *Medieval Islamic Political Thought.* Edinburgh: Edinburgh University Press, 2004.

———. "*Al-Riḍā*" = "On the Meaning of the ʿAbbāsid Call to *al-Riḍā.*" In C.E. Bosworth et al. (eds.). *The Islamic World from Classical to Modern Times: Essays in Honor of Bernard Lewis*, pp. 95–111. Princeton, NJ: Darwin Press, 1989.

———. *Slaves on Horses: The Evolution of the Islamic Polity.* Cambridge: Cambridge University Press, 1980.

——— and M. Hinds. *God's Caliph: Religious Authority in the First Centuries of Islam.* Cambridge: Cambridge University Press, 1986.

Daniel, E.L. "Balʿamī's *Tārīkh*" = "Manuscripts and Editions of Balʿamī's *Tarjamah-i Tārīkh-i Ṭabarī.*" *JRAS* New Series 2 (1990), 282–321.

———. "Balʿamī's Account of Early Islamic History." In Farhad Daftary and Josef W. Meri (eds). *Culture and Memory in Medieval Islam*, pp. 163–189. London: I.B. Tauris, 2003.

Al-Dāraquṭnī, ʿAlī b. ʿUmar. *Kitāb ʿIlal al-ḥadīth.* Ed. Maḥfūẓ al-Raḥmān Zayn Allāh al-Salafī. Riyadh: Dār Ṭayba, 1405 H.

———. *Sunan.* Beirut: Dār al-Kutub al-ʿIlmiyya, 1417/1996.

Al-Dārimī, ʿAbdallāh b. ʿAbd al-Raḥmān. *Sunan.* Damascus: Maṭbaʿat al-Iʿtidāl, 1349 H.

Al-Dhahabī, Muḥammad b. Aḥmad Shams al-Dīn. *Al-Kāshif fī maʿrifat man lahu riwāya fī l-kutub al-sitta.* Ed. Muḥammad ʿAwāma. Jeddah: Dār al-Qibla li-l-Thaqāfa al-Islāmiyya, 1413/1992.

———. *Mīzān al-iʿtidāl fī naqd al-rijāl.* Ed. ʿAlī Muḥammad al-Bijāwī. Beirut: Dār al-Maʿrifa li-l-Ṭibāʿa wa-l-Nashr, 1382/1963.

———. *Al-Mughnī fī l-ḍuʿafāʾ*. Ed. Nūr al-Dīn al-ʿItr. N.p., n.d.

———. *Siyar aʿlām al-nubalāʾ*. Ed. Shuʿayb al-Arnāʾūṭ. Beirut: Muʾassasat al-Risāla, 1982–1985.

———. *Tadhkirat al-ḥuffāẓ*. 1) Hyderabad. Dāʾirat al-Maʿārif al-ʿUthmāniyya, 1333 H. 2) Beirut. Dār Iḥyāʾ al-Turāth al-ʿArabī, n.d.

———. *Taʾrīkh al-Islām wa-ṭabaqāt al-mashāhīr wa-l-aʿlām*. Ed. ʿUmar ʿAbd al-Salām Tadmurī. Beirut: Dār al-Kitāb al-ʿArabī, 1408–1421/1988–2000.

Al-Dīnawarī = Aḥmad b. Dāwūd, Abū Ḥanīfa al-Dīnawarī. *Al-Akhbār al-ṭiwāl*. Ed. ʿAbd al-Munʿim ʿĀmir. Cairo: Dār Iḥyāʾ al-Kutub al-ʿArabiyya, 1960.

Donner, F.M. "Muzayna." *EI*², 7:824a–825a.

———. *Narratives of Islamic Origins: The Beginnings of Islamic Historical Writing* [*Studies in Late Antiquity and Early Islam*, no. 14]. Princeton, NJ: Darwin Press, 1998.

Dozy, R. *Supplément aux Dictionnaires Arabes*. Leiden: E.J. Brill, 1881.

———. *Vêtements = Dictionnaire détaillé des noms des vêtements chez les arabes*. Leiden/Paris: E.J. Brill, 1845.

Al-Dūlābī, Muḥammad b. Aḥmad Abū Bishr. *Al-Dhurriyya al-ṭāhira al-nabawiyya*. Ed. Saʿd al-Mubārak Ḥasan. Kuwait: Al-Dār al-Salafiyya, 1407 H.

Dunlop, D.M. "Balʿamī." *EI*², 1:984a–984b.

Duri, ʿAbd al-ʿAzīz. "Al-Fikra al-mahdiyya bayn al-daʿwa al-ʿAbbāsiyya wa-l-ʿaṣr al-ʿAbbāsī al-awwal." In Wadād al-Qāḍī (ed), *Studia Arabica et Islamica: Festschrift for Iḥsān ʿAbbās on his Sixtieth Birthday*, pp. 123–132. Beirut: American University of Beirut Press, 1981.

Elad, A. *The ʿAbbāsid Army = Characteristics of the Development of the ʿAbbāsid Army (Especially Ahl-Khurāsān and al-Abnāʾ Units) With Emphasis on the Reign of Al-Amīn and al-Maʾmūn*. PhD dissertation, The Hebrew University, 1986 (in Hebrew).

———. "Abū ʿAwn, ʿAbd al-Malik b. Yazīd al-Khurāsānī." *EI*³, s.v.

———. "The Dome of the Rock" = "Why did ʿAbd al-Malik Build the Dome of the Rock? A Re-Examination of the Muslim Sources." In Julian Raby and Jeremy Johns (eds.), *Bayt al-Maqdis: ʿAbd al-Malik's Jerusalem*, pp. 241–308. Oxford: Oxford University Press (Oxford Studies in Islamic Art No. 9), 1992.

———. "Early Muslim Historiography" = "Community of Believers of 'Holy Men' and 'Saints' or Community of Muslims? The Rise and Development of Early Muslim Historiography." *JSS* 47 (2002), 241–308.

———. "The Ethnic Composition of the ʿAbbāsid Revolution: A Reevaluation of Some Recent Research." *JSAI* 24 (2000), 246–326.

———. "The First ʿAbbāsid *Mahdī*" = "The Caliph Abū l-ʿAbbās al-Saffāḥ, the First ʿAbbāsid *Mahdī*." In Ezra Fleischer, Mordechai A. Friedman, and Joel A. Kraemer (eds.), *Masʾat Moshe: Studies in Jewish and Islamic Culture Presented to Moshe Gil*, pp. 9–55. Jerusalem and Tel-Aviv: Bialik Institute, 1998 (in Hebrew).

———. "The *Ḥadīth* of al-Mahdī" = "The Struggle for the Legitimacy of Authority as Reflected in the *Ḥadīth* of al-Mahdī." In John Nawas (ed.). *ʿAbbāsid Studies II. Occasional Papers of the School of ʿAbbāsid Studies*, pp. 39–96. Leuven: Peeters, 2010.

———. "Historical Writing" = "The Beginnings of Historical Writing by the Arabs: The Earliest Syrian Writers on the Arab Conquests." *JSAI* 28 (2003), 65–152.

———. *Jerusalem* = *Medieval Jerusalem and Islamic Worship: Holy Places, Ceremonies, Pilgrimage*. Leiden: E.J. Brill, 1995.

———. "al-Maʾmūn's Army" = "*Mawālī* in the Composition of al-Maʾmūn's Army: A Non-Arab Takeover?" In Monique Bernards and John Nawas (eds.). *Patronate and Patronage in Early and Classical Islam*, pp. 278–325. Leiden-Boston: E.J. Brill, 2005.

———. "The Rebellion of Muḥammad b. ʿAbdallāh b. al-Ḥasan b. al-Ḥasan (Known as al-Nafs al-Zakiyya) in 145/762." In J.E. Montgomery (ed.), *ʿAbbasid Studies* (*Orientalia Lovaniensia Analecta 135*), pp. 147–198. Leuven: Peeters, 2004.

———. "The Southern Golan in the Early Muslim Period: The Significance of Two Newly Discovered Milestones of ʿAbd al-Malik." *Der Islam* 76 (1999), 33–88.

———. "Transition" = "Aspects of the Transition from the Umayyad to the ʿAbbāsid Caliphate." *JSAI* 19 (1995), 89–132.

———. "Wāsiṭ" = "The Siege of Wāsiṭ (132/749): Some Aspects of ʿAbbāsid and ʿAlīd Relations at the Beginning of ʿAbbāsid Rule. In Moshe Sharon (ed.). *Studies in Islāmic History and Civilization in Honour of Professor David Ayalon*, pp. 59–90. Jerusalem and Leiden: Cana Publishing House-E.J. Brill, 1986.

Al-Fākihī, Muḥammad b. Isḥāq b. al-ʿAbbās Abū ʿAbdallāh. *Akhbār Makka*. Ed. ʿAbd al-Malik ʿAbdallāh Duhaysh. Beirut[2]: Dār Khiḍr, 1414 H.

———. *Kitāb al-Muntaqā fī akhbār Umm al-Qurā*. Ed. Ferdinand Wüstenfeld. Leipzig: 1858–1861. (Photocopy: Beirut. Khayyāṭ, 1964).

Al-Fasawī = Yaʿqūb b. Sufyān, Abū Yūsuf al-Fasawī. *Kitāb al-Maʿrifa wa-l-taʾrīkh*. Ed. Akram Ḍiyāʾ al-ʿUmarī. Beirut[2]: Muʾassasat al-Risāla, 1401/1981.

Al-Fīrūzābādī, Muḥammad b. Yaʿqūb Abū Ṭāhir. *Al-Maghānim al-muṭāba fī maʿālim Ṭāba*. Ed. Ḥamad Muḥammad al-Jāsir. Riyadh: Dār al-Yamāma li-l-Baḥth wa-l-Tarjama wa-l-Nashr, 1389/1969. [*Nuṣūṣ wa-Abḥāth Jughrāfiyya wa-Taʾrīkhiyya ʿan Jazīrat al-ʿArab*, no. 11].

Fleischhammer, M. *Kitāb al-Aghānī* = *Die Quellen des Kitāb al-aġānī*. Wiesbaden: Harrassowitz, 2004.

Fragmenta Historicorum Arabicorum [*Kitāb al-ʿUyūn wa-l-ḥadāʾiq*]. Ed. M.J. De Goeje. Leiden: E.J. Brill, 1871.

Friedmann, Y. *Prophecy Continuous: Aspects of Aḥmadī Religious Thought and its Medieval Background*. New Delhi[2]: Oxford University Press, 2003.

Gil, M. *A History of Palestine, 634–1099*. Trans. from Hebrew by Ethel Broido. Cambridge: Cambridge University Press, 1992.

Gleave, R. "Ja'far al-Ṣādeq." *EIr*, 14:349–356 ("Life"; "Teachings").

Goitein, S.D. "The Origin of the Vizierate and its True Character." In idem, *Studies in Islamic History and Institutions*, pp. 168–196. Leiden: E.J. Brill, 1966.

Goldziher, I. *Muslim Studies.* Ed. Samuel M. Stern. London: George Allen and Unwin, 1967.

Griffini, E. "Arabischer Handschriften" = "Die jüngste ambrosianische Sammlung arabischer Handschriften." ZDMG 69 (1915), 63–88.

Günther, S. *Maqātil* = *Quellenuntersuchungen zu den "Maqātil aṭ-Ṭālibiyyīn" des Abū l-Farağ al-Iṣfahānī (gest.356/967)*: ein Beitrag zur Problematik der mündlichen und schriftlichen Überlieferung in der mittelalterlichen arabischen Literatur. Zurich/ New York: G. Olms, 1991.

———. "Medieval Arabic Author" = "'... *nor have I learned it from any book of theirs'.* Abū l-Faraj al-Iṣfahānī: A Medieval Arabic Author at Work." In R. Brunner, M. Gronke et al. (eds.). *Islamstudien Ohne Ende. Festscrift für Werner Ende zum 65. Geburtstag*, pp. 139–153. Würzburg. Deutsche Morgenländische Gesellschaft, 2002.

———. "New Results in the Theory of Source Criticism in Medieval Arabic Literature." *Al-Abhath* 42 (1994), 3–15.

Al-Hādī ilā l-Ḥaqq, Yaḥyā b. al-Ḥusayn b. al-Qāsim b. Ibrāhīm. *Kitāb al-Aḥkām fī l-ḥalāl wa-l-ḥarām.* Ed. 'Alī b. Aḥmad b. Abī Ḥarīsa. Sana'a: Maktabat al-Yaman al-Kubrā, 1410/1990.

Ḥājjī Khalīfa, Muṣṭafā b. 'Abdallāh. *Kashf al-ẓunūn 'an asāmī l-kutub wa-l-funūn.* Beirut: Dār al-Kutub al-'Ilmiyya, 1413/1992.

Al-Ḥākim al-Naysābūrī, Muḥammad b. 'Abdallāh b. Ḥamdawayh. *Al-Madkhal ilā l-Ṣaḥīḥ.* Ed. Rabī' Hādī 'Umayr al-Madkhalī. Beirut: Mu'assasat al-Risāla, 1404 H.

———. *Al-Mustadrak.* 1) Ed. Yūsuf al-Mar'ashlī. Beirut: Dār al-Ma'rifa, 1406 H. 2) Ed. Muṣṭafā 'Abd al-Qādir 'Aṭā. Beirut: Dār al-Kutub al-'Ilmiyya, 1411/1990.

Al-Ḥalabī, 'Alī b. Burhān al-Dīn. *Insān al-'uyūn fī sīrat al-Amīn al-Ma'mūn* [Known as *al-Sīra al-Ḥalabiyya*]. Beirut: Dār al-Ma'rifa, 1400 H.

Halm, H. *Shi'a Islam: From Religion to Revolution.* Princeton, NJ: Wiener Publishers, 1997.

Al-Ḥarbī[?], Ibrāhīm b. Isḥāq b. Bashīr b. 'Abdallāh al-Marwazī. *Kitāb al-Manāsik wa-amākin ṭuruq al-ḥajj wa-ma'ālim al-Jazīra.* Ed. Ḥamad Muḥammad al-Jāsir. Riyadh: Dār al-Yamāma li-l-Baḥth wa-l-Nashr, 1969. [*Nuṣūṣ wa-Abḥāth Jughrāfiyya wa-Ta'rīkhiyya 'an Jazīrat al-'Arab*, no. 9].

Ḥasan, Muḥammad. *Al-Mahdī fī l-Islām.* Cairo: Dār al-Kitāb al-'Arabī, 1373/1953.

Hasson, I. "al-Zubayr b. al-'Awwām." EI^2, 11:549a–551a.

Al-Ḥaṭṭāb al-Ru'aynī, Muḥammad b. Muḥammad b. 'Abd al-Raḥmān Abū 'Abdallāh. *Mawāhib al-jalīl fī sharḥ mukhtaṣar khalīl.* Ed. Zakariyyā' 'Umayrāt. Beirut: Dār al-Kutub al-'Ilmiyya, 1416/1995.

Al-Haytamī, Aḥmad b. Muḥammad b. Muḥammad b. ʿAlī b. Ḥajar Shihāb al-Dīn al-Saʿdī. *al-Mukhtaṣar = Al-Qawl al-mukhtaṣar fī ʿalāmāt al-mahdī l-muntaẓar*. Ed. Muḥammad ʿAzab. Cairo: Dār al-Ṣaḥwa li-l-Nashr, 1407/1986.

———. *Al-Ṣawāʿiq al-muḥriqa ʿalā ahl al-rafḍ wa-l-ḍalāl wa-l-zandaqa*. Ed. ʿAbd al-Raḥmān b. ʿAbdallāh al-Turkī and Kāmil Muḥammad al-Kharrāṭ. Beirut: Muʾassasat al-Risāla, 1997.

Al-Haythamī, ʿAlī b. Abī Bakr Nūr al-Dīn. *Majmaʿ al-zawāʾid*. Beirut: Dār al-Kutub al-ʿIlmiyya, 1408/1988.

Al-Ḥāzimī, Muḥammad b. Mūsā. *Al-Amākin aw mā ittafaqa lafẓuhu wa-iftaraqa musammāhu min al-amkina*. Ed. Ḥamad Muḥammad al-Jāsir. Riyadh: Dār al-Yamāma li-l-Baḥth wa-l-Tarjama wa-l-Nashr, 1415 H.

El-Hibri, T. *Reinterpreting Islamic Historiography: Hārūn al-Rashīd and the Narrative of the ʿAbbāsid Caliphate*. Cambridge: Cambridge University Press, 1999.

Hillebrand, C. *The Umayyad Caliphate = The History of al-Ṭabarī*. Vol. 26: *The Waning of the Umayyad Caliphate*. Albany: State University of New York Press, 1989.

Al-Ḥillī, al-Ḥasan b. ʿAlī b. Dāwūd. *Rijāl Ibn Dāwūd*. Ed. Muḥammad Ṣādiq Āl Baḥr al-ʿUlūm. Najaf: Al-Maṭbaʿa al-Ḥaydariyya, 1392/1972.

Al-Ḥillī, al-Ḥasan b. Sulaymān. *Mukhtaṣar baṣāʾir al-darajāt*. Najaf: Al-Maṭbaʿa al-Ḥaydariyya, 1370/1950.

Al-Ḥillī, al-Ḥasan b. Yūsuf b. ʿAlī b. al-Muṭahhar. *Khulāṣat al-aqwāl fī maʿrifat al-rijāl*. Ed. Jawād al-Qayyūmī. [Qumm?]: Muʾassasat Nashr al-Faqāha, 1417 H.

———. *Muntahā l-maṭlab fī taḥqīq al-madhhab*. Mashhad: Majmaʿ al-Buḥūth al-Islāmiyya, 1412 H.

———. *Al-Mustajād min Kitāb al-Irshād*. Qumm: Maktabat Āyatullāh al-ʿUẓmā l-Marʿashī l-Najafī, 1406 H.

Al-Ḥimyarī, Muḥammad b. ʿAbd al-Munʿim. *Kitāb al-Rawḍ al-miʿṭār fī khabar al-aqṭār*. Ed. Iḥsān ʿAbbās. Beirut: Maktabat Lubnān, 1975.

Hinz, W. *Islamische Masse und Gewichte*. Leiden: E.J. Brill, 1955.

Al-Ḥiṣnī, Abū Bakr b. Muḥammad b. ʿAbd al-Muʾmin al-Ḥusaynī Taqī l-Dīn. *Dafʿ shubhat man shabbaha wa-tamarrada wa-nasaba dhālika ilā l-Sayyid al-jalīl al-Imām Aḥmad*. Ed. Muḥammad Zāhid b. al-Ḥasan al-Kawtharī. Cairo: Al-Maktaba al-Azhariyya li-l-Turāth, n.d.

Hodgson, M.S. "How did the Early Shīʿa Become Sectarian." *JAOS* 75 (1951), 1–13.

———. "Djaʿfar al-Ṣādiḳ," *EI*², 2:374a–375b.

Hoyland, Robert (trans., ed.). *Theophilus of Edessa's Chronicle and the Circulation of Historical Knowledge in Late Antiquity and Early Islam*. Liverpool: Liverpool University Press, 2011.

Ibn al-Abbār, Muḥammad b. ʿAbdallāh b. Abī Bakr al-Quḍāʿī Abū ʿAbdallāh. *Al-Muʿjam fī aṣḥāb al-Qāḍī l-Imām Abī ʿAlī l-Ṣadafī.* Madrid: Rojas, 1886.

Ibn ʿAbd al-Barr = Yūsuf b. ʿAbdallāh b. Muḥammad b. ʿAbd al-Barr Abū ʿUmar al-Qurṭubī. *Al-Intiqāʾ fī faḍāʾil al-thalātha al-aʾimma al-fuqahāʾ.* Beirut: Dār al-Kutub al-ʿIlmiyya, n.d.

———. *Al-Istī ʿāb fī maʿrifat al aṣḥāb.* Ed. ʿAlī Muḥammad al-Bijāwī. Beirut: Dār al-Jīl, 1412 H.

———. *Tajrīd al-Tamhīd li-mā fī l-Muwaṭṭā min al-maʿānī wa-l-asānīd.* Ed. Muṣṭafā b. Aḥmad al-ʿAlawī and Muḥammad ʿAbd al-Kabīr al-Bakrī. Al-Maghrib [sic]: Wizārat ʿUmūm al-Awqāf wa-l-Shuʾūn al-Islāmiyya, 1387 H.

Ibn ʿAbd Rabbihi, Aḥmad b. Muḥammad. *Kitāb al-ʿIqd al-farīd.* Ed. Aḥmad Amīn, Aḥmad al-Zayn, Ibrāhīm al-Abyārī. Cairo: Maṭbaʿat Lajnat al-Taʾlīf wa-l-Tarjama wa-l-Nashr, 1940–1953.

Ibn Abī l-Dunyā, ʿAbdallāh b. Muḥammad b. ʿUbayd al-Qurashī. *Kitāb al-Iʿtibār wa-aʿqāb al-surūr wa-l-aḥzāb.* Ed. Najm ʿAbd al-Raḥmān Khalaf. Amman: Dār al-Bashīr, 1413/1993.

———. *Makārim al-akhlāq.* Ed. Majdī l-Sayyid Ibrāhīm. Cairo: Maktabat al-Qurʾān li-l-Ṭabʿ wa-l-Nashr wa-l-Tawzīʿ, n.d.

Ibn Abī l-Ḥadīd, ʿAbd al-Ḥamīd b. Hibat Allāh b. Muḥammad Abū Ḥāmid. *Sharḥ Nahj al-balāgha.* Ed. Muḥammad Abū l-Faḍl Ibrāhīm. Cairo: Dār Iḥyāʾ al-Kutub al-ʿArabiyya, 1959–1964.

Ibn Abī Ḥātim al-Rāzī, ʿAbd al-Raḥmān b. Muḥammad b. Idrīs al-Tamīmī. *ʿIlal al-ḥadīth.* Ed. Muḥibb al-Dīn al-Khaṭīb. Beirut: Dār al-Maʿrifa, 1405 H.

———. *Kitāb al-Jarḥ wa-l-taʿdīl.* Beirut. Dār Iḥyāʾ al-Turāth al-ʿArabī, 1371–1373/1952–1953. [Reprint of Hyderabad: Dāʾirat al-Maʿārif al-ʿUthmāniyya, 1952.]

Ibn Abī Shayba = ʿAbdallāh b. Muḥammad b. Ibrāhīm (Abū Shayba) Abū Bakr. *Kitāb al-Muṣannaf.* Ed. Kamāl Yūsuf al-Ḥūt. Riyadh: Maktabat al-Rushd, 1409 H.

Ibn ʿAdī = ʿAbdallāh b. ʿAdī Abū Aḥmad al-Jurjānī. *Al-Kāmil fī ḍuʿafāʾ al-rijāl.* Ed. S. Zakkār and Yaḥyā Mukhtār al- Ghazzāwī. Beirut[3]: Dār al-Fikr, 1409/1988.

Ibn al-ʿAdīm, ʿUmar b. Aḥmad. *Bughyat al-ṭalab fī taʾrīkh Ḥalab.* Ed. Suhayl Zakkār. Damascus: Maṭābiʿ Dār al-Baʿth, 1408/1988.

———. *Zubdat al-ḥalab min taʾrīkh Ḥalab.* Ed. Sāmī l-Dahhān. Damascus: Al-Maʿhad al-Faransī bi-Dimashq li-l-Dirāsāt al-ʿArabiyya, 1370/1951.

Ibn al-Aṣbagh = ʿArrām b. al-Aṣbagh al-Sulamī. "Jibāl Tihāma" = "Kitāb Asmāʾ jibāl Tihāma wa-sukkanihā wa-mā fīhā min al-ashjār wa-mā fīhā min al-miyāh." In ʿAbd al-Salām Muḥammad Hārūn (ed.), *Nawādir al-makhṭūṭāt,* vol. 8, pp. 383–441. Cairo: Maṭbaʿat Lajnat al-Taʾlīf wa-l-Tarjama wa-l-Nashr, 1955.

Ibn ʿAsākir, ʿAlī b. al-Ḥasan Abū l-Qāsim. *Taʾrīkh Madīnat Dimashq*. Ed. ʿUmar b. Gharāma al-ʿAmr(aw)ī. Beirut: Dār al-Fikr, 1415/1995–2001. [See also Ibn Manẓūr, *al-Mukhtaṣar*].

Ibn Aʿtham al-Kūfī = Aḥmad b. Aʿtham al-Kūfī Abū Muḥammad. *Kitāb al-Futūḥ*. 1) Hyderabad: Dāʾirat al-Maʿārif al-ʿUthmāniyya, 1388–1395/1968–1975 2) Ed. ʿAlī Shīrī. Beirut: Dār al-Aḍwāʾ li-l-Ṭibāʿa wa-l-Nashr, 1411 H.

Ibn al-Athīr, ʿAlī b. Muḥammad ʿIzz al-Dīn. *Al-Kāmil fī l-taʾrīkh*. 1) Ed. Carl Johan Tornberg. Leiden: E.J. Brill, 1863–1871. 2) Reprint. Beirut: Ed. Carl Johan Tornberg. Dār Ṣādir-Dār Beirut, 1402/1982.

———. *Al-Lubāb fī tahdhīb al-ansāb*. Beirut: Dār Ṣādir, n.d.

———. *Usd al-ghāba fī tamyyīz al-ṣaḥāba*. 1) Cairo: Jamʿiyyat al-Maʿārif al-Miṣriyya, 1280–1286 H. 2) Beirut: Dār al-Kitāb al-ʿArabī, n.d.

Ibn Bābawayh al-Qummī, ʿAlī b. al-Ḥusayn b. Mūsā (al-Shaykh al-Ṣadūq's father). *Al-Imāma wa-l-tabṣira min al-ḥayra*. Qumm: Madrasat al-Imām al-Mahdī, 1404 H.

Ibn Bābawayh al-Qummī, Muḥammad b. ʿAlī b. al-Ḥusayn b. Mūsā, (al-Shaykh al-Ṣadūq). *ʿIlal al-sharāʾiʿ wa-l-aḥkām*. Najaf: Al-Maktaba al-Ḥaydariyya wa-Maṭbaʿatuhā, 1966.

———. *Al-Amālī*. Qumm: Markaz al-Ṭibāʿa wa-l-Nashr fī Muʾassasat al-Baʿtha, 1417 H.

———. *Kamāl (Ikmāl) al-dīn wa-tamām (itmām) al-niʿma fī ithbāt al-rajʿa*. Ed. ʿAlī Akbar al-Ghifārī. [Qumm?]: Muʾassasat al-Nashr al-Islāmī, 1405 H.

———. *Al-Khiṣāl fī l-akhlāq*. Ed. ʿAlī Akbar al-Ghifārī. Qumm: Manshūrāt Jamāʿat al-Mudarrisīn fī Qumm, 1403 H.

———. *ʿUyūn akhbār al-Riḍā*. Ed. Ḥusayn al-Aʿlamī. Beirut: Maṭābiʿ Muʾassasat al-Aʿlamī, 1404/1984.

Ibn Durayd, Muḥammad b. al-Ḥasan Abū Bakr al-Azdī. *Kitāb al-Ishtiqāq*. Ed. ʿAbd al-Salām Muḥammad Hārūn. Cairo[2]: Maṭbaʿat al-Khānjī, 1399/1979.

Ibn Farḥūn, Ibrāhīm b. ʿAlī b. Muḥammad al-Yaʿmurī l-Mālikī. *Al-Dībāj al-mudhhab fī aḥkām al-madhhab*. Beirut: Dār al-Kutub al-ʿIlmiyya, 1417/1996.

Ibn Ḥabīb, Muḥammad b. Ḥabīb. "al-Mughtālīn" = "Asmāʾ al-mughtālīn fī l-jāhiliyya wa-l-Islām wa-asmāʾ man qutila min al-shuʿarāʾ." In ʿAbd al-Salām Muḥammad Hārūn (ed.). *Nawādir al-makhṭūṭāt*, vol. 6: pp. [105]–278. Cairo[2]: Muṣṭafā l-Bābī l-Ḥalabī, 1973.

———. *Kitāb al-Muḥabbar*. Ed. Ilse Lichtenstaedter. Hyderabad: Dāʾirat al-Maʿārif al-ʿUthmāniyya, 1942.

———. *Kitāb al-Munammaq fī akhbār Quraysh*. Ed. Khūrshīd Aḥmad Fāriq. Beirut: ʿĀlam al-Kutub, 1405/1985.

Ibn Ḥajar = Aḥmad b. ʿAlī Abū l-Faḍl Ibn Ḥajar al-ʿAsqalānī. *al-Alqāb = Nuzhat al-albāb fī l-alqāb*. Ed. ʿAbd al-ʿAzīz b. Muhammad Ṣāliḥ al-Sadīdī. Riyadh: N.p., 1989.

———. *Fatḥ al-bārī fī sharḥ Ṣaḥīḥ al-Bukhārī*. Ed. Muḥammad Fuʾād ʿAbd al-Bāqī and Muḥibb al-Dīn al-Khaṭīb. Beirut: Dār al-Maʿrifa, 1379 H.

———. *Al-Iṣāba fī tamyīz al-Ṣaḥāba*. 1) Ed. ʿAlī Muḥammad al-Bijāwī. Beirut: Dār al-Jīl, 1412/1992. 2) Ed. ʿĀdil Aḥmad ʿAbd Mawjūd and ʿAlī Muḥammad Muʿawwāḍ. Beirut: Dār al-Kutub al-ʿIlmiyya, 1415/1995.

———. *Lisān al-mīzān*. Beirut: Muʾassasat al-Aʿlamī li-l-Maṭbūʿāt, 1390/1971

———. *Muqaddimat fatḥ al-Bārī*. Beirut: Dār Iḥyāʾ al-Turāth al-ʿArabī, 1408/1988.

———. *Tahdhīb al-tahdhīb*. 1) Hyderabad: Dāʾirat al-Maʿārif al-ʿUthmāniyya, 1325–1327 H. 2) Beirut: Dār al-Fikr, 1404/1984.

———. *Taʿjīl al-manfaʿa bi-zawāʾid rijāl al-aʾimma al-arbaʿa*. Ed. Ikrām Allāh Imdād al-Ḥaqq. Beirut: Dār al-Kitāb al-ʿArabī, n.d.

———. *Taqrīb al-tahdhīb*. 1) Ed. Muḥammad ʿAwāma. Damascus[?]: Dār al-Rashīd, 1406/1986. 2) Ed. Muṣṭafā ʿAbd al-Qādir ʿAṭā. Beirut: Dār al-Kutub al-ʿIlmiyya, 1415/1995.

Ibn Ḥamza al-Ḥusaynī l-Shāfiʿī, Muḥammad b. ʿAlī b. al-Ḥasan Abū l-Maḥāsin. *Man lahu riwāya = Al-Ikmāl fī dhikr man lahu riwāya fī Musnad al-Imām Aḥmad min al-rijāl siwā man dhukira fī Tahdhīb al-kamāl*. Ed. ʿAbd al-Muʿṭī Amīn Qalʿajī. Karachi: Jāmiʿat al-Dirāsāt al-Islāmiyya, n.d.

Ibn Ḥamza al-Ṭūsī, Muḥammad b. ʿAlī ʿImād al-Dīn Abū Jaʿfar. *Al-Thāqib fī l-manāqib*. Ed. Nabīl Riḍā ʿAlwān. Qumm²: Muʾassasat Anṣāriyya li-l-Ṭibāʿa wa-l-Nashr, 1412 H.

———. *Al-Wasīla ilā nayl al-faḍīla*. Ed. Muḥammad al-Ḥassūn. Qumm: Maktabat Āyatullāh al-ʿUẓmā l-Marʿashī l-Najafī, 1408 H.

Ibn Ḥanbal = Aḥmad b. Ḥanbal. *Faḍāʾil al-saḥāba*. Ed. Waṣī Allāh Muḥammad ʿAbbās. Beirut: Muʾassasat al-Risāla, 1403/1983.

———. *Al-ʿIlal*. Beirut: Al-Maktab al-Islāmī, 1408 H.

———. *Musnad*. Beirut. Dār Ṣādir, n.d. [Reprint of Būlāq, 1313 H.]

Ibn Ḥazm, ʿAlī b. Aḥmad b. Saʿīd Abū Muḥammad. *Al-Iḥkām fī uṣūl al-aḥkām*. Cairo: Dār al-Ḥadīth, 1404 H.

———. *Jamharat ansāb al-ʿArab*. Ed. ʿAbd al-Salām Muḥammad Hārūn. Cairo: Dār al-Maʿārif, 1962.

Ibn Ḥibbān = Muḥammad b. Ḥibbān b. Aḥmad al-Bustī l-Tamīmī. *Kitāb al-Majrūḥīn min al-muḥaddithīn al-ḍuʿafāʾ wa-l-matrūkīn*. Ed. Maḥmūd Ibrāhīm Zāyid. Aleppo: Dār al-Waʿy, 1395–1412/1975–1992.

———. *Mashāhīr ʿulamāʾ al-amṣār*. Ed. Marzūq ʿAlī Ibrāhīm. El-Mansoura: Dār al-Wafāʾ li-l-Ṭibāʿa wa-l-Nashr wa-l-Tawzīʿ, 1411 H.

——— *Ṣaḥīḥ*. Ed. Shuʿayb al-Arnāʾūṭ. Beirut: Muʾassasat al-Risāla, 1414/1993.

———. *Kitāb al-Thiqāt*. Hyderabad: Dāʾirat al-Maʿārif al-ʿUthmāniyya, 1393–1403/1973–1983.

Ibn Hishām, ʿAbd al-Malik. *al-Sīra al-nabawiyya*. Ed. Muḥammad Muḥyī l-Dīn ʿAbd al-Ḥamīd. Cairo: Maktabat Muḥammad ʿAlī Ṣubayḥ, 1383/1963.

Ibn al-ʿImād al-Hanbalī, ʿAbd al-Ḥayy b. Aḥmad b. Muḥammad. *Shadharāt al-dhahab fī akhbār man dhahab*. Ed. ʿAbd al-Qādir al-Arnāʾūṭ and Maḥmūd al-Arnāʾūṭ. Beirut: Dār Ibn Kathīr, 1406–1416/1986–1995.

Ibn ʿInaba, Aḥmad b. ʿAlī b. al-Ḥusayn b. ʿAlī b. Muhannā Jamāl al-Dīn al-Ḥasanī. *ʿUmdat al-ṭālib fī ansāb āl Abī Ṭālib*. Ed. Muḥammad Ḥasan Āl al-Ṭālaqānī. Najaf: Al-Maṭbaʿa al-Ḥaydariyya, 1380/1961.

Ibn al-Jawzī, ʿAbd al-Raḥmān b. ʿAlī b. Muḥammad Abū l-Faraj. *Kitāb al-Ḍuʿafāʾ wa-l-matrūkīn*. Ed. ʿAbdallāh al-Qāḍī. Beirut: Dār al-Kutub al-ʿIlmiyya, 1406 H.

———. *Kitāb al-Mawḍūʿāt*. Ed. ʿAbd al-Raḥmān Muḥammad ʿUthmān. Medina: N.p., 1386/1966.

———. *Al-Muntaẓam fī taʾrīkh al-mulūk wa-l-umam*. Ed. Muḥammad Muṣṭafā ʿAbd al-Qādir ʿAṭā. Beirut: Dār al-Kutub al-ʿIlmiyya, 1412/1992.

———. *Ṣafwat al-ṣafwa*. Ed. Maḥmūd Fākhūrī and Muḥammad Rawwās Qalʿajī. Beirut^{2}: Dār al-Maʿrifa, 1399/1979.

Ibn al-Kalbī, Hishām b. Muḥammad b. al-Sāʾib. *Jamharat al-nasab*. 1) Ed. W. Caskel. Leiden: E.J. Brill, 1966. 2) Ed. Nājī Ḥasan. Beirut: ʿĀlam al-Kutub, 1407/1986. 3) Ed. Maḥmūd Firdaws al-ʿAẓm. Damascus: Dār al-Yaqẓa al-ʿArabiyya, [1983?]–1986.

———. *Nasab Maʿadd wa-l-Yaman al-kabīr*. Ed. Nājī Ḥasan. Beirut: ʿĀlam al-Kutub/ Maktabat al-Nahḍa al-ʿArabiyya, 1408/1988.

Ibn Kathīr, Ismāʿīl b. ʿUmar Abū l-Fidāʾ. *Al-Bidāya wa-l-nihāya fī l-taʾrīkh*. 1) Cairo: Maṭbaʿat al-Saʿāda, 1351–1358/1932–1939. 2) Ed. ʿAlī Shīrī. Beirut: Dār Iḥyāʾ al-Turāth al-ʿArabī, 1408/1988.

Ibn Khālawayh, al-Ḥusayn b. Aḥmad Abū ʿAbdallāh. *Al-Ḥujja fī l-qirāʾāt al-sabʿ*. Ed. ʿAbd al-ʿĀl Sālim Mukarram. Beirut^{4}: Dār al-Shurūq, 1401 H.

Ibn Khaldūn, ʿAbd al-Raḥmān b. Muḥammad b. Muḥammad. *Kitāb al-ʿIbar wa-dīwān al-mubtadaʾ wa-l-khabar fī ayyām al-ʿArab wa-l-ʿAjam wa-l-Barbar wa-man ʿāṣarahum min dhawī l-sulṭān al-akbar.* 1) Beirut: Muʾassasat al-Aʿlamī li-l-Maṭbūʿāt, 1391/1971. 2) Beirut: Dār al-Kitāb al-Lubnānī, 1956–1961.

Ibn Khallikān, Aḥmad b. Muḥammad b. Abī Bakr Abū l-ʿAbbās Shams al-Dīn. *Wafayāt al-aʿyān wa-anbāʾ abnāʾ al-zamān*. Ed. Iḥsān ʿAbbās. Beirut: Dār al-Thaqāfa, 1968–1972.

Ibn Khayyāṭ al-ʿUṣfurī, Khalīfa. *Ṭabaqāt*. 1) Ed. Suhayl Zakkār. Beirut: Dār al-Fikr li-l-Ṭibāʿa wa-l-Nashr wa-l-Tawzīʿ, 1414/1993. 2) Ed. Akram Ḍiyāʾ al-ʿUmarī. Riyadh^{2}: Dār Ṭayba, 1402/1982.

———. *Taʾrīkh Khalīfa b. Khayyāṭ*. 1) Ed. Suhayl Zakkār. Beirut: Dār al-Fikr li-l-Ṭibāʿa wa-l-Nashr wa-l-Tawzīʿ, 1414/1993. 2) Ed. Akram Ḍiyāʿ al-ʿUmarī. Najaf: Maṭbaʿat al-Ādāb, 1386/1967.

Ibn Maʿīn, Yaḥyā. *Taʾrīkh*. Ed. ʿAbdallāh Aḥmad Ḥasan. Beirut: Dār al-Qalam li-l-Ṭibāʿa wa-l-Nashr wa-l-Tawzīʿ, n.d.

Ibn Mākūlā, ʿAlī b. Hibat Allāh. *Al-Ikmāl fī rafʿ al-irtiyāb ʿan al-muʾtalif wa-l-mukhtalif min al-asmāʾ wa-l-kunā wa-l-ansāb*. Vols. 1–6. Ed. ʿAbd al-Raḥmān b. Yaḥyā l-Muʿallimī. Hyderabad: Dāʾirat al-Maʿārif al-ʿUthmāniyya, 1381–1386/1962–1967. Vol. 7. Beirut. Dār al-Kutub al-ʿIlmiyya, 1411/1990.

Ibn Manẓūr, Muḥammad b. Mukarram. *Lisān al-ʿArab.* Beirut: Dār Ṣādir Dār Bayrūt, 1375/1956.

———. *Mukhtaṣar Taʾrīkh Madīnat Dimashq.* Damascus: Dār al-Fikr li-l-Ṭibāʿa wa-l-Nashr wa-l-Tawzīʿ, 1404–1411/1984–1990.

Ibn al-Murajjā = Al-Musharrāf b. al-Murajjā Abū l-Maʿālī l-Maqdisī. *Faḍāʾil Bayt al-Maqdis wa-l-Khalīl wa-faḍāʾil al-Shām.* Ed. O. Livne-Kafri. Shfarʿam: Al-Mashreq, 1995.

Ibn al-Nadīm, Muḥammad b. Isḥāq Abū l-Faraj. *Al-Fihrist.* 1) Ed. Riḍā Tajaddud. Tehran: N.p. [1971]. 2) English translation: B. Dodge. *The Fihrist of al-Nadīm: A Tenth Century Survey of Muslim Culture.* New York: Columbia University Press, 1970.

Ibn al-Najjār, Muḥammad b. Maḥmūd b. al-Ḥasan al-Baghdādī. *Dhayl taʾrīkh Baghdād.* Ed. Muṣṭafā ʿAbd al-Qādir ʿAṭā. Beirut: Dār al-Kutub al-ʿIlmiyya, 1417/1997.

Ibn Nāṣir al-Dīn, Muḥammad b. ʿAbdallāh b. Muḥammad Shams al-Dīn al-Dimashqī. *Tawḍīḥ al-mushtabih fī ḍabṭ asmāʾ al-ruwāt wa-ansābihim wa-alqābihim wa-kunāhum.* Ed. Muḥammad Nuʿaym al-ʿIrqsūsī. Beirut[2]: Muʾassasat al-Risāla, 1414/1993.

Ibn Qāniʿ = ʿAbd al-Bāqī b. Qāniʿ b. Marzūq b. Wāthiq Abū l-Ḥusayn al-Umawī (*mawlāhum*). *Muʿjam al-ṣaḥāba.* Ed. Ṣalāḥ b. Sālim al-Miṣrātī. Medina: Maktabat al-Ghurabāʾ al-Athariyya, 1418 H.

Ibn Qayyim al-Jawziyya, Muḥammad b. Abī Bakr b. Ayyūb al-Ḥanbalī l-Dimashqī. *Tuḥfat al-mawdūd bi-aḥkām al-mawlūd.* Ed. Muḥammad Ṣubḥī Ḥasan Ḥallāq. Cairo: Maktabat Ibn Taymiyya, 1420/1999.

Ibn Qutayba, ʿAbdallāh b. Muslim. *Gharīb al-ḥadīth.* Ed. ʿAbdallāh al-Jubūrī. Qumm: Dār al-Kutub al-ʿIlmiyya, 1408 H.

———. *Kitāb al-Maʿāṛif.* 1) Ed. Ferdinand Wüstenfeld. Göttingen: Vandenhoeck und Ruprecht, 1850. 2) Ed. Tharwat ʿUkāsha. Cairo[4]: Dār al-Maʿārif, 1981.

———. *Taʾwīl mukhtalif al-ḥadīth.* Ed. Muḥammad Zuhayr al-Najjār. Beirut: Dār al-Jīl, 1393/1972.

———. *ʿUyūn al-akhbār.* Cairo: Dār al-Kutub, 1924–1930.

Ibn Saʿd = Muḥammad b. Saʿd b. Manīʿ. *Al-Qism al-mutammim li-tābiʿī ahl al-Madīna wa-man baʿdahum min rubʿ al-ṭabaqa al-thālitha ilā muntaṣaf al-ṭabaqa al-sādisa.* Ed. Ziyād Muḥammad Manṣūr. Medina[2]: Maktabat al-ʿUlūm wa-l-Ḥikam, 1408/1987.

———. *Al-Ṭabaqāt al-kubrā.* Ed. Iḥsān ʿAbbās. Beirut: Dār Ṣādir li-l-Ṭibāʿa wa-l-Nashr, 1958.

Ibn Sayyid al-Nās, Muḥammad b. Muḥammad Abū l-Fatḥ. *ʿUyūn al-athar fī funūn al-maghāzī wa-l-shamāʾil wa-l-siyar.* Beirut: Muʾassasat ʿIzz al-Dīn li-l-Ṭibāʿa wa-l-Nashr, 1406/1986.

Ibn Shabba = ʿUmar b. Shabba Abū Zayd al-Numayrī. *Taʾrīkh al-Madīna al-munawwara.* Ed. Fahīm Muḥammad Shaltūt. Jeddah [?]. N.p., [date of introduction is 1399/1979].

Ibn Shaddād, Muḥammad b. ʿAlī b. Ibrāhīm ʿIzz al-Dīn. *Al-Aʿlāq al-khaṭīra fī dhikr umarāʾ al-Shām wa-l-Jazīra*. Vol. 1, part 2. Ed. Yaḥyā Zakariyyāʾ ʿAbbāra. Damascus: Wizārat al-Thaqāfa, 1991.

Ibn Shāhīn, ʿUmar b. Aḥmad b. ʿUthmān Abū Ḥafṣ. *Nāsikh al-ḥadīth wa-mansūkhuhu*. Ed. Samīr b. Amīn al-Zuhayrī. Al-Zarqāʾ: Maktabat al-Manār, 1408/1988.

Ibn Shahrāshūb, Muḥammad b. ʿAlī. *Maʿālim al-ʿulamāʾ*. Qumm: N.p., n.d.

———. *Manāqib āl Abī Ṭālib*. Najaf: al-Maṭbaʿa al-Ḥaydariyya, 1376/1956.

Ibn al-Shiḥna, Muḥammad. *Taʾrīkh Ḥalab*. Ed. K. Ohta. Tokyo, 1990.

Ibn Taghrī Birdī = Yūsuf b. Taghrī Birdī Abū l-Maḥāsin. *Al-Nujūm al-zāhira fī mulūk Miṣr wa-l-Qāhira*. Cairo: Maṭbaʿat Dār al-Kutub al-Miṣriyya, 1929–1930.

Ibn Ṭāʾūs, ʿAlī b. Mūsā b. Jaʿfar Abū l-Qāsim Ibn Ṭāʾūs. *al-ʿAmal al-mashrūʿ = Jamāl al-usbūʿ bi-kamāl al-ʿamal al-mashrūʿ*. Ed. Jawād Qayyūmī l-Iṣfahānī. N.p.: Maṭbaʿat Akhtar Shamāl, 1371 H.

———. *Al-Iqbāl bi-l-aʿmāl al-ḥasana fīmā yuʿmal marra fī l-sana*. Ed. Jawād al-Qayyūmī l-Iṣfahānī. [Qumm?]: Maktabat al-Aʿlām al-Islāmī, 1416 H.

———. *Al-Tashrīf bi-l-minan fī l-taʿrīf bi-l-fitan (al-maʿrūf bi-l-Malāḥim wa-l-fitan)*. Iṣfahān: N.p., 1416 H.

———. *Al-Yaqīn fī ikhtiṣāṣ mawlānā ʿAlī (ʿalayhi al-salām) bi-imrat al-muʾminīn*. Ed. al-Anṣārī. Qumm: Muʾassasat Dār al-Kutub [al-Jazāʾirī] li-l-Ṭibāʿa wa-l-Nashr, 1413 H.

Ibn Taymiyya, Aḥmad b. ʿAbd al-Ḥalīm b. ʿAbd al-Salām Abū l-ʿAbbās. *Minhāj al-sunna al-nabawiyya fī naqḍ al-Shīʿa wa-l-Qadariyya*. Ed. Muḥammad Rashād Sālim. N.p.: Muʾassasat Qurṭuba, 1406 H.

Ibn Zanjala, ʿAbd al-Raḥmān b. Muḥammad Abū Zurʿa. *Ḥujjat al-qirāʾāt*. Ed. Saʿīd al-Afghānī. Beirut[2]: Muʾassasat al-Risāla, 1402/1982.

Ibn al-Zubayr, al-Rashīd. *Book of Gifts and Rarities (Kitāb al-Hadāyā wa-l-tuḥaf)*. Trans. Ghāda al-Hijjāwī l-Qaddūmī. Cambridge, MA: Harvard University Press, 1996.

———. *Kitāb al-Dhakhāʾir wa-l-tuḥaf*. Ed. Muḥammad Ḥamīdullāh. Kuwait: Dāʾirat al-Maṭbūʿāt wa-l-Nashr, 1959. See also al-Zubayrī.

Al-Irbilī, ʿAlī b. ʿĪsā b. Abī l-Fatḥ. *Kashf al-ghumma fī maʿrifat al-aʾimma*. Beirut[2]: Dār al-Aḍwāʾ, 1405/1985.

Al-ʿIṣāmī, ʿAbd al-Malik b. Ḥusayn b. ʿAbd al-Malik al-Makkī. *Simṭ al-nujūm al-ʿawālī fī anbāʾ al-awāʾil wa-l-tawālī*. Cairo: al-Maktaba al-Salafiyya, 1380 H.

Al-Iṣfahānī, Aḥmad b. ʿAbdallāh b. Aḥmad Abū Nuʿaym. *Ḥilyat al-awliyāʾ wa-ṭabaqāt al-aṣfiyāʾ*. 1) Ed. Muṣṭafā ʿAbd al-Qādir ʿAṭā. Cairo: Maṭbaʿat al-Saʿāda, 1351–1357/1932–1938. 2) Beirut: Dār al-Fikr, 1418/1997.

———. *Kitāb al-Ḍuʿafāʾ*. Ed. Fārūq Ḥamāda. Casablanca: Dār al-Thaqāfa, 1405/1984.

Al-Iṣfahānī, ʿAlī b. al-Ḥusayn b. Muḥammad Abū l-Faraj. *Kitāb al-Aghānī*. 1) Būlāq, 1284–1285 H. 2) Cairo: Dār al-Kutub al-Miṣriyya, 1345–1381/1927–1961 (vols. 1–16); Cairo: Al-Hayʾa al-Miṣriyya al-ʿĀmma li-l-Taʾlīf wa-l-Kitāb, 1389–1394//1970–1974 (vols. 17–24); Ed. Ibrāhīm al-Abyārī. Cairo: Dār al-Shaʿb, 1394–1399/1974–1979 (vols. 25–30).

———. *Maqātil al-ṭālibiyyīn*. Ed. Aḥmad Ṣaqr. Cairo: N.p., 1368/1949.

Al-Iṣfahānī, Muḥammad b. al-Ḥasan b. Muḥammad al-Fāḍil al-Hindī Bahāʾ al-Dīn. *Kashf al-lithām ʿan qawāʿid al-aḥkām*. Qumm: Maktabat Āyatullāh al-ʿUẓmā l-Marʿashī l-Najafī, 1405 H.

Al-Isfarāʾīnī, Ṭāhir b. Muḥammad Abū l-Muẓaffar. *Al-Tabṣīr fī l-dīn wa-tamyīz al-firqa al-nājiya ʿan l-firaq al-hālikīn*. Ed. Kamāl Yūsuf al-Ḥūt. Beirut: ʿĀlam al-Kutub, 1983.

Jafri, Ḥusain M. *Origins and Early Development of Shīʿa Islam*. London and New York: Longman, 1979.

Al-Jāḥiẓ, ʿAmr b. Baḥr Abū ʿUthmān. *Kitāb al-Bayān wa-l-tabyīn*. Ed. ʿAbd al-Salām Muḥammad Hārūn. Cairo: Maktabat al-Khānjī, 1388/1968.

Al-Jahshiyārī, Muḥammad b. ʿAbdūs, Abū ʿAbdallāh. *Kitāb al-Wuzarāʾ wa-l-kuttāb*. Ed. Muṣṭafā l-Saqā, Ibrāhīm al-Abyārī and ʿAbd al-Ḥafīẓ Shalabī Cairo: Muṣṭafā l-Bābī l-Ḥalabī, 1357/1938.

Al-Jāsir, Ḥamad Muḥammad. *Bilād Yanbuʿ. Lamaḥāt taʾrīkhiyya jughrāfiyya wa-inṭibāʿāt khāṣṣa*. Riyadh: Dār al-Yamāma li-l-Baḥth wa-l-Tarjama wa-l-Nashr, 1966.

Al-Jawāhirī, Muḥammad. *Rijāl = Al-Mufīd min muʿjam rijāl al-ḥadīth*. Qumm²: Maktabat al-Maḥallātī, 1424 H.

Al-Jumaḥī, Muḥammad b. Sallām b. ʿUbaydallāh. *Ṭabaqāt fuḥūl al-shuʿarāʾ*. Ed. Maḥmūd Muḥammad Shākir. Jeddah: Dār al-Madanī, n.d.

Kaḥḥāla, ʿUmar Riḍā. *Muʿjam al-muʾallifīn*. Damascus. Al-Maktaba al-ʿArabiyya, 1957–1961. [Reprinted: Beirut: Dār Iḥyāʾ al-Turāth al-ʿArabī [1993?].]

Al-Kalāʿī, Sulaymān b. Mūsā Abū l-Rabīʿ. *Al-Iktifāʾ bi-mā taḍannahu min maghāzī Rasūl Allāh wa-l-thalātha al-khulafāʾ*. Ed. Muḥammad Kamāl al-Dīn ʿIzz al-Dīn ʿAlī. Beirut: ʿĀlam al-Kutub, 1417/1997.

Al-Kashshī, Muḥammad b. ʿUmar b. ʿAbd al-ʿAzīz. *Rijāl = Maʿrifat akhbār al-rijāl*. 1) Bombay. N.p., 1317/1899. 2) Karbalāʾ-al-Najaf: Maṭbaʿat al-Ādāb, n.d.

Kazi, A.K. and J.G. Flynn (trans). *Muslim Sects and Divisions: The Section on Muslim Sects in Kitab al-Milal wa l-Nihal by Muhammad b. ʿAbdul-al-Karīm Shahrastani (d. 1153)*. London: Kegan Paul International, 1984.

Kennedy, H. *The Early Abbasid Caliphate: A Political History*. London: Croom Helm, 1981.

———. *al-Manṣūr and al-Mahdī = The History of al-Ṭabarī*. Vol. 29: *al-Manṣūr and al-Mahdī*. Albany: State University of New York Press, 1990.

———. *The Prophet and the Age of the Caliphates: The Islamic Near East from the Sixth to the Eleventh Century*. London and New York: Longman, 1986.

Khadduri, Majid. *Islamic Law of Nations. Shaybānī's Siyar Translated with an Introduction, Notes, and Appendices*. Baltimore: Johns Hopkins University Press, 1966.

Al-Khaṭī, ʿAlī Najal Muḥammad Āl Sayf. *Wafāt al-imām al-Ḥasan b. ʿAlī*... In *Majmūʿa wafayāt al-aʾimma wa-yalīhi wafāt al-Sayyida Zaynab*. Beirut: Dār al-Balāgha, 1412 H.

Al-Khaṭīb al-Baghdādī, Aḥmad b. ʿAlī b. Thābit Abū Bakr. *Al-Kifāya fī ʿilm al-riwāya*. Ed. Aḥmad ʿUmar Hāshim. Beirut: Dār al-Kitāb al-ʿArabī, 1405/1985.

———. *Taʾrīkh Baghdād*. 1) Cairo: N.p., 1349/1931. 2) Ed. Muṣṭafā ʿAbd al-Qādir ʿAṭā. Beirut: Dār al-Kutub al-ʿIlmiyya, 1417/1997.

Al-Khazrajī = Aḥmad b. ʿAbdallāh al-Khazrajī l-Anṣārī l-Yamanī. *Khulāṣat tadhhīb tahdhīb al-Kamāl fī asmāʾ al-rijāl*. Ed. ʿAbd al-Fattāḥ Abū Ghudda. Aleppo[4]: Maktab al-Maṭbūʿāt al-Islāmiyya, 1411 H.

Khouri, R.G. *Ibn Lahīʿa = ʿAbd Allāh Ibn Lahīʿa (97–174/715–790): juge et grand maître de l'école égyptienne: avec édition critique de l'unique rouleau de papyrus arabe conservé à Heidelberg*. Wiesbaden: Harrassowitz, 1986.

Al-Khūʾī, Abū l-Qāsim al-Mūsawī. *Rijāl = Muʿjam rijāl al-ḥadīth wa-tafḍīl ṭabaqāt al-ruwāt*. [Qumm[5]?]: Markaz Nashr al-Thaqāfa al-Islāmiyya, 1413/1992.

———. *Kitāb al-Ṭahāra*. Qumm[3]: Dār al-Hādī, 1410 H.

Al-Kindī, Muḥammad b. Yūsuf Abū ʿUmar. 1) *Kitāb al-Wulāt wa-kitāb al-quḍāt*. Ed. R. Guest. Beirut, 1908 and Leiden, 1912. 2) *Wulāt Miṣr*. Ed. Ḥusayn Naṣṣār. Beirut: Dār Beirut/Dār Ṣādir, 1379/1959.

Kister, M.J. "The Battle of the Ḥarra: Some Socio-Economic Aspects." In Miriam Rosen-Ayalon (ed.). *Studies in Memory of Gaston Wiet*, pp. 33–49. Jerusalem: Hebrew University, 1977.

———. "Ḳuḍāʿa." *EI*[2], 5:315a.

———. "The Massacre of the Banū Qurayẓa: A Re-Examination of a Tradition." *JSAI* 8 (1986), 61–96.

Kohlberg, E. *Ibn Ṭāwūs = A Medieval Muslim Scholar at Work: Ibn Ṭāwūs and his Library*. Leiden: E.J. Brill, 1992 [*Islamic Philosophy Theology and Science: Texts and Studies*, vol. 12].

———. "*Muḥaddath* in Twelver Shīʿism." In *Studia Orientalia Memoriae D. H. Baneth Dedicata*, pp. 39–47. Jerusalem: Magnes Press, 1979.

———. "Muḥammad b. ʿAlī Zayn al-ʿĀbidīn." *EI*[2], 7:397b–400a.

———. "Mūsā al-Kāẓim." *EI*[2], 7:645a–648b.

———. "An Unusual Shīʿī *Isnād*." *IOS* 5 (1975), 142–149. [Reprinted in idem, *Belief and Law in Imāmī Shīʿism*, no. 8. Aldershot, Hampshire, UK: Variorum, 1991.]

Al-Kūfī, Muḥammad b. Sulaymān al-Qāḍī. *Manāqib al-Imām amīr al-muʾmnīn ʿAlī b. Abī Ṭālib ʿalayhi al-salām*. Ed. Muḥammad Bāqir al-Maḥmūdī. N.p: Majmaʿ Iḥyāʾ al-Thaqāfa al-Islāmiyya, 1412 H.

Al-Kulaynī, Muḥammad b. Yaʿqūb Abū Jaʿfar. *al-Kāfī = Al-Uṣūl min al-kāfī*. Ed. ʿAlī Akbar al-Ghifārī. Tehran[3]: Dār al-Kutub al-Islāmiyya, 1388 H.

Al-Kūrānī, ʿAlī l-ʿĀmilī. *Muʿjam aḥādīth al-Imām al-Mahdī*. Qumm: Muʾassasat al-Maʿārif al-Islāmiyya, 1411 H.

Al-Kutubī, Muḥammad b. Shākir. *Fawāt al-wafayāt wa-l-dhayl ʿalayhā*. Ed. Iḥsān ʿAbbās. Beirut: Dār Ṣādir, 1974.

Landau-Tasseron, E. "Arabia." In Chase F. Robinson (ed.). *The New Cambridge History of Islam*. Vol. 1: The Formation of the Islamic World, Sixth to Eleventh Centuries, pp. 397–447. Cambridge: Cambridge University Press, 2010.

———. *Biographies* = *The History of al-Ṭabarī*. Vol. 39: *Biographies of the Prophet's Companions and Their Successors*. Albany: State University of New York Press, 1998.

———. *al-Mujaddid* = "The 'Cyclical Reform': A Study of the *Mujaddid* Tradition." *Studia Islamica* 70 (1989), 79–113.

———. "Reconstruction" = "On the Reconstruction of Lost Sources." *Al-Qanṭara* 25 (2004), 45–91.

Lane, E.W. *An Arabic-English Lexicon*. London: Williams and Norgate, 1863.

Lassner, J. "Provincial Administration under the Early ʿAbbāsids: Abū Jaʿfar al-Manṣūr and the Governors of the Ḥaramayn." *Studia Islamica* 49 (1979), 39–54.

———. *The Shaping of ʿAbbāsid Rule*. Princeton, NJ: Princeton University Press, 1980.

Lecker, M. *The Banū Sulaym: A Contribution to the Study of Early Islam*. Jerusalem: Hebrew University (The Max Schloessinger Memorial Series, Monographs 4), 1989.

———. "The Markets of Medina (Yathrib) in Pre-Islamic and Early Islamic Times." *JSAI* 6 (1985), 133–147. [Reprinted in idem, *Jews and Arabs in Pre-and Early Islamic Arabia*, no. 8. London: Variorum, 1998.]

———. *Muḥammad and the Jews*. Jerusalem: Yad Izhak Ben-Zvi and the Hebrew University of Jerusalem, 2014 [in Hebrew].

———. *Muslims, Jews and Pagans: Studies on Early Islamic Medina*. Leiden: E.J. Brill, 1995.

———. "Sulaym." *EI*², 9:817a–818b.

———. "Wāqidī's Account on the Status of the Jews of Medina: A Study of a Combined Report." *JNES* 54 (1995), 15–32. [Reprinted in idem, *Jews and Arabs in Pre-and Early Islamic Arabia*, no. 7. London: Variorum, 1998.]

———. "Al-Zuhrī" = "Biographical Notes on Ibn Shihāb al-Zuhrī." *JSS* 41 (1996), 21–63.

Leder, S. *al-Haiṯam ibn ʿAdī* = *Das Korpus al-Haiṯam ibn ʿAdī (st. 207/822): Herkunft, Überlieferung, Gestalt früher Texte der aḫbār Literatur*. Frankfurt am Main: Vittorio Klostermann, 1991.

———. "ʿUmar b. Shabba." *EI*², 10:826b–827b.

Le Strange, G. *The Lands of the Eastern Caliphate*. Elibron Classics Series. Adamant Media Corporation, 2006 [Facsimile of Cambridge: Cambridge University Press, 1905].

Al-Madāʾinī, ʿAlī b. al-Ḥasan Abū l-Ḥasan. "Kitāb al-Murdifāt min Quraysh." In ʿAbd al-Salām Muḥammad Hārūn (ed.). *Nawādir al-Makhṭūṭāt*, 2:58–80. Cairo²: Muṣṭafā l-Bābī l-Ḥalabī, 1392/1972.

Madelung, W. "'Abdallāh b. al-Zubayr and the Mahdī." *JNES* 40 (1981), 291–306.

———. "The *Hāshimiyyāt* of al-Kumayt and Hāshimī Shi'ism." *Studia Islamica* 70 (1989), 5–26.

———. "al-Mahdī." *EI*², 5:1230b–1238a.

———. "Al-Mughīriyya." *EI*², 7:347b–348b.

———. *Al-Qāsim b. Ibrāhīm = Der Imām al-Qāsim Ibn Ibrāhīm und die Glaubenslehre der Zaiditen.* Berlin: Walter de Gruyter, 1965.

———. "The Sufyānī between Tradition and History." *Studia Islamica* 63 (1986), 5–48.

———. "A Treatise of the Sharīf al-Murtaḍā on the Legality of Working for the Government (*Mas'ala fī l-'amal ma'a l-sulṭān*). *BSOAS* 43 (1980), 18–31.

———. "Yaḥyā b. 'Abdallāh." *EI*², 11:242a–243b.

———. "Zayd b. 'Alī b. al-Ḥusayn." *EI*², 11:473b–474b.

———. "Zaydiyya." *EI*², 11:477b–481a.

Madelung, see also *Akhbār a'immat al-zaydiyya.*

Al-Maḥmūdī, Muḥammad Bāqir. *Nahj al-sa'āda fī mustadrak nahj al-balāgha*. Beirut: Dār al-Ta'āruf li-l-Maṭbū'āt, 1396 A.H.

Al-Majlisī, Muḥammad Bāqir. *Biḥār al-anwār*. Beirut: Mu'assasat al-Wafā'/Dār Iḥyā' al-Turāth al-'Arabī, 1403/1983.

Al-Malaṭī, Yūsuf b. Mūsā b. Muḥammad Abū l-Maḥāsin Jamāl al-Dīn. *Al-Mu'taṣar min al-mukhtaṣar min mushkil al-āthār*. Hyderabad²: Dā'irat al-Ma'ārif al-'Uthmāniyya, 1362 H.

Al-Māmaqānī, Ḥasan b. 'Abdallāh. *Rijāl = Kitāb tanqīḥ al-maqāl fī aḥwāl al-rijāl.* Najaf: Al-Maṭba'a al-Murtaḍawiyya, 1350–1353 H.

Al-Maqdisī, Muḥammad b. 'Abd al-Wāḥid b. Aḥmad al-Ḥanbalī Abū 'Abdallāh. *Al-Aḥādīth al-mukhtāra* (*aw: al-Mustakhraj min al-aḥādīth al-mukhtāra mimmā lam yukharrijhu al-Bukhārī wa-Muslim fī Ṣaḥīḥayhimā*). Ed. 'Abd al-Malik 'Abdallāh b. Duhaysh. Mecca: Maktabat al-Nahḍa al-Ḥadītha, 1410 H.

Al-Maqqarī, Aḥmad b. Muḥammad. *Nafḥ al-ṭīb min ghuṣn al-Andalus al-raṭīb wa-dhikr wazīrihā Lisān al-Dīn Ibn al-Khaṭīb.* Ed. Iḥsān 'Abbās. Beirut: Dār Ṣādir, 1968.

Al-Maqrīzī, Aḥmad b. 'Alī Taqī l-Dīn. *Imtā' al-asmā' bi-mā li-l-Nabī min al-aḥwāl wa-l-amwāl wa-l-ḥafada wa-l-matā'.* Ed. Muḥammad 'Abd al-Ḥamīd al-Namīsī. Beirut: Dār al-Kutub al-'Ilmiyya, 1420/1999.

———. *Kitāb al-Muqaffā l-kabīr.* Ed. Muḥammad al-Ya'lāwī. Beirut: Dār al-Gharb al-Islāmī, 1411/1991.

———. *Kitāb al-Nizā' wa-l-takhāṣum fīmā bayna Banī Umayya wa-Banī Hāshim.* 1) Ed. Geerhardus Vos. Leiden: E.J. Brill, 1888. 2) Ed. Ḥusayn Mu'nis. Cairo: Dār al-Ma'ārif, 1988.

Al-Maqrīzī, see also Bosworth, *al-Maqrīzī.*

Al-Mar'ashī, al-Ḥusayn b. Aḥmad. *Ghurar al-siyar.* Ed. Suhayl Zakkār. Beirut: Dār al-Fikr li-l-Ṭibā'a wa-l-Nashr wa-l-Tawzī', 1417/1996.

Margoliouth, D.S. *Lectures on Arabic Historians*. Calcutta: University of Calcutta, 1930. [Reprinted Delhi, 1977.]

Al-Marzubāṇī, Muḥammad b. ʿImrān b. Mūsā Abū ʿUbaydallāh. *Muʿjam al-shuʿarāʾ*. Ed. Fritz Krenkow. Cairo: Maktabat al-Quds, 1354 H.

———. *Al-Muwashshaḥ*. Ed. ʿAlī Muḥammad al-Bijāwī. Cairo: Dār Nahḍat Miṣr, 1965.

Al-Masʿūdī, ʿAlī b. al-Ḥasan b. ʿAlī Abū l-Ḥasan. *Murūj al-dhahab wa-maʿādin al-jawhar*. 1) Ed. Charles Pellat. Beirut: Al-Jāmiʿa al-Lubnāniyya, 1966–1979. 2) Ed./trans. A.J.B. Pavet de Courteille, et al. Paris, 1861–1877.

———. *Kitāb al-Tanbīh wa-l-ishrāf*. (BGA, vol. 8). Ed. Michael J. De Goeje. Leiden: E.J. Brill, 1894.

Al-Māzandarānī, Muḥammad Ṣāliḥ. *Sharḥ uṣūl al-Kāfī*. Ed. ʿAlī ʿĀshūr. Beirut: Dār Iḥyāʾ al-Turāth al-ʿArabī li-l-Ṭibāʿa wa-l-Nashr wa-l-Tawzīʿ, 1421/2000.

Mazor, A. "al-Qudāmī" = "The *Kitāb Futūḥ al-Shām* of al-Qudāmī as a Case Study for the Transmission of Traditions About the Conquest of Syria." *Der Islam* 74 (2008), 17–45.

McAuliffe, Jane Dammen (trans.). *ʿAbbāsid Authority = The History of al-Ṭabarī*. Vol. 28: *ʿAbbāsid Authority Affirmed: The Early Years of al-Manṣūr A.D. 753–763/A.H. 136–145*. Albany: State University of New York Press, 1995.

Mitter, U. "Origin and Development of the Islamic Patronate." In Monique Bernards and John Nawas (eds). *Patronate and Patronage in Early and Classical Islam*, pp. 70–133. Leiden: E.J. Brill, 2005.

Al-Mizzī, Yūsuf b. ʿAbd al-Raḥmān b. Yūsuf Abū l-Ḥajjāj. *Tahdhīb al-kamāl fī asmāʾ al-rijāl*. Ed. Bashshār ʿAwwād Maʿrūf. Beirut: Muʾassasat al-Risāla, 1985–1992.

Modarressi, H. *Tradition and Survival: A Bibliographical Survey of Early Shīʿite Literature*. Vol. 1. Oxford: Oneworld Publications, 2003.

Moezzi-Amir, M.A. *The Divine Guide in Early Shiʿism: The Sources of Esotericism in Islam*. Trans. David Streight. Albany: State University of New York Press, 1994.

Momen, M. *An Introduction to Shīʿī Islam: The History and Doctrine of Twelver Shīʿism*. New Haven and London: Yale University Press, 1985.

Moscati, S. "Le massacre des Umayyades dans l'histoire et dans les fragments poétiques." *Archiv Orientalni* 18 (1950), 88–115.

———. "La rivolta di ʿAbd al-Ǧabbār." *Rendiconti della Reale Accademia dei Lincei, Classe di scienze morali, storiche e filologiche* (1947): 613–615.

———. "Wāsiṭ" = "Il Tradimento di Wasit." *Le Muséon* 64 (1951), 177–186.

Motzki, A.H. "The Prophet and the Cat. On Dating Mālik's *Muwaṭṭā* and Legal Traditions." *JSAI* 22 (1998), 18–83.

Al-Mubārakfūrī, Muḥammad ʿAbd al-Raḥmān b. ʿAbd al-Raḥīm Abū l-ʿAlā. *Tuḥfat al-aḥwadhī bi-sharḥ Jāmiʿ al-Tirmidhī*. Beirut: Dār al-Kutub al-ʿIlmiyya, 1410/1990.

Al-Mubarrad, Muḥammad b. Yazīd. *al-Kāmil = Al-Kitāb al-kāmil*. Ed. W. Wright. Leipzig: F.A. Brockhaus, 1864.

Mughulṭāy see al-Bakjarī l-Ḥikrī.

Al-Munajjid, Ṣalāḥ al-Dīn. *Bayna al-khulafāʾ wa-l-khulaʿāʾ fī l-ʿaṣr al-ʿAbbāsī*. Beirut[2]: Dār al-Kitāb al-Jadīd, 1974.

Al-Munāwī, Muḥammad ʿAbd al-Raʾūf. *Fayḍ al-qadīr sharḥ al-Jāmiʿ al-ṣaghīr min aḥādīth al-Bashīr al-Nadhīr*. Beirut: Dār al-Kutub al-ʿIlmiyya, 1415/1994.

Munt, T.H.R. *The Holy City of Medina: Sacred Space in Early Islamic Arabia* (Cambridge Studies in Islamic Civilization). New York: Cambridge University Press, 2014.

———. "Ibn Zabāla" = "Writing the History of an Arabian Holy City: Ibn Zabāla and the First Local History of Medina." *Arabica* 59 (2012), 1–34.

Muslim = Muslim b. al-Ḥajjāj al-Naysābūrī. *Ṣaḥīḥ*. Ed. Muḥammad Fuʾād ʿAbd al-Bāqī. Beirut: Dār Iḥyāʾ al-Turāth al-ʿArabī, n.d.

Al-Muṭahhar b. Ṭāhir = Al-Muṭahhar b. Ṭāhir al-Maqdisī. *Kitāb al-Badʾ wa-al-taʾrīkh*. Paris: Ernest Leroux, 1899–1916.

Al-Muttaqī l-Hindī, ʿAlī b. ʿAbd al-Malik. *Kanz al-ʿummāl fī sunan al-aqwāl wa-l-afʿāl*. Ed. Bakrī Ḥayyānī and Ṣafwat al-Saqqā. Beirut: Muʾassasat al-Risāla, 1409/1989.

Nagel, T. "Muḥammad b. ʿAbdallāh" = "Ein früher Bericht über den Aufstand von Muḥammad b. ʿAbdallāh im Jahre 145 h." *Der Islam* 46 (1970), 227–262.

Al-Najafī, Muḥammad Ḥasan. b. Bāqir. *Jawāhir al-kalām fī sharāʾiʿ l-Islām*. Tehran: Dar al-Kutub al-Islāmiyya, 1367–1404 H.

Najam, Haider. "Idrīs b. ʿAbdallāh" = "The Community Divided: A Textual Analysis of the Murders of Idrīs b. ʿAbdallāh (d. 175/791)." *JAOS* 128 (2008), 459–475.

Al-Najāshī, Aḥmad b. ʿAlī Abū l-ʿAbbās al-Asadī l-Kūfī. *Rijāl = Fihrist muṣannifī l-Shīʿa al-mushtahar bi-Rijāl al-Najāshī*. Ed. Mūsā l-Shabīrī l-Zanjānī. Qumm[5]: Muʾassasat al-Nashr al-Islāmī, 1416 H.

Al-Nasāʾī, Aḥmad b. Shuʿayb Abū ʿAbd al-Raḥmān. *Kitāb al-Ḍuʿafāʾ wa-l-matrūkīn*. Beirut: Dār al-Maʿrifa li-l-Ṭibāʿa wa-l-Nashr wa-l-Tawzīʿ, 1406/1986.

———. *Man lam yarwi ʿanhu ghayr wāḥid*. Ed. Maḥmūd Ibrāhīm Zāyid. Beirut: Dār al-Maʿrifa, 1406 H.

———. *Al-Sunan al-Kubrā*. Ed. ʿAbd al-Ghaffār Sulaymān al-Bundārī and Sayyid Kisrawī Ḥasan. Beirut: Dār al-Kutub al-ʿIlmiyya, 1411/1991.

Al-Nawawī, Yaḥyā b. Sharaf Abū Zakariyyāʾ. *Sharḥ al-Nawawī ʿalā Ṣaḥīḥ Muslim*. Beirut: Dār al-Kitāb al-ʿArabī, 1407/1987.

Al-Nawbakhtī, al-Ḥasan b. Mūsā Abū Muḥammad. *Kitāb Firaq al-shīʿa*. Ed. H. Ritter. Istanbul: Maṭbaʿat al-Dawla, 1931.

Newman, A.J. *The Formative Period of Twelver Shīʿism: Ḥadīth as Discourse Between Qum and Baghdad*. Richmond: Curzon, 2000.

Nöldeke, T. "Der Chalif Manṣūr." *Orientalische Skizzen*, pp. 126–134. Berlin: Paetel, 1892 (English translation, idem. *Sketches from Eastern History*, pp. 120–129. London-Edinburgh: A. and C. Black, 1892.)

Noth, A. "Der Charakter der ersten grossen Sammlungen von Nachrichten zur frühen Kalifenzeit." *Der Islam* 67 (1971), 168–199.

Nuʿaym b. Ḥammād al-Marwazī. *Kitāb al-Fitan.* Ed. Suhayl Zakkār. Beirut: Dār al-Fikr li-l-Ṭibāʿa wa-l-Nashr wa-l-Tawzīʿ, 1993.

Nubdha = Anonymous. *Nubdha min kitāb al-taʾrīkh li-l-muʾallif al-majhūl min al-qarn al-ḥādī ʿashar* (Arabskii anonim 11 veka). Ed. P.A. Griaznevich. Moscow. Dār al-Nashr li-l-Ādab al-Sharqiyya, 1960.

Al-Nuʿmānī, Muḥammad b. Ibrāhīm. *Kitāb al-Ghayba.* Ed. Fāris Ḥassūn Karīm. Qumm: Anwār al-Hudā, 1422 H.

Al-Nūrī l-Ṭabarsī, Ḥusayn b. Muḥammad. *Khātimat Mustadrak al-wasāʾil.* Qumm: Muʾassasat Āl al-Bayt li-Iḥyāʾ al-Turāth, 1416 H.

———. *Mustadrak al-wasāʾil wa-mustanbaṭ al-masāʾil.* Beirut: Muʾassasat Āl al-Bayt li-Iḥyāʾ al-Turāth, 1408 H.

———. *Nafas al-Raḥmān fī faḍāʾil Sayyidinā Salmān.* Ed. Jawād al-Qayyūmī l-Iṣfahānī. N.p: Muʾassasat al-Āfāq, 1411 H.

Al-Nuwayrī, Aḥmad b. ʿAbd al-Wahhāb. *Nihāyat al-arab fī funūn al-adab.* Cairo: Dār al-Kutub al-Miṣriyya, 1923–1998.

Omar, F. *The ʿAbbāsid Caliphate 132/750–170/786.* Baghdad: National Printing and Publishing Co., 1969.

———. "Al-Rasāʾil al-mutabādala bayna al-Manṣūr wa-Muḥammad Dhī l-Nafs al-Zakiyya." *Majallat al-ʿArab* 5, no. 1 (1970), pp. 17–36. [Also published under the title: "Mawqif al-ʿalawiyyīn al-siyāsī min al-ʿAbbāsiyyīn: al-mawqif kamā taʿkisuhu al-rasāʾil al-mutabādala bayna al-Manṣūr wa-Muḥammad al-Nafs al-Zakiyya." In *Buḥūth fī l-taʾrīkh al-ʿAbbāsī*, pp. 92–110. Beirut/Baghdad: Dār al-Qalam li-l-Ṭibāʿa/Maktabat al-Nahḍa, 1977.]

———. "Some Aspects of the Relation between the ʿAbbāsids and the Ḥussaynid Branch of the ʿAlids 132–193/750–809 A.D." *Arabica* 22 (1975), 170–179. [Reprinted in idem, *Abbāsiyyāt: Studies in the History of the Early ʿAbbāsids*, no. 10, pp. 115–134. Baghdad, 1976.]

Peacock, A.C.S. *Balʿamī* = *Medieval Islamic Historiography and Political Legitimacy: Balʿamī's Tārīkhnāma.* London and New York: Routledge, 2007.

Poonawala, Ismail K. (trans.). *The History of al-Ṭabarī.* Vol. 9: *The Last Years of the Prophet.* Albany: State University of New York Press, 1990.

Al-Qāḍī, Wadād. "The Earliest 'Nābita' and the Paradigmatic 'Nawābit.'" *Studia Islamica* 78 (1993), 27–61.

Al-Qāḍī l-Nuʿmān, al-Nuʿmān b. Muḥammad b. Manṣūr. *Sharḥ al-akhbār fī faḍāʾil al-aʾimma al-aṭhār.* Ed. Muḥammad al-Ḥusaynī l-Jalālī. Qumm: Muʾassasat al-Nashr al-Islāmī, n.d.

Al-Qalqashandī, Aḥmad b. ʿAlī Abū l-ʿAbbās. *Ṣubḥ al-aʿshā fī ṣināʿat al-inshā.* Ed. Yūsuf ʿAlī Ṭawīl. Damascus: Dār al-Fikr, 1987.

Al-Qazwīnī, ʿAbd al-Karīm b. Muḥammad al-Rāfiʿī. *Al-Tadwīn fī akhbār Qazwīn*. Ed. ʿAzīz Allāh al-ʿUṭāridī. Beirut: Dār al-Kutub al-ʿIlmiyya, 1987.

Al-Quḍāʿī, Muḥammad b. Salāma. *Musnad al-Shihāb*. Ed. Ḥamdī ʿAbd al-Majīd al-Salafī. Beirut: Mu'assasat al-Risāla, 1405/1985.

Al-Qummī, ʿAbbās b. Muḥammad Riḍā. *Al-Anwār al-bahiyya fī tawārīkh al-ḥujaj al-ilāhiyya*. Qumm: Mu'assasat al-Nashr al-Islāmī, 1417 H.

———. *Kitāb al-Kunā wa-l-alqāb*. Tehran: Maktabat al-Ṣadr, n.d.

Al-Rabaʿī, Muḥammad b. ʿAbdallāh b. Aḥmad b. Sulaymān b. Zabr. *Mawlid al-ʿulamā' = Ta'rīkh mawlid al-ʿulamā' wa-wafayātihim*. Ed. ʿAbdallāh b. Aḥmad b. Sulaymān al-Ḥamad. Riyadh: Dār al-ʿĀṣima, 1410 H.

Raddatz, H.P. "Sufyān al-Thawrī." *EI*², 9:770b–772a.

al-Rāshid, Saʿd b. ʿAbd al-ʿAzīz. *Darb Zubaydah: The Pilgrim Road from Kufa to Mecca*. Riyadh: Riyadh University Libraries, 1980. [Expanded Arabic translation: Riyadh: Dār al-Waṭan al-ʿArabī li-l-Nashr wa-l-Tawzīʿ, 1993.]

Al-Rāwandī, Saʿīd b. ʿAbdallāh Quṭb al-Dīn. *Al-Kharā'ij wa-l-jarā'iḥ fī muʿjizāt al-nabī wa-l-a'imma ʿalayhim al-salām*. Qumm: Mu'assasat al-Imām al-Mahdī, 1409 H.

Robinson, C. F. and A. Marsham. "ʿAbdallāh b. ʿAlī" = "The Safe-Conduct for the Abbasid ʿAbd Allāh b. ʿAlī (d. 764)." *BSOAS* 70 (2007), 247–281.

Rosenthal, F. *A History of Muslim Historiography*. Leiden: E.J. Brill, 1968.

Al-Ṣafadī, Khalīl b. Aybek Ṣalāḥ al-Dīn. *Al-Wāfī bi-l-wafāyāt*. 1) Various editors. Beirut: Al-Maʿhad al-Almānī li-l-Abḥāth al-Sharqiyya, 2008–2009 (Vols. 3, 15, 18, 21, 22, 27 2) Beirut: Dār Iḥyā' al-Turāth, 1420/2000 (Vols. 2, 4, 5, 6, 8, 12, 17, 19, 24).

Al-Ṣaffār, Muḥammad b. al-Ḥasan b. Farrūkh Abū Jaʿfar. *Baṣā'ir al-darajāt al-kubrā fī faḍā'il āl Muḥammad*. Ed. Mīrzā Muḥsin Kūcheh Bāghī. Tehran: Manshūrāt Mu'assasat al-Aʿlamī, 1404 H.

Al-Sakhāwī, Muḥammad b. ʿAbd al-Raḥmān Abū l-Khayr and/or Abū ʿAbdallāh. *Al-Tuḥfa al-laṭīfa fī ta'rīkh al-Madīna al-sharīfa*. Beirut: Dār al-Kutub al-ʿIlmiyya, 1993.

Al-Ṣāliḥī l-Shāmī, Muḥammad b. Yūsuf. *Subul al-hudā wa-l-rashād fī sīrat khayr al-ʿibād*. Ed. ʿĀdil Aḥmad ʿAbd al-Mawjūd and ʿAlī Muḥammad Muʿawwaḍ. Beirut: Dār al-Kutub al-ʿIlmiyya, 1414/1993.

Al-Samʿānī, ʿAbd al-Karīm b. Muḥammad b. Manṣūr Abū Saʿd al-Tamīmī. *Al-Ansāb*. 1) Hyderabad: Dā'irat al-Maʿārif al-ʿUthmāniyya, 1962–1982. 2) Ed. ʿAbdallāh ʿUmar al-Bārūdī. Beirut: Dār al-Jinān li-l-Ṭibāʿa wa-l-Nashr wa-l-Tawzīʿ, 1408/1988.

Al-Samhūdī, ʿAbdallāh b. Shihāb al-Dīn Abū l-Maḥāsin. *Wafā' al-wafā' bi-akhbār Dār al-Muṣṭafā*. Ed. Qāsim al-Sāmarrā'ī. London-Beirut. Al-Furqān Islamic Heritage Foundation, 1422/2001.

Al-Sarakhsī, Muḥammad b. Aḥmad b. Suhayl Abū Bakr. *Kitāb al-Mabsūṭ*. Cairo: Maṭbaʿat al-Saʿāda, [1324]–1331 H.

———. *Sharḥ al-siyar al-kabīr*. Ed. Ṣalāḥ al-Dīn al-Munajjid. Cairo: Maṭbaʿat Miṣr, 1960.

Al-Sayyid, Riḍwān. "al-Nafs al-Zakiyya" = *al-Jamāʿa wa-l-mujtamaʿ wa-l-dawla: sulṭa al-idīyūlūjiyyā fī l-majāl al-siyāsī l-ʿArabī l-Islāmī.* Al-Faṣl al-Rābiʿ: "*Muḥammad al-Nafs al-Zakiyya, daʿwatuhu wa-kitābuhu fī l-siyar.*" Beirut: Dār al-Kitāb al-ʿArabī, 1418/1997.

Schacht, J. "Abū Ḥanīfa." *EI*², 1:123a–124b.

Sezgin, F. *Geschichte des Arabischen Schrifttums*. Vol. I. Leiden. E.J. Brill, 1967.

Al-Shabastarī, ʿAbd al-Ḥusayn. *al-Imām al-Ṣādiq = Al-Fāʾiq fī ruwāt wa-aṣḥāb al-Imām al-Ṣādiq*. Qumm: Muʾassasat al-Nashr al-Islāmī, 1418 H.

Al-Shāfiʿī, Muḥammad b. Idrīs. *Kitāb al-Umm*. Beirut: Dār al-Fikr, 1400/1980.

Al-Shahrastānī, Muḥammad b. ʿAbd al-Karīm. *al-Milal wa-l-niḥal.* Ed. Muḥammad Sayyid al-Kīlānī. Beirut: Dār al-Maʿrifa, 1404 H.

Al-Shahrastānī, see also Kazi and Flynn.

Al-Shāhrūdī, ʿAlī l-Namāzī. *Rijāl = Mustadrakāt ʿilm rijāl al-ḥadīth.* Tehran: Ḥaydarī, 1414 H.

———. *Safīna = Mustadrak Safīnat al-Biḥār*. Ed. Ḥasan b. ʿAlī l-Namāzī. Qumm: Muʾassasat al-Nashr al-Islāmī, 1419 H.

Al-Shākirī, Ḥusayn. *Mawsūʿat al-Muṣṭafā wa-l-ʿitra.* Qumm: Nashr al-Hādī, 1417 H.

Sharon, M. *Black Banners from the East: The Establishment of the ʿAbbāsid State. Incubation of a Revolt.* Jerusalem/Leiden: Magnes Press/E.J. Brill, 1983.

———. *Revolt: The Social and Military Aspects of the ʿAbbāsid Revolution*. Jerusalem: Max Schloessinger Memorial Fund, Hebrew University, 1990.

Al-Shawkānī, Muḥammad b. ʿAlī b. Muḥammad. *Fatḥ al-qadīr al-jāmiʿ bayn fannay al-riwāya wa-l-dirāya min ʿilm al-tafsīr.* Beirut: Dār al-Fikr, 1401/1981.

———. *Nayl al-awṭār min aḥādīth sayyid al-akhyār sharḥ muntaqā l-akhbār.* Beirut: Dār al-Jīl, 1973.

Al-Shaykh al-Mufīd, Muḥammad b. Muḥammad b. al-Nuʿmān al-ʿUkbarī l-Baghdādī. *Kitāb al-Amālī.* Ed. Ḥusayn al-Ustādh Walī and ʿAlī Akbar al-Ghifārī. Beirut: Dār al-Mufīd li-l-Ṭibāʿa wa-l-Nashr wa-l-Tawzīʿ, 1414/1993.

———. *Al-Fuṣūl al-ʿashara fī l-ghayba.* Beirut: Dār al-Mufīd li-l-Ṭibāʿa wa-l-Nashr wa-l-Tawzīʿ, 1414/1993.

———. *Kitāb al-Ikhtiṣāṣ*. Ed. ʿAlī Akbar al-Ghifārī and Maḥmūd al-Zarandī. Beirut²: Dār al-Mufīd li-l-Ṭibāʿa wa-l-Nashr wa-l-Tawzīʿ, 1414/1993.

———. *Al-Irshād fī maʿrifat ḥujaj Allāh ʿalā l-ʿibād.* Beirut: Dār al-Mufīd li-l-Ṭibāʿa wa-l-Nashr wa-l-Tawzīʿ, 1414/1993. English trans. I.K.A. Howard, *Kitab al-Irshad: The Book of Guidance*. London: Muhammadi Trust, 1981.

———. *Al-Masāʾil al-Jārūdiyya*. Ed. Muḥammad Kāẓim Mudīr Shānjī. Beirut²: Dār al-Mufīd li-l-Ṭibāʿa wa-l-Nashr wa-l-Tawzīʿ, 1414/1993.

al-Shaykh al-Ṣadūq, see Ibn Bābawayh al-Qummī.

Sibṭ Ibn al-Jawzī, Yūsuf b. Kizoghlū. *Mirʾāt al-zamān fī taʾrīkh al-aʿyān*. MS. London: British Library Add. 23,277.

———. *Tadhkirat al-khawāṣṣ min al-umma bi-dhikr khaṣāʾiṣ al-aʾimma.* Tehran: Maktabat Nīnawā l-Ḥadītha, n.d.

Sourdel, D. "La biographie d'Ibn al-Muqaffaʿ d'après les sources anciennes." *Arabica* 1 (1954), 307–323.

———. "Ibn al-Furāt." *EI*², 3:767a–768b.

———. "La Politique religieuse du Calife ʿAbbāside al-Maʾmūn." *Revue des Études Islamiques* 30 (1962), 27–48.

———. *Le vizirat ʿabbāside de 749 à 936 (132 à 324 de l'hégire).* Damascus: Institut français de Damas, 1959–1960.

Strothmann, R. "Die Literatur der Zaiditen." *Der Islam* 1 (1910), 354–368.

———. *Das Staatsrecht der Zaiditen.* Strassburg: Karl J. Trübner, 1912.

———. "Zaydiyya" = "al-Zaidīya." *EI*¹, 8:1196b–1198b.

Al-Sulamī, Yūsuf b. Yaḥyā b. ʿAlī b. ʿAbd al-ʿAzīz al-Maqdisī l-Shāfiʿī. *ʿIqd al-durar fī akhbār al-muntaẓar.* Beirut: Dār al-Kutub al-ʿIlmiyya, 1403/1983.

Al-Suyūṭī, ʿAbd al-Raḥmān b. Abī Bakr Jalāl al-Dīn. *Al-Dībāj ʿalā Ṣaḥīḥ Muslim b. al-Ḥajjāj.* Ed. Abū Isḥāq al-Ḥuwayrī l-Atharī. Al-Khubar (Saudi Arabia): Dār Ibn ʿAffān, 1416/1996.

———. *Al-Durr al-manthūr fī l-tafsīr bi-l-maʾthūr.* 1) Tehran. N.p., 1377 H. 2) Beirut: Dār al-Maʿrifa li-l-Ṭibāʿa wa-l-Nashr, n.d.

———. *Al-Muzhir fī ʿulūm al-lugha wa-anwāʿihā.* Ed. Fuʾād ʿAlī Manṣūr. Beirut: Dār al-Kutub al-ʿIlmiyya, 1998.

———. *Taʾrīkh al-Khulafāʾ.* Cairo: N.p., 1305 H.

———. *Al-ʿUrf al-wardī bi-akhbār al-Mahdī.* In idem, *al-Ḥāwī li-l-fatāwī*, vol. 2, pp. 57–87. Beirut: Dār al-Kutub al-ʿIlmiyya, 1402/1982.

Al-Ṭabarānī, Sulaymān b. Aḥmad b. Ayyūb Abū l-Qāsim. *Al-Aḥādīth al-ṭiwāl.* Ed. Ḥamdī ʿAbd al-Majīd al-Salafī. Baghdād: Maṭbaʿat al-Umma, 1404/1983.

———. *al-Awsaṭ* = *Al-Muʿjam al-awsaṭ.* Ed. Ṭāriq b. ʿAwaḍ Allāh b. Muḥammad and al-Muḥsin b. Ibrāhīm al-Ḥusaynī. Cairo: Dār al-Ḥaramayn, 1415 H.

———. *Al-Kabīr* = *Al-Muʿjam al-kabīr.* Ed. Ḥamdī b. ʿAbd al-Majīd al-Salafī. Mosul²: Maktabat al-ʿUlūm wa-l-Ḥikam, 1404/1983.

Al-Ṭabarī = Muḥammad b. Jarīr b. Yazīd al-Ṭabarī. *Taʾrīkh al-rusul wa-l-mulūk.* 1) Ed. Michael J. De Goeje. Leiden: E.J. Brill, 1879–1901. [Reprinted: Leiden: E.J. Brill, 1964.] 2) Persian version by Abū ʿAlī Muḥammad Balʿamī. Translated by H. Zotenberg under the title *Chronique de… Tabari, traduit sur la version persane d'Abou-ʿAlî Mohammed Belʿamî.* Paris: Imprimérie impériale, 1867–1874.

———. *History of Al-Ṭabarī* (English translation) see Bosworth, *The ʿAbbāsid Caliphate in Equilibrium*; Hillenbrand, *The Umayyad Caliphate;* Kennedy, *al-Manṣūr and al-Mahdī*; McAuliffe, *ʿAbbāsid Authority*; Poonawala, *Last Years of the Prophet*; Tasseron, *Biographies*; see also Williams.

———. *Jāmiʿ al-bayān ʿan taʾwīl al-Qurʾān*. Ed. Ṣidqī Jamīl al-ʿAṭṭār. Beirut: Dār al-Fikr li-l-Ṭibāʿa wa-l-Nashr wa-l-Tawzīʿ, 1415/1995.

Al-Ṭabarī, Muḥammad b. Jarīr b. Rustum al-Ṭabarī (al-Imāmī). *Dalāʾil al-imāma*. Qumm: Markaz al-Ṭibāʿa wa-l-Nashr fī Muʾussasat al-Baʿtha, 1413 H.

———. *Manāqib* = *Nawādir al-muʿjizāt fī manāqib al-aʾimma al-hudāt*. Qumm: Muʾassasat al-Imām al-Mahdī, 1410 H.

Al-Ṭabarsī, al-Faḍl b. al-Ḥasan. *Iʿlām al-warā bi-aʿlām al-hudā*. Qumm: Muʾassasat Āl al-Bayt li-Iḥyāʾ al-Turāth, 1417 H.

Al-Ṭabāṭabāʾī, ʿAlī b. Muḥammad. *Riyāḍ al-masāʾil fī bayān aḥkām al-sharʿ bi-l-dalāʾil*. Qumm: Muʾassasat al-Nashr al-Islāmī, 1422 H.

Al-Tafrishī, Muṣṭafā. *Naqd al-rijāl*. Qumm: Muʾassasat Āl al-Bayt li-Iḥyāʾ al-Turāth, 1418 H.

Al-Tanūkhī, al-Muḥassin b. ʿAlī Abū ʿAlī. *Kitāb al-Faraj baʿda al-shidda*. Ed. ʿAbbūd al-Shālijī. Beirut: Dār Ṣādir, 1978.

———. *Nishwār al-muḥāḍara wa-akhbār al-mudhākara*. Ed. ʿAbbūd al-Shālijī. Beirut: Dār Ṣādir, 1971–1973.

Al-Thaqafī l-Kūfī, Ibrāhīm b. Muḥammad b. Saʿīd b. Hilāl. *Kitāb al-Ghārāt*. Ed. Jalāl al-Dīn al-Ḥusaynī l-Armawī l-Muḥaddith. N.p: Maṭbaʿat Bahman, n.d.

Al-Ṭihrānī, Āghā Buzurg. *Al-Dharīʿa ilā taṣānīf al-shīʿa*. Vol. 2: Najaf. Maktabat al-Gharī[?], 1355 H. Vol. 4: Tehran: 1360 H. Vol. 6: Tehran: Chāpkhāne-yi Bānk-i Millī, 1365 H. Vol. 22: Najaf and Tehran: Al-Maktaba al-Islāmiyya, 1393/1974. Vol. 25: Najaf and Tehran: Al-Maktaba al-Islāmiyya, 1398/1978.

Traini, R. "La corrispondenza tra al-Manṣūr e Muḥammad an-Nafs az-zakiyyah." *Annali dell'Istituto Universitario Orientale di Napoli.* N.S., 14 (1964), 773–798.

Tucker, W.F. "ʿAbdallāh ibn Muʿāwiya and the Janāḥiyya: Rebels and Ideologues of the Late Umayyad Period." *Studia Islamica* 51 (1980), 39–57.

———. "Bayān b. Samʿān and the Bayāniyya: Shīʿite Extremists of Umayyad Iraq." *Muslim World* 65 (1975), 241–253.

———. "Manṣūriyya" = "Abū Manṣūr al-ʿIjlī and the Manṣūriyya: A Study in Medieval Terrorism." *Der Islam* 54 (1977), 66–76.

———. "Mughīriyya" = "Rebels and Gnostics, al-Mughīra Ibn Saʿīd and the Mughīriyya." *Arabica* 22 (1975), 33–47.

Al-Ṭurayḥī, Fakhr al-Dīn b. Muḥammad b. ʿAlī. *Majmaʿ al-baḥrayn wa-maṭlaʿ al-nayyirayn*. Ed. Aḥmad al-Ḥusaynī. N.p²: Maktabat al-Nashr wa-l-Thaqāfa al-Islāmiyya, 1408 H.

Al-Ṭūsī, Muḥammad b. al-Ḥasan Abū Jaʿfar. *Kitāb al-Amālī*. Qumm: Dār al-Thaqāfa, 1414 H.

———. *Fihrist*. Ed. Jawād al-Qayyūmī. [Qumm?]: Muʾassasat Nashr al-Faqāha, 1417 H.

———. *al-Ghayba*. Ed. ʿIbād Allāh al-Ṭihrānī and ʿAlī Aḥmad Nāṣiḥ. Qumm: Muʾassasat al-Maʿārif al-Islāmiyya, 1411 H.

———. *Ikhtiyār maʿrifat al-rijāl*. Ed. Mahdī l-Rajāʾī. Qumm: Muʾassasat Āl al-Bayt, 1404 H.

———. *Al-Istibṣār fīmā ukhtulifa min al-akhbār*. Ed. Ḥasan al-Kharsān. Qumm: Dār al-Kutub al-Islāmiyya, 1363 H.

———. *Al-Khilāf fī l-aḥkām* [also known by *Masāʾil al-khilāf fī l-aḥkām*]. Ed. Sayyid ʿAlī l-Khurāsānī et al. Qumm: Muʾassasat al-Nashr al-Islāmī, 1407–1417 H.

———. *Rijāl al-Ṭūsī*. Ed. Jawād al-Qayyūmī l-Iṣfahānī. Qumm: Muʾassasat al-Nashr al-Islāmī, 1415 H.

Al-Ṭūsī, see also Ibn Ḥamza al-Ṭūsī.

Al-Tustarī, Muḥammad Taqī. *Rijāl* = *Qāmūs al-rijāl*. Qumm: Muʾassasat al-Nashr al-Islāmī, 1425 H.

Al-ʿUmarī, ʿAlī b. Muḥammad b. ʿAlī b. Muḥammad al-ʿAlawī. *Ansāb* = *Al-Majdī fī ansāb al-Ṭālibiyyīn*. Ed. Aḥmad al-Mahdawī l-Dāmighānī. Qumm: Maktabat Āyatullāh al-ʿUẓmā l-Marʿashī l-Najafī (Maṭbaʿat Sayyid al-Shuhadāʾ ʿalayhi al-salām), 1409 H.

Al-ʿUqaylī, Muḥammad b. ʿAmr b. Mūsā b. Ḥammād Abū Jaʿfar al-Makkī. *Kitāb al-Ḍuʿafāʾ*. Ed. ʿAbd al-Muʿṭī Amīn Qalʿajī. Beirut: Dār al-Kutub al-ʿIlmiyya, 1418 H.

Veccia Vaglieri, L. V. "Ibrāhīm b. ʿAbdallāh." *EI*², 3:983r–985r.

Van Arendonk, C. *L'Imamat Zaidite* = *Les Debut de l'imāmat Zaidite au Yémen* (French trans. by J. Ryckmans). Leiden: E.J. Brill, 1960.

Van Berchem, M. *CIA* = *Matériaux pour un Corpus Inscriptionum Arabicarum*. Part 2. *Syrie du Sud*: Vol. 1. *Jérusalem Ville*. Vol. 2: *Jérusalem Ḥaram*. Cairo: Imprimerie de l'Institut Français d'Archéologie Orientale, 1922.

Van Ess, J. "The Kāmilīya" = "Die Kāmilīya: Zur Genese einer häresiographischen Tradition." *Die Welt des Islams* 27 (1988), 141–153 [English trans.: Gwendolyn Goldbloom, "The Kāmilīya: On the Genesis of a Heresiographical Tradition." In Etan Kohlberg (ed.). *Shīʿism*. The Formation of the Classical Islamic World, general editor Lawrence I. Conrad, vol. 32, pp. 209–219. Burlington, VT: Ashgate, 2003.]

———. "Une lecture à rebours de l'histoire du muʿtazilism." *REI* 47 (1979): 19–69.

———. *Theologie und Gesellschaft im. 2 und 3. Jahrhundert Hidschra. Eine Geschichte des religiösen Denkens im frühen Islam*. Berlin and New York: Walter de Gruyter, 1991–1995.

Van Vloten, G. "Zur Abbasidengeschichte." *ZDMG* 52 (1898), 213–222.

Wakīʿ, Muḥammad b. Khalaf b. Ḥayyān. *Quḍāt* = *Akhbār al-quḍāt*. Cairo: Maṭbaʿat al-Istiqāma, 1366/1947.

Al-Wāqidī, Muḥammad b. ʿUmar. *Kitāb al-Maghāzī*. Ed. Marsden Jones. London: Oxford University Press, 1966.

Watt, M. *The Formative Period of Islamic Thought*. Edinburgh: Edinburgh University Press, 1973.

Wellhausen, J. *The Arab Kingdom and Its Fall.* Trans. M.G. Weir. Beirut: Khayyat's Reprints, 1963.

Williams, John Alden (tr.) Al-Tabari—The Early Abbasi Empire. Cambridge and New York: Cambridge University Press, vol. I, 1988; vol. II, 1989.

Al-Yaʿqūbī, Aḥmad b. Abī Wāḍiḥ. *Taʾrīkh.* 1) Ed. Martijn Th. Houtsma. Leiden: E.J. Brill, 1882. 2) Beirut: Dār Ṣādir/Dār Beirut, 1379/1960.

Yāqūt, Shihāb al-Dīn Abū ʿAbdallāh al-Rūmī l-Ḥamawī. *Muʿjam al-buldān.* 1) Ed. Ferdinand Wüstenfeld. Leipzig: F.A. Brockhaus, 1866–1877. 2) Beirut: Dār Ṣādir, 1955–1957.

———. *Udabāʾ = Kitāb Irshād al-arīb ilā maʿrifat al-adīb (al-maʿrūf bi-Muʿjam al-udabāʾ aw ṭabaqāt al-udabāʾ).* 1) Ed. David S. Margoliouth. London/Cairo: Luzac/ Maṭbaʿa Hindiyya, 1923–1931 [E.J.W. Gibb Memorial Series no. 6]. 2) Ed. Aḥmad Farīd al-Rifāʿī. Cairo: Maktabat ʿĪsā l-Bābī l-Ḥalabī, 1355–1357/1936–1937. 3) Ed. Iḥsān ʿAbbās. Beirut: Dār al-Gharb al-Islāmī, 1993.

Al-Zabīdī. *Tāj al-ʿarūs.* Beirut: Dār Ṣādir, 1966. [Reprint of Cairo: Būlāq, 1306 H.]

Zaman, M.Q. "al-Nafs al-Zakiyya" = "The Nature of Muḥammad al-Nafs al-Zakiyya's Mahdiship: A Study of Some Reports in Iṣbahānī's *Maqātil.*" *Hamdard Islamicus* 13 (1990), 59–65.

———. *Religion and Politics under the Early ʿAbbāsids. The Emergence of the Proto-Sunnī Elite.* Leiden: E.J. Brill, 1997.

———. "Wazīr." *EI*², 11:185a–188a.

Al-Zirbāṭī, Ḥusayn al-Ḥusaynī. *Muḥammad al-Bāqir = Bughyat al-ḥāʾir fī aḥwāl awlād al-Imām al-Bāqir ʿalayhi al-salām.* Qumm: Dār al-Tafsīr (Ismāʿīliyān), 1417 H.

Al-Ziriklī, Khayr al-Dīn. *Al-Aʿlām.* Beirut⁵: Dār al-ʿIlm li-l-Malāyīn, 1980.

Al-Zubayr b. Bakkār = Al-Zubayr b. Bakkār b. ʿAbdallāh b. Muṣʿab. *al-Muwaffaqiyyāt = Al-Akhbār al-muwaffaqiyyāt.* Ed. Sāmī l-Makkī l-ʿĀnī. Baghdad: N.p., 1392/1972.

———. *Jamharat nasab Quraysh wa-akhbārihā.* Ed. Maḥmūd Muḥammad Shākir. Cairo: N.p., 1381 H.

Al-Zubayrī, Muṣʿab b. ʿAbdallāh. *Kitāb Nasab Quraysh.* Ed. Évariste Lévi-Provençal. Cairo³: Dār al-Maʿārif, 1953.

Al-Zurqānī, Muḥammad b. ʿAbd al-Bāqī b. Yūsuf Abū ʿAbdallāh al-Miṣrī. *Sharḥ al-Mawāhib al-laduniyya.* Beirut: Dār al-Kutub al-ʿIlmiyya, 1411 H.

General Index

ʿAbbād, family 328
ʿAbbād b. ʿAbdallāh b. al-Zubayr 335, 338
ʿAbbād b. Ḥamza b. ʿAbdallāh b. al-Zubayr 329
ʿAbbād b. Kathīr 262n164
al-ʿAbbās b. ʿAbd al-Muṭṭalib 32n81, 149n28, 219, 359, 390, 407
al-ʿAbbās b. al-Ḥasan b. al-Ḥasan b. al-Ḥasan 118
al-ʿAbbās b. ʿĪsā l-ʿUqaylī 389, n66
al-ʿAbbās b. al-Qāsim 166, 167, 168, 301
al-ʿAbbās b. ʿUbaydallāh b. Muḥammad b. ʿUmar 259
al-ʿAbbās b. ʿUthmān 150
ʿAbbāsī(s)
- ascendance of 78, 83, 84, 87, 107n22, 135, 136, 248, 386
- revolution 2, 84, 86, 87, 455
- viziers 78, 137, 141, 238

ʿAbd al-Aʿlā b. Aʿyan 64, 65, 83
ʿAbd al-Aʿlā b. ʿUbaydallāh b. Muḥammad b. Ṣafwān 300
ʿAbdallāh b. ʿAbdallāh b. ʿAbd al-ʿAzīz 281
ʿAbdallāh b. ʿAbd al-ʿAzīz b. ʿAbdallāh 8, 281
ʿAbdallāh b. ʿAbd al-Malik b. Marwān 20
ʿAbdallāh b. ʿAbd al-Raḥmān b. al-Ḥārith 287
ʿAbdallāh b. Abī Farwa 155, 156, 390
ʿAbdallāh b. Abī ʿUbayda b. ʿAbdallāh b. Zamʿa 323n67, 413
ʿAbdallāh b. ʿAdī b. Ḥāritha b. Rabīʿa Abū ʿAdī 166, 274
ʿAbdallāh b. ʿAlī b. ʿAbdallāh b. al-ʿAbbās 60, 77, 78, 88, 169, 170, 172n15, 194n120, 381n29, 385n45
ʿAbdallāh b. ʿAlī (Zayn al-ʿĀbidīn) b. al-Ḥusayn b. ʿAlī b. Abī Ṭālib 89, 89n152
ʿAbdallāh b. ʿĀmir al-Aslamī al-Madanī 354
ʿAbdallāh b. ʿĀmir b. Kurayz b. Khālid b. ʿUqba b. Abī Muʿayṭ 397n96
ʿAbdallāh b. ʿAmr b. ʿAbd al-Raḥmān Abū Muḥammad al-Warrāq 68n67
ʿAbdallāh b. ʿAmr b. ʿUthmān b. ʿAffān 121n117, 321n60
Abdallāh b. ʿĀṣim b. al-Mundhir b. al-Zubayr 321n62
ʿAbdallāh b. ʿAṭāʾ b. Yaʿqūb 228, 307
ʿAbdallāh b. ʿAyyāsh al-Makhzūmī 288
ʿAbdallāh b. Burayda 308
ʿAbdallāh b. Dāwūd b. al-Ḥasan b. al-Ḥasan b. ʿAlī b. Abī Ṭālib 118, 123, 369n26
ʿAbdallāh b. Dhakwān Abū l-Zinād 48n152
ʿAbdallāh b. al-Faḍl b. al-Rabīʿ 462
ʿAbdallāh b. al-Ḥasan b. al-Furāt 77, 78
ʿAbdallāh b. al-Ḥasan b. al-Ḥasan b. ʿAlī b. Abī Ṭālib, passim
ʿAbdallāh b. al-Ḥasan b. al-Ḥasan b. al-Ḥasan b. ʿAlī b. Abī Ṭālib 118
ʿAbdallāh b. al-Ḥasan b. al-Ḥusayn 25, 270n209
ʿAbdallāh b. ʿImrān b. Abī Farwa 346, 381, 402, 404, 408
ʿAbdallāh b. Isḥāq b. al-Qāsim b. Isḥāq b. ʿAbdallāh 256, 396
ʿAbdallāh b. Ismāʿīl b. ʿAbdallāh b. Jaʿfar b. Abī Ṭālib 199, 255, 257, 401
ʿAbdallāh b. Jaʿfar b. ʿAbd al-Raḥmān b. al-Miswar b. Makhrama al-Zuhrī 63, 67, 80, 133, 164, 302, 304, 385n45
ʿAbdallāh b. Jaʿfar b. Abī Ṭālib 104n7, 375
- family of 254

ʿAbdallāh b. Jazʾ 134
ʿAbdallāh b. Khālid, family of 322
ʿAbdallāh b. Lahīʿa 130
ʿAbdallāh b. Masʿūd 194, 203
ʿAbdallāh b. Muʿāwiya b. Jaʿfar b. Abī Ṭālib 426n3
- mawlā of 198, 200, 258
- rebellion of 385, 414, 428, 429n17

ʿAbdallāh (al-Ashtar) b. Muḥammad b. ʿAbdallāh b. al-Ḥasan b. al-Ḥasan 12, 91, 142, 143, 236, 380
ʿAbdallāh b. Muḥammad b. ʿAbd al-Raḥmān b. Ṣafwān al-Jumaḥī 200
ʿAbdallāh b. Muḥammad b. Masʿada 142, 143n238
ʿAbdallāh b. Muḥammad b. ʿUmar b. ʿAlī b. Abī Ṭālib 72, 88n152, 199, 261, 263, 268, 374, 401

ʿAbdallāh b. Muḥammad b. Yazdād, Abū Ṣāliḥ 179
ʿAbdallāh b. al-Mundhir b. al-Mughīra 322
ʿAbdallāh b. Mūsā b. ʿAbdallāh b. al-Ḥasan b. al-Ḥasan 23, 30, 36, 218
ʿAbdallāh b. Muṣʿab b. Thābit b. ʿAbdallāh b. al-Zubayr 314, 315, 316, 334, 338, 341n149, 400
ʿAbdallāh (al-Akbar) b. Nāfiʿ b. Thābit b. ʿAbdallāh b. al-Zubayr 320, 381, 395
ʿAbdallāh (al-Aṣghar) b. Nāfiʿ b. Thābit b. ʿAbdallāh b. al-Zubayr 320, 381, 395
ʿAbdallāh b. al-Najāshī 431, 433, 434
ʿAbdallāh b. al-Rabīʿ b. ʿUbaydallāh al-Ḥārithī 110, 170n10, 381, 384n45, 385n45
ʿAbdallāh b. Shaybān b. ʿAbd al-Malik b. Mismaʿ 141
ʿAbdallāh b. Ṭāʾūs 26
ʿAbdallāh b. ʿUmar b. ʿAbdallāh Abū ʿAdī al-ʿAblī 22n30, 168, 273–274, 284
ʿAbdallāh b. ʿUmar b. Ḥafṣ b. ʿĀṣim 277
ʿAbdallāh b. ʿUmar b. al-Qāsim 8, 276, 381, 382
ʿAbdallāh b. Yazīd b. Hurmuz 274, 359, 360n90
ʿAbdallāh b. Zamʿa 19n12
ʿAbdallāh b. al-Zubayr b. al-ʿAwwām 39, 241, 281, 288, 323, 328, 331, 332, 335
family of 314, 326, 327, 338
ʿAbdallāh b. al-Zubayr b. ʿUmar b. Dirham al-Zubayrī [*mawlāhum*], 322, 382
ʿAbd al-ʿAzīz b. ʿAbdallāh b. ʿAbdallāh b. ʿUmar b. al-Khaṭṭāb 8, 265, 280, 281
ʿAbd al-ʿAzīz b. ʿAbdallāh b. ʿAṭāʾ b. Yaʿqūb 307
ʿAbd al-ʿAzīz b. Abī l-Ṣaʿba al-Madanī 198n149
ʿAbd al-ʿAzīz b. Abī Salama b. ʿUbaydallāh b. ʿAbdallāh 279, 307n410, 396
ʿAbd al-ʿAzīz al-ʿAbsī *see* Abū Dhufāfa
ʿAbd al-ʿAzīz b. Ibrāhīm b. ʿAbdallāh b. Muṭīʿ al-ʿAdawī 283
Abd al-ʿAzīz b. ʿImrān b. ʿAbd al-ʿAzīz, Ibn Abī Thābit 32, 58, 63, 67n65, 149, 151, 305, 306, 307, 382, 383, 384, 385n45, 391, 413, 414, 415, 416n155, 417, 418
ʿAbd al-ʿAzīz b. Marwān 129n165, 131
ʿAbd al-ʿAzīz b. Muḥammad b. ʿAbd al-ʿAzīz 307n409
ʿAbd al-ʿAzīz b. Muḥammad b. ʿUbayd b. Abī ʿUbayd al-Darāwardī 29, 164, 348, 378, 385
ʿAbd al-ʿAzīz b. Saʿīd b. Saʿd b. ʿUbāda al-Khazrajī 110n37, 284, 346
ʿAbd al-Ḥamīd b. ʿAbd al-ʿAzīz b. ʿAbdallāh b. ʿAbdallāh 8
ʿAbd al-Ḥamīd b. Jaʿfar b. ʿAbdallāh b. [Abī] al-Ḥakam al-Awsī al-Anṣārī 153, 163, 294, 344, 351n47, 371, 384n45, 385, 420n172
ʿAbd al-Jabbār b. ʿAbd al-Raḥmān al-Azdī 85, 86, 87
ʿAbd al-Jabbār [b. Aḥmad] (qāḍī) 5n17
ʿAbd al-Jabbār b. Saʿīd b. Sulaymān b. Nawfal 88n151, 297, 298
ʿAbd al-Malik b. Abī Zuhayr b. ʿAbd al-Raḥmān al-Thaqafī 168, 356
ʿAbd al-Malik b. Mismaʿ b. Mālik b. Mismaʿ 140, 141
ʿAbd al-Malik b. Shihāb [b. Mismaʿ?] 141
ʿAbd al-Malik b. Yaḥyā b. ʿAbbād b. ʿAbdallāh b. al-Zubayr 338
ʿAbd al-Malik b. Yazīd al-Azdī Abū ʿAwn 2, 97, 455n120
ʿAbd al-Raḥmān b. ʿAbdallāh b. Abī ʿUbayda 323n67
ʿAbd al-Raḥmān b. ʿAbdallāh b. ʿUtba b. ʿAbdallāh b. Masʿūd 194
Abd al-Raḥmān b. Abī l-Mawālī 51, 119, 122, 347, 348n37, 360, 361n95, 386
ʿAbd al-Raḥmān b. Abī l-Ṣaʿba al-Madanī 198n149
ʿAbd al-Raḥmān b. Abī Salama b. ʿUbaydallāh 281
ʿAbd al-Raḥmān b. Abī l-Zinād 303
ʿAbd al-Raḥmān b. ʿAmr b. Ḥabīb 64
ʿAbd al-Raḥmān b. al-Faḍl b. ʿAbd al-Raḥmān b. al-ʿAbbās 80n113, 81
ʿAbd al-Raḥmān b. Ḥarb 138
ʿAbd al-Raḥmān b. al-Ḥārith b. Hishām al-Makhzūmī 138, 287n297, 288, 291n323
ʿAbd al-Raḥmān b. Ibrāhīm b. ʿAbdallāh b. Muṭīʿ 283
ʿAbd al-Raḥmān b. al-Mughīra al-Ḥizāmī 244n53

ʿAbd al-Raḥmān b. Muḥammad b. ʿAbd al-Malik al-Kindī 228n108, 339n138
ʿAbd al-Raḥmān b. Muḥammad b. Abī Bakr b. ʿAbdallāh 138n209, 179
ʿAbd al-Raḥmān b. al-Qāsim 365
ʿAbd al-Raḥmān b. ʿUmar b. al-Khaṭṭāb, family of 282
ʿAbd al-Raḥmān b. ʿUthmān b. ʿAbd al-Raḥmān al-Makhzūmī 137, 138
ʿAbd al-Raḥmān b. Yūnus Abū Muslim 197n148
ʿAbd al-Raḥmān b. Yūsuf b. Kharrāsh 161n86, 367
ʿAbd al-Ṣamad b. ʿAlī b. ʿAbdallāh b. al-ʿAbbās 66, 282, 284
ʿAbd al-ʿUzzā, Banū 273, 295
ʿAbd al-Wahhāb b. Yaḥyā b. ʿAbbād b. ʿAbdallāh b. al-Zubayr 318, 334, 422
ʿAbd al-Wāḥid b. Abī ʿAwn al-Dawsī 303–304, 360
ʿAbd al-Wāḥid b. Sulaymān b. ʿAbd al-Malik 70, 71, 72n82
ʿĀbida bt. Shuʿayb b. ʿAbdallāh b. ʿAmr b. al-ʿĀṣ (ʿĀbida al-Ḥasnāʾ) 156, 157
Abraham 181n54, 243n52, 244n53, 437n49, 460
ʿAbs, Banū 133, 134
Abū l-ʿAbbās al-Filasṭīnī 59, 386, 387
Abū ʿAbd al-Raḥmān al-Humānī 178
Abū ʿAmr b. Nuʿaym, family of 352, 353
Abū ʿAwn, *mawlā* of al-Miswar b. Makhrama al-Zuhrī 304
Abū Ayyūb al-Khūzī 87
Abū Bakr b. ʿAbdallāh b. Muḥammad b. Abī Sabra 159, 293, 295, 296 297
Abū Bakr b. Abī Quḥāfa, family of 284
Abū Bakr b. al-Ḥasan b. al-Ḥasan 117
Abū Bakr b. Ḥamza b. ʿAbdallāh b. al-Zubayr 329
Abū Bakr b. ʿUmar b. Ḥafṣ b. ʿĀṣim 277, 278
Abū Dhufāfa 133, 134, 136, 137
Abū Habbār al-Muzanī 138, 250, 349, 396, 420
Abū Ḥamza al-Khārijī 167n121, 323n67, 388n58, 389, 398
  revolt of 388, 389
Abū Ḥanīfa al-Nuʿmān b. Thābit 46n149, 222, 363, 364, 371, 372
  school of 186
Abū Ḥunayn 360, 361, 387, 417, 418n163
Abū Hurayra 35, 55n28, 328n88, 385n47
Aḥmad b. Ibrāhīm b. al-Ḥasan b. Ibrāhīm al-Ḥasanī, Abū l-ʿAbbās 182, 185n71
Abū l-Aḥwaṣ (poet) 136
Abū l-ʿĀṣ b. Umayya, Banū 32, 270, 272
Abū l-Aṣamm 194
Abū l-Azhar al-Tamīmī 109, 116, 119, 146, 381, 404
Abū l-Faraj al-Iṣfahānī 7, 23, 32, 36, 61, 62, 63, 90, 161, 224, 247n72, 308, 316, 358, 367, 372, 386, 388n59
  Kitāb al-aghānī 389, 393, 395n87, 417, 423n194
  Maqātil al-Ṭālibiyyīn 7, 61, 73, 142, 163, 247n72, 320, , 375, 377n10, 385, 398, 402, 422, 452
Abū l-Ḥajjāj al-Minqarī 212
Abū l-Khaṣīb Marzūq 156
Abū l-Khaṭṭāb 440
Abū Lahab 166, 168, 301
Abū Muslim 72, 84, 91n163, 172n15, 200n160, 247, 248, 399
Abū Naṣr al-Bukhārī, Sahl b. ʿAbdallāh al-Nassāba 17, 18n11, 25n44, 25n47, 26n51, 165, 241, 242n42, 254, 259, 267, 334n123
Abū Nuʿaym 369n26
Abū l-Qalammas *see* ʿUthmān b. ʿUbaydallāh b. ʿAbdallāh
Abū Rāfiʿ 36, 122, 242n39, 390
Abū l-Sāj 23
Abū Salama al-Khallāl 66, 69, 82–88, 190, 218n55, 280, 425, 441, 458
Abū Salama al-Muṣabbiḥī 408
Abū Salama b. ʿUbaydallāh b. ʿAbdallāh b. ʿUmar b. al-Khaṭṭāb 281
Abū l-Yaqẓān *see* ʿĀmir b. Ḥafṣ
Abū Ṭālib 174
  family of 21, 108, 142
Abū ʿUbayda b. ʿAbdallāh b. Zamʿa 19, 20n18, 323n67
Abū Wajza al-Saʿdī 22n29, 271n210
Abū Zayd b. Abī l-Ghamr 365
al-Abwāʾ 60, 61n47, 69, 70, 72, 79, 84, 88, 90, 174, 175, 218n55, 249n82, 263, 377, 400, 402, 407, 416, 425, 441, 451, 454n117
adab 9, 12, 98n197

ʿAdan (Aden) 96, 329n91
ʿAdī b. Kaʿb, Banū 276, 361
ʿAdī b. Nawfal b. ʿAbd Manāf, family of 275
Aḥjār al-Zayt 36, 37, 63n52, 68, 83, 218–221, 441n70, 441n72
Ahl al-Bayt (CD data base) 11
ahl al-bayt 2, 65, 432
ahl Khurāsān 73, 83, 86, 87, 97, 102, 108, 109n33, 116, 120, 151, 170n7, 194, 195, 210, 213, 222, 223n82, 250, 455
ahl al-Shām 108, 132, 133, 170, 194, 272, 386
Aḥmad b. ʿAbdallāh b. Muḥammad b. ʿUmar b. ʿAlī b. Abī Ṭālib 261
Aḥmad b. ʿAbd al-ʿAzīz 63
Aḥmad b. Abī Khaythama 23n37
Aḥmad b. ʿĀʾidh b. Ḥabīb 188n86
Aḥmad b. Ḥanbal 122
Aḥmad b. al-Ḥārith b. al-Mubārak al-Kharrāz 50n3, 69, 76n98, 90n160, 367, 368n21, 388, 423, 424
Aḥmad b. Ḥasan al-Shāmī 184n67
Aḥmad b. al-Ḥusayn b. Hārūn (al-Muʾayyad) 182n60
Aḥmad b. Ibrāhīm b. Aḥmad al-ʿAmmī, Abū Bishr 262n159
Aḥmad (al-Mukhtafī) b. ʿĪsā (al-Mubārak) b. ʿAbdallāh b. Muḥammad 81, 263n168, 264, 267
Aḥmad b. ʿĪsā b. Zayd b. ʿAlī b. al-Ḥusayn b. ʿAlī b. Abī Ṭālib 237n14
Aḥmad b. Isḥāq (tr.) 366n15
Aḥmad b. Muḥammad b. ʿAbd al-ʿAzīz 307n409
Aḥmad b. Muḥammad b. Masʿada 143n238
Aḥmad b. Muḥammad b. Saʿīd 161n86, 367n20, 419n166, 443
Aḥmad b. Saʿīd (tr.) 30n69, 49n2, 375, 376
Aḥmad al-Shāmī of Ṣanʿāʾ 184n67
Aḥmad b. Sulaymān al-Ṭūsī (tr.) 280n262
ʿĀʾidh b. Ḥabīb b. al-Mallāḥ 23n35, 187, 410n134
ʿĀʾisha bt. Ṭalḥa b. ʿUmar b. ʿUbaydallāh 118n105
ʿĀʾisha bt. ʿUthmān b. ʿAffān 335n127
Akhbār al-ʿAbbās 52, 70, 399
ʿAkk, tribe 315
ʿalāmāt (signs) 39
al-ʿalāmāt al-khams (the five signs) 40
ʿAlī, Banū 143, 144, 302
ʿAlī b. al-ʿAbbās b. al-Ḥasan b. al-Ḥasan b. al-Ḥasan 118, 123n133
ʿAlī b. ʿAbd al-Ḥamīd b. ʿUbayd 387, 417, 418
ʿAlī b. Abī ʿAqīl Muḥammad b. ʿAbdallāh 268
ʿAlī b. Abī l-Ghanāʾim Muḥammad 374n1
ʿAlī b. Abī Ṭālib 2, 42, 88, 122n126, 165, 184, 219n59, 223, 263n164, 272, 318, 333, 339, 375n2, 390, 426, 429, 433, 435, 437, 444, 452n107
  dweling 21
  followers 128
  praises of 50n6, 185
  reign of 43, 346
ʿAlī b. Abī Ṭālib b. Sarḥ 35, 218n51, 422
ʿAlī b. al-Ḥasan b. al-Ḥasan b. al-Ḥasan 36, 118, 218
ʿAlī (Zayn al-ʿĀbidīn) b. al-Ḥusayn b. ʿAlī b. Abī Ṭālib 89n151, 159n80, 173, 242, 246, 253, 254n109, 426, 430, 435, 436, 453, 464n155
alms 262, 298, 429
  voluntary 98, 346
  see also ṣadaqāt
ʿAlī b. al-Ḥusayn b. ʿAlī b. Ḥamza 247n72
ʿAlī b. Ibrāhīm b. al-Ḥasan b. al-Ḥasan 116, 123n133
ʿAlī b. Ismāʿīl b. Ṣāliḥ b. ʿAlī 136
ʿAlī b. Mālik b. Khaytham (Khuthaym?) b. ʿIrāk al-Ghifārī 353
ʿAlī b. Muḥammad b. ʿAbdallāh b. al-Ḥasan b. al-Ḥasan 127, 128, 132
ʿAlī b. Muḥammad b. ʿAlī b. Muḥammad al-ʿAlawī, al-ʿUmarī 265, 266
ʿAlī b. Muḥammad b. Sulaymān al-Nawfalī 380n26
ʿAlī b. Muḥammad b. Sulaymān b. ʿAlī b. ʿAbdallāh b. al-ʿAbbās 142, 380
ʿAlī b. al-Muṭṭalib b. ʿAbdallāh b. al-Muṭṭalib al- Makhzūmī 283, 292
ʿAlī l-Riḍā (Imām) 78, 176, 399, 400
ʿAlī b. Ṣāliḥ b. Ṣāliḥ b. Ḥayy (Ḥayyān) 138
ʿAlī b. ʿUbaydallāh b. Muḥammad b. ʿUmar b. ʿAlī b. Abī Ṭālib 260, 402
  Kitāb al-Aqḍiya 260
ʿAlwa al-Kurāʿa [Karrāʿa?] 136n202
amān 81, 85, 105, 132, 144, 167, 171, 172n15, 173, 190, 204, 209, 210, 217, 226, 236, 254, 255, 261, 262, 290, 299, 303, 307, 352, 369, 463

al-Amar 319n52
al-Aʿmash *see* Sulaymān b. Mihrān
Amat al-Wahhāb bt. ʿAmr b. Musāḥiq b. ʿAbdallāh b. Makhrama 297
al-Amīn (Caliph) Muḥammad b. ʿAbdallāh b. Hārūn 7n26, 23n37, 75n92, 151n40, 302n379, 340n145, 341n145, 462
Amīna bt. Khuḍayr 310, 319
Amīna bt. Muḥammad 310n4
Amīna bt. Muṣʿab 310n4
Amīna, Umm Isḥāq b. Ṭalḥa 121n117
ʿĀmir b. Ḥafṣ (Abū l-Yaqẓān) 69, 70, 90n160, 122, 171n13
ʿĀmir b. Ṣaʿṣaʿa, Banū 356, 411
ʿĀmir b. Wāthila Abū l-Ṭufayl 34
ʿAmr b. al-ʿĀṣ 129, 156, 157
ʿAmr b. ʿAwn 420
ʿAmr b. Bishr al-Sakūnī 339n138
ʿAmr b. ʿUbayd 4, 78, 101n203, 125n145, 364
al-Anbār 102
Anṣār 2, 7, 105, 107, 147, 152, 154, 165n105, 186, 230, 234, 253n105, 326, 343–345, 361, 362, 364, 464
Antichrist (al-Dajjāl) 203n172
Antipatris *see* Nahr Abī Fuṭrus
ʿAqīl b. Abī Ṭālib, Banū 2, 268, 401
al-ʿAqīqī *see* Yaḥyā b. al-Ḥasan al-Nassāba
al-Āqūl 169n1
Arazi, A. 103n2, 324
arīf (n. *irāfa*) 129n167
Arqam b. Abī l-Arqam (ʿAbd Manāf) b. Asad 292
ʿArrām b. al-Aṣbagh al-Sulamī 228n108, 285n289, 339n138, 346, 347n21
Asad, Banū 19, 310, 322, 361
Asad b. al-Marzubān 197, 206
  Mosque of 197n148
Ashrāf: of Quraysh 106, 298
  of Medina 369
  of Syria 135
ʿĀṣim b. al-Mundhir b. al-Zubayr b. al-ʿAwwām 5n20, 321, 336n131
ʿĀṣim b. ʿUmar b. al-Khaṭṭāb 276
Aslam, Banū 168, 343, 347, 348, 354, 362
Asmāʾ bt. ʿAbd al-Raḥmān b. Abī Bakr 176n32
Asmāʾ bt. Abī Bakr b. ʿAbdallāh b. Ṣāliḥ b. ʿAbdallāh b. al-Zubayr 326, 340
Asmāʾ bt. ʿAqīl b. Abī Ṭālib 259
Asmāʾ bt. al-Ḥasan b. ʿAbdallāh b. ʿUbaydallāh b. al-ʿAbbās 157, 158, 208, 225
Asmāʾ bt. al-Ḥusayn b. ʿAbdallāh b. ʿUbaydallāh b. ʿAbbās 319, 422
Asmāʾ bt. Jaʿfar al-Ṣādiq 250
Asmāʾ bt. Muḥammad b. Abī Bakr 201n163
Asmāʾ bt. Muṣʿab b. Thābit b. ʿAbdallāh b. al-Zubayr 341
Asmāʾ bt. Salama b. ʿUmar b. Abī Salama al-Makhzūmī 101n203
ʿAssāma (ʿUsāma?) b. ʿAmr al-Maʿāfirī 128, 132
ʿAṭāʾ b. ʿAbdallāh b. ʿAṭāʾ b. Yaʿqūb 307
al-Athaba 329
ʿĀtika bt. ʿAbd al-Malik b. al-Ḥārith b. Khālid 21, 229
ʿĀtika bt. al-Faḍl b. ʿAbd al-Raḥmān 65, 81
ʿĀtika bt. Yazīd b. Muʿāwiya 149
al-Aʿwar al-Kalbī 445n86
al-Aʿwaṣ 100, 201
ʿAwn b. Mālik b. Mismaʿ b. Mālik 141
ʿAwn b. Muḥammad b. ʿAlī b. Abī Ṭālib 25n45, 270n209
Ayalon, D. 102n206
ʿayn
  ʿAyn ʿAskar 328
  ʿAyn al-Ḍariyya, 104n6
    al-Muhd (Nahd?) 328
  ʿAyn al-Nahd 329
  ʿAyn al-Najafa 329
  ʿAyn al-Riḍā 339
  ʿAyn al-Rubuḍ (Rubḍ?) 329
  ʿAyn Rustān 88n152, 261
ʿayn *see* spy/ies
Ayyām al-ʿArab 12n41, 99, 205
ʿAyyāsh b. Abī Rabīʿa 287
Ayyūb b. Ḥasan al-Rāfiʿī 329
Ayyūb b. Salama b. ʿAbdallāh b. al-Walīd b. al-Walīd 162, 289, 290, 368, 397n96
Ayyūb b. ʿUmar b. Abī ʿAmr b. Nuʿaym 352n50, 397
Azhar b. Saʿd b. Nāfiʿ al-Sammān, Abū Bakr 140, 357, 387, 397, 398, 399

Bāb al-Khawkha 150
Bāb Banī Salima 196n132, 203

Bādhām (or Bādhān), *mawlā* Umm Hāni' bt. Abī Ṭālib 35
Badr 121, 271
battle of 153, 165n105, 175, 222n78, 253n105
Badr al-Dīn Badal b. Ismāʿīl al-Tibrīzī 183
Baghdad 7n26, 78, 81, 106n18, 109n33, 117n91, 122, 131, 138, 160n82, 169, 178n39, 182n60, 185–186, 197, 206, 216, 217n47, 222, 227, 237n17, 239, 245, 260n145, 285n284, 295, 296, 299, 317, 318, 319, 338, 369, 371, 384, 390, 396, 399, 405n123, 419, 455n119
Bāhila, Banū 140, 398, 357, 362
Bahz b. Imru' al-Qays b. Buhtha b. Sulaym 351
Bākhamrā 127, 136, 252, 461
Bakkār b. ʿAbdallāh b. Muṣʿab b. Thābit 24n38, 315–318, 333, 340
Bakr, Banū 343, 354, 362
al-Bakrī 21, 209, 327, 328, 331n104, 339n138, 379, 393
al-Balādhurī 54, 55, 89, 100n202, 122, 158n78, 162, 170n7, 206, 210, 226, 255, 266, 285, 290, 335, 368, 373
Ansāb al-ashrāf 54
Balʿamī 30, 31, 86, 87, 177n37, 189, 190–193
Ta'rīkhnāma 190, 192
al-Balqā' 135, 135n196
Baqīʿ al-Gharqad 196, 203n172, 221, 223n85
Baqīʿ al-Zubayr 325, 326, 327
al-barīd 95
al-Baṣra 4–5, 44n137, 124, 125n141, 136–141, 143–144, 146–147, 162, 167, 171, 194, 197, 218n47, 227, 229n110, 237–239, 253n105, 266, 282, 285n284, 288, 302, 313, 321, 325, 336n131, 341, 349, 358–360, 363, 369, 387, 399, 420
Bassām b. Ibrāhīm, revolt of 458
al-Baṭḥā' 23n35, 201, 379
al-Bathna 20, 24
Baṭn Iḍam 319
Baṭn Nakhl 407
Bayān b. Samʿān 54
al-Baydā' 38, 355
black flags from Khurāsān 42, 44
al-Bughaybigha 104n7
al-Buḥturī 136n202, 137
Bukayr b. Māhān 52
Bukhārā 31, 86
Busr b. Saʿīd 33
Buṭḥān 203, 329
Byzantium 9, 317n38, 340n145

Caesarea 202
Camel, Battle of 323, 333
Conrad, L.I. 9
Cook, D. 3n10, 10n35, 28n65, 34, 37, 39, 41, 425, 429n17, 439n61, 447n95, 452
Covenant of the Children of Israel 435

Ḍabba, tribe 101
al-Ḍaḥḥāk b. ʿUthmān b. ʿAbdallāh b. Khālid b. Ḥizām 322
dāʿī (pl. *duʿāt*) 82, 85, 86n143, 195n128, 218n55, 458, 459
Damascus 113, 135, 262, 288n304
al-Dāmigha (The Irrefutable) 182, 183
Daniel, E.L. 191–192, 193n111, 193n112
Dār ʿAmr 326
Dār Banū Salima 149
Dār al-Ḥijāra 326
Dār al-Makhba' 450
Dār Marwān 104n6, 115, 150–151, 210, 383
Dār al-Mundhir b. al-Zubayr 326
Dār Muṣʿab b. al-Zubayr 326
Dār Rayṭa 450
Dār ʿUrwa b. al-Zubayr 326, 327
Dār Uways b. Saʿd b. Abī Sarḥ al-ʿĀmirī 149
Dār Yazīd b. ʿAbd al-Malik 107n22, 149
al-Ḍariyya 104n6, 297
daʿwa
ʿAbbāsī 17n5, 52, 61n47, 70, 86, 87, 109, 190, 195, 197, 441
of the Banū Ḥasan b. ʿAlī 128
Dāwūd b. ʿAbdallāh (Abū l-Karrām) b. Muḥammad b. ʿAlī 29, 377, 385
Dāwūd b. ʿAlī b. ʿAbdallāh b. al-ʿAbbās 77, 269n207, 270n207, 272, 273, 295, 458, 459
Dāwūd b. al-Ḥasan b. al-Ḥasan b. ʿAlī b. Abī Ṭālib 117, 118, 123
Dāwūd b. ʿĪsā b. Mūsā b. Muḥammad b. ʿAlī 340
Dāwūd b. Karrāz al-Bāhilī 195
Daylam 317, 334
Dayr al-ʿĀqūl 169n1

De Goeje, M.J. 127n159, 310, 376n7
Dhū l-Ḥulayfa 201n163
Dhū l-Khushub 88, 298n356
dībāj (brocade) 121n116, 160nn82, 83
al-Dībāj al-Mudhhab 366
al-Dībāj *see* Muḥammad b. ʿAbdallāh b. ʿAmr b. ʿUthmān
Diʿbil 183n65
Diḥya b. Muṣʿab (Muʿaṣṣab?) b. al-Aṣbagh b. ʿAbd al-ʿAzīz 129n166
dīwān al-ʿaṭāʾ 164, 303
dīwān al-khātam 455
Donner, F.M. 9, 11n40
Ḍubayʿa, Banū 140
Dunlop, D.M. 191

Egypt 26, 33, 43, 99, 113, 124, 125, 127–132, 169, 228, 258, 275, 325, 360
Euphrates 57, 120n112

al-Fadak 88
al-Faḍl b. ʿAbd al-Raḥmān b. al-ʿAbbās b. Rabīʿa al-Hāshimī 64, 65, 80–82
al-Faḍl b. Dukayn 145n5, 294
al-Faḍl b. Sahl 171n11
al-Faḍl b. Ṣāliḥ b. ʿAlī 93
al-Faḍl b. Sulaymān al-Hāshimī 227, 356
Fākhita bt. Fulayḥ b. Muḥammad b. al-Mundhir b. al-Zubayr 25, 26n48, 334
al-Fākihī 167n118
Akhbār Makka 398
Fāliḥ b. Maʿmar Abū l-Shadāʾid al-Fazārī 226, 355, 411
Faraj the eunuch 151
Farsh Malal 19, 334
Farsh Suwayqa 19, 21, 24, 334
Fāṭima bt. ʿAbdallāh b. Muḥammad b. ʿUmar b. ʿAlī b. Abī Ṭālib 21, 261n154
Fāṭima bt. ʿAlī b. Abī Ṭālib 447
Fāṭima bt. ʿAmr 172
Fāṭima bt. al-Ḥasan b. al-Ḥasan b. ʿAlī b. Abī Ṭālib 25, 255, 265n180, 289
Fāṭima bt. al-Ḥusayn b. ʿAlī b. Abī Ṭālib 121, 270, 397
Fāṭima bt. Jaʿfar b. Muṣʿab b. al-Zubayr 312, 336n130
Fāṭima bt. Muḥammad (the Prophet's daughter) 2, 57, 97, 172, 173, 185, 261n156, 285n289, 390, 426, 428–430, 445, 456, 464
Fāṭima bt. Muḥammad b. ʿAbdallāh b. al-Ḥasan 223
Fāṭima bt. al-Mundhir b. al-Zubayr 329
Fāṭima bt. al-Qāsim b. Muḥammad b. Jaʿfar b. Abī Ṭālib 336, 341
Fāṭima bt. Saʿīd b.ʿUqba 23n35, 379, 419
Fāṭima bt. ʿUbaydallāh b. Muḥammad b. ʿUmar b. ʿAlī b. Abī Ṭālib 259
Fāṭima bt. al-Walīd b. ʿUtba b. Rabīʿa b. ʿAbd Shams 172, 227, 274
Fāṭima bt. Yaʿqūb b. al-Faḍl 81n121
Fāṭima's scroll (*muṣḥaf Fāṭima*) 429, 430, 430n27, 436, 438, 440, 442
fatwā (pl. *fatāwā*) 364, 366, 367
al-Fayd 104n6, 196, 200
Fazāra, Banū 222n78, 355
Firaq al-Shīʿa 440
fitna 81, 219n59, 221, 442, 448
al-Fiṭyawn, Banū 345
Fleichhammer, M. 9
Fulayḥ b. Sulaymān b. Abī l-Mughīra b. Ḥunayn 283, 284, 346
al-Furʿ 279, 285n289, 327–329, 332, 330n103, 332, 333, 339m138, 463

al-Ghāba 230n116, 325, 327
al-Ghāḍirī 100, 125n141, 408
Ghassān b. ʿAlī b. ʿAbd al-Ḥamīd 416
Ghaṭafān, Banū 114, 134, 150, 355
Ghifār b. Mulayl, Banū 208, 209, 343, 351, 352n50, 353, 354, 359, 360n89, 362
Ghurar al-siyar 181
Görke, A. 9, 10n35
Günther, S. 9, 388n59, 394, 423, 424n198

Habbār b. al-Aswad 323n67
Ḥabīb b. al-Mallāḥ 21n29, 23n35, 410n134
al-Ḥadāʾiq al-wardiyya fī manāqib aʾimmat al-Zaydiyya see Ḥumayd b. Aḥmad al-Muḥallī
al-Hādī (Caliph) Mūsā b. Muḥammad b. ʿAbdallāh 22, 26n51, 30, 50, 81, 118n102, 212n36, 251, 266, 280n263, 296, 315n30, 337
Ḥaḍramawt 131
Ḥafṣ b. ʿUmar 110
Ḥafṣa bt. ʿImrān b. Ibrāhīm b. Muḥammad 25, 270n209
ḥajj 70, 93, 106, 109, 116, 119n111, 126n148, 229, 230, 250, 315, 434, 462

leader of 70, 71, 72n82, 159n80, 240, 266, 302n379, 341n145
route 103, 107n22, 200
al-Ḥajjāj b. Yūsuf 106, 235, 241, 430
al-Ḥakam b. Ṣadaqa b. Nizār 178
Ḥakīm b. ʿAyyāsh *see* al-Aʿwar al-Kalbī
Ḥalab 136
Ḥamad al-Jāsir 319n53
Ḥammād b. ʿUthmān b. Muḥammad b. Khālid b. al-Zubayr 164, 197, 237, 238, 313, 314, 359, 419, 428
Ḥammāda bt. Muʿāwiya b. ʿAbdallāh b. Jaʿfar b. Abī Ṭālib 255, 256n120, 257
Ḥammām Ṣaʿba *see* Ibn Abī l-Ṣaʿba, bath house (*ḥammām*) of
Ḥamza b. ʿAbdallāh b. Muḥammad (al-Bāqir) 250
Ḥamza b. ʿAbdallāh b. al-Zubayr 328, 329, 335, 336, 361
Ḥamza b. ʿAbd al-Muṭṭalib 174, 212
Ḥamza b. Jaʿfar b. Muṣʿab b. al-Zubayr 136n130, 336n130
Ḥamza b. Mālik b. al-Haytham al-Khuzāʿī 197
ḥarba 163, 345, 385
al-Ḥarbī [Ibrāhīm b. Isḥāq?] 22, 23, 160n84
al-Ḥārith *al-munajjim* 171n11
al-Ḥārith b. al-ʿAbbās 158
al-Ḥārith b. ʿAbdallāh b. ʿAyyāsh 288
al-Ḥārith b. ʿAbd al-Raḥmān b. Saʿd b. Abī Dhubāb al-Dawsī 201n164
al-Ḥārith b. ʿĀmir (al-ʿAyyāsh) b. ʿAbd al-Raḥmān b. al-Ḥārith b. Hishām 291n323
al-Ḥārith b. ʿAmr b. Muzayqāʾ 344
al-Ḥārith b. al-Ḥifār 156, 381n31, 390
al-Ḥārith b. Isḥāq 151, 200, 201n164, 360, 387, 415, 417, 418
al-Ḥārith b. Kaʿb, Banū 52, 53, 107, 109
al-Ḥārith b. Surayj 429n17
al-Ḥārith b. Zuhra b. Kilāb, Banū 305
al-Ḥarra 219
Battle of 113, 220, 221, 323, 360
summit of 147n19
Ḥarrat Wāqim 220, 330n99
Hārūn b. Mūsā b. ʿAbdallāh b. Muḥammad a l-Farwī 304n, 308, 316, 388–390
Hārūn al-Rashīd (Caliph) 22n30, 24n38, 82, 107n22, 136n203, 138, 176, 203, 235, 240, 245, 263, 280n263, 292, 297, 315–317, 320, 329, 337, 338, 340n145, 368, 455, 456n123
Hārūn b. Saʿd al-ʿIjlī 364, 372, 373
al-Ḥasan b. ʿAbdallāh al-Jazzār 187
al-Ḥasan b. ʿAlī b. Abī Ṭālib, Banū 234
al-Ḥasan (al-Afṭas) b. ʿAlī b. ʿAlī b. al-Ḥusayn b. ʿAlī b. Abī Ṭālib 164, 165, 248n75, 253, 254
al-Ḥasan b. al-Ḥasan b. ʿAlī b. Abī Ṭālib 24, 104n7, 116, 117n95, 117n97, 118, 121, 123, 145n4, 157, 190, 271, 335, 429, 430, 434, 440
sister of 157
al-Ḥasan b. Ḥusayn al-ʿUranī 187
al-Ḥasan b. Jaʿfar b. al-Ḥasan b. al-Ḥasan 117
al-Ḥasan b. Muʿāwiya b. ʿAbdallāh b. Jaʿfar b. Abī Ṭālib 154, 165–168, 227, 255, 269, 274
al-Ḥasan b. Sahl b. Nawbakht *al-munajjim* 171n11
al-Ḥasan b. Ṣāliḥ b. Ṣāliḥ b. Ḥayy (Ḥayyān) 371
al-Ḥasan b. Zayd, Abū Dalfāʾ 183n65
al-Ḥasan b. Zayd b. al-Ḥasan b. ʿAlī b. Abī Ṭālib 20n19, 32n81, 93, 94, 96, 143, 229, 242–244, 245n57, 284, 295, 321, 337, 338n134, 353n52, 376, 393, 401, 402, 407, 408, 460, 461
Hāshim, Banū 57, 60, 90, 93, 172, 175, 190, 273, 301, 340, 426, 430, 435
leadership of 49, 52, 80, 432, 434
meeting of 60, 62, 65, 69, 70–74, 78, 79, 174, 441
struggles 48
Hāshimiyya (faction) 2, 52, 86n143, 87, 106, 427n27
Hāshimiyya (near al-Kūfa) 97, 109n33, 116n87, 118, 119, 120n112, 122, 127, 146n9, 169, 171, 234, 241
Hawāzin, Banū 358
al-Haytham b. ʿAdī 119, 278n246, 369n26
al-Haytham b. Shuʿba al-Nahshalī l-Tamīmī 195
Ḥayyān (Riyāḥ b. ʿUthmān's grandfather) 113n57
Hazārmard 142, 143n240, 198, 203, 206, 279
al-Ḥazra 24
al-Ḥijāz 23, 44n137, 60n45, 87, 88n152, 99, 103, 249, 261, 266, 295, 297, 331, 350, 454, 458
Ḥimṣ 135

Hind (India) 171n13
Hind bt. Abī ʿUbayda b. ʿAbdallāh (al-Akbar) b. Zamʿa 18n8, 19–21, 171n13, 323n67, 334, 374n2
Hind, the Prophet's wife *see* Umm Salama
al-Ḥīra 94n175, 457n126, 458, 459
Hishām b. ʿAbdallāh b. Abī ʿUbayda 323n67
Hishām b. ʿAbd al-Malik (Caliph) 25n45, 103, 128n165, 135, 270n209, 289, 290, 333, 336
Hishām b. ʿAmr b. Bisṭām b. Sufayḥ 90, 91, 94
Hishām b. Ayyūb b. Salama 291
Hishām b. Ibrāhīm b. Hishām b. Rāshid 228, 399, 400
Hishām b. Muḥammad b. al-Sāʾib al-Kalbī 177, 179–181, 431–433, 445n86
Hishām b. Muḥammad b. ʿUrwa b. Hishām b. ʿUrwa 206
Hishām b. ʿUmāra b. al-Walīd b. ʿAdī b. al-Khiyār 106, 161, 162, 206, 279n248, 290, 321, 325n72, 328, 329, 337, 363, 364, 367–369, 391, 423
Hishām b. al-Walīd 275n231
Ḥiyār Banī l-Qaʿqāʿ 133–135
Hodgson, M. 452n112, 454, 457n127
Ḥubāba bt. ʿĀmir b. ʿAbdallāh b. ʿĀmir b. Bishr 118n105
Ḥumayd b. ʿAbdallāh b. Abī Farwa 308, 389
Ḥumayd b. Abī l-Ṣaʿba al-Madanī 198n149
Ḥumayd b. Aḥmad al-Muḥallī l-Hamdānī 182, 183, 184n67
Ḥumayd b. Qaḥṭaba 96n183, 99, 125, 193, 194n119, 195, 197, 206, 207, 210, 213–216, 355
al-Ḥumayma 266, 403, 408
Ḥunayn, Battle of 165, 253
al-Ḥusayn b. ʿAlī b. Abī Ṭālib 40, 47, 185, 192, 224n87, 313n16, 428, 447n95
Banū 246
al-Ḥusayn b. ʿAlī b. al-Ḥasan b. al-Ḥasan b. al-Ḥasan, *ṣāḥib al-Fakhkh* 118n102, 160n83, 235, 265
al-Ḥusayn b. Ṣakhr 299
al-Ḥusayn b. Yazīd (tr.) 403, 408
al-Ḥusayn b. Zayd b. ʿAlī b. al-Ḥusayn b. ʿAlī b. Abī Ṭālib 200, 248n78, 248n79, 251, 376, 406n126, 464
Ḥuyay b. Hāniʾ al-Maʿāfirī Abū Qabīl 43, 44

Ibn Abī ʿAlqama *see* Hārūn b. Mūsā b. ʿAbdallāh
Ibn Abī ʿAtīq al-Bakrī 121n117
Ibn Abī Dhiʾb Muḥammad b. ʿAbd al-Raḥmān 178, 179, 411n135
Ibn Abī Ḥātim al-Rāzī 372
Ibn Abī l-Mawālī ʿAbd al-Raḥmān 119, 122, 171n13, 386
Ibn Abī l-Ṣaʿba, bath house (*ḥammām*) of 198
Ibn Abī Thābit *see* ʿAbd al-ʿAzīz b. ʿImrān
Ibn Abī ʿUyayna 183n65
Ibn Abrūd 162, 408
Ibn Aflaḥ, *dār* of 196, 203
Ibn ʿĀʾisha *see* ʿUbaydallāh b. Muḥammad b. Ḥafṣ
Ibn Daʾb *see* ʿĪsā b. Yazīd
Ibn al-ʿAdīm 136
Ibn Aʿtham al-Kūfī 77
Ibn Bābawayh l-Qummī 459
Ibn Dāḥa, Ibrāhīm b. Sulaymān 68, 79, 80n109
Ibn Ḥabīb Muḥammad 54
Ibn Ḥajar Aḥmad b. ʿAlī al-ʿAsqalānī 373, 411, 412
Ibn al-Ḥārithiyya 52
Ibn Ḥazm ʿAlī b. Aḥmad 80, 141, 158, 167, 279, 282, 306, 321
Ibn Ḥibbān Muḥammad 294, 372
Ibn Ḥubayn Lane (zuqāq) 149
Ibn ʿInaba 18, 27, 240, 241, 246, 267
ʿUmdat al-ṭālib 18
Ibn al-Jawzī ʿAbd al-Raḥmān b. ʿAlī 95
Ibn Khuḍayr Ibrāhīm b. Muṣʿab b. Muṣʿab b. al-Zubayr 114, 155, 163, 211, 225, 237, 310n5, 311, 353, 398n101
Ibn Lahīʿa 34, 43
Ibn Mayyāda 114n67, 150
Ibn al-Muqaffaʿ 144
Ibn al-Murajjā 17n3
Ibn al-Nadīm 179, 298, 424
ibn sabiyya (son of a slave woman) 25n44, 58, 59, 172, 335n129, 443, 444
see also umm walad
Ibn Shabba ʿUmar 7, 63, 211n31, 219, 224, 388, 394, 402, 409, 413, 420, 422
Ibn Taghrī Birdī 86

Ibn Ṭā'ūs ʿAbdallāh b. Ṭā'ūs b. Kaysān 27, 48n152
Ibn Ṭā'ūs ʿAlī b. Mūsā b. Jaʿfar 463, 464
Ibn Taymiyya 57
Ibn Zabāla *see* Muḥammad b. al-Ḥasan b. Zabāla
Ibrāhīm b. ʿAbdallāh b. ʿAṭā' b. Yaʿqūb 307
Ibrāhīm b. ʿAbdallāh b. al-Ḥasan 25n45, 85, 121, 134, 136, 197, 228n110, 270n209, 372
Ibrāhīm b. ʿAlī b. Harama 32
Ibrāhīm b. ʿAlī b. al-Ḥasan b. ʿAlī b. Abī Rāfiʿ 36, 390
Ibrāhīm b. al-Ḥasan b. al-Ḥasan 117n92, 127, 145
Ibrāhīm b. Hishām 151n40, 430
Ibrāhīm b. Isḥāq al-Ḥarbī 22n32
Ibrāhīm b. Ismāʿīl b. Ibrāhīm b. al-Ḥasan 116
Ibrāhīm (*Khalīl Allāh*) *see* Abraham
Ibrāhīm b. Jaʿfar b. Muṣʿab b. al-Zubayr 206, 312, 341n148
Ibrāhīm (al-Imām) b. Muḥammad b. ʿAlī b. ʿAbdallāh b. al-ʿAbbās 32n81, 69, 70, 71, 72, 79, 82, 83m131, 251, 376n6, 403, 408
Ibrāhīm b. Muḥammad b. ʿAbdallāh b. al-Mudabbir 23n37
Ibrāhīm b. Muḥammad b. ʿAbdallāh (Abū l-Karrām) b. Muḥammad 25n46, 32n81, 64, 66n63, 71, 376, 400, 403, 408
Ibrāhīm b. Muḥammad b. ʿAbd al-ʿAzīz 280n263, 307n409
Ibrāhīm b. Muḥammad b. Ibrāhīm b. Ṭalḥa 285
Ibrāhīm b. Muṣʿab b. Muṣʿab *see* Ibn Khuḍayr
Ibrāhīm b. Muṣʿab b. ʿUmāra b. Ḥamza b. Muṣʿab b. al-Zubayr 319, 341, 400
Ibrāhīm b. Ṭalḥa b. ʿUmar b. ʿUbaydallāh b. Maʿmar 285
Ibrāhīm b. Yaʿqūb b. ʿUmar b. Saʿd b. Abī Waqqāṣ 305
Ibrāhīm b. Ziyād b. ʿAnbasa b. Saʿīd 391, 405, 408
iddiʿā' 301n377
Idrīs (al-Akbar) b. ʿAbdallāh b. al-Ḥasan 21, 124, 229, 234
Idrīs (al-Aṣghar) b. ʿAbdallāh b. al-Ḥasan 21
al-Ifāda fī ta'rīkh al-a'imma al-sāda 185n71, 186
Ifrīqiya (North Africa) 131n174, 143
ʿIjliyya 4, 436, 438, 440
Ikhshīdīs 78
ʿilm, Prophet's 435
Ilyās b. ʿUbaydallāh b. Muḥammad b. ʿUmar 260
imāmate 55n25, 399
  Shīʿī theory of 10n97, 11
ʿImrān b. ʿAbd al-ʿAzīz b. ʿUmar b. ʿAbd al-Raḥmān b. ʿAwf 306
ʿImrān b. Rabīʿa 129n167
iqṭāʿ 320n54, 325
ʿIrāk b. Mālik 154
al-ʿIrāq 5, 26, 53, 54, 84, 94, 95, 96, 99, 100, 103, 104n6, 108, 116, 119n107, 119n111, 122, 124, 127, 132, 137, 145, 155, 170, 171, 178, 194n120, 196, 201n164, 213, 222, 234, 235, 237, 239, 241, 252, 255, 266, 280, 283n275, 286, 292, 299, 300n369, 310, 322, 325, 360, 369, 386, 400, 418n164, 428, 440, 448, 463
al-ʿIrq 317
ʿĪsā b. ʿAbdallāh b. Muḥammad b. ʿUmar b. ʿAlī 8, 13, 50, 64, 80, 91n162, 164, 221, 233, 252, 253, 259, 263, 377, 401, 403, 405, 407, 447
ʿĪsā b. ʿAlī b. ʿAbdallāh b. al-ʿAbbās 26, 92n166
ʿĪsā b. al-Ḥusayn al-Marwazī l-Warrāq 316
ʿĪsā b. Jaʿfar b. Abī Jaʿfar al-Manṣūr 280n263, 316
ʿĪsā b. Lahīʿa b. ʿUqba b. Firʿān 130
ʿĪsā b. Mūsā l-Khurāsānī 24n37
ʿĪsā b. Mūsā b. Muḥammad b. ʿAlī l-ʿAbbāsī 23n35, 26, 31, 66, 92, 106, 107n22, 108, 110, 140, 143, 153, 154, 162, 166, 167, 193, 194n118, 195–204, 207–210, 215, 222, 225–228, 233, 245, 255, 257–260, 262, 285, 293, 295, 299, 343, 353, 355n67, 356n67, 360–360, 368, 376, 401, 411, 460
ʿĪsā b. Yazīd b. Da'b b. Bakr, Ibn Da'b 50n6, 76n98
ʿĪsā b. Zayd b. ʿAlī b. al-Ḥusayn b. ʿAlī 46, 47n149, 65, 139, 154, 163, 200n157, 210, 214, 251, 252, 449
Isḥāq b. ʿAbdallāh b. ʿAbd al-ʿAzīz b. ʿAbdallāh 281
Isḥāq b. ʿAbdallāh b. ʿAṭā' b. Yaʿqūb 228
Isḥāq b. ʿAmmār b. Ḥayyāsh 464

Isḥāq b. al-Ḥasan b. al-Ḥasan b. ʿAlī 117
Isḥāq b. Ibrāhīm b. Dīnār 348
Isḥāq b. Ibrāhīm b. al-Ḥasan b. al-Ḥasan b. ʿAlī 116, 123n133
Isḥāq b. Jaʿfar al-Ṣādiq 243
Ismāʿīl (Abraham's son) 181n54
Ismāʿīl b. ʿAbdallāh b. Jaʿfar b. Abī Ṭālib 256, 450
Ismāʿīl b. Abī ʿAmr b. Nuʿaym b. Māhān 208, 351n48, 352
Ismāʿīl b. Ayyūb b. Salama 291
Ismāʿīl b. Ibrāhīm b. al-Ḥasan b. al-Ḥasan b. ʿAlī 116, 123n133, 384n43
Ismāʿīl b. Ibrāhīm b. Hūd 102n206
Ismāʿīl b. Jaʿfar al-Ṣādiq 249
Ismāʿīl b. Jaʿfar b. Ibrāhīm b. Muḥammad b. ʿAlī 23n35, 229n110, 250, 375, 378, 379, 409, 410
Ismāʿīl b. Ṣāliḥ b. ʿAlī al-ʿAbbāsī 136n203
Ismāʿīl b. Umayya b. ʿAmr b. Saʿīd b. al-ʿĀṣ 269n207, 270
Ismāʿīl b. Yaʿqūb al-Taymī 391, 416n155

Jaʿfar (al-Ṣādiq) 3, 38, 41, 45, 47n150, 48, 55–57, 61n47, 63, 67–69, 70–73, 77, 93, 176, 181n54, 187, 188, 215, 221, 235, 343, 361, 425, 426, 432, 443, 463
  animosities 254, 361
  esoteric knowledge 66, 69, 72, 78, 380, 436, 437, 439, 440, 444, 445, 461
  estate of 228, 230, 243, 244, 399, 460
  followers 123, 141, 156, 162, 240, 247, 251, 261, 268, 284, 351, 358, 368, 370, 384, 390, 392, 419, 438
  prophecies 175, 217, 218, 377
  quietism 83, 217, 457
  shīʿa of 459, 462
  swearing alliagnece 241, 458
  unique qualities 79, 80, 83, 433, 434, 442
  wife 65
Jaʿfar b. ʿAbdallāh b. ʿAlī b. Yazīd b. Rukāna 275, 276n232, 392, 405, 408
Jaʿfar b. ʿAbdallāh b. ʿAṭāʾ b. Yaʿqūb 307
Jaʿfar b. al-Ḥasan b. al-Ḥasan b. ʿAlī b. Abī Ṭālib 117, 123n133, 266, 430
Jaʿfar b. Ḥanẓala al-Bahrānī 169, 170
Jaʿfar b. Ibrāhīm al-Jaʿfarī 415
Jaʿfar b. Muḥammad b. ʿAlī b. al-Ḥusayn *see* Jaʿfar (al-Ṣādiq)
Jaʿfar b. Muḥammad b. al- Ashʿath al-Khuzāʿī 2n7, 64, 380, 455, 456
Jaʿfar b. Muḥammad b. Ismāʿīl b. al-Faḍl b. ʿAbdallāh 80
Jaʿfar b. Muḥammad b. Masʿada 143n238
Jaʿfar b. Muḥammad b. ʿUmar b. ʿAlī b. Abī Ṭālib 259
Jaʿfar b. Muṣʿab b. al-Zubayr 312, 336
Jaʿfar b. Sulaymān b. ʿAlī b. ʿAbdallāh b. al-ʿAbbās 136, 227, 228, 266, 274, 295, 296, 308, 353, 366
al-Jafr 297
Jafr (secret knowledge) 436, 437n49, 438
Jāhiliyya 6, 105, 135n200, 149n28, 172, 174, 181n52, 189, 290, 324, 344, 349n43, 355n65
Jahm b. ʿUthmān 351, 392, 419
al-Jāmiʿ al-kāfī fī fiqh al-Zaydiyya 186–188
al-Jawwāniyya 329, 330
al-Jazīra 124, 127n157, 154, 169, 170, 323n67
Jerusalem 9, 151n38
Jubayr b. ʿAbdallāh al-Sulamī 350
Juhayna, Banū 22, 32, 154, 168, 196n132, 198, 207, 208n9, 210, 211, 212, 343, 346–348, 354, 362, 386
Jumaḥ, Banū 299, 301, 359, 361
al-Junayd b. Khālid b. Huraym al-Taghlibī 86n143
al-Jurf 202, 225, 307n404, 325
Jurjān 296
Juynboll, G.H.A. 9, 10n35

Kābul 143
Kaltham (Kulthum / Kalthum) b. al-Mundhir al-Kalbī 130, 319
Kathīr b. al-Ḥuṣayn al-ʿAbdī or al-ʿAbdarī 154, 196, 255
Kathīr b. al-Ṣalt 110, 359
al-Kattānī *see* Muḥammad b. Yaḥyā b. ʿAlī b. ʿAbd al-Ḥamīd
Khadīja bt. ʿAlī (Zayn al-ʿĀbidīn) b. al-Ḥusayn b. ʿAlī b. Abī Ṭālib 259
Khadīja bt. Muṣʿab b. Thābit b. ʿAbdallāh b. al-Zubayr 341
Khadīja bt. ʿUbaydallāh b. Muḥammad b. ʿUmar b. ʿAlī b. Abī Ṭālib 259

Khadīja bt. ʿUmar b. Muḥammad (al-Bāqir) b. ʿAlī 214, 448
Khaftān 160
Khālid b. ʿAbdallāh al-Qasrī 54, 108, 111, 127
Khālid b. Barz b. Kāmil b. Barz 135
Khālid b. Ḥizām, family of 336
Khālid b. Kathīr (b. Abī l-ʿAwrāʾ) 86n143
Khālid b. al-Mukhtār 188
Khālid b. Muṣʿab (Khuḍayr) b. Muṣʿab b. al-Zubayr 312, 329
Khālid b. Saʿīd b. Rabīʿa b. Ḥubaysh al-Ṣadafī 128, 129n167, 130
Khālid b. ʿUthmān b. Khālid b. al-Zubayr b. al-ʿAwwām 313, 333
Khandaq 147, 148n22, 195n125, 200n160, 203n169, 205, 207–209, 347, 350, 351
Khārija b. ʿUdwān, Banū 20n19, 392
Khārijī/s 20n19, 27, 43, 60, 141, 167n21, 323n67, 388n58, 389, 392, 393, 398, 433, 434
Khaṭṭāb, Banū 283
Khawla bt. Manẓūr 335
Khawwāt b. Bukayr b. Khawwāt 145, 344
Khawwāt b. Jubayr b. al-Nuʿmān 344
Khaytham (Khuthaym) b. ʿIrāk b. Mālik al-Ghifārī 154
al-Khayzurān 292
Khāzim b. Khuzayma al-Tamīmī l-Nahshalī 195n139
Khazraj, Banū 147, 165n105, 220n64, 222n78, 225n91, 253n105, 344n10, 346
  women of 345n11
al-Khiḍr 42
Khubayb b. ʿAbdallāh b. al-Zubayr 335
Khubayb b. Thābit b. ʿAbdallāh b. al-Zubayr 319, 320, 395
Khuḍayr *see* Muṣʿab b. Muṣʿab b. al-Zubayr b. al-ʿAwwām
Khurāsān 2, 30, 31, 42, 44, 61n47, 70, 71, 72, 77, 85, 86, 87, 94, 97, 98, 99, 100, 103, 108, 124, 125n141, 158, 171, 194n120, 247, 248, 272, 286, 349n42, 399, 400, 429n17, 455, 456
Khuwaylid al-Zubayr b. al-ʿAwwām 323n67, 334
Kinda, Banū 110, 111n45, 359
Kitāb Fāṭima 430
Kitāb al-Maṣābīḥ 182, 183, 184n67, 185n71
Kohlberg, E. 10, 62n47, 83n131, 248n78, 248n79, 453n115, 459n132
kufʾ (pl. *akfāʾ*) 340
al-Kūfa 42, 44, 46, 52–53, 82, 96, 101n203, 110, 118–119, 120n112, 124, 125n141, 137–139, 146n9, 169, 194, 200, 218n55, 222, 252n101, 266, 286n295, 288, 325, 360, 369–370, 372n47, 431n29, 438, 441, 443, 445n86, 452n107, 458, 459, 461
  Bridge 120
  Kunāsat 440
Kulthum bt. Wahb b. ʿAbd al-Raḥmān b. Wahb 334, 422
Kurdīn *see* Mismaʿ b. ʿAbd al-Malik b. Mismaʿ
Kuthayyir ʿAzza 19n17, 379n19, 393, 415

Landau-Tasseron, E. 9
Lecker, M. 149n28, 202n165, 203n169, 204n173
al-luʿanāʾ 172
Lubāba bt. ʿUbaydallāh b. al-ʿAbbās b. ʿAbd al-Muṭṭalib 263n168

Maʿbad b. al-Khalīl al-Maraʾī 86n143
al-Madāʾinī ʿAlī b. Muḥammad Abū l-Ḥasan 50, 64, 68, 69, 77, 78, 85n139, 86, 87, 99, 125, 133, 136, 137, 161, 200, 201, 202n167, 206, 210, 367, 368, 388n59, 423, 424
Madelung, W. 2, 10, 28n65, 34, 35n94, 39, 43, 44, 186, 234, 333, 445n86
Madhād 147, 296, 350
al-Maghrib 124, 234, 235
al-Mahdī (Caliph) Muḥammad b. ʿAbdallāh b. Muḥammad 2, 18, 24n38, 28, 30, 31, 50, 81, 106, 117, 132, 133, 137, 170, 176, 212n36, 217, 228, 230, 236, 238, 240, 255, 292, 297, 299, 315, 320, 337, 338, 340, 359, 368, 389n66, 460
Mahdī 4, 17, 28, 29, 32–36, 39, 40, 42n127, 43, 45, 52, 59, 371, 439, 385, 444–446, 450, 456, 460
  Ibn al-Ḥanafiyya as 428
  Jaʿfar al-Ṣādiq as 451
  Nafs Zākiya as 44, 49, 51, 53–55, 58, 61, 65, 66n61, 69, 71, 76, 78, 375, 378, 442
Maḥmūd b. Maʿmar b. Fāliḥ (Abū l-Shadāʾid) al-Fazārī 410

Mahra, Banū 109n33
Makhzūm, Banū 101n203, 110, 283, 287, 288n304, 289, 291, 361
al-Maktaba al-Shāmila (CD data base) 11
Malaḥ 339
malāḥim 43, 221
Mālik b. Anas 18n8, 33, 286, 288, 308, 363, 364–367
Mālik b. Aʿṣur, Banū 357n75
al-Māmaqānī Ḥasan b. ʿAbdallāh 459
Maʿmar b. Fāliḥ (Abū l-Shadāʾid) 392
al-Maʾmūn (Caliph) ʿAbd Allāh b. Hārūn al-Rashīd 7, 45, 130, 136, 151n40, 171n11, 176, 177, 179, 206n3, 254n109, 298, 317, 341n145, 400
al-Manṣūr (Caliph) ʿAbdallāh b. Muḥammad b. ʿAlī passim
al-Maqām (in Mecca) 38
al-Maqrīzī Aḥmad b. ʿAlī Taqī l-Dīn 73, 128n165
Maqṣūra 115n71, 150
al-Marʿashī al-Ḥusayn b. Aḥmad 181
Māriya the Copt 173
Market of the Firewood Sellers 197
Marw 86, 176, 400
Marwān b. al-Ḥakam (Caliph) 94n175, 129, 309
Marwān b. Muḥammad b. Marwān b. al-Ḥakam (Caliph) 53, 58, 59, 70, 78, 93, 104n7, 127, 170, 386, 398, 408
Masʿada b. Ṣadaqa 142n238
al-Masjid al-Ḥarām 75
Maslama b. Hishām b. ʿAbd al-Malik 289
Mawhūb b. Rashīd (Rushayd) b. Ḥayyān 152, 357, 411
maymana 154, 251, 266n188, 403
Māzin, Banū 326
Mazor, A. 9
McAuliffe, J.D. 100n202, 178, 186n74, 310, 413n148
Mecca 22, 38, 40, 60n45, 62n47, 70, 72, 74, 75, 93, 98, 116, 146, 147, 154
  mosque of 160n83, 165–169, 172n15, 174, 190, 200, 201, 211n25, 227, 229, 238, 240, 250, 254n109, 255, 263n164, 266, 269, 274, 286–288, 291, 295, 299, 307, 315, 327, 353, 369, 389, 421, 460, 461
Medina 4, 39, 120, 124, 140, 148, 155, 162–168, 226
  inhabitnats of 3, 107, 152, 186, 201, 225, 233, 252, 257, 261, 299, 361, 449
  dignitaries of 93, 106, 149, 156–158, 204, 236, 275, 278, 290, 305, 322, 337, 353
  economy 103, 105, 336
  governors of 25, 59, 89, 90, 94, 104n7, 107–114, 145, 161–162, 197, 212n36, 227, 229, 237, 243, 246, 263, 265, 269, 272, 280n263, 281, 282n269, 284, 288, 291, 295, 296, 302, 305, 314–317, 334, 338, 347, 353n52, 366, 368, 383, 407, 417, 430, 454n115, 458, 461
  Jewish tribes of 325, 330n99
  mosque of 159, 230n121, 300, 389, 391
  praises of 324
  primary school of 329
  qāḍī of 110, 154, 277, 286, 293, 295, 398, 299, 367, 383
  tribal structure of 6–8, 150, 151
  and passim
Messiah 37, 39, 106, 439, 445
  see also Mahdī
Minā 433
al-Miqdād b. ʿAbdallāh (al-Aṣghar) b. Wahb b. Zamʿa 323n67
al-Miqdād b. ʿAmr 202n165
miʿrāj 17n3
Miskīn b. ʿUmar (tr.) 408
Mismaʿ b. ʿAbd al-Malik b. Mismaʿ b. Mālik Abū Sayyār [?] 140, 141, 162, 384n45, 387, 394
Mismaʿ b. Muḥammad b. Shaybān b. Mālik b. Mismaʿ 140, 194
Moezzi, A. 10, 40–42, 47n150, 451, 452
Moscati, S. 85n136
Motzki, A.H. 9
mountains: ʿA.l.j. 143
  al-Ashʿar 22n34
  Āra 285n289
  Juhayna 25, 347
  Salʿ 149n28, 202, 203n169, 204, 207, 208, 212, 225
  Quds 285n289
  Ṭaraf al-Qadūm 201, 202n167, 304
  Uḥud 304, 330n99

Mourad, S. 9
mu'adhdhin 420
al-Muʿallā, Banū 326, 440n67
al-Muʿallā b. Khunays 76n76, 458
Muʿāwiya b. ʿAbdallāh b. Jaʿfar b. Abī Ṭālib 154, 196, 210, 255, 256
Muʿāwiya b. Abī Sufyān 33, 129n165, 172n15, 230n116, 327, 347n26
Muʿāwiya b. Ḥudayj al-Juhanī 33
Muʿāwiya b. ʿUbaydallāh b. Yasār Abū ʿUbaydallāh 132
al-Mubārak *see* ʿĪsā (al-Mubārak) b. ʿAbdallāh b. Muḥammad b. ʿUmar
al-Mubayyiḍa 154
al-Mughīra b. ʿAbdallāh b. ʿUmar b. Makhzūm, family of 287
al-Mughīra b. ʿAbd al-Raḥmān 288
al-Mughīra b. al-Fazʿ 197
al-Mughīra b. Khubayb b. Thābit b. ʿAbdallāh b. al-Zubayr 319, 320n54
al-Mughīra b. Saʿīd 28n65, 54–57
al-Mughīriyya 4, 54–56, 443, 444
muhājirūn 165n105, 186, 285n105
Muhallabī, family 143, 144, 198
Muḥammad (al-Arqaṭ) b. ʿAbdallāh b. ʿAlī b. Abī Ṭālib 71
Muḥammad b. ʿAbdallāh b. ʿAbd al-ʿAzīz b. ʿAbdallāh 281
Muḥammad b. ʿAbdallāh b. ʿAbd al-Muṭṭalib (The Prophet) 1, 2, 10, 17n3, 28, 30, 33, 37, 122, 185, 186, 201n163, 210, 216, 220, 230, 235, 244, 276, 323, 343, 375, 378m18, 384n44, 390, 407, 426n2, 427, 428, 443, 450, 456n123, 462, 464
  battles of 147, 153, 165, 202n165, 207, 253, 275n230, 303, 319n52, 412
  companion of 40, 344
  family of 41, 57, 62n47, 76, 106, 172, 174, 184, 285n289, 431, 432, 452, 456
  flag 447
  granting estates 325, 352n50
  knowledge of 435
  ṣadaqāt of 88n152, 88n152, 241, 242n49
  signs of 45
  sword 212, 436, 438, 439
  relics of 438, 440
  weapons (*silāḥ*) 140, 435–438
  wives 225, 244n54, 292n325, 429n17
Muḥammad b. ʿAbdallāh b. Abī ʿUbayda 323n67
Muḥammad b. ʿAbdallāh b. ʿAmr b. Saʿīd b. al-ʿĀṣ 269
Muḥammad (al-Dībāj) b. ʿAbdallāh b. ʿAmr b. ʿUthmān b. ʿAffān 25n45, 69, 97, 119, 121, 122, 171, 270n209, 271–273, 393n82, 414
Muḥammad b. ʿAbdallāh b. ʿAnbasa, Abū Jabra 166, 269
Muḥammad b. ʿAbdallāh b. al-Ḥasan b. al-Ḥasan b. ʿAlī b. Abī Ṭālib (al-Nafs al-Zakiyya) 187
  Sīra fī ahl al-baghy 187
  Kitāb al-Siyar 27n55, 47, 186, 187, 189, and passim
Muḥammad b. ʿAbdallāh (Abū l-Karrām [Kirām?]) b. Muḥammad b. ʿAlī 80, 201, 222, 257n129, 258, 377, 406, 408
Muḥammad b. ʿAbdallāh b. Muḥammad b. ʿAqīl 199, 268, 401
Muḥammad b. ʿAbdallāh b. Muḥammad b. ʿUmar b. ʿAlī 72, 88n152, 199, 261, 263, 268
Muḥammad b. ʿAbdallāh b. Muslim al-Zuhrī 12, 29, 378, 385
Muḥammad b. ʿAbd al-ʿAzīz b. ʿUmar al-Zuhrī 306, 307, 367, 383, 384n45, 397n95
Muḥammad b. ʿAbd al-Raḥmān Abū l-Yaḥāmīm 282
Muḥammad b. ʿAbd al-Raḥmān b. al-Mughīra b. al-Ḥārith 294, 295, 363n1
Muḥammad b. ʿAbd al-Wāḥid b. ʿAbdallāh b. Abī Farwa 156n67, 208n9, 208n10
Muḥammad b. Abī l-ʿAbbās al-Saffāḥ 26, 89, 92n166, 195, 196, 198, 203, 210, 340, 347
Muḥammad b. Abī Bakr b. ʿUmar b. Ḥafṣ b. ʿĀṣim 168, 278
Muḥammad b. Abī Ḥarb *see* Ibn Abī Ḥarb
Muḥammad b. ʿAjlān b. Hurmuz 18n8, 161, 227, 274, 360, 363n1, 367
Muḥammad b. ʿAlī b. ʿAbdallāh b. al-ʿAbbās 20, 52, 53, 71
Muḥammad (Ibn al-Ḥanafiyya) b. ʿAlī b. Abī Ṭālib 379n19, 427, 428, 444
Muḥammad b. ʿAlī b. Ḥamza b. al-Ḥasan b. ʿUbaydallāh 117n92, 117n95, 117n97, 123n133, 247

Muḥammad b. ʿAlī l-Ḥasanī, Abū ʿAbdallāh 186
Muḥammad (al-Bāqir) b. ʿAlī b. al-Ḥusayn b. ʿAlī b. Abī Ṭālib 37, 54, 56n29, 173, 176n32, 181n54, 236, 242, 248, 308, 427n10, 426, 432, 435, 427, 456
Muḥammad (al-Jawād) b. ʿAlī (al-Riḍā) b. Mūsā 446
Muḥammad b. Bashīr (tr.) 178
Muḥammad b. Bashīr Abū Jaʿfar al-Zāhid 178n39
Muḥammad b. Bashīr b. ʿAṭāʾ b. Marwān al-Kindī, al-Wāʿiẓ 178n39
Muḥammad b. Bashīr al-Khārijī 20n19, 392, 393
Muḥammad b. Bashīr al-Qazzāz 178n39
Muḥammad b. Dāwūd b. ʿĪsā b. Mūsā 302n379, 340
Muḥammad b. al-Ḥasan al-Shaybānī 186
Muḥammad b. al-Ḥasan b. al-Ḥasan b. ʿAlī 117
Muḥammad b. al-Ḥasan b. al-Ḥusayn b. ʿAlī b. al-Ḥusayn 38
Muḥammad b. al-Ḥasan b. Zabāla 161n84, 389, 401, 411–413, 418n164
Muḥammad b. Ibrāhīm b. al-Ḥasan b. al-Ḥasan 117
Muḥammad b. Ibrāhīm b. Muḥammad b. ʿAlī 25n45, 92n166, 196n133, 262n164, 270, 273
Muḥammad b. ʿImrān b. Ibrāhīm b. Muḥammad b. Ṭalḥa 101n202, 286, 365, 383, 402, 408
Muḥammad b. Ismāʿīl b. Jaʿfar b. Ibrāhīm b. Muḥammad 160n84, 267, 343, 375, 378, 384n43, 385, 413–415
Muḥammad b. Jaʿfar al-Ṣādiq 247
Muḥammad b. Jaʿfar b. Ibrāhīm b. Muḥammad b. ʿAlī 378, 415
Muḥammad b. Jaʿfar b. Muṣʿab b. al-Zubayr 313
Muḥammad b. Jaʿfar b. al-Walīd 385
Muḥammad b. Khālid b. ʿAbdallāh al-Qasrī 100n202, 108, 111, 112, 132, 133, 149, 151n40, 156, 211, 237, 277, 293, 311
Muḥammad b. Khālid b. Ismāʿīl al-Makhzūmī 126n146
Muḥammad b. Manṣūr b. Yazīd al-Murādī 187
Muḥammad b. al-Mundhir b. al-Zubayr b. al-ʿAwwām 321, 331, 332
Muḥammad b. Saʿd b. Nāfiʿ 156, 357, 382n37, 388, 393, 397
Muḥammad b. Ṣafwān 299
Muḥammad b. al-Sāʾib al-Kalbī 35, 432
Muḥammad b. Ṣāliḥ b. ʿAbdallāh b. Mūsā b. ʿAbdallāh 23
Muḥammad b. Sulaymān b. ʿAlī b. ʿAbdallāh b. al-ʿAbbās 138n209, 265, 266, 380n26, 454n115
Muḥammad b. ʿUbaydallāh b. Muḥammad b. ʿUmar b. ʿAlī b. Abī Ṭālib 259
Muḥammad b. ʿUmar b. ʿAlī b. Abī Ṭālib 72, 258, 259, 265n10, 374
Muḥammad b. ʿUthmān b. Muḥammad b. Khālid b. al-Zubayr 164, 237, 238, 313, 314, 359, 419
Muḥammad b. ʿUthmān b. ʿUbaydallāh 279, 280
Muḥammad b. Yaḥyā b. ʿAbdallāh b. al-Ḥasan 24n38, 92n165
Muḥammad b. Yaḥyā b. ʿAlī b. ʿAbd al-Ḥamīd b. ʿUbayd 416n159, 58, 82, 178, 179, 387, 391, 415–418
Muḥammad b. Yaḥyā b. Saʿīd b. Farrūkh al-Qaṭṭān 161, 367, 383, 384
Muḥammad b. Yaḥyā (tr.) 63, 64
Muḥammad b. Yaʿqūb b. ʿUtba al-Thaqafī 304
Muḥammad b. Yazdād b. Suwayd 179
Muḥammad b. Zayd b. ʿAlī b. al-Ḥusayn 199, 200, 251, 252, 257, 276, 401, 406, 408
al-Mujāḥ 327, 328
Mujāhid b. Jabr al-Makkī 40
al-Mulāmis b. Khuzayma 129n167
Mulayka bt. al-Ḥasan b. al-Ḥasan b. ʿAlī b. Abī Ṭālib 206, 312, 313n16, 336, 341
al-Mundhir b. Muḥammad b. al-Mundhir b. al-Zubayr b. al-ʿAwwām 320, 321
al-Mundhir b. al-Zubayr b. ʿAbd al-Raḥmān b. Habbār 323n67, 326
al-Muraysīʿ 320, 330
Mūsā b. ʿAbd al-ʿAzīz b. ʿUmar b. ʿAbd al-Raḥmān b. ʿAwf 306

Mūsā b. ʿAbdallāh b. al-Ḥasan b. al-Ḥasan b. ʿAlī b. Abī Ṭālib 21n29, 22, 23, 44, 115n70, 116, 123n133, 127, 133, 146n9 [?], 155, 213–217, 228n110, 229n111, 235–240, 243, 245n57, 254, 256, 267, 310, 315, 349, 375, 379, 384n43, 405, 408, 409, 410n134, 413–415, 418, 448, 451
wife of 229n112
Mūsā b. ʿAbdallāh b. Mūsā b. ʿAbdallāh b. al-Ḥasan b. al-Ḥasan 380, 418
Mūsā b. Jaʿfar (al-Ṣādiq) b. Muḥammad b. ʿAlī 176 216, 217, 218n53, 236, 288, 399, 446
Muṣʿab b. ʿAbdallāh b. Muṣʿab b. Thābit al-Zubayrī 227, 238, 274n227, 297n355, 298, 332, 337, 342, 353n52, 391
Muṣʿab b. Thābit b. ʿAbdallāh b. al-Zubayr b. al-ʿAwwām 314–316, 330, 341
Muṣʿab b. ʿUthmān b. Muṣʿab b. ʿUrwa b. al-Zubayr 340
Musaddid 161, 367
Muṣallā l-Janāʾiz 151n40
al-Musayyab b. al-Zuhayr al-Ḍabbī 101, 102
muṣḥaf Fāṭima see *Fāṭima's scroll*
Muslim b. ʿUqba al-Murrī 106, 107, 113, 114, 151, 323n67
Musliya, Banū 52
Mutakallim 462
al-Muʿtaṣim (Caliph), Muḥammad b. Hārūn al-Rashīd 280n263, 302n379
al-Mutawakkil (Caliph), Jaʿfar b. Muḥammad b. Hārūn al-Rashīd 22–24
al-Mutawakkil b. Abī l-ʿAjwa (al-Faḥwa?) 308
Muʿtazila 4, 48, 74n87, 78, 101n203, 364n4, 443
Muṭṭalib, Banū 275, 334
Muzāḥim (market) 149n28
Muzayna, Banū 168, 339n138, 343, 347–349, 354, 362, 386

Nadhīr b. Yazīd b. Khālid 112, 133, 149
Nāfiʿ b. Thābit b. ʿAbdallāh b. al-Zubayr 36, 320, 326, 395
Nāfiʿ, *mawlā* Ibn ʿUmar 48
Nafīs b. Muḥammad 326
Nafīsa bt. al-Ḥasan b. ʿAlī b. Abī Ṭālib 335
Nagel, T. 61n47, 174–177, 394, 422, 441n70
Nahr Abī Fuṭrus (Antipatris) 131
Najaf 453, 457
Namira, Banū 328
naqb (pl. *anqāb*) 204
Naqb Wāqim 329
naqīb 2n7, 455
al-Nāṭiq bi-l-Ḥaqq, Abū Ṭālib Yaḥyā b. al-Ḥusayn 48n152, 182n60, 185, 186, 190
Nawfal b. al-Ḥārith b. ʿAbd al-Muṭṭalib 260
Nawfal b. Musāḥiq 298
Nawfal, Banū 275
Nuʿaym b. Ḥammād 34, 39, 40, 43, 44
Numayr, Banū 356, 362

Omar, F. 61n47, 85n138, 174, 175, 177, 183, 454

Peacock, A.C.S. 190, 192
Pharaoh 185
poetry (*shiʿr*) 12, 20n19, 50, 82, 98n197, 136n202, 152, 179, 238, 240n30, 265, 315, 342, 355n67, 357, 373, 381, 384, 389, 392, 393, 410n134, 416, 417
madīḥ 270, 271n210, 393n82

Qadariyya 363n1
Qaḥṭaba b. Shabīb 53, 85, 197, 485
qāʾim 37–39, 41, 59, 439n61, 443–446, 452
al-Qalansuwa (in Jund Filasṭīn) 131
qalansuwa miṣriyya 148n26
muḍarraba 148
al-Qaʿqāʿ b. Khulayd b. Jazʾ 134n189
Qarība bt. Rukayḥ (ʿAbdallāh?) b. Abī ʿUbayda b. ʿAbdallāh 21, 334
al-Qāsim b. al-ʿAbbās b. Muḥammad b. Muʿattib b. Abī Lahab 167, 168, 301
al-Qāsim b. ʿAbdallāh b. ʿAmr b. ʿUthmān b. ʿAffān 25n45, 270n209
al-Qāsim b. Abī ʿAqīl Muḥammad b. ʿAbdallāh b. Muḥammad 268
al-Qāsim b. al-Ḥasan b. al-Ḥasan b. ʿAlī 199
al-Qāsim b. al-Ḥasan b. Zayd b. ʿAlī b. al-Ḥusayn 199n156, 200, 201, 222, 245, 401
al-Qāsim b. Isḥāq b. ʿAbdallāh b. Jaʿfar b. Abī Ṭālib 166, 167, 168, 250, 256, 396

al-Qāsim b. al-Muṭṭalib al-ʿIjlī 35
qaṣr 329, 330
Qaṣr al-ʿAqīq 328
Qaṣr Ibn Hubayra 120n112
Qaṣr Sulaymān b. ʿAbd al-Malik 202
Qinnasrīn 134, 135
Qirqīsiyā 323
al-Qubba al-Khaḍrāʾ (The Green Dome in Baghdād) 185
Quḍāʿa, Banū 109, 347n26, 348, 359, 385
Qudāma b. Mūsā b. ʿUmar b. Qudāma b. Maẓʿūn 300
Qudayd 328n85, 330
Battle of 167, 323, 336n130
Qūhistān 86
quietism (*quʿūd*) *see* Jaʿfar (al-Ṣādiq), quietism of
Quraysh/Qurashī, family 156, 158, 166, 175, 196n134, 200, 234, 260, 268, 295, 331, 337, 391
Qurayṭ b. ʿAbdallāh, family of 152, 357n74, 392, 411

Rabʿa b. Rashdān, Banū 33, 379
al-Rabadha 98, 109n33, 116, 119, 120–121, 127, 235, 236, 239, 271, 286, 290, 291, 325, 343, 347, 378, 365, 369, 386, 464
al-Rabīʿ b. Ḥabīb 21n29, 188
al-Rabīʿ b. Yūnus 112n56, 133, 156, 238
Rabīʿa b. ʿAbdallāh b. ʿAṭāʾ b. Yaʿqūb 307
Rabīʿa b. Ḥubaysh al-Ṣadafī 129n165
Rabīʿa, *mawlā* of Banū Sibāʿ 309
al-Rāfiḍa / *rāfiḍī* 372, 373
Rajāʾ b. Ḥaywa al-Kindī 113
Rāqid 17, 18n8
al-Raqqa 160n82, 280n263, 315, 317
Rashīd (Rushayd?) b. Ḥayyān b. Abī Sulaymān b. Samʿān 152, 357, 392
Rāshidūn 276, 425
Rāsib, Banū 138
Raushan, M. 192, 193
Rayṭa bt. ʿAbdallāh b. ʿAbd al-Madān 20
al-Rayy 31, 124, 170, 194n120, 234, 286
Revolt of the blacks (*al-sūdān*) 284, 296, 297n353, 407, 408, 415, 416n155, 417, 422
ridda, wars 203
riwāya 282n270, 389n66, 396n94, 400
Riyāḥ b. ʿUthmān 95, 107, 108, 111, 112, 115, 145, 211, 246, 272, 296, 300, 305, 307, 311, 398n101
Rizām 108, 111, 112, 133, 149, 237, 405
Rubayḥa bt. Muḥammad b. ʿAbdallāh al-Qurashiyya 291, 292n325
Rukāna b. ʿAbd Yazīd b. Hāshim al-Qurashī 276
Rukn (in Mecca) 38
Ruqayya bt. ʿAbdallāh b. al-Ḥasan b. al-Ḥasan b. ʿAlī b. Abī Ṭālib 4
Ruqayya bt. ʿAbdallāh b. al-Zubayr 335n127
Ruqayya bt. ʿAmr b. ʿUthmān 121n117
Ruqayya bt. al-Ḥasan b. ʿAlī, Umm Salama 335
Ruqayya (al-Ṣughrā) bt. Muḥammad b. ʿAbdallāh b. ʿAmr al-Dībāj 25n45, 121, 270n209, 272, 273
Ruqayya bt. Mūsā b. ʿAbdallāh 267, 379, 384, 409, 413–415

Saʿd b. ʿAbd al-Ḥamīd b. Jaʿfar 345, 386, 392, 419
Saʿd b. ʿUbāda 346
ṣadaqa/ ṣadaqāt 88n152, 159, 241, 242n40, 280n263, 284, 285n289, 295n342, 296, 338, 340, 346, 429, 430
Ṣadif, Banū 129n165, 191
al-Ṣafadī Khalīl b. Aybek Ṣalāḥ al-Dīn 424
Ṣafar 19
safaṭ ("basket of knowledge") 427, 447, 448
see also ṣundūq
al-Saffāḥ Abū l-ʿAbbās (Caliph) ʿAbdallāh b. Muḥammad b. ʿAlī 17, 20, 28n64, 31, 32n78, 51–53, 63, 65, 66, 78, 79, 84, 85, 88, 93, 104, 301, 345n12, 441n70, 441n72
appointments of 109, 143n241, 291
Arab descent 59
as Mahdi 106
granting estates 248, 261, 298n356
mother of 170n10
period of 60, 89, 107, 355, 457–459
policy of 108
swearing allegiance 90
wife of 243, 244
Sāfila 147, 327n82
Ṣāḥib al-Shāma 160n83

Sahl b. ʿAqīl b. Ismāʿīl 420
Sahl b. Bishr 370, 420
Sahm, Banū 130
Saʿīd b. Abī Sufyān al-Ṣayrafī 155
Saʿīd b. Kathīr b. ʿUfayr 131
Saʿīd b. Sulaymān b. Nawfal b. Musāḥiq b. ʿAbdallāh 297, 298
Saʿīd b. ʿUqba b. Shaddād b. Umayya al-Juhanī 44, 45, 229n110, 378–380, 414, 415
Salama b. Aslum al-Juhanī 32–35, 379
Ṣāliḥ b. ʿAlī b. ʿAbdallāh b. al-ʿAbbās 69, 72, 79n109, 113, 137n203, 144
Ṣāliḥ b. Muʿāwiya b. ʿAbdallāh b. Jaʿfar b. Abī Ṭālib 255, 289
Salima, Banū 147, 147, 148n21, 149, 345
  Bāb 196, 203, 345
Salm b. Qutayba b. Muslim 98, 170, 194, 227n102
  see also ʿUqba b. Salm al-Hunāʾī
Sāmānīs 191
Samarqand 31, 222
al-Sāmarrāʾ 23, 179
al-Samhūdī 20n18, 151n40, 219, 220, 222, 319n52, 330n99, 389, 412
Ṣanʿāʾ 182n60, 184, 185n71, 187, 370, 422n185
sappers (*faʿala*) 195, 207n7
al-Sarāt 329, 462
al-Sāya 339
Sayāla 22
Sayf b. ʿUmayra al-Nakhaʿī l-Kūfī 456, 457n125
Sayyid 52, 134n190, 154, 344
Sayyid, R. 47, 183, 184, 186–189
Schacht, J. 9n32, 371
Sezgin, F. 412
Shaddād b. Umayya 378
al-Shahrastānī 440
Shajara 201
Sharon, M. 84, 445n86
Shiʿb Fazāra 215
Shihāb al-Dīn al-Marʿashī 374n1
Shihāb b. ʿAbd al-Malik b. Mismaʿ 141
Shujāʿ, Banū 211, 212, 223, 343, 347, 350
shurṭa 163, 282n169, 286n295
  head of (*ṣāḥib al-shurṭa*) 29n66, 85, 101, 128n163, 162, 211, 252, 279, 281, 291, 310n5, 311, 314, 345, 385, 416, 455
Sibṭ b. al-Jawzī 95, 179–181
  Tadhkirat al-khawwāṣ 179
Ṣiffīn, Battle of 344, 390
Sijistān 288, 371, 433
al-Sind 12, 26, 86n143, 91, 96, 124, 142, 143, 150, 171n13, 198, 236, 267, 380
Siqāyat Sulaymān b. ʿAbd al-Malik 201, 202
Solomon/Sulaymān (King) 179, 235
Spuler, B. 191
spy(ies), ʿAbbāsīs (*ʿayn*) 97, 98, 110n37, 239, 284, 346, 349n42
al-sūdān (revolt of, in Medina) *see* revolt of the blacks (*al-sūdān*)
Sudayf b. Maymūn 301
Sufyān al-Thawrī 100n202, 262n164, 268, 363, 364, 370, 371, 386n50
Sufyān b. Muʿāwiya b. Yazīd b. al-Muhallab b. Abī Ṣufra 143, 144
Sulaym, Banū 325, 339, 343, 349n43, 350, 351, 354, 362, 392, 419
Sulaymān b. ʿAbdallāh b. al-Ḥasan b. al-Ḥasan 21, 229, 235
Sulaymān b. ʿAbdallāh b. [Muḥammad b.?] Abī Sabra 296, 297
Sulaymān b. ʿAbd al-Malik (Caliph) 134, 135n200, 202, 241, 242, 321n60, 332
Sulaymān b. ʿAlī b. ʿAbdallāh b. al-ʿAbbās 143, 144, 227, 265n179, 267, 341, 416
Sulaymān b. ʿĀṣim b. al-Mundhir 321n62
Sulaymān b. ʿAyyāsh al-Saʿdī 20n19, 22n29, 271n210, 342, 392, 393, 404
Sulaymān b. Dāwūd b. al-Ḥasan b. al-Ḥasan 117, 123n133, 408
Sulaymān b. Fulayḥ b. Sulaymān 284
Sulaymān b. Hārūn (tr.) 436
Sulaymān b. al-Ḥasan b. al-Ḥasan 117
Sulaymān b. Ḥayyān Abū Khālid al-Aḥmar 371
Sulaymān b. Khālid al-Aqṭaʿ 438
Sulaymān b. Mihrān (al-Aʿmash) 101n203, 363n1
Sulaymān b. Muḥammad al-Sārī 138, 420
Sulaymān b. Mujālid 420
Sulaymān b. Nahīk (tr.) 249n80
al-Ṣūlī 82
ṣundūq, the Prophet's 427
  see also *safaṭ*
supernatural, powers 18, 60, 67, 72, 79, 380, 431, 433, 434, 441, 448, 450, 456, 460–462
sutūr 159, 161n84

Suwayqa 22–24, 33, 46, 228, 240, 274n225, 393, 394, 410n134
Syria (al-Shām) 38, 99, 100, 103, 108, 113, 114, 124, 125n141, 127, 132–137, 154, 169, 170, 184n67, 194, 198, 200n160, 211n25, 216n45, 235, 237, 238, 272, 287, 303, 386

Tabāla 288
al-Ṭabarī 7, 8, 30, 31, 36, 44n137, 86, 87, 95, 96, 102, 140, 142, 163, 164, 169, 175, 177–181, 185, 189–193, 206, 221, 227, 229, 239, 240, 253, 257, 259, 269, 275, 276, 291, 297, 300, 305, 311, 315–318, 337, 341, 346, 358, 375, 380–385, 389, 391–400, 403, 407, 408, 413–418, 421, 461
  Taʾrīkh al-rusul wa-l-mulūk 7, 30, 163, 175, 189, 407–410, 422
Ṭabaristān 124, 234
Ṭabāṭibā *see* Ibrāhīm b. Ismāʿīl b. Ibrāhīm b. al-Ḥasan
Ṭāhir b. Muḥammad b. ʿAbdallāh b. Muḥammad b. ʿAqīl 268
Ṭāhir b. Muḥammad (al-Nafs al-Zakiyya) b. ʿAbdallāh 25, 334
Ṭāʾif 165, 168, 202n167, 242n39, 274, 278, 282n269, 284, 347, 348, 354, 356, 362
Tāj al-Dīn Muḥammad b. al-Qāsim b. al-Ḥusayn b. Maʿiyya al-Ḥasanī l-Ḥillī l-Dībājī 24n37
Ṭālibī, family 1, 72, 194, 200, 229, 252n102, 267, 268, 374, 429
Ṭayyʾ 296
Thābit b. ʿAbdallāh b. al-Zubayr 328, 330–332, 335
  family of 330
Thaniyyat al-Wadāʿ 209n16, 211, 221, 225
Thaqīf, Banū 356
Thumāma b. al-Walīd b. al-Qaʿqāʿ b. Khulayd 137
Tiberias 277
al-Tihāma 285n289, 288
al-Ṭihrānī Āghā Buzurg 24n37, 264
Traini, R. 174, 175, 177, 181–183
Ṭūkh al-Khayl 132
al-ṭulaqāʾ 172
Tumāḍir bt. Manẓūr b. Sayyār b. ʿAmr al-Fazārī 335
al-ṭuradāʾ 172
al-Turāth (CD data base) 11
al-Ṭūs 286
Ṭuwwa 132

ʿUbayd b. Ḥunayn 283n275
ʿUbaydallāh b. Abī Salama b. ʿUbaydallāh b. ʿAbdallāh 281
ʿUbaydallāh b. Abī ʿUbayda b. ʿAbdallāh b. Zamʿa 323n67
ʿUbaydallāh b. ʿAmr b. Abī Dhiʾb (Hishām) b. Shuʿba 294
ʿUbaydallāh b. Muḥammad b. Ḥafṣ b. ʿUmar b. Mūsā 421
ʿUbaydallāh b. Muḥammad b. Ṣafwān b. ʿUbaydallāh 299
ʿUbaydallāh b. Muḥammad b. ʿUmar b. ʿAlī b. Abī Ṭālib 259, 402, 404
ʿUbaydallāh b. Muḥammad b. ʿUmar b. ʿAlī b. al-Ḥusayn b. ʿAlī 260n145
ʿUbaydallāh b. ʿUmar b. Ḥafṣ b. ʿĀṣim b. ʿUmar 161, 278, 279n248, 294n336, 367
ʿUmar b. ʿAbd al-ʿAzīz (Caliph) 113, 225, 328n88
ʿUmar b. ʿAbd al-ʿAzīz b. ʿAbdallāh b. ʿAbdallāh b. ʿUmar 265
ʿUmar b. Abī ʿAmr b. Nuʿaym b. Māhān al-Ghifārī 352, 353, 393, 397
ʿUmar b. ʿAlī b. Abī Ṭālib, Banū 258
ʿUmar b. ʿĀṣim b. al-Mundhir b. al-Zubayr b. al-ʿAwwām 321
ʿUmar b. al-Furāt al-Kātib al-Baghdādī 78
ʿUmar b. Ḥafṣ al-Muhallabī *see* Hazārmard
ʿUmar b. Ḥafṣ b. ʿĀṣim b. ʿUmar b. al-Khaṭṭāb 277
ʿUmar b. Ḥafṣ b. ʿUthmān b. Qabīṣa b. Abī Ṣufra 380
ʿUmar b. Muḥammad b. ʿUmar b. ʿAlī b. Abī Ṭālib 199, 260, 401
ʿUmar b. Rāshid 149n31, 393, 421, 422
ʿUmar b. Shabba Abū Zayd al-Numayrī 7, 8, 17n1, 36, 63, 64, 67, 70, 72, 76, 82, 152, 163, 164, 178, 179, 200, 206, 228, 229n111, 237, 246n65, 253, 256, 257, 259, 264, 267, 274, 289, 308, 314, 319n48, 325, 241, 343, 345, 353, 357, 370, 374, 375, 377, 383–386, 392, 422, 460
ʿUmarī (ʿAlīd family) 2, 71–73, 76, 88, 250, 260, 262, 361, 401

ʿUmayr b. Bayān al-ʿIjlī 440
ʿUmayriyya *see* ʿIjliyya
Umayya, Banū 8n65, 77, 269, 445n86
commanders 194, 198
dynasty 28n65
period 61n47, 188, 409
rebellion against 371, 453
rule 453
Umm ʿAbdallāh bt. ʿAbdallāh b. Muḥammad b. ʿUmar 261
Umm ʿAbdallāh bt. Abī Sabra b. Abī Ruhm 298
Umm ʿAbdallāh bt. al-Ḥasan b. ʿAlī 175n32, 427n6, 464n155
Umm al-Dardāʾ 113n57
Umm Farwa bt. al-Qāsim b. Muḥammad b. Abī Bakr 176n32, 250
Umm Hāniʾ bt. Abī Ṭālib 35
Umm al-Ḥasan *see* Nafīsa bt. al-Ḥasan
Umm al-Ḥasan bt. ʿAbd al-Malik b. Yaḥyā b. ʿAbbād 340
Umm al-Ḥasan bt. Jaʿfar b. Ḥasan b. Ḥasan b. ʿAlī 265, 266
Umm al-Ḥasan bt. Mūsā b. ʿAbdallāh 409n130
Umm al-Ḥasan bt. ʿUbaydallāh b. Muḥammad b. ʿUmar 260
Umm Hāshim bt. Jaʿfar b. Jaʿda b. Hubayra al-Makhzūmī 259
Umm al-Ḥusayn bt. ʿAbdallāh b. Muḥammad (al-Bāqir) b. ʿAlī 221, 260, 361, 363, 403, 406, 447, 448
Umm ʿĪsā bt. ʿAbdallāh b. Muḥammad b. ʿUmar b. ʿAlī 261n154
Umm ʿIyāl 285
Umm Kulthūm bt. ʿAbdallāh b. al-Ḥasan 21
Umm Kulthūm bt. al-Ḥasan b. Zayd 243, 244
Umm Kulthūm bt. Ibrāhīm b. Muḥammad b. ʿAlī 280n257
Umm Kulthūm bt. Muḥammad b. ʿUmar b. ʿAlī 259
Umm Kulthūm bt. Mūsā b. ʿAbdallāh b. al-Ḥasan 239
Umm Kulthum / Kulthūm bt. Wahb 318, 319n48
Umm Salama (Hind the Prophet's wife) 244n 53, 292n325
Umm Salama bt. Muḥammad b. al-Ḥasan b. al-Ḥasan 25, 464n155
Umm Salama bt. Muḥammad b. Ṭalḥa b. ʿAbdallāh 229n112, 409, 414, 415
Umm Salama bt. Yaʿqūb b. Salama 289
Umm Salama *see* Ruqayya bt. al-Ḥasan b. ʿAlī
umm walad 59n40, 259, 261, 267, 335n129
see also ibn sabiyya
ʿumūma 427
ʿUqba b. Salm b. Nāfiʿ al Hunāʾī, al-Azdī 98, 196n132, 198, 210, 347, 402
ʿUqba b. Shaddād b. Umayya al-Juhanī 33, 379
ʿUrwa b. al-Zubayr 324, 327, 328, 329n92, 397n96
dār 325
family of 321, 337, 338, 340
ʿUṣayya b. Yaqẓa, Banū 350n44
al-ʿUshayra 88n152, 261
ʿUthmān b. ʿAbdallāh b. ʿAṭāʾ b. Yaʿqūb 307
ʿUthmān b. ʿAffān (Caliph) 43, 156, 316, 325, 318n31, 388, 390
ʿUthmān b. Ḥayyān 113, 114
ʿUthmān b. Ibrāhīm b. Muḥammad b. Muʿādh al-Taymī 168, 285
ʿUthmān b. Muḥammad b. Khālid b. al-Zubayr 74, 153, 155, 162–164, 237, 238, 313, 314, 337, 349, 359
ʿUthmān b. al-Mundhir b. Muṣʿab b. ʿUrwa b. al-Zubayr 340
ʿUthmān b. Saʿd b. Nāfiʿ 357, 388, 397
ʿUthmān b. ʿUbaydallāh b. ʿAbdallāh, Abū l-Qalammas 153, 155, 163, 197, 198, 205, 279, 280–282

van Arendonk, C. 3, 47n152, 126n147, 174n22, 182, 184n67, 279n248, 308n414, 372
Van Ess, J. 3, 27n56, 42, 126n147, 187n78, 274n227, 400n111

Wādī l-ʿAqīq 202n165, 203n170, 210n22, 325, 328, 329, 330
Wādī Fāḍija 312, 313
Wādī l-Farsh 19
Wādī l-Khayf 20
Wādī Malal 19, 24
Wādī Murr 319
Wādī l-Qurā 169, 320n55, 330, 331n104
Wafāʾ b. Zayd b. al-Aṣbagh b. Zayd 131n174
Wahb b. ʿAbdallāh (al-Aṣghar) b. Wahb b. Zamʿa 323n67

al-Walīd b. ʿAbd al-Malik (Caliph) 113, 135, 241, 242n40, 288n304, 298
al-Walīd b. Hishām b. Qaḥdham b. Sulaymān b. Dhakwān 370
al-Walīd b. ʿUtba 274n227, 275
al-Walīd b. Yazīd (Caliph) 52n15, 58, 60, 65, 73, 81, 135n197
Wallāda bt. al-ʿAbbās b. Jazʾ b. al-Ḥārith b. Zuhayr al-ʿAbsī 134
al-Wāqidī, Muḥammad b. ʿUmar 27n57, 48n152, 51, 54, 55n24, 67, 115, 119, 122, 146, 148, 180, 212, 287, 295, 303, 329, 365, 366, 386
Wāqim 206, 220, 329–330
Wāṣil b. ʿAṭāʾ 4, 363
Wāsiṭ 53, 84, 124, 179, 372, 397n98, 399, 420
waṣiyya 428
Watt, M. 54
Williams, J.A. 21n25, 207n7
Wirdān, *mawlā* of ʿAmr b. al-ʿĀṣ 129n165

Yaḥyā b. ʿAbdallāh b. al-Ḥasan b. al-Ḥasan 115, 234, 315–318, 333
Yaḥyā b. ʿAbdallāh b. Muḥammad b. ʿUmar b. ʿAlī 263
Yaḥyā b. Ḥamza b. ʿAbdallāh b. al-Zubayr 336
Yaḥyā b. al-Ḥasan b. Jaʿfar al-ʿUbaydalī l-ʿAqīqī al-Nassāba 30n69, 247, 254n108, 267, 374n2, 375n5, 376, 377, 389, 419n166
Yaḥyā b. al-Ḥusayn b. Hārūn Abū Ṭālib al-Nāṭiq bi-l-Ḥaqq 185, 186
Yaḥyā b. Saʿīd b. Farrūkh al-Qaṭṭān 161, 367
Yaḥyā b. al-Zubayr b. ʿAbbād b. Ḥamza 338
Yaḥyā b. ʿUrwa b. al-Zubayr 329, 332
al-Yamāma 32n81, 159, 165, 168, 280n263, 285, 288n299
  Battle of 315
Yamūt b. al-Muzarriʿ 21n29, 23n35, 393, 394n85, 410n134
  Akhbār wa-mulaḥ wa-ādāb 393
Yanbuʿ 261n158, 346, 347
  Yanbuʿ district 21, 347
Yaʿqūb b. ʿAbdallāh b. ʿAṭāʾ b. Yaʿqūb 307
Yaʿqūb b. al-Ḥasan b. al-Ḥasan 117
Yaʿqūb b. al-Qāsim b. Muḥammad b. Yaḥyā al-Taymī 318, 422
Yaʿqūb b. ʿArabī (tr.) 75n90, 139
Yaʿqūb b. Dāwūd (ʿAbbāsī vizier) 137, 141, 238
Yaʿqūb b. Ibrāhīm b. al-Ḥasan b. al-Ḥasan 117
Yaʿqūb b. Shayba 43
Yaʿqūb b. ʿUtba al-Thaqafī 304n389
al-Yaʿqūbī Aḥmad b. Wāḍiḥ 24n37, 87, 158n76, 196
Yarmūk, battle of 33, 287n299
Yazīd b. ʿAbdallāh b. Zamʿa 323n67
Yazīd b. Abī Ḥabīb Suwayd al-Azdī 43
Yazīd b. Ḥātim al-Muhallabī 128, 132
Yazīd b. Muʿāwiya b. ʿAbdallāh b. Jaʿfar b. Abī Ṭālib 39, 113, 154, 215, 255, 287
Yazīd b. ʿUmar b. Hubayra 53, 84, 88, 104n6, 135n197, 172n15, 440
Yemen (al-Yaman) 38, 43, 96, 99n200, 110, 124, 165, 166, 167–168, 184n67, 250, 256, 274, 288, 309, 315, 351, 381, 392, 396
Yūsuf b. Abī ʿAmr b. Nuʿaym b. Māhān 352

Zāb, Battle of 78, 385n45
zakāt 340, 463
Zamʿa b. al-Aswad, family of 20n18, 323n67, 334
Zaman, M.Q. 5, 59n39, 363
Zandaqa / al-Zanādiqa 81, 338, 428
Zayd b. ʿAlī b. al-Ḥusayn b. ʿAlī b. Abī Ṭālib 46, 251, 372, 376, 427, 429, 430, 445
Zayd b. al-Aṣbagh b. ʿAbd al-ʿAzīz 129, 131n174
Zayd b. Ḥasan 19n18, 393n81
Zayd, the *mawlā* of Mismaʿ b. ʿAbd al-Malik b. Mismaʿ 140, 394
Zaydī rebellion 47n150
Zaydiyya 4, 46–78, 189, 372, 399, 433, 438, 440, 443
Zayn al-ʿĀbidīn see ʿAlī b. al-Ḥusayn
Zaynab bt. ʿAbdallāh b. al-Ḥasan b. al-Ḥasan 21, 118, 223, 266, 414
Zaynab bt. ʿAbdallāh b. Muḥammad b. ʿUmar 261n154
Zaynab bt. Abī Rāfiʿ 390n72
Zaynab bt. ʿAlī b. ʿAbdallāh b. al-ʿAbbās 265n180

Zaynab bt. Muḥammad (al-Nafs al-Zakiyya) b. ʿAbdallāh b. al-Ḥasan 25, 26, 89, 92n166, 106, 196, 340
Zaynab bt. Muḥammad (al-Bāqir) b. ʿAlī b. al-Ḥusayn 196, 247, 259, 340
Zaynab bt. Mūsā b. ʿAbdallāh b. al-Ḥasan 415
Zaynab bt. ʿUmar b. Abī Salama b. ʿAbd al-Asad al-Makhzūmī 101n202
Ziyād b. ʿUbaydallāh b. ʿAbdallāh b. ʿAbd al-Madān al-Ḥārithī 52, 53, 90, 95, 104n7, 107–109, 115, 288, 293, 295, 346, 387
Zotenberg, H. 190n94, 192
Zubayda bt. Jaʿfar b. al-Manṣūr 107n22
al-Zubayr b. ʿĀṣim b. al-Mundhir b. al-Zubayr b. al-ʿAwwām 321
al-Zubayr b. Bakkār b. ʿAbdallāh b. Muṣʿab 17n6, 20n19, 22n29, 23, 106, 113n58, 146n9, 152n45, 167n18, 242n39, 259n139, 271n210, 297n355, 298, 311n5, 314n23, 315–317, 320, 321n61, 327–333, 337, 338, 340–342, 369, 373, 391–393, 395, 412n145, 417, 430
al-Zubayr b. Hishām 318n42
al-Zubayr b. Khubayb b. Thābit b. ʿAbdallāh b. al-Zubayr 310, 319, 330, 341n149, 400n118
Zuhra, Banū 101n202, 150, 302, 303, 305, 307, 309, 360, 383, 391
Zurayq, Banū 326
Zurayqa 136n202